A NORTON CRITICAL EDITION

William Langland
PIERS PLOWMAN

THE DONALDSON TRANSLATION
MIDDLE ENGLISH TEXT
SOURCES AND BACKGROUNDS
CRITICISM

Edited by

ELIZABETH ROBERTSON
UNIVERSITY OF COLORADO AT BOULDER

and

STEPHEN H. A. SHEPHERD
LOYOLA MARYMOUNT UNIVERSITY

W • W • NORTON & COMPANY • *New York* • *London*

W. W. Norton & Company has been independent since its founding in 1923, when William Warder Norton and Mary D. Herter Norton first published lectures delivered at the People's Institute, the adult education division of New York City's Cooper Union. The Nortons soon expanded their program beyond the Institute, publishing books by celebrated academics from America and abroad. By mid-century, the two major pillars of Norton's publishing program—trade books and college texts—were firmly established. In the 1950s, the Norton family transferred control of the company to its employees, and today—with a staff of four hundred and a comparable number of trade, college, and professional titles published each year—W. W. Norton & Company stands as the largest and oldest publishing house owned wholly by its employees.

The text of this book is composed in Fairfield Medium
with the display set in Bernhard Modern.
Composition by Binghamton Valley Composition, LLC.
Manufacturing by the Courier Companies—Westford Division.
Production Manager: Benjamin Reynolds.

Library of Congress Cataloging-in-Publication Data

Langland, William, 1130?–1400?
[Piers the Plowman]
Piers Plowman: the Donaldson translation, select authoritative Middle English text, sources and backgrounds, criticism / William Langland; edited by Elizabeth Robertson and Stephen H. A. Shepherd.
p. cm. — (A Norton critical edition)
Includes bibliographical references.

ISBN 0–393–97559–2 (pbk.)

1. Langland, William, 1330?–1400? Piers the Plowman—Criticism, Textual.
2. Langland, William, 1330?–1400? Piers the Plowman—Sources. 3. Langland,
William, 1330?–1400? Piers the Plowman.   4. Christian pilgrims and pilgrimages—
Poetry. 5. Christian poetry, English (Middle) 6. Visions—Poetry. 7. Dreams—
Poetry. I. Robertson, Elizabeth Ann, 1951– II. Shepherd, Stephen H. A.
III. Donaldson, E. Talbot (Ethelbert Talbot), 1940– IV. Title. V. Series.

PR2013.D6 2004
821'.1—dc22   2004057578

W. W. Norton & Company, Inc., 500 Fifth Avenue, New York, N.Y. 10110-0017
www.wwnorton.com
W. W. Norton & Company Ltd., Castle House,
75/76 Wells Street, London W1T 3QT

2 3 4 5 6 7 8 9 0

for C. David Benson
teacher, mentor, friend

Contents

Preface

Elizabeth Kirk once remarked that there are some books that should never be read for the first time. *Piers Plowman* might be said to be one of those books. One of the masterpieces of the Middle Ages, this fourteenth-century English poem can repeatedly frustrate the reader. It is difficult to follow the plot—as Elizabeth Salter and Derek Pearsall tell us, "Langland is not committed to a narrative structure in any continuous way"[1]—and once a thread emerges, it then leads nowhere in particular or digresses into new sets of ideas and narratives. Nominally, the poem is a dream vision—but it proves to comprise not one, but eight dreams, with two additional dreams within dreams. It is also a pilgrimage that has several protagonists and multiple quests. It resists closure, ending with the search with which it began. Although it is known as a personification allegory, it refuses to keep the allegorical and the literal separate. As Kirk and Judith Anderson write, "it is not the sort of allegory we find in the fifteenth-century play *Everyman*, where personifications seem intended to reduce moral and religious ideas that would otherwise be abstract or difficult to something simple and plain. Quite the contrary: it uses allegory to make the reader think harder and face more problems."[2] It is written in a conventional alliterative medium, but it does not always conform to the technical expectations of that medium; for example, it has lines longer than the traditional alliterative line, it alliterates nouns with seemingly inconsequential words such as prepositions, it eschews the ornate and specialized vocabulary characteristic of alliterative gems such as *Sir Gawain and the Green Knight, Morte Arthure*, and the *Wars of Alexander*. According to Derek Pearsall, "the structure of the poem is associative and idiosyncratic, the very sequence of materials often difficult to understand, its handling of dream and allegory shifting, inconsistent, opportunistic; what appears to be its main ordering structure, [the main character, Will's, search for] . . . Dowel Dobet and Dobest, turns out to be a façade, and the central theophanic character, Piers Plowman, a mystery; characters emerge, disappear, re-emerge, problems are taken up and dropped unsolved. By any standards but its own it is near to artistic breakdown."[3]

In addition, the poem's textual history is complex (a situation not necessarily unrelated to the exigencies of its reading). It is known in three versions called the A-, B-, and C-versions—and a fourth, the Z-, has been proposed. The exact relationship among the versions of the poem is uncertain, although it is generally accepted that A, a shorter version, precedes

1. Elizabeth Salter and Derek Pearsall, eds. *Piers Plowman* (Evanston, Ill.: York Medieval Texts, 1969), p. 32.
2. Elizabeth Kirk and Judith Anderson, Introduction to *Piers Plowman: An Alliterative Verse Translation by E. Talbot Donaldson* (New York: W.W. Norton and Company, 1990), p. ix.
3. Derek Pearsall, *Old and Middle English Poetry* (New York: Routledge, 1977), p. 178.

B and that C is a revision of B, one that clarifies the theology and politics of the previous version. It is also uncertain who wrote the poem, although it is attributed to the narrator of the poem who seems to call himself William Langland. Based on internal evidence offered by the poem, a rough biography has been proposed, although in actuality there is scant evidence for any biography at all. The author might have been born around 1325 and must have died after 1388.[4] The life of the author would thus have spanned the reigns of Edward III (1327–1377) and Richard II (1377–1399). The A-version is dated by some between 1365 and 1370 and the C-text in the early 1390s. If these datings are correct, and if the poem is the product of a single author writing over a long period of time (rather than, for example, someone producing many versions of a poem at the same time for multiple audiences), the poet then wrote, and rewrote, his majestic poem across some twenty years of his life. The poem carries within it the marks of the tumultuous events of those years—the political, economic, and emotional aftermath of the Great Plague of 1348–1349, including the so-called Peasants' Revolt of 1381, the death of Edward III, and the troubled reign of Richard II, the Hundred Years' War, and the religious controversies spurred by the followers of Wycliffe known as the Lollards.

Our lack of specific information about the poet further complicates our understanding of his work. There are hints within the poem about the supposed biography of the author. Some argue that William Langland hides his name acrostically in the phrase "I have lived in land," said I, "my name is Long Will" (xv.152). The "autobiographical passage" of the C-text (reprinted in this Norton Critical Edition, p. 363) tells us that the narrator, Will, is married to Kit, has a daughter named Calotte, and that he is a cleric in minor orders who was paid to pray for the souls of others. As compelling as these details seem to be as autobiography, we must remember that they are presented within a fiction. The poet may have been named Will, but the human will is also an allegorical entity in the poem. One fifteenth-century note (appended at the end of the C-text of *Piers Plowman* preserved in Dublin Trinity College MS. 212 [D.4.1]) attributes the poem to the son of one Stacy de Rokayle, a member of the gentry who owned land at Shipton-under-Wychwood, but support for this attribution is tentative. As yet, we know little or nothing at all about this author except what we can discern from the text. The original dialect of the poem suggests the poet came from west Worcestershire near the Malvern Hills he mentions in the Prologue (1.5). His profound knowledge of, and engagement with, the cultural life of London tells us he was more than an occasional visitor, however, to the metropolis; indeed, like his contemporary Geoffrey Chaucer, he is quintessentially a London poet—but unlike Chaucer, Langland is a poet of all of London, not just of the court.

As has long been recognized by historians, the poem is a compendium of fourteenth-century culture, and its very richness contributes to the challenges it poses to its readers. It embraces every aspect of that life from the most mundane (life in the local pub) to the most abstract (the meaning of imagination). Because it is so richly embedded, the poem requires a close reading that includes not just intellectual, literary, and theological learning, but knowledge of a wide variety of cultural realms that infuse the

4. See further the essay by Ralph Hanna, printed herein, p. 591.

poem's language—the legal, the theological, the domestic, the ecclesiastical, the political, the economic, the mercantile, the material, and the spiritual. From that perspective, the Sources and Backgrounds section of this Norton Critical Edition helps reveal for first-time readers of *Piers Plowman* the vital encyclopedic imagination of the poet; at the same time, it is one of the glories of this work that references to other texts can never solve the poem's own profound engagement with its culture.

Notwithstanding its inherent difficulties, the (perhaps deliberate) obscurity of the poet, and its daunting cultural range, this poem was extremely popular in its own time, as more than fifty surviving manuscripts attest. It was read widely by Langland's contemporaries and became well known enough that it was called upon as a rallying point for the leaders of the so-called Peasants' Revolt.[5] Some think that the C-text revisions, generally viewed as theologically and politically more conservative than the B-text, reflect the poet's dismay that it was so read. Yet its encompassing vision allowed for widely divergent understandings of it, then, later, and now. In the Renaissance, it did not find its way into print until 1550, during the reign of Edward VI, but did so then because it was favored for its supposed proto-Protestant sentiments. Distance has allowed us to see that the poem's density offers possibilities for many kinds of readers with a variety of political and theological positions, yet its primary emphasis is traditional, orthodox, and conservative; if it has a mission, it is reformist rather than revolutionary.

That said, its poetics is radical and visionary. Knowledgeable advocates of the poem would insist that its confusions are commensurate with its visionary apprehension of social and theological reality. Like many great poems, *Piers Plowman* invites the reader to discover, as William Blake would say, the "infinite" beneath the appearance of convention and ideology, once the "doors of perception were cleansed."[6] The honesty of this poem lies in the recognition that such transformations of perceptions of society and its institutions require strenuous mental, emotional, and imaginative—and for Langland—spiritual effort. The poem has the potential to change one's life. It is difficult to read this poem without reexamining how you know what you know and how and why you believe what you believe. It challenges complacency of all kinds—from the intellectual to the emotional. As Kirk and Anderson write, "it is also a profound exploration of the processes of human thought, which drove one frustrated and fascinated student to calling it a 'poem that hurts your mind,' because it makes the reader think more probingly about the assumptions of its society and of the reader's own society than most texts require."[7] It is filled with indignation for the suffering of others, and scathing scrutiny not only of the failures of others, but also of one's own capacity for self-deception; at the same time, its unstinting examination of self and world is infused throughout with compassion. These are just some of the reasons why one might wish to read the work of an unknown poet, who never settled on a final version of a poem, and whose work is so difficult to follow.

It may help readers to engage with the poem if they come to accept that

5. See Sources and Backgrounds, p. 484.
6. William Blake, "The Marriage of Heaven and Hell," Plate 14, in *William Blake: The Complete Poems*, ed. Alicia Ostriker (New York: Penguin Books, 1977), p. 188.
7. Kirk and Anderson, p. vii.

frustration and incompleteness are an essential part of experiencing the poem; indeed they are fundamental to it, for the poem's goal is not so much to disseminate Christian ideals, as to make those Christian ideals immanent in every moment of daily life. A reader can be drawn into the text in such a way that she or he becomes the protagonist on a quest slowly developing in understanding and frustrated in a search for truth. Along with Will, the reader encounters a variety of domains, including a variety of institutions (the Church, the schools, the marketplace, etc.) that offer conflicting and multiple perspectives. The poet's "cast of thought is one that refuses to approach a problem from one point of view without putting that perspective to the test against the most cogent alternatives known to him."[8] Its difficulties are like those of postmodernism—except for the urgency of the faith that impels the quest for meaning.

Even the textual history of the poem contributes to its urgent probing. The great number of surviving manuscripts of the poem and the successive versions they seem to represent need not appear to be so bewildering if one sees in this record of variation a record also of a poem which refused to stop becoming. And whether this was because a single author, or subsequent copyists, or a combination, drove this movement is less important to decipher than to see in the condition of the poem's preservations the integrity of a material reenactment of its interior insistence on repeating, reassessing, renaming, redefining, rejecting, reaccepting, and rereading the salvific life.

In some ways the poem is quite simple. Holy Church tells us at the beginning that God has provided all beings with three basic necessities, food, drink, and clothing (I.17–26). The poem unfolds by exploring how and why it is that those necessities are no longer equally available to all. Society is impelled by its individuals' needs to recover these gifts; in Langland's vision they should be recovered for everyone equally. Hence the needs of the poor permeate the poem—but just as the poor are shown to be needy, so are the rich. Need in the end is shown to be material and spiritual, and the two domains are irrevocably intertwined. Fulfillment of need can finally only be sought in God's love—something only briefly and imperfectly experienced in the temporal world, but a love that urgently needs to be sought. Unity can never last; transcendence can only be glimpsed; quests take place without movement and must constantly be reinitiated. The technique of the poem is integral to its themes: a reader must go through the poem not just to find its meanings, but also to experience them.

For these and other reasons, a translation of the poem alone cannot suffice to convey its riches. Within brief passages, single lines, or even single words, the poet makes language shimmer with multiplicity and variety. To engage the poem's experiential qualities, the reader needs to delve into the Middle English. In examining the original language, the reader will find, in Blakean terms, that the imagination is "unfettered," released from conventions, dogma, and the doctrinal. Take, for example, "Treuthe is tresore the triest on erthe" (I.137). The poet loves puns, and in "triest" is a typical example with the triple referents of "tree," "three," and "true"—

8. Kirk and Anderson, p. xii.

that is, the tree of the Cross, the Trinity, and abstract Truth.[9] The line thus offers three forms of meaning—the doctrinal (the Trinity), the affective (meditation on the Cross), and the abstract (the most pure truth), where all three lead to the same place but must be experienced differently; at the same time; none can exist without the other two. Elsewhere, the author's complexity is conveyed less in individual words than in the development of thought over a few lines. For example, the narrator begins an allegorical pilgrimage to truth at the beginning of the poem, but interrupts the pilgrimage to plough a field (in Passus VI). The ploughing itself becomes the pilgrimage. At other moments, the poet will provide images of uncommon lyrical beauty that cannot be adequately conveyed in translation, such as his image of God's love as a plant weighed down to earth with desire for humanity (I.152ff). The poem stretches the resources of language and style in such various and unpredictable ways that a full appreciation of its poetics can only finally be gleaned through engaging it in its original language. Through such an engagement the reader can come to appreciate Langland's brilliant transformation of theological truths that have become commonplace and weakened by power and acquisitiveness into the dynamism of love.

Acknowledgments

This edition came into being at the request of Judith Anderson and Elizabeth Kirk, who originally asked Elizabeth Robertson and C. David Benson to take up the work unfinished by E. Talbot Donaldson; that is, to combine his edition of the B-text of *Piers Plowman* with their finalized translation of that text and to provide sources and backgrounds to complete a Norton Critical Edition of this magnificent poem. As this project has developed, this proposed structure has inspired new work. We have shifted from Donaldson's B-text to producing one of our own close to it and more closely aligned with the translation. The attendees of the 1995 National Endowment for the Humanities (NEH) Chaucer-Langland Institute in Boulder, Colorado, using their own teaching experiences as a guide, also recommended and encouraged such a project. Late after C. David Benson decided to leave the project, Stephen Shepherd agreed to take over his position. We, therefore, are extremely grateful to C. David Benson for his generous contributions to the foundations of our work. In addition, this project could never have been completed without the meticulous long hours word-processing and proofreading by Colleen Anderson at the University of Colorado. Another selfless and extremely helpful contributor to this project is Anna Baldwin, who offered suggestions for the Sources and Backgrounds section.[1] We are also grateful to Derek Pearsall for his response to our selections. In the initial stages of the project, Jessica Staheli worked tirelessly and intelligently gathering secondary sources and permissions for

---

9. Maureen Quilligan discusses this pun and Langland's delight in polysemy in her *The Language of Allegory: Defining the Genre* (Ithaca: Cornell UP, 1979). For students wishing to pursue this kind of study of Langland's polysemy, the best sources are the *Oxford English Dictionary* (OED) and the *Middle English Dictionary* (MED).

1. We are eager to recommend Anna Baldwin's *A Guidebook to Piers Plowman* (London: Palgrave Macmillan, 2007), which includes summaries of each passus as well as reading and essay options.

the sources and backgrounds to the text. Later graduate assistance was helpfully provided by Eric I. Turner and Melanie Haupt. We would like to thank the Graduate Committee on Arts and Humanities at the University of Colorado, the Council on Research and Creative Work of the University of Colorado, and Loyola Marymount University for contributing to the resources a collaboration of this kind requires. We would like to acknowledge George Kane's generosity in allowing us to use his text and for his helpful advice at the initial stages of this project. We would also like to thank Judith Anderson and Elizabeth Kirk for help and encouragement throughout the project. We would also like to thank Shelli Shepherd and Jeffrey Robinson for their kind and perspicacious contributions to the completion of the volume. We are grateful to Carol Bemis for her extraordinary patience and thoughtfulness about the production of this text. We have dedicated this volume to the teacher, mentor, and friend who has introduced so many to this wonderful poem. We are honored to make the fine work of so distinguished a scholar as E. Talbot Donaldson available to undergraduates. Any royalties for this book will go to the scholarship fund in his name in the hope that future students will continue to recognize his brilliant contributions to medieval studies.

Note to the Second Impression

If ever there was an edition produced by a committee, this is it: like the poem itself, this edition will continue to be revised and developed, and we welcome suggestions for improvement.

  We are grateful to those who provided suggestions for the second impression, including Linda Georgiana and James Goldstein. Above all we owe a special debt to Ralph Hanna and Traugott Lawler for their generous provision of astute and extensive comments.

Elizabeth Robertson
Stephen H. A. Shepherd
Boulder, Colorado, and Los Angeles, California
October, 2007

Reading Middle English†

The original dialect of *Piers Plowman* appears to have been that of the South West Midlands (comprising mainly Gloucestershire, Herefordshire, and Worcestershire, and which includes the Malvern Hills area mentioned in the *Prologue*). The text of the Middle English version presented in this Norton Critical Edition is, however, written in a less westerly Midlands dialect, reflecting the preponderance of manuscripts of the B-version which emanate from the environs of London—and quite possibly also reflecting the author's own move to London, where his poem was copied and distributed by many interested readers. The comments below apply to Midland English, but cannot always account for individual scribal habits.

I. The Sounds of Middle English: General Rules

The following general analysis of the sounds of Middle English will enable the reader who has not time for detailed study to read Middle English aloud so as to preserve some of its most essential characteristics, without, however, giving heed to many important details. The next section, "Detailed Analysis," is designed for the reader who wishes to go more deeply into the pronunciation of Middle English. Middle English differs from Modern English in three principal respects: (1) the pronunciation of the long vowels *a, e, i* (or *y*), *o*, and *u* (spelled *ou, ow*); (2) the fact that Middle English final *e* is often sounded; and (3) the fact that all Middle English consonants are sounded.

1. LONG VOWELS

Middle English vowels are long when they are doubled (*aa, ee, oo*) or when they are terminal (*he, to, holy*); *a, e,* and *o* are long when followed by a single consonant plus a vowel (*name, mete, note*). Middle English vowels are short when they are followed by two consonants.

Long *a* is sounded like the *a* in Modern English "father": *maken, madest.*

Long *e* may be sounded like the *a* in Modern English "name" (ignoring the distinction between the close and open vowel): *be, swete.*

Long *i* (or *y*) is sounded like the *i* in Modern English "machine": *lif, whit, myn, holy.*

Long *o* may be sounded like the *o* in Modern English "note" (again ignoring the distinction between the close and open vowel): *do, brode.*

Long *u* (spelled *ou, ow*) is sounded like the *oo* in Modern English "goose": *house, now.* Note that in general Middle English long vowels are pronounced like long vowels in modern languages other than English. Short vowels and diphthongs, however, may be pronounced as in Modern English.

2. FINAL E

Final *e* is sounded like the *a* in Modern English "sofa." It is commonly silent before words beginning with a vowel or *h*.

† Reprinted, with adaptation, from E. Talbot Donaldson's account in M. H. Abrams et al., eds., *The Norton Anthology of English Literature*, 7th ed., 2 vols. (New York: W. W. Norton & Company, 2000), I: 15–18, with permission of W. W. Norton & Company.

3. CONSONANTS

Middle English consonants are pronounced separately in all combinations—*gnawen*: *g-nawen*; *knowe*: *k-nowe*; *write*: *w-rite*; *folk*: *fol-k*. In a simplified system of pronunciation the combination *gh* as in *night* or *thought* may be treated as if it were silent.

II. The Sounds of Middle English: Detailed Analysis

I. SIMPLE VOWELS

Sound	Pronunciation	Example
long *a* (spelled *a, aa*)	*a* in "father"	*maken, madest*
short *a*	*o* in "hot"	*happe*
long *e* close (spelled *e, ee*)	*a* in "name"	*be, depe*
long *e* open (spelled *e, ee*)	*e* in "there"	*mete, eet*
short *e*	*e* in "set"	*bisette*
final-*e*	*a* in "sofa"	*large*
long *i* (spelled *i, y*)	*i* in "machine"	*I, lif, myne*
short *i*	*i* in "in"	*wit*
long *o* close (spelled *o, oo*)	*o* in "note"	*do, roos*
long *o* open (spelled *o, oo*)	*oa* in "broad"	*go, woo*
short *o*	*o* in "oft"	*potel*
long *u* when spelled *ou, ow*	*oo* in "goose"	*house, power*
long *u* when spelled *u*	*u* in "pure"	*vertue*
short *u* (spelled *u, o*)	*u* in "full"	*ful, love*

Doubled vowels and terminal vowels are always long, whereas single vowels before two consonants other than *th* and *ch* are always short. The vowels *a*, *e*, and *o* are long before a single consonant followed by a vowel: *nāmë*, *sēkë* (sick), *hōly*. In general, words that have descended into Modern English reflect their original Middle English quantity: *lǐven* (to live), but *līf* (life).

The close and open sounds of long *e* and long *o* may often be identified by the Modern English spellings of the words in which they appear. Original long close *e* is generally represented in Modern English by *ee*: "sweet," "knee," "teeth," "see" have close *e* in Middle English, but so does "be"; original long open *e* is generally represented in Modern English by *ea*: "meat," "heath," "sea," "great," "breath" have open *e* in Middle English. Similarly, original long close *o* is now generally represented by *oo*: "soon," "food," "good," but also "do," "to"; original long open *o* is represented either by *oa* or by *o*: "coat," "boat," "moan," but also "go," "bone," foe," "home." Notice that original close *o* is now almost always pronounced like the *oo* in goose, but that original open *o* is almost never so pronounced; thus it is often possible to identify the Middle English vowels through Modern English sounds.

The nonphonetic Middle English spelling of *o* for short *u* has been preserved in a number of Modern English words ("love," "son," "come"), but in others *u* has been restored: "sun" (sonne), "run" (ronne).

For the treatment of final *e*, see "General Rules," "Final *e*" (p. xvii).

2. DIPHTHONGS

Sound	Pronunciation	Example
ai, ay, ei, ay	between *ai* in "aisle" and *ay* in "day"	*faire, lay, heigh, sweyved*
au, aw	*ou* in "out"	*penaunce, lawe*
eu, ew	*ew* in "few"	*seweth*
oi, oy	*oy* in "joy"	*boy, soiled*
ou, ow	*ou* in "thought"	*thoughte, lowe*

Note that in words with *ou* and *ow* that in Modern English are sounded with the *ou* of "about," the combination indicates not the diphthong but the simple vowel long *u* (see "Simple Vowels," above).

3. CONSONANTS

In general, all consonants except *h* were always sounded in Middle English, including consonants that have become silent in Modern English such as the *g* in *gnaw*, the *k* in *knight*, the *l* in *folk*, and the *w* in *write*. In noninitial *gn*, however, the *g* was silent as in Modern English "sign." Initial *h* was silent in short common English words and in words borrowed from French and may have been almost silent in all words. The combination *gh* as in *night* or *thoughte* was sounded like the *ch* of German *ich* or *nach*. Note that Middle English *gg* represents both the hard sound of "dagger" and the soft sound of "bridge."

III. Parts of Speech and Grammar

1. NOUNS

The plural and possessive of nouns end in *es*, formed by adding *s* or *es* to the singular: *werk, werkes; preyer, preyeres*; a final consonant is frequently doubled before *es*: *God, Goddes; hed, heddes*. A common irregular plural is *eyen* (spelled variously, including *eyn, yen, iyen, eghne, eyghen*—"eyes").

2. PRONOUNS

Where they appear, the chief differences from Modern English are as follows:

Modern English	Middle English
I	*I, Y, Ich*
you (singular)	*thow, thou* (subjective); *thee* (objective)
her	*hir(e), her(e)*
its	*his*
you (plural)	*ye* (subjective); *yow* (objective)
their	*her(e)*
them	*hem*

In formal speech, the second person plural is often used for the singular. The possessive adjectives *my* and *thy* take *n* before a word beginning with a vowel or *h*: *thyne ende, myn herte*.

3. ADJECTIVES

Adjectives ending in a consonant sometimes (though not consistently) add final *e* when they stand before the noun they modify and after another modifying word such as *the, this, that,* or nouns or pronouns in the possessive: *a good hors,* but *the (this, my, the kinges) goode hors.* They also may add *e* when standing before and modifying a plural noun, a noun in the vocative, or any proper noun.

Adjectives are compared by adding *er(e)* for the comparative, *est(e)* for the superlative. Sometimes the stem vowel is shortened or altered in the process: *faire, fairer, fairest; low, lower, lowest.*

4. ADVERBS

Adverbs are formed from adjectives by adding *e, ly,* or *liche;* the adjective *fair* thus yields *faire,* and *fairliche; wikked* yields *wikkedly.*

5. VERBS

Middle English verbs, like Modern English verbs, are either "weak" or "strong." Weak verbs form their preterites and past participles with a *t* or *d* suffix and preserve the same stem vowel throughout their systems, although it is sometimes shortened in the preterite and past participle: *love, loved; here, herde; mete, mette.* Strong verbs do not use the *t* or *d* suffix, but vary their stem vowel in the preterite and past participle: *take, toke, taken; fynde, fonde, founden.*

The inflectional endings are the same for Middle English strong verbs and weak verbs except in the preterite singular and the imperative singular. In the following paradigms, the weak verbs *loven* (to love) and *heren* (to hear), and the strong verbs *taken* (to take) and *gynnen* (to begin) serve as models.

	Present Indicative	*Preterite Indicative*
I	*love, here*	*loved(e), herde*
	take, gynne	*took, gan*
thou	*lovest, herest*	*lovedest, herdest*
	takest, gynnest	*tooke, gonne*
he, she, it	*loveth, hereth*	*loved(e), herde*
	taketh, gynneth	*took, gan*
we, ye, they	*love(n) (th), here(n) (th)*	*loved(e) (en), herde(n)*
	take(n) (th), gynne(n) (th)	*tooke(n), gonne(n)*

The present plural ending *eth* is southern, whereas the *e(n)* ending is Midland. In the weak preterite, when the ending *e* gave a verb three or more syllables, it was frequently dropped. Note that in certain strong verbs like *gynnen* there can be two distinct stem vowels in the preterite.

	Present Subjunctive	*Preterite Subjunctive*
Singular	*love, here*	*lovede, herde*
	take, gynne	*tooke, gonne*
Plural	*love(n), here(n)*	*lovede(n), herde(n)*
	take(n), gynne(n)	*tooke(n), gonne(n)*

In verbs like *gynnen*, which have two stem vowels in the indicative preterite, the vowel of the plural and of the second person singular is used for the preterite subjunctive.

The imperative singular of most weak verbs is *e*: (*thou*) *love*; (*thou*) *drynke*. The imperative plural of all verbs is either *e* or *eth*: (*ye*) *love*(*th*), *here*(*th*), *take*(*th*), *gynne*(*th*).

The infinitive of verbs is *e* or *en*: *love*(*n*), *here*(*n*), *take*(*n*), *gynne*(*n*).

The past participle of weak verbs is the same as the preterite without inflectional ending: *loved*, *herd*. In strong verbs the ending is either *e* or *en*: *take*(*n*), *gonne*(*n*). The prefix *y-* often appears on past participles: *y-loved*, *y-herd*, *y-take*(*n*).

Reading Langland's Alliterative Verse†

Piers Plowman is written in the so-called "alliterative long line," a direct descendant of the alliterative poetry of Anglo-Saxon England. This form was still being used by poets in the North and West and was brought to its fullest development in the jeweled craftsmanship of Langland's contemporary, the poet of *Pearl* and *Sir Gawain and the Green Knight*, but it became a lost tradition after the fifteenth century when it was superseded by the iambic pentameter line introduced by Chaucer. Such verse does not normally rhyme. Nor does it have a standard number of syllables and a regularly repeated alternation between stressed and unstressed syllables, of the kind we are used to in most English poetry. Instead, each line contains at least four major stressed syllables, with varying numbers of unstressed syllables distributed among them; the stressed words are bound together by a pattern in which, ideally, at least three of them begin with the same sound.[1] The Dreamer-narrator's first picture of the dream world (Pro. 14–19) in Middle English, which is translated on page 3 offers a good example:

> As *I* bi*h*elde into the *e*st, an *h*iegh to the sonne,
> I seigh a *t*oure on a *t*oft, *t*rielich y-maked,
> A *d*epe *d*ale binethe, a *d*ongeon thereinne
> With *d*epe *d*yches and *d*erke and *d*redful of sight.
> A *f*aire *f*elde *f*ul of *f*olke *f*onde I there bytwene,
> Of alle *m*aner of *m*en, the *m*ene and the riche,
> Worchyng and *w*andryng as the *w*orlde asketh.

---

† Reprinted, with adaptations, from William Langland, *Piers Plowman: An Alliterative Verse Translation by E. Talbot Donaldson* ed. Elizabeth D. Kirk and Judith H. Anderson (New York: W. W. Norton and Company, 1990), pp. ix–x, with permission of W. W. Norton & Company.

1. In this system, the letters *v* and *f* count as the same letter, but the sounds *s* and *sh*, or *ch* and *k*, do not. Any vowel or diphthong alliterates with any other, or with a word that begins with the letter *h*, especially in words in which, as in many modern British dialects, the *h* is lightly stressed or even not pronounced at all.

Notes on the Middle English Texts

Editorial Procedures

All unreprinted editions of Middle English texts in this Norton Critical Edition have been prepared from manuscripts, incunabulae, or photographic reproductions thereof. þ and ȝ have been modernized (the former to *th* and the latter to *gh, y,* or *z*), as has the use of *u* and *v, i* and *j*; abbreviations are expanded silently. Word-division, punctuation, and capitalization are editorial. Otherwise, and excepting the correction of mechanically obvious scribal errors, the orthography of the base texts has not been regularized. In the texts in the *Sources and Backgrounds* section where this may present difficulties, we have employed marginal glosses or explanatory footnotes—and persistently difficult words and potential "false friends" (such as *the*, "thee/you") are reglossed roughly every 100 lines. Editorial emendations to the base texts that go beyond the correction of mechanically obvious errors are placed within square brackets; unless otherwise indicated, omissions are made silently.

This Middle English Text of Piers Plowman

The original plan of this dual-language edition was to reprint selections from the standard (indeed, monumental) scholarly edition of the B-Text by George Kane and E. Talbot Donaldson, printed by the Athlone Press (the edition is commonly known as "Kane-Donaldson"); this was the edition upon which the translation was, in principle, based. We intended to print as much of the text as the press would generously allow, about 40 percent. It became evident, however, that to print anything less than the entire Middle English text would do an injustice to Donaldson's translation, as well as to new readers' perception of the original poet's assiduous excellence. A comparison of Donaldson's translation with Kane-Donaldson reveals, moreover, that (in addition to new punctuation) Donaldson did not always follow Kane-Donaldson's choice of readings from the large number of manuscripts that he and Kane had to consult in their effort to decide which manuscript, if any, had the best claim to recording what are most likely the author's original words (as opposed to those substituted by later copyists). There are hundreds of such variations. Most by far are minor, often introduced to render a sustainable alliterative vocabulary in the translation: for instance, Passsus III, line 2, where Donaldson chooses a common manuscript reading, "before," over Kane-Donaldson's "to." Other variations stand to alter the interpretation of the text substantially: thus, in the Prologue, line 17, Donaldson rejects Kane-Donaldson's trenchant conjectural emendation to "bond[age]" from "bondemen" (serfs, husbandmen), and retains "bondmen." Another example: at Passus V, line 20, where in Kane-Donaldson the dreamer speaks of the uprooting of trees that betokens that "dedly synne . . . shal fordoon hem (them) alle," Donaldson, following the minority reading of two *Piers* manuscripts, changes "them" to to the more alarming "us."

Any facing-page complement to Donaldson's translation that is to make better comparative sense to students must then reflect not Kane-Donaldson but "Donaldson's Kane-Donaldson." For more advanced students interested in the complex history and theory of editing *Piers Plowman*, such a complementary Middle English edition, when compared against Kane-Donaldson, may help to uncover differences of opinion between the two great scholars that have otherwise gone unrecorded.

For this edition, Stephen Shepherd selected as the base text the copy of *Piers Plowman* preserved in Oxford, Bodleian Library, Manuscript Laud misc. 581. Amongst editors of the poem this manuscript is given the identifying sigil "L." For their base text, Kane-Donaldson chose manuscript W (Cambridge, Trinity College, MS B.15.17), but believed L to be the next-best choice, and acknowledged its "superior originality" and its avoidance of the "150 more group errors" reproduced in W (p. 214); indeed, the Athlone edition resorts to many of L's readings in its emendations. Selecting L enables us to present an "authoritative" edition without reproducing Kane-Donaldson, and yet one that is close enough to Donaldson's translation to make a high proportion of emendation unnecessary. Where we have had to introduce changes to the base text, it is usually to accommodate, where reasonably unambiguous, Donaldson's acceptance of Kane-Donaldson emendations, and these changes, sourced in Kane-Donaldson, are marked with the usual square brackets. The spelling within emendations has been changed to reflect the usual forms of the L text. We have endeavored to punctuate the edition in a fashion that corresponds as closely as possible to that of the translation, and we have silently resolved the contents of Latin and French quotations to match their counterparts in the translation. Paragraphing and other breaks in the text have also been aligned with the translation.

Note on the Translation†

The translator of *Piers Plowman*, even more than translators of other works, is faced with the temptation to make the poem simpler and clearer than it actually is. To some extent this is inevitable. A translator cannot translate without making up his mind one way or another about certain things that are open to debate, and Donaldson's Chaucer students will never forget his setting them translation exercises, accompanied by scathing remarks about the futility of putting Middle English that doesn't make sense into modern English that doesn't make sense either. But a translator who lets his translation turn into a reinterpretation, a glorified gloss, has sacrificed something central to the character of Langland's poem. Furthermore, the impact of Langland's style depends on his abrupt juxtaposition of words from widely divergent levels of diction and on the graphic sharpness of his often sardonic wording. He is concrete where the translator wants to be abstract and particular in the very midst of discussing the general. His syntax is sometimes contorted, not simply in ways that are natural in Middle English (in which case it should be translated into equally natural-sounding modern English) but also in ways that create special effects or juxtapositions. A translation constantly threatens to

† Reprinted from William Langland, *Piers Plowman: An Alliterative Verse Translation by E. Talbot Donaldson*, ed. Elizabeth D. Kirk and Judith H. Anderson (New York: W. W. Norton & Company, 1990), pp. xv–xvi, with permission of W. W. Norton & Company.

become blander, more uniform, less complex and compelling than its original. Donaldson's particular concern as a translator was to avoid these dangers as fully as possible. He did not want to tame the poem.

A second and related concern of his was to observe as closely as possible the actual constraints of Langland's alliterative meter. He found during the ten years he worked on the translation that, whereas one would suppose these two goals to be in tension with each other, in practice the more strictly he kept to the poem's formal demands, the better he could resist the temptation to rewrite, tidy, and rationalize it. Perhaps keeping faith with Langland's form gives a kind of distance that is good protection against trying to make the poem too much one's own, the poem Langland might have written if he had been somebody else.

The translation is entirely Donaldson's, and the editors have regarded the translation itself as outside their charge, except for the correction of an insignificant number of actual typographical errors or omissions in his finished manuscript. It should also be noted that he was working with his and George Kane's own edition of the poem, including line numbering, and that the translation will differ accordingly from translations of other editions * * *. The notes, however, are our own, and he must not be held responsible for them, except where he had already annotated passages that appear in *The Norton Anthology of English Literature*, fifth edition (1986).[1]

* * *

Using This Edition†

The Gloss

Words appear in the Gloss at the back of the book if they fall into one of the following categories: (1) important concepts or names of allegorical figures that need more explanation than can readily be confined to a note; (2) modern cognates of Middle English words that have lost some pertinent meaning or connotation of the word they translate or have acquired further, potentially misleading ones; (3) names of places and people or terms for officials, institutions, and the like that recur frequently.

In every case these words are footnoted on their first occurrence in the text (or on the first occasion when a meaning not self-evident to the modern reader is involved). Where the Gloss entry is fuller than the footnote gloss, the footnote adds "(Gloss)" or, if substantially fuller, "see Gloss." On subsequent occurrences in a new *Passus* or after a substantial interval, the word is followed by an asterisk if the Gloss is relevant.

Foreign Words and Biblical References

Much annotation in the edition concerns the Latin words and lines, and the occasional French, that Langland scatters through his English. Where

---

1. In the present Norton Critical Edition, further typographical errors have been corrected, some new notes have been added, and many of the notes made by Kirk and Anderson have been retained, some augmented, and some streamlined [*Editors*].

† Reprinted from William Langland, *Piers Plowman: An Alliterative Verse Translation by E. Talbot Donaldson*, ed. Elizabeth D. Kirk and Judith H. Anderson (New York: W. W. Norton & Company, 1990), pp. xxv–xxvii, with permission of W. W. Norton & Company.

such words are sifted into an English sentence, the translation leaves them in their original language and translates them in a footnote. Where the whole line is in Latin, it is translated and italicized in the text itself, and the translator has deliberately used a more archaic and formal kind of language, suggestive of the King James Bible or of the liturgy, to mark the contrast with Langland's own style. As in the Kane-Donaldson edition, where the Latin line is an integral part of Langland's statement, it is given its own line number; where it is a parenthetical citation of authority, it is indented and given no number of its own and is referred to by the number of the line before, followed by the letter *a*.

Langland generally quoted from memory or used manuscripts now considered faulty, and as a result his passages often vary somewhat from modern editions of the Bible or of the other works on which he draws. He sometimes attributes a verse to one source when it is actually from another, as commonly happens in a manuscript culture where few people own their own copies of books, so that to "know" a text means to remember it. Biblical references in the notes are to the Vulgate, the Latin Bible, current in Langland's time, and they follow its numbering rather than that of the King James Bible, since it is closer to Langland's citations and since many of them are to the Apocrypha or deuterocanonical books, biblical works not included in Protestant Bibles. Donaldson's text and the notes always translate what Langland has, rather than what he should have, written, however: thus Langland's line is translated where it differs from the official Vulgate text. Biblical verses in the text are expanded in the notes only if their gist is unlikely to be clear from Langland's citation.

Books of the Latin Vulgate

OLD TESTAMENT

(Note: the footnotes contain the more familiar names and forms of names of books in the Protestant Bible, Apocrypha, or deuterocanonical books: for example, "Chronicles," "Song of Solomon," "1 Samuel," and "Tobit," rather than "Paralipomenon," "Canticle of Canticles," "1 Kings," and "Tobias," respectively. To facilitate cross-reference, both are given below; the more familiar form comes first, preceded by its abbreviation.)

Gen.	Genesis
Exod.	Exodus
Lev.	Leviticus
Num.	Numbers
Deut.	Deuteronomy
Josh.	Joshua
Judg.	Judges
Ruth	Ruth
1 Sam.	1 Samuel; also 1 Kings
2 Sam.	2 Samuel; also 2 Kings
1 Kings	1 Kings; also 3 Kings
2 Kings	2 Kings; also 4 Kings
1 Chron.	1 Chronicles; Vulgate: 1 Paralipomenon
2 Chron.	2 Chronicles; Vulgate: 2 Paralipomenon
Ezra	Ezra; also 1 Esdras

Neh.	Nehemiah; also 2 Esdras
Tobit	Tobit; Vulgate: Tobias
Judith	Judith
Esther	Esther
Job	Job
Ps.	Psalms
Prov.	Proverbs
Eccl.	Ecclesiastes
Song. Sol.	Song of Solomon; Vulgate: Canticle of Canticles; also popularly, Song of Songs
Wisd.	Wisdom; also Wisdom of Solomon
Ecclus.	Ecclesiasticus; also Sirach
Isa.	Isaiah; Vulgate: Isaias
Jer.	Jeremiah; Vulgate: Jeremias
Lam.	Lamentations
Baruch	Baruch
Ezek.	Ezekiel; Vulgate: Ezechiel
Dan.	Daniel
Hos.	Hosea; Vulgate: Osee
Joel	Joel
Amos	Amos
Obad.	Obadiah; Vulgate: Abdias
Jonah	Jonah; Vulgate: Jonas
Micah	Micah; Vulgate: Micheas
Nahum	Nahum
Hab.	Habakkuk; Vulgate: Habacuc
Zeph.	Zephaniah; Vulgate: Sophonias
Haggai	Haggai; Vulgate: Aggeus
Zech.	Zechariah; Vulgate: Zacharias
Mal.	Malachi; Vulgate: Malachias
1 Macc.	1 Maccabees; Vulgate: 1 Machabees
2 Macc.	2 Maccabees; Vulgate: 2 Machabees

NEW TESTAMENT

Matt.	Matthew	1 Tim.	1 Timothy
Mark	Mark	2 Tim.	2 Timothy
Luke	Luke	Tit.	Titus
John	John	Phil.	Philemon
Acts	Acts	Heb.	Hebrews
Rom.	Romans	Jam.	James
1 Cor.	1 Corinthians	1 Pet.	1 Peter
2 Cor.	2 Corinthians	2 Pet.	2 Peter
Gal.	Galatians	1 John	1 John
Eph.	Ephesians	2 John	2 John
Phil.	Philippians	3 John	3 John
Col.	Colossians	Jude	Jude
1 Thess.	1 Thessalonians	Rev.	Revelation; Vulgate: Apocalypse
2 Thess.	2 Thessalonians		

Abbreviations

The following are the principal abbreviations used in the footnotes, head-notes, and bibliographies (for abbreviations in biblical references, see the tables beginning on p. xxv).

BRUO	*A Biographical Register of the University of Oxford to A. D. 1500*
c.	*circa*
cf.	*compare*
CHLMP	*Cambridge History of Later Medieval Philosophy*
E & S	*Essays and Studies*
EC	*Essays in Criticism*
ed.	*edition/editor*
EETS	*Early English Text Society (Oxford University Press): ES Extra Series; OS Original Series; SS Supplementary Series*
ELH	*English Literary History*
ES	*English Studies*
esp.	*especially*
ff.	*and following*
fol.	*folio*
fols.	*folios*
JEGP	*Journal of English and Germanic Philology*
l.	*line*
ll.	*lines*
LSE	*Leeds Studies in English*
ME	*Middle English*
MED	*Middle English Dictionary*
MERELGR	*Medieval English and Religious and Ethical Literature: Essays in Honour of G. H. Russell,* ed. Gregory Kratzmann and James Simpson (Woodbridge, Suffolk: D. S. Brewer, 1988)
MESGK	*Medieval English Studies presented to George Kane,* ed. Edward Donald Kennedy, Ronald Waldron, and Joseph S. Wittig (Woodbridge, Suffolk: D.S. Brewer, 1988)
MLR	*Modern Language Review*
MS	*manuscript*
MSS	*manuscripts*
N & Q	*Notes and Queries*
n	*(foot)note*
NM	*Neuphilologische Mitteilungen*
no.	*number*
nos.	*numbers*
OED	*Oxford English Dictionary*
p.	*page*
PMLA	*Publications of the Modern Language Association of America*
pp.	*pages*
PQ	*Philological Quarterly*
r.	*recto (front; right-hand page of an open book)*
RES	*Review of English Studies*

SB	*Studies in Bibliography*
SP	*Studies in Philology*
TRHS	*Transactions of the Royal Historical Society*
v.	*verso (back; left-hand page of an open book)*
vol.	*volume*
vols.	*volumes*
YES	*The Yearbook of English Studies*
YLS	*Yearbook of Langland Studies*

The Text of
PIERS PLOWMAN

Prologue†

In a somer seson whan soft was the sonne
I shope me in shroudes as I a shepe were;
In habite as an heremite unholy of workes
Went wyde in this world, wondres to here.
5 [Ac] on a May mornyng, on Malverne Hulles,
Me byfel a ferly, of fairy me thoughte:
I was wery forwandred and went me to reste
Under a brode banke bi a bornes side,
And as I lay and lened and loked in the wateres
10 I slombred in a slepyng, it sweyved so merye.
Thanne gan I to meten a merveilouse swevene
That I was in a wildernesse, wist I never where;
[Ac] as I bihelde into the est, an hiegh to the sonne,
I seigh a toure on a toft, trielich y-maked,
15 A depe dale binethe, a dongeon thereinne,
With depe dyches and derke and dredful of sight.
A faire felde ful of folke fonde I there bytwene,
Of alle maner of men, the mene and the riche,
Worchyng and wandryng as the worlde asketh.
20   Some put hem to the plow, pleyed ful selde,
In settyng and in sowyng swonken ful harde;
Wonnen that wastours with glotonye destruyeth.
And some putten hem to pruyde, apparailed hem thereafter,
In contenaunce of clothyng comen disgised.
25 In prayers and in penance putten hem manye,
Al for love of owre Lorde lyveden ful streyte,
In hope for to have Heveneriche blisse—
As ancres and heremites that holden hem in here selles,
Coveiten nought in contré to kairen aboute,
30 For no likerous liflode her lykam to plese.
And somme chosen [hem to] chaffare—they [cheveden] the bettere,
As it semeth to owre syght that suche men thryveth.
And somme murthes to make as mynstralles conneth
And geten gold with here glee, [gilteles], I leve.
35 Ac japers and jangelers, Judas chylderen,
Feynen hem fantasies and foles hem maketh,
And han here witte at wille to worche yif [hem liste].
That Poule precheth of hem I [dar] nought preve it here:
Qui loquitur turpiloquium [is Luciferes hyne].

---

† Text of Oxford, Bodleian Library, MS Laud misc. 581, printed with permission of the Bodleian Library. Edited by Stephen H. A. Shepherd and Elizabeth Robertson. For further details about the edition, see p. xxii.

Prologue

In a summer season when the sun was mild
I clad myself in clothes as I'd become a sheep;
In the habit of a hermit unholy of works[1]
Walked wide in this world, watching for wonders.
And on a May morning, on Malvern Hills,[2]   5
There befell me as by magic a marvelous thing:
I was weary of wandering and went to rest
At the bottom of a broad bank by a brook's side,
And as I lay lazily looking in the water
I slipped into a slumber, it sounded so pleasant.   10
There came to me reclining there a most curious dream
That I was in a wilderness, nowhere that I knew;
But as I looked into the east, up high toward the sun,
I saw a tower on a hill-top, trimly built,
A deep dale beneath, a dungeon tower in it,   15
With ditches deep and dark and dreadful to look at.
A fair field full of folk I found between them,
Of human beings of all sorts, the high and the low,
Working and wandering as the world requires.
    Some applied themselves to plowing, played very rarely,   20
Sowing seeds and setting plants worked very hard;
Won what wasters gluttonously consume.
And some pursued pride, put on proud clothing,
Came all got up in garments garish to see.
To prayers and penance many put themselves,   25
All for love of our Lord lived hard lives,
Hoping thereafter to have Heaven's bliss—
Such as hermits and anchorites[3] that hold to their cells,
Don't care to go cavorting about the countryside,
With some lush livelihood delighting their bodies.   30
And some made themselves merchants—they managed better,
As it seems to our sight that such men prosper.
And some make mirth as minstrels can
And get gold for their music, guiltless, I think.
But jokers and word jugglers, Judas' children,[4]   35
Invent fantasies to tell about and make fools of themselves,
And have whatever wits they need to work if they wanted.
What Paul preaches of them I don't dare repeat here:
Qui loquitur turpiloquium[5] is Lucifer's henchman.

---

1. The speaker might intend to imply he was dressed as a shepherd or simply in a sheep skin. For Langland's opinion of hermits, see lines 28–30 below.
2. These hills in the west of England overlook a broad plain that seems to encompass the core of the country as one looks toward London.
3. Both are vowed to a religious life of solitude; anchorites were enclosed, whereas hermits could wander. (Gloss: the function of the Gloss at the end of this Norton Critical Edition is explained in the section "Using This Edition," p. xxiv)
4. Minstrels who entertain with jokes and fantastic stories are regarded as descendants of Christ's betrayer, Judas.
5. "Who speaks filthy language": not Paul, though; cf. Eph. 5:3–4.

40   Bidders and beggeres fast aboute yede
     [Til] her bely and her bagge [were bretful] y-crammed;
     [Flite thanne] for here fode, foughten atte ale.
     In glotonye, God it wote, gon hij to bedde,
     And risen [up] with ribaudye, tho Roberdes knaves.
45   Slepe and sleuthe seweth hem evre.
       Pilgrymes and palmers plighted hem togidere
     To seke Seynt James and seyntes in Rome.
     Thei went forth in here wey with many wise tales,
     And hadden leve to lye al here lyf after.
50   I seigh somme that seiden thei had y-sought seyntes:
     To eche a tale that thei tolde here tonge was tempred to lye
     More than to sey soth—it semed bi here speche.
     Heremites on an heep with hoked staves
     Wenten to Walsyngham, and here wenches after.
55   Grete lobyes and longe that loth were to swynke
     Clotheden hem in copis to ben knowen fram othere
     And shopen hem heremites, here ese to have.
     I fonde there freris—alle the four ordres—
     [Prechynge] the peple for profit of [the wombe],
60   Glosed the Gospel as hem good lyked;
     For coveitise of copis, construed it as thei wolde.
     Many of this Maistres mowe clothen hem at lykyng,
     For here money and [here] marchandise marchen togideres.
     Sith Charité hath be chapman and chief to shryve lordes,
65   Many ferlis han fallen in a fewe yeris.
     But Holy Chirche and hij holde better togideres,
     The moste myschief on molde is mountyng [up] faste.
       There preched a pardonere as he a prest were,
     Broughte forth a bulle with bishopes seles,
70   And seide that hymself myghte assoilen hem alle
     Of falshed of fastyng, of vowes y-broken.
     Lewed men leved hym wel and lyked his wordes,
     Comen up knelyng to kissen his [bulle].
     He bonched hem with his brevet and blered here eyes,

Beadsmen[6] and beggars bustled about   40
Till both their bellies and their bags were crammed to the brim;
Staged flytings[7] for their food, fought over beer.
In gluttony, God knows, they go to bed,
And rise up with ribaldry, those Robert's boys.[8]
Sleep and sloth[9] pursue them always.   45
    Pilgrims and palmers[1] made pacts with each other
To seek out Saint James[2] and saints at Rome.
They went on their way with many wise stories,
And had leave to lie all their lives after.
I saw some that said they'd sought after saints: 50
In every tale they told their tongues were tuned to lie
More than to tell the truth—such talk was theirs.
A heap of hermits with hooked staffs
Went off to Walsingham,[3] with their wenches behind them.
Great long lubbers that don't like to work   55
Dressed up in cleric's dress to look different from other men
And behaved as they were hermits, to have an easy life.
I found friars there—all four of the orders[4]—
Preaching to the people for their own paunches' welfare,
Making glosses[5] of the Gospel that would look good for themselves;   60
Coveting copes,[6] they construed it as they pleased.
Many of these Masters may clothe themselves richly,
For their money and their merchandise[7] march hand in hand.
Since Charity[8] has proved a peddler and principally shrives lords,
Many marvels have been manifest within a few years.   65
Unless Holy Church and friars' orders hold together better,
The worst misfortune in the world will be welling up soon.
    A pardoner[9] preached there as if he had priest's rights,
Brought out a bull[1] with bishop's seals,
And said he himself could absolve them all   70
Of failure to fast, of vows they'd broken.
Unlearned men believed him and liked his words,
Came crowding up on knees to kiss his bull.
He banged them with his brevet[2] and bleared their eyes,

---

6. Wheedlers, or possibly those who said prayers for others at a price.
7. Contests in which the participants took turns insulting each other, preferably in verse.
8. I.e., robbers.
9. Not just laziness but irresponsibility more generally; see Gloss.
1. Virtually professional pilgrims who took advantage of the hospitality offered them to go on traveling year after year. Strictly speaking, "palmers" were pilgrims who had been to Jerusalem or who had made lifelong commitments to pilgrimage (Gloss).
2. I.e., his shrine at Compostela, in Galicia, Spain (Gloss).
3. English town, site of a famous shrine to the Virgin Mary (Gloss).
4. In Langland's day there were four orders of friars in England: Franciscans, Dominicans, Carmelites, and Augustinians.
5. Interpretations.
6. Monks', friars', and hermits' long cloaks.
7. *Masters*: Masters of divinity. The "merchandise" sold by the friars for money is shrift; that is, confession and remission of sins, which by canon law cannot be sold.
8. The ideal of the friars, as stated by St. Francis, was simply love, i.e., charity.
9. An official empowered to pass on from the pope temporal indulgence for the sins of people who contributed to charitable enterprises—a function frequently abused; see Gloss.
1. Papal license to act as a pardoner, endorsed by the local bishop (Gloss).
2. Pardoner's license.

75 And raughte with his ragman rynges and broches.
    Thus [ye] geven [yowre] golde glotones to kepe,
    And leneth [it] loseles that lecherye haunten.
    Were the bischop y-blissed and worth bothe his eres,
    His seel shulde nought be sent to deceyve the peple.
80 —It is naught by the bischop that the boy precheth,
    [Ac] the parisch prest and the pardonere parten the silver
    That the [povere peple] of the parisch sholde have yif thei nere.
        Persones and parisch prestes pleyned hem to the bischop
    That here parisshes were pore sith the pestilence-tyme,
85 To have a lycence and a leve at London to dwelle,
    And syngen there for symonye, for silver is swete.
    Bischopes and Bachelers, bothe Maistres and Doctours,
    That han cure under Criste and crounyng in tokne
    And signe that thei sholden shryven here paroschienes,
90 Prechen and prey for hem, and the pore fede,
    Liggen in London in Lenten an elles.
    Somme serven the kyng and his silver tellen,
    In Cheker and in Chancerye chalengen his dettes
    Of wardes and wardmotes, weyves and streyves.
95 And some serven as servantz lordes and ladyes
    And in stede of stuwardes sytten and demen.
    Here Messe and here matynes and many of here Oures
    Arn don undevoutlych: drede is at the laste
    Lest Crist in constorie acorse ful manye.
100   I parceyved of the power that Peter had to kepe
    To bynde and to unbynde as the Boke telleth,
    How he it left with love as owre Lorde hight
    Amonges foure vertues, [moste vertuous of alle],
    That "cardinales" ben called—and closyng yatis
105 There Crist is in kyngdome, to close and to shutte,
    And to opne it to hem and Hevene blisse shewe.
    Ac of the cardinales atte courte that caught of that name
    And power presumed in hem a pope to make

And raked in with his parchment-roll rings and brooches.   75
Thus you give your gold for gluttons' well-being,
And squander it on scoundrels schooled in lechery.
If the bishop were blessed and worth both his ears,
His seal should not be sent out to deceive the people.
—It's nothing to the bishop that the blackguard preaches,   80
And the parish priest and the pardoner split the money
That the poor people of the parish would have but for them.
    Parsons and parish priests complained to the bishop
That their parishes were poor since the pestilence-time,[3]
Asked for license and leave to live in London,   85
And sing Masses there for simony,[4] for silver is sweet.
Bishops and Bachelors, both Masters and Doctors,[5]
Who have cures under Christ and their crowns shaven
As a sign that they should shrive their parishioners,
Preach and pray for them, and provide for the poor,   90
Take lodging in London in Lent and other seasons.
Some serve the king and oversee his treasury,
In the Exchequer and in Chancery[6] press charges for debts
Involving wards' estates and city-wards,[7] waifs and strays.
And some like servants serve lords and ladies   95
And in the stead of stewards[8] sit and make judgments.
Their Masses and their matins and many of their Hours[9]
Are done undevoutly: there's dread that in the end
Christ in his consistory[1] will condemn full many.
    I pondered on the power that Peter had in keeping   100
To bind and unbind as the Book tells,[2]
How he left it with love as our Lord commanded
Among four virtues, most virtuous of all,
That are called "cardinals"—and closing gates[3]
Of the kingdom of Christ, who may close and lock them,   105
Or else open them up and show Heaven's bliss.
But as for the cardinals at court that thus acquired their name
And presumed they had the power to appoint a pope

3. Since 1349, England had suffered a number of epidemics of the plague, the "Black Death," which
   had caused famine and depopulated the countryside. Cf. p. 427.
4. Buying and selling the functions, spiritual powers, or offices of the Church for money. Wealthy
   persons, especially in London, set up foundations to pay priests to sing Masses for their souls and
   those of their relatives (Gloss). Cf. p. 443.
5. *Bachelors*: i.e., bachelors of divinity; elsewhere, may also mean a novice knight; see Gloss. *Doctors*:
   Doctors of Divinity, most commonly, but can also mean medical doctors in some contexts.
6. The Exchequer was a royal commission that received revenue and audited accounts; Chancery
   dealt with petitions addressed to the king. Both typically had bishops or other clerics among their
   officers, if not at their heads.
7. The king was guardian of an underage heir ("ward") to the holdings of one of his major noblemen
   and could claim dues from the subdivisions of a city ("city-wards"), lost property, and strayed cattle
   (or, according to another interpretation, the property of deceased aliens with no legitimate heirs).
8. The managers of large households or estates.
9. Clerics organized their day around seven canonical "hours," or periods of liturgical prayer called
   offices, of which matins was the first (Gloss).
1. Literally, a bishop's court or the senate of cardinals convened by the pope to deliberate on church
   affairs.
2. Matt. 16:18–20 recounts Christ's giving Peter and the succeeding popes this authority to make
   pronouncements on earth that will also be binding in Heaven.
3. The four cardinal virtues are prudence, temperance, justice, and fortitude and are distinguished
   from the three "theological" virtues of faith, hope, and charity; Langland plays below on the fact
   that "cardinal," from Latin *cardo*, "hinge" (hence "gates"), is also the term for the superior group
   of ecclesiastics who, from 1179, had acquired the power to elect the pope.

To han [the] power that Peter hadde—inpugnen I
    nelle,
110   For in love and letterure the eleccioun bilongeth:
Forthi I can and can naughte-of courte speke more.
   Thanne come there a kyng, knyghthod hym ladde,
Might of the comunes made hym to regne.
And thanne cam Kynde Wytte, and clerkes he made
115   For to conseille the kyng and the comune save.
The kyng and knyghthode and clergye bothe
Casten that the comune shulde [here communes]
    fynde.
The comune contreved of Kynde Witte craftes,
And for profit of alle the poeple plowmen ordeygned
120   To tilie and travaile as trewe lyf asketh.
The kynge and the comune and Kynde Witte the thridde
Shope lawe and lewté eche [lyf] to knowe his owne.
Thanne loked up a lunatik—a lene thing withalle—
125   And knelyng to the kyng, clergealy he seyde:
"Crist kepe the, sire Kyng, and thi kyngriche
And lene the lede thi londe so Leuté the lovye,
And for thi rightful rewlyng be rewarded in Hevene."
And sithen in the eyre an hiegh an angel of Hevene
130   Jangle ne jugge that justifie hem shulde,
But suffren and serven; forthi seyde the angel:
"'Sum rex. Sum princeps!'   —Neutrum fortasse
    deinceps.

O, qui jura, regis,   Cristi specialia regis.
Hoc quod agas melius,   justus es esto pius.
135   Nudum jus a te,   vestiri vult pietate.
Qualia vis metere,   talia grana sere.
Si jus nudatur,   nudo de jure metatur.
Si seritur pietas,   de pietate metas."
Thanne greved hym a Goliardeys, a gloutoun of wordes,
140   And to the angel an heigh [answered] after:
"Dum rex a regere dicatur nomen habere
Nomen habet sine re nisi studet jura tenere."
Thanne [comsed] alle the comune crye in vers of Latin
To the kynges conseille—construe hoso wolde:

Who should have the power that Peter had—well I'll not impugn
    them,
For the election belongs to love and to learning: 110
Therefore I can and cannot speak of court further.
    Then there came a king, knighthood accompanied him,
Might of the community[4] made him a ruler.
And then came Kind Wit, and he created clerks[5]
To counsel the king and keep the commons safe.   115
The king in concert with knighthood and with clergy as well
Contrived that the commons should provide their commons[6] for
    them.
The commons with Kind Wit contrived various crafts,
And for profit of all the people appointed plowmen
To till and to toil as true life requires.   120
The king and the commons and Kind Wit the third
Defined law and lewté[7] for every kind of life, known limits.
Then a lunatic looked up—a lean one at that—
And counseled the king with clerkly words, kneeling before him: 125
"Christ keep you, sir King, and the kingdom you rule
And grant you to lead your land so that Lewté loves you,
And for your righteous ruling be rewarded in Heaven."
And after in the air on high an angel of Heaven
Came low to speak in Latin, for illiterate men lacked
The jargon or the judgment to justify themselves,   130
But can only suffer and serve; therefore said the angel:
"'I'm a king. I'm a prince!' —*Neither perhaps when you've gone*
    hence.
You, King, who're here to save   the special laws that King Christ gave.
To do this better you will find   it's well to be less just than kind.
By you law's naked truth   wants to be clothed in ruth.[8]   135
Such seeds as you sow,   such a crop will grow.
If you strip law bare,   bare law will be your share.
If you sow pity,   you'll be sitting pretty."[9]
Then a Goliard[1] grew angry, a glutton of words,
And to the angel on high answered after: 140
"Since the name of king, rex, comes from regere, 'to rule,'
Unless he law directs, he's a wright without a tool."[2]
Then all the commons commenced to cry in Latin verse
To the king's council—let who will construe it:

---

4. *Might*: in Middle English, "might" simply means the strength necessary to do a particular thing, not necessarily overwhelming force. *Community*: the important Middle English word *commune*, *communes* has three meanings Langland plays on in this passage: (1) the community taken as a whole; (2) the common people; (3) the food that supports the community; see Gloss.
5. *Kind Wit*: natural acumen, good sense, experiential knowledge; see Gloss. *Clerks*: clerics, intellectuals; see Gloss.
6. The first occurrence of *commons* in this line means "common people"; the second, food.
7. Justice, as distinct from the law as such; see Gloss.
8. Pity. Cf. pp. 486–88.
9. The Latin verses seem to have been current in Langland's time. Many such jingles have distinctive internal rhyme; when this is so, they have been printed with a space between the half-lines.
1. A wandering student or cleric; goliards wrote songs and poetry, often satirical or ribald and attacking the clerical establishment. By relating the word to "glutton," Langland plays on its derivation from Old French *gale*, "throat."
2. *Wright*: workman, maker. The Latin couplet is contemporary.

145   *"Precepta regis   sunt nobis vincula legis."*
       With that ran there a route of ratones at ones,
      And smale mys with hem, mo then a thousande,
      Comen to a conseille for here comune profit;
      For a cat of a courte cam whan hym lyked
150   And overlepe hem lyghtlich and laughte hem at his wille,
      And pleyde with hem perilouslych, and possed aboute.
      "For doute of dyverse [dedes] we dar noughte wel loke,
      And yif we grucche of his gamen he wil greve us alle,
      Cracche us or clowe us and in his cloches holde.
155   That us lotheth the lyf or he lete us passe.
      Myghte we with any witte his wille withstonde
      We myghte be lordes aloft and lyven at owre ese."
      A raton of renon, most renable of tonge,
      Seide for a sovereygne [salve] to [hem alle].
160   "I have y-sein segges," quod he, "in the cité of London
      Beren bighes ful brighte abouten here nekkes,
      And some colers of crafty werk; uncoupled thei wenden
      Bothe in wareine and in waste, where hem leve lyketh;
      And otherwhile thei aren elleswhere, as I here telle.
165   Were there a belle on here beigh, bi Jhesu, as me thynketh,
      Men myghte wite where thei went and [here weye rowme].
      And right so," quod that ratoun, "reson me sheweth
      To bugge a belle of brasse or of brighte sylver
      And knitten [it] on a colere for owre comune profit
170   And hangen it upon the cattes hals; thanne here we mowen
      Where he ritt or rest or [rowmeth] to playe.
      And yif him list for to laike thenne loke we mowen
      And peren in his presence therwhile hym plaie liketh.
      And yif him wrattheth be y-war and his weye shonye."
175   Alle this route of ratones to this reson thei assented,
      Ac tho the belle was [y-brought] and on the beighe hanged
      There ne was ratoun in alle the route, for alle the rewme of Fraunce,
      That dorst have y-bounden the belle aboute the cattis nekke
      Ne hangen aboute [his] hals, al Engelonde to wynne;
180   [Ac] helden hem unhardy and here conseille feble,
      And leten here laboure lost, and alle here longe studye.
      A mous that moche good couthe, as me [tho] thoughte,
      Stroke forth sternly and stode biforn hem alle,
      And to the route of ratones reherced these wordes:
185   "Though we culled the catte, yut sholde ther come another
      To cracchy us and al owre kynde though we croupe under benches.
      Forthi I conseille alle the comune to lat the catte worthe,
      And be we never so bolde the belle hym to shewe.
      [The while he caccheth conynges he coveiteth nought owre
         caroyne,
190   But fet hym al with venesoun—defame we hym nevere.
      For better is a litel losse than a longe sorwe:

"What the king ordains   is to us the law's chains."[3]   145
　　With that there ran a rabble of rats together,
And little mice along with them, no less than a thousand,
Came to a council for their common profit;
For a cat of court came when he pleased
And leapt lightly over them and when he liked seized them,   150
And played with them perilously, and pushed them about.[4]
"For dread of various deeds we hardly dare move,
And if we grumble at his games he will grieve us all,
Scratch us or claw us or catch us in his clutches.
So that we'll loathe life before he lets us go.   155
If by any wit we might withstand his will
We could be lofty as lords and live at our ease."
A rat of renown, most ready of tongue,
Said as a sovereign salve for them all:
"I've seen creatures," he said, "in the city of London   160
Bear chains full bright about their necks,
And collars of fine craftsmanship;[5] they come and go without leashes
Both in warren and in wasteland, wherever they please;
And at other times they are in other places, as I hear tell.
If there were a bell to clink on their collars, by Christ, I think   165
We could tell where they went and keep well out of their way.
And right so," said the rat, "reason tells me
To buy a bell of brass or of bright silver
And clip it on a collar for our common profit
And hang it over the cat's head; then we'd be able to hear   170
Whether he's riding or resting or roving out to play.
And if he desires sport we can step out
And appear in his presence while he's pleased to play.
And if he's angry we'll take heed and stay out of his way."
This whole convention of vermin was convinced by this advice,   175
But when the bell was brought and bound to the collar
There was no rat in the rabble, for all the realm of France,
That dared bind the bell about the cat's neck
Or hang it over his head, to win all England;
But they held themselves faint-hearted and their whole plan foolish,   180
And allowed all their labor lost, and all their long scheming.
A mouse that knew much good, as it seemed to me then,
Strode forth sternly and stood before them all,
And to the rats arrayed there recited these words:
"Though we killed the cat, yet there would come another   185
To scratch us and all our kind though we crept under benches.
Therefore I counsel all the commons to let the cat alone,
And let's never be so bold as to show the bell to him.
While he's catching conies[6] he doesn't crave our flesh,
But feeds himself on rich food—let's not defame him.   190
For a little loss is better than a long sorrow:

3. A metrical version of a Roman legal maxim.
4. Langland gives an original twist to the familiar fable about "belling the cat." Cf. p. 488.
5. The rat conflates the gold chains of office worn by city magnates with the collars of dogs.
6. Rabbits.

The mase amonge us alle though we mysse a schrewe].
For I herde my sire seyn, is sevene yere y-passed,
There the catte is a kitoun, the courte is ful elyng.
195 That witnisseth Holi Write, whoso wil it rede:
Ve terre ubi puer rex est, etc.
For may no renke there rest have for ratones bi nyghte,
[And] many mannes malt we mys wolde destruye,
And also ye route of ratones rende mennes clothes
200 Nere [the] cat of [the] courte that can yow overlepe.
For had ye rattes yowre [reyke], ye couthe nought reule yowreselve.
I sey for me," quod the mous, "I se so mykel after,
Shal never the cat ne the kitoun bi my conseille be greved—
Ne carpyng of this coler, that costed me nevre.
205 And though it had coste me catel, biknowen it I nolde—
But suffre as hymself wolde to [sleen that] hym liketh,
Coupled and uncoupled to cacche what thei mowe.
Forthi uche a wise wighte I warne wite wel his owne."
—What this meteles bemeneth, ye men that be merye,
210 Devine ye, for I ne dar, bi dere God in Hevene.
Yit hoved there an hondreth in houves of selke
Serjauntz it semed that serveden atte barre,
Plededen for penyes and [pounded] the lawe,
And nought for love of owre Lorde unlese here lippes onis:
215 Thow myghtest better mete myste on Malverne Hulles
Than gete a "momme" of here mouthe but monoy were shewed.
Barones an burgeis and bondemen als
I seigh in this assemblé, as ye shul here after;
Baxsteres and brewesteres and bocheres manye,
220 Wolle websteres and weveres of lynnen,
Taillours, tynkeres, and tolleres in marketes,
Masons, mynours, and many other craftes.
Of alkin libbyng laboreres lopen forth somme,
As dykers and delveres that doth here dedes ille,
225 And dryven forth the [longe] day with *"Dieu save dame Emme."*
Cokes and here knaves crieden, "Hote pies, hote!
Gode gris [and] gees! Go we dyne, go we!"
Taverners until hem tolde the same:
"White wyn of Oseye and wyn of Gascoigne,
230 Of the Ryne and of the Rochel, the roste to defye."
Al this seigh I slepyng, and sevene sythes more.

We'd all be muddling through a maze though we'd removed one foe.
For I heard my sire say, seven years ago,
Where the cat is a kitten, the court is wholly wretched.
That's how Holy Writ reads, whoever wants to look: 195
Woe to the land where the king is a child![7]
For no creature may rest quiet because of rats at night,
And many a man's malt we mice would destroy,
And also you rabble of rats would ruin men's clothing
If it weren't for the court-cat that can outleap you.   200
For if you rats held the reins, you couldn't rule yourselves.
I speak for myself," said the mouse, "I foresee such trouble later,
That by my counsel neither cat nor kitten shall be grieved—
And let's have no carping of this collar, that cost me nothing.
And though it had cost me money, I'd not admit it had—   205
But suffer as himself wishes to slay what he pleases,
Coupled and uncoupled let them catch what they will.
Therefore I warn every wise creature to stick to what's his own."
—What this dream may mean, you men that are merry,
You divine, for I don't dare, by dear God in Heaven.   210
Yet scores of men stood there in silken coifs
Who seemed to be law-sergeants[8] that served at the bar,
Pleaded cases for pennies and impounded[9] the law,
And not for love of our Lord once unloosed their lips:
You might better measure mist on Malvern Hills   215
Than get a "mum" from their mouths till money's on the table.
Barons and burgesses[1] and bondmen also
I saw in this assemblage, as you shall hear later;
Bakers and brewers and butchers aplenty,
Weavers of wool and weavers of linen,   220
Tailors, tinkers, tax-collectors in markets,
Masons, miners, many other craftsmen.
Of all living laborers there leapt forth some,
Such as diggers of ditches that do their jobs badly,
And dawdle away the long day with *"Dieu save dame Emme."*[2]   225
Cooks and their kitchen-boys kept crying, "Hot pies, hot!
Good geese and pork! Let's go and dine!"
Tavern-keepers told them a tale of the same sort:
"White wine of Alsace and wine of Gascony,
Of the Rhine and of La Rochelle, to wash the roast down with."   230
All this I saw sleeping, and seven times more.

---

7. Eccl. 10:16.
8. *Coifs*: Silk scarves were a lawyer's badge of office. *Law-sergeants*: important lawyers.
9. *Impounded*: detained in legal custody. *Pennies*: fairly valuable coins in medieval England (Gloss).
1. Town-dwellers who had full rights as the citizens of a municipality (Gloss). In contrast, barons were members of the higher aristocracy, and bondmen were peasants who held their land from a lord in return for customary services or rent.
2. "God save Dame Emma": presumably a popular song.

Passus I

What this montaigne bymeneth, and the merke dale,
And the felde ful of folke I shal yow faire schewe.
A loveli ladi of lere, in lynnen y-clothed,
Come down fram [the] castel and called me faire
5   And seide, "Sone, slepestow? Sestow this poeple,
How bisi thei ben abouten the mase?
The moste partie of this poeple that passeth on this erthe,
Have thei worschip in this worlde, thei wilne no better:
Of other hevene than here holde thei no tale."
10 I was aferd of her face, theigh she faire were,
And seide, "Mercy, madame, what [may] this [bymene]?"
"The toure up the toft," quod she, "Treuthe is thereinne,
And wolde that ye wroughte as his worde techeth.
For he is fader of feith, fourmed yow alle
15 Bothe with fel and with face, and yaf yow fyve wittis
Forto worschip hym therwith the while that ye ben here.
And therfore he hyghte the erthe to help yow uchone
Of wollen, of lynnen, of lyflode at nede,
In mesurable manere to make yow at ese;
20 And comaunded of his curteisye in comune three thinges:
Arne none nedful but tho, and nempne hem I thinke
And rekne hem bi resoun—reherce thow hem after.
That one is vesture from chele the to save;
[That other is] mete atte mele for myseise of thiselve,
25 And drynke whan thow dryest—ac do nought out of resoun
That thow worth the werse whan thow worche shuldest.
For Loth in his lifdayes for likyng of drynke
Dede bi his doughtres that the Devel lyked,
Delited hym in drynke as the Devel wolde,
30 And lecherye hym laught and lay bi hem bothe,
And al he witt it wyn, that wikked dede.
        Inebriamus eum vino, dormiamusque cum eo,
            Ut servare possimus de patre nostro semen.
Thorw wyn and thorw women there was Loth acombred
And there gat in glotonye gerlis that were cherlis.
Forthi drede delitable drynke and thow shalt do the bettere:
35 Mesure is medcyne though thow moche yerne.
It is naught al gode to the goste that the gutte axeth
Ne liflode to thi likam [that leef is to thi soule.
Lef naught thi likam] for a lyer him techeth:
That is the wrecched worlde wolde the bitraye;
40 For the Fende and thi flesch folweth togidere,
And that [shendeth] thi soule: [sette] it in thin herte,

Passus† I

What this mountain means, and the murky dale,
And the field full of folk I shall clearly tell you.
A lady lovely of look, in linen clothes,
Came down from the castle and called me gently,
And said, "Son, are you asleep? Do you see these people,   5
How busy they're being about the maze?
The greatest part of the people that pass over this earth,
If they have well-being in this world, they want nothing more:
For any heaven other than here they have no thought."
I was afraid of her face, fair though she was,   10
And said, "Mercy, madam, what may this mean?"
"The tower on the hill-top," she said, "Truth¹ is within it,
And would have you behave as his words teach.
For he is father of faith, formed you all
Both with skin and with skull, and assigned you five senses   15
To worship him with while you are here.
And therefore he ordered the earth to help each one of you
With woolens, with linens, with livelihood at need,
In a moderate manner to make you at ease;
And of his kindness declared three things common to all: 20
None are necessary but these, and now I will name them
And rank them in their right order—you repeat them after.
The first is vesture to defend you from the cold;
The second is food at fit times to fend off hunger,
And drink when you're dry—but don't drink beyond reason   25
Or you will be the worse for it when you've work to do.
For Lot in his lifetime because he liked drink
Did with his daughters what the Devil found pleasing,
Took delight in drink as the Devil wished,
And lechery laid hold on him and he lay with them both,   30
Blamed it all on the wine's working, that wicked deed.
　　Let us make him drunk with wine, and let us lie with him,
　　　*that we may preserve seed of our father.*²
By wine and by women there Lot was overcome
And there begot in gluttony graceless brats.
Therefore dread delicious drink and you'll do the better:
Moderation is medicine no matter how you yearn.   35
It's not all good for your ghost³ that your gut wants
Nor of benefit to your body that's a blessing to your soul.
Don't believe your body for it does the bidding of a liar:
That is this wretched world that wants to betray you;
For the Fiend and your flesh both conform to it,   40
And that besmirches your soul: set this in your heart,

---

† *Passus*—Latin "step"—is the word the poet uses for the sections of his poem, which is conceived as a journey or pilgrimage.
1. Langland plays on three meanings of the term "Truth": (1) fidelity, integrity—as in modern "troth"; (2) reality, actuality, conformity with what is; (3) God, the ultimate truth; see Gloss.
2. Gen. 19:32.
3. Spirit.

And for thow sholdest ben ywar I wisse the the beste."
　　"[A], madame, mercy," quod I, "me liketh wel yowre wordes.
Ac the moneye [on] this molde that men so faste holdeth,
45 Telle me to whom that tresore appendeth?"
"Go to the Gospel," quod she, "that God seide hymselven
Tho the poeple hym apposed with a peny in the temple
Whether thei shulde [worship therwith Sesar the kyng].
And [he] axed of hem of whome spake the lettre
50 'And the ymage ilyke that thereinne stondeth?'
'Caesaris,' thei seide, 'we sen hym wel uchone.'
'Reddite Caesari,' quod God, 'that Caesari bifalleth,
Et que sunt Dei Deo, or elles ye done ille.'
For [rightfulliche] Reson shulde rewle yow alle,
55 And Kynde Witte be wardeyne yowre welthe to kepe
And tutour of youre tresore and take it yow at nede,
For housbonderye and [he] holden togideres."
　　Thanne I frained hir faire, for Hym that hir made,
"[The] dongeoun in the dale that dredful is of sighte,
60 What may it be to mene, madame, I yow biseche?"
"That is the Castel of Care: whoso cometh therinne
May banne that he borne was to body or to soule.
Therinne wonieth a wighte that Wronge is y-hote,
Fader of falshed, [he] founded it hymselve.
65 Adam and Eve he egged to ille,
Conseilled Caym to kullen his brother;
Judas he japed with Juwen silver,
And sithen on an eller honged hym after.
He is letter of love, and lyeth hem alle;
70 That trusten on his tresor [bitrayed are] sonnest."
　　Thanne had I wonder in my witt what womman it were
That such wise wordes of Holy Writ shewed,
And [hailsed] hir on the hieghe name, ar heo thennes yeode,
What she were witterli that wissed me so faire.
75 "Holi Cherche I am," quod she, "thow oughtest me to knowe:
I underfonge the firste and the feyth [the] taughte.
[Thow] broughtest me borwes my biddyng to fulfille,
And to love me lelly the while thi lyf dureth."
Thanne I [kneled] on my knees and cryed hir of grace,
80 And preyed hir pitousely prey for my synnes,
And also kenne me kyndeli on Criste to bileve,

And so that you should yourself be wary I'm giving this advice."
"Ah, madam, mercy," said I, "your words much please me.
But the money minted on earth that men are so greedy for,
Tell me to whom that treasure belongs?"   45
"Go to the Gospel," she said, "that God himself spoke
When the people approached him with a penny* in the temple
And asked whether they should worship⁴ with it Caesar the king.
And he asked them to whom the inscription referred
'And the image also that is on the coin?'   50
'*Caesaris*,'⁵ they said, 'we can all see it clearly.'
'*Reddite Caesari*,' said God, 'what *Caesari* belongs,⁶
And *quae sunt Dei Deo*, or else you do wrong.'
For rightfully Reason⁷ should rule you all,
And Kind Wit* be keeper to take care of your wealth   55
And be guardian of your gold to give it out when you need it,
For economy⁸ and he are of one accord."
    Then I questioned her courteously, in the Creator's name,
"The dungeon in the dale that's dreadful to see,
What may it mean, madam, I beseech you?"   60
"That is the Castle of Care: whoever comes into it
Will be sorry he was ever born with body and soul.
The captain of the castle is called Wrong,
Father of falsehood, he founded it himself.
Adam and Eve he egged to evil,   65
Counseled Cain to kill his brother;
He made a joke out of Judas with Jewish silver,⁹
And afterwards on an elder tree hanged him high.
He's a molester of love, lies to every one;
Those who trust in his treasure are betrayed soonest."   70
    Then I wondered in my wits what woman it might be
Who could show from Holy Scripture such wise words,
And I conjured her in the high name, ere she went away,
To say who she really was that taught me so well.
"I am Holy Church," she said, "you ought to know me: 75
I befriended you first and taught the faith to you.
You gave me gages¹ to be guided by my teaching
And to love me loyally while your life lasts."
Then kneeling on my knees I renewed my plea for grace,
Prayed piteously to her to pray for my sins,   80
And advise me how I might find natural faith² in Christ,

4. "Worship" in Middle English often means religious celebration, but the worship of God is only one instance of showing the appropriate honor and respect to someone or something; the word can therefore be used about objects other than God.
5. Caesar's.
6. "Render unto Caesar"; "to Caesar." In the next line the Latin clause means "What are God's unto God." See Matt. 22:15–21.
7. Langland distinguishes the role of reason, as the distinctive human capacity to reach truth by discursive reasoning, from the functions of a number of other related mental processes and sources of truth (for example, from Kind Wit in the next line); see Gloss.
8. I.e., prudent management.
9. For the fall of Adam and Eve, see Gen. 3; for Cain's murder of Abel, see Gen. 4. In the next lines, for Judas' betrayal of Jesus, see Matt. 26:14–16; for his death (line 68), see Matt. 27:3–6.
1. I.e., pledges (at baptism).
2. The root Middle English phrase for this state is "kynde knowynge": see Gloss under "kind." Cf. lines 138–68 below.

That I mighte worchen his wille that wroughte me to man.
"Teche me to no tresore, but telle me this ilke,
How I may save my soule, that seynt art y-holden?"
85   "Whan alle tresores aren tried, Trewthe is the best.
I do it on *Deus Caritas* to deme the sothe.
It is as derworth a drewery as dere God hymselven.
[For] whoso is trewe of his tonge, telleth none other,
And doth the werkis therwith, and wilneth no man ille,
90   He is a god bi the Gospel, agrounde and aloft,
And also ylike to owre Lorde bi Seynte Lukes wordes.
The clerkes that knoweth this shulde kenne it aboute,
For Cristene and uncristne clameth it uchone.
Kynges and knightes shulde kepe it bi resoun,
95   Riden and rappe down in reumes aboute,
And taken *transgressores* and tyen hem faste
Til Treuthe had y-termyned her trespas to the ende.
[For David in his dayes dubbed knightes
And did hem swere on here swerde to serve Trewthe evere.]
100   That is the professioun appertly that appendeth for knyghtes,
And nought to fasten a Fryday in fyve score wynter,
But holden with him and with hir that [asken the] treuthe,
And never leve hem for love ne for lacchyng of [yiftes],
And whoso [passeth] that poynte [is] apostata in [his] ordre.
105   [And] Criste, kingene kynge, knighted ten,
Cherubyn and seraphin, suche sevene and anothre;
Yaf hem myghte in his majesté—the murger hem thoughte—
And over his mene meyné made hem archangeles,
Taughte hem bi the Trinitee Treuthe to knowe,
110   To be buxome at his biddyng—he bad hem noughte elles.
Lucifer with legiounes lerned it in Hevene,
[And was the lovelokest of lighte after owre Lorde
Til] he brake buxumnesse—his blisse gan he tyne
And fel fro that felawship in a fendes liknes
115   Into a depe derke helle, to dwelle there forevre,
And mo thowsandes with him than man couthe noumbre,
Lopen out with Lucifer in lothelich forme,
For thei leveden upon [Lucifer] that lyed in this manere:
Ponam pedem in aquilone et similis ero altissimo.
120   And alle that hoped it mighte be so, none Hevene mighte hem holde,
But fellen out in fendes liknesse [ful] nyne dayes togideres,
Til God of his goodnesse gan [garte the Hevene to stekye],
And [stable and stynte], and stonden in quiete.

That I might obey the command of him who made me man.
"Teach me of no treasure, but tell me this one thing,
How I may save my soul, sacred as you are?"
"When all treasures are tried, Truth* is the best.   85
I call on *Deus caritas*[3] to declare the truth.
It's as glorious a love-gift as dear God himself.
For whoever is true of his tongue, tells nothing untrue,
Does his work with truth, wishes no man ill,
He is a god by the Gospel, on ground and aloft,   90
And also like our Lord by Saint Luke's words.[4]
Clerks who've been taught this text should tell it all about,
For Christians and non-Christians lay claim to it both.
To keep truth kings and knights are required by reason,*
And to ride out in realms about and beat down wrong-doers,   95
Take *transgressores*[5] and tie them up tight
Until Truth has determined their trespass in full.
For David in his days when he dubbed knights[6]
Made them swear on their swords to serve Truth forever.
That is plainly the profession that's appropriate for knights,   100
And not to fast one Friday in five score winters,
But to hold with him and with her who ask for truth,
And never leave them for love nor through a liking for presents,
And whoever passes that point is an apostate to his order.
    For Christ, King of Kings, created ten orders,[7]   105
Cherubim and seraphim, seven such and another;
Gave them might* in his majesty—the merrier they thought it—
And over his household he made them archangels,
Taught them through the Trinity how Truth may be known,
And to be obedient to his bidding—he bade nothing else.   110
Lucifer with his legions learned this in Heaven,
And he was the loveliest of light after our Lord
Till he broke obedience—his bliss was lost to him
And he fell from that fellowship in a fiend's likeness
Into a deep dark hell, to dwell there forever,   115
And more thousands went out with him than any one could count,
Leaping out with Lucifer in loathly shapes,
Because they believed Lucifer who lied in this way:
I shall set my foot in the north and I shall be like the most high.[8]
And all that hoped it might be so, no Heaven could hold them,   120
But they fell out in fiend's likeness fully nine days together,
Till God of his goodness granted that Heaven settle,
Become stationary and stable, and stand in quiet.

3. "God [is] love": 1 John 4:8.
4. Not Luke, but see 1 John 4:16 and cf. Ps. 81:6. See, however, related ideas in Luke 18:18 and 6:35.
   The phrase "a god by the Gospel" is Langland's; what he means by it will be a recurrent theme.
5. Transgressors: the Latin word appears at Isa. 53:12.
6. Behind the idea that King David created knighthood probably lies his selection of officers for his
   army (1 Chron. 12:18) translated into chivalric terms; like other heroes, he was typically portrayed
   in the Middle Ages as a chivalric figure, just as God's creation of the angels, below, is pictured in
   terms of a medieval aristocratic household.
7. I.e., ten orders of heavenly beings: seraphim, cherubim, thrones, dominions, virtues, powers, prin-
   cipalities, archangels, angels, and the nameless order that fell with Lucifer.
8. Cf. Isa. 14:13–14, which has "throne" (*sedem*) where Langland has "foot" (*pedem*).

Whan thise wikked went out wonderwise thei fellen,
125 Somme in eyre, somme in erthe, and somme in helle depe,
Ac Lucifer lowest lith of hem alle.
For pryde that he pult out his peyne hath none ende.
And alle that worche with wronge wenden hij shulle
After her deth-day and dwelle with that shrewe.
130 Ac tho that worche wel, as holi writt telleth,
And enden, as I ere seide, in Treuthe that is the best
Mowe be siker that her soule shal wende to Hevene
Ther Treuthe is in Trinitee, and troneth hem alle.
Forthi I sey as I seide ere, bi sighte of thise textis
135 Whan alle tresores arne y-tried, Treuthe is the beste.
Lereth it this lewde men, for lettred men it knowen,
That Treuthe is tresore the triest on erthe."
    "Yet have I no kynde knowing," quod I, "yet mote ye kenne me
        better
By what craft in my corps it comseth and where."
140 "Thow doted daffe," quod she "dulle arne thi wittes:
To litel Latyn thow lernedest, lede, in thi youthe.
        Heu michi, quia sterilem   duxi vitam juvenilem.
It is a kynde knowyng that kenneth in thine herte
For to lovye thi Lorde lever than thiselve,
No dedly synne to do, dey though thow sholdest.
145 This I trowe be treuthe: who can teche the better,
Loke thow suffre hym to sey, and sithen lere it after.
For thus witnesseth his worde: worcheth thow thereafter.
For Trewthe telleth that love is triacle of Hevene.
May no synne be on him sene that useth that spise.
150 And alle his werkes he wroughte with love as him liste;
And lered it Moises for the levest thing, and moste like to
        Hevene,
And also the plente of pees, moste precious of vertues.
For Hevene myghte noughte holden it, [so hevy it semed],
Tyl it hadde of the erthe yeten [itselve].
155 And whan it haved of this folde flessh and blode taken,
Was nevere leef upon lynde lighter therafter,
And portatyf and persant as the poynt of a nedle
That myghte non armure it lette, ne none heigh walles.
Forthi is Love leder of the Lordes folke of Hevene,
160 And a mene as the maire is bitwene the [comune] and the [kyng].
Right so is Love a ledere and the lawe shapeth
Upon man for his mysdedes—the merciment he taxeth.
And for to knowe it kyndely, it comseth bi myght,
And in the herte there is the hevede, and the heigh welle.
165 For in kynde knowynge in herte there [comseth] a myghte,
And that falleth to the Fader that formed us alle,
Loked on us with love and lete his sone deye

When these wicked ones went out they fell in wondrous wise,
Some in air, some on earth, some deep in hell,   125
But Lucifer lies lowest of them all.
For pride that puffed him up his pain has no end.
And all that work with wrong will surely make their way
After their death-day to dwell with that wretch.
But those who wish to work well, as holy words direct,   130
And who end, as I said earlier, in Truth that is the best
May be certain that their souls will ascend to Heaven
Where Truth is in Trinity, bestowing thrones on all who come.
Therefore I say as I said before, by the sense of these texts
When all treasures are tried, Truth is the best.   135
Let unlearned men be taught this, for learned men know it,
That Truth is the trustiest treasure on earth."
    "Yet I've no natural knowledge,"[9] said I, "you must teach me more
        clearly
Through what force faith is formed in my body and where."
"You doting dolt," said she, "dull are your wits: 140
Too little Latin you learned, lad, in your youth.
    Alas, I repine   for a barren youth was mine.[1]
It's a natural knowledge that's nurtured in your heart
To love your Lord more dearly than you love yourself,
To do no deadly sin though you should die for it.
This I trust is truth: whoever can teach you better,   145
Look to it that you let him speak, and learn it after.
For thus his word witnesses: do your work accordingly.
For Truth tells us that love is the trustiest medicine in Heaven.
No sin may be seen on him by whom that spice is used.
And all the deeds he[2] pleased to do were done with love;   150
And he taught it to Moses as a matchless thing, and most like
        Heaven,
And also the plant of peace, most precious of virtues.
For Heaven might not hold it,[3] so heavy it seemed,
Till it had with earth alloyed itself.
And when it had of this earth taken flesh and blood,   155
Never was leaf upon linden lighter thereafter,
And portable and piercing as the point of a needle:
No armor might obstruct it, nor any high walls.
Therefore Love is leader of the Lord's people in Heaven,
And an intermediary as the mayor is between community and king.   160
Just so Love is a leader by whom the law's enforced
Upon man for his misdeeds—he measures the fine.
And to know this naturally, it's nourished by a power
That has its head in the heart, and its high source.
For a natural knowledge* in the heart is nourished by a power   165
That's let fall by the Father who formed us all,
Looked on us with love and let his son die

---

9. Instinctive or experiential knowledge; Langland's phrase, a recurrent and important one, is "kynde knowynge"; see Gloss under "kind."
1. Proverbial.
2. I.e., Truth.
3. I.e., love, which, as the passage goes on, becomes embodied in Christ.

Mekely for owre mysdedes, to amende us alle.
And yet wolde he hem no woo that wroughte hym that peyne,
170 But mekelich with mouthe mercy he bisoughte—
To have pité of that poeple that peyned hym to deth.
Here myghtow see ensamples in hymselve one,
That he was mightful and meke, and mercy gan graunte
To hem that hongen him an heigh and his herte thirled.
175   Forthi I rede [the] riche haveth reuthe [on] the povere:
Though ye be [myghty] to mote, beth meke in yowre werkes,
For the same [mesure] that ye mete, amys other elles,
Ye shullen ben weyen therwyth whan ye wende hennes.
    Eadem mensura qua mensi fueritis remecietur
        vobis.
For though ye be trewe of yowre tonge and trewliche wynne
180 And as chaste as a childe that in cherche wepeth,
But if ye loven lelliche and lene the poure
[Of] such goed as God yow sent godelich parteth,
Ye ne have na more meryte in Masse ne in Houres
Than Malkyn of hire maydenhode that no man desireth.
185 For James the gentil [joigned] in his bokes
That faith withoute the faite is [feblere than nought],
And as ded as a [dorenayle] but yif the [dede] folwe.
    Fides sine operibus mortua est.
Chastité withoute charité worth cheyned in helle!
It is as lewed as a laumpe that no lighte is inne.
190 Many chapeleynes arne chaste, ac charité is awey.
Aren [none hardere] than hij whan thei ben avaunced—
Unkynde to her kyn and to alle Cristene,
Chewen here charité and chiden after more—
Such chastité withouten charité worth cheyned in helle!
195 [Ye] curatoures [that] kepen [yow] clene of [yowre body],
[Ye] ben acombred with coveitise—[ye] konne nought [out crepe],
So harde hath Avarice y-hasped [yow] togideres.
That is no treuthe of the Trinité but treccherye of helle:
And lernyng to lewde men the latter for to dele,
200 [For] this wordes ben wryten in the [Evangelye]:
Date et dabitur vobis, for I dele yow alle.
That is the lokke of love [that] lateth oute my grace
To conforte the careful acombred with synne.
Love is leche of Lyf, and nexte owre Lorde selve,
205 And also the graith gate that goth into Hevene.

Meekly for our misdeeds, to amend us all.
Yet he⁴ did not ask harm on those who hurt him so badly,
But with his mouth meekly made a prayer for mercy—   170
For pity for those people who so painfully killed him.
Here you may see examples in himself alone,
How he was mighty* and meek, and bade mercy be granted
To those who hanged him high and pierced his heart.
    Therefore I implore rich persons to have pity on the poor: 175
Though you're mighty men at law, be meek in your deeds,
For the same measure you mete out, amiss or otherwise,
You shall be weighed with it when you go hence.
    *With the same measure that ye mete it shall be measured to you
        again.*⁵
For though you are true of your tongue and truly earn your profits
And are as chaste as a child crying at a church service,   180
Unless you really love and relieve the poor
And share in a goodly way such goods as God sends you,
You have no more merit in Mass nor in Hours*
Than Malkin for her maidenhead that no man desires.⁶
For James the gentle⁷ enjoined in his books   185
That faith without works is worse than nothing,
And as dead as a doornail unless the deed goes with it.
    *Faith without works is dead.*⁸
Let chastity without charity be chained in hell!
It's as lifeless as a lamp that has no light in it.
Many chaplains are chaste, but their charity is missing.   190
None are harder of heart than they are when they're promoted—
Unkind to their kin and to all Christian people,
Chew up their charity and chide for more—
May such chastity without charity be chained in hell!
You curates who keep yourselves clean of your bodies,   195
You're encumbered with covetousness—you can't escape it,
So hard has Avarice hasped you together.
That's no truth of the Trinity but treachery of hell:
And a lesson to unlearned men to delay their alms-giving,
For in the Evangel we find these very words: 200
*Date et dabitur vobis,*⁹ for I endow you all.
That is the love-latch that lets my grace out
To comfort the care-worn overcome with sin.
Love is Life's doctor,* and next¹ our Lord himself,
And also the strait² street that goes straight to Heaven.   205

4. I.e., Christ, not the Father as in the sentence before. In such slippery transitions from one subject to another, Langland takes advantage of the greater flexibility of Middle English syntax; and usually, as here, the transition reflects an important connection of ideas, in this case the relationship between God's action and Christ's.
5. Luke 6:38.
6. Malkin: traditionally a name for a slut, here for a woman who would be a slut if she could but who is still a virgin only because she is too undesirable.
7. "Gentil" in Middle English kept the connection between gentle qualities and the ideals associated with the chivalric or "gentle" class (Gloss).
8. Jas. 2:26.
9. "Give and it shall be given unto you": Luke 6:38.
1. Next to.
2. I.e., narrow; see Matt. 7:13–14.

Forthi I sey as I seide ere, by [sighte of thise] textis,
Whan alle tresores ben y-tryed, Treuthe is the beste.
Now have I tolde the what Treuthe is—that no tresore is bettere—
I may no lenger lenge the with: now loke the owre Lord."

Passus II

Yet I [kneled] on my knees and cryed hir of grace
And seide, "Mercy, madame, for Marie love of hevene,
That bar [the] blisful barne that boughte us on the Rode,
Kenne me bi somme crafte to knowe the fals."
5 "Loke uppon thi left half, and lo, where he standeth,
Bothe Fals and Favel and here feres manye."
I loked on my left half as the lady me taughte
And was war of a womman [wonderli] y-clothed.
Purfiled with pelure, the fynest upon erthe;
10 Y-crounede with a corone—the kyng hath non better.
Fetislich hir fyngres were fretted with golde wyre,
And thereon [riche] rubyes, as red as any glede,
And diamantz of derrest pris, and double manere
     safferes,
Orientales and ewages envenymes to destroye.
15 Hire robe was ful riche, of red scarlet engreyned,
With ribanes of red golde and of riche stones.
Hire arraye me ravysshed—suche ricchesse saw I nevere.
I had wondre what she was and whas wyf she were.
  "What is this womman," quod I, "so worthily atired?"
20 "That is Mede the mayde, hath noyed me ful oft
And y-lakked my lemman—that Lewté is hoten—
And bilowen [hym] to lordes that lawes han to kepe.
In the Popis paleys she is pryvé as myself,
But Sothenesse othenesse wolde nought so, for she is a bastarde,
25 For fals was hire fader—that hath a fykel tonge
And nevere sothe seide sithen he come to erthe.
And Mede is manered after hym, as [men of] kynde [carpeth]:
     Qualis pater talis filius. Bona arbor bonum fructum facit.
I aughte ben herre than she: I cam of a better.
Mi fader the grete God is, and grounde of alle graces,
30 O God withoute gynnynge, and I his gode doughter,

Therefore I say as I said before, by the sense of these texts,
When all treasures are tried, Truth is the best.
Now that I've told you what Truth is—there's no treasure better—
I may delay no longer now: our Lord look after you."

Passus II

Still kneeling on my knees I renewed my plea for grace
And said, "Mercy, madam, for Mary's love in heaven,
Who bore the blissful babe that bought[1] us on the Cross,
Teach me some talent to distinguish the false."
"Look on your left side, and lo, where he stands,   5
Both False and Favel[2] and lots of fellows of theirs."
I looked on my left side as the lady told me
And was aware of a woman wonderfully dressed.
Her gown was faced with fur, the finest on earth;
Crowned with a coronet—the king has none better.   10
Her fingers were filigreed fancifully with gold,
And rich rubies on them, as red as hot coals,
And diamonds most dear of cost, and two different kinds of
      sapphires,
Pearls and precious water-stones[3] to repel poisons.
Her robe was most rich, dyed with red-scarlet,[4]   15
With ribbons of red gold and with rich stones.
Her array ravished me—I'd seen such riches nowhere.
I wondered who she was and whose wife she might be.
    "Who is this woman," said I, "so worthily attired?"
"That is Meed[5] the maid who has harmed me very often   20
And maligned my lover—Lewté* is his name—
And has told lords who enforce laws lies about him.
In the Pope's palace she's as privileged as I am,
But Soothness[6] would not have it so, for she is a bastard,
And her father was false—he has a fickle tongue   25
And never told the truth since the time he came to earth.
And Meed has manners like his, as men say is natural:
    Like father, like son. A good tree brings forth good fruit.[7]
I ought to be higher than she: I came of better parentage.
My father is the great God, the giver of all graces,
One God without beginning, and I'm his good daughter,   30

---

1. Redeemed.
2. "Lying"; it is the name of characters representing deceit in Old French literature, but also occurs as an actual English proper name.
3. Water-sapphires, not the same as sapphire itself, but often used as a jewel. Medieval lapidaries attributed specific healing powers to many precious stones.
4. A fine, rich cloth, not necessarily always dyed red, so the phrase is not redundant; "red" in the next line is a traditional intensifier in the expression "red-gold," where it means "rich, bright," rather than the color red. Her robe and rubies might recall the scarlet woman of Rev. 17.
5. "Reward, recompense, the profit motive": The range of contradictory meanings, positive and negative, the term can involve (such as bribery, gift, just compensation, and heavenly salvation) emerges as the scene advances; how Meed should be defined will be a prime subject of Passus II–IV (Gloss). Cf. p. 485.
6. Truth, truthfulness, fidelity.
7. The first phrase is proverbial; the second, from Matt. 7:17.

And hath yove me Mercy to marye with myself,
And what man be merciful and lelly me love
Shal be my lorde and I his leef, in the heighe Hevene;
And what man taketh Mede—myne hed dar I legge—
35 That he shal lese for hir love a [lompe] of *caritatis*.
How construeth David the kynge of men that [caccheth] mede
And men of this molde that meynteneth treuthe,
And how ye shal save yowself? The Sauter bereth witnesse:
Domine, quis habitabit in tabernaculo tuo? etc.
40 And now worth this Mede y-maried al to a mansed schrewe,
To one Fals Fikel-Tonge—a fendes biyete.
Favel thorw his faire speche hath this folke enchaunted,
And al is Lyeres ledyng that [lady] is thus y-wedded.
Tomorwe worth y-made the maydenes bruydale;
45 There mighte thow wite if thow wolt which thei ben alle
That longeth to that lordeship, the lasse and the more.
Knowe hem there if thow canst, and kepe [the from hem alle],
And lakke hem nought but lat hem worth til Lewté be justice
And have powere to punyschen hem—thanne put forth thi resoun.
Now I bikenne the Criste," quod she, "and his clene
50   moder,
And lat no conscience acombre the for coveitise of Mede."
   Thus left me that lady liggyng aslepe,
And how Mede was y-maried in meteles me thoughte—
That alle the riche retenauns that regneth with False
55 Were boden to the bridale on bothe two sydes,
Of alle maner of men, the mene and the riche;
To marie this maydene was many man assembled,
As of knightes and of clerkis and other comune poeple,
As sysours and sompnours, shireves and here clerkes,
60 Bedelles and baillives and brokoures of chaffre,
Forgoeres and vitaillers and vokates of the Arches—
I can nought rekene the route that ran aboute Mede.
Ac Symonye and Cyvile and sisoures of courtes
Were moste pryvé with Mede of any men, me thoughte.
65 Ac Favel was the first that fette hire out of boure
And as a brokour broughte hir to be with Fals enjoigned.

And he's granted me that I might marry Mercy as my own,
And any man who's merciful and loves me truly
Shall be my lord and I his love, aloft in Heaven;
And the man who takes Meed—I'll bet my head on it—
Shall lose for her love a lump of *caritatis*.[8]   35
What does David the King declare of men that crave meed
And of the others on earth who uphold truth,
And how you shall save yourselves? The Psalter[9] bears witness:
Lord, who shall dwell in thy tabernacle? etc.
And now this Meed is being married to a most accursed wretch,   40
To one False Fickle-Tongue—a fiend begot him.
Favel through his fair speech has these folk under enchantment,
And it's all by Liar's leadership that this lady is thus wedded.
Tomorrow will be made the maiden's bridal;
If you wish you may witness there who they all are   45
That belong to that lordship, the lesser and the greater.
Acquaint yourself with them if you can, and keep clear of them all,
And don't malign them but let them be until Lewté* becomes justice
And has power to punish them—then put forth your evidence.
Now I commend you to Christ," said she, "and to Christ's pure
     mother,   50
And don't let your conscience be overcome by coveting Meed."
   Thus that lady left me lying asleep,
And how Meed was married was shown me in a dream—
How all the rich retinue that rule with False
Were bidden to the bridal for both sides of the match,   55
Of all manner of men, the moneyless and the rich;
To marry off this maiden many men were assembled,
Including knights and clerks and other common people,
Such as assizers* and summoners,* sheriffs and their clerks,
Beadles and bailiffs and brokers of merchandise,   60
Harbingers and hostelers and advocates of the Arches[1]—
I can't reckon the rabble that ran about Meed.
But Simony and Civil[2] and assizers of courts
Were most intimate with Meed of any men, I thought.
But Favel was the first that fetched her from her bedroom   65
And like a broker brought her to be joined to False.

---

8. *Lump*: the word had in Middle English the same down-to-earth connotations as in modern English.
   Of "caritatis": "Of love"; Langland plays on the difference between two aspects of love: desire and
   "charity," disinterested love. To speak of measuring love by the lump is characteristic of Langland's
   shifting registers of language, which force, sometimes startlingly, a sharpened awareness of words
   and their meanings where familiarity has obscured them.
9. The Book of Psalms, or a separate volume containing them. They were collectively attributed to
   King David. The next line is from Ps. 14:1.
1. All these are officials whose functions made them particularly open to bribery. Assizers were
   members of the assize or inquest that was the ancestor of the modern jury ("assizers of courts" in
   line 63); summoners were the officials who served summonses to the ecclesiastical courts; sheriffs
   were the king's chief administrators in each shire; beadles were manorial officials who summoned
   to court and collected fines; bailiffs were the chief representatives of the lords of the manor;
   harbingers were responsible for requisitioning on the spot, on the king's behalf, materials and
   labor needed for such projects as building. "The Arches": The Archbishop of Canterbury's court
   in London, Bow Street.
2. *Simony*: buying and selling the functions, spiritual powers, or offices of the Church (Gloss). *Civil*:
   i.e., civil (as opposed to criminal) law, especially noted for its bribery and corruption in the later
   Middle Ages (Gloss). Cf. p. 443.

Whan Symonye and Cyvile seigh here beire wille
Thei assented for silver to sei as bothe wolde.
Thanne lepe Lyer forth and seide, "Lo, here a chartre
70 That Gyle with his gret othes gaf hem togidere."
And preide Cyvile to se and Symonye to rede it.
Symonye and Cyvile stonden forth bothe
And unfoldeth the feffement that Fals hath y-maked;
Thus bigynneth thes gomes to greden ful heigh:
    Sciant presentes et futuri, etc.
75 "Witeth and witnesseth that wonieth upon this erthe
That Mede is y-maried more for here goodis
Than for ani vertue or fairenesse or any free kynde.
Falsenesse is faine of hire for he wote hire riche,
And Favel with his fikel speche feffeth bi this chartre
80 To be prynces in pryde and Poverté to dispise,
To bakbite and to bosten and bere fals witnesse,
To scorne and to scolde and sclaundere to make,
Unboxome and bolde to breke the Ten Hestes;
And the Erldome of Envye and [Yre] togideres,
85 With the Chastelet of Chest and Chateryng oute of resoun,
The Counté of Coveitise and alle the costes aboute,
That is Usuré and Avarice—alle I hem graunte
In bargaines and in brokages with al the Borghe of Theft,
[With] al the lordeship of Lecherye in lenthe and in brede,
90 As in werkes and in wordes and waitynges with eies,
And in [wenes] and in wisshynges and with ydel thoughtes,
There as wille wolde and werkmanship failleth."
Glotonye he gaf hem eke and grete othes togydere,
And alday to drynke at dyverse tavernes,
95 And there to jangle and to jape, and jugge here evene-Cristene;
And in fastyngdayes to frete ar ful tyme were,
And thanne to sitten and soupen til slepe hem assaille,
And bredun as burgh-swyn, and bedden hem esily,
Tyl sleuth and slepe slyken [here] sides;
100 And thanne Wanhope to awake [hem] so, with no wille to amende,
For he leveth be lost—this is here last ende.
"And thei to have and to holde and here ieyres after
A dwellyng with the Devel, and dampned be forevre,
With al the purtenaunces of Purgatorie, into the pyne of helle,
105 Yeldyng for this thinge at one yeres ende
Here soules to Sathan, to suffre with hym peynes,
And with him to wonye [in] wo whil God is in Hevene."
In witnesse of which thing Wronge was the first,

When Simony and Civil saw the couple's wish
They assented for silver to say as both wanted.
Then Liar leaped forth and said, "Lo, here's a charter
That Guile with his great oaths has given them jointly."   70
And he prayed Simony to inspect it and Civil to read it.
Simony and Civil both stand forth
And unfold the conveyance that False has made;
Then these characters commence to cry on high:
    Let men now living and those to come after know, etc.[3]
"Let all who are on earth hear and bear witness   75
That Meed is married more for her property
Than for any goodness or grace or any goodly parentage.
Falseness fancies her for he knows she's rich,
And Favel with his fickle speech enfeoffs[4] them by this charter
That they may be princes in pride and despise Poverty,   80
Backbite and boast and bear false witness,
Scorn and scold and speak slander,
Disobedient and bold break the Ten Commandments;
And the Earldom of Envy and Ire together,
With the Castelet[5] of Quarreling and uncurbed Gossip,   85
The County of Covetousness and the countryside about,
That is Usury and Avarice—all I grant them
In bargainings and brokerings with the Borough of Theft,
With all the Lordship of Lechery in length and in breadth,
As in works and in words and with watching of eyes,   90
And in wild wishes and fantasies and with idle thoughts,
When to do what their wills would they want[6] the strength."
Gluttony he gave them too and great oaths together,
And to drink all day at diverse taverns,
And to jabber there and joke, and judge their fellow-Christians;   95
And to gobble food on fasting days before the fitting[7] time,
And then to sit supping till sleep assails them,
And grow portly as town-pigs, and repose in soft beds,
Till sloth and sleep sleek their sides;
And then they'll wake up with Wanhope,[8] with no wish to amend,   100
For he believes he's lost—this is their last fortune.
"And they to have and to hold and their heirs after them
A dwelling with the Devil, and be damned forever,
With all the appurtenances of Purgatory, into the pain of hell,
Yielding for this thing at some year's end   105
Their souls to Satan, to suffer pain with him,
And to live with him in woe while God is in Heaven."
To witness which thing Wrong was the first,

---

3. The formula for the beginning of a charter, or a "conveyance," a common legal document, often
   conveying rights or property.
4. I.e., he grants them territory as a feudal lord does, not as an outright gift but specifically to be
   held by them as his liegemen, in return for military and other service.
5. I.e., little castle.
6. Lack.
7. Fasts required abstinence from certain foods for specified periods of time. Some fasts ended in
   midafternoon.
8. Despair, considered the ultimate development of sloth (Gloss).

And Pieres the pardonere of Paulynes doctrine,
110 Bette the bedel of Bokynghamshire,
Rainalde the reve of Rotland sokene,
Munde the mellere and many moo other.
"In the date of the Devel this dede [is asseled]
Bi sighte of Sire Symonye and Cyvyles leve."
115   Thenne tened hym Theologye whan he this tale herde,
And seide to Cyvile, "Now sorwe [on thi bokes],
Such [weddyng] to worche to wratthe with Treuthe;
And ar this weddyng be wroughte, wo the bityde!
For Mede is *mulier*—of Amendes engendreth—
120 And God [graunted] to gyf Mede to Treuthe,
And thow hast gyven hire to a gyloure, now God gyf the sorwe!
[The] tixt telleth the nought so, Treuthe wote the sothe,
For *dignus est operarius* his hyre to have.
And thow hast fest hire to Fals—fy on thi lawe!
125 For al by lesynges thow lyvest and lecherouse werkes.
Symonye and thiself schenden Holi Cherche;
The notaries and yee noyeth the peple.
Ye shul abiggen it bothe, bi God that me made!
Wel ye witen, wernardes, but if yowre witte faille,
130 That Fals is [feyntlees] and fikel in his werkes,
And [as] a bastarde y-bore of Belsabubbes kynne.
And Mede is *mulier,* a mayden of gode:
[She] myghte kisse the kynge for cosyn an she wolde.
Worcheth bi wisdome and bi witt also:
135 Ledeth hire to Londoun there lawe is y-shewed—
If any lawe wil loke thei ligge togederes.
And [if the Justice] jugge hir to be joigned with Fals,
Yet beth war of [the] weddyng, for witty is Truthe,
And Conscience is of his conseille and knoweth yow uchone,
140 And if he fynde yow in defaute and with Fals holde,
It shal bisitte yowre soules ful soure atte laste."
    Hereto assenteth Cyvile, ac Symonye ne wolde
Tyl he had silver for his [seles] and [signes of] notaries.
Thanne fette Favel forth floreynes ynowe
145 And bad Gyle "[Go] gyve golde al aboute,
And namelich to the notaries, that hem none ne faille,
And feffe False Witnes with floreines ynowe,
For he may Mede amaistrye and maken at my wille."
Tho this golde was gyve, grete was the thonkynge

And Piers the pardoner of Pauline doctrine,[9]
Bart the beadle of Buckinghamshire,   110
Reynold the reeve[1] of Rutland district,
Mund the miller and many more besides.
"In the date of the Devil this deed is sealed
In sight of Sir Simony and with Civil's approval."
   Then Theology grew angry when he heard all this talk,   115
And said to Civil, "Now sorrow on your books,
To permit such a marriage to make Truth angry;
And before this wedding is performed, may it befall you foul!
Since Meed is *mulier*[2]—Amends is her parent—
God granted to give Meed to Truth,   120
And you've bestowed her on a deceiver, now God send you sorrow!
The text does not tell you so,[3] Truth knows what's true,
For *dignus est operarius*[4] to have his hire.
And you've fastened her to False—fie on your law!
For you live wholly by lies and by lecherous acts.   125
Simony and yourself are sullying Holy Church;
The notaries[5] and you are noxious to the people.
You shall both make amends for it, by God that made me!
You know well, you wastrels, unless your wits are failing,
That False is unflaggingly fickle in his deeds,   130
And like a bastard born of Beelzebub's kindred.
And Meed is *mulier,* a maiden of property:
She could kiss the king for cousin if she wished.
Work with wisdom and with your wit as well:
Lead her to London where law is determined—   135
If it's legally allowable for them to lie together.
And if the Justice judges it's right to join her with False,
Yet be wary of the wedding, for Truth is wise and discerning,
And Conscience[6] is of his council and knows all your characters,
And if he finds that you've offended and are one of False's followers, 140
It shall beset your souls most sourly in the end."
   Civil assents to this, but Simony was unwilling
Till he had silver for his seals and the stamps of the notaries.
Then Favel fetched forth florins[7] enough
And bade Guile, "Go give gold all about,   145
And don't neglect the notaries, see that they need nothing.
And fee False Witness with florins enough,
For he may overmaster Meed and make her obey me."
When this gold had been given, there was great thanking

---

9. A puzzling phrase, which may refer to the "crutched" or "Pauline" friars (but friars were not usually pardoners) or possibly to the clerics so common around St. Paul's Cathedral in London.
1. *Bart*: Langland has "Bette," which, since it cannot be a woman's name, may be a form of "Batty," a nickname for Bartholomew; *Reeve*: the superintendent of a large farming estate.
2. Literally, "woman"; technically, a woman of legitimate birth.
3. I.e., scripture does not support their plan.
4. "Worthy is the laborer": Luke 10:7.
5. Medieval notaries could, like modern ones, be officials charged with drawing up or attesting to important documents; a notary could also simply be an important person's clerk or secretary.
6. The term in Middle English included not only moral conscience, just as in modern English, but also awareness in a broader sense; the meaning of Conscience, like that of Meed, shifts and expands in his encounter with her and with Reason (Gloss).
7. Gold coins (Gloss).

150 To Fals and to Favel for her faire yiftes.
     And comen to conforte fram care the Fals,
     And seiden, "Certis cesse shal we nevere
     Til Mede be thi wedded wyf thorw [wit] of us alle,
     For we have Mede amaistried with owre mery speche
155 That she graunteth to gon with a gode wille
     To Londoun to loke yif that lawe wolde
     Jugge yow joyntly in joye for evere."
     Thanne was [Fals] fayne and Favel as blithe,
     And leten sompne alle segges in schires aboute,
160 And bad hem alle be bown, beggeres and othere,
     To wenden wyth hem to Westmynstre to witnesse this dede.
     Ac thanne cared thei for caplus to kairen hem thider;
     [Thanne fette Favel] folus [of the beste];
     Sette Mede upon a schyreve shodde al newe;
165 And Fals sat on a sisoure that softlich trotted,
     And Favel on [Faire Speche, feyntlich] atired.
     Tho haved notaries none; annoyed thei were
     For Symonye and Cyvile shulde on hire fete gange.
     Ac thanne swore Symonye and Cyvile bothe
170 That sompnoures shulde be sadled and serve hem uchone:
     "And lat apparaille this provisoures in palfreis wyse;
     Sire Symonye hymselven shal sitte upon here bakkes.
     Denes and suddenes, drawe yow togideres,
     Erchdekenes and officiales and alle yowre regystreres,
175 Lat sadel hem with silve owre synne to suffre
     As avoutrie and devoses and derne usurye,
     To bere bischopes aboute, abrode in visytynge.
     Paulynes pryvés, for pleyntes in the consistorie,
     Shul serve myself, that Cyvile is nempned.
180 And [lat] carte-sadel the comissarie; owre carte shal he [drawe],
     And fecchen us vytailles at *fornicatores*.
     And maketh of Lyer a longe carte, to lede alle these othere,
     As [fobbes] and faitours that on here fete rennen."
     Fals and Favel fareth forth togideres,
185 And Mede in the myddes and alle thise [meynee] after.
     I have no tome to telle the taille that hem folweth,
     Of many maner man that on this molde libbeth;
     Ac Gyle was forgoer and gyed hem alle.
          Sothenesse seigh hym wel and seide but a litel,

To False and Favel for their fair gifts.   150
And they all came to comfort False from the care that afflicted him,
And said, "Be sure we shall never cease our efforts
Till Meed is your wedded wife through wit of us all,
For we've overmastered Meed with our merry speech
So that she grants to go with a good will   155
To London to learn whether law would
Judge you jointly in joy forever."
Then False felt well pleased and Favel was glad,
And they sent to summon all men in shires about,
And bade them all be ready, beggars and others,   160
To go with them to Westminster[8] to witness this deed.
And then they had to have horses to haul them thither;
Then Favel fetched foals of the best;
Set Meed on a sheriff shod all new;
And False sat on an assizer* that softly trotted,   165
And Favel on Fair Speech, clad in feigning clothes.
Then notaries had no horses, and were annoyed also
Because Simony and Civil should walk on foot.
But then Simony swore and Civil as well
That summoners* should be saddled and serve them all: 170
"And let these provisors[9] be put into palfrey's harness;
Sir Simony himself shall sit on their backs.
Deans and subdeans,[1] you draw together,
Archdeacons and officials and all your registrars,[2]
Let them be saddled with silver to suffer our sins   175
Such as adultery and divorce and clandestine usury,
To bear bishops about, abroad on visitations.
Pauline's people,[3] for complaints in the consistory,*
Shall serve myself, Civil is my name.
And let the commissary[4] be cart-saddled and our cart pulled by him,   180
And he must fetch us victuals from *fornicatores*.[5]
And make a long cart of Liar, loaded with all the rest,
Such as twisters and tricksters that trot on their feet."
False and Favel fare forth together,
And Meed in the midst and her serving men behind.   185
I've no opportunity to tell of the tail of the procession,
Of many manner of men that move over this earth;
But Guile was foregoer and guided them all.
    Soothness* saw them well and said but a little,

8. An area (now part of London) famous for its courts of justice.
9. Clerics nominated to their benefices directly by the pope (going over the head of the local and national hierarchy); petitions for such offices were regularly accompanied by bribes.
1. Like the secular officials above, these and the officers in the next line are clerics whose functions were thought to make them particularly open to bribery. *Deans*: clerics who were either the head of the body of priests attached to a cathedral or (if a rural dean) in charge of a group of parishes under a bishop. *Subdeans*: parish priests, chosen to assist the bishop in administering church discipline in a portion of the diocese.
2. *Archdeacons*: The bishop's second in command, in charge of part of the diocese; *Officials*: The presiding judges of an archbishop's, bishop's, or archdeacon's court. *Registrars*: bishops' notaries.
3. *Visitations*: bishop's official inspection tours of his diocese. *Pauline's people*: A problem phrase; see the note to line 109 above.
4. The bishop's official representative in part of his diocese, who can act for him in his absence and who presides over the bishop's court.
5. Fornicators.

190 And priked [forth on] his palfrey and passed hem alle
And come to the Kynges courte and Conscience it tolde,
And Conscience to the Kynge carped it after.
"By Cryst!" quod the Kynge, "and I cacche myghte
Fals or Favel or any of his feres,
195 I wolde be wroke of tho wrecches that worcheth so ille,
And don hem hange by the hals, and alle that hem meynteneth.
Shal nevre man of molde meynprise the leste,
But righte as the lawe wil loke, late falle on hem alle,"
And comanded a constable that come atte furst
200 To "attache tho tyraunts, for eny [tresore], I hote;
[Fettereth Falsenesse fast] for enykynnes yiftes,
And gurdeth of Gyles hed—lat hym go no furthere;
And bryngeth Mede to me maugré hem alle.
[Symonye and Cyvile, I sende hem to warne
205 That Holy Cherche for hem worth harmed for evere].
[And yif ye lacche Lyer, late hym nought ascapen
Er he be put on the pilorye, for eny preyere, I hote]."
       Drede atte dore stode and the dome herde,
And how the kynge comaunded constables and serjants
210 Falsenesse and his felawschip to fettren an to bynden.
Thanne Drede went wightliche and warned the Fals
And bad hym flee for fere and his felawes alle.
[Thanne] Falsenesse for fere fleigh to the freres;
And Gyle doth hym to go agast for to dye.
215 Ac marchants mette with hym and made hym abide
And bishetten hym in here shope to shewen here ware,
Apparailled hym as a prentice the poeple to serve.
Lightlich lyer lepe awey thanne,
Lorkynge thorw lanes, tolugged of manye:
220 He was nawhere welcome for his manye tales,
Over al y-howted and y-hote trusse,
Tyl pardoneres haved pité and pulled hym into house;
Wesshen hym and wyped hym and wonden hym in cloutes,
And sente hym on Sondayes [with seles] to [cherche],
225 And gaf pardoun for pens poundmel aboute.
Thanne loured leches and lettres thei sent
That he sholde wonye with hem wateres to loke.
Spiceres spoke with hym to spien here ware,
For he couth [on] here craft and knewe many gommes.
230 Ac mynstralles and messageres mette with hym ones
And helden hym an half-yere and ellevene dayes.
Freres with faire speche fetten hym thennes;
For knowyng of comeres coped hym as a frere.
Ac he hath leve to lepe out as oft as hym liketh,
And is welcome whan he wil, and woneth wyth hem
235   oft.

And pressed ahead on his palfrey and passed them all   190
And came to the King's court and told Conscience* about it,
And Conscience recounted it to the King afterward.
"By Christ!" said the King, "if I can catch
False or Favel or any of his fellows,
I'll be avenged on those villains that act so viciously,   195
And have them hanged by the neck, and all who support them.
Shall no bondsman be allowed to go bail for the least,
But whatever law will allot, let it fall on them all."
And he commanded a constable that came straightway
To "detain those tyrants, despite their treasure, I say;   200
Fetter Falseness fast no matter what he gives you,
And get Guile's head off at once—let him go no farther;
And bring Meed to me no matter what they do.
Simony and Civil, I send to warn them
That their actions will hurt Holy Church forever.   205
And if you lay hand on Liar, don't let him escape
Before he's put in the pillory, for any prayer he makes."
    Dread stood at the door and heard this declaration,
How the King commanded constables and sergeants
That Falseness and his fellowship should be fettered and bound.   210
Then Dread came away quickly and cautioned False
And bade him flee for fear and his fellows too.
Then Falseness for fear fled to the friars;
And Guile in dread of death dashed away fast.
But merchants met with him and made him stay   215
And shut him up in their shop to show their wares,
Appareled him as an apprentice to wait on purchasers.
Lightly Liar leapt away then,
Lurking through lanes, belabored by many:
Nowhere was he welcome for his many tales,   220
Everywhere hunted out and ordered to pack,
Till pardoners* took pity and pulled him indoors;
Washed him and wiped him and wound him in cloths,
And sent him on Sundays with seals[6] to church,
Where he gave pardon for pennies* by the pound about.   225
Then doctors* were indignant and drafted letters to him
That he should come and stay with them to examine urine.
Apothecaries wanted to employ him to appraise their wares,
For he was trained in their trade and could distinguish many gums.[7]
But minstrels and messengers met with him once   230
And had him with them half a year and eleven days.
Friars with fair speech fetched him thence;
To keep him safe from the curious they coped him as a friar.[8]
But he has leave to leap out as often as he pleases,
And is welcome to come when he wants, and he stays with them
    often.   235

6. A pardoner needed the bishop's seal on the document that gave him license, in a particular diocese or district, to preach and collect money for indulgences.
7. I.e., gums used as perfumes, spices, or medicines.
8. Clothed him in a friar's cloak.

Alle fledden for fere and flowen into hernes;
Save Mede the mayde na mo durst abide.
Ac trewli to telle she trembled for drede
And ek wept and wronge whan she was attached.

Passus III

Now is Mede the maide and namo of hem alle
With bedellus and with bayllyves brought bifor the Kyng.
The Kyng called a clerke—[I can] nought his name—
To take Mede the mayde and make hire at ese.
5   "I [wil] assaye hir myself and sothelich appose
What man of this [worlde] that hire were leveste.
And if she worche bi witte and my wille folwe
I wil forgyve hir this gilte, so me God help."
Curteysliche the clerke thanne, as the Kyng hight,
10   Toke Mede bi the middel and broughte hir into chaumbre;
[Ac] there was myrthe and mynstralcye Mede to plese.
They that wonyeth in Westmynstre [worschipe] hir alle.
Gentelliche with joye the justices somme
Busked hem to the boure there the birde [dwelleth],
15   [Conforted] hire kyndely by Clergise leve,
And seiden, "Mourne nought, Mede, ne make thow no sorwe,
For we [wil] wisse the Kynge and thi wey shape
To be wedded at thi wille, and where the leve liketh,
For al Conscience caste [and] craft, as I trowe."
20   Mildeliche Mede thanne mercyed hem alle
Of theire gret goodnesse, and gaf hem uchone
Coupes of clene golde and coppis of silver,
Rynges with rubies and ricchesses manye,
The leste man of here meyné a Motoun of golde.
25   Thanne laughte thei leve, this lordes, at Mede.
With that comen clerkis to conforte hir the same
And beden hire be blithe: "For we beth thine owne
Forto worche thi wille [while thi lyf lasteth]."
Hendeliche heo thanne bihight hem the same
30   To love [hem] lelli and lordes [hem] make,
And in the consistorie atte courte [callen hire] names.
"Shal no lewdnesse [hym] lette, the leode that I lovye,
That he ne worth first avanced, for I am biknowen
There konnyng clerkes shul clokke bihynde."
35   Thanne come there a confessoure coped as a frere;
To Mede the mayde [mekeliche he louted]
And seide ful softly, in shrifte as it were,
"Theigh [lered] men and [lewed] had leyne by the bothe,

All fled for fear and flew into corners;
Except for Meed the maid none remained there.
But truly to tell she trembled for dread
And twisted about tearfully when she was taken into custody.

Passus III

Now Meed* the maid alone among them all
Is brought before the King by beadles and bailiffs.[1]
The King called a clerk—I can't recall his name—
To take Meed the maid and make her at home.
"I will sound her out myself and ask straightforwardly   5
What man of this world she would prefer.
And if she works with wit and follows my will
I will forgive her her guilt, so God help me."
Courteously the clerk then, as the King commanded,
With his arm around her waist led her away to a chamber;   10
But there was mirth and minstrelsy that Meed might be pleased.
Those who work at Westminster* worship her all.
Gently with joy the justices together
Bustle to the bedroom where the bride dwells,
Comforted her kindly with Clergy's* permission,   15
And said, "Don't mourn, Meed, or make any sorrow,
For we'll take care of the King and clear your way
To be wedded as you will, whatever you please,
For all Conscience's* calculations and craftiness, I'm sure."
Mildly Meed then made her thanks to them all   20
For their great goodness, and gave them each one
Cups of clean gold and copes sewn with silver,
Rings with rubies and riches aplenty,
The lowest lad of the household a Lamb of gold.[2]
Then they took their leave, these lords, of Lady Meed.   25
With that came clerks* to comfort her also,
And bade her be blithe: "For we'll be your men
And work your will while your life lasts."
She replied to this promise pleasantly, saying to them
That she would love them loyally and make lords of them,   30
And in the consistory* at court call out their names.
"No stupidity shall stop him, the scholar I love,
From being first advanced, for I am recognized
Where clever clerks like cripples bring up the rear."
Then there came a confessor coped as a friar;   35
To Meed the maid meekly he bowed
And said very softly, in shrift as it were,
"Though learned men and unlearned had both lain with you,

1. *Beadle*: server of summonses to the manorial court; *Bailiff*: chief representative of the lord of the manor.
2. A French gold coin, so called because it bore—ironically in the context—the image of the Lamb of God. Here Meed's behavior fits her simplest definition as bribery, and the insistence on her scarlet clothing (one of whose associations is with whores and with the Whore of Babylon in the Book of Revelation) is a notable element in her developing meaning. Cf. p. 372.

And [theigh Falsehede] haved y-folwed the al this [fyftene] wyntre,
40 I shal assoille the myselve for a seme of whete,
And also be thi [baudekyn] and bere wel thi message
Amonges [clerkes] and [knightes], Conscience to [felle]."
Thanne Mede for here mysdedes to that man kneled
And shrove hire of hire shrewednesse—shamelees, I trowe;
45 Tolde hym a tale and toke hym a noble
Forto ben hire bedeman and hire [baude] als.
Thanne he assoilled hir sone and sithen he seyde,
"We han a wyndowe a-wirchyng wil [stonden] us wel heigh;
Woldestow glase that gable and grave thereinne thi name,
50 Siker sholde thi soule be Hevene to have."
      "Wist I that," quod [the] womman, "I wolde nought spare
For to be yowre frende, frere, and faille yow nevre—
Whil ye love lordes that lechery haunteth
And lakketh nought ladis that loveth wel the same.
55 It is a freleté of flesche—ye fynde it in bokes—
And a course of kynde, wherof we komen alle.
Who may scape the sklaundre, the skathe is sone amended:
It is synne of [the] sevene sonnest relessed.
Have mercy," quod Mede, "of men that it haunte,
60 And I shal kevre yowre kirke, yowre cloystre do maken,
Wowes do whitten and wyndowes glasen,
Do peynten and purtraye [who payed] for the makynge,
That evry segge shal [see] I am sustre of yowre hous."
      Ac God to alle good folke suche gravynge defendeth—
65 To writen in wyndowes of here wel-dedes,
On aventure pruyde be peynted there and pompe of the worlde.
For [God] knoweth thi conscience and thi kynde wille
And thi coste—and thi coveitise, and who the catel
          oughte.
Forthi I lere yow lordes, leveth suche [wrytynge],
70 To writen in wyndowes of yowre wel-dedes,
Or to greden after Goddis men whan ye [gyve] doles,
An aventure ye han yowre hire here and youre Hevene als.
          Nesciat sinistra quid faciat dextra.
"Lat noughte thi left half, late no rathe,
Wyte what thow worchest with thi right syde."
75 For thus bit [God in] the Gospel gode men do here almesse.—
      Meires and maceres that menes ben bitwene
The Kynge and the comune to kepe the lawes,
To punyschen on pillories and pynynge-stoles
Brewesteres and bakesteres, bocheres and cokes;
80 For thise aren men on this molde that moste harme worcheth

And though Falsehood had followed you all these fifteen winters,
I shall absolve you myself for a seam[3] of wheat,   40
And also be your go-between and bear your message well
To ecclesiasts and knights at court, to chop Conscience down."
Then Meed knelt to that man for the misdeeds she'd done
And shrove herself of her sins—shameless, I think;
Told him a tale and tipped him a noble[4]   45
To be her beadsman[5] and her go-between as well.
Then he absolved her swiftly and said thereafter,
"We've a window being worked on that will cost us a lot;
If you'd glaze that gable and engrave your name there,
Your soul should be certain to have Heaven."   50
    "If I were sure of that," said the woman, "I would spare nothing
To be your friend, friar, and fail you never—
As long as you love lords that practice lechery
And don't malign ladies that love it well too.
It's a frailty of the flesh—you find it in books—   55
And a natural enough urge, innate in our kind.
If you can escape the scandal, the scar is soon healed:
It's the sin of the seven soonest remitted.
Have mercy," said Meed, "on men that practice it,
And I'll find funds for your church roof, provide you with a cloister, 60
Have your walls white-washed and your windows glazed,
And have painted and portrayed who paid for the work,
So that every soul shall see I'm a sister of your house."
    But God forbids such engraving to all good people—
Inscribing in stained glass the story of their beneficence,   65
Lest pride be portrayed there and pomp of this world.
For God can see your conscience and the kindness of your will
And the cost to you—and your covetousness, and whom the capital
        belonged to.
Therefore learn from me, you lords, to leave off such writing,
Inscriptions on stained glass of the story of your gifts,   70
Or to go calling for God's men when you give alms,
For fear you have your hire here and your Heaven as well.
    Let not the left hand know what the right hand is doing.[6]
"Let not your left hand, late or early,
Be aware what work you do with your right hand."
For thus God in the Gospel bids good men give their alms.—   75
    Mayors and mace-bearers[7] that are intermediaries between
The King and the commons* in keeping the laws,
Who should punish on pillories and pining-stools[8]
Brewers and bakers, butchers and cooks;
For these are the ones in the world who work most harm   80

3. A pack-horse load.
4. A gold coin worth eighty pennies.
5. I.e., to say prayers for her.
6. Matt. 6:3.
7. The mace, or staff of office, was carried before a public official and symbolized his power; the mace was originally a weapon of war.
8. Chairs on which criminals or other kinds of offenders (usually women) were exposed to public shame.

To the pore peple that parcelmele buggen;
For they poysoun the peple priveliche and oft
Thei rychen thorw regraterye and rentes hem buggen
With that the pore people shulde put in here wombe:
85   For toke thei on trewly, thei tymbred nought so heighe,
Ne boughte non burgages—be ye ful certeyne.
Ac Mede the mayde the maire hath bisoughte
Of alle suche sellers sylver to take,
Or presents withoute pens as peces of silver,
90   Ringes or other ricchesse the regrateres to maynetene:
"For my love," quod that lady, "love hem uchone
And soffre hem to selle somdele ayeins resoun."
—Salamon the sage a sarmoun he made
For to amende maires and men that kepen [the] lawes,
95   And [toke hym] this teme that I telle thynke:
Ignis devorabit tabernacula eorum qui libenter accipiunt munera,
        etc.
Amonge this lettered ledes this Latyn is to mene
That fyre shal falle and [forbrenne at the laste]
The [house] and the [home] of hem [that] desireth
100 Yiftes or yeres-yyves bicause of here offices.—
    The Kynge fro conseille cam and called after Mede
And ofsent hir alswythe; [serjauntz hir fette]
[And] broughten hir to bowre with blisse and with joye.
Curteisliche the kynge thanne comsed to telle;
105 To Mede the mayde melleth thise wordes:
"Unwittily, womman, wroughte hastow oft.
Ac worse wroughtestow nevre than tho thow Fals toke.
But I forgyve [the] that gilte and graunte the my grace
Hennes to thi deth-day: do so namore.
110 I have a knyghte, Conscience, cam late fro biyunde;
Yif he wilneth the to wyf, wyltow hym have?"
"Ye, lorde," quod that lady, "Lorde forbede elles!
But I be holely at yowre heste, lat hange me sone!"
    Thanne was Conscience calde to come and appiere
115 Bifor the Kynge and his conseille, clerkes and othere.
Knelynge, Conscience to the Kynge louted
What his wille were and what he do shulde.
"Woltow wedde this womman yif I wil assente?
For she is fayne of thi felawship, for to be thi make."
120 Quod Conscience to the Kynge, "Cryst it me forbede!

To the poor people that purchase small portions;
Because they poison the people privily and often
They get rich through their retail-sales and buy rental property
With what the poor people should be putting in their bellies:
For if their earnings were honest, their houses were less high,   85
And they'd buy no borough-freeholds[9]—you can be sure of that.[1]
But Meed the maid has made a plea to the mayor
To accept silver from all such sellers,
Or presents of unminted metal such as medals of silver,
Rings or other riches on behalf of retailers: 90
"For my love," said that lady, "love them each one
And suffer them to sell at prices somewhat unreasonable."
—Solomon the sage[2] had something to say
To amend mayors and men that administer the laws,
And took this as his text that I intend to repeat: 95
*Fire shall consume the tabernacles of those who willingly accept bribes,
etc.*[3]
Among these lettered lords this Latin signifies
That fire shall fall on and conflagration consume
The house and home of any who desires
Presents to be proffered him as perquisites of his office.—   100
     The King came from council and called for Meed
And sent for her straightway; sergeants fetched her
And brought her to his bower with bliss and with joy.
Courteously the King commenced to speak;
To Meed the maid in this manner he spoke: 105
"Unwisely, woman, you have worked often.
But worse work you never did than when you took False.
But I forgive you that guilt and grant you my grace
From now to your death-day: do so no more.
I have a knight called Conscience, has come lately from abroad;   110
If he wants you for his wife, will you have him?"
"Yes, lord," said that lady, "Lord forbid else!
If I'm not wholly at your behest, have me hanged!"
     Then Conscience was called to come and appear
Before the King and his council, clerks and others.   115
Kneeling to the King, Conscience questioned him humbly
What his will was and what he should do.
"Will you have this woman if I will assent?
For she craves your company, to become your mate."
Said Conscience to the King, "Christ forbid it!   120

---

9. This kind of landownership was the securest and most lucrative way of owning rental property:
   the owner owns the land and the tenements built on it outright, or at least has life-ownership of
   them—unlike many owners of buildings in a town who had a mere lease on the land itself and
   therefore had to pay rent to someone else for the land under their own buildings.
1. This sentence, which began at line 76, is neither a "complete sentence" by the standards of modern
   grammar nor logically connected with the immediate dramatic situation between Meed and the
   friar. Such passages recur in Langland, reflecting the associative energy of his thought, sometimes
   overwhelming surface coherence. They are characteristic of the way his poetry reproduces the
   urgency and spontaneous probing of a mind yoking many variables together and pursuing them
   with the passion of conversation and argument, rather than of more formal rhetoric.
2. Old Testament king, David's successor, supposed author of the "Wisdom Books" in the Bible; see
   "Sapience" in Gloss.
3. Job 15:34.

Ar I wedde suche a wyf, wo me bityde!
She is frele of hir feith, fykel of here speche;
[She] maketh men mysdo many score tymes.
[In] truste of hire tresore [she teneth] ful manye.
125 Wyves and widewes wantounes she techeth,
Lereth hem leccherye that loveth hire yiftes.
Yowre fadre she felled thorw fals biheste,
Apoysounde popis, [apeired] Holi Cherche.
Is naught a better baude, bi hym that me made,
130 Bitwene Hevene and helle, in erthe though men soughte.
She is tikil of hire taile, talwis of hir tonge,
As comune as [the] cartwey to eche a knave that walketh,
To monkes, to mynstralles, to meseles in hegges.
Sisoures and sompnoures, suche men hir preiseth.
135 Shireves of shires were shent yif she nere.
She doth men lese here londe and here lyf bothe;
She leteth passe prisoneres and payeth for hem ofte,
And gyveth the gailers golde and grotes togideres
To unfettre the Fals, fle where hym lyketh.
140 [She] taketh the trewe bi the toppe and tieth hym faste
And hangeth hym for hatred that harme dede nevre.
To be cursed in consistorie she counteth noughte a [bene];
For she copeth the comissarie and coteth his clerkis
She is assoilled as sone as hirself liketh.
145 [She] may neighe as moche do in a moneth one
As yowre secret seel in syx score dayes.
She is privé with the pope—provisoures it knoweth;
Sire Symonye and hirselve seleth [the] bulles.
She blesseth thise bisshopes [if] they be lewed;
150 [Provendres], persones, and prestes [she] meynteneth
To [holde] lemmannes and lotebies alle here lif-dayes,
And bringen forth barnes ayein forbode lawes.
There she is wel with the kynge, wo is the rewme!
For she is favorable to the Fals and fouleth Trewthe ofte.
155 Bi Jhesus, with here jeweles yowre justices she shendeth
And lith ayein the lawe, and letteth hym the gate
That feith may noughte have his forth, here floreines go so thikke.

Before I wed such a wife, woe betide me!
She is frail and unfaithful, fickle of her speech;
She makes men misbehave many score times.
In trust of her treasure she troubles a great many.
Wives and widows she teaches wantonness, 125
Gives them lessons in lechery who love her gifts.
She felled your father through false promises,[4]
Poisoned popes, impaired Holy Church.[5]
There's not a better go-between, by him that made me,
Between Heaven and hell, though one searched the whole earth. 130
Her tail is ticklish, her tongue is too ready,
She's as common as the cartway to comers and goers,
To monks, to messengers, to leper-men in hedges.
Assizers* and summoners,* such men prize her.
Sheriffs of shires would be shamed but for her. 135
She makes men lose their lives and their land both;
She permits prisoners to go free, pays for their release,
And gives the jailers gold and groats[6] together
To unfetter the False, to flee where he likes.
She takes the true man by the top and ties him up fast 140
And hangs him out of hatred who has harmed no one.
To be excommunicated in the consistory* she doesn't care a bean;
Because she gives copes to the commissary[7] and coats to his clerks
She is absolved as soon as she herself pleases.
She may almost as much do in a month only 145
As your secret seal in six score days.
She's privileged with the Pope—provisors* know it;
She and Sir Simony put the seals on the bulls.[8]
She blesses bishops she knows to be ignorant;
Prebendaries,[9] parsons, and priests she supports 150
To maintain mistresses and concubines all their mortal days,
And to bring forth bastards forbidden by law.
Where she stands well with the King, woe to the realm!
For she is favorable to False and befouls Truth often.
By Jesus, with her jewels she corrupts your justices 155
And tells lies against the law, and lays down obstacles
So that faith may not go freely forth, her florins* rain so thick.

---

4. At the date when this passage was written, the king was Edward III, whose father, Edward II, was murdered in prison, after his wife and her lover led a revolt and forced him to resign the throne; however, no story ascribing his death to bribery survives. (Meed gives her version of her dealings with Edward and his father below.) Here, as often, Langland comments on specific historical events as well as on the more general referents for his allegorical analysis. Cf. p. 485.
5. The phrase "poisoned popes" refers to the Emperor Constantine, who, when he converted to Christianity and made it the official religion of the Roman Empire, allegedly gave the pope temporal rulership and lands, thus, according to a later passage in the poem, "poisoning" the Church; see XV.557–61. (This gift, the "Donation of Constantine," was actually an eighth-century forgery.)
6. A silver coin worth four pennies, no small sum.
7. The bishop's official representative in part of his diocese, who can act for him in his absence and who presides over the bishop's court.
8. For an abbey to hold an election of an abbot, or for a bishop to appoint a cleric to hold a benefice, a letter of permission from the king under his personal seal was needed. But if an individual or a religious order wanted to circumvent this provision, a timely bribe to the papal court could cause the king's order to be preempted by a papal bull (Gloss) appointing the briber.
9. Priests holding a special stipend usually resulting from their having a function at a cathedral above and beyond whatever ordinary parish position they also held.

She ledeth the lawe as hire list and lovedayes maketh,
And doth men lese thorw hire love that lawe myghte wynne—
160 The maze for a mene man though he mote hir evre,
Lawe is so lordeliche and loth to make ende;
Withoute presents or pens [he] pleseth wel fewe.
Barounes and burgeys she bryngeth in sorwe,
And alle the comune in kare that coveyten lyve in trewthe.
165 Clergye and coveitise she coupleth togideres.
This is the lyf of that lady, now Lorde yif hir sorwe!
And alle that meynteneth here men, meschaunce hem bityde!
For pore men mowe have no powere to pleyne hem though thei smerte,
Suche a maistre is Mede amonge men of gode."
170   Thanne morned Mede and mened hire to the Kynge,
To have space to speke, spede if she myghte.
The Kynge graunted hir grace with a gode wille.
"Excuse the yif thow canst: I can namore seggen,
For Conscience acuseth the to congey the for evere."
175 "Nay, lorde," quod that lady, "leveth hym the worse
Whan ye wyten witterly where the wronge liggeth.
There that myschief is [moste], Mede may helpe.
And thow knowest, Conscience, I cam nought to chide,
Ne deprave thi persone with a proude herte.
180 Wel thow wost, [Conscience]—but yif thow wolt gabbe—
Thow hast hanged on myne half ellevene tymes,
And also griped my golde [and] gyve it where the liked.
Whi thow wratthest the now wonder me thynketh.
Yit I may—as I myghte—menske the with yiftes
185 And mayntene thi manhode more than thow knoweste.
Ac thow hast famed me foule bifor the Kynge here,
For kulled I nevere no kynge ne conseilled therafter,
Ne dede as thow demest—I do [it] on the Kynge.
In Normandye was he noughte noyed for my sake,
190 Ac thow thiself sothely shamedest hym ofte,
Crope into a kaban for colde of thi nailles,
Wendest that wyntre wolde have lasted evere,
And draddest to be ded for a dym cloude,
And hiedest homeward for hunger of thi wombe.
195 Without pité, piloure, pore men thow robbedest
And bere here bras at thi bakke to Caleys to selle,
There I lafte with my lorde his lyf for to save.
I made his [meyné] meri and mornyng lette;
I batered hem on the bakke and bolded here hertis
200 And dede hem hoppe for hope to have me at wille.
Had I ben marschal of his men, bi Marie of Hevene,

She leads the law as she likes and arranges lovedays,[1]
And makes men lose for love of her so that lawyers may profit—
A maze for a poor person though he pleads forever,   160
Law is so lordly and loath to make an end;
Without presents or silver pennies* he pleases very few.
Barons and burgesses* she brings into sorrow,
And all the commons into care that crave to live in truth.
Clergy and covetousness she couples together.   165
This is the life of that lady, now Lord give her sorrow!
And all that maintain her men, let mischance betide them!
For poor men have no power to plead though they smart,
Such a master Meed is among men of property."
    Then Meed mourned and lamented to the King,   170
To have a chance to challenge the charges Conscience made.
The King granted her grace with a good will.
"Excuse yourself if you can: I can say no more,
For Conscience accuses you to cut you off from court forever."
    "No, lord," said that lady, "believe him the less   175
Until you realize rightly where the wrong lies.
Where misery prevails most, Meed may help.
And you can be sure, Conscience, I didn't come here to quarrel,
Nor to disparage you personally in the pride of my heart.
And you're well aware, Conscience—unless you wish to lie—   180
That you've relied on my largesse lots of times,
And also grasped my gold and given it where you pleased.
It's a wonder to me why you're waxing angry now.
I'm still able—as I always was—to honor you with gifts
And to maintain your manhood more than you admit.   185
But you've defamed me foully before the King here,
For I never killed any king or counseled others to,
Or carried on as you declare—I call the King to witness.
In Normandy in my name he was not injured,
But you yourself for sure shamed him often,   190
Crept into a cabin for cold of your toes,
Worried that winter would last for ever,
And dreaded your death from a dark cloud,
And hurried homeward for hunger of your belly.[2]
Without pity, pillager, you plundered poor men   195
And bore their brass on your back to Calais to sell,[3]
While I stayed longer with my sire to save his life.
I made his fighting men merry and stopped their mourning;
I banged them on their backs and emboldened their hearts
And had them hopping for hope to have me at will.   200
If I'd been marshall of his men, by Mary of Heaven,

1. Manor courts set aside certain days to try to reconcile adversaries in a negotiated settlement; this laudable aim was too often achieved by bribery rather than by genuine resolution of the conflict.
2. A good example of a passage where Conscience is being conceived of as consciousness or awareness more generally than merely ethical conscience; Meed accuses him of being what makes the soldiers realize they are cold, hungry, and frightened. See also note 4 below.
3. The English army scavenged its way back to Calais to embark for home. "Brass" (i.e., copper pans) was probably typical of the little left in fought-over villages; "Calais," a major commercial center, was in English hands and prosperous.

I durst have leyde my lyf, and no lasse wedde,
He shulde have be lorde of that londe a lengthe and a brede,
And also kyng of that kitthe his kynne for to helpe,
205   The leste brolle of his blode a barounes pere.
Cowardliche thow, Conscience, conseiledest hym thennes
To leven his lordeship for a litel silver
That is the richest rewme that reyne overhoveth.
    It bicometh a kynge that kepeth a rewme
210   To yive mede to men that mekelich hym serveth,
To alienes, to alle men, to honoure hem with yiftes.
Mede maketh hym biloved and for a man holden.
Emperoures and erlis and al manere lordes
[Thorwgh] yiftes han yonge men to [yerne] and to ride.
215   The Pope and [his] prelatis presentz underfongen,
And medeth men hemselven to meyntene here lawes.
Servauntz for her servise—we seth wel the sothe—
Taken mede of here maistre as thei mowe acorde.
Beggeres for here biddynge bidden [of] men mede;
220   Mynstralles for here murthe mede thei aske.
The kynge hath mede of his men to make pees in londe;
Men that [kenne clerkes] crave of hem mede;
Prestis that precheth the poeple to gode
Asken mede and masse-pans and here mete [als];
225   Alkynnes crafty men craven mede for here prentis;
[Mede and marchandise] mote nede go togideres;
No wighte, as I wene, withoute mede may libbe."
    Quatz the Kynge to Conscience, "Bi Criste, as me thynketh
Mede is wel worthi, [me thynketh,] the maistrye to have."
230   "Nay!" quod Conscience to the Kynge, and kneled to the erthe,
"There aren two manere of Medes, my lorde, [bi] yowre leve:
That one God of his grace graunteth in his blisse
To tho that wel worchen whil thei ben here.
The prophete precheth therof, and put it in the Sautere:
    Domine, quis habitabit in tabernaculo tuo?
235   'Lorde, who shal wonye in thi wones with thine holi seyntes,
Or resten on thi holy hilles?' This asketh David,
And Davyd assoileth it hymself as the Sauter telleth:
    Qui ingreditur sine macula et operatur justiciam.
'Tho that entren of o colour and of on wille
And han wroughte werkis with righte and with reson,
240   And he that ne useth naughte the lyf of usurye,
And enfourmeth pore [peple] and pursueth treuthe.'

I'd have dared lay my life, and no less a pledge,
He'd have been lord of that land in length and in breadth,
And also king of that country to raise his kin's estate,
The least brat of his blood a baron's peer.   205
Cowardly, Conscience, you counseled him thence
To leave his lordship for a little silver
Which is the richest realm that the rain falls on.[4]
    It becomes a king who takes care of a realm
To give meed to men who meekly serve him,   210
To aliens,[5] to all men, to honor them with gifts.
Meed makes him beloved and his manhood esteemed.
Emperors and earls and all kinds of lords
With gifts get young men to gallop on their errands.
The Pope and his prelates expect to get presents,   215
And they give meed to men to maintain their laws.
Servants for their service—we see well the truth—
Take meed from their masters as they may agree.
Beggars for the prayers they bid[6] beg men for meed;
Minstrels for their mirth demand their meed.   220
The king has meed from his men to make peace in the land;
Tutors that teach clerks trust to receive meed;
Priests that preach to the people good behavior
Ask for meed and mass-pennies and their meals as well;
All kinds of craftsmen crave meed for their apprentices;[7]   225
Meed and merchandise must go together;
No life, as I believe, can last without meed."
    Said the King to Conscience, "By Christ, it strikes me
Meed has argued so ably, I think she has the upper hand."
    Kneeling to the King on knees, "No!" said Conscience.   230
"Meed must be counted of two kinds, sir King, by your leave:
The first God of his grace grants in his bliss
To those who work well while they are here.
The prophet preaches of this, and put it in the Psalter:*
    Lord, who shall abide in thy tabernacle?[8]
'Lord, who shall inhabit your home with your holy saints,   235
Or rest on your holy hills?' David asks this,
And David resolves it himself as the Psalter tells:
    He that enters without spot and works justice.[9]
'Those who enter of one color[1] and of one will
And have done their work with right and with reason,
And he who does not lead his life making loans for usury,   240
But who informs poor people and pursues truth.'

4. Edward III waged a disastrous campaign against France from October 1359 to May 1360, in which a winter of severe hardship, topped off by the "Black Monday" hailstorm of April 14, led Edward to sign a treaty giving up his claim to the French crown and most of his French territories except Aquitaine, receiving in return only the large ransom paid for King John of France (the "little silver" of line 207). The "dark cloud" in line 193 probably refers to the "Black Monday" storm.
5. Perhaps mercenary soldiers or perhaps other foreigners who are useful to him in dealing with foreign affairs or commercially in trade or banking.
6. Pray.
7. I.e., the fee craftsmen charge for training apprentices.
8. Ps. 14:1.
9. Ps. 14:2.
1. I.e., without spot.

> *Qui pecuniam suam non dedit ad usuram et munera super*
> *innocentem.*

And alle that helpeth the innocent and halt with the rightful,
Withoute mede doth hem gode and the trewthe helpeth
Suche manere men, my lorde, shal have this furst mede
245 Of God at a grete nede whan thei gone hennes.
        There is [a] mede mesurelees that maistres desireth;
To meyntene mysdoers mede thei take;
And thereof seith the Sauter in a Salmes ende:
> *In quorum manibus iniquitates sunt; dextera eorum repleta est muneribus.*
250 And he that gripeth her [giftes], so me God helpe,
Shal abie it bittere, or the Boke lyeth.
Prestes and parsones that plesynge desireth,
That taketh mede and moné for Messes that thei syngeth,
[Shal have] mede [on this molde that] Mathew [hath graunted]:
> *Amen, amen, receperunt mercedem suam.*
255   That laboreres and lowe [lewed] folke taketh of her maistres,
It is no manere mede but a mesurable hire.
In marchandise is no mede, I may it wel avowe:
It is a permutacioun apertly, a penyworth for an othre.
        Ac reddestow nevere *Regum*, thow recrayed Mede,
260 Whi [that] venjaunce fel on Saul and on his children?
God sent to Saul bi Samuel the prophete
That Agag of Amaleke and al his peple aftre
Shulde deye for a dede that done had here ealdres.
'Forthi,' seid Samuel to Saul, 'God hymself hoteth [the]
265 Be boxome at his biddynge his wille to fulfille.
Wende to Amalec with thyn oste and what thow fyndest there slee it.
Biernes and bestes, brenne hem to ded;
Wydwes and wyves, wommen and children,
Moebles and unmoebles, and al that thow myghte fynde
270 Brenne it—bere it noughte awey, be it nevere so riche.
For mede ne for moné loke thow destruye it.
Spille it and spare it noughte, thow shalt spede the bettere.'
And for he coveyted her catel and the Kynge spared,
Forbare hym and his bestes bothe, as the Bible witnesseth,
275 Otherwyse than he was warned of the prophete,
God seide to Samuel that Saul shulde deye
And al his sede for that synne shenfullich ende.
Such a myschief Mede made the Kynge to have
That God hated hym for evere and alle his eyres after.
280 The *culorum* of this cas kepe I noughte to shewe;
An aventure it noyed [me], none ende wil I make;
For so is this worlde went with hem that han powere

He that puts not out his money to usury nor takes rewards against
    the innocent.[2]
And all that help the innocent and hold with the righteous,
Without meed give aid to them and help the truth,
Such manner of men, my lord, shall have this first meed
From God at their great need when they go hence.   245
    There is a meed immeasurable that men in power desire;[3]
To maintain misdoers they accept men's meed;
And the Psalter in a Psalm's end speaks of them:
In whose hands are iniquities; their right hand is full of bribes.[4]
And he that grasps their gifts, so God help me,   250
Shall bear a bitter cost for them, or the Book lies.
Priests and parsons who want pampered lives,
Who take meed and money for Masses that they sing,
Will have reward in this world as Matthew has granted them:
    Verily, verily, they have received their reward.[5]
    What laborers and lowly folk unlearned get from their masters,   255
It is in no manner meed but a measurable hire.
There is no meed in merchandise, I may well assert it:
It is a plain permutation, one pennyworth for another.
    But have you never read *Regum,*[6] you wretched Meed,
Why that vengeance fell on Saul and on his children?   260
God sent to Saul by Samuel the prophet
To say that Agag of Amalek and all his people as well
Should die for a deed done by their forebears.
'Therefore,' said Samuel to Saul, 'God himself commands you
To be obedient to his bidding and fulfill his will.   265
Go to Amalek with your host and whatever you find there slay it.
Both men and beasts, burn them to death;
Widows and wives, women and children,
Furniture and farmsteads, whatever you find there
Burn it—don't bear it away, be it never so rich.   270
Despite meed or money make sure you demolish it.
Destroy it and spare it not, you will speed the better.'
But because he coveted their cattle and spared the King,
Forbore him and his beasts both, as the Bible witnesses,
Otherwise than he was warned by the prophet,   275
God said to Samuel that Saul must die
And all his seed for that sin shamefully end.
Such a mischance Meed made the King have
That God hated him always and all his heirs as well.
The *culorum*[7] of this case I don't care to show;   280
Lest I should have harm from it, I will make no end;
For so wags the world with those who wield power

2. Ps. 14:5.
3. Conscience here begins to describe the second kind of meed.
4. Ps. 25:10.
5. Matt. 6:5.
6. "[The Book] of Kings": see 1 Sam: 15.
7. "Conclusion": from *saeculorum,* which, in the phrase in *saecula saeculorum,* "for ever and ever," concludes many prayers.

That whoso seyth hem sothes is sonnest y-blamed.
I, Conscience, knowe this, for Kynde Witt me it taughte,
285 That Resoun shal regne and rewmes governe,
And righte as Agag hadde happe shul somme.
Samuel shal sleen hym and Saul shal be blamed
And David shal be diademed and daunten hem alle,
And one Cristene kynge kepen [us echone].
290 Shal namore Mede be maistre [on erthe],
Ac Love and Lowenesse and Lewté togederes,
Thise shul be maistres on molde [trewe men] to save,
And whoso trespasseth ayein Treuthe or taketh ayein his wille,
Leuté shal don hym lawe and no lyf elles.
295 Shal no serjaunt for [that] servyse were a silke howve
Ne no pelure in his [panelon] for pledyng atte barre.
Mede of mysdoeres maketh many lordes
And over lordes lawes [ledeth] the rewmes.
Ac Kynde Love shal come yit and Conscience togideres
300 And make of Lawe a laborere; suche love shal arise
And such a pees amonge the peple and a parfit trewthe
That Jewes shal wene in here witte—and waxen wonder glade—
That Moises or Messie be come into [myddel] erthe,
And have wonder in here hertis that men beth so trewe.
305 Alle that bereth baslarde, brode swerde or launce,
Axe other hachet or eny wepne ellis,
Shal be demed to the deth but if he do it smythye
Into sikul or to sithe, to schare or to kulter.
    Conflabunt gladios suos in vomeres, etc.
Eche man to pleye with a plow, pykoys or spade,
310 Spynne or sprede donge—or spille hymself with sleuthe.
Prestes and parsones with *Placebo* to hunte
And dyngen upon David eche a day til eve.
Huntynge or haukynge if any of hem use,
His boste of his benefys worth bynome hym after.
315 Shal neither kynge ne knyghte, constable ne meire,
[Overcarke] the comune ne to the courte sompne
Ne put hem in panel to don hem plighte here treuthe.
But after the dede that is don one dome shal rewarde

That whoever furnishes them with facts is the first to be blamed.[8]
Because Kind Wit* taught me, I, Conscience, know this,
That Reason shall reign and rule all realms,   285
And just as Agag had shall happen to some.
Samuel shall slay him and Saul shall be blamed
And David shall be diademed and dominate them all,
And one Christian king care for each one of us.
Meed shall no more be master on earth,   290
But Love and Lowliness and Lewté* together,
These shall be governors on this ground to guard true men,
And whoever trespasses against Truth or takes things against his will,
No living man but Lewté shall apply the law to him.
For such service shall no sergeant[9] wear a silk scarf   295
Nor face his cap with fur for defending clients.
Meed of misdoers makes many lords
And over lords' laws she leads the realm.
But Kind Love[1] shall come yet and Conscience with him
And make a laborer of Law; such love shall arise   300
And such a peace among the people and a perfect trust
That Jews shall judge in their wit—and be joyful at heart—
That Moses or Messiah has come to middle earth,
And have marvel in their minds that men are so true.
All that arm themselves with broad sword, with spear or dagger,   305
Axe or hatchet or any other weapon,
Shall be doomed to death unless they reduce it
To sickle or to scythe, to plowshare or to coulter.[2]
     They shall beat their swords into plowshares, etc.[3]
Each man shall play with a plow, pickax or spade,
Spin or spread dung—or spoil himself in sloth.   310
Priests and parsons with *Placebo* shall hunt
And ding upon David[4] each day till evening.
On hunting or on hawking[5] if any of them go,
The living he delights in he shall lose straightway.
Shall neither king nor knight, constable nor mayor,   315
Lay such care upon the commons as to make them come to court
And put them in a panel and have them plight their oaths.[6]
But by the facts evinced in evidence one verdict shall award

---

8. It is not clear whether Conscience will not finish the *story* (or if so how its ending could have harmed him) or will not draw any *conclusions* from it (presumably because doing so would be too direct a criticism of the King's own behavior, though it is not clear just how).
9. I.e., law-sergeant, barrister-at-law, an important lawyer.
1. Natural, innate, instinctive love; see Gloss under "Kind."
2. *Coulter*: part of a plow.
3. Isa. 2:4.
4. *Placebo*: "I will please [the Lord]": Ps. 114:9; *Ding upon David*: i.e., say their Psalter continuously (the Psalms being attributed to King David).
5. Hunting and hawking were forbidden to clerics, though widely indulged in all the same.
6. Serving on such panels was considered a great hardship, not simply because this function, like jury duty today, was time consuming. Instead of assessing evidence, medieval "jurors" took oaths vouching for the credibility of one of the parties to the lawsuit. This would be a demanding enough responsibility at the best of times, but under the problematical conditions of medieval "justice" (of which Langland is so critical) jurors were often subjected to great pressures in the form of bribes, threats, or even blackmail. It is understandable that as late as the fifteenth century it was not uncommon for an individual facing legal proceedings to have more faith in trial by ordeal or combat than in a jury.

Mercy or no mercy, as Treuthe [may] acorde.
320 Kynges courte and comune courte, consistorie and chapitele,
Al shal be but one courte and one [buyrn] be justice:
[That] worth Trewe Tonge, a tidy man that tened me nevere.
Batailles shal non be, ne no man bere wepne,
And what smyth that ony [smytheth] be smyte therwith to dethe.
         Non levabit gens contra gentem gladium, etc.
325 And er this fortune falle fynde men shal the worste
By syx sonnes and a schippe and half a shef of arwes;
And the myddel of a mone shal make the Jewes to torne,
And Saracenes for that sighte shulle synge *Gloria in excelsis,*
For Makomet and Mede myshappe shal that tyme;
330 For *melius est bonum nomen quam divicie multe.*"
         Also wroth as the wynde wex Mede in a while:
"I can no Latyn?" quod she. "Clerkis wote the sothe.
Se what Salamon seith in Sapience-Bokes:
'That yiveth yiftes, [taketh yeme], the victorie wynneth,
335 And moche worschip [hath] therwith,' as holi wryt telleth:
Honorem adquiret qui dat munera, etc."
"I leve wel, lady," quod Conscience, "that thi Latyne be trewe,
Ac thow art like a lady that redde a lessoun ones,
Was *omnia probate,* and that plesed here herte
340 For that lyne was no lenger atte leves ende.
Had [she] loked that [left] half and the lef torned,
[She] shulde have founden [felle] wordis folwyng therafter:
Quod bonum est tenete—Treuthe that texte made.
And so [mysferde] ye, madame: ye couthe namore fynde
345 Tho ye [soughte] Sapience, sittynge in youre studie.
This tixte that ye han tolde were [trewe] for lordes,
Ac yow failled a cunnyng clerke that couthe the lef have torned.
And if ye seche Sapience eft, fynde shal ye that folweth,
A ful teneful tixte to hem that taketh mede:
350 *Animam autem aufert accipientium, etc.*
And that is the taille of the tixte of that [teme] ye schewed,
That theighe we wynne worschip and with mede have victorie,
The soule that the soude taketh bi so moche is bounde."

Mercy or no mercy, as Truth may agree.
King's court and common court, consistory* and chapter,[7]   320
All will be but one court and one man be justice:
That will be True Tongue, a tidy man who never troubled me.
There shall be no battles, and no man bear weapon,
And the smith that smithies[8] any shall be smitten to death with it.
    Nation shall not lift up sword against nation, etc.[9]
And before this fortune befalls men shall find the worst   325
By six suns and a ship and half a sheaf of arrows;
And the middle of a moon shall make the Jews convert,
And for that sight Saracens shall sing *Gloria in excelsis*,
For to Makomet and Meed mishap shall come that time;
For *better is a good name than great riches.*"[1]   330
    Meed at that moment grew as mad as the wind:
"I know no Latin?" said she. "Clerks know the truth.
See what Solomon says in his Sapience-Book:[2]
'They that give gifts, take heed, are granted the victory,
And much worship as well,' as holy words tell: 335
He will acquire honor who gives gifts, etc."[3]
"I can well believe, lady," said Conscience, "that your Latin is good,
But you are like a lady that read a lesson once,
It was *omnia probate*,[4] and that pleased her heart
Since the line was no longer at the leaf 's end.   340
If she'd looked overleaf on the lefthand side,
She would have found fell words following thereafter:
Quod bonum est tenete[5]—a text that Truth made.
And that was your mistake, madam: you could find no more written
When you searched Sapience, sitting in your study.   345
The text you have told us would be true for lords,
But you lacked a clever clerk that could have turned the page.
And if you search Sapience again, you shall find what follows,
A most troublesome text to those that take meed:
But he steals the spirit of those who accept.[6]   350
And that is the tail of the text that you tried to quote,
That though we win worship and with meed have the victory,
The soul that accepts the gift by so much is enslaved."

---

7. "King's court" and "common court" were the courts for criminal and civil cases, respectively; "consistory" was the bishop's court; "chapter" was the deliberative and adjudicative meeting of the members of a monastery or convent, or of the canons (priests) attached to a cathedral.
8. Forges.
9. Isa. 2:4. The meaning of the images in the cryptic prophecy that follows has been much debated; the important point is its Apocalyptic character. Riddling prophecies are frequent at this period.
1. *Gloria in excelsis*: "Glory [to God] in the highest": Luke 2:11. *Makomet*: Mohammed, the founder of Islam. *Better is a good name than great riches*: Prov. 22:1.
2. Four biblical "Wisdom Books" are attributed to King Solomon. This one is the Book of Wisdom or the Wisdom of Solomon, which, along with Ecclesiasticus, is now considered canonical by Catholics but not by Protestants. The other two are Proverbs and Ecclesiastes.
3. Prov. 22:9.
4. "Prove [i.e., test] all things": 1 Thess. 5:21.
5. "Hold that which is good": 1 Thess. 5:21.
6. Prov. 22:9; see line 336 above.

Passus IV

"Cesseth!" [seyde] the Kynge. "I suffre yow no lengere.
Ye shal saughtne, forsothe, and serve me bothe.
Kisse hir," quod the Kynge, "Conscience, I hote."
"Nay, bi Criste," quod Conscience, "congeye me for evere.
5 But Resoun rede me therto, rather wil I deye."
"And I comaunde the," quod the Kynge to Conscience thanne,
"Rape the to ride and Resoun thow fecche.
Comaunde hym that he come my conseille to here.
For he shal reule my rewme and rede me the beste
10 [Of Mede and of mo othere—what man shal hire wedde];
And acounte with the, Conscience, so me Cryst helpe,
How thow lernest the peple, the lered and the lewede."
"I am fayne of that forwarde," seyde the freke thanne,
And ritte righte to Resoun and rowneth in his ere,
15 [Seyde him] as the Kynge [sente] and sithen toke his leve.
"I shal arraye me to ride," quod Resoun. "Reste the a while,"
And called Catoun his knave, curteise of speche,
And also Tomme-Trewe-Tonge-Telle-Me-No-Tales-
Ne-Lesyng-To-Lawghe-Of-For-I-Loved-Hem-Nevere.
20 "Sette my sadel uppon Suffre-Til-I-Se-My-Tyme,
And lete warrok [hym] wel with [witful] gerthes.
Hange on hym the hevy brydel to holde his hed lowe,
For he wil make 'wehe' tweye er [we] be there."
Thanne Conscience uppon his caple kaireth forth faste
25 And Resoun with hym ritte, rownynge togideres
Whiche maistries Mede maketh on this erthe.
One Waryn Wisdom and Witty his fere
Folwed hem faste, [for thei] haved to done
In the Cheker and [in] Chauncerie, to be discharged of thinges,
30 And riden fast for Resoun shulde rede hem the beste
For to save [hemselven] fro shame and fram harmes.
[Ac] Conscience knewe hem wel—thei loved
        coveitise—
And bad Resoun ride faste and recche of her noither.
"There aren wiles in here wordes and with Mede thei dwelleth.
35 There as wratthe and wranglyng is, there wynne thei silver,
Ac there is love and lewté [hem liketh] noughte come there.
        Contricio et infelicitas in vijs eorum, etc.
Thei ne gyveth noughte of [good feith, wot God the sothe.]

Passus IV

"Stop it!" said the King. "I'll stand for this no longer.
You shall settle your dispute, I say, and serve me both.
Kiss her," said the King, "Conscience, I command you."
"No, by Christ," said Conscience, "you can banish me from court.
Unless Reason recommends it, I will rather die."   5
"And I command you," said the King to Conscience then,
"Ride off right now and bring Reason here.
Command him to come and consult on this affair.
For he shall rule my realm and direct me what's best
About Meed and other matters—what man shall wed her;   10
And account with you, Conscience, so Christ help me,
How you lead my liegemen, learned and unlearned."
"I am glad of that agreement," Conscience gave answer,
And went straight away to Reason and whispered in his ear,
Told him what the King intended and then took his leave.   15
"I'll get ready to ride," said Reason. "Rest for a while,"
And called Cato his servant,[1] courteous of speech,
And also Tom-True-Tongue-Tell-Me-No-Tales-
Nor-Lies-To-Laugh-At-For-I-Loved-Them-Never.[2]
"Set my saddle upon Suffer-Till-I-See-My-Time,   20
And get him well girded with girths of wit.
Hang the heavy bridle on him to hold his head low,
For he will whinny 'weehee' twice before we get there."
Then Conscience on his colt canters forth fast
And Reason rides with him, reckoning together   25
What machinations Meed makes on this earth.
One Warren Wisdom and Witty[3] his fellow
Followed them fast, for they had business
In the Exchequer and in Chancery,[4] to be discharged of suits,
And they ride fast because Reason could direct them the best   30
How to save themselves from shame and harms.
But Conscience was well acquainted with them—they loved
    covetousness—
And bade Reason ride fast and reckon with neither.
"There are wiles in their words and with Meed is their home.
Where wrath and wrangling are, there they rake in silver,   35
But where love and lewté* are they don't like to come.
    Grief and unhappiness in their ways, etc.[5]
They give no respect to good faith, God knows the truth.

1. Dionysius Cato, supposed author of the *Distichs of Cato*, an early fourth-century collection of maxims, one of the first books studied in medieval grammar schools; here the name suggests the relationship between Reason and elementary education.
2. Reason depends partly on the quality of the raw material available to him to work on, as well as (next line) on the patience to wait until a problem has reached the point where it can be solved by rational analysis.
3. The morally ambiguous potential of these forms of intelligence may be clearer in the context of the Gloss entry "wit."
4. The government body that dealt with petitions addressed to the king.
5. Ps. 13:3; the Latin in line 37a is from the same verse.

Non est timor dei ante oculos eorum, etc.
For thei wolde do more for a [dyner or a] dozeine [capons]
Than for love of owre Lorde or alle hise leve seyntes.
40 Forthi, Resoun, lete hem ride, tho riche, bi hemselven,
For Conscience [knowe thei] noughte ne Cryst, as I trowe."
And thanne Resoun rode faste the righte heighe gate
As Conscience hym kenned til thei come to the Kynge.
Curteisliche the Kynge thanne come ayein Resoun
45 And bitwene hymself and his sone sette hym on benche,
And wordeden wel wyseli a gret while togideres.
    Thanne come Pees into [the] parlement and put forth a bille,
How Wronge ayeines his wille had his wyf taken,
And how he ravisshed Rose, Reginoldes love,
50 And Margarete of hir maydenhode, maugré here chekis,
"Bothe my gees and my grys his gadelynges feccheth.
I dar noughte for fere of hym fyghte ne chyde.
He borwed of me Bayard [and] broughte hym nevre [ayein],
Ne no ferthynge therfore for naughte I couthe plede.
55 He meyneteneth his men to morther myne hewen,
Forstalleth my feyres, fighteth in my chepynge,
Breketh up my [berne dores], bereth aweye my whete
And taketh me but a taile for ten quarteres of otes.
And yet he bet me therto and lyth bi my mayde.
60 I nam noughte hardy for hym uneth to loke."
    The Kynge knewe he seide sothe, for Conscience hym tolde,
That Wronge was a wikked luft and wroughte moche sorwe.
Wronge was afered [tho] and Wisdome he soughte,
To make [his] pees with his pens—and profered
      hym manye
65 And seide, "Had I love of my lorde the Kynge, litel wolde I recche
Theighe Pees and his powere pleyned [hem] evre."
Tho wan Wisdome and sire Waryn the Witty
For that Wronge had y-wroughte so wikked a dede,
And warned Wronge tho with suche a wyse tale:
70 "Whoso worcheth bi wille wratthe maketh ofte,
I seye it bi [myself], thow shalt it wel fynde,
But if Mede it make, thi myschief is uppe,
For bothe thi lyf and thi londe lyth in his grace."
Thanne wowed Wronge Wisdome ful yerne
75 To make his pees with his pens, handi-dandi payed.
[Thanne] Wisdome and Witte wenten togideres
And toke Mede myd hem mercy to winne.
Pees put forth his hed and his panne blody:
"Wythouten gilte, God it wote, gat I this skathe."

The fear of God is not before their eyes, etc.
For they'd do more for a dinner or a dozen capons
Than for the love of our Lord and all his beloved saints.
Therefore, Reason, let them ride, those rich men, by themselves,   40
For they have no care for Conscience or Christ, as I think."
Then Reason took the high road, riding fast
As Conscience counseled him till they came to the King.
Courteously the King then came to meet Reason
And between himself and his son set him on the bench,   45
And they exchanged wise words a long while together.
   Then came Peace into the parliament and presented a plea,
How regardless of his resistance Wrong had seized his wife,
And how he ravished Rose, Reginald's widow,
And Margaret of her maidenhead, no matter how she struggled,   50
"Both my fowls and my farrows fall prey to his followers.
I don't dare for fear of him fight or complain.
He borrowed Bayard[6] from me and never brought him back,
And I got no farthing[7] for him for any plea I made.
He encourages his company to kill my hired hands,   55
Preempts what I have to sell, harasses me in my bargaining,
Breaks down my barn doors, bears away my wheat
And leaves only a talley in return for ten quarters of oats.[8]
And then he beats me to boot and lies by my maid.
Because of him I hardly have the heart to stir."   60
   The King knew he was telling truth, for Conscience told him so,
That Wrong was a wicked wretch who wrought much sorrow.
Therefore Wrong grew afraid and felt out Wisdom,
If he would make peace for him with his pennies—and he proffered
      him many
And said, "If I had the love of my lord the King, little would I care   65
Though Peace and his party pled at law forever."
Then Wisdom and Warren Witty both won money
Because Wrong had committed so criminal an act,
And they went to warn Wrong with this wise advice:
"Whoever works wilfully will often stir up anger,   70
I say it for myself, you'll see it's true,
Unless Meed makes amends, mischance will come upon you,
For both your life and your land lie in his grace."
Whereupon Wrong wooed Wisdom most eagerly
To make his peace with his pennies, paid out handy-dandy.[9]   75
Then Wisdom and Wit[1] went together
And led Meed along with them to get leniency for him.
Peace put forth his head with his pate all bloodied:
"Without guilt, God knows, I got this wound."

6. A common and proverbial name for a horse.
7. A coin worth a quarter of a medieval penny.
8. *Talley*: A receipt in the form of a stick notched to indicate the amount owed; the stick was then
   split so each party had half. In practice, recipients of talleys, like Peace, too generally had the
   bitter experience of never seeing their money. *Ten quarters*: eighty bushels.
9. I.e., surreptitiously. In the game "Handy-dandy," one player shakes something between his two
   hands and then suddenly closes them, leaving the other player to guess which hand the object is
   now in; similarly, Wrong passes Wisdom the money without anyone seeing what is in the hands.
1. Mental capacity, intellectual ability; see Gloss.

80 Conscience and the comune [knewen] the sothe,
    Ac Wisdom and Witte were about faste
    To overcome the Kynge with catel yif thei myghte.
    The Kynge swore bi Crist and bi his crowne bothe
    That Wronge for his werkis sholde wo tholye,
85 And comaunded a constable to casten hym in yrens:
    "[He shal] noughte this sevene yere seen his feet ones!"
    "God wot," quod Wysdom, "that were naughte the beste.
    And he amendes mowe make, late Meynprise hym have
    And be borwgh for his bale and biggen hym bote,
90 Amende that [mysdede] and evermore the bettere."
    Witt acorded therwith and [witnessede] the same:
    "Bettere is that bote bale adoun brynge
    Than bale be y-bette and bote nevere the bettere."
    Thanne gan Mede to [meken] here, and mercy she bisought
95 And profred Pees a present al of pure golde.
    "Have this [of me, man]" quod she, "to amende thi skathe,
    For I wil wage for Wronge, he wil do so namore."
    Pees thanne [pitously] prayed to the Kynge
    To have mercy on that man that mysdid hym so ofte.
100 "For he hath waged me wel, as Wisdome hym taughte,
    I forgyve hym that gilte with a goode wille.
    So that [ye] assent, I can seye no [more].
    For Mede hath made me amendes, I may namore axe."
    "Nay!" quod the Kynge tho, "so me Cryst helpe,
105 Wronge wendeth noughte so awaye [ar] I wite more.
    For loupe he so lightly [awey], laughen he wolde
    And [ofte] the balder be to bete myne hewen.
    But Resoun have reuthe on hym, he shal rest in [the] stokkes
    As longe as [I lyve], but Lowenesse hym borwe."
110 Somme men redde Resoun tho to have reuthe on that schrewe
    And for to conseille the Kynge and Conscience after
    That Mede moste be meynpernour—Resoun thei bisoughte.
    "Rede me noughte," quod Resoun, "no reuthe to have
    Til lordes and ladies lovien alle treuthe
115 And haten al harlotrye, to heren it or to mouthen it;
    Tyl Pernelles purfil be put in here hucche,
    And childryn cherissyng be [chastised] with yerdes,
    And harlotes holynesse be holden for an [hethynge];
    Til clerken coveitise be to clothe the pore and to fede;
120 And religious romares *Recordare* in here cloistres
    As Seynt Benet hem bad, Bernarde and Fraunceys;
    And til prechoures prechyng be preved on hemselven;
    Tyl the Kynges conseille be the comune profyte;

Conscience and the commons* could perceive the truth,   80
But Wisdom and Wit went about trying
To overcome the King with cash if they could.
The King swore by Christ and by his crown both
That Wrong should be punished properly in payment for his deeds,
And commanded a constable to cast him in irons: 85
"He shall not see his feet once in seven years!"
"Why, God knows," said Wisdom, "that wouldn't be wise.
If he may make amends, let Bail manumit[2] him
And put up pledges for his crimes and purchase recompense,
Amend that misdeed and be evermore the better."   90
Wit agreed with this and his words advised the same:
"Better that betterment blot out badness
Than for badness to be beaten and betterment no better."
Then Meed began to humble herself, and asked for mercy
And proffered Peace a present all of pure gold.   95
"Have this from me, man," said she, "to amend your hurt,
For I will warrant well and truly, Wrong will do so no more."
Then Peace piteously prayed to the King
For mercy on that man who misdid him so often.
"Because he's compensated me well, as Wisdom counseled him,   100
I forgive him his guilt with a good will.
So long as you assent, I can say no more.
Since Meed has made me amends, I may ask nothing further."
"No!" cried the King, "so Christ help me,
Wrong will not run off so before the record's all before me.   105
If he got off so easily, then all he'd do is laugh
And often be the bolder to beat my servants.
Unless Reason has ruth on him, he'll remain in the stocks
As long as I live, unless Lowliness[3] go bail for him."
Some people appealed to Reason then to have pity on that scoundrel   110
And to counsel the King and Conscience as well
That Meed might be his bailsman—thus they begged Reason.
"Don't speak to me," said Reason, "of showing any pity
Till lords and ladies all love truth
And scorn all scurrility, to speak it or hear it;   115
Till Parnel's[4] proud finery is put away in her chest,
And the cherishing of children is chastised with rods,[5]
And scoundrels' sanctity is considered of no value;
Till clerkly covetousness is to clothe and feed the poor;
And religious roamers *Recordare*[6] in their cloisters   120
As Saint Benedict* bade them, Bernard* and Francis;[7]
And till preachers' preaching is proved on themselves;
Till the King's counsel is the common profit;

---

2. I.e., free.
3. *Ruth*: pity. *Lowliness*: humility (Gloss).
4. I.e., Pernelle, a woman's name, here used generically.
5. I.e., until children are not spoiled.
6. "religious": (Gloss). "*Recordare*": "Remember": the first word of the Offertory in the Mass.
7. *St. Benedict* (480?–543?): founder of the Benedictine Order, whose Rule influenced most subsequent Western monastic orders. *St. Bernard of Clairvaux* (1091–1153): founder of the Cistercian
Order. *St. Francis*: founder of the Franciscan Order (1182–1226).

Tyl bisschopes baiardes ben beggeres chambres,
125   Here haukes and her houndes helpe to pore religious;
And til Seynt James be soughte there I shal assigne,
That no man go to Galis but if he go for evere.
And alle Rome-renneres for robberes of byyende
Bere no silver over see that signe of Kynge sheweth,
130   Noyther [grotes ne golde y-grave with Kynges coyn],
Uppon forfeture of that fee whoso fynt hym at Dovere,
But if it be marchaunt or his man or messagere with lettres,
Provysoure or prest or penaunt for his synnes.
And yet," quod Resoun, "bi the Rode, I shal no reuthe have
135   While Mede hath the maistrye in [the] moot halle.
Ac I may shewe ensaumples as I se other:
I sey it bi myself, and it so were
That I were kynge with crowne, to kepen a rewme,
Shulde nevere wronge in this worlde that I wite myghte
140   Ben unpunisshed in my powere, for peril of my soule,
Ne gete my grace [thorwgh] giftes, so me God [helpe],
Ne for no Mede have mercy but mekenesse it [made],
For *Nullum Malum* the man mette with *Impunitum*
And badde *Nullum Bonum* be *Irremuneratum.*
145   Late yowre confessoure, sire Kynge, construe this [yow on Englissh],
And yif ye worken it in werke, I wedde myne eres
That Lawe shal ben a laborere and lede a-felde donge,
And Love shal lede thi londe as the lief lyketh."
      Clerkes that were confessoures coupled hem togideres
150   Alle to construe this clause and for the Kynges profit,
Ac noughte for conforte of the comune ne for the Kynges soule.
For I seighe Mede in the moot-halle on men of lawe wynke
And thei lawghyng lope to hire, and lafte Resoun manye.
Waryn Wisdome wynked uppon Mede
155   And seide, "Madame, I am yowre man, whatso my mouth jangleth;
I falle in floreines," quod that freke, "an faile speche
            ofte."
Alle rightful recorded that Resoun treuthe tolde.
[Kynde] Witt acorded therwith and comended his wordes,
And the moste peple in the [moot-]halle, and manye of the grete,
160   And leten Mekenesse a maistre and Mede a mansed schrewe.
Love lete of hir lighte and Lewté yit lasse
And seide it so [loude] that [Sothenesse] it herde,
"Whoso wilneth hir to wyf for welth of her godis,
But he be knowe for a kokewolde, kut of my nose."
165   Mede mourned tho and made hevy chere
For the moste comune of that courte called hire an hore.

Till bishops' bay horses become beggars' chambers,[8]
Their hawks and their hounds help to poor religious houses;   125
And till Saint James* is sought where I shall assign,
And no man go to Galicia[9] unless he goes for ever.
And all Rome-runners for robbers abroad
Take no silver overseas that shows the King's sign,[1]
Neither groats* nor gold engraved with the King's mark,   130
Upon forfeiture of those funds if he's found at Dover,
Unless it's a merchant or his man or a messenger with letters,
Provisor* or priest or penitent for his sins.
And yet," said Reason, "by the Rood,[2] I shall render no mercy
While Meed maintains her mastery in the court of law.   135
But I can show examples as I see them here and there:
I say it for myself, if it so were
That I were king with crown, a kingdom's ruler,
No wrong in my realm that I recognized as such
Should go unpunished in my power, for peril of my soul,   140
Nor get my grace with gifts, so God help me,
Nor have mercy for any Meed unless meekness caused it,
For a man named *Nullum Malum* met with *Impunitum*
And bade *Nullum Bonum* be *Irremuneratum*.[3]
Let your confessor, sir King, construe you this in English,   145
And if you put it into practice, I'll pledge my ears
That Law will be a laborer and load dung onto fields,
And Love will lead your land as you like best."
    Clerks who were confessors conferred together
To construe this clause all for the King's profit,   150
But not for comfort of the commons or for the King's soul.
For I saw Meed in the meeting-hall wink at men of law
And laughing they leapt to her, and many left Reason.
Warren Wisdom winked at Meed
And said, "Madam, I am your man, whatever my mouth blabs;   155
I'm flustered by florins,"* said that fellow, "and my tongue falters
    often."
All righteous people recorded that Reason spoke the truth.
Kind Wit* accorded with this and commended his words,
As did most of the people in the palace, and a good part of the great,
And agreed that Meekness was a master and Meed a cursed slut.   160
Love allowed her of little worth and Lewté yet less
And said it so loud that Soothness* heard it,
"Whoever wants her for wife for wealth of her goods,
If he doesn't come to be called a cuckold, cut off my nose."
Meed moped then and made heavy cheer   165
Because most of the commons in that court called her a whore.

---

8. I.e., till bishops spend their money on housing beggars rather than on fine horses.
9. Part of Spain, site of the famous pilgrimage center of St. James at Compostela.
1. "Rome-runners" is the subject of the verb "take," whose indirect object is "for robbers abroad."
   The immense sums paid to the pope annually were a burning issue, which had been protested in
   Parliament in 1376; they had been estimated as five times the royal revenue.
2. Cross, crucifix (Gloss).
3. Behind the chopped Latin is the widely quoted dictum of Pope Innocent III, "The just judge is
   he . . . who leaves no evil [*Nullum Malum*] unpunished [*Impunitum*] and no good [*Nullum
   Bonum*] unrewarded [*Irremuneratum*]."

Ac a sysoure and a sompnoure sued hir faste,
And a schireves clerke byschrewed al the route:
"For ofte have I," quod he, "holpe yow atte barre,
170   And yit yeve ye me nevere the worthe of a russhe."
The Kynge called Conscience and afterwardes Resoun
And recorded that Resoun had rightfullich schewed,
And mowdilich uppon Mede with myghte the Kynge loked,
And gan wax wrothe with lawe, for Mede almoste had shent it,
175   And seide, "Thorw yowre lawe as I leve I lese many chetes.
Mede overmaistrieth lawe and moche treuthe letteth.
Ac Resoun shal rekene with yow yif I regne any while,
And deme yow, bi this day, as ye han deserved.
Mede shal noughte meynprise yow, bi the Marie of Hevene!
180   I wil have Leuté in lawe, and lete be al yowre janglyng!
And as moste folke witnesseth wel, Wronge shal be
                  demed."
Quod Conscience to the kynge, "But the comune wil assent,
It is ful hard, bi myn hed, hereto to brynge it,
[And] alle yowre lige leodes to lede thus evene."
185   "By hym that raughte on the Rode," quod Resoun to the Kynge,
But if I reule thus yowre rewme, rende out my guttes—
Yif ye bidden Buxomnes be of myne assente."
"And I assent," seith the Kynge, "by Seynte Marie my lady!
Be my conseille comen of clerkis and of erlis.
190   Ac redili, Resoun, thow shalt noughte [reyke hennes];
For as longe as I lyve, lete the I nelle."
"I am aredy," quod Resoun, "to reste with yow evere;
So Conscience be of [yowre] conseille, I kepe no bettere."
"I graunt [gladlye]," quod the Kynge, "Goddes forbode it faile!
195   Als longe as [I lyve], lyve we togideres."

Passus V

The Kyng and his knightes to the kirke wente
To here matynes [and Masse and to the mete] after.
Thanne waked I of my wynkynge, and wo was withalle
That I ne hadde sleped sadder and y-seighen more.
5   Ac er I hadde faren a fourlonge feyntise me hente
That I ne myghte ferther a foot for defaute of slepynge.
[I] sat softly adown and seide my Bileve,
And so I babeled on my bedes, thei broughte me a-slepe.
   Thanne [mette me] moche more than I bifore tolde,
10   For I say the felde ful of folke that I bifore of seyde,

But an assizer* and a summoner* pursued her fast,
And a sheriff 's clerk cursed one and all:
"For I have often," he said, "helped you at the bar,[4]
And yet you never gave me a gift as good as a bean."   170
The King called Conscience and afterward Reason
And recorded that Reason had rightfully spoken,
And awesomely and angrily he cast his eye on Meed,
And his wrath was aroused with law, for Meed had almost ruined it,
And he said, "Through your law I believe I lose many reversions.[5]   175
Meed overmasters law and much obstructs the truth.
But Reason will reckon with you if I reign for any time,
And judge you justly, by this day, just as you deserve.
Meed shall not make bail for you, by Mary in Heaven!
I will have Lewté in law, and let be all your arguing!   180
By the judgment most people here have passed, let punishment fall
    on Wrong."
Said Conscience to the King, "Unless the commons* will assent,
It's very hard, by my head, actually to effect this,
And to arbitrate equitably for all your liegemen."
"By him that was crucified on the Cross," said Reason to the King,   185
Unless I rule your realm thus, rip out my guts—
If you bid Obedience be of my party."
"And I assent," said the King, "by Saint Mary my lady!
Let my council come of clerks and earls.
But Reason, you shall not readily retire from here;   190
As long as I live, I'll not let you go."
"I'm ready," said Reason, "to remain with you always;
So long as Conscience belongs to your council, I care for nothing else."
"I agree gladly," said the King, "God forbid otherwise!
As long as I live let's live together."   195

Passus V

Accompanied by his knights the King came to church
To hear matins and Mass, and went to meat[1] after.
Then my slumber ceased, and I was sorry when I woke
That I'd not slept more soundly and seen more.
But before I'd gone a furlong faintness overcame me   5
And I couldn't walk a foot further for lack of sleep.
I sat down softly and said my Creed,[2]
And I babbled on my beads and they brought me to sleep.
    Then I dreamed much more than I mentioned before,
For I saw the field full of folk that I told you of before,   10

4. I.e., in court.
5. Disputed property that reverts to the king. When Meed bribes every representative of the legal
   system to get indictments for treason, felony, or disputed inheritances dismissed, the Crown loses
   reversions.
1. Food, nourishment.
2. The basic formulation of Christian belief, which every Christian was supposed to know by heart.
   The liturgy provided several formulations for use at different times of the church year. Cf. p. 373.

And how Resoun gan arrayen hym alle the reume to preche
And with a Crosse afor the Kynge comsed thus to techen.
He preved that thise pestilences was for pure synne,
And the southwest wynde on Saterday at evene
15   Was pertliche for pure pryde, and for no poynt elles.
Piries and plomtrees were puffed to the erthe
In ensample, ye segges, ye shulden do the bettere;
Beches and brode okes were blowen to the grounde
[And] torned upward her tailles, in tokenynge of drede
20   That dedly synne ar Domesday shal fordon [us] alle.
Of this matere I myghte mamely ful longe
Ac I shal seye as I saw, so me God helpe,
How pertly afor the poeple Resoun gan to preche.
He bad Wastoure go worche what he best couthe
25   And wynnen his wastyng with somme manere crafte.
And preyed Peronelle her purfyle to lete
And kepe it in hir cofre for catel at hire nede.
Thomme Stowue he taughte to take two staves
And fecche Filice home fro the wyven pyne.
30   He warned Watt his wyf was to blame
That hire hed was worth a marke [and] his hode noughte a grote.
[He] bad Bette kut a bow other tweyne
And bete Betoun therwith but if she wolde worche.
He charged chapmen to chasten her childeren:
35   "Late no wynnynge forweny [hem] whil thei be yonge,
Ne for no pousté of pestilence plese hem noughte out of resoun.
My syre seyde so to me and so did my dame,
That 'the levere childe, the more lore bihoveth.'
And Salamon seide the same that Sapience made:
     Qui parcit virge odit filium.
40   'Whoso spareth the sprynge spilleth his children.'"
And sithen he preyed prelatz and prestes togideres,
"That ye prechen to the peple, preve it on yowreselven,
And doth it in dede, it shal drawe yow to good.
[Lyve] as ye leren us: we shal leve yow the bettere."
45   And sithen he radde religioun here reule to holde,
"Leste the Kynge and his conseille yowre comunes appayre
And ben stuwardes of yowre stedes til ye be [stewed] bettre."
And sithen he conseilled the Kynge [his] comune to lovye:
"It is thi tresore if tresoun ne were, and triacle at thi nede."
50   And sithen he prayed the Pope have pité on Holi Cherche,

And how Reason arrayed himself to preach the whole realm a sermon
And with a Cross before the King thus commenced his teaching.
He proved that these pestilences were caused purely by sin,
And the southwestern wind on Saturday at evening[3]
Occurred obviously because of pride, and for no cause else.   15
Peartrees and plumtrees were puffed to the ground
In meaning, you men, you must do better;
Beeches and broad oaks were blown to the earth
And turned their tails upward, betokening dread
That deadly sin before Doomsday should undo us all.   20
I might mumble of this matter for a long time
But I shall say as I saw, so God help me,
How standing in the people's sight Reason started his sermon.
He bade Waster get to work at what he knew best
And win back what he'd wasted with some kind of work.   25
And he prayed Parnel[4] to put away her robe's embroidery
And keep it in her closet in case she needed money.
He taught Tom Stowe to take two sticks
And fetch Felice home from where females are punished.[5]
He warned Wat his wife was to blame   30
That her head was worth a mark[6] and his hood not a groat.*
He bade Bart cut a bough or two
And beat Betty with it unless she got busy at her chores.
He charged chapmen[7] to chastise their children:
"Don't let your plentiful profits pamper them in youth,   35
And out of fear of the pestilence's power don't please them overmuch.
My sire said to me and so did my dame,
'The more you dote on your dear child, the more discipline he needs.'
And Solomon said the same in Sapience-Book:*
    He that spareth the rod hateth his son.[8]
'Whoever spares the switch spoils his children.'"   40
And then he prayed prelates and priests together,
"What you preach to the people, practice it yourselves,
And do it in deed, it shall do you good.
Live the lessons you teach us: we'll believe you the more."
And then he directed religious* to obey their rule strictly,   45
"Lest the King and his council curtail your rations
And be stewards in your stead till you learn to restrain yourselves."
And then he counseled the King to hold his commons in love:
"It's your treasure and treacle[9] at need if treason's not involved."
And then he prayed the Pope to have pity on Holy Church,   50

---

3. *Pestilences*: since 1349, England had suffered a number of epidemics of the plague. Cf.
   p. 427.*Southwestern wind . . . Saturday at evening*: a storm on January 15, 1362, severe enough
   for mention in several chronicles.
4. A woman's name.
5. *Tom Stowe*: the name, like those in the next few lines, is generic, comparable to the modern "John
   Smith." *Two sticks . . . females are punished*: women were punished for being shrewish wives, dis-
   honest tradespeople, etc., by being plunged in water on a "ducking stool"; presumably Tom is to
   fetch his wife home and beat her (with the "two sticks") himself instead of relying on the community to discipline her.
6. Equivalent to 160 pennies, several weeks' wages.
7. Merchants, tradesmen.
8. Prov. 13:24.
9. A powerful medicine.

And er he gyve any grace governe firste hymselve.
"And ye that han lawes to [loke], late treuthe be yowre coveytise
More than golde or other gyftes if ye wil God plese.
For whoso contrarieth treuthe, he telleth in the Gospel,
55   *Amen dico vobis, nescio vos.*
And ye that seke Seynte James and seintes [at] Rome,
Seketh Seynt Treuthe, for he may save yow alle.
Qui cum Patre et Filio: that feire hem bifalle
That suweth my sermon." And thus seyde Resoun.
60   Thanne ran Repentance and reherced his teme
And gert Wille to wepe water with his eyen.
      Peronelle Proude-Herte platte hir to the erthe
And lay longe ar she loked, and "Lorde, mercy!" cryed,
And byhighte to hym that us alle made
65   She shulde unsowen hir serke and sette there an heyre
To affaiten hire flessh that fierce was to synne.
"Shal nevere heighe herte me hente but holde me lowe
And suffre to be myssayde—and so did I nevere.
But now wil I meke me and mercy biseche
70   [Of] al [that] I have [had envye] in myne herte."
      Lecchoure seyde, "Allas!" and [to] owre Lady cryed
To make mercy for his misdedes bitwene God and [hym],
With that he shulde the Saterday sevene yere thereafter
Drynke but myd the doke and dyne but ones.
75   Envye with hevy herte asked after scrifte
And carefullich [his coupe] he comsed to shewe.
He was as pale as a pelet, in the palsye he semed.
[He was] clothed in a caurimaury—I couthe it noughte discreve—
[A] kirtel and [a] kourteby, a knyf bi his syde.
80   Of a freres frokke were the forsleves.
As a leke hadde y-leye longe in the sonne
So loked he with lene chekes, lourynge foule.
His body was to-bolle for wratthe that he bote his lippes
And [wrothliche he wroth his fiste], to wreke hymself he thoughte
85   With werkes or with wordes whan he seighe his tyme.
Eche a worde that he warpe was of an addres tonge;
Of chydynge and of chalangynge was his chief lyflode,
With bakbitynge and bismer and beryng of fals witnesse.
This was al his curteisye where that evere he shewed hym.
90   "I wolde ben y-shryve," quod this schrewe, "and I for shame durst.
I wolde be gladder, bi God, that Gybbe had meschaunce
Than thoughe I had this woke y-wonne a weye of Essex chese.
I have a neighbore neyghe me, I have ennuyed hym ofte
[And blamed hym bihynde his bakke to brynge hym in fame.
95   To apeyre hym bi my powere, pursued wel ofte]

And before he granted any forgiveness to govern himself.
"And you that look after the laws, let truth be your aim
More than gold or gifts if you will gratify God.
For whoever is contrary to truth, he tells in the Gospel,
Verily I say unto you, I know you not.[1]   55
And you that seek Saint James* and saints at Rome,
Seek Saint Truth, for he can save you all.
Qui cum Patre et Filio:[2] fair befall them
That are swayed by my sermon." And thus spoke Reason.
 Then Repentance ran forth and repeated his theme   60
And made Will[3] weep water from his eyes.
 Parnel Proud-Heart fell prone to the ground
And lay long before she looked up and cried, "Lord, mercy!"
And made her promise to him that created us all
That she would unsew her shirt and set a haircloth within   65
To vanquish her flesh that was fiercely sinful.
"High heart shall never overcome me but I'll hold myself low
And suffer myself to be slandered—and I never did so before.
But now I'll make myself meek and beg for mercy
From all of whom I've had envy in my heart."   70
 Lecher said, "Alas!" and to our Lady cried
To stand between himself and God and beseech mercy for his sins,
Provided he should on Saturdays seven years thereafter
Drink only with the duck and dine but once.
 Envy with heavy heart asked for shrift   75
And grieving for his guilt began his confession.
He was pale as a sheep's pelt, appeared to have the palsy.
He was clothed in a coarse cloth—I couldn't describe it—
A tabard[4] and a tunic, a knife tied to his side.
Like those of a friar's frock were the foresleeves.   80
Like a leek that had lain long in the sun
So he looked with lean cheeks, louring foully.
His body was so blown up for anger that he bit his lips
And shook his fist fiercely, he wanted to avenge himself
With acts or with words when he saw his chance.   85
Every syllable he spat out was of a serpent's tongue;
From chiding and bringing charges was his chief livelihood,
With backbiting and bitter scorn and bearing false witness.
This was all his courtesy wherever he showed himself.
"I'd like to be shriven," said this scoundrel, "if shame would let me. 90
By God, I'd be gladder that Gib had bad luck
Than if I'd won this week a wey[5] of Essex cheese.
I've a neighbor dwelling next door, I've done him harm often
And blamed him behind his back to blacken his name.
I've done my best to damage him day after day   95

---

1. Matt. 25:12.
2. "Who with the Father and the Son [lives and reigns for ever and ever]": the traditional formula of praise to God with which the sermon concludes. This may suggest that "Saint Truth" is particularly associated with the Holy Spirit within the Trinity.
3. The human will; but "Will" is also, according to several later passages, the name of the Dreamer.
4. A loose, sleeveless jacket, worn over the tunic.
5. A very large measure.

And lowen on hym to lordes to don hym lese his silver,
And made his frendes ben his foon thorw my false tonge.
His grace and his good happes greveth me ful sore.
Bitwene [meyné and meyné] I make debate ofte
100　That bothe lyf and lyme is lost thorw my speche.
Whan I [mette] him in market that I moste [hated]
I [hailsed] hym hendeliche as I his frende were:
He is doughtier than I—I dar [none harme don hym].
Ac hadde I maystrye and myghte [I wolde murthere hym for evere].
105　Whan I come to the kirke and sholde knele to the Rode
[To] preye for the pople as the prest techeth,
For pilgrimes, for palmers, for alle the poeple after,
Thanne I crye on my knees that Cryste yif [him] sorwe
That bar awey my bolle and my broke schete.
110　Awey fro the auter turne I myn eyghen
And biholde how [Heyné] hath a newe cote;
[Thanne I wisshe] it were myne and al the webbe after.
And of [his] lesynge I laughe—that [lighteth] myn herte,
And for [his] wynnynge I wepe and waille the tyme.
115　[I] deme [men ther] hij don ille, [yet] I do wel worse;
Whoso undernymeth me hereof, I hate hym dedly after.
I wolde that uche a wyght were my knave,
[And] whoso hath more than I, that angreth [myn herte].
Thus I lyve lovelees lyke a luther dogge
120　That al my [brest] bolneth for bitter of my galle.
I myghte noughte eet many yeres as a man oughte
For envye and yvel wille is yvel to defye.
May no sugre ne swete thinge asswage my swellynge
Ne no *diapenidion* dryve it fro myne herte,
125　Ne noyther schrifte ne shame, but hoso schrape my mawe?"
　　"Yus, redili," quod Repentaunce, and radde hym to the beste;
"Sorwe [for] synnes is savacioun of soules."
"I am sori," quod [Envye]. "I am but selde other,
And that maketh me [so mat], for I ne may me venge.
130　Amonges burgeyses have I be [biggynge] at Londoun
And gert Bakbitinge be a brocoure to blame mennes ware.
Whan he solde and I noughte, thanne was I redy
To lye and to loure on my neighbore and to lakke his chaffare.
I wil amende this yif I may, thorw myghte of God almyghty."
135　　Now awaketh Wratthe, with two whyte eyen,
And nyvelynge with the nose and his nekke hangynge.
"I am Wrath," quod he. "I was sumtyme a frere,
And the coventes gardyner, for to graffe ympes.
On limitoures and listres lesynges I ymped
140　Tyl thei bere leves of low speche, lordes to plese,

And lied to lords about him to make him lose money,
And turned his friends into his foes with my false tongue.
His good luck and his glad lot grieve me greatly.
Between household and household I often start disputes
So that both life and limb are lost for my speech.   100
When I met the man in market that I most hated
I fondled him affectionately as if I were a friend of his:
He is stronger than I am—I don't dare harm him.
But if I had might and mastery I'd murder him once for all.
When I come to the kirk[6] and kneel before Christ's Cross   105
To pray for the people as the priest teaches,
For pilgrims, for palmers,* for all the people after,
Then crouching there I call on Christ to give him sorrow
That took away my tankard and my torn sheet.[7]
Away from the altar I turn my eyes   110
And notice how Heinie has a new coat;
Then I wish it were mine and all the web[8] it came from.
And when he loses I laugh—that lightens my heart,
And when he wins I weep and wail the time.
I condemn men when they do evil, yet I do much worse;   115
Whoever upbraids me for that, I hate him deadly after.
I wish that every one were my servant,
And if any man has more than I, that angers my heart.
So I live loveless like a loathsome dog
So that all my breast is blown up for bitterness of spirit.   120
For many years I might not eat as a man ought
For envy and ill will are hard to digest.
Is there any sugar or sweet thing to assuage my swelling
Or any *diapenidion*[9] that will drive it from my heart,
Or any shrift or shame, unless I have my stomach scraped?"   125
    "Yes, readily," said Repentance, directing him to live better;
"Sorrow for sins is salvation for souls."
"I am sorry," said Envy. "I'm seldom anything else,
And that makes me so miserable, since I may not avenge myself.
I've been among burgesses* buying at London   130
And made Backbiting a broker to blame men's wares.
When he sold and I didn't, then I was ready
To lie and lour at my neighbor and belittle his merchandise.
I will amend this if I may, by might of God almighty."
    Now Wrath rouses himself, rubbing his white eyes,   135
Sniveling at his nose and his neck-flesh hanging.
"I am Ire," said he. "I have been a friar,
And the convent's gardener, making grafts on trees.
I grafted lies on limiters and on lectors[1] too
Till they put out leaves of lowly speech, pleasing to lords,   140

6. Church.
7. The loss of Envy's tankard and torn sheet, and his fury at it, are not explained in the text or by modern scholars.
8. I.e., bolt of cloth.
9. "Sugar-stick," a medicine. Sugar, scarce and precious in the Middle Ages, was used to treat illness.
1. *Limiters*: friars licensed by a bishop to preach (and collect donations) in a given area. *Lectors*: friars who taught in universities. The next few lines detail their activities. Cf. p.456.

And sithen thei blosmed obrode in boure to here shriftes.
And now is fallen therof a frute that folke han wel levere
Schewen her schriftes to hem than shryve hem to her persones.
And now persones [han] parceyved that freres parte with
     hem
145 Thise possessioneres preche and deprave freres;
And freres fyndeth hem in defaute, as folke bereth witnes,
That whan thei preche the poeple in many place aboute,
I, Wrath, walke with hem and wisse hem of my bokes.
Thus thei speken of spiritualté that eyther despiseth other
150 Til thei be bothe beggers and by my spiritualté libben,
Or elles alle riche and riden; [I, Wrath, rest nevere
That I ne moste folwe this folke], for suche is my grace.
I have an aunte to nonne and an abbesse bothe.
Hir were levere swowe or swelte than soeffre any peyne.
155 I have be cook in hir kichyne and the covent served
Many monthes with hem and with monkes bothe.
I was the priouresses potagere and other poure ladyes
And made hem joutes of jangelynge—that dame Johanne was a bastard,
And Dame Clarice a knightes doughter, ac a kokewolde was hire syre,
160 And Dame Peronelle a prestes file—'Priouresse worth she nevere
For she had childe in chiri-tyme: al owre chapitere it wiste!'
Of wykked wordes I, Wrath, here wortes i-made
Til 'Thow lixte!' and 'Thow lixte!' lopen oute at ones,
And eyther hitte other under the cheke.
165 Hadde thei had knyves, bi Cryst, her eyther had killed other.
(Seynt Gregorie was a gode pope and had a gode forwit
That no priouresse were prest, for that he [purveyede].
Thei had thanne ben *infamis* the firste day, thei can so yvel hele
     conseille.)
Amonge monkes I mighte be, ac many tyme I shonye,
170 For there ben many felle frekis my feres to aspye,
Bothe prioure an sup-prioure and owre *pater abbas*
And if I telle any tales thei taken hem togyderes
And do me faste Frydayes to [therf] bred and to water;
And am chalanged in the chapitelhous as I a childe were,
175 And baleised on the bare ers and no breche bitwene.
Forthi have I no lykyng, [leve me], with tho leodes to
     wonye.
I ete there unthende fisshe and fieble ale drynke.

And then they blossomed abroad in bedrooms to hear shrifts.
And now a fruit has fallen from this that folk had much rather
Show their sins to them than be shriven by their parsons.
And now that parsons have perceived that friars get part of their
    revenue
These possessioners[2] preach disparagement of friars;   145
And friars find parsons deficient, as folk bear witness,
So that when friars preach to the people in places all about,
I, Wrath, run alongside them and read them my books.
Thus they speak of spirituality and each despises the other
Till they both become beggars and live by my spirituality,   150
Or else all become rich and ride; I, Wrath, rest never
But must follow these folk, for such is my grace.
I have an aunt who's a nun and an abbess at that.
She'd rather faint or fall dead than feel any pain.
I've been cook in her kitchen and the convent's servant   155
Many months with them and with monks as well.
I prepared stews for the prioress[3] and other poor ladies
And served them juicy suggestions—that Dame Joan was a bastard,
And Dame Clarice a knight's daughter, but her daddy was a cuckold,
And Dame Parnel a priest's wench—'She'll never be prioress   160
For she had a child in cherry-time: our whole chapter[4] knows it!'
With vicious verbiage I, Wrath, cooked their vegetables
Till 'You lie!' and 'You lie!' leapt out at once,
And each hit the other under the cheek.
Had they had knives, by Christ, they'd have killed each other.   165
(Saint Gregory[5] was a good pope and had good foresight
When he provided that the priesthood should be closed to prioresses.
They would have been *infamis*[6] then and there, they keep secrets so
    badly.)
I might live among monks, but mostly I shun it,
For there are many fierce fellows there to ferret out my deeds,   170
Both prior and sub-prior and our *pater abbas*[7]
And if I tell any tales they take counsel together
And make me fast Fridays on flat bread and water;
And I'm challenged like a child in the chapterhouse,
And lambasted on the bare arse and no breeches between.   175
Therefore it's no pleasure, I promise you, to live in those people's
    house.
I eat unwholesome fish there and the ale I drink is weak.

---

2. Priests in possession of a parish whose inhabitants' donations supported them. (These donations were not optional but an annual tax of 10 percent—thus called "tithes," from Old English *teotha*, "tenth"—levied on the income of each parishioner from labor or business and, if he or she owned land, on the increase derived from the earth, such as crops, livestock born within the year, etc. The tithes were supposed to support the priest, maintain the church, and help the poor.) Parish clergy were consequently hostile to friars trying to horn in on either their functions or their income.
3. The second in command of a convent, or the mother superior of a smaller or secondary convent dependent on the first. Cf. p. 454.
4. *Cherry-time*: i.e., in cherry season. *Chapter*: governing body of a convent or monastery.
5. Not St. Gregory the Great* but Gregory IX, who, in the thirteenth century, had a collection of papal decrees made.
6. "Infamous." Presumably Wrath means they would be in violation of their priestly office by telling the secrets of the confessional.
7. "Father Abbot." The prior and sub-prior are the abbot's second and third in command, particularly responsible for order and discipline.

Ac otherwhile whan wyn cometh, whan I drynke at eve,
I have a fluxe of a foule mouthe wel fyve dayes after;
180 Al the wikkednesse that I wote bi any of owre bretheren
I [coughe] it [up] in owre cloistre that al [the] covent wote it."
   "Now repent the," quod Repentaunce, "and reherce thow nevre
Conseille that thow cnowest—bi contenaunce ne bi [speche].
— And drynke noughte over-delicatly, ne to depe noyther,
185 That thi wille [ne thi wit] to wrath myghte torne.
Esto sobrius," he seyde, and assoilled me after,
And bad me wilne to wepe, my wikkednesse to amende.
   Thanne cam Coveytise; can I hym noughte descryve,
So hungriliche and holwe Sire [Hervy] hym loked.
190 He was bitel-browed and baber-lipped also with two blered eyghen;
And [lyk] a letheren purs lolled his chekes
Wel sydder than his chyn—thei chiveled for elde.
And as a [bondmannes] bacoun his berde was [y-shave];
With an hode on his hed, a hatte above,
195 In a [torne] tabarde of twelve wynter age.
But if that a lous couthe [lepe, I leve and I trowe],
She sholde noughte have walked on that welche, so was it thredebare.
"I have ben coveytouse," quod this caityve, "I biknowe it here.
For some tyme I served Symme atte [Nok],
200 And was his prentis y-plighte his profit to wayte.
First I lerned to lye a leef other tweyne:
Wikkedlich to weye was my furst lessoun,
To Wy and to Wynchestre I went to the faire
With many manere marchandise as my maistre me highte.
205 Ne had the grace of gyle y-go amonge my ware
It had be unsolde this sevene yere, so me God helpe.
Thanne drowe I me amonges draperes my donet to lerne,
To drawe the [lyst] alonge, the lenger it semed.
Amonge the riche rayes I rendred a lessoun:
210 [Proched] hem with a [paknedele] and plaited hem togyderes,
And put hem in a presse and pyned hem therinne
Tyl ten yerdes or twelve tolled out threttene.
My wyf was a [wynnestere], and wollen cloth made
[And] spak to [the spynnestere] to spynnen it [softe].
215 The pounde that she payed by poised a quarteroun more
Than myne owne auncere [whan I] weyghed treuthe.
I boughte hir barlymalte; she brewe it to selle.

But once in a while when wine comes, when I drink in the evening,
I have a flux of a foul mouth for five days after;
All the nastiness I know about any of our brothers   180
I cough it up in our cloister so the whole convent knows it."
    "Now repent," said Repentance, "and don't reveal ever
Secrets you've discovered—neither by your speech nor look.
Don't drink with too much delight, nor too deeply either,
Lest your will and your wits be overwhelmed by wrath.   185
Esto sobrius," he said, and absolved me[8] after,
And bade me will to weep, to amend my wickedness.
    Then came Covetousness; I can't describe him,
So hungrily and hollow Sir Harvey[9] looked.
He was beetle-browed and blubber-lipped with two bleary eyes;   190
And like a leather purse lolled his cheeks
Over his chops beneath his chin—they churned from age.
And like a bondsman's bacon his beard was shaved;[1]
With a hood on his head, a hat on top,
In a torn tabard of twelve winters' age.   195
Unless a louse could really leap, believe you me,
She wouldn't go walking on that weave, it was so threadbare.
"I've been covetous," said that caitiff, "I confess it here.
For some time I served Sim at the Nook,
And was pledged as his apprentice to promote his profits.   200
First I learned to lie a leaf or two:[2]
How to weigh wickedly was my first lesson,
To Wye and to Winchester I went to the fair
With many kinds of merchandise as my master bade me.
If the grace of guile hadn't gone among my wares   205
They'd have been unsold these seven years, so God help me.
Then I went to school with fabric-salesmen to study my primer,[3]
To stretch the selvage out to make it seem longer.
Among costly striped cloths I recorded a lesson:
Pierced them with a packneedle and pleated them together,   210
Pinned them in a press and put them on the rack
Till ten yards or twelve would extend to thirteen.[4]
My wife was a bread-winner; she made woolen cloth
And said to the spinster that she should spin it soft.
The pound that she paid by passed by a quarter   215
What my own scale showed when I weighed something honestly.[5]
I bought her barleymalt; she brewed it for sale.

---

8. *Esto sobrius*: "Be sober"; 1 Pet. 5:8. *Absolved me*: The first-person pronouns here and in the next line are clearly present in the manuscripts. One explanation of them is that they mark the greater participation of the Dreamer (Will) in this part of the scene—the part concerned with Wrath— or in the scene from here on.
9. "Sir" implies rank or priesthood, but neither Covetousness' name nor his title has been explained by scholars.
1. The bondsman's cheaper bacon still had bristles on the rind.
2. I.e., a page at a time.
3. I.e., the "donet," the fourth-century grammar by Donatus, which was one of the first schoolbooks a student encountered. Hence, metaphorically, the beginner's lesson in any craft or discipline.
4. Sir Harvey uses some kind of frame for stretching cloth illegally.
5. She cheats the spinner by weighing the wool with what is supposed to be a pound weight but is really one and a quarter. She wants softly twisted wool because it can be stretched afterwards to go further.

Peny-ale and podyng-ale she poured togideres
For laboreres and for low folke—that lay by hymselve.
220 The best [in my bedchambre] lay [by the walle],
And whoso bummed therof boughte it therafter,
A galoun for a grote, God wote na lesse,
[Whan] it cam in cupmel—this crafte my wyf used.
Rose the regratere was hir righte name:
225 She hath holden hokkerye [ellevene wynter].
Ac I swere now, so the ik, that synne wil I lete
And nevere wikkedliche weye ne wikke chaffare use,
But wenden to Walsyngham, and my wyf als,
And bidde the Rode of Bromeholme brynge me oute of dette."
    "Repentestow the evere?" quod Repentance, "ne restitucioun
230   madest?"
"Yus, ones I was herberwed," quod he, "with an hep of chapmen.
I roos whan thei were arest and y-rifled here males."
"That was no restitucioun," quod Repentance, "but a robberes thefte;
Thow haddest better worthy be hanged therfore."
"I wende ryflynge were restitucioun, for I lerned nevere
235   rede on boke,
And I can no Frenche, in feith, but of the ferthest ende of Norfolke."
"Usedestow evere usurie," quod Repetaunce, "in alle thi
      lyftyme?"
"Nay, sothly," he seyde, "save in my youthe.
I lerned amonge Lumbardes and Jewes a lessoun
240 To wey pens with a peys and pare the hevyest
And lene it for love of the crosse to legge a wedde and lese it.
Suche dedes I did wryte yif he his day breke.
I have mo maneres thorw rerages than thorw *miseretur et
    commodat*."
I have lent lordes and ladyes my chaffare

Penny-ale and pudding-ale she poured together
For laborers and low folk—that lay off by itself.[6]
The best in my bedchamber was stored by the wall,   220
And whoever had a taste of it bought it thereafter,
A gallon for a groat,* God knows for no less,
When she served it out cup by cup—such craftiness she had.[7]
Rose the retailer was her right name:
She's lived the life of a huckster eleven years.   225
But now I swear, so may I thrive, I shall forgo sin
And never set my scales falsely or sell bad wares,
But make my way to Walsingham,* and my wife as well,
And call on the Cross of Bromholm to clear me of debt."[8]
  "Did you ever repent?" said Repentance, "or
      make restitution?"   230
"Yes, once I was at an inn," he answered, "with a heap of peddlers.
I rose when they were at rest and rifled their bags."
"That was no restitution," said Repentance, "but a robber's theft;
Actually you ought rather to have been hanged for that."
"I thought rifling was restitution, for I never learned
      to read,   235
And I know no French, in faith, but of the farthest end of Norfolk."[9]
"Did you ever practice usury," asked Repentance, "in all your
      lifetime?"
"No, I'm sure," he said, "except in my youth.
I learned a lesson among Lombards and Jews[1]
To put pennies on a scale and then pare the heaviest   240
And lend it for love of the cross and lose it for the pawn.[2]
Such mortgages I made him sign if he missed his day.
I've more manors through forfeiture than through *miseretur et
      commodat.*"[3]
I've lent lords and ladies my wares

6. She sets off by itself a mixture of the better, thicker ("pudding") ale adulterated with the thinnest (penny a gallon) to pass off on the cheaper customers (at the price of the better, of course).
7. I.e., it is so much better than the common mix that everyone prefers it, and by doling it out in separate cupfuls, probably with an inaccurate measure, she clears four pennies a gallon for it.
8. The Priory of St. Andrew at Bromholm, near Walsingham, had what was believed to be a miracle-working crucifix containing a fragment of the True Cross; Sir Harvey's prayer, which echoes the petition for forgiveness in the Lord's Prayer ("Forgive us our debts as we forgive our debtors"), has an ironically financial ring.
9. I.e., no French at all, far Norfolk being a remote region with a distinctive dialect. (Avarice seems to think the all-too-unfamiliar word "restitution" is French.) Cf. the third poem, p. 431.
1. Though the medieval economy had come to depend heavily on financing through loans for interest, usury (as opposed to compassionate, interest-free loans) was still strictly forbidden by the Church. Consequently, business had made itself dependent on financiers from whom loans (or loans thinly disguised as something else) could be obtained, especially from Jews and from certain international bankers and merchants, primarily from Lombardy. The thriving business these financiers conducted also made them (with typical social irrationality) hated scapegoats and fueled the development of anti-Semitism in the later Middle Ages. Various ways to circumvent the prohibition against taking interest were devised. One, associated with the same groups and mentioned in the next lines, was to clip some of the metal from coins and melt it down; thus (l. 247) Avarice lends coins that have all lost part of their edge.
2. Another way of getting around the ban on usury was to lend on security of a pawn (or a manor, in line 243) worth considerably more than the loan and hope that the borrower would default and lose the pawn. Sir Harvey makes the borrower sign a contract with no grace period if the payment is late ("such mortgages," in line 242). *For love of the cross:* i.e., for the money—coins were marked with a cross—instead of for charity, which is the true meaning of the Cross.
3. "[A good man] showeth favor and lendeth": Ps. 111:5—i.e., through compassionately helping the needy without asking interest.

245   And ben her brocour after and boughte it myself.
       Eschaunges and chevesances, with suche chaffare I dele,
       And lene folke that lese wol a lyppe at every noble.
       And with Lumbardes lettres I ladde golde to Rome,
       And toke it by taille here and tolde hem there lasse."
250   "Lentestow evere lordes for love of her mayntenaunce?"
       "Ye, I have lent lordes loved me nevere after,
       And have y-made many a knyghte bothe mercere and drapere
       That payed nevere for his prentishode noughte a peire gloves."
       "Hastow pité on pore men that [for pure nede] borwe?"
255   "I have as moche pité of pore men as pedlere hath of cattes
       That wolde kille hem yf he cacche hem myghte for coveitise of here
           skynnes."
       "Artow manlyche amonge thi neighbores of thi mete and
           drynke?"
       "I am holden," quod he, "as hende as hounde is in kychyne;
       Amonges my neighbores namelich such a name Ich have."
260   "Now [but thow repente the rather]," quod Repentance,
       "[God lene the nevre grace] thi good wel to bisette,
       Ne thine [heires] after the have joye of that thow wynnest,
       Ne thi excecutours wel bisett the silver that thow hem levest;
       And that was wonne with wronge with wikked men be despended,
265   For were I frere of that hous there gode faith and charité is,
       I nolde cope us with thi catel ne owre kyrke amende,
       Ne have a peny to my pitaunce of thyne, [for pyne of my soule],
       For the best boke in owre hous theighe brent golde were the leves,
       And I wyst wytterly thow were suche as thow telleth.
           Servus es alterius cum fercula pinguia queris;
           Pane tuo pocius: vescere liber eris.
270   Thow art an unkynde creature: I can the noughte assoille
       Til thow make restitucioun," [quod Repentance], "and rekne
           with hem alle;
       And sithen that Resoun rolle it in the regystre of Hevene
       That thow hast made uche man good, I may the noughte assoille.
           Non dimittitur peccatum donec restituatur ablatum.
       For alle that hath of thi good, have God my trouthe,
275   Is holden at the Heighe Dome to helpe the to restitue.
       And whoso leveth [that I lye], loke in the Sauter-glose,
       In *Miserere mei Deus*, where I mene treuthe.
           Ecce enim veritatem dilexisti, etc.
       Cum sancto sanctus eris: construe me that on Englische."

And been their broker afterwards and bought it back myself.[4]   245
Bills of exchange and borrowers' notes, that's my business,
And I lend money to people who lose a lip from every noble.*
And with Lombards' letters I delivered gold to Rome,
And procured it on credit here and counted out less there."[5]
"Did you ever lend to lords for love of their patronage?"   250
"Yes, I've lent to lords who loved me never after,
And I've made many a knight both mercer and draper[6]
That never paid for his apprenticeship a single pair of gloves."
"Do you have pity on poor men that borrow purely for need?"
"I've as much pity on poor men as a peddler has on cats   255
Who'd kill 'em if he could catch 'em because he craves their
     skins."
"Are you a generous man among your neighbors with your meat and
     drink?"
"I'm accounted as kindly," said he, "as a cur in the kitchen;
Especially with people living near me I'm reputed as such."
     "Now unless you repent properly," said Repentance,   260
"May God never give you grace to dispose your goods well,
Nor your heirs after you to have joy from what you win,
Nor your executors to bestow well the silver that you leave them;
And may what was won with wrong be spent by wicked men,
For if I were a friar of that friary where good faith and charity are,   265
I'd not use your cash for copes or for the cost of church-repair,
Or take as my portion one penny of yours, for peril of my soul,
For the best book in our house though its leaves were burnished gold,
If I were surely persuaded that you are such as you say.
     Greed for rich dishes makes you another's slave;
     Eat your own bread: it will your freedom save.[7]
You're an unnatural creature: I cannot absolve you   270
Until you make restitution," said Repentance, "and have a reckoning
     with them all;
And until Reason enrolls it in the register of Heaven
That you've made every man good, I may not absolve you.
     The sin is not remitted until the theft has been returned.[8]
For any one who has any of your goods, as God has my troth,
Is obligated at the High Doom[9] to help you restore it.   275
And if any one believes I'm lying, look in the Psalter*-gloss,
In *Miserere mei Deus,*[1] whether my remarks are true.
     For behold thou hast loved truth, etc.[2]
Cum sancto sanctus eris:[3] construe that in English for me."

---

4. Another way of concealing interest-taking was to lend the borrower goods, not money, and then
   buy the goods back at much less than their value (hence the reference in lines 252–53 to making
   knights into mercers and drapers).
5. Lombardy bankers developed an early equivalent of the international letter of credit; Sir Harvey
   can get a letter of credit that is worth more in one place than he has to pay for it in another.
6. *Mercer:* a dealer in textiles and cloth-making. *Draper:* one in the business of cloth-making.
7. No source for this Latin couplet has been found.
8. St. Augustine (see Gloss), Epistle 153, section 20.
9. Judgment, verdict; the "High Doom" is Doomsday, the Day of Judgment at the Second Coming
   of Christ (Gloss).
1. "Have mercy on me, O God": Ps. 50:3.
2. Ps. 50:8.
3. "With the holy thou wilt be holy": Ps. 17:26.

Thanne wex that shrewe in wanhope and walde have
   hanged himself
280 Ne hadde Repentaunce the rather reconforted hym in this manere:
   "Have mercye in thi mynde and with thi mouth biseche it.
       Misericordia eius super omnia opera eius, etc.
   And al the wikkednesse in this worlde that man myghte worche or
       thynke
   Ne is no more to the mercye of God than [amyd] the see a glede.
       *Omnis iniquitas quantum ad misericordiam dei est quasi sintilla in
           medio maris.*
   Forthi have mercy in thi mynde, and marchandise, leve it,
285 For thow hast no good grounde to gete the with a wastel
   But if it were with thi tonge or ellis with thi hondes.
   For the good that thow hast geten bigan al with falsehede.
   And as longe as thow lyvest therwith thow yeldest noughte but
       borwest.
   And if thow wite nevere ne whom [ne where] to restitue,
290 Bere it to the bisschop and bidde hym of his grace
   Bisette it hymselve as best is for thi soule.
   For he shal answere for the at the Heygh Dome—
   For the and for many mo that man shal yif a rekenynge
   What he lerned yow in Lente—leve thow none other—
295 And what he lent yow of owre Lordes good to lette yow fro synne."
       Now bigynneth Glotoun for to go to schrifte
   And kaires hym to kirke-ward his coupe to schewe.
   Ac Beton the brewestere bad hym good morwe
   And [heo] axed of hym whiderward he wolde.
300 "To Holi Cherche," quod he, "forto here Masse,
   And sithen I wil be shryven and synne namore."
   "I have gode ale, gossib," quod she, "Glotown, wiltow assaye?"
   "Hastow," [quod he], "any hote spices?"
   "I have peper and [pioné] and a pounde of garlike,
305 A ferthyngworth of fenel seed for fastyng dayes."
   Thanne goth Glotoun in, and grete othes after.
   Cessé the [sowestere] sat on the benche,
   Watte the warner and his wyf bothe,
   Tymme the tynkere and tweyne of his [knaves],
310 Hikke the hakeneyman and Hugh the nedeler,
   Clarice of Cokkes Lane and the clerke of the cherche,
   Sire Piers of Pridie and Peronelle of Flaundres,
   Dawe the dykere and a dozeine other,
   A ribibour, a ratonere, a rakyer of Chepe,
315 A ropere, a redyngkyng and Rose the [disshere],
   Godfrey of Garlekehithe and Gryfin the Walsh,

Then that wretch was overwhelmed with wanhope* and would have
    hanged himself
Except that Repentance swiftly consoled him in this way: 280
"Keep mercy in your mind and with your mouth beseech it.
    His mercy is over all his works, etc.[4]
And all the wickedness in this world that one could do or
    think
Is no more to the mercy of God than a spark amid the sea.
    All iniquity compared to the mercy of God is like a spark in the
       middle of the sea.[5]
Therefore have mercy in your mind, and as for merchandise, leave it,
For you haven't enough honest earnings to buy a loaf of bread   285
Unless you went to work with your tongue or with your hands.
For the goods you have gotten began all with falsehood.
And as long as you live with them you don't lighten your debt but
    borrow.
And if you can't remember to what man or where you must restore them,
Bear them to the bishop and beg him of his grace   290
To bestow them himself where it shall prove best for your soul.
For he shall answer for you at the High Doom—
For you and for many more that man shall give a reckoning
What lessons he taught you in Lent—believe nothing else—
And what he gave you of our Lord's goods to guard you from sin."   295
    Now Glutton begins to go to shrift
And takes his way towards the Church to tell his sins.
But Betty the brewer bade him good morning
And she asked him where he was going.
"To Holy Church," he said, "to hear Mass,   300
And then I shall be shriven and sin no more."
"I've got good ale, old friend," she said. "Glutton, will you try it?"
"Have you," he asked, "any hot spices?"
"I have pepper and peony and a pound of garlic,
A farthingworth* of fennel seed[6] for fasting days."   305
Then Glutton goes in, and great oaths after.
Cissy the seamstress was sitting on the bench,
Wat the warren-keeper[7] and his wife too,
Tim the tinker and two of his servants,
Hick the hackneyman and Hugh the needle-seller,   310
Clarice of Cock's Lane[8] and the clerk* of the church,
Sir Piers of Pridie and Parnel of Flanders,
Dave the ditch-digger and a dozen others,
A rebeck-player,[9] a rat-catcher, a street-raker of Cheapside,
A rope-maker, a redingking and Rose the dish vendor,   315
Godfrey of Garlickhithe and Griffin the Welshman,

---

4. Ps. 144:9.
5. Common statement derived from St. Augustine.
6. *Peony*: considered a spice in the Middle Ages. *Fennel seed*: this herb was believed to be good for
   getting rid of wind and staving off hunger.
7. An official responsible for overseeing and protecting a game-preserve.
8. Clarice (and Parnel of the next line) are prostitutes.
9. *Rebeck-player*: fiddle-player. *Street-raker*: a scavenger—hence street-cleaner—of Cheapside, a section
   of London. What a "redingking" (line 315) was is not known, possibly a reeding, or thatching, master.

[Of] upholderes an hepe erly bi the morwe
Geven Glotoun with glad chere good ale to hansel.
    Clement the cobelere cast of his cloke
320 And atte "New Faire" nempned it to selle.
Hikke the [hostellere] hitte his hood after
And badde Bette the bochere ben on his side.
There were chapmen y-chose this chaffare to preise:
Whoso haveth the hood shuld have amendes of the cloke.
325 [Tho] risen up in rape and rouned togideres
And preised these penyworthes apart bi hemselve.
[There were othes an heep, whoso it herde].
Thei couth noughte bi her conscience acorden [togideres]
Tyl Robyn the ropere [arise thei bisoughte]
330 And nempned hym for a noumpere that no debate nere.
Hikke the hostellere [thanne] hadde the cloke
In covenaunte that Clement shulde the cuppe fille
And have Hikkes hode [the] hostellere, and holde hym y-served;
And whoso [repenteth] rathest shulde arise after
335 And grete Sire Glotoun with a galoun ale.
There was laughyng and louryng and "Let go the cuppe!"
[Bargaines and beverages bigan to arise]
And seten so til evensonge and songen umwhile
Tyl Glotoun had y-globbed a galoun an a [gille].
340 His guttis gunne to [gothelen] as two gredy sowes;
He pissed a potel in a Paternoster while,
And blew [the] rounde ruwet at his rigge-bon ende
That alle that herde that horne held her nose after
And wissheden it had be wexed with a wispe of firses.
345 He [hadde no strengthe to] stonde er he his staffe hadde,
And thanne gan he go liche a glewmannes bicche
Somme tyme aside and somme tyme arrere,
As whoso leyth lynes forto lacche [with] foules.
[Ac] whan he drowgh to the dore, thanne dymmed his eighen;
350 He [thrumbled] on the thresshewolde an threwe to the erthe.
Clement the cobelere caughte hym bi the myddel
Forto lifte hym alofte and leyde him on his knowes.
Ac Glotoun was a gret cherle and a grym in the liftynge,
And coughed up a caudel in Clementis lappe.
355 Is non so hungri hounde in Hertfordschire

A heap of old-clothesmen early in the morning
Gladly treated Glutton to drinks of good ale.
    Clement the cobbler took the cloak off his back
And put it up as a prize for a player of "New Fair."[1]   320
Then Hick the ostler[2] took off his hood
And bade Bart the butcher to be on his side.
Then peddlers were appointed to appraise the goods:
For his cloak Clement should get the hood plus compensation.
They went to work quickly and whispered together   325
And appraised these prize items apart by themselves.
There were heaps of oaths for any one to hear.
They couldn't in conscience come to an agreement
Till Robin the roper was requested to rise
And named as an umpire so no quarrel should break out.   330
Then Hick the ostler had the cloak
In covenant that Clement should have the cup filled
And have Hick the ostler's hood, and call it a deal;
The first to regret the agreement should get up straightway
And greet Sir Glutton with a gallon of ale.   335
There was laughing and louring and "Let go the cup!"
They began to make bets and bought more rounds
And sat so till evensong[3] and sang sometimes
Till Glutton had gulped down a gallon and a gill.[4]
His guts began to grumble like two greedy sows;   340
He pissed four pints in a Paternoster's length,[5]
And on the bugle of his backside he blew a fanfare
So that all that heard that horn held their noses after
And wished it had been waxed up with a wisp of gorse.[6]
He had no strength to stand before he had his staff in hand,   345
And then he made off moving like a minstrel's bitch[7]
Sometimes sideways and sometimes backwards,
Like someone laying lines to lime birds with.[8]
But as he started to step to the door his sight grew dim;
He fumbled for the threshold and fell on the ground.   350
Clement the cobbler caught him by the waist
To lift him aloft and laid him on his knees.
But Glutton was a large lout and a load to lift,
And he coughed up a custard in Clement's lap.
There's no hound so hungry in Hertfordshire   355

1. This was a game in which two participants exchanged items in their possession that were not of equal value and hence involved a cash payment by the player who put up the less valuable object. Clement puts up his cloak and Hick his hood; each chooses an agent to represent him in the evaluation of the objects, which is conducted by peddlers. Hick is represented by Bart, but since the evaluators are unable to agree, Robin is named as an umpire. It is decided that Hick should have Clement's cloak and Clement Hick's hood, but that Clement should receive a cup of ale as well, or perhaps the money for a cup of ale, which he would then share with all the participants. A fine of further ale would be placed on either of the men who grumbled at the exchange.
2. I.e., stableman (called "hackneyman" above, implying a stable of horses primarily for hire).
3. Vespers, the evening prayer service said just before sunset.
4. A quarter pint.
5. I.e., the time it takes to say the Paternoster, the Lord's Prayer.
6. *Waxed up*: i.e., sealed. *Gorse*: a spiny shrub. Contrast with lines 506–9 below.
7. I.e., a trained dog performing some feat (probably walking on her hind legs) with difficulty.
8. Birds were caught by smearing a sticky substance ("lime") on strings or twigs; someone doing this systematically over an area would turn right and left or move forward and back.

Durst lape of [that] levynges, so unlovely [it] smaughte.
　　With al the wo of this worlde his wyf and his wenche
Baren hym home to his bedde and broughte hym therinne.
And after al this excesse he had an accidie
360　That he slepe Saterday and Sonday til sonne yede to reste.
Thanne waked he of his wynkyng and wiped his eyghen,
The fyrste worde that he warpe was, "Where is the bolle?"
His [wyf edwyted] hym tho [of wykkednesse and synne],
And Repentance righte so rebuked hym that tyme.
365　"As thow with wordes and werkes hast wroughte yvel in thi lyve,
Shryve the and be shamed therof, and shewe it with thi mouth."
"I, Glotoun," quod the gome, "gylti me yelde:
That I have trespassed with my tonge, I can noughte telle how ofte;
Sworen Goddes soule [and his sydes] and 'so God me help!'
370　There no nede ne was nyne hundreth tymes.
And overseye me at my sopere and sometyme at nones,
That I, Glotoun, girt it up er I hadde gone a myle,
And y-spilte that myghte be spared and spended on somme hungrie;
Overdelicatly on [feste] dayes drunken and eten bothe;
375　And sat sometyme so longe there that I slepe and ete at ones;
For love of tales in tavernes to drynke the more I [hyed;
Fedde me bifor] none whan fastyng dayes were."
"This shewyng shrifte," quod Repentance, "shal be meryte to the."
And thanne gan Glotoun grete and gret doel to make
380　For his lither lyf that he lyved hadde,
And avowed fast, for hunger or for thurst:
"Shal nevere fisshe on the Fryday defien in my wombe
Tyl Abstinence myn aunte have yive me leve,
And yit have I hated hir al my lyftyme."
385　　Thanne come Sleuthe al bislabered with two slymy eighen.
"I most sitte [to be shryven], or elles shulde I nappe;
I may noughte stonde ne stoupe ne withoute a stole knele.
Were I broughte abedde, but if my taille-ende it made,
Sholde no ryngynge do me ryse ar I were rype to dyne."
390　He bygan *Benedicite* with a bolke and his brest knocked,
Roxed and [remed] and rutte atte laste.
"What! Awake, renke," quod Repentance, "and rape the to shrifte."
"If I shulde deye bi this day, [I drede me sore].
I can noughte parfitly my Paternoster as the prest it syngeth,
395　But I can rymes of Robyn Hood and Randolf Erle of Chestre,
Ac neither of owre Lorde ne of owre Lady the leste that evere was
　　made.
I have made vowes fourty and foryete hem on the morne.
I parfourned nevre penaunce as the prest me highte,
Ne ryghte sori for my synnes, [so thee I], yet was I nevere.
400　And yif I bidde any bedes but if it be in wrath
That I telle with my tonge is two myle fro myne herte.

That would dare lap up that leaving, so unlovely the taste.
  With all the woe in this world his wife and his maid
Brought him to his bed and bundled him in it.
And after all this excess he had a fit of sloth
So that he slept Saturday and Sunday till the sun set. 360
When he was awake and wiped his eyes,
The first word he spoke was, "Where is the bowl?"
His spouse scolded him for his sin and wickedness,
And right so Repentance rebuked him at that time.
"As with words as well as with deeds you've done evil in your life, 365
Shrive yourself and be ashamed, and show it with your mouth."
"I, Glutton," he began, "admit I'm guilty of this:
That I've trespassed with my tongue, I can't tell how often;
Sworn by God's soul and his sides and 'So God help me!'
When there was no need for it nine hundred times. 370
And over-stuffed myself at supper and sometimes at midday,
So that I, Glutton, got rid of it before I'd gone a mile,
And spoiled what might have been saved and dispensed to the hungry;
Over-indulgently on feast days I've drunk and eaten both;
And sometimes sat so long there that I slept and ate at once; 375
To hear tales in taverns I've taken more drink;
Fed myself before noon on fasting days."
"This full confession," said Repentance, "will gain favor for you."
Then Glutton began to groan and to make great lament
For the life he had lived in so loathsome a way, 380
And vowed he would fast, what for hunger or for thirst:
"Shall never fish on Friday be fed to my belly
Till Abstinence my aunt has given me leave,
And yet I have hated her all my lifetime."
  Then came Sloth all beslobbered with two slimy eyes. 385
"I must sit to be shriven, or else I shall nap;
I can neither stand nor stoop nor kneel without a stool.
If I were tucked into my bed, unless my tail-end caused it,
No bell-ringing should make me rise before I was ready to dine."
He began *Benedicite*⁹ with a belch and knocked his breast, 390
Stretched and sighed and snored at the last.
"What! Wake up, sir," said Repentance, "and speedily shrive yourself."
"If I should die on this day, my dread would be great.
I can't say my Paternoster perfectly as the priest sings it,
But I know rhymes of Robin Hood and Randolph Earl of Chester,¹ 395
But neither of our Lord nor our Lady the least that was ever
    made.
I've made forty vows and forgotten them next morning.
I never performed the penance as the priest enjoined me,
Nor really sorry for my sins, so thrive I, I was never yet.
And if I pray any prayer that's not prompted by wrath 400
What I tell with my tongue is two miles from my heart.

9. "Bless me": the first words of a formal confession.
1. This is thought to be the earliest known reference to vernacular narratives about Robin Hood. The context suggests that the "Earl of Chester" (there were several) is the one who became a popular hero about 1200 for resisting taxation. The first *historical* reference to Robin Hood is in a roll of 1230 where he is named a fugitive.

I am occupied eche day, haliday and other,
With ydel tales atte ale and otherwhile in cherches;
Goddes peyne and his passioun ful [pure] selde thynke I thereon.
405 I visited nevere fieble men ne fettered [men] in puttes.
I have levere here an harlotrie or a somer game of souteres,
Or lesynges to laughe at and belye my [neighbores],
Than al that evere Marke made, Mathew, Johan, and Lucas.
Vigilies and fastyng dayes, alle thise late I passe,
410 And ligge abedde in Lenten an my lemman in myn armes
Tyl matynes and Masse be do, and thanne [moste] to the freres;
Come I to *Ite missa est* I holde me y-served.
I nam noughte shryven sometyme, but if sekenesse it make,
Nought tweies in two yere, and thanne [telle I] up gesse.
415 I have be prest and parsoun passynge thretti wynter,
Yete can I neither sol-fe ne synge ne seyntes lyves rede;
But I can fynde in a felde or in a fourlonge an hare
Better than in *Beatus vir* or in *Beati omnes*
Construe [clausemele] and kenne it to my parochienes.
420 I can holde lovedayes [or] here a reves rekenynge
Ac in Canoun ne in Decretales I can noughte rede a lyne.
Yif I bigge and borwe [aughte], but yif it be y-tailled,
I foryete it as yerne, and yif men me it axe,
Sixe sithes or sevene I forsake it with othes.
425 And thus tene I trewe men ten hundreth tymes,
And my servauntz sometyme: her salarye is bihynde;
Reuthe is to here rekenynge whan we shal rede [acomptes]:
So with wikked wille and wraththe my werkmen I paye.
Yif any man doth me a benfait or helpeth me at nede,
430 I am unkynde ayein his curteisye and can noughte understonde it,
For I have and have hadde somedele haukes maneres;
I nam noughte lured with love but there ligge aughte under the thombe.
The kyndenesse that myne evene-Cristene kidde me farnere,
Sixty sythes, I, Sleuthe, have foryete it sith,
435 In speche and in sparynge of speche; y-spilte many a tyme
Bothe flesche and fissche and many other vitailles;
Bothe bred and ale, butter, melke, and chese
Forsleuthed in my servyse til it myghte serve no man.
I ran aboute in youthe and yaf me noughte to lerne
440 And evere sith be beggere [by cause of my] sleuthe."
Heu michi, quia sterilem   vitam duxi juvenilem.

I'm occupied every day, holy days and others,
With idle tales over ale and at other times in church;
God's pain and his passion I seldom put my mind on.
I never visited feeble men nor fettered men in prison.   405
I'd sooner hear scurrility or a summer game of shoemakers,[2]
Or lyings to laugh at and belie my neighbors,
Than all the books Mark ever made, Matthew, John, and Luke.
Vigils and fasting days, I forget them all,
And lie abed in Lent making love to my mistress   410
Till matins and Mass are done, and then must hurry to the friars;[3]
If I make it by *Ite missa est*[4] I feel meritorious.
Sometimes I'm not shriven, unless sickness causes it,
Twice in two years, and then I tell my sins by guess-work.
I've been a priest and parson passing thirty years now,   415
Yet I can't either sing or chant sol-fa[5] or read saints' lives;
But in a field or a furlong I can find a hare
Better than I can in *Beatus vir* or *Beati omnes*[6]
Construe clause by clause and make it clear to my parishioners.
I can hold lovedays* or hear a reeve's* reckoning   420
But neither in Canon nor in Decretals[7] can I read a line.
If I acquire something on credit, unless there's a clear record of it,
I disremember it immediately, and if a man asks me for it,
Six times or seven I swear it's not my debt.
And thus I trouble true men ten hundred times,   425
And my servants sometimes: their salary's in arrears;
It's heart-rending to hear the reckoning when we must read accounts:
Thus with such wicked will and wrath I pay my workmen's wages.
If any man does me a good turn or helps me at need,
I'm unkind in return for his courtesy and cannot understand it,   430
For I have and always have had some of a hawk's manners;
I'm not lured with love unless something's lying under the thumb.[8]
The kindness that my fellow-Christians accorded me years ago,
Sixty times since, I, Sloth, have forgotten it,
In speaking and in sparing to speak; I've spoiled many times   435
Both flesh and fish and many other victuals;
Both bread and ale, butter, milk, and cheese
For sloth went sour in my service till they could serve no one.
I ran about in youth and was a rebel against learning
And have ever since been a beggar because of my sloth."   440
Alas, I repine   for a barren youth was mine.[9]

2. Games were played to celebrate midsummer, but the reference to shoemakers has not been
   explained.
3. Friars offered late Masses and other services for those too lazy to attend regular parish services,
   another source of friction between friars and ordinary parish priests.
4. "Go, Mass is finished": the last words of the Mass.
5. *Sol-fa*: the names of the fourth and fifth notes of the octave, which were used in teaching music;
   Sloth cannot learn to chant the various parts of the liturgy with their different cadences.
6. The first words of several instructive psalms: "Blessed [is] the man": Ps. 1 and 111; "Blessed [are]
   all [who]": Ps. 127.
7. *Canon*: probably canon (or ecclesiastical) law, or possibly the canonical books of the Bible. *Decretals*: collections of canon law by Gratian and by later authorities.
8. Trained hawks were used for hunting. They were recalled by whirling a lure on a line that indicated
   food in the falconer's hand.
9. A proverb used by Langland earlier: I.141a.

"Repentestow the naughte?" quod Repentance, and righte with that
    he swowned
Til *Vigilate* the veille fette water at his eyghen
And flatte it on his face and faste on hym criede,
And seide, "Ware the, [for] Wanhope wolde the bitraye.
445 'I am sori for my [synne],' sey to thiselve,
And bete thiselve on the breste and bidde hym of grace,
For is no gult here so grete that his goodnesse [is] more."
Thanne sat Sleuthe up and seyned hym swithe,
And made avowe tofore God, for his foule sleuthe,
450 "Shal no Sondaye be this sevene yere, but sykenesse it [make],
That I ne shal do me er day to the dere cherche
And heren matines and Masse as I a monke were.
Shal none ale after mete holde me thennes
Tyl I have evensonge herde: I behote to the Rode.
455 And yete wil I yelde ayein, if I so moche have,
Al that I wikkedly wan sithen I wytte hadde,
And though my liflode lakke, leten I nelle
That eche man shal have his ar I hennes wende;
And with the residue and the remenaunt, bi the Rode of Chestre,
460 I shal seke Treuthe ar I se Rome."
    Robert the Robbere on *Reddite* lokede,
And for ther was noughte [wherwith], he wepe swithe sore.
Ac yet the synful shrewe seyde to hymselve,
"Cryst that on Calvarye uppon the Crosse deydest,
465 Tho Dismas my brother bisoughte [the] of grace,
And haddest mercy on that man for *Memento* sake,
So rewe on this robbere that *Reddere* ne have,
Ne nevere wene to wynne with crafte that I owe;
But for thi mykel mercy mitigacioun I biseche:
470 Dampne me noughte at Domesday for that I did so ille."
What bifel of this feloun I can noughte faire schewe.
Wel I wote he wepte faste water with his eyen
And knowleched his [coupe] to Cryst yete eftsones,
That *Penitentia* his pyke he shulde polsche newe
475 And lepe with hym over londe al his lyftyme,
For he had leyne bi *Latro*, Luciferes aunte.
    Thanne had Repentaunce reuthe and redde hem alle to knele.
"I shal biseche for al synful owre Saveoure of grace
To amende us of owre mysdedes: do mercy to us alle,
480 [God] that of thi goodnesse gonne the worlde make,
And of naughte madest aughte, and man moste liche to thiselve,
And sithen suffredest [hym] to synne, a sikenesse to us alle,
And al for the best, as I bileve, whatevere the Boke telleth.
O felix culpa, O necessarium peccatum Ade, etc.

"Do you repent?" said Repentance, and right away he
    swooned
Till *Vigilate*[1] the vigil-keeper fetched water from his eyes
And flicked it on his face and cried fast to him,
Saying, "Beware, for Wanhope* wants to betray you.
'I'm sorry for my sin,' say to yourself,   445
And beat yourself on the breast and beg him for grace,
For there's no guilt here so great but his goodness is more."
Then Sloth sat up and made the sign of the Cross,
And vowed before God, for his foul sloth,
"No Sunday shall pass for seven years, unless sickness causes it,   450
That I shall not direct my steps before daylight to the dear church
And hear matins and Mass as if I'd taken a monk's vows.
Shall no ale after meals hold me away
Till I have heard evensong: I swear my oath to the Cross.
And yet I shall restore, if I still have so much,   455
All the ill gains I've got since I was first granted wits,
And though I lack livelihood I'll leave nothing undone
So that each man shall have what's his before I go hence;
And with the residue and the remnant, by the Rood of Chester,[2]
I shall seek Truth before I see Rome."   460
    Robert the Robber looked upon *Reddite*,[3]
And because he had nothing wherewith, he wept most sorrowfully.
But yet the sinful scoundrel said to himself,
"Christ that on Calvary on the Cross died,
When Dismas my brother begged thee for grace,   465
And thou haddest mercy on that man for *Memento's* sake,[4]
So have ruth on this robber that has no *Reddere*,[5]
And never hopes to earn what he owes by honest labor;
But for thy much mercy I beseech mitigation:
Damn me not at Doomsday* because I did such evil."   470
What befell of this felon I cannot fully show.
Well I know he wept water with his eyes
And acknowledged himself culpable to Christ yet again,
That *Penitentia* should polish his pike[6] afresh
And leap with him over land all his lifetime,   475
For he had lain with *Latro*,[7] Lucifer's aunt.
    Then Repentance had pity and prayed them all to kneel.
"I shall beseech for all sinners our Savior for grace
To amend us for our misdeeds: grant mercy to us all,
God that of thy goodness gavest the world being,   480
And of nothing madest everything, and man most like thyself,
And then sufferedest him to sin, a sickness to us all,
And yet for the best, as I believe, whatever the Book says.
O happy guilt, O necessary sin of Adam, etc.[8]

1. "Watch": Matt. 26:41.
2. A famous Cross ("Rood") on an island in the river Dee off Chester.
3. "Render [therefore to all their dues]": Rom. 13:7.
4. "Remember [me when thou comest into thy kingdom]": Luke 23:42; the words to Christ on the
   Cross of the penitent thief, identified as Dismas in the apocryphal Gospel of Nicodemus.
5. "[Goods to] return": see line 461 above.
6. *Penitentia*: penitence. *Pike*: a staff with an iron point or spike, particularly associated with pilgrims.
7. Thief.
8. From the Easter Eve liturgy.

For thourgh that synne thi sone sent was to erthe
485 And bicam man of a mayde mankynde to save,
And madest thiself with thi sone and us synful yliche;
     Faciamus hominem ad ymaginem et similitudinem nostram;
         Et alibi, Qui manet in caritate in Deo manet et Deus in eo.
And sith with thi self sone in owre sute deydest
On Gode Fryday for mannes sake at ful tyme of the daye,
There thiself ne thi sone no sorwe in deth feledest
490 But in owre secte was the sorwe and thi sone it ladde.
     Captivam duxit captivitatem.
The sonne for sorwe therof les syghte for a tyme,
Aboute mydday whan moste lighte is and meletyme of seintes;
Feddest with thi fresche blode owre forfadres in derknesse.
     Populus qui ambulabat in tenebris vidit lucem magnam.
The lighte that lepe oute of the, Lucifer [it] blent,
495 And blewe alle thi blissed into the blisse of Paradise.
The thrydde daye [therafter] thow yedest in owre sute;
A synful Marie the seighe ar Seynte Marie thi dame,
And al to solace synful thow suffredest it so were.
     Non veni vocare justos set peccatores ad penitenciam.
And al that Marke hath y-made, Mathew, Johan, and Lucas,
500 Of thyne doughtiest dedes were don in owre armes.
     Verbum caro factum est et habitavit in nobis.
And bi so moche, [it] semeth, the sikerere we mowe
Bydde and biseche, if it be thi wille,
That art owre fader and owre brother, be merciable to us,
And have reuthe on thise ribaudes that repente hem [so] sore
505 That evere thei wratthed the in this worlde in worde, thoughte, or dedes."
Thanne hent Hope an horne of *Deus tu conversus vivificabis nos*
And blew it with *Beati quorum remissae sunt iniquitates,*
That alle seyntes [for synful] songen at ones,
"*Homines et jumenta salvabis quemadmodum multiplicasti*
     misericordiam tuam, Deus."
510   A thousand of men tho thrungen togyderes,
Criede upward to Cryst and to his clene moder
To have grace to go [to] Treuthe—[God leve that thei moten]!
Ac there was wyghte non so wys the wey thider couthe,
But blustreden forth as bestes over bankes and hilles

For through that sin thy son was sent to earth
And became man of a maid to save mankind,   485
And thou madest thyself with thy son like us sinful men;
> *Let us make man in our image and likeness; And elsewhere,*
> *Who dwelleth in love dwelleth in God and God in him.*[9]
And since then with thy own son thou sufferedest death in our sect[1]
On Good Friday for man's sake at full time of the day,[2]
Where neither thyself nor thy son felt sorrow in death
But in our sect was the sorrow and thy son led it.   490
> *He led captivity captive.*[3]
The sun for sorrow of this lost sight for a time,
About midday when there's most light and mealtime of saints;[4]
Thou feddest with thy fresh blood our forefathers in darkness.
> *People that walked in darkness have seen a great light.*[5]
The light that leapt out of thee blinded Lucifer,
And blew all thy blessed into the bliss of Paradise.   495
The third day thereafter thou walkedest in our sect;
A sinful Mary[6] saw thee before Saint Mary thy mother,
And all to solace sinners thou sufferedest it so to be.
> *I came not to call the righteous but sinners to repentance.*[7]
And all that Mark made record of, Matthew, John, and Luke,
About thy doughtiest deeds was done in our armor.   500
> *The Word was made flesh and dwelt among us.*[8]
And by so much, it seems, the more surely we may
Beg and beseech, if it be thy will,
Who art our father and our brother, be merciful to us,
And have ruth on these rogues that repent so sorely
That they ever angered thee on this earth in word, thought, or deed."   505
Then Hope took hold of a horn of *Deus tu conversus vivificabis nos*[9]
And blew it with *Beati quorum remissae sunt iniquitates,*[1]
So that all the saints sang for sinners at once,
"*Men and animals thou shalt save inasmuch as thou hast multiplied thy*
> *mercy, O God.*"[2]
A thousand men then thronged together,   510
Cried upward to Christ and to his clean mother
To have grace to go to Truth—God grant they might!
But there was no one so wise as to know the way thither,
But they blundered forth like beasts over banks and hills

9. (1) Gen. 1:26; (2) 1 John 4:16.
1. The expressions "in our sect" (i.e., as a member of our group—here and line 496) and "in our armor" (line 500) refer to Christ's putting on human nature in the Incarnation and acting as one of us. Cf. Langland's treatment of the Crucifixion in Passus XVIII.
2. The time of Christ's death (the "ninth hour" in the Gospels) had come to be identified with noon.
3. Eph. 4:8.
4. This image links the Crucifixion of Christ and the bread and wine of Communion (Lord's Supper), which is a re-enactment of it. Christ's blood was thought to have flowed into hell to rescue the patriarchs and prophets who lived before his coming ("our forefathers," l. 493); Langland's image of this blood as food suggests not only Communion but a common image of the Atonement, the pelican that was believed to wound its breast to feed its children with its blood.
5. Isa. 9:2.
6. The repentant Mary Magdalene: Mark 16:9, John 20:1–18.
7. Luke 5:32.
8. John 1:14.
9. "O God, you will turn and give us life": from the Mass.
1. "Blessed [are they] whose transgressions are forgiven": Ps. 31:1.
2. Ps. 35:7–8.

515 Til late was and longe, that thei a lede mette
    Apparailled as a paynym in pylgrymes wyse.
    He bare a burdoun y-bounde with a brode liste,
    In a withewyndes wise y-wounden aboute.
    A bolle and a bagge he bare by his syde.
520 An hundreth of ampulles on his hatt seten,
    Signes of Synay and shelles of Galice,
    And many a cruche on his cloke and keyes of Rome,
    And the vernicle bifore, for men shulde knowe
    And se bi his signes whom he soughte hadde.
525 This folke frayned hym [faire] fro whennes he come.
    "Fram Synay," he seyde, "and fram [the] Sepulcre.
    In Bethleem, and in Babiloyne, I have ben in bothe;
    In Ermonye, in Alisaundre, in many other places.
    Ye may se bi my signes that sitten on myn hatte
530 That I have walked ful wyde in wete and in drye
    And soughte gode seyntes for my soules helth."
    "Knowestow oughte a corseint," [quod thei], "that men calle Treuthe?
    Coudestow aughte wissen us the weye where that wy dwelleth?"
    "Nay, so [God glade me]," seide the gome thanne.
535 "I [ne] seygh nevere palmere with pike ne with scrippe
    Axen after hym er now in this place."
        "Peter!" quod a plowman, and put forth his hed.
    "I knowe hym as kyndely as clerke doth his bokes.
    Conscience and Kynde Witte kenned me to his place
540 And deden me suren hym sikerly to serve hym forevere,
    Bothe to sowe and to sette the while I swynke myghte.
    I have ben his folwar al this fourty wyntre,
    Bothe y-sowen his sede and sued his bestes,
    Withinne and withouten wayted his profyt,
545 [I-dyked] and [i-dolve], i-do that [he] hoteth.
    Sometyme I sowe and sometyme I thresche,
    In tailoures crafte and tynkares crafte, what Treuthe can devyse.
    I weve an I wynde and do what Treuthe hoteth.
    For thoughe I seye it myself, I serve hym to paye.
550 Ich have myn huire [of hym] wel, and otherwhiles more.
    He is the prestest payer that pore men knoweth.
    He ne withhalt non hewe his hyre that he ne hath it at even.
    He is as low as a lombe and loveliche of speche.
    And yif ye wilneth to wite where that [wye] dwelleth,
555 I [wol] wisse yow [wel right] the weye to his place."

Till they met a man, many hours later   515
Appareled like a pagan[3] in pilgrims' manner.
He bore a stout staff with a broad strap around it,
In the way of woodbine wound all about.
A bowl and a bag he bore by his side.
A hundred holy water phials were set on his hat,   520
Souvenirs of Sinai and shells of Galicia,
And many a cross on his cloak and keys of Rome,
And the vernicle in front, so folk should know
By seeing his signs what shrines he'd been to.[4]
These folk asked him fairly from whence he came.   525
"From Sinai," he said, "and from the Holy Sepulchre.
Bethlehem, Babylon, I've been to both;
In Armenia, in Alexandria,[5] in many other places.
You can tell by the tokens attached to my hat
That I've walked far and wide in wet and in dry   530
And sought out good saints for my soul's health."
"Did you ever see a saint," said they, "that men call Truth?
Could you point out a path to where that person lives?"
"No, so God save me," said the fellow then.
"I've never known a palmer* with knapsack or staff   535
To ask after him ere now in this place."
     "Peter!"[6] said a plowman, and put forth his head.
"We're as closely acquainted as a clerk and his books.
Conscience* and Kind Wit* coached me to his place
And persuaded me to swear to him I'd serve him forever,   540
Both to sow and set plants so long as I can work.
I have been his follower all these forty winters,
Both sowed his seed and overseen his cattle,
Indoors and outdoors taken heed for his profit,
Made ditches and dikes, done what he bids.   545
Sometimes I sow and sometimes I thresh,
In tailor's craft and tinker's, whatever Truth can devise.
I weave wool and wind it and do what Truth says.
For though I say it myself, I serve him to his satisfaction.
I get good pay from him, and now and again more.   550
He's the promptest payer that poor men know.
He withholds no worker's wages so he's without them by evening.
He's as lowly as a lamb and lovely of speech.
And if you'd like to learn where that lord dwells,
I'll direct you on the road right to his palace."   555

3. I.e., outlandishly. (Langland's word, *paynym*, was especially associated with Saracens, i.e., Arabs.)
4. *Holy water phials*: a pilgrim to Canterbury collected a phial of holy water from St. Thomas' shrine; collecting another every time one passed through Canterbury was a mark of a professional pilgrim. *Sinai*: souvenirs from the Convent of St. Katharine on Sinai. *Shells*: the emblem of St. James* at Compostela, in Galicia. *Cross*: a commemorative item from trips to the Holy Land. *Keys*: the sign of St. Peter's keys, from Rome. *Vernicle*: a copy of the image of Christ's face preserved on a cloth, another famous relic from Rome. It was believed to have appeared after Veronica gave her headcloth to Christ, as he was going to execution, to wipe his face on.
5. *Holy Sepulchre*: a church near Cairo on the site where Mary lived during the Flight into Egypt. *Armenia*: presumably to visit Mt. Ararat, where the Ark is said to have landed. *Alexandria*: the site of the martyrdom of St. Catherine and St. Mark.
6. I.e., an oath "By St. Peter!"

"Ye, leve Pieres," quod this pilgrymes, and profered hym huire.
"Nay, bi [the peril of] my [soule]!" quod Pieres, and gan forto swere:
"I nolde fange a ferthynge for Seynt Thomas shryne.
Treuthe wolde love me the lasse a longe tyme thereafter.
560 Ac ye [that] wilneth to wende wel, this is the weye thider:
Ye mote go thourgh Mekenesse, bothe men and wyves,
Tyl ye come into Conscience that Cryst wite the sothe
That ye loven owre Lorde God levest of alle thinges,
And thanne yowre neighbores nexte—in non wise apeyre,
565 Otherwyse than thow woldest [men] wroughte to thiselve.
And so boweth forth bi a broke, Beth-Buxum-Of-Speche,
Tyl ye fynden a forth, Yowre-Fadres-Honoureth;
    Honora patrem et matrem, etc.
Wadeth in that water and wascheth yow wel there
And ye shul lepe the lightloker al yowre lyftyme.
570 So shaltow se Swere-Noughte-But-If-It-Be-For-Nede-
And-Namelich-An-Ydel-The-Name-Of-God-Almyghti.
Thanne shaltow come by a crofte, but come thow noughte thereinne:
[The] crofte hat Coveyte-Noughte-Mennes-Catel-Ne-Her-Wyves-
Ne-None-Of-Her-Servauntes-That-Noyen-Hem-Myghte.
575 Loke ye breke no bowes there but if it be yowre owne.
Two stokkes there stondeth, ac stynte ye noughte there:
They hat Stele-Noughte [and] Slee-Noughte: stryke forth by bothe;
Leve hem on thi left halfe and loke noughte thereafter.
And holde wel thyne haliday heighe til even.
580 Thanne shaltow blenche at a bergh, Bere-No-False-Witnesse:
He is frithed in with floreines and other [fees] many.
Loke thow plukke no plante there for peril of thi soule.
Thanne shal ye se Sey-Soth-So-It-Be-To-Done-
In-No-Manere-Ellis-Naughte-For-No-Mannes-Biddyng.
585 Thanne shaltow come to a courte as clere as the sonne.
The mote is of mercy, the manere aboute;
And alle the wallis ben of witte to holden wille oute.
[The kerneles ben of] Crystendome [that] kynde to save,
Boterased with Bileve-So-Or-Thow-Beest-Noughte-y-Saved;
590 And alle the houses ben hiled, halles and chambres,
With no lede but with Love-And-[Lowenesse]-As-Bretheren-[Of-O-
    Wombe].
The brugge is of Bidde-Wel-The-Bette-May-Thow-Spede.
Eche piler is of penaunce, of preyeres to seyntes;
Of almesdedes ar the hokes that the gates hangen on.
595 Grace hatte the gateward, a gode man forsothe;

"Yes, friend Piers,"[7] said these pilgrims, and proffered him pay.
"No, by the peril of my soul!" said Piers, and swore an oath:
"I wouldn't take a farthing's fee for Saint Thomas' shrine.[8]
Truth would love me the less a long time after.
But you that are anxious to be off, here's how you go: 560
You must go through Meekness, both men and women,
Till you come into Conscience[9] that Christ knows the truth
That you love our Lord God of all loves the most,
And next to him your neighbors—in no way harm them,
Otherwise than you'd have them behave to you.   565
And so follow along a brook's bank, Be-Modest-Of-Speech,
Until you find a ford, Do-Your-Fathers-Honor;
     Honor thy father and thy mother, etc.[1]
Wade in that water and wash yourselves well there
And you'll leap the lighter all your lifetime.
So you shall see Swear-Not-Unless-It-Is-For-Need-   570
And-Namely-Never-Take-In-Vain-The-Name-Of-God-Almighty.
Then you'll come to a croft,[2] but don't come into it:
The croft is called Covet-Not-Men's-Cattle-Nor-Their-Wives-
And-None-Of-Your-Neighbor's-Serving-Men-So-As-To-Harm-Them.
See that you break no boughs there unless they belong to you.   575
Two wooden statues stand there, but don't stop for them:
They're called Steal-Not and Slay-Not: stay away from both;
Leave them on your left hand and don't look back.
And hold well your holiday until the high evening.[3]
Then you shall blench at a barrow,[4] Bear-No-False-Witness: 580
It's fenced in with florins and other fees aplenty.
See that you pluck no plant there for peril of your soul.
Then you shall see Speak-The-Truth-So-It-Must-Be-Done-
And-Not-In-Any-Other-Way-Not-For-Any-Man's-Asking.
Then you shall come to a castle shining clear as the sun.   585
The moat is made of mercy, all about the manor;
And all the walls are of wit* to hold will out.
The crenelations are of Christendom to save Christiankind,
Buttressed with Believe-So-Or-You-Won't-Be-Saved;
And all the houses are roofed, halls and chambers,   590
Not with lead but with Love-And-Lowness-As-Brothers-Of-One-
     Womb.
The bridge is of Pray-Properly-You-Will-Prosper-The-More.
Every pillar is of penance, of prayers to saints;
The hooks are of almsdeeds that the gates are hanging on.
The gate-keeper's name is Grace, a good man indeed;   595

7. I.e., Peter, hence the particular appropriateness of his swearing by St. Peter (line 537), a connection that Langland will exploit in a variety of ways.
8. The shrine of St. Thomas at Canterbury was famous for the gold and jewels offered by important pilgrims.
9. A good example of a place where the meaning "consciousness," rather than ethical "conscience," is dominant (Gloss).
1. Exod. 20:12. Beginning in lines 563–64 with the two "great" commandments (Matt. 22:37–39), Piers's directions include most of the commandments of Exod. 20. Cf. p. 369.
2. A small enclosed field, or a small agricultural holding worked by a tenant.
3. A holiday—i.e., a holy day—lasted until sunset ("high evening"); it was not supposed to be used for work, and drinking and games were forbidden, at least until after attendance at church services.
4. A low hillock or a burial mound.

Hys man hatte Amende-Yow, for many man [he] knoweth.
Telleth hym this tokene: 'Treuthe [wote] the sothe;
I parfourned the penaunce the preest me enjoyned
And am ful sori for my synnes and so I shal evere
600   Whan I thinke thereon, theighe I were a pope.'
Biddeth Amende-Yow meke him til his maistre ones
To wayve up the wiket that the womman shette
Tho Adam and Eve eten apples unrosted.
      Per Evam cunctis clausa est et per Mariam Virginem iterum
            patefacta est.
For he hath the keye and the clikat though the kynge slepe.
605   And if Grace graunte the to go in in this wise
Thow shalt see in thiselve Treuthe sitte in thine herte
In a cheyne of charyté as thow a childe were,
To suffre hym and segge noughte ayein thi sires wille.
      Ac bewar thanne of Wrath, that wikked shrewe,
610   [For] he hath envye to hym that in thine herte sitteth,
And pukketh forth pruyde to prayse thiselven;
The boldnesse of thi bienfetes maketh the blynde thanne,
And [so] worstow dryven oute as dew and the dore closed,
Kayed and clikated, to kepe the withouten,
615   Happily an hundreth wyntre ar thow eft entre.
Thus myght thow lesen his love to late wel by thiselve,
And [get it ayein thorugh] grace [ac thorugh no gifte ellis].
Ac there ar sevene sustren that serven Treuthe evere
And aren porteres of the posternes that to the place longeth.
620   That one hat Abstenence, and Humilité another;
Charité and Chastité ben [her] chief maydenes;
Pacience and Pees moche poeple thei helpeth;
Largenesse the lady let in ful manye;
Heo hath hulpe a thousande oute of the Develes ponfolde.
625   [Ac] who is sibbe to this [sustren], so me God helpe,
He is wonderliche welcome and faire underfongen.
But if ye be syb to summe of thise sevene
It is ful harde, bi myne heved, for any of yow alle
To geten ingonge at any gate there but grace be the more."
630   "Bi Cryst," quod a cutpurs, "I have no kynne there."
"Ne I," quod an ape-warde, "bi aughte that I knowe."
"Wite God," quod a wafrestre, "wist I this for sothe,
Shulde I nevere ferthere a fote for no freres prechyng."
"Yus!" quod Pieres the Plowman, and pukked [hym] to gode.
635   "Mercy is a maydene there hath myghte over hem alle,
And she is syb to alle synful, and her sone also,
And thorughe the helpe of hem two—hope thow none other—
Thow myghte gete grace therebi so thow go bityme."
"By seynt Poule!" quod a pardonere, "paraventure I be noughte knowe
      there;

His man is called Amend-Yourself, for he knows many men.
Say this sentence to him: 'Truth sees what's true;
I performed the penance the priest gave me to do
And I'm sorry for my sins and shall be so always
When I think thereon, though I were a pope.'   600
Pray Amend-Yourself mildly to ask his master once
To open wide the wicket-gate that the woman shut
When Adam and Eve ate unroasted apples.
    *Through Eve it was closed to all and through the Virgin Mary it was
        opened again.*[5]
For he keeps the latchkey though the king sleep.
And if Grace grants you to go in in this way   605
You shall see in yourself Truth sitting in your heart
In a chain of charity as though you were a child again,[6]
To suffer your sire's will and say nothing against it.
    But beware lest Anger ambush you, that arrant wretch,
For he has hatred for him who has his seat in your heart,   610
And he puffs you up with pride to praise yourself;
Confidence in your kind deeds makes you become blind then,
And so you'll be duly driven out and the door closed,
Latched and locked, to leave you outside,
Perhaps a hundred years before you enter again.   615
Thus you might lose his love through lauding yourself,
And get it back again through grace and through no gift else.
But there are seven sisters that serve Truth always
Who are guards of the gates that go into the place.
One is called Abstinence, Humility another;   620
Charity and Chastity are the chief maidens;
Patience and Peace proffer help to many people;
Largesse the lady lets in full many;
She has helped a thousand out of the Devil's pound.
But whoever is sib to these sisters, so God help me,   625
Is wonderfully welcomed and warmly received.
Unless you can claim kinship with some of these seven
It's very hard, by my head, for any of you all
To get admission at any gate unless grace prevails."
"By Christ," cried a pickpocket, "I have no kin there."   630
"Nor I," said an ape-trainer, "for anything I know."
"God knows," said a cake-seller, "if I were sure of this,
I wouldn't go a foot further for any friar's preaching."
"Yes!" said Piers Plowman, and prodded him for his good.
"Mercy is a maiden there that has dominion over them all,   635
And she is sib to all sinners, and her son as well,
And through the help of these two—think nothing else—
You might get grace there if you go in time."
"By Saint Paul!" said a pardoner,* "possibly I'm not known
        there;

5. From a service commemorating the Virgin Mary.
6. *In a chain of charity*: either Truth is bound by (that is, constrained by) *caritas*, "love," or Truth is enthroned, adorned with *cantos* like a chain of office. *As though you were a child again*: cf. Mark 10:15: "Whosoever shall not receive the kingdom of God as a little child, he shall not enter therein." This childlike quality is here envisaged as total submissiveness (line 608).

I wil go fecche my box with my brevettes and a bulle with bisshopes
640   lettres."
"By Cryst!" quod a comune womman, "thi companye wil I folwe.
Thow shalt sey I am thi sustre." I ne wot where thei bicome.

Passus VI

"This were a wikked way but whoso hadde a gyde
That [myghte] folwen us eche a fote": thus this folke hem mened.
Quatz Perkyn the Plouman, "Bi Seynt Peter of Rome!
I have an half-acre to erye bi the heighway;
5   Hadde I eried this half-acre and sowen it after,
I [wolde] wende with yow and the way teche."
"This were a longe lettynge," quod a lady in a sklayre.
"What sholde we wommen worche therewhiles?"
"Somme shal sowe sakke for shedyng of the whete.
10   And ye lovely ladyes, with youre longe fyngres,
That ye han silke and sendal to sowe whan tyme is
Chesibles for chapelleynes cherches to honoure.
Wyves and wydwes, wolle and flex spynneth;
Maketh cloth, I conseille yow, and kenneth so yowre doughtres.
15   The nedy and the naked, nymmeth hede how hij liggeth:
Casteth hem clothes [for colde], for so [wol] Treuthe.
For I shal lene hem lyflode but yif the londe faille
As longe as I lyve, for the Lordes love of Hevene.
And alle manere of men that thorw mete and drynke lybbeth,
20   Helpith hym to worche wightliche that wynneth yowre fode."
"Bi Crist!" quod a knyghte [tho], "[thow kennest] us the best.
Ac on the teme, trewly, taughte was I nevere.
Ac kenne me," quod the knyghte, "and [I wole konne erie]."
"Bi Seynt Poule," quod Perkyn, "[for] ye profre yow so [lowe]
25   I shal swynke and swete and sowe for us bothe,
And [eke laboure] for thi love al my lyftyme,
In covenaunt that thow kepe Holi Kirke and myselve
Fro wastoures and fro wykked men that [wolde me destruye].
And go hunte hardiliche to hares and to foxes,
30   To bores and to [buckes] that breketh adown myne hegges,
And go affaite the faucones wilde foules to kille,
For suche cometh to my croft and croppeth my whete."
Curteislich the knyghte thanne comsed thise wordes:
"By my power, Pieres, I plighte the my treuthe
35   To fulfille this forward thowgh I fighte sholde.
Als longe as I lyve I shal the mayntene."
"Ye, and yit a poynt," quod Pieres, "I preye yow of more:
Loke ye tene no tenaunt but Treuthe wil assent,

I'll go fetch my box with my brevets[7] and a bull* with bishop's
    letters."   640
"By Christ!" said a common woman,[8] "I'll keep you company.
You shall say I am your sister." I don't know what became of them.

Passus VI

"This would be a bewildering way unless we had a guide
Who could trace our way foot by foot": thus these folk complained.
Said Perkin[1] the Plowman, "By Saint Peter of Rome!
I have a half-acre to plow by the highway;
If I had plowed this half-acre and afterwards sowed it,   5
I would walk along with you and show you the way to go."
"That would be a long delay," said a lady in a veil.
"What ought we women to work at meanwhile?"
"Some shall sew sacks to stop the wheat from spilling.
And you lovely ladies, with your long fingers,   10
See that you have silk and sendal to sew when you've time
Chasubles[2] for chaplains for the Church's honor.
Wives and widows, spin wool and flax;
Make cloth, I counsel you, and teach the craft to your daughters.
The needy and the naked, take note how they fare: 15
Keep them from cold with clothing, for so Truth wishes.
For I shall supply their sustenance unless the soil fails
As long as I live, for the Lord's love in Heaven.
And all sorts of folk that feed on farm products,
Busily abet him who brings forth your food."   20
"By Christ!" exclaimed a knight then, "your counsel is the best.
But truly, how to drive a team has never been taught me.
But show me," said the knight, "and I shall study plowing."
"By Saint Paul," said Perkin, "since you proffer help so humbly,
I shall sweat and strain and sow for us both,   25
And also labor for your love all my lifetime,
In exchange for your championing Holy Church and me
Against wasters and wicked men who would destroy me.
And go hunt hardily hares and foxes,
Boars and bucks that break down my hedges,   30
And have falcons at hand to hunt down the birds
That come to my croft[3] and crop my wheat."
Thoughtfully the knight then spoke these words:
"By my power, Piers, I pledge you my word
To uphold this obligation though I have to fight.   35
As long as I live I shall look after you."
"Yes, and yet another point," said Piers, "I pray you further:
See that you trouble no tenant unless Truth approves,

7. Pardoner's credentials.
8. I.e., a prostitute.
1. A nickname for Piers or Peter.
2. *Sendal*: a thin, rich form of silk. *Chasubles*: garments worm by priests to celebrate Mass.
3. A small enclosed field.

And thowgh ye mowe amercy [him], late Mercy be taxoure,
40   And Mekenesse thi mayster maugré medes chekes.
And thowgh pore men profre yow presentis and yiftis,
Nym it naughte, an aventure ye mowe it naughte deserve.
For thow shalt yelde it ayein at one yeres ende
In a ful perillous place, purgatorie it hatte.
45   And mysbede noughte thi [bondeman]—the better may thow spede;
Thowgh he be thyn underlynge here, wel may happe in Hevene
That he worth worthier sette, and with more blisse:
      Amice, ascende superius.
For in charnel atte chirche cherles ben yvel to knowe,
Or a knighte fram a knave; knowe this in thin herte.
50   And that thow be trewe of thi tonge, and tales that thow hatie
But if thei ben of wisdome or of witt, thi werkmen to chaste.
Holde with none harlotes ne here noughte her tales,
And nameliche atte mete suche men eschue,
For it ben the Develes disoures—I do the to understande."
55   "I assente, bi Seynt Jame," seyde the knighte thanne,
"Forto worche bi thi [worde] the while my lyf dureth."
"And I shal apparaille me," quod Perkyn, "in pilgrimes wise
And wende with yow [the wey] til we fynde Treuthe."
[He] cast on [his] clothes, y-clouted and hole,
60   [His] cokeres and [his] coffes for colde of [his] nailles,
And [hanged his] hoper at [his] hals in stede of a scrippe:
"A busshel of bredcorne brynge me therinne,
For I wil sowe it myself and sitthenes wil I wende
To pylgrymage as palmers don pardoun forto have.
65   Ac whoso helpeth me to erie or [any thinge swynke]
Shal have leve, bi owre Lorde, to lese here in hervest,
And make [him] mery theremydde, maugré whoso bigruccheth it.
And alkyn crafty men that konne lyven in treuthe,
I shal fynden hem fode that feithfulliche libbeth,
70   Save Jakke the jogeloure and Jonet of the stues,
And Danyel the dys-playere and Denote the baude,
And Frere Faytoure and folke of his ordre,
And Robyn the rybaudoure for his rusty wordes.
Treuthe tolde me ones and bad me tellen it [forth]:
75   *Deleantur de libro viventium*: I shulde noughte dele with hem,
For Holi Cherche is hote of hem no tythe to [aske].
Quia cum justis non scribantur.
They ben ascaped good aventure, now God hem amende."
      Dame-Worche-Whan-Tyme-Is Pieres wyf highte;
His doughter highte Do-Righte-So-Or-Thi-Dame-Shal-The-Bete;
80   His sone highte Suffre-Thi-Sovereynes-To-Haven-Her-Wille-
Deme-Hem-Noughte-For-If-Thow-Doste-Thow-Shalt-It-Dere-Abugge-

And though you may amerce[4] him, let Mercy set the fine,
And Meekness be your master no matter what Meed does.   40
And though poor men proffer you presents and gifts,
Don't accept them, for it's uncertain that you deserve to have them.
For at some set time you'll have to restore them
In a most perilous place called purgatory.
And treat no bondman badly—you'll be the better for it;   45
Though here he is your underling, it could happen in Heaven
That he'll be awarded a worthier place, one with more bliss:
      Friend, go up higher.[5]
For in the charnelhouse[6] at church churls are hard to distinguish,
Or a knight from a knave; know this in your heart.
And see that you're true of your tongue, and as for tales—hate them   50
Unless they have wisdom and wit for your workmen's instruction.
Avoid foul-mouthed fellows and don't be friendly to their stories,
And especially at your repasts shun people like them,
For they tell the Fiend's fables—be very sure of that."
"I assent, by Saint James," said the knight then,   55
"To work by your word while my life lasts."
"And I shall apparel myself," said Perkin, "in pilgrims' fashion
And walk along the way with you till we find Truth."
He donned his working-dress, some darned, some whole,
His gaiters and his gloves to guard his limbs from cold,   60
And hung his seed-holder behind his back instead of a knapsack:
"Bring a bushel of bread-wheat for me to put in it,
For I shall sow it myself and set out afterwards
On a pilgrimage as palmers* do to procure pardon.
And whoever helps me plow or work in any way   65
Shall have leave, by our Lord, to glean my land in harvest-time,
And make merry with what he gets, no matter who grumbles.
And all kinds of craftsmen that can live in truth,
I shall provide food for those that faithfully live,
Except for Jack the juggler and Jonette from the brothel,   70
And Daniel the dice-player and Denot the pimp,
And Friar Faker and folk of his order,
And Robin the ribald for his rotten speech.
Truth told me once and bade me tell it abroad:
Deleantur de libro viventium:[7] I should have no dealings with them, 75
For Holy Church is under orders to ask no tithes[8] of them.
For let them not be written with the righteous.[9]
Their good luck has left them, the Lord amend them now."
    Dame-Work-When-It's-Time-To was Piers's wife's name;
His daughter was called Do-Just-So-Or-Your-Dame-Will-Beat-You;
His son was named Suffer-Your-Sovereigns-To-Have-Their-Will-   80
Condemn-Them-Not-For-If-You-Do-You'll-Pay-A-Dear-Price-

4. Punish with a fine, the amount of which is at the discretion of the judge.
5. Luke 11:10
6. A crypt for dead bodies.
7. "Let them be blotted out of the book of the living": Ps. 68:29.
8. Because the money they make is not legitimate income or increase derived from the earth; there-
    fore they do not owe the tithes, or 10 percent taxes, due the Church.
9. Ps. 68:29.

Late-God-y-Worth-Withal-For-So-His-Worde-Techeth.
"For now I am olde and hore and have of myn owen,
To penaunce and to pilgrimage I wil passe with thise other;
85   Forthi I wil, or I wende, do wryte my biqueste:
'In Dei nomine, amen,' I make it myselven.
He shal have my soule that best hath [deserved] it,
And [defend it] fro the Fende—for so I bileve—
Til I come to his acountes, as my Credo me [techeth]—
90   To have relees and remissioun on that rental I leve.
The kirke shal have my caroigne and kepe my bones,
For of my corne and catel he craved the tythe:
I payed it hym prestly for peril of my soule;
[He is] holden, I hope, to have me in [mynde]
95   And mengen [me] in his memorye amonge alle Crystene.
My wyf shal have of that I wan with treuthe, and nomore,
And dele amonge my [frendes] and my dere children.
For thowgh I deye todaye, my dettes ar quitte;
I bare home that I borwed ar I to bedde yede.
100 And with the residue and the remenaunte, bi the Rode of Lukes,
I wil worschip therwith Treuthe bi my lyve,
And ben his pilgryme atte plow for pore mennes sake.
My plow-[pote] shal be my pykstaf and [putte at] the rotes
And helpe my culter to kerve and clense the forwes."
105   Now is Perkyn and [the] pilgrymes to the plowe faren.
To erie this halve-acre holpyn hym manye.
Dikeres and delveres digged up the balkes;
Therewith was Perkyn apayed and preysed hem [yerne].
Other werkemen there were that wroughten ful [faste]:
110 Eche man in his manere made hymself to done,
And some to plese Perkyn piked up the wedes.
At heighe pryme Peres lete the plowe stonde
To oversen hem hymself; whoso best wroughte
Shulde be huyred therafter, whan hervest-tyme come.
115 Thanne seten somme and songen atte nale
And hulpen erie [the] half-acre with "How! trolli-lolli!"
"Now bi the peril of my soule!" quod Pieres al in pure tene,
"But ye arise the rather and rape yow to worche,
Shal no greyne that [here] groweth glade yow at nede,
120 And though ye deye for dole, the Devel have that [recche]!"
Tho were faitoures aferde and feyned hem blynde;
Somme leyde here legges aliri as suche [lorelles] conneth
And made her mone to Pieres, [how thei myghte noght werche]:
"We have no lymes to laboure with, Lorde, y-graced be ye;
125 Ac we preye for yow, Pieres, and for yowre plow bothe,

Let-God-Have-His-Way-With-All-Things-For-So-His-Word-Teaches.
"For now I am old and hoary and have something of my own,
To penance and to pilgrimage I'll depart with these others;
Therefore I will, before I go away, have my will written: 85
'*In Dei nomine, amen*,'[1] I make this myself.
He shall have my soul that has deserved it best,
And defend it from the Fiend—for so I believe—
Till I come to his accounting, as my Creed teaches me—
To have release and remission I trust in his rent book.   90
The kirk* shall have my corpse and keep my bones,
For of my corn and cattle it craved the tithe:
I paid it promptly for peril of my soul;
It is obligated, I hope, to have me in mind
And commemorate me in its prayers among all Christians.   95
My wife shall have what I won with truth, and nothing else,
And parcel it out among my friends and my dear children.
For though I die today, my debts are paid;
I took back what I borrowed before I went to bed.
As for the residue and the remnant, by the Rood of Lucca,[2]   100
I will worship Truth with it all my lifetime,
And be his pilgrim at the plow for poor men's sake.
My plowstaff shall be my pikestaff and push at the roots
And help my coulter to cut and cleanse the furrows."
    Now Perkin and the pilgrims have put themselves to plowing.   105
Many there helped him to plow his half-acre.
Ditchers and diggers dug up the ridges;
Perkin was pleased by this and praised them warmly.
There were other workmen who worked very hard:
Each man in his manner made himself a laborer,   110
And some to please Perkin pulled up the weeds.
At high prime[3] Piers let the plow stand
To oversee them himself; whoever worked best
Should be hired afterward, when harvest-time came.
Then some sat down and sang over ale   115
And helped plow the half-acre with "Ho! trolly-lolly!"[4]
"Now by the peril of my soul!" said Piers in pure wrath,
"Unless you get up again and begin working now,
No grain that grows here will gladden you at need,
And though once off the dole you die let the Devil care!"   120
Then fakers were afraid and feigned to be blind;
Some set their legs askew as such loafers can
And made their moan to Piers, how they might not work:
"We have no limbs to labor with, Lord, we thank you;
But we pray for you, Piers, and for your plow as well,   125

1. "In the name of God, amen": customary beginning of a will.
2. *Residue and remnant*: land had to be left to one's natural heirs, though up to one third of personal property (the "residue and remnant") could be left to the Church for Masses for the testator or other purposes; the other two thirds had to go to the family, one to the widow and the other to the children. Piers's arrangements seem to leave the wife considerably more latitude. *Rood of Lucca*: an ornate crucifix at Lucca in Italy was a popular object of pilgrimage.
3. Nine in the morning, or after a substantial part of the day's work has been done, since laborers start so early.
4. Presumably the refrain of a popular song. (Note similarly musical loafers in Pro. 224–25.)

That God of his grace yowre grayne multiplye,
And yelde yow of yowre almesse that ye yive us here,
For we may noughte swynke ne swete, suche sikenesse us eyleth."
    "If it be soth," quod Pieres, "that ye seyne, I shal it sone asspye.
130 Ye ben wastoures, I wote wel, and Treuthe wote the sothe,
And I am his [holde] hyne and [aughte] hym to warne
Which thei were in this worlde his werkemen appeyred.
Ye wasten that men wynnen with travaille and with tene.
Ac Treuthe shal teche yow his teme to dryve,
135 Or ye shal ete barly bred and of the broke drynke;
But if he be blynde [or] broke-legged, or bolted with yrnes—
[Thei] shal ete [as good as I, so me God helpe],
Tyl God of his goodnesse [grace gare hem to arise].
Ac ye myghte travaille as Treuthe wolde and take mete and huyre
140 To kepe kyne in the felde, the corne fro the bestes,
Diken or delven or dyngen uppon sheves,
Or helpe make morter, or bere mukke afelde.
In lecherye and in losengerye ye lyven, and in sleuthe,
And al is thorw suffrance that venjaunce yow ne taketh.
145 Ac ancres and heremytes that eten but at nones
And namore er morwe, myne almesse shul thei have,
And of my catel to cope hem with—that han cloistres and cherches.
Ac Robert Renneaboute shal [righte] noughte have of myne,
Ne 'Posteles' but they preche conne and have powere of the
      bisschop.
150 They shal have payne and potage and [a pitaunce biside],
For it is an unresonable religioun that hath righte noughte of certeyne."
Thanne gan Wastoure to wrath hym and wolde have y-foughte;
To Pieres the Plowman he profered his glove.
A Brytonere, a braggere, a bosted Pieres als,
155 And bad hym go pissen with his plow, [pyvysshe] schrewe.
"Wiltow or neltow, we wil have owre wille
Of thi flowre and of thi flessche, fecche whan us liketh,
And make us myrie [therwith], maugré thi chekes."
Thanne Pieres the Plowman pleyned hym to the knyghte
160 To kepe hym, as covenaunte was, fram cursed shrewes,
"And fro this wastoures wolveskynnes that maketh the worlde dere,
For [thei] waste and wynnen noughte, and [tho worth nevere]
Plenté amonge the poeple therwhile my plow liggeth."
Curteisly the knyghte thanne, as his kynde wolde,
165 Warned Wastoure and wissed hym bettere:
"Or thow shalt abugge by the lawe, by the ordre that I bere!"
"I was nought wont to worche," quod Wastour, "now wil I nought
      bigynne!"
And lete lighte of the lawe and lasse of the knyghte,
And sette Pieres at a pees and his plow bothe,
170 And manaced [him] and his men yif thei mette eftsone.
    "Now by the peril of my soule!" quod Pieres, "I shal apeyre yow alle."
And houped after Hunger that herd hym atte firste.

That God of his grace make your grain multiply,
And reward you for whatever alms you will give us here,
For we can't strain and sweat, such sickness afflicts us."
   "If what you say is so," said Piers, "I'll soon find out.
I know you're ne'er-do-wells, and Truth knows what's right,   130
And I'm his sworn servant and so should warn him
Which ones they are in this world that do his workmen harm.
You waste what men win with toil and trouble.
But Truth shall teach you how his team should be driven,
Or you'll eat barley bread and use the brook for drink;   135
Unless you're blind or broken-legged, or bolted[5] with iron—
Those shall eat as well as I do, so God help me,
Till God of his goodness gives them strength to arise.
But you could work as Truth wants you to and earn wages and bread
By keeping cows in the field, the corn from the cattle,   140
Making ditches or dikes or dinging on sheaves,
Or helping make mortar, or spreading muck afield.
You live in lies and lechery and in sloth too,
And it's only for suffrance that vengeance has not fallen on you.
But anchorites and hermits that eat only at noon   145
And nothing more before the morrow, they shall have my alms,
And buy copes at my cost—those that have cloisters and churches.
But Robert Runabout shall have no rag from me,
Nor 'Apostles' unless they can preach and have the bishop's
    permission.
They shall have bread and boiled greens and a bit extra besides,   150
For it's an unreasonable religious life that has no regular meals."
Then Waster waxed angry and wanted to fight;
To Piers the Plowman he proffered his glove.
A Breton, a braggart, he bullied Piers too,
And told him to go piss with his plow, peevish wretch.   155
"Whether you're willing or unwilling, we will have our will
With your flour and your flesh, fetch it when we please,
And make merry with it, no matter what you do."
Then Piers the Plowman complained to the knight
To keep him safe, as their covenant was, from cursed rogues,   160
"And from these wolfish wasters that lay waste the world,
For they waste and win nothing, and there will never be
Plenty among the people while my plow stands idle."
Because he was born a courteous man the knight spoke kindly to Waster
And warned him he would have to behave himself better: 165
"Or you'll pay the penalty at law, I promise, by my knighthood!"
"It's not my way to work," said Waster, "I won't
    begin now!"
And made light of the law and lighter of the knight,
And said Piers wasn't worth a pea or his plow either,
And menaced him and his men if they met again.   170
   "Now by the peril of my soul!" said Piers, "I'll punish you all."
And he whooped after Hunger who heard him at once.

---

5. I.e., shackled.

"Awreke me of thise wastoures," quod he, "that this worlde schendeth."
Hunger in haste tho hent Wastour bi the mawe
175 And wronge hym so bi the wombe that [al watered] his eyen.
He buffeted the Britoner aboute the chekes
That he loked like a lanterne al his lyf after.
He bette hem so bothe he barste nere here guttes.
Ne hadde Pieres with a pese lof preyed [hym bileve]
180 They hadde ben [dede and] dolven, ne deme thow non other.
"[Lete] hem lyve," he seyde, "and lete hem ete with hogges,
Or elles benes and bren y-baken togideres."
Faitoures for fere flowen into bernes
And flapten on with flayles fram morwe til even,
185 That Hunger was nought so hardy on hem forto loke.
For a potful of peses that Peres hadde y-maked
An heep of heremites henten hem spades
And ketten here copes and courtpies hem made
And wenten as werkemen [to wedynge] and [mowynge],
190 And dolven [drit] and [donge] to dryve aweye Hunger.
Blynde and bedreden were botened a thousande;
That seten to begge sylver sone were thei heled,
For that was bake for Bayarde was bote for many hungry,
And many a beggere for benes buxome was to swynke,
195 And eche a pore man wel apayed to have pesen for his huyre,
And what Pieres preyed hem to do as prest as a sperhauke.
And thereof was Peres proude and put hem to werke,
And yaf hem mete [and money] as [thei] myghte [asserve].
Thanne hadde Peres pité and preyed Hunger to wende
200 Home into his owne erd and holden hym there [evere].
"I am wel awroke now of wastoures thorw thi myghte.
Ac I preye the, ar thow passe," quod Pieres to Hunger,
"Of beggeres and of bidderes what best be [to] done?
For I wote wel, be thow went, thei wil worche ful ille;
205 Myschief it maketh thei beth so meke nouthe,
And for defaute of her fode this folke is at my wille.
[And] they are my blody bretheren, for God boughte us alle.
Treuthe taughte me ones to lovye hem uchone
And to helpen hem of alle thinge [after that] hem nedeth.
210 Now wolde I witen, [if thow wistest], what were the best
An how I myghte amaistrien hem and make hem to worche."
"Here now," quod Hunger, "and holde it for a wisdome:
Bolde beggeres and bigge that mowe her bred biswynke,
With houndes bred and hors bred holde up her hertis,
215 [And] abate hem with benes for bollyng of her wombe—
And yif the gomes grucche, bidde hem go swynke,
And he shal soupe swettere whan he it hath deservid.
And if thow fynde any freke that fortune hath appeyred

"Avenge me on these vagabonds," said he, "that vex the whole world."
Then Hunger in haste took hold of Waster by the belly
And gripped him so about the guts that his eyes gushed water.   175
He buffeted the Breton about the cheeks
That he looked like a lantern all his life after.
He beat them both so that he almost broke their guts.
Had not Piers with a pease loaf[6] prayed him to leave off
They'd have been dead and buried deep, have no doubt about it.   180
"Let them live," he said, "and let them feed with hogs,
Or else on beans and bran baked together."
Fakers for fear fled into barns
And flogged sheaves with flails from morning till evening,
So that Hunger wouldn't be eager to cast his eye on them.   185
For a potful of peas that Piers had cooked
A heap of hermits laid hands on spades
And cut off their copes and made short coats of them
And went like workmen to weed and to mow,
And dug dirt and dung to drive off Hunger.   190
Blind and bedridden got better by the thousand;
Those who sat to beg silver were soon healed,
For what had been baked for Bayard[7] was boon to many hungry,
And many a beggar for beans obediently labored,
And every poor man was well pleased to have peas for his wages,   195
And what Piers prayed them to do they did as sprightly as
     sparrowhawks.
And Piers was proud of this and put them to work,
And gave them meals and money as they might deserve.
Then Piers had pity and prayed Hunger to take his way
Off to his own home and hold there forever.   200
"I'm well avenged on vagabonds by virtue of you.
But I pray you, before you part," said Piers to Hunger,
"With beggars and street-beadsmen[8] what's best to be done?
For well I know that once you're away, they will work badly;
Misfortune makes them so meek now,   205
And it's for lack of food that these folk obey me.
And they're my blood brothers, for God bought* us all.
Truth taught me once to love them every one
And help them with everything after their needs.
Now I'd like to learn, if you know, what line I should take   210
And how I might overmaster them and make them work."
"Hear now," said Hunger, "and hold it for wisdom:
Big bold beggars that can earn their bread,
With hounds' bread and horses' bread hold up their hearts,
And keep their bellies from swelling by stuffing them with beans—   215
And if they begin to grumble, tell them to get to work,
And they'll have sweeter suppers once they've deserved them.
And if you find any fellow-man that fortune has harmed

6. The cheapest and coarsest grade of bread, the food of those who cannot get better.
7. Generic name for a horse; a bread made of beans and bran, the coarsest category of bread, was
   used to feed horses and hounds, but was eaten by people when need was great.
8. Paid prayer-sayers.

[With fyre or with] fals men, fonde thow suche to cnowe.
220 Conforte [hem] with thi catel, for Crystes love of Hevene;
Love hem and lene hem—so lawe of [Kynde] techeth.
    Alter alterius onera portate.
And alle maner of men that thow myghte asspye
That nedy ben [or naked and nought han to spende,
With mete or with moné lat make hem fare the bettre].
225 Love hem and lakke hem noughte; late God take the venjaunce.
Theigh thei done yvel, late thow God aworthe:
Michi vindictam et ego retribuam.
And if thow wil be graciouse to God, do as the Gospel techeth,
And [bilove] the amonges low men: so shaltow lacche grace."
    Facite vobis amicos de mamona iniquitatis.
"I wolde nought greve God," quod Piers, "for al the good on grounde!
230 Mighte I synnelees do as thow seist?" seyde Pieres thanne.
"Ye, I bihote the," quod Hunger, "or ellis the Bible lieth:
Go to Genesis the gyaunt, engendroure of us alle:
In sudore and swynke thow shalt thi mete tilye
And laboure for thi lyflode, and so owre Lorde hyghte.
235 And Sapience seyth the same—I seigh it in the Bible.
Piger propter frigus no felde nolde tilye;
He shal [go] begge and bidde and no man bete his hunger.
Mathew with mannes face [moutheth] thise wordis:
'*Servus nequam* had a mnam, and for he [nolde it use],
240 He had maugré of his maistre for evermore after,
And binam [hym] his mnam for he ne wolde worche,
And yaf [it hym in haste] that [hadde] ten [bifore];
And [sithen] he seyde that [his servauntz] it herde,
He that hath shal have, and helpe there [nede is],
245 And he that nought hath shal nought have and no man hym helpe,
And that he weneth wel to have I wil it hym bireve.'
Kynde Witt wolde that eche a wyght wroughte,
Or in [techynge] or [tellynge] or travaillynge [of hondes],
Contemplatyf lyf or actyf lyf; Cryst wolde [it als].
250 The Sauter seyth in the Psalme of *Beati omnes,*
The freke that fedeth hymself with his feythful laboure,
He is blessed by the Boke in body and in soule."
Labores manuum tuarum, etc.
"Yet I prey yow," quod Pieres, "*pour charité,* and ye kunne

Through fire or through false men, befriend him if you can.
Comfort such at your own cost, for the love of Christ in Heaven;   220
Love them and relieve them—so the law of Kind[9] directs.
     Bear ye one another's burdens.[1]
And all manner of men that you may find
That are needy or naked and have nothing to spend,
With meals or with money make them the better.
Love them and don't malign them; let God take vengeance.   225
Though they behave ill, leave it all up to God:
Vengeance is mine and I will repay.[2]
And if you want to gratify God, do as the Gospel teaches,
And get yourself loved by lowly men: so you'll unloose his grace."
     Make to yourselves friends of the mammon of unrighteousness.[3]
"I would not grieve God," said Piers, "for all the goods on earth!
Might I do as you say without sin?" said Piers then.   230
"Yes, I give you my oath," said Hunger, "or else the Bible lies:
Go to Genesis the giant, engenderer of us all:[4]
In sudore[5] and slaving you shall bring forth your food
And labor for your livelihood, and so our Lord commanded.
And Sapience* says the same—I saw it in the Bible.   235
Piger propter frigus[6] would plow no field;
He shall be a beggar and none abate his hunger.
Matthew with man's face[7] mouths these words:
'Entrusted with a talent, *servus nequam*[8] didn't try to use it,
And earned his master's ill-will for evermore after,   240
And he took away his talent who was too lazy to work,
And gave it to him in haste that had ten already;
And after he said so that his servants heard it,
He that has shall have, and help when he needs it,
And he that nothing has shall nothing have and no man help him,   245
And what he trusts he's entitled to I shall take away.'
Kind Wit* wants each one to work,
Either in teaching or tallying or toiling with his hands,
Contemplative life or active life; Christ wants it too.
The Psalter says in the Psalm of *Beati omnes*,[9]   250
The fellow that feeds himself with his faithful labor,
He is blessed by the Book in body and in soul."
The labors of thy hands, etc.[1]
"Yet I pray you," said Piers, "*pour charité*,[2] if you know

9. Nature (Gloss).
1. Gal. 6:2.
2. Rom. 12:19.
3. Luke 16:9.
4. This puzzling epithet has been explained on the grounds that Genesis is the longest book (except for Psalms) in the Bible, and that it recounts the creation of mankind.
5. "In the sweat [of thy face shalt thou eat bread]": Gen. 3:19.
6. "The sluggard [will not plow] by reason of the cold": Prov. 20:4.
7. Each of the four Evangelists had his traditional pictorial image, derived partly from the faces of the four creatures in Ezekiel's vision (Ezek. 1:5–12), and partly from those of the four beasts of the Apocalypse (Rev. 4:7). Matthew was represented as a winged man; Mark, a lion; Luke, a winged ox; and John, an eagle.
8. *Talent*: a unit of money. *Servus nequam*: "The wicked servant": Luke 19:22; see lines 17–27.
9. "Blessed [are] all [who]": Ps. 127:1.
1. Ps. 127:2.
2. "For charity."

Eny leef of lechecraft, lere it me, my dere.
255 For somme of my servauntz and myself bothe
Of al a wyke worche nought, so owre wombe aketh."
"I wote wel," quod Hunger, "what sykenesse yow eyleth.
Ye han maunged over-moche: that maketh yow grone,
Ac I hote the," quod Hunger, "as yow thyne hele wilnest,
260 That thow drynke no day ar thow dyne somwhat.
Ete noughte, I hote the, ar Hunger the take
And sende the of his sauce to savoure with thi lippes;
And kepe some tyl sopertyme, and sitte nought to longe;
Arise up ar appetit have eten his fulle.
265 Lat nought Sire Surfait sitten at thi borde;
[Love] him nought for he is [a lechoure] and likerous of tonge,
And after many manere metes his maw is [alonged].
And yif thow diete the thus, I dar legge myne [armes]
That Phisik shal his furred [hode] for his fode selle
270 And his cloke of Calabre with alle the knappes of golde,
And be fayne, bi my feith, his phisik to lete
And lerne to laboure with londe [lest] lyflode [hym faille].
[There are mo lieres than] leches—Lorde, hem amende!—
Thei do men deye thorw here drynkes ar destiné it wolde."
275 "By Seynt [Pernele]," quod Pieres, "thise aren profitable wordis.
[This is a lovely lessoun; Lorde it the foryelde!
Wende now whan thow wolt, that wel be thow evere!"]
"Byhote God!" quod Hunger, "hennes ne wil I wende
Til I have dyned bi this day and y-dronke bothe."
280 "I have no peny," quod Peres, "poletes forto bigge,
Ne neyther gees ne grys; but two grene cheses,
A fewe cruddes and creem and [a cake of otes],
[A lof] of benes and bran y-bake for my fauntis.
And yet I sey, by my soule, I have no salt bacoun
285 Ne no kokeney, bi Cryst, coloppes forto maken,
Ac I have percil, and [poret], and many [plante koles],
And eke a cow and a kalf, and a cart-mare
To drawe afelde my donge the while the drought lasteth.
Bi this lyflode [I] mot lyve til Lammasse tyme
290 Bi that I hope to have hervest in my croft.
Thanne may I dighte thi dyner as [the] dere liketh."
Alle the pore peple pesecoddes fetten;
Benes and baken apples thei broughte in her lappes,
Chibolles and chervelles and ripe chiries manye,
295 And profred Peres this present to plese with Hunger.
Hunger eet [this] in hast and axed after more.
Thanne pore folke for fere fedde Hunger yerne,
With grene poret and pesen, to [peysen hym] thei thoughte.

Any modicum of medicine, teach me it, dear sir.
For some of my servants and myself as well   255
For a whole week do no work, we've such aches in our stomachs."
"I'm certain," said Hunger, "what sickness ails you.
You've munched down too much: that's what makes you groan,
But I assure you," said Hunger, "if you'd preserve your health,
You must not drink any day before you've dined on something.   260
Never eat, I urge you, ere Hunger comes upon you
And sends you some of his sauce to add savor to the food;
And keep some till suppertime, and don't sit too long;
Arise up ere Appetite has eaten his fill.
Let not Sir Surfeit sit at your table;   265
Love him not for he's a lecher whose delight is his tongue,
And for all sorts of seasoned stuff his stomach yearns.
And if you adopt this diet, I dare bet my arms
That Physic for his food will sell his furred hood
And his Calabrian[3] cloak with its clasps of gold,   270
And be content, by my troth, to retire from medicine
And learn to labor on the land lest livelihood fail him.
There are fewer physicians than frauds—reform them, Lord!—
Their drinks make men die before destiny ordains."
"By Saint Parnel,"[4] said Piers, "these are profitable words.   275
This is a lovely lesson; the Lord reward you for it!
Take your way when you will—may things be well with you always!"
"My oath to God!" said Hunger, "I will not go away
Till I've dined this day and drunk as well."
"I've no penny," said Piers, "to purchase pullets,   280
And I can't get goose or pork; but I've got two green cheeses,
A few curds and cream and a cake of oatmeal,
A loaf of beans and bran baked for my children.
And yet I say, by my soul, I have no salt bacon
Nor any hen's egg, by Christ, to make ham and eggs,   285
But scallions aren't scarce, nor parsley, and I've scores of cabbages,
And also a cow and a calf, and a cart-mare
To draw dung to the field while the dry weather lasts.
By this livelihood I must live till Lammass[5] time
When I hope to have harvest in my garden.   290
Then I can manage a meal that will make you happy."
All the poor people fetched peasepods;[6]
Beans and baked apples they brought in their skirts,
Chives and chervils and ripe cherries aplenty,
And offered Piers this present to please Hunger with.   295
Hunger ate this in haste and asked for more.
Then poor folk for fear fed Hunger fast,
Proffering leeks and peas, thinking to appease him.

---

3. Of gray fur (a special imported squirrel fur).
4. Who St. Pemelle was is obscure; the A and B manuscripts and editions other than Kane-Donaldson read, "By Saint Paul."
5. The harvest festival, August 1 (the name derived from Old English *hiaf*, loaf), when a loaf made from the first wheat of the season was offered at Mass.
6. Peas in the pod. These, like most foods in the next lines, are early crops.

By that it neighed nere hervest newe corne cam to chepynge.
300   Thanne was folke fayne and fedde Hunger with the best;
With good ale as Glotoun taughte [thei] gerte [hym to] slepe.
Tho wolde Wastour nought werche but [wandred] aboute,
Ne no begger ete bred that benes inne were,
But of coket or clerematyn, or elles of clene whete,
305   Ne none halpeny ale in none wise drynke,
But of the best and of the brounest that [brewesteres] selle.
Laboreres that have no lande to lyve on but her handes
[Deyneth] nought to dyne a-day nyght-olde wortes.
May no peny-ale hem paye, ne no pece of bakoun,
310   But if it be fresch flesch other fische fryed,
And that *chaud* or *plus chaud* for chillyng of here mawe.
But if he be hieghlich huyred ellis wil he chyde;
That he was werkman wrought [warie] the tyme.
Ayeines Catones conseille comseth he to jangle:
315   *Paupertatis onus pacienter ferre memento.*
He greveth hym ayeines God and gruccheth ayeines Resoun,
And thanne curseth he the kynge and al [the] conseille after
Suche lawes to loke laboreres to [chaste].
Ac whiles Hunger was her maister there wolde none of hem
          chyde
320   Ne stryve ayeines [the] statut, so sterneliche he loked.
Ac I warne yow werkemen, wynneth while ye mowe,
For Hunger hiderward hasteth hym faste.
He shal awake with water wastoures to chaste;
Ar fyve [yere] be fulfilled suche famyn shal aryse.
325   Thorwgh [flode] and thourgh foule wederes frutes shul faille,
And so [seith] Saturne and sent yow to warne:
Whan ye se the [mone] amys and two monkes hedes,
And a mayde have the maistrie, and [multiplye] bi eight,
Thanne shal Deth withdrawe and Derthe be justice,
330   And Dawe the dyker deye for hunger,
But if God of his goodnesse graunt us a trewe.

And now harvest drew near and new grain came to market.[7]
Then poor people were pleased and plied Hunger with the best;   300
With good ale as Glutton taught they got him to sleep.
Then Waster wouldn't work but wandered about,
And no beggar would eat bread that had beans in it,
But the best bread or the next best, or baked from pure wheat,
Nor drink any half-penny ale[8] in any circumstances,   305
But of the best and the brownest that barmaids sell.
Laborers that have no land to live on but their hands
Deign not to dine today on last night's cabbage.
No penny-ale can please them, nor any piece of bacon,
But it must be fresh flesh or else fried fish,   310
And that *chaud* or *plus chaud*[9] so it won't chill their bellies.
Unless he's hired at high wages he will otherwise complain;
That he was born to be a workman he'll blame the time.
Against Cato's* counsel he commences to murmur:
Remember to bear your burden of poverty patiently.[1]   315
He grows angry at God and grumbles against Reason,
And then curses the king and all the council after
Because they legislate laws that punish laboring men.[2]
But while Hunger was their master there would none of them
      complain
Or strive against the statute,[3] so sternly he looked.   320
But I warn you workmen, earn wages while you may,
For Hunger is hurrying hitherward fast.
With waters he'll awaken Waster's chastisement;
Before five years are fulfilled such famine shall arise.
Through flood and foul weather fruits shall fail,   325
And so Saturn[4] says and has sent to warn you:
When you see the moon amiss and two monks' heads,
And a maid have the mastery, and multiply by eight,[5]
Then shall Death withdraw and Dearth be justice,
And Daw the diker[6] die for hunger,   330
Unless God of his goodness grants us a truce.

---

7. Presumably as the new harvest approaches, merchants who have been holding grain for the highest prices release it for sale, since prices are about to tumble.
8. Ale even weaker than Rose the retailer's watery penny-ale; in line 309, laborers are too fussy and will no longer accept even penny-ale.
9. "Hot" or "very hot."
1. From Cato's *Distichs*, a collection of pithy phrases used to teach Latin to beginning students.
2. Like so many governments, late fourteenth-century England responded to inflation and the bargaining power of the relatively scarce laborers with wage and price freezes, which had their usual lack of effect. One way landowners, desperate to obtain enough laborers, tried to get around the wage-laws was by offering food as well as cash. Cf. p. 428.
3. I.e., anti-inflationary legislation.
4. Planet thought to influence the weather, generally perceived as hostile.
5. This cryptic prophecy, like the one at III.323–27, has never been satisfactorily explained; the basic point is that it is Apocalyptic.
6. A laborer who digs dikes and ditches.

Passus VII

Treuthe herde telle herof and to Peres he sent
To taken his teme and tulyen the erthe,
And purchaced hym a pardoun *a poena et a culpa*,
For hym and for his heires for evermore after;
5   And bad hym holde hym at home and eryen his leyes,
And alle that halpe hym to erie or to sowe,
Or any [maner] myster that myghte Pieres [helpe],
Pardoun with Pieres Plowman Treuthe hath y-graunted.
Kynges and knyghtes that kepen Holy Cherche
10   And ryghtfullych in [reume] reulen the peple
Han pardoun thourgh purgatorie to passe ful lyghtly,
With patriarkes and prophetes in paradise to be felawes.
Bisshopes y-blessed, yif thei ben as thei
        shulden,
Legistres of bothe lawes, the lewed therewith to preche
15   And inasmoche as thei mowe amende alle synful,
Aren peres with the Apostles—thus pardoun Piers sheweth—
And at the Day of Dome atte [here] deyse to sytte.
Marchauntz in the margyne hadden many yeres
Ac none *a poena et a culpa* the Pope nolde hem graunte,
20   For thei holde nought her halidayes as Holi Cherche techeth,
And for thei swere by her soule and "so God moste [hem] helpe!"
Ayein clene conscience her catel to selle.
Ac under his secret seel Treuthe sent hem a lettre
[And bad hem] bugge boldely [what] hem best liked
25   And sithenes selle it ayein and save the wynnyge,
And [make] mesondieux theremyde and myseysé [to] helpe,
Wikked wayes wightlich hem amende,
And do bote to brugges that tobroke were,
Marien maydenes or maken hem nonnes,
30   Pore peple [bedreden] and prisounes [in stokkes],
Fynden hem here fode [for oure Lordes love of Hevene],
Sette scoleres to scole or to somme other craftes,
Releve Religioun and renten hem bettere.
"And I shal sende yow myselve Seynt Michel myn [angel]
35   That no devel shal yow dere ne fere yow in yowre deying.
And witen yow fro wanhope, if ye wil thus worche

Passus VII

Truth heard tell of this and sent word to Piers
To take his team and till the earth,
And procured him a pardon *a poena et a culpa*,[1]
For him and for his heirs for evermore after;
And bade him hold at home and plow his land,   5
And any one who helped him plow or sow,
Or any kind of craft that could help Piers,
Pardon with Piers Plowman Truth has granted.
Kings and knights that keep Holy Kirk* safe
And in the realm rightfully rule the people   10
Have pardon to pass through purgatory quickly,
With patriarchs and prophets to be fellows in paradise.
Those who've been blessed as bishops, if they embody what they
    should,
And are expert in either law,[2] to preach each to the ignorant
And inasmuch as they may amend all sinners,   15
Are peers with the Apostles—thus Piers's pardon reads—
And on the Day of Doom* at their dais they will sit.
Merchants in the margin[3] had many years' grace
But the Pope would grant them no pardon *a poena et a culpa*,
Because they don't hold their holy days as Holy Church teaches,   20
And because they swear by their souls and "so may God help!" them
Against good conscience to get their goods sold.
But under his secret seal[4] Truth sent them a letter
And bade them buy boldly whatever best pleased them
And sell it again and save such profit as they made,   25
And have hospitals built with it to help the unfortunate,
Or apply it to repairing roads that are in poor condition,
Or to build bridges that have broken down,
Or marry off maidens or make them nuns,[5]
Poor people bedridden and prisoners in stocks,   30
Provide them with their food for our heavenly Lord's love,
Send scholars to school or set them to a craft,
Relieve religious orders and give them larger incomes.
"And I shall myself send you my angel Saint Michael
So that when you die no devil shall do you harm or scare you.   35
And if you will work thus, I'll ward off wanhope* from you

---

1. This pardon has remained one of the most controversial elements of the poem. "From punishment and from guilt" is a formula indicating an absolute pardon. Strictly speaking, remissions obtained by pilgrimages (and pardons dispensed by pardoners in return for donations) could remit only the *punishment* for sin; note that even Truth's pardon does both only for some people (not, for example, for merchants, lines 18–19 below). Christ alone, through the Atonement, had the power to absolve repentant sinners from the *guilt* and delegated it to St. Peter and to the Church through the apostolic succession (lines 15–17 below) to be dispensed in the sacrament of confession and in penance. (This pardon also covers, according to another legal formula in the next line, Piers's heirs, which ordinary pardons could not.) The belief, however, that indulgences (especially those obtained from the Pope himself) absolved guilt as well as punishment was widespread.
2. Canon and civil law.
3. I.e., as a further clause added to the margin of an original document.
4. Personal, not public, seal authorizing a document, e.g., the stamp of a signet ring.
5. I.e., provide dowries without which a woman whose family cannot provide for her can neither marry nor enter a convent.

And sende yowre sowles in safté to my seyntes in joye."
Thanne were marchauntz mery; many wepten for joye
And preyseden Pieres the Plowman that purchaced this bulle.
40   Men of lawe lest pardoun hadde—[leve thow none other]!—
For the Sauter saveth hem noughte such as taketh yiftes,
And namelich of innocentz that none yvel ne kunneth.
          Super innocentem munera non accipies.
Pledoures shulde peynen hem to plede for such [and] helpe.
Prynces and prelates shulde paye for her travaille:
          A regibus et principibus erit merces eorum.
45   Ac many a justice an juroure wolde for Johan do more
Than *pro Dei pietate* [pleden atte the barre].
Ac he that spendeth his speche and speketh for the pore
That is innocent and nedy and no man appeireth,
Conforteth hym in that cas, [coveiteith noght his] yiftes,
50   [Ac] for owre Lordes love [lawe for hym sheweth],
Shal no devel at his ded-day deren hym a myte
That he ne worth sauf [sikerly]; the Sauter bereth witnesse,
          Domine, quis habitabit in tabernaculo tuo?
Ac to bugge water ne wynde ne witte ne fyre the fierthe,
55   Thise foure the Fader of Hevene made to this folde in comune;
Thise ben Treuthes tresores trewe folke to helpe,
That nevere shal wax ne wanye withoute God hymselve.
Whan thei drawen on to [the deth] and indulgences wolde have,
[His] pardoun is ful petit at [his] partyng hennes
That any mede of mene men for motyng taketh.
60   Ye legistres and lawyeres, [yif I lye witeth Mathew]:
          Quodcumque vultis ut faciant vobis homines, facite eis.
Alle lybbyng laboreres that lyven [by] her hondes
That trewlich taken and trewlich wynnen
And lyven in love and in lawe, for her lowe hertis
[Hadde] the same absolucioun that sent was to Peres.
65   Beggeres [and] bidderes ne beth noughte in the bulle
But if the suggestioun be soth that shapeth hem to begge.
For he that beggeth or bit, but if he have nede,
He is fals with the Fende and defraudeth the nedy,
And also bigileth the gyver ageines his wil.
70   For if he wist he were noughte nedy he wolde yive that another
That were more nedy; so the nediest shuld be hulpe.
Catoun kenneth [me] thus, and the Clerke of the *Stories*.

And send your souls in safety to my saints in joy."
Then merchants were merry; many wept for joy
And praised Piers the Plowman that procured them this bull.[6]
    Men of law had least pardon—believe nothing else!—   40
For the Psalter* grants no salvation to such as take gifts,
And especially from innocent people who purpose no evil.
    Thou shalt not take rewards against the innocent.[7]
Advocates should undertake to help them with their pleas.
Princes and prelates should pay for their labor:
    From kings and princes will be their reward.[8]
But many a justice and juror would for John do more   45
Than *pro Dei pietate*[9] plead at the bar.
But he that spends his speech speaking for the poor man
Who is innocent and has need and is harming no one,
He that comforts him in that case, covets no gifts from him,
But for our Lord's love expounds law for him,   50
No devil at his death-day shall do him any harm
So that he will not be surely safe; the Psalter bears witness,
    Lord, who shall dwell in thy tabernacle?[1]
But to buy water or wind or wit* or fire the fourth,
These four the Father of Heaven formed for this earth in common;
These are Truth's treasures to help true folk,   55
Which will never wax or wane without God's word.
When he draws near to death and would have indulgences,
His pardon is most paltry at his parting hence
That accepts from poor people any pay for his pleading.
You lawyers and legal experts, if I lie blame Matthew: 60
    Whatsoever ye would that men should do to you, do ye to them.[2]
All living laborers that live by their hands
That truly take and truly earn
And live in love and in law, for their low hearts
Had the same absolution that was sent to Piers.
Of beggars and street-beadsmen[3] the bull makes no mention   65
Unless there's a real reason that renders them beggars.
For whoever asks for alms, unless he has need,
Is as false as the Fiend and defrauds the needy,
And also beguiles the giver against his will.
For if he were aware he was not needy he would give his alms   70
To another that was more needy; thus the neediest should have help.
Cato* counsels me thus, as does the Clerk of the *Historia*.[4]

---

6. There was much debate about whether merchants exercised a legitimate function in society, since
they did not create anything, but made money from redistributing the work of others. In the following lines, Langland takes the position that their trade has intrinsic moral hazards, but defends
the function itself. *Bull*: (Gloss).
7. Ps. 14:5.
8. Source unknown, but cf. Ecclus. 38:2.
9. *John* (line 45): a representative commoner; "justice and juror" will "do more" for him: presumably
because he will pay (unlike the "poor man" in line 47). *Pro Dei pietate*: "For love of God."
1. Ps. 14:1.
2. Matt. 7:2.
3. Paid prayer-sayers.
4. *Histona Scholastica* (Scholastic History) of Peter Comestor, an account of major events in the
Bible.

Cui des videto is Catounes techyng.
And in the *Stories* he techeth to bistowe thyn almes:
Sit elemosina in manu tua donec studes cui
75   *des.*
Ac Gregori was a gode man and bad us gyven alle
That asketh for his love that us alle leneth.
    Non eligas cui miserearis ne forte pretereas illum qui
       meretur accipere, quia incertum est pro quo
       Deo magis placeas.
For wite ye nevere who is worthi, ac God wote who hath nede.
In hym that taketh is the treccherye, if any tresoun walke.
80   For he that yiveth yeldeth and yarketh hym to reste;
And he that biddeth borweth and bryngeth hymself in dette.
For beggeres borwen evermo and her borgh is God almyghti
To yelden hem that yiveth hem, and yet usuré more.
    Quare non dedisti pecuniam meam ad mensam, ut
       ego veniens cum usuris exegissem illam?
Forthi biddeth nought, ye beggeres, but if ye have nede;
85   For whoso hath to buggen hym bred, the Boke bereth witnesse,
He hath ynough that hath bred ynough, though he have nought elles.
    Satis dives est qui non indiget pane.
(Late usage be yowre solace of seyntes lyves redyng.)
The Boke banneth beggarie and blameth hem in this manere:
Junior fui etenim senui, et non vidi justum derelictum nec semen
    eius querens panem.
90   For [thei] lyve in no love ne no lawe holde;
[Thei] wedde [no] wommen that [thei] with delen
But as wilde bestis with "wehe!" worthen uppe and worchen,
And bryngeth forth barnes that bastardes men calleth;
Or [his] bakke, or [his] bone, [thei] breketh in his youthe,
95   [And] sitthe gon faiten with [here] fauntes for evermore after.
There is moo mysshape peple amonge thise beggeres
Than of alle [othere] maner men that on this molde [wandreth].
Thei that lyve thus here lyf mowe lothe the tyme
That evere [thei were men] wrought whan [thei] shal hennes fare.
100   Ac olde men and hore that helplees ben of strengthe,
And women with childe that worche ne mowe,
Blynde and [bedreden] and broken her membres
That taketh this myschief mekelych, as meseles and othere,
Han as pleyne pardoun as the plowman hymself;
105   For love of her lowe hertis owre Lorde hath hem graunted
Here penaunce and here purgatorie, here [is opene on] erthe.
    "Pieres," quod a prest tho, "thi pardoun most I rede,
For I wil construe eche clause and kenne it the on Englich."
And Pieres at his preyere the pardoun unfoldeth,

Cui des videto[5] is Cato's teaching.
And in the *Historia* he tells how to bestow your alms:
Let your alms remain in your hand until you are sure to whom you are
    giving.   75
But Gregory was a good man and bade us give to every one
That asks us for his love that gives us everything.
    Do not choose whom you pity lest by chance you pass over him who
        deserves to receive, since it is uncertain for whose sake you will
        please God more.[6]
For you never know who is worthy, but God knows who has need.
The treachery is in him that takes, if betrayal is involved.
For giving presents is repayment that brings the giver peace of mind;   80
But the beggar is a borrower who brings more debt on himself.
For beggars are borrowers whose bond is God almighty
To pay their debts to their donors, and in addition interest.
    Wherefore then gavest thou not my money into the bank, that
        at my coming I might have required it with usury?[7]
Therefore beg not, you beggars, unless it be for need;
For whoever has wherewith to buy bread, the Book bears witness,   85
He has enough who has bread enough, though he has nothing more.
    He is rich enough who does not lack bread.[8]
(It's a comforting custom to read accounts of saints.)[9]
The Book curses all beggars and blames them in this way:
I have been young and now have become old; and I have not seen the
    righteous forsaken nor his seed begging bread.[1]
For they live in no love and think no law binds them;   90
They wed no women with whom they deal
But like wild beasts with "weehee!" mount and go to work,
And bring forth a brood that bear the name of bastard;
Or they break a child's back, or a bone, in his youth,
And go forth as fakers with their brats for evermore after.   95
There are more misshapen people among these beggars
Than among all other manner of men that move upon this earth.
Thus they that lead their lives so may loathe the time
That they were ever made men when they must go hence.
But men old and hoary that are helpless of strength,   100
And women with child for whom work is impossible,
Blind and bedridden and broken-limbed people
Who take their misery meekly, leper-men and others,
Have as plenary pardon[2] as the plowman himself;
For love of their low hearts our Lord has granted them   105
Their penance and their purgatory in full plenty on earth.
    "Piers," said a priest then, "your pardon must I read,
For I'll explain each paragraph to you and put it in English."
And Piers unfolds the pardon at the priest's prayer,

---

5. "See to whom you give."
6. Not from Pope Gregory the Great* but from St. Jerome's* Commentary on Eccl. 11:6.
7. Luke 19:23.
8. From St. Jerome's Epistles.
9. Presumably because they show how God provides for those whose trust in him is complete.
1. Ps. 36:25.
2. As complete a pardon (i.e., a *poena et a culpa*) as Piers.

110   And I bihynde hem bothe bihelde al the bulle.
      Al in two lynes it lay, and nought a [lettre] more,
      And was writen right thus in witnesse of treuthe:
      Et qui bona egerunt ibunt in vitam eternam;
      Qui vero mala in ignem eternum.
115   "Peter!" quod the prest tho, "I can no pardoun fynde—
      But 'Do wel, and have wel,' and God shal have thi sowle,
      And 'Do yvel, and have yvel,' [and] hope thow non other
      [But] after thi ded-day the Devel shal have thi sowle."
      And Pieres for pure tene pulled it atweyne
120   And seyde, "*Si ambulavero in medio umbre mortis*
            non timebo mala; quoniam tu mecum es.
      I shal cessen of my sowyng and swynk nought so harde,
      Ne about my [bileve] so bisi be namore.
      Of preyers and of penaunce my plow shal ben herafter,
125   And wepen whan I shulde [werche], though whete bred me faille.
      The prophete his payn ete in penaunce and in sorwe
      By that the Sauter seith, [and] so dede other manye.
      That loveth God lelly, his lyflode is ful esy.
            Fuerunt michi lacrime mee panes die ac nocte.
      And but if Luke lye, he lereth us [another]
130   [Bi foules that are] nought bisy aboute the [bely-joye]:
      '*Ne soliciti sitis,*' he seyth in the Gospel,
      And sheweth us bi ensamples us selve to wisse.
      The foules [in] the [firmament], who fynt hem at wynter?
      [Whan the frost freseth fode hem bihoveth],
135   Have thei no gernere to go to, but God fynt hem alle."
      "What!" quod the prest to Perkyn, "Peter, as me thinketh,
      Thow art lettred a litel. Who lerned the on boke?"
      "Abstinence the abbesse myne a b c me taughte,
      And Conscience come [after] and kenned me [bettre]."
      "Were thow a prest, Pieres," quod he, "thow mighte preche [when the
140   liked]
      As devynour in devynyté, with *Dixit insipiens* to thi teme."
      "Lewed lorel!" quod Pieres, "litel lokestow on the Bible;
      On Salomones sawes selden thow biholdest."
            Ejice derisores et jurgia, cum eis ne crescant.
      The prest and Perkyn apposeden eyther other,
145   And thorw here wordes [I] awoke and waited aboute,
      And seighe the sonne [evene] south sitte that tyme,
      Metelees and monelees on Malverne Hulles.
      Musyng on this meteles, [a myle-waye] Ich yede.
      Many tyme this meteles hath maked me to studye
150   Of that I seigh slepyng, if it so be myghte,

And I behind them both beheld all the bull.*   110
In two lines it lay, and not a letter more,
And was worded this way in witness of truth:
They that have done good shall go into life everlasting;
And they that have done evil into everlasting fire.[3]
"Peter!" said the priest then, "I can find no pardon here—   115
Only 'Do well, and have well,' and God will have your soul,
And 'Do evil, and have evil,' and hope nothing else
But that after your death-day the Devil will have your soul."
And Piers for pure wrath pulled it in two
And said, *"Though I walk in the midst of the shadow of death*   120
I will fear no evil; for thou art with me.[4]
I shall cease my sowing and not work so hard,
Nor be henceforth so busy about my livelihood.
My plow shall be of penance and of prayers hereafter,
And I'll weep when I should work, though wheat bread fails me.   125
The prophet[5] ate his portion in penance and sorrow
As the Psalter says, and so did many others.
Who loves God loyally, his livelihood comes easy.
     My tears have been my bread day and night.[6]
And unless Luke lies, he finds another lesson for us
In birds that are not busy about their belly-joy: 130
'Ne soliciti sitis,'[7] he says in the Gospel,
And shows us examples by which to school ourselves.
The fowls in the firmament, who feeds them in winter?
When the frost freezes they forage for food,
They have no granary to go to, but God feeds them all."   135
"What!" said the priest to Perkin, "Peter, it would seem
You are lettered a little. Who lessoned you in books?"
"Abstinence the abbess taught me my a b c,
And Conscience* came after and counseled me better."
"If you were a priest, Piers," said he, "you might preach when you
          pleased   140
As a doctor of divinity, with *Dixit insipiens*[8] as your text."
"Unlearned lout!" said Piers, "you know little of the Bible;
Solomon's sayings are seldom your reading."
     Cast out the scorners and contentions with them, lest they increase.[9]
The priest and Perkin opposed each other,
And through their words I awoke and looked everywhere about,   145
And saw the sun sit due south at that time,
Meatless and moneyless on Malvern Hills.
Musing on my dream, I walked a mile-way.
Many a time my dream has made me study
What I saw sleeping, if it might so be,   150

3. From the Athanasian Creed, based on Matt. 25:31–46. Cf. p.374.
4. Ps. 23:4.
5. David, whose Psalm is quoted below.
6. Ps. 41:4.
7. "Take no thought [for your life]": Matt. 6:25; also Luke 12:22.
8. "The fool hath said [in his heart, There is no God]": Ps. 13:1.
9. Prov. 22:10.

And also for Peres [love] the Plowman ful pensyf in herte,
And which a pardoun Peres hadde alle the peple to conforte,
And how the prest impugned it with two propre wordes.
Ac I have no savoure in songewarie, for I se it ofte faille.
155 Catoun and canonistres conseilleth us to leve
To sette sadnesse in songewarie, for *"Somnia ne cures."*
Ac for the boke Bible bereth witnesse
How Danyel devyned the dremes of a kynge—
That Nabugodonosor [nempneth thise] clerkis—
160 Daniel seyde, "Sire Kynge, thi [swevene is to mene]
That unkouth knyghtes shul come thi kyngdom to [cleyme]:
Amonges lowere lordes thi londe shal be departed."
As Danyel devyned, in dede it felle after:
The Kynge lese his lordship and [lasse] men it hadde.
165 And Joseph mette merveillously how the mone and the sonne
And the ellevene sterres hailsed hym alle.
Thanne Jacob jugged Josephes swevene:
"Beau fils," quod his fader, "for defaute we shullen—
I myself and my sones—seche the for nede."
170 It bifel as his fader seyde in Pharaoes tyme
That Joseph was justice Egipte to loken;
It bifel as his fader tolde, his frendes there hym soughte.
     And al this maketh me on meteles to thynke
And how the prest preved no pardoun to Do-Wel,
175 And demed that Do-Wel indulgences [passeth],
Biennales and triennales and bisschopes lettres.—
Do-wel at the Day of Dome is dignelich underfongen:
[He] passeth al the pardoun of Seynt Petres cherche!
Now hath the Pope powere pardoun to graunte
180 [The peple] withouten eny penaunce to passen [to joye]?
This is [a leef of] owre bileve, as lettered men us techeth.
     Quodcumque ligaveris super terram erit ligatum et in celis,
          etc.
And so I leve lelly—Lordes forbode ellis!—
That pardoun and penaunce and preyeres don save
Soules that have synned sevene sithes dedly.
185 Ac to trust to thise triennales, trewly, me thinketh
Is nought so syker for the soule, certis, as is Do-Wel.
Forthi I rede yow renkes that riche ben on this erthe
Uppon trust of yowre tresoure triennales to have,
Be ye nevere the balder to breke the Ten Hestes,
190 And namelich ye maistres, mayres and jugges,

And for love of Piers the Plowman most pensive in heart,
And what a pardon Piers had for the people's comfort,
And how the priest impugned it with two proper words.
But I've no delight in dream-lore, for it lets us down often.
Cato* and canon-lawyers counsel us to cease					155
Assigning certainty to dream-lore, for "*Somnia ne cures.*"[1]
But because the Bible book bears witness
How Daniel divined the dreams of a king—
Nebuchadnezzar,[2] as these clerks name him—
Daniel said, "Sir King, your dream signifies					160
That strange soldiers shall come to seize your kingdom:
Among lower lords your land will be divided."
As Daniel divined, in deed it happened after:
The King lost his lordship and lesser men had it.
Moreover, Joseph dreamed marvelously how the moon and the sun		165
And the eleven stars all hailed him.
Then Jacob judged Joseph's dream:
"*Beau fils,*"[3] said his father, "for famine we shall—
I myself and my sons—seek you for need."
It befell as his father said in Pharaoh's time					170
That Joseph was justice with jurisdiction over Egypt;
It befell as his father said, his friends sought him there.[4]
     All this makes me muse on dreams
And how the priest proved no pardon to Do-Well,
And deemed that Do-Well by-passes indulgences,[5]				175
Biennial Masses and triennial Masses and bishops' letters.[6]—
Do-Well at the Day of Doom* is deferentially received:
He passes by all the pardon of Saint Peter's church!
Now does the Pope possess power to grant such a pardon
That people may pass without penance to joy?					180
This is a leaf of our belief, as lettered men teach us.
     Whatsoever thou shalt bind on earth shall be bound in Heaven,
          etc.[7]
And so I believe loyally—Lord forbid otherwise!—
That pardon and penance and prayers will save
Souls that have sinned seven times deadly.
But to trust to these triennials, truly, I think					185
Is not so certain for the soul, surely, as is Do-Well.
Therefore I admonish you men that have money on earth
And trust through your treasure to have triennials,
Be you never the bolder to break the Ten Commandments,
And mainly you masters, mayors and judges,					190

1. "Pay no attention to dreams."
2. Daniel interpreted dreams for Nebuchadnezzar in Dan. 2 and 4 and for his son Belshazzar in Dan. 5; the poet seems to be conflating the two (or three) incidents.
3. "Fair son."
4. Joseph's dream occurs in Gen. 37:9–10, but the interpretation the poet attributes to Jacob is based on subsequent events, not on Jacob's reaction at the time.
5. Formal remissions of the temporal or purgatorial punishment for sin (not the *guilt*—see VII.3, note), issued by pardoners or earned by pilgrimage or certain acts of worship.
6. *Biennial* and *triennial Masses*: said for the soul of a deceased person for two, or for three, years after the death of the beneficiary. *Bishops' letters*: letters authorizing pardoners to preach indulgences (like the pardoner in Pro. 72–82).
7. Matt. 16:19.

That han the welthe of this worlde—and for wyse men ben
    holden—
To purchace pardoun and the Popis bulles,
At the dredeful dome whan ded shullen rise
And comen alle bifor Cryst acountis to yelde,
195 How thow laddest thi lyf here and his [lawe] keptest,
[What] thow dedest day bi day the dome wil reherce.
A poke ful of pardoun there, ne Provinciales lettres,
Theigh ye be founde in the fraterneté [amonge] the foure ordres
And have indulgences doublefolde, but if Do-Wel yow help,
200 I sette yowre patentes and yowre [pardoun] at one pies hele.
Forthi I conseille alle Cristene to crye God mercy,
And Marie his moder be owre mene bitwene,
That God gyve us grace ar we gone hennes
Suche werkes to werche while we ben here
205 That after owre deth-day Do-Wel reherce
At the Day of Dome we dede as he highte.

Passus VIII

Thus y-robed in russet I rowmed aboute
Al a somer sesoun for to seke Do-Wel,
And frayned ful oft of folke that I mette
If ani wighte wiste where Do-Wel was at inne,
5 And what man he mighte be of many man I axed.
Was nevere wighte as I went that me wisse couthe
Where this lede lenged, lasse ne more,
Tyl it bifel on a Fryday two freres I mette,
Maistres of the Menoures, men of grete witte.
10 I hailsed hem hendely as I hadde lerned
And preyed hem *pour charitee*, ar thei passed forther,
If thei knewe any contré or costes [aboute],
"Where that Do-Wel dwelleth, doth me to wytene.
For [ye] ben men on this molde that moste wyde walken,
15 And knowen contrees and courtes and many kynnes places,
Bothe prynces paleyses and pore mennes cotes,
And Do-Wel and Do-Yvel, where thei dwelle bothe."
"[Marie!]" quod the [maistres, "amonges us he dwelleth],
And evere hath, as I hope, and evere shal hereafter."

That have the wealth of this world—and are thought to be wise
    men—
To purchase pardon and the Pope's bulls,
At the dreadful doom* when dead men shall arise
And all come before Christ and account to him,
How you led your life here and kept the letter of the law,   195
What you did day by day the doom will record.
A poke full of pardon there, nor Provincial's letters,[8]
Though you're found in the fraternity among the four orders[9]
And have indulgences doublefold, unless Do-Well helps you,
I count your patents and your pardon not worth a pie's heel.[1]   200
Therefore I counsel all Christians to cry to God for mercy,
And to Mary his mother to be our mean between,
That God give us grace before we go hence
To work such works while we are here
That after our death-day Do-Well will report   205
At the Day of Doom we did what he bade.

Passus VIII

Thus robed in russet[1] I roamed about
A whole summer season searching for Do-Well,
And I asked very frequently of folk that I met
If any one knew where Do-Well made his home,
And many a man I asked what man he might be.   5
There was never any one as I went that was able to tell me
Where that fellow could be found, not the first inkling,
Till it befell on a Friday I fell in with two friars,
Masters* of the Minorites,[2] men of great intelligence.
I hailed them as handsomely as I had been taught   10
And prayed them, *pour charité*,[3] before they parted from me,
If they knew any neighborhood, near or far,
"Where Do-Well dwells, do please tell me.
For you walk most widely of worldly men,
And know countries and courts and many kinds of places,   15
Both princes' palaces and poor men's cottages,
And Do-Well and Do-Evil, where they dwell both."
"Mary!" said the masters, "he dwells among us,
And always has, as I hope, and always will hereafter."

8. *Poke*: a small bag or sack, especially those carried by poor travelers, pilgrims, or beggars. *Provincial's letters*: letters from the Provincial, or head of a province (i.e., of a regional group of houses of a religious order), which appointed a lay person a "confrater," or honorary brother, of the order within that region, and conferred the privileges of the order on him or her or, sometimes, on whole families.
9. In Langland's day there were four orders of friars in England: Franciscans, Dominicans, Carmelites, and Augustinians.
1. *Patents*: papal licenses or indulgences. *Pie's heel*: the crust left at the broad end of the slice when the rest has been eaten.
1. Coarse woolen cloth, commonly reddish, worn by workers and by those, such as hermits, adopting an ascetic life; this fits with the clothes the Dreamer puts on in the Prologue "as I'd become a sheep" (or a shepherd).
2. The Friars Minor or Franciscans.
3. "For charity."

20   *"Contra!"* quod I as a clerke and comsed to disputen.
    "Sepcies in die cadit justus.
    Sevene sythes, seith the Boke, synneth the rightful;
    And whoso synneth, I sey, [certes] me thinketh
    [That] Do-Wel and Do-Yvel mow nought dwelle togideres.
    Ergo he nys naught alway [at home] amonge yow freres.
25   He is otherwhile elliswhere, to wisse the peple."
    "I shal sey the, my sone," seide the frere thanne,
    "How sevene sithes the sad man on the day synneth.
    By a forbisene," quod the frere, "I shal the faire shewe.
    Lat brynge a man in a bote amydde a brode water:
30   The wynde and the water and the [waggynge of the bote]
    Maketh the man many a tyme to falle and to stonde.
    For stonde he nevere so styf, he stombleth [in the waggynge],
    Ac yit is he sauf and sounde, and so hym bihoveth,
    For yif he ne arise the rather and raughte to the stiere,
35   The wynde wolde wyth the water the bote overthrowe.
    Thanne were [the mannes] lyf loste thourgh lacchesse of hymself.
    [Right] thus it [fareth]," quod the frere, "bi folke here on erthe.
    The water is likned to the worlde that wanyeth and wexeth;
    The godis of this grounde aren like to the grete wawes,
40   That as wyndes and [wateres] walweth aboute.
    The bote is likned to [the] body that brutel is of kynde,
    That thorugh the Fende and thi flessh and the [false] worlde
    Synneth the sad man [sevene sythes a day].
    Ac dedly synne doth he nought; for Do-Wel hym [helpeth],
45   That is charité the champioun, chief help ayein synne.
    For he strengtheth [the] to stonde and stereth [thi] soule
    [That] thowgh thi body bow as bote doth in the water,
    Ay is thi soule sauf but [thow] thiself wole
    [Folwe thi flesshes wille and the Fendes after,
50   And] do dedly synne and drenche [thiselve].
    God wole suffre wel thi sleuthe yif thiself lyketh,
    For he yaf the to Yeres-yyve to yeme wel thiselve,
    Witte [and] fre wille, to every wyghte a porcioun,
    To fleghyng foules, to fissches, and to bestes,
55   Ac man hath moste therof and moste is to blame,
    But if he worche wel therwith as Do-Wel hym techeth."
       "I have no kynde knowyng," quod I, "to conceyve yowre wordes,
    Ac if I may lyve and loke, I shal go lerne bettere."
    "I bikenne the Cryst," [quod he], "that on the Crosse deyde."
60   And I seyde, "The same save yow fro myschaunce
    And yive yow grace on this grounde good men to worthe."
       Thus I went widewhere [Do-Wel to seke,
    And as I wente by a wode, walkyng myn one],
    Blisse of [the] briddes [abide me made],
65   And vnder a lynde vppon a launde lened I a stounde

"*Contra!*"⁴ said I like a clerk and commenced to argue.   20
"*Seven times a day falleth the just man.*⁵
Seven times, says the Book, sins the righteous;
And if someone sins, I say, it seems certain to me
That Do-Well and Do-Evil cannot dwell together.
*Ergo*⁶ he is not always at home among you friars.
He's occupied at times elsewhere, educating the people."   25
"I shall show you, my son," said the friar then,
"How the steadiest man sins seven times a day.
By an example," said the friar, "I shall show you clearly.
Let a man be brought in a boat amid a broad expanse of water:
The wind and the water and the wobbling of the boat   30
Will make the man many a time fall and stand.
For though he stands ever so stiffly, he stumbles from the motion,
And yet he is safe and sound, and so it behooves him be,
For if he doesn't arise right away and reach for the helm,
The wind and the water will overwhelm the boat.   35
Then the man's life would be lost through his laziness alone.
Just so it fares," said the friar, "with folk here on earth.
The water that wanes and waxes is likened to the world;
The goods of this ground are like the great waves,
For like water in the wind they welter about.   40
The boat is likened to the body that is brittle by nature,
So that through the Fiend and the flesh and the false world
The steadfast man sins seven times a day.
But he does not do deadly sin; for Do-Well helps him,
That is charity the champion, chief help against sin.   45
For he strengthens you to stand and steers your soul
So that though your body turns about like a boat in the water,
Your soul is always safe unless you yourself will
Follow your flesh's will and the Fiend's as well,
And do deadly sin and drown yourself.   50
God will gladly suffer your sloth if you yourself wish it,
For he gave you a New Year's gift with which to guide yourself,
Wit* and free will, to every wight⁷ a portion,
To flying fowls, to fishes, and to beasts,
But man has most of it and is most to blame,   55
Unless he works well with it as Do-Well teaches."
    "I have no natural knowledge,"* said I, "to understand your words,
But if I may live and go on looking, I shall learn better."
"I commend you to Christ," said he, "who was crucified on Cross."
And I said, "The same save you from misfortune   60
And give you grace on this ground to become good men."
    Thus I fared far and wide trying to find Do-Well,
And as I went by a wood, walking alone,
The merry melody of birds made me abide,
And on a lea under a linden I lay down a while   65

4. "On the contrary": a technical term of objection in scholarly argument.
5. Prov. 24:16.
6. "Therefore": technical term of resolution in scholarly argument.
7. Creature.

To [lerne] the layes [the] lovely foules made.
Murthe of her mouthes made me to slepe.
The merveillousest meteles mette me thanne
That ever [dremed drighte] in [doute], as I wene.
70 A moche man as me thoughte and lyke to myselve
Come and called me by my kynde name.
"What artow," quod I tho, "that thow my name knowest?"
"That thow wost wel," quod he, "and no wyghte bettere."
"Wote I what thow art?" [quod I]. "Thought," seyde he thanne.
75 I have suwed the sevene yere; sey thow me no rather?"
"Art thow Thought?" quod I tho. "Thow couthest me [telle]
Where that Do-Wel dwelleth and do me [to wisse]."
"Do-Wel," [quod he], "and Do-Bet and Do-Best the thridde
Aren three faire vertues and beth naughte fer to fynde.
80 Whoso is [meke of his mouth, mylde of his speche],
Trewe of his tonge and of his two handes,
And thorugh his laboure or his londe his lyflode wynneth,
Trusti of his tailende, taketh but his owne,
And is nought dronkenlew ne dedeignous, Do-Wel hym folweth.
85 Do-Bet doth ryght thus, ac he doth moche more.
He is as low as a lombe, and loveliche of speche;
[Whiles he hath ought of his owne he helpeth ther nede is].
The bagges and the bigurdeles, he hath to-broken hem alle,
That the Erl Avarous [hadde, or] his heires,
90 And with Mammonaes moné he hath made hym frendes,
And is ronne into Religioun and hath rendred the
        Bible,
And precheth to the poeple Seynt Poules wordes:
Libenter suffertis insipientes, cum sitis ipsi sapientes.
'[Ye wise] suffreth the unwise with yow forto libbe
95 And with gladde wille doth hem gode, for so God yow hoteth.'
Do-Best is above bothe and bereth a bisschopes crosse;
Is hoked [at] that one ende to [holde men in good lif].
A pyke is on that potente to pulte adown the wikked
That wayten any wikkednesse Do-Wel to tene.
100 And [as] Do-Wel and Do-Bet amonges hem ordeigned,
[They han crouned] one to be kynge to kepin hem [alle],
That yif Do-Wel [and] Do-Bet did ayein Do-Best,
[And were unbuxome at his biddyng and bolde to don ille],
Thanne [sholde] the kynge come and casten hem in [prisone,
105 And putten hem ther in penaunce withoute pité or grace],
But if Do-Best bede for hem, thei to be there forevere.
Thus Do-Wel and Do-Bet and Do-Best the thridde
Crouned one to be kynge, [and by her conseille werchen];
And reule the Reume bi [rede of hem alle],
110 And none other wise but as thei thre assented."
    I thonked Thought tho that he me thus taughte.

To learn the lays the lovely fowls made.
Mirth of their mouths made me go to sleep.
The most marvelous dream came to me then
That ever any hero had in danger, I think.
A large man who looked to me much like myself   70
Came and called me by my christened name.
"Who are you," I asked then, "who know my name?"
"That you know well enough," said he, "and no one better."
"Do I know who you are?" I asked. "Thought," said he then.
"I've pursued you seven years; haven't you seen me before?"   75
"Are you Thought?" said I then. "I think you could tell me
Where Do-Well dwells and direct me to him."
"Do-Well," said he, "and Do-Better and Do-Best the third
Are three fair virtues and are not far to find.
Whoever is meek of his mouth, mild of his speech,   80
True of his tongue and of his two hands,
And through his labor or his land earns his livelihood,
Trustworthy of his tail-end, takes only what is his,[8]
And is not drunken or disdainful, Do-Well is with him.
Do-Better does the same, but he does much more.   85
He's lowly as a lamb, lovely of speech;
While he has anything of his own he helps where there's need.
The bags and the strongboxes, he's broken them all,
That the Earl Avarice had, or his heirs,
And with Mammon's[9] money he has made himself friends,   90
And has taken residence in religious houses and has rendered the
    Bible,
And preaches to the people Saint Paul's words:
Ye suffer fools gladly, seeing ye yourselves are wise.[1]
'You wise ones, allow the unwise to live with you
And with glad will do them good, for so God commands.'   95
Do-Best is above both and bears a bishop's crozier
That has a hook at one end to hold men in good lives.
A spike is on that staff to shove down the wicked
That lie in wait devising villainy with which to vex Do-Well.
And as Do-Well and Do-Better decided between them,   100
They have crowned one to be king and keep watch over them all,
That if Do-Well and Do-Better did anything against Do-Best,
And were disobedient to his bidding and bold to do evil,
Then the king should come and cast them in prison,
Put them there in penance without pity or grace,   105
Unless Do-Best recommends mercy, to remain there forever.
Thus Do-Well and Do-Better and Do-Best the third
Crowned one to be king: their counsel would guide him;
And he should rule the realm by direction of them all,
And not in any other way but as those three agreed."   110
    I thanked Thought then that he thus taught me.

8. This line is based on an untranslatable pun: *tailende/tail-ende.* The first means "talleying, keeping
   accounts"; the second, "tail-end," is a sexual allusion.
9. In the New Testament, riches, often personified as the demon of greed (a basic passage is Luke
   16:1–13).
1. 2 Cor. 11:19.

"Ac yete savoureth me nought thi seggyng, [so me God help:
More kynde knowynge] I coveite to lerne,
How Do-Wel, Do-Bet, and Do-Best don amonges the peple."
"But Witte conne wisse the," quod Thought, "where tho
115 thre dwelle,
Ellis [noot no man] that now is alyve."
Thoughte and I thus thre days we yeden
Disputyng uppon Do-Wel day after other.
[Ac] ar we were ywar with Witte gan we mete.
120 He was longe and lene, liche to none other;
Was no pruyde on his apparaille ne poverté noyther;
Sadde of his semblaunt and of [a] soft [speche].
I dorste meve no matere to make hym to jangle,
But as I bad Thought tho be mene bitwene,
125 And [to] put forth somme purpos to proven his wittes,
What was Do-Wel fro Do-Bet and Do-Best fram hem bothe,
Thanne Thought in that tyme seide thise wordes:
"Where Do-Wel [and] Do-Bet and Do-Best ben in londe,
Here is Wille wolde y-wyte yif Witte couthe teche hym;
130 And whether he be man or [no] man this man wolde aspye,
And worchen as thei thre wolde; this is his entente."

Passus IX

"Sire Do-Wel dwelleth," quod Witte, "nought a day hennes,
In a castel that Kynde made of foure kynnes thinges.
Of erthe and eyre is it made, medled togideres,
With wynde and with water wittily enjoyned.
5 Kynde hath closed thereinne, craftily withalle,
A lemman that he loveth like to hymselve:
Anima she hatte: [to hir hath envye]
A proude pryker of Fraunce, *princeps huius mundi*,
And wolde winne hir awey with wyles and he myghte.
10 Ac Kynde knoweth this wel and kepeth hir the bettere,
And hath do hir with Sire Do-Wel, duke of this marches;
Do-Bet is hir damoisele, Sire Do-Weles doughter,
To serve this lady lelly bothe late and rathe.
Do-Best is above bothe, a bisschopes pere:
15 That he bit mote be do; he [boldeth] hem alle;
Anima that lady is ladde bi his lerynge.
Ac the constable of [the] castel, that kepeth [hem alle],
Is a wys knighte withal; Sire Inwitte he hatte,
And hath fyve feyre sones bi his first wyf:

"But still I've no savor in your sayings, so help me God:
More natural knowledge I need to learn,
How Do-Well, Do-Better, and Do-Best do among the people."
"Unless Wit* can tell you this," said Thought, "where those
    three live,   115
Otherwise no one knows that is now alive."
Thought and I thus three days we walked
Debating about Do-Well day after day.
But before we were aware we met with Wit.
He was long and lean, like no one else;   120
There was no pride in his apparel nor poorness either;
Of a soft speech and sober of appearance.
I dared mention no matter that would make him wrangle,
But as I bade Thought then to be an intermediary between us,
And to put forth some proposition that would prove his wits,   125
How Do-Well differed from Do-Better and Do-Best from them both,
Then at that time Thought said these words:
"Where Do-Well and Do-Better and Do-Best live in the country,
Here is Will who'd wish to learn if Wit knew how to teach him;
And whether he is man or no man this man would discover,   130
And work as they three would wish; this is his intention."

Passus IX

"Sir Do-Well dwells," said Wit, "not a day from here,
In a castle that Kind made of four kinds of things.[1]
It is made of earth and of air all mingled together,
With wind and with water woven cleverly together.
Kind has enclosed therein, cunningly enough,   5
A lady he loves who's like himself:
Anima[2] is her name: there lusts after her
A haughty horseman of France, *princeps huius mundi*,[3]
Who would win her away with wiles if he could.
Kind, knowing this, keeps most careful watch over her,   10
And has domiciled her with Sir Do-Well, duke of these borders;
Do-Better is her damsel, Sir Do-Well's daughter,
And serves this lady loyally both late and early.
Do-Best is above both, a bishop's peer:
What he bids must be done; he emboldens them all;   15
What Dame Anima does is at Do-Best's instruction.
But the constable[4] of the castle, who keeps guard over them all,
Is a wise knight withal; Sir Inwit[5] is his name.
He has five fair sons by his first wife:

---

1. *Kind*: (Gloss). *Four kinds of things*: the four basic elements—earth, air, fire, and water—out of which the creation is made.
2. "The soul" (Gloss). The line above is ambiguous in Middle English and could also mean "A lady he loves as much as himself."
3. "The prince of this world" (a title for the Devil).
4. The governor or warden of a royal castle.
5. Basically, "mind, understanding, rational power," but often "moral awareness, conscience" as well (Gloss).

20 Sire Se-Wel, and Say-Wel, and Here-Wel the hende,
    Sire Worche-Wel-Wyth-Thine Hande, a wighte man of strengthe,
    And Sire Godfrey Go-Wel, gret lordes [alle].
    Thise [sixe] ben sette to save this Lady Anima
    Tyl Kynde come or sende to [kepe] hir [hymselve]."
25   "What kynnes thyng is Kynde?" quod I "Canstow me telle?"
    "Kynde," quod [he], "is creatour of alle kynnes [bestes],
    Fader and fourmour, [the firste of alle thynges],
    And that is the gret God that gynnynge had nevere,
    Lorde of lyf and of lyghte, of lysse and of peyne.
30 Angeles and al thing aren at his wille,
    Ac man is hym moste lyke of marke and of [shape].
    For thorugh the worde that he [warp] wexen forth bestes,
    [And al at his wille was wrought with a speche],
              Dixit et facta sunt,
    [Save man that he made ymage] to hymself
35 And Eve of [Adam] his ribbe-bon withouten eny mene.
    For he was synguler hymself and seyde 'Faciamus,'
    As who seith, 'More mote hereto than my worde one.
    My myghte mote helpe now with my speche.'
    Righte as a lorde sholde make lettres, and hym lakked parchemyn,
40 Though he couth write nevere so wel [and] he had [a] penne,
    The lettre, for al the lordship, I leve were nevere y-maked.
    And so it semeth bi hym [there he seide in the Bible],
    Faciamus hominem ad imaginem nostram.
    He moste worche with his worde and his witte shewe.
    And in this manere was man made thorugh myghte of God
45   almighti,
    With his worde and werkemanschip, and with lyf to laste.
    And thus God gaf hym a goost of the Godhed of Hevene,
    And of his grete grace graunted hym blisse,
    Lyf that ay shal last, [and] al [his] lynage after.
50 That is the Castel that Kynde made: Caro it hatte,
    And is as moche to mene as man with a soule.
    That he wrought with werke and with worde bothe;
    Thorugh myghte of the majesté man was y-maked.
    Inwit and alle wittes [enclosed] ben therinne,
55 For love of the lady Anima, that lyf is y-nempned.
    Overal in mannes body [heo] walketh and wandreth,
    Ac in the herte is hir home and hir moste reste;
    Ac Inwitte is in the hed, and to the herte he loketh:
    What Anima is lief or loth, he [let] hir at his wille;
60 For after the grace of God the grettest is Inwitte.
       Moche wo worth that man that mysreuleth his inwitte,
    And that be glotouns, globbares—her god is her wombe.
          Quorum deus venter est.
    For thei serven Sathan her soule shal he have;

Sir See-Well, and Say-Well, and Hear-Well the courteous,   20
Sir Work-Well-With-Your-Hands, a man of wondrous strength,
And Sir Godfrey Go-Well, great lords all.
To these six is assigned the safety of Lady Anima
Till Kind come or send for her to keep her himself."
   "What kind of thing is Kind?" said I. "Can you tell me?"   25
"Kind," said he, "is creator of all kinds of beasts,
Father and former, the first of all things,
And that is the great God that had beginning never,
Lord of life and of light, of relief and of pain.
Angels and all things are at his command,   30
But man is most like him in mien and in shape.
For beasts came into being by the breath of his word,
And they all as he willed had life at his speech,
     He spoke and they were created,[6]
Except man that he made in the image of himself
And Eve of Adam's rib-bone without any intermediary.   35
For he was singular himself and said '*Faciamus,*'[7]
As if to say, 'There must be more for this than my word alone.
My might* must help along with my speech.'
Just as a lord would write a letter, but if he lacked paper,
Though he could write ever so readably and had a pen ready to hand,   40
The letter, for all his literacy, I believe would not be written.
And so it seems to have been with him when he said in the Bible,
Let us make man in our image.
He must both work with his word and show his wit as well.
And in this manner man was made through the might of God
     almighty,   45
With his word and with his workmanship, and with life to last.
And thus God gave him a soul from the Godhead of Heaven,
And of his great grace granted him bliss,
Life that shall last forever, and all his lineage as well.
That is the castle that Kind made: *Caro*[8] is its name,   50
Which is to mean as much as man with a soul.
Both with work and with word he created him;
Through the might of the majesty man was made.
Inwit* and all wits* are enclosed therein,
For love of that lady Anima, as life is called.   55
She walks and wanders everywhere in man's body,
But in his heart is her home and her chief place of rest;
But Inwit is in the head, and he looks to the heart:
Whether Anima is lief[9] or loath, he leads her at his will;
For after the grace of God the greatest is Inwit.   60
   Much woe has that man who misuses his inwit,
And such are gluttons, guzzlers—their god is their belly.
     Whose god is their belly.[1]
Since they serve Satan he shall have their souls;

6. Ps. 148:5.
7. "Let us make [man in our image]": Gen. 1:26; the whole sentence appears in line 43.
8. Literally, "Flesh"; by extension, a human being.
9. Willing, glad.
1. Phil. 3:19.

That liveth synful lyf here, her soule is liche the Devel;
65   And alle that lyven good lyf aren like God almighti.
        Qu manet in caritate in Deo manet, etc.
Allas, that drynke shal fordo that God dere boughte,
And doth God forsaken hem that he shope to his liknesse.
        Amen dico vobis, nescio vos; Et alibi,
            Et dimisi eos secundum desideria eorum,
[Fauntes and] foles that fauten inwitte,
[Holy Cherche is owynge to helpe hem and save
70   And] fynden hem that hem fauted—and faderelees children,
And wydwes that han noughte wherwith to wynnen hem her fode,
Madde men and maydenes that helplees were:
Alle thise lakken inwitte and lore [hem] bihoveth.
Of this matere I myghte make a longe tale,
75   And fynde fele witnesses amonges the foure doctours;
And that I lye nought of that I lere the, Luke bereth witnesse.
Godfader and godmoder that sen her godchildren
At myseise and at mischief and mowe hem amende
Shal [purchace] penaunce in purgatorie but yif thei hem helpe.
80   For more bilongeth to the litel barne ar he the lawe knowe
Than nempnyng of a name, and he nevere the wiser.
Shulde no Crystene creature crien atte yate
Ne faille payn ne potage, and prelates did as thei shulden.
A Juwe wolde noughte se a Juwe go jangelyng for defaute
85   For alle the moebles on this molde and he amende it mighte.
Allas, that a Crestene creature shal be unkynde til another
Sitthen Juwes, that we jugge Judas felawes,
Ayther of hem helpeth other of that that hym nedeth.
Whi [ne wol] we Cristene of Cristes good be as kynde?
90   [So] Juwes [shul] ben owre loresmen shame to us alle!
The comune for her unkyndenesse, I drede me, shul abye;
Bisschopes shul be blamed for beggeres sake.
He is [jugged with] Judas that yiveth a japer silver
And biddeth the begger go for his broke clothes.
        Proditor est prelatus cum Juda qui patrimonium Cristi minus
            distribuit; Et alibi, Perniciosus dispensator est qui res
                pauperum Cristi inutiliter consumit.
95   He doth nought wel that doth thus, ne drat nought God almighty,
Ne loveth nought Salamones sawes that Sapience taughte.
        Inicium sapiencie timor Domini.
That dredeth God, he doth wel; that dredeth hym for love
And [dredeth hym] nought for drede of venjaunce doth therfore the bettere.

Those who live sinful lives here, their souls are like the Devil;
And all who lead good lives here are like God almighty.   65
   He that dwelleth in love dwelleth in God, etc.[2]
Alas, that drink shall destroy what God dearly paid for,
And cause him to cast off those he created in his likeness.
   Verily I say unto you, I know you not; And elsewhere,
     And I gave them up unto their own lusts,[3]
Infants and idiots in whom inwit is lacking,[4]
Holy Church is obligated to help and save them
And provide them with what they fail in—and fatherless children,   70
And widows that have nothing wherewith to win their food,
Mad men and maidens that would be helpless:
All these lack inwit and must have direction.
Of this matter I might make a long story,
And find sufficient texts among the four doctors;[5]   75
And that this lesson is no lie, Luke bears witness.[6]
Godfathers and godmothers who see their godchildren
In misfortune and in mischance and yet might assist them
Shall get penance in purgatory unless they provide help.
For more belongs to the little child before he learns the law   80
Than being named with a name,[7] and he never the wiser.
No Christian creature would cry at the gate
Or be deprived of bread and pottage if prelates did as they should.
A Jew would not see a Jew go chattering for need
For all the goods on this ground if he might give him help.   85
Alas, that any Christian creature should be unkind to his fellow
Since Jews, that we judge Judas' fellows,
Each of them helps the other with whatever he needs.
Why are we Christians not as kind with Christ's goods?
That Jews should show us good examples is a shame to us all!   90
It will cost the commons* dear for their unkindness,* I fear;
Bishops shall be blamed for beggars' sakes.
He is judged with Judas that gives a jester silver
And bids the beggar be off for his bedraggled clothing.
   A traitor with Judas is the prelate who fails to distribute
     Christ's patrimony; And elsewhere, He is a pernicious
     steward who wastes the things of Christ's poor.[8]
He does not well that does this, nor dreads God almighty,   95
Nor loves the sayings of Solomon in his Sapience-Book.
   The fear of the Lord is the beginning of wisdom.[9]
Who dreads God, he does well; who dreads him for love
And dreads him not for dread of vengeance does thereby better.

2. 1 John 4:16.
3. Matt. 25:12; Ps. 80:13.
4. Wit moves on from drunks who have voluntarily destroyed their *inwit* to other groups who lack
   rational understanding through no fault of their own and must be provided for. Here *inwit* cannot
   mean "conscience" (Gloss).
5. St. Ambrose* (340?–397), St. Augustine* (354–430), St. Jerome* (340?–420), and St. Gregory
   the Great* (540?–604) were considered the four major early theologians and commentators of the
   Western Church (Gloss).
6. There is nothing pertinent in Luke; Langland may have had in mind Acts 6:1 or Jas. 1:27.
7. I.e., christened.
8. Religious maxims of conjectural origin.
9. Ps. 110:10; Ecclus. 1:16.

He doth best that withdraweth hym, by day and bi nyghte,
100   To spille any speche or any space of tyme.
       Qui offendit in verbo in omnibus est reus.
      [Tynynge] of tyme, Treuthe wote the sothe,
      Is moste y-hated [upon] erthe of hem that [ben] in Hevene,
      And sitthe to spille speche, that spyre is of grace,
      And Goddes gleman, and a game of Hevene.
105   Wolde nevere the faithful fader his fithel were untempred!
      Ne his gleman a gedelyng, a goer to tavernes.
      To alle trew tidy men that travaille desyren,
      Owre Lorde loveth hem and lent, loude other stille,
      Grace to go to hem and [ofgon] her lyflode.
       Inquirentes autem Dominum non minuentur omni bono.
110   [Do-Wel] in this worlde is [trewe wedded libbing folk],
      For thei mote worche and wynne and the worlde susteyne.
      For of her kynde thei come that confessoures ben nempned,
      Kynges and knightes, kayseres and [clerkes];
      Maydenes and martires out of o man come.
115   The wyf was made the [wye] for to help worche.
      And thus was wedloke y-wrought with a mene persone
      First bi the faderes wille and the frendes conseille,
      And sytthenes bi assent of hemself as thei two myghte acorde.
      And thus was wedloke y-wroughte, and God hymself it made.
120   In erthe the Hevene is, hymself was the witnesse.
      Ac fals folke, faithlees, theves and lieres,
      Wastoures and wrecches, out of wedloke, I trowe,
      Conceyved ben in [cursed] tyme, as Caym was on Eve
      [After that Adam and heo eten the apple].
125   Of such synful shrewes the Sauter maketh mynde.
       Concepit in dolorem et peperit iniquitatem.
      And alle that come of that Caym come to yvel ende.
      For God sent to [Seth] and seyde bi an angel,
      'Thyne issue in thyne issue, I wil that thei be wedded,
      And nought thi kynde with Caymes y-coupled ne y-spoused.'
130   Yet [Seth] ayein the sonde of owre Saveoure of Hevene

He does best who desists, day and night,
From squandering any speech or any space of time.   100
    Who offends in one point is guilty of all.[1]
And Truth knows what's true: time that is wasted
On earth is most hated by those who are in Heaven,
And then the squandering of speech, which is the sprout of grace,
And God's music-maker, and a merriment of Heaven.
The faithful father would never wish that his fiddle were untuned!   105
Nor his gleeman[2] a gadabout, a goer to taverns.
All sincere and steady men who desire to work,
Our Lord loves them and allows, great or small,
Grace to go with them and let them gain their livelihood.
    They that seek the Lord shall not want any good thing.[3]
    Do-Well in this world is wedded people who live truly,   110
For they must toil to take their bread and to sustain the world.
For those who are called confessors come of their kind,
Kings and kaisers,[4] clerks and knights;
Maidens and martyrs from one man have their being.
The woman was made meet[5] to help the man work.   115
And thus marriage was made with an intermediate person's help[6]
First by the father's will and the friends' counsel,
And then by their own assent as they two might agree.
And in this way wedlock was wrought, and it was God who made it.
Its Heaven is on earth, as he himself bore witness.[7]   120
But false folk, faithless, thieves and liars,
Wasters and worthless men, out of wedlock, I think,
Are conceived in cursed time, as Cain was on Eve
After Adam and she had eaten the apple.[8]
Of such sinful scoundrels the Psalter makes mention.   125
    He hath conceived sorrow and brought forth injustice.[9]
And all that came from that Cain came to evil ends.
For God sent to Seth[1] and said by an angel,
'I will that you wed your issue with your issue,
And that your kin with Cain's be not coupled nor married.'
Yet Seth against the stricture of our Savior in Heaven   130

1. Jas. 2:10.
2. Minstrel (*glee*: music, melody).
3. Ps. 33:11.
4. Emperors (from Latin *Caesar*). "Confessor": one who heroically makes an avowal of faith.
5. *One man*: i.e., Adam. *Meet*: suitable, fitting.
6. I.e., arranging a marriage must start with negotiations between intermediaries, relatives and friends if not an actual go-between; the consent of the parties themselves (line 118) is the last step, rather than the first. "Thus" here means "in the following manner."
7. Behind this line lie God's creation of Eve (Gen. 2:18–25) and Christ's first miracle, changing water into wine, at the wedding at Cana (John 2:1–11). It is more specifically based, however, on the wedding Mass, which states both that God "hallowed wedlock by a great sacrament, thereby foreshadowing, in the marriage bond, Christ's union with the Church," and that God "endowed this primal fellowship of [Adam and Eve] with the one and only blessing not forfeited either in the punishment of the first sin or under sentence of the flood."
8. Medieval legend, such as that reflected in an apocryphal *Life of Adam and Eve* (source unclear), held that Cain was conceived during a time of penitence and fasting; sexual intercourse was just as definitely forbidden at such times as it was outside of marriage.
9. Ps. 7:15.
1. God's command to Seth, Adam's third son, is not in Genesis, but appears in Peter Comestor's *Historia*, an account of major events in the Bible. Biblical commentators, however, interpreted the forbidden marriages in Gen. 6 between "the sons of God" and "the daughters of men" as between Seth's kin and Cain's.

Caymes kynde and his kynde coupled togideres
Tyl God wratthed [with here] werkis and suche a worde seyde:
'That I maked man now it me athynketh.'
   Penitet me fecisse hominem.
And come to Noe anon and bad hym nought lette:
135 'Swithe go shape a shippe of shides and of bordes.
Thiself and thi sones three and sithen yowre wyves,
Buske yow to that bote and bideth ye therinne
Tyl fourty dayes be fulfilled, that flode have y-wasshen
Clene awey the cursed blode that Caym hath y-maked.
140 Bestes that now ben shulle banne the tyme
That evere that cursed Caym come on this erthe.
Alle shal deye for his dedes bi [dounes] and bi hulles,
And the foules that fleeghen forth with other bestes,
Excepte oneliche of eche kynde a couple
145 That in [the] shyngled shippe shul ben y-saved.'
Here abought the barne the belsyres gultes,
And alle for her forfadres ferden the worse.
The Gospel is here-ageine in o degré, I fynde:
   Filius non portabit iniquitatem patris, et
      pater non portabit iniquitatem filij.
150 Ac I fynde if the fader be false and a shrewe,
That somdel the sone shal have the sires tacches.
Impe on an ellerne and if thine apple be swete
Mochel merveile me thynketh, and more of a schrewe
That bryngeth forth any barne but if he be the same
155 And have a savoure after the sire—selde seestow other.
   Numquam colligunt de spinis vuas nec de tribulis fycus.
And thus thourw cursed Caym cam care uppon erthe,
And al for thei wrought wedlokes ayein [the] wille [of God].
Forthi have thei maugré for here mariages that marye so
      her childeren.
For some as I se now, soth forto telle,
160 For coveitise of catel unkyndeliche ben wedded.
[A] careful concepcioun cometh of suche mariages,
As bifel of the folke that I bifore of tolde.
For goode shulde wedde goode though hij no good hadde.
'I am *via et veritas*,' seith Cryst, 'I may avaunce alle.'
165 It is an oncomely couple, bi Cryst, as me thinketh,
To yyven a yonge wenche to [a yolde] feble,
Or wedden any widwe for welth of hir goodis,
That nevere shal barne bere but if it be in armes.
[In jelousie, joyelees, and janglynge on bedde]
170 Many peire sithen the pestilence han plight [hem] togideres.
The fruit that thei brynge forth aren foule wordes;
Have thei no children but cheste [and choppes] bitwene.
Though thei don hem to Donmowe, but if the Devel help,

Coupled his kin with the kin of Cain,
Till God grew angry with their behavior and uttered this sentence:
'That I made man it now makes me sorry.'
    I repent that I made man.[2]
And he came to Noah anon and bade him not delay:
'Quickly go build a boat of boards and planks.   135
Yourself and your three sons and also your wives,
Set yourselves up in that ship and stay inside it
Till forty days have been fulfilled and the flood has washed
Clean away the cursed blood that Cain has made.
Beasts that now breathe shall upbraid the time   140
That ever cursed Cain came upon earth.
All shall die for his deeds on downs and hills,
And the fowls that fly forth along with other beasts,
Save for a single couple of every sort that there is
That in the shingled ship shall be saved.'   145
Here the grandchild was made guilty for the grandfather's sins,
And all for his forefather fared the worse.
The Gospel is against this in some degree, I find:
The son shall not bear the iniquity of the father, neither shall the
    father bear the iniquity of the son.[3]
But I find if the father is false and a scoundrel,   150
That to some degree the son shall have his sire's faults.
Graft applewood on an alder and if your apple is sweet
It would seem to me most marvelous, and more so if a scoundrel
Should bring forth any brat who does not behave the same
And smack of his sire—you seldom see otherwise.   155
    Men never gather grapes of thorns nor figs of thistles.[4]
And thus through cursed Cain care came upon earth,
And all for marriages they made against the commands of God.
Therefore those have misfortune in marriages that thus marry off
    their children.
For some as I see now, to speak the truth,
In hope of making money marry unnaturally.   160
Care-ridden conception comes of such marriages,
As befell the folk that I before spoke of.
For good folk should wed good folk though goods they have none.
'I am *via et veritas*,'[5] says Christ, 'I can advance you all.'
It is an uncomely couple, by Christ, I think,   165
When a young wench is wedded to a worn-out gaffer,
Or any widow wedded for the wealth she possesses,
Who will never bear a baby unless it be in her arms.
In jealousy, joyless, and in jangling abed
Many a pair since the pestilence have pledged their vows.   170
The fruit that they bring forth are foul words;
They have no children but chafing and exchanges of blows.
Though they dare go to Dunmow, unless the Devil helps them,

---

2. Gen. 6:7. The lines following refer to Gen. 6–7.
3. Not the Gospel but Ezek. 18:20.
4. Matt. 7:16.
5. "The way and the truth": John 14:6.

To folwen after the flicche, fecche thei it nevere;
175 But thei bothe be forsworne that bacoun thei tyne.
Forthi I conseille alle Crystene coveite nought be wedded
For coveitise of catel ne of kynrede riche.
Ac maydenes and maydenes macche yow togideres,
[Widwers] and [widwes] worcheth the same.
180 For no londes but for love loke ye be wedded,
And thanne gete ye the grace of God and good ynogh to lyve with.
And every maner seculer [man] that may nought continue
Wysly go wedde and war [the] fro synne,
For leccherye in likyng is lymeyerde of helle.
185 Whiles thow art yonge [and yepe] and thi wepne [yet] kene,
Wreke the with wyvynge yif thow wil ben excused.
　　　Dum sis vir fortis, ne des tua robora scortis.
　　　Scribitur in portis: 'Meretrix est janua mortis.'
Whan ye have wyved, bewar and worcheth in tyme,
Nought as Adam and Eve whan Caym was engendred.
For in untyme trewli bitwene man and womman
190 Ne shulde no [bedbourde] be; but if thei bothe were clene
Of lyf and and of [love] and [of lawe also],
That derne dede do no man ne sholde.
[Ac] if thei leden thus her lyf, it [liketh] God almighti,
For he made wedloke firste and himself it seide:
　　　Bonum est ut unusquisque uxorem suam habeat propter
　　　　fornicacionem.
195 That othergatis ben geten for gedelynges ben holden,
As false folke, fondelynges, faitoures and lyars
Ungracious to gete goode or love of the poeple,
Wandren [as wolves], and wasten [if] thei mowe;
Ayeines Do-Wel thei don yvel and the Devel [plese],
200 And after her deth-day shulle dwelle with the same,
But God gyve hem grace here hemself to amende.
　　Do-Wel, my [dere], is to don as lawe techeth,
To love [and to lowe thee and no lyf to greve;
Ac to love and to lene], leve me, that is Do-Bet;
205 To yiven and to yemen bothe yonge and olde,
To helen and to helpen, is Do-Best of alle.
[Thanne is] Do-Wel to drede, and Do-Bet to suffre,
And so cometh Do-Best [aboute] and bryngeth adoun Mody,
And that is wikked wille that many werke shendeth
210 And dryveth away Do-Wel thorugh dedliche synnes."

To vie for the flitch, they'll never fetch it home;
Unless they both lie under oath they'll lose that bacon.[6] 175
Therefore I counsel all Christians not to crave to be married
For a fat fortune or family connections.
But virgins and virgins should make vows with one another,
And widowers and widows should wed in the same way.
For no lands but for love look to it that you marry, 180
And then you'll get the grace of God and goods enough to live with.
And every manner of secular man that cannot remain continent
Wisely go wed and ward off sin,
For fantasies of the flesh are the Fiend's lures.
While you're young and yeasty and your weapon yet keen, 185
Work it out in wiving if you would be excused.
　　While you've strength galore,　don't waste it on a whore.
　　For o'er the door is writ this lore:　'A whore is death's door.'[7]
When you've wedded, be wary and work in season,
Not as Adam and Eve when Cain was engendered.
For truly in unfitting time between men and women
There should be no bed-games; unless they're both clean 190
Of life and of love and of law as well,
The deed done in the dark should be done by no one.
But if they lead their lives thus, it delights God almighty,
For he first devised marriage and referred to it himself:
　　It is good for every man to have his own wife on account of
　　　　fornication.[8]
Those conceived outside wedlock are considered worthless, 195
False folk, foundlings, fakers and liars
Without grace to gain property or get people's love,
Wander like wolves, wasting what they may;
Against Do-Well they do evil and give the Devil pleasure,
And after their death-day will go dwell with him, 200
Unless God gives them grace to amend themselves here.
　　Do-Well, my dear sir, is to do as law teaches,
To behave lovingly and humbly and harm no person;
But to love and to lend aid, believe me, that's Do-Better;
To protect and provide for people young and old, 205
To heal them and to help them, is Do-Best of all.
Then is Do-Well to dread, and Do-Better to suffer,
And so Do-Best comes about and brings down Obstinate,
And that is wicked will who spoils work constantly
And drives away Do-Well with deadly sins." 210

---

6. The Dunmow flitch (a cured side of bacon) was awarded to the couple who after a year of marriage could claim no quarrels, no regrets, and the desire, if freed from their vows, to remarry one another.
7. The Latin couplet is traditional. Cf. Prov. 29:3, 7:27.
8. 1 Cor. 7:2.

Passus X

Thanne hadde witte a wyf—was hote Dame Studye—
That lene was of [lyke] and of [lowe chere].
She was wonderly wroth that Witte me thus taughte,
And al starynge Dame Studye sternelich seyde:
5   "Wel, artow wyse, [Wit," quod she], "any wysdomes to telle
To flatereres or to folis that frantyk ben of wittes?"
And blamed hym and banned hym and badde hym be stylle,
With suche wise wordes to wissen any sottes,
And seyde "*Noli mittere*, man, margerye-perlis
10   Amanges hogges that han hawes at wille.
Thei don but dryvele theron; draffe were hem levere
Than al the precious perré that in Paradys wexeth.
I sey it bi suche," quod she, "that sheweth bi her werkes
That hem were lever londe and lordship on erthe,
15   Or ricchesse, or rentis, and reste at her wille,
Than alle the sothe sawes that Salamon seyde evere.
Wisdome and witte now is nought worth a [russhe]
But if it be carded with coveytise as clotheres [don] here wolle.
Whoso can contreve deceytes an conspire wronges
20   And lede forth a loveday to latte [the] treuthe,
He that suche craftes can to conseille is clepid;
Thei lede lordes with lesynges and bilyeth treuthe.
Job the gentel in his gestes witnesseth
That wikked men thei welden the welthe of this worlde,
25   And that thei ben lordes of eche a londe that oute of lawe libbeth.
        Quare impij vivunt bene? Bene est omnibus qui prevaricantur et
            inique agunt?
The Sauter seyth the same bi suche that don ille.
        Ecce ipsi peccatores habundantes in seculo; optinuerunt
            divicias.
'Lo,' seith Holy Letterrure, 'whiche lordes beth this shrewes!'
Thilke that God moste gyveth, leste good thei deleth,
And moste unkynde to the comune that moste catel weldeth.
        Que perfecisti destruxerunt; justus autem, etc.
30   Harlotes for her harlotrye may have of her godis,
And japeres and jogeloures and jangelers of gestes,
Ac he that hath Holy Writte ay in his mouth,
And can telle of Tobye and of the twelve Apostles,
Or prechen of the penaunce that Pilat wrought
35   To Jhesu the gentil that Jewes todrowe
[On crosse upon Calvarye, as clerkes us techeth],
Litel is he loved [or lete by] that suche a lessoun [techeth],
Or daunted or drawe forth, I do it on God hymself.

Passus X

Then Wit had a wife—her name was Dame Study—
Who was lowly of look and lean of her body.
She was very vexed that Wit informed me thus,
And scowling Dame Study sternly said:
"Well, aren't you wise, Wit," she said, "to speak any wisdom   5
To flatterers or fools that are frenzied in their wits?"
And upbraided him and blamed him and bade him be still,
And to stop speaking to sots such wise words,
And said, "*Nolite mittere*, man, margery-pearls¹
Among hogs that have husks at their will.   10
All they do is dirty them; they'd rather have swill
Than all the precious pearls that Paradise grows.
I say it of such," she said, "that show by their actions
That they'd liefer have land and lordship on earth,
Or riches, or revenue, or rest when they please,   15
Than all the true saws Solomon spoke in his life.
Wisdom and wit now are not worth a rush
Unless they're carded with covetousness as cloth-makers card wool.²
Whoever can construct frauds and conspire in wrongs
And direct a loveday* to disable the truth,   20
Whoever's capable of such craft is called to council;
They influence lords with lies and make liars of the facts.
Job the gentle* generalizes in his story
That wicked men wield the wealth of this world,
And that those who live outside the law are lords of every land.   25
    Wherefore do the wicked live? Wherefore are all they happy
      *that deal very treacherously?*³
The Psalter* says the same of such as do evil.
    Behold these are the sinners who prosper in the world; they
      *increase in riches.*⁴
'See,' says Holy Scripture, 'what sorts of lords these scoundrels are!'
Those whom God gives most to, the least they give in turn,
And the most unkind to the community are those with most money.
    *What thou hast made they have destroyed; but the just man, etc.*⁵
    Ribalds for their ribaldry may relish their gifts,   30
And jesters and jugglers and jabberers of tales,
But he who has Holy Writ always in his mouth,
And can tell of Tobit⁶ and of the twelve Apostles,
Or preach of the pain that Pilate caused
To Jesu the gentle whom the Jews stretched   35
Upon a Cross on Calvary, as clerks teach us,
Little is he loved or listened to that teaches such a lesson,
Or caressed or comforted, I call God to witness.

---

1. *Nolite mittere*: "Cast not [pearls before swine]": Matt. 7:6. *Margery*: "pearl" (Latin *margarita*).
2. *Rush*: a straw, a trifle. *Card wool*: wool is carded before spinning with a comb-like tool.
3. Job 21:7; Jer. 12:1.
4. Ps. 72:12.
5. Ps. 10:4.
6. The Book of Tobias, included in the Catholic Bible but later regarded as apocryphal by Protestants.

But tho that feynen hem folis and with faityng libbeth
40 Ayein the lawe of owre Lorde, and lyen on hemselve,
Spitten and spewen and speke foule wordes,
Drynken and dryvelen and do men for to gape,
Lickne men and lye on hem that leneth hem no yiftes,
Thei conne namore mynstralcye ne musyke men to glade
45 Than Munde the Mylnere of *Multa fecit Deus.*
Ne [holpe hir] harlotrye, have God my treuthe,
[Wolde] nevere kyng ne knight ne [chanoun] of Seynt Poules
Yyve hem to her Yeres-yive the [value] of a grote.
Ac [mynstralcye and murthe] amonges men is nouthe
50 Leccherye, losengerye, and loseles tales;
Glotonye and grete othes—[thise aren games nowadayes],
Ac if thei carpen of Cryst, this clerkis and this lewed,
Atte mete in her murthes whan mynstralles ben stille,
Thanne telleth thei of the Trinité [how two slow the thridde],
55 And bringen forth a balled resoun, taken Bernard to witnesse,
And putten forth a presumpsioun to preve the sothe.
Thus thei dryvele at her deyse the Deité to knowe,
And gnawen God [in] the gorge whan her gutte is fulle.
Ac the careful may crye and carpen at [the] yate,
60 Bothe afyngred and athurst, and for chele quake;
Is none to nymen [in ne] his noye to amende,
But [hunsen] hym as an hounde and hoten hym go thennes.
Litel loveth he that lorde that lent hym al that blisse
That thus parteth with the pore a parcel whan hym nedeth.
65 Ne were mercy in mene men more than in riche
Mendinantz meteles mighte go to bedde.
God is moche in the gorge of thise grete maystres,
Ac amonges mene men his mercy and his werkis.
And so seith the Sauter: [seke it in *Memento*].
   *Ecce, audivimus eam in Effrata; invenimus eam in campis
   silve.*
70 Clerkes and [kete] men carpen of God faste
And have [hym] moche in [her] mouthe—ac mene men in herte.
   Freres and faitoures han founde [up] suche questiouns
To plese with proude men sithen the pestilence tyme;
And prechen at Seint Poules for pure envye of clerkis
75 That folke is noughte fermed in the feith ne fre of her goodes,
Ne sori for her synnes, so is pryde waxen
In religioun and in alle the rewme, amonges riche and pore,
That preyeres have no power [thise pestilences] to lette.
[For God is def nowadayes and deyneth noughte us to here,
80 That gerles for oure gultes he forgrynt hem alle].

But those who feign to be fools and get a fraudulent living
Against the law of our Lord, and lie about themselves,   40
Spit and spew and speak foul words,
Drink and drivel and draw men's guffaws,
Caricature people and calumniate those who don't care to tip them,
They know no more minstrelsy nor music to gladden men
Than Mund the Miller knows of *Multa fecit Deus*.[7]   45
If lewdness didn't lend its aid, the Lord have my troth,
Would never king nor knight nor canon of Saint Paul's[8]
Give them a New Year's gift of a groat's* value.
But minstrelsy and mirth among men nowadays
Are filthiness, flatteries, and foolish tales;   50
Gluttony and great oaths—these are games nowadays,
But if they discourse of Christ, these clerks and laymen,
At meals in their mirth when minstrels are still,
Then they tell of the Trinity how two slew the third,[9]
And bring a threadbare argument to bear, take Bernard* to witness,   55
And proffer an assumed probability as a proof of the truth.
Thus they drivel on the dais a definition of Godhead,
And set their teeth in God's gorge when their guts are full.
But the care-worn may cry and clamor at the gate,
Famished and faint with thirst, and freezing for cold;   60
There is no one to ask him in nor offer help for his harm,
But they curse him like a cur and bid him clear out.
Little does he love that Lord who lends him all that bliss
That parcels out to the poor such a portion in his need.
If there weren't more mercy in low men than among the rich   65
Mendicants might go meatless to bed.
God is much in the gullet of these great masters,*
But among lowly men are his mercy and his works.
And so the Psalter says: seek it in *Memento*.[1]
      Lo, we heard of it at Ephrath; we found it[2] *in the fields of the*
            wood.
Clerks and clever men converse glibly of God   70
And have him much in their mouths—but lowly men in heart.
      Friars and frauds have devised such questions
To please proud men with since the pestilence time;
And they preach at Saint Paul's[3] in pure envy of the clergy
So that folk are not firm in their faith nor free with their goods,   75
Nor are sorry for their sins, so has pride increased
In religious orders and in all the realm, among rich and poor,
That prayers have no power to prevent these pestilences.
For God is deaf nowadays and does not deign to hear us,
So that for our guilts he grinds girls and boys to death.   80

7. "God hath done many things": Ps. 39:6.
8. *Canon*: one of a group of privileged (and well-paid) priests attached to a cathedral and constitut-
   ing its ruling body under a dean. *Saint Paul's*: the cathedral of the city of London.
9. The possibility that the Crucifixion is the murder of one member of the Trinity by the other two is
   being made a blasphemous after-dinner joke.
1. "Remember": Ps. 131:1.
2. I.e., a place for the Lord (Ps. 131:6).
3. The Cross outside St. Paul's Cathedral was a major preaching place in London.

And yette the wrecches of this worlde is none y-war bi other,
Ne for drede of the Deth withdrawe nought her pryde,
Ne beth plentyuous to the pore as pure charité wolde,
But in gaynesse and in glotonye for-glotten her goode,
85   And breken noughte to the beggar as the Boke techeth.
         Frange esurienti panem tuum, etc.
And the more he wynneth and welt welthes and ricchesse
And lordeth in [ledes], the lasse good he deleth.
Thobye [techeth] nought so: take hede, ye riche,
How the Boke-Bible of hym bereth witnesse:
         Si tibi sit copia, habundanter tribue; si autem exiguum, illud
            impertiri stude libenter.
90   Whoso hath moche spene manliche, so meneth Thobie,
And whoso litel weldeth, [wisse] him therafter,
For we have no lettre of owre lyf how longe it shal dure.
Suche lessounes lordes shulde lovie to here,
And how he myghte moste meyné manliche fynde,
95   Nought to fare as a fitheler or a frere forto seke festes,
Homelich at other mennes house and hatyen her owne.
Elyng is the halle, uche daye in the wyke,
There the lorde ne the lady liketh noughte to sytte.
Now hath uche riche a reule to eten bi hymselve
100 In a pryvé parloure for pore mennes sake,
Or in a chambre with a chymneye, and leve the chief
         halle
That was made for meles men to eten inne.
And al to spare to spille that spende shal another.
I have y-herde hiegh men, etyng atte table,
105 Carpen as thei clerkes were of Cryste and of his mightes,
And leyden fautes uppon the Fader that fourmed us alle,
And carpen ayeine [clergye] crabbed wordes:
'Whi wolde owre Saveoure suffre suche a worme in his blisse
That [biwyled] the womman and the [wye] after,
110 Thorw whiche [werke and wil] thei went to helle,
And al her sede for here synne the same deth suffred?
Here lyeth yowre lore,' thise lordes gynneth dispute,
'Of that ye clerkes us kenneth of Cryst by the Gospel:
Filius non portabit iniquitatem patris, etc.
115 Whi shulde we that now ben for the werkes of Adam
Roten and torende? Resoun wolde it nevere!'
         Unusquisque portabit onus suum, etc.
Suche motyves thei moeve, this maistres, in her glorie,
And maken men in mysbileve that muse moche on her wordes.
Ymaginatyf herafterward shal answere to yowre purpos.
120 Augustyne to suche argueres he telleth hem this teme:
Non plus sapere quam oportet.
Wilneth nevere to wite whi that God wolde

And yet worldly wretches will not beware from watching others,
Nor for dread of the Death withdraw their pride,
Nor give plentifully to the poor as pure charity asks,
But in gluttony and gay living guzzle down their wealth,
And break no bread for the beggar as the Book teaches.   85
    Deal thy bread to the hungry, etc.[4]
And the more he wins and wields worldly riches
And lords it over his landsmen, the less good he gives.
Tobit teaches not so: take heed, you rich,
How the Bible-Book bears witness of him:
    If thou hast abundance, give thine alms accordingly; if thou
        hast but a little, take care even so to bestow that willingly.[5]
Whoever has received much should bestow much, so says Tobit,   90
And whoever's been allotted little, limit himself accordingly,
For we've no document that defines the duration of our life.
Such lessons lords should love to hear,
And how they might most liberally look after the largest household,
And not fare like a fiddler or friar seeking feasts,   95
At home in other men's houses and hating his own.
Unhappy is the hall, every day in the week,
Where the lord and the lady have no liking to sit.
Now has each rich man a rule to eat by himself
In a private parlor to avoid poor men,   100
Or in a chamber with a chimney-corner, and leave the chief hall
    empty
That was made for men to eat their meals in.
And all to spare and to save what some one else will spend.
I have heard high-born men, eating at the table,
Discourse like clerks on Christ and his powers,   105
And impute faults to the Father that formed us all,
And carp against clergy with crabbed words:
'Why would our Savior suffer such a worm in his bliss
That fooled the female and her fellow after,
Through which work and will they went to hell,   110
And all their seed for that sin suffered the same death?
Here your learning lies,' these lords start to argue,
'If what you clerks claim is true of Christ in the Gospel:
The son shall not bear the iniquity of the father, etc.[6]
Why should we who live now for the works of Adam   115
Go to rot and ruin? Reason forbids it!'
    Every man shall bear his own burden, etc.[7]
Such matters they mouth, these masters,* in their boasting,
And make men believe amiss who muse on their words.
Imaginative* hereafter shall answer to your purpose.
Such arguers Augustine* answers with this text: 120
Know no more than is necessary.[8]
Never wish to learn why it was God's will

4. Isa. 58:7.
5. Tob. 4:9.
6. Ezek. 18:20: repeats IX. 149.
7. Gal. 6:5.
8. No exact source in Augustine is known, but see Rom. 12:3

Suffre Sathan his sede to bigyle,
Ac bileve lelly in the lore of Holi Cherche,
125 And preye hym of pardoun and penaunce in thi lyve,
And for his moche mercye to amende [us] here.
For alle that wilneth to wyte the [whyes] of God almighty,
I wolde his eye were in his ers, and his [hele] after—
That evere [eft] wilneth to wite whi that God wolde
130 Suffre sathan his sede to bigile
Or Judas the [Juwe] Jhesu bytraye.
Al was as [he] wolde—Lorde, y-worschiped be thow!—
And al worth as thow wolte what so we dispute.
And tho that useth this havelounes to blende mennes wittes
135 What is Do-Wel fro Do-Bet, now def mote he worthe,
Sitthe he wilneth to wyte whiche thei ben [alle].
But if he lyve in the [leste degré] that longeth to Do-Wel,
For I dar ben his bolde borgh that Do-Bet wil he nevere,
Theigh Do-Best drawe on hym day after other."
140   And whan that Witte was y-war [how his wyf] tolde,
He bicome so confus he couth noughte [mele],
And as doumbe [as a dore] drowe hym [aside].
And for no carpyng I couth, ne knelyng to the grounde,
I myghte gete no greyne of his grete wittis,
145 But al laughyng he louted and loked uppon Studye
In signe that I shulde biseche hir of grace.
And whan I was war of his wille, to his wyf gan I [knele]
And seyde, "Mercy, madame, yowre man shal I worthe
As longe as I lyve, bothe late and rathe,
150 Forto worche yowre wille the while my lyf dureth,
With that ye kenne me kyndely to knowe
        what is Do-Wel."
    "For thi mekenesse, man," quod she, "and for thi mylde speche,
I shal kenne the to my cosyn that Clergye is hoten.
He hath wedded a wyf withinne this syx [wykes]
155 Is sybbe to the sevene artz; Scripture is hir name.
Thei two, as I hope, after my [bisechynge]
Shullen wissen the to Do-Wel, I dar [wel] undertake."
    Thanne was I also fayne as foule of faire morwe,
Gladder than the gleman that golde hath to yifte,
160 And axed hir the heigheweye where that Clergye dwelte.
"And telle me some token [to hym], for tyme is that I wende."
    "Axe the heighewaye," quod she, "hennes to Suffre-
Bothe-Wel-And-Wo, yif that thow wolt lerne;
And ryde forth by Ricchesse—ac rest thow naught therinne,
165 For if thow couplest the [with hym], to Clergye comestow nevere.
And also the [longe] launde, that Leccherye hatte,
Leve hym on thi left halve a large myle or more
Tyl thow come to a courte, Kepe-Wel-Thi-Tonge-
Fro-Lesynges-And-Lither-Speche-And-Likerouse-Drynkes.

To suffer Satan to deceive his seed,
But believe loyally in the lore of Holy Church,
And pray him for penance and pardon in your lifetime,   125
And that for the muchness of his mercy he may amend us here.
For any one who wants to learn the whys of God almighty,
I wish his eye were in his arse, and his heel as well—
Whoever again wants to know why it was God's wish
To suffer Satan to deceive his seed   130
Or Judas the Jew to prepare Jesus' betrayal.
All was as he willed—Lord, worship be unto you!—
And all will be as you wish whatever we say.
And whoever tries these tactics to trick men's minds
How Do-Well differs from Do-Better, now deafness come upon him,   135
Since he's eager to understand who they all are.
Unless he lives in the lowest degree that belongs to Do-Well,
I'll boldly put up a bond for him that he'll Do-Better never,
Though day after day Do-Best aim at him."
    And when Wit was aware what his wife was saying,   140
He became so confused he couldn't speak,
And as dumb as a doornail drew to the side.
And for no words I knew, nor for kneeling to the ground,
I might garner no grain of his great wits,
But all grinning he grimaced and glanced at Study   145
As a sign that I should beseech her of grace.
And when I was aware what he wanted I knelt to his wife
And said, "Mercy, madam, your man shall I be
As long as I live, both late and early,
And work your will while my life lasts,   150
If you consent to counsel me how I may comprehend Do-Well
        naturally."*
    "For your meekness, man," said she, "and for your mild speech,
I shall acquaint you with my cousin—Clergy* is his name.
He has wedded a wife within these six weeks
Who is sib to the seven arts; she is called Scripture.[9]   155
These two, as I hope, after my request
Will direct you to Do-Well, I dare well warrant it."
    Then was I as blithe as a bird on bright morning,
Merrier than a minstrel whom men have given gold,
And asked her the highway to where Clergy dwelt.   160
"And tell me how to introduce myself, for it's time I went."
    "Ask for the highway," said she, "from here to Suffer-
Both-Welfare-And-Woe, if you wish to learn;
And ride on past Riches—don't rest there,
For if you keep company with him, you'll never come to Clergy.   165
And also the long pastureland, Lechery by name,
Leave it on your left hand a long mile or more
Till you come to a castle, Keep-Well-Your-Tongue-
From-Lies-And-Loose-Speech-And-Delicious-Drinks.

9. Knowledge of scripture presupposed the "seven arts" that formed the basic curriculum in medieval
   education. They consist of the trivium (grammar, rhetoric, and logic) and the quadrivium (arithmetic, geometry, astronomy, and music).

170   Thanne shaltow se Sobreté and Sympleté-Of-Speche,
     That eche wighte be in wille his witte the to shewe.
     And thus shaltow come to Clergye that can many thinges.
     Saye hym this signe: I sette hym to scole;
     And that I grette wel his wyf—for I wrote hir [the Bible],
175   And sette hir to *Sapientia* and to the Sauter glose.
     Logyke I lerned hir, and [al the lawe after],
     And alle the musouns in musike I made hir to knowe.
     Plato the Poete, I put hym fyrste to boke;
     Arestotle and other moo to argue I taughte.
180   Grammer for gerles I garte first wryte,
     And bette hem with a baleis, but if thei wolde lerne.
     Of alkinnes craftes I contreved toles,
     Of [carpenteres and] kerveres; [I kenned first] masouns
     And lerned hem level and lyne, though I loke dymme.
185   Ac Theologie hath tened me ten score tymes.
     The more I muse thereinne, the mistier it semeth,
     And the depper I [devyned], the derker me [thoughte];
     It is no science forsothe forto sotyle inne;
     [Ne were the love that lith therinne, a wel lewed thing it were].
190   Ac for it let best by Love, I love it the bettre,
     For there that Love is leder, ne [lacketh] nevere grace.
     Loke thow love lelly yif the lyketh Do-Wel,
     For Do-Bet and Do-Best ben [drawen] of Loves [scole].
     In other science it seyth (I saye it in Catoun):
195   *Qui similat verbis nec corde est fidus amicus,*
     Tu quoque fac simile; sic ars deluditur arte.
     'Whoso gloseth as gylours don, go me to the same;
     And so shaltow false folke and faythlees bigyle.'
     This is Catounes kennyng to clerkes that he lereth.
200   Ac Theologye techeth nought so, whoso taketh yeme;
     He kenneth us the contrarye, ayein Catones wordes,
     [And biddeth] us be as bretheren and [blissen] owre enemys,
     And loven hem that lyen on us, and lene hem [at her nede],
     And do good ayeines yvel; God hymself it hoteth.
         Dum tempus est operemur bonum ad omnes, maxime autem
            ad domesticos fidei.
205   Poule preched the peple that parfitnesse loved
     To do good for Goddes love and gyven men that asked,
     And [sovereynelyche] to suche that sueth owre Bileve.
     And alle that lakketh us or lyeth owre Lorde techeth us to lovye,
     And nought to greven hem that greveth us; God [that forbedeth].
         Michi vindictam et ego retribuam.
210   Forthi loke thow lovye as longe as thow durest,
     For is no science under sonne so sovereyne for the soule.
       Ac astronomye is an harde thynge, and yvel forto knowe;
     Geometrie and geomesye is ginful of speche;
     Whoso thenketh werche with tho [thre] thryveth ful late,

Then you shall see Sobriety and Sincerity-Of-Speech,   170
So that every one will be willing to share his wits with you.
Then you will come to Clergy who knows many kinds of things.
Repeat this password: I put him in school;
And that you bring best wishes for his wife—I wrote the Bible for her,
And set her studying *Sapientia** and the Psalter* gloss.   175
She learned logic from me, and all the law after,
And with all the measures in music I made her acquainted.
Plato* the Poet, I put him first to reading;
Aristotle and many others too I taught how to argue.
Grammar books for brats I first brought into being,   180
And beat them with a broom, anybody who wouldn't learn.
For all kinds of crafts I contrived tools,
For carpenters and carvers; I first counseled masons
And taught them level and line, though my sight's a little dim.
    But Theology has troubled me ten score times.   185
The more I muse on it, the mistier it seems,
And the deeper I divined, the darker I thought it;
It's surely no science to argue subtly in;
If it weren't for the love that lies in it, it would be a lame study.
But since it allows so much to Love, I love it the better,   190
For wherever Love is leader, there's no lack of grace.
Be sure to love loyally if you'd like to Do-Well,
For Do-Better and Do-Best are drawn from Love's school.
In other sciences it says (I saw it in Cato*):
If some one dissembles in words and is not a good friend at heart,   195
You do the same: thus art's deceived by art.
'If some one glozes* as the guileful do, give him back the same;
And thus you'll fool folk who are faithless and false.'
This is Cato's counsel to clerks he teaches.
But Theology does not teach this, if you take heed;   200
He counsels us the contrary, against Cato's words,
And bids us be like brothers and bless our enemies,
And love those that lie about us, and lend them help at need,
And do good against evil; God himself commands it.
    While we have time, let us do good unto all men, especially
        unto them who are of the household of faith.[1]
Paul who loved perfectness preached the people   205
To do good for God's love and give to men who asked,
And especially to such as subscribe to our Creed.
And our Lord teaches us to love all that lie about us or slander us,
And not to grieve them that grieve us: God forbids that.
    Vengeance is mine and I will repay.[2]
Therefore look to it that you love as long as you last,   210
For no science under sun is so salutary for the soul.
    But astrology is a hard subject, not easy to understand;
Geometry and geomancy[3] are full of juggling terms;
Whoever thinks to work with those three thrives full late,

1. Gal. 6:10.
2. Rom. 12:19; cf. Deut. 32:35.
3. Divination by means of lines and figure.

215 For sorcerye is the sovereyne boke that to [that] science longeth.
Yet ar there fybicches in [forelles] of fele mennes makyng,
Experimentz of alkamye [of Albertes makyng,
Nigromancie and perimancie the Pouke to raise].
If thow thinke to Do-Wel, dele therwith nevere.
220 Alle thise [sciences] I myself sotiled and ordeyned,
And founded hem formest, folke to deceyve.
Telle Clergye thise tokenes, and [to] Scripture after,
To conseille the kyndely to knowe what is Do-Wel."
   I seide, "Graunt mercy, madame," and mekeliche hir grette,
225 And went wightlich [my wey] withoute more lettynge,
And [er] I come to Clergye [coude I] nevere stynte.
[I] gret the good man as [the goode wyf] me taughte,
And afterwardes [his] wyf—[I] worshiped hem bothe,
And tolde [hire] the tokenes that me taughte were.
230 Was nevere gome uppon this grounde, sith God made [Hevene],
Fairer underfongen ne frendeloker at ese
Than myself sothly, sone so he wist
That I was of Wittis hous and with his wyf Dame Studye.
[Curteisly Clergye colled me and kiste,
235 And asked how Wit ferde and his wyf Studye].
I seyde to hem sothely that sent was I thider
Do-Wel and Do-Bet and Do-Best to lerne.
   "It is a comune lyf," quod Clergye, "on Holy Cherche to bileve
With alle the artikles of the feithe that falleth to be knowe.
240 And that is to bileve lelly, bothe lered and lewed,
On the grete God that gynnyng had nevere,
And on the sothfaste Sone that saved mankynde
Fro the dedly deth and the Develes power
Thorwgh the helpe of the Holy Goste, the whiche is of bothe;
245 Three [propre] persones, ac nought in plurel noumbre,
For al is but on God and eche is God hymselve:
   Deus pater, Deus filius, Deus Spiritus Sanctus.
God the Fader, God the Sone, God Holi Goste of bothe,
Maker of [man and his make] and of bestes bothe.
Austyn the olde hereof he made bokes,
250 And hymself ordeyned to sadde us in bileve.
Who was his autour? Alle the foure Evangelistes,
And Cryst clepid hymself so, the [Scripture] bereth witnesse.
   Ego in Patre, et Pater in me est, et qui videt me
         videt et Patrem meum.
Alle the clerkes under Cryst ne couthe this assoille,
But thus it bilongeth to bileve to lewed that willen do wel,
255 For had nevere freke fyne wytte the feyth to dispute,
Ne man had no merite myghte it ben y-proved.

For sorcery is the sovereign book those sciences deal with.   215
Yet there is claptrap bound in covers composed by many men,
Experiments of alchemy of Albert's devising,
Necromancy and perimancy[4] to make the Devil appear.
If you're disposed to Do-Well, never deal with these.
All these sciences I myself established and developed,   220
And was their first founder, that they might fool people.
Tell these tokens to Clergy, and to Scripture as well,
That they will answer to your asking how inwardly to know Do-Well."
   I said, "Many thanks, madam," and meekly saluted her,
And went quickly on my way without further delay,   225
And before I came to Clergy I could never stop.
I greeted the good man as the good wife taught me,
And afterwards his wife—I was respectful to both,
And told her the tokens that had been taught to me.
Never man that moved on this earth, since God made Heaven,   230
Was made more warmly welcome or more wonderfully at ease
Than I myself surely, as soon as he knew
That I was of Wit's house and with his wife Dame Study.
Courteously Clergy kissed and embraced me,
And asked how Wit was and his wife Study.   235
I told them truly that I'd been sent to them
To learn of Do-Well and Do-Better and Do-Best too.
   "It's a common[5] life," declared Clergy, "to believe in Holy Church
With all the articles of faith that ought to be known.
And that is to believe loyally, both learned and layman,   240
In the great God that had no beginning ever,
And in the soothfast* Son that saved mankind
From the deadly death and the Devil's power
Through the help of the Holy Ghost, who is of both;
Three perfect persons, but not in plural number,   245
For all are but one God and each is God himself:
   God the Father, God the Son, and God the Holy Ghost.
God the Father, God the Son, God Holy Ghost of both,
Maker of man and his mate and of animals too.
Augustine* the old hereof made books,
And he himself established this to make us sure in our faith.   250
Who was his authority? All the four Evangelists,
And Christ called himself so, the Scripture bears witness.
   *I am in the Father, and the Father in me, and he that seeth me
      seeth also my Father.*[6]
All the clerks under Christ could not explain this,
But so it belongs to the belief of unlettered men that wish to do well,
For no clerk ever had wit acute enough to discuss faith's reasons,   255
And man would have no merit if it might be proved.

4. *Albert the Great* (1193?–1280): a major scholastic philosopher and teacher of St. Thomas
(1225?–1274); his major work in the sciences gave him the reputation of being a magician. *Necromancy* and *perimancy* (i.e., pyromancy) are forms of magic based on contacts with the dead and
on patterns in fire, respectively.
5. In common, communal; i.e., not peculiar to particular individuals.
6. John 14:9–11.

Fides non habet meritum ubi humana racio prebet experimentum.
[So] is Do-Bet to suffre for thi soules helth
Al that the Boke bit by Holy Cherche techyng.
And that is, man, bi thi mighte, for mercies sake,
260   Loke thow worche it in werke that thi worde sheweth;
Suche as thow semest in syghte, be in assay y-founde,
        Appare quod es vel esto quod appares.
And lat nobody be bi thi beryng bygyled,
But be suche in thi soule as thow semest withoute.
Thanne is Do-Best to be bolde to blame the gylty,
265   Sithenes thow seest thiself as in soule clene;
Ac blame thow nevere body and thow be blameworthy;
        Si culpare velis,   culpabilis esse cavebis;
        Dogma tuum sordet   cum te tua culpa remordet.
God in the Gospel grymly repreveth
Alle that lakken any lyf and lakkes han hemselve.
        Quid consideras festucam in oculo fratris tui, trabem in
            oculo tuo?
'Why mevestow thi mode for a mote in thi brotheres eye
270   Sithen a beem in thine owne ablyndeth thiselve—
        Ejice primo trabem de oculo tuo—
Whiche letteth the to loke lasse other more?'
I rede eche a blynde bosarde do bote to hymselve,
As parsones and parissh prestes that preche shulde and teche
Alle manere men to amenden by here myghte.
275   This tixte was tolde yow to ben war ar ye taughte
That ye were suche as ye seyde to salve with othere.
For Goddis worde wolde nought be loste, for that worcheth evere;
[Though] it availled nought the comune, it myghte availle yowselven.
Ac it semeth now sothly to [syght of the worlde]
280   That Goddes worde worcheth naughte on [wyse] ne on lewede
But in suche a manere as [Mathew] meneth in the Gospel.
        Dum cecus ducit cecum ambo in foveam cadunt.
Lewed men may likne yow thus, that the beem lithe in
            yowre eyghen,
And the festu is fallen for yowre defaute
In alle manere men thourgh mansed prestes.
285   The Bible bereth witnesse that alle the [barnes] of Israel
Byttere aboughte the gultes of two badde prestes,
Offyn and Fynes; for her coveytise
Archa Dei myshapped, and Ely brake his nekke.
Forthi ye corectoures, claweth heron and corecteth fyrst yowselven,
290   And thanne mowe ye [manliche] seye, as David made the Sauter,
Existimasti inique quod ero tui similis,

Faith has no merit where human reason supplies the proof.[7]
So Do-Better is to suffer for your soul's health
All that the Book bids by Holy Church's teaching.
And that is, man, according to your might, for mercy's sake,
See to it that you put into practice what's proclaimed by your word;   260
Such as you seem to sight, be found in assay,
  Seem what you are and be what you seem.[8]
And let nobody be beguiled by your behavior,
But be such in your soul as you seem outside.
Then is Do-Best to be bold in blaming the guilty,
Since you see yourself to be clean in soul;   265
But never blame anybody if you are blameworthy;
  If you wish to blame, see that you're free of shame;
  Your teaching fails when your own sin prevails.[9]
God in the Gospel grimly reproves
All who find fault with others and have faults themselves.
  Why beholdest thou the mote that is in thy brother's eye, but
    considerest not the beam that is in thine own eye?[1]
'What makes you mad about a mote in your brother's eye
When your own bears a beam that is blinding you—   270
  First cast the beam out of thine own eye—
And stopping you from seeing things small or large?'
I advise every blind booby to better himself,
Such as parsons or parish priests that should preach and teach
And amend all manner of men as much as they can.
This text was told you so that before teaching you'd make sure   275
You were such as you said when you offer salve to others.
Yet God's word would not be wasted, for it works always;
Though it meant nothing to the community, it might avail yourselves.
But surely it seems now to the sight of the world
That God's word is not working on wise men or on ignorant   280
Except in such a manner as Matthew mentions in the Gospel.
  If the blind lead the blind both shall fall into the ditch.[2]
Unlettered people may apply this parable to you: the beam lies in
    your eyes,
And for your misbehavior the mote has made blind
All kinds of human creatures because of cursed priests.
  The Bible bears witness that everybody in Israel   285
Paid a bitter price for two bad priests' guilts,
Hophni and Phinehas; for their covetousness
Mishap befell *Archa Dei*,[3] and Ely broke his neck.
Therefore you correctors, clutch this hard and correct yourselves first,
And then you may say sturdily, as David's Psalter puts it,   290
Thou thoughtest unjustly that I would be such an one as thyself, but

7. The Latin pronouncement is St. Gregory's.*
8. Saying quoted by such well-known biblical commentators of the Middle Ages as Thomas Aquinas.
9. Source unknown. Literal translation of the second line: "Your teaching is foul when your sin gnaws at you."
1. *Mote*: a speck. *Beam*: a large piece of wood. *Why beholdest thou . . . in thine own eye*: Matt. 7:3; the quotation three lines below is verse 5.
2. Matt. 15:14.
3. "The Ark of God": 1 Sam. 4:11, 18.

arguam te et statuam contra faciem tuam.
Thanne shal borel clerkes ben abasched to blame yow or to greve,
And carpen noughte as thei carpen now, and calle yow doumbe houndes:
     Canes non valentes latrare—
And drede to wratthe yow in any worde yowre werkemanship to lette,
295   And be prestiore at yowre prayere than for a pounde of nobles,
And al for yowre holynesse; have ye this in herte.
[Amonges rightful religious this rule shulde be holde.
Gregory the grete clerke and the goode Pope
Of religiouns the rule reherseth in his *Moralia,*
300   And seith it in ensample that thei shulde do therafter:
'Whan fisshes faillen the flode or the fressh water,
Thei deye for drought, whan thei drye ligge;
Right so by religioun, it roileth and sterveth
That out of covent and cloistre coveiten to libbe.'
305   For if Hevene be on this erthe and ese to any soule,
It is in cloistre or in scole, by many skiles I fynde.
For in cloistre cometh no man to carpe ne to fighte,
But al is buxumnesse there and bokes, to rede and to lerne].
In scole there is scorne but if a clerke wil lerne,
310   And grete love and lykynge, for eche [loweth hym to] other,
Ac now is Religioun a ryder, a [rennere] bi stretes,
A leder of lovedayes and a londe-bugger,
A priker on a palfray fro [place] to maner,
An heep of houndes at his ers as he a lorde were,
And but if his knave knele that shal his
315   cuppe brynge,
He loureth on hym and [lakketh] hym, 'Who [lered] hym curteisye?'
Litel had lordes to donn to yyve londe fram her heires
To religious that have no reuthe though it reyne on here auteres.
In many places ther [thei] persones ben, be [thei purelich]
     at ese,
320   Of the pore have thei no pité, and that is [pure chartre].
Ac thei leten hem as lordes, her londe lith so brode.
Ac there shal come a kyng and confesse yow religiouses,
And bete yow as the Bible telleth, for brekynge of yowre reule,
And amende monyales, monkes, and chanouns,
325   And putten hem to her penaunce, *Ad pristinum statum ire;*
And barounes with erles beten hem thorugh *Beatus virres* techynge;
[Bynymen] that here barnes claymen and blame yow foule.
     Hij in curribuset et hij in equis ipsi obligati sunt, etc.
And thanne freres in here freitoure shal fynden a keye
Of Costantynes coffres in which is the catel

I will reprove thee and set them in order before thy face.[4]
Then shall bare-witted clerks be abashed to blame or vex you,
And to carp as they carp now, and call you dumb hounds:
    Dogs not able to bark—[5]
And be afraid to anger you with any word that hinders your works,
And move more promptly at your prayer than for a pound of nobles,*   295
And all for your holiness; hold this in heart.
Among righteous religious orders this rule should be kept.
Gregory* the great clerk and the good Pope
Rehearses in his *Moralia*[6] the rule of religious orders
And says this as an example that they should act on: 300
'When fishes leave the salt flood or the fresh water,
They die for drought, lying on the dry ground;
Right so religious, they rot and die
When they crave to escape life in cloister and convent.'
    For if Heaven be on this earth and ease to any soul,   305
It is in cloister or in school, on many counts I find.
For in cloister no man comes to quarrel or to fight,
But there all is obedience and books, to read and to learn.
There is scorn in school if a clerk will not learn,
And great love and liking, for each bows low to the other,   310
But now Religion* is a rider, a runner through the streets,
A leader of lovedays* and a land-buyer,
One who pricks his palfrey from market place to manor,
A heap of hounds at his arse as if he were a lord,
And unless his body-servant bend his knee when he brings him the
    cup,   315
He glowers at him and grumbles, 'Where did he get his manners?'
Lords were of little wisdom to take land from their heirs
For religious who have no ruth though it rain on their altars.
In many places where they are parsons, if they have peace and
    comfort,
They have no pity on the poor, and that's their plenary charter.[7]   320
And they behave like lords, their lands stretch so far.
But there shall come a king and confess you religious,
And beat you as the Bible tells, for breaking your rule,
And amend members of your orders, monks, nuns, and canons,
And put them to their penance, *Ad pristinum statum ire;*[8]   325
And barons with earls shall beat them with *Beatus vir*'s[9] teaching;
Confiscate what their children claim and condemn you foully.
    Some trust themselves to chariots and some to horses, etc.[1]
And then friars in their refectory shall find a key
To Constantine's coffers that contain the money

4. Ps. 49:21.
5. Isa. 56:10.
6. One of his best-known works, a commentary on Job pointing moral applications.
7. A deed conferring absolute ownership. Clergy here attacks monks who become absentee parish
   priests when lay lords leave landed property to monastic orders.
8. "To go [back] to their original state": i.e., the state of the primitive church before it owned wealth
   and property.
9. *Beatus vir*: "Blessed [is] the man" (Ps. 1:1).
1. Ps. 19:8–9; the verses continue, "but we shall call upon the name of the Lord our God. They have
   been bound and have fallen, but we have risen."

330   That Gregories godchildren [ungodly] dispended.
      And thanne shal the Abbot of Abyndoun and alle his issu for evere
      Have a knokke of a kynge, and incurable the wounde.
      That this worth soth, seke ye that oft over-se the Bible:
            Quomodo cessauit exactor! quievit tributum! Contrivit Dominus
                 baculum impiorum et virgam
                 dominancium cedencium plaga insanabili.
      Ac ar that kynge come Cayme shal awake,
335   Ac Do-Wel shal dyngen hym adoune and destruyen his myghte."
            "Thanne is Do-Wel and Do-Bet," quod I, "*dominus* and
                 knighthode?"
            "I nel nought scorne," quod Scripture, "but if scryveynes lye,
      Kynghod ne knyghthod, by naught I can awayte,
      Helpeth nought to Heveneward [at] one [yeres] ende,
340   Ne ricchesse, [ne rentes], ne reauté of lordes.
      Poule preveth it inpossible, riche men [in] Hevene;
      Salamon seith also that sylver is worst to lovye.
            Nichil iniquius quam amare pecuniam.
      And Caton kenneth us to coveiten it naught but as nede techeth.
            Dilige denarium set parce dilige formam.
      And patriarkes and prophetes and poetes bothe
345   Wryten to wissen us to wilne no ricchesse
      And preyseden poverté with pacience; the [Apostle] bereth witnesse
      That thei han heritage in Hevene, and bi trewe righte,
      There riche men no righte may clayme, but of reuthe and grace."
            "*Contra!*" quod I, "bi Cryste, that can I repreve!
350   And preve it bi [the Pistel that Peter is nempned]:
      That is baptized beth sauf, be he riche or pore."
            "That is *in extremis*," quod Scripture. "[As] Saracenes and Jewes
      Mowen be saved so, and [so] is owre byleve;
      That [arn] uncristene in that cas may crysten an hethen,
355   And for his lele byleve, whan he the lyf tyneth,
      Have the heritage [in] Hevene as [an heigh] Crystene.
      Ac Crysten men withoute more may nought come to Hevene,
      For that Cryst for Cristen men deyde and confermed the lawe
      That whoso wolde and wylneth with Cryste to aryse
            Si cum Cristo surrexistis, etc.
360   He shulde lovye and lene and the lawe fulfille.
      That is, love thi lorde God levest above alle,
      And after alle Crystene creatures, in comune eche man other;
      And thus bilongeth to lovye that leveth to be saved.
      And but we do thus in dede ar the Daye of Dome,
365   It shal bisitten us ful soure the silver that we kepen,

That Gregory's godchildren have ungodly dispended.   330
And then the Abbot of Abingdon and all his issue forever[2]
Shall have a cut from a king, and incurable the wound.
That this shall turn out true, test it, you frequent readers of the Bible:
> *How hath the oppressor ceased! the tribute ceased! The Lord*
> *hath broken the staff of the wicked and the sceptre of*
> *the rulers who cut with an incurable wound.*[3]
And before that king comes Cain shall awake,
But Do-Well shall dash him down and destroy his might."   335
   "Then is Do-Well and Do-Better," said I, "*dominus*[4] and
      knighthood?"
   "I'll not be scornful," said Scripture; "unless legal sticklers lie,
Can neither kinghood nor knighthood, as far as I can see,
Help at all toward Heaven when one's hour comes,
Nor riches, nor revenue, nor royal lord's estate.   340
Paul proves it impossible, rich men in Heaven;
Solomon also says that silver is the worst thing to love.
> *There is not a more wicked thing than to love money.*[5]
And Cato* counsels us not to covet it except as need teaches.
> *Love the penny but be sparing of love for its beauty.*
And patriarchs and prophets and poets too
Wrote works to warn us not to wish for riches   345
And praised poverty with patience; the Apostle bears witness
That the poor have heritage in Heaven, and by true right,
While rich men may not claim right, but only mercy and grace."
   "*Contra!*"* I cried, "by Christ, that I can refute!
And prove it by the Epistle that bears Peter's name: 350
Whoever is baptized will be saved, be he rich or poor."
   "That is *in extremis*,"[6] said Scripture. "Saracens and Jews
May be saved so, and so we believe;
Non-Christians may in that case christen a heathen,
And for his loyal belief, when his life is lost,   355
He may have heritage in Heaven like a high Christian.
But Christians cannot without something more come to Heaven,
Because Christ died for Christian men and confirmed the law
That whoever wishes and wills to arise with Christ
> *If ye be risen with Christ, etc.*[7]
He should love and lend help and fulfill the law's commands.   360
That is, love your Lord God as dearest love of all,
And then all Christian creatures, in common each man other;
And thus it behooves him to love that hopes to be saved.
And unless we do this in deed before the Day of Doom,*
The silver that we save will beset us most sourly,   365

---

2. *Constantine*: the emperor who allegedly gave the Pope temporal rulership and lands when he made Christianity the official religion of the Roman Empire. *Gregory's godchildren*: monks, so called because Gregory the Great* was a monk. *Abingdon*: one of the wealthiest abbeys in England.
3. Isa. 14:4–6.
4. Lord[ship].
5. Ecclus. 10:10.
6. "At the point of death."
7. Col. 3:1.

And owre bakkes that moth-eten be, and sen beggers go
    naked,
Or delyte in wyn and wylde foule and wote any in defaute,
For every Cristene creature shulde be kynde til other,
And sithen hethen to helpe in hope of amendement.
370 God hoteth bothe heigh and lowe that no man hurte other,
And seith, 'Slee nought that semblable is to myne owen liknesse
But if I sende the sum tokne,' and seith, '*Non moechaberis*,'
Is slee nought but suffre, and [so] for the beste,
[For *michi vindictam et ego retribuam*].
375 'I shal punysshen hem in purgatorie or in the putte of helle
Uche man for his mysdedes but mercy it lette.'"
    "This is a longe lessoun," quod I, "and litel am I the wyser;
Where Do-Wel is or Do-Bet derkelich ye shewen.
Many tales ye tellen that Theologye lerneth,
380 And that I man made was and my name y-entred
In the legende of lyf longe er I were,
Or elles unwriten for wikkednesse as Holy Writ wytnesseth.
    Nemo ascendit ad Celum nisi qui de
        celo decendit.
I leve it wel, bi owre Lorde, and on no letterure bettere.
For Salamon the sage that *Sapience* [made]
385 God gaf hym grace of witte and alle his godes after
[To rule the reume and riche to make];
He demed wel and wysely as Holy Writte telleth;
Aristotle and he, who wissed men bettere?
Maistres that of Goddis mercy techen men and prechen
390 Of here wordes thei wissen us for wisest as in here tyme,
And al Holi Cherche holdeth hem bothe [in helle]!
And if I shulde worke bi here werkes to wynne me Hevene,
That for her werkes and witte now wonyeth in pyne,
Thanne wroughte I unwysely, whatsoevere ye preche.
395 Ac of fele witty, in feith, litel ferly I have
Though her goste be ungraciouse God for to plese.
For many men on this molde more sette here hertis
In good than in God; forthi hem grace failleth—
At here moste myschief [mercy were the beste],
400 [Whan thei shal lyf lete, a lippe of Goddes grace]—
As Salamon dede and such other that shewed gret wittes,
Ac her werkes, as Holy Wrytte seyth, was evere the contrarye.
Forthi wyse-witted men and wel-y-lettred clerkes
As thei seyen hemself selden done therafter
    Super cathedram Moysi, etc.
405   Ac I wene it worth of many as was in Noes tyme
Tho he shope that shippe of shides and bordes:

And our overcoats that are moth-eaten, while we behold beggars go
    naked,
Or delight in wine and wild fowl when we're aware of one in need,
For all Christian creatures should be kind to each other,
And then help heathen in hope of amending them.
God orders both high and low that no one hurt another,   370
And says, 'Slay none that is similar to my own likeness
Unless I send you some token,' and says, '*Non moechaberis*,'[8]
That is, slay not but suffer, for so is the best,
For *vengeance is mine and I will repay*.[9]
'I shall punish in purgatory or in the pit of hell   375
Each man for his misdeeds unless mercy prevents it.' "
    "This is a long lesson," said I, "and I'm little the wiser;
Where Do-Well is or Do-Better you disclose darkly.
Many tales you tell that are taught by Theology,
And that I was made man and my name entered   380
In the ledger of life long before I was,
Or else unwritten for doing wrong as Holy Writ witnesses.
    No man hath ascended up to Heaven but he that came down
        from Heaven.[1]
I believe this well, by our Lord, and no letter better.
For Solomon the sage that wrote *Sapientia**
God gave him grace of wit and all goods as well   385
To rule the realm and make rich his people;
He judged well and wisely as Holy Writ tells;
Aristotle* and he, who taught men better?
Masters* that teach men and preach God's mercy to them
Instruct us with their sayings as for the sagest in their time,   390
And all Holy Church holds them both in hell![2]
And if I should work by their words to win myself Heaven,
Who for their works and wit are now walled up in hell,
Then I'd be working unwisely, whatever you preach.
But of many wise men, in truth, little marvel I have   395
That their spirits have no power by which to please God.
For many men on this earth more set their hearts
On goods than in God; therefore grace fails them—
At the moment of greatest misery mercy would be best,
When they must leave life, a lump of God's grace—   400
As it was with Solomon and such others as showed great intelligence,
But their works, as Holy Writ witnesses, were always the contrary.
Therefore wise-witted men and well-learned clerks
As they say themselves seldom act accordingly
    In Moses' seat, etc.[3]
    But I think it is with a number now as it was in Noah's time   405
When he built that boat of boards and planks:

8. "Thou shalt not commit adultery," which Langland renders "slay not" in the next line, thus conflating the fifth and sixth commandments: Exod. 20:13–14, Luke 18:20.
9. Rom. 12:19; cf. Deut. 32:35.
1. John 3:13.
2. The fate of the "Righteous Heathen," a category that includes righteous pagans and biblical figures who lived before Christ, was a recurrent concern in the Middle Ages. Cf. pp.415 ff.
3. Matt. 23:2: the verse continues, "have sat the Scribes and the Pharisees."

Was nevere wrighte saved that wrought theron, ne other
  werkman elles,
But briddes and bestes and the blissed Noe,
And his wyf with his sones and also here wyves;
410 Of wrightes that it wroughte was none of hem y-saved;
God lene it fare nought so bi folke that the feith techen
Of Holi Cherche, that herberwe is, and Goddes hous to save
And shelden us fram shame therinne as Noes shippe did bestes—
And men that maden it amydde the flode adreynten.
415 The *culorum* of this clause curatoures is to mene
That ben carpenteres Holy Kirke to make for Crystes owne bestes:
      Homines et jumenta salvabis, Domine, etc.
[At Domesday the deluvye worth of deth and fyre at ones;
Forthi I conseille yow clerkes, of Holy Kirke the wrightes,
Worcheth ye as ye sen y-write, lest ye worthe noght therinne].
420   On Gode Fridaye, I fynde, a feloun was y-saved
That had lyved al his lyf with lesynges and with thefte,
And for he biknewe on the Crosse and to Cryste shrof hym
He was sonnere saved than Seynt Johan Baptiste
[Or] Adam or Isaye or eny of the prophetes
425 That hadde y-leine with Lucyfer many longe yeres;
A robbere was y-raunceouned rather than thei alle
Withouten penaunce of purgatorie to perpetuel blisse.
Thanne Marye Magdaleyne [who myghte do] worse?
Or who [dide] worse than David that Uries deth conspired,
430 Or Poule the Apostle that no pitee hadde
Moche Crystene kynde to kylle to deth?
And [now] ben [suche] as sovereynes wyth seyntes in Hevene,
Tho that wroughte wikkedlokest in worlde tho thei were,
And tho that wisely wordeden and wryten many bokes
435 Of witte and of wisdome with dampned soules wonye.
That Salamon seith I trowe be soth and certeyne of us alle:
      Sunt justi atque sapientes et opera eorum in manu
          Dei sunt.
'There aren witty and wel-libbyng ac her werkes ben y-hudde
In the hondes of almighty God;' and he wote the sothe
Wher for love a man worth allowed there and his lele werkes,
440 Or elles for his yvel wille [and] envye of herte
And be allowed as he lyved so: for bi lyther men knoweth the gode;
And wherby wote men whiche is whyte if alle thinge blake were,
And who were a gode man but if there were some shrewe?
Forthi lyve we forth with lither men; I leve fewe ben gode,

No carpenter who came to work on it was saved, nor any kind of
    workman,
But birds and beasts and the blessed Noah,
And his wife and his sons and also their wives;
None of the carpenters who constructed it came to be saved;   410
God forbid it fare thus with the folk who teach the faith
Of Holy Church, our harborage, and God's house to save
And shield us from shame as Noah's ship did beasts—
And that the men who made it amid the sea drowned.
The *culorum*[4] of this clause refers to ecclesiastics   415
Who are carpenters to build Holy Kirk* for Christ's own beasts:
    O Lord, thou preservest men and beasts, etc.[5]
At Doomsday will come a deluge of death and fire together;
Therefore I counsel you clerks, carpenters of Holy Church,
Work the way you've seen it written, lest you not be one who's in it.
    On Good Friday, I find, a felon was saved   420
That had lived all his life with lies and theft,
And because he confessed on the Cross and shrove himself to Christ
He was sooner saved than Saint John the Baptist
Or Adam or Isaiah or any of the prophets
That had lain with Lucifer many long years;   425
A robber was ransomed rather than them all
Without punishment in purgatory to perpetual bliss.[6]
Than Mary Magdalene who might do worse?[7]
Or who did worse than David who devised Uriah's death,
Or Paul the Apostle who pitilessly   430
Killed all kinds of Christian people?[8]
But now such are sovereigns with saints in Heaven,
Those who worked most wickedly when they were on earth,
And those who spoke their minds most wisely and wrote many books
Of wit and wisdom dwell with damned souls.   435
What Solomon says I think is true and certain of us all:
    *There are righteous and wise men and their works are in the hand
        of God.*[9]
'There are witty and well-living but their works are hidden
In the hands of almighty God;' and he knows the truth
Whether a man will be let in there for love and for his loyal deeds,
Or else for his evil will and envy of heart   440
And let in because he lived so: for by the wicked men learn the good;
And whereby would men know what white is if everything were black,
And what a good man was like unless there were some scoundrels?
Therefore let's live along with evil men; I believe few are good,

4. "Conclusion."
5. Ps. 35:7.
6. Luke 23:39–43. St. John the Baptist is listed with the Old Testament figures because, though he
    baptized Christ (Matt. 3), he was killed by Herod before Christ saved mankind (Matt. 14:1–12).
7. Mary Magdalene (Luke 8:2) was associated with the sinner of Luke 7:37–50 and with the sister
    of Lazarus and of Martha, whom Jesus praised because she chose "the better part" of sitting at his
    feet (Luke 10:38–42). She was regarded as the archetypal corrupt but repentant woman.
8. King David, when he desired Bathsheba, orchestrated things so that her husband Uriah was killed
    in battle (2 Sam. 11). Before his conversion to Christianity, St. Paul was a zealous persecutor of
    Christians, especially the first martyr, Stephen (Acts 7:57–59).
9. Eccl. 9:1

445 For *'quant oportet vient en place, il ny ad que pati.'*
And he that may al amende have mercy on us alle.
For sothest worde that evere God seyde was tho he seyde
    Nemo bonus.
[And yet have I foryete ferther of fyve wittes techyng
That] Clergye tho of Crystes mouth commended was it litel,
450 For he seyde to Seynt Peter and to suche as he loved,
    Dum steteritis ante Reges et presides nolite cogitare.
'Though ye come bifor kynges and clerkes of the lawe,
Beth noughte [afered of that folke], for I shal [gyve yow tonge],
[Kunnynge and clergie to conclude hem alle].'
Davyd maketh mencioun he spake amonges kynges
455 And mighte no kynge overcome hym as bi kunnyng of speche.
But witte ne wisdome wan nevere the maystrye
Whan man was at myschief withoute the more grace.
The doughtiest doctour and devynoure of the Trinitee
Was Augustyn the olde, and heighest of the foure;
460 Sayde thus in a sarmoun—I seigh it writen ones—
*'Ecce ipsi idiote rapiunt Celum ubi nos sapientes
    in inferno mergimur.'*
And is to mene to Englisshmen, more ne lasse,
Aren none rather y-ravysshed fro the righte byleve
Than ar this cunnynge clerkes that conne many bokes,
465 Ne none sonner saved ne sadder of bileve
Than plowmen and pastoures and pore comune laboreres,
Souteres and sheperdes: suche lewed jottes
Percen with a Paternoster the paleys of Hevene,
And passen purgatorie penaunceles at her hennes-partyng
470 Into the [parfit] blisse of Paradys for her pure byleve
That inparfitly here knewe and eke lyved.
Yee, men knowe clerkes that han cursed the tyme
That evere thei couth [konne on boke] moore than *Credo in Deum
    Patrem*
And pryncipaly her Paternoster; many a persone hath wisshed.
475 I se ensamples myself, and so may many another,
That servauntes that serven lordes selden falle in arrerage,
But tho that kepen the lordes catel, clerkes and reves.
Right so lewed [laboreres] and of litel knowyng
Selden falle so foule and so fer in synne
480 As clerkes of Holi Kirke that kepen Crystes tresore,
The which is mannes-soule-to-save, as God seith in the Gospel:
    Ite vos in vineam meam."

For 'when necessity comes near, there's nothing to do but suffer.'[1]   445
And may he that amends everything have mercy on us all.
For the most certain thing God ever said was when he said
    Nemo bonus.[2]
And yet further I've forgotten from five wits'[3] teaching
That Clergy* was ever commended by Christ's words,
For he said to Saint Peter and such as he loved,   450
    When you shall stand before rulers and kings take no thought.[4]
'Though you come before kings and clerks of the law,
Be not afraid of that folk, for I shall lend you tongue,
Cunning and clergy to confound them all.'
David makes mention he spoke among kings
And no king could overcome him in cunning of speech.[5]   455
But neither wit nor wisdom ever won a victory
When man was in misfortune without the more grace.
The doughtiest doctor and diviner of the Trinity
Was Augustine* the old, and highest of the four;[6]
He said this in a sermon—I saw it written once—   460
'Behold the ignorant themselves seize Heaven while we wise men are
    sunk in hell.'[7]
And this is to mean to Englishmen, the mighty and the small,
Are none more readily ravished from the right belief
Than are these clever clerks that quote many books,
Or none sooner saved or surer in their faith   465
Than plowmen and pasture-men and poor common laborers,
Shoemakers and shepherds: such ignorant dolts
Pierce with a Paternoster* the palace of Heaven,
And pass through purgatory penanceless at their parting hence
Into the perfect bliss of Paradise for their pure faith   470
Who led imperfect lives here and had little knowledge.
Aye, men recall clerks who have cursed the time
That they ever cared to construe more in a book than *Credo in Deum*
    Patrem[8]
And especially their Paternoster; many a parson has wished it.
I see examples myself, and so may many others,   475
That servants who serve lords seldom fall in arrears,
But those who keep the lord's accounts, such as clerks and reeves.*
Just so unlettered laborers and of little knowing
Seldom fall so foully and so far into sin
As clerks of Holy Kirk that keep Christ's treasure,   480
Which is man's-soul-to-save, as God says in the Gospel:
    Go ye into my vineyard."[9]

---

1. This saying, which Langland gives in a mixture of Latin and French, is proverbial.
2. "No one [is] good [save one, that is, God]": Luke 18:19.
3. The five senses: sight, hearing, touch, taste, and smell.
4. Mark 13:9, 11.
5. Ps. 118:46.
6. The four doctors: St. Ambrose,* St. Augustine,* St. Jerome,* and St. Gregory the Great.*
7. Not from a sermon by Augustine, but from his *Confessions*, VIII, 8.
8. "I believe in God, the Father [Almighty]": the beginning of the Apostles' Creed.
9. Matt. 20:4.

Passus XI

Thanne Scripture scorned me and a skile tolde,
And lakked me in Latyne, and lighte by me she sette,
And seyde "*Multi multa sciunt et seipsos nesciunt.*"
Tho wepte I for wo and wratth of her speche,
5   And in a wynkyng [worth til I wex] aslepe.
     A merveillouse meteles mette me thanne
That I was ravisshed right there—Fortune me fette
And into the londe of longynge [and love] she me broughte,
And in a myroure that hight Mydlerd she mad me to biholde.
10   Sitthen she sayde to me, "Here myghtow se wondres,
And knowe that thow coveytest and come therto, paraunter."
Thanne hadde Fortune folwyng hir two faire damoyseles;
Concupiscentia-Carnis men called the elder mayde,
And Coveytise-of-Eyes [that other was y-called].
15   Pryde-of-Parfyte-Lyvynge pursued hem bothe
And badde me for my contenaunce acounte
          Clergye lighte.
Concupiscentia-Carnis colled me aboute the nekke
And seyde, "Thow art yonge and yepe and hast yeres ynowe
For to lyve longe and ladyes to lovye,
20   And in this myroure thow myghte se myrthes ful manye
That leden the wil to lykynge al thi lyftyme."
The secounde seide the same: "I shal suwe thi wille;
Til thow be a lorde and have londe leten the I nelle,
That I ne shal folwe thi felawship if Fortune it lyke."
25   "He shal fynde me his frende," quod Fortune therafter;
"The freke that folwed my wille failled nevere blisse."
Thanne was there one that highte Elde that hevy was of
          chere:
"Man," quod he, "if I mete with the, bi Marie of Hevene,
Thow shalt fynde Fortune the faille at thi moste nede,
30   And *Concupiscentia-Carnis* clene the forsake;
Bitterliche shaltow banne thanne, bothe dayes and nightes,
Coveytise-of-Eyghe that evere thow hir knewe;
And Pryde-of-Parfyt-Lyvynge to moche peril the brynge."
     "Yee? Recche the nevere," quod Recchelesnes, stode forth
          in ragged clothes.
35   "Folwe forth that Fortune wole; thow hast wel fer til Elde.
A man may stoupe tymes ynow whan he shal tyne the croune.
'*Homo proponit,*' quod a poete, and Plato he hyght,
And '*Deus disponit,*' quod he; lat God done his wille.
If Trewthe wil witnesse, it be wel do Fortune to folwe;
40   *Concupiscentia-Carnis* ne Coveityse-of-Eyes
Ne shal nought greve the gretly, ne bigyle the, but thow wolt."

Passus XI

Then Scripture scorned me and spoke her mind,
And belittled me in Latin, and made light of me,
And said, *"Many men know many things and don't know themselves."*[1]
Then I wept at her words, for woe and for anger,
And grew drowsy and dozed off into a deep sleep.[2]   5
   A most marvelous dream came to me then
That I was fetched away forcibly—Fortune seized me
And into the land of longing and love she brought me,
And made me look into a mirror called Middle Earth.
Afterwards she said to me, "In this you might see wonders,   10
And recognize what you really want and reach it, perhaps."
Then Fortune had following her two fair damsels;
Concupiscentia-Carnis[3] men called the elder maid,
And Covetousness-of-Eyes the other was called.
Pride-of-Perfect-Living pursued them both   15
And said that for appearance's sake I should pay small heed to
    Clergy.*
Concupiscentia-Carnis clasped me about the neck
And said, "You are young and yeasty and have years enough ahead
To live a long life and make love to ladies,
And in this mirror you might see mirths by the score   20
That will lead you to delight all your lifetime."
The second said the same: "I shall serve your pleasure;
Till you're a lord and have land I'll not leave you ever,
But will follow in your fellowship if Fortune pleases."
"He shall find me his friend," said Fortune then;   25
"The fellow that followed my will never failed to have bliss."
Then was there one called Old Age that was unhappy of
    countenance:
"Man," said he, "if I meet you, by Mary of Heaven,
You'll find Fortune failing you at your greatest need,
And *Concupiscentia-Carnis* will clean forsake you;   30
Your curses will be bitter, both day and night,
For Covetousness-of-Eyes, that ever you knew her;
And Pride-of-Perfect-Living will put you in great danger."
   "Yes? Don't take him seriously," said Recklessness, standing forth
    in ragged clothes.
"Follow whatever Fortune wills; you've far to go till Age.   35
It's time enough for a man to stoop when he starts going bald.
'*Man proposes,*' said a poet then, and Plato* was his name,
'*And the Deity disposes,*'[4] said he; let God do his will.
If Truth will witness, it's well done to follow Fortune;
Concupiscentia-Carnis and Covetousness-of-Eyes   40
Will not grieve you greatly nor, unless you wish, beguile you."

---

1. The opening of a popular monastic meditation on penance and forgiveness.
2. Here begins a dream within a dream, which runs to XI.405.
3. "Lust of the Flesh": 1 John 2:16 warns against "the lust of the flesh and the lust of the eye,* and
   the pride of life, . . . [which are] not of the Father, but . . . of the world."
4. Proverbial, ultimately deriving from Prov. 16:9.

"Yee, farewel Phippe," quod Fauntelté, and forth gan me drawe
Til *Concupiscentia-Carnis* acorded alle my werkes.
"Allas, eye!" quod Elde and Holynesse bothe,
45 "That witte shal torne to wrecchednesse for Wille to have his lykyng!"
Coveityse-of-Eyghes conforted me anon after
And folwed me fourty wynter and a fyfte more,
That of Do-Wel ne Do-Bet no deyntee me thoughte.
I had no lykynge, leve me, the leste of hem to knowe.
50 Coveytyse-of-Eyes cam ofter in mynde
Than Do-Wel or Do-Bet amonge my dedes alle.
Coveytise-of-Eyes conforted me ofte.
"Have no conscience," [quod she], "how thow come to gode.
Go confesse the to sum frere, and shewe hym thi synnes.
55 For whiles Fortune is thi frende, freres wil the lovye,
And [festne] the [in] her fraternité and for the biseke
To her Priour Provyncial a pardoun forto have,
And preyen for the pol bi pol yif thow be *pecuniosus.*"
      Set pena pecuniaria non sufficit pro spiritualibus delictis.
   By wissynge of this wenche I [did], here wordes were so swete,
60 Tyl I [foryede] youthe and yarn into elde.
And thanne was Fortune my foo for al hir faire biheste,
And poverté pursued me and put me lowe.
And tho fonde I the frere aferde and flyttynge bothe,
Ayeines owre firste forward, for I seyde I nolde
65 Be buryed at her hous but at my parissh cherche.
For I herde onys how Conscience it tolde:
[At kirke] there a man were crystened by kynde he shulde be buryed.
And for I seyde thus to freres, a fool thei me helden,
And loved me the lasse for my lele speche.
70 Ac yet I cryed on my confessoure that helde hymself so kunnyng,
"By my feith, frere," quod I, "ye faren lyke thise woweres
That wedde none wydwes but forto welde here godis.
Righte so, by the Rode, roughte ye nevere
Where my body were buryed bi so ye hadde my silver.
75 Ich have moche merveille of yow, and so hath many another,
Why yowre covent coveyteth to confesse and to burye
Rather than to baptise barnes that ben catekumelynges.
Baptizyng and burying, bothe ben ful nedeful,
Ac moche more merytorie, me thynke, it is to baptize.
80 For a baptized man may, as maistres telleth,
Thorugh contricioun [clene] come to the heigh Hevene,
     Sola contricio delet peccatum.
Ac a barne withoute bapteme may nought so be saved:
     Nisi quis renatus fuerit.
Loke, ye lettred men, whether I lye or noughte."

"Yes, farewell, Phip,"[5] said Childishness, and drew me forth with him
Till *Concupiscentia-Carnis* accorded to all my deeds.
"Oh, alas!" said Old Age and Holiness both,
"That wit will turn to wretchedness so Will may have his pleasure!"   45
Covetousness-of-Eyes comforted me straightway
And followed me forty winters and a fifth more,
So that I didn't give a damn for Do-Well and Do-Better.
I had no liking, believe me, to learn the least thing about them.
Covetousness-of-Eyes came more often in my mind   50
Than Do-Well or Do-Better did among all my doings.
Covetousness-of-Eyes comforted me often.
"Have no scruple," she said, "how you succeed to wealth.
Go find some friar to confess to, and fill him with your sins.
For while Fortune is your friend, friars will love you,   55
And embrace you in their brotherhood and ask a boon for you
From their Prior Provincial to get a pardon for you,
And they'll pray for you pate by pate if you're *pecuniosus*."[6]
     Pecunial punishment does not suffice for spiritual sins.[7]
   So sweet were this wench's words I did what she said
Till my young days were done and I'd drifted into age.   60
And then Fortune was my foe for all her fair promises,
And poverty pursued me and put me low.
And then I found the friar afraid and fickle, too,
Contrary to our first compact, because I said I wouldn't
Be buried at their house but at my parish church.   65
For I had heard once how Conscience said it:
A man's body should be rightly buried at the church he was baptized in.
And since I said this to friars, they considered me a fool,
And loved me the less for my legitimate speech.
And yet I confronted my confessor who fancied himself so clever,   70
"By my faith, friar," I said, "I find you like a wooer
Who will wed no woman before her wealth's in his control.
Just so, by the Cross, you couldn't possibly care less
Whose earth covered my corpse once you'd acquired my silver.
I am much amazed at you, and so are many others,   75
Why your fraternity prefers to confess men and bury them
Rather than christen converts and other fit candidates.
Baptizing and burying, both are necessary,
But there's much more merit, it seems to me, in baptizing.
For a baptized man may, as masters* relate,   80
Through contrition come clean to the high Heaven,
     Contrition alone destroys sin.[8]
But without baptism a baby may not be saved:
     Unless a man be reborn.[9]
Look, you learned men, whether I lie or not."

---

5. A childish form of Philip.
6. *Prior Provincial*: head of a regional group of houses of a religious order. *Pate by pate*: i.e., head by
   head, each friar individually. *Pecuniosus*: "rich."
7. Based on canon law.
8. Theological tenet.
9. John 3:5.

And Lewté [loughe] on me [for] I loured [on the frere].

85   "Wherfore lourestow?" quod Lewté, and loked on me harde.

"Yif I durste," quod I, "amonges men this meteles avowe!"

"Ye, bi Peter and bi Poule!" quod he, and [toke] hem bothe to witnesse:

*"Non oderis fratres secrete in corde tuo, set publice argue
      illos."*

"Thei wol alleggen also," quod I, "and by the Gospel preven:

90   *Nolite judicare quemquam."*

"And wherof serveth lawe," quod Lewté, "if no lyf undertoke
      it—

Falsenesse ne faytrye? For sumwhat the Apostle seyde,

Non oderis fratrem.

And in the Sauter also seithe David the prophete,

95   *Existimasti inique quod ero tui similis etc.*

It is *licitum* for lewed men to [legge] the sothe

If hem lyketh and leste—eche a lawe it graunteth

Excepte parsones and prestes and prelates of Holy Cherche.

It falleth noughte for that folke no tales to telle—

100   Though the tale were trewe—and it touched synne.

Thinge that al the worlde wote, wherfore shuldestow spare

[To] reden it in retoryke to arate dedly synne?

Ac be neveremore the fyrste the defaute to blame;

Thoughe thow se yvel sey it noughte fyrste; be sorye it nere
      amended.

105   Thinge that is pryvé, publice thow it nevere.

Neyther for love laude it nought ne lakke it for envye.

      Parum lauda; vitupera parcius."

"He seith sothe," quod Scripture tho, and skipte an heigh and
      preched.

Ac the matere that she meved, if lewed men it knewe,

The lasse, as I leve, lovyen thei wolde

110   [The bileve of owre Lord that lettred men techeth].

This was her teme and her tyxte—I toke ful gode hede—

"Multi to a maungerye and to the mete were sompned,

And whan the peple was plenere comen the porter unpynned the
      yate

And plukked in *pauci* priveliche and lete the remenaunt go rowme."

115   Al for tene of her tyxte trembled myn herte

And in a were gan I waxe and with myself to dispute

Whether I were chosen or nought chosen; on Holi Cherche I thoughte,

That underfonge me atte fonte for one of Goddis chosne.

For Cryste cleped us alle, come if we wolde,

120   Sarasenes and scismatikes and so he dyd the Jewes,

      O vos omnes sicientes venite, etc.

And Lewté* laughed at me because I was louring at the friar.
"Why are you louring?" said Lewté, and looked at me hard.   85
"If I only dared," I declared, "tell this dream among men!"
"Yes, by Peter and by Paul!" said he, and took them both to witness:
Thou shalt not hate the brothers secretly in thy heart, but rebuke them
     publicly."[1]
"They'll produce a passage too," said I, "a proof from the Gospel:
Do not judge any one."[2]   90
"And what purpose does law possess," said Lewté, "if no one reproves
     them—
Falseness and fraudulence? For that's why the Apostle said,
Thou shall not hate the brother [*secretly*].
And in the Psalter also says David the prophet,
Thou thoughtest unjustly that I would be such an one as thyself, etc.[3]   95
It's *licitum*[4] for laymen to allege what's true
If they'd like to and elect to—every law allows it
Except for parsons and priests and prelates of Holy Church.
It's not proper for such people to publish any stories—
Even though the tale were true—if it touched on sin.   100
What the whole world's aware of, why should you hesitate
To write about it in a book to rebuke deadly sin?
But never be the first to blame bad behavior;
Though you see evil don't be the first to say so; be sorry it's not
     amended.
A matter that's not manifest, don't you make it known.   105
Neither laud it for love nor belittle it for malice.
     Be spare in your praise; be more spare in your blame."[5]
"He speaks the truth," said Scripture then, and skipped on high and
     preached.
But the topic that she treated, if untaught men knew it,
The less, I believe, their love would be
For the belief of our Lord that lettered men teach.   110
This was her topic and her text—I took careful note—
"*Multi* were bidden to a marriage, to take meat at the feast,
And when the folk were fully assembled the porter unfastened the
     gate
And passed *pauci*[6] in privately and let the rest go packing."
All troubled by her text I trembled at heart   115
And grew gloomy in mind and began to argue with myself
Whether I was chosen or not chosen; on Holy Church I thought,
Who had befriended me at the font for one of God's chosen.
For Christ called us all, come if we would,
Saracens and schismatics and also the Jews,   120
     O all ye that thirst come, etc.[7]

1. Lev. 19:17.
2. Matt. 7:1.
3. Ps. 49:21.
4. "Licit, lawful."
5. From the Roman Seneca, a Stoic philosopher and dramatist.
6. *Multi* (line 112): "many." *Pauci*: "few": Matt. 22:1–14; the Latin words occur in verse 14, "Many are called, but few are chosen."
7. *Saracens*: a general word for pagans, not just Moslems. *Schismatics*: heretics. *O all ye that thirst come, etc*: Isa. 55:1.

And badde hem souke for synne [saufté] at his breste,
And drynke bote for bale, brouke it whoso myghte.
"Thanne may alle Crystene come," quod I, "and cleyme there entré
By the blode that he boughte us with, and thorugh baptesme after:
    Qui crediderit et baptizatus fuerit, etc.
125 For though a Crystene man coveyted his Crystenedome to reneye,
Rightfulliche to renye no resoun it wolde.
For may no cherle chartre make ne his [chatel] selle
Withouten leve of his lorde: no lawe wil it graunte.
Ac he may renne in arrerage and rowme so fro home
130 And as a reneyed caityf recchelesly [rowmeth] aboute.
Ac Resoun shal rekne with hym [and rebuken hym at the
    laste,
And Conscience acounte with hym] and casten hym in arrerage,
And putten [hym] after in prisone—in purgatorie to brenne;
For his arrerages rewarden hym there, [right] to the Daye of Dome,
135 But if Contricioun [wol] come and crye bi his lyve
Mercy for his mysdedes, with mouth [and] with herte."
    "That is soth," seyde Scripture; "may no synne lette
Mercy alle to amende and Mekenesse hir folwe;
For they beth, as owre bokes telleth, above Goddes werkes:
    Misericordia eius super omnia opera eius."
140 "Yee? Baw for bokes," quod one was broken oute of helle,
"[I], Troianus, a trewe knyghte, [take] witnesse at a pope
How [I] was ded and dampned to dwellen in pyne
For an uncristene creature; clerkis wyten the sothe
That al the clergye under Cryste [ne] mighte me cracche fro helle,
145 But onliche love and leauté and my lawful domes.
Gregorie wist this wel and wilned to my soule
Savacioun for sothenesse that he seigh in my werkes.
And [for] he wepte and wilned [that I] were [saved],
[Graunted me worth] grace [thorugh his grete wille].
150 Wythouten any bede-byddynge his bone was underfonge,
And I saved, as ye may se, withoute syngyng of Masses,
By love and by lernyng of my lyvyng in treuthe,
Broughte me fro bitter peyne there no biddyng myghte."
    Lo, ye lordes, what leuté did by an Emperoure of Rome
155 That was an uncrystene creature, as clerkes fyndeth in bokes;
Nought thorw preyere of a pope, but for his pure treuthe
Was that Sarasene saved, as Seynt Gregorie bereth witnesse.
Wel oughte ye lordes that lawes kepe this lessoun to have in mynde
And on Troianus treuth to thenke, and do treuthe to the peple.
160 [This matere is merke for many, ac, men of Holy Cherche,

And bade them for their sins suck safety at his breast,
And drink remedy for wrong-doing, revel in it who would.
"Then may all Christians come," said I, "and claim entry there
By the blood that he bought us with, and through baptism after:
    He that believeth and is baptized, etc.[8]
For though a Christian man craved to deny his Christianity,   125
Reason would never acknowledge that he might deny it rightfully.
For no churl may make a charter or put his chattels up for sale
Without leave of his lord: no law will grant it.
But he may run in arrears and go roving from home
And roam around recklessly like a runaway prisoner.   130
But Reason shall have a reckoning with him and rebuke him in the
    end,
And Conscience account with him and convict him of debt,
And then put him in prison—to burn in purgatory;
And reward him there for his arrears, right to the Day of Doom,*
Unless Contrition will come and cry in his lifetime   135
For mercy for his misdeeds, with mouth and with heart."
    "That is true," said Scripture; "no sin may prevent
Mercy from amending everything if Meekness go with her;
For they are both, as our books say, above God's works:
    His mercy is above all his works."[9]
"Yeah? Bah for books," said one who'd broken out of hell,   140
"I, Trajan,[1] a true knight, take witness of a pope
How I was dead and damned to dwell in torment
As an unchristian creature; clerks know the truth
That all the clergy* under Christ couldn't snatch me from hell,
But only love and lawfulness and my law-abiding judgments.   145
Gregory was well aware of this and willed to my soul
Salvation for the steadfast truth he saw in my deeds.
And because he wept and wished that I would be saved,
Grace was granted me for the great force of his wishes.
Without special prayers his plea was heeded,   150
And I saved, as you may see, without singing of Masses,
By love and by his learning of my living in truth.
This plucked me out of bitter pain where no praying might."[2]
    Lo, you lords, what lawfulness did for an Emperor of Rome
That was an unchristian creature, as clerks* find in books;   155
Not through prayer of a pope, but purely for his truth
Was that Saracen saved, as Saint Gregory bears witness.
Well ought you lords that keep the laws have this lesson in mind
And think of Trajan's truth, and administer truth to the people.
This matter is murky for many, but, men of Holy Church,   160

8. Mark 16:16.
9. Ps. 144:9.
1. The Roman Emperor Trajan was renowned for his dedication to justice. The story of his being
    saved, even though a pagan, by the intervention of St. Gregory the Great* was widely told in the
    Middle Ages as a solution to the problem of how God deals with the "righteous heathen," and as
    proof that pagans who are sufficiently dedicated to virtues known to them can be saved by the spe-
    cial mercy of God. See p.416.
2. Where Trajan's speech stops and a different one begins (by a speaker who quotes Trajan in line
    171) is unclear.

The *Legenda Sanctorum* yow lereth more largere than I yow telle.
Ac thus lele love and lyvyng in truthe
Pulte out of pyne a paynym of Rome.
Y-blissed be truthe that so brak helle yates
165 And saved the Sarasene from Sathanas power,
Ther no clergye ne couthe, ne konnyng of lawes.
Love and leuté is a lele science,
For that is the boke blissed of blisse and of joye.
God wroughte it and wrote it with his owne fynger,
170 And took it Moises upon the mounte alle men to lere].
"Lawe withouten love," quod Troianus, "leye there a bene!"
Or any science under sonne, the sevene artz and alle,
But if thei ben lerned for owre Lordes love, loste is alle the tyme,
For no cause to cacche silver thereby, ne to be called a mayster,
175 But al for love of owre Lorde and the bet to love the peple.
For Seynte Johan seyde it, and soth aren his wordes:
         Qui non diligit manet in morte.
Whoso loveth noughte, leve me, he lyveth in deth-deyinge.
And that alle manere men, enemys and frendes,
Loven her eyther other and lene hem as herselve.
180 Whoso leneth noughte he loveth noughte, [Lorde] wote the sothe,
And comaundeth eche creature to confourme hym to lovye
[Her evene-Cristene as hemself] and here ennemys after.
For hem that hateth us is owre meryte to lovye,
And [sovereynelyche] pore peple; here prayeres may us helpe.
185 For owre joye and owre [juwele], Jhesu Cryst of Hevene,
In a pore mannes apparaille pursueth us evere,
And loketh on us in her liknesse—and that with lovely chere—
To knowen us by owre kynde herte and castyng of owre eyen
Whether we love the lordes here byfor [the] Lorde of blisse;
190 And exciteth us bi the Evangelye that when we maken festes
We shulde noughte clepe owre kynne therto, ne none kynnes riche:
Cum facitis convivia nolite invitare amicos.
"Ac calleth the careful therto, the croked and the pore;
For yowre frendes wil feden yow, and fonde yow to quite,
Yowre festynge and yowre faire yifte; uche frende quyteth so other.
195 Ac for the pore I shal paye, and pure wel quyte her travaille
That yiveth hem mete or moneye and loveth hem for my sake."
    [Alle myghte God have made riche men if he wolde],
[Ac] for the best ben somme riche and somme beggers and pore.
For alle are we Crystes creatures and of his coffres riche,
200 And bretheren as of o blode, as wel beggares as erles.
For on Calvarye of Crystes blode Crystenedome gan sprynge,
And blody bretheren we bycome there of o body y-wonne,
As *quasi modo geniti* gentil men uche one,

The *Legenda Sanctorum*[3] tells the lesson at greater length than I.
But thus lawful love and living in truth
Pulled out of pain a pagan of Rome.
Blessed be truth that so broke hell's gates
And saved the Saracen from Satan's power,   165
Where no clergy could, nor competence in law.
Love with lawfulness is a reliable science,
For they are the blessed book of bliss and of joy.
God first fashioned it and with his own finger wrote it,
And gave it to Moses on the mountain that all men might learn it.[4]   170
"Law without love," said Trajan, "that's worth less than a bean!"
Or any science under sun, the seven arts and all,
Unless they're learned for our Lord's love, the labor's all lost,
Not for some craft to acquire silver by, or to be called a master,*
But all for the love of our Lord and to love the people better.   175
For Saint John said it, and his sayings are true:
      Who loveth not abideth in death.[5]
Whoever loves not, believe me, he lives in death-dying.
And let folk of all factions, whether friends or enemies,
Love each other and help each other as they would themselves.
Whoever lends no help loves not, the Lord knows the truth,   180
And he commands every creature to conform himself to love
Other Christians as himself and his enemies as well.
For whoever hates us it's our merit to love,
And especially poor people; their prayers may help us.
For our joy and our jewel, Jesus Christ of Heaven,   185
In a poor man's apparel pursues us always,
And looks on us in their likeness—and with lovely countenance—
To find out by our friendly heart and on whom we fix our eyes
Whether we love the lords here before the Lord of bliss;
And he urges us in the Evangel that when we hold feasts   190
We should not ask our kin to come, nor any kind of rich men:
When thou makest feasts call not thy friends.[6]
"But call the care-worn to them, the crippled and the poor;
For your friends will feed you, find ways to pay you back,
For your feasting and fair gift; each friend thus repays the other.
But I shall pay for the poor, and requite the pains they take   195
Who give them meals and money and love men for my sake."
      God might have made all men rich if he'd wished,
But it's for the best that some be rich and some beggars and poor.
For we are all Christ's creatures and his coffers make us rich,
And brothers of one blood, as well beggars as earls.   200
For of Christ's blood on Calvary Christendom sprang,
And we became blood brothers there in the body that won us,
As *quasi modo geniti*[7] gentlemen all,

3. A popular collection of saints' lives (literally, "Readings of Saints"). See p.416.
4. God gave the Ten Commandments to Moses on Mt. Sinai, writing them on two tablets of stone (Exod. 32:15–16).
5. 1 John 3:14.
6. Luke 14:12; Langland's next four lines are based on Luke 14:13–14.
7. "As newborn babes": 1 Pet. 2:2. This text opens the Introit, or beginning of the main part of the Mass, for the Sunday Mass after Easter.

No beggere ne boye amonges us but if it synne made:
    Qui facit peccatum servus est peccati etc.
205 In the Olde Lawe, as [the] lettre telleth, "Mennes sones" men called us
Of Adames issue and Eve, ay til God-man deyde;
And after his resurreccioun *Redemptor* was his name,
And we his bretheren, thourgh hym y-bought, bothe riche and pore.
Forthi love we as leve [children] shal, and uche man laughe up
    other,
210 And of that eche man may forbere, amende there it nedeth,
And every man helpe other, for hennes shal we alle:
    Alter alterius onera portate.
And be we noughte unkynde of owre catel, ne of owre kunnynge neyther,
For noet no man how neighe it is to be y-nome fro bothe.
Forthi lakke no lyf other though he more Latyne knowe,
215 Ne undernym noughte foule, for is none withoute faute.
For whatevere clerkis carpe of Crystenedome or elles,
Cryst to a comune woman seyde, in [comen] at a feste,
That *fides sua* shulde saven hir and salven hir of synnes.
Thanne is byleve a lele helpe, above logyke or lawe.
220 Of logyke ne of lawe in *Legenda Sanctorum*
Is litel allowaunce made, but if bileve hem helpe;
For it is overlonge ar logyke any lessoun assoille,
And lawe is loth to lovye but if he lacche sylver.
Bothe logyke and lawe, that loveth noughte to lye,
225 I conseille alle Crystene cleve noughte theron to sore,
For sum wordes I fynde y-wryten were of Faithes techyng,
That saved synful men, as Seynt Johan bereth wytnesse:
    Eadem mensura qua mensi fueritis, remecietur vobis.
Forthi lerne we the lawe of love as owre Lorde taughte;
230 And as Seynte Gregory seide, for mannes soule helthe
    Melius est scrutari scelera nostra quam naturas rerum.
    Why I move this matere is moste for the pore;
For in her lyknesse owre Lorde ofte hath ben y-knowe.
Witnesse in the Paske wyke, whan he yede to Emaus;
235 Cleophas ne knewe hym naughte that he Cryste were
For his pore paraille and pylgrymes wedes,
Tyl he blessed and brak the bred that thei eten.
So bi his werkes thei wisten that he was Jhesus,
Ac by clothyng thei knewe hym noughte, [so caitifliche he
    yede].
240 And al was in ensample, [sotheliche], to us synful here
That we shulde be low and loveliche, [and lele ech man to other],
And [paciente as pylgrymes], for pylgrymes ar we alle.
And in the apparaille of a pore man and pilgrymes lyknesse
Many tyme God hath ben mette amonge nedy peple,

No beggar or bad-boy is among us unless he were bred by sin:
    Whosoever committeth sin is the servant of sin.[8]
In the Old Law, as the letter tells, men called us "Men's sons"   205
Of Adam's issue and of Eve, always till God-man died;
And after his resurrection *Redemptor*[9] was his name,
And we his brothers, bought by him, both rich and poor.
Therefore let us love like dear children, each man laughing with the
    other,
And with what each man may spare, amend where there's need,   210
And every man help other, for we all must go hence:
    Bear ye one another's burdens.[1]
And let us not be miserly of our money, nor of our minds either,
For no man knows how near's the time he'll be denied both.
Therefore blame nobody else though he has better Latin,
And rebuke no one bitterly, for nobody's without fault.   215
For whatever comment clerks make on Christendom and such,
Christ said to a common woman who'd come in at a feast
That *fides sua*[2] should save her and absolve her of her sins.
Then belief is a reliable help, more than logic or law.
For logic and for law in *Legenda Sanctorum*   220
Is little allowance made, unless belief assists them;
For it's overlong before logic resolves a lesson's meaning,
And law is loath to love before he lays hand on silver.
Both logic and law, if you do not love to lie,
I counsel all Christians not to cling to them too hard,   225
For I find a phrase written that was of Faith's teaching,
That saved sinful men, as Saint John bears witness:
With the same measure ye mete, it shall be measured to you.[3]
Therefore let's learn the law of love as our Lord taught;
And as Saint Gregory* said, for man's soul's health   230
It is better to examine our sins than the natures of things.[4]
    Why I'm making much of this matter is mostly for the poor;
For in their likeness our Lord has often let himself be seen.
Witness in Easter week, when he went to Emmaus;
Cleophas could not tell that it was Christ who came   235
Because of his poor apparel and pilgrim's clothes,
Till he blessed and broke the bread that they ate.[5]
Thus by his works they became aware that he was Jesus,
But by clothing they could not recognize him, he came dressed so
    wretchedly.
And this was all an example, surely, to us sinful here   240
That we should be lowly and loving, and loyal to each other,
And patient like pilgrims, for pilgrims are we all.
And in the apparel of a poor man and in pilgrim's likeness
Many a time God has been met among needy people,

8. John 8:34.
9. "Redeemer."
1. Gal. 6:2.
2. "Her faith": Luke 7:50 (which reads, "thy faith").
3. Not John but Matt. 7:2.
4. A common maxim, for which no exact source in Gregory has been identified.
5. The appearance of the resurrected Christ is recounted in Luke 24:13–32.

245 There nevere segge hym seigh in secte of the riche.
Seynt Johan and other seyntes were seyne in pore clothynge,
And as pore pilgrymes preyed mennes godis,
Jhesu Cryste on a Jewes doughter alyghte, gentil woman though she
    were
Was a pure pore mayde and to a pore man wedded.
250 Martha on Marye Magdeleyne an huge pleynte she made
And to owre Saveour self seyde thise wordes:
"Domine non est tibi cure quod soror mea reliquit me sola ministrare?"
And hastiliche God answered, and eytheres wille [lowed],
Bothe Marthaes and Maries, as Mathew bereth witnesse.
255 Ac poverté God put bifore, and preysed it the bettre:
    "Maria optimam partem elegit, que non
      anfertur ab ea."
And alle the wyse that evere were, by aughte I can aspye,
Preysen poverté for best lyf if pacience it folwe,
And bothe bettere and blisseder by many folde than ricchesse.
Although it be soure to suffre, there cometh swete after.
260 As on a walnot withoute is a bitter barke,
And after that bitter barke, be the shelle aweye,
Is a kirnelle of conforte kynde to restore.
So is after poverté or penaunce pacientlyche y-take:
Maketh a man to have mynde in Gode and a grete wille
265 To wepe and to wel bydde, wherof wexeth mercy,
Of which Cryst is a kirnelle to conforte the soule.
And wel sykerer he slepyth, the [segge] that is pore,
And lasse he dredeth deth, and in derke to be robbed
Than he that is righte ryche; Resoun bereth wytnesse:
    Pauper, ego, ludo dum tu, dives, meditaris.
270 Although Salamon seide, as folke seeth in the Bible,
Divicias nec paupertates, etc.
Wyser than Salamon was bereth witnesse and taughte
That parfyte povert was no possessioun to have,
And lyf moste lykynge to God, as Luke bereth witnesse;
    Si vis perfectus esse, vade et vende, etc.
275 And is to mene to men that on this molde lyven,
Whoso wil be pure parfyt mote possessioun
    forsake,
Or selle it, as seith the Boke, and the sylver dele
To beggeres that begge and bidden for Goddes love.
For failled nevere man mete that myghtful God served;
280 As David seith in the Sauter, to suche that ben in wille
To serve God godeliche ne greveth hym no penaunce:
    Nichil inpossibile volenti,
Ne lakketh nevere lyflode, lynnen ne wollen:

Where none ever encountered him clad in the costume of the rich.   245
Saint John and other saints were seen in poor clothing,
And as poor pilgrims prayed men for their goods,
Jesus Christ alighted in a Jew's daughter, and though she was a gentle
    woman
She was a most impoverished maid and married to a poor man.[6]
Martha made a great complaint about Mary Magdalene   250
And to our Savior himself said these words:
"Lord, dost thou not care that my sister hath left me to serve alone?"[7]
And God answered hastily, allowing each her way,
Both Martha and Mary, as Matthew bears witness.
But poverty God placed ahead, and praised it for the better: 255
    "Mary hath chosen the best part, which shall not be taken
        away from her."
And all the wise men that ever were, from what I can tell,
Praise poverty as the best life if patience accompany it,
And both better and blesseder by many times than riches.
Although it's sour to suffer, there comes a sweetness afterward.
As on a walnut on the outside is a bitter bark,   260
And under that bitter bark, once the shell's been removed,
Is a kernel of comfort that can restore health.
So it is after poverty or penance have been patiently suffered:
They make a man put his mind on God and move him to wish eagerly
To weep and to pray well, from which there wells up mercy,   265
Of which Christ is a kernel to comfort the soul.
And far sounder sleep is sent to the poor man,
And he dreads death less, and darkness with its robbers
Than he that wields much wealth; let the witness be Reason:
    I, the poor man, play while you, the rich, are anxious.[8]
Although Solomon* said, as folk see in the Bible,   270
Neither riches nor poverty, etc.[9]
A man wiser than Solomon was bore witness and taught
That perfect poverty was to have no possessions,
And a life that God likes most, as Luke bears witness;
    If thou wilt be perfect, go and sell, etc.[1]
And this means to men that move over this earth,   275
Whoever wishes to be wholly perfect has to give up all his
    possessions,
Or sell them, as the Book says, and dispense his silver
To beggars who for God's love beg and bid their prayers.
For meat never failed any man who served mighty* God;
As David says in the Psalter,* such as desire   280
To serve God goodly are grieved by no penance:
    Nothing shall be impossible to him who desires,[2]
Nor does he ever lack livelihood, linen or woolen:

---

6. The account of the Annunciation is in Luke 1:26–38, but the notion that Mary was genteel and
   poor comes from medieval tradition.
7. Luke 10:40 (line 255a is from Luke 10:42).
8. Proverbial.
9. Prov. 30:8: the verse reads, "give me neither poverty nor riches. . . ."
1. Not Luke but Matt. 19:21; the *wiser* man in line 272 is Jesus.
2. Matt. 17:19.

Inquirentes autem dominum non minuentur omni
          bono.
If prestes weren [wise], thei wolde no sylver take
For Masses ne for matynes—noughte her mete of usureres,
285 Ne neither kirtel ne cote, theigh they for colde shulde deye,
And thei her devor dede, as David seith in the Sauter:
          Judica me, deus, et discerne causam meam.
Spera in deo speketh of prestes that have no spendyng sylver,
That yif thei travaille trewlich and trusten in God almighti,
Hem shulde lakke no lyflode, noyther wollen ne lynnen.
290 And the title that thei take ordres by telleth ye ben avaunced.
Thanne nedeth noughte yow to [nyme] sylver for Masses that ye syngen,
For he that toke yow yowre tytle shulde take yow yowre wages,
Or the bisshop that [blessed] yow [and enbawmed youre fyngres].
For made nevere no kynge no knyghte but he hadde catel to spende
295 As bifel for a knighte, or fonde hym for his strengthe.
It is a careful knyghte, and of a caytyve kynges makynge,
That hath no londe ne lynage riche ne good loos of his handes.
The same I segge, for sothe, by alle suche prestes
That han noyther kunnynge ne kynne, but a croune
          one,
300 And a tytle, a tale of noughte, to his lyflode at myschief.
He [oughte no] bileve, as I leve, to lacche thorw his
          croune,
[More than cure] for konnyng or "knowen for clene of
          berynge."
A chartre is chalengeable byfor a chief justice:
If false Latyne be in [the] lettre, the lawe it inpugneth,
305 Or peynted parenterlinarie, parceles over-skipped.
The gome that gloseth so chartres for a goky is holden.
So is it a goky, by God, that in his Gospel failleth,
Or in Masse or in matynes maketh any defaute:
Qui offendit in uno in omnibus est reus, etc.
310 And also in the Sauter seyth Davyd to overskippers:
Psallite Deo nostro; psallite quoniam rex terre
          Deus Israel; psallite sapienter.
The bisshop shal be blamed bifor God, as I leve,
That crouneth suche Goddes knightes that conneth nought *sapienter*
Synge ne Psalmes rede ne segge a Messe of the day.
315 Ac never neyther is blamelees, the bisshop ne the chapleyne;
For her eyther is endited and that of *Ignorantia*

But they that seek the Lord shall not be deprived of any good
          thing.[3]
If priests were wise, they would take no silver
For Masses or for matins*—nor take meat from usurers,
Nor either kirtle[4] or coat, though the cold killed them,   285
If they did their duty, as David says in the Psalter:
          Judge me, O God, and distinguish my cause.[5]
Spera in deo[6] speaks of priests that have no silver to spend,
That if they toil truly and trust in God almighty,
They should lack no livelihood, neither linen nor woolen.
And the title that you take in orders tells that you've been preferred.   290
Then you need accept no silver for singing Masses,
For he should award you your wages who awarded you your title,
Or else the bishop that blessed you and put balm on your fingers.[7]
For a king would make no man a knight unless he'd money to spend
As was fitting for a knight, or else he'd fund him for his prowess.   295
It's an uneasy knight, made by an ignoble king,
That has no property or rich parentage or prowess of his deeds.
I say the same, be sure, of all such priests
That have neither keen minds nor kindred, but a tonsured crown
          only,
And a title, a useless trifle, to trust to when one's needy.   300
He ought to rely on no more livelihood, I believe, because of his
          tonsure,
Than a church-living for his learning and for being "allowed of good
          behavior."
A charter is challengeable before a chief justice:
If false Latin is in the language, the law impugns it,
Or if there's lettering between the lines, or passages left out.   305
Whoever handles a charter so is held to be a goose.
So is he a goose, by God, that's faulty in Gospel-reading,
Or makes any mistake in Mass or in matins:
Who offends in one point is guilty in all.[8]
And also in the Psalter David says to over-skippers: 310
Sing praise to our God; sing praise since the king of the world is the
          God of Israel; sing praises wisely.[9]
The bishop shall be blamed before God, I believe,
That names those as God's knights who cannot *sapienter*[1]
Sing or read Psalms or say a Mass of the day.
But neither shall be blameless, the bishop or the chaplain;   315
For each one is an offender and the charge is *Ignorantia*

---

3. Ps. 33:11.
4. A knee-length tunic.
5. Ps. 42:1.
6. "Trust in God": Ps. 36:3.
7. The question of whether priests should be paid for their services (and, if so, by whom) was a
    burning issue in Langland's time. The person responsible for certifying one's fitness to be a priest
    and consecrating him as such (*blessed you and put balm on your fingers*—line 293) would be the
    bishop.
8. Jas. 2:10.
9. Ps. 46:7–8.
1. "Wisely."

Non excusat episcopos nec idiotes prestes.
This lokynge on lewed prestes hath don me lepe fram poverté
The whiche I preyse, there pacyence is, more parfyt than
          ricchesse.
320 Ac moche more in metynge thus with me gan one dispute,
And slepynge I seigh al this, and sithen cam Kynde
And nempned me by my name and bad me nymen hede
And thorw the wondres of this worlde wytte for to take.
And on a mountaigne that Mydelerd hyghte—as me tho thoughte—
325 I was fette forth, by [forbisenes] to knowe
Thorugh eche a creature Kynde my creatoure to lovye.
I seigh the sonne and the see and the sonde after
And where that bryddes and bestes by here make thei yeden,
Wylde wormes in wodes and wonderful foules
330 With flekked fetheres and of fele coloures.
Man and his make I myghte [se] bothe,
Poverté and plenté, bothe pees and werre,
Blisse and bale, bothe I seigh at ones,
And how men token Mede and Mercy refused.
335 Resoune I seighe sothly suen alle bestes,
In etyng, in drynkynge, and in engendrynge of kynde,
And after course of concepcioun, none toke kepe
          of other,
As whan thei hadde ryde in rotey tyme anon [reste thei] therafter;
Males drowen hem to males [al mornyng] bi hemself,
340 And [femelles to femelles ferded and drowe].
There ne was cow ne cow-kynde that conceyved hadde
That wolde belwe after [bole]—ne bore after sowe.
Bothe horse and houndes and alle other bestes
Medled noughte wyth here makes, [save man allone].
345 Briddes I bihelde that in buskes made nestes—
Hadde nevere wye witte to worche the leest.
I hadde wonder at whom and where the pye
[Lerned] to legge the stykkes in whiche she leythe and bredeth.
There nys wrighte, as I wene, shulde worche hir neste to paye;
350 If any masoun made a molde therto, moche wonder it were.
And yet me merveilled more how many other briddes
Hudden and hileden her egges ful derne
[For men sholde hem nought fynde whan thei there-fro wente.
In mareys and mores manye hudden her egges]
355 For fere of other foules and for wylde bestis.
And some troden, [I took kepe], and on trees bredden,
And broughten forth her bryddes so al above the grounde.
And some bryddes at the bille thorwgh brethynge
          conceyved,

Non excusat episcopos nec uneducated priests.[2]
This look at unlearned priests has made me leap away from poverty
Which I praise, when it's in patience's company, as more perfect than
        riches.
Yet much more in my dream some one[3] thus argued with me,   320
And sleeping I saw all this, and soon Kind* came
And named me by name and bade me note carefully
And through the wonders of this world my wits should be sharpened.
And on a mountain called Middle Earth—as it seemed to me then—
I was lifted aloft, to learn by examples   325
To love Kind my creator through every creature of his.
I saw the sun and the sea and the sand after
And where birds and beasts moved beside their mates,
Wild worms in woods and wonderful fowls
With flecked feathers and of various colors.   330
Man and his mate I might see both,
Poverty and plenty, both peace and war,
Bliss and bitterness, both I saw at once,
And how men took Meed* and dismissed Mercy.
I saw how steadily Reason stayed with all beasts,   335
In eating, in drinking, in engendering of species,
And after intercourse caused conception, they took scant heed of
        each other,
As when he'd ridden her in rutting time at once they rested thereafter;
Males withdrew with males all mourning by themselves,
And females with females flocked and herded.   340
There was no cow or cow-kind that had conceived in her womb
That would bellow for a bull—nor boar for a sow.
Both horses and hounds and all other beasts
Would not meddle with their mates, save man alone.
I beheld birds building nests in bushes—   345
No man's imagination could make a match for the simplest.
I wondered from whom and where the magpie
Learned to lay the sticks in which she lays and breeds.
No carpenter could, I think, copy her nest correctly;
If any mason made a mold for it, it would be most wonderful.   350
Yet I marveled more of many other birds
How secretly they screened and concealed their eggs
So that folk should not find them when they flew away.
In marshes and on moors many hid their eggs
For fear of other fowls and for wild beasts.   355
And some trod, I took note, on trees where they bred,
And brought forth their birdlings high above the ground.
And some birds brought about conception by breathing through their
        bills,

2. The Middle English word translated as "uneducated" is actually *idiotes*, "idiots." The Latin means
   "Ignorance does not excuse bishops nor" (no known source).
3. The identity of *some one*, the next speaker, is controversial. Various speakers have been suggested,
   including Scripture (whom Trajan originally interrupted) and Recklessness, a character who
   appears only briefly in this version of the poem (XI.34).

And some kauked; I toke kepe how pekokes bredden.
360 Moche merveilled me what maister thei hadde,
And who taughte hem on trees to tymbre so heigh
There noither buirn ne beste may her briddes rechen.
And sythen I loked upon the see and so forth upon the sterres;
Many selcouthes I seygh ben nought to seye nouthe.
365 I seigh floures in the fritthe and her faire coloures
And how amonge the grene grasse grewe so many hewes,
And somme soure and some swete; selcouthe me thoughte.
Of her kynde and her coloure to carpe it were to longe.
        Ac that moste moeved me and my mode chaunged
370 That Resoun rewarded and reuled alle bestes
Save man and his make; many tyme, [me thoughte],
No resoun hem [ruled, neither riche ne pore].
[Thanne I rebuked Resoun] and righte til hymselven I seyde,
"I have wonder [in my wit], that witty art holden,
375 Why thow ne suwest man and his make that no mysfait hem folwe."
And Resoun arated me, and seyde, "Recche the nevere
Whi I suffre or nought suffre: thiself hast nought to done.
Amende thow it if thow myghte, for my tyme is to abyde.
Suffraunce is a sovereygne vertue and a swyfte venjaunce.
380 Who suffreth more than God?" quod he. "No gome, as I leve.
He mighte amende in a minute-while al that mysstandeth.
Ac he suffreth for somme mannes good, and so is owre bettre.
[Holy Writ," quod that wye, "wisseth men to suffre.
        Propter Deum subiecti estote omni creature.
385 Frenche men and fre men affaiteth thus here children:
Bele vertue est suffrance; mal dire est petite vengeance;
Bien dire et bien suffrir fait lui suffrable a bien venir.
Forthi I rede," quod Resoun, "thow rule thi tonge bettre.
And er thow lakke my lif loke thyn be to preise.
For is no creature under Crist can formen hymselven,
390 And if a man myghte make laklees hymself,
Ech a lif wolde be laklees—leve thow none other.
Ne thow shalt fynde but fewe fayne wolde here
Of here defautes foule bifore hem reherced].
The wyse and the witty wrote thus in the Bible:
395 *De re que te non molestat noli certare.*
For be a man faire or foule, it falleth noughte forto lakke
The shappe ne the shafte that God shope hymselve.
For al that he [wrought] was wel y-do, as Holy Writ witnesseth,
        Et vidit Deus cunta que fecerat, et erant valde
                bona.
And badde every creature in his kynde encrees,
400 Al to murthe with man that most woo tholye
In fondynge of the flesshe and of the Fende bothe.
For man was made of suche a matere he may nought wel astert

And some copulated by cauking;[4] I noticed how peacocks bred.
I marveled much what master they had,   360
And who brought them to build nests on branches so high
That their birdlings were above the reach both of beasts and men.
And later I looked upon the sea and so aloft to the stars;
I saw many marvels I must not speak of now.
I saw flowers in the field and their fair colors   365
And how among the green grass grew so many hues,
And some sour and some sweet; it seemed wonderful to me.
To discuss their kinds and colors would keep me too long.
    But what most moved me and changed my mood
Was that Reason respected and ruled all beasts   370
But man and his mate; many times, I thought,
No reason ruled them, neither rich nor poor.
And then I rebuked Reason and said right to his face,
"It seems strange to me why you, who are considered so intelligent,
Don't follow man and his mate so they don't misbehave."   375
And Reason scolded me, and said, "It's no concern of yours
What I permit and don't permit: mind your own business.
You amend whatever you may, for my time is yet to come.
Sufferance is a sovereign virtue and a swift vengeance.
Who suffers more than God?" he asked. "No man, as I believe.   380
He might in a minute's time amend all that is amiss.
But he suffers for some man's sake, and so it's better for us.
Holy Scripture," said that person, "instructs men to suffer.
    Be ye subject to every creature for God's sake.[5]
Frenchmen and good family men thus try to fashion their children: 385
Forbearance is a virtue fair;   malediction but a vengeance spare;
Pleasant mien and answer   kind bring the forbearing peace of mind.[6]
Therefore I direct you," said Reason, "to rule your tongue better.
And before you belittle my life see that your life merits praise.
For there is no creature under Christ that can form himself,
And if a man might make himself wholly without fault,   390
Everybody would be blameless—believe nothing else.
And you'll find but a few who'd feel happy to hear
A list of their foul faults reviewed in their presence.
The wise and the witty once wrote in the Bible:
In a thing that does not trouble you strive not.[7]   395
For whether a man is foul or fair, it's not fitting to libel
The favor or the form that God fashioned himself.
For all he wrought was well wrought, as Holy Writ witnesses,
    And God saw all things that he had made, and they were very
        good.[8]
And he commanded every creature to increase in its kind,
All to make man merry who must suffer woe   400
From the tempting of the flesh and from the Fiend as well.
For man was made from such a matter that he may not escape

4. Copulating or "treading" as birds do, with the male mounting the female's back.
5. 1 Pet. 2:13.
6. These French verses are evidently contemporary with Langland.
7. Ecclus. 11:9.
8. Gen. 1:31.

That ne sometymes hym bitit to folwen his kynde.
Catoun acordeth therewith: *nemo sine crimine vivit.*
405   Tho caughte I coloure anon and comsed to ben aschamed,
And awaked therwith; wo was me thanne
That I in meteles ne myghte more have y-knowen.
Thanne seyde I to myself, "[Slepyng, hadde I grace]
[To wit] what Do-Wel is, [ac wakyng, nevere]."
410   And as I caste up myn eyghen, one loked on me.
"[What is Do-Wel?" quod that wighte]. "Ywisse, sire," I seide,
"To se moche and suffre more, certes, is Do-Wel."
"Haddestow suffred," he seyde, "slepyng tho thow were,
Thow sholdest have knowen that Clergye can, and conceived
          more thorugh Resoun.
415   For Resoun wolde have reherced the righte as Clergye saide;
Ac for thine entermetyng here artow forsake.
Philosophus esses si tacuisses.
Adam, wiles he spak nought, had Paradys at wille,
Ac whan he mameled aboute mete and entermeted to knowe
The wisdom and the witte of God, he was put fram blisse.
420   And right so ferde Resoun bi the: thow with rude speche
Lakkedest and losedest thinge that longed [the] nought to done.
Tho hadde he [litel] lykynge forto lere the more.
Pruide now and presumpcioun paraventure wole the appele
That Clergye thi compaignye ne kepeth nought to sue.
425   Shal nevere chalangynge ne chydynge chaste a man so sone
As shal shame, and shenden hym, and shape hym to amende.
For lat a dronken daffe in a dyke falle,
Late hym ligge, loke noughte on hym, til hym [list] to ryse,
For though Resoun rebuked hym thanne, [reccheth hym nevere;
430   Of Clergie ne of his conseille he counteth noght a russhe.
To blame or to bete hym thanne] it were but pure synne.
Ac whan nede nymeth hym up, for [nede] lest he sterve,
And shame shrapeth his clothes and his shynes wassheth,
Thanne wote the dronken daffe wherfore he is to blame."
435   "Ye seggen soth!" quod I. "Ich have y-seyne it ofte.
There smitte no thinge so smerte ne smelleth so [foule]
As shame: there he sheweth him [him shonyeth every man].
Why ye wisse me thus," quod I, "was for I rebuked
          Resoun."
"Certes," quod he, "that is soth," and shope hym forto walken,
440   And I aros up right with that and [reverenced] hym [faire,
And if his wille were, he wolde] telle me his name.

So that some times it betides him to follow his nature.
Cato* accords with this: *Nemo sine crimine vivit*."⁹
Then at once my face flushed and I began to feel ashamed,   405
And awaked therewith;¹ I was woeful then
That I might have learned a larger lesson as I lay dreaming.
Then I said to myself, "Sleeping, I had grace
To learn what Do-Well is, but waking, never."
And as I lifted my eyes aloft, some one was looking at me.   410
"What is Do-Well?" said that person. "Well, sir," I said,
"To see much and suffer more surely is Do-Well."
"If you'd suffered," he said, "when you were sleeping just now,
You would have acquired Clergy's knowledge, and conceived more
        through Reason.
For Reason would have reviewed all that Clergy revealed to you;   415
But for your interference you have been forsaken.
*You would have been a philosopher if you had remained silent.*²
While Adam held his tongue, he had Paradise to play in,
But when he fussed about food and fancied he might learn
The wisdom and the wit of God, he was turned away from bliss.
And Reason behaved right so with you: you with rude speech   420
Praised and dispraised things of which you were not a proper judge.
Then he felt small satisfaction in instructing you further.
Now pride and presumption will perhaps bring charges against you,
So that Clergy will no longer care to keep company with you.
Never shall challenging and chiding chasten a man so quickly   425
As shame will, and shatter him, and make him shape up.
For if a drunken fool falls in a ditch,
Let him lie, don't look at him, till he feels like getting up,
For though Reason rebuked him then, he'd not react to it;
For Clergy and his counsel he couldn't care less.   430
To blame him or to beat him then were but a waste of time.
But when necessity snatches him up, lest he expire for need,
And shame scrapes his clothes and washes his shins clean,
Then finally the drunken fool feels why he is to blame."
"You speak truth!" said I. "I've seen it often.   435
Nothing strikes as sharply or smells as foul
As shame: where he shows up he's shunned by everybody.
Why you counsel me thus," I declared, "was because I rebuked
        Reason."
"Certainly," he said, "that is so," and started to walk,
And I arose right then and reverently addressed him,   440
And if it were his will, he would tell me his name.

9. "No one lives without fault": Cato's *Distichs*.
1. The dream within a dream ends here.
2. Boethius (480?–524), *The Consolation of Philosophy*, II, prose 7. The *Consolation* was one of the
   most influential philosophical treatises in the Middle Ages.

Passus XII

"I am Ymagynatyf," quod he; "Idel was I nevere
Thoughe I sitte bi myself, in sikenesse ne in helthe,
I have folwed the, in feithe, this fyve and fourty wyntre
And many tymes have moeved the to [mynne] on thine ende,
5   And how fele fernyeres are faren, and so fewe to come,
And of thi wylde wantounesse [whiles] thow yonge were—
To amende it in thi myddel age, lest mighte the [faylle]
In thyne olde elde that yvel can suffre
Poverté or penaunce, or preyeres bidde:
      Si non in prima vigilia nec in secunda, etc.
10   Amende the while thow myghte—thow hast ben warned ofte
With poustees of pestilences, with poverté and with angres;
And with thise bitter baleyses God beteth his dere childeren:
      Quem diligo castigo, etc.
And David in the Sauter seith of suche that loveth Jhesus,
      Virga tua et baculus tuus, ipsa me consolata sunt, etc.
'Although thow stryke me with thi staffe, with stikke or with yerde,
15   It is but murth as for me, to amende my soule.'
And thow medlest the with makynges and myghtest go sey thi Sauter,
And bidde for hem that yiveth the bred, for there ar
      bokes ynowe
To telle men what Do-Wel is, Do-Bet and Do-Best bothe
And prechoures to preve what it is, of many a peyre freres."
20   I seigh wel he sayde me soth, and somwhat me to excuse
Seid, "Catoun conforted his sone that, clerke though he were,
To solacen hym sumtyme—[so] I do whan I make:
Interpone tuis interdum gaudia curis.
And of holy men I herde," quod I, "how thei otherwhile
Pleyden the parfiter [in here prayeres after].
25   Ac if there were any wight that wolde me telle
What were Do-Wel and Do-Bet, and Do-Best atte laste,
Wolde I nevere do werke but wende to Holi Cherche
And there bydde my bedes but whan Ich eet or slepe."
"Poule in his Pistle," quod he, "preveth what is Do-Wel:
Fides, spes, caritas, et maior horum, etc.
30   'Feith, hope, and charitee, and alle ben good,
And saven men sundry tymes, ac none so sone as charité.'
For he doth wel, withoute doute, that doth as Lewté techeth.
That is, if thow be man maried, thi make thow lovye
And lyve forth as lawe wole while ye lyven bothe.
35   Right so, if thow be religious, renne thow nevere ferther
To Rome ne to Rochemadore, but as thi reule techeth,
And holde the under obedyence that heighwey is to Hevene.

Passus XII

"I am Imaginative,"[1]* said he; "I was never idle
Though I sit by myself, in sickness nor in health,
I've followed you, in faith, these forty-five winters
And many times have moved you to have mind on your end,
And how many are your yesteryears, and so few yet to come,   5
And of your wild wantonness when you were young—
To amend it in your middle age, lest might* fail you
In your old age that ill can endure
Poverty or penance, or pray to good effect:
    If not in the first watch nor in the second, etc.[2]
Amend yourself while you may—you have been warned often   10
By pangs of pestilence, by poverty and ailments;
And with these bitter brooms God beats his dear children:
    Whom I love I castigate, etc.[3]
And in the Psalter* David says of such as love Jesus,
    Thy rod and thy staff, they comforted me.[4]
'Although you strike me with your staff, with stick or with rod,
It's merely mirth to me, to amend my soul.'   15
And you meddle with making verse and might go say your Psalter,
And pray for them that provide your bread, for there are plenty of
    books
To tell men what Do-Well is, Do-Better and Do-Best both
And preachers to explain it all, of many a pair of friars."
I saw well he spoke the truth, and somewhat to excuse myself   20
Said, "Cato* comforted his son, clerk* though he was,
To solace himself sometimes—so I do when I write:
Interpose some pleasures at times among your cares.
And I've heard it said of holy men, how they now and then
Played to be more perfect in their prayers afterward.
But if there were any one who would tell me   25
What Do-Well and Do-Better were, and Do-Best at the last,
I would never do any work but wend to Holy Church
And stay there saying prayers save when I ate or slept."
"Paul in his Epistle," said he, "explains what Do-Well is:
Faith, hope, charity, and the greatest of these, etc.[5]
'Faith, hope, and charity, and all are good,   30
And save men sundry times, but none so soon as charity.'
For he does well, without doubt, who does what Lewté* teaches.
That is, if you're a married man, you must love your mate
And live as law requires as long as you both live.
Right so, if you're a religious,* never run any further   35
To Rome or to Rochemadour,[6] save as your rule teaches,
And hold yourself under obedience that's highway to Heaven.

1. Not "imagination" in the modern sense, but the power to form mental images of things in the exterior world or in the past.
2. Cf. Luke 12:38: the idea is that the Lord *will* come and should find his servants ready.
3. Rev. 3:19; cf. Prov. 3:12.
4. Ps. 22:4. See p. 370.
5. 1 Cor. 13:13.
6. These were popular pilgrimage places.

And if thow be mayden to marye and mighte wel contynue,
Seke thow nevere seynt forther for no soule helthe.
40 [Lo], what made Lucyfer to lese the heigh Hevene,
Or Salamon his sapience, or Sampson his strengthe?
Job the Jewe his joye dere aboughte;
Arestotle and other mo, Ypocras and Virgyle,
Alisaundre that al wan, elengelich ended.
45 Catel and Kynde Witte was combraunce to hem alle;
Felyce hir fayrnesse fel hir al to sklaundre
And Rosamounde right so reufully bysette
The bewté of hir body—in badnesse she dispended.
Of many suche I may rede, of men and of wommen,
50 That wyse wordes wolde shewe, and worche the contrarye;
     Sunt homines nequam bene de virtute loquentes.
And riche renkes right so gaderen and sparen,
And tho men that thei moste haten mynistren it atte laste.
And for thei suffren and se so many nedy folkes
And love hem nought as owre lorde bytte, lesen her soules.
     Date, et dabitur vobis.
55 [So catel and Kynde Wit acombreth ful manye—
Wo is hym that hem weldeth but he hem wel despende!
     Scientes et non facientes varijs flagellis vapulabunt.
Sapience, seith the Boke, swelleth a mannes soule:
     Sapienca inflat, etc].
And ricchesse right so but if the rote be trewe.
Ac grace is a grasse [therfore] tho grevaunces to abate.
60 Ac grace ne groweth noughte [til good wil yeve reyne];
Pacience-And-Poverté the place is there it groweth,
And in lele lyvynge men and in lyf holy,
And thorugh the gyfte of the Holy Goste as the Gospel telleth:
     Spiritus ubi vult spirat.
     Clergye and Kynde Witte comth of sighte and techynge
65 As the Boke bereth witnesse to buirnes that can rede:
     Quod scimus loquimur, quod vidimus testamur.
Of *quod scimus* cometh Clergye, [a] connynge of hevene,
And of *quod vidimus* cometh Kynde Witte, of sighte of dyverse peple.
Ac grace is a gyfte of God and of gret love spryngeth;
Knewe nevere clerke how it cometh forth, ne Kynde Witte the weyes.
     Nescit aliquis unde venit aut quo vadit.
70 Ac yit is Clergye to comende, and Kynde Witte bothe,
And namely Clergye, for Crystes love that of Clergye is rote.
For Moyses witnesseth that God wrote for to wisse the peple

And if you're man or maid unmarried and might well continue so,
Seek no saint further for your soul's health.
Lo, what made Lucifer lose the high Heaven,   40
Or Solomon his sapience, or Samson his strength?[7]
Job the Jew bought his joy dearly;
Aristotle and others too, Hippocrates and Virgil,
Alexander who won everything—all ended badly.
Wealth and Kind Wit* weakened them all;   45
Felicia for her fairness fell into contempt
And Rosamond right so ruinously employed
The beauty of her body—in badness she squandered it.[8]
Of many such I may read, of men and of women,
That could speak wise words, and worked the contrary;   50
        They are worthless men speaking well of virtue.[9]
And just so prosperous people pile up money and hoard it,
And those men that they most hate administer it in the end.
And since they let themselves see so many needy folk
And don't love them as our Lord bade, they lose their souls.
        Give, and it shall be given unto you.[1]
So wealth and Kind Wit weaken many—   55
Woe to him who has them unless he employ them well!
        Those who know and act not they shall beat with many whips.[2]
Sapience, the Book says, swells a man's soul:
        Knowledge puffeth up, etc.[3]
And right so do riches unless they rise from a true root.
But grace is a herb-grass therefor that gives relief for these ailments.
But grace does not grow until good will brings rain;   60
Patience-And-Poverty is the place where it grows,
And in men who live lives lawful and holy,
And through the gift of the Holy Ghost as the Gospel tells:
        The spirit bloweth where it will.[4]
    Clergy* and Kind Wit come of seeing and studying
As the Book bears witness to anybody who can read: 65
        We speak what we know, we testify what we have seen.[5]
Of *quod scimus* comes Clergy, heavenly comprehension,
And of *quod vidimus* comes Kind Wit, of what various men have seen.
But grace is a gift of God and springs from great love;
No clerk ever knew how it comes forth, nor Kind Wit its ways.
        No one knoweth whence it cometh or whither it goeth.[6]
Yet Clergy is to be commended, and Kind Wit too,   70
And especially Clergy, for love of Christ who's Clergy's root.
For Moses records that God wrote to direct the people

7. Solomon was led by his foreign wives into building shrines to pagan gods (I Kings 11:2–4); Samson was betrayed by Delilah (Judg. 16:4–21).
8. The prosperity of Job led God to permit Satan to test him by taking everything from him and inflicting undeserved suffering on him. The classical and medieval figures Aristotle, Hippocrates, Virgil, Alexander the Great, Felice, and Rosamond all die violent deaths.
9. From a Latin epigram that had become proverbial in Langland's time.
1. Luke 6:38.
2. Luke 12:47.
3. 1 Cor. 8:1.
4. John 3:8.
5. John 3:11: "what we know" (*quod scimus*), "what we have seen" (*quod vidimus*).
6. John 3:8.

In the Olde Lawe as the lettre telleth, that was the lawe of Jewes,
That what woman were in avoutrie taken, [wher] riche or pore,
75 With stones men shulde hir stryke and stone hir to deth.
A womman as we fynden was gulty of that dede,
Ac Cryste of his curteisye thorw Clergye hir saved.
For thorw carectus that Cryst wrot the Jewes knewe
  hemselven
Gultier as afor God, and gretter in synne,
80 Than the woman that there was, and wenten awey for schame.
[Thus Clergye there] conforted the womman.
Holy Kirke knoweth this, that Crystes wrytyng saved;
So Clergye is conforte to creatures that repenten,
And to mansed men myschief at her ende.
85 For Goddes body myghte noughte be of bred withouten Clergye,
The which body is bothe bote to the rightful
And deth and dampnacioun to hem that dyeth yvel,
As Crystes [carectes] conforted and bothe coupable shewed,
The womman that the Jewes [jugged] that Jhesus thoughte to save.
  Nolite judicare et non judicabimini.
90 Right so Goddes body, bretheren, but it be worthily taken
Dampneth us atte Daye of Dome as the carectes dede the Jewes.
Forthi I conseille the for Cristes sake Clergye that thow lovye;
For Kynde Witte is of his kyn, and neighe cosynes bothe
To owre Lorde, leve me; forthi love hem, I rede.
95 For bothe ben as miroures to amenden owre defautes
And lederes for lewed men and for lettred bothe.
  Forthi lakke thow nevere logyke, lawe, ne his custumes,
Ne countreplede clerkes, I conseille the forevre.
For as a man may nought se that mysseth his eyghen,
100 Namore can no klerke but if he caught it first thorugh bokes.
Although men made bokes, the maistre [was God],
And Seynt Spirit the saumplarye and seide what men sholde write.
And right as syghte serveth a man to se the heighe strete,
Right so [lereth] letterure lewed men to resoun.
105 And as a blynde man in bataille bereth wepne to fighte
And hath none happ with his axe his enemye to hitte,
Namore kan a kynde-witted man, but clerkes hym teche,
Come for al his kynde witte to Crystendome and be saved;
Whiche is the coffre of Crystes tresore, and clerkes kepe the keyes,
110 To unlouken it at her lykynge, and to the lewed peple
Yyve mercy for her mysdedes if men it wole aske
Buxomelich and benygneliche, and bidden it of grace.
Archa Dei, in the Olde Lawe, Levites it kepten.
Hadde nevere lewed man leve to leggen honde on that chest,
115 [But he were preste or prestes sone, patriarke or prophete.
Saul, for he sacrifised, sorwe hym bityde,

In the Old Law as the letter tells, that was the law of Jews,
That whatever woman was taken in adultery, whether rich or poor,
Men should strike her with stones and stone her to death.[7]   75
A woman as we find was guilty of that deed,
But Christ of his courtesy used Clergy to save her.[8]
For through the characters that Christ wrote the Jews confessed
      themselves
Guiltier before God, and more gravely in sin,
Than the woman that was there, and went away for shame.   80
Thus Clergy there comforted the woman.
Holy Church recognizes that by his writing Christ rescued her;
So Clergy is comfort to creatures that repent,
And to unremorseful men mischief at their ending.
For God's body could not be of bread without Clergy,   85
And that body is both betterment to the righteous
And death and damnation to those who die wicked,
As Christ's characters both comforted and convicted of guilt,
The woman whom the Jews judged that Jesus thought to save.
      Judge not and ye will not be judged.[9]
Just so God's body, brethren, unless it be worthily taken   90
Damns us at the Day of Doom* as the characters did the Jews.
Therefore I counsel you for Christ's sake to give Clergy your love;
For Kind Wit is of his kindred, and both close cousins
Of our Lord, believe me; therefore love them, I say.
For both are like looking-glasses in which we learn to cure our faults   95
And leaders for unlearned men and lettered men as well.
    Therefore do not belittle logic, law, nor its customs,
Nor contradict clerks, I counsel you forever.
For as a man may not see who is missing his eyesight,
No more can any clerk know unless he acquired it first in books.   100
Although men made books, the master was God,
And the Holy Spirit the exemplar who said what men should write.
And just as sight serves a man so he can see the high street,
Just so by literature unlearned men learn to reason.
And as a blind man in battle who bears a weapon to fight   105
Has no luck with his axe to hit his enemy,
No more can a kind-witted man, unless clerks teach him,
Come for all his kind wit to Christendom and be saved;
And that's the coffer of Christ's treasure, and clerks have the keys,
To unlock it when they like, and to unlearned people   110
Give mercy for their misdeeds if men will request it
Humbly and whole-heartedly, and ask it of grace.
Levites in the Old Law looked after *Archa Dei*.[1]
No unlearned man had leave to lay hand on that chest,
Unless he were a priest or a priest's son, patriarch or prophet.   115
Because Saul performed a sacrifice, sorrow came upon him,

7. Deut. 22:23–24.
8. John 8:3–11.
9. Matt. 7:1.
1. "The Ark of God"; see 1 Sam. 13:12 on Saul (line 116 below) and 2 Sam. 6:6–7 on the unsancti-
   fied touching of the sacred Ark containing the stone tablets God gave Moses, on which the Ten
   Commandments were written (lines 118–20). *Levites*: see n. 3, p. 269

And his sones also for that synne myscheved;
And manye mo other men, that were no Levites,
That with *Archa Dei* wenten in worschip and reverence,
120 And leyden hand theron to liften it up, loren here lif after.
      Forthi I conseille alle creatures no Clergie to dispise,
Ne sette shorte bi here science, whatso thei don
          hemselve.
Take we here wordes at worth, for here witnesse be trewe.
And medle nought moche with hem to moeven any wrathe,
125 Lest cheste chafe us to choppe ech man other.
          Nolite tangere christos meos.]
For Clergye is kepere under Cryst of Hevene:
Was there nevere [kyng ne] knyghte but Clergye hym made.
Ac Kynde Witte cometh of alkynnes sightes,
Of bryddes and of bestes, of tastes of treuthe.
130 [Devynours] toforn us [viseden and markeden]
The selkouthes that thei seighen, her sones for to teche.
And helden it an heighe science, her wittes to knowe;
Ac thorugh her science, sothely, was nevere no soule y-saved
Ne broughte by her bokes to blisse ne to joye.
135 For alle her kynde [knowyng] come but of dyverse sightes.
Patriarkes and prophetes repreved her science
And seiden her wordes ne her wisdomes [was] but a folye;
As to the Clergye of Cryst, counted it but a trufle:
          Sapiencia huius mundi stulticia apud Deum.
      For the heighe Holi Goste Hevene shal tocleve
140 And love shal lepe out after into this lowe erthe,
And clennesse shal cacchen it, and clerkes shullen it fynde:
Pastores loquebantur ad invicem.
He speketh there of riche men right nought ne of right
          witty,
Ne of lordes that were lewed men, but of the hexte lettred oute:
          Ibant magi ab oriente.
145 If any frere were founde there, Ich yif the fyve shillynges.
Ne in none beggares cote was that barne borne
But in a burgeys place, of Bethlem the best.
          *Set non erat ei locus in diversorio, et pauper non habet
              diversorium.*
To pastours and to poetes appiered [the] aungel
And bad hem go to Bethlem, Goddis burth to honoure,
150 And songe a songe of solas, *Gloria in excelsis Deo.*
[Riche men rutte tho, and in here reste were,
Tho it shone to sheperdes, a shewer of blisse].
Clerkes knewe it wel and comen with here presentz

And his sons also suffered from that sin;
And many more men, too, who were not Levites,
Who walked with *Archa Dei* in worship and reverence,
And laid hand on it to lift it, lost their lives afterward.   120
    Therefore I counsel all Christians not to condemn Clergy,
Nor make light of clerks' learning, no matter what the clerks are like
    themselves.
Let's assume their words are worthy, for they're witnessed by truth.
And let's not meddle with them much to move anyone to wrath,
Lest ill will so heat us all that we hit out at one another.   125
    Touch not mine anointed.[2]
For Clergy is caretaker under Christ of Heaven:
There could never be king nor knight unless Clergy made him.
But Kind Wit* comes of all kinds of observations,
Of birds and of beasts, of bits of truth.
Diviners before our time surveyed and made note   130
Of the strange things they saw to teach their sons about them.
And considered it a high science, the skill they possessed;
But through such science, in truth, was never one soul saved
Nor brought by their books to bliss or to joy.
For all their natural knowledge came from nothing but observations.   135
Patriarchs and prophets reproved their science
And said their words and their wisdom were merely folly;
Compared to Christ's Clergy they accounted it as trifling:
    The wisdom of this world is foolishness with God.[3]
    For the high Holy Ghost shall hew through Heaven
And love shall leap out into this low earth,   140
And cleanness shall catch it, and clerks shall find it:
The shepherds were talking one to another.[4]
He makes no mention of rich men there nor of men of common
    sense,
Nor of lords that were unlettered, but of the most learned anywhere:
    There came wise men from the east.[5]
If any friar was found there, I'll bet five shillings.   145
That baby was not born in a beggar's cottage
But in a burgess'* house, the best in Bethlehem.
    *But there was no room for him in the inn, and a poor man has no
    inn.*[6]
To shepherds and sages the angel showed himself
And ordered them on to Bethlehem to honor God's birth,
And they sang a song of solace, *Gloria in excelsis Deo.*[7]   150
Rich men then were sound asleep, snoring in their beds,
When it shone to shepherds, a shower of bliss.
Clerks were well aware what it was and came with their presents

2. Ps. 104:15.
3. 1 Cor. 3:19.
4. Luke 2:15.
5. Matt. 2:1.
6. Luke 2:7; that a poor man cannot afford an inn (and that, therefore, if Joseph and Mary were try-ing to get a room, they cannot have been poor) is Langland's addition. The passage reflects a major controversy in Langland's time about whether Christ was poor.
7. "Glory to God in the highest": Luke 2:14.

And deden her homage honourablely to hym that was almyghty.
155 Why I have tolde [the] al this, I toke ful gode hede
How thow contraryedest Clergye with crabbed wordes,
How that lewed men lightloker than lettred were saved,
Than clerkes or kynde-witted men of Crystene peple.
And thow seidest soth of somme, ac se in what manere.
160 Take two stronge men and in Themese caste hem,
And bothe naked as a nedle, her none [sadder] than other;
That one [can] connynge—and can swymmen and dyven.
That other is lewed of that laboure—lerned nevere swymme.
Which trowestow of tho two in Themese is in
     moste drede,
165 He that nevere ne dyved ne nought can of swymmynge,
Or the swymmere, that is sauf bi so hymself lyke,
There his felaw flet forth as the flode lyketh,
And is in drede to drenche, that nevere dede swymme?"
"That swymme can nought," I seide, "it semeth to my wittes."
170 "Right so," quod the renke, "resoun it sheweth
That he that knoweth clergye can sonner aryse
Out of synne and be sauf, though he synne ofte,
If hym lyketh and lest, than any lewed, lelly.
For if the clerke be konnynge he knoweth what is synne,
175 And how contricioun withoute confessioun conforteth the soule,
As thow seest in the Sauter in Psalme one or tweyne
How contricioun is commended, for it caccheth awey synne:
Beati quorum remisse sunt iniquitates, et quorum tecta sunt
     [peccata].
And this conforteth uch a clerke and kevereth hym fram wanhope
In which flode the Fende fondeth a man hardest,
180 There the lewed lith stille and loketh after Lente,
And hath no contricioun ar he come to shryfte, and thanne can
     he litel telle,
[But] as his loresman [lereth] hym bileveth and troweth,
And that is after person or parisch prest, and paraventure [unconnynge]
To lere lewed men, as Luk bereth witnesse:
185 *Dum cecus ducit cecum, etc.*
Wo was hym marked that wade mote with the lewed!
Wel may the barne blisse that hym to boke sette,
That lyvynge after letterure saved hym lyf and soule:
Dominus pars hereditatis meae is a meri verset
190 That has take fro Tybourne twenti stronge theves.
There lewed theves ben lolled up, loke how thei be saved!
The thef that had grace of God on Gode Fryday, as thow speke,

And did their homage honorably to him who was almighty.
Why I have told you all this, I took careful note   155
How you contradicted Clergy with crabbed words,
How with less difficulty than learned men unlearned men were saved,
More easily than clerks or kind-witted men of Christian people.[8]
And you spoke the truth of some, but see in what manner.
Take two strong men and toss them in the Thames,[9]   160
And both naked as a needle, neither sturdier than the other;
One has acquired competence—he can swim and dive.
The other does not know how—he never learned to swim.
Which of those two do you think feels most threatened in the
      Thames,
He who has no notion of swimming and never dived,   165
Or the swimmer, who is safe so long as he himself pleases,
While his companion's carried on as the current pleases,
And is in dread of drowning, the one that never did swim?"
"The one who can't swim," I said, "it seems to my wits."
"Precisely," said that personage, "so it appears by reason   170
That he that's had a clerk's education can sooner arise
Out of sin and be safe, though he sins often,
If he feels it urgent upon him, than uneducated people.
For if the clerk is clever he can tell what sin is,
And how contrition without confession comforts the soul,   175
As you see in the Psalter in a Psalm or two
How contrition is commended, for it clears away sin:
*Blessed are they whose transgressions are forgiven, and whose [sins] are
      covered.*[1]
And this comforts each clerk* and recalls him from wanhope*
Which is the flood in which the Fiend fastens hardest on a man,
While the unlearned man lies still and looks toward Lent,   180
And has no contrition before he comes to confession, and can then
      tell but little,
But what his instructor teaches he trusts and believes,
And that's from a parson or parish priest, and perhaps incompetent
To give lessons to unlearned men, as Luke bears witness:
When the blind lead the blind, etc.[2]   185
Woe was marked out for him that must go wading with the ignorant!
A young man may much thank him who first made him read books,
So that living by written lore delivered him body and soul:
Dominus pars hereditatis meae[3] is a merry little verse
That has taken out of Tyburn twenty flagrant thieves.   190
While unlettered thieves are locked up, look how they're set free![4]
The thief that had grace of God on Good Friday, as you mentioned,[5]

---

8. In X.448–82.
9. The large tidal river along which London is situated. London's principal river.
1. Ps. 31:1.
2. Matt. 15:14, but Luke 6:39 is similar.
3. "The Lord is the portion of mine inheritance": Ps. 15:5.
4. *Tyburn*: place of public execution in London. *Twenty flagrant thieves*: Langland refers to the "neck verse"; if a criminal could show he had a clerical education by reading a passage in a Latin Bible, his life (or neck) was spared because a cleric was accountable to the Church, not to the State's criminal law.
5. In X.420–27 and also in V.461–70.

—Was for he yelte hym creaunt to Cryst and
    knewleched hym gulty,
And grace axed of God, [that graith is hem evere]
195 That boxomeliche biddeth it and ben in wille to amenden hem.
Ac though that thef had Hevene, he hadde none heigh blisse,
As Seynt Johan and other seyntes that asserved hadde bettere.
Right as sum man yeve me mete and sette me amydde the
    flore;
Ich have mete more than ynough, ac nought so moche worship
200 As tho that seten atte syde table or with the sovereignes of the halle,
But as a begger, bordelees, bi myself on the grounde.
So it fareth bi that feloun that a Gode Fryday was saved:
He sitte neither with Seynt Johan, Symonde, ne Jude,
Ne wyth maydenes ne with martires ne [with mylde] wydwes,
205 But by hymself as a soleyne, and served on the erthe.
For he that is ones a thef is evermore in daungere,
And as lawe lyketh, to lyve or to deye:
De peccato propiciato noli esse sine metu.
And forto serven a seynt and such a thef togyderes,
It were noyther resoun ne right to rewarde hem bothe aliche.
210 And right as Troianus the trewe knyght tilde nought depe in helle
That owre Lorde ne had hym lightlich oute, so leve I the thef be
    in Hevene.
For he is in the lowest of Hevene, if owre bileve be trewe,
And wel loselyche he lolleth there by the lawe of Holy Cherche:
Quia reddit unicuique juxta opera sua.
[Ac] why that one thef on the crosse creaunt hym yelt
215 Rather than that other thef, though thow wolde appose,
Alle the clerkes under Cryst ne couthe the skil assoille:
Quare placuit? Quia voluit.
    And so I sey by the, that sekest after the whyes,
And aresonedest Resoun—a rebukyng, as it were,
[And willest of briddes and of bestes, and of here bredynge to
    knowe,
220 Why somme be alow and somme aloft, thi lykyng it were];
And of the floures in the fryth and of her feire hewes,
Whereof thei cacche her coloures, so clere and so brighte,
And of the stones and of the sterres; thow studyest, as I leve,
How evere beste or brydde hath so breme wittes.
225 Clergye ne Kynde Witte ne knewe nevere the cause,
Ac Kynde knoweth the cause hymselve, no creature elles.
He is the pyes patroun and putteth it in hire ere
That there the thorne is thikkest to buylden and brede;
And Kynde kenned the pecok to cauken in swich a [wise].
230 [Kynde] kenned Adam to knowe his pryvé membres,
And taughte hym and Eve to hylien hem with leves.
Lewed men many tymes maistres thei apposen

—That was because he yielded himself conquered to Christ and
    acknowledged his guilts,
And prayed God for grace, who always readily grants it
To those that humbly ask for it and are in will to amend themselves.   195
But though that thief had Heaven, he had no high bliss,
Such as Saint John and other saints who had deserved better.
Just as some man might give me food and set me in the middle of the
    floor;
I would have more than enough meat, but not so much honor
As those that sat at the side table or held sway in the hall,   200
But like a beggar, not at the board, but by myself on the ground.
So it fares with that felon that won salvation on Good Friday:
He sits neither with Saint John, Simon, nor Jude,[6]
Nor with maidens nor with martyrs nor with meek widows,
But by himself solitary, and served on the earth.   205
For he who has been once a thief is evermore in danger,
And as law likes, to live or to die:
Be not without fear for a sin propitiated.[7]
And to serve a saint and such a thief together,
It would be neither reasonable nor right to regard them both alike.
And just as Trajan the true knight was not entombed so deep in hell   210
So that our Lord didn't have him lightly out, so I believe the thief is
    in Heaven.
For he is lodged in the lowest part of Heaven, if our belief is true,
And most loosely he loiters there by the law of Holy Church:
Since he rendereth to each according to his works.[8]
But why that one thief on the cross there yielded himself recreant
Rather than that other thief, though you demand an answer,   215
All the clerks under Christ couldn't give the reason:
Why did it please him? Because he wished it.[9]
   And so I say of you, who seek for the whys,
And adduce reasons against Reason—rebuke him, as it were,
And want to know about birds and beasts, and of their breeding
    habits,
Why some stay low and some go aloft you'd like to learn;   220
And of the flowers in the field and of their fair hues,
Whence they come by their colors, so clear and so bright,
And of the stones and of the stars; you study, I believe,
How every beast or bird has such brilliant wits.
Clergy or Kind Wit could never know the cause,   225
But Kind* knows the cause himself, no creature else.
He is the magpie's patron and put it in her ear
To build and to breed where the thorn bush is thickest;
And Kind taught the peacock to copulate in such a way.
Kind caused Adam to be conscious of his privy parts,   230
And taught him and Eve to hide them with leaves.
Many times ignorant men demand of masters*

---

6. These saints were among the original twelve Apostles.
7. Ecclus. 5:5.
8. Ps. 61: 13. Cf. the story of Aigolandus, p. 415.
9. Cf. Ps. 134:6: "Whatsoever the Lord wished [*voluit*], that did he."

Why Adam ne hiled nought firste his mouth that eet the apple
Rather than his lykam alow: lewed axen thus clerkes.
235 Kynde knoweth whi he dede so, ac no clerke elles.
Ac of briddes and of bestes men by olde tyme
Ensamples token and termes, as telleth this poetes,
And that the fairest foule foulest engendreth,
And feblest foule of flyght is that fleegheth or swymmeth.
240 And that is the pekok and the pohenne [with her proude fetheres,
Bitokneth right riche men that regne here on erthe.
For pursue a pekok or a pohenne to cacche,
They may not flee fer ne ful heighe neither];
For the traillyng of his taille overtaken is he sone.
245 And his flesshe is foule flesshe, and his feet bothe,
And unlovelich of ledene, and laith for to here.
Right so the riche, if he his ricchesse kepe
And deleth it nought tyl his deth-day, the taille [is al of] sorwe.
Right as the pennes of the pecok payned hym in his flighte,
250 So is possessioun payne of pens and of nobles
To alle hem that it holdeth til her taille be plukked.
And though the riche repente thanne and birewe the tyme
That evere he gadered so grete and gaf thereof so litel,
Though he crye to Cryst thanne with kene wille, I leve
255 His ledne be in owre Lordes ere lyke a pyes [chiterynge].
And whan his caroigne shal come in cave to be buryed
I leve it flaumbe ful foule the folde al aboute,
And alle the other ther it lyth envenymed thorgh his attere.
By the [po feet] is understonde, as I have lerned in Avynet,
260 Executoures, fals frendes that fulfille nought his wille
That was writen, and thei witnesse, to worche right as it
          wolde;
Thus the poete preves the pecok for his fetheres;
So is the riche [reverenced] bi resoun of his godis.
The larke that is a lasse foule is more lovelich of ledne,
265 And wel awey of wenge swifter than the pecok,
And of flesch by fele folde fatter and swetter.
To lowe-lybbyng men the larke is resembled.
Arestotle the grete clerke suche tales he telleth.
Thus he lykneth in his *Logyk* the leste foule oute.
270 And where he be sauf or nought sauf the sothe wote no Clergye,
Ne of Sortes ne of Salamon no scripture can telle.
Ac God is so good, I hope that sitth he gaf hem wittis
To wissen us [wyes] therewith that [wisshen] to be saved—
And the better for her bokes to bidden we ben holden—
275 That God for his grace gyve her soules reste,
For lettred men were lewed yut ne were lore of
          her bokes."
"Alle thise clerkes," quod I tho, "that on Cryst leven,
Seggen in her sarmones that noyther Sarasenes ne Jewes

Why Adam didn't first hide his mouth that ate the apple
Rather than his body below: ignorant men thus badger clerks.
Kind can tell why he did so, and no clerk else.   235
But from birds and beasts men born in former times
Derived patterns and parables, as these poets tell,
And that the fairest fowl breeds in the foulest manner,
And is the feeblest fowl of flight of those that fly or swim.
And that is the peacock and the peahen with their proud feathers,   240
Which represent rich men who reign here on earth.
For if you pursue a peacock or a peahen so as to catch them,
They may not fly far nor very high either;
For the trailing of his tail he is overtaken quickly.
And his flesh is foul flesh, and his feet foul too,   245
And his language is unlovely, loathsome to hear.
Right so the rich man, if he keeps his riches hoarded up
And does not dole them out until his death-day, the tail is of sorrow.
Just as the plumes of the peacock impede him in his flight,
So there is an impediment in possession of pennies* and nobles*   250
To all those who hold on to them until their tails are plucked.
And though the rich man repent then and start to rue the time
That he ever gathered such a great amount and gave away so little,
Though he cry to Christ then with keen will, I believe
His language will sound in our Lord's ear like a magpie's chattering.   255
And when his corpse comes to be enclosed in the grave
I believe it will infect foully all the field around it,
And all the others where it lies will be imbued with its poison.
By the peacock's feet are figured, as I have found in Avienus,[1]
Executors, false friends that don't fulfill his will   260
Which was written, and they were witnesses, for them to work as it
        directed;
Thus the poet points out the peacock for his feathers;
So is the rich man reverenced by reason of his goods.
The lark that is a littler bird is more lovely of voice,
And far away of wing swifter than the peacock,   265
And fatter of flesh, and many times more flavorsome.
The lark is likened to low-living men.
Aristotle* the great scholar tells stories such as these.
Thus in his *Logic* he draws this likeness from the littlest fowl there is.
And whether he is saved or not saved is surely known to no Clergy,   270
Nor of Socrates[2] nor of Solomon* no scripture can tell.
But God is so good, I hope that since he gave them wits
With which to make us men wise who wish to be saved—
And we are obliged by their books the better to pray—
That God of his grace give their souls rest,   275
For learned men would be unlettered still if it weren't for the lore of
        their books."
"All these clerks," I declared then, "that believe in Christ's teaching,
Say in their sermons that neither Saracens nor Jews

1. A writer of Latin fables (fourth century).
2. The Greek philosopher (470?–399 B.C.) and leading figure in the Dialogues of his pupil Plato.

Ne no creature of Cristes lyknesse withouten Crystendome
    worth saved."
280   "*Contra!*" quod Ymagynatyf tho, and comsed for to loure,
And seyde, "*Salvabitur vix justus in die judicii;*
Ergo salvabitur," quod he, and seyde namore Latyne.
"Troianus was a trewe knyghte and toke nevere Cristendome,
And he is sauf, so seith the boke, and his soule in Hevene.
285   For there is fullyng of fonte and fullyng in blode-shedyng,
And thorugh fuire is fullyng, and that is ferme bileve:
    Advenit ignis divinus, non comburens sed illuminans, etc.
Ac trewth that trespassed nevere ne transversed ayeines his lawe,
But lyveth as his lawe techeth, and leveth there be no bettere,
And if there were he wolde amende, and in suche wille deyeth—
290   Ne wolde nevere trewe God but [trewe] treuth were allowed.
And where it worth [of treuth] or nought, the [worth of] bileve is grete,
And an hope hangyng therinne to have a mede for his treuth;
    For *DEUS dicitur quasi Dans Eternam Uitam Suis, hoc est, fidelibus.*
    Et alibi, Si ambulavero in medio umbre mortis.
The glose graunteth upon that vers a gret mede to treuthe.
295   And witt and wisdome," quod that wye, "was sommetyme tresore
To kepe with a comune: no katel was holde bettere,
And moche murth and manhod." And right with that he vanesched.

Passus XIII

And I awaked therewith, witles nerehande,
And as a freke that [fey] were forth gan I walke
In manere of a mendynaunt, many a yere after.
And of this metyng many tyme moche thought I hadde,
5 First how Fortune me failled at my moste nede,
And how that Elde manaced me, myght we evere meten;
And how that freris folwed folke that was riche,
And [poeple] that was pore at litel prys thei sette,
And no corps in her kirkeyerde ne in her kyrke was buryed
10   But quikke he biquethe hem aughte or shulde helpe quyte her
      dettes,
And how this coveitise overcome clerkes and prestes,
And how that lewed men ben ladde, but owre Lorde hem helpe,
Thorough unkonnyng curatoures to incurable peynes;
And how Pthat Ymagynatyf in dremeles me tolde

Nor any creature of Christ's likeness can be saved without
    Christendom."
    "*Contra!*"* exclaimed Imaginative then, and commenced to frown,   280
And said, "*Salvabitur vix justus in die judicii*;
Ergo salvabitur,"[3] said he, and spoke no more Latin.
"Trajan was a true knight and never took Christendom,
And he is safe, the book says, and his soul in Heaven.
For there is baptism both at the font and by blood-shedding,   285
And through fire there is baptism, and that's our firm belief:
    Then came a divine fire, not burning but illuminating, etc.[4]
But truth that never trespassed nor transgressed against his law,
But lives as his law teaches, and believes there is no better,
And if there were he would adopt it, and in such a will dies—
Would never true God wish but true truth were allowed.[5]   290
And whether it's witness of truth or not, the worth of belief is great,
And a hope is hanging in it to have reward for his truth;
For *DEUS* is to say *Dans Eternam Vitam Suis,*[6] *that is, to the faithful.*
    And elsewhere, If I walk through the midst of the shadow of death.
The gloss upon that verse grants a great reward to truth.[7]
And wit and wisdom," said that man, "was once a treasure   295
To keep a community with: no capital was held better,
And such mirth and manhood." And with that he vanished.

Passus XIII

And with that I woke up, my wits almost gone,
And like some one under a spell I started to walk
In the manner of a mendicant,[1] many a year after.
And about this dream of mine many times I had much thought,
First how Fortune failed me at my greatest need,   5
And how Old Age menaced me, if we might ever meet;
And how friars followed after folk that were rich,
And people that were poor they prized but little,
And in their kirks* or kirkyard no corpse was buried
Unless while alive he left them something or helped lighten their
    debts,   10
And how this covetousness overcame clerks* and priests,
And how laymen are led, unless our Lord helps them,
Through incompetent curates[2] to incurable pains;
And how Imaginative told me in my dream

3. "The righteous man will scarcely be saved in the day of judgment; therefore he *will* be saved": line 281 comes from 1 Peter 4:18.
4. From the liturgy for Pentecost; the line refers to the tongues of fire in which the Holy Ghost descended on the Apostles: Acts 2:1–4. The *baptism* of blood is martyrdom, the *baptism* of fire is direct illumination by the Holy Ghost.
5. The line may be paraphrased, "The true God couldn't possibly want anything other than that real integrity be recognized and provided for."
6. "God"; "giving eternal life to his own." "V" and "U" are interchangeable in Latin scripts.
7. *And elsewhere . . . shadow of death*: Ps. 22:4: the verse continues, "I will fear no evil: for thou art with me." See p. 370. *Gloss*: the *Glossa Ordinaria,* the traditional medieval commentary on the Bible, which explains "with me" as "that is, in the heart, by faith, so that after the shadow of death I will be with thee."
1. A friar, who lives by begging.
2. Assistant or deputy priests.

15   Of Kynde and of his connyng, and how curteise he is to bestes,
      And how lovynge he is to [eche lyf], on londe and on water—
      Leneth he no lyf lasse ne more,
      [For alle] creatures that crepen [or walken] of kynde ben engendred;
      And sitthen how Ymagynatif seyde, "*Vix salvabitur justus,*"
20   And whan he had seyde so how sodeynelich he passed.
      I lay down longe in this thoughte, and atte laste I slepte,
      And as Cryste wolde there come Conscience to conforte me that tyme,
      And bad me come to his courte, with Clergye sholde I dyne.
      And for Conscience of Clergye spake I come wel the rather.
25   And there I [mette] a Maistre—what man he was I neste—
      That lowe louted and loveliche to Scripture.
      Conscience knewe hym wel and welcomed hym faire.
      Thei wesshen and wypeden and wenten to the dyner.
      Ac Pacience in the paleis stode in pilgrymes clothes
30   And preyde mete [*pour*] *charité* for a pore heremyte.
      Conscience called hym in and curteisliche seide,
      "Welcome, wye, go and wasshe, thow shalt sitte sone."
         This Maister was made sitte as for the moste worthy,
      And thanne Clergye and Conscience and Pacience cam after.
35   Pacience and I were put to be macches,
      And seten by owreselve at a syde borde.
      Conscience called after mete, and thanne cam Scripture
      And served hem thus sone of sondry metes manye,
      Of Austyn, of Ambrose, of alle the foure Evangelistes.
            Edentes et bibentes que apud eos sunt.
40   Ac [of thise men] this Maister ne his man no manere flessh [ete],
      Ac thei ete mete of more coste, mortrewes and potages.
      Of that men myswonne thei made hem wel at ese,
      Ac her sauce was oversoure and unsavourely grounde
      In a morter *Post mortem* of many bitter peyne,
45   But if thei synge for tho soules and wepe salt teres:
            Vos qui peccata hominum comeditis, nisi pro eis lacrimas et
               oraciones, effuderitis ea que in delicijs comeditis in tormentis
               evometis.
      Conscience curteisly tho comaunded Scripture
      Bifor Pacience bred to brynge, [bitynge apart],
      And me that was his [mette other mete bothe].
      He sette a soure lof tofor us and seyde, "*Agite poenitenciam,*"
50   And sith he drough us drynke, *Diu perseverans*,
      "As longe," quod [he], "as [lyf] and lycame may dure."
      "Here is propre service," quod Pacience. "Ther fareth no prynce bettere."
      [And he broughte us of *beati quorum* of *Beatus Virres* makynge,

Of Kind* and of his cleverness, and how courteous he is to beasts,   15
And how loving he is to every creature alive, on land and on water—
He allots to no living thing more or less than to another,
For all creatures that creep or walk of Kind are engendered;
And so on to how Imaginative said, "*Vix salvabitur justus*,"³
And when he had said so how suddenly he vanished.   20
I lay long in this thought, and at the last I slept,
And as Christ willed there came Conscience* to comfort me then,
And bade me come to his court, to dine in company with Clergy.*
And because Conscience mentioned Clergy I came all the sooner.
And there I met a Master*—I'd no idea what man he was—   25
Who bowed down deeply and deferentially to Scripture.
Conscience was well acquainted with him and welcomed him warmly.
They washed their hands and wiped them and then went to dinner.
But Patience stood in the palace yard in pilgrim's clothes
And prayed for food *pour charité*⁴ for a poor hermit.   30
Conscience called him in and courteously said,
"Welcome, sir, go and wash, we shall sit soon."
    This Master was made to sit in the place of most honor,
And then Clergy and Conscience and Patience came after.
Patience and I were placed as companions for dinner,   35
And sat by ourselves at a side table.
Conscience called for food, and then came Scripture
And served them thus soon with many sorts of dishes,
Of Augustine,* of Ambrose,* of all the four Evangelists.
    *Eating and drinking what things are among them.*⁵
But of these men this Master nor his man ate no manner of flesh,   40
But fed on food more costly, viands stewed and thick soups.
With what men miswon they made themselves easy,
But their sauce was oversour and unsavorly ground
In a mortar *Post mortem*⁶ of many bitter pains,
Unless they sing for those souls and weep salt tears: 45
    You who feast upon men's sins, unless you pour out tears and
        prayers for them, you shall vomit up among
        *torments the food which you feast on now among pleasures.*⁷
Conscience courteously then commanded Scripture
To bring bread before Patience, seated below them,
And to me his messmate more sorts of food as well.
He set a sour loaf before us and said, "*Agite poenitentiam*,"⁸
And then he drew us drink, *Diu perseverans*,⁹   50
"As long," said he, "as life lasts and body draws breath."
"This is proper service," said Patience. "No prince could fare better."
And he brought us some *beati quorum* made by *Beatus Vir*,¹

---

3. "The righteous man will scarcely be saved." In XII.281–82.
4. "For charity."
5. Luke 10:7.
6. "After death."
7. Source unknown.
8. "Do penance": Matt. 3:2. It is not clear why Scripture, who earlier was Clergy's wife and here seems to act as hostess, has become male, but the manuscripts all agree on this.
9. "Persevering a long while," i.e., to the end; cf. Matt. 10:22.
1. "Blessed [are they] whose [transgressions are forgiven]"; "Blessed [is] the man [unto whom the Lord imputeth not sin]": Ps. 31:1–2; line 54a also comes from the first verse of this Psalm.

And thanne a messe of other mete of *Miserere*
    Mei Deus],
      Et quorum tecta sunt peccata,
55 In a dissh of derne shrifte, *Dixi et confitebor tibi*
"Brynge Pacience some pitaunce pryveliche," quod Conscience,
And thanne had Pacience a pitaunce, *Pro hoc orabit ad te omnis*
    sanctus in tempore opportuno;
And Conscience conforted us and carped us mery tales:
    Cor contritum et humiliatum, Deus, non despicies.
    Pacience was proude of that propre service
60 And made hym muirth with his mete, ac I morned evere
For this Doctoure on the heigh dese dranke wyn so faste:
    Ve vobis qui potentes estis ad bibendum vinum!
He eet many sondry metes, mortrewes and puddynges,
Wombe-cloutes, and wylde braune, and egges y-fryed with grece.
Thanne seide I to myself so Pacience it herde,
65 "It is nought foure dayes that this freke, bifor the Den of Poules,
Preched of penaunces that Poule the Apostle suffred:
In fame and frigore and flappes of scourges.
    Ter cesus sum et a Judeis quinquies quadragenas, etc.
Ac o worde thei overhuppen at ech a tyme that thei preche
70 That Poule in his Pistel to al the peple tolde:
    Periculum est in falsis fratribus.
Holy Writ bit men be war—I wil nought write it here
On Englisch an aventure it sholde be reherced to ofte,
And greve therewith that good ben—ac gramarienes shul rede:
    Unusquisque a fratre se custodiat, quia ut dicitur
      periculum est in falsis fratribus.
Ac I wist nevere freke that as a frere yede bifor men on Englissh
75 Taken it for [his] teme and telle it withouten glosynge.
Thei prechen that penaunce is profitable to the soule,
And what myschief and malese Cryst for man tholed,
"Ac this Goddes gloton," quod I, "with his gret chekes
Hath no pyté on us pore—he performeth yvel
80 That he precheth [and] preveth nought to pacience," I tolde,
And wisshed witterly, with wille ful egre,
That disshes [and] dobleres bifor this ilke Doctour
Were moltoun led in his maw—and Mahoun amyddes.
"I shal jangle to this jurdan with his just wombe,
85 [And appose hym] what penaunce is, of which he preched rather."
Pacience parceyved what I thought, and [preynte] on me to be stille,
And seyde, "Thow shalt se thus sone, whan he may no more,

And then a serving of another mixture made by *Miserere Mei*
    Deus,[2]
     And whose sins are covered,
In a salver of secret shrift, *Dixi et confitebor tibi*[3]   55
"Bring Patience an extra portion privately," said Conscience,
And then Patience had a portion, *Pro hoc orabit ad te omnis*
    sanctus in tempore opportuno;[4]
And Conscience comforted us with his cheerful conversation:
    A contrite and humbled heart, O God, thou wilt not despise.[5]
   Patience was proud of that proper service
And made merry at his meal, but I mourned ever   60
Because this Doctor* on the high dais[6] drank wine so fast:
    Woe to you that are mighty to drink wine![7]
He munched many sorts of foods, mutton stews and puddings,
Eggs fried in fat, and tripe, and flesh of wild boar.
Then I said to myself so that Patience heard me,
"It was not four days ago that this friar, before the Dean* of Paul's,[8] 65
Preached of penances that Paul the Apostle suffered:
In fame et frigore[9] and flailings with whips.
    Thrice was I beaten and of the Jews five times forty, etc.
But one verse they always leap over whenever they preach
That Paul in his Epistle told the people everywhere: 70
    There is danger in false brothers.[1]
Holy Writ directs men to beware—I will not write it here
In English lest perhaps it should be too often repeated,
And thereby grieve those that are good—but grammarians shall read:
    Let each one guard himself from a brother, as it is said that
       there is danger in false brothers.
But I never knew a fellow dressed as a friar before men in English
Take this as his text and talk about it without glozing.*   75
They preach that penance is profitable to the soul,
And what strong pain and distress Christ stood for man's sake,
"But this God's glutton," said I, "with his great cheeks
Has no pity on us poor—he performs badly
What he preaches and practices no patience," I said,   80
And I hoped most heartily, with a full hateful will,
That the platters and plate placed before this Doctor
Would turn to molten lead in his midriff—and Mahoun[2] in the midst.
"I shall prate to this pisspot with his plump belly,
And press him to say what penance is, of which he preached earlier." 85
Patience perceived what my purpose was, and winked at me to be still,
And said, "You will see soon enough, when he can eat no more,

2. "Have mercy on me. God": Ps. 50:3.
3. "I have said and I will confess to thee": Ps. 31:5.
4. "For this shall every one that is holy pray unto thee in an opportune time": Ps. 1:6.
5. Ps. 50:19.
6. Important people sat at the head table on a raised dais at the end of the hall in which meals were
   served.
7. Isa. 5:22.
8. The cathedral of the city of London.
9. "In hunger and thirst": 2 Cor. 11:27; the next line is 2 Cor. 11:24–25.
1. 2 Cor. 11:26. The pun on "brother" and "friar" (both called *frater* in Latin), on which Langland
   plays in this line and in line 73a, was well established.
2. I.e., Mohammed: a Christian name for the Devil, because of popular belief that Mohammed was
   the Moslems' God rather than their prophet.

He shal have a penaunce in his paunche, and puffe at ech a worde,
And thanne shullen his guttis godele, and he shal galpen after.
90   For now he hath dronken so depe he wil devyne sone,
And preven it by her Pocalips and passioun of Seynt Auereys
That neither bacoun ne braune, blanmangere ne mortrewes,
Is noither fisshe no flesshe but fode for a penaunte;
And thanne shal he testifye of a Trinitee and take his felawe to witnesse
95   What he fonde in a [forel of] a freres lyvyng,
And but if the fyrst lyne be lesyng, leve me nevere after.
And thanne is tyme to take and to appose this Doctoure
Of Do-Wel and of Do-Bet, and if Do-Best be any penaunce."
      And I sete stille as Pacience seyde, and thus sone this Doctour
100   (As rody as a rose [roddede] his chekes)
Coughed and carped, and Conscience hym herde
And tolde hym of a Trinité and toward us he loked.
"What is Do-Wel, sire Doctour?" quod I. "Is Do-[Best] any
      penaunce?"
"Do-Wel," quod this Doctour, and [dranke after],
105   "Do non yvel to thine evene-Crystene, nought by thi powere."
"By this day, sire Doctour," quod I thanne, "be ye nought in Do-Wel!
For ye han harmed us two in that ye eten the puddyng,
Mortrewes and other mete—and we no mussel hade.
And if ye fare so in yowre fermorie, ferly me thinketh
But chest be there charité shulde be, and yonge childern dorste
110   pleyne,
I wolde permute my penaunce with yowre, for I am in poynte to Do-
      Wel."
Thanne Conscience curteisliche a contenaunce he made
And preynte upon Pacience to preie me to be stille,
And seyde hymself, "Sire Doctour, and it be yowre wille,
115   What is Do-Wel and Do-Bet? Ye devynours knoweth."
"Do-Wel," quod this Doctour, "do as clerkes techeth;
[That travailleth to teche othere, I holde it for a Do-Bet];
And Do-Best doth hymself so as he seith and precheth:
        Qui facit et docuerit magnus vocabitur in regno
            celorum."
"Now thow, Clergye," quod Conscience, "[carpe] what is Do-Wel."
120   "I have sevene sones," he seyde, "serven in a castel
There the Lorde of Lyf wonyeth, to leren [hem] what is Do-Wel.
Til I se tho sevene and myself acorden,
I am unhardy," quod he, "to any wyght to preve it.
For one Pieres the Ploughman hath inpugned us alle
125   And sette alle sciences at a soppe save love one,
And no tixte ne taketh to meyntene his cause

He will have a penance in his paunch, and puff at every word,
And then his guts will grumble, and he'll begin to belch.
For now he's drunk so deep he'll soon start divining for us,   90
And prove it by their Apocalypse and the passion of Saint Aurea³
That neither bacon nor brawn, blankmanger⁴ nor stew,
Is either fish or flesh, but food for a penitent;
And then he'll testify of a Trinity and take his fellow to witness
What he found in some volume about a friar's way of life,   95
And unless the first line is a lie, believe me never.
And that's the moment for your move to make him give an answer
About Do-Well and Do-Better, and whether Do-Best is any penance."
   And I sat still as Patience said, and soon this Doctor
(As red as a rose reddened his cheeks)   100
Coughed and cleared his throat, and Conscience heard him
And told him of a Trinity and looked toward us.
"What is Do-Well, sir Doctor?"* said I. "Is Do-Best⁵ any penance?"
"Do-Well," said this Doctor, and drank after,
"Perform no injury to your fellow-Christians, as far as you can avoid it."   105
"By this day, sir Doctor," said I, "then you don't Do-Well!
For you have harmed us two in that you ate the pudding,
Marrow bones and other meat—and no morsel for us.
And if that's how you behave in your hospital, I'd think it a wonder
If charity's not changed to contention there, if young children dared
      complain,   110
I'd like to replace my penance with yours, for I'm in purpose to Do-
      Well."
Then Conscience courteously cast a glance in my direction
And winked at Patience to imply he should pray me to keep quiet,
And said himself, "Sir Doctor, if it is your will,
What is Do-Well and Do-Better? You divines know."   115
"Do-Well," said this Doctor, "do as clerks teach;
Whoever tries to teach others, I take that for Do-Better;
And Do-Best does himself just so as he says and preaches:
      *Who shall do and teach he shall be called great in the kingdom of
            Heaven.*"⁶
"Now, Clergy," said Conscience, "you declare what Do-Well is."
"I have seven sons,"⁷ he said, "who serve in a castle   120
Where the Lord of Life lives, so they may learn Do-Well.
Until I see those seven and myself agree,
I am unconfident," said he, "to define it for any one.
For one Piers the Plowman has impugned us all
And says no study is worth a straw except for love alone,   125
And takes no text to sustain his case

---

3. The "Apocalypse of Gluttons" of Walter Map was a satire on greed, a parody of the Book of Revelation; Langland's puzzling "Seint Avereys" is translated as Saint Aurea, who, according to Vincent
   of Beauvais' popular medieval Encyclopedia, drank only "what she could distil from cinders."
4. This popular dish seems to have contained eggs, cream, and sugar and probably (especially in view
   of the next line) chicken and almonds.
5. Most manuscripts have "Do-Well" here.
6. Matt. 5:19.
7. The seven liberal arts (see p. 147, n .9).

But *Dilige Deum* and *Domine, quis habitabit,*
And [demeth] that Do-Wel and Do-Bet aren two infinites,
Whiche infinites with a feith fynden oute Do-Best,
130   Which shal save mannes soule: thus seith Piers the Ploughman."
"I can nought heron," quod Conscience, "ac I knowe Pieres.
He wil nought ayein Holy Writ speken, I dar wel undertake."
"Thanne passe we over til Piers come and preve this in dede.
Pacience hath be in many place and parauntre cnoweth
135   That no clerke ne can, as Cryst bereth witnesse:
        Pacientes vincunt, etc."
    "[At] yowre preyere," quod Pacyence tho, "so no man displese hym,
Disce" quod he, "*doce, dilige inimicos.*
Disce and Do-Wel, *doce* and Do-Bet, [*dilige* and Do-Best]:
[Thus lered me ones a lemman—Love was hir name].
140   'With wordes and with werkes,' quod she, 'and wille of thyne herte,
Thow love lelly thi soule al thi lyftyme.
And so thow lere the to lovye, for the Lordes love of Hevene,
Thine enemye in al wyse eveneforth with thiselve.
Cast coles on his hed [of] al kynde speche;
145   Bothe with [werke] and with [worde] fonde his love to wynne;
And lay on hym thus with love til he laghe on the.
And but he bowe for this betyng, blynde mote he worthe!'
Ac for to fare thus with thi frende foly it were,
For he that loveth the lelly lyte of thyne coveiteth.
150   Kynde love coveiteth noughte no catel but speche.
With half a laumpe-lyne in Latyne, *Ex vi transitionis,*
I bere [there in a bouste], fast y-bounde, Do-Wel
In a signe of the Saterday that sette firste the kalendare,
And al the witte of the Wednesday of the nexte wyke after;
155   The myddel of the mone is the mighte of bothe.
And herewith am I welcome, there I have it with me.
Undo it; late this Doctour deme if Do-Wel be therinne.
For bi hym that me made, mighte nevere poverté,
Miseise ne myschief ne man with his tonge,
160   Colde ne care, ne compaignye of theves,
Ne noither hete ne haille ne non helle pouke,
Ne noither fuire ne flode ne fere of thine enemy
Tene the eny tyme and thow take it with the.
        Caritas nichil timet.
[And eke have God my soule, and thow wilt it crave,
165   There nys neither emperour ne emperesse, erl ne baroun,
Pope ne patriarke that pure reson ne shal the make
Maister of alle tho men thorugh myght of this redels,
Nought thorugh wicchecrafte but thorugh wit; and thow wilt thiselve

But *Dilige Deum* and *Domine, quis habitabit,*[8]
And declares that Do-Well and Do-Better are two unfinished things,
Which unfinished things with a faith will find out Do-Best,
Which will save man's soul: thus says Piers the Plowman."   130
"I know nothing of this," said Conscience, "but I know Piers.
He will not argue against Holy Writ, I dare answer for it."
"Then let this pass until Piers comes and explains it in person.
Patience has been in many places and perhaps he knows
What no clerk can, as Christ bears witness: 135
  The patient overcome, etc."[9]
 "At your prayer," said Patience then, "provided it displeases no one,
Disce" said he, "*doce, dilige inimicos.*[1]
Disce and Do-Well, *doce* and Do-Better, *dilige* and Do-Best:
I learned this from a lover once—Love was her name.
'With words and with works,' she said, 'and will of your heart,   140
Look that you love your soul faithfully all your lifetime.
And so learn to love, for the Lord of Heaven's sake,
Your enemy in every way even as you love yourself.[2]
Cast coals on his head of all kind speech;
Both with work and with word strive to win his love;   145
And lay on him with love until he laughs with you.
And unless he bows for this beating, let blindness come upon him!'
But to fare thus with your friend would be folly indeed,
For he who loves you loyally wants little that is yours.
Natural love needs no return but speech.   150
With half a lamp-line in Latin, *Ex vi transitionis,*
I bear in a box, fast bound there, Do-Well
In a sign of the Saturday that first started the calendar,
And all the wit of the Wednesday of the next week after;
The middle of the moon is the might of both.[3]   155
And herewith I am welcome, when I have it with me.
Undo it; let this Doctor see if Do-Well is inside.
For by him that made me, might never poverty,
Misease nor mischief nor man with his tongue,
Cold nor care, nor company of thieves,   160
Nor either heat or hail or any devil of hell,
Nor either fire or flood or fear of your enemy
Trouble you at any time if you take it with you.
  Charity fears nothing.[4]
And also God have my soul, if you will ask it,
There is neither emperor nor empress, earl nor baron,   165
Pope nor patriarch who will not for pure reason make you
Master of all those men through might of this riddle,
Not through witchcraft but through wit;* if you wish yourself

8. "Love God": Matt. 22:37; "Lord, who shall dwell": Ps. 14:1.
9. Proverbial, but cf. Matt. 10:22.
1. "Learn, teach, love your enemies"; cf. Luke 6:35.
2. See Matt. 5:43–48; for line 144, Prov. 25:21–22 and Rom. 12:20–21.
3. *Ex vi transitionis:* "by the power of the transition (or transitivity)," a grammatical term. *The middle . . . of both:* Patience's riddle, like several earlier enigmatic prophecies, has never been fully explained; nor does the reader have to figure it out, since we will learn what is in Patience's bundle in the next *Passus.*
4. Cf. 1 John 4:18, 1 Cor. 13:7–8.

Do kynge and quene, and alle the comune after
170   Yeve the al that thei may yeve—as the for best yemere;
And as thow demest wil thei do alle here dayes after:
        Pacientes vincunt]."
"It is but a dido," quod this Doctour, "a dysoures tale:
Al the witt of this worlde and wighte mennes strengthe
Can nought [parfornen] a pees bytwene the Pope and his enemys,
175   Ne bitwene two Cristene kynges can no wighte pees make
Profitable to ayther peple;" and put the table fro hym,
And toke Clergye and Conscience to conseille, as it were,
That Pacience tho moste passe, "for pilgrimes kunne wel lye."
Ac Conscience carped loude and curteislich seide,
180   "Frendes, fareth wel," and faire spake to Clergye,
"For I wil go with this gome if God wil yive me grace,
And be pilgryme with Pacience til I have proved more."
"What!" quod Clergye to Conscience, "ar ye coveitouse nouthe
After yeres-yyves or yiftes, or yernen to rede redeles?
185   I shal brynge yow a Bible, a Boke of the Olde Lawe,
And lere yow if yow lyke the leest poynte to knowe
That Pacience the pilgryme parfitly knewe nevere."
"Nay, bi Cryste," quod Conscience to Clergye, "God the foryelde;
For al that Pacience me profreth proude am I litel.
190   Ac the wille of the wye and the wille [of] folke here
Hath moeved my mode to mourne for my synnes.
The good wille of a wighte was nevre boughte to the fulle,
For there nys no tresore therto—to a trewe wille.
Haved nought [Marye] Magdeleigne more for a boxe of salve
Than Zacheus for he seide, '*Dimidium bonorum meorum do*
195   *pauperibus,*'
And the pore widwe for a peire of mytes
Than alle tho that offreden into *Gazophilacium?*"
Thus curteislich Conscience congeyde fyrst the frere,
And sithen softliche he seyde in Clergyes ere:
200   "Me were lever, by owre Lorde, and I lyve shulde,
Have Pacience parfitlich than half thi pakke of bokes."
Clergye to Conscience no congeye wolde take,
But seide ful sobreliche, "Thow shalt se the tyme
Whan thow art wery for-walked, wilne me to consaille."
205   "That is soth," seyde Conscience, "so me God helpe,
If Pacience be owre partyng felawe and pryvé with us bothe,
There nys wo in this worlde that we ne shulde amende;
And confourmen kynges to pees, and alkynnes londes,
Sarasenes and Surré, and so forth alle the Jewes,
210   Turne into the trewe feith and intil one byleve."
"That is soth," [seyde] Clergye, "I se what thow menest.
I shal dwelle as I do, my devore to shewen,
And confermen fauntekynes other folke y-lered,

To make king and queen, and all the commons* after
Give you all that they can give—to you as best of governors;   170
And do as you decide they will do all their days after:
    The patient overcome."
"It's just a joke," said this Doctor, "a jester's story:
All the wisdom of this world and the work of strong men
Cannot produce a peace between the Pope and his enemies,[5]
Nor can any compass a peace between two Christian kings   175
Profitable to either's people." And he pushed the table from him,
And took Clergy and Conscience to counsel, as it were,
That Patience must be made to part then, "for pilgrims often lie."
But Conscience cried aloud and courteously said,
"Friends, farewell," and spoke fairly to Clergy,   180
"For if God will give me grace I will go with this man,
And be a pilgrim with Patience till I've experienced more."
"What!" said Clergy to Conscience, "are you covetous now
Of fees or favors, or feel inclined to solve riddles?
I shall bring you a Bible, a Book of the Old Law,   185
And if you like I'll help you learn the least point in it
That Patience the pilgrim never perfectly knew."
"No, by Christ," said Conscience to Clergy, "God requite you;
For all that Patience has to proffer me my pride is but small.
But the will of that one, and the will of people here   190
Have moved my mind to mourn for my sins.
No currency could ever fully buy a creature's good will,
For no treasure's value is equal to it—to a true will.
Did not Mary Magdalene get more for a box of salve
Than Zacchaeus for saying, '*Dimidium bonorom meorum do
    pauperibus*,'[6]   195
And the poor widow profit more from a pair of half-farthings*
Than all those that made offerings into *Gazophilacium*?"[7]
First Conscience said farewell to the friar most courteously,
And second he spoke softly in Clergy's ear:
"I would liefer, by our Lord, if my life lasts,   200
Have Patience perfectly than half your pack of books."
Clergy would not consent to bid Conscience farewell,
But said most soberly, "You shall see the time
When you're worn out from walking, you'll wish for my advice."
"That is so," said Conscience, "so God help me,   205
If Patience were our partner and imparted his thoughts to us both,
There is no woe in this world that we could not amend;
And cause kings to want peace, and all kinds of lands,
Saracens and Syria, and so forth all the Jews,
Turn them to the true faith and to one creed."   210
"That is so," said Clergy. "I see what you mean.
I shall dwell here as I do, doing my duty,
And inform young folks or folks with learning,

5. At this date there were two competing popes (the "Great Schism").
6. "The half of my goods I give to the poor": Luke 19:8. On Mary Magdalene's salve, see Luke 7:36–50.
7. "The treasury": Luke 21:1–4.

Tyl Pacience have preved the and parfite the maked."
215 Conscience tho with Pacience passed, pilgrymes as it were.
Thanne had Pacience, as pylgrymes han, in his poke vittailles:
Sobreté and symple speche and sothfaste byleve,
To conforte hym and Conscience if they come in place
There unkyndenesse and coveytise is, hungrye contrees bothe.
220 And as thei went by the weye—of Do-Wel thei carped—
Thei mette with a mynstral as me tho thoughte.
Pacience apposed hym and preyed he sholde telle
To Conscience what crafte he couthe, an to what contree he wolde.
    "I am a mynstral," quod that man, "my name is *Activa Vita*
225 Alle ydel Ich hatye, for of 'actyf' is my name.
A wafrere, wil ye wite, and serve many lordes,
[Ac] fewe robes I fonge, or furred gounes.
Couthe I lye to do men laughe, thanne lacchen I shulde
Other mantel or money amonges lordes mynstralles.
230 Ac for I can noither tabre ne trompe ne telle none gestes
Farten ne fythelen at festes, ne harpen,
Jape ne jogly ne gentlych pype,
Ne noyther sailly ne [sautrye], ne synge with the gyterne,
I have none gode gyftes of thise grete lordes,
235 For no bred that I brynge forth, save a beneson on the Sonday
Whan the prest preyeth the peple her Paternoster to bidde
For Peres the Plowman and that hym profite wayten.
And that am I, Actyf, that ydelnesse hatye.
For alle trewe travaillours and tilieres of the erthe
240 Fro Mychelmesse to Mychelmesse I fynde hem with wafres.
Beggeres and bidderes of my bred craven,
Faitoures and freres and folke with brode crounes.
I fynde payne for the pope and provendre for his palfrey,
And I hadde nevere of hym, have God my treuthe,
245 Noither provendre ne parsonage yut of the popis yifte,
Save a pardoun with a peys of led and two pollis amydde.
Hadde Iche a clerke that couthe write I wolde caste hym a bille
That he sent me under his seel a salve for the pestilence,
And that his blessyng and his bulles bocches mighte destroye:
        In nomine meo demonia ejicient, et super egros manus imponent,
        et bene habebunt.
250 And thanne wolde I be prest to peple paste for to make,
And buxome and busy aboute bred and drynke
For hym and for alle his, fonde I that his pardoun
Mighte lechen a man as [me thinketh] it shulde.
For sith he hath the powere that Peter hadde, he hath the potte with
        the salve:

Till Patience has proved you and brought you to perfectness."
Then Conscience departed with Patience, like a pair of pilgrims.   215
Then Patience had, as pilgrims do, packed food in his bag:
Sobriety and sincere speech and steadfast belief,
To comfort himself and Conscience if they should come to places
Where unkindness or covetousness is, hungry countries both.
And as they went on their way discussing Do-Well together,   220
They met with a minstrel as it seemed to me then.
Patience approached him and prayed him to tell
Conscience what craft he practiced, and to what country he was bound.
    "I am a minstrel," said that man, "my name is *Activa Vita**8
I hate everything idle, for from 'active' is my name.   225
A wafer-seller, if you want to know, and I work for many lords,
But I've few robes as my fee from them, or fur-lined gowns.
If I could lie to make men laugh, then I might look to get
Either mantle or money among lords' minstrels.
But because I can neither play a tabor9 nor a trumpet nor tell any stories 230
Nor fart nor fiddle at feasts, nor play the harp,
Joke nor juggle nor gently pipe,
Nor dance nor strum the psaltery,1 nor sing to the guitar,
I have no good gifts from these great lords,
For any bread I bring forth, except a blessing on Sundays   235
When the priest prays the people to say their Paternoster*
For Piers the Plowman and those who promote his profit.
And that is I, Active, who hate idleness.
For all true toilers and tillers of the earth
From Michaelmas to Michaelmas2 I feed them with wafers.   240
Beggars and beadsmen* crave bread from me,
Fakers and friars and folk with shaven heads.
I supply food to the pope and provender to his palfrey,
And I never had from him, God have my word,
Neither prebend3 nor parsonage yet from the pope's gift,   245
Except a pardon with a piece of lead and a pair of heads in the middle.4
If I had a clerk* that could write I'd compose a letter to him
That he should send me under his seal a salve for the pestilence,
And that his blessing and his bulls might bring an end to boils:
    In my name shall they cast out demons, and they shall lay
        *hands on the sick, and they shall be well.*5
And then I'd be quick to prepare pastries for the people,   250
And be bustling and busy about bread and drink
For him and for all his men, if I found that his pardon
Might cure a man as it seems to me it should.
For since he has the power that Peter had, he has the pot with the
    salve:

8. "Active Life," life engaged with the ongoing affairs of the world, as opposed to the "contemplative life," dedicated to prayer. Cf.pp.400ff.
9. Small drum.
1. Stringed instrument.
2. The feast of St. Michael, September 29, associated with the coming of fall and the end of the growing year.
3. Stipend paid to a canon, a priest attached to a cathedral.
4. The seal on a papal pardon was made of lead, stamped with the heads of St. Peter and St. Paul.
5. Mark 16:17–18.

Argentum et aurum non est michi, quod autem habeo tibi do;
    in nomine Domini, surge et ambula.

Ac if mighte of miracle hym faille it is for men ben
255   nought worthy
To have the grace of God, and no gylte of the pope.
For may no blyssyng done us bote but if we wil amende,
Ne mannes Masse make pees amonges Cristene peple
Tyl pruyde be purelich fordo, and that thourgh payn defaute.
260 For ar I have bred of mele ofte mote I swete,
And ar the comune have corne ynough, many a colde mornyng.
So ar my wafres ben y-wrought moche wo I tholye.
Alle Londoun, I leve, liketh wel my wafres,
And lowren whan thei lakken it; it is nought longe y-passed
265 There was a carful comune whan no carte come to toune
With [bake] bred fro [Stratford]; tho gan beggeres wepe
And werkmen were agaste a litel; this wil be thoughte longe:
In the date of owre Dryghte, in a drye Apprile,
A thousande and thre hondreth tweis thretty and ten,
270 My wafres there were gesen whan Chichestre was Maire."
    I toke gode kepe, by Cryst, and Conscience bothe,
Of Haukyn the Actyf Man and how he was y-clothed.
He hadde a cote of Crystendome, as Holy Kirke bileveth,
Ac it was moled in many places with many sondri plottes,
275 Of pruyde here a plotte, and there a plotte of unboxome speche,
Of scornyng and of scoffyng and of unskilful berynge;
As in aparaille and in porte proude amonges the peple;
Otherwyse than he hath with herte or syghte shewynge [hym];
Willynge that alle men wende he were that he is noughte,
280 Forwhy he bosteth and braggeth with many bolde othes;
And inobedient to ben undernome of any lyf lyvyng;
And so syngulere by hymself as to syghte of the poeple
Was none suche as hymself, ne none so [pope]-holy;
Y-habited as an hermyte, an ordre by hymselve,
285 Religioun *sanz* reule and resonable obedience;
Lakkyng lettred men and lewed men bothe;
In lykyng of lele lyf and a lyer in soule;
With inwit and with outwitt ymagenen and studye,
As best for his body be, to have a [bolde] name;
290 And entermeten hym over al ther he hath nought to done;
Wilnyng that men wende his witte were the best,
[Or for his crafty konnynge, or of clerkes the wisest,
Or strengest on stede, or styvest under gerdel,
And lovelokest to loken on and lelest of werkes,
295 And none so holy as he, ne of lif clenner,
Or fairest of feitures of forme and of shafte,

Silver and gold have I none, but what I have I give to thee;
   In the name of the Lord, rise and walk.[6]
But if the power to perform miracles fails him it's because people are
   not worthy   255
To have the grace of God, and no guilt of the pope.
For no blessing may benefit us unless we better our lives,
Nor any man's Mass make peace among Christian people
Till pride is utterly cast out, and that through absence of bread.
For before I have made bread from meal I must often sweat,   260
And before the commons* have corn enough, many a cold morning.
So before my wafers are made I suffer much woe.
All London, I believe, like my wafers well,
And lour when they lack them; it is not long since
There was a commons full of care when no cart came to town   265
With baked bread from Stratford;[7] then beggars wept
And workmen were a bit aghast; this will be long remembered:
In the date *Anno Domini*, in a dry April,
A thousand and three hundred twice thirty and ten,
My wafers were wanting when Chichester was mayor."[8]   270
   I took close heed, by Christ, and Conscience did too,
Of Hawkin the Active Man and how he was dressed.
He had a coat of Christendom, as Holy Kirk* believes,
But it was soiled with many spots in sundry places,
Here a spot of insolent speech, and there a spot of pride,   275
Of scorning and of scoffing and unsuitable behavior;
As in apparel and deportment proud among the people;
Presenting himself as something more than he seems or is;
Wishing all men would think him what he is not,
And so he boasts and brags with many bold oaths;   280
And impatient of reproof from any person living;
And himself so singular as to seem to the people
As if there were none such as himself, nor none so pope-holy;
In the habit of a hermit, an order by himself,
A religious* *sans*[9] rule or reasonable obedience;   285
Belittling lettered men and unlettered both;
Pretending to like lawful life and a liar in soul;
With inwit and with outwit[1] to imagine and study,
As it would be best for his body, to be thought a bold man;
And interfere everywhere where he has no business;   290
Wishing every one to be assured his intellect was the best,
Or that he was most clever at his craft, or a clerk of greatest wisdom,
Or strongest on steed, or stiffest below the belt,
And loveliest to look at and most lawful of deeds,
And none so holy as he, nor any cleaner of life,   295
Or fairest of features in form and in shape,

---

6. *The pot with the salve*: the pope's power to absolve sins is portrayed as a pot of medicine he can
   dole out. *Silver and gold . . . rise and walk*: Acts 3:6.
7. The town of Stratford-atte-Bowe was a major supplier of bread to London.
8. *Anno Domini*: in the year of our Lord. *My wafers . . . was mayor*: there actually was a scarcity of
   food in 1370 when John de Chichestre was mayor.
9. "Without."
1. The ability to perceive and observe, the exterior equivalent of inwit (Gloss).

And most sotil of songe, other sleighest of hondes,
And large to lene, loos thereby to cacche],
And if he gyveth oughte pore gomes, telle what he deleth;
300 Pore of possessioun in purse and in coffre;
And as a lyon on to loke, and lordeliche of speche;
Baldest of beggeres; a bostour that nought hath,
In towne and in tavernes tales to telle,
And segge thinge that he nevere seigh and for soth sweren it;
305 Of dedes that he nevere dyd demen and bosten;
And of werkes that he wel dyd witnesse and seggen,
"Lo, if ye leve me nought or that I lye wenen,
Axeth at hym or at hym, and he yow can telle
What I suffred and seighe and some tymes hadde,
310 And what I couth and knewe, and what kynne I come of."
Al he wolde that men wiste of werkes and of wordes
Which myghte plese the peple and praysen hymselven.
    Si hominibus placerem, Christi servus non essem; Et
        alibi, Nemo potest duobus dominis servire.
"Bi Criste!" quod Conscience tho, "thi best cote, Haukyn,
Hath many moles and spottes; it moste ben y-wassh."
315 "Ye, whoso toke hede," quod Haukyn, "byhynde and bifore,
What on bakke, and what on bodyhalf, and by the two sydes,
Men sholde fynde many frounces and many foule plottes."
And he torned hym as tyte and thanne toke I hede
It was fouler by fele folde than it firste semed.
320 It was bidropped with wratthe and wikked wille,
With envye and yvel speche, entysyng to fyghte,
Lyinge and [lakkyng], and leve tonge to chyde;
Al that he wist wykked by any wighte tellen it,
And blame men bihynde her bakke and bydden hem meschaunce;
325 And that he wist bi Wille tellen it Watte,
And that [by] Watte [he] wiste, Wille wiste it after,
And made of frendes foes thorugh a false tonge.
"Or with myghte of mouthe or thorugh mannes strengthe
Avenge me fele tymes, other frete myselve [wythinne];
330 As a shepster shere [y-shrewed myn evene-Cristen]:
    Cuius maledictione os plenum est et amaritudine; sub lingua
        eius labor et dolor; Et alibi, Filij hominum,
        dentes eorum arma et sagitte et lingua eorum
        gladius acutus.
There is no lyf that I lovye lastyng any while;
For tales that I telle no man trusteth to me.
And whan I may nought have the maistrye, with malencolye [y-take],
That I cacche the crompe, the cardiacle some tyme,
335 Or an ague in suche an angre, and some tyme a fevre
That taketh me al a twelfmoneth, tyl that I dispyse
Lechecrafte [of] owre Lorde and leve on a wicche,
And segge that no clerke ne can—ne Cryste, as I leve—

And most splendid at song, or most skillful of hands,
And glad to give generously, to get praise thereby,
And if he gives to poor people, proclaims what he's giving;
Poor of possession in purse and in coffer;   300
And like a lion to look at, and lordly of speech;
Boldest of beggars; a boaster who has nothing,
In town and in taverns telling his tales,
And speaking of something he never saw and swearing it true;
Of deeds that he never did discoursing and boasting;   305
And for works that he did well he calls witnesses and says,
"Look, if you don't believe me or think I'm lying to you,
Ask him or him, and he can tell you
What I suffered and saw and some times had,
And what I knew or could calculate, and what kindred I came from." 310
He wished that men were aware of all his words and deeds
That might please the people and bring praise to himself.
    If I pleased men, I should not be the servant of Christ; And
        elsewhere, No man can serve two masters.[2]
"By Christ!" said Conscience then, "your best coat, Hawkin,
Has many spots and stains; it should be washed."
"Yes, if any one took heed," said Hawkin, "behind and in front,   315
What on the back, what over the belly, and on both sides,
He would find many filthy places and many foul spots."
And when he turned himself at that time I took note
That it was far filthier than at first it seemed.
It was splattered with spleen and stubborn will,   320
With envy and evil speech, asking for fights,
Lying and libeling, a tongue that loved to scold;
Spread abroad any bad thing anybody told him,
And blame men behind their backs and wish them bad luck;
And what he learned from Will would tell it to Wat,   325
And what he learned from Wat, Will would soon know it,
And made foes of friends with a false tongue.
"Either with what my mouth could manage or with man's strength
Avenge myself many times, or munch my insides;
Cursed my fellow-Christians like sharp shears cutting wool: 330
    Whose mouth is full of cursing and of bitterness; under his
        tongue is travail and grief; And elsewhere, The sons
        of men, their teeth are arms and arrows and their
        tongue is a sharp sword.[3]
No one living loves me lasting any while;
For the tales that I tell no one trusts me.
And when I can't make myself master, melancholy overcomes me,
So that I catch a stomach-cramp, or occasionally heartburn,
Or an ague in so great an anger, or at other times a fever   335
That takes hold on me a whole twelvemonth, until I despise
The treatment our Lord tenders and put my trust in a witch,
And say no clerk—nor Christ, I believe—can cure me so well

2. Gal. 1:10; Matt. 6:24.
3. Ps. 98:7; Ps. 56:5.

218   PIERS PLOWMAN

To the souter of Southwerke or of Shordyche Dame
     Emme.
340 [For] Goddes worde [ne grace] gaf me nevere bote,
     But thorw a charme had I chaunce, and my chief hele."
     I wayted wisloker and thanne was it soiled
     With lykyng of lecherye as by lokyng of his eye.
     For uche a mayde that he mette he made hir a signe
345 Semynge to synneward, and some he gan taste
     Aboute the mouth, or bynethe bygynneth to grope,
     Tyl eytheres wille waxeth kene and to the werke yeden,
     As wel in fastyng days [as] Frydayes and forboden nyghtes
     And as [lief] in Lente as oute of Lente, alle tymes ylyche;
350 Suche werkes with hem [were] nevere oute of sesoun
     Tyl thei myghte namore, and thanne had merye tales
     And how that lechoures lovyen, laughen, an japen,
     And of her harlotrye and horedome in her elde tellen.
         Thanne Pacience parceyved of poyntes his cote
355 Was colmy thorw coveityse and unkynde desyrynge.
     More to good than to God the gome his love caste,
     And ymagyned how he it myghte have
     With false mesures and mette, and with false witnesse;
     Lened for love of the wedde, and loth to do treuthe;
360 And awaited thorwgh [wittes wyes] to bigile;
     And menged his marchaundyse and made a gode moustre:
     "The worste within was—a gret witte I lete hit.
     And if my neighbore had any hyne or any beste elles
     More profitable than myne, many sleightes I made—
365 How I myghte have it al my witte I caste,
     And but I it had by other waye, atte laste I stale it,
     Or pryviliche his purse shoke, unpiked his lokkes.
     Or by nyght or by day aboute was Ich evere
     Thorwgh gyle to gadren the good that Ich have.
370 Yif I yede to the plow, I pynched so narwe
     That a fote londe or a forwe fecchen I wolde
     Of my nexte neighbore—nymen of his erthe.
     And if I rope, overreche, or yaf hem red that ropen,
     To seise to me with her sykel that I ne sewe nevre.
375 And [what body] borweth of me [aboughte] the tyme
     With presentes priveliche, or payed somme certeyne;
     So walde he or nought wolde he, wynnen I wolde.
     And bothe to kyth and to kyn unkynde of that Ich hadde;
     And whoso cheped my chaffare, chiden I wolde
380 But he profred to paye a peny or tweyne
     More than it was worth, and yet wolde I swere
     That it coste me moche more—swore manye othes.
     In haly dayes at Holi Cherche whan Ich herde Masse
     Hadde [I] nevere wille, wot God, witterly to biseche
385 Mercye for my mysdedes, that I ne morned more
     For losse of gode, leve me, than for my lykames giltes.

As the shoemaker of Southwark or the Shoreditch woman, Dame
    Emma.
For neither God's word nor his grace ever gave me help,   340
But through a charm my cure occurred, and I recovered my health."
I watched it more warily and then saw it was soiled
With lecherous leanings and looks from the eye.
For every maid that he met he made her a gesture
Suggesting sin, and some he would savor   345
About the mouth, or beneath begin to grope,
Till their wills grow keen together and they get to work,
As well on fasting days as Fridays and forbidden nights
And as lief in Lent as out of Lent, all times alike;[4]
Such works with them were never out of season   350
Till they might do no more, and then told merry tales
And at how lechers make love, laugh, and joke,
And in their old age tell of their whoring and wenching.
    Then Patience perceived other spots on his coat,
Dirt caused by covetousness and craving unnaturally.   355
The man had his mind more on money than on God,
And he imagined how he might have it
By falsifying weights and measures, or by false witness;
Lent money for love of the collateral, and loath to deal honestly;
And watched for ways by which his wits might cheat men;   360
And mixed his merchandise around and made it look good:
The worst pieces were placed underneath—that seemed a proper trick.
And if my neighbor had a hired hand or else a beast of some sort
More profitable than mine, I made many plans—
How I might have it was all I thought about,   365
And unless I got hold of it some other way, in the end I stole it,
Or emptied his purse privily, picked his locks.
Both by night and by day I'd always be busy
Getting through guile the goods that I own.
And if I went to the plow, I pinched so close   370
That I'd infringe by a foot or a furrow on the land
Of my nearest neighbor—nab a bit of his field.
And if I reaped, I'd overreach, or tell my reapers to,
And have them seize with their sickles some grain I'd never sown.
And anybody who borrowed from me bought the favor dearly   375
With private presents, or payments on account;
So no matter what might happen to him, I always made money.
And both to kith and to kin I was unkind with what I had;
And whoever purchased my produce, I'd complain to him
Unless he proffered to pay a penny* or two   380
More than it was worth, and yet I would swear
That it cost me much more—swore many oaths.
On holy days in Holy Church when I heard Mass
No desire swayed me, God knows, to beseech sincerely
Mercy for my misdeeds, but I mourned more   385
For my goods gone astray, believe me, than for guilts of my body.

4. Sexual intercourse was forbidden on many days of the year, for example, on fast days during Lent
and Advent and on the nights before religious feasts, as well as during pregnancy and menstruation.

As if I had dedly synne done, I dred nought that so sore
As when I lened and leved it lost—or longe ar it were
      payed.
So if I kydde any kyndenesse myn even-Cristene to helpe
390 Upon a cruel coveityse [my conscience] gan hange.
And if I sent over see my servauntz to Bruges,
Or into Pruslonde my prentys my profit to wayten,
To marchaunden with [my] monoye and maken [here] eschaunges,
Mighte nevere me conforte in the menetyme,
395 Noither Messe ne matynes, ne none manere sightes;
Ne nevere penaunce perfourned ne Paternoster seyde
That my mynde ne was more on my gode in a doute
Than in the grace of God and his grete helpes."
      Ubi thesaurus tuus, ibi et cor tuum.
[Yet glotoun with grete othes his garnement hadde soiled,
400 And foule beflobered it, as with fals speche,
As there no nede was Goddes name an ydel;
Swore therby swithe ofte and al biswatte his cote;
And more mete eet and dronke than kynde myghte defye,
"And caughte siknesse sometyme for my surfaites ofte
405 And thanne I dradde to deye in dedly synne,"
That into wanhope is worth and wende naught to be saved,
The whiche is sleuthe so slow that may no sleightes helpe it,
Ne no mercy amenden the man that so deieth].
[Ac] which ben the braunches that bryngeth a man to sleuth?
410 [Is whan man] morneth noughte for his mysdedes ne maketh no
      sorwe;
Ac penaunce that the prest enjoigneth perfourneth yvel;
Doth none almesdede; dret hym of no synne;
Lyveth ayein the Bileve and no lawe holdeth.
Uch day is haliday with hym, or an heigh ferye,
415 And if he aughte wole here it is an harlotes tonge.
Whan men carpeth of Cryst or of clennesse of soule,
He wexeth wroth and wil noughte here but wordes of myrthe.
Penaunce and pore men and the passioun of seyntes,
He hateth to here thereof, and alle that it telleth.
420 Thise ben the braunches, beth war, that bryngeth a man to wanhope.
Ye lordes and ladyes and legates of Holi Cherche
That fedeth foles-sages, flatereres and lyeres,
And han likynge to lythen hem [in hope] to do yow to lawghe—
      Ve vobis qui ridetis, etc.—
And yiveth hem mete and mede, and pore men refuse,
425 In yowre deth-deyinge, I drede me sore
Lest tho thre maner men to moche sorwe yow brynge.
      *Consencientes et agentes
          pari pena punientur.*
Patriarkes and prophetes, prechoures of Goddes wordes,

And if I'd done any deadly sin, I'd not dread that so sorely
As when I'd made a loan and believed it lost—or it was long before
    repayment.
And if I performed any friendly act to help my fellow-Christians
Upon a cruel covetousness my conscience hung.   390
And if I sent my servants overseas to Bruges,
Or my apprentice to Prussia to profit my affairs,⁵
To buy merchandise with my money and make exchange for it here,
Nothing might comfort me in the meantime,
Neither Mass nor matins, nor anything I might see;   395
Nor ever performed a penance or said my Paternoster*
When my mind was not more on my goods in jeopardy
Than on the grace of God and his great helps."
    *Where your treasure is, there is your heart also.*⁶
Yet the glutton's garment was soiled with great oaths,
And sloppily beslobbered, as with speaking falsely,   400
Where no need was taking God's name in vain;
Used it constantly in cursing and so sweat-covered his coat;
And ate and drank more at meals than nature might digest,
"And sometimes suffered sickness for surfeiting myself
And then I dreaded to die in deadly sin,"   405
So that supposing he could not be saved he sank into wanhope,*
And that is sloth* so sluggish that no skills can help it,
Nor any mercy amend the man who dies in it.
But what are the ways by which one comes to wanhope?
When a man does not mourn for his misdeeds or make sorrow for
    them;   410
But performs poorly the penance the priest enjoins;
Does no almsdeeds; dreads no sin;
Lives contrary to the Creed and cares for no law.
Every day is a holiday with him, or a high feast,
And if he will hear anything it is a ribald's tongue.   415
When men discuss Christ or cleanness of spirit,
He is angry and will hear only words of mirth.
Penance and poor men and the passion of saints,
He hates to hear of, and all that tell about them.
These are the ways, beware, by which one comes to wanhope.   420
You lords and ladies and legates of Holy Church
Who feed fool-sages, flatterers and liars,
And like to listen to them in hope to laugh at them—
    Woe unto you that laugh, etc.—⁷
And give them fees and favors, and refuse poor men,
In your death-dying, I dread sorely   425
Lest those three sorts of men thrust you into great sorrow.
    *Those who consent and those who do [it] will be punished with the
      same penalty.*⁸
Patriarchs and prophets, preachers of God's words,

5. *Bruges*: the center of the cloth industry in Flanders. *Or my apprentice . . . my affairs*: Prussia
(northern Germany) was a major distributor of English cloth to eastern Europe.
6. Matt. 6:21.
7. Luke 6:25: the verse continues "now, for ye shall mourn and weep."
8. The Latin line is a legal maxim.

Saven thorw her sarmoun mannes soule fram helle;
Right so [flatereres] and foles aren the Fendes disciples
430　To entice men thorw her tales to synne and harlotrye.
Ac clerkes that knowen Holy Wryt shulde kenne lordes
What David seith of suche men, as the Sauter telleth:

> *Non habitabit in medio domus mee qui facit superbiam et qui*
> *loquitur iniqua.*

Shulde none harlote have audience in halle ne in [chambre]
There wise men were, witnesseth Goddes wordes,
435　Ne no mysproude man amonges lordes ben allowed.
[Clerkes and knightes welcometh kynges mynstralles,
And for love of here lorde litheth hem at festes;
Much more, me thynketh, riche men sholde
Have beggeres bifore hem, the whiche ben Goddes mynstralles
440　As he seith hymself; Seynt Johan bereth witnesse:

> *Qui vos spernit me spernit.*

Forthi I rede yow riche, reveles whan ye maketh,
For to solace youre soules swich mynstralles to have:
The povere for a fool-sage sittyng at thi table,
And a lered man to lere the what owre Lord suffred
445　For to save thi soule from Sathan thyn enemy,
And fithele the withoute flaterynge of Good Friday the storye,
And a blynd man for a bordeour, or a bedrede womman
To crie a largesse bifore our Lord, youre good loos to shewe.
Thise thre maner mynstralles maketh a man to laughe,
450　And in his deeth-deyinge thei don him gret confort
That bi his lyve lithed hem and loved hem to here.
Thise solaceth the soule til hymself be falle
In a welhope, for he wroughte so, amonges worthi seyntes,
There] flateres and foles thorw her foule wordes
455　Leden tho that [lithed] hem to Luciferes feste
With *Turpiloquio,* a lay of sorwe, and Luciferes fithele.
　　Thus Haukyn the Actyf Man hadde y-soiled his cote
Til Conscience acouped hym thereof, in a curteise manere,
Whi he ne hadde wasshen it or wyped it with a brusshe.

Passus XIV

"I have but one hatere," quod Haukyn. "I am the lasse to blame
Though it be soiled and selde clene: I slepe thereinne on nightes;
And also I have an houswyf, hewen, and children—

> *Uxorem duxi et ideo non possum venire—*

That wolen bymolen it many tyme maugré my chekes.
5　It hath ben laved in Lente and oute of Lente bothe
With the sope of sykenesse that seketh wonder depe,

Save with their sermons men's souls from hell;
Just so flatterers and fools are the Fiend's disciples
To entice men with their tales to sin and ribaldry.   430
But clerks well-read in Holy Writ should report to lords
What David says of such men, as the Psalter tells:
> He who worketh pride and speaketh iniquities shall not dwell
>   within my house.[9]
A lewd man should not have audience in hall nor in chamber
Where wise men are, God's words witness,
Nor any light-minded man be allowed among lords.   435
Clerks and knights welcome king's minstrels,
And for love of their lord listen to them at feasts;
Much more, it seems to me, rich men should
Have beggars before them, who shall be God's minstrels
As he says himself; Saint John bears witness: 440
> He who despiseth you despiseth me.[1]
Therefore I remind you rich men, when you make your revels,
To solace your souls have such minstrels:
A poor person for a fool-sage placed at your table,
And a learned man from whom to learn what our Lord suffered
To save your soul from Satan your enemy,   445
And without flattering fiddle for you Good Friday's story,
And a blind man for a banterer, or a bedridden woman
To ask alms for you before our Lord, to exhibit your good fame.
A man is made to laugh by minstrels like these three,
And in his death-dying they do him great comfort   450
Who in his lifetime listened to them and loved to hear them.
These solace his soul until he himself has fallen
In a wellhope,[2] since he did so well, among worthy saints,
While flatterers and fools through their foul words
Lead those that listen to them to Lucifer's feast   455
With Turpiloquio,[3] a lay of sorrow, and Lucifer's fiddle.
    Thus Hawkin the Active Man had soiled his coat
Till Conscience questioned him, in a courteous manner,
Why he had not washed it or whisked it with a brush.

Passus XIV

"I have only one whole outfit," said Hawkin. "I am the less to blame
Though it is soiled and seldom clean: I sleep in it at night;
And also I have a housewife, hired help, and children—
> I have taken a wife and therefore I cannot come[1]—
Who will often spill on it and spoil it despite anything I do.
It's been laundered in Lent and out of Lent as well   5
With the soap of sickness that searches very deep,

9. Ps. 100:7.
1. Luke 10:16.
2. The opposite of "wanhope."*
3. "Filthy language."
1. Luke 14:20.

And [lathered] with the losse of catel forto [me loth were]
[To agulte] God or gode man bi aughte that I wiste,
And [sithe] was shryven of the preste, that [for my synnes] gave me
10 To penaunce pacyence, and pore men to fede,
Al for coveitise of my Crystenedome, in clennesse to kepen it.
And couthe I nevere, by Cryste, kepen it clene an houre,
That I ne soiled it with syghte or sum ydel speche,
Or thorugh werke or thorugh worde or wille of myn herte—
15 That I ne flober it foule fro morwe tyl eve."
        "And I shal kenne the," quod Conscience, "of Contricioun
           to make
That shal clawe thi cote of alkynnes filthe:
        Cordis contricio, etc.
Do-Wel [shal] wasshen it and wryngen it thorw a wys confessour:
        Oris confessio, etc.
Do-Bet shal beten it and bouken it as brighte as any scarlet,
20 And engreynen it with good wille and Goddes-Grace-To-Amende-The,
And sithen sende the to Satisfaccioun, for to [sonnen] it after:
        Satisfaccio.
[Do-Best shal kepe it clene from unkynde werkes].
Shal nevere [myx] bimolen it ne moth after biten it,
Ne fende ne false man defoulen it in thi lyve.
25 Shal none heraude ne harpoure have a fairere garnement
Than Haukyn the Actyf Man, and thow do by my techyng,
Ne no mynstral be more worth amonges pore and riche
Than [Haukyn wil] the wafrere, [which is] *Activa Vita*."
        "And I shal purveye the paste," quod Pacyence, "though no plow
           erie,
30 And floure to fede folke with as best be for the soule;
Though nevere greyne growed, ne grape uppon vyne,
Alle that lyveth and loketh lyflode wolde I fynde,
And that ynough; shal none faille of thinge that hem nedeth:
        Ne solliciti sitis, etc.; volucres celi Deus pascit, etc.;
            pacientes vincunt, etc.
Thanne laughed Haukyn a litel and lightly gan swerye:
35 "Whoso leveth yow, by owre Lorde, I leve noughte he be blissed."
"No?" quod Pacyence paciently, and out of his poke hente
Vitailles of grete vertues for al manere bestes
And seyde "Lo, here lyflode ynough, if owre byleve be trewe.
For lente nevere was lyf but lyflode were shapen
40 Wherof [and] wherfore [and] whereby to lybbe.
Firste the wylde worme under weet erthe,
Fissch to lyve in the flode, and in the fyre the crykat,
The corlue by kynde of the eyre—moste clennest flesch of
        bryddes,
And bestes by grasse and by greyne and by grene rotis,
45 In menynge that alle men myghte the same

And lathered with the loss of property till I was loath at heart
To aggrieve God or good man in any way I knew,
And so was shriven by the priest, who for my sins assigned me
Patience as my penance, and to feed poor men,   10
All to take care of my Christendom, to keep it in cleanliness.
And I could never, by Christ, keep it clean an hour,
That I didn't soil it with sight or with some idle speech,
Or by work or by word or by will of my heart—
That I don't make it all messy from morning till evening."   15
    "And I shall teach you," Conscience told him, "how Contrition may
        be used
To scrape your coat clean of all kinds of filth:
    Contrition of heart, etc.
Do-Well will wash it and wring it with a wise confessor:
    Confession of mouth, etc.
Do-Better will scrub it and scour it till no scarlet could be brighter,
And dye it with God's-Grace-To-Amend-Yourself and with good will,   20
And then send you to Satisfaction, to let the sun bleach it:
    Satisfaction.[2]
Do-Best will keep it clean from unkind deeds.
Then no filth shall defile it nor any moth devour it,
Nor either fiend or false man befoul it in your lifetime.
No herald nor harper will have a fairer garment   25
Than Hawkin the Active Man, if you act according to my teaching,
Nor any minstrel be held more worthy among poor and rich
Than will Hawkin the waferer, who is Activa Vita."[3]
    "And I'll provide you with dough," said Patience, "though no plow
        tills,
And flour to feed folk with as may be best for the soul;   30
Though grain never grew, nor grape upon vine,
I'd allot livelihood to all that live and move,
And that enough; none shall lack what's necessary to them:
    Have no care, etc.; God feedeth the fowls of the air, etc.; the
        patient overcome, etc."[4]
Then Hawkin laughed a little and swore a light oath:
"Whoever believes you, by our Lord, I don't believe he's blessed."   35
"No?" said Patience patiently, and pulled out of his bag
Victuals of great virtue for all kinds of beasts
And said, "Lo, here's livelihood enough, if what we believe is true.
For none was ever lent life unless livelihood was arranged
Whereof and wherefore and whereby to live.   40
First the wild worm under wet earth,
Fish to live in the flood, and in the fire the cricket,
The curlew whose kind is to live on air—his flesh the cleanest among
        birds,
And beasts on grass and on grain and on green roots,
Meaning that all men might likewise   45

2. Contrition, confession, and satisfaction are the three parts of the sacrament of penance; satisfaction refers to the penance of prayers or works the sinner is enjoined to perform by the priest in confession.
3. Waferer: wafer-maker. Activa Vita: "Active Life."
4. Matt. 6:25–26; Ps. 41:4; proverbial, but cf. Matt. 10:22.

Lyve thorw lele byleve [as owre Lord] witnesseth:
> *Quodcumque pecieritis a Patre in nomine meo, etc.;*
> *Et alibi, Non in solo pane vivit homo set*
> *in omni verbo quod procedit de ore Dei."*

But I [listnede and] loked what lyflode it was
[That Pacience so preysed, and of his poke hente]
50 A pece of the Paternoster [and pofrede us alle].
[And thanne was it] *fiat voluntas tua* [sholde fynde us alle].
"Have, Haukyn," quod Pacyence, "and ete this whan the hungreth,
Or whan thow clomsest for colde, or clyngest for
    drye.
Shal nevere gyves the greve, ne grete lordes wrath,
Prisone ne peyne, for *pacientes vincunt.*
55 Bi so that thow be sobre of syghte and of tonge,
In [ondynge] and in handlyng, and in alle thi fyve wittis,
Darstow nevere care for corne ne cloth ne for drynke,
Ne deth drede [ne Devel], but deye as God lyketh
Or thorw honger or thorw hete, at his wille be it;
60 For if thow lyvest after his lore, the shorter lyf the better:
> *Si quis amat Cristum mundum non diligit istum.*

For thorw his breth bestes wexen and abrode yeden:
> *Dixit, et facta sunt, etc.*

Ergo thorw his breth [bothe] men and bestes lyven,
As Holy Writ witnesseth whan men segge her graces:
> *Aperis tu manum tuam et imples omne animal*
>   *benediccione.*

It is founden that fourty wynter folke lyved withouten tulying,
65 And oute of the flynte spronge the flode that folke and bestes dronke.
And in Elyes tyme Hevene was y-closed
That no reyne ne rone—thus rede men in bokes
That many wyntres men lyveden and no mete ne tulyeden.
Sevene slepe, as seith the Boke, sevene hundreth wynter
70 And lyveden withoute lyflode, and atte laste thei woken.
And if men lyved as mesure wolde, shulde neveremore be
    defaute
Amonges Cristene creatures, if Crystes wordes ben trewe.
Ac unkyndnesse *caristiam* maketh amonges Crystene peple,
[Other] plenté maketh pruyde amonges pore and riche.
75 Ac mesure is so moche worth it may noughte be to dere.
For the meschief and the meschaunce amonges men of Sodome

Live through loyal belief as our Lord witnesses:
>*Whatsoever ye shall ask from the Father in my name, etc.;*
>*And elsewhere, Man doth not live by bread alone but*
>*by every word that proceedeth from the mouth of God.*"⁵
But I listened and looked to see what livelihood it was
That Patience so praised, and he pulled from his bag
A piece of the Paternoster* and proffered it to us all.   50
And so it was *fiat voluntas tua*⁶ that would feed us all.
"Have some, Hawkin," said Patience, "and eat it when you're hungry,
Or when your teeth chatter for chill, or you chew your cheek for
    thirst.
Shall never handcuffs harm you, nor anger of great lords,
Prison or pain, for *patientes vincunt.*⁷
So long as you're restrained in speech and in looking,   55
In inhaling odors and in handling things, in all your five senses,
You need never care for corn⁸ nor for clothes or drink,
Nor dread death nor Devil, but die as God pleases
Either through hunger or through heat, at his will be it;
For if you live by his lore, the shorter life the better: 60
>*If any one loves Christ he does not love this world.*⁹
For by his breath beasts grew and walked abroad:
>*He spoke, and they were made, etc.*¹
Therefore by his breath both men and beasts live,
As Holy Writ's words witness when men say their graces:
>*Thou openest thine hand and fittest every living being with*
>   *blessing.*²
It is found that forty winters folk lived without plowing,
And out of the flint sprang the flood that folk and beasts drank.³   65
And in Elijah's era Heaven was closed
So that no rain rained—thus men read in books
That men lived for many winters without minding the plow.
Seven slept, as the Book says, seven hundred winters
And lived without livelihood, and at the last they woke.⁴   70
And if men lived as moderation would, there should nevermore be
    shortages
Among Christian creatures, if Christ's words are true.
But unkindness makes *caristiam*⁵ among Christian people,
Or plenty makes pride among poor and rich.
But moderation is worth so much that it may not cost too dear.   75
For the mischance and misery among men of Sodom

5. John 14:13; Matt 4:4.
6. "Thy will be done": Matt. 6:10 (the Lord's Prayer); see also Matt. 26:39, Christ in the Garden of
    Gethsemane.
7. "The patient overcome."
8. Wheat, i.e., food.
9. Proverbial.
1. Ps. 148:5.
2. Ps. 144:16, commonly used in saying grace before meals.
3. Num. 20:11.
4. *Heaven was closed*: for the Hebrew prophet Elijah (l. 66), 1 Kings 17:1, Jas. 5:17. *Seven slept . . .
    at the last they woke*: the Seven Sleepers of Ephesus were Christians walled up in a cave during the
    persecutions of the Emperor Decius and miraculously wakened under the Emperor Theodosius
    (448 A.D.).
5. "Dearth, scarcity." For this line and the next, cf. the first poem on p. 431.

Wex thorw plenté of payn and of pure sleuthe.
    Ociositas et habundancia panis peccatum turpissimum nutrivit.
For [men] mesured nought hemself of [mete] and [drynke],
Diden dedly synne that the Devel lyked,
80 Vengeaunce fel upon hem for her vyle synnes;
[So] thei sonken into helle, tho citees uchone.
Forthi mesure we us wel, and make [we] faithe owre
     scheltroun,
And thorw faith cometh contricioun, Conscience wote wel,
Whiche dryveth awey dedly synne and doth it to be venial.
85 And though a man myghte noughte speke, contricioun myghte hym save
And brynge his soule to blisse, so that feith bere witnesse
That whiles he lyved he bileved in the lore of Holy Cherche.
Ergo contricioun, feith, and conscience is kyndelich Do-Wel,
And surgienes for dedly synnes whan shrifte of mouth failleth.
90 Ac shrifte of mouth more worthy is if man be [inliche] contrit,
For shrifte of mouth sleeth synne, be it nevere so dedly—
Per confessionem to a prest *peccata occiduntur*—
There contricioun doth but dryveth it doun into a venial synne,
As David seith in the Sauter: *Et quorum tecta sunt peccata.*
95 Ac satisfaccioun seketh oute the rote and bothe sleeth and voideth,
And as it nevere had y-be, to nought bryngeth dedly synne
That it nevere eft is seen ne sore, but semeth a wounde y-heled."
    "Where woneth Charité," quod Haukyn. "I wiste nevere in
     my lyve
[Wye] that with hym spake as wyde as I have passed."
100   "There parfit treuthe and povere herte is, and pacience of tonge,
There is Charitee the chief, chaumbrere for God hymselve."
    "Whether Paciente Poverté, "quod Haukyn, "be more plesaunte to
     owre Drighte
Than ricchesse rightfulliche y-wonne and resonablelich y-spended?"
    "Ye? *Quis est ille?* quod Pacience, "quik, *laudabimus eum!*
105 Though men rede of richchesse right to the worldes ende,
I wist nevere renke that riche was, that whan he
     rekne sholde,
Whan it drow to his deth-day, that he ne dred hym sore,
And that atte rekenyng in arrerage fel rather than oute of dette,
There the pore dar plede—and preve by pure resoun—
110 To have allowaunce of his lorde: by the lawe he it cleymeth.
Joye that nevere joye hadde of rightful jugge he axeth,
And seith 'Lo, briddes and bestes that no blisse ne knoweth
And wilde wormes in wodes, thorw wyntres thow hem grevest
And makest hem welnyegh meke and mylde for defaute,
115 And after thow sendest hem somer, that is her sovereigne joye
And blisse to alle that ben, bothe wilde and tame.'
Thanne may beggeres as bestes after bote waiten

Came about through abundance of bread and because of pure sloth.
   Idleness and abundance of bread nourished the basest sin.[6]
Since men were immoderate in their meat and drink,
Did deadly sin that the Devil found pleasing,
Vengeance fell on them for their vile sins;   80
So they sank into hell, those cities each one.
Therefore let us live with moderation, and let's make faith our
      defense,
And through faith comes contrition, Conscience knows well,
Which drives away deadly sin and reduces it to venial.[7]
And though a man might not speak, contrition might save him   85
And bring his soul to bliss, so long as faith bears witness
That while he lived he believed in the lore of Holy Church.
*Ergo** contrition, faith, and conscience naturally comprise Do-Well,
And they're surgeons for deadly sins when shrift of mouth is lacking.
But shrift of mouth is worth more if a man is truly contrite, 90
For shrift of mouth slays sin, be it never so deadly—
Per confessionem to a priest *peccata occiduntur*[8]—
While contrition does nothing but drive it down into a venial sin,
As David says in the Psalter:* *Et quorum tecta sunt peccata.*[9]
But satisfaction searches out the root and both slays and purges,   95
And as if it had never been about, brings deadly sin to naught
So that it's never again seen or sore, but seems a wound healed."
   "Where does Charity dwell?" asked Hawkin. "I don't remember in
      my life
Any one that spoke with him, as widely as I've traveled."
   "Where perfect truth and poor heart are, and patience of tongue,   100
There Charity chiefly lives, chamberlain for God himself."
   "Is Patient Poverty," Hawkin asked, "more pleasing to
      our Lord
Than riches earned righteously and reasonably spent?"
   "Yes? *quis est ille?*" Patience exclaimed, "quick, *laudabimus eum!*[1]
Though men read about riches right to the world's end,   105
I never knew any one who was rich that when he had to make his
      reckoning,
When he drew to his death-day, his dread was not great,
And that at the reckoning he fell into arrears rather than out of debt,
Where a poor man dares plead—and prove by pure reason—
To have a lenience of his lord: he has a legal claim to it.   110
From a righteous judge he asks for joy who has been joyless always,
And says, 'Lo, birds and beasts that are barred from bliss
And wild worms in woods, through winters you grieve them
And make them almost meek and mild for hunger,
And afterward you send them summer, which is their sovereign joy   115
And bliss to all who have being, both wild and tame.'
Then may beggars like beasts look for better treatment

6. A common observation correlating with the description of Sodom in Ezek. 16:49; for the destruction of Sodom and Gomorrah, see Gen. 18:20–19:25.
7. "Venial" sin, a slight or unwitting offense, does not damn the sinner; "deadly" sin, if not confessed
   and forgiven, does.
8. "Through confession," "sins are slain."
9. "And whose sins are covered": Ps. 31:1.
1. "Who is that man?" "We shall praise him!"

That al her lyf han lyved in langour and in defaute;
But God sent hem sometyme some manere joye,
120   Other here or elleswhere, Kynde wolde it nevere.
For to wrotherhele was he wroughte that nevere was joye shaped.
Angeles that in helle now ben hadden joye sometyme,
And Dives in deyntees lyved and in *douce vie*.
Righte so Resoun sheweth that tho [renkes] that were [lordes]—
125   And her [ladyes] also—lyved her lyf in murthe.
Ac God is of a wonder wille, by that Kynde Witte sheweth,
To yive many men his mercymonye ar he it have deserved.
Right so fareth God by some riche: reuthe me it thinketh,
For thei han her hyre here an Hevene as it were,
130   And gret lykyng to lyve withoute laboure of body,
And whan he deyeth ben disalowed, as David seith in the Sauter.

> *Dormierunt et nichil invenerunt. Et alibi, Velud*
> *sompnium surgencium, Domine, in civitate tua*
> *et ad nichilum rediges, etc.*

Allas, that ricchesse shal reve and robbe mannes soule
Fram the love of owre Lorde at his laste ende!
Hewen that han her hyre afore aren evermore nedy.
135   And selden deieth he out of dette that dyneth ar he deserve it,
And til he have done his devor and his dayes journé.
For whan a werkman hath wroughte, thanne may men se the sothe
What he were worthi for his werke, and what he hath deserved,
And nought to fonge bifore for drede of disalowynge.
140   So I segge by yow riche, it semeth nought that ye shulle
Have Hevene in yowre [herberwyng] and Hevene herafter
Right as a servaunt taketh his salarye bifore and sitth wolde clayme
> more
As he that none hadde and hath huyre atte laste.
It may nought be, ye riche men, or Matheu on God lyeth:

> *De delicijs ad delicias deficile est transire.*

145   Ac if [ye] riche have reuthe and rewarde wel the pore,
And lyven as lawe techeth, done leuté to alle,
Criste of his curteysie shal conforte yow atte laste
And rewarde alle dowble ricchesse that reuful hertes habbeth.
And as an hyne that hadde his hyre ar he bygonne,
150   And whan he hath done his devor wel men doth hym other bounté,
Yyveth hym a cote above his covenaunte, righte so Cryst yiveth Hevene
Bothe to riche and to noughte riche that rewfullich
> lybbeth;
And alle that done her devor wel han dowble hyre for her travaille,
Here foryyvenesse of her synnes and Hevene blisse after.
155   Ac it nys but selde y-seyn as by holy seyntes bokes
That God rewarded double reste to any riche wye.
For moche murthe is amonges riche, as in mete and
> clothyng,
And moche murthe in Maye is amonges wilde bestes;

Who have lived all their lives languishing and hungry;
Unless God sent them sometime some kind of joy,
Either here or elsewhere, Kind* would never wish it.   120
For he was born to bitter fate for whom no bliss was shaped.
Angels who are now in hell once had joy,
And Dives lived in delight and *douce vie*.[2]
Just so Reason* judges that those gentlemen who were lords—
And their ladies as well—lived their lives in mirth.   125
But God has a curious custom, according to Kind Wit,*
Of giving many men their remuneration before they've earned it.
Just so God deals with some rich men: it seems to me a pity,
Since they have their hire here and Heaven as it were,
And great delight in living without labor of their bodies,   130
And when they die they are disallowed, as David says in the Psalter.*
        *They have slept and found nothing. And elsewhere, As the
            dream of them that awake, O Lord, in thy city even
            to nothing wilt thou reduce, etc.*[3]
Alas, that riches shall rob and ravish man's soul
From the love of their Lord in their last hour!
Hired hands that are paid ahead are evermore needy.
And seldom does he die out of debt who dines before he deserves to, 135
And until he's done his duty and his day's work.
For when a workman has done his work, then one can see truly
What his work was worth, and what he has deserved,
And not to fetch pay in advance for fear of rejection.
So I say about you rich, it doesn't seem you ought   140
To have Heaven in your home here and Heaven hereafter
Just as a servant who gets his salary in advance and later insists on
        more
Like one who had none and has hire at last.
It may not be, you rich men, or Matthew lies of God:
    It is difficult to cross from delights to delights.[4]
And if you rich people have pity and keep the poor well fed,   145
And live just as law enjoins, doing justice to them all,
Christ of his courtesy will comfort you in the end
And reward with double wealth all whose hearts well with pity.
And as a hired hand that had his hire before he began work,
And when he has done his duty well men do him other kindness,   150
Give him a coat beyond the contract, just so Christ gives Heaven
Both to the prosperous and the not prosperous who show pity in their
        lives;
And all who do their duty well have double pay for their labors,
Here on earth forgiveness of their sins and Heaven's bliss hereafter.
    But it is but seldom seen in holy saints' books   155
That God rewarded double rest to any rich man.
For there is much mirth among the rich, what with their meals and
        clothing,
And much mirth is in May among wild beasts;

2. *Dives*: see Luke 16:19–24. *Douce vie*: "an easy, pleasurable life."
3. Ps. 75:6; Ps. 72:20.
4. Cf. Matt 19:23–24, probably as transmitted through the Epistles of St. Jerome.*

And so forth whil somer lasteth her solace dureth.
160   Ac beggeres aboute midsomer bredlees thei soupe,
And yit is wynter for hem worse, for wete-shodde thei gange,
Afyrst sore and afyngred and foule y-rebuked
And arated of riche men that reuthe is to here.
Now, Lorde, sende hem somer and some manere joye,
165   Hevene after her hennes-goynge that here han suche defaute.
For alle myghtest thow have made none mener
            than other
And yliche witty and wyse, if the wel hadde lyked.
And have reuthe on thise riche men that rewarde noughte thi prisoneres;
Of the good that thow hem gyvest *ingrati* ben manye.
170   Ac God of thi goodnesse gyve hem grace to amende.
For may no derth ben hem dere, drouth ne weet,
Ne noyther hete ne haille have thei here hele;
Of that thei wilne and wolde wanteth hem nought here.
Ac pore peple, thi prisoneres, Lorde, in the put of myschief,
175   Conforte tho creatures that moche care suffren,
Thorw derth, thorw drouth, alle her dayes here.
Wo in wynter tymes for wantyng of clothes,
And in somer tyme selde soupen to the fulle.
Conforte thi careful, Cryst, in thi ryche,
180   For how thow confortest alle creatures clerkes bereth witnesse:
        Convertimini ad me et salvi eritis.
Thus *in genere* of his genitrice Jhesu Cryst seyde
To robberes, and to reveres, to riche and to pore,
[To hores, to harlotes, to alle maner poeple].
Thow taughtest hem in the Trinitee to take baptesme
185   And be clene thorw that crystennynge of alle kynnes [synne].
And [if] us fel thorw folye to falle in synne after,
Confessioun and knowlechyng and cravyng thi mercy
Shulde amende us as many sithes as man wolde desire.
Ac if the [Pouke] wolde plede here-ayeine and punyssh us in
            conscience,
190   [We] shulde take the acquitance as quik and to the Qued schewe it:
        Pateat, etc.: Per passionem Domini.
And putten of so the Pouke, and preven us under borwe.
Ac the perchemyn of this patent of poverté be moste,
And of pure pacience and parfit bileve.
Of pompe and of pruyde the parchemyn decorreth,
195   And principaliche of alle peple but thei be pore of herte.
Ellis is al an ydel, al that evere we [diden],
[Paternoster] and penaunce and pilgrimage to Rome,
But owre spences and spendyng sprynge of a trewe welle,
Elles is al owre laboure loste—lo, how men writeth

And so forth while summer lasts their solace continues.
But beggars about midsummer have breadless suppers,   160
And yet winter is worse for them, for they walk wetshod,
Faint from thirst and from hunger and foully abused
And berated by rich men that it's heart-rending to hear.
Now, Lord, send them some summer and some kind of joy,
Heaven after they go hence who are here in much need.   165
For thou mightest have made all men so that none was more needy
    than another
And all alike witty and wise, if that had well pleased thee.
And have mercy on these rich men that don't maintain thy prisoners;
For the good thou hast given them *ingrati*⁵ are many.
But God of thy goodness give them grace to amend.   170
For may no dearth do them harm, drought nor wet,
Nor either heat or hail if they have their health;
Of what they wish for and would have they are wanting nothing here.
But poor people, thy prisoners, Lord, in the pit of misery,
Comfort those creatures whom many cares afflict,   175
Dearth and drought, all their days here.
Woe in winter times for want of clothing,
And in summertime seldom sup till they're full.
Comfort thy care-worn, Christ, in thy kingdom,
For how thou comfortest all creatures clerks bear witness: 180
    *Ye will be turned to me and ye will be saved.*⁶
Thus *in genere*⁷ of his gentle* kind* Jesus Christ said
To pillagers, to plunderers, to rich and to poor,
To whores, to whoremongers, to all kinds of people.
Thou taughtest them in the Trinity to take baptism
And through christening be clean of all kinds of sin.   185
And if through our folly it befell us to fall into sin afterward,
Confession and acknowledging and craving thy mercy
Should amend us as many times as any man would desire.
And if the Devil should debate against this and disturb us in our
    consciences,
We should quickly take the acquittance and accost the Fiend with it: 190
    *Let it be known, etc.: Through the passion of the Lord.*⁸
And so repel our Opponent, and prove ourselves under protection.
But the parchment for these letters patent must be made of poverty,
And of pure patience and perfect belief.
When made of pomp and of pride the parchment crumbles,
And in practice for all people unless they're poor of heart.   195
Otherwise all is in vain, all that we ever did,
Paternoster and penance and pilgrimage to Rome,
Unless our expenses and dispensing spring of a true well,
Otherwise is all our labor lost—lo, how men write

5. "Ungrateful"; cf. Luke 6:35.
6. Isa. 45:22.
7. "In a way [characteristic]."
8. The opening phrase imitates a public letter or document from the king putting on record a contract or right (called "letters patent" in line 192). In this case the "acquittance" of line 190 (the "receipt," as it were), showing that Christ has paid sinners' debt to the Devil, is the release demonstrating the Devil has lost his claim to them.

200 In fenestres atte freres—if fals be the foundement.
Forthi Crystene sholde ben in comune riche, none coveitouse for
    hymselve.
For sevene synnes that there ben assaillen us evere;
The Fende folweth hem alle and fondeth hem to helpe,
Ac with ricchesse [tho ribaudes] rathest men bigyleth,
205 For there that richesse regneth reverence folweth,
And that is plesaunte to pryde in pore and in riche.
[Ac] the riche is reverenced by resoun of his richchesse,
There the pore is put bihynde, and paraventure can more
Of witte and of wysdom that fer awey is better
210 Than ricchesse or reauté, and rather y-herde in Hevene.
For the riche hath moche to rekene, and righte softe walketh;
The heigh waye to Hevene-ward oft ricchesse letteth:
    Ita inpossibile diviti, etc.
There the pore preseth bifor the riche with a pakke at his rugge:
    Opera enim illorum sequuntur illos,
Batauntliche, as beggeres done, and baldeliche he craveth
215 For his poverté and his pacience a perpetuel blisse:
    Beati pauperes quoniam ipsorum est regnum Celorum.
[Ac] pryde in ricchesse regneth rather than in poverté;
[Or] in the maister [or] in the man some mansioun he hath.
Ac in poverté there pacyence is, pryde hath no myghte,
Ne none of the sevene synnes sitten ne mowe there longe,
220 Ne have powere in poverté, if pacyence it folwe.
For the pore is ay prest to plese the riche
And buxome at his byddyng for his broke loves,
And buxomenesse and boste [ben] evermore at werre,
And ayther hateth other in alle manere werkes.
225   If Wratthe wrastel with the pore he hath the worse ende,
For if they pleyne [the fiebler is the pore];
And if he chyde or chatre hym chieveth the worse,
[For lowliche he loketh, and loveliche is his speche
That mete or monoy of othere men mote asken.
230   And if Glotonye greve Poverté he gadereth the lasse,
For his rentes ne wil naught reche no riche metes to bigge;
And though his glotonye be to good ale, he goth to colde beddyng,
And his heved unheled, unesiliche y-wrye
For whan he streyneth hym to strecche, the strawe is his shetes.
235 So for his glotonye and his grete sleuthe he hath a grevous penaunce,
That is weyllowey wan he waketh and wepeth for colde,
And sometyme for his synnes; so he is nevere merye
Withoute mournynge amonge, and meschief to bote].
   And if Coveitise cacche the pore, thei may nought come togideres,
240 And by the nekke namely her none may hente other;
For men knoweth wel that Coveitise is of a kene wille
And hath hondes and armes of a longe lengthe,

On windows they provide the friars with—if the foundation is false.   200
Therefore Christians should be rich in common, none covetous for
    himself.
For there are seven sins[9] that are always assailing us;
The Fiend follows them all and tries to foster them,
But with riches those ribalds most readily beguile men,
For where riches reign acts of reverence follow,   205
And that is pleasing to pride in poor and in rich.
But the rich is given reverence by reason of his riches,
Where the poor is pushed back, and perhaps has more
Of wit and of wisdom that are far away better
Than riches or royalty, and heard more readily in Heaven.   210
For the rich has much to reckon with, and walks right softly;
The highway toward Heaven is often blocked by riches:
    Thus it is impossible for a rich man, etc.[1]
While the poor presses ahead with a pack on his back:
    For their works follow them,[2]
Blatantly, as beggars do, and boldly he craves
For his poverty and patience a perpetual bliss: 215
    Blessed are the poor for theirs is the kingdom of Heaven.[3]
    But pride reigns in riches rather than in poverty;
Either in the master or in his man he maintains some lodging.
But in poverty where patience lives pride has no might,
And none of the seven sins may sit there for long,
Or have power in poverty, if patience accompany it.   220
For the poor is always prepared to please the rich
And is obedient to his bidding for the breadcrumbs he gives,
And obedience and boastfulness must be evermore at war,
And each hates the other in all sorts of acts.
    If Wrath wrestles with the poor he derives the less from it,   225
For if they put in a complaint at law the poor is the weaker;
And if he chides or chafes he achieves the less,
For he looks lowly and his language is pleasant
Who must ask other men for his meals or money.
    And if Gluttony grieves Poverty he gains the less by it,   230
For his revenue will not reach far enough to buy rich foods;
And though his gluttony be for good ale, he goes to a cold bed,
With his head exposed, inadequately covered
For when he stretches to his full extent, the straw is his sheets.
So for his gluttony and great sloth he has a grievous penance,   235
Which is a world of woe when he wakes and weeps for cold,
And sometimes for his sins; so he is never merry
Without mourning mixed in, and misery as well.
    And if Covetousness catch the poor, they may not come together,
And notably by the neck may neither grasp the other;   240
For it's common knowledge that Covetousness has a keen will
And has hands and arms of a great length,

---

9. Pride, lechery, envy, avarice, wrath, gluttony, and sloth.
1. Cf. Matt. 19:23–24.
2. Rev. 14:13.
3. Cf. The familiar Beatitude in Matt 5:3, but Luke 6:20 is closer.

And Poverté nis but a petit thinge, appereth nought to his navle,
And lovely layke was it nevere bitwene the longe and
    the shorte.
245 And though Avarice wolde angre the pore, he hath but litel myghte,
For Poverté hath but pokes to putten in his godis,
There Avarice hath almaries and yren-bounde coffres.
And whether be lighter to breke? Lasse boste it maketh
A beggeres bagge than an yren-bounde coffre.
250   Lecherye loveth hym nought, for he yeveth but lytel sylver
Ne doth hym noughte dyne delycatly ne drynke wyn oft.
A strawe for the stuwes! it stode nought, I trowe,
Had thei none [haunte] but of pore men; her houses were
    untyled.
And though Sleuthe suwe Poverté, and serve nought God to paye,
255 Mischief is [ay a mene] and maketh hym to thynke
That God is his grettest helpe, and no gome elles,
And his servaunt, as he seith, and of his sute bothe.
And where he be or be noughte, he bereth the signe of
    poverté
And in that secte owre Saveoure saved al mankynde.
260 Forthi al pore that paciente is [of pure right] may claymen,
After her endynge here, Hevene-riche blisse.
Moche hardier may he axen that here myghte have his wille
In londe and in lordship and likynge of bodye
And for Goddis love leveth al an lyveth as a beggere.
265 And as a mayde for mannes love her moder forsaketh,
Hir fader and alle her frendes, and folweth hir make—
Moche is [that] mayde to lovie of [a man] that such one taketh,
More than a mayden is that is maried thorw brokage
As bi assent of sondry partyes, and sylver to bote,
270 More for coveitise of [catel] than kynde love of bothe—
So it [preveth] bi eche a persone that possessioun forsaketh
And put hym to be pacient, and Poverté weddeth,
The which is sybbe to God hymself—so [neigh is Poverté].
    "Have God my trouthe," quod Haukyn, "[I here yow] preyse faste
    Poverté.
275 What is Poverté, Pacience," quod he, "proprely to mene?"
    "Paupertas" quod Pacience, *"est odibile bonum, remocio curarum,*
    possessio sine calumpnia, donum Dei, sanitatis mater,
    absque solicitudine semita, sapiencie temperatrix,
    negocium sine dampno, incerta fortuna, absque solicitudine felicitas."
    "I can nought construe," quod Haukyn, "ye moste kenne this on
    Englisch."
    "[Al this] in Englisch," quod Pacyence, "it is wel harde wel to Expounen,
Ac somdel I shal seyne it, by so thow understonde.
280 Poverté is the first poynte that Pryde moste hateth.
Thanne is it good by good skil, al that agasteth Pryde.

And Poverty's just a puny thing, appears not up to his navel,
And there was never satisfactory sport between the short and the
    long.
And though Avarice would anger the poor, he has but little power,   245
For Poverty has only packs to put his goods in,
While Avarice has huge chests and iron-bound coffers.
And which is easier to break open? Less uproar is made
By a beggar's bag than an iron-bound coffer.
    Lechery loves him not, for he has little silver to spend   250
And sits not down to dine delicately nor drinks wine often.
A straw for the stews!⁴ they'd not be standing, I think,
If their only patrons were poor men; there'd be no roofs upon their
    houses.
And though Sloth pursues Poverty, and serves not God's pleasure,
Misery is always an intermediary and makes him think   255
That God is his greatest help, and after God no one,
And he is his servant, as he says, and of the same household.
And whether he serves him or serves him not, he bears the sign of
    poverty
And in that livery our Lord delivered all mankind.
Therefore any poor man who is patient may claim by pure right,   260
After his ending here, Heaven-kingdom's bliss.
Much more confidently may he claim it that could have his will here
In land and in lordship and delights of the body
And leaves it all for God's love and lives like a beggar.
And as a maid forsakes her mother for a man's love,   265
Her father and all her friends, and follows her mate—
Much is that maid to be loved by the man who weds her,
More than a maiden is who is married through brokerage
As by assent of sundry parties, and silver thrown in,
More for the sake of money than the mutual love of the pair—   270
So it proves with every person who forsakes possession
And applies himself to be patient, and weds Poverty,
Who is sib⁵ to God himself—so close is Poverty."
    "May God have my troth," said Hawkin, "I hear you praise Poverty
    much.
What is Poverty, Patience," said he, "properly defined?"   275
"*Poverty,*" said Patience, "*is a hateful good, a removal from cares,*
    a possession without impropriety, a gift of God, mother of
    health, a narrow path without anxiety, nurse of wisdom, a
    business without loss, an uncertain fortune, felicity without care."⁶
    "I can't construe this," Hawkin told him, "you must translate it into
    English."
    "All this in English," said Patience, "is very hard to expound,
But I shall explain some of it, so you may understand.
Poverty is the principal point that Pride hates most.   280
Then it's good for a good reason, whatever grieves Pride.

---

4. Houses of prostitution (literally, baths).
5. Kindred.
6. The Latin lines in the original text come from a collection of classical maxims repeated in the
    Middle Ages. Phrases in this definition recur like refrains in lines 287–320a.

Righte as contricioun is confortable thinge, Conscience wote wel,
And a sorwe of hymself and a solace to the sowle,
So Poverté propreliche penaunce [is to the body
285   And joye to pacient povere], pure spiritual helthe,
[And contricioun confort and *cura animarum*;
Ergo paupertas est odibile bonum].
Selde sitte Poverté the sothe to declare,
Or as justyce to jugge men enjoigned is no pore,
290   Ne to be maire above men, ne mynystre under kynges;
Selden is any pore yput to punysshen any peple.
Ergo Poverté and pore men parfornen the comaundement
Nolite judicare quemquam.
          Remocio curarum.
Selde is any pore [right] riche but of rightful
          heritage.
295   Wynneth he naught with weghtes fals ne with unseled mesures,
Ne borweth of his neghbores but that he may wel
          paye;
          Possessio sine calumpnia.
The [fourthe] is a fortune that florissheth the soule
Wyth sobreté fram al synne and also yit more;
It affaiteth the flesshe fram folyes ful manye,
300   A collateral conforte, Crystes owne yifte:
          Donum Dei.
The fyfte is moder of [myght and of mannes] helthe,
[A frende in alle fondynges, of foule yveles leche],
And for the [lewde] evere [yliche] a lemman of al clennesse:
          Sanitatis mater.
The sexte is a path of pees; ye, thorw the pas of Altoun
305   Poverté myghte passe withoute peril of robbyng.
For there that Poverté passeth, pees folweth after,
And evere the lasse that he [lede], the [lighter] he is of herte:
          [*Cantabit paupertas coram latrone viator*,
And an hardy man of herte amonge an hepe of theves].
Forthi seith Seneca *Paupertas est absque solicitudine semita.*
310   The seveneth is welle of wisdome, and fewe wordes sheweth
For lordes alloweth hym litel or lysteneth to his reson;
He tempreth the tonge to treuthe-ward [that] no tresore coveiteth:
          Sapiencie temperatrix.
The eigteth is a lele laborere and loth to take more
Than he may wel deserve, in somer or in wynter;
315   And [though he] chaffareth he chargeth no losse mowe he charité
          wynne: *Negocium sine dampno.*
The nyneth is swete to the soule, no sugre swettere,
For Pacyence is payn for Poverté hymselve.
And sobreté swete drynke and good leche in sykenesse.

Just as contrition is a comforting thing, Conscience well knows,
And a sorrow in itself and a solace to the soul,
So Poverty is properly penance to the body
And a joy to patient poor, pure spiritual health,   285
And contrition is comfort and *cura animarum*;[7]
Therefore poverty is a hateful good.
Seldom does Poverty sit to decide the truth,
Or is assigned the job of justice to make judgments on men,
Nor made mayor over men, or a minister under kings;   290
Seldom is any poor man compelled to punish any people.
Therefore Poverty and poor men perform the commandment
Do not judge any one:[8]
    A removal from cares.
Seldom does a poor man become really rich save by rightful
    inheritance.
He wins nothing with false weights nor with unlicensed measures,   295
He borrows nothing from his neighbors but what he knows he can
    repay:
    A possession without impropriety.
The fourth is a fortune from which the soul flourishes
With sobriety from all sin and also still more;
It diverts the flesh from manifold follies,
A collateral comfort, Christ's own gift: 300
    A gift of God.
The fifth is mother of might and of man's health,
A physician for foul ills, a friend in all temptations,
And for an unlearned man ever alike a lover wholly clean:
    Mother of health.
The sixth is a path of peace; yes, through the pass of Alton[9]
Poverty might pass without peril from robbers.   305
For where Poverty passes, peace follows after,
And ever the less his load is, the lighter he is of heart:
    Poverty will sing on his journey in the face of the thief,[1]
And a man hardy of heart among a heap of thieves.
Therefore Seneca says *Poverty is a narrow path without anxiety.*[2]
The seventh is a well of wisdom, with few words to speak   310
For lords make little allowance for him nor listen to his opinion;
He tempers his tongue toward the truth who covets no treasure:
    Nurse of wisdom.
The eighth is a lawful labor and loath to take more
Than he may surely deserve, in summer or in winter;
And though he negotiates he regrets no loss if he can gain charity: 315
    A business without loss.
The ninth is sweet to the soul, no sugar sweeter,
For Patience comprises bread for Poverty himself,
And sobriety is sweet drink and a good physician in sickness.

---

7. "The healing of souls."
8. Matt. 7:1.
9. This piece of road on the Hampshire-Surrey border was famous for its robbers.
1. From the Roman satirist Juvenal: Satire X.22.
2. The Roman dramatist and philosopher Seneca (4 B.C.—A.D. 65) expresses similar views, but a specific source for this line has not been identified in his work.

Thus lered me a lettred man for owre lordes love, [Seint Austyn]:
320 A blissed lyf withouten bysynesse [for body and soule:]
  Absque solicitudine felicitas.
Now God that al good gyveth graunt his soule reste
That thus fyrst wrote to wyssen men what Poverté was to mene."
  "Allas," quod Haukyn the Actyf Man tho, "that after my
    crystendome
I ne hadde ben ded and dolven for Do-Weles sake!
325 So harde it is," quod Haukyn, "to lyve and to do synne.
Synne suweth us evere," quod he, and sori gan wexe,
And wepte water with his eyghen, and weyled the tyme
That evere he dede dede that dere God displesed;
Swowed and sobbed and syked ful ofte
330 That evere he hadde londe or lordship, lasse other more,
Or maystrye over any man mo than of hymself.
"I were nought worthy, wote God," quod Haukyn, "to were any
    clothes,
Ne noyther sherte ne shone, save for shame one
To kevre my caroigne," quod he, and cryde mercye faste
335 And wepte and weyled; and therewith I awaked.

Passus XV

Ac after my wakyng it was wonder longe
Ar I couth kyndely knowe what was Do-Wel,
And so my witte wex and wanyed til I a fole were.
And somme lakked my lyf—allowed it fewe—
5 And leten for a lorel, and loth to reverencen
Lordes or ladyes or any lyf elles,
As persones in pellure with pendauntes of sylver;
To serjauntz ne to suche seyde noughte ones,
"God loke yow, lordes," ne louted faire,
10 That folke helden me a fole; and in that folye I raved
Tyl Resoun hadde reuthe on me and rokked me aslepe,
Tyl I seigh, as it sorcerye were, a sotyl thinge withal,
One withouten tonge and teeth tolde me whyder I shulde,
And wherof I cam and of what kynde. I conjured hym atte laste
15 If he were Crystes creature, for Crystes love me to tellen.
  "I am Crystes creature," quod he, "and [of his kynne a partye],
In Crystes courte i-knowe wel and [Crystene in many a place].
Is noyther Peter the Porter ne Poule with his fauchoune
That wil defende me the dore—dynge Ich nevre so late,
20 At mydnyght, at mydday, my voice so is y-knowe
That eche a creature of his courte welcometh me fayre."

Thus for our Lord's love Saint Augustine,* a lettered man, taught me:
A blessed life without busy cares for body and for soul: 320
    Felicity without care.
Now God who gives all good grant his soul rest
Who first composed this to explain to men what Poverty meant."
  "Alas," said Hawkin the Active Man then, "that after my
    christening
I hadn't died and been buried deep for Do-Well's sake!
So hard it is," said Hawkin, "to live and to do sin.   325
Sin pursues us always," said he, and began to grow sorrowful,
And wept water with his eyes, and bewailed the time
That ever he'd done deed that displeased dear God;
Swooned and sobbed and sighed full often
That he'd ever had land or lordship, less or more,   330
Or been master over any man more than of himself.
"I would not be worthy, God knows," said Hawkin, "to wear any
    clothes,
Neither shirt nor shoes, except for shame alone
To cover my cadaver," said he, and cried fast for mercy
And wept and wailed; and therewith I awoke.   335

Passus XV

But after my waking it was wondrous long
Before I'd enough natural knowledge* to understand what Do-Well was,
And so my wits waxed and waned till I went out of my mind.
And some scorned my life—few would sanction it—
And looked on me as a lazy loafer, one loath to do honor   5
To lords or ladies or any other living person,
Such as people in fur-pieces with pendants of silver;
To sergeants* and to such I said not once,
"God look you, lords," nor would lowly bow,
So that folk held me a fool; and in that folly I raved   10
Till Reason had ruth[1] on me and rocked me asleep,
Till I saw, as if it were sorcery, a subtle[2] thing withal,
One without tongue or teeth told me where I should go,
And where I came from and of what kind.* I conjured him at the last
If he were Christ's creature, for Christ's love to tell me.   15
  "I am Christ's creature," he said, "and a kinsman of his household,
Known well in Christ's court and to Christians in many a place.
Neither Peter the Porter nor Paul with his falchion[3]
Refuses to admit me at the door—no matter how late I knock,
At midnight, at midday, my voice is so well known   20
That every creature in his court welcomes me fairly."

1. Pity.
2. The Middle English word primarily implies something immaterial rather than something not obvious.
3. *Peter*: St. Peter is the "porter" of Heaven because he holds the keys (Matt. 16:19); *Paul*: St. Paul was represented with a sword, i.e., a falchion, perhaps because he was executed with one, or perhaps to symbolize the "sword of the spirit" (Eph. 6:7).

"What ar ye called," quod I, "in that courte amonges Crystes
    peple?"
"The whiles I quykke the corps," quod he, "called am I *Anima*;
And whan I wilne and wolde, *Animus* Ich hatte.
25 And for that I can and knowe, called am I *Mens*;
And whan I make mone to God, *Memoria* is my name.
And whan I deme domes and do as Treuthe techeth,
Thanne is *Ratio* my right name, Resoun an Englissh.
And whan I fele that folke telleth, my firste name is *Sensus*,
30 And that is wytte and wisdome, the welle of alle craftes.
And whan I chalange or chalange noughte, chepe or refuse,
Thanne am I Conscience y-calde, Goddis clerke and his notarie;
And whan I love lelly owre Lorde and alle other,
Thanne is lele love my name, and in Latyn *Amor*.
35 And whan I [flee] fro the flesshe and forsake the caroigne,
Thanne am I spirit specheles: *Spiritus* thanne Ich hatte.
Austyn and Isodorus, ayther of hem bothe,
Nempned me thus to name; now thow myghte chese
How thow coveitest to calle me, now thow knowest alle my names."
    Anima pro diversis accionibus diversa
        nomina sortitur: Dum vivificat corpus Anima est;
        dum vult Animus est; dum scit Mens est;
        dum recolit Memoria est; dum judicat Racio est;
        dum sentit Sensus est; dum negat
        vel consentit Consciencia est; dum amat Amor est;
        dum spirat Spiritus est.
40   "Ye ben as a bisshop," quod I, al bourdynge that tyme,
"For bisshopes y-blessed thei bereth many names,
Presul and *Pontifex* and *Metropolitanus*,
And other names an hepe, *Episcopus* and *Pastor*."
    "That is soth," seyde he, "now I se thi wille:
45 Thow woldest knowe and kunne the cause of alle her names,
And of myne, if thow myghtest, me thinketh by thi speche."
    "Ye, syre," I seyde, "by so no man were greved,
Alle the sciences under sonne and alle the sotyle craftes,
I wolde I knewe and couth, kyndely, in myne herte."
50   "Thanne artow inparfit," quod he, "and one of Prydes knyghtes.
For such a luste and lykynge Lucifer fel fram Hevene.
    Ponam pedem meum in aquilone et similis ero
        altissimo.

"What are you called in that court," said I, "among Christ's
   people?"
"While I breathe breath in the body," said he, "I am called *Anima*;[4]
And when I will and wish, *Animus* is my name.
And because I'm capable of knowing, I am called *Mens*;   25
And when I make moan to God, *Memoria* is my name.
When I arbitrate issues and act as Truth teaches,
Then *Ratio* is my right name, Reason* in English.
And when I feel what folk tell, my first name is *Sensus*,
And that is wit* and wisdom, the well of all skills.   30
And when I challenge or don't challenge, choose or reject,
Then I'm called Conscience, God's clerk and his notary;
And when I love loyally our Lord and all others,
Then is loyal love my name, and in Latin *Amor*.
And when I flee from the flesh and forsake the body,   35
Then I'm a spirit speechless: then *Spiritus* is my name.
Augustine* and Isidore,[5] each of the two,
Named me with these names; now you might choose
By which you'd care to call me, now you're acquainted with them all."

    Anima is distinguished by various names according to its
       various actions: When it vivifies the body it is Life;
       when it wills it is Soul; when it knows it is Mind;
       when it recollects it is Memory; when it judges it is
       Reason; when it feels it is Sense; when it denies or
       consents it is Conscience; when it loves it is Love;
       when it expires it is Spirit.[6]

"You remind me of a bishop," said I, making a joke,   40
"For those blessed as bishops bear many names,
Praesul and *Pontifex* and *Metropolitanus*,
And a whole heap of others, *Episcopus* and *Pastor*."[7]

    "That is so," he said, "now I see your will:
You would like to learn everything that lies behind their names,   45
And behind mine, if you might, it seems to me from your words."

    "Yes, sir," I said, "so long as no one takes offense,
All the sciences under the sun and all the subtle arts,
I'd like to know them naturally, natively, in my heart."

    "Then you are imperfect," said he, "and are one of Pride's knights. 50
For a wish and a longing like this Lucifer fell from Heaven.
    I shall place my foot in the north and I shall be like the most
       high.[8]

4. The names of *Anima* ("Soul") indicate the soul's various functions: as *Anima*, "Principle of Life or
Being"; as *Animus*, "Will"; as *Mens*, "Mind"; as *Memoria*, "Memory" (but also see "Imaginative"*);
as *Ratio*, "Reason";* as *Sensus*, "Sense," or "Perception"; as *Conscientia*, "Conscience";* as *Amor*,
"Love"; as *Spiritus*, "Spirit." Precisely what the terms mean and how they should be translated is
a matter of debate.
5. Isidore of Seville (c. 560–636), Bishop of Seville and author of a massive encyclopedic work called
Etymologies.
6. From Isidore, whose definitions were widely consulted in the Middle Ages.
7. Medieval titles for a bishop or archbishop reflecting various pagan, governmental, and biblical
functions that contributed historically to the defining of the office. *Praesul*: the leader of the sacred
dances and ritual; *Pontifex*: literally, "bridge-builder," one of the Roman titles for a high priest; *Metropolitanus*: head of a province, based in its central or "mother" city; *Episcopus*: overseer; *Pastor*:
shepherd.
8. Cf. Isa. 14:13–14.

It were ayeynes Kynde," quod he, "and alkynnes resoun
That any creature shulde kunne al excepte Cryste
    one.
Ayein such Salomon speketh and dispiseth her wittes,
And seith, *Sicut, qui mel comedit multum, non est ei bonum,*
    sic qui scrutator est maiestatis opprimitur
55   *a gloria.*
To Englisch men this is to mene that mowen speke and here,
The man that moche hony eteth, his mawe it engleymeth,
And the more that a man of good mater hereth,
But he do therafter it doth hym double scathe.
60 '*Beatus est,*' seith Seynt Bernard, '*qui scripturas legit,*
Et verba vertit in opera fullich to his powere.'
Coveytise to kunne and to knowe science
[Adam and Eve putte out of Paradys].
    Sciencie appetitus hominem inmortalitatis gloriam
      spoliavit.
And righte as hony is yvel to defye and engleymeth the mawe,
65 Right so that thorw resoun wolde the rote knowe
Of God and of his grete myghtes his graces it letteth.
For in the lykyng lith a pryde, and a lycames coveitise,
Ayein Crystes conseille and alle clerkes techyng,
That is *Non plus sapere quam oportet sapere.*
70   Freres and fele other Maistres that to the lewed men prechen,
Ye moeven materes inmesurables to tellen of the Trinité,
That ofte tymes the lewed peple of her bileve douten.
Bettere [it] were [by] mony Doctoures [by-leven] such techyng,
And tellen men of the Ten Comaundementz and touchen the sevene
    synnes,
And of the braunches that burgeouneth of hem and bryngeth men
75   to helle,
And how that folke in folyes myspenden her fyve wittes,
As wel freres as other folke folilich spenen
In housyng, in haterynge, and [in] hiegh clergye shewynge
More for pompe than for pure charité; the poeple wote the sothe.
80 That I lye nought, loo, for lordes ye plesen,
And reverencen the riche the rather for her sylver:
    Confundantur omnes qui adorant sculptilia; Et
      alibi, Ut quid diligitis vanitatem et queritis
      mendacium?
Go to the glose of the verse, ye grete clerkes,
If I lye on yow to my lewed witte, ledeth me to brennynge!
For as [me thynketh] ye forsaketh no mannes almesse,
85 Of usureres, of hores, of avarous chapmen,
And louten to this lordes that mowen lene yow nobles

It would go against Kind,"* he said, "and against all kinds of reason
That any creature's knowledge should include everything but Christ's
    alone.
Solomon speaks against such and despises their wits,
And says, *Just as, if someone eats much honey, it is not good for
    him, so he who is an examiner of majesty is overwhelmed by
    its glory.*[9]   55
This is to mean to English men who may speak and hear,
The man who eats much honey, his maw is cloyed,
And the more good matter that a man hears,
It does him double harm unless he does what it says.
'*Beatus est*,' says Saint Bernard,* '*qui Scripturas legit*,   60
Et verba vertit in opera[1] fully to his power.'
Desire to understand and be skilled in sciences
Put Adam and Eve out of Paradise.
    *The appetite for knowledge despoiled man of the glory of
        immortality.*[2]
And just as honey is hard to digest and overloads the stomach,
Right so any one who with his reason would derive the root   65
Of God and of his great powers will find his graces diminished.
For pride inheres in his interest, and an appetite of the body,
Against Christ's counsel and all clerks'* teaching,
Which is *Know no more than you need to know.*[3]
    Friars and many other Masters* who give ignorant men sermons,   70
You argue incomprehensible issues when you talk of the Trinity,
That the faith of unlearned folk is frequently tinged with doubt.
For many Doctors* it would be better to leave behind such teaching,
And tell men of the Ten Commandments and touch on the seven
    sins,[4]
And of the branches that burgeon from them and bring men to
    hell,   75
And how folk on follies misspend their five senses,
As well friars as other folk foolishly spend
On housing, on habiliments, on showing off high learning
More for pomp than for pure charity; the people know the truth.
And that I'm not lying, look, for it's lords you please,   80
And you reverence the rich more readily for their money:
    *Confounded be all they that worship graven images; And
        elsewhere, So why do you love vanity and seek after
        mendacity?*[5]
Go to the gloss[6] on that verse, you great clerks,
And if I lie about you in my lack of learning, lead me to be burned!
For I feel that you refuse to take alms from no one,
Not from usurers or whores or avaricious merchants,   85
And you bow low to these lords that may allot you nobles

9. Prov. 25:27.
1. "Blessed is he . . . who reads the Scriptures and turns their words into works."
2. Also from St. Bernard.
3. Rom. 12:3.
4. Pride, lechery, envy, avarice, wrath, gluttony, and sloth.
5. Ps. 96:7; Ps. 4:3.
6. The *Glossa Ordinaria*, the traditional medieval commentary on the Bible, interprets the "graven
    images" as lies and as transitory objects of desire.

Ayeine yowre reule and religioun: I take recorde at Jhesus
That seide to his disciples, *'Ne sitis personarum acceptores.'*
Of this matere I myghte make a longe Bible,
90 Ac of curatoures of Crystene peple, as clerkes bereth witnesse,
I shal tellen it for treuth sake; take hede whoso lyketh.
As holynesse and honestete oute of Holi Cherche [spryngeth]
Thorw lele-libbyng men that Goddes lawe techen,
Right so out of Holi Cherche alle yveles spredeth
95 There inparfyt presthod is, prechoures and techeres.
And se it by ensample in somer tyme on trowes
There somme bowes ben leved and somme bereth none.
There is a myschief in the more of suche manere [stokkes];
Right so parsones and prestes and prechoures of Holy Cherche
100 Aren rote of the righte faith to reule the peple;
Ac there the rote is roten, Reson wote the sothe,
Shal nevre floure ne frute [wexe] ne faire leef be grene.
Forthi wolde ye lettred leve the leccherye of clothynge,
And be kynde, as bifel for clerkes, and curteise of Crystes goodes,
105 Trewe of yowre tonge and of yowre taille bothe,
And hatien to here harlotrye, and [aughte] to underfonge
Tythes of untrewe thinge y-tilied or chaffared,
Lothe were lewed men but thei yowre lore folwed
And amenden hem that [thei] mysdon more for yowre ensamples
110 Than forto prechen and preve it nought—ypocrysie it semeth,
For ypocrysie in Latyn is lykned to a [lothelich] dongehul
That were bysnewed with snowe, and snakes wythinne,
Or to a wal that were whitlymed and were foule wythinne.
Right so prestes, prechoures, and prelates [manye],
115 Ye aren enblaunched with *belles paroles* and with [*belles*] clothes,
Ac yowre werkes and yowre wordes thereunder aren ful [wolveliche].
   Johannes Crysostomus of clerkes [carpeth] and prestes:
Sicut de templo omne bonum progreditur, sic de templo omne
   malum procedit. Si sacerdocium integrum fuerit, tota floret ecclesia;
   si, autem, coruptum fuerit, omnium fides marcida est. Si
   sacerdocium fuerit in peccatis, totus populus convertitur ad
   peccandum. Sicut cum videris arborem pallidam et marcidam,
   intelligis quod vicium habet in radice, ita cum videris populum
   indisciplinatum et irreligiosum, sine dubio sacerdocium eius non est
   sanum.
If lewed men wist what this Latyn meneth,
120 And who was myn auctor, moche wonder me thinketh
But if many a prest [forbere] here baselardes and here broches
[And bere] bedes in her hande and a boke under her arme.
Sire Johan and Sire Geffray hath of sylver [a gerdel],
A basellarde or a ballokknyf with botones overgylte,

Against your rule and religion: I find recorded of Jesus
That he said to his disciples, *'Ne sitis personarum acceptores.'*[7]
Of this matter I might make a whole Bible,
But of curators of Christian people, as clerks bear witness,   90
I shall tell it for truth's sake; take heed whoever wishes.
As holiness and honesty spring out of Holy Church
Through lawful-living men that teach the law of God,
Just so out of Holy Church all evils spread
Where there is imperfect priesthood, preachers and teachers.   95
And for an example see how on trees in summer time
There are some boughs that bear leaves and some bear none.
There is some sickness in the root of such sorts of trees;
Just so parsons and priests and preachers of Holy Church
Are the root of the right faith to rule the people;   100
But where the root is rotten, Reason knows the truth,
Shall never flower nor fruit grow nor fair leaf be green.
Therefore if you lettered men would leave your lechery for clothing,
And, as befitted clerks, be kind and courteous with Christ's goods,
True of your tongue and of your tail too,   105
And hate to hear indecency, or ever to accept
Tithes[8] of things untruly gotten by tillage or barter,
Then unlearned men would not be loath to learn from your teaching
And would amend what they do amiss more for your examples
Than if you fail to practice what you preach—that seems hypocrisy,   110
For in a Latin text hypocrisy is likened to a loathsome dunghill
Spread over with snow outside, and snakes inside it,
Or to a wall that's been white-washed and is foul underneath.[9]
Just so priests, preachers, and many prelates too,
You appear bleached with *belles paroles* and with *belles* clothes,[1] 115
But your works and your words are most wolf-like underneath.
    John Chrysostomus comments on clerks and priests:
Just as from the temple all good emanates, so from the temple all
    evil emanates. If the priesthood has been unspotted, the whole
    church flourishes; if, however, it has been corrupted, every-
    one's faith is withered. If the priesthood has been involved in
    sin, the whole population is turned toward sinning. Just as
    when you see a tree faded and withered, you know it has a
    defect in its root, so when you see a people undisciplined and
    irreligious, without doubt the priesthood is not healthy.[2]
If unlearned men were aware what this Latin means,
And what man was my authority, it would seem to me much wonder   120
Unless many priests began to forbear their brooches and shortswords
And bore beads in their hands and a book under their arms.
Sir John and Sir Geoffrey have a silver girdle,
A shortsword or a snickersnee with splendid gilt buttons,

7. "Be not unjust regarders of persons"; Jas. 2:1; Deut. 1:17.
8. Taxes due the Church.
9. Cf. Matt. 23:27, where the comparison is to a "white sepulchre" with bones and stench inside.
1. "Lofty, fine words," "beautiful clothes."
2. St. John Chysostom (c. 345–407) was one of the greatest of the Fathers of the Eastern (Greek)
   Church—hence his "great" authority (l. 120). But the passage is actually not his but from an
   unknown Latin author often mistaken for him; cf. Isa. 24:2.

125   Ac a portous that shulde be his plow, *Placebo* to segge—
     Hadde he nevre [saved] sylver therto [for spendyng at ale];
     [He syngeth service bokelees, seith it with ydel wille].
     Allas, ye lewed men, moche lese ye on prestes!
     Ac thinge that wykkedlich is wonne and with false sleigthes,
130   Wolde nevere witte of witty God but wikked men it hadde,
     The which aren prestes inparfit and prechoures after sylver,
     Sectoures and sudenes, somnoures and her lemmannes,
     This that with gyle was geten ungraciouslich is spended.
     So harlotes and hores ar hulpen with such goodis
135   [Ac] Goddes folke for defaute therof forfaren and spillen.
     Curatoures of Holy Kirke as clerkes that ben averouse,
     Lightlich that they leven loselles it habbeth,
     Or [endeth] intestate, and thanne—[entreth] the bisshop!
     And maketh murthe therewith and his [meyné] bothe;
140   And [nempneth hym] a nygarde that no good myghte asspare
     To frende ne to fremmed—'The Fende have his soule!
     For a wrecched hous he helde al his lyftyme,
     And that he spared and bispered, spene we in murthe!'
     By lered, by lewed, that loth is to spende,
145   Thus gone her godes be the goste faren.
     Ac for good men, God wote, gret dole men maken,
     And bymeneth good mete-yyveres, and in mynde haveth
     In prayers and in penaunces, and in parfyt charité."
        "What is charité," quod I tho. "A childissh thinge," he seide.
          Nisi efficiamini sicut parvuli non intrabitis in regnum
            celorum.
150   "Withouten fauntelté or foly, a fre liberal wille."
        "Where shulde men fynde such a frende with so fre an herte?
     I have lyved in londe," quod I, "my name is Longe Wille,
     And fonde I nevere ful charité, bifore ne bihynde.
     Men beth mercyable to mendynantz and to pore,
155   And wolen lene there thei leve lelly to ben payed.
     Ac charité that Poule preyseth best, and most plesaunte to owre
        Saveoure—
     Non inflatur, non ambiciosa, non querit que sua sunt—
     I seigh nevere such a man, so me God helpe,
     That he ne wolde aske after his, and otherwhile coveyte
160   Thinge that neded hym nought, and nyme it if he myghte.
     Clerkis kenne me that Cryst is in alle places,
     Ac I seygh hym nevere sothly but as myself in a miroure.
        Hic in enigmate, tunc facie ad faciem.
     And so I trowe trewly, by that men telleth of [it],
     [Charité] is nought championes fyghte ne chaffare as I trowe."
     "Charité," quod he, "ne chaffareth noughte ne chalengeth,
165   ne craveth.
     As proude of a peny as of a pounde of golde,

But a prayerbook that should be his plow to repeat *Placebo*—   125
He's never saved silver to buy one because of spending on ale;
He sings the service without a book, says it with idle mind.
Alas, you unlearned men, you lose much on priests!
But whatever is wickedly won and with false tricks,
Would never the wisdom of wise God but wicked men should have it,   130
Such as imperfect priests and those who preach for money,
Executors and subdeans,* summoners* and their mistresses,
What was gotten with guile is ungraciously expended.
Thus whoremongers and whores are helped with such goods
But God's folk are enfeebled and founder for lack of them.   135
Curators of Holy Kirk such as clerks that are avaricious,
What they leave behind low-living men lightly spend,
Or else they end intestate, and then—enter the bishop!
And he makes merry with it and his henchmen do too;
And they name him a no-good that spared no goods   140
For friend or for foreigner—'The Fiend have his soul!
For he held a wretched household all his lifetime,
And what he saved and stored away, let's spend it in mirth!'
With learned, with unlearned, who are loath to spend,
That's how their goods go when their spirit's gone hence.   145
But for good men, God knows, men greatly mourn,
And lament good meat-givers, and keep them in remembrance
In prayers and in penances, and in perfect charity."
    "What is charity?" I asked then. "A childish thing," he said.
        Unless ye become as little children ye shall not enter into
            the kingdom of Heaven.[3]
"Without a child's fantasy or folly, a free liberal will."   150
    "Where should one find such a friend with so free a heart?
I have lived in land," said I, "my name is Long Will,[4]
And I never found full charity, before nor behind.
Men are merciful to mendicants and to poor men,
And will lend money when they believe they can rely on repayment.   155
But charity that Paul praises best, and most pleasing to our
        Savior—
Is not puffed up, is not ambitious, seeketh not her own—[5]
I saw never such a man, so God help me,
Who would not ask for what is his, and at other times covet
A thing he had no need for, and nab it if he could.   160
Clerks proclaim to me that Christ is in all places,
But I never saw him surely except as myself in a mirror.
        Here darkly, then face to face.[6]
And so I trust truly, from what men tell about it,
Charity is neither what champions fight for nor exchangeable for cash."
    "Charity," said he, "neither makes exchanges nor challenges, nor
        does it crave.   165
As pleased with a penny* as with a pound of gold,

3. Matt. 18:3.
4. In this passage, "lived in land" and "Long Will" have been thought by some modern critics to play
on the name of the (supposed) author, William Langland. Cf. pp. 573 ff.
5. 1 Cor. 13:4–5.
6. 1 Cor. 13:12.

And is as gladde of a goune of a graye russet
As of a tunicle of Tarse or of trye scarlet.
He is gladde with alle gladde, and good tyl alle wykked
170   And leneth and loveth alle that owre Lorde made.
Curseth he no creature ne he can bere no wratthe,
Ne no lykynge hath to lye ne laughe men to scorne.
Al that men seith, he let it soth and in solace taketh,
And alle manere meschiefs in myldenesse he suffreth.
175   Coveiteth he none erthly good, but Heveneriche blisse."
        "Hath he any rentes or ricchesse or any riche frendes?"
        "Of rentes ne of ricchesse ne reccheth he nevere,
For a frende that fyndeth hym failled hym nevere at nede:
Fiat voluntas tua fynt hym evermore,
180   And if he soupeth [eteth] but a soppe of *Spera-in-Deo*.
He can purtreye wel the Paternoster and peynte it with *Aves*
And otherwhile is his wone to wende in pilgrymage
There pore men and prisones liggeth, her pardoun to have;
Though he bere hem no bred, he bereth hem swetter lyflode;
185   Loveth hem as owre Lorde biddeth and loketh how thei fare.
And whan he is wery of that werke thanne wil he sometyme
Labory in a lavendrye wel the lengthe of a myle,
And yerne into youthe and yepliche [seke]
Pryde with al the appurtenaunce, and pakken hem togyderes,
190   And bouken hem at his brest and beten hem clene,
And leggen on longe with *Laboravi in gemitu meo*,
And with warme water at his eyghen wasshen hem after.
Thanne he syngeth whan he doth so, and sometyme wepyng,
Cor contritum et humiliatum, Deus, non despicies."
        "By Cryst! I wolde that I knewe hym," quod I, "no creature
195   levere."
        "Withouten helpe of Piers Plowman," quod he, "his persone
            seestow nevere."
        "Where clerkes knowen hym," quod I, "that kepen Holy Kirke?"
        "Clerkes have no knowyng," quod he, "but by werkes and bi
            wordes.
Ac Piers the Plowman parceyveth more depper
200   That is the wille and wherfore that many wyghte suffreth:
        Et vidit Deus cogitaciones eorum.
For there ar [pure] proude-herted men paciente of tonge
And boxome as of berynge to burgeys and to lordes,
And to pore peple han peper in the nose,
And as a lyoun he loketh there men lakketh his werkes.
205   For there ar beggeres and bidderes, bedmen as it were,
Loketh as lambren and semen lyf-holy,

And as glad for a gown of a gray russet
As for a jacket cut from Tarsia cloth or from costly scarlet.[7]
He's glad with all who're glad, and good to all wicked
And loves and lends help to all that our Lord made.   170
He curses no creature and he can harbor no anger,
And has no liking to lie or laugh men to scorn.
All that men say, he assumes it's true and accepts without question,
And all sorts of distress he suffers with mildness.
He covets no earthly good, but Heaven's bliss."   175
　　"Has he any income or assets or any rich friends?"
　　"In income and assets he has no interest,
For a friend provides for him who never failed him at need:
Fiat voluntas tua[8] provides for him always,
And if he sups he eats but a snack of *Spera-in-Deo*.[9]   180
He can portray well the Paternoster* and paint it with *Aves*[1]
And he is accustomed occasionally to come as a pilgrim
To where poor men and prisoners lie, to ask pardon from them;
Though he bears them no bread, he bears them sweeter sustenance;
He loves them as our Lord bids and looks after their welfare.   185
And when he's weary of that work then he will sometimes
Labor in a laundry the length of a mile-walk,
And burst into youth's bailiwick and briskly seek out
Pride with all its appurtenances, and pack them together,
And bang them against his breast and beat them clean,   190
And lay on long with *Laboravi in gemitu meo*,[2]
And with warm water from his eyes wash them after.
Then he sings when he does so, and sometimes weeping,
A contrite and humbled heart, God, thou wilt not despise."[3]
　　"By Christ! I wish he were my acquaintance," said I, "no creature
　　　　sooner."   195
　　"Without help of Piers Plowman," said he, "you'll not see his
　　　　person ever."
　　"Do clerks that keep Holy Kirk know him?" I asked.
　　"Except by works and words," said he, "clerks have no way of
　　　　knowing.
But Piers the Plowman perceives more deeply
What is the will and wherefore that many a one suffers: 200
　　And God saw their thoughts.[4]
For there are purely proud-hearted men patient of tongue
And bland in their behavior to burgesses* and lords,
And for poor people have pepper in their nose,[5]
And look like a lion when men belittle their deeds.
For there are beggars and prayer-bidders, beadsmen* as it were,   205
Who look like lambs and seem life-holy,

7. *Russet*: a poor fabric; *Tarsia cloth . . . scarlet*: costly ones.
8. "Thy will be done": Matt. 6:10 (the Lord's Prayer). Note this is the "livelihood" Patience had in his poke, XIV.50.
9. "Hope-in-God": Ps. 41:6.
1. Prayers beginning "Hail [*Ave*] Mary": cf. Luke 1:28.
2. "I have labored in groaning": Ps. 6:7.
3. Ps. 50:19.
4. Luke 11:17 reads, "He [Jesus] saw their thoughts."
5. Proverbial expression meaning "treat with contempt," i.e., respond as if they were an irritant.

Ac it is more to have her mete [on] such an esy manere
Than for penaunce and parfitnesse, the poverté that such taketh.
Therefore by coloure ne by clergye knowe shaltow hym nevere,
210 Noyther thorw wordes ne werkes, but thorw wille one,
And that knoweth no clerke, ne creature in erthe
But Piers the Plowman, *Petrus id est Christus.*
For he [lyveth] noughte in lolleres ne in lande-leperes hermytes,
Ne at ancres there a box hangeth; alle suche thei faiten.
215 Fy on faitoures and *in fautores suos!*
     For charyté is Goddis champioun and as a good chylde hende,
And the meryest of mouth at mete where he sitteth.
The love that lith in his herte maketh hym lyghte of speche
And is compenable and confortatyf as Cryst bit hymselve:
     Nolite fieri sicut ypocrite tristes.
220 For I have seyn hym in sylke and sommetyme in russet,
Bothe in grey and in grys and in gulte herneys,
And as gladlich he it gaf to gomes that it neded.
Edmonde and Edwarde eyther were kynges
And seyntes y-sette, [stille] charité hem folwed.
225 I have seyne charité also syngen and reden,
Ryden and rennen in ragged wedes,
Ac biddyng as beggeres bihelde I hym nevere.
Ac in riche robes rathest he walketh,
Y-called and y-crimiled and his crowne shave.
230 And in a freres frokke he was y-founde ones,
Ac it is [fern and fele yere] agoo, in Fraunceys tyme.
In that secte sitthe to selde hath he be knowen.
Riche men he recomendeth and of her robes taketh,
That withouten wyles leden [wel] her lyves.
     Beatus est dives qui, etc.
235 In kynges courte he cometh ofte there the conseille is trewe,
Ac if Coveityse be of the conseille he wil nought come therinne.
In courte among [the comune] he cometh but selde
For braulyng and bakbytyng and beryng of fals witnesse.
In the constorie bifor the comissarie he cometh nought ful ofte,
240 For her lawe dureth overlonge but if thei lacchen sylver,
And matrimoigne for monye maken, and unmaken,

But it's more to get their meals in a manner so easy
Than for penance or perfectness, the poverty they adopt.
Therefore by color[6] nor by clergy you'll never come to know him,
Neither through words nor works, but through will alone,   210
And no clerk knows that, nor creature on earth
But Piers the Plowman, *Petrus id est Christus*.[7]
For he does not live in lollers or land-leaping hermits,
Nor with anchorites* where a box[8] hangs; all such are frauds.
Fie on fakers and *in fautores suos!*[9]   215
    For charity is God's champion and as a good child courteous,
And the merriest of mouth at meals where he sits.
The love that lies in his heart makes him lively of speech,
And he is companionable and comforting as Christ bids himself:
    Be not sad as the hypocrites.[1]
For I have seen him in silk and sometimes in russet,   220
Both in gray cloth and gay fur and in gilt harness,
And he'd hand it over happily to any one who needed it.
Edmund and Edward each was a king[2]
And they're established as saints, charity pursued them so steadily.
I have also seen charity sing and read,   225
Ride and run in ragged clothes,
But behaving like a beggar I never beheld him.
But in rich robes he most readily walks,
With skullcap and curled hair and his crown shaven.[3]
And in a friar's frock he was found once,   230
But it was many years far, far gone, in Francis'* time.
In that sect since he's been too seldom known.
He has regard for rich men and takes robes from them,
Those who without wiles lead well their lives.
    Blessed is the rich man who, etc.[4]
He comes often to the king's court where the council is true,   235
But if Covetousness is in the council he will not come there.
Among the commons in court he comes only rarely
Because of brawling and backbiting and bearing of false witness.
In the consistory* before the commissary[5] he comes not very often,
For their lawsuits last overlong unless they get silver,   240
And for money they make marriage, and unmake it too,

6. I.e., appearance.
7. "Peter, that is, Christ." This brief line brings together crucial images, including these: 1 Cor. 10:4 calls Christ "the rock (*petra*)" from which we drink spiritually as the Israelites in the desert drank from a spring Moses brought forth by striking a rock (Num. 20:1–13); in Matt. 16:18, Christ gives Simon the name Peter and calls him the "rock" on which the church will be built; "Piers" is a form of the name *Petrus*, or Peter.
8. *Lollers*: lazy freeloaders, a term of contempt later (but not at this date) applied to the heretical proto-Protestant followers of John Wycliffe (1320?–1384). *Land-leaping hermits*: hermits who don't stay put in their hermitages. *Box*: i.e., alms-box (anchorites, who were solitaries, were not supposed to go out begging).
9. "On their protectors."
1. Matt 6:16.
2. *Edmund*: Edmund the Martyr was King of East Anglia (died 870). *Edward*: Edward the Confessor (died 1066).
3. I.e., he is most appropriately made an abbot or bishop; lines 244–48 remark how rarely he is seen in a position of ecclesiastical authority.
4. Ecclus. 31:8: the verse continues, "is found without stain."
5. The bishop's official representative in part of his diocese, who can act for him in his absence and who presides over the bishop's court.

And that Conscience and Cryst hath y-knitte faste
Thei undon it [undignely], tho doctours of lawe.
[Amonges erchebisshopes and bisshopes, for beggares sake,
245 For to wonye with hem his wone was sometyme,
And Cristes patrimoigné to the pore parcelmele dele;
Ac Avarice hath the keyes now and kepeth for his kynnesmen,
And for his sectoures and his servauntz, and some for here children].
Ac I ne lakke no lyf, but Lorde amende us alle,
250 And gyve us grace, good God, charité to folwe.
For whoso myghte mete with hym, such maneres hym eyleth
Noyther he blameth ne banneth, bosteth ne prayseth,
Lakketh ne loseth, ne loketh up sterne,
Craveth ne coveiteth ne crieth after more:
        In pace in idipsum dormiam, etc.
255 The moste lyflode that he lyveth by is love in Goddis passioun;
Noyther he biddeth ne beggeth ne borweth to yelde.
Misdoth he no man, ne with his mouth greveth.
        Amonges Cristene men this myldnesse shulde laste
In alle manere angres, have this at herte
260 That though thei suffred al this, God suffred for us more
In ensample we shulde do so, and take no venjaunce
Of owre foes that doth us falsenesse; that is owre Fadres wille.
For wel may every man wite if God hadde wolde hymselve,
Sholde nevere Judas ne Juwe have Jhesu don on Rode,
265 Ne han martired Peter ne Poule, ne in prisoun holden.
Ac he suffred in ensample that we shulde suffre also,
And seide to suche that suffre wolde,
['*Pacientes vincunt verbi gratia,*'] and [verred] ensamples manye.
[Lo], in *Legenda Sanctorum*, the lyf of holy seyntes,
270 What penaunce and poverté and passioun thei suffred,
In hunger, in hete, in al manere angres.
Antony and Egidie and other holi fadres
Woneden in wildernesse amonge wilde bestes,
Monkes and mendynauntz, men bi hemselve,
275 In spekes an spelonkes, selden speken togideres.
Ac noyther Antony ne Egidy ne hermite that tyme
Of liouns ne of leoperdes no lyflode ne toke,
But of foules that fleeth: thus fynt men in bokes.
Excepte that Egydie after an hynde cryede,
280 And thorw the mylke of that mylde best the man was susteyned;
[Ac] day by day had he hir nought his hunger forto slake,
But selden and sondrie tymes, as seith the boke and techeth.
Antony adayes aboute none-tyme
Had a bridde that broughte hym bred that he by lyved,

And what Conscience* and Christ have knit fast together
They disrespectfully undo it, those doctors of law.
Among archbishops and bishops, for beggars' sake,
It was once his wont to dwell with them   245
And apportion to the poor Christ's patrimony;
But Avarice has the keys now and keeps it for his kinsmen,
And for his executors and his servants, and some for their children.
But I belittle no living person, but Lord amend us all,
And give us grace, good God, to follow charity.   250
For whoever might meet with him, his manners are such
That he neither blames nor berates, boasts nor praises,
Libels nor lauds, nor looks up sternly,
Craves nor covets nor cries for more:
       In peace in the selfsame I shall sleep, etc.[6]
The largest livelihood that he lives on is love in God's passion;   255
He neither begs nor beseeches nor borrows at interest.
He mistreats no man, nor lets his mouth grieve him.
       Among Christian men this mildness should endure
In all kinds of ills, have this at heart
That though they suffered all this, God suffered for us more   260
In example that we should do the same, and take no vengeance
On our foes who do us falseness; that is our Father's will.
For every one may know well that if God had willed himself,
Should never Judas nor Jew have put Jesus on the Cross,
Nor have martyred Peter or Paul, nor held them prisoners.   265
But he suffered in example that we should suffer also,
And said to such as were willing sufferers,
'Patientes vincunt verbi gratia,'[7] and advanced many examples.
       Lo, in *Legenda Sanctorum*,[8] the life of holy saints,
What penance and poverty and passion they suffered,   270
In hunger, in heat, in all sorts of vexations.
Antony and Egidius[9] and other holy fathers
Had their homes in the wilderness among wild animals,
Monks and mendicants, men by themselves,
In crevices and caves, conversed seldom together.   275
But neither Antony nor Egidius nor any hermit then
From lions or leopards would accept livelihood,
But from fowls that fly: thus men find in books.
Except that Egidius had a hind[1] he'd call for,
And through the milk of that mild beast the man was sustained;   280
But he did not have her every day to assuage his hunger,
But seldom and at scattered times, as the book says and teaches.
Every day Antony about high noon
Had a bird that brought him bread that he lived on,

6. Ps. 4:9: the verse continues, "and I shall find rest."
7. "The patient overcome through grace of the word."
8. *Saints' Lives.*
9. The stories of these (and the other famous hermits mentioned in the next lines) appear in the *Legenda Aurea, The Golden Legend*, a collection of saints' lives. *Antony*: St. Anthony, an early hermit
   in the desert (died 356), was believed to be the founder of monasticism; *Egidius*: (St. Giles) was a
   Greek who became a hermit in southern France (died 700).
1. A female deer.

285 And though the gome hadde a geste God fonde hem bothe.
Poule *primus heremita* had parroked hymselve
That no man mighte hym se for mosse and for leves.
Foules hym fedde fele wynteres withalle,
Til he founded freres of Austines ordre—[or ellis freres lyen].
290 Poule after his prechyng panyers he made,
And wan with his hondes that his wombe neded.
Peter fisched for his fode, and his felawe Andrewe;
Some thei solde and some thei sothe and so thei lyved bothe.
And also Marie Magdeleyne by mores lyved and dewes,
295 Ac moste thorw [meditacioun], and mynde of God almighty.
I shulde nought this sevene dayes seggen hem alle
That lyveden thus for owre Lordes love manye longe yeres.
Ac there ne was lyoun ne leopart that on laundes wenten,
Noyther bere ne bor ne other best wilde,
300 That ne fel to her feet and fauned with the tailles;
And if thei couth han y-carped, by Cryst, as I trowe,
Thei wolde have fedde that folke bifor wilde foules.
[For al the curteisye that bestes konne thei kidde that
folk ofte,
In likkyng and in lowynge, ther thei on laundes yede].
305 Ac God sent hem fode bi foules and by no fierse bestes,
In menynge that meke thinge mylde thinge shulde fede.
[Right so] religious ryghtful men shulde fynde,
And lawful men to lyf-holy men lyflode brynge;
And thanne wolde lordes and ladyes be loth to agulte,
310 And to take of her tenauntz more than Treuth wolde,
Fonde thei that freres wolde forsake her almesses,
And bidden hem bere it there it was y-borwed.
For we [by] Goddes [bihestes] abiden alwey
Tyl briddes brynge us [wherby] we shulde lyve.
315 For had ye potage and payn ynough and peny-ale to drynke
And a messe theremydde of o manere kynde,
Ye had right ynough, ye religious, and so yowre reule me
tolde:

*Numquid, dicit Job, rugiet onager cum herbam habuerit aut mugiet bos
cum ante plenum presepe steterit? Brutorum animalium natura te
condempnat, quia cum eis pabulum commune sufficiat; ex adipe
prodijt iniquitas tua.*

If lewed men knewe this Latyn thei wolde loke whom thei
yeve,
320 And avyse hem bifore a fyve dayes or sexe
Or thei amortesed to monkes or [monyales] her rentes.

And though the good man had a guest God provided for them both.   285
Paul *primus heremita*[2] had penned himself up
So that no man might see him for moss and for leaves.
Fowls fed him all his food for many a winter,
Till he founded friars of Austin's* order—or else friars lie.
After his preaching Paul practiced basket-making,[3]   290
And earned with his hands what his stomach had need of.
Peter fished for his food, like his fellow Andrew;[4]
They sold some and stewed some and so they both lived.
And also Mary Magdalene[5] lived on meals of roots and dews,
But mostly through meditation, with her mind on God almighty.   295
In seven days I'd not succeed in speaking of them all
Who lived thus for our Lord's love many long years.
But there was no lion or leopard that lived in the woods,
Neither bear nor boar nor wild beast of other kind,
That didn't fall to their feet and fawn with their tails;   300
And if they could have communicated, by Christ, as I think,
They would have fed that folk before wild fowls did.
For all the courtesy that animals have they often showed those
     people,
By licking, by lowing, where they walked along through the woods.
But God sent them food by fowls and not by fierce beasts,   305
Meaning that the meek should maintain the mild.
Right so righteous men should maintain religious* orders,
And lawful men bring livelihood to life-holy men;
And then lords and ladies would be loath to transgress,
And to take from their tenants more than Truth would allow,   310
If they found that friars would refuse their alms,
And bid them bring it back to where it had been borrowed.
For by God's will we are waiting always
Till birds bring us wherewithal by which to live.
For if you had pottage and a piece of bread and penny-ale to drink 315
And a single serving of some sort of food,
You would have right enough, you religious,* and so your rule told
     me:
*Says Job, Will the wild ass bray when he hath grass or the ox low
     when he standeth before a full manger? The nature of brute
     animals condemns you, since common food suffices with
     them; from fat your iniquity proceeds.*[6]
If unlearned men knew this Latin they'd look hard at whom they give
     to,
And reflect beforehand five or six days   320
Before they resigned their revenues to religious men and women.

2. "The first hermit": St. Paul of Thebes (died 342), who is also supposed to have supported himself
   by making baskets. The Austin Friars claimed him (not without controversy) as their founder.
3. This Paul is St. Paul the Apostle—he, however, made tents, not baskets (Acts 18:3); Langland, like
   other medieval writers, may be confusing the two Pauls.
4. The Apostles Peter and Andrew, his brother, were fishermen when Jesus called them (Matt. 4:18).
5. The repentant sinner and follower of Jesus in the New Testament. According to medieval legend
   she lived in solitude for thirty years in the wilderness of southern France.
6. The first sentence is from Job 6:5. The second, which could be Langland's own, comments on the
   biblical text.

Allas, lordes and ladyes, lewed conseille have ye,
To yyve fram yowre eyres that yowre ayeles yow lefte,
And [bisette] to bidde for yow to such that ben riche,
325   And ben founded and feffed eke to bidde for other.
Who perfourneth this prophecye of the peple that now lybbeth,
Dispersit, dedit pauperibus?
If any peple perfourme that texte it ar this pore freres,
For that thei beggen abouten in buildynge thei spene,
330   And on hemself sum and such as ben her laboreres;
And of hem that habbeth thei taken and yyve hem that ne habbeth.
Ac clerkes and knyghtes and comuneres that ben riche,
Fele of yow fareth as if I a forest hadde
That were ful of faire trees, and I fonded and caste
335   How I myghte mo therinne amonges hem sette.
Right so, ye riche, ye robeth that ben riche
And helpeth hem that helpeth yow and yiveth there no nede is,
As whoso filled a toune [ful] of a fressh ryver
And went forth with that water to woke with Themese.
340   Right so, ye riche, ye robeth and fedeth
Hem that han as ye han—hem ye make at ese.
Ac Religious that riche ben shulde rather feste beggeres
Than burgeys that riche ben, as the Boke techeth:
    Quia sacrilegium est res pauperum non pauperibus dare.
    Item, peccatoribus dare est demonibus immolare.
    Item, monache, si indiges et accipis, pocius das
    quam accipis; si, autem, non eges
    et accipis rapis. Porro, non indiget monachus
    si habeat quod nature sufficit.
Forthi I conseille alle Cristene to confourmen hem to Charité,
345   For Charité withoute chalengynge unchargeth the soule,
And many a prisone fram purgatorie thorw his preyeres delyvreth.
Ac there is a defaute in the folke that the faith kepeth,
Wherfore folke is the feblere and nought ferme of bilieve.
As in Lussheborwes is a lyther alay, and yet loketh he lyke a sterlynge;
350   The merke of that moné is good, ac the metal is fieble;
And so it fareth by some folke now; thei han a faire speche,
Croune and crystendome, the Kynges merke of Hevene,
Ac the metal, that is mannes soule, [myd] synne is foule alayed.
Bothe lettred and lewede beth allayed now with synne
355   That no lyf loveth other, ne owre Lorde, as it semeth,
For thorw werre and wykked werkes and wederes [unsesonable]
Weder-wise shipmen and witti clerkes also
Han no bilieve to the lifte ne to the [lodesterre].
Astrymyanes alday in her arte faillen
360   That whilum warned bifore what shulde falle after.
Shipmen and sheperdes that with shipp wenten
Wisten by the walkene what shulde bityde;
As of wederes and wyndes thei warned men ofte.

Alas, lords and ladies, there's little wisdom in your counsel,
To alienate from your heirs what your ancestors left you,
And employ it to get prayers from people who are rich,
And who are founded and funded to pray for others.   325
Who performs the prophecy of people now living,
He hath dispersed, he hath given to the poor?[7]
If any people perform that text it is these poor friars,
For what they get by begging about they use for building expenses,
And spend some on themselves and on such as are their laborers;   330
And they take from them that have and give to them that have not.
But commoners who've acquired money and rich clerks and knights,
Many of you are apt to act as if I had a forest
That was full of fair trees, and I devised a plan
How I might plant more among those that were there.   335
Right so, you rich, you give robes to those who're rich
And help whoever helps you and give to them who have no need,
Like someone who filled a cask full from a fresh river
And went forth with that water to wet down the Thames.
Right so, you rich, you give robes and food   340
To those who have as you have—it is they whom you ease.
But religious who are rich should rather feast beggars
Than burgesses* that live in abundance, as the Book teaches:
> *Since it is sacrilege not to give to the poor what is theirs.*
>> *Likewise, to give to sinners is to sacrifice to devils.*
>> *Likewise, monk, if you are in need and receive, you*
>> *give rather than receive; if, however, you are not in*
>> *need and receive, you are stealing. Further, the monk*
>> *lacks nothing who has what suffices to nature.*[8]
Therefore I counsel all Christians to conform themselves to Charity,
For without challenging the debt Charity discharges the soul of it,   345
And through his prayers many a prisoner is freed from purgatory.
But there is a deficiency in the folk who supervise the faith,
By which lay folk become the feebler and not firm of belief.
As in Luxemburgs[9] is a base alloy, and yet they look like sterling;
The mark of that money is good, but the metal is inferior;   350
And so it fares with some folk now; they have a fair speech,
Shaven crown and christening, the King of Heaven's mark,
But the metal, that is man's soul, is much alloyed with sin.
Both learned and unlearned are alloyed now with sin
So that no living creature loves another, nor our Lord, as it seems,   355
For through war and wicked works and unseasonable weather
Weather-wise shipmen and witty* clerks as well
Can no longer rely on the sky aloft or on the lodestar.
Every day astronomers prove unable in their craft
Which used once to warn before what should happen later.   360
Shipmen and shepherds who set out to earn their wages
Saw by the sky what should befall;
About weather and winds they warned people often.

7. Ps. 111:9.
8. Statements deriving from St. Jerome,* who was associated with asceticism in the Middle Ages.
9. Substandard coins made in Luxembourg.

Tilieres that tiled the erthe tolden her maistres,
365 By the sede that thei sewe, what thei selle mighte,
And what to leve and to lyve by, the londe was so trewe.
Now failleth the folke of the flode, and of the londe bothe,
Sheperdes and shipmen, and so do this tilieres.
Noither thei kunneth ne knoweth one cours bifor another.
370 Astrymyanes also aren at her wittes ende;
Of that was calculed of the element, the contrarie thei fynde.
Gramer, the grounde of al, bigyleth now children
For is none of this newe clerkes, whoso nymeth hede,
That can versifye faire ne formalich enditen,
375 Ne nought on amonge an hundreth that an auctour can construe,
Ne rede a lettre in any langage but in Latyn or in Englissh.
Go now to any degré, and but if Gyle be mayster,
[And, as usher under hym to fourmen us alle,
Flaterere his felawe, ferly me thynketh].
380 Doctoures of decres and of divinité maistres,
That shulde konne and knowe alkynnes clergye,
And answere to argumentz, and [assoille] a *Quodlibet*—
I dar nought seggen it for shame—if suche weren apposed
Thei shulde faillen in her philosofye and in phisyk bothe.
385   Wherfore I am afered of folke of Holi Kirke,
Lest thei overhuppen, as other don, in offices and in houres.
Ac if thei overhuppe—as I hope noughte—owre byleve suffiseth,
As clerkes in Corpus Cristi Feste singen and reden
That *sola fides sufficit* to save with lewed peple.
390 And so may Sarasenes be saved, Scribes and [Grekis].
Allas, thanne, but owre loresmen lyven as thei leren us,
And for her lyvynge that lewed men be the lother God agulten.
For Sarasenes han somwhat semynge to owre bileve,
For thei love and bileve in o [Lord] almighty,
395 And we lered and lewede in on God bileveth;
[Cristene and uncristene in on God bileveth].
Ac one Makometh, a man, in mysbileve
Broughte Sarasenes of Surré, and se in what manere.
This Makometh was a Crystene man, and for he moste noughte be
        pope,
400 Into Surré he soughte, and thorw his sotil wittes
Daunted a dowve, and day and nyghte hir fedde.
The corne that she cropped he caste it in his ere,
And if he amonge the poeple preched or in places come,
Thanne wolde the colver come to the clerkes ere
405 Menynge as after meet; thus Makometh hir enchaunted,
And dide folke thanne falle on knees, for he swore in his prechynge

Tillers who tilled the earth could tell their masters,
From the seed that they sowed, what they might sell at market,   365
And what to let be and what to live on, the land was so true.
Now the land fails folk, and the flood does too,
Shepherds and shipmen, and so with these plowmen.
They can't interpret or distinguish one tendency from another.
Astronomers also are at the end of their wits;   370
What they've calculated about the element, the contrary occurs.
Grammar, the ground of all, now beguiles children
For there's not one of these new clerks, if you note carefully,
That can versify fairly or formally compose,
Nor one out of a hundred who can understand an author,   375
Or read a letter in any language but Latin or English.
Go now to any degree,[1] and unless Guile is the master,*
And, as an usher[2] under him to discipline us all,
Flatterer his fellow, I'd find it a wonder.
Doctors of decretals[3] and masters of divinity,   380
Who should be cognizant and competent in all kinds of learning,
And answer to arguments, and handle a *Quodlibet*[4]—
I dare not say it for shame—if such were examined
They should fail in their philosophy and in physics both.
    Therefore I am afraid for folk of Holy Church,   385
Lest, like some others, they leap over their offices and hours.*
But if they overleap[5]—as I hope they don't—our faith suffices,
As clerks in the Feast of Corpus Christi sing and read
That *sola fides sufficit*[6] to save ignorant people with.
And so may Saracens be saved, Scribes and Greeks.   390
Alas, then, but those we learn from live the way they teach us,
And for their living that unlearned men be the loather to offend God.
For the Saracens' creed is somewhat similar to ours,
For they love and believe in one Lord almighty,
And we learned and unlearned believe in one God;   395
Christians and unchristians all believe in one God.
But one Mohammed, a man, into misbelief
Brought Saracens of Syria, and see in what way.
This Mohammed was a Christian man, and because he might not be
        pope,
He set off for Syria, and with his subtle wits   400
Tamed a turtledove, and fed her all times of day and night.
The corn that she cropped he cast it in his ear,
And if he preached among the people or in places he came to,
Then the culver[7] would come to the clerk's ear
Intent on taking food; thus Mohammed enticed her,   405
And made folk fall on their knees, for he swore in his sermons

---

1. I.e., look at the program of study leading to a degree at any level of the educational system.
2. An assistant teacher.
3. Authorities on papal decrees.
4. "Suppose [that]": the opening formula in a scholarly debate or exercise.
5. *Offices*: periods of liturgical prayer. *Overleap*: "skip over parts of."
6. "Faith alone suffices": from a hymn sung on Corpus Christi. The point at issue is whether a service conducted by a priest who skips segments of it is invalid.
7. Dove.

That the colver that come so come fram God of Hevene
As messager to Makometh, men forto teche.
And thus thorw wyles of his witte and a whyte dowve,
410 Makometh in mysbileve men and wommen broughte,
That lered there and lewed yit lyven on his lawes.
And sitth owre Saveoure suffred the Sarasenes so bigiled
Thorw a Crystene clerke acursed in his soule—
Ac for drede of the deth I dar nought telle treuthe,
415 How Englissh clerkes a colver feden that Coveityse hatte,
And ben manered after Makometh that no man useth treuth.
    Ancres and hermytes and monkes and freres
Peren to Apostles thorw her parfit lyvynge.
Wolde nevere the Faithful Fader that his ministres sholde
420 Of tyrauntz that teneth trewe men taken any almesse,
But done as Antony did, Dominik and Fraunceys,
[Bothe] Benet and Bernarde, the which hem firste taughte
To lyve bi litel and in lowe houses by lele mennes almesse.
Grace sholde growe and be grene thorw her good lyvynge,
425 And folkes sholde fynde, that ben in dyverse sykenesse,
The better for her byddynges in body and in soule.
Her preyeres and her penaunces to pees shulde brynge
Alle that ben at debate, and bedemen were trewe.
    Petite et accipietis, etc.
'Salt saveth catel,' seggen this wyves:
    Vos estis sal terre, etc.
430 The hevedes of Holi Cherche, and thei holy were,
Cryst calleth hem salt for Crystene soules.
    Et si sal evanuerit, in quo salietur?
Ac fressh flessh other fissh, whan it salt failleth,
It is unsavory, forsoth, y-sothe or y-bake;
So is mannes soule, sothly, that seeth no good ensaumple
435 Of hem of Holy Cherche that the heigh weye shulde teche
And be gyde and go bifore as a good baneoure,
And hardy hem that bihynde ben and yive hem good evydence.
Ellevene holy men al the worlde torned
Into lele byleve; the lightloker, me thynketh,
440 Shulde al maner men, we han so manye maistres,
Prestes and prechoures, and a pope above,
That Goddes salt shulde be to save mannes soule.
    Al was hethenesse sometyme, Ingelond and Wales
Til Gregory gerte clerkes to go here and preche.
445 Austyn [the Kynge crystened] at Caunterbury,
And thorw myracles, as men may rede, al that marche he torned
To Cryst and to Crystendome, and Crosse to honoure,

That the culver that came so came from God in Heaven
As a messenger to Mohammed, that he might teach men.[8]
And thus through wiles of his wit and through a white dove,
Mohammed brought into misbelief men and women,   410
So that learned there and unlearned still believe in his laws.
And since our Savior allowed Saracens to be so beguiled
By a Christian clerk accursed in his soul—
But for dread of the death I dare not speak the truth,
How English clerks feed a culver that is called Covetousness,   415
And have manners like Mohammed's so that no man honors truth.
    Anchorites* and hermits* and monks and friars
Are peers with the Apostles for their perfect living.
Would never the Father of Faith wish to find his ministers
Taking alms from tyrants that harass true men,   420
But doing as Antony[9] did, Dominic* and Francis,*
Both Benedict* and Bernard,* who taught them first
To live on little and in low houses by lawful men's alms.
Grace should grow and be green through their good lives,
And folk should feel, who suffer various sicknesses,   425
Both in body and in soul the better for their prayers.
Their prayers and their penances should bring peace among
All those who are at odds, if only beadsmen* were true.
    Seek and you shall receive, etc.[1]
'Salt saves cattle,' say these wives:
    Ye are the salt of the earth, etc.
The heads of Holy Church, if they were holy,   430
Christ calls them salt for Christian souls.
    And if the salt have lost its savor, wherewith shall it be salted?[2]
But fresh flesh or fish, when they lack salt,
Are unsavory, to be sure, whether stewed or baked;
So is man's soul, indeed, that sees no good example
Of those of Holy Church who should teach the high way   435
And be guides and go before like a good standard-bearer,
And hearten those behind and offer clear examples for them.
Eleven holy men converted all the world
Into the right religion; the more readily, I think,
Should all manner of men be converted, we have so many masters,   440
Priests and preachers, and a pope on top,
That should be God's salt to save man's soul.
    At one time all was heathenness, England and Wales,
Till Gregory* caused clerks to come here and preach.
Augustine[3] christened the King at Canterbury,   445
And through miracles, as men may read, made all that region turn
To Christ and Christendom, and to hold the Cross in honor,

---

8. The legend that Mohammed was a lapsed Christian who faked appearances of the Holy Ghost as
   a dove was widespread in the Middle Ages.
9. For Antony, see line 272 above; St. Dominic, St. Francis' contemporary, was the founder of the
   Dominican Friars.
1. Cf. Matt. 7:7.
2. This line and 429a above: Matt. 5:13.
3. Not St. Augustine of Hippo* but the Augustine sent to convert the English in 597; the King he
   converted was Ethelbert of Kent.

And fulled folke faste and the faith taughte
More thorw miracles than thorw moche prechynge;
450 As wel thorw his werkes as with his holy wordes
[Enformed] hem what fullynge and faith was to mene.
Cloth that cometh fro the wevyng is nought comly to were
Tyl it is fulled under fote or in fullyng-stokkes,
Wasshen wel with water and with taseles cracched,
455 Y-touked and y-tented, and under tailloures hande.
And so it fareth by a barne that borne is of wombe:
Til it be crystened in Crystes name and confermed of the bisshop
It is hethene as to Hevene-ward, and helpelees to the soule.
'Hethene' is to mene after heth and untiled erthe,
460 As in wilde wildernesse wexeth wilde bestes
Rude and unresonable, rennenge without [keperes].
    Ye nymmen wel how Matheu seith how a man made a feste.
He fedde hem with no venysoun ne fesauntes y-bake,
But with foules that fram hym nolde, but folwed his whistellynge:
    Ecce altilia mea et omnia parata sunt.
465 And wyth calves flesshe he fedde the folke that he loved.
The calfe bytokeneth clennesse in hem that kepeth lawes,
For as the cow thorw kynde mylke the calf norissheth til an oxe,
So love and lewté lele men susteyneth,
And maydenes and mylde men mercy desiren
470 Right as the cow calf coveyteth swete mylke;
So [menen] rightful men [after] mercy and treuthe.
[And by the hande-fedde foules is folke understonde
That loth ben to lovye withouten lernyng of ensaumples.
Right as capons in a courte cometh to mennes whistellynge,
475 In menynge after mete folweth men that whistellen,
Right so rude men that litel reson conneth
Loven and bileven by lettred mennes doynges,
And by here wordes and werkes wened and trowen;
And as tho foules to fynde forde after whistellynge,
480 So hope thei to have Hevene thorugh here whistellynge.
And by the man that made the feste the Majesté bymeneth,
That is God of his grace, giveth alle men blisse.
With wetheres and with wondres he warneth us with a whistellere
Where that his wille is to worshipen us alle,
485 And feden us and festen us for evermore at ones].
    Ac who beth that excuseth hem that aren persounes and
            prestes,
That hevedes of Holy Cherche ben, that han her wille here,
Withoute travaille the tithe del that trewe men biswynkyn?
Thei wil be wroth for I write thus, ac to witnesse I take,

And busily baptized people and brought them to the faith
More through miracles than through much preaching;
As well with his works as with his holy words   450
Taught them what baptism betokened and told them of the faith.
Cloth that comes from weaving is not comely to wear
Till it's fulled under foot or in fulling-frames,
Washed well with water and carded with teasels,
Stretched on tenters, and tinted, and placed in tailor's hand.[4]   455
And so it must be with a baby that is born of a womb:
Till it's christened in Christ's name and confirmed by the bishop
It is heathen as regards Heaven, and helpless of soul.
'Heathen' has its meaning from heath and untilled earth,
As wild beasts wax in the wilderness   460
Rude and unreasonable, running without keepers.
   You remember well how Matthew tells of a man who made a feast.
He fed them with no venison nor pheasants he'd had baked,
But with fowls that would not go from him, but followed his whistling:
   Behold my fatlings and all things are ready.[5]
And with calves' flesh he fed the folk that he loved.   465
The calf betokens cleanness in those that keep the laws,
For as the cow through kindly milk nourishes the calf into an ox,
So love and lewté* sustain lawful men,
And maidens and mild men desire mercy
Just as the cow's calf covets sweet milk;   470
So righteous men's minds move toward mercy and truth.
And by the hand-fed fowls those folk are betokened
Who are loath to love without learning from examples.
Just as capons in a courtyard come to men's whistling,
Intent on finding food follow men that whistle,   475
Right so rude men whose reasoning power is small
Learn to love and believe through lettered men's doings,
And on what they profess and perform they found their own beliefs;
And as those fowls hope to find food after the whistling,
So they hope to have Heaven on hearing their whistling.   480
And by the man that made the feast the Majesty is signified,
That is God of his grace who gives all men bliss.
With weathers and wonders he warns us with a whistler
Where it is his will to work honor for us,
And feed us and feast us for evermore in one body.   485
   But who are they that excuse themselves that are parsons and
      priests,
Who are the heads of Holy Church, who have their pleasure here,
Without travail the tenth part of what true men produce by working?
They will be wrathful because I write thus, but I have ready witness,

4. Cloth after weaving went through a process ("fulling") of scouring, cleansing, and thickening by being treaded or put through a mill. Then it was dried in a stretching frame on tenterhooks to make sure it came out even and square (line 455) and had the nap rubbed up with combs called teasels (line 454).
5. The parable of the wedding feast is in Matt. 22:1–14, but the tame birds are not in the biblical story.

490 Bothe Mathew and Marke and *Memento-Domine* David:
      Ecce, audivimus eam in Effrata, etc.
    What pope or prelate now perfourneth that Cryst highte,
      Ite in universum mundum et predicate, etc.?
    Allas that men so longe shulde byleve [on Makometh],
    So many prelates to preche as the pope maketh—
    Of Nazareth, of Nynyve, of Neptalim and Damaske,
    That thei ne went as Cryst wisseth, sithen thei wil [have]
495   name,
    To be pastours and preche the passioun of Jhesus,
    And as hymself seyde, so to lyve and deye:
      Bonus pastor animam suam ponit, etc.
    And seyde it in savacioun of Sarasenes and other;
    For Crystene and uncristene Cryst seide to prechoures,
500 *Ite vos in vineam meam, etc.*
    And sith that this Sarasenes, Scribes and [Grekis],
    Han a lippe of owre Byleve, the lightloker me thynketh
    Thei shulde torne whoso travaille wolde to teche hem of the Trinité.
      Querite, et invenietis, etc.
    [For alle paynymes prayeth and parfitly bileveth
505 In o grete God, and his grace asken,
    And make here mone to Makometh here message to
        shewe.
    Thus in a feith leve that folke, and in a fals mene,
    And that is routhe for rightful men that in the rewme wonyen,
    And a peril to the pope and prelatis that he maketh
510 That bere bisshopes names of Bedleem and Babiloigne.
        Whan the heigh Kyng of Hevene sente his sone to erthe
    Many myracles he wroughte men for to turne,
    In ensaumple that men sholde se by sadde resoun
    Men myghte nought be saved but thorugh mercy and grace,
515 And thorugh penaunce and passioun and parfit bileve.
    And bicam man of a mayde and *Metropolitanus*,
    And baptised and bishyned with the blode of his herte
    Alle that wilned and wolde with inwit bileve it.
    Many a seynt sithen hath suffred to deye
520 Al for to enfourme the faith; in fele contrees deyeden,
    In Ynde, in Alisaundre, in Ermonye and Spayne,
    In doleful deth deyeden for here faith.
    In savacioun of mannes soule Seynt Thomas was y-martired;
    Amonges unkynde Cristene for Cristes love he deyde,
525 And for the right of al this rewme and alle rewmes Cristene.

Both Matthew and Mark and *Memento-Domine* David:[6]   490
    Behold, we have heard of it in Ephratah, etc.
What pope or prelate now performs what Christ bade,
    Go ye into the whole world and preach, etc.?[7]
Alas that for so long men should believe in Mohammed,
When the pope makes so many prelates to preach about—
Of Nazareth, of Nineveh, of Nephthali and Damascus,[8]
Let them travel there, as Christ teaches, since they've taken the
    name,   495
In order to be pastors and preach the passion of Jesus,
And as himself said, so to live and die:
    The good shepherd layeth down his life, etc.[9]
And said it in salvation of Saracens and others;
For Christians and unchristians Christ said to preachers,
Go ye into my vineyard, etc.[1]   500
And since these Saracens, Scribes and Greeks,
Have a clause of our Creed,[2] the quicker I think
They'd turn to it if someone troubled to teach them of the Trinity.
    Seek, and ye shall find, etc.[3]
For all pagans pray and have a perfect belief
In one great God whose grace they ask for,   505
And they make their moan to Mohammed to show their message to
    him.
Thus that folk believe in a faith and in a false mediary,
And that is ruth for righteous men who reside in the kingdom,
And a peril to the pope and the prelates he makes
Who bear bishops' names of Bethlehem and Babylon.   510
    When the high King of Heaven sent his son to earth
He made many miracles to turn men to him,
In example that men should see that by sober reason
Men might not be saved but through mercy and grace,
And through penance and passion and perfect belief.   515
And he became man of a maid and *Metropolitanus*,[4]
And baptized and made brilliant with the blood of his heart
All who wished and would with inwit* believe it.
Many a saint since has suffered to die
All to found the faith; in various countries died,   520
In India, in Alexandria, in Armenia and Spain,
With doleful death died for their faith.
In salvation of man's soul Saint Thomas was martyred;[5]
Among unkind Christians for Christ's love he died,
And for the right of all this realm and all the realms of Christendom.   525

6. "Remember-Lord": Ps. 131:1; line 490a is verse 6.
7. Mark 16:15; cf. Matt. 28:19.
8. The pope sometimes created bishops *in partibus infidelium* ("in pagan territory"); that is, as heads of imaginary dioceses in non-Christian lands, such as the places named here. They were commonly just fictitious jobs with real incomes, intended as a reward for other activities.
9. John 10:11.
1. Matt. 20:4.
2. Moslems, Jews, and such Greek philosophers as Aristotle* believe in one God, and so already share the central doctrine of Christianity.
3. Matt. 7:7.
4. "Chief bishop" (literally, "archbishop"); see line 42 above.
5. Presumably, in view of line 528, St. Thomas of Syria.

Holy Cherche is honoured hieghlich thorugh his deying;
He is a forbisene to alle bisshopes, and a bright myroure,
And sovereynliche to swich that of Surré bereth the name,
And naught to hippe aboute in Engelonde to halwe mennes auteres,
530   And crepe in amonges curatoures, confessen ageyne the lawe:
        Nolite mittere falsem in messem alienam.
Many man for Crystes love was martired amonges Romanyes
Er Crystendome was knowe there, or any Crosse honoured].
It is reuth to rede how rightwis men lyved,
How thei defouled her flessh, forsoke her owne wille,
535   Fer fro kitth and fro kynne yvel y-clothed yeden,
Badly y-bedded, no boke but conscience,
Ne no richchesse but the Rode to rejoyse hem inne.
        Absit nobis gloriari nisi in Cruce Domini Nostri, etc.
And tho was plenté and pees amonges pore and riche,
And now is routhe to rede how the red noble
540   Is reverenced or the Rode, receyved for the worthier
Than Crystes Crosse that overcam deth and dedly synne.
And now is werre and wo, and whoso why axeth:
For coveityse after crosse: the croune stant in golde!
Bothe riche and religious, that rode thei honoure
545   That in grotes is y-grave and in golde nobles.
For coveityse of that crosse [clerkes] of Holy Kirke
Shul [overtourne] as Templeres did; the tyme approcheth faste.
[Mynne] ye nought, wyse men, how tho men honoured
More tresore than treuthe: I dar nought telle the sothe;
550   Resoun and rightful dome tho religious [dampned].
Right so, ye clerkes, for yowre coveityse er [come aughte] longe
Shal thei demen *dos ecclesiae* and [depose yow for yowre
        pryde].
        Deposuit potentes de sede, etc.
Yif Knyghthod and Kynde Wytte and [the] Commune [and] Conscience
Togideres love lelly, leveth it wel, ye bisshopes,
555   The lordeship of londes [lese ye shal] for evere,
And lyven as *Levitici* as owre lorde yow techeth:
        Per primicias et decimas, etc.
    Whan Costantyn of curteysye Holy Kirke dowed
With londes and ledes, lordeshipes and rentes,
An angel men herde an heigh at Rome crye,
560   'Dos ecclesiae this day hath y-dronke venym
And tho that han Petres powere arn apoysoned alle.'
A medecyne mote therto that may amende prelates.

Holy Church is honored highly by his dying;
He sets an example to all bishops, serving as a bright mirror,
And especially to such whose name says they're of Syria,
That they should not hop about England as altar-consecrators,
Creeping in among curates to hear confessions illegally: 530
    Put not thy sickle unto another's grain.[6]
Many a man for Christ's love was martyred among the Romans
Before Christendom was countenanced there, or any Cross honored.
It is ruth to read how righteous men lived,
How they defouled their flesh, forsook their own desires,
Went far from kith and kin clad in poor garments,   535
Badly bedded, no book but conscience,
And no riches but the Rood* to rejoice in.
    Let it not be for us to glory except in the Cross of our Lord, etc.[7]
And then there was plenty and peace among poor and rich,
And now it's ruth to read how the red noble*
Is reverenced before the Rood, received as worthier   540
Than Christ's Cross that overcame death and deadly sin.
And now there's war and woe, and whoever wants to know why:
For covetousness for a cross:[8] the crown stands in gold!
Both rich and religious, that rood they honor
That is engraved on groats and on gold nobles.   545
For covetousness for that cross clerks of Holy Church
Shall overturn as Templars did;[9] the time approaches fast.
Don't you remember, you wise men, how those men honored
Treasure more than truth: I dare not tell what's true;
By reason and rightful judgment those religious* were damned.   550
Just so, you clerks, for your covetousness it can't be long
Before they shall condemn *dos ecclesiae*[1] and put you down for your
    pride.
    He hath put down the mighty from their seat, etc.[2]
If Conscience and the Commons* and Kind Wit* and Knighthood
Love together loyally, believe it well, you bishops,
Your lordship over lands you shall lose forever,   555
And live like *Levitici*[3] as our Lord teaches you:
    By first fruits and tithes, etc.[4]
    When Constantine of his courtesy granted Holy Kirk* endowment
Of lands and landsmen, lordships and revenues,
Men heard an angel on high cry at Rome,
'*Dos ecclesiae* this day has drunk venom   560
And those that have Peter's power are poisoned all.'
A medicine must be found for this that may amend prelates.

6. Deut. 23:25.
7. Gal. 6:14.
8. This and subsequent puns turn on the fact that coins had a cross stamped on one side; nobles*
   and groats* (l. 545) had a king's crown on the other.
9. The fabulously wealthy order of Knights Templars was suppressed in 1312 in a tremendous scandal.
1. "The worldly endowment of the church."
2. Luke 1:52.
3. "Levites": members of the Old Testament tribe of Levi charged with the care of the Temple.
4. The Latin words Langland uses occur in Deut 12:6. This text was used to argue that priests should
   be supported by the tithes and donations of the people, not by wealth of their own.

That sholden preye for the pees, possessioun hem letteth;
Take her landes, ye lordes, and let hem lyve by dymes.
565 If possessioun be poysoun and inparfit hem make
[Charité] were to dischargen hem for Holi Cherche sake,
And purgen hem of poysoun or more perile falle.
Yif presthod were parfit, the peple solde amende
That contrarien Crystes lawe and Crystendome dispise.
570 Every bisshop that bereth Crosse, by that he is holden
Thorw his provynce to passe and to his peple to shewe hym,
Tellen hem and techen hem on the Trinité to bileve,
And feden hem with gostly fode and gyve [nedy folk to fynden].
[Ac Ysay of yow spekethe and Ozias bothe,
575 That no man sholde be bisshop but if he hadde bothe
Bodily fode and gostly fode to] gyve there it nedeth:

> In domo mea non est panis neque vestimentum et ideo nolite
> constituere me regem.

Ozias seith for such that syke ben and fieble
> Inferte omnes decimas in orreum meum ut cibus in
> domo mea.

Ac we Crystene creatures that on the Crosse byleven
580 Aren ferme as in the faith—Goddes forbode elles!—
And han clerkes to kepen us therinne and hem that shal come after.
And Jewes lyven in lele lawe; owre Lorde wrote it hymselve
In stone for it stydfast was and stonde sholde evre.
> Dilige deum et proximum is parfit Jewen lawe.

And toke it Moyses to teche men til Messye
585   come,
And on that lawe thei [leve] and leten it the beste.
And yit knewe thei Cryst that Crystendome taughte,
[And] for a parfit prophete that moche peple saved
Of selcouth sores: thei seyne it ofte,
590 Bothe of myracles and mervailles, and how he men fested
With two fisshes an fyve loves fyve thousande peple,
And bi that maungerye [thei] mighte wel se that Messye he semed;
And whan he luft up Lazar that layde was in grave
And under stone ded and stanke; with styf voys hym called:
> Lazare, veni foras!

595 Dede hym rise and rowme right bifor the Juwes.
Ac thei seiden and sworen with sorcerye he wroughte,
And studyeden to stroyen hym, and stroyden hemself,
And thorw his pacyence her powere to pure nought
        he broughte:
> Pacientes vincunt.

Danyel of her undoynge devyned and seyde
600 Cum sanctus sanctorum veniat cessabit unxio vestra.

Those that should pray for peace, their possessions impede them;
Take their lands, you lords, and let them live by tithes.
If possession is poison and makes imperfect clergy   565
It would be charity to discharge them of it for Holy Church's sake,
And purge them of poison before more peril arises.
If priesthood were perfect, the people should amend
Who act contrary to Christ's law and despise Christendom.
Every bishop that bears a Cross, by that he is bound   570
To pass through his province and let his people see him,
And talk to them and teach them to believe in the Trinity,
And feed them with spiritual food and provide for needy folk.
But Isaiah speaks of you and Hosea as well,
That no man should be a bishop but he who had both   575
Bodily food and spiritual food to confer on those who need it:
    *In my house is neither bread nor clothing and therefore make me
        not king.*[5]
Hosea says for such as are sick and weak
*Bring all the tithes into my storehouse that there might be food in mine
      house.*[6]
    But we Christian creatures whom the Cross inspires
Are firm in the faith—God forbid else!—   580
And have clerks to keep us in it and those who shall come after.
And Jews live in legitimate law; our Lord wrote it himself
In stone because it was steadfast and should stand forever.
Dilige deum et proximum[7] is perfect Jewish law.
And he entrusted it to Moses to teach men until Messiah should
    come,   585
And in that law they believe and look on it as the best.
Yet they were acquainted with Christ who taught Christendom,
And knew him for a perfect prophet who purged many persons
Of strange sicknesses: they saw it often,
Both miracles and marvels, and how he made men a feast   590
And fed with two fishes and five loaves five thousand people,
And by that marvel they might see that he seemed Messiah;
And when he lifted up Lazarus that was laid in grave
And under stone dead and stank; with stout voice he called him:
    Lazarus, come forth![8]
Made him rise and rove about right before the Jews.   595
But they said and swore that he worked with sorcery,
And studied how they might destroy him, and destroyed themselves,
And through his patience their power was brought down to pure
    nothing:
    The patient overcome.[9]
Daniel divined their undoing and said
When the holy of holies comes your anointing shall cease.[1]   600

5. Isa. 3:7.
6. Not Hosea but Mal. 3:10.
7. "Love God and thy neighbor": Deut. 6:5, Lev. 19:18; cf. Matt. 22:37, 39–40.
8. John 11:43.
9. Proverbial, but cf. Matt. 10:22.
1. Cf. Dan. 9:24, 26; i.e., when the Messiah comes, the special relationship between God and the
Jews will be superseded.

And yet wenen tho wrecches that he were *pseudopropheta*,
And that his lore be lesynges, and lakken it alle,
And hopen that he be to come that shal hem releve,
Moyses eft or Messye here maisteres yet devyneth.
605 Ac Pharesewes and Sarasenes, Scribes, and Grekis
Aren folke of on faith: the Fader God thei honouren.
And sitthen that the Sarasenes and also the Jewes
Konne the firste clause of owre bileve, *Credo in Deum Patrem
omnipotentem*,
Prelates of Crystene provynces shulde preve if thei myghte
610 Lere hem litlum and lytlum *et in Jesu Christum filium*,
Tyl thei couthe speke and spelle *et in Spiritum Sanctum*,
[Recorden] it and [rendren] it with *remissionem peccatorum
Carnis resurrectionem et vitam aeternam. Amen.*"

Passus XVI

"Now faire falle yow," quod I tho, "for yowre faire shewynge!
For Haukynnes love the Actyf Man evere I shal yow lovye.
Ac yet I am in a were what Charité is to mene."
"It is a ful trye tree," quod he, "trewly to telle.
5 Mercy is the more therof; the myddel stokke is Reuthe;
The leves ben lele wordes, the lawe of Holy Cherche;
The blosmes beth boxome speche and benygne lokynge.
Pacience hatte the pure tre, and Pore-Symple-Of-Herte,
And so thorw God and good men groweth the frute Charité."
10 "I wolde travaille," quod I, "this tree to se twenty hundreth myle,
And forto have my fylle of that frute forsake al other saulee.
Lorde!" quod I, "if any wighte wyte whideroute it groweth?"
"It groweth in [a] gardyne," quod he, "that God made hymselven—
Amyddes mannes body the more is of that stokke.
15 Herte hatte the erber that it in groweth,
And *Liberum Arbitrium* hath the londe to ferme
Under Piers the Plowman, to pyken it and to weden it."
"Piers the Plowman!" quod I tho, and al for pure joye
That I herde nempne his name anone I swouned after
20 And laye longe in a love-dreme; and atte laste me thoughte
That Pieres the Plowman al the place me shewed,
And bad me toten on the tree, on toppe and on rote.
With thre pyles was it underpighte; I perceyved it sone.
"Pieres," quod I, "I preye the, whi stonde thise piles here?"
"For wyndes, wiltow wyte," quod he, "to witen it fram
25   fallyng:

And yet those poor wretches suppose that he was *pseudopropheta*,[2]
And that his lore was a lie, and belittle it all,
And hope that he is to come who shall rehabilitate them all,
A second Moses or Messiah their masters foretell.
But Pharisees and Saracens, Scribes and Greeks   605
Are folk of one faith: God the Father they honor.
And since the Saracens and also the Jews
Know the first clause of our Creed, *Credo in Deum Patrem
    omnipotentem,*
Prelates of Christian provinces should experiment if they might
Lay on little by little *et in Jesu Christum filium,*   610
Till they could speak and spell *et in Spiritum Sanctum,*
Commit it to memory and repeat it with *remissionem peccatorum
Carnis resurrectionem et vitam aeternam. Amen.*"[3]

Passus XVI

"Now fair befall you," said I then, "for your fair explanation!
For Hawkin the Active Man's love I shall always love you.
But I am still bewildered about what Charity means."
"To tell the truth," said he, "it is a tree of great excellence.
Mercy is the master root; the main trunk is pity;   5
The leaves are lawful words, the law of Holy Church;
The blossoms are obedient speech and benevolent looks.
Patience is the tree's plain name, and Poor-Simple-Of-Heart,
And so through God and good men grows its fruit Charity."
"I would travel to see this tree," said I, "twenty hundred miles,   10
And to have my fill of that fruit forsake all other victuals.
Lord!" said I, "if any one knows whereabouts it grows?"
"It grows in a garden," said he, "that God made himself—
In the midst of man's body the trunk's root makes its home.
Heart is what the orchard's called in which it grows,   15
And *Liberum Arbitrium*[1] has the land to farm
Under Piers Plowman, to plant it and weed it."
"Piers the Plowman!" said I then, and all for pure joy
That I'd heard his name named anon I swooned after
And lay long in a love-dream;[2] and at the last I thought   20
That Piers the Plowman showed all the place to me,
And told me to gaze at the tree, at its top and at its root.
It was propped up with three poles; I perceived it at once.
"Piers," said I, "I pray you, why do these poles stand here?"
"Because of winds, if you will know," said he, "to ward it from
    falling: 25

2. "A false prophet."
3. These Latin phrases and clauses are all from the Apostles' Creed: "I believe in God, the Father Almighty"; "and Jesus Christ, his Son"; "and in the Holy Ghost"; "the forgiveness of sins, the resurrection of the body, and the life everlasting. Amen."
1. "Free Will."
2. A second "dream within a dream" begins here and runs to line 167.

Cum ceciderit justus non collidetur, quia
        Dominus supponit manum suam—
And in blowyng tyme abite the floures but if this piles helpe.
The worlde is a wykked wynde to hem that wolden treuthe.
Coveityse cometh of that wynde and crepeth amonge the leves
And forfret neigh the frute thorw many faire sightes.
30   Thanne with the firste pyle I palle hym down, *Potencia Dei Patris.*
The flesshe is a fel wynde, and in flourynge tyme
Thorw lykyng and lustes so loude he gynneth blowe
That it norissheth nice sightes and [another] tyme wordes
And wikked werkes therof, wormes of synne,
35   And forbiteth the blosmes right to the bare leves.
Thanne sette I to the secounde pile, *Sapiencia Dei Patris,*
That is the passioun and the power of owre Prynce Jhesu.
Thorw preyeres and penaunces and Goddes passioun in mynde
I save it til I se it rypen and somdel y-fruited.
40   And thanne fondeth the Fende my fruit to destruye
With alle the wyles that he can and waggeth the rote
And casteth up to the croppe unkynde neighbores,
Bakbiteres [brewe]-cheste, brawleres and chideres,
And leith a laddre thereto—of lesynges aren the ronges—
45   And feccheth away my floures sumtyme afor bothe myn eyhen.
Ac *Liberum Arbitrium* letteth hym sometyme,
That is lieutenant to loken it wel by leve of myselve:
        Videatis qui peccat in Spiritum Sanctum
            numquam remittetur; hoc est idem qui
            peccat per liberum arbitrium non repugnat.
Ac whan the Fende and the Flesshe forth with the Worlde
Manasen byhynde me my fruit for to fecche,
50   Thanne *Liberum Arbitrium* laccheth the thridde [planke]
And palleth adown the Pouke purelich thorw grace
And helpe of the Holy Goste, and thus have I the maystrie."
        "Now faire falle yow, Pieres," quod I, "so faire ye discryven
The powere of this postes and her propre [myghtes].
55   Ac I have thoughtes a threve of this thre piles,
In what wode thei woxen and where that thei growed,
For alle ar thei aliche longe, none lasse than other,
And to my mynde—as me thinketh—on o more thei growed;
And of o gretnesse and grene of greyne thei semen."
60   "That is soth," seide Pieres, "so it may bifalle.
I shal telle the as tite what this tree hatte.
The grounde there it groweth, goodnesse it highte;
And I have tolde the what highte the tree: the Trinité it meneth."
And egrelich he loked on me, and therfore I spared
65   To asken hym any more therof, and badde hym ful fayre
"To [devyse] the fruit that so faire hangeth."
        "Here now bineth," quod he tho, "if I nede hadde,

When the just man shall fall he shall not be bruised, for the
    Lord putteth his hand under him—[3]
And in blossom time they bite the blooms unless these props help.
The World is a wicked wind to those who want truth.
Covetousness comes from that wind and creeps in among the leaves
And threatens to devour the fruit through many fair shows.
Then with the first pole I pound him down, *Potentia Dei Patris.*[4]   30
The Flesh is a fierce wind, and in flowering time
Through lusts and delights so loud begins to blow
That it nourishes naughty sights and at another time words
And wicked works that come from them, worms of sin,
And they bite the blossoms down to the bare leaves.   35
Then I seize the second prop, *Sapientia Dei Patris,*[5]
That is the passion and the power of our Prince Jesu.
Through prayers and penances and God's passion in mind
I save it till I see it ripened and somewhat fruited.
And then the Devil endeavors to destroy my fruit   40
With all the wiles that he knows he works to shake the root
And casts clear to the top unkind neighbors,
Strife-breeding backbiters, brawlers and chiders,
And he lays a ladder to it—lies are its rungs—
And sometimes fetches away my flowers before my very eyes.   45
But *Liberum Arbitrium* waylays him sometimes,
Who is my lieutenant to look after it well by leave of myself:
    You may see that whoever sinneth against the Holy Spirit it
      will not be forgiven him; this is the same as whoever
      sinneth by free will doth not fight back.[6]
But when the Fiend and the Flesh reinforced by the World
Menace behind me to make off with my fruit,
Then *Liberum Arbitrium* lifts the third post   50
And dashes down the Devil directly through grace
And help of the Holy Ghost, and thus I have the victory."
    "Now fair befall you, Piers," I said, "so fairly you describe
The power of these posts and their particular strengths.
But I have thoughts by the thousand about these three props,   55
Within what wood they grew and whence they came,
For they are all alike long, none littler than another,
And to my mind—it seems to me—they must have grown from one root;
And they seem of one size and of the same green hue."
    "That is so," said Piers, "and such may be the case.   60
I shall tell you at this time what the tree is called.
The ground it grows in, goodness is its name;
And I have told you what the tree is called: it betokens the Trinity."
And he looked at me irritably, and therefore I refrained
From asking him any more about it, and bade him very courteously   65
"To define the fruit that hangs so fairly on it."
    "Here now beneath," said he then, "if I had need of it,

---

3. Ps. 36: 24.
4. "The Power of God the Father."
5. "The Wisdom of God the Father."
6. Cf. Matt. 12:32.

Matrymonye I may nyme, a moiste fruit withalle.
Thanne Contenence is [nere] the croppe as Calwey bastarde.
70 Thanne bereth the croppe kynde fruite and clenneste of alle,
Maydenhode, angeles peres, and [arst] wole be ripe
And swete withoute swellyng—soure worth it nevere."
I prayed Pieres to pulle adown an apple, and he wolde,
And suffre me to assaye what savoure it hadde.
75 And Pieres caste to the croppe, and thanne comsed it to crye;
And wagged Wydwehode, and it wepte after;
And whan [he] meved Matrimoigné it made a foule noyse.
I had reuth whan Piers rogged, it gradde so reufulliche.
For evere as thei dropped adown the Devel was redy
80 And gadred hem alle togideres, bothe grete and smale,
Adam and Abraham, and Ysay the prophete,
Sampson and Samuel and Seynt Johan the Baptiste,
Bar hem forth boldely, nobody hym letted,
And made of holy men his horde *in limbo inferni*,
85 There is derkenesse and drede and the Devel maister.
And Pieres for pure tene that o pile he laughte
And hitte after hym, happe how it myghte,
Filius bi the Fader wille, and frenesse of *Spiritus Sancti*
To go robbe that Raggeman and reve the fruit fro hym.
90   And thanne spakke *Spiritus Sanctus* in Gabrieles mouthe
To a mayde that highte Marye, a meke thinge withalle,
That one Jhesus a justice sone moste jouke in her chambre
Tyl *plenitudo temporis*, [tyme] comen were
That Pieres fruit floured and fel to be ripe.
95 And thanne shulde Jhesus juste therefore bi juggement of armes
Whether shulde fonde the fruit, the Fende or hymselve.
The mayde myldeliche tho the messager graunted
And seyde hendelich to hym, "Lo me, his handemayden
For to worchen his wille withouten any synne."
   Ecce ancilla Domini; fiat michi
      secundum verbum tuum.
100 And in the wombe of that wenche was he fourty wokes
Tyl he wex a faunt thorw her flessh and of fightyng couthe
To have y-foughte with the Fende ar ful tyme come.
And Pieres the Plowman parceyved plenere tyme
And lered hym lechecrafte his lyf for to save
105 That, thowgh he were wounded with his enemye, to warisshe hymself,
And did hym assaye his surgerye on hem that syke were

I might pick Matrimony, a moist fruit withal.
Then Continence comes near the top like a Cailloux bastard.[7]
Then at the very crown comes its native fruit and cleanest of all,   70
Maidenhood, angels' pears, and earliest to be ripe
And sweet without swelling—its savor never sour."[8]
I prayed Piers to pluck down an apple, if he would,
That I might have an opportunity to test what taste it had.
And Piers threw something to the summit, and that started to cry;   75
And he made Widowhood waver, and it wept then;
And when he moved Matrimony it made a foul noise.
I had pity when Piers shook it, so piteously it cried.
And ever as they dropped down the Devil was ready
And gathered them all together, both great and small,   80
Adam and Abraham, and Isaiah the prophet,
Samson and Samuel and Saint John the Baptist,
He bore them off boldly, nobody stopped him,
And made his hoard of holy men *in limbo inferni*,[9]
Where there's darkness and dread and the Devil is master.   85
And Piers for pure rage picked up that one post
And hit after him, happen how it might,
Filius by the Father's will, and favor of *Spiritus Sancti*[1]
To go rob that Ragman[2] and wrest the fruit from him.
    And then spoke *Spiritus Sanctus*[3] in Gabriel's mouth   90
To a maid named Mary, a meek thing withal,
That one Jesus a justice's son must sojourn in her chamber
Till *plenitudo temporis*,[4] full time should come
That Piers's fruit flowered and befell to be ripe.
And then Jesus should joust for it by judgment of arms   95
Which one should fetch the fruit, the Fiend or himself.
Mildly the maid then submitted to the messenger
And said to him humbly, "Lo, I am his handmaiden
To work his will without any sin."
    Behold the handmaid of the Lord; let it be done to me
        according to thy word.[5]
And in the womb of that wench was he forty weeks   100
Till he was born a boy from her body and grew bold to fight,
And would have fought with the Fiend before the time had fully come.
And Piers the Plowman perceived the proper time
And made him skilled in medicine that he might save his life
So that, though he was hurt by his enemy, he might heal himself;   105
And he had him assay his surgery on such as were sick

---

7. A grafted ("bastard") pear from Burgundy, reputed as especially sweet.
8. The image of the tree is used in multiple ways to represent, first, a fixed state with three conditions (assault by the world, the flesh, and the devil), then the Trinity and its distinct functions, and then the hierarchy of married chastity, continence or widowhood, and virginity. Finally, the tree introduces a historical sequence.
9. "In the border region of hell." Limbo was thought to be the abode after death of the righteous who lived before the Christian Redemption, e.g., the biblical figures in lines 81–82 above.
1. "The Son"; "the Holy Ghost."
2. A name for the Devil.
3. "The Holy Ghost."
4. "The fullness of time"; Gal. 4:4.
5. Luke 1:38.

Til he was parfit practisoure [if] any peril fulle.
And soughte oute the syke and [salved blynde and crokede],
And comune wommen converted and [clensed of synne],
110   [And syke and synful bothe so] to good torned:
        Non est sanis opus medicus, set in
            firmis.
Bothe meseles and mute, and in the menysoun blody,
Ofte he heled suche—he ne helde [it] for no maistrye,
Save tho he leched Lazar that hadde y-leye in grave
Quatriduanus quelt, quykke did hym walke.
115   Ac [ar] he made the maistrye *maestus coepit esse*
And wepte water with his eyghen; there seyen it manye.
Some that the sighte seyne saide that tyme
That he was leche of lyf and lorde of heigh hevene.
Jewes jangeled thereayeyne [that] jugged lawes
120   And seide he wroughte thorw wicchecrafte and with the Develes mighte:
        Demonium habes, etc.
"Thanne ar ye cherles," [chidde Jhesus], "and yowre children bothe,
And Sathan yowre saveoure; yowre selve now ye witnessen.
For I have saved yowself and yowre sones after,
Yowre bodyes, yowre bestes, and blynde men holpen,
125   And fedde yow with [two] fisshes and with fyve loves,
And left baskettes ful of broke mete bere awey whoso wolde."
And mysseide the Jewes manliche, and manaced hem to bete,
And knokked on hem with a corde and caste adown her stalles
That in cherche chaffareden, or chaungeden any moneye;
130   And seyde it in sighte of hem alle, so that alle herden:
"I shal overtourne this temple and adown throwe,
And in thre dayes after edifye it newe,
And make it as moche, other more, in alle manere poyntes
As evere it was, and as wyde; wherfore I hote yow
135   Of preyeres and of parfitnesse this place that ye callen."
        Domus mea domus oracionis vocabitur.
Envye and yvel wille [erne] in the Jewes.
Thei casten and contreveden to kulle hym whan thei mighte;
Uche daye after other theire tyme thei awaited
Til it bifel on a Fryday, a litel bifor Paske.
140   The Thorsday byfore, there he made his [cene],
Sittyng atte sopere, he seide thise wordes:
"I am solde thorw [som] of yow: he shal the tyme rewe
That evere he his Saveoure solde for sylver or elles."
Judas jangeled thereayein, ac Jhesus hym tolde,
145   It was [hymself] sothely, and seide, *"Tu dicis."*
Thanne went forth that wikked man and with the Jewes mette,

Till he was a perfect practitioner if any peril should arise.
And he hunted out the ill and healed blind and maimed,
And converted common women and cleansed them of sin,
And so steered toward the good sick and sinful both: 110
> They that are healthy do not need a physician, but they that are
> sick.[6]
Both leper-men and mutes, and men with bloody bowels,
Often he healed such—he held it no great feat,
Save when he gave life to Lazarus that had lain in his grave
Quatriduanus[7] cold, caused him to walk alive.
But before he performed the feat *maestus coepit esse*[8]   115
And wept water with his eyes; many there saw it.
Some that saw the sight said at that time
That he was healer of life's hurts and lord of high heaven.
Jews who judged laws jangled against him
And said he worked with witchcraft and with the Devil's power: 120
> *Thou hast a devil, etc.*[9]
"Then you are churls," Jesus chided them, "and your children too,
And Satan your savior; your own selves now bear witness.
For I have saved yourselves and your sons as well,
Your bodies, your beasts, and given blind men help,
And fed you with two fishes and with five loaves,   125
And left baskets of broken meat for him to bear away who wished."[1]
And he rebuked the Jews boldly, and threatened to beat them,
And lashed them with a length of rope and leveled the stalls
Of those who made of church a market, or changed money there;[2]
And said it in sight of all, so that all heard it: 130
"I shall overturn this temple and tear it down,
And in three days after have it built anew,[3]
And build it every bit as big, or bigger, in all ways
As it ever was, and as wide; wherefore I bid you
To pronounce this a place of prayers and of perfectness."   135
> *My house shall be called the house of prayer.*[4]
Envy and wicked will welled up in the Jews.
They took counsel and conspired to kill him when they might;
From this day to that day they waited their time
Till it befell on a Friday, a little before Passover.
The Thursday before that, there where he made his repast,   140
Sitting at supper, he said these words:
"I am sold by a certain one of you: he shall rue the time
That ever he sold his Savior for silver or goods."
Judas objected to this, but Jesus told him,
It was surely himself, and said, *"Tu dicis."*[5]   145
Then that wicked man went forth and met with the Jews,

6. Matt. 9:12.
7. "For the space of four days": John 11:39.
8. "He began to be sorrowful"; cf. John 11:35: "Jesus wept."
9. John 10:20, which reads "he hath," rather than "thou hast."
1. Matt. 14:16–20.
2. Matt. 21:12.
3. John 2:19.
4. Matt. 21:13.
5. "Thou sayest it": Matt. 26:25; on lines 142–43, see Matt. 26:21–24.

And tolde hem a tokne how to knowe with Jhesus,
And which tokne to this day to moche is y-used—
That is kissyng and faire contenaunce, and unkynde wille.
150 And [thus] was with Judas tho that Jhesus bytrayed:
"Ave, Rabbi," quod that ribaude, and right to hym he yede,
And kiste hym to be caught thereby and kulled of the Jewes.
Thanne Jhesus to Judas and to the Jewes seyde,
"Falsenesse I fynde in thi faire speche
155 And gyle in thi gladde chere, and galle is in thi lawghyng.
Thow shalt be myroure to manye men to deceyve,
Ac [to] the [worldes ende] thi wikkednesse shal worth upon thiselve:
       Necesse est ut veniant scandala; ve homini
             illi per quem scandalum venit.
Thow I bi tresoun be y-take, [to] yowre [Jewen] wille,
Suffreth my Postles in pays and in pees gange."
160 On a Thoresday in thesternesse thus was he taken—
Thorw Judas and Jewes Jhesus was [y-nome]
That on the Fryday folwynge, for mankynde sake,
Justed in Jerusalem, a joye to us alle.
On Crosse upon Calvarye Cryst toke the bataille
165 Ayeines Deth and the Devel; destruyed her botheres myghtes,
Deyde and Deth fordid, and daye of nyghte made.
       And I awaked therewith and wyped myne eyghen,
And after Piers the Plowman pryed and stared,
Estwarde and westwarde, I awayted after faste,
170 And yede forth as an ydiote, in contré to aspye
After Pieres the Plowman—many a place I soughte.
And thanne mette I with a man a myd-Lenten Sondaye,
As hore as an hawethorne, and Abraham he highte.
I frayned hym first fram whennes he come
175 And of whennes he were, and whider that he thoughte.
       "I am Feith," quod that freke, "it falleth noughte to lye,
And of Abrahames hous an heraud of armes.
I seke after a segge that I seigh ones,
A ful bolde bacheler; I knewe hym by his blasen."
       "What bereth that buirn," quod I tho, "so blisse the
180   bityde?"
       "Thre leodes in o lith, non lenger than other,
Of one mochel and myghte, in mesure and in lengthe.
That one doth, alle doth, and eche doth by his one.
The firste hath mighte and majestee, maker of alle thinges;
185 *Pater* is his propre name, a persone by hymselve.
The secounde of that sire is Sothfastnesse, *Filius*,
Wardeyne of that witte hath; was evere withoute gynnyng.
The thridde hatte the Holy Goost; a persone by
             hymselve,
The lighte of alle that lyf hath a londe and a watre,

And settled on a signal by which to single out Jesus,
And to this day that trick is too much used—
That is kissing and friendly countenance, and unkind will.
And this was Judas' way when he betrayed Jesus: 150
"Ave, Rabbi,"⁶ said that reprobate, and walked right to him,
And kissed him so he might be caught and killed by the Jews.
Then Jesus spoke to Judas and to the Jews as well:
"Falsehood I find in your fair speech
And guile in your glad cheer, and gall is in your laughter.   155
You shall be a mirror to many for men's deception,
But to the world's end your wickedness shall work upon yourself:
    For it must needs be that scandals come; but woe to that
        man by whom the scandal cometh.⁷
Though I am taken by treason, so you Jews may attain your wish,
Permit my Apostles to pass in peace where they will."
On a Thursday in a thickening light thus was Jesus captured—   160
Through Judas and Jews Jesus was taken
Who on the Friday following, for mankind's sake,
Jousted in Jerusalem, a joy to us all.
On Cross upon Calvary Christ took the battle
Against Death and the Devil; destroyed the power of both,   165
Died and destroyed Death, and made day of night.
    And I awaked with that and wiped my eyes,
And after Piers the Plowman I peered and stared,
Eastward and westward, I never once stopped looking,
And so set forth like an idiot, searching through the country   170
For Piers the Plowman—in many a place I sought him.
And then I met with a man on a mid-Lenten Sunday,
As hoar as a hawthorn, and Abraham was his name.
I asked him first whence he came
And of what land he was, and where he was heading.   175
    "I am Faith," said that fellow, "it's not fitting to lie,
And a herald of arms of Abraham's house.
I'm seeking for a certain man that I saw once,
A very bold bachelor;* by his blazon⁸ I knew him."
    "What blazon does that warrior wear," said I then, "so well betide
        you?"   180
    "Three beings in one body, none bigger than the others,
Of one size and strength, the same in girth and length.
What one does, all do, and each does by himself.
The first has might and majesty, maker of all things;
Pater is his proper name, one person by himself.   185
The second is from that sire, Soothfastness, Filius,⁹
Warden of all that have wits; he was always without beginning.
The third goes by the name of the Holy Ghost; again, one person by
        himself,
The light of all that have life on land and on water,

6. "Hail, Rabbi [i.e., Master]": Matt. 26:49.
7. Matt. 18:7.
8. A heraldic shield identifying a warrior. On Abraham's allegorical status, cf. p. 371.
9. Pater: "Father"; Filius: "Son."

190 Confortoure of creatures; of hym cometh al blisse.
So thre bilongeth for a lorde that lordeship claymeth:
Myghte and a mene [his owne myghte to knowe]
(Of [hymselve] and of his servaunt) and what [suffreth hem] bothe.
So God, that gynnyng hadde nevre but tho hym good thoughte,
195 Sent forth his sone as for servaunt that tyme
To occupien hym here til issue were spronge,
That is, children of Charité, and Holi Cherche the moder.
Patriarkes and prophetes and aposteles were the chyldren,
And Cryst and Crystenedome and Crystene, Holy Cherche,
200 In menynge that man moste on o God bileve,
And there hym lyked, and [he] loved, in thre persones hym
        shewed.
And that it may be so and soth [sheweth it] manhode:
Wedloke and widwehode with virgynyté y-nempned,
In toknynge of the Trinité, was taken oute of o man,
205 Adam, owre aller fader. Eve was of hymselve,
And the issue that thei hadde, it was of hem bothe,
And either is otheres joye in thre sondry persones,
And in hevene and here one syngulere name.
And [thus] is mankynde [and] manhede of matrimoigné y-spronge,
210 And bitokneth the Trinité and trewe bileve.
Mighte is [in] matrimoigné that multiplieth the erthe,
And bitokneth trewly, telle if I dorste,
He that firste fourmed al, the Fader of Hevene.
The Sone, if I durst seye, resembleth wel the wydwe:
        Deus meus, Deus meus, ut quid dereliquisti me?
215 That is, creatour wex creature to knowe what was bothe.
As widwe withoute wedloke was nevre yete y-seye,
Na more myghte God be man but if he moder hadde.
So wydwe withoute wedloke may noughte wel stande,
Ne matrimoigné withoute moillerye is nought moche to preyse.
        Maledictus homo qui non reliquit semen in Israel.
220 Thus in thre persones is perfitliche [pure] manhede,
That is man and his make and moillere children,
And is nought but gendre of o generacioun bifor Jhesu Cryst in
        Hevene:
So is the Fader forth with the Sone, and Fre Wille of bothe,
        Spiritus procedens a Patre et Filio,
Which is the Holy Goste of alle, and alle is but o God.
225   Thus in a somer I hym seigh as I satte in my porche;
I ros up and reverenced hym and right faire hym grette.
Thre men, to my syghte, I made wel at ese,
Wesche her feet and wyped hem, and afterward thei eten
Calves flesshe and cake-brede, and knewe what I thoughte.

Comforter of creatures; all bliss comes of him.   190
So three things belong to a lord that lays claim to lordship:
Might* and a means to make his own might known
(That is, of himself and his servant) and what accedes to them both.
So God, who never had beginning but when it seemed good to him,
Sent forth his son as a servant at that time   195
To occupy himself here till issue had sprung,
That is, children of Charity, and Holy Church the mother.
Patriarchs and prophets and apostles were the children,
And Christ and Christendom and Christians, Holy Church,
In meaning that man must believe in one God,   200
And where it pleased him, if love prompted him, he appeared in three
        persons.
And that it may be seen as certain is showed by manhood:
What is called wedlock and widowhood along with virginity,
To betoken the Trinity, were taken out of one man,
Adam, father of us all. Eve came from his body,   205
And the issue that they had, it came from them both,
And either is the other's joy in three separate persons,
And in heaven and here have only one single name.
And thus mankind and manhood have sprung from matrimony,
And betoken the Trinity and true belief.   210
There is might in matrimony that multiplies the earth,
And it betokens truly, if I dared tell it here,
Him who first formed all, the Father of Heaven.
The Son, if I dared say it, much resembles the widow:
        My God, my God, why hast thou forsaken me?[1]
That is, creator became creature so he could know what both were.   215
As a widow without wedlock was never yet seen,
No more might God be man unless a mother bore him.
So widow without wedlock may not well be,
Nor matrimony without children is not much to be praised.
        Cursed is the man who has not left his seed in Israel.[2]
Thus manhood separate, as a thing by itself, subsists in three persons,   220
That is man and his mate and from marriage their children,
And it is nothing but one kind and its kindred before Jesus Christ in
        Heaven:
So the Son comes forth from the Father, and Free Will from both,
        The Spirit proceeding from the Father and the Son,[3]
Which is the Holy Ghost of all of them, and all are but one God.
        Thus in a summertime I saw him as I sat on my porch;   225
I rose up and reverenced him and greeted him right fairly.
Three men, to my sight, I made well at ease,
Washed their feet and wiped them, and afterwards they ate
Calf's flesh and cake-bread, and could see what I thought.

---

1. Matt. 27:46: Christ's words on the Cross; cf. Ps. 21:2.
2. From the apocryphal Gospel of the Nativity of Mary, chap. 2.
3. From the Athanasian Creed (see p. 373). A number of theologians influential in medieval thought, including Sts. Augustine,* Bernard,* and Bonaventure (1221–1274), associate the human faculty of will with the Holy Ghost, or Holy Spirit.

Ful trewe tokenes bitwene us is, to telle whan me
230   lyketh.
Firste he fonded me if I, [Feith], loved bettere
Hym or Ysaak myn ayre, the which he highte me kulle.
He wiste my wille by hym—he wil me it allowe.
I am ful syker in soule therof, and my sone bothe.
235 I circumcised my sone sitthen for his sake,
Myself and my meyné; and alle that male were
Bledden blode for that Lordes love, and hope to blisse the tyme.
Myn affiaunce and my faith is ferme in this bilieve
For hymself bihighte to me—and to myne issue bothe—
240 Londe and lordship and lyf withouten ende.
To me, and to myn issue, more yete he me graunted,
Mercy for owre mysdedes as many tyme as we asken:
        Quam olim Abrahe promisisti et semini eius.
And sith he sent me to seye I sholde do sacrifise
And done hym worshipe with bred and with wyn bothe,
245 And called me fote of his faith, his folke forto save
And defende hem fro the Fende, folke that on me leneden.
Thus have I ben his heraude here and in helle,
And conforted many a careful that after his comynge wayten,
And thus I seke hym," he seide, "for I herde seyne late
250 Of a [buyrn] that baptised hym—Johan Baptiste was his name—
That to patriarkes and prophetes and other peple in derknesse
Seyde that he seigh here that sholde save us alle:
        Ecce agnus dei, etc."
    I hadde wonder of his wordes and of his wyde clothes,
For in his bosome he bar a thyng that he blissed evere.
255 And I loked on his lappe; a lazar lay thereinne
Amonges patriarkes and profetes pleyande togyderes.
"What awaytestow," quod he, "and what woldestow
        have?"
"I wolde wyte," quod I tho, "what is in yowre lappe."
"Loo," quod he, and lete me se. "Lorde, mercy!" I seide.
260 "This is [a] present of moche prys; what prynce shal it have?"
"It is a preciouse present," quod he, "ac the Pouke it hath attached,
And me theremyde," quod that man. "May no wedde us quite
Ne no buyrn be owre borwgh, ne bryng us fram his daungere—
Oute of the Poukes pondfolde no meynprise may us fecche—
265 Tyl he come that I carpe of: Cryst is his name
That shal delyvre us some daye out of the Develes powere
And bettere wedde for us [wage] than we ben alle worthy,
That is lyf for lyf; or ligge thus evere
Lollynge in my lappe tyl such a lorde us fecche."
270 "Allas," I seyde, "that synne so longe shal lette
The myghte of Goddes mercy that myght us alle amende."

There are most trustworthy tokens between us, to tell of when I
    please.[4]   230
First he tested me to find whether I, Faith, loved better
Him or Isaac my heir, whom he bade me kill.[5]
Through him he learned what my will was—he will allow it to me.
I'm fully certain in my soul of this, and my son as well.
I circumcised my son for his sake later,   235
Myself and my servants; and all such as were male
Bled blood for that Lord's love, and hope to bless the time.
I feel full confidence and faith in this belief
For he himself promised me—and my issue too—
Land and lordship and life without end.   240
And yet he granted me more, and my issue as well,
Mercy for our misdeeds as many times as we ask it:
    As thou hast formerly promised to Abraham and to his seed.[6]
And then he sent to me to say that I should do sacrifice
And worship him with bread and with wine both,
And called me foot of his faith, to bring his folk to safety   245
And defend them from the Fiend, folk who leaned on me.
Thus I have been his herald both here and in hell,
And comforted many care-worn who count on his coming,
And so I seek him," he said, "for I heard it said lately
By somebody who baptized him—John the Baptist was his name—   250
Who to patriarchs and prophets and other people in darkness
Said that he saw one here who should save us all:
    Behold the Lamb of God, etc."[7]
    Then I wondered at his words and at his wide clothes,
For in his bosom he bore a thing that he blessed constantly.
And I looked in his lap;[8] a leper lay therein   255
Among patriarchs and prophets playing together.
"What are you eyeing so eagerly," he asked, "and what do you hope to
    have?"
"I'd like to learn," said I then, "what's lying in your lap."
"Look," he said, and let me see. "Lord, mercy!" I cried.
"This is a present of great price; what prince shall receive it?"   260
"It is a precious present, but the Fiend has placed a lien on it,
And on me as well," said that man. "No pledge may release us
And nobody can go bail for us, or bring us from his sway—
No bailsman can fetch us free out of the Devil's pound—
Till he comes whom I'm describing: Christ is his name   265
Who shall some day deliver us out of the Devil's power
And pay a better price for us than we people are all worth,
That is life for life; or else lie thus forever
Lolling in my lap till such a lord fetch us."
    "Alas," said I, "that sin shall so long obstruct   270
The might of God's mercy that might amend us all."

4. Gen. 18:1–16. The three angels entertained by Abraham, who brought him God's promise of the
   birth of Isaac, were interpreted in the Middle Ages as a representation of the Trinity.
5. Gen. 22:1–19.
6. Cf. Luke 1:55.
7. John 1:29.
8. The fold of a robe over the chest to form a pouch; therefore, the bosom. Cf. Luke 16:22–23.

I wepte for his wordes; with that sawe I another
Rapelich renne forth the righte waye [we] went.
I affrayned hym fyrste fram whennes he come,
275   What he highte, and whider he wolde, and wightlich he tolde.

Passus XVII

"I am *Spes*, [a spye," quod he], "and spire after a knyghte
That toke me a maundement upon the Mounte of Synay
To reule alle rewmes with: I bere the writte [right] here."
"Is it asseled?" I seyde. "May men se thi lettres?"
5   "Nay," he sayde, "I seke hym that hath the sele to kepe,
And that is Crosse and Crystenedome, and Cryst thereon to hange;
And whan it is asseled [therwith], I wote wel the sothe,
That Lucyferes lordeship laste shal no lenger.
[And thus my lettre meneth; ye mowe knowe it al]."
10   "Late se thi lettres," quod I, "we mighte the lawe knowe."
[He plokked] forth a patent, a pece of an harde roche
Wheron was writen two wordes on this wyse y-glosed:
Dilige deum et proximum tuum,
This was the tixte trewly—I toke ful gode yeme.
15   The glose was gloriousely writen with a gilte penne:
In hijs duobus mandatis tota lex pendet et prophete.
     "Is here alle thi lordes lawes?" quod I. "Ye, leve me," he seyde.
"Whoso worcheth after this writte I wil undertaken
Shal nevere devel hym dere, ne deth in soule greve;
20   For though I seye it myself, I have saved with this charme
Of men and of wommen many score thousandes."
     "He seith soth," seyde this heraud. "I have [founded] it ofte.
Lo, here in my lappe that leved on that charme,
Josue and Judith and Judas Macabeus,
25   Ye, and sexty thousande bisyde forth that ben nought seyen here."
     "Yowre wordes aren wonderful," quod I tho. "Which of yow is trewest
And lelest to leve on for lyf and for soule?
Abraham seith that he seigh holy the Trinité,
Thre persones in parcelles, departable fro other,
30   And alle thre but o God; thus Abraham me taughte;
And hath saved that bileved so and sory for her synnes,
He can noughte segge the somme, and some aren in his lappe.
What neded it [now] a newe lawe to [brynge]
Sith the fyrst sufficeth to savacioun and to blisse?

I wept for his words; with that I saw another man
Running rapidly along the same road we were taking.
I asked him first from whence he came,
Who he was, and whither he went, and at once he told me.   275

Passus XVII

"I am *Spes*, a spy,"[1] said he, "and seek tidings of a knight
Who gave me a commandment upon the Mount of Sinai[2]
To rule all realms with: I have the writ right here."
"Is it sealed?" I said. "May one see your letters?"
"No," he said, "I seek him who has the seal in keeping,   5
And that is Cross and Christendom, and Christ to hang on it;
And when it is sealed therewith, I know well the truth,
That Lucifer's lordship shall last no longer.[3]
And that's my letter's meaning; you may know it all."
"Let's see your letters," said I, "it may be a law we know."   10
He pulled out a diploma, a piece of a hard rock[4]
Whereon were written two words with this gloss as well:
Love God and thy neighbor,[5]
This was the text truly—I took careful heed.
The gloss was gloriously written with a gilt pen: 15
On these two commandments hang all the law and the prophets.
   "Are these all your lord's laws?" said I. "Yes, believe me," he said.
"If one works by this writing I will guarantee
No devil will do him harm, nor death grieve him in his soul;
For though I say so myself, I have saved with this charm   20
Both of men and of women many score thousands."
   "He tells the truth," said this herald.[6] "I have tested it often.
Look, here in my lap are some who believed in that charm,
Joshua and Judith and Judas Maccabeus,[7]
Yes, and sixty thousand more than these who are not seen here."   25
   "Your words are wonderful," said I. "Which of you is truest
And best to believe for body and soul?
Abraham says that he saw all of the Trinity,
Its components three persons, each partable from the other,
And all three only one God; thus Abraham taught me;   30
And he has saved those that so believed and were sorry for their sins,
He cannot state the sum, and some are in his lap.[8]
What need was there now to bring on a new law
Since the first is sufficient for salvation and bliss?

1. *Spes*: "hope"; *spy*: scout.
2. Where God gave the Ten Commandments to Moses (Exod. 19–20), who here represents Hope, as Abraham represents Faith.
3. A writ is not operative until it has the seal, or stamped imprint, of the issuing authority. Christ hanging on the Cross is the "seal" of the Ten Commandments because he came "not to destroy, but to fulfill," the Law (Matt 5:17), thus ending the Devil's domination over mankind.
4. The Ten Commandments were given to Moses engraved on stone.
5. This summary of Jewish law was endorsed by Christ in line 16 (Matt. 22:37–39).
6. I.e., Abraham.
7. Heroes of the Old Testament Book of Joshua and the Apocryphal books of Judith and Maccabees.
8. Cf. Luke 16:22–23 on the lap, or bosom, of Abraham.

35 And now [comseth] *Spes* and speketh—that hath aspied the lawe—
And telleth noughte of the Trinitee that toke hym his lettres,
To byleve and lovye in o Lorde almyghty
And sitthe, right as myself, so lovye alle peple.
The gome that goth with o staf he semeth in gretter hele
40 Than he that goth with two staves, to syghte of us alle.
And righte so, by the Rode, Resoun me sheweth
It is lyghter to lewed men [o] lessoun to knowe
Than for to techen hem two—and to harde to lerne the leest.
It is ful harde for any man on Abraham byleve
45 And wel awey worse yit for to love a shrewe.
It is lightor to leve in thre lovely persones
Than for to lovye and lene as wel lorelles as lele.
Go thi gate!" quod I to *Spes*, "so me God helpe,
Tho that lerneth thi lawe wil litel while usen it."
50   And as we wenten thus in the weye, wordyng togyderes,
Thanne seye we a Samaritan, sittende on a mule,
Rydynge ful rapely the right weye we yeden,
Comynge fro a cuntré that men called Jerico;
To a justes in Jherusalem he [jaced] awey faste.
55 Bothe the heraud and Hope and he mette at ones
Where a man was wounded and with theves taken.
He myghte neither steppe ne stonde ne stere fote ne handes,
Ne helpe hymself sothely, for semivyf he semed,
And as naked as a nedle, and none helpe aboute.
60 Feith had first sighte of hym, ac he flegh on syde
And nolde nought neighen hym by nyne londes lengthe.
Hope cam hippyng after, that hadde so y-bosted
How he with Moyses maundement hadde many men y-holpe,
Ac whan he hadde sighte of that segge, asyde he gan hym drawe,
65 Dredfully, by this day, as duk doth fram the faucoun.
Ac so sone so the Samaritan hadde sighte of this lede
He lighte adown of Lyard and ladde hym in his hande,
And to the wye he went his woundes to biholde,
And parceyved bi his pous he was in peril to deye
70 And but if he hadde recovrere the rather, that rise shulde he nevre.
[And breide to his boteles and bothe he atamede];
Wyth wyn and with oyle his woundes he wasshed,
Enbawmed hym and bonde his hed, and in his [barm] hym layde,
And ladde hym so forth on Lyard, to *Lex Cristi*, a graunge
75 Wel six myle or sevene biside the Newe Market;
Herberwed hym at an hostrye and to the hostellere called:
"Have, kepe this man," [quod he], "til I come fro the justes.
And lo here sylver," he seyde, "for salve to his woundes."
And he toke hym two pans, to lyflode as it were,
And seide, "What he speneth more [for medcyn] I make the good
80   hereafter,
For I may nought lette," quod that leode and Lyarde he bistrydeth

And now *Spes* speaks up—who has spied out the law—   35
And tells nothing of the Trinity's entrusting him with his letters,
To believe in and love one Lord almighty
And then, just as I should myself, so love all people.
One who steps with one staff seems in better health
Than he who steps with two staves, it seems to all our eyes.   40
Since that's the case, by the Cross, Reason declares to me
It is easier for ignorant men to understand one lesson
Than to teach them two—and the least too hard to learn.
It's very hard for any man to believe what Abraham says
And it's even harder to love an evil person.   45
It's less hard to believe in three lovely persons
Than to love and lend help to both lawless and just.
Go your way!" said I to *Spes*, "so God help me,
Those that learn your law will not long follow it."
      And as we went thus on our way, talking with one another,   50
Then we saw a Samaritan,⁹ sitting on a mule,
Riding very rapidly the road we were taking,
Coming from a country that men call Jericho;
To a jousting in Jerusalem he jogged along fast.
Both the herald and Hope and he met together   55
Where a man was wounded and waylaid by thieves.
He might neither step nor stand nor stir foot or hand,
Nor help himself at all, for he seemed half-alive,
And as naked as a needle, and no help about.
Faith had first sight of him, but he fled aside   60
And would not come as near to him as nine fields' length.
Hope came hopping after, he who had boasted so
How he with Moses' commandment had helped many men,
But when he saw the sight of that man, he sheered aside,
As full of dread, by this day, as a duck that sees a falcon.   65
But as soon as the Samaritan caught sight of this man
He alighted from Lyard¹ and led him by hand,
And came close to the man to take account of his wounds,
And perceived by his pulse that he was in peril of death
And unless he had succor soon, he should never arise.   70
And he stepped swiftly to his bottles and unstopped them both;
He washed his wounds with wine and with oil,
Put balm on his head, and a bandage, and bore him in his arms,
And brought him, lying on Lyard, to *Lex Christi*,² a farm
Some six miles or seven beside the New Market;   75
Put him up at an inn and called the inn-keeper:
"Keep this man," said he, "in your care till I come from the jousts.
And look, here's silver," he said, "for salve for his wounds."
And he paid him two pennies,* expenses for his living,
And said, "What more he spends for medicine I'll make good
      later,   80
For I cannot stay," said that man and he bestrode Lyard

9. For the parable of the good Samaritan see Luke 10:30–36. Langland changes some elements of
    the story, such as the Samaritan's going *to* Jerusalem, not away from it.
1. Common name for a horse.
2. "The law of Christ"; see Gal. 6:2: "Bear ye one another's burdens, and so fulfill the law of Christ."

And raped hym to [ryde the righte waye to Jherusalem].
   Faith [folwed] after faste and fonded to mete hym,
And *Spes* spaklich hym spedde, spede if he myghte,
85 To overtake hym and talke to hym ar thei to toun come.
And whan I seygh this I sojourned noughte but shope me to renne
And suwed that Samaritan that was so ful of pité,
And graunted hym to ben his [gome]. "Gramercy," he seyde,
"Ac thi frende and thi felawe thow fyndest me at nede."
90 And I thanked hym tho, and sith [thus] I hym tolde
How that Feith fleigh awey, and *Spes* his felaw bothe,
For sighte of the sorweful man that robbed was with theves.
"Have hem excused," quod he; "her help may litel availle.
May no medcyn [under mone] the man to hele brynge,
95 Neither Feith ne fyn hope, so festred ben his woundis,
Without the blode of a barn borne of a mayde.
And be he bathed in that blode, baptised as it were,
And thanne plastred with penaunce and passioun of that babi,
He shulde stonde and steppe, ac stalworth worth he nevre
100 Tyl he have eten al the barn and his blode y-dronke.
For went nevere wy in this worlde thorw that wildernesse
That he ne was robbed or rifled, rode he there or yede,
Save Faith [and myselve] and *Spes* [his felaw],
And thiself now and such as suwen owre werkis.
105 For [an outlawe is] in the wode, and under banke lotyeth,
And may uch man se, and gode merke take
Who is bihynde and who bifore and who ben on hors;
For he halt hym hardyer on horse than he that is a-fote.
For he seigh me that am Samaritan suwen Feith and his felaw
110 On my caple that hatte *Caro*—of mankynde I toke it—
He was unhardy, that harlot, and hudde hym *in inferno*.
Ac ar this day thre dayes I dar undertaken
That he worth fettred, that feloune, fast with cheynes,
And nevre eft greve grome that goth this ilke gate:
    O mors, ero mors tua, etc.
And thanne shal Feith be forester here and in this fritth
115   walke
And kennen [out-comen] men that knoweth noughte the contré
Which is the weye that Ich went, and wherforth to Jherusalem.
And Hope the [hostellere] shal be there the man lith an helynge;
And alle that fieble and faynt be, that Faith may nought teche,
120 Hope shal lede hem forth with love, as his lettre telleth,
And hostel hem and hele thorw Holi Cherche
    bileve
Tyl I have salve for alle syke; and thanne shal I retourne
And come ayein bi this contree and confort alle syke
That craveth it or coveiteth it and cryeth thereafter.
125 For the barne was born in Bethleem that with his blode shal save
Alle that lyveth in Faith and folweth his felawes techynge."

And rode hastily the road right to Jerusalem.
    Faith followed after fast and did his very best to catch him,
And *Spes* sped smartly to see if he might
Overtake him and talk with him before the trail came to town.   85
And when I saw this I did not stay but bestirred myself
And pursued that Samaritan that was so full of pity,
And offered him to be his man. "Many thanks," he said,
"But your friend and your fellow you will find me at need."
And I thanked him then, and thereupon I told him   90
How Faith fled away, and his fellow *Spes* too,
At the sight of that sorrowful man that was set upon by thieves.
"They can be excused," said he; "they could not help much.
No medicine under the moon can restore the man to health,
Neither Faith nor fine hope, so festered are his wounds,   95
Without the blood of a babe born of a maid.
If he is bathed in that blood, baptized as it were,
And then given plasters of penance and passion of that baby,
He should stand and step, but full strength will not return
Till he has eaten all the babe and drunk of his blood.   100
For no one in the world ever went through that wilderness
Who was not rifled or robbed, whether riding or walking,
Save Faith and myself and *Spes* his companion,
And yourself now and such as shall follow our works.
For an outlaw is in the wood, lurking under the hillside,   105
And may see each man, and mark with care
Who is behind and who in front and who are on horse;
For he who is on horse acts braver than any one on foot.
Because he saw me that am Samaritan pursue Faith and his fellow
On my mount that is called *Caro*³—I acquired it from mankind—   110
He was faint-hearted, that outlaw, and hid *in inferno*.⁴
But before three days from this day I dare guarantee
That he will be fettered, that felon, fast with chains,
And never again grieve any one who goes along this road:
        *O death, I will be thy death, etc.*⁵
And then shall Faith walk these wooded fields and serve as forester
        here   115
And teach those who come into this country but cannot discover
Which is the way that I went, and whither to Jerusalem.
And Hope shall be inn-keeper where the man lies recovering;
And all who are feeble and faint, whom Faith may not teach,
Hope shall lead them along with love, as his letter tells him,   120
And put them up at his inn and heal them through belief in Holy
        Church
Till I have salve for all sick; and then I shall return
And come again through this country and comfort all the sick
Who crave it or covet it and cry after it.
For the babe was born in Bethlehem who will save with his blood   125
All that live in Faith and follow his fellow's teaching."

3. "The Flesh": this is the horse called Lyard earlier.
4. "In hell."
5. Hos. 13:14.

    "A, swete syre," I seyde tho, "wher I shal byleve?—
(As Feith and his felawe enfourmed me bothe)—
In thre persones departable that perpetuel were evere,
130 And alle thre but o God? thus Abraham me taughte.
And Hope afterwarde, he bad me to lovye
O God wyth al my good, and alle gomes after
Lovye hem lyke myselve, ac owre Lorde above alle."
    "After Abraham," quod he, "that heraud of armes,
135 Sette faste thi faith and ferme bileve;
And as Hope highte the, I hote that thow lovye
Thyn evene-Crystene evermore, eveneforth with thiself.
And if Conscience carpe there-ayein, or Kynde Witte oyther,
Or heretykes with argumentz, thin honde thow [hem] shewe.
140 For God is after an hande; y-here now and knowe it.
The Fader was fyrst as a fyst with o fynger foldynge
Tyl hym [liked] and lest to unlosen his fynger,
And [profred] it forth as with a paume to what place it sholde.
The paume is [the pith of] the hande, and profreth forth the fyngres
145 To mynystre and to make that myghte of hande knoweth.
And bitokneth trewly, telle whoso liketh,
The Holy Gost of Hevene: he is as the paume.
The fyngres that fre ben to folde and to serve
Bitokneth sothly the Sone that sent was til erthe,
150 That toched and tasted, atte techynge of the paume,
Seynt Marie, a mayde, and mankynde laughte:
      Qui conceptus est de Spiritu Sancto, etc.
The fader is thanne as a fust with fynger to touche—
      Quia omnia traham ad me ipsum, etc.—
Al that the paume parceyveth profitable to fele.
Thus ar thei alle but one, as it an hande were,
155 And thre sondry sightes in one shewynge,
The paume for he putteth forth fyngres and the fust bothe.
Right so, redily Reson it sheweth
How he that is Holy Goste Sire and Sone preveth.
And as the hande halt harde and al thynge faste
160 Thorw foure fyngres and a thombe forth with the paume,
Righte so the Fader and the Sone and Seynt Spirit the thridde
Halt al the wyde worlde within hem thre,
Bothe welkne and the wynde, water and erthe,
Hevene and helle and al that [is therinne].
165 Thus it is—nedeth no man to trowe non other—
That thre thinges bilongeth in owre [Fader] of Hevene
And aren serelepes by hemself; asondry were [thei] nevre;
Namore [may a hande] meve withouten fyngeres.
And as my fust is ful honde y-folde togideres,
170 So is the Fader a ful God, formeour and shepper.
      Tu fabricator omnium, etc.

"Ah, sweet sir," I said then, "which shall I believe?—
(For Faith and his fellow have informed me both)—
In three perpetual persons who are partable from each other,
Yet all three only one God? thus Abraham taught me.   130
And afterward Hope, he bade me to love
One God with all my might, and all men after
Love them like myself, but our Lord above all."
    "After Abraham," said he, "that herald of arms,
Set fast your faith and firm belief;   135
And just as Hope enjoined you, I enjoin you to love
Your fellow-Christian men evermore, as much as yourself.
And if Conscience complain about this, or Kind Wit either,
Or heretics with arguments, show your hand to them.
For God is as a hand; now hear this and know it.   140
The Father was first like a fist with one finger folded
Till he felt it was fitting to unfold his finger,
And he put it forth as with a palm to whatever place it should go.
The palm is the vital part of the hand, and puts forth the fingers
To administer and to make what the hand's might conceives of.   145
And it betokens truly, tell it if you like,
The Holy Ghost of Heaven: he is like the palm.
The fingers that are free to fold and to serve
Betoken surely the Son that was sent to earth,
Who touched and tasted, at teaching of the palm,   150
Saint Mary, a maid, and took mankind upon him:
        Who was conceived of the Holy Ghost, etc.[6]
Then is the Father like a fist with a finger to touch—
        I will draw all things to myself, etc.[7]—
All that the palm perceives is profitable to feel.
Thus are they all only one, as if it were a hand,
And three separate things seen in a single apparition,   155
The palm because he puts the fingers forth and makes the fist too.
Right so, Reason readily shows this
How he who is the Holy Ghost fulfills both Sire and Son.
And as the hand holds hard and fast to all things
Through four fingers and a thumb put forth by the palm,   160
Just so the Father and the Son and Holy Spirit the third
Hold the whole wide world within the three of them,
Both welkin[8] and the wind, water and earth,
Heaven and hell and all that is therein.
Thus it is—no man need now believe anything different—   165
That three things belong in our Father of Heaven
And are each separate by themselves; sundered were they never;
No more may a hand move without fingers.
And as my fist is a full hand folded together,
So is the Father a full God, former and creator.   170
        Thou maker of all things, etc.[9]

6. From the Apostles' Creed.
7. John 12:32.
8. I.e., the sky.
9. From the medieval Latin hymn "Jesus, Savior of Mankind" ("*Jesu salvator saeculi*").

Al the myghte myd hym is in makyng of thynges.
The fyngres fourrmen a ful hande to purtreye or peynten;
Kervynge and compassynge [is] crafte of the fyngres.
Right so is the Sone the science of the Fader
175 And ful God as is the Fader, no febler ne no better.
The paume is purelich the hande, hath power bi hymselve
Otherwyse than the wrythen fuste or werkmanschip of fyngres.
For the paume hath powere to put oute alle the joyntes
And to unfolde the fuste, [for hym it bilongeth,
180 And receyve that the fyngres recheth and refuse bothe
Whan he feleth the fuste and] the fyngres wille;
So is the Holy Goste God, nother gretter ne lasse
Than is the Sire [or] the Sone and in the same myghte,
And alle [thre] but o God, as is myn hande and my fyngres.
185 Unfolden or folden, my fuste and myn paume
Al is but an hande, howso I torne it.
Ac who is herte in the hande, evene in the myddes,
He may receyve right noughte; Resoun it sheweth.
For the fyngres that folde shulde and the fuste make,
190 For peyne of the paume, powere hem failleth
To clicche or to clawe, to clyppe or to holde.
Were the myddel of myn honde y-maymed or y-persshed
I shulde receyve righte noughte of that I reche myghte;
Ac though my thombe and my fyngres bothe were to-shullen,
195 And the myddel of myn hande withoute maleese,
In many kynnes maneres I myghte myself helpe,
Bothe meve and amende, though alle my fyngres oke.
Bi this skil," [he seyde], "I se an evydence
That whoso synneth in the Seynt Spirit assoilled worth he nevre,
200 Noither here ne elleswhere, as I herde telle:
         Qui peccat in Spiritum Sanctum, etc.
For he prikketh God as in the paume, [*qui*] *peccat in Spiritum Sanctum.*
For God the Fader is as a fuste; the Sone is as a fynger;
The Holy Goste of Hevene, [he] is as the pawme.
So whoso synneth in Seynt Spirit, it semeth that he greveth
205 God that he grypeth with, and wolde his grace quenche.
     [For] to a torche or a tapre the Trinitee is lykned,
As wex and a weke were twyned togideres,
And thanne a fyre flaumende forth oute of bothe.
And as wex and weyke and [warme] fyre togyderes
210 Fostren forth a flaumbe and a feyre leye
[That serveth thise swynkeres to se by anightes],
So doth the Sire and the Sone and also *Spiritus Sanctus*
Fostren forth amonges folke love and bileve
That alkyn Crystene clenseth of synnes.
215 And as thow seest sometyme sodeynliche a torche,

The whole force is from him for the forging of things.
The fingers form a full hand to portray or paint;
Carving and sketching are the craft of the fingers.
Just so is the Son the skill of the Father
And full God as the Father is, no feebler and no better.   175
The palm is perfectly the hand, has power by itself
Aside from the folded fist or the functioning of the fingers.
For the palm has power to push out the knuckles
And to unfold the fist, for his function it is,
And to receive what the fingers reach for or to refuse it   180
When he feels the fist's and the fingers' will;
So is the Holy Ghost God, neither greater nor less
Than the Sire is or the Son and of the same power,
And all three only one God, like my hand and my fingers.
Whether folded or unfolded, my fist and my palm   185
Are all only one hand, however I turn it.
But whoever is hurt in the hand, in its very middle,
He may clasp nothing securely; Reason declares it.
For the fingers that should fold and form the fist,
From pain in the palm, the power fails them   190
To clutch or to claw, to clasp or to hold.
If the middle of my hand were maimed or pierced
I could wield no whit of what I might reach;
But though my thumb and my fingers were both thick-swollen,
And the middle of my hand was maimed in no way,   195
There are many means by which I might help myself,
Both move and make amends, though all my fingers ached.
By this example," he said, "I see an indication
That whoso sins against the Holy Spirit shall not have absolution,
Either here or elsewhere, as I have heard tell: 200
    Who sinneth against the Holy Spirit, etc.
For he pricks God as in the palm, *qui peccat in Spiritum Sanctum.*[1]
For God the Father is like a fist; the Son is like a finger;
The Holy Ghost of Heaven, he is like the palm.
For whoso sins against the Holy Spirit, it seems that he hurts
God in what he grasps things with, and thus his grace is quenched.[2]   205
    For to a torch or a taper the Trinity is likened,
As if wax and a wick were twined together,
And then a fire flaming forth from both.
And as wax and wick and warm fire together
Foster forth a flame and a fair blaze   210
That gives light to these laborers when they labor at night,
So do the Sire and the Son and also *Spiritus Sanctus*[3]
Foster forth among the folk faith and belief
Which makes all kinds of Christians clean of their sins.
And as sometimes you see suddenly a torch,   215

1. The Latin clause repeats line 200a, both already translated in line 199. Langland follows Mark 3:29. The meaning of this verse, which makes offending the Holy Ghost more serious than any other offense, was a long-standing subject of discussion.
2. Analogies attempting to explain the Trinity were common in medieval religious writings. For example, the Trinity is compared to a candle in the *Legenda Aurea* XXXVII.
3. "The Holy Spirit."

The blase thereof y-blowe out, yet brenneth the weyke—
Withoute leye or lighte [lith fyre in the macche]—
So is the Holy Gost God and grace withoute mercy
To alle unkynde creatures that coveite to destruye
220 Lele love other lyf that owre Lorde shapte.
And as glowande gledes gladieth noughte this werkmen
That worchen and waken in wyntres nightes
As doth a kex or a candel that caughte hath fyre and blaseth,
Namore doth Sire ne Sone ne Seynt Spirit togyderes
225 Graunteth no grace ne forgifnesse of synnes
Til the Holi Goste gynne to glowe and to blase,
So that the Holy Goste gloweth but as a glede [unglade]
Tyl that lele love ligge on hym and blowe.
And thanne flaumbeth he as fyre on Fader and on *Filius*
230 And melteth her myghte into mercy, as men may se in wyntre
Ysekeles in eveses thorw hete of the sonne
Melteth in a mynut-while to myst and to watre.
So grace of the Holy Goste the grete myghte of the Trinité
Melteth into mercy to mercyable—and to non other.
235 And as wex withouten more on a warme glede
Wil brennen and blasen be thei togyderes,
And solacen hem that may [nought] se, that sitten in derkenesse,
So wole the Fader foryif folke of mylde hertes
That reufulliche repenten and restitucioun make,
240 Inasmoche as thei mowen amenden and payen;
And if it suffice noughte for assetz that in suche a wille deyeth,
Mercy for his mekenesse wil make good the remenaunte.
And as the weyke and fyre wil make a warme flaumbe
For to myrthe men with that in merke sitten,
245 So wil Cryst of his curteisye, and men crye hym mercy,
Bothe foryive and foryete, and yet bidde for us
[Fro] the Fader of Hevene foryyvenesse to have.
Ac hew fyre at a flynte fowre hundreth wyntre,
Bot thow have towe to take it with, tondre or broches,
250 Al thi laboure is loste, and al thi longe travaille;
For may no fyre flaumbe make faille it his kynde.
So is the Holy Gost God and grace withouten mercy
To alle unkynde creatures: Cryst hymself witnesseth:
     Amen dico vobis, nescio vos, etc.
   Be unkynde to thin evene-Cristene and al that thow canst bidden,
255 Delen and do penaunce, day and nyghte, evere,
And purchace al the pardoun of Pampiloun and Rome,
And indulgences ynowe, and be *ingratus* to thi kynde,
The Holy Goste hereth the nought ne helpe may the—by resoun.
For unkyndenesse quencheth hym that he can noughte shyne
260 Ne brenne ne blase clere, for blowynge of unkyndenesse.

When its blaze has been blown out, the wick still burns—
Without flame or flare fire lingers in the wick—
So is the Holy Ghost God and grace without mercy
To all unkind creatures that covet to destroy
Loyal love or life that our Lord created.   220
And as glowing gleeds⁴ don't gladden these workmen
Who work and wake on winter nights
As a torch does or a taper that's taken fire and blazes,
No more do Sire and Son and Holy Spirit together
Grant any grace or forgiveness of sins   225
Till the Holy Ghost begins to glow and to blaze,
So that the Holy Ghost glows only like a gleed without flame
Till loyal love lies on him and blows.
And then he flames like fire on Father and on *Filius*⁵
And melts their might into mercy, as men may see in winter   230
Icicles on eaves through heat of the sun
Melt in a minute's time to mist and to water.
So grace of the Holy Ghost melts the great might of the Trinity
Into mercy for merciful men—and melts it for no others.
And as wax on a warm gleed without more fuel   235
Will burn and blaze if they blend together,
And bring solace to those sitting in darkness, seeing nothing,
So will the Father forgive folk of mild hearts
Who ruefully repent and make restitution,
Inasmuch as they may make amends and repayments;   240
And if assets are insufficient for one who dies in such a will,
The mercy that his meekness earns will make good the remnant.
And as the wick and fire will make a warm flame
To make men glad who must sit in the dark,
So will Christ of his courtesy, if men cry mercy of him,   245
Both forgive and forget, and further pray for us
From the Father of Heaven to have forgiveness.
But strike fire from a flint four hundred winters,
Unless you have tow to take fire from it, tinder or taper,
All your labor is lost, and all your long slaving;   250
For no fire may burst into flame if it lacks kindling.
So is the Holy Ghost God and grace without mercy
To all unkind creatures: Christ himself bears witness:
    *Verily I say unto you, I know you not, etc.*⁶
  Be unkind to your fellow-Christians and any prayers you can make,
Hand out alms and do acts of penance forever, day and night,   255
And purchase all the pardon of Pamplona⁷ and of Rome,
And indulgences enough, and be *ingratus*⁸ to your kind,*
The Holy Ghost will not hear you or help you—and with reason.
For unkindness quenches him so that he cannot shine
Or burn or blaze bright, for the blowing of unkindness.   260

4. I.e., coals.
5. "Son."
6. Matt. 25:12: Christ's words at the Last Judgment, rejecting the sinners at his left hand.
7. The bishop of Pamplona in Spain was famous for issuing batches of indulgences.
8. *Indulgences:* formal remissions of the temporal or purgatorial punishment for sin. *Ingratus:*
"unkind, ungrateful."

Poule the Apostle preveth wher I lye:
    Si linguis hominum loquar, etc.
Forthy beth war, ye wyse men, that with the worlde deleth;
That riche ben and resoun knoweth, reuleth wel yowre soule;
Beth noughte unkynde, I conseille yow, to yowre evene-Crystene.
265 For many of yow riche men, bi my soule, men telleth,
Ye brenne but ye blaseth noughte; that is a blynde bekene:
    Non omnis qui dicit Domine, Domine, intrabit, etc.
[Mynne ye nought, riche men, to which a myschaunce]
Dives deyed, dampned for his unkyndenesse
Of his mete and his moneye to men that it neded?
270 Uch a riche, I rede, rewarde at hym take
And gyveth yowre good to that God that grace of ariseth.
For that ben unkynde to his, hope I none other
But, thei dwelle there Dives is dayes withouten ende.
Thus is unkyndenesse the contrarie that quencheth, as it were,
275 The grace of the Holy Gooste, Goddes owne kynde.
For that Kynde dothe unkynde fordoth, as these cursed theves,
Unkynde Cristene men, for coveityse and envye
Sleeth a man for his moebles, wyth mouth or wyth handes.
For that the Holy Goste hath to kepe, tho harlotes destroyeth,
280 The which is lyf and love, the leye of mannes bodye.
For every manere good man may be likned
[To a torche] or a tapre to reverence the Trinitee,
And who morthereth a good man, me thynketh by myn inwyt,
He fordoth the levest lyghte that owre Lorde loveth.
285 Ac yut in mo maneres men offenden the Holy Goste;
Ac this is the worste wyse that any wighte myghte
Synnen ayein the Seynt Spirit, assenten to destruye
For coveityse of any kynnes thinge that Cryst dere boughte.
How myghte he axe mercy, or any mercy hym helpe,
290 That wykkedlich and willefullich wolde mercy anynte?
Innocence is nexte God and nyghte and day it crieth
"Venjaunce, venjaunce! foryive be it nevere
That shent us and shadde owre blode—forshapte us, as it
    [semed]:
    Vindica sanguinem justorum!
Thus 'Venjaunce, venjaunce!' verrey charité asketh.
And sith Holi Cherche and Charité chargeth this so
295   sore,
Leve I nevre that owre Lorde [at the laste ende]
Wil love that [lyf that lakketh] charité,
Ne have pité for any preyere there that he pleyneth."
    "I pose I hadde synned so and shulde now deye,
300 And now am sory that so the Seint Spirit agulte,
Confesse me and crye his grace, [Cryst] that al made,

Paul the Apostle proves I'm not lying:

If I speak with the tongues of men, etc.[9]

Therefore beware, you wise men, who deal with worldly matters;

You that are rich and can reason well, rule your souls well;

Be not unkind, I counsel you, to your fellow-Christians.

For many of you rich men, by my soul, men tell, 265

You burn but you blaze not; that is a blind beacon:

Not every one that saith Lord, Lord, shall enter, etc.[1]

Don't you remember, you rich men, in what misadventure

Dives[2] died, damned for his unkindness

In denying meat* and money to men that had need of them?

I urge every rich man to take heed of him 270

And give your good to that God from whom grace arises.

For those that are unkind to his,[3] I have no other hope

But that they'll dwell where Dives is days without end.

Thus is unkindness the contrary quality that quenches, as it were,

The grace of the Holy Ghost, God's own kind. 275

For what Kind* creates unkind kills, like those cursed thieves,

Unkind Christian men, for covetousness and envy

Murder a man for his possessions, by word of mouth or with hands.

For what the Holy Ghost has in his keeping, these evil ones destroy,

And that is life and love, the firelight of man's body. 280

For every manner of good man may well be likened

To a torch or a taper to reverence the Trinity,

And whoever murders a good man, my inwit* seems to tell me,

He puts out the precious light that our Lord loves most dearly.

But yet in more manners men offend the Holy Ghost; 285

But this is the worst way that any one might

Sin against the Holy Ghost, assent to destroy

For covetousness of any kind of thing what Christ bought dear.

How might he ask mercy, or any mercy help him,

Who would wickedly and wilfully do away with mercy? 290

Innocence is nearest God and night and day it cries

"Vengeance, vengeance! forgiven be it never

To those who sullied us and shed our blood—as it seemed, unmade
   us:

Revenge the blood of the just![4]

Thus 'Vengeance, vengeance!' full charity demands.

And since this is a point of prime importance to Holy Church and
   Charity, 295

I do not believe that our Lord will ever at the last moment

Love that life that is lacking in charity,

Nor have pity for any prayer that his plaints may make."

   "Suppose I had sinned so and was soon to die,

And now regret my guilty act against the Holy Spirit, 300

Confess myself and cry for grace from Christ who made all,

9. 1 Cor. 13:1: the verse continues, "and of angels, but have not charity, I am become as sounding brass or a tinkling cymbal."
1. Matt. 7:21.
2. See Luke 16:19–24.
3. I.e., to God's people.
4. Cf. Rev. 6:9–10.

And myldliche his mercy axe, myghte I noughte be saved?"
"Yus," seide the Samaritan, "so thow myghte repente
That rightwisnesse thorw repentance to reuthe myghte torne.
305   Ac it is but selden y-seye, there sothenesse bereth witnesse,
Any creature that is coupable afor a kynges justice
Be raunsoned for his repentaunce there alle resoun hym dampneth.
For there that partye pursueth, the pele is so huge,
That the kynge may do no mercy til bothe men acorde
310   And eyther have equité, as Holy Writ telleth:
        Numquam dimittitur peccatum, etc.
Thus it fareth bi suche folke that [folwen] al her [wille],
Evel lyven and leten noughte til lyf hem forsake.
[Drede of desperacioun thanne dryveth awey grace
That mercy in here mynde may noughte thanne falle];
315   Good hope that helpe shulde to wanhope torneth—
Nought of the nounpowere of God, that he ne is myghtful
To amende al that amys is and his mercy grettere
Than alle owre wykked werkes, as Holi Writ telleth:
        Misericordia eius super omnia opera eius—
Ac ar his rightwisnesse to reuthe tourne some restitucioun bihoveth;
320   His sorwe is satisfaccioun for [swich] that may noughte paye.
      Thre thinges there ben that doth a man by strengthe
Forto fleen his owne hous, as Holy Wryt sheweth.
That one is a wikked wyf that wil nought be chasted;
Her fiere fleeth fro hyr for fere of her tonge.
325   And if his hous be unhiled and reyne on his bedde
He seketh and seketh til he slepe drye.
And whan smoke and smolder smyt in his syghte,
It doth hym worse than his wyf or wete to slepe;
For smoke and smolder [smerteth] his eyen
330   Til he be blere-nyed or blynde, and [the borre] in the throte;
Cougheth and curseth that Cryst gyf [hym] sorwe
That sholde brynge in better wode or blowe it til it brende.
Thise thre that I telle of ben thus to understonde:
The wyf is owre wikked flesshe that wil nought be chasted
335   For kynde cleveth on hym evere to contrarie the soule;
And thowgh it falle it fynt skiles [that] 'Freleté it made,'
And 'That is lightly foryeven and foryeten bothe
To man that mercy asketh and amende thenketh.'
The reyne that reyneth there we reste sholde
340   Ben sikenesses and sorwes that we suffren [oughte],
As Powle the Apostle to the peple taughte:
        Virtus in infirmitate perficitur.
And thowgh that men make moche deol in her angre
And inpacient in here penaunce, pure resoun knoweth
That thei han cause to contrarie by kynde of her sykenesse;
345   And lightlich owre Lorde at her lyves ende
Hath mercy on suche men that so yvel may suffre.

And mildly ask his mercy, might I not be saved?"
"Yes," said the Samaritan, "you might so repent
That righteousness might turn to ruth because of repentance.
But it is seldom seen, where truth serves as witness,   305
That any creature convicted before a king's justice
Is ransomed for his repentance where all reason damns him.
For where the injured party prosecutes, so ponderous is the charge,
That the king may grant no mercy till both men accord
And each has equity, as Holy Writ tells: 310
      The sin is never remitted, etc.[5]
Thus it fares with such folk who follow all their will,
Live evilly and don't leave off till life forsakes them.
Dread rising from despair then drives away grace
So that mercy may not come to their minds at that time;
Good hope that should help alters to wanhope*—   315
Not from any impotence of God, as if he had not the power
To amend all that is amiss and his mercy greater
Than all our wicked works, as Holy Writ witnesses:
      His mercy is above all his works[6]—
But before his righteousness turns to ruth some restitution is needed;
His sorrow is satisfaction for such a one as may not pay.   320
    There are three things that make a man by force
To flee from his own house, as Holy Writ shows.
The first one is a shrewish wife who will not be chastised;
Her mate flees her for fear of her tongue.
And if his house's roof has holes in it and it rains on his bed   325
He looks and looks till he can lie down dry.
And when his eyes smart from smoke from a smoldering fire,
It's even worse than his wife or his wet bed;
For smoke and smut smart in his eyes
Till he's blear-eyed or blind, and a burr in his throat;   330
He coughs and curses and asks Christ to give him sorrow
That should have brought in better wood or blown it till it blazed.
These three that I speak of are thus understood:
The wife is our wicked flesh that will not be chastised
Because nature cleaves to it to contravene the soul;   335
And though it falls it finds excuses that 'Frailty caused it,'
And 'That is fast forgotten and forgiven too
To a man who asks for mercy and means to amend.'
The rain that rains where we should rest in bed
Consists of sickness and sorrows that we should suffer,   340
As Paul the Apostle put it to the people:
      Virtue is perfected in sickness.[7]
And though men make much complaint in their anger
And take their tribulations impatiently, true reason recognizes
That they have cause to act contrariwise on account of their sickness;
And at their lives' end our Lord has little trouble   345
In having mercy on such men whom such misery afflicts.

5. St. Augustine, Epistle 153, section 20.
6. Ps. 144:9.
7. 2 Cor. 12:9.

Ac the smoke and the smolder that smyt in owre eyghen,
That is coveityse and unkyndenesse that quencheth Goddes mercy;
For unkyndenesse is the contrarie of alkynnes resoun.
350   For there nys syke ne sori ne non so moche wrecche
That he ne may lovye and hym lyke and lene of his herte
Goed wille, and good worde bothe, wisshen and willen
Alle manere men mercy and foryifnesse,
And lovye hem liche hymself, and his lyf amende.
355   I may no lenger lette," quod he, and Lyarde he pryked
And went away as wynde, and therewith I awaked.

Passus XVIII

Wolle-ward and wete-shoed went I forth after
As a reccheles renke that [reccheth of no wo],
And yede forth lyke a lorel, al my lyftyme,
Tyl I wex wery of the worlde and wylned eft to slepe,
5   And lened me to a Lenten, and longe tyme I slepte,
Rested me there, and rutte faste, tyl *Ramis-Palmarum*.
      Of gerlis and of *"Gloria, laus!"* gretly me dremed
And how *"Osanna!"* by orgonye olde folke songen
[And of Crystes passioun and penaunce the peple that of-raughte].
10   One semblable to the Samaritan and somedel to Piers the Plowman
Barfote on an asse bakke botelees cam pryke
Wythoute spores other spere: spakliche he loked,
As is the kynde of a knyghte that cometh to be dubbed,
To geten [hym] gylte spores [and] galoches y-couped.
15   Thanne was Faith in a fenestre and cryde, "A, *fili David!*"
As doth an heraude of armes whan aunturos cometh to justes.
Olde Juwes of Jerusalem for joye thei songen,
      "Benedictus qui venit in nomine Domini."
Thanne I frayned at Faith what al that fare bement,
And who sholde jouste in Jherusalem. "Jhesus," he seyde,
20   "And fecche that the Fende claymeth, Piers fruit the Plowman."
"Is Piers in this place?" quod I; and he preynte on me:
"This Jhesus of his gentrice wole juste in Piers armes,
In his helme and in his haberjoun, *humana natura*,
That Cryst be nought biknowe here for *consummatus Deus*.
25   In Piers paltok the Plowman this priker shal ryde,
For no dynte shal hym dere as *in deitate Patris*."

But the smoke and the smolder that our eyes smart from,
That is covetousness and unkindness that quench God's mercy;
For unkindness is the contrary of every kind of reason.
For no one is so sick or so much a wretch   350
That he may not love if he likes and deliver from his heart
Good will, good words too, wish and will
To all manner of men mercy and forgiveness,
And love them like himself, and lead a better life.
I may delay no longer," said he, and spurred Lyard hard   355
And went away like wind, and I awoke with that.

Passus XVIII

Wool-chafed and wet-shoed I went forth after
Like a careless creature unconscious of woe,
And trudged forth like a tramp, all the time of my life,
Till I grew weary of the world and wished to sleep again,
And lay down till Lent, and slept a long time,   5
Rested there, snoring roundly, till *Ramis-Palmarum.*[1]
    I dreamed chiefly of children and cheers of *"Gloria, laus!"*[2]
And how old folk to an organ sang *"Hosanna!"*
And of Christ's passion and pain for the people he had reached for.
One resembling the Samaritan and somewhat Piers the Plowman   10
Barefoot on an ass's back bootless came riding
Without spurs or spear: sprightly was his look,
As is the nature of a knight that draws near to be dubbed,
To get himself gilt spurs and engraved jousting shoes.
Then was Faith watching from a window and cried, *"A, fili David!"*   15
As does a herald of arms when armed men come to joust.
Old Jews of Jerusalem joyfully sang,
    "Blessed is he who cometh in the name of the Lord."[3]
And I asked Faith to reveal what all this affair meant,
And who was to joust in Jerusalem. "Jesus," he said,
"And fetch what the Fiend claims, the fruit of Piers the Plowman."   20
"Is Piers in this place?" said I; and he pierced me with his look:
"This Jesus for his gentleness* will joust in Piers's arms,
In his helmet and in his hauberk, *humana natura,*[4]
So that Christ be not disclosed here as *consummatus Deus.*[5]
In the plate armor of Piers the Plowman this jouster will ride,   25
For no dint will do him injury as *in deitate Patris."*[6]

1. Palm Sunday (literally, "branches of palms"): this part of the poem reflects the biblical account of Christ's entry into Jerusalem.
2. "Glory, praise [and honor]": the first words of an anthem sung by children in medieval religious processions on Palm Sunday.
3. Matt. 21:9: on the first Palm Sunday, crowds greeted Christ crying "Hosanna [l. 8] to the son of David [l. 15]" and the present line.
4. *Hauberk*: coat of mail. *Humana natura*: "human nature," which Christ assumed in order to redeem humanity.
5. The perfect (three-personed) God.
6. "*Dint*: blow. *In deitate Patris*: "in the godhead of the Father": as God, Christ could not suffer, but as man, he could.

"Who shal juste with Jhesus," quod I, "Juwes or Scribes?"
"Nay," quod [Feith, ac the] Fende and Fals-Dome-[To-Deye].
Deth seith he shal fordo and adown brynge
30 Al that lyveth or loketh in londe or in watere.
Lyf seyth that he [lyeth] and leyth his lif to wedde
That for al that Deth can do, within thre dayes [to walke]
And fecche fro the Fende Piers fruite the Plowman,
And legge it there hym lyketh, and Lucifer bynde,
35 And forbete and adown brynge bale deth for evere,
        O mors, ero mors tua.
Thanne cam Pilatus with moche peple, *sedens pro tribunali*,
To se how doughtilich Deth sholde do, and deme her botheres righte.
The Juwes and the justice ayeine Jhesu thei were,
And al [the] courte on hym cryde, *"Crucifige!"* sharpe.
40 Tho put hym forth a [peloure] bifor Pilat and seyde,
"This Jhesus of owre Jewes temple japed and dispised,
To fordone it on o day and in thre dayes after
Edefye it eft newe—here he stant that seyde it—
And yit maken it as moche in al manere poyntes.
45 Bothe as longe and as large, bi loft and by grounde."
"Crucifige!" quod a cacchepolle, "[he kan of wicchecrafte]!"
"Tolle! tolle!" quod another, and toke o kene thornes
And bigan of [grene] thorne a gerelande to make,
And sette it sore on his hed and seyde in envye,
50 *"Ave, Rabbi,"* quod that Ribaude, and threw redes at hym;
Nailled hym with thre nailles naked on [a] Rode,
And poysoun on a pole thei put up to his lippes
And bede hym drynke his deth [to lette and] his dayes [lengthe],
And [seyde], "Yif that thow sotil be, help now thiselven.
55 If thow be Cryst and kynges sone, come downe of the Rode!
Thanne shul we leve that Lyf the loveth and wil nought lete the deye."
        "Consummatum est," quod Cryst and comsed forto swowe,
Pitousliche and pale as a prisoun that deyeth.
The Lorde of Lyf and of Lighte tho leyed his eyen togideres.
60 The daye for drede withdrowe and derke bicam the sonne;
The wal wagged and clef and al the worlde quaved.
Ded men for that dyne come out of depe graves
And tolde whi that tempest so longe tyme dured:
"For a bitter bataille," the ded bodye sayde;
65 "Lyf and Deth in this derknesse, her one fordoth her other.
Shal no wighte wite witterly who shal have the maystrye
Er Sondey aboute sonne rysynge"; and sank with that til erthe.
Some seyde that he was Goddes sone that so faire deyde:

"Who shall joust with Jesus," said I, "Jews or Scribes?"[7]
"No," said Faith, "but the Fiend and False-Doom*-To-Die.
Death says he will undo and drag down low
All that live or look upon land or water.   30
Life says that he lies, and lays his life in pledge
That for all that Death can do, within three days he'll walk
And fetch from the Fiend the fruit of Piers the Plowman,
And place it where he pleases, and put Lucifer in bonds,
And beat and bring down burning death forever,   35
    O death, I will be thy death."[8]
Then Pilate came with many people, *sedens pro tribunali,*[9]
To see how doughtily Death should do, and judge the rights of both.
The Jews and the justice were joined against Jesus,
And all the court cried upon him, *"Crucifige!"*[1] loud.
Then a plaintiff appeared before Pilate and said,   40
"This Jesus made jokes about Jerusalem's temple,
To have it down in one day and in three days after
Put it up again all new—here he stands who said it—
And yet build it every bit as big in all dimensions,
As long and as broad both, above and below."   45
"Crucifige!" said a sergeant, "he knows sorcerer's tricks."
"Tolle! tolle!"[2] said another, and took sharp thorns
And began to make a garland out of green thorn,
And set it sorely on his head and spoke in hatred,
"Ave, Rabbi," said that wretch, and shot reeds[3] at him;   50
They nailed him with three nails naked on a Cross,
And with a pole put a potion up to his lips
And bade him drink to delay his death and lengthen his days,
And said, "If you're subtle, let's see you help yourself.
If you are Christ and a king's son, come down from the Cross!   55
Then we'll believe that Life loves you and will not let you die."
    "Consummatum est,"[4] said Christ and started to swoon,
Piteously and pale like a prisoner dying.
The Lord of Life and of Light then laid his eyelids together.
The day withdrew for dread and darkness covered the sun;   60
The wall wavered and split and the whole world quaked.
Dead men for that din came out of deep graves
And spoke of why that storm lasted so long:
"For a bitter battle," the dead body said;
"Life and Death in this darkness, one destroys the other.   65
No one will surely know which shall have the victory
Before Sunday about sunrise"; and sank with that to earth.
Some said that he was God's son that died so fairly:

---

7. "Scribes" were persons who made a very strict, literal interpretation of the Old Law and hence
   rejected Christ's teaching of the New.
8. Hos. 13:14.
9. "Sitting as a judge": Matt. 27:19.
1. "Crucify!": John 19:6.
2. "Away with him, away with him!": John 19:15.
3. *Ave, Rabbi*: "Hail, Rabbi [i.e., Master]": Matt. 26:49; these are actually the words Judas spoke when
   he kissed Christ in order to identify him to the arresting officers. *Reeds*: arrows, probably small ones
   intended to hurt rather than to kill.
4. "It is finished": John 19:30.

Vere Filius Dei erat iste.
And somme saide he was a wicche: "Good is that we assaye
70   Where he be ded or noughte ded, doun er he be taken."
Two theves also tholed deth that tyme
Uppon a crosse bisydes Cryst; so was the comune lawe.
A cacchepole cam forth and craked bothe her legges
And her armes after of eyther of tho theves.
75   Ac was no boy so bolde Goddes body to touche;
For he was knyghte and kynges sone, Kynde foryaf that tyme
That non harlot were so hardy to leyne hande uppon hym.
      Ac there cam forth a knyghte with a kene spere y-grounde
Highte Longeus as the lettre telleth, and longe had lore his sighte;
Bifor Pilat and other peple in the place he
80   hoved,
Maugré his many tethe, he was made that tyme
To [justen with Jhesus, this blynde Juwe Longeus].
For alle thei were unhardy that hoved on hors or stode,
To touche hym or to taste hym or take hym down of Rode,
85   But this blynde bacheler [that] bar hym thorugh the herte.
The blode spronge down by the spere and unspered [his] eyen.
Thanne fel the knyghte upon knees and cryed [Jhesu] mercy.
"Ayeyne my wille it was, Lorde, to wownde yow so sore."
He seighed and sayde, "Sore it me athynketh.
90   For the dede that I have done, I do me in yowre grace,
Have on me reuth, rightful Jhesu!" and right with that he wept.
      Thanne gan Faith felly the fals Juwes dispise,
Called hem caytyves, acursed forevere.
"For this foule vyleynye, venjaunce to yow [falle]!
95   To do the blynde bete [the dede], it was a boyes conseille.
Cursed [caytyves], knighthod was it nevere
To [bete a body y-bounde with any bright wepne].
The gree yit hath he geten for al his grete wounde,
For yowre champioun chivaler, chief knyght of yow alle,
100 Yelt hym recreaunt [remyng], right at Jhesus wille.
For be this derkenesse y-do, Deth worth [y-vanquisshed],
And ye lordeynes han y-lost, for Lyf shal have the maistrye;
And yowre fraunchise that fre was, fallen is in thraldome;
And ye cherles and yowre children chieve shal ye nevre,
105 Ne have lordship in londe ne no londe tylye,
But al bareyne be and [by] usurye [lybben],
Which is lyf that owre Lorde in alle lawes acurseth.
Now yowre good dayes ar done as Danyel prophecyed;
Whan Cryst cam her kyngdom the croune shulde [lese]:
      Cum veniat sanctus sanctorum cessabit unxio vestra.
110 What for fere of this ferly and of the fals Juwes

Truly this was the Son of God.[5]
And some said he was a sorcerer: "We should see first
Whether he's dead or not dead before we dare take him down."   70
Two thieves were there that suffered death that time
Upon crosses beside Christ; such was the common law.
A constable came forth and cracked both their legs
And the arms afterward of each of those thieves.
But no bastard was so bold as to touch God's body there;   75
Because he was a knight and a king's son, Nature decreed that time
That no knave should have the hardiness to lay hand on him.
     But a knight with a sharp spear was sent forth there
Named Longeus[6] as the legend tells, who had long since lost his sight;
Before Pilate and the other people in that place he waited on his
          horse,   80
For all that he might demur, he was made that time
To joust with Jesus, that blind Jew Longeus.
For all who watched there were unwilling, whether mounted or afoot,
To touch him or tamper with him or take him down from the Cross,
Except this blind bachelor* that bore him through the heart.   85
The blood sprang down the spear and unsparred[7] his eyes.
The knight knelt down on his knees and begged Jesus for mercy.
"It was against my will, Lord, to wound you so sorely."
He sighed and said, "Sorely I repent it.
For what I here have done, I ask only your grace,   90
Have mercy on me, rightful Jesu!" and thus lamenting wept.
     Then Faith began fiercely to scorn the false Jews,
Called them cowards, accursed forever.
"For this foul villainy, may vengeance fall on you!
To make the blind beat the dead, it was a bully's thought.   95
Cursed cowards, no kind of knighthood was it
To beat a dead body with any bright weapon.
Yet he's won the victory in the fight for all his vast wound,
For your champion jouster, the chief knight of you all,
Weeping admits himself worsted and at the will of Jesus.   100
For when this darkness is done, Death will be vanquished,
And you louts have lost, for Life shall have the victory;
And your unfettered freedom has fallen into servitude;
And you churls and your children shall achieve no prosperity,
Nor have lordship over land or have land to till,   105
But be all barren and live by usury,
Which is a life that every law of our Lord curses.
Now your good days are done as Daniel prophesied;
When Christ came their kingdom's crown should be lost:
     When the Holy of Holies comes your anointing shall cease.[8]
What for fear of this adventure and of the false Jews   110

5. Matt. 27:54.
6. Longeus (usually Longinus) appears in the apocryphal Gospel of Nicodemus, which provided
   Langland with the material for much of his account of Christ's despoiling of hell. Cf. p. 375.
7. Opened (with a pun on ME *spere*, n.: spear, bar, screen; and *speren*, v.: to lock, bar, close, enclose,
   store, imprison, exclude, block, or spear).
8. Cf. Dan. 9:24, probably via the liturgy for Advent.

I drowe me in that derkenesse to *Descendit-ad-Inferna*
And there I sawe sothely *secundum Scripturas*
[Where] out of the west coste a wenche, as me thoughte,
Cam walkynge in the wey—to helle-ward she loked.
115 Mercy hight that mayde, a meke thynge withalle,
A ful benygne buirde, and boxome of speche.
Her suster as it semed cam softly walkyng
Evene, out of the est, and westward she loked,
A comely creature [and a clene]: Treuth she highte.
120 For the vertue that hir folwed, aferd was she nevere.
Whan this maydenes mette, Mercy and Treuth,
Eyther axed other of this grete wonder,
Of the dyne and of the derknesse, and how the daye rowed,
And which a lighte and a leme lay befor helle.
125   "Ich have ferly of this fare, in feith," seyde Treuth,
"And am wendyng to wyte what this wonder meneth."
    "Have no merveille," quod Mercy, "myrthe it bytokneth.
A mayden that hatte Marye, and moder without felyng
Of any kynnes creature, conceyved thorw speche
130 And grace of the Holy Goste; wex grete with childe;
Withouten [wommen] wem into this worlde she brought hym.
And that my tale be trewe, I take God to witnesse,
Sith this barn was bore ben thirti wynter passed,
Which deyde and deth tholed this day aboute mydday.
135 And that is cause of this clips that closeth now the sonne,
In menynge that man shal fro merkenesse be drawe
The while this lighte and this leme shal Lucyfer ablende.
For patriarkes and prophetes han preched herof often
That man shal man save thorw a maydenes helpe,
140 And that was tynt thorw tre, tree shal it wynne,
And that Deth doun broughte, deth shal releve."
    "That thow tellest," quod Treuth, "is but a tale of waltrot.
For Adam and Eve and Abraham with other,
Patriarkes and prophetes that in peyne liggen,
145 Leve thow nevere that yone lighte hem alofte brynge,
Ne have hem out of helle—[holde] thi tonge, Mercy!
It is but a trufle that thow tellest. I, Treuth, wote the sothe,
For that is ones in helle, out cometh it nevere.
Job the [parfit] patriarke reproveth thi sawes:
    Quia in inferno nulla est redempcio."
150   Thanne Mercy ful myldly mouthed thise wordes:
"Thorw experience," quod she, "I hope thei shal be saved,
For venym fordoth venym, [ther fecche I evydence
That Adam and Eve have shul bote].
For of alle venymes foulest is the scorpioun:
155 May no medcyne [amende] the place there he styngeth
Tyl he be ded and do therto—the yvel he destroyeth,

I withdrew in that darkness to *Descendit-ad-Inferna*[9]
And there I saw surely *secundum Scripturas*[1]
Where out of the west a wench, as I thought,
Came walking on the way—she looked toward hell.
Mercy was that maid's name, a meek thing withal,   115
A most gracious girl, and goodly of speech.
Her sister as it seemed came softly walking
Out of the east, opposite, and she looked westward,
A comely creature and cleanly: Truth was her name.
Because of the virtue that followed her, she was afraid of nothing.   120
When these maidens met, Mercy and Truth,
Each of them asked the other about this great wonder,
And of the din and of the darkness, and how the day lowered,
And what a gleam and a glint glowed before hell.
    "I marvel at this matter, by my faith," said Truth,   125
"And am coming to discover what this queer affair means."
    "Do not marvel," said Mercy, "it means only mirth.
A maiden named Mary, and mother without touching
By any kind of creature, conceived through speech
And grace of the Holy Ghost; grew great with child;   130
With no blemish to her woman's body brought him into this world.
And that my tale is true, I take God to witness,
Since this baby was born it has been thirty winters,
Who died and suffered death this day about midday.
And that is the cause of this eclipse that is closing off the sun,   135
In meaning that man shall be removed from darkness
While this gleam and this glow go to blind Lucifer.
For patriarchs and prophets have preached of this often
That man shall save man through a maiden's help,
And what a tree took away a tree shall restore,[2]   140
And what Death brought down a death shall raise up."
    "What you're telling," said Truth, "is just a tale of nonsense.
For Adam and Eve and Abraham and the rest,
Patriarchs and prophets imprisoned in pain,
Never believe that yonder light will lift them up,   145
Or have them out of hell—hold your tongue, Mercy!
Your talk is mere trifling. I, Truth, know the truth,
For whatever is once in hell, it comes out never.
Job the perfect patriarch disproves what you say:
    Since in hell there is no redemption."[3]   150
    Then Mercy most mildly uttered these words:
"From observation," she said, "I suppose they shall be saved,
Because venom destroys venom, and in that I find evidence
That Adam and Eve shall have relief.
For of all venoms the foulest is the scorpion's: 155
No medicine may amend the place where it stings
Till it's dead and placed upon it—the poison is destroyed,

9. "He descended into hell": from the Apostles' Creed.
1. "According to the Scriptures."
2. The first tree bore the fruit that Adam and Eve ate, thereby damaging mankind; the second tree is
   the Cross on which Christ was crucified, thereby redeeming mankind.
3. Cf. Job 7:9.

The fyrst venymouste, thorw [vertue] of hymself.
So shal this deth fordo—I dar my lyf legge—
Al that Deth dyd furste thorw the Develles entysynge.
160 And right as [the gylour] thorw gyle [bigyled man formest],
So shal grace that bigan [al] make a good [ende
And bigyle the gylour—and that is good] sleighte:
     Ars ut artem falleret."
"Now suffre we," seyde Treuth. "I se as me thinketh
Out of the nippe of the north, nought ful fer hennes,
165 Rightwisnesse come rennynge—reste we the while,
For [heo] wote more than we—[heo] was er we bothe."
    "That is soth," seyde Mercy, "and I se here bi southe
Where Pees cometh playinge in pacience y-clothed.
Love hath coveyted hir longe: leve I none other
170 But [Love] sent hir some lettre, what this lighte bymeneth
That overhoveth helle thus: [she] us shal telle."
Whan Pees in pacience y-clothed approched nere hem tweyne,
Rightwisnesse hir reverenced for her riche clothyng
And preyed Pees to telle hir to what place she wolde,
175 And in her gay garnementz whom she grete thoughte.
    "My wille is to wende," quod she, "and welcome hem alle
That many day myghte I noughte se for merkenesse of synne.
Adam and Eve and other moo in helle,
Moyses and many mo [merye] shal [synge],
180 And I shal daunce therto: do thow so, sustre.
For Jhesus justed wel, joye bygynneth dawe.
      Ad vesperum demorabitur fletus, et ad matutinum leticia.
Love that is my lemman suche lettres me sente
That Mercy my sustre and I mankynde shulde save,
And that God hath forgyven and graunted me, Pees, and Mercy
185 To be mannes meynpernoure for everemore after.
Lo, here the patent," quod Pees: *"In pace in idipsum:*
And that this dede shal dure, *dormiam et requiescam."*
    "What? Ravestow," quod Rightwisnesse. "Or thow art right
      dronke.
Levestow that yonde lighte unlouke myghte helle
190 And save mannes soule? Sustre, wene it nevre.
At the bygynnynge God gaf the dome hymselve
That Adam and Eve and alle that hem suwed
Shulde deye dounerighte and dwelle in pyne after
If that thei touched a tre and the [trees] fruite eten.
195 Adam afterward ayeines his defence
Frette of that fruit and forsoke as it were
The love of owre Lorde and his lore bothe,
And folwed that the Fende taughte and his [flesshes] wille
Ayeines Resoun. I, Rightwisnesse, recorde thus with Treuth,
200 That her peyne be perpetuel and no preyere hem helpe;
Forthi late hem chewe as thei chose, and chyde we nought, sustres,
For it is botelees bale, the bite that thei eten."

The first effect of the venom, through the virtue it possesses.
So shall this death destroy—I dare bet my life—
All that Death did first through the Devil's tempting.
And just as the beguiler with guile beguiled man first,   160
So shall grace that began everything make a good end
And beguile the beguiler—and that's a good trick:
    A trick by which to trick trickery."[4]
    "Now let's be silent," said Truth. "It seems to me I see
Out of the nip of the north, not far from here,
Righteousness come running—let's wait right here,   165
For she knows far more than we—she was here before us both."
    "That is so," said Mercy, "and I see here to the south
Where Peace clothed in patience comes sportively this way.
Love has desired her long: I believe surely
That Love has sent her some letter, what this light means   170
That hangs over hell thus: she will tell us what it means."
When Peace clothed in patience approached near them both,
Righteousness did her reverence for her rich clothing
And prayed Peace to tell her to what place she was going,
And whom she was going to greet in her gay garments.   175
    "My wish is to take my way," said she, "and welcome them all
Whom many a day I might not see for murk of sin.
Adam and Eve and the many others in hell,
Moses and many more will merrily sing,
And I shall dance to their song: sister, do the same.   180
Because Jesus jousted well, joy begins to dawn.
    Weeping may endure for a night, but joy cometh in the morning.[5]
Love who is my lover sent letters to tell me
That my sister Mercy and I shall save mankind,
And that God has forgiven and granted me, Peace, and Mercy
To make bail for mankind for evermore after.   185
Look, here's the patent," said Peace: "*In pace in idipsum:*
And that this deed shall endure, *dormiam et requiescam.*"
    "What? You're raving," said Righteousness. "You must be really
      drunk.
Do you believe that yonder light might unlock hell
And save man's soul? Sister, don't suppose it.   190
At the beginning God gave the judgment himself
That Adam and Eve and all that followed them
Should die downright and dwell in torment after
If they touched a tree and ate the tree's fruit.
Adam afterwards against his forbidding   195
Fed on that fruit and forsook as it were
The love of our Lord and his lore too,
And followed what the Fiend taught and his flesh's will
Against Reason. I, Righteousness, record this with Truth,
That their pain should be perpetual and no prayer should help them;   200
Therefore let them chew as they chose, and let us not chide, sisters,
For it's misery without amendment, the morsel they ate."

4. From a medieval Latin hymn.
5. Ps. 29:6.

"And [I] shal preve," quod Pees, "her peyne mote have ende,
And wo into wel mowe wende atte laste;
205 For had thei wist of no wo, wel had thei noughte knowen;
For no wighte wote what wel is that nevere wo suffred,
Ne what is hote hunger that had nevere defaute.
If no nyghte ne were, no man, as I leve,
Shulde wite witterly what day is to mene.
210 Shulde nevere righte riche man that lyveth in reste and ese
Wyte what wo is ne were the deth of kynde.
So God, that bygan al, of his good wille
Bycam man of a mayde mankynde to save
And suffred to be solde to see the sorwe of deyinge,
215 The which unknitteth al kare and comsynge is of reste,
For til *modicum* mete with us, I may it wel avowe,
Wote no wighte, as I wene, what is 'ynough' to mene.
Forthi God of his goodnesse the fyrste gome Adam
Sette hym in solace and in sovereigne myrthe,
220 And sith he suffred hym synne sorwe to fele,
To wite what wel was—kyndelich to knowe it.
And after God auntred hymself, and toke Adames kynde,
To [se] what he hath suffred in thre sondri places,
Bothe in Hevene and in erthe, and now til helle he thynketh,
225 To wite what al wo is that wote of al joye.
So it shal fare bi this folke: her foly and her synne
Shal lere hem what langour is—and lisse withouten ende.
Wote no wighte what werre is there that pees regneth,
Ne what is witterly wel til 'Weyllowey!' hym teche."
230   Thanne was there a wighte with two brode eyen:
Boke highte that beupere, a bolde man of speche.
"By Godes body," quod this Boke, "I wil bere witnesse
That tho this barne was y-bore there blased a sterre
That alle the wyse of this worlde in o witte acordeden
235 That such a barne was borne in Bethleem citee
That mannes soule sholde save and synne destroye.
And alle the elementz," quod the Boke, "herof bereth witnesse.
That he was God that al wroughte, the walkene firste shewed:
[The hostes] in Hevene token *stella comata*
240 And tendeden hir as a torche to reverence his birthe.
The lyghte folwed the Lorde into the lowe erthe.
That water witnessed that he was God for he went on it;
Peter the Apostel parceyved his gate
And as he went on the water wel hym knewe and seyde,
       'Jube me venire ad te super aquas.'
245 And lo, how the sonne gan louke her lighte in herself
Whan she seye hym suffre that sonne and se made.
The erthe for hevynesse that he wolde suffre
Quaked as quykke thinge, and al biquasht the roche.

"And I shall prove," said Peace, "that their pain must end,
And in time trouble must turn into well-being;
For had they known no woe, they'd not have known well-being;   205
For no one knows what well-being is who was never in woe,
Nor what is hot hunger who has never lacked food.
If there were no night, no man, I believe,
Could be really well aware of what day means.
Never should a really rich man who lives in rest and ease   210
Know what woe is if it weren't for natural death.
So God, who began everything, of his good will
Became man by a maid for mankind's salvation
And allowed himself to be sold to see the sorrow of dying.
And that cures all care and is the first cause of rest,   215
For until we meet *modicum*,⁶ I may well avow it,
No man knows, I suppose, what 'enough' means.
Therefore God of his goodness gave the first man Adam
A place of supreme ease and of perfect joy,
And then he suffered him to sin so that he might know sorrow,   220
And thus know what well-being is—to be aware of it naturally.
And afterward God offered himself, and took Adam's nature,
To see what he had suffered in three separate places,
Both in Heaven and on earth, and now he heads for hell,
To learn what all woe is like who has learned of all joy.   225
So it shall fare with these folk: their folly and their sin
Shall show them what sickness is—and succor from all pain.
No one knows what war is where peace prevails,
Nor what is true well-being till 'Woe, alas!' teaches him."
    Then was there a wight⁷ with two broad eyes: 230
Book was that beaupere's⁸ name, a bold man of speech.
"By God's body," said this Book, "I will bear witness
That when this baby was born there blazed a star
So that all the wise men in the world agreed with one opinion
That such a baby was born in Bethlehem city   235
Who should save man's soul and destroy sin.
And all the elements," said the Book, "hereof bore witness.
The sky first revealed that he was God who formed all things:
The hosts in Heaven took *stella comata*⁹
And tended her like a torch to reverence his birth.   240
The light followed the Lord into the low earth.
The water witnessed that he was God for he walked on it;
Peter the Apostle perceived his walking
And as he went on the water knew him well and said,
    '*Bid me come unto thee on the water.*'¹
And lo, how the sun locked her light in herself   245
When she saw him suffer that made sun and sea.
The earth for heavy heart because he would suffer
Quaked like a quick thing, and the rock cracked all to pieces.

6. A small quantity.
7. Creature, person.
8. "Fine fellow": Book's two broad eyes suggest the Old and New Testaments.
9. "Hairy star," i.e., comet.
1. Matt. 14:28.

Lo, helle mighte noughte holde, but opened tho God tholed,
250 And lete oute Symondes sones to seen hym hange on Rode.
And now shal Lucifer leve it, thowgh hym loth thinke,
For [Jhesus as a] geaunt with a gynne [cometh yonde]
To breke and to bete dounn [alle] that ben ayeines [hym],
[And to have out of helle alle that hym liketh].
255 And I, Boke, wil be brent but Jhesus rise to lyve
In alle myghtes of man and his moder gladye,
And conforte al his kynne, and out of care brynge,
And al the Juwen joye unjoignen and unlouken;
And but thei reverencen his Rode and his Resurexioun
260 And bileve on a newe lawe, be lost lyf and soule."
      "Suffre we," seide Treuth, "I here and se bothe
A spirit speketh to helle and bit unspere the yatis."
         Attollite portas.
      A voice loude in that lighte to Lucifer cryeth,
"Prynces of this place, unpynneth and unlouketh,
265 For here cometh with croune that Kynge is of Glorie."
Thanne syked Sathan and seyde to [helle],
"Suche a lyghte ayeines owre leve Lazar it fette:
Care and combraunce is comen to us alle.
If this Kynge come in mankynde wil he fecche
270 And lede it ther [Lazar is], and lyghtlych me bynde.
Patriarkes and prophetes han parled herof longe,
That such a lorde and a lyghte shulde lede hem alle hennes."
      "Lysteneth," quod Lucifer, "for I this lorde knowe;
Bothe this lorde and this lighte, is longe ago I knewe hym.
275 May no deth [this lorde] dere, ne no develes queyntise,
And where he wil is his waye—ac war hym of the periles.
If he reve me my righte he robbeth me by maistrye.
For by right and bi resoun tho renkes that ben here
Bodye and soule ben myne, bothe gode and ille.
280 For hymself seyde that Sire is of Hevene,
Yif Adam ete the apple, alle shulde deye
And dwelle with us develes: this thretynge [Drighten] made.
And [sitthen] he that Sothenesse is seyde thise wordes,
And sitthen I [was] seised sevene [thousande] wyntre,
285 I leve that lawe nil naughte lete hym the leest."
      "That is sothe," seyde Sathan, "but I me sore drede
For thow gete hem with gyle and his gardyne breke,
And in semblaunce of a serpent sat on the appel tre
And eggedest hem to ete, Eve by hirselve,

Lo, hell might not hold, but opened when God suffered,
And let out Simeon's sons[2] to see him hang on Cross.   250
And now shall Lucifer believe it, loath though he is,
For Jesus like a giant with an engine[3] comes yonder
To break and beat down all that may be against him,
And to have out of hell every one he pleases.
And I, Book, will be burnt unless Jesus rises to life   255
In all the mights* of a man and brings his mother joy,
And comforts all his kin, and takes their cares away,
And all the joy of the Jews disjoins and disperses;
And unless they reverence his Rood* and his Resurrection
And believe on a new law, be lost body and soul."   260
    "Let's be silent," said Truth, "I hear and see both
A spirit speaks to hell and bids the portals be opened."
        Lift up your gates.[4]
    A voice loud in that light cried to Lucifer,
"Princes of this place, unpin and unlock,
For he comes here with crown who is King of Glory."   265
Then Satan[5] sighed and said to hell,
"Without our leave such a light fetched Lazarus away:[6]
Care and calamity have come upon us all.
If this King comes in he will carry off mankind
And lead it to where Lazarus is, and with small labor bind me.   270
Patriarchs and prophets have long prated of this,
That such a lord and a light should lead them all hence."
    "Listen," said Lucifer, "for this lord is one I know;
Both this lord and this light, it's long ago I knew him.
No death may do this lord harm, nor any devil's trickery,   275
And his way is where he wishes—but let him beware of the perils.
If he bereaves me of my right he robs me by force.
For by right and by reason the race that is here
Body and soul belongs to me, both good and evil.
For he himself said it who is Sire of Heaven,   280
If Adam ate the apple, all should die
And dwell with us devils: the Lord laid down that threat.
And since he who is Truth himself said these words,
And since I've possessed them seven thousand winters,
I don't believe law will allow him the least of them."   285
    "That is so," said Satan, "but I'm sore afraid
Because you took them by trickery and trespassed in his garden,
And in the semblance of a serpent sat upon the apple tree
And egged them to eat, Eve by herself,

2. Simeon had been told by the Holy Ghost that "he should not see death" before he had seen "the
   Lord's Christ" (Luke 2:26). The apocryphal Gospel of Nicodemus reports that Simeon's sons were
   raised from death at the time of Jesus' Crucifixion.
3. A device, probably thought of as a gigantic slingshot.
4. The first words of Psalm 23:9, which reads in the Latin Bible, "Lift up your gates, O princes, and
   be ye lifted up, ye everlasting doors, and the King of Glory shall come in."
5. Langland, following a tradition also later reflected in Milton's *Paradise Lost*, pictures hell as populated by a number of devils: Satan, Lucifer (line 273ff.), who began the war in Heaven and
   tempted Eve; Goblin (line 293); Belial (line 321); and Ashtoreth (line 404). Lucifer the rebel angel
   naturally became identified with the word "Satan," which in the Old Testament had originally
   meant an evil adversary; many of the other devils are displaced gods of pagan religions.
6. For Christ's raising of Lazarus from the dead, cf. John 11.

290 And toldest hir a tale, of tresoun were the wordes;
And so thow haddest hem oute, and hider atte laste."
"It is noughte graythely geten there gyle is the rote,
For God wil nought be bigiled," quod Gobelyn, "ne bijaped.
We have no trewe title to hem, for thorwgh tresoun were thei
        dampned."
295 "Certes I drede me," quod the Devel, "leste Treuth [do] hem fecche.
This thretty wynter, as I wene, he [went aboute] and
        preched.
I have assailled hym with synne, and sometyme y-asked
Where he were God or Goddes sone: he gaf me shorte answere.
And thus hath he trolled forth [lyke a tidy man] this two and thretty
        wynter.
300 And whan I seighe it was so, slepyng I went
To warne Pilates wyf what dones man was Jhesus,
For Juwes hateden hym and han done hym to deth.
I wolde have lengthed his lyf, for I leved yif he deyede
That his soule wolde suffre no synne in his syghte.
305 For the body, whil it on bones yede, aboute was evere
To save men fram synne yif hemself wolde.
And now I se where a soule cometh [seyllynge hiderward]
With glorie and with grete lighte; God it is, I wote wel.
I rede we flee," quod [the Fende], "faste alle hennes.
310 For us were better noughte be than biden his syghte.
For thi lesynges, Lucifer, loste is al owre praye.
Firste thorw the we fellen fro Hevene so heigh:
For we leved thi lesynges [we lopen out alle.
And now for thi laste lesynge] y-lore we have Adam,
315 And al owre lordeship, I leve, a londe and [in helle]."
        Nunc princeps huius mundi ejicietur foras.
Efte the lighte bad unlouke and Lucifer answered,
        "*Quis est iste?*
What lorde artow?" quod Lucifer. The lighte sone seide,
        "*Rex Glorie.*
[The] lorde of myghte and of mayne and al manere vertues:
        Dominus Virtutum.
Dukes of this dym place, anon undo this yates
320 That Cryst may come in, the Kynges sone of Hevene."
And with that breth helle brake with Beliales barres;
For any wye or warde wide [opened] the yatis.
Patriarkes and prophetes, *populus in tenebris,*
Songen Seynt Johanes songe, *Ecce agnus Dei.*
325 Lucyfer loke ne myghte, so lyghte hym ableynte.
And tho that owre [Lorde] loved into his lighte he laughte,

And told her a tale with treasonous words;   290
And so you had them out, and hither at the last."
"It's an ill-gotten gain where guile is at the root,
For God will not be beguiled," said Goblin, "nor tricked.
We have no true title to them, for it was by treason they were
    damned."
    "Certainly I fear," said the Fiend, "lest Truth fetch them out.   295
These thirty winters, as I think, he's gone here and there and
    preached.
I've assailed him with sin, and sometimes asked
Whether he was God or God's son: he gave me short answer.
And thus he's traveled about like a true man these two and thirty
    winters.
And when I saw it was so, while she slept I went   300
To warn Pilate's wife what sort of man was Jesus,
For outlaws hated him and have put him to death.
I would have lengthened his life, for I believed if he died
That his soul would suffer no sin in his sight.
For the body, while it walked on its bones, was busy always   305
To save men from sin if they themselves wished.
And now I see where a soul comes descending hitherward
With glory and with great light; God it is, I'm sure.⁷
My advice is we all flee," said the Fiend, "fast away from here.
For we had better not be at all than abide in his sight.   310
For your lies, Lucifer, we've lost all our prey.
Through you we fell first from Heaven so high:
Because we believed your lies we all leapt out.
And now for your latest lie we have lost Adam,
And all our lordship, I believe, on land and in hell."   315
    *Now shall the prince of this world be cast out.*⁸
Again the light bade them unlock, and Lucifer answered,
    *"Who is that?*⁹
What lord are you?" said Lucifer. The light at once replied,
    "The King of Glory.
The Lord of might* and of main and all manner of powers:
    The Lord of Powers.
Dukes of this dim place, at once undo these gates
That Christ may come in, the Heaven-King's son."   320
And with that breath hell broke along with Belial's bars;
For any warrior or watchman the gates wide opened.
Patriarchs and prophets, *populus in tenebris,*¹
Sang Saint John's song, *Ecce agnus Dei.*²
Lucifer could not look, the light so blinded him.   325
And those that our Lord loved his light caught away,

7. In Matt. 27:19, Pilate's wife warns Pilate because of a dream to "have nothing to do with that just man [Jesus]." Langland has the Fiend admit to having caused the dream in order that Pilate's wife should persuade her husband not to harm Jesus and thus keep him safe on earth and ensure that he not come to visit hell and despoil it.
8. John 12:31. "Prince of this world" is a title for the Devil.
9. This phrase and the next two translated from the Latin come directly or loosely from Ps. 23:8, following immediately on the words quoted in line 262a.
1. "People in darkness": Matt. 4:16, citing Isa. 9:2.
2. "Behold the Lamb of God": John 1:36.

And seyde to Sathan, "Lo, here my soule to amendes
For alle synneful soules, to save tho that ben worthy.
Myne thei be and of me—I may the bette hem clayme.
330 Although Resoun recorde, and right of myself,
That if thei ete the apple alle shulde deye,
I bihyghte hem nought here helle for evere.
For the dede that thei dede, thi deceyte it made;
With gyle thow hem gete agayne al resoun.
335 For in my paleys, Paradys, in persone of an addre,
Falseliche thow fettest there thynge that I loved.
Thus ylyke a lusarde with a lady visage
Thevelich thow me robbedest; the Olde Lawe graunteth
That gylours be bigiled, and that is gode resoun:
    Dentem pro dente et oculum pro oculo.
340 *Ergo* soule shal soule quyte and synne to synne wende,
And al that man hath mysdo, I, man, wyl amende.
Membre for membre [was amendes] bi the Olde Lawe,
And lyf for lyf also, and by that lawe I clayme
Adam and al his issue at my wille herafter.
345 And that Deth in hem fordid, my deth shal releve
And bothe quykke and quyte that queynte was thorw synne.
And that grace gyle destruye good feith it asketh.
So leve it noughte, Lucifer, ayeine the lawe I fecche hem,
But bi right and by resoun raunceoun here my lyges.
    Non veni solvere legem sed adimplere.
350 Thow fettest myne in my place [maugré] al resoun
Falseliche and felounelich; gode faith me it taughte
To recovre hem thorw raunceoun and bi no resoun elles.
So that with gyle thow gete thorw grace it is y-wone.
Thow, Lucyfer, in lyknesse of a luther addere
355 Getest by gyle tho that God loved;
And I, in lyknesse of a leode, that lorde am of Hevene,
Graciouslich thi gyle have quytte: go gyle ayeine gyle!
And as Adam and alle thorw a tre deyden
Adam and alle thorwe a tree shal torne ayeine to lyve,
360 And gyle is bigyled and in his gyle fallen:
    Et cecidit in foveam quam fecit.
Now bygynneth thi gyle ageyne the to tourne,
And my grace to growe ay gretter and wyder.
The bitternesse that thow hast browe, brouke it thiselven
That art doctour of deth, drynke that thow madest.
365   For I that am Lorde of Lyf, love is my drynke
And for that drynke today I deyde upon erthe.
I faughte so me threstes yet for mannes soule sake.
May no drynke me moiste ne my thruste slake

And he said to Satan, "Lo, here's my soul in payment
For all sinful souls, to save those that are worthy.
Mine they are and of me—I may the better claim them.
Although Reason records, and right of myself,   330
That if they ate the apple all should die,
I did not hold out to them hell here forever.
For the deed that they did, your deceit caused it;
You got them with guile against all reason.
For in my palace, Paradise, in the person of an adder,   335
You stole by stealth something I loved.
Thus like a lizard with a lady's face[3]
Falsely you filched from me; the Old Law confirms
That guilers be beguiled, and that is good logic:
    A tooth for a tooth and an eye for an eye.[4]
*Ergo** soul shall requite soul and sin revert to sin,   340
And all that man has done amiss, I, man, will amend.
Member for member was amends in the Old Law,
And life for life also, and by that law I claim
Adam and all his issue at my will hereafter.
And what Death destroyed in them, my death shall restore   345
And both quicken[5] and requite what was quenched through sin.
And that grace destroy guile is what good faith requires.
So don't believe it, Lucifer, against the law I fetch them,
But by right and by reason here ransom my liegemen.
    I have not come to destroy the law but to fulfill it.[6]
You fetched mine in my place unmindful of all reason   350
Falsely and feloniously; good faith taught me
To recover them by reason and rely on nothing else.
So what you got with guile through grace is won back.
You, Lucifer, in likeness of a loathsome adder
Got by guile those whom God loved;   355
And I, in likeness of a mortal man, who am master of Heaven,
Have graciously requited your guile: let guile go against guile!
And as Adam and all died through a tree
Adam and all through a tree return to life,
And guile is beguiled and grief has come to his guile: 360
    And he is fallen into the ditch which he made.[7]
And now your guile begins to turn against you,
And my grace to grow ever greater and wider.
The bitterness that you have brewed, imbibe it yourself
Who are doctor of death, the drink you made.
    For I who am Lord of Life, love is my drink   365
And for that drink today I died upon earth.
I struggled so I'm thirsty still for man's soul's sake.
No drink may moisten me or slake my thirst

---

3. In medieval art the Devil tempting Eve was sometimes represented as a snake (see the "serpent" of line 288) and sometimes as a lizard with a female human face, standing upright.
4. Matt. 5:38, citing Exod. 21:24.
5. Revitalize.
6. Matt. 5:17
7. Ps. 7:16.

Tyl the vendage falle in the Vale of Josephath,
370 That I drynke righte ripe must, *Resurrectio mortuorum*.
And thanne shal I come as a kynge crouned with angeles
And han out of helle alle mennes soules.
Fendes and fendekynes bifore me shulle stande
And be at my biddynge, whereso [best] me lyketh.
375 [Ac] to be merciable to man thanne, my kynde it asketh.
For we beth bretheren of blode, but noughte in baptesme alle.
Ac alle that beth myne hole bretheren in blode and in baptesme
Shal noughte be dampned to the deth that [dureth] withouten ende.
        Tibi soli peccavi, etc.
It is nought used in erthe to hangen a feloun
380 Ofter than ones, though he were a tretour,
And yif the kynge of that kyngedome come in that tyme
There [a] feloun thole sholde deth or otherwyse [juwyse],
Lawe wolde he yeve hym lyf if he loked on hym.
And I that am Kynge of Kynges shal come suche a tyme
385 There dome to the deth dampneth al wikked,
And yif lawe wil I loke on hem, it lithe in my grace
Whether thei deye or deye noughte for that thei deden ille.
Be it any thinge aboughte, the boldenesse of her synnes,
I may do mercy thorw [my] rightwisnesse and alle my wordes trewe;
And though Holi Writ wil that I be wroke of hem that
390   deden ille,
        Nullum malum inpunitum, etc.
Thei shul be clensed clereliche and [kevered] of her synnes
In my prisoun purgatorie til *Parce!* it hote.
And my mercy shal be shewed to manye of my [halve]-bretheren,
For blode may suffre blode bothe hungry and akale,
395 Ac blode may nought se blode blede but hym rewe:
        *Audivi archana verba que non licet homini
            loqui.*
Ac my rightwisnesse and right shal reulen al helle
And mercy al mankynde bifor me in Hevene.
For I were an unkynde kynge but I my kynde holpe,
And namelich at such a nede ther nedes helpe bihoveth.
        Non intres in judicium cum servo tuo.
400 Thus bi lawe," quod owre Lorde, "lede I wil fro hennes
Tho [ledes] that [I] loved and leved in my comynge;
And for thi lesynge, Lucifer, that thow lowe til Eve,
Thow shalt abye it bittre"—and bonde hym with cheynes.
Astaroth and al the route hidden hem in hernes;
405 They dorste noughte loke on owre Lorde, the [leste] of hem alle,

Till vintage time befall in the Vale of Jehoshaphat,[8]
When I shall drink really ripe wine, *Resurrectio mortuorum*.[9]   370
And then I shall come as a king crowned with angels
And have out of hell all men's souls.
Fiends and fiendkins shall stand before me
And be at my bidding, where best it pleases me.
But to be merciful to man then, my nature requires it.   375
For we are brothers of one blood, but not in baptism all.
And all that are both in blood and in baptism my whole brothers
Shall not be damned to the death that endures without end.
        Against thee only have I sinned, etc.[1]
It is not the custom on earth to hang a felon
Oftener than once, even though he were a traitor,   380
And if the king of the kingdom comes at that time
When a felon should suffer death or other such punishment,
Law would he give him life if he looks upon him.
And I who am King of Kings shall come in such a time
Where doom* to death damns all wicked,   385
And if law wills I look on them, it lies in my grace
Whether they die or do not die because they did evil.
And if it be any bit paid for, the boldness of their sins,
I may grant mercy through my righteousness and all my true words;
And though Holy Writ wills that I wreak vengeance on those that
        wrought evil,   390
        No evil unpunished, etc.[2]
They shall be cleansed and made clear and cured of their sins
In my prison purgatory till *Parce!*[3] says 'Stop!'
And my mercy shall be shown to many of my half-brothers,
For blood-kin may see blood-kin both hungry and cold,
But blood-kin may not see blood-kin bleed without his pity: 395
        *I heard unspeakable words which it is not lawful for a man to
            utter.*[4]
But my righteousness and right shall rule all hell
And mercy rule all mankind before me in Heaven.
For I'd be an unkind king unless I gave my kin help,
And particularly at such a time when help was truly needed.
        Enter not into judgment with thy servant.[5]
Thus by law," said our Lord, "I will lead from here   400
Those I looked on with love who believed in my coming;
And for your lie, Lucifer, that you lied to Eve,
You shall buy it back in bitterness"—and bound him with chains.
Ashtoreth and all the gang hid themselves in corners;
They dared not look at our Lord, the least of them all,   405

8. On the evidence of Joel 3:2, 12, the site of the Last Judgment was thought to be the Vale of
   Jehoshaphat.
9. "The resurrection of the dead": from the Nicene Creed.
1. Ps. 50:6.
2. "[He is a just judge who leaves] no evil unpunished [and no good unrewarded]": not from the Bible,
   but from Pope Innocent III's tract *Of Contempt for the World*; see IV.143–44.
3. "Spare!"
4. In 2 Cor. 12:4, St. Paul tells how in a vision he was snatched up to Heaven, where he heard things
   that may not be repeated among men.
5. Ps. 142:2.

But leten hym lede forth what hym lyked and lete what hym liste.
    Many hundreth of angeles harpeden and songen,
        Culpat caro purgat caro, regnat Deus Dei caro.
Thanne piped Pees of poysye a note:
        Clarior est solito post maxima nebula phebus; Post
            inimicicias clarior est et amor.
    "After sharpe shoures," quod Pees, "moste shene is the sonne;
410 Is no weder warmer than after watery cloudes;
Ne no love levere, ne lever frendes,
Than after werre and wo whan Love and pees be maistres.
Was nevere werre in this worlde ne wykkednesse so kene
That Love, and hym luste, to laughynge ne broughte.
415 And pees thorw pacience alle perilles [stoppeth]."
"Trewes!" quod Treuth, "thow tellest us soth, bi Jhesus!
Clippe we in covenaunt and uch of us cusse other."
"And lete no peple," quod Pees, "perceyve that we chydde;
For inpossible is no thyng to hym that is almyghty."
420 "Thow seist soth," seyde Ryghtwisnesse, and reverentlich hir kyste,
Pees, and Pees [hire], *per saecula saeculorum:*
        Misericordia et Veritas obviaverunt sibi; Justicia et Pax osculate
            sunt.
Treuth tromped tho and songe *Te Deum Laudamus,*
And thanne luted Love in a loude note:
        Ecce quam bonum et quam iocundum, etc.
Tyl the daye dawed this damaiseles [carolden]
425 That men rongen to the Resurexioun, and right with that I waked
And called Kitte my wyf and Kalote my doughter:
"Ariseth and reverenceth Goddes ressurrexioun,
And crepeth to the the Crosse on knees, and kisseth it for a juwel,
For Goddes blissed body it bar for owre bote,
430 And it afereth the Fende, for suche is the myghte
May no grysly gost glyde there it shadweth."

Passus XIX

Thus I awaked and wrote what I had dremed,
And dighte me derely and dede me to cherche
To here holy the Masse and to be houseled after.
In myddes of the Masse tho men yede to Offrynge
5 I fel eftsones aslepe, and sodeynly me mette
That Pieres the Plowman was paynted al blody
And come in with a Crosse bifor the comune peple,

But let him lead away what he liked and leave what he wished.
  Many hundreds of angels harped and sang,
    Flesh sins, flesh redeems, flesh reigns as God of God.[6]
Then Peace piped a note of poetry:
    As a rule the sun is brighter after the biggest cloud; After
      hostilities love is brighter.[7]
  "After sharp showers," said Peace, "the sun shines brightest;
No weather is warmer than after watery clouds;   410
Nor any love lovelier, or more loving friends,
Than after war and woe when Love and peace are masters.
There was never war in this world nor wickedness so sharp
That Love, if he liked, might not make a laughing matter.
And peace through patience puts an end to all perils."   415
"Truce!" said Truth, "you tell the truth, by Jesus!
Let's kiss in covenant and each of us clasp other."
"And let no people," said Peace, "perceive that we argued;
For nothing is impossible to him that is almighty."
"You speak the truth," said Righteousness, and reverently kissed her,   420
Peace, and Peace her, *per saecula saeculorum:*[8]
    Mercy and Truth have met together; Righteousness and Peace have
      kissed each other.[9]
Truth sounded a trumpet then and sang *Te Deum Laudamus,*[1]
And then Love strummed a lute with a loud note:
    Behold how good and how pleasant, etc.[2]
Till the day dawned these damsels caroled,
When bells rang for the Resurrection, and right then I awoke   425
And called Kit my wife and Calote my daughter:
"Arise and go reverence God's resurrection,
And creep to the Cross on knees, and kiss it as a jewel,
For God's blessed body it bore for our good;
And it frightens the Fiend, for such is its power   430
That no grisly ghost may glide in its shadow."

Passus XIX

Then I roused and wrote the record of my dream,
And clothed myself carefully and came to the church
To hear the whole Mass and receive the Eucharist after.
In the middle of the Mass when men went to the Offering[1]
I slipped into sleep again, and straightway I dreamed   5
That Piers the Plowman was painted all bloody
And came in with a Cross before the common people,

6. From a medieval Latin hymn.
7. These Latin verses are from Alain of Lille, a late twelfth-century poet and philosopher.
8. "Forever and ever" (the liturgical formula).
9. Ps. 84:11.
1. "We praise thee, God" (a celebrated Latin hymn, associated with religious feast days and occasions of public rejoicing).
2. Ps. 132:1: the verse continues, "[it is] for brothers to dwell in unity!"
1. The point in the Mass when the worshipers make their offerings (unlike its modern counterpart, the medieval congregation went forward in procession to do so) is also the point at which the priest places on the altar the bread and wine that will become the body and blood of Christ.

And righte lyke in alle lymes to owre Lorde Jhesu.
And thanne called I Conscience to kenne me the sothe:

10   "Is this Jhesus the juster," quod I, "that Juwes did to deth,
Or it is Pieres the Plowman? Who paynted hym so rede?"
Quod Conscience, and kneled tho, "Thise aren Pieres armes,
His coloures and his cote-armure, ac he that cometh so blody
Is Cryst with his Crosse, conqueroure of Crystene."

15   "Why calle ye hym Cryst, sithenes Juwes [called] hym Jhesus?
Patriarkes and prophetes prophecyed bifore
That alkyn creatures shulden knelen and bowen
Anon as men nempned the name of God Jhesu.
Ergo is no name to the name of Jhesus,

20   Ne none so nedeful to nempne by nyghte ne by daye.
For alle derke develles aren adradde to heren it,
And synful aren solaced and saved bi that name.
And ye callen hym Cryst; for what cause, telleth me,
Is 'Cryst' more of myghte and more worthy name

25   Than 'Jhesu' or 'Jhesus" that al owre joye come of?"
       "Thow knowest wel," quod Conscience, "and thow konne resoun,
That knyghte, kynge, conqueroure may be o persone.
To be called a knighte is faire, for men shal knele to hym;
To be called a kynge is fairer, for he may knyghtes make;

30   Ac to be conquerour called, that cometh of special grace,
And of hardynesse of herte and of hendenesse,
To make lordes of laddes of londe that he wynneth
And fre men foule thralles that folweth nought his lawes.
The Juwes that were gentil men Jhesu thei dispised,

35   Bothe his lore and his lawe; now ar thei lowe cherlis.
As wyde as the worlde is, wonyeth there none
But under tribut and taillage, as tykes and cherles.
And tho that bicome Crysten by conseille of the Baptiste
Aren frankeleynes, fre men, thorw fullyng that thei toke

40   And gentel men with Jhesu, for Jhesus was y-folled
And uppon Calvarye on Crosse y-crouned Kynge of Jewes.
It bicometh to a kynge to kepe and to defende
And conquerour of [his] conquest his lawes and his large.
And so ded Jhesus the Jewes: he justified and taughte hem

45   The lawe of lyf that last shal evere,
And fended fram foule yveles, feveres and fluxes,
And fro fendes that in hem was, and fals bileve.
Tho was he Jhesus of Jewes called, gentel prophete,
And kynge of her kyngdome, and croune bar of thornes.

50   And tho conquered he on Crosse as conquerour noble;
Myght no deth hym fordo ne adown brynge
That he ne aros and regned and ravysshed helle.
And tho was he conquerour called of quikke and of ded,
For he yaf Adam and Eve, and other mo, blisse

And most like in all limbs to our Lord Jesu.[2]
And then I called to Conscience to answer my question truly:
"Is this Jesus the jouster," I asked, "that Jews put to death,   10
Or is it Piers the Plowman? Who painted him so red?"
Conscience, upon his knees, replied, "These are Piers's arms,
His colors and his coat-armor, but he that comes so bloody
Is Christ with his Cross, conqueror of Christians."
    "Why do you call him Christ, since Jews called him Jesus?   15
Patriarchs and prophets prophesied before
That all kinds of creatures should incline and kneel
As soon as they heard some one speak the name of God Jesu.
*Ergo** there is no name like the name of Jesus,
Nor none so needful to name by night and by day.   20
For all dark devils are in dread to hear it,
And the sinful are solaced and saved by that name.
And you call him Christ; for what cause, tell me,
Is 'Christ' of more might* and a more worthy name
Than 'Jesu' or 'Jesus' whom all our joy came from?"   25
    "Surely you know," said Conscience, "if you're of sound mind,
That knight, king, conqueror can be one person.
To be named a knight is fair, for men shall kneel to him;
To be called a king is fairer, for he can make knights;
But to be called a conqueror, that comes by special grace,   30
And from hardiness of heart and from heart-felt courtesy,
To make lads lords of the lands he wins
And foul slaves of free men who will not follow his laws.
The Jews who were gentle* men held Jesus in scorn,
Both his lore and his law; now are they low churls.   35
As wide as the world is, not one of them lives
But under tribute and taxation, like ragtag curs and churls.
And those who became Christians by counsel of the Baptist
Are franklins,[3] free men, from the baptism they received
And gentle men with Jesu, for Jesus was baptized   40
And on the Cross on Calvary crowned King of the Jews.
It befits a conquering king to keep watch and to defend
His laws and his liegemen in the lands of his conquest.
And so Jesus did with the Jews: he dispensed justice and taught them
The law of life that shall last forever,   45
And defended them from foul ills, fevers and fluxes,
And from fiends that were in them, and from false belief.
Then he was called Jesus by the Jews, gentle prophet,
And king of their kingdom, and bore the crown of thorns.
And then he conquered on the Cross like a noble conqueror;   50
No death could destroy him or dash him down
So that he did not arise and reign and ravage hell.
And then he was called conqueror by the quick[4] and the dead,
For he gave Adam and Eve bliss, and others as well

2. Medieval legend portrayed Pope Gregory* celebrating Mass and seeing, at the moment he put the
   bread on the altar, the figure of the crucified Christ hovering over it.
3. Free landowners, as opposed to serfs; by the fourteenth century, members of the gentry.
4. Living.

55 That longe hadde leyne bifore as Lucyferes cherles,
    [And toke Lucifer the lothely that lord was of helle
    And bond hym as he is bounde with bondes of yren.
    Who was hardier than he? His herte blode he shadde
    To maken alle folke free that folwen his lawe].
60 And sith he [yeveth] largely alle his lele lyges
    Places in Paradys at her partynge hennes,
    He may wel be called conquerour, and that is 'Cryst' to mene.
    Ac the cause that he cometh thus with Crosse of his passioun
    Is to wissen us therewyth that whan that we ben tempted,
65 Therwith to fyghte and fenden us fro fallyng into synne,
    And se bi his sorwe that whoso loveth joye
    To penaunce and to poverté he moste putten hymselven,
    And moche wo in this worlde willen and suffren.
       Ac to carpe more of Cryst and how he come to that name,
70 Faithly forto speke, his firste name was Jhesus.
    Tho he was borne in Bethleem, as the Boke telleth,
    And cam to take mankynde, kynges and aungeles
    Reverenced hym [righte] faire with richesse of erthe.
    Angeles out of Hevene come knelyng and songe
         Gloria in excelsis deo, etc.
75 Kynges come after, kneled and offred [sense],
    Mirre and moche golde, withouten [mercede] askynge
    Or any kynnes catel, but [knowleched] hym soevereigne
    Bothe of sonde, sonne, and see, and sithenes thei went
    Into her kyngene kyth, by conseille of angeles.
80 And there was that worde fulfilled the which thow of speke:
         Omnia celestia terrestria flectantur in hoc nomine Ihesu.
    For alle the angeles of Hevene at his burth kneled,
    And al the witte of the worlde was in tho thre kynges.
    Resoun and [rightwisnesse] and reuth thei offred;
    Wherfore and whi wyse men that tyme,
85 Maistres and lettred men, Magy hem called.
    That o kynge cam with resoun kevered under sense.
    The secounde kynge sitthe sothliche offred
    Rightwisnesse under red golde, resouns felawe;
    Golde is likned to leuté that last shal evere
90 And resoun to [richels]—to righte and to treuthe.
    The thridde kynge tho cam knelyng to Jhesu
    And presented hym with pitee, apierynge by myrre;
    For mirre is mercy to mene and mylde speche of tonge.
    [Ertheliche] honest thinges was offred thus at ones
95 Thorw thre kynne kynges knelynge to Jhesu.
       Ac for alle thise preciouse presentz owre Lorde Prynce Jhesus
    Was neyther kynge ne conquerour til he [comsed] wexe
    In the manere of a man, and that by moche sleight,
    As it bicometh a conquerour to konne many sleightes,

That had before lain long as Lucifer's churls, 55
And he took Lucifer the loathsome who was lord of hell
And bound him as he is bound with bonds of iron.
Who was hardier than he? He shed his heart's blood
To make all folk free who follow his law.
And since he allots liberally to all his loyal liegemen 60
Places in Paradise at their parting hence,
He may well be called a conqueror, and that is what 'Christ' means.[5]
But the cause of his coming thus with the Cross of his passion
Is to teach us by that token that when we face temptation,
To fight against it and defend ourselves from falling into sin, 65
And to see by his sorrow that whoso loves joy
Must apply himself to penance and to poverty, too,
And in this world must wish for much woe to suffer.
    But to discuss Christ further and how he came to that name,
To tell the facts faithfully, his first name was Jesus. 70
When he was born in Bethlehem, as the Book tells,
And came to take mankind, kings and angels
Reverenced him right fairly with riches of the earth.
Angels out of Heaven came kneeling and sang
    Glory to God in the highest, etc.[6]
Kneeling kings came afterwards, carrying incense to him, 75
Myrrh and much gold, unmindful of reward
Or any kind of requital, but proclaimed him sovereign
Both of sand, sun, and sea, and set out after
For the kingdoms they came from, counseled by angels.
And there was that word fulfilled that you spoke of: 80
    All things heavenly and earthly should bow at this name of Jesu.[7]
For all the angels of Heaven kneeled at his birth,
And all the wisdom of the world was in those three kings.
Reason and righteousness and ruth were their offerings;
Wherefore and why wise men at that time,
Masters and lettered men, said that Magi was their name. 85
The first king came with reason under cover of incense.
The second king then came carrying as his offering
Reason's fellow, righteousness, under cover of red gold;
Gold is likened to lawfulness that shall last forever
And incense represents reason—so right goes with truth.[8] 90
The third king kneeling then came close to Jesus
And presented him with pity, appearing as myrrh;
For myrrh means mercy and mild speech of tongue.
Honest earthly things were thus offered at once
By kings of three kingdoms who came kneeling to Jesu. 95
    But for all these precious presents our Lord Prince Jesu
Was neither king nor conqueror till he commenced to grow
In the manner of a man, and one with much skill,
As it becomes a conqueror to call on many skills,

5. Literally, "Christ" means "the anointed."
6. Luke 2:14.
7. Phil. 2:10, already referred to in lines 15–17 above.
8. The translation departs from the Kane-Donaldson edition (KD), which here might be translated literally, "For it [gold] shall turn treason to right and to truth." For Donaldson's reading, see KD p. 161.

100 And many wyles and witte, that wil ben a leder.
     And so did Jhesu in his dayes whoso [dorste] telle it;
     Sumtyme he suffred, and sumtyme he hydde hym,
     And sumtyme he faughte faste, and fleigh otherwhile,
     And sometyme he gaf good and graunted hele bothe,
105 Lyf and lyme; as hym lyste, he wrought
     As kynde is of a conquerour; so comsed Jhesu
     Tyl he had alle hem that he fore bledde.
     In his juventé, this Jhesus atte Juwen feste,
     Water into wyn tourned, as holy writ telleth.
110 And there bigan God of his grace to Do-Wel.
     For wyn is lykned to lawe and lyf of holynesse,
     And lawe lakked tho, for men loved nought her enemys,
     And Cryst conseilleth thus, and comaundeth bothe,
     Bothe to lered and to lewed, to lovye owre enemys.
115 So atte feste firste as I bifore tolde
     Bygan God of his grace and goodnesse to Do-Wel,
     And tho was he cleped and called nought [onliche] Cryst but Jhesu,
     A [fauntekyne] ful of witte, *Filius Mariae*.
     For bifor his moder Marie made he that wonder,
120 That she furste and formest ferme shulde bilieve
     That he thorw grace was gete and of no gome elles.
     He wrought that bi no witte, but thorw worde one,
     After the kynde that he come of; there comsed he Do-Wel.
         And whan he was woxen more, in his moder absence,
125 He made lame to lepe, and yave lighte to blynde,
     And fedde with two fisshes and with fyve loves
     Sore afyngred folke, mo than fyve thousande.
     Thus he conforted carful and caughte a gretter name
     The whiche was Do-Bet, where that he went.
130 For defe thorw his doynges and dombe speke [and herde],
     And alle he heled and halpe that hym of grace asked.
     And tho was he called in contré of the comune peple
     For the dedes that he did *Fili David Jhesus.*
     For David was doughtiest of dedes in his tyme;
135 The berdes tho songe, *'Saul interfecit mille et David decem milia,'*
     Forthi the contré there Jhesu cam called hym *Fili David,*
     And nempned hym of Nazereth; and no man so worthi
     To be kaisere or kynge of the Kyngedome of Juda,
     Ne over Juwes justice as Jhesus was hem thoughte.
140 [Hereof] Caiphas hadde envye, and other of the Jewes,
     And forto doun hym to deth day and nyghte thei casten.
     Kulleden hym on crosse-wyse at Calvarie on Fryday,
     And sithen buryden his body, and beden that men sholde

And to wield many wiles and tricks, one who will be a leader.   100
And Jesus did so in his days, if one dared tell it;
Sometimes he suffered, and sometimes he hid,
And sometimes he fought fiercely, and fled at other times,
And sometimes he gave goods and granted health both,
Life and limb; as he liked, he worked   105
In the way that a conqueror works; so Jesus went about it
Till he had all them for whom he bled.
This Jesus at a Jew's feast, when he was just a boy,
Turned water into wine, as holy words relate.[9]
And there God of his grace began to Do-Well.   110
For wine is likened to law and to life-holiness,
And law was lacking then, for men loved not their enemies,
And Christ counsels thus, and commands as well,
Both learned and unlearned, to love our enemies.
So first at that feast that I referred to before   115
Of his grace and goodness God began to Do-Well,
And then the custom was to call him not only Christ but Jesu,
Young fry full of wisdom, *Filius Mariae*.[1]
For before his mother Mary he performed that miracle,
So that she first and foremost should firmly believe   120
That he was begotten by grace and not begotten of man.
He performed that with no subtle sleight, but by speech alone,
According to the kin he came of; there he commenced Do-Well.
    And when he'd grown more mature, in his mother's absence,
He made lame leap about, and gave light to blind,   125
And fed with two fishes and with five loaves
Near-famished folk, more than five thousand.[2]
Then he comforted those full of care and acquired a greater name
Which was Do-Better, wherever he went.
For by his doing the deaf heard and the dumb spoke,   130
And he healed and helped all who asked him for grace.
And then he was called in the country by the common people
For the deeds that he did *Fili David Jesus*.[3]
For David was doughtiest of deeds in his time;
Then the maidens sang, '*Saul interfecit mille et David decem milia*,'[4]   135
Therefore the country Jesus came into called him *Fili David*,
And named him of Nazareth; and no man so worthy
To be kaiser* or king of the Kingdom of Judah,
Or justice over the Jews as they thought Jesus was.
Caiaphas[5] was envious of him, along with other Jews,   140
Who to do him to death day and night conspired.
They killed him cross-wise on Calvary on Friday,
And buried his body, and bade that men should

---

9. Jesus' first miracle, at the wedding at Cana, John 2:1–11.
1. *Fry*: this term translates "fauntkyn," which has the same connotation as the modern "small fry." *Filius Mariae*: "Son of Mary."
2. See, for example, Isa. 35:6, Luke 9:10–13, John 9, and Mark 8:22–26.
3. "Jesus, son of David": Matt. 21:9.
4. "Saul hath slain his thousands and David his ten thousands": 1 Sam. 18:7.
5. The high priest who condemned Jesus in the Jewish trial before he was handed over to the Romans: Matt. 26:3, 57–68.

Kepen it fro night-comeres, with knyghtes y-armed,
145 For no [frende] shulde [it] fecche; for prophetes hem tolde
That that blessed body of burieles shulde rise
And gone into Galilé, and gladen his Apostles
And his moder Marie; thus men bifore [devyned].
The knyghtes that kepten it biknewe it hemselven
150 That angeles and archangeles, ar the day spronge,
Come knelynge to the corps and songen
[*Christus Rex resurgens*, and it aros after],
Verrey man bifor hem alle, and forth with hem he yede.
The Jewes preyed hem pees, and [preyed] the knyghtes
155 Telle the comune that there cam a compaignye of his Aposteles
And bywicched hem as thei woke and awey stolen it.
Ac Marie Magdeleyne mette hym bi the wey
Goynge toward Galilé in Godhed and manhed
And lyves and lokynge, and she aloude cryde
160 In eche a compaignye there she cam, '*Christus resurgens!*'
Thus cam it out that Cryst overcam, rekevered and lyved:
     Sic oportet Christum pati et intrare, etc.
For that [womman] witeth may noughte wel be conseille.
   Peter parceyved al this and pursued after
Bothe James and Johan, Jhesu for to seke,
165 Taddé and ten mo, with Thomas of Ynde.
And as alle thise wise wyes weren togideres
In an hous al bishette and her dore y-barred
Cryst cam in—and al closed, bothe dore and yates—
To Peter and to his Aposteles, and seyde, '*Pax vobis*'
170 And toke Thomas by the hande and taughte hym to grope
And fele with his fyngres his flesshelich herte.
Thomas touched it, and with his tonge seyde,
     '*Dominus meus et Deus meus.*
Thow art my Lorde, I bileve, God Lorde Jhesu;
Thow deydest and deth tholedest, and deme shalt us alle,
175 And now art lyvynge and lokynge and laste shalt evere.'
Crist carped thanne, and curteislich seyde,
'Thomas, for thow trowest this and trewliche bilevest it,
Blessed mote thow be, and be shalt for evere.
And blessed mote thei be, in body and in soule,
180 That nevere shal se me in sighte, as thow [seest] nouthe,
And lellich bileven al this; I love hem and blesse hem:
     Beati qui non viderunt et crediderunt.'
And whan this dede was done Do-Best he taughte,
And yaf Pieres [pardoun], and [power] he graunted,

Keep it from night-comers, in care of armed knights,
So that no friend could fetch it; for prophets had foretold   145
That that blessed body should rise from its burying-place
And go into Galilee, and gladden his Apostles
And his mother Mary; thus men prophesied before.
The knights assigned to keep it safe conceded themselves
That angels and archangels, ere the day dawned,   150
Came kneeling to the corpse and in chorus sang
Christus Rex resurgens,[6] and it arose thereafter
Veritable man before them all, and went forth with them.
The Jews besought the knights' silence, saying that they should
Tell the commoners that there came a company of his Apostles   155
And bewitched them as they kept watch and stole away with it.
But Mary Magdalene met him on the road
Going toward Galilee[7] in Godhood and in manhood
And alive and alert, and loudly she cried
To every company she encountered, '*Christus resurgens!*'   160
Thus it came out that Christ overcame, recovered and lived:
    Ought Christ thus to suffer and to enter, etc.[8]
For what a woman knows may not well remain secret.
    Peter perceived all this and pursued after
To seek Jesus, as did James and John as well,
And Thaddeus and ten others, with Thomas of India.[9]   165
And as all these wise ones were together
All shut up in a house whose doors were barred
Christ came in—and all were closed, both doors and gates—
To Peter and to his Apostles, and said, '*Pax vobis*'.[1]
And he took Thomas by the hand and taught him to probe   170
And feel with his fingers his fleshly heart.
Thomas touched it, and with his tongue he said,
    '*My Lord and my God.*
You are my Lord, I believe, God Lord Jesu,
Who died and endured death, and shall judge us all,
And are now alive in all limbs and shall last forever.'   175
Then Christ replied courteously, declaring to him,
'Thomas, because you trust in this and truly believe it,
Blessed may you be, and shall be forever.
And blessed may they be, in body and in soul,
Who shall never see the sight of me, as you see now,   180
And loyally believe all this; I love them and bless them:
    Blessed are they who have not seen and have believed.'
And when this deed was done he put Do-Best in train,
And gave Piers pardon, and he granted power to him,

6. "Christ the King is risen"; Rom. 6:9. For the guards and the fear that the disciples would steal the body and say that Christ was risen, see Matt. 27:62–66.
7. John 20:11–18, but she meets him at the sepulchre; in Matt. 28:1–8 she and "the other Mary" are told to say to the disciples that Jesus will meet them in Galilee.
8. Luke 24:26: the Latin verse reads, "Ought not Christ to have suffered these things and thus to enter into his glory?"
9. James, John, Thomas, and Thaddeus (Matt. 10:2–4) were Apostles; according to tradition, Thomas became the Apostle to India (Legenda Aurea, chap. 5).
1. "Peace [be] unto you": this Latin phrase and the next two (lines 172a, 181a) come from John 20:19, 28, 29.

Myghte men to assoille of alle manere synnes,
185 [To alle manere men mercy and forgyfnes,]
In covenant that thei come and knewleche to paye
To Pieres pardon the Plowman, 'Redde quod debes.'
Thus hath Pieres powere, be his pardoun payed,
To bynde and to unbynde bothe here and elles,
190 And assoille men of alle synnes, save of dette one.
Anone after an heigh up into Hevene
He went, and wonyeth there, and wil come atte laste
And rewarde hym righte wel that reddit quod debet,
Payeth parfitly, as pure trewthe wolde,
195 And what persone payeth it nought punysshen he thinketh,
And demen hem at Domesdaye, bothe quikke and ded,
The gode to Godhede and to grete joye,
And [wikked] to wonye in wo withouten ende."
    Thus Conscience of Crist and of the Crosse carped
200 And conseilled me to knele therto; and thanne come, me thoughte,
One Spiritus Paraclitus to Pieres and to his felawes.
In lyknesse of a lightnynge he lyghte on hem alle
And made hem konne and knowe alkyn langages.
I wondred what that was, and wagged Conscience,
205 And was afered [for] the lyghte, for in fyres lyknesse
Spiritus Paraclitus overspradde hem alle.
Quod Conscience and kneled, "This is Crystes messager
And cometh fro the grete God; Grace is his name.
Knele now," quod Conscience, "and if thow canst synge
210 Welcome hym and worshipe hym with Veni Creator Spiritus."
Thanne songe I that songe; so did many hundreth,
And cryden with Conscience, "Help us, [Cryst], of Grace!"
    Thanne bigan Grace to go with Piers Plowman,
And conseilled hym and Conscience the comune to sompne:
215 "For I wil dele todaye and dyvyde grace
To alkynnes creatures that kan her fyve wittes,
Tresore to lyve by to her lyves ende,
And wepne to fyghte with that wil nevre faille.
For Antecryst and his al the worlde shal greve,
220 And acombre the, Conscience, but if Cryst the helpe.
And fals prophetes fele, flatereres and glosers,
Shullen come and be curatoures over kynges and erlis;
And pryde shal be Pope, Prynce of Holy Cherche,
Coveytyse and Unkyndenesse cardinales hym to lede.
225 Forthi," quod Grace, "er I go I wil gyve yow tresore,
And wepne to fighte with whan Antecryst yow assailleth."

Might* to absolve all men of all manner sins,
To all manner of men mercy and forgiveness,   185
On condition that they come and confess the debt they owe
To Piers the Plowman's pardon, *'Redde quod debes.'*
Thus Piers has power, once his pardon is paid,
To bind and unbind both here and elsewhere,[2]
And absolve men of all sins, save only of debt.   190
And soon afterward on high up into Heaven
He went, where he dwells, and will come at the last
And reward him right well who *reddit quod debet*,[3]
Makes perfect payment, as pure truth wishes,
And intends to punish any people who do not pay their debt,   195
And judge them at Doomsday,* both the dead and the living,
The good to Godhead and to great joy,
And the wicked to woe, without end to dwell there."
    Thus Conscience discoursed of Christ and of the Cross
And said I should kneel to it; then came, it seemed to me,   200
One *Spiritus Paraclitus*[4] to Piers and to his fellows.
In likeness of lightning he lighted on them all
And made them speak and understand all sorts of languages.
I wondered what that was, and nudged Conscience,
And was frightened for the light, for in fire's likeness   205
Spiritus Paraclitus overspread them all.
Conscience kneeling counseled me, "This is Christ's messenger
And he comes from the great God; Grace is his name.
Kneel now," commanded Conscience, "and if you can sing
Welcome him and worship him with *Veni Creator Spiritus*."[5]   210
Then I sang that song; so did many hundreds,
And cried with Conscience, "Help me, Christ, with Grace!"
    Then Grace began to go with Piers Plowman,
And counseled him and Conscience to call the commons* together:
"For today I will distribute and divide up grace   215
To all kinds of creatures that claim five wits,*
Treasure to live by to their lives' end,
And weapons to fight with that will never fail.
For Antichrist[6] and his followers will grieve all the world,
And crush you, Conscience, unless Christ helps you.   220
And flocks of false prophets, flatterers and cheats,
Shall come and have the cure of souls of kings and earls;
And pride shall be Pope, Prince of Holy Church,
Covetousness and Unkindness cardinals to lead him.
Therefore," said Grace, "before I go I'll give you treasure,   225
And a weapon to fight with when Antichrist attacks you."

---

2. For Christ's gift of authority to Peter, see Matt. 16:19. "Pay what thou owest" (line 187): Matt. 18:28; cf. Rom. 13:7.
3. "Pays what he oweth" (see preceding note).
4. The Holy Ghost, also called "the Comforter": see John 14:26. The Dreamer, who was attending Easter Mass, now finds himself in the midst of the feast of Pentecost, which commemorates the descent of the Holy Ghost on the Apostles.
5. "Come, Creator Spirit [the Holy Ghost]": from a Latin hymn sung on Pentecost.
6. A false Christ, the great opponent of Christ at the end of time: 1 John 2:18, 22; the idea was a major element in late medieval Apocalyptic thought.

And gaf eche man a grace to gye with hymselven
That ydelnesse encombre hym nought, envye ne pryde:
    Divisiones graciarum sunt, etc.
Some [wyes] he yaf wytte with wordes to shewe,
230 [To wynne with truthe that] the worlde asketh,
As prechoures and prestes and prentyce of lawe:
Thei lelly to lyve by laboure of tonge,
And bi witte to wissen other as Grace hem wolde teche.
And some he kenned crafte and kunnynge of syghte
235 [By] sellyng and buggynge her bylyf to wynne.
And some he lered to laboure [on londe and on water,
And lyve by that laboure] a lele lyf and a trewe.
And somme he taughte to tilie, to [coke] and to thecche,
To wynne with her lyflode by lore of his techynge;
240 And some to dyvyne and divide, noumbres to kenne;
And some to [kerve or] compas, and coloures to make;
And some to se and to saye what shulde bifalle
Bothe of wel and of wo, [and bewar before],
As astronomyenes thorw astronomye and philosophres wyse;
245 And some to ryde and to recoevre that unrightfully was wonne:
He wissed hem wynne it ayeyne thorw wightnesse of handes,
And fecchen it fro fals men with Folvyles lawes.
And some he lered to lyve in longynge to ben hennes,
In poverté and in [pacience], to preye for alle Crystene,
250 And alle he lered to be lele and eche a crafte love other,
[Ne no boste ne] debate [be] amonge hem [alle].
"Thowgh some be clenner than somme, ye se wel," quod
    Grace,
That [alle crafte and konnyng] cometh of my yifte.
Loke that none lakke other, but loveth alle as bretheren;
255 And who that moste maistries can be myldest of berynge.
And crouneth Conscience kynge, and maketh Crafte yowre stuward,
And after Craftes conseille clotheth yow and
    fede.
For I make Pieres the Plowman my procuratour and my reve,
And regystrere to receyve *redde quod debes.*
260 My prowor and my plowman Piers shal ben on erthe,
And for to tulye Treuthe, a teme shal he have."
    Grace gave Piers a teme, foure gret oxen.
That on was Luke, a large beste and a lowe-chered,
And Marke, and Mathew the thrydde, myghty bestes bothe;
265 And joigned to hem one Johan, most gentil of alle,
The prys nete of Piers plow, passyng alle other.
And Grace gave Pieres of his goodnesse foure stottis,
Al that his oxen eryed they to harwe after.
On hyghte Austyne, and Ambrose another,

And he gave each man a grace to guide himself with
So that idleness would not overcome him, nor envy or pride:
    There are divisions of graces, etc.[7]
And certain ones he gave wisdom which their words would show,
And so to win with honesty what the world requires,   230
Such as preachers and priests and apprentices of the law:
They to live lawfully by labor of their tongue,
And with their intelligence teach others as Grace would teach them.
And some he taught the skill to assess what they saw
So that they might support themselves by selling and buying.   235
And some learned from him to labor on land and on water,
And by that labor live a lawful life and true.
And some he taught to till, to cock hay and to thatch,
And earn their livelihood by the lore he taught them;
And some to divine and divide, to be well-versed in numbers;   240
And some to make sculptures or sketches, or skillfully mix colors;
And some to foresee and to say what should occur
Both of well-being and of woe, and beware in advance,
Such as astronomers with astronomy and wise philosophers;
And some to ride out and recover what had been wrongfully seized: 245
He instructed them to restore it through strength of their hands,
And fetch it from false men with Folville's laws.[8]
And some learned from him to live in longing to be hence,
In poverty and in patience, praying for all Christians,
And he taught them all to live by law and each craft to love the other,   250
That no swaggering or dissension be seen among them all.
"Though some are cleaner than some others, you see well," said
    Grace,
"That competence in every craft comes from my gift.
See that nobody blames his fellow, but like brothers love each other;
And he who is master of the most crafts be mildest of bearing.   255
And crown Conscience king, and make Craftsmanship your steward,
And according to Craftsmanship's counsels clothe and feed
    yourselves.
For I make Piers Plowman my proxy and my reeve,*
And registrar to receive *redde quod debes*.[9]
My purveyor and my plowman Piers shall be on earth,   260
And in order to till Truth, a team shall he have."
    Grace gave Piers a team, four great oxen.
The first was Luke, a large beast with lowly mien,
And Mark, and Matthew the third, mighty beasts both;
And joined to them one John, most gentle* of all,   265
The prize ox of Piers's plow, surpassing all the others.[1]
And Grace of his goodness gave Piers four horses,
To harrow afterward all that his oxen plowed.
One had the name Austin,* and Ambrose* another,

7. 1 Cor. 12:4: the verse continues, "but the same Spirit [in each]."
8. "Folville's law" had become a proverbial expression for taking the law into one's own hands.
9. "Pay what thou owest."
1. The oxen, the traditional animals to pull a plow, are the four Evangelists, Luke being traditionally represented as an ox.

270   Gregori the grete clerke and [the gode] Jerome.
        Thise foure the feithe to teche [folwed] Pieres teme
        And harwed in an handwhile al Holy Scripture,
        Wyth two harwes that thei hadde, an olde and a newe:
            Id est, Vetus Testamentum et Novum.
        And Grace gave [Piers] greynes, cardynales vertues,
275   And sewe it in mannes soule and sithen he tolde her names.
        Spiritus prudentiae the firste seed hyghte,
        And whoso eet that ymagyne he shulde,
        Ar he did any dede, devyse wel the ende;
        And lerned men a ladel bugge with a longe stele,
280   That cast for to [kele] a crokke to save the fatte aboven.
        The secounde seed highte *Spiritus Temperantiae.*
        He that ete of that seed hadde suche a kynde
        Shulde nevere mete ne [meschief] make hym to swelle;
        Ne sholde no scorner oute of skyl hym brynge;
285   Ne wynnynge ne welthe of wordeliche ricchesse,
        Waste worde of ydelnesse ne wykked speche meve;
        Shulde no curyous clothe comen on hys rugge,
        Ne no mete in his mouth that Maister Johan spiced.
        The thridde seed that Pieres sewe was *Spiritus Fortitudinis,*
290   And whoso eet of that seed hardy was evre
        To suffre al that God sent, sykenesse and angres.
        Myghte no [lyer with lesynges] ne losse of worldely catel
        Maken hym, for any mournynge, that he nas merye in soule,
        And bolde and abydynge bismeres to suffre.
295   And playeth al with pacyence, and *Parce mihi, Domine,*
        And covered hym under conseille of Catoun the wyse:
            Esto forti animo cum sis dampnatus inique.
        The fierthe seed that Pieres sewe was *Spiritus Justitiae,*
        And he that eet of that seed shulde be [evene] trewe
        With God, and nought agast but of gyle one.
300   For gyle goth so pryvely that good faith otherwhile
        [Shal] noughte ben aspyed [thorugh] *Spiritus Justitiae.*
        Spiritus Justiciae spareth noughte to spille [the gulty]
        And forto correcte the kynge yif [the kynge] falle in gylte.
        For counteth he no kynges wratthe whan he in courte sitteth;
305   To demen as a domes-man adradde was he nevre,
        Noither of duke ne of deth, that he ne dede lawe,
        For present or for preyere or any prynces lettres.
        He dede equité to alle eveneforth his powere.
          Thise foure sedes Pieres sewe and sitthe he did hem harwe
310   Wyth Olde Lawe and Newe Lawe that love myghte wexe
        Amonge the foure vertues, and vices destroye.

Gregory* the great clerk and the good Jerome.*   270
To teach the faith these four followed Piers's team
And in an instant harrowed all Holy Scripture,
With two harrows that they had, an old and a new:
    That is, the Old Testament and the New.[2]
And Grace gave Piers seed-grain, cardinal virtues,[3]
And sowed it in man's soul and then spoke their names.   275
Spiritus prudentiae[4] was the first seed's name,
And whoever ate of that would use imagination,
Before he did any deed, discern well the end;
And he taught men to select a ladle with a long handle,
Contrived for keeling a crock to save the fat on top.   280
The second seed was called *Spiritus Temperantiae.*[5]
He who ate of that seed had such a nature
That neither feast nor famine should effect a swelling of his maw;
Nor should any scorner disturb his even temper;
Nor should wealth of worldly riches nor winning of money   285
Nor any worthless idle word nor wicked speech move him;
Should no conspicuous cloak come upon his back,
Nor any meat* in his mouth that Master John had spiced.
The third seed that Piers sowed was *Spiritus Fortitudinis,*[6]
And whoever ate of that seed was always hardy   290
To suffer all that God sent, sickness and miseries.
No liar with his lies nor loss of worldly good
Might make him, for any mourning, other than merry in soul,
And steadfast and steady to withstand slanders.
He replies to all with patience, and *Parce mihi, Domine,*[7]   295
And took cover under the counsel of Cato* the wise:
    Be of strong mind since ye are damned unjustly.
The fourth seed that Piers sowed was *Spiritus Justitiae,*[8]
And he that ate of that seed should be even-handed and true
With God, and aghast of nothing save of guile alone.
For guile goes so secretly that good faith sometimes   300
Shall not be observed by *Spiritus Justitiae.*
Spiritus Justitiae does not spare to scourge the guilty
And to correct the king if the king is caught in guilt.
For he takes account of no king's wrath when his court is in session;
He never dreaded to hand down decisions of justice,   305
Not for duke or for death, so that he did not dispense law,
For present or for prayer or for any prince's letters.
He did equity to all insofar as he was able.
    Piers sowed these four seeds and then saw to their harrowing
With Old Law and New Law so that love might increase   310
Among the four virtues, and bring vices to destruction.

2. I.e., all Scripture is to be interpreted by correlating every part of it with both the Old and the New
   Testaments, a traditional practice in medieval exegesis. No source has been identified for this Latin
   phrase.
3. "Prudence, temperance, justice, and fortitude."
4. "The Spirit of prudence."
5. "The Spirit of temperance."
6. "The Spirit of fortitude."
7. "Spare me, Lord": cf. Job 7:16.
8. "The Spirit of justice."

"For comunelich in contrees kammokes and wedes
Fouleth the fruite in the felde there thei growe togyderes,
And so don vices vertues; [forthy," quod Piers],
315   "Harweth alle that kunneth kynde witte bi conseille of this doctours,
And tulyeth [to] her techynge the cardinale vertues."
"Ayeines thi greynes," quod Grace, "bigynneth for to ripe,
Ordeigne the an hous, Piers, to herberwe in thi cornes."
"By God, Grace," quod Piers, "ye moten gyve tymbre,
320   And ordeyne that hous ar ye hennes wende."
And Grace gave hym the Crosse, with the [garland] of thornes,
That Cryst upon Calvarye for mankynde on pyned.
And of his baptesme and blode that he bledde on Rode
He made a maner morter, and Mercy it highte.
325   And therewith Grace bigan to make a good foundement,
And watteled it and walled it with his [peyne] and his passioun;
And of al Holy Writ he made a rofe after;
And called that hous Unité, Holi Cherche on Englisshe.
And whan this dede was done, Grace devised
330   A carte hyghte Cristendome to carye [home] Pieres sheves,
And gaf hym caples to his carte, Contricioun and Confessioun;
And made presthode hay-warde the while hymself went
As wyde as the worlde is, with Pieres to tulye Treuthe
[And the Lond of Bileve, the lawe of Holy Cherche].
335   Now is Pieres to the plow, Pruyde it aspyde
And gadered hym a grete oest to greven, he thinketh,
Conscience and al Crystene and cardinale vertues,
Blowe hem doune and breke hem and bite atwo the mores.
And sent forth Surquydous, his serjaunt of armes,
340   And his spye Spille-Love, one Speke-Yvel-Byhynde.
Thise two come to Conscience and to Crystene peple
And tolde hem tydynges—that tyne thei shulde
[The sedes] that [Sire] Pieres [sewe], the cardynal vertues.
"And Pieres berne worth broke; and thei that ben in Unité
345   Shulle come out, Conscience, and yowre two caples,
Confessioun and Contricioun, and yowre carte the Byleve
Shal be coloured so queyntly and kevered under owre sophistrie
That Conscience shal noughte knowe [who is
        Crystene or hethen],
Ne no maner marchaunt that with moneye deleth
350   Where he wynne wyth righte, with wronge, or with usuré."
With suche coloures and queyntise cometh Pryde y-armed
With the lorde that lyveth after the luste of his body,
"To wasten on welfare and on wykked [lyvynge]
Al the worlde in a while thorw owre witte," quod Pruyde.
355   Quod Conscience to alle Crystene tho, "My conseille is to wende
Hastiliche into Unyté and holde we us there.
Preye we that a pees were in Piers berne the Plowman.

"For commonly in the country crabgrass and weeds
Harm the grain when they grow on the same ground together,
And so do vices virtues; therefore," said Piers,
"All that claim kind wit* harrow with the counsel of these doctors,*   315
And according to their teaching till the cardinal virtues."
"Before your grain," said Grace, "begins to ripen,
Prepare yourself a house, Piers, to put your crops in."
"By God, Grace," said Piers, "you must give timber,
And arrange for that house ere you go hence."   320
And Grace gave him the Cross, with the garland of thorns,
That Christ suffered on at Calvary for mankind's sake.
And from his baptism and the blood that he bled on the Cross
He made a kind of mortar, and Mercy was its name.
And with it Grace began to make a good foundation,   325
And wattled it and walled it with his[9] pain and his passion;
And out of all Holy Writ he made a roof afterward;
And he called that house Unity, Holy Church in English.
And when this deed was done, Grace designed a cart
That is called Christendom to carry home Piers's sheaves,   330
And let him have horses to haul his cart, Contrition and Confession;
And made priesthood hedge-warden while he himself went
As wide as the world is, with Piers to plow Truth
And the Land of Belief, the law of Holy Church.
    Now Piers has gone to the plow, Pride observed it   335
And gathered himself a great host to begin an attack
On Conscience and all Christians and cardinal virtues,
Blow them down and break them and bite the roots in two.
And he sent forth Presumption, his sergeant-at-arms,
And his spy Spoil-Love, one Speak-Evil-Behind.   340
These two came to Conscience and to Christian people
And told them tidings—they'd be constrained to forgo
The seeds that Sir Piers sowed, the cardinal virtues.
"And Piers's barn will be broken down; and they that abide in Unity
Shall come out, Conscience, and your two cart-horses,   345
Confession and Contrition, and your cart the Faith
Shall be camouflaged so cleverly and covered by our sophistry
So that Conscience will not be able to discriminate between a
      Christian and a heathen,
And no manner of merchant who deals with money will know
Whether he wins it with right, with wrong, or with usury."   350
With such coloring and cleverness Pride comes armed
With the lord who lives for delight of his body,
"To lay waste on welfare[1] and wicked living
All the world in a while through our wit," said Pride.
Said Conscience to all Christians then, "My counsel is to go   355
Hastily into Unity and let's hold ourselves there.
Let's pray that there be peace in Piers Plowman's barn.

---

9. I.e., Christ's. "Wattle and daub" is the term for a method of construction in which twigs, etc., mixed
  with clay, are used to fill in the spaces between posts. Piers's "barn" closely resembles the great
  tithe-barns of the period, which in turn greatly resemble country churches in their construction.
1. I.e., living well.

For witterly, I wote wel we beth noughte of strengthe
To gone agayne Pryde but Grace were with us."
360   And thanne cam Kynde Wytte Conscience to teche,
And cryde and comaunded al Crystene peple
For to delven a dyche depe aboute Unité
That Holy Cherche stode in [holynesse] as it a pyle [were].
Conscience comaunded tho al Crystene to delve
365   And make a muche mote that myghte ben a strengthe
To helpe Holy Cherche and hem that it kepeth.
Thanne alkyn Crystene save comune wommen
Repenteden and [forsoke] synne, save they one,
And [a sisoure and a sompnoure] that were forsworen ofte;
370   Wytynge and willefully with the false helden,
And for sylver were forswore—sothely thei wist it!
There nas no Crystene creature that kynde witte hadde,
Save schrewes one suche as I spak of,
That he ne halpe a quantité holynesse to wexe,
375   Somme thorw bedes byddynge and some [by pylgrymages]
And other pryvé penaunce, and some thorw penyes delynge.
And thanne welled water for wikked werkes
Egerlich ernynge out of mennes eyen.
Clennesse of the comune and clerkes clene lyvynge
380   Made Unité, Holi Cherche, in holynesse to stonde.
     "I care noughte," quod Conscience, "though Pryde come nouthe.
The lorde of luste shal be letted al this Lente, I hope.
Cometh," quod Conscience, "ye Cristene, and dyneth,
That han laboured lelly al this Lente tyme.
385   Here is bred y-blessed, and Goddes body therunder.
Grace thorw Goddes worde gave Pieres power,
[Myghte] to maken it, and men to ete it after
In helpe of her hele onys in a moneth,
Or as ofte as they hadden nede, tho that hadde y-payed
390   To Pieres pardoun the Plowman *redde quod debes.*"
     "How?" quod al the comune. "Thow conseillest us to yelde
Al that we owen any wyghte ar we go to housel?"
"That is my conseille," quod Conscience, "and cardynale vertues;
[Or] uche man foryyve other, and that wyl the
          Paternoster:
     Et dimitte nobis debita nostra, etc.
395   And so to ben assoilled and sithen ben houseled."
     "Ye? bawe!" quod a brewere. "I wil nought be reuled,
Bi Jhesu, for al yowre janglynge, with *Spiritus Justitiae,*
Ne after Conscience, by Cryste, whil I can selle
Bothe dregges and draffe, and drawe it at on hole
400   Thikke ale and thinne ale; for that is my kynde!
And noughte hakke after holynesse. Holde thi tonge,
          Conscience!

For certainly, I'm sure we are not strong enough
To go against Pride unless Grace is with us."
And then Kind Wit* came to give Conscience instructions,   360
And cried out and commanded all Christian people
To dig a ditch deep around Unity
That Holy Church might stand in holiness as if it were a fort.
Then Conscience commanded all Christians to dig
And make a big moat that might be a defense   365
To help Holy Church and all who guard it.
Then all kinds of Christians except common women
Repented and forsook sin, except only them,
And an assizer* and a summoner* who were forsworn often;
Wittingly and willfully they held with the false,   370
And were forsworn for silver—and surely knew the truth!
There was no Christian creature that had kind wit,
Except for such wicked ones as I spoke of,
Who did not to some extent help holiness to grow,
Some by saying prayers and some by pilgrimages   375
And other private penance, and some by giving pennies* away.
And then there welled up water for wicked deeds
Issuing harshly out of men's eyes.
Cleanness of the commons* and clerks' clean living
Made Unity, Holy Church, to stand in holiness.   380
    "I care not," said Conscience, "though Pride come now.
The lord of lust shall be thwarted all this Lent, I hope.
Come," said Conscience, "you Christians, and dine,
You who have labored loyally all this Lenten time.
Here is blessed bread, and God's body thereunder.   385
Grace through God's word gave Piers power,
Might* to make it, so men might eat it after
To help their health once every month,
Or as often as they had need, those who had paid
To Piers the Plowman's pardon *redde quod debes*."[2]   390
    "How's that?" said all the commons. "You counsel us to repay
All we owe any man ere we go to Mass?"
"That is my counsel," said Conscience, "and cardinal virtues;
Or else each man forgive the other, and that's what the Lord's Prayer
        asks:
    And forgive us our debts, etc.[3]
And so to be absolved and then receive the Eucharist."   395
    "Yes? bah!" said a brewer. "I will not be ruled,
By Jesus, for all your jangling, by *Spiritus Justitiae*,[4]
Nor by Conscience, by Christ, while I can sell
Both dregs and draff,[5] and draw from one hole
Thick ale and thin ale; that's the kind of man I am!   400
And I won't go hacking[6] after holiness. Hold your tongue,
        Conscience!

2. "Pay what thou owest."
3. The verse continues, "as we forgive our debtors."
4. "The Spirit of justice."
5. The refuse left after brewing.
6. I.e., riding on a horse.

Of *Spiritus Justiciae* thow spekest moche an ydel."
"Caytyve!" quod Conscience. "Cursed wrecche!
Unblessed artow, brewere, but if the God helpe.
405 But thow lyve by lore of *Spiritus Justitiae*,
The chief seed that Pieres sewe, y-saved worstow nevre.
But Conscience [be thi] comune and cardynale vertues,
Leve it wel, [thow art] loste, bothe lyf and soule."
    "Thanne is many [a] man y-lost," quod a lewed vycory.
410 "I am a curatour of Holy Kyrke, and come nevre in my tyme
Man to me that me couth telle of cardinale vertues,
Or that acounted Conscience at a cokkes fether.
I knewe nevre cardynal that he ne cam fro the pope,
And we clerkes whan they come, for her comunes payeth,
For her pelure and her palfreyes mete, and piloures that hem
415   folweth.
The comune *clamat cotidie*, eche a man to other,
'The contré is the curseder that cardynales come inne,
And there they ligge and lenge, moste lecherye there regneth.'
Forthi," quod this vicori, "be verrey God, I wolde
420 That no cardynal come amonge the comune peple,
But in her holynesse holden hem stille
At Avynoun amonge the Juwes—*Cum sancto sanctus eris, etc.*—
Or in Rome as here rule wole, the reliques to kepe;
And thow, Conscience, in Kynges courte, and shuldest nevre come
    thennes;
425 And Grace that thow gredest so of, gyour of alle clerkes;
And Pieres [the Plowman] with his newe plow and his olde
Emperour of al the worlde, that alle men were Cristene.
Inparfyt is that pope that al peple shulde helpe
And [soudeth] hem that sleeth suche as he shulde save.
430 [Ac] wel worth Piers the Plowman that [pursueth] God in doyng:
Qui pluit super justos et injustos at ones,
And sent the sonne to save a cursed mannes tilthe
As bryghte as to the best man [or] to the beste woman.
Righte so Pieres the Plowman peyneth hym to tulye
435 As wel for a wastour and wenches of the stuwes
As for hymself and his servauntz, save he is firste y-served.
[So blessed be Piers the Plowman that peyneth hym to tulye],
And travailleth and tulyeth for a tretour also sore
As for a trewe tydy man al tymes ylyke.
440 And worshiped be he that wroughte al, bothe good and wykke,
And suffreth that synful be til some tyme that thei repente.
And [Piers] amende the pope that pileth Holy Kirke
And cleymeth bifor the kynge to be keper over Crystene,
And counteth nought though Crystene ben culled and robbed,
445 And fynt folke to fyghte and Cristene blode to spille
Ayeyne the Olde Lawe and Newe Lawe, as Luke [bereth witnesse]:

Of *Spiritus Justitiae* you speak a lot of nonsense."
"Scoundrel!" said Conscience. "Cursed wretch!
Unblessed are you, brewer, unless God be your help.
Unless you live by the lore of *Spiritus Justitiae*,   405
The chief seed that Piers sowed, you shall never be saved.
Unless Conscience is your commons* and cardinal virtues,
Believe it well, you will be lost, both body and soul."
    "Then is many a man lost," remarked an ignorant vicar.
"I am a curator of Holy Kirk,* and there came never in my time   410
To me any man that could tell me about cardinal virtues,
Or that counted Conscience as worth a cock's feather.
I never knew a cardinal that did not come from the pope,
And we clerks when they come pay the cost of their provisions,
Of their furs and their palfreys' food, and the pillagers that follow
    them.   415
The commons *clamat cotidie*,[7] each man to other,
'The country is the curseder that cardinals come into,
And where they loll about and linger, most lechery reigns there.'
Therefore," said this vicar, "by very God, I wish
That no cardinal would come among the common people,   420
But in their holiness hold themselves still
In Avignon among the Jews—*Cum sancto sanctus eris, etc.*[8]—
Or in Rome as their rule directs, to watch over the relics;
And you, Conscience, in the King's court, and should never come
    away;
And Grace that you go crying of should be guide of all clerks;   425
And Piers the Plowman with his new plow and his old
Emperor of all the world, so that all men might be Christians.
Imperfect is that pope who should give all people help
And pays soldiers to slay such as he should save.
But long live Piers Plowman whose deeds are like God's: 430
Who raineth upon the just and the unjust at once,[9]
And sends the sun to save a cursed man's harvest
As bright as to the best man or the best woman.
Just so Piers the Plowman takes pains to plow
As well for a waster and wenches of the brothel   435
As for himself and his servants, except he is served first.
So blessed be Piers the Plowman who takes such pains to plow,
And tills and toils for a traitor just as hard
As for a man of true integrity all times alike.
And worshiped be he who wrought all, both good and evil,   440
And suffers the sinful till such time as they repent.
And may Piers amend the pope who pillages Holy Church
And over the king claims to be keeper of Christians,
And does not care though Christians are killed and robbed,
And pays people to fight and spill Christian blood   445
Against the Old Law and the New Law, as Luke bears witness:

7. "Cry out daily."
8. "With the holy thou wilt be holy": Ps. 17:26. Jews as moneylenders were thought to be essential to
supporting the court of the pope at Avignon, during the period of the "Great Schism" (1378–1417),
when there were two popes.
9. Matt. 5:45.

Non occides; michi vindictam, etc.
It semeth by so hymself hadd his wille
That he ne reccheth righte noughte of al the remenaunte.
And Cryst of his curteisye the cardinales save
450 And tourne her witte to wisdome and to wele of soule.
For the comune," quod this curatour, "counten ful litel
The conseille of Conscience or cardinale vertues
But if [it sowne] as by syghte somwhat to wynnynge.
Of gyle ne of gabbynge gyve thei nevere tale,
455 For *Spiritus Prudentiae* amonge the peple is gyle,
And alle tho faire vertues as vyces thei semeth.
Eche man sotileth a sleight synne forto hyde
And coloureth it for a kunnynge and a clene lyvynge."
Thanne loughe there a lorde; and, "By this lighte," sayde,
460 "I halde it ryghte and resoun of my reve to take
Al that myne auditour or elles my stuwarde
Conseilleth me by her acounte and my clerkes wrytynge.
With *Spiritus Intellectus* they [toke] the reves rolles,
And with *Spiritus Fortitudinis* fecche it, [wol he, nol he]."
465 And thanne come there a kynge, and bi his croune seyde:
"I am kynge with croune the comune to reule,
And Holy Kirke and clergye fro cursed men to defende.
And if me lakketh to lyve by the lawe wil I take it
There I may hastlokest it have, for I am hed of lawe;
470 Ye ben but membres, and I above alle.
And sith I am yowre aller hed, I am yowre aller hele
And Holy Cherche chief help, and chiftaigne of the comune.
And what I take of yow two, I take it atte techynge
Of *Spiritus Justitiae*, for I jugge yow alle.
475 So I may baldely be houseled for I borwe nevere,
Ne crave of my comune but as my kynde
      asketh."
      "In condicioun," quod Conscience, "that thow [the comune]
      defende
And rule thi rewme in resoun, [as right wol] and treuth,
[Have] thow may [thyn askynge], as thi lawe asketh.
      Omnia tua sunt ad defendendum, set non ad deprehendendum."
480 The vyker hadde fer home, and faire toke his leve,
And I awakned therewith and wrote as me mette.

Passus XX

Thanne as I went by the way whan I was thus awaked,
Hevy-chered I yede, and elynge in herte.
I ne wiste where to ete ne at what place,

Thou shalt not kill; vengeance is mine, etc.[1]
It seems as if as long as he himself has his will
He takes no heed at all of any one else.
And Christ of his courtesy save the cardinals
And turn their wit into wisdom and into wealth of spirit.   450
For the commons," said this curate, "account very little
The counsel of Conscience or cardinal virtues
Unless it appears to promise a profit of some kind.
Deceit and double-dealing don't disturb them at all,
For *Spiritus Prudentiae*[2] among the people is guile,   455
And all those fair virtues seem like vices to them.
Each man schemes up a stratagem to conceal sin
And makes it appear as politic or a proper mode of action."
Then a lord laughed: "By this light," he said,
"I hold it right and reasonable to receive from my reeve*   460
All that my auditor or else my steward
Counsels me to take by their accounts and my clerk's books.
With *Spiritus Intellectus*[3] they took the reeve's records,
And with *Spiritus Fortitudinis*[4] I'll fetch it, willy-nilly."
And then there came a king, and by his crown he spoke: 465
"I am king with crown to rule the commonwealth,
And to defend Holy Kirk and clergy from cursed men.
And if I lack enough to live on the law will I take it
Where I may have it quickest, for I am head of law;
You are only members, and I am over all.   475
Since I am head of you all, I am healer of you all
And chief help for Holy Church, and chieftain of the commons.
And what I take of you two, I take it by instruction
Of *Spiritus Justitiae,* for I am judge of you all.
So I may boldly receive communion for I'm in no man's debt,   475
Nor do I crave anything of my commons save what's required by my
      nature."
    "On condition," said Conscience, "that you defend the
      commonwealth
And rule your realm with reason, as right and truth demand,
You may have what you ask for, as your law declares.
    All things are yours for defense, but not for plunder."[5]
This vicar's home was far away, and he fairly took his leave,   480
And I awakened therewith and wrote what I had dreamed.

Passus XX

Then as I walked on my way when I'd awakened thus,
Heavy-hearted I went, and anguished in spirit.
I didn't know where to eat nor at what place I might,

1. Exod. 20:13, Luke 18:20, Deut. 32:35, Heb. 10:30.
2. "The Spirit of prudence."
3. "The Spirit of understanding, the intellectual spirit."
4. "The Spirit of fortitude."
5. Apparently a legal tenet (line 479).

And it neighed nyeghe the none and with Nede I mette
5   That afronted me foule, and faitour me called.
      "Coudestow noughte excuse the, as dede the kynge and other,
     That thow toke to thi bylyf, to clothes and to sustenance,
     [Was] by techynge and by tellynge of *Spiritus*
          Temperantiae,
     And thow nome namore than Nede the taughte?
10   And Nede ne hath no lawe, ne nevre shal falle in dette,
     For thre thynges he taketh his lyf for to save:
     That is mete whan men hym werneth and he no moneye
          weldeth,
     Ne wyght none wil ben his borwe, ne wedde hath none to legge;
     And he [cacche] in that cas, and come thereto by sleighte,
15   He synneth noughte sothelich that so wynneth his fode.
     And though he come so to a clothe and can no better
          chevysaunce,
     Nede anonrighte nymeth hym under meynpryse.
     And if hym lyst for to lape, the lawe of kynde wolde
     That he dronke at eche diche ar he [deye] for thurste.
20   So nedé at grete nede may nymen as for his owne
     Wythoute conseille of Conscience or cardynale vertues,
     So that he suwe and save *Spiritus Temperantiae.*
     For is no vertue by fer to *Spiritus Temperantiae,*
     Neither *Spiritus Justitiae* ne *Spiritus Fortitudinis*
25   For *Spiritus Fortitudinis* forfaiteth ful oft;
     He shal do more than mesure many tyme and ofte,
     And bete men over bitter and somme [body] to litel,
     And greve men gretter than goode faith it wolde.
     And *Spiritus Justitiae* shal juggen, wol he nol he,
30   After the kynges conseille, and the comune lyke.
     And *Spiritus Prudentiae* in many a poynte shal faille
     Of that he weneth wolde falle if his wytte ne were;
     Wenynge is no wysdome ne wyse ymagynacioun:
          Homo proponit et Deus disponit;
     [God] governeth alle good vertues.
35   Ac Nede is next hym for anon he meketh
     And as low as a lombe for lakkyng of that hym nedeth;
     [For Nede maketh nedé fele nedes lowe-herted].
     [Philosophres] forsoke wele for they wolde be nedy
     And woneden [wel elengelich] and wolde noughte be riche.
40   And God al his grete joye gostliche he left,
     And cam and toke mankynde and bycam nedy.
     So nedy he was, as seyth the Boke in many sondry places,
     That he seyde in his sorwe on the selve Rode:
     'Bothe fox and foule may fleighe to hole and crepe
45   And the fisshe hath fyn to flete with to reste;
     There nede hath y-nome me that I mote nede abyde

And as noon drew near Need stood before me
And accosted me discourteously, and called me a fraud.   5
   "Couldn't you excuse yourself, like the king and the others,
That what you got to go on living with, garments and sustenance,
Amounted to no more than *Spiritus Temperantiae*[1] recommended to
      you,
And you nabbed nothing else but what Need told you to?
And Need has no law, and shall never fall in debt,   10
For there are three things that he takes to save his life:
That is food when men refuse him it and he finds no money in his
      purse,
And none will stand surety for him, and he can supply no pledge;
If in that case he cadges something, acquires it by sleight,
Surely he doesn't sin who so gets his food.   15
And though he comes thus to some clothing and can make no better
      bargain,
Need shall straightway serve as his bondsman.
And if he'd like to lap water, nature's law decrees
That he drink at every ditch before he dies of thirst.
So needy in his great need may take what's necessary for him   20
Without counsel of Conscience or cardinal virtues,
So long as he pursue and preserve *Spiritus Temperantiae*.
For there's no virtue to be preferred to *Spiritus Temperantiae*,
Neither *Spiritus Justitiae* nor *Spiritus Fortitudinis*[2]
For *Spiritus Fortitudinis* offends very often;   25
He'll do more than moderation asks many a time and oft,
And beat this body over bitterly and that body too little,
And inflict greater grief on men than good faith wishes.
And *Spiritus Justitiae* will judge, willy-nilly,
According to the king's counsel if it's the commons'* pleasure.   30
And *Spiritus Prudentiae*[3] will fail in many a particular
Of what he supposes would happen if it weren't for his wit;
Such supposing is not wisdom nor sage prognostication:
      Man proposes and God disposes;[4]
God governs all good virtues.
   But Need is next him for he soon knows meekness   35
And is lowly as a lamb for lack of what he needs;
For Need by necessity makes needy men feel humble.
Philosophers forsook wealth for they wished to be needy
And lived most wretched lives and looked for no riches.
And God's spirit would forgo all his great joy,   40
And he came and took mankind[5] and became needy.
He was so needy, as the Book says in many sundry places,
That he spoke this speech in his sorrow on the Cross:
'The fowl may fly and the fox creep to a hole
And the fish swim with his fin to find his rest;   45
While need grips me so narrowly that I must needs remain

1. "The Spirit of temperance."
2. "Spirit of justice"; "Spirit of fortitude."
3. "Spirit of prudence."
4. Proverbial, ultimately deriving from Prov. 16:9.
5. I.e., human nature.

And suffre sorwes ful sowre that shal to joye tourne.'
Forthi be noughte abasshed to byde and to be nedy
Syth he that wroughte al the worlde was wilfullich nedy,
50 Ne never none so nedy, ne poverere deyde."
       Whan Nede had undernome me thus anon I felle aslepe
And mette ful merveillously that in mannes forme
Antecryst cam thanne and al the croppe of Treuthe
Torned it [tyte] up-so-doune and overtilte the rote,
55 And [made] Fals sprynge and sprede and spede mennes nedes.
In eche a contré there he cam he cutte awey Treuthe
And gert Gyle growe there as he a god were.
Freres folwed that fende, for he yaf hem copes,
And religiouse reverenced hym and rongen here belles,
60 And al the covent forth cam to welcome [a] tyraunt
And alle hise as wel as hym, save onlich folis,
Which folis were wel lever to deye
[Than to lyve] lengore sith [Leuté] was so rebuked,
And a fals fende Antecriste over alle folke regned.
65 And that were mylde men and holy that no myschief dredden
Defyed al falsenesse and folke that it used.
And what kynge that hem conforted, knowynge [here gyle],
They cursed, and her conseille, were it clerke or lewed.
Antecriste hadde thus sone hundredes at his banere,
70 And Pryde [bar] it bare, boldely aboute,
With a lorde that lyveth after lykynge of body,
That cam ayein Conscience, that kepere was and gyoure
Over kynde Crystene and cardynale vertues.
"I conseille," quod Conscience tho, "cometh with me, ye foles,
75 Into Unyté, Holy Cherche, and holde we us there,
And crye we to Kynde that he come and defende us
Foles fro this Fendes lymes for Piers love the Plowman.
And crye we to alle the comune that thei come to Unité
And there abide and bikere ayein Beliales children."
80 Kynd Conscience tho herde and cam out of the planetes
And sent forth his forejoures, fevres and fluxes,
Coughes and cardiacles, crampes and tothaches,
Rewmes and radegoundes and roynouse scalles,
Byles and bocches and brennyng agues,
85 Frenesyes and foule yveles; forageres of Kynde
Hadde y-prykked and prayed polles of peple.
Largelich a legioun [loste] her lyf sone.
There was "Harrow and help! here cometh Kynde
With Deth that is dredful to undone us alle!"
90 The lorde that lyved after lust tho alowde cryde
After Conforte, a knyghte, to come and bere his banere:
"Alarme! Alarme!" quod that lorde, "eche lyf kepe his owne!"
Thanne mette this men—ar mynstralles myghte pipe

And suffer sorrow most sour that shall turn to joy.'[6]
Therefore don't be abashed to abide and to be needy
Since he who was the world's creator was willfully needy,
And never was there any so needy, and none died poorer."   50
    When Need had scolded me so I fell asleep at once
And dreamed most marvelously that in man's form
Antichrist came then and cut Truth's branches,
Quickly turned the tree upside down and tore up the roots,
And made False spring up and spread and support men's needs.   55
In every country where he came he cut away Truth
And got Guile to grow there as if he were a god.
Friars followed that fiend, for he gave them copes,*
And religious orders did him reverence and rang their bells,
And all the convent came to welcome a usurper   60
And all his followers as well as him, save only fools,
Which fools would prefer far more to die
Than to live any longer since Lewté* was so despised,
And a false fiend Antichrist put all folk beneath his rule.
And mild men and holy whom no misery frightened   65
Defied all falseness and folk who practiced it.
And what king gave comfort to the false, conscious of their guile,
These others cursed, and his counselors, whether clerks or laymen.
Antichrist thus soon had hundreds at his banner,
And Pride bore it presumptuously, displaying it about,   70
With a lord who lived for delight of his body,
Who came against Conscience, the keeper and the guide
Of Christian kindred and of cardinal virtues.
"I counsel," said Conscience then, "come with me, you fools,
Into Unity, Holy Church, and let's hold ourselves there,   75
And let's cry out to Kind* that he come and defend us
Fools from these Fiend's limbs for love of Piers the Plowman.[7]
And let's cry to all the commons* to come into Unity
And abide there and strike blows against Belial's children."[8]
Kind heard Conscience then and came out of the planets   80
And sent forth his foragers, fevers and fluxes,
Coughs and cardiac ailments, cramps and toothaches,
Rheums and running sores and rankling scurvy,
Boils and blisters and burning agues,
Frenzies and foul disorders; foragers of Kind   85
Had pricked and preyed upon people's skulls.
A number large as a legion straightway lost their lives.
There were howls of "Help! here comes Kind
With Death that is dreadful to undo us all!"
The lord who lived for delight then cried aloud   90
For a knight called Comfort to come bear his banner:
"Alarm! Alarm!" said that lord, "each man look out for himself!"
Then these men met—before minstrels could pipe

---

6. Langland is paraphrasing Matt. 8:20, words not, however, spoken from the Cross.
7. Here, as in lines 61–63 above, Langland echoes 1 Cor. 1:22–29, especially "For the foolishness of
   God is wiser than men. . . . God chose what is foolish in the world to shame the wise."
8. A major devil.

And ar heraudes of armes hadden descreved lordes—
95   Elde the hore; he was in the vauntwarde
And bare the banere bifor Deth; by righte he it claymed.
Kynde come after with many kene sores
As pokkes and pestilences, and moche poeple shente.
So Kynde thorw corupciouns kulled ful manye.
100 Deth cam dryvende after and al to doust passhed
Kynges and knyghtes, kayseres and popes.
Lered ne lewed, he let no man stonde
That he hitte evene that evere stired after.
Many a lovely lady and [here] lemmanes-knyghtes
105 Swouned and swelted for sorwe of Dethes dyntes.
Conscience of his curteisye [tho] Kynde he bisoughte
To cesse and suffre and see where thei wolde
Leve Pryde pryvely and be parfite Cristene.
And Kynde cessed [sone], to se the peple amende.
110   Fortune gan flateren thenne tho fewe that were alyve
And byhight hem longe lyf, and Lecherye he sent
Amonges al manere men, wedded and unwedded,
And gadered a gret hoste al agayne Conscience.
This lecherye leyde on with a laughyng chiere
115 And with pryvé speche and peynted wordes,
And armed hym in ydelnesse and in hiegh berynge.
He bare a bowe in his hande and manye [brode] arwes,
Weren fethered with faire biheste and many a false truthe.
With his untydy tales he tened ful ofte
120 Conscience and his compaignye, of Holi [Kirke] the techeres.
Thanne cam Coveityse and caste how he myghte
Overcome Conscience and cardynal vertues,
And armed hym in avaryce and hungriliche lyved.
His wepne was al-wiles, to wynnen and to hyden;
125 With glosynges and with gabbynges he gyled the peple.
Symonye hym [suwede] to assaille Conscience,
And [pressed on] the [pope], and prelates thei maden
To holden with Antecryste, her temperaltés to save.
And come to the kynges conseille as a kene baroun
130 And [knokked] Conscience in courte afor hem alle;
And gart Gode Feith flee, and Fals to abide,
And boldeliche bar adown with many a brighte noble
Moche of the witte and wisdome of Westmynster Halle.
He jugged til a justice and justed in his ere
And overtilte al his treuthe with "Take this up
135   amendement."
And to the Arches in haste he yede anone after
And torned Civile into Symonye, and sitthe he toke the Official.
For a [menyvere mantel] he made lele matrimonye

Or heralds of arms had identified lords—
Old Age the hoary; he was in the vanguard   95
And bore the banner before Death; he claimed it by right.
Kind came after with many cutting sores
Such as poxes and pestilence, and brought many people to ruin.
So Kind with bodily corruptions killed very many.
Death came driving after him and dashed all to dust   100
Companies of kings and knights, kaisers and popes.
Learned or unlearned, he let no man stand
That he hit squarely who ever stirred afterward.
Many a lovely lady and their lover-knights
Sank down swooning for sorrow of Death's blows.   105
Then Conscience of his courtesy craved of Kind
To cease and abstain and see whether they would
Leave Pride privily and be proper Christians.
And Kind ceased straightway, to see the people amend.
    Then Fortune began to flatter those few that were alive   110
And promised them long life, and sent Lechery out
Among all manner of men, married and unmarried,
And gathered a great host all against Conscience.
This Lechery laid on with a laughing face
And with privy speech and painted words,   115
And armed himself in idleness and in arrogant bearing.
He bore a bow in his hand with many broad arrows
Which were feathered with fair promise and many a false betrothal.
With unseemly stories he distressed very often
Conscience and his company, Holy Kirk's teachers.   120
Then Covetousness came and considered how he might
Overcome Conscience and cardinal virtues,
And armed himself in avarice and lived hungrily.
His weapon was all-wiles, to win money and hide it;
With glozings* and garblings he beguiled the people.   125
Simony* pursued him to assail Conscience,
And put pressure on the pope, and they appointed prelates
As allies of Antichrist, to hold safe their temporalities.[9]
And he came to the King's Council like a keen baron
And cuffed Conscience in court before them all;   130
And made Good Faith flee, and False to abide,
And boldly bore down with many a bright coin
Much of the wit and wisdom of Westminster Hall.[1]
He jogged to a justice and jousted in his ear
And overturned all his integrity with "Take this and think better of
    me."   135
And for the Arches[2] in haste he headed afterward
And turned Civil* into Simony,* and then subverted the Official.[3]
For a miniver[4] mantle he made true matrimony

9. Their worldly possessions.
1. Where the law courts were.
2. The Archbishop of Canterbury's court in London.
3. The presiding judge of an ecclesiastical court. The sense is that Simony's wealth subordinates Civil
   Law by bribing court officers.
4. A white or light gray fur.

Departen ar Deth cam and devos shupte.
140 "Allas!" quod Conscience and cried, "wolde Criste of his grace
That Coveityse were Cristene that is so kene a fighter,
And bolde and bidyng while his bagge lasteth."
And thanne lowgh Lyf and leet dagge his clothes
And armed hym in haste in harlotes wordes,
145 And helde Holynesse a jape and Hendenesse a wastour,
And lete Leuté a cherle and Lyer a fre man.
Conscience and [his] conseille, he counted it folye.
Thus relyed Lyf for a litel fortune
And pryked forth with pryde; preyseth he no vertue,
150 [And] careth noughte how Kynde slow, and shal come atte laste
And culle alle erthely creature save Conscience one.
Lyf leep asyde and laughte hym a lemman.
"Heel and I," quod he, "and Hieghnesse of Herte
Shal do the noughte drede noyther Deth ne Elde,
155 And [so] foryete sorwe, and yyve noughte of synne."
This lyked Lyf, and his lemman Fortune,
And geten in her glorie a gadelyng atte laste,
One that moche wo wroughte, Sleuthe was his name.
Sleuthe wex wonder yerne and sone was of age
160 And wedded one Wanhope, a wenche of the stuwes.
Her syre was a sysour that nevre swore treuthe,
One Thomme Two-Tonge, ateynte at uch a queste.
This Sleuthe [wex sleigh] of werre and a slynge made,
And threwe Drede-Of-Dyspayre a dozein myle aboute.
165 For care Conscience tho cryed upon Elde
And bad hym fonde to fyghte and afere Wanhope.
And Elde hent Good Hope, and hastilich he shifte hym,
And wayved awey Wanhope, and with Lyf he fyghteth.
And Lyf fleigh for fere to Fysyke after helpe
170 And bisoughte hym of socoure, and of his salve hadde,
And gaf hym golde good woon that gladded his herte.
And thei gyven hym agayne, a glasen houve.
Lyf leved that lechecrafte lette shulde Elde
And dryven awey Deth with dyas and dragges.
175 And Elde auntred hym on Lyf, and atte laste he hitte
A fisicien with a forred hood that he fel in a palsye,
And there deyed that doctour ar thre dayes after.
    "Now I see," seyde Lyf, "that surgerye ne fisyke
May noughte a myte availle to medle ayein Elde."
180 And in hope of his hele gode herte he hente
And rode so to Revel, a ryche place and a merye—
The Companye of Conforte men cleped it sumtyme—
    And Elde after [hym], and over myne heed yede,
And made me balled bifore and bare on the croune;
185 So harde he yede over myn hed it wil be seen evre.

Divide before Death came and fashioned divorces.
   "Alas!" said Conscience and cried, "would Christ of his grace   140
That Covetousness were a Christian since he's so keen a fighter,
And stout-hearted and steadfast while his purse-strings hold."
And then Life laughed and let his clothing be slashed[5]
And in haste armed himself in whoreson's words,[6]
And judged Holiness a joke and Gentleness* a waster,   145
And alleged that Lewté* was a churl and Liar a gentleman.
Conscience and his counsel, he accounted them folly.
Thus for a little luck Life revived
And pricked forth with pride; he praises no virtue,
And cares not how Kind slew folk, and shall come at the last   150
And kill all earthly creatures save Conscience alone.
Life leapt aside and selected a mistress.
"Health and I," said he, "and Highness of Heart
Shall induce you to have no dread of either Death or Age,
And so forget sorrow, and have no sense of sin."   155
Life liked this, and his love Fortune,
And at last they begot in their gloating a graceless brat,
One who caused much care and was called Sloth.
Sloth matured with wondrous speed and was soon of age
And wedded one Wanhope,* a wench of the brothel.   160
Her sire was an assizer* who never swore truthfully,
One Tom Two-Tongue, convicted at every inquest.
This Sloth grew skilled in war and made himself a sling,
And threw Dread-Of-Despair a dozen miles about.
Then Conscience in his care called upon Old Age   165
And said he should strive to fight and scare away Wanhope.
And Old Age took Good Hope, and hastily he stationed him,
And drove Wanhope away, and he fights with Life.
And Life fled for fear to Physic for help
And besought succor from him, and had some of his salve,   170
And gave him gold aplenty which gladdened his heart.
And they gave him a gift in return, a glass helmet.[7]
Life believed that medicine would delay Old Age
And drive away Death with drugs and prescriptions.
And Old Age ventured against Life, and he hit at the last   175
A physician in a furred hood so that he fell in a palsy,
And there that doctor died before three days passed.
   "Now I see," said Life, "that surgery and medicine
Cannot do any good at all against Old Age."
And in hope for his health he grew hardy of heart   180
And so rode off to Revel, a rich place and a merry one—
The Company of Comfort men called it once.
   And Old Age came after him, and went over my head,
And made me both bald in front and bare on the crown;
So hard he went over my head it will always be evident.   185

5. It was fashionable to have the hems and borders of clothes "slashed" or cut into elaborate decorative shapes.
6. Indecent language.
7. I.e., something that purports to provide protection but does not.

"Sire evel-y-taughte Elde," quod I, "unhende go with the!
Sith whanne was the way over [mennes] hedes?
Haddestow be hende," quod I, "thow woldest have asked leve."
   "Ye, leve, lordeyne?" quod he, and leyde on me with age,
190 And hitte me under the ere; unethe may Ich here.
He buffeted me aboute the mouthe and bett out my [wangtethe]
And gyved me in goutes; I may noughte go at large.
And of the wo that I was in my wyf had reuthe
And wisshed ful witterly that I were in Hevene.
195 For the lyme that she loved me fore and leef was to fele
On nyghtes namely whan we naked were,
I ne myght in no manere maken it at hir wille,
So Elde and [heo] sothly hadden it forbeten.
And as I seet in this sorwe I say how Kynde passed
200 And Deth drowgh niegh me; for drede gan I quake,
And cried to Kynde, "Out of care me brynge?
Loo, Elde the hoore hath me biseye.
Awreke me if yowre wille be, for I wolde ben hennes."
   "Yif thow wilt ben y-wroken, wende into Unité,
205 And holde the there evre tyl I sende for the,
And loke thow conne somme crafte ar thow come thennes."
"Conseille me, Kynde," quod I. "What crafte is best to lerne?"
"Lerne to love," quod Kynde, "and leve alle othre."
"How shal I come to catel so, to clothe me and to fede?"
210 "And thow love lelly lakke shal the nevre
[Wede] ne wordly [mete] whil thi lyf lasteth."
And by conseille of kynde I comsed to rowme
Thorw Contricioun and Confessioun tyl I cam to Unité.
And there was Conscience constable Cristene to save,
215 And biseged [sikerly] with sevene grete gyauntz
That with Antecrist helden hard ayein Conscience.
Sleuth with his slynge an hard saut he made.
Proude prestes come with hym; [passyng an hundreth],
In paltokes and pyked shoes, [purses and] longe knyves,
220 Comen ayein Conscience; with Coveityse thei helden.
   "By [the] Marie!" quod a mansed preste of the marche of Yrlonde.
"I counte namore Conscience bi so I cacche sylver
Than I do to drynke a draughte of good ale,"
And so seide sexty of the same contreye,
225 And shoten ayein with shotte, many a shef of othes,
And brode hoked arwes, "Goddes herte and his nayles!"
And hadden almost Unyté and Holynesse adowne.
   Conscience cryed, "Helpe, Clergye, or ellis I falle
Thorw inparfit prestes and prelates of Holi Cherche!"
230 Freres herden hym crye and comen hym to helpe,
Ac for thei couth noughte wel her craft Conscience forsoke
      hem.

"Mister bad-mannered Age," I said, "may mischief go with you!
Since when was the highway over men's heads?
If you had any courtesy," I said, "you would have asked leave."
    "What, leave, lazy loafer?" he said, and laid on me with age,
And hit me under the ear; I can hardly hear.   190
He buffeted me about the mouth and beat out my molars
And fettered me with fits of gout; I'm not free to go far.
And of the woe that I was in my wife had pity
And wished most warmly that I were in Heaven.
For the limb that she loved me for and liked to feel   195
Notably at night when we were naked in bed,
I might by no means make it do her will,
So Old Age with her aid had beaten it down.
And as I sat in this sorrow I saw Kind* passing by
And Death drew near me; dread made me quake,   200
And I cried to Kind, "Can you bring me out of care?
Lo, Old Age the hoary has attended to me.
Avenge me if you see fit, for I would fain be hence."
    "If vengeance is what you want, wend your way into Unity,
And hold yourself there always till I send for you,   205
And see you learn a craft to carry on before you come thence."
"Counsel me, Kind," said I. "What craft is best to learn?"
"Learn to love," said Kind, "and leave all other crafts."
"How can I get my keep thus, and clothe and feed myself?"
"If you love folk faithfully you shall find you never lack   210
Worldly food or clothes to wear while your life lasts."
And by counsel of Kind I commenced to roam
Through Contrition and Confession until I came to Unity.
And there Conscience was constable⁸ to save Christian people,
And was strongly besieged by seven great giants⁹   215
That held with Antichrist hard against Conscience.
Sloth with his sling made a savage assault.
Proud priests came with him; a pack bigger than a hundred,
In paltoks and peaked shoes, purses and long knives,¹
Came against Conscience; they held with Covetousness.   220
    "By the Mary!" cried a cursed priest from a far corner of Ireland.
"I make no more of Conscience while I amass silver
Than I do of drinking a draught of good ale,"
And so said sixty of the same country,
And shot shots in attack, many a sheaf of oaths,   225
And broad hooked arrows, "God's heart and his nails!"
And almost had Unity and Holiness down.
    Conscience cried, "Help, Clergy, or I'll fall
Because of imperfect priests and prelates of Holy Church!"
Friars heard him cry out and came to help him,   230
But because they did not know their craft well Conscience rejected
    them.

8. The governor or warden of a royal castle.
9. I.e., the Seven Deadly Sins.
1. Cloaks and fashionable pointed shoes, as well as purses and daggers, are accoutrements appropri-
    ate to dangerous soldiers rather than to priests.

Nede neghed tho nere and Conscience he tolde
That thei come for coveityse, to have cure of soules,
"And for thei arn poure, paraventure, for patrimoigné hem failleth,
235   Thei wil flatre to fare wel folke that ben riche.
And sithen thei chosen chele and cheytifté,
Lat hem chewe as thei chese, and charge hem with no cure.
For lomer he lyeth that lyflode mote begge
Than he that laboureth for lyflode and leneth it beggeres.
240   And sithen freres forsoke the felicité of erthe
Lat hem be as beggeres or lyve by angeles fode."
Conscience of this conseille tho comsed for to laughe,
And curteislich conforted hem and called in alle freres
And seide, "Sires, sothly welcome be ye alle
245   To Unité and Holi Cherche; ac on thyng I yow preye:
Holdeth yow in Unyté, and haveth none envye
To lered ne to lewed, but lyveth after yowre rewle.
And I wil be yowre borghe: ye shal have bred and clothes
And other necessaries anowe; yow shal no thyng [lakke]
250   With that ye leve logyk and lerneth for to lovye.
For love laft thei lordship, bothe londe and scole,
Frere Fraunceys and Dominyk, for love to ben holy.
And if ye coveyteth cure, Kynde wil yow [telle]
That in mesure God made alle manere thynges,
255   And sette it at a certeyne and at a syker noumbre.
And nempned [hem] names, and noumbred the sterres:
    Qui numerat multitudinem stellarum et omnibus eis nomina
        vocat.
Kynges and knyghtes that kepen and defenden
Han officers under hem, and uch of hem [a] certeyne:
And if thei wage men to werre, thei write hem in noumbre;
Wil no tresorere [take] hem [wages], travaille thei nevre so
260   sore,
[But thei ben nempned in the noumbre of hem that ben y-waged].
Alle other in bataille ben y-holde bribours,
Pilours and pykehernois, in eche a [parissh] y-cursed.
Monkes and monyals, and alle men of religioun,
265   Her ordre and her reule wil to han a certeyne noumbre
Of lewed and of lered; the lawe wol and axeth
A certeyn for a certeyne, save onelich of freres.
Forthi," quod Conscience, "by Cryst, Kynde Witte me telleth
It is wikked to wage yow; ye wexeth out of noumbre.
270   Hevene hath evene noumbre and helle is without noumbre.
Forthi I wolde witterly that ye were in the registre
And yowre noumbre undre notarie sygne, and noyther mo ne lasse."
    Envye herd this and heet freres to go to scole
And lerne logyk and lawe and eke contemplacioun,
275   And preche men of Plato, and preve it by Seneca

Then Need drew near and announced to Conscience
That they came for covetousness, to have cure of souls,
"And since they are poor, perhaps, having no patrimony,
To fare well they will flatter folk that are rich.   235
And since they elected to live a life of cold and hardship,
Let them chew as they chose, uncharged with cure of souls.
For he who must beg his livelihood lies more often
Than he who labors for his livelihood and lets beggars share it.
And forasmuch as they forsook the felicity of earth   240
Let them be like beggars and live by angel's food."
At this counsel Conscience then commenced to laugh,
And comforted them courteously and called in all friars
And said, "Sirs, you are all surely welcome
To Unity and Holy Church; but one thing I pray you: 245
Hold yourselves in Unity, and have no envy
Of learned or unlearned, but live by your rule.
And I will give you my guarantee: you shall get bread and clothing
And other necessities enough; you'll not lack anything
If you leave off studying logic and learn to love.   250
For love they left their lordship, both land and school,
Friar Francis* and Dominic,* for love of holiness.
And if you covet cure of souls, Kind will tell you
That in moderation God made all manner of things,
And established them in a certain and settled number.   255
And named them names, and numbered the stars:
     Who numbereth the multitude of the stars and calleth their names
          to them all.[2]
Kings who protect the kingdom with their company of knights
Have officers under them, each a settled number:
And if they pay men to make war, they mark them down in a roster;
No paymaster will pay them wages, though they fight like proper
     soldiers,   260
Unless their names are noted among the number of the hired.
All others in battle are held to be thieves,
Pillagers and plunderers, in every parish cursed.
Monastic men and women, all members of religious orders,
Each order has its rule that asks a settled number   265
Of lettered and unlettered; the law desires and demands
A certain number for a certain sort, save only with friars.
Therefore," said Conscience, "by Christ, Kind Wit* tells me
It is wicked to pay your wages; you're waxing out of number.
Heaven has even number and hell is without number.[3]   270
Therefore I would strongly wish that you were in the register
And your number under a notary's seal, and neither more nor less."
     Envy heard this and ordered friars to go to school
And learn logic and law and also contemplation,
And preach to men about Plato, and support it by Seneca[4]   275

2. Ps. 146:4.
3. Indefinite number was perceived in the Middle Ages as imperfect and threatening; Job 10:22
   describes limitless number as being orderless, and Rev. 20:8 calls the number of the devil limitless. Matt. 10:30 and Rev. 7:4–8 describe God's providence as numbering everything precisely.
4. A Roman philosopher, whose sayings were popular in the Middle Ages.

That alle thinges under Hevene oughte to ben in comune.
And yit he lyeth, as I leve, that to the lewed so precheth,
For God made to men a lawe and Moyses it taughte:
Non concupisces rem proximi tui.
280 And evele is this y-holde in parisches of Engelonde,
For parsones and parish prestes that shulde the peple shryve
Ben curatoures called to knowe and to hele,
Alle that ben her parisshiens penaunce to enjoigne
And be ashamed in her shrifte; ac shame maketh hem
          wende
285 And fleen to the freres as fals folke to Westmynstre
That borweth and bereth it thider and thanne biddeth frendes
Yerne of foryifnesse, or lenger yeres lene.
Ac whil he is in Westmynstre he wil be bifore
And make hym merye with other mennes goodis.
290 And so it fareth with moche folke that to freres shryveth,
As sysours and excecutours; thei [shal yeve the] freres
A parcel to preye for hem, and [pleye with] the remenaunt,
And suffre the ded in dette to the Day of Dome.
Envye herfore hated Conscience,
295 And freres to philosofye he fonde hem to scole,
The while Coveytise and Unkyndenesse Conscience assailled.
      In Unité, Holy Cherche, Conscience helde hym
And made Pees porter to pynne the yates
Of alle tale-tellers and tyterers in ydel.
300 Ypocrisye and [hij] an hard saut thei made:
Ypocrysie atte yate hard gan fighte
And wounded wel wykkedly many [a] wise techer
That with Conscience acorded and cardinale vertues.
Conscience called a leche that coude wel shryve:
305 "Go salve tho that syke ben, thorw synne y-wounded."
Shrifte shope sharpe salve and made men do penaunce
For her mysdedes that thei wroughte hadden,
And that Piers [pardoun] were payed, *redde quod debes.*
Somme lyked noughte this leche, and lettres thei sent
Yif any surgien were [in] the sege that softer couth
310   plastre.
Sire Lief-To-Lyve-In-Leccherye lay there and groned;
For fastyng of a Fryday he ferde as he wolde deye.
"Ther is a surgiene in [the] sege that soft can handle,
And more of phisyke bi fer and fairer he plastreth;
315 One Frere Flaterere is phisiciene and surgiene."
Quod Contricioun to Conscience, "Do hym come to Unyté,
For here is many a man herte thorw Ypocrisie."
      "We han no nede," quod Conscience. "I wote no better leche
Than persoun or parissh prest, penytancere or bisshop,
320 Save Piers the Plowman that hath powere over alle

That all things under Heaven ought to be held in common.
I believe that he lies, who so preaches to unlearned men,
For God made a law for men and Moses taught it:
Thou shalt not covet thy neighbor's goods.[5]
But this is poorly preserved in parishes of England,   280
For parsons and parish priests who are supposed to shrive the people
Are called curates because they should know and cure them,
Assign penance to all people who are their parishioners
And make them ashamed in their shrift; but shame makes them go
    off
And flee to the friars as false folk go to Westminster[6]   285
Who borrow money and bear it there and bid importunately
Their friends to forgive the debt, or grant a further term.
But while he is in Westminster he will keep busy
And make himself merry with other men's goods.
And so it fares with many folk who confess themselves to friars,   290
Such as assizers* and executors; they will assign the friars
A portion of the estate to pray for them, and play with the remainder,
And leave the dead man in debt until the Day of Doom.*
Envy hereupon hated Conscience
And gave fellowships to friars to study philosophy in school,   295
While Covetousness and Unkindness came to attack Conscience.
   In Unity, Holy Church, Conscience held himself
And appointed Peace porter to bar the gates
To all tale-tellers and tattlers of gossip.
With their help Hypocrisy made a hard assault: 300
Hypocrisy at the gate began a grim fight
And wounded most maliciously many a wise teacher
Who'd been in accord with Conscience and cardinal virtues.
Conscience called a doctor who could give good shrift:
"Go give salve to those that are sick whom sin has wounded."   305
Shrift composed a sharp salve and made men do penance
For the dubious deeds that they had done before,
And that Piers's pardon might be paid, *redde quod debes.*[7]
Some did not like this surgeon, and they sent letters
To see if there were a doctor in the siege that applied softer
    compresses.   310
Sir Love-To-Live-In-Lechery lay there and groaned;
From fasting on Friday he fared as he would die.
"There is a surgeon in the siege who has a soft touch,
And knows far more about physic and fashions gentler remedies;
One Friar Flatterer is both physician and surgeon."   315
Said Contrition to Conscience, "Have him come into Unity,
For we have here many a man hurt by Hypocrisy."
   "We have no need," said Conscience. "I know no better doctor
Than parson or parish priest, penitencer[8] or bishop,
Except for Piers the Plowman who has power over all   320

5. Exod. 20:17: the Latin Bible has "house" (*domum*) where Langland has "thing" (*rem*)—i.e., translated more freely, "good(s)."
6. Where the law courts were.
7. "Pay what thou owest."
8. Confessor.

And indulgence may do but if dette lette it.
I may wel suffre," seyde Conscience, "syn ye desiren,
That Frere Flaterer be fette and phisike yow syke."
The Frere herof herde and hyed faste
325   To a lorde for a lettre leve to have
To curen as a curatour; and cam with his [lettre]
Baldly to the bisshop and his brief hadde
In contrees there he come in confessiouns to here;
And cam there Conscience was and knokked atte yate.
330   Pees unpynned it, was porter of Unyté,
And in haste asked what his wille were.
"In faith," quod this Frere, "for profit and for helthe
Carpe I wolde with Contricioun and therfore come I hider."
"He is sike," seide Pees, "and so ar many other.
335   Ypocrisie hath herte hem; ful harde is if thei kevre."
      "I am a surgien," seide the [Frere], "and salves can make.
Conscience knoweth me wel, and what I can do
        bothe."
      "I preye the," quod Pees tho, "ar thow passe ferther,
What hattestow? I preye the hele noughte thi name."
340   "Certes," seyde his felow, "Sire *Penetrans domos*."
      "Ye? Go thi gate," quod Pees. "Bi God, for al thi
        phisyk,
But thow conne somme crafte, thow comest nought herinne.
I knewe such one ones, noughte eighte wynter passed,
Come in thus y-coped at a courte there I dwelt,
345   And was my lordes leche and my ladyes bothe.
And at the last this limitour, tho my lorde was out,
He salved so owre wommen til somme were with childe."
      Hende Speche het Pees opene the yates.
"Late in the Frere and his felawe, and make hem faire chere.
350   He may se and here [here], so it may bifalle,
That Lyf thorw his lore shal leve Coveityse
And be adradde of Deth, and withdrawe hym fram Pryde
And acorde with Conscience, and kisse her either
        other."
Thus thorw Hende Speche entred the Frere,
355   And cam to Conscience, and curteisly hym grette.
      "Thow art welcome," quod Conscience. "Canstow hele the syke?
Here is Contricioun," quod Conscience, "my cosyn, y-wounded.
Conforte hym," quod Conscience, "and take kepe to his sores.
The plastres of the persoun and poudres biten to sore;
360   [And] lat hem ligge overlonge, and loth is to chaunge hem.
Fro Lenten to Lenten he lat his plastres bite."
      "That is overlonge," quod this limitour, "I leve, I shal amende it."

And may deal out indulgences unless debt prevents it.
I may well consent," said Conscience, "because you desire it,
That Friar Flatterer be fetched and give physic to you sick."
The Friar heard hereof and hurried fast
To a lord for a letter to allow him leave   325
To have a cure like a curate;⁹ and he came with his letter
Boldly to the bishop and went back with his authority
To hear confession in any countries that he came into;
And he came to where Conscience was and clapped at the gate.
Peace, porter of Unity, prepared to open up   330
And asked in haste what he wanted there.
"In faith," said the Friar, "for profit and health
I would converse with Contrition and therefore I came here."
"He is sick," said Peace, "and so are many others.
Hypocrisy has hurt them; they'll not easily recover."   335
    "I am a surgeon," said the Friar, "and skilled at mixing salves.
Conscience is well acquainted with me, and knows how competent I
        am."
    "I pray you," said Peace then, "before you proceed further,
What are you called? I request you not to conceal your name."
    "Certainly," said this fellow, "Sir *Penetrans domos.*"¹   340
    "Yes? Well, you can go away again," said Peace. "By God, for all
        your medicine,
Unless you're competent in some craft, you're not coming in here.
I knew such a one once, not eight winters ago,
Who came in thus coped to a court where I lived,
And served as surgeon for both our sire and our dame.   345
And at the last this limiter,² when my lord was out,
He salved our women so till some were with child."
    Courteous Speech called on Peace to cast open the gates.
"Let the Friar and his fellow in, and give them fair welcome.
He may see and hear here, it may happen so,   350
That Life through his lore will leave Covetousness
And be in dread of Death, and withdraw from Pride
And become accorded with Conscience, so that they'll kiss each
        other."
Thus because of Courteous Speech the Friar was called in,
And came to Conscience, and courteously greeted him.   355
    "You are welcome," said Conscience. "Can you heal the sick?
Here is Contrition," said Conscience, "my cousin, wounded.
Comfort him," said Conscience, "and take care of his injuries.
The compresses of the parson and his powders bite too sorely;
And he lets them lie too long, and is reluctant to change them.   360
From Lenten to Lenten he lets his remedies bite."
    "That's too long, I believe," said this limiter, "I'll amend it."

9. A friar was not authorized to beg in a parish in competition with the parish priest without permission, but permission could be obtained from the lay lord of the area.
1. "Sir House-Penetrator." 2 Tim. 3:6 reads "For of these [men] are those who penetrate houses (*penetrant domos*) and lead captive simple women burdened with sins, who are led to manifold desires."
2. I.e., friar.

And goth and gropeth Contricioun and gaf hym a
    plastre
Of "a pryvé payement and I shal praye for yow
365   [And] for alle that ye ben holde to al my lyftyme,
And make [of] yow [*Memoria*] in Masse and in matynes,
As freres of owre fraternité, for a litel sylver."
Thus he goth and gadereth and gloseth there he shryveth
Tyl Contricioun hadde clene foryeten to crye and to wepe
370   And wake for his wykked werkes as he was wont to done.
For confort of his confessour contricioun he lafte,
That is the [sovereyne] salve for alkyn synnes.
   Sleuth seigh that, and so did Pryde,
And come with a kene wille Conscience to assaille.
375   Conscience cryde eft [Clergye to helpe],
And [bad] Contricioun [come] forto kepe the yate.
   "He lith [adreynt] and dremeth," seyde Pees, "and so do many
    other.
The Frere with his phisik this folke hath enchaunted,
And [doth men drynke dwale]: thei drede no synne."
380   "Bi Cryste," quod Conscience tho, "I wil bicome a pilgryme,
And walken as wyde as the wordle [renneth]
To seke Piers the Plowman, that Pryde [myghte] destruye,
And that freres hadde a fyndyng that for nede flateren
And contrepleteth me, Conscience; now Kynde me avenge,
385   And sende me happe and hele til I have Piers the Plowman."
And sitthe he gradde after Grace til I gan awake.

And he sets out to search Contrition's wounds and prescribes a
    remedy
Of "a privy payment and I shall pray for you
And for all that you're beholden to all my lifetime,   365
And make a *Memoria* for you at Mass and at matins,*
As friars of our fraternity, for a little silver."[3]
Thus he goes about gathering cash and glozing[4] those he shrives
Until Contrition had clean forgotten to cry and to weep
And wake for his wicked works as he was wont to do.   370
Because of the comfort his confessor gave he abandoned contrition,
Which is the sovereign salve for sins of every kind.
    Sloth saw that, and so did Pride,
And came to attack Conscience with a keen will.
Conscience cried again to Clergy to help,   375
And bade Contrition come to keep the gate.
    "He lies drowned in dream," said Peace, "and so do many
    others.
The Friar with his physic has enchanted the folk here,
And given them a drugged drink: they dread no sin."
    "By Christ," said Conscience then, "I will become a pilgrim,   380
And walk as wide as the world reaches
To seek Piers the Plowman, who might expunge Pride,
And see that friars had funds who flatter for need
And contradict me, Conscience; now Kind avenge me,
And send me heart and health till I have Piers the Plowman."   385
And Conscience cried for Grace until I became wakeful.

Appendix

The "Autobiographical" Passage from the C-Version†

The C-text, the last of the three versions of *Piers Plowman*, contains a passage often thought to be autobiographical. The poet who made the C-version prefixed to the Confession of the Seven Deadly Sins (Passus V of the B-text) an apology by the Dreamer, "Long Will," who is at once long, or tall, and long on willing, or, arguably, willful. While there is no conclusive historical evidence for doing so, readers of *Piers Plowman* have generally regarded this passage as a source of information about the real author, about whom we otherwise know so little. Scholarship has determined that the way of life it describes is plausible, as well as compatible with the way the poem portrays the Dreamer and with the character of the poem itself. Throughout all the versions of the poem, the Dreamer manifests grave concern about whether a writer's way of life is justifiable in a world where there is such need for practical service and where religious

---

3. *Memoria*: remembrance; i.e., "I'll pray for you." In the Mass, the commemoration of the dead begins, "*Memento*" ("Remember"). *For a little silver*: the Friar offers to sell Contrition the spiritual benefits that accrue to a member of his order of friars.
4. I.e., deceiving.
† Introduction and text reprinted from Elizabeth Kirk and Judith Anderson. William Langland, *Piers Plowman: An Alliterative Verse Translation by E. Talbot Donaldson*, ed. Elizabeth D. Kirk and Judith H. Anderson (New York: W. W. Norton & Company, 1990), pp. 243–47, with permission of W. W. Norton & Company.

tradition offers such definite answers to basic human questions. (*Passus* XI.84–106a and *Passus* XII.1–28 are crucial to these issues.) The account of the Dreamer's life in the C-text seems to be the poem's final word on the subject. (Talbot Donaldson translated the Dreamer's apology in the following passage from lines 1–104 of the C-text in Huntington Library MS HM 143.)

Thus I awoke, as God's my witness, when I lived in Cornhill,[1]
Kit and I in a cottage, clothed like a loller,[2]
And little beloved, believe you me,
Among lollers of London and illiterate hermits.
For I wrote rhymes of those men as Reason* taught me.   5
For as I came by Conscience* I met with Reason,
In a hot harvest time when I had my health,
And limbs to labor with, and loved good living,
And to do no deed but to drink and sleep.
My body sound, my mind sane, a certain one accosted me;   10
Roaming in remembrance, thus Reason upbraided me:
"Can you serve," he said, "or sing in a church?
Or cock hay with my hay-makers, or heap it on the cart,
Mow it or stack what's mown or make binding for sheaves?
Or have a horn and be a hedge-guard and lie outdoors at night,   15
And keep my corn in my field from cattle and thieves?
Or cut cloth or shoe-leather, or keep sheep and cattle,
Mend hedges, or harrow, or herd pigs or geese,
Or any other kind of craft that the commons* needs,
So that you might be of benefit to your bread-providers?"   20
"Certainly!" I said, "and so God help me,
I am too weak to work with sickle or with scythe,
And too long,[3] believe me, for any low stooping,
Or laboring as a laborer to last any while."
"Then have you lands to live by," said Reason, "or relations with
    money   25
To provide you with food? For you seem an idle man,
A spendthrift who thrives on spending, and throws time away.
Or else you get what food men give you going door to door,
Or beg like a fraud on Fridays[4] and feastdays in churches.
And that's a loller's life that earns little praise   30
Where Rightfulness rewards men as they really deserve.
He shall reward every man according to his works.[5]
Or are you perhaps lame in your legs or other limbs of your body,

1. An area of London associated with vagabonds, seedy clerics, and people at loose ends. Cf. p. 420.
2. Idler, vagabond. The term was eventually applied to the proto-Protestant followers of John Wycliffe. It is unlikely that Langland has this meaning in mind, but many post-Reformation readers thought that he did. "Kit": B.XVIII.426 refers to "Kit my wife and Calote [i.e., Colette] my daughter." The Dreamer seems to be someone with clerical training who has received consecration into minor clerical orders (such as that of deacon) but who is not a priest. Even priests came to be required to observe celibacy only gradually, and lesser clerics could marry, although marriage blocked their further advancement in the Church.
3. I.e., tall, perhaps with a pun on willfulness. The Dreamer is called "Long Will" in Passus XV.152 of the B-text. The questions the dreamer has just been asked echo the interrogations of wanderers under the Statutes of Labourers. Cf. p. 428.
4. Fast days, because Christ was crucified on a Friday.
5. Matt. 16:27; cf. Ps. 61:12.

Or maimed through some misadventure, so that you might be excused?"
   "When I was young, many years ago,
My father and my friends provided me with schooling,   35
Till I understood surely what Holy Scripture meant,
And what is best for the body as the Book tells,
And most certain for the soul, if so I may continue.
And, in faith, I never found, since my friends died,
Life that I liked save in these long clothes.[6]   40
And if I must live by labor and earn my livelihood,
The labor I should live by is the one I learned best.
    [*Abide*] *in the same calling wherein you were called.*[7]
And so I live in London and upland[8] as well.
The tools that I toil with to sustain myself
Are Paternoster* and my primer, *Placebo* and *Dirige*,[9]   45
And sometimes my Psalter* and my seven Psalms.
These I say for the souls of such as help me.
And those who provide my food vouchsafe, I think,
To welcome me when I come, once a month or so,
Now with him, now with her, and in this way I beg   50
Without bag or bottle but my belly alone.
   And also, moreover, it seems to me, sir Reason,
No clerk should be constrained to do lower-class work.
For by the law of Leviticus[1] that our Lord ordained
Clerks with tonsured crowns should, by common understanding,   55
Neither strain nor sweat nor swear at inquests,
Nor fight in a vanguard and defeat an enemy:
    Do not render evil for evil.[2]
For they are heirs of Heaven, all that have the tonsure,
And in choir and in churches they are Christ's ministers.
    The Lord is the portion of my inheritance. And elsewhere,
      Mercy does not constrain.[3]
It is becoming for clerks to perform Christ's service,   60
And untonsured boys be burdened with bodily labor.
For none should acquire clerk's tonsure unless he claims descent
From franklins[4] and free men and folk properly wedded.
Bondmen and bastards and beggars' children—
These belong to labor; and lords' kin should serve   65
God and good men as their degree requires,
Some to sing Masses or sit and write,
Read and receive what Reason ought to spend.

---

6. The long dress of a cleric, not limited to actual priests.
7. 1 Cor. 7:20, with variations.
8. North of London, in rural country.
9. "I will please [the Lord]" and "Make straight [my way]": Ps. 114:9 and Ps. 5:9. *Placebo* and *Dirige* are the first words of hymns based on two of the seven "penitential" Psalms that were part of the regular order of personal prayer. The "primer" was the basic collection of private prayers for lay people.
1. Lev. 21 sets restrictions on members of the priesthood.
2. 1 Thess. 5:15, with variations.
3. I.e., "mercy is not restricted": source unknown; the quotation above is from Ps. 15:5.
4. Free men. By this date, the term did not just mean non-serfs but designated landowners who were becoming members of the gentry class yet were not knights. The distinction Langland seems to make in this line between franklins and free men may reflect the rising status of certain families of "freedmen," the original meaning of the word "franklins."

But since bondmen's boys have been made bishops,
And bastards' boys have been archdeacons,   70
And shoemakers and their sons have through silver become knights,
And lords' sons their laborers whose lands are mortgaged to them—
And thus for the right of this realm they ride against our enemies
To the comfort of the commons* and to the king's honor—
And monks and nuns on whom mendicants must depend   75
Have had their kin named knights and bought knight's-fees,[5]
And popes and patrons have shunned poor gentle* blood
And taken the sons of Simon Magus[6] to keep the sanctuary,
Life-holiness and love have gone a long way hence,
And will be so till this is all worn out or otherwise changed.   80
Therefore proffer me no reproach, Reason, I pray you,
For in my conscience I conceive what Christ wants me to do.
Prayers of a perfect man and appropriate penance
Are the labor that our Lord loves most of all.
    "*Non de solo*," I said, "forsooth *vivit homo*,   85
Nec in pane et in pabulo;[7] the Paternoster witnesses
Fiat voluntas Dei[8]—that provides us with everything."
    Said Conscience, "By Christ, I can't see that this lies;
But it seems no serious perfectness to be a city-beggar,
Unless you're licensed to collect for prior or monastery."   90
    "That is so," I said, "and so I admit
That at times I've lost time and at times misspent it;
And yet I hope, like him who has often bargained
And always lost and lost, and at the last it happened
He bought such a bargain he was the better ever,   95
That all his loss looked paltry in the long run,
Such a winning was his through what grace decreed.
        The kingdom of Heaven is like unto treasure hidden in a
            field.
        The woman who found the piece of silver, etc.[9]
So I hope to have of him that is almighty
A gobbet of his grace, and begin a time
That all times of my time shall turn into profit."   100
    "And I counsel you," said Reason, "quickly to begin
The life that is laudable and reliable for the soul."
    "Yes, and continue," said Conscience, and I came to the church.[1]

5. The estate a knight held from his overlord in return for military service was called his "fee."
6. See Gloss, under "simony."
7. "Not solely [by bread] doth man live, neither by bread nor by food": the verse continues, "but by
   every word that proceedeth out of the mouth of God": Matt. 4:4, with variations; cf. Deut. 8:3.
8. "God's will be done." The Lord's Prayer (the "Paternoster") reads, "Thy will be done" (Matt. 6:10).
9. Matt. 13:44; Luke 15:9–10. Both passages come from parables that compare finding the kingdom
   of Heaven to risking everything you have to get the one thing that matters most.
1. The four lines that follow this passage connect it to the beginning of the second dream (the B-text's
   Passus V): "And to the church I set off, to honor God; before the Cross, on my knees, I beat my
   breast, sighing for my sins, saying my Paternoster, weeping and wailing until I fell asleep."

SOURCES AND BACKGROUNDS

Scriptural and Religious

From The Douai Bible†

Moses and the Ten Commandments[1]

* * *

19:1   In the third month of the departure of Israel out of the land of Egypt, on this day they came into the wilderness of Sinai:

2   For departing out of Raphidim, and coming to the desert of Sinai, they camped in the same place, and there Israel pitched their tents over against the mountain.

3   And Moses went up to God: and the Lord called unto him from the mountain, and said: "Thus shalt thou say to the house of Jacob, and tell the children of Israel:

4   " 'You have seen what I have done to the Egyptians, how I have carried you upon the wings of eagles, and have taken you to myself.

5   " 'If therefore you will hear my voice, and keep my covenant, you shall be my peculiar possession above all people: for all the earth is mine.

6   " 'And you shall be to me a priestly kingdom, and a holy nation.' These are the words thou shalt speak to the children of Israel."

7   Moses came, and calling together the elders of the people, he declared all the words which the Lord had commanded.

* * *

20:1   And the Lord spoke all these words:

2   "I am the Lord thy God, who brought thee out of the land of Egypt, out of the house of bondage.

3   "Thou shalt not have strange gods before me.

4   "Thou shalt not make to thyself a graven thing, nor the likeness of any thing that is in heaven above, or in the earth beneath, nor of those things that are in the waters under the earth.

5   "Thou shalt not adore them, nor serve them: I am the Lord thy God, mighty, jealous, visiting the iniquity of the fathers upon the children, unto the third and fourth generation of them that hate me:

* * *

---

† All selections reprinted from *The Holy Bible . . . Douay Version* (Baltimore, Maryland, 1900). The Douai (or Douai/Douay-Rheims) version of the Bible, originally published between 1582 and 1610 as a Roman Catholic alternative to Protestant English translations, represents a close translation of the Latin Vulgate, the official Bible with which Langland would have been most familiar.

1. Exodus 19:1–7 (cf. *Piers Plowman* Passus XVII, where Langland identifies Moses with Hope, recollecting Moses' biblical role as guardian of the Israelites' future); 20:1–17 (cf. *Piers Plowman* Passus V, lines 560–584); 24:12 (cf. *Piers Plowman* Passus XVII, lines 1–19).

369

7   "Thou shalt not take the name of the Lord thy God in vain: for the Lord will not hold him guiltless that shall take the name of the Lord his God in vain.

8   "Remember that thou keep holy the sabbath day.

9   "Six days shalt thou labor, and shalt do all thy works.

10   "But on the seventh day is the sabbath of the Lord thy God: thou shalt do no work on it, thou nor thy son, nor thy daughter, nor thy manservant, nor thy maidservant, nor thy beast, nor the stranger that is within thy gates.

11   "For in six days the Lord made heaven and earth, and the sea, and all things that are in them, and rested on the seventh day: therefore the Lord blessed the seventh day, and sanctified it.

12   "Honor thy father and thy mother, that thou mayst be long lived upon the land which the Lord thy God will give thee.

13   "Thou shalt not kill.

14   "Thou shalt not commit adultery.

15   "Thou shalt not steal.

16   "Thou shalt not bear false witness against thy neighbor.

17   "Thou shalt not covet thy neighbor's house: neither shalt thou desire his wife, nor his servant, nor his handmaid, nor his ox, nor his ass, nor any thing that is his."

*   *   *

24:12   And the Lord said to Moses: "Come up to me into the mount, and be there: and I will give thee tables of stone, and the law, and the commandments which I have written: that thou mayst teach them."

*   *   *

Psalm 22[1]

1   The Lord ruleth me: and I shall want nothing.

2   He hath set me in a place of pasture.
He hath brought me up, on the water of refreshment:

3   He hath converted my soul.
He hath led me on the paths of justice, for his own name's sake.

4   For though I should walk in the midst of the shadow of death, I will fear no evils, for thou art with me.
Thy rod and thy staff, they have comforted me.

5   Thou hast prepared a table before me, against them that afflict me.
Thou hast anointed my head with oil; and my chalice which inebriateth me, how goodly is it!

6   And thy mercy will follow me all the days of my life.
And that I may dwell in the house of the Lord unto length of days.

The Good Samaritan[1]

*   *   *

25   And behold a certain lawyer stood up, tempting [Jesus], and saying, "Master, what must I do to possess eternal life?"

1. Psalm 23 in other Bibles. Cf. *Piers Plowman* Passus VII, lines 111–121; and Passus XII, line 293.
1. Luke 10:25–37. Cf. *Piers Plowman* Passus XVII, lines 50 ff.

26   But he said to him: "What is written in the law? How readest thou?"

27   He answering, said: "'Thou shalt love the Lord thy God with thy whole heart, and with thy whole soul, and with all thy strength, and with all thy mind: and thy neighbor as thyself.'"[2]

28   And he said to him: "Thou hast answered right: this do, and thou shalt live."

29   But he, willing to justify himself, said to Jesus: "And who is my neighbor?"

30   And Jesus answering, said: "A certain man went down from Jerusalem to Jericho, and fell among robbers, who also stripped him, and having wounded him went away, leaving him half dead.

31   "And it chanced, that a certain priest went down the same way: and seeing him, passed by.

32   "In like manner also a Levite,[3] when he was near the place and saw him, passed by.

33   "But a certain Samaritan[4] being on his journey, came near him; and seeing him, was moved with compassion.

34   "And going up to him, bound up his wounds, pouring in oil and wine: and setting him upon his own beast, brought him to an inn, and took care of him.

35   "And the next day he took out two pence, and gave to the host, and said: 'Take care of him: and whatsoever thou shalt spend over and above, I, at my return, will repay thee.'

36   "Which of these three, in thy opinion, was neighbor to him that fell among the robbers?"

37   But he said: "He that shewed mercy to him." And Jesus said to him: "Go and do thou in like manner."

*   *   *

Paul's Allegory of Abraham[1]

3:1   O senseless Galatians, who hath bewitched you that you should not obey the truth, before whose eyes Jesus Christ hath been set forth, crucified among you?

2   This only would I learn of you: Did you receive the Spirit by the works of the law, or by the hearing of faith?

3   Are you so foolish, that, whereas you began in the Spirit, you would now be made perfect by the flesh?

4   Have you suffered so great things in vain? If it be yet in vain.

---

2. The lawyer quotes Deuteronomy 6:5 and Leviticus 19:18; cf. Matthew 22:37, 39, 40, and *Piers Plowman* Passus XVII, lines 10–14.

3. See n.3, p 269.

4. There was considerable enmity between the Samaritans and the Jews of Judea (cf. Luke 9:52–56), and so Jesus' account of this Samaritan's mercy is especially admonishing.

1. St. Paul's Epistle to the Galatians 3:1–9; 4:21–31. Paul's main concern is the question of whether Christians should observe Jewish law in such matters as circumcision. In a bold allegoresis, Paul turns the Hebrew bible (Old Testament) story of the sons of Abraham on its head. Traditionally, Ishmael, Abraham's son by Hagar the slave woman, was held to be the father of the non-Jewish peoples of the Arab world; Isaac, Abraham's son by his wife Sarah, was the patriarch of the Jews, God's chosen people. But now, according to Paul, the Christians are the chosen people, following a new version of the law, based on faith in Christ, while the Jews are the new outcast heirs of Ishmael. There is much of Paul's technique of reassigning traditional allegorical interpretations in Langland's own work—for instance, in the variations between Will's two dreams about the Tree of Charity, Passus XVI, lines 1–166. For Langland's identification of Abraham with Faith, see the same passus, lines 172–179.

5   He therefore who giveth to you the Spirit, and worketh miracles among you; doth he do it by the works of the law, or by the hearing of the faith?

6   As it is written: "Abraham believed God, and it was reputed to him unto justice."[2]

7   Know ye therefore, that they who are of faith, the same are the children of Abraham.

*   *   *

4:21   Tell me, you that desire to be under the law, have you not read the law?

22   For it is written that Abraham had two sons: the one by a bond-woman, and the other by a free woman.[3]

23   But he who was of the bondwoman was born according to the flesh: but he of the free woman, was by promise.

24   Which things are said by an allegory. For these are the two testaments. The one from Mount Sinai, engendering unto bondage; which is Hagar.

25   For Sinai is a mountain in Arabia, which hath affinity to that in Jerusalem which now is, and is in bondage with her children.

26   But that Jerusalem, which is above, is free: which is our mother.

27   For it is written: "Rejoice thou barren that bearest not: break forth and cry, thou that travailest not: for many are the children of the desolate, more than of her that hath a husband."[4]

28   Now we, brethren, as Isaac was, are the children of the promise.

29   But as then he, that was born according to the flesh, persecuted him that was after the spirit; so also it is now.

30   But what saith the scripture? "Cast out the bondwoman and her son; for the son of the bondwoman shall not be heir with the son of the free woman."[5]

31   So then, brethren, we are not the children of the bondwoman, but of the free: by the freedom wherewith Christ has made us free.

The Whore of Babylon[1]

*   *   *

1   And there came one of the seven angels, who had the seven vials, and spoke with me, saying: "Come, I will show thee the condemnation of the great harlot, who sitteth upon many waters.

2   With whom the kings of the earth have committed fornication; and they who inhabit the earth, have been made drunk with the wine of her whoredom."

3   And he took me away in spirit into the desert. And I saw a woman sitting upon a scarlet colored beast, full of names of blasphemy, having seven heads and ten horns.

4   And the woman was clothed round about with purple and scarlet,

2. Genesis 15:6.
3. Genesis 16:15–21:2.
4. Isaiah 54:1.
5. Genesis 21:10.
1. Apocalypse (the Book of Revelation) 17. Cf. the description of Lady Meed, *Piers Plowman* Passus II, starting at line 7; Langland's account may also allude to Alice Perrers, about whom see p. 485.

and gilt with gold, and precious stones and pearls, having a golden cup in her hand, full of the abomination and filthiness of her fornication.

5 And on her forehead a name was written: A mystery; Babylon the great, the mother of the fornications, and the abominations of the earth.

6 And I saw the woman drunk with the blood of the saints, and with the blood of the martyrs of Jesus. And I wondered, when I had seen her, with great admiration.

7 And the angel said to me: "Why dost thou wonder? I will tell thee the mystery of the woman, and of the beast which carrieth her, which hath the seven heads and ten horns.

8 "The beast, which thou sawest, was, and is not, and shall come up out of the bottomless pit, and go into destruction: and the inhabitants on the earth (whose names are not written in the book of life from the foundation of the world) shall wonder, seeing the beast that was, and is not.

* * *

18 "And the woman which thou sawest is the great city, which hath kingdom over the kings of the earth."[2]

* * *

The Athanasian Creed†

(1) Whoever wills to be saved, before all things it is necessary that he hold the catholic faith: (2) which faith, unless everyone shall have kept whole and undefiled, without doubt he will perish eternally.

(3) Now the catholic faith is this, that we worship one God in Trinity, and Trinity in Unity, (4) neither confounding the Persons, nor dividing the substance: (5) for there is one Person of the Father, another Person of the Son, another Person of the Holy Spirit; (6) but the Godhead of the Father, of the Son, and of the Holy Spirit is one, the Glory equal, the Majesty coeternal.

(7) Such as the Father is, such is the Son, and such is the Holy Spirit: (8) the Father uncreated, the Son uncreated, the Holy Spirit uncreated; (9) the Father infinite, the Son infinite, the Holy Spirit infinite; (10) the Father eternal, the Son eternal, the Holy Spirit eternal; (11) and yet not three eternals, but one eternal; (12) as also not three uncreated, nor three infinites, but one uncreated, and one infinite. (13) So likewise is the Father almighty, the Son almighty, the Holy Spirit almighty; (14) and yet not three almighties, but one almighty. (15) So the Father is God, the Son God, and the Holy Spirit God; (16) and yet not three Gods, but one God. (17) So

---

2. Conventionally the great city ("Babylon the great") is understood as a metaphor for pagan Rome, but can also be understood as the corruption of any worldly city in contrast to the perfection of the heavenly city, the New Jerusalem; Langland associates Lady Meed with London (Passus II, line 156 ff.).

† Translated by Stephen H. A. Shepherd from *Enchiridion Symbolorum*, ed. Henricus Denziger, rev. Adolfus Schönmetzer (New York: Herder, 1967), pp. 40–42. Also known as the *Quicumque Vult* from its opening words, this profession of faith and definition of correct belief was in the Middle Ages regularly recited in early Sunday services. This Creed (as distinct from the Apostles' and Nicene Creeds) is named after St. Athanasius (d. 373) but was probably penned after his death. Cf. *Piers Plowman*, Passus X, lines 232–243, and the speeches of Faith and Spes in Passus XVI and XVII.

the Father is Lord, the Son Lord, and the Holy Spirit Lord; (18) and yet not three Lords but one Lord: (19) for just as we are compelled by Christian truth to acknowledge every Person by Himself to be both God and Lord, (20) so are we forbidden by the catholic religion to say there are three Gods or three Lords.

(21) The Father is made of none, neither created nor begotten; (22) the Son is of the Father alone, not made nor created, but begotten; (23) the Holy Spirit is of the Father and the Son, not made nor created nor begotten, but proceeding. (24) So there is one Father, not three Fathers; one Son, not three Sons; and one Holy Spirit, not three Holy Spirits. (25) And in this Trinity there is none before or after, none greater or less, (26) but the whole three Persons are coeternal together and coequal. (27) So that in all things, as is said above, the Trinity in Unity and the Unity in Trinity is to be worshipped. (28) He therefore who wills to be saved, let him think thus of the Trinity.

(29) But it is necessary to eternal salvation that he also believe faithfully the Incarnation of our Lord Jesus Christ. (30) The right faith, therefore, is that we believe and confess that our Lord Jesus Christ, the Son of God, is God and man: (31) as God, of the substance of the Father begotten before time; as man, of the substance of His mother born in time; (32) perfect God, perfect man consisting of a reasoning soul and human flesh; (33) equal to the Father according to His Godhead, inferior to the Father according to His humanity; (34) who, although He is God and man, yet He is not two, but one Christ; (35) one however not by conversion of the Godhead in the flesh, but by taking of the manhood in God; (36) one altogether not by mingling of substance but by unity of Person. (37) For as the reasoning soul and flesh is one man, so God and Man is one Christ. (38) Who suffered for our salvation, descended into hell,[1] on the third day rose again from the dead, (39) ascended into heaven, sits at the right hand of the Father, from whence He shall come to judge the living and the dead. (40) At whose coming all men shall rise again with their bodies, and shall give account for their own works; (41) and those who have done good, shall go into life eternal, and those who indeed have done evil, into eternal fire.

(42) This is the catholic faith: which except a man shall have believed faithfully and firmly, he cannot be saved.

---

1. For an elaborative legend of Christ's descent into hell, see the selection from the *Gospel of Nicodemus*, p. 375.

From the Gospel of Nicodemus†

[*The Harrowing of Hell*]¹

"Sen he° was slike° and was bot° man — *i.e, Lazarus / such / but*
To the,° Satanas, we° say, — *thee / i.e., we devils*
Wenes° thou, wrtht,° to maister° than — *do you think / ?wretch / conquer*
Both God and man verray?° — *true*
1325 Trowes thou that thou close° him can — *enclose*
That he ne sall° win oway,° — *shall / away*
That his pouer servand fro the wan²
And° was dampned° for ay?°" — *and (who) / damned / ever*
Than answered Satanas:
1330 "Of him have I no drede,
I knaw° wele what he was — *know*
And what life he gan lede;° — *did lead*

His fourty dayes when he had fast,
That tyme him tempid° I; — *tempted*
1335 And to the Jews counsailes I cast
That thai suld ger him dy;³
When Pilat wald° that he had past,° — *wished / passed (free)*
I egged him egerly,
Till he was hanged at the last
1340 With other theves him by;
And thatfore als° I yow say, — *also*
Ordans° for him a stede,° — *prepare / place*
He cumes heder° this day, — *hither*
By this° I hald° hym dede." — *By now / consider*

1345 Thus als° thai gan togeder chide,° — *as / argue*
A voice spak loud and clere:
"Ye princes, I bid ye opin wide
Yowre endless° yates° here, — *everlasting / gates*
The King of Blis now in sall glide."
1350 And than spac Lucifere:
"Satanas, turn him ogayn° this tide,° — *away from / time*
Als thou lufes° me dere." — *love*
Than Satanas sperd° the Yates — *barred*
And his felows he cald:
1355 "Haldes him thareout algates,° — *at all costs*
Or we forever be thrald!"° — *enslaved*

---

† Reprinted, with new punctuation and glosses, from *The Middle English "Harrowing of Hell" and "Gospel of Nicodemus,"* ed. William Henry Hulme, Early English Text Society, Extra Series 100 (London, 1907), pp. 108–120 (text of London, British Library, MS Cotton Galba E. IX). The MS dates from the end of the fourteenth century.
1. The *Gospel of Nicodemus* has a Greek and Latin heritage that goes at least as far back as the beginning of the fifth century. It is an important apocryphal source for Christian lore concerning Christ's redemption of worthy pre-Christian souls confined to Hell. Cf. Langland's treatment of the episode, Passus XVIII.
2. He who (once before) won away from you his poor servant (Lazarus).
3. That they should make him die.

Than said saint David thare he lay,
Unto thai° sayntes all, *those*
"In erth lifand thus gan I say
1360 Als I se now byfall;
That God has made, this es° the day, *is*
Mak joy tharin we sall;
Brasen° yates he brac° for ay *brass / broke*
And iren barres ful small;° *into fragments*
1365 Fro waies° of wilsumnes,° *ways / bewilderment*
I tald, he has tham taken;
I se now suth° it es, *true*
He has us noght forsaken."

Than on this wise said Ysai:° *(cf. Isa. 14: 9–20)*
1370 "Whils° I had life in land, *While*
On this same maner than said I,
Whoso kowth° understand: *could*
'Ded men that in thaire graves ly
Sall rise and be lifand,° *living*
1375 Al sall mak joy and melody
That erth has in his hand.'
Eftsones° I said alsswa° *likewise / also*
To Ded,° 'Whare es thi might, *Death*
Sen he fetches us tharfra?'
1380 No° see I all this right." *now*

A voice spak than ful hidosely,
Als it war thonors° blast: *thunder's*
"Undo yowre yates bilive,° bid I! *quickly*
Thai may no langer last:
1385 The King of Blis cumes in yow by."
Than Hell a voice upkast:
"What es he that thai say° in hy?° *speak of / loudly*
He sall be set° ful fast." *constrained*
Than said David, "Ye ne wate° *know*
1390 How that I said thus right,° *correctly*
'He es lord of grete state,
In batayle mekill° of might;' *great*

"The King of Blis, trewly I tell,
Right at thi° yates standes; *thy*
1395 He has bihalden° fro° hevyn to hell *seen / from*
The sorow of his servandes.
Tharfore undo, thou fende so fell,° *fierce*
Thi yates right with thi handes,
The King of Blis cumes in ful snell° *quickly*
1400 To bring us fro thi bandes° *bonds*
Thurgh might of his godhede."
Than Jhesus strake° so fast, *proceeded*

The yates in sunder° yede°   *two / went*
And iren bandes al brast.°   *burst apart*

1405   He kyd° that he was mekill of might,   *made known*
The fendes pousté° he felled,   *power*
All lemid° that lathly° lake° of light   *gleamed / hateful / pit*
That with mirknes° was melled.°   *darkness / mixed*
When all the saintes saw that sight
1410   That in that dongon dwellid,
None durst speke a word on hight,°   *loudly*
Bot ilk° one softly tellid.°   *each / spoke*
"Welkum, Lord, untill us,
Ful lang here has us° thoght;°   *to us / it seemed*
1415   Blisced mot thou be, Jhesus,
Ful dere thou has us boght."

He lowsed° than thaire° bandes all   *loosened / their*
That lang had bunden° bene,°   *bound / been*
He made tham fre that are° ware thrall,   *formerly*
1420   O° care he clensed tham clene;   *of*
The fendes that saw slike° light bifall   *such*
Ware° none bifore was sene   *where*
Said, "We er clomsed° grete and small   *stunned*
With° yone° caytef° so kene."   *by / that / wretch*
1425   Ane sais that mikel him dredes:
"What ertou schewes slike might[4]
And es so mekill° in dedes   *powerful*
And semes so litell in sight?

"Sen thou was man, on what manere
1430   Was godhede° in the hid?°   *divinity / hidden*
Was thou noght ded? What dose° thou here?   *do*
Slike maistris° never was kyd;°   *power / made known*
We fendes war all ful fayn° in fere°   *happy / together*
When the Jews to ded° the° did;   *death / thee*
1435   How ertou put to slike powere,
And slike tene° us bytid?°   *suffering / befallen*
The sawles that us war° sent   *were*
Has thou won hethin° oway,   *hence*
Thou has us schamly schent°   *ruined*
1440   And prived° us of oure pray."°   *deprived / prey*

Than Jhesus sone° toke Satanas,   *immediately*
That are° was lord and sire,   *formerly*
And him in thraldom bunden has
To brin° in endles fire.   *burn*
1445   Than said the fendes that with him was
Ful of anger and of ire,

4. What are you that shows such might?

"Satan, thou has us lorn,° allas!   *destroyed*
Thou did noght oure desire;
We bad the lat him ga°   *go*
1450 And noght to cum herein;
Oure° he feches us fra,°   *what is ours / from us*
Oure court waxes° ful thin;   *grows*

"Thou Duke of Ded,° leder° fro live,   *Death / leader*
Hething° of goddes angels,   *mockery*
1455 Ogains° that strang° how durst thou strive   *against / strong man*
That us thus frekly° felles?°   *boldly / strikes down*
Thou hight° to bind him here bilive,°   *promised / readily*
It es noght als thou telles;
Till endles ded he will the° drive   *thee*
1460 And all that with the dwelles;
When thou the Jews gan stir
That thai suld ger° him dy,   *make*
Thou suld enquere and spir°   *investigate*
First if he war worthi;

1465 "And if that he had done none ill,
Thou suld have gert° tham blin;°   *made / stop*
Whi suld thou bring a man us till
In wham was sene° no syn?   *seen*
All has thou lost now by this skill°   *reason*
1470 The wightes° that war herein,   *people*
And thou thaire paines sall ay fulfill
With wo never out to wyn;°   *make way*
That we wan thurgh the tre
When Eve the fruit had etyn,
1475 Ilk° dele° ogayn has he   *every / part*
Now with the Rode-Tre° getyn."°   *Rood-Tree; i.e., the Cross / got*

Jhesus than spac with voice ful clere
To the sayntes that he has soght:
"Cumes unto me, my childer° dere,   *children*
1480 That my° liknes war wroght;   *in my*
Ye that for syn war presond° here,   *imprisoned*
To blis ye sall be broght."
Than all tha saintes drogh to him nere
And thanked him in thaire thoght;
1485 On Adam his hand he laid—
And he on knese° gan fall—   *knees*
"Pese be to the," he sayd,
"And to thi childer all."

Adam said than, and for joy gret,
1490 "Lord, I sall wirschip the,
Fro my famen° thou has me fett°   *enemies / fetched*
In blis to bide and be,
In sorows sere° whare I was sett   *many*

To my sare wald thou se;°   *attend*
1495 Me will thou lede withowten let°   *hindrance*
Fro pine thurgh thi peté;°   *pity*
Thou fendes° us that we ne fall   *defend*
Till pine° that es pereles;°   *pain / without equal*
Makes joy, ye saintes all,
1500 And thankes his grete gudenes."°   *goodness*

All patriarkes and ilk prophete
And other saintes all
Fell doun on knese bifor his fete
Smertly° both grete and small: *promptly*
1505 "Lord, thou es cumen our bales° to bete;°   *sorrows / remedy*
Evermore serve the we sall.
That° thou thurgh prophecy gan hete°   *That which / promise*
We se it now bifall:
Ded° thurgh° ded es destroid.°   *Death / through / destroyed*
1510 Lord, lovyng° be unto the,   *praise*
All es noght° that us noyed,°   *nothing / vexed*
That war thralles er° made fre."   *are*

By the right hand gan he Adam take
And blisced him right thare,
1515 He led him fro that lathly° lake   *hateful*
And all that with him ware.
Saint David than ful baldly spake,
Als thai fro hell gan fare:°   *depart*
"A new sang° till oure Lord ye make,   *song*
1520 Als I myself said are;°   *before*
He that has bene wirkand°   *performing*
Mervailes omang us here,
He has save his right hand
To him and his powere;

1525 "Ful mekely has he schewed his might
Omang all Cristen men,
He has techid ilka° werdly° wight°   *each / earthly / being*
His rightwisnes to ken."°   *know*
Thus all tha sayntes thanked him right
1530 That slike lane° wald tham len:°   *loan / lend*
"Blisced be he that cumes als he hight,°   *promised*
In the name of God. Amen."
Ilk prophet thus gan tell
Of thaire awin° prophecy   *own*
1535 How he suld° hery° hell,   *should / harrow*
How he suld for tham dy.

Thus als thai unto welthis° went   *prosperity*
That war won out of wa,
A sang thai said with ane assent
1540 That was this: "Alleluya!"

By the hand oure Lord has Adam hent,°   *seized*
With Michell he bad him ga:
Thai toke the way with gude° entent   *good*
Unto paradise ful thra.°   *boldly*
1545   Michaell resaived° tham sone°   *received / at once*
That war to him bikend,°   *entrusted*
In blis he has tham done°   *put*
That lastes withouten end.

*   *   *

From Fasciculus Morum†

Envy and Bread

Now to the virtue of charity we direct our attention, which virtue in every
way upbraids and opposes reprehensible envy and its followers. For as
much as envy delights in evil, so much charity delights in good. And therefore it is a most strong combatant against envy. * * * We should know that
according to John 14 it is said: "God is love." Since God is charity,[1] no vice
can exist with it.

*   *   *

We should know that against spiritual hunger Christ comes like an affec-
tionate mother to feed us. For He says himself in John 6, "I am that bread
of life . . . which come down from heaven." And note that there are five
loaves of bread, with which He fed five thousand men,[2] and still feeds us.
The first is the bread of the poor, coarse and simple, which is made from
barley or peas or beans, which feeds many with difficulty. And it is the
bread of contrition, which for many is too harsh; the Psalmist says, "My
tears have been my bread day and night."[3] But this loaf will be divided into
three bites, that is into remorse for past sins, present, and future. The second loaf is of confession; the Psalmist says, ". . . rise up after you have
been resting, you who eat the bread of sorrow,"[4] as if he says, you who have
contrition do not delay too much but hurriedly rise to confession. This loaf
has three qualities: first it must be consumed in haste so that it does not
spoil, second in cleanness so that it does not get soiled, and third with discretion so that one does not lose one's appetite. The third loaf is of
penance and satisfaction, of which the Psalm says, "Ashes like bread I
ate."[5] Whatever in fact is touched by ashes is made bitter. In this way
penance in time here is bitter, but elsewhere is sweet. And this loaf is

---

† Translated by Stephen H. A. Shepherd from Siegfried Wenzel, ed. and trans., *Fasciculus Morum:
   A Fourteenth-Century Preacher's Handbook* (University Park, U of Pennsylvania P, 1989), pp. 175,
   257. *Fasciculus Morum* ("A Bundle of Moral Matters," composed c. 1300) is a treatise on the seven
   deadly sins designed to provide preachers with assistance in formulating spiritual arguments
   through richly associative, scripturally based analogies between vices and virtues—a traditional
   technique with which Langland was obviously familiar. Cf. *Piers Plowman* Passus V, lines 75ff.,
   Passus VI, lines 253ff., Passus VIII, lines 45–50; and Passus XVI, lines 1–9.
1. Both "charity" and "love" are suitable translations of the source Latin word, *caritas*.
2. John 6:9–12.
3. Psalm 42:3.
4. Psalm 127:2.
5. Psalm 102:9.

divided in three: in fasting, prayer, and, almsgiving. * * * The fourth loaf is perseverance without lapsing; about which Isaiah [30:23] says, "The bread of the crop of the earth will be plenteous and fat." He calls it "plenteous" on account of its generous desire to satisfy, and "fat" on account of its desire to persevere and not relapse. And this loaf is divided in three, that is in compassion with the death of Christ, in consideration of one's own danger, and in caution about future evil. The fifth loaf is of the Eucharist. And it is the bread of lords, that is those who overcome their own sins and chastise and dominate them. And therefore it is the bread of life, of which John 6 says, "He who eats this bread will live forever." And it is similarly divided in three: in purity of heart, constancy of faith, and perseverance in good works.

From Pearl†

I

1

Pearl, that a prince is well content
To give a circle of gold to wear,
Boldly I say, all orient
Brought forth none precious like to her;
So comely in every ornament,
So slender her sides, so smooth they were,
Ever my mind was bound and bent
To set her apart without a peer.
In a garden of herbs I lost my dear;
Through grass to ground away it shot;
Now, lovesick, the heavy loss I bear
Of that secret pearl without a spot.

2

Since in that spot it sped from me so,
Often I watched and wished for that grace
That once was wont to banish woe
And bless with brightness all my days;
That clutches my heart in cruel throe
And causes my blood to rage and race,
Yet sweeter songs could no man know
Than silence taught my ear to trace;
And many there came, to think of her face

† From Marie Borroff, trans., *Pearl: A New Verse Translation* (New York: W. W. Norton & Company, 1977), pp. 1–3, 31. Reprinted by permission of W. W. Norton & Company. *Pearl* is an anonymous fourteenth-century alliterative dream vision produced at the same time as *Piers Plowman*. With Gower, Chaucer, and Langland, the *Pearl*-poet has been called by John Burrow a "Ricardian" poet, that is, one of the poets writing under the reign of Richard II (1377–1399). Characteristic of the *Pearl*-poet's richly associative work is his use of ornate courtly vocabulary, a progressive accretion of significance to a single symbol, and a careful interlocking of stanzas through repetition of words and refrains. Notice the difference between the opening of *Piers Plowman* and this poem. Here, the dreamer falls asleep and finds himself in a supernatural otherworld rather than a reflection of his own world.

With cover of clay so coldly fraught:
O earth, you mar a gem past praise,
My secret pearl without a spot.

3

That spot with spice must spring and spread
Where riches rotted in narrow room;
Blossoms white and blue and red
Lift now alight in blaze of noon;
Flower and fruit could never fade
Where pearl plunged deep in earthen tomb,
For the seed must die to bear the blade
That the wheat may be brought to harvest home.[1]
Good out of good to all and some:
Such a seed could never have come to nought
Nor spice in splendor spare to bloom
From that precious pearl without a spot.

4

To that especial spot I hied
And entered that same garden green
In August at a festive tide
When corn is cut with scythe-edge keen.
On the mound where pearl went tumbling wide,
Leaf vied with leaf in shade and sheen:
Gillyflower and ginger on every side
And peonies peerless blooming between.
But fairer yet, and all unseen,
Was the fragrance that my senses sought;
There, I know, is the dear demesne
Of my precious pearl without a spot.

5

Before that spot with head inclined
I stretched my hand in stark despair;
My heart lamented, deaf and blind,
Though reason reconciled my care.
I mourned my pearl so close confined
With thoughts in throng contending there;
Comfort of Christ might come to mind
But wretched will would not forbear.
I fell upon that flower-bed fair;
Such odor seized my brain distraught
I slipped into slumber unaware,
On that precious pearl without a spot.

1. John 12:24.

II

1

My soul forsook that spot in space
And left my body on earth to bide.
My spirit sped, by God's good grace,
On a quest where marvels multiplied.
I knew not where in the world it was,
But I saw I was set where cliffs divide;
A forest flourished in that place
Where many rich rocks might be descried.
The glory that flashed there far and wide
Eye could not credit, nor mind invent;
Pure cloth-of-gold were pale beside
Such rich and rare embellishment.

2

Embellished were those hills in view
With crystal cliffs as clear as day
And groves of trees with boles as blue
As indigo silks of rich assay;
The leaves, like silver burnished new,
Slide rustling rife on every spray;
As shifts of cloud let sunshine through,
They shot forth light in shimmering play.
The gravelstones that strewed the way
Were precious pearls of orient;
The beams of the sun but blind and grey
Beside such bright embellishment.

3

Amid those hills embellished bright
My sorrows fled in full retreat;
Fragrance of fruits with great delight
Filled me like food that mortals eat.
Birds of all colors fanned in flight
Their iridescent pinions fleet,
But lute or lyre, by craft or sleight,
Could not make music half so sweet,
For while in time their wings they beat
In glad accord their voices blent;
With more of mirth might no man meet
Than hear each brave embellishment.

4

So all embellished was the land
Where Fortune bears me on my way;
No tongue is worthy to command
Fit words those splendors to display.

I walked along with bliss at hand;
No slope so steep to make me stay;
The further, the fairer the pear trees stand,
The spice-plants spread, the blossoms sway,
And hedgerows run by banks as gay
As glittering golden filament;
I came to the shore of a waterway:
Dear God, what brave embellishment!

5

Embellishing those waters deep,
Banks of pure beryl greet my gaze;
Sweetly the eddies swirl and sweep
With a rest and a rush in murmuring phrase;
Stones in the stream their colors steep,
Gleaming like glass where sunbeam strays,
As stars, while men of the marshlands sleep,
Flash in winter from frosty space;
For every one was a gem to praise,
A sapphire or emerald opulent,
That seemed to set the pool ablaze,
So brilliant their embellishment.

* * *

XIII[2]

1

"Jesus on his faithful smiled
And said, 'God's kingdom shall be won
By him who seeks it as a child,
For other entry-right is none.
Harmless, steadfast, undefiled,
Unsullied bright to gaze upon,
When such stand knocking, meek and mild,
Straightway the gate shall be undone.
There is the endless bliss begun
That the jeweler sought in earthly estate
And sold all his goods, both woven and spun,
To purchase a pearl immaculate.[3]

2

"This immaculate pearl I tell you of,
The jeweler gave his wealth to gain,
Is like the realm of heaven above;
The Father of all things said it plain.
No spot it bears, nor blemish rough,

2. Having met a maiden bedecked with pearls—probably the dreamer's deceased daughter—the dreamer is instructed by her on the criteria for salvation [*Editors*].
3. Matthew 13:45–46.

But blithe in rondure ever to reign,
And of righteousness it is prize and proof:
Lo, here on my breast it long has lain;
Bestowed by the Lamb so cruelly slain,
His peace to betoken and designate;
I bid you turn from the world insane
And purchase your pearl immaculate."

3

"Immaculate pearl whom white pearls crown,
Who bear," said I, "the pearl of price,
Who fashioned your form? Who made your gown?
Oh, he that wrought it was most wise!
Such beauty in nature never was known;
Pygmalion never painted your eyes,
Nor Aristotle, of long renown,
Discoursed of these wondrous properties,
Your gracious aspect, your angel guise,
More white than the lily, and delicate:
What duties high, what dignities
Are marked by the pearl immaculate?"

4

"My immaculate Lamb, my destiny sweet,"
Said she, "who can all harm repair,
He made me his mate in marriage meet,
Though once such a match unfitting were.
When I left your world of rain and sleet
He called me in joy to join him there:
'Come hither, my dove without deceit,
For you are spotless, past compare.'[4]
He gave me strength, he made me fair,
He crowned me a virgin consecrate,
And washed in his blood these robes I wear,[5]
And clad me in pearls immaculate."

5

"Immaculate being, bright as flame,
In royalties set and sanctified,
Tell me now, what is that Lamb
That sought you out to become his bride?
Over all others you pressed your claim
To live in honor with him allied,
Yet many a noble and worthy dame
For Christ's dear sake has suffered and died;
And you have thrust those others aside
And reserved for yourself that nuptial state,

4. Song of Solomon 4:7; 5:2.
5. Revelation 7:13–14.

Yourself all alone, so big with pride,
A matchless maid and immaculate?"

XIV

I

"Immaculate," came her answer clear,
"Unblemished am I, my peers among;
So much I claim with honor here,
But matchless—there you have it wrong.
We all are brides of the Lamb so dear,
One hundred and forty-four thousand strong,
In Apocalypse the words appear
As John beheld it and told with tongue.[6]
Thousands on thousands, virgins young,
He saw on Mount Sion in sacred dream,
Arrayed for the wedding in comely throng
In the city called New Jerusalem.

* * *

XX

I

Moved by delight of sight and sound,
My maddened mind all fate defied.
I would follow her there, my newly found,
Beyond the river though she must bide.
I thought that nothing could turn me round,
Forestall me, or stop me in mid-stride,
And wade I would from the nearer ground
And breast the stream, though I sank and died.
But soon those thoughts were thrust aside;
As I made for the river incontinent
I was summoned away and my wish denied:
My Prince therewith was not content.

2

It contented him not that I, distraught,
Should dare the river that rimmed the glade;
Though reckless I was, and overwrought,
In a moment's space my steps were stayed.
For just as I started from the spot
I was reft of my dream and left dismayed;
I waked in that same garden-plot,
On that same mound my head was laid.
I stretched my hand where Pearl had strayed;
Great fear befell me, and wonderment;

6. Revelation 14:1.

And, sighing, to myself I said,
"Let all things be to his content."

3

I was ill content to be dispossessed
Of the sight of her that had no peer
Amid those scenes so bright and blessed;
Such longing seized me, I swooned, or near;
Then sorrow broke from my burning breast;
"O honored Pearl," I said, "how dear
Was your every word and wise behest
In this true vision vouchsafed me here.
If you in a garland never sere.
Are set by that Prince all-provident,
Then happy am I in dungeon drear
That he with you is well content."

4

Had I but sought to content my Lord
And taken his gifts without regret,
And held my place and heeded the word
Of the noble Pearl so strangely met,
Drawn heavenward by divine accord
I had seen and heard more mysteries yet;
But always men would have and hoard
And gain the more, the more they get.
So banished I was, by cares beset,
From realms eternal untimely sent;
How madly, Lord, they strive and fret
Whose acts accord not with your content!

5

To content that Prince and well agree,
Good Christians can with ease incline,
For day and night he has proved to be
A Lord, a God, a friend benign.
These words came over the mound to me
As I mourned my Pearl so flawless fine,
And to God committed her full and free,
With Christ's dear blessing bestowing mine,
As in the form of bread and wine
Is shown us daily in sacrament;
O may we serve him well, and shine
As precious pearls to his content.

Amen.

JULIAN OF NORWICH

From A Book of Showings to the Anchoress Julian of Norwich[†]

[*The First Revelation*]

CHAPTER 3

And when I was xxx[th] yere old and a halfe, God sent me a bodily sicknes, in the which I ley iii daies and iii nyghtes. And on the iiii nyght I toke all my rightes of holie church and went not to have leven tyll day.[1] And after this I lay two daies and two nightes. And on the third night I weenied often tymes to have passed,[2] and so wenyd thei that were with me. And yet in this I felt a great louthsomnes[3] to die, but for nothing that was in earth that me lyketh to leve for,[4] ne for no payne that I was afrayd of, for I trusted in God of his mercie. But it was for I would have leved to have loveved[5] God better and longer tyme that I might by the grace of that levyng have the more knowing and lovyng of God in the blisse of heaven. For my thought all that tyme that I had leved heer so litle and so shorte in regard of that endlesse blesse. I thought, "Good Lorde, may my levyng no longar be to thy worshippe?"

And I understode in my reason and by the feelyng of my paynes that I

---

† From *The Showings of Julian of Norwich*, A Norton Critical Edition, ed. Denise N. Baker (New York: W. W. Norton & Company, 2005), pp. 6–14, 124–25. Reprinted by permission of W. W. Norton & Company. The note that follows is reprinted from M. H. Abrams and Stephen Greenblatt, et al., eds., *The Norton Anthology of English Literature*, 7th ed. (New York: W. W. Norton & Company, 2000), 2 vols., I, pp. 1355–56, with permission of W. W. Norton & Company.

The "Showings," or "Revelations" as they are also called, were sixteen mystical visions received by the woman known as Julian of Norwich. The name may be one that she adopted when she became an anchoress in a cell attached to the church of St. Julian that still stands in that town on the northeast coast of England. An anchorite (m.) or anchoress (f.) is a religious recluse confined to an enclosure, which he or she has vowed never to leave. At the time of such an enclosing the burial service was performed, signifying that the enclosed person was dead to the world and that the enclosure corresponded to a grave. The point of this confinement was, of course, to pursue more actively the contemplative or spiritual life. * * * We know very little about [Julian] except what she tells us in her writings. About the date of her visions, however, she is very precise. They occurred, she tells us, at the age of thirty and a half on May 13, 1373. * * *

A Book of Showings survives in a short and a long version. The longer text, from which the following excerpts are taken, was the product of fifteen and more years of meditation on the meaning of the visions in which much had been obscure to Julian. Apparently the mystical experiences were never repeated, but through constant study and contemplation the showings acquired a greater clarity, richness, and profundity as they continued to be turned over in a mind both gifted with spiritual insight and learned in theology. * * *

Julian's interpretations of her showings owe much to the orthodox theology of her time, but they are colored by her experience and temperament as an individual woman. The blood of Christ reminds her of water dripping from the eaves of a house and the scales of herring. One of her favorite adjectives is "homely," which signifies the ease, intimacy, and familiarity of being at home. Thus God is "homely" with her, and she with him in the way a great lord may condescend to be on intimate and familiar terms with one of his servants in spite of the distance that separates them. Julian's book is one of many distinguished mystical texts, both English and Continental, composed during the late Middle Ages, for example, Walter Hilton's *The Scales of Perfection* or the anonymous *Cloud of Unknowing*, brilliant works of instruction for those who would follow the mystical way. Julian's work, however, is unique in its combination of intellectual and stylistic eloquence and the homeliness of its imagery and feeling.

1. I received all my rites of holy church and believed that I would not live until day.
2. I expected often times to have passed away.
3. Loathsomeness, unwillingness.
4. That pleases me to live for.
5. Lived to have loved.

should die, and I ascentyd[6] fully with all the will of myn hart to be at God's will. Thus I indured till day, and by then was my bodie dead from the miedes[7] downward as to my feeling. Then was I holpen to be set upright, undersett with helpe,[8] for to have the more fredom of my hart to be at God's will and thinkyng on God while my life laste. My curate was sent for to be at my ending, and before he cam I had set up my eyen[9] and might not speake. He set the crosse before my face and sayd, "I have brought the image of thy Saviour. Looke ther upon and comfort thee ther with."

My thought I was well, for my eyen was sett upright into heaven, where I trusted to come by the mercie of God. But nevertheles I ascentyd to sett my eyen in the face of the crucyfixe if I might, and so I dide, for my thought I might longar dure to looke even forth then right up.[1] After this my sight began to feyle.[2] It waxid as darke aboute me in the chamber as if it had ben nyght, save[3] in the image of the crosse, wher in held a comon light, and I wiste not how.[4] All that was beseid the crosse was oglye and ferfull[5] to me as it had ben much occupied with fiendes. After this the over part of my bodie began to die so farforth that unneth I had anie feeling.[6] My most payne was shortnes of breth and faielyng[7] of life. Then went I verily to have passed.[8]

And in this sodenly all my paine was taken from me, and I was as hole,[9] and namely, in the over parte of my bodie, as ever I was befor. I merveiled of this sodeyn change, for my thought that it was a previe working of God and not of kynd.[1] And yet by feeling of this ease I trusted never the more to have lived, ne the feeling of this ease was no full ease to me, for me thought I had lever have ben delivred of this world,[2] for my hart was wilfully set ther to.

Then cam sodenly to my mynd that I should desyer the second wound of our Lordes gifte and of his grace that my bodie might be fulfilled with mynd and feeling of his blessed passion, as I had before praied. For I would that his paynes were my paynes, with compassion and afterward langyng[3] to God. This thought me that I might with his grace have the woundes that I had before desyred. But in this I desyred never no bodily sight ne no maner schewing of God, but compassion as me thought that a kynd sowle[4] might have with our Lord Jesu, that for love would become a deadly man. With him I desyred to suffer, livyng in my deadly bodie, as God would give me grace.

---

6. Assented.
7. Middle.
8. Helped to sit upright, supported with help.
9. Raised up my eyes. *Curate*: parish priest.
1. For I thought I might longer endure to look forward rather than upward.
2. Fail.
3. Except. *Waxid*: grew.
4. Ordinary light, and I knew not how.
5. Beside the Cross was ugly and fearful.
6. Upper part of my body began to die to a great extent that scarcely I had any feeling.
7. Failing.
8. Then thought I truly to have passed away.
9. Whole. *Sodenly*: suddenly.
1. For I thought that it was a secret work of God and not of nature. *Merveiled*: marveled.
2. I thought I would rather have been delivered out of this world.
3. Longing.
4. Except compassion that I thought a natural and empathetic soul. The adjective *kind* in Middle English means both "natural" and "kind."

Revelation I

CHAPTER 4

And in this sodenly I saw the reed bloud rynnyng downe from under the garlande, hote and freyshely, plentuously and lively, right as it was[1] in the tyme that the garland of thornes was pressed on his blessed head. Right so both God and man, the same that sufferd for me, I conceived truly and mightly that it was him selfe that shewed it me without anie meane.[2]

And in the same shewing sodeinly the Trinitie fulfilled my hart most of joy, and so I understode it shall be in heaven without end to all that shall come ther. For the Trinitie is God, God is the Trinitie. The Trinitie is our maker. The Trinitie is our keper. The Trinitie is our everlausting lover. The Trinitie is our endlesse joy and our bleisse by our Lord Jesu Christ and in our Lord Jesu Christ. And this was shewed in the first syght and in all, for wher Jhesu appireth[3] the blessed Trinitie is understand as to my sight.

And I sayd, "Benedicite, Dominus."[4] This I sayd for reverence in my menyng with a mightie voyce. And full greatly was I a stonned for wonder and marvayle that I had that he that is so reverent and so dreadfull will be so homely[5] with a synnfull creature liveing in this wretched flesh. Thus I toke it for that tyme that our Lord Jhesu of his curteys love would shewe me comfort before the tyme of my temptation, for me thought it might well be that I should by the sufferance[6] of God and with his keping be tempted of fiendes before I should die. With this sight of his blessed passion, with the Godhead that I saw in my understanding, I knew well that it was strenght inough to me, ye, and to all creaturs livyng that sould be saved against all the fiendes of hell and against all ghostely[7] enemies.

In this he brought our Ladie Sainct Mari[8] to my understanding. I saw her ghostly in bodily lykenes,[9] a simple mayden and a meeke, yong of age, a lit-tle waxen above a chylde, in the stature as she was when she conceivede.[1] Also God shewed me in part the wisdom and the truth of her sowle, wher in I understode the reverent beholding that she beheld her God that is her maker, marvayling with great reverence that he would be borne of her that was a symple creature of his makyng. For this was her marvayling, that he that was her maker would be borne of her that was made. And this wis-dome and truth, knowing the greatnes of her maker and the littlehead[2] of her selfe that is made, made her to say full meekely to Gabriell, "Loo me here, God's handmayden."[3] In this syght I did understand verily that she is more then all that God made beneth her in wordines and in full-

---

1. Hot and fresh, plenteously and vigorously, just as it was. *Rynnyng*: running.
2. Any intermediary.
3. Appears.
4. "Blessed be thou, Lord."
5. So revered and awe-inspiring will be so familiar or intimate. Julian often refers to God's homely or homelike intimacy with humanity as well as his courteous, more formal relationship. *Stonned*: astonished.
6. Permission. As Julian will reveal later, the fiend is himself powerless, but God allows him to tempt humankind. *Curteys*: courteous.
7. Spiritual.
8. St. Mary, the mother of Jesus.
9. In a spiritual manner in bodily likeness. Some of Julian's showings seem to be midway between sen-sory visions or auditions and incorporeal revelations.
1. Conceived Jesus.
2. Littleness.
3. Mary's response to the angel Gabriel's announcement that she would be the mother of the Son of God.

head,[4] for above her is nothing that is made but the blessed manhood of Christ as to my sight.

CHAPTER 5

In this same tyme that I saw this sight of the head bleidyng, our good Lord shewed a ghostly sight of his homely lovyng.[5] I saw that he is to us all thing that is good and comfortable to our helpe. He is oure clothing that for love wrappeth us and wyndeth us, halseth us and all becloseth us,[6] hangeth about us for tender love that he may never leeve us. And so in this sight I saw that he is all thing that is good as to my understanding.

And in this he shewed a little thing, the quantitie of an haselnott, lying in the palme of my hand, as me semide,[7] and it was as rounde as a balle. I looked theran with the eye of my understanding and thought, "What may this be?" And it was answered generaelly thus: "It is all that is made." I marvayled how it might laste, for me thought it might sodenly have fallen to nawght[8] for littlenes. And I was answered in my understanding: "It lasteth and ever shall, for God loveth it. And so hath all thing being by the love of God."

In this little thing I saw iii properties. The first is that God made it; the secund, that God loveth it; the thirde, that God kepyth it. But what behyld I, verely, the maker, the keper, the lover. For till I am substantially unyted[9] to him, I may never have full reste ne verie blisse, that is to say, that I be so fastned to him that ther be right nought[1] that is made betweene my God and me.

This little thing that is made, me thought it might have fallen to nought for littlenes. Of this nedeth us to have knowledge that us lyketh nought all thing that is made for to love and have God that is unmade.[2] For this is the cause why we be not all in ease of hart and of sowle: for we seeke heer rest in this thing that is so little wher no reste is in. And we know not our God that is almightie, all wise, and all good, for he is verie reste.

God will be knowen, and him lyketh that we rest us in him. For all that is beneth him suffyseth not[3] to us. And this is the cause why that no sowle is in reste till it is noughted[4] of all thinges that is made. When she is wilfully noughted for loue, to have him that is all, then is she able to receive ghostly reste.

And also our good Lord shewed that it is full great plesaunce to him that a sely sowle come to him naked, pleaynly and homely.[5] For this is the kynde dwellyng of the sowle by the touchyng of the Holie Ghost,[6] as by the understandyng that I have in this schewying. "God, of thy goodnes geve me thy

4. In worthiness and fullness.
5. A spiritual sight of his intimate love. *Bleidyng*: bleeding.
6. Enfolds us, embraces us, and entirely encloses us.
7. As it seemed to me. *Haselnott*: hazelnut.
8. Naught, nothing.
9. United in substance or essence. Julian explains this ontological union between God and humans in Revelation XIV, chapters 53–56.
1. Nothing at all.
2. Of this we need to have knowledge so that all created things do not please us except to love and have God who is uncreated.
3. Suffices not, is not adequate.
4. Stripped.
5. It is a very great pleasure to him that a blessed soul come to him stripped naked, plainly and intimately.
6. The natural dwelling of the soul by the contact or influence of the Holy Spirit.

selfe, for thou art inough to me, and I maie aske nothing that is lesse that maie be full worshippe to thee. And if I aske anie thing that is lesse, ever me wanteth,[7] but only in thee I have all." And these wordes of the goodnes of God be full lovesum to the sowle and full neer touching the will[8] of our Lord, for his goodnes fulfillith all his creaturs and all his blessed workes without end. For he is the endlesshead[9] and he made us only to him selfe, and restored us by his precious passion, and ever kepeth us in his blessed love. And all this is of his goodnes.

* * *

FROM CHAPTER 7

* * *

And in alle that tyme that he schewd thys that I have now seyde in gostely syght, I saw the bodely syght lastyng of the plentuous bledyng of the hede. The grett droppes of blode felle downe fro under the garlonde lyke pelottes semyng as it had comynn oute of the veynes.[1] And in the comyng oute they were browne rede, for the blode was full thycke. And in the spredyng abrode they were bryght rede. And whan it camme at the browes,[2] ther they vanysschyd. And not wythstonding, the bledyng contynued tylle many thynges were sene and understondyd. Nevertheles, the feyrhede and the lyvelyhede continued in the same bewty and lyvelynes.[3]

The plentuoushede is lyke to the droppes of water that falle of the evesyng of an howse[4] after a grete shower of reyne that falle so thycke that no man may nomber them with no bodely wyt. And for the roundnesse they were lyke to the scale of heryng[5] in the spredyng of the forhede. Thes thre thynges cam to my mynde in the tyme: pelettes for the roundhede in the comyng oute of the blode, the scale of heryng for the roundhede in the spredyng, the droppes of the evesyng of a howse for the plentuoushede unnumerable.

Thys shewyng was quyck and lyvely and hydows[6] and dredfulle and swete and lovely. And of all the syght that I saw, this was most comfort to me, that oure good Lorde, that is so reverent and dredfulle, is so homely and so curteyse. And this most fulfyllyd me with lykyng and syckernes in soule.[7]

And to the understondyng of thys he shewde thys open example. It is the most wurschypp that a solempne kyng or a gret lorde may do to a pore servante yf he wylle be homely with hym and, namely, yf he shew it hym selfe of a fulle true menyng and with a glad chere boyth in prevyte and opynly.[8] Than thyngkyth thys pore creature thus: "Loo, what myght thys noble lorde do more wurschyppe and joy to me than to shew to me that

7. Ever I am lacking, unsatisfied.
8. Are very lovely to the soul and closely conforming to the will.
9. Endlessness.
1. Pellets seeming to have come out of the veins.
2. Came to the eyebrows.
3. Fairness and liveliness continued in the same beauty and liveliness.
4. Eaves of a house.
5. Herring.
6. Hideous.
7. With pleasure and certainty in the soul.
8. A glad expression in private and in public. Julian presents her comprehensive interpretation of this example of the lord and servant in Revelation XIV, chapter 51.

am so lytylle thys marvelous homelynesse? Verely, it is more joy and lykyng to me than if he gave me grett geftes and wer hym selfe strange[9] in maner." This bodely exsample was shewde so hygh that thys mannes hart myght be ravyssched[1] and almost foryet hym selfe for joy of thys grette homelynesse.

Thus it faryth by oure Lorde Jhesu and by us, for verely it is the most joy that may be, as to my syght, that he that is hyghest and myghtyest, noblyest and wurthyest, is lowest and mekest, homlyest and curtysest. And truly and verely this marvelous joy shalle be shew us all when we shall see hym. And thys wille oure good Lorde that we beleve and trust, joy and lyke, comfort us and make solace as we may with his grace and with his helpe in to the tyme that we see it verely. For the most fulhede of joy that we shalle have, as to my syght, ys thys marvelous curtesy and homelynesse of oure Fader, that is oure maker, in oure Lorde Jhesu Crist, that is oure Broder and oure Savior.

But this marvelous homelynesse may no man know in this lyfe, but yf he have it by specialle schewyng of oure Lorde or of gret plenty of grace inwardly yeven[2] of the Holy Gost. But feyth and beleve with charyte deserve the mede,[3] and so it is had by grace. For in feyght with hope and cheryte[4] oure lyfe is groundyd. The shewyng, made to whom that God wylle, pleynely techyth the same, openyd and declaryd with many prevy poyntes[5] be longyng to our feyth and beleve, which be wurshipfull to be knowen. And whan the shewyng which is yeven for a tyme is passyde and hydde, than fayth kepyth it by grace of the Holy Goste in to our lyvys ende.[6] And thus by the shewyng it is none other than the feyth, ne lesse ne more, as it may be seene by oure Lordes menyng in the same matter by than it come to the last ende.

*   *   *

[*Conclusion*]

CHAPTER 86

This boke is begonne by Goddys gyfte and his grace, but it is nott yett performyd[1] as to my syght. For charyte pray we alle to gedyr with Goddes wurkyng, thankyng, trustyng, enjoyeng, for this wylle oure good Lord be prayde by the understandyng that I toke in alle his owne menyng and in the swete wordes where he seyth fulle merely, *I am grownd of thy besechyng.*[2] For truly I saw and understode in oure Lordes menyng that he shewde it, for he wyll have it knowyn more than it is. In whych knowyng he wylle geve us grace to love hym and cleve to hym, for he beholde his hevynly tresure and solace in hevynly joye, in drawyng of oure hartes fro sorow and dark-nesse whych we are in.

---

9. Aloof.
1. Ravished or carried away in spirit. This term is often used in Middle English texts to describe the state of mystical or contemplative union with God.
2. Given.
3. Reward.
4. For in faith with hope and charity. These three theological virtues are instilled by grace freely given by the Holy Spirit.
5. Secret points.
6. Lives' end.
1. Completed, accomplished.
2. Revelation XIV, chapter 41.

And fro the tyme that it was shewde, I desyerde oftyn tymes to wytt in what was oure Lord's menyng. And xv yere after and mor I was answeryd in gostly understondyng, seyeng thus, "What, woldest thou wytt thy Lordes menyng in this thyng? Wytt it wele, love was his menyng. Who shewyth it the? Love. Wherfore shewyth he it the? For love. Holde the therin, thou shalt wytt more in the same. But thou schalt nevyr witt therin other withoutyn ende."

Thus was I lernyd that love is oure Lordes menyng. And I sawe fulle surely in this and in alle that or God made us he lovyd us, whych love was nevyr slekyd[3] ne nevyr shalle. And in this love he hath done alle his werkes. And in this love he hath made alle thynges profytable to us. And in this love oure lyfe is evyr lastyng. In oure makyng we had begynnyng, but the love wher in he made us was in hym fro without begynnyng, in whych love we have oure begynnyng. And alle this shalle we see in God with outyn ende.

Deo gracias.[4]

Explicit liber revelacionum Julyane ana[c]orite Norwyche, cuius anime propicietur Deus.[5]

MARGERY KEMPE

From The Book of Margery Kempe†

[*The Birth of Her First Child and Her First Vision*]

1. When this creature was twenty years of age or somewhat more, she was married to a worshipful burgess and was with child within a short

---

3. Slackened, diminished. *Or:* before.
4. Thanks be to God.
5. Here ends the book of revelations of Julian, anchorite of Norwich, upon whose soul God have mercy.

† From *The Book of Margery Kempe,* A Norton Critical Edition, ed. and trans. Lynn Staley (New York: W. W. Norton & Company, 2001), pp. 6–8, 91–95. Reprinted by permission of W. W. Norton & Company. The note that follows is reprinted from M. H. Abrams and Stephen Greenblatt, et al., eds., *The Norton Anthology of English Literature,* 7th ed. (New York: W. W. Norton & Company, 2000), 2 vols., I, pp. 366–67, with permission of W. W. Norton & Company.

    The Book of Margery Kempe is the spiritual autobiography of a medieval [married woman] telling of her struggles to carry out instructions for a holy life that she claimed to have received in personal visions from Christ and the Virgin Mary. The assertion of such a mission by a married woman, the mother of fourteen children, was in itself sufficient grounds for controversy; in addition, Kempe's outspoken defense of her visions as well as her highly emotional style of religious expression embroiled her with fellow citizens and pilgrims and with the church, although she also won both lay and clerical supporters. Ordered by the archbishop of York to swear not to teach in his diocese, she courageously stood up for her freedom to speak her conscience.

    * * * At about the age of twenty she married John Kempe, a well-to-do fellow townsman. After the traumatic delivery of her first child—the rate of maternal mortality in childbirth was high—she sought to confess to a priest whose harsh, censorious response precipitated a mental breakdown, from which she eventually recovered through the first of her visions. * * * These visions recurred during the rest of her life, and her noisy weeping at such times made her the object of much scorn and hostility. Her orthodoxy was several times examined, as in her famous encounter with the archbishop of York, but her unquestioning acceptance of the church's doctrines and authority, and perhaps also her status as a former mayor's daughter, shielded her against charges of heresy.

    * * * Kempe was illiterate and acquired her command of Scripture and theology from sermons and other oral sources. Late in her life, she dictated her story in two parts to two different scribes. * * *

    * * * Kempe tells of her visit to the famous anchoress [Julian of Norwich—see p. 388]; the two women talked, and Julian seems to have understood and approved of Kempe's way of life.

time, as nature would. And, after she had conceived, she was labored with great attacks of illness until the child was born, and then, what for the labor she had in childing and for the sickness going before, she despaired of her life, thinking she might not live. And then she sent for her ghostly father, for she had a thing in conscience which she had never shown before that time in all her life. For she was ever hindered by her enemy, the devil, evermore saying to her that, while she was in good health, she needed no confession but could do penance by herself alone,[1] and all should be forgiven, for God is merciful enough. And therefore this creature oftentimes did great penance in fasting on bread and water and other deeds of alms with devout prayers, except she would not show this sin in confession. And, when she was at any time sick or troubled, the devil said in her mind that she should be damned, for she was not shriven of that sin. Wherefore, after her child was born, she, not trusting her life, sent for her ghostly father, as was said before, in full will to be shriven[2] of all her lifetime as nearly as she could. And, when she came to the point to say that thing which she had so long concealed, her confessor was a little too hasty and began sharply to reprove her before she had fully said her intent, and so she would no more say for aught he might do.

And anon, for the dread she had of damnation on the one side and his sharp reproving on that other side, this creature went out of her mind and was wonderfully vexed and labored with spirits for half a year, eight weeks and some odd days. And in this time she saw, as she thought, devils open their mouths, all inflamed with burning flames of fire as if they should have swallowed her in, sometimes menacing her, sometimes threatening her, sometimes pulling her and hailing her both night and day during the foresaid time. And also the devils cried upon her with great threats and bade her that she should forsake her Christianity, her faith, and deny her God, his mother, and all the saints in heaven, her good works and all good virtues, her father, her mother, and all her friends. And so she did. She slandered her husband, her friends and her own self; she spoke many a reproving word and many a harsh word; she knew no virtue nor goodness; she desired all wickedness; just as the spirits tempted her to say and do, so she said and did. She would have killed herself many a time because of her stirrings and have been damned with them in hell. And as a witness thereof she bit her own hand so violently that it was seen all her life afterward. And also she tore the skin on her body against her heart grievously with her nails, for she had no other instruments, and worse she would have done, save she was bound and kept with strength both day and night so that she might not have her will.

And, when she had long been labored in these and many other temptations, so that men thought she should never have escaped nor lived, then on a time, as she lay alone and her keepers were away from her, our merciful Lord Christ Jesus, ever to be trusted, worshiped be his name, never

---

Modern scholars have linked that way of life to patterns of late medieval religious experience. In particular, she exemplifies the affective piety advocated by the Franciscans, which emphasized the importance of love through a direct experiential knowledge of Christ by every Christian. *The Book of Margery Kempe* is a remarkable record of the powerful and potentially liberating effect this doctrine exercised on the fifteenth-century laity and on women in particular.

1. Auricular confession, or confessing to a priest, was central to the sacrament of penance, but some people, the Lollard followers of John Wyclif, who were seen as heretics, felt that the penitent needed no intermediary between the soul and God.
2. Confessed.

forsaking his servant in time of need, appeared to his creature, who had forsaken him, in likeness of a man, most seemly, most beautiful, and most amiable that ever might be seen with man's eye, clad in a mantle of purple silk, siting upon her bedside, looking upon her with so blessed a countenance that she was strengthened in all her spirits, said to her these words: "Daughter, why have you forsaken me, and I forsook never you?"

And anon, as soon as he had said these words, she saw verily how the air opened as bright as any lightning, and he rose up into the air, not right hastily and quickly, but fairly and easily so that she might well behold him in the air until it was closed again. And anon the creature was stabled in her wits and in her reason as well as ever she was before, and prayed her husband, as soon as he came to her, that she might have the keys of the buttery in order to take her meat and drink as she had done before. Her maidens and her keepers counseled him that he should deliver her no keys, for they said she would but give away such good as there was, for she knew not what she said, or so they thought. Nevertheless, her husband, ever having tenderness and compassion for her, commanded they should deliver to her the keys. And she took her meat and drink as her bodily strength would serve her and knew her friends and her household and all others who came to her to see how our Lord Jesus Christ had wrought his grace in her, so blessed may he be who ever is near in tribulation. When men think he is far from them, he is full near by his grace. Afterward, this creature did all other occupations that fell to her to do wisely and soberly enough, save she knew not verily the draught of our Lord.

*   *   *

[From Chapter 52: Margery Is Examined before the Archbishop of York]

*   *   *

On the next day she was brought into the Archbishop's chapel, and there came many of the Archbishop's household, despising her, calling her "lollard" and "heretic," and swearing many a horrible oath that she should be burnt. And she, through the strength of Jesus, said again to them, "Sirs, I fear you shall be burnt in hell without end unless you amend yourselves of your swearing of oaths, for you keep not the commandments of God. I would not swear as you do for all the good of this world."

Then they went away as if they were ashamed. She then, making her prayer in her mind, asked grace so to conduct herself that day as was most pleasant to God and profit to her own soul and good example to her fellow Christians. Our Lord, answering her, said it should be right well. At the last, the said Archbishop came into the chapel with his clerks, and sharply he said to her, " 'Why go you in white? Are you a maiden?"

She, kneeling on her knees before him, said, "No, sir, I am no maiden; I am a wife."

He commanded his household to fetch a pair of fetters and said she should be fettered, for she was a false heretic. And then she said, "I am no heretic, nor shall you prove me one."

The Archbishop went away and let her stand alone. Then she made her prayers to our Lord God almighty to help her and succor her against all her enemies, ghostly and bodily, a long while, and her flesh trembled and quaked wonderfully so that she was fain to put her hands under her clothes so that it should not be espied.

Afterward the Archbishop came again into the chapel with many worthy clerks, among which was the same doctor who had examined her before and the monk who had preached against her a little time before in York. Some of the people asked whether she were a Christian woman or a Jew; some said she was a good woman, and some said no. Then the Archbishop took his seat, and his clerks also, each of them in his degree, many people being present. And in the time while the people were gathering together and the Archbishop taking his seat, the said creature stood all behind, making her prayers for help and succor against her enemies with high devotion, so long that she melted all into tears. And at the last she cried loudly therewith, so that the Archbishop and his clerks and many people had great wonder of her, for they had not heard such crying before. When her crying was passed, she came before the Archbishop and fell down on her knees, the Archbishop saying full roughly unto her, "Why weep you so, woman?"

She, answering, said, "Sir, you shall wish some day that you had wept as sorely as I."

And then anon, after the Archbishop put to her the Articles of our Faith, to which God gave her grace to answer well and truly and readily without any great study so that he might not blame her, then he said to the clerks, "She knows her faith well enough. What shall I do with her?"

The clerks said, "We know well that she knows the Articles of the Faith, but we will not suffer her to dwell among us, for the people have great faith in her dalliance, and perhaps she might pervert some of them."

Then the Archbishop said unto her, "I am badly informed of you; I hear said you are a right wicked woman."

And she said again, "Sir, so I hear said that you are a wicked man. And, if you are as wicked as men say, you shall never come into heaven unless you amend yourself while you are here."

Then he said full roughly, "Why, you, what say men of me?"

She answered, "Other men, sir, can tell you well enough."

Then said a great clerk with a furred hood, "Peace, you speak of yourself and let him be."

Afterward said the Archbishop to her, "Lay your hand on the book here before me and swear that you shall go out of my diocese as soon as you may."

"No, sir," she said, "I pray you, give me leave to go again into York to take my leave of my friends."

Then he gave her leave for one day or two. She thought it was too short a time, wherefore she said again, "Sir, I may not go out of this diocese so hastily, for I must tarry and speak with good men before I go, and I must, sir, with your leave, go to Bridlington[1] and speak with my confessor, a good man, who was the good prior's confessor, who is now canonized."[2]

---

1. Bridlington was the site of the cult of St. John of Bridlington (d. 1379), who was prior of the house of Augustinian Canons there.
2. William Sleighholme was confessor to St. John of Bridlington.

Then said the Archbishop to her, "You shall swear that you shall neither teach nor challenge the people in my diocese."[3]

"No, sir, I shall not swear," she said, "for I shall speak of God and reprove those who swear great oaths wheresoever I go, unto the time that the pope and holy church have ordained that no man shall be so hardy to speak of God, for God almighty forbids not, sir, that we shall speak of him. And also the gospel makes mention that, when the woman had heard our Lord preach, she came before him with a loud voice and said, 'Blessed be the womb that bore you and the teats that gave you suck.'[4] Then our Lord said again to her, 'Forsooth so are they blessed that hear the word of God and keep it.' And therefore, sir, I think that the gospel gives me leave to speak of God."

"A, sir," said the clerks, "here know we well that she has a devil within her, for she speaks of the gospel."[5]

Immediately a great clerk brought forth a book and laid Saint Paul for his part against her that no woman should preach.[6]

She, answering thereto, said, "I preach not, sir, I go in no pulpit. I use but communication and good words, and that will I do while I live."

Then said a doctor who had examined her beforetime, "Sir, she told me the worst tales of priests that ever I heard."

The bishop commanded her to tell that tale.

"Sir, by your reverence, I spoke but of one priest by way of example, who as I have learned went wayward in a wood through the sufferance of God for the profit of his soul until the night came upon him. He, destitute of his lodging, found a fair garden, in which he rested that night, having a fair pear tree in the midst all flourished with flowers and embellished, and blooms full delectable to his sight, where came a bear, great and violent, ugly to behold, shaking the pear tree and knocking down the flowers. Greedily this grievous beast ate and devoured those fair flowers. And, when he had eaten them, turning his tail end in the priest's presence, voided them out again at the shameful part.

"The priest, having great abomination of that loathly sight, conceiving great heaviness for doubt of what it might mean, on the next day wandered forth on his way all heavy and pensive and fortuned to meet with a seemly aged man, like a palmer or a pilgrim, who inquired of the priest the cause of his heaviness. The priest, rehearsing the matter before written, said he conceived great dread and heaviness when he beheld that loathly beast befoul and devour such fair flowers and blooms and afterward so horribly devoid them before him at his tail end, and he not understanding what this might mean.

"Then the palmer, showing himself the messenger of God, thus addressed him, 'Priest, you yourself are the pear tree, somewhat flourishing and flowering through saying your service and administering the sacraments, though you do so undevotedly, for you take full little heed how you say your matins[7] and your service, just so it is blabbered to an end. Then go you to your mass without devotion, and for your sin have you full little

---

3. Women were prohibited from preaching. Julian of Norwich draws a careful distinction between teaching and preaching.
4. Luke 11.27–28.
5. Lollards were known as "Bible men and women."
6. 1 Corinthians 14.34–35.
7. The service that, with lauds, is the first of the canonical hours of morning prayer.

contrition. You receive there the fruit of everlasting life, the sacrament of the altar, in full feeble disposition. Afterward all the day after you misspend your time, you give yourself to buying and selling, chopping and changing, as if you were a man of the world. You sit at the ale, giving yourself to gluttony and excess, to lust of your body, through lechery and uncleanness. You break the commandments of God through swearing, lying, detraction, and backbiting, and the use of other such sins. Thus by your misgovernance, like the loathly bear, you devour and destroy the flowers and blooms of virtuous living to your endless damnation and many men's hindering unless you have grace from repentance and amending.'"

Then the Archbishop liked well the tale and commended it, saying it was a good tale. And the clerk who had examined her beforetime, in the absence of the Archbishop, said, "Sir, this tale smites me to the heart."

The foresaid creature said to the clerk, "A, worshipful doctor, sir, in the place where my dwelling is mostly, is a worthy clerk, a good preacher, who boldly speaks against the misgovernance of the people and will flatter no man. He says many times in the pulpit, 'If any man is evil pleased with my preaching, note him well, for he is guilty.' And right so, sir," said she to the clerk, "fare you by me, God forgive it you."

The clerk knew not well what he might say to her. Afterward the same clerk came to her and prayed her for forgiveness that he had been so against her. Also he prayed her specially to pray for him. And then anon after, the Archbishop said, "Where shall I find a man who might lead this woman from me?"

Quickly many young men started up, and every man said, "My Lord, I will go with her."

The Archbishop answered, "You are too young; I will not have you."

Then a good sober man from the Archbishop's household asked his Lord what he would give him if he should lead her. The Archbishop offered him five shillings, and the man asked for a noble. The Archbishop, answering, said, "I will not spend so much on her body."

"Yes, good sir," said the said creature, "our Lord shall reward you right well again."

Then the Archbishop said to the man, "See, here is five shillings, and lead her fast out of this country."

She, kneeling down on her knees, asked his blessing. He, praying her to pray for him, blessed her and let her go.

Then she, going again to York, was received by many people and by full worthy clerks, who delighted in our Lord who had given her, not lettered, wit and wisdom to answer so many learned men without villainy or blame. Thanks be to God.

WALTER HILTON

From the Epistle on the Mixed Life†

* * *

Two maner° states there ben° in Hooli Chirche bi   *kinds of / are*
the whiche Cristen soules plesen° God and geten   *please*
hem[1] the blis of hevene: that oon° is bodili, and that   *one*
othir is goostli.°   *spiritual*
  Bodili wirchynge° longeth° principali to worldli men   *endeavor / pertains*
or women, the whiche han levfulli wordeli goodes,[2]
and wilfulli usen wordeli bysinesses. Also it longeth to
alle yonge bigynnynge men whiche comen newe out of
wordli synnes to the service of God, for to make hem
able to goosteli wirkynge, and for to breke doun the
unbuxumnesse° of the body bi reson and bi such bod-   *lack of discipline*
ili werchynge, that it myght be souple° and redi, and   *compliant*
not moche contrarious to the spirit [in] goosteli
wirchinge. For, as Seint Poul seith, as woman was
maad° for man and not man for woman,[3] riyt° so bodili   *made / just*
worchynge was maad for goosteli and not goostli for
bodili. Bodili wirchynge gooth° bifore, and goosteli   *goes*
cometh aftir. So seith Seynt Poul: *Non quod prius spir-*
ituale, sed quod prius animale, deinde spirituale[4]—
"goosteli werk cometh not first, but first cometh bodili
werk that is doon bi the bodi, and sithen° cometh   *later*
goostli werk aftir."
  And this is the cause whi it bihoveth° to be so: for   *behooves*
we aren born in synne and in corrupcioun of the
flesch, bi the whiche we aren blynded and so ovreleid°   *overburdened*
that we have neithir the gostli knowynge of God bi
liyt° of undirstondynge, ne goostli felynge° of Hym bi   *illumination / awareness*
clene° desire of lovnge; and forthi° we mai not   *pure / therefore*
sodeynli stirte° oute of this myrk° pitte of this fleschli   *escape / dark*
corrupcion into that goostli light—for we mai not suf-
fre it ne beere° it for sikenesse of oure silf—[no] more   *endure*
thanne we mai with oure bodili iyen,° whanne thei   *eyes*
aren sore, bihoolde the sight of the sonne. And therfore we mosten° abide and worche bi proces of tyme,   *must*
first bi bodili werkes bisili,° unto° wee ben discharged   *actively / until*

---

† Text of Lambeth Palace Library MS 472, fol. 194ʳ ff., printed with permission of Lambeth Palace
Library; paragraphing and emendation modeled on the edition of S.J. Ogilvie-Thompson, *Walter*
Hilton's "Mixed Life" edited from Lambeth Palace MS 472 (Salzburg, 1986). Hilton (d. 1396), an
Augustinian Canon who lived in Nottinghamshire, is best known for his work *The Scale of Perfec-*
tion, a somewhat mystical account of the process of gaining closer spiritual access to God. The
present text takes the form of a letter written to a devout man who is nevertheless also wealthy and
of considerable influence; his is necessarily a "mixed" life, a combination of the secular works of
the active life and the private devotions of the contemplative life. Cf. Langland's treatment of
Activa Vita in *Passus* XIV and the "autobiographical" passage from the C-text, p. 363.
1. Obtain for themselves.
2. Secular people who rightfully possess temporal goods.
3. See Ephesians 5:22–25.
4. 1 Corinthians 15:46.

of this hevy birthene° of synne the whiche letteth° us *burden / prevents*
fro° goostli wirkynge, and to° oure soule be sumwhat *from / until*
clensed from grete outeward synnes and abled° to *enabled*
goosteli werk.

Bi this bodili worchynge that I speke of mai thou
undirstonde al maner of good werkes that thi soule
dooth° bi the wittes° and the membres of thi bodi unto *does / senses*
thisilf,° as [in] fastynge, wakynge,° and in refreyning of *yourself / keeping vigil*
thi fleschli lustis° bi othir penaunce doynge,° or to *desires / performing*
thyn even-Cristen° bi fulfillinge of the Dedes of *fellow Christian(s)*
Merci, bodili or goosteli,[5] or unto God bi suffrynge of
all maner [bodili] myscheves° for the love of riytwise- *harms*
nesse.° Alle thise werkes doon in trouthe, bi charité,° *righteousness / love*
plesen God—withouten the which, thei aren nought.° *nothing*
Thanne whoso desireth for to be occupied goostli, it is
siker° and profitable to him that he be first wel *certain*
assaied° a longe tyme in this bodili worchynge, for *tried*
thise bodili deedes aren a tokene and a schewynge° of *demonstration*
moral vertues, withouten whiche a soule is not able
for to worche goostli.

Breke° down first pride in bodili berynge,° and also *Break / carriage*
withinne thyn herte thenkynge, boostynge, and
rosynge[6] of thisilf and of thi deedes, presumynge of
thisilf, veyn° likynge in thisilf of ony thynge that God *vain*
hath sent to thee, bodili or goostli. Breke doun also
envie and wrath ayens thyn even-Cristen, whethir he
be riche or pore, good or badde, that thou hate him
not ne have disdeyn of him wilfulli, nothir° in word *neither*
ne° in deede. Also breke doun covetise° of wordli *nor / covetousness*
good, that thou for hooldynge [or] getynge° or savynge *acquiring*
of it offende not thi conscience, ne breke not charité
to God and to thyn even-Cristene for love of no wordli
good, but° that thou getist to kepe it and spende it *i.e., unless*
withoute love and veyn likynge of it, as resoun asketh,
in worschipe of God and help of thyne even-Cristen.
Breke doune as moche as thou mai fleschli likynges,
eithir in accidie° or in bodili eese,° or glotonie, or *sloth / ease, laziness*
leccherie. And thanne, whanne thou hast be° wel *been*
travueiled° and wel assaied in alle siche° bodili *exercised / such*
werkes, than mai thou bi grace ordayne° thee to *direct*
goostli worchynge.

Grace and goodnesse of oure Lord Ihesu Crist, that
He hath schewid to thee in withdrawynge of thyn
herte fro love and likynge of wordeli vanité and use of
fleschi synnes, and in turnynge of thi wille entierli° to *entirely*

5. Hilton refers, respectively, to the Seven Spiritual Works of Mercy (admonishing the sinner, instructing the ignorant, counseling the doubtful, comforting the sorrowful, bearing wrongs patiently, forgiving all injuries, and praying for the living and the dead); and the Seven Corporal Works of Mercy (feeding the hungry, giving drink to the thirsty, harboring the stranger, clothing the naked, comforting the sick, visiting the prisoner, and burying the dead).

6. Thinking highly, boasting, and praising.

His service and His plesaunce,° bringeth into [my] *pleasure*
herte moche matire to love Him [in] His merci. And
also it stireth° me greteli to strengthe° thee in the good *stirs, prompts / encourage*
purpos and in thi worchying that thou haste bigunne,
for to brynge it to a good eende yif° that I coude,° and *even if / could*
principalli for God, and sith° for tendre affeccioun of *then*
love which thou haste to me, if° I be a wrecche° and *although / miscreant*
unworthi.

I knowe weel° the desire of thyn herte, that thou *well*
yernest° gretli to serve oure Lord bi goostli occupa- *desire*
cioun al holli, withoute lettynge° or trobolynge° [of] *hindrance / tribulation*
wordeli bisynesse, that thou myghtest come bi grace
to more knowynge and goosteli feelynge° of God and *awareness*
of goostli thynges. This desire is good, as I hope—and
of God, for it is sette unto Hym in charité speciali.
Nevertheless it is for to restreyne and rulen bi discre-
cion as anemptis outeward worchynge aftir the staat
that thou art inne,[7] for charité unruled turneth sumtyme into vice. And forthi it is seid in hooli writte, *ordi-*
navit in me caritatem[8]—that is to seie oure Lord,
yevynge° to me charité sette it in ordre and in rule, *giving*
that it schulde not be lost thorugh° myn undiscre- *because of*
cioun. Riyt so, this charité and this desire that oure
Lord hath yeven° of his merci to thee is for to rulen *given*
and ordaynen hou thou schal pursue it aftire thi
degree asketh,[9] and aftir the lyvynge° that thou hast *way of life*
used bifore this tyme, and aftire the grace of vertues
that thou now haste.

Thou schalt not uttirli folwen thi desire for to leven° *leave behind*
occupacioun and bisynesse of the world—which aren
nedefull° to usen in rulynge of thi silf and of alle oth- *necessary*
ere that aren undir thi kepynge—and yeve thee hooli° *wholly*
to goostli occupaciouns of praiers and meditaciouns,
as it were a frere° or a monk or anothir man that were *friar*
not bounden to the world bi children and servantes, as
thou art; for it falleth° not to thee, and yif thou do soo, *is fitting*
thou kepest not the ordre of charité. Also, yif ° thou *if*
woldest leven uttirli goostli occupacion—nameli now
aftir the grace that God hath yeven unto thee—and
sette thee hooli to the bisynesse of the world to fulfillynge of werkes of actif ° lyf as fulli as an-nothir man *active*
that nevere feeled devocion, thou levest the ordre of
charité, for thi staat° asketh for to doo bothe, eche of *social condition*
hem in dyvers° tyme. Thou schalt meedele° the *different / mix*
werkes of actif liyf with goostli werkes of lif contemplatif; and thanne doost thou weel. For thou

---

7. You have to restrain that desire and govern it with discretion, and suit its outward expression to
your state in life.
8. Song of Solomon 2:4.
9. According to your (social) condition.

schalt oo tim° with Martha[1] be bisi for to rule and   *time*
governe thi household, thi children, thi servantes, thi
neighbors, thi tenauntes: yif thei doo weel, comfort
hem therinne and helpe hem; yef thei doon yuvele,°   *wickedly*
for to teche hem and amende hem and chastice hem.
And thou schalt also loke° and knowen° wideli that thi   *see to it / make known*
thynges and thi wordeli goddes be rightfully keped bi
thi servauntes governynge and truli spended,°   *utilized*
that
thou mygth the more plentevousli fulfille the deedes
of merci with hem unto thi even-Cristene. [Anothir
tyme] thou schal with Maria leve bisinesse of the
world and sitten down at the feet of oure Lord, bi
mekenesse, in praiers and in hooli thoughtis and in
contemplacion of Him as He yeveth thee grace. And so
schalt thou goon from the toon° to the tothir medfulli°   *one / meritoriously*
and fulfille hem bothe; and thanne kepist thou weel
the ordre of charité.

Nevertheless, that thou have no wondir of this that
I seie,° therfore I schal telle and declare to thee a litil   *say*
of this more openli. Thou schalt understonde that
theer is three maner of lyvynge. Oon is actif; another
is contemplatyf; the thredde is maad of bothe, and
that is medeled.

Actif liyf aloone longeth° to wordeli men and   *pertains*
women whiche are lewed, [fleschli, rude and bois-
tous][2] in knowyng of goostli occupacioun, for thei fee-
len no savour° in devocion bi fervour of love as othere   *delight*
men doon, ne thei can no skile[3] of it. And yit nevertheless, thei have drede of God and of the peynes° of   *punishments*
helle—therefore, thei fleen synne—and they have
desire for to plese God and for to come to hevene; and
thei have a good wille to her° even-Cristene. Unto   *their*
thise men it is needful and spedful° to usen the werkes   *beneficial*
of actif liyf as bisili as thei mai in heelpe of hemself and
of hire even-Cristene, for thei can not elles° doon.°   *otherwise / do*

Contemplatif liyf aloone longeth to siche° men and   *such*
women that for the love of God forsaken alle open
synnes of the world and of here flesch and alle bisynesse, charges,° and governaunces of wordli goodes,   *burdens*
and maken hemself pore and naked to the bare nede
of the bodili kynde° and fleen° fro sovereynté of alle   *nature / flee*
othere men to the service of God. Unto thise men it
longeth for to travaile and ocupie hem inwardli for to
gete thorugh the grace of oure Lord clennesse° of   *purity*
herte and pees° in conscience bi destroiynge of synne   *peace*
and receyvynge of vertues, and so for to come to con-

---

1. *Martha* was conventionally used as a symbol of the active life, as opposed to *Mary* (*Maria*), a symbol of the contemplative life. Cf. Luke 10:38–42.
2. Uneducated, physical, rough, and clumsy.
3. Have no discriminating knowledge.

templacioun; which clennesse mai not be haad withoute grete exercise of bodi and contynuel traveil of
spirit in devoute praieres, fervent desires, and goostli
meditacions.

The thridde liyf, that is medelid, longith speciali to
men of holi chirche, as to prelates and othire curates
whiche have cure° and sovereynté over othere men for   *spiritual care*
to teche and for to rule hem, bothe here bodies and
principali here soules, in fulfillynge of the deedes of
merci, bodili and goostli. Unto thise men it longeth
sumtyme [to] usen werkes of actif lif, in help and
sustenaunce of hemsilf and of here suggettis° and of   *subjects*
othere also, and sumtyme for to leven al manere bisynesse outeward and yeve hem unto praieres and meditacions, redynge of hooli writ, and to othere goostli
occupacions aftir that thei feele hemsilf disposed.

Also it longeth generaly [to] sum temporal men, the
which have sovereynté with moche avere° of worldli   *wealth*
goodis and haven also as it were lordschipe overe othere men, for to governe and sustene hem as a fadir
hath over his children, a maister over his servauntes,
and a lord overe his tenantes—the whiche men have
also receyved of oure [Lordis yift,° grace of] devocioun,   *gift*
and in partie° savouure of goostli occupacioun. Unto   *part*
thise men also longeth medeled lif that is bothe actif
and contemplatif.

For yf thise men, standynge° the charge and the   *as long as lasts*
boond whiche thei han° take,° wolen° leeve uttirli the   *have / taken / want to*
bisynesse of the world, the whiche oweth° skilfulli° for *ought / wisely*
to be used in fulfillynge of here° chaarge, and holi   *their*
gyve hem to contemplatif liyf, thei doon not weel,° for   *well, properly*
thei kepen not the ordre of charité. For charité * * *
lieth bothe in love of God and of thin evene-Cristene
* * *. For he that, for the love of God in contemplacion, leveth the love of his even-Cristene and dooth
not to hem as he oughte whanne he is bounden
therto, he fulfillith not charité. Also * * * whoso hath
more reward to° werkes of actif liyf and to bisynesse   *concern for*
of the world that for the love of his even-Cristene he
leeveth goostly occupacion uttirli, aftir that God [hath
disposed] hym thereto, he fulfilleth not fully charité:
this is the seiynge of Gregor.[4]

Forthi oure Lord, for to stirre summe to use this
medeled liyf, took upon Himself the persoone of sich°   *such*
manere men, bothe of prelates of hooli chirche and
othere sich as aren disposid as I have seid, and gave
hem ensample bi His own worchynge that thei
schulden usen this medeled liyf as he dide. O° tyme   *One*

---

4. St. Gregory ("The Great," c. 540–604); the allusion is possibly to Gregory's Homily XIII in *Homi-
liarum in Evangelia, Libri II.*

He comouned° with men and medeled with men,   *communed*
schewynge to hem His deedes of merci, for He
taughte the uncouth° and unkunynge° bi His pre-   *uneducated / ignorant*
chynge, He vesited the sike and heeled hem of here
sooris,° He fede the hongry, and He comforted the   *sicknesses*
sori.° And another tyme He lefte the conversacion of   *distressed*
alle wordeli men and of His disciples also, and wente
into dissert° upon the hillis and contynued alle the   *desert*
nyghte in praieres aloone, as the gospel seith. This
medeled liyf schewed oure Lord [in Himsilf] to
ensample of⁵ alle othere that han taken the charge of
this medeled liyf; that thei schulde oon tyme yeve hem
to bisynesse of wordli thynges at resonable neede, and
to the werkes of actif liyf in profite of here even-
Cristene which thei have cure of, and anothir tyme
yeve hem hooli to devocion and to contemplacion in
praieres and in meditacion.

✳ ✳ ✳

From The Abbey of the Holy Ghost†

Heer biginneth a tretis that is clept° *The Abbey of*   *called*
the Holy Gost; that is, concience of monnes° herte°   *man's / heart*
schulde ben° in this abbey most.   *be*

Mi deore° brethren and sustren, I seo° wel that   *dear / see*
monie° wolde ben in religion° but thei mowe not for   *many / religious orders*
povert or for age or for drede of heore kun¹ or for bond
of mariage. And therfore I make her° a book of reli-   *here*
gion of herte—that is, of the Abbeye of the Holi
Gost—that alle tho° that mouwe° not ben in [bodili]   *those / can*
religion thei mowe ben in gostly.° A Jesu, merci!   *spiritual*
Where may this abbey and this religion best ben
i-founded? Certes,° nevere so wel ne so semely° as in a   *Certainly / appropriately*
place that is clept Concience. Now behoveth° hit°   *behooves / it*
thenne at the biginnynge, that the place of the concience be clanset thorw wys clansynge.² The Holi
Gost schal senden adoun° twey° maidens ful con-   *down / two*
nynge:° that on is clept Rihtwisnesse, and that other   *knowledgeable*
Love-of-Clannesse.³ Theose tweyne schul° caste from   *will*
the concience and from the herte alle manere fulthus°   *impurities*
of foule thoughtes and of foule yeornynges.° And   *desires*

---

5. As an example for.
† Text of Oxford, Bodleian Library MS. Eng. Poet. a.l (the "Vernon Manuscript"), fols. 359ʳᵃ–360ʳᵇ.
   Printed by permission of the Bodleian Library. This very large manuscript, dated c.1380–1400, also
   contains a version of *Piers Plowman*, along with many other pious and devotional texts. For a helpful account of related texts and editions, see Julia Boffey, " 'The Charter of the Abbey of theHoly
   Ghost' . . ." *YES* 33 (2003), pp. 120–130. The architectonic and personifying allegory of the somewhat mystical *Abbey* is not as sophisticated as that employed by Langland, but reveals aspects of
   the figurative literary milieu with which he and his readers would have been familiar.
1. They cannot because of poverty or advanced age or fear of censure from their family.
2. Cleansed through wise cleansing.
3. One is called Righteousness, and the other Love-of-Purity.

whon° the place of the concience is wel i-clanset, then *when*
schal the foundement° beon maad large and deep.° *foundation / deep*
And that schul twey maydens make: that on is clept
Mekenesse° that schal make the foundement deep *Meekness, Humility*
thorw louhnesse° of hireself, and that other is clepett *humility*
Poverté,° that maketh hit large and wyd above and *Poverty*
casteth out of the hert al that is of eorthliche° thinges *physical*
and worldlich° thouhtes that thei that have erthliche *worldly*
goodes with love thei ne faste not heore hertes
theron.[4] And theose ben cleped Pore-in-Spirit; of
wyuche° God speketh in the godspel° and seith that *whom / gospel*
heoren° is the kindom of hevene: *Beati pauperes spir-* *theirs*
itu quoniam ipsorum est regnum celorum.[5] Blessed is,
thenne, that religioun that is foundet uppon povert
and uppon mekenesse.

This abbey also schal be set uppon a good riveer° *river*
of teeres,° for everi citee and abbey that ben set on *tears*
goode riveres ben the more at ese and the more deli-
ciouse.° On such a river was the Marie Maudeleyn *delightful*
i-sett and i-foundet,[6] and therfore graces and richesses
comen fulliche° al at hire wille. And therfore seith *fully*
David: *Fluminis impetus letificat civitatem Dei*[7]—that
is to seye, "The goode river maketh the citee likyng° *pleasing*
of God, for hit is clene and siker° and riche of alle *honest*
goode marchaundises. Riht so the river of teres
clanseth Godes cité—that is, monnes soule, the wyuche
is Godes; and the holy men seyn° that the fulthe° of *say / impurity*
synne departeth° richesses° of° vertues and of alle *takes away / value / from*
goode thewes.° And whon the foundement is maad,° *deeds / built*
then schul come twey dameseles, Boxumnesse° on *Obedience*
that on half, and Merciful on that other half, for to
rere° the walles an° heigh and make hem stalworthe° *raise / on / sturdy*
with a freo herte, largeliche yevynge to the pore and to
the meseysé.[8] For whon we don° eny goode dedes of *do*
charité thorw grace of good entente, als° moni goode *as*
stones we leggen° on ure° housyng in the blisse of *lay / our*
hevene, i-fastned togederes with the love of God and
of ur even-Cristne.° We reden that Salomon made *fellow Christians*
his housynge of grete precious stones.[9] Theos
precious stones ben almesdedes° and holi werkes that *deeds of charity*
schul be bounden togederes with quiklym° of love and *cement*
studefast beleeve° and therfore seith David the *faith*
prophet, *Omnia opera eius in fide*[1]—that is to seyen,

---

4. So that those with worldly goods not set their hearts lovingly upon those goods.
5. "Blessed are the poor in spirit; for theirs is the kingdom of heaven," Matthew 5:3.
6. Mary Magdalen stood by the Cross at the Crucifixion and was later one of the women who dis-covered Christ's empty tomb; in her sorrowful devotion she was then the first person to whom the risen Christ appeared (see Mark 16:5). In the Middle Ages, this Mary was admired as a tearful model of penitent and contemplative endeavor.
7. "There is a river, the streams whereof shall make glad the city of God," Psalm 46:4.
8. A liberal heart, giving generously to the poor and the needy.
9. See 1 Kings 7.
1. "And all his works are done in truth," Psalm 33:4.

"Alle his werkes be don in studefast beleeve. And as a wal may not fastnen° withouten ciment or morter, right so no werkes that we do are nought° worth to God ne° noteful to ur soules but° thei be don in the love of God and in trewe beleeve. An therfore al that we sinful don is loren° til that we amenden us. Seththe° Damisele Sufferaunce and Damisele Fort[2] schul reysen° up the pilers and undersetten° heom° so studfastlich and so stalworthlich that no wynd of wordes ne of non angres° ne of gostliche fondynges° ne of fleschliche° lustes, the innore ne the ottere,° ne mai hem doun casten.

 Aftur this behoveth hit that the cloistre be maad of foure corners—for-whi° hit is cleped the cloystre, for hit closeth and steketh° and warliche° schal be loken.° Mi deore bretheren and sustren, yif ye wollen holden° ow° in gostlich religion, holdeth ow withinne and steketh yor yates° and so warliche kepeth the wardes° of yor cloistre that non other° fondinges, non innore, mowe have eny entré to maken thi sylence to bren° or sturen° the to synne. Steke° thin eyen from foule sightes, thin eren from foule heringes,° thy mouth from foule speches and from unclene lauhtres,° thin herte from foule thoghtes, thin honden° from foule hondlynges, and thi neose° from uvele° smellynges.

 Schrift° schal make the chapightre hous,[3] Predi-cacion thi fretore,[4] Orisoun° thi chapel, Contempla-cion thi dortur,° that schal beo reised on heigh with heighe yeornynges° and with love quikingus° to God. Contemplacion is a devout risyng up of the herte, with brennynde° love in God to dwellen, and of His dely-ces° for to heeren, and of his halewes° sumdel tasten of the swetnesse that Godes i-chosene schul haven in hevene. Rihtfulnesse schal beo thi fermorer,° Devo-cion thi cellerer; Meditacion schal make thi gerneer.° And whon thin houses of offys° ben maad, thenne behoveth hit that the Holi Gost sette° the covent of graces and of vertues. And thenne schal the Holi Gost of this religion be wardeyn and visitor, the wyuche° God the Fader foundet thorw His miht.° As David seith, *Fundavid eam altissimus*;[5] that is, the heighe God the Fader foundede this religioun, the Sone throw His wisdom ordeyned hit. As Seint Poul wit-nesseth and seith, *Quae a deo sunt ordinatae sunt*;[6] that is, the heighe God hath maad hit, the Sone ruleth hit, the Holi Gost kepeth hit, and visyteth hit—and

hold up
nothing
nor / i.e., unless

lost
Then
raise / anchor / them

tribulations / temptations
bodily / outer

for which reason
fixes / vigilantly / locked
keep
you
gates
guards / i.e, external

inflame / stir / Set
things heard

jokes / hands
nose / evil, foul

Confession
Prayer
dormitory
desires / stirrings

burning
beauties / blessed ones

infirmary officer
granary-keeper
departments
provide

which
power

---

2. Damsel Patient Endurance and Damsel Fortitude.
3. The chapter house would be the usual meeting place for the abbey.
4. Preaching (will make) your refectory.
5. "And the highest himself has established her," Psalm 87:5.
6. "That is, those authorities that exist have been instituted by God," Romans 13:1.

that synge° we in holi churche: *Veni, creator spiritus,*   *sing*
mentes tuorum visita imple superna gracia que tu
creasti pectora[7]—"Come thou, Holi Gost, ther hertes
of thyne thou visyte and folfulle° the brestes with thi   *imbue*
grace that thou hast i-foormed."°   *created*

    The gode° Ladi Charité, as heo° is most worthi   *good / she*
beforen alle othere, schal ben abbesse of this seli°   *holy, wondrous*
abbeye. And as thei that ben in religion° schul nothing   *religious orders*
don ne siggen° ne gon into no studé° ne taken ne yiven   *say / study, meditation*
withoute leve° of heore° abbesse, riht so gostliche ne   *permission / their*
schulle none of suche thinges be don withoute leve
of Charité. For thus comaundeth Seint Poul: *Omnia*
vestra in caritate fiant"[8]—that is, "What ye don or
seyen or thenken° with herte, al ye mosten hit don in   *intend*
love and in charité" A,° deore° brethren and sustren,   *Ah, Oh / dear*
that her is an hard comaundement! But hit is notful°   *important*
for ur soules that ur thouhtes and ur wordes and ur
werkes ben onliche° don for the love and in the love   *only*
of God. Weilawei,° yif I dar° seye, for mony ben in   *Alas / dare*
religion and gon to seche° religion, tho that doth not   *seek*
after the comaundement of Seynt Poul, ne after the
counseil of the gode Ladi Charité that is abbesse of
this seli religion. And therfore thei leose muche tyme
of heor meede and echen gretliche heore peynes but
yif thei amenden hem.[9]

    Therfore leve° bretheren and sustren, beoth ever-   *dear*
more waker° and war,° and in alle yor werkes thenketh   *alert / aware*
bisyliche,° whatso ye don, that hit be for the love of   *diligently*
God and in His love.

    The Ladi Wisdam schal beo prioresse,° for heo is   *chief nun*
worthi: *nam prior omnium creatura est sapiencia*[1]—
that is, "Aller furst° is wisdam i-maked," and throw   *ahead of all*
the lore and the counseyl of this prioresse we schul
don al that we don. And thus seith David: "*Omnia in*
sapiencia tu fecisti"[2]—that is, "that° thou hast i-maked   *that which*
thow hast hit maad avisiliche."°   *thoughtfully*

    The Goode Ladi Mekenesse that ever maketh hire-
self iliche° lowe and under al othere schal beo sub-   *equally*
prioresse; hire schalt thou honouren and worschipen
with buxumnesse.

    A, Jhesu! blesset is that abbey.

❊   ❊   ❊

---

7. This is one of the most famous and frequently sung of hymns, commonly known by the first three
   words of the Latin as quoted here.
8. "Let all your things be done with charity," 1 Corinthians 16:14.
9. They will lose much time from the period of their reward (in heaven) and draw out their pains (in
   purgatory) unless they correct themselves.
1. "Before them all was wisdom created," Ecclesiasticus 1:4.
2. "In wisdom hast thou made them all," Psalm 104:24.

From The Castle of Love†

[*The Four Daughters of God*]

35	On Englisch Ichul° mi resun° schowen,	*I shall / argument*
	For him that con not i-knowen	
	Nouther French ne Latyn.	
	On Englisch Ichulle tellen him	
	Wherfore the world was i-wrouht,	
40	Theraftur how he° was bitauht°	*(i.e., the world) / given to*
	Adam ure° fader, to ben° his,	*our / be*
	With al the merthe of paradys,	
	To wonen° and welden° to such ende,	*dwell in / rule*
	Til that he scholde to hevene wende;°	*go*
45	And hou sone he hit for-les;°	*lost*
	And seththen,° hou hit for-bouht° wes	*afterwards / redeemed*
	Thorw° the heighe kynges Sone,	*through*
	That here on eorthe wolde come	
	For His sustren° that were to-boren°	*sisters / at odds with one another*
50	And for a prison° that was forloren,°	*prisoner (i.e., Adam) / lost*
	And hou He made, as ye schul heeren,	
	That heo° i-custe° and sauht° weren;°	*they / kissed / reconciled / were*
	And to whuche° a castel He alihte°	*which / descended*
	Tho° he wolde here for us fihte°—	*when / fight*
55	That the Marie° bodi wes—°	*Virgin Mary's / was*
	Ther He alihte and His in° ches.	*dwelling place / chose*

✻ ✻ ✻

71	Thauh° hit on Englisch be dim and derk,	*although*
	Ne nabbe° no savur° bifore a clerk,°	*nor does it have / taste / scholar*
	For lewed° men that luitel° connen°	*unlearned / little / know*
	On Englisch hit is thus bi-gonnen.°	*begun*

✻ ✻ ✻

	Foure douhtren° hedde° the kyng,	*daughters / had*
290	And to uchone° sunderlyng°	*each one / separately*
	He yaf ° a dole° of his fulnesse,°	*gave / portion / abundance*
	Of his miht and of his wysnesse,	
	As wolde bifallen° to uch° on—	*befall / each*
	And yit° was al the folnesse° on,°	*yet / fullness / unified*
295	That to himself bilay;°	*belongs*
	Withoute whom he ne mai	
	His kindom with pees° wysen,°	*peace / rule*
	Ne with rihte° hit justisen.°	*justice / govern*
	Good is to nempnen° hem° forthi.°	*name / them / therefore*
300	The furste° doughter hette° Merci—	*first / is called*

---

† Reprinted, with new glosses and punctuation, from *The Minor Poems of the Vernon MS*, ed. Carl Horstmann, EETS 98 (London, 1892), Part 1, pp. 356–69. There are several different English versions of the debate among the four daughters of God, including the early thirteenth-century *Sawles Warde*. This version (note its emphasis on English) dates from around 1300, and derives ultimately from the Anglo-Norman *Chateau d'Amour* by Robert Grosseteste, composed in the first half of the thirteenth century. Cf. *Piers Plowman*, Passus XVIII, lines 110ff.

The kynges eldeste doughter heo° is;   *she*
That other hette Soth,° iwis;°   *truth / indeed*
The thridde° soster is cleped° Right;   *third / called*
Pees hette the feorthe aplight.°   *assuredly*
305 Withouten theos foure, with worschipe°   *honor*
Mai no kyng lede gret lordschipe.
   This kyng, as thou herdest ar° this,   *before*
Hedde a thral° that dude° amis,   *servant (i.e., Adam) / did*
That for his gult strong and gret
310 With his lord was so i-vet,°   *at enmity*
That thorw besiht° of riht dom°   *legal provision / judgment*
To strong prison was i-don°   *constrained*
And bitaken° to alle his fon,°   *given / enemies*
That sore° him pyneden,° everichon;°   *sorely / tormented / everyone*
315 That of no thing heo nedden° onde°   *had not / desire*
Bote° him to habben under honde;°   *except / control*
Heo him duden° in prisun of deth,   *put*
And pyneden him sore withouten meth.°   *mercy*

De Misericordia°   Concerning Mercy

Merci that anon i-seigh;°   *saw*
320 Hit eode° hire herte swithe° neih,°   *went / very / near*
Ne mai hire no thing lengore holde;°   *restrain*
Byforen the kyng comen heo wolde
To schewen forth hire resoun
And to dilyvere the prisoun:°   *prisoner*
325 "Understond," quath heo,° "Fader myn!"   *she*
Thow wost° that I am doughter thyn,   *know*
And am ful of boxumnes,°   *humility*
Of milce° and of swetnes,   *mildness*
And al Ich habbe, Fader, of ° the.°   *from / thee*
330 I beoseche° that thou here° me,   *beg / hear*
That the [sorful°] wrecche prisoun°   *sorrowful / prisoner*
Mote° come to sum raunsum   *may*
That amidden alle his fon
In strong prison thou hast i-don.°   *put*
335 He him made agulte,° thulke° unwreste,°   *sin / that / wretched one*
And biswikede° him thorw heor° feire beheste,°   *beguiled / their / promise*
And seiden him° yif he wolde the Appel ete,   *i.e., to him*
That whon° he hedde° al i-ete,   *when / had*
He scholde habbe al the miht of Gode
340 Of the Treo° that him was forbode;   *Tree*
And begylen him therof and he° luytel roughten°—   *they / cared*
For falshede° ever-yite° he souhten.   *falsehood / still, ever*
And falshede hem i-yolde° be,   *given*
And the wrecche prisun i-sold to me!
345 For thow art kyng of boxumnes,
Of milce and of swetnes,
And I thi douhter alre° eldest,   *of all*
Over alle the othere beldest;°   *most bold*

Nevere I thi douhter neore°   *should be*
350 Bote milce toward him were.
Milce and merci he schal have,
Thorw milce Ichulle the prisun crave;
For thin owne swete pité°   *pity*
I schal him bringe to saveté°   *safety*
355 Thi milce for him I crie evermore,
And have of him milce and ore!"°   *pardon*

De Veritate°   *Concerning Truth*

Anon whon Soth this i-seigh,
Hou° Merci, hire soster, hir herte beigh°   *heart / bowed*
And wolde this thral of prisun bringe
360 That Rihte hedde° him i-demet° withouten endinge,   *had / sentenced*
Al° heo° chaunged hire mood,   *Wholly / she*
And biforen the kyng she stood:
"Fader, I the biseche, herkne to me!
I ne may forbere° to telle hit the°   *refuse / to thee*
365 Hou hit me thinketh a wonder thing
Of Merci, my suster, wilnyng,
That wolde with hire milsful° sarmon°   *merciful / sermon*
Dilivere the thral out of prison
That swithe agulte, ther Ich hit seih,[1]
370 And tolde hit to Riht that stood me neih.
Fader, Ich sigge° the° forthi: *tell / thee*
Thou ouhtes nought to heere Merci,
Of no boone° that heo bisecheth the   *request*
Bote Riht and Sooth ther-mide° be.   *there at hand*
375 And thow lovest soth and hatest lees,°   *lies*
For of thi fulnesse i-comen Ich wes;°   *was*
And eke thow art kyng rihtwys,°   *just*
And Merci° herte so reuthful° is   *Mercy's / compassionate*
That, yif heo mai save with hire mylde speche
380 Al that heo wole fore biseche,
Never shal be misdede° abouht°—   *misdeed / paid for*
And thou, kyng, schalt be douted° right nouht.   *feared*
Thou art also so trewe a kyng,
And stable of thought in alle thyng;
385 Forthi me thinketh Merci wilneth wough°   *harm*
And speken toyeynes° Right inough°   *against / (more than) enough*
For° Riht con° hym in prison bynde   *because / was able*
He oughte nevere milce to fynde—
Milce and Merci he hath forloren!—
390 He was warned therof biforen.
Whi scholde me° helpe thulke° mon   *people / this*
That nedde° of himself pité non?   *had not*
His dom he mot habbe as Soth con sugge,°   *say*
And al his misdede abugge.°"   *pay for*

1. Who very much sinned, as I saw it.

De Justicia°   *Concerning Rightful Justice*

395   Riht i-herde° this talkyng;   *heard*
      Anon heo° sted bifore the kyng: *she*
      "Thi doughtur," heo seith, "I am, I wot° bi thon,°   *know / this*
      For thou art king, riht domesmon;°   *judge*
      The beth rihte domes mitte,²
400   Alle thine werkes beth ful of witte.°   *wisdom*
      This thral of whom my sustren deeth° mene,°   *make / lament*
      Hath deservet° as at ene;°   *deserved (to be punished) / once for all*
      For in tyme, while that he freo° wes,   *free*
      He hedde with him bothe Merci and Pees°   *peace*
405   And Soth and Right he hedde bo,°   *both*
      And with his wille he wente hem fro
      And tyed hym to wraththe° and wough,°   *wrath / woe*
      To wreccheddam° and serwe inough,°   *wretchedness / sorrow*
      So that, yif Riht geth,°   *succeeds*
410   He schal evere tholyen° deth;   *suffer*
      For tho° thow him the heste° hightest,°   *when / command / commandedest*
      Thorw Soth thou him the deth dightest,°   *deemed*
      And I myself him gaf the dom,
      As sone as he hedde the gult i-don;
415   For Soth bereth witnesse therto,
      And elles nedde° I no dome i-do.   *hadn't*
      Yif he in court biforen us were,
      The dom° thou scholdest sone i-here.   *judgment*
      For Riht ne spareth for to jugge
420   Whatsoevere Soth wol sugge;
      Thorw wisdam heo° demeth alle   *she*
      As whole to his gult bifalle."
      Soth and Riht, lo° thus heo° suggeth,°   *behold / they / say*
      And this thral to dethe juggeth;
425   Never nouther ne speketh him good,
      Ne non that Merci understood
      Ac as a Mon mis-i-rad°   *badly advised*
      On uche half he is misbilad.°   *mistreated*
      Ne helpeth him nothing wherso he wende,
430   That his fo fetteth° him in uche ende   *fetches*
      And i-strupt° him al startnaked°   *stripped / naked*
      Of might and strengthe al bare i-maked;
      Him and al that of him sprong,
      He dude a theuwedam° vyl° and strong   *dominion / evil*
435   And made agulten° swithe° i-lome.°   *do wrong / very / often*
      And Riht com after with hire dome;
      Withouten Merci and Pees heo° con jugge   *she*
      Ever after° that Soth wol sugge;   *according to*
      Ne Pees mot not mid hem° be,   *them*
440   Out of londe heo° mot° fle,°   *she / must / flee*
      For pees bileveth° in no londe   *remains*
      Wher ther is werre, nuy,° and onde,°   *trouble / malice*

      2. Right judgments are with you.

Ne merci mot not among hem live,
Ac both heo° beth of londe i-drive.[3]   *they*
445 Nis ther nout° in world bileved°   *nothing / left behind*
    That nis destrued° and todreved°   *destroyed / dispersed*
    And dreynt,° forloren,° and fordemed,°   *drowned / lost / condemned*
    But eighte soulen that weren i-yemed°   *protected*
    In the schup° and that weoren heo   *ship (ark)*
450 Noe and his sones threo,
    And heore wyves that heo hedden bifore;
    Of al the worlde nas beleved more.
    Careful° herte him° oughte come°   *(a) sorrowful / to whom / to come*
    That thencheth° uppon the dredful dome.   *thinks*
455 And al hit is thorw Riht and Soth
    That withouten Pees and Merci doth.

De Pace°   *Concerning Peace*

    So that Pees a° last up-breek°   *at / came forward*
    And thus to hire Fader speek:
    "I am thi doughter saught° and some,°   *at peace / in agreement*
460 And of thi fulnesse am i-come.
    Tofore° the° my playnt I make: *Before / you*
    Mi two sustren me habbeth forsake,
    Withouten me heo° doth heore° dom,   *they / their*
    Ne merci among hem° nought ne com   *them*
465 For no thing that I mighte do.
    Ne moste Merci hem come to,
    Ne for none kunnes° fey°   *kind of / fee*
    Ne moste Ich hem come neygh,°   *near*
    Ak° that dom is al heore owen.   *but*
470 Forthi Ich am of londe° i-flowen,°   *from the land / fled*
    And wole with the° lede my lyf;   *thee*
    Ever o° that ilke° stryf   *until / same*
    That among my sustren is i-wake,
    Thorw sauhtnesse° mowe sum ende take—   *reconciliation*
475 Ac what is hit ever the bet[4]
    That Riht and Soth ben i-set°   *settled (in accord)*
    But heo° wite° wel pees?   *they / know*
    Rihtes mester° hit is and wes   *duty*
    In uche° dom pees to maken;   *each*
480 Schal I thenne beo forsaken
    Whon everiche good for me° is wrouht   *i.e., my sake*
    And to habben° me bithouht?°   *acquire / brought to mind*
    Ne he me lovede nevere to fere°   *as a companion*
    That Merci my suster nul° not here.   *would*
485 Off us foure, Fader, Ichul° telle the   *I will*
    Hou me thinketh hit oughte to be.
    Whon the foure beth togedere i-sent
    To don an evene juggement,
    And schul thorw skil alle and some

---

3. But both (peace and mercy) are driven from the land.
4. What good is it.

490 Yiven° and demen evene° dome,   *give / equal*
 Ther ne oughte no dome forth gon
 Er then the foure ben aton;°   *unanimous*
 Aton heo moten atstonden° alle   *stand*
 And loken seththen° hou dom wol falle.   *then*
495 Be° us foure this I telle: *about*
 We beoth° not alle of on spelle;°   *are / pronouncement*
 Bothe Ich and Merci,
 We beclepeth° the dom forthi;°   *appeal / therefore*
 Hit is al as Right and Soth wol deme;
500 Merci° ne me nis° hit not qweme.° *(to) Mercy / is not / pleasing*
 Withouten us ther is bale° to° breme;° *sorrow / too / grim*
 Forthi, Fader, thow nime° yeme!°   *take / heed*
 Of uche goodschipe Pees is ende,
 Ne fayleth ne weole° ther heo wol lende,° *wealth / remain*
505 Ne wisdam nis not worth an hawe°   *straw*
 Ther Pees fayleth to felawe°   *unite*
 And hose° Pees loveth withouten gabbe,° *whoso / without deception*
 Pees withouten ende he schal habbe.
 Mi word oughte ben of good reles°   *efficacy*
510 For thou art Kyng and Prince—of Pes.
 Forthi thou oughtest to here me,
 And Merci my suster that clepeth to the,
 That the thral, the prisoun,
 Mote come to sum Raunsoun.
515 Ure wille, Fader, thou do sone
 And here ure rihte bone!°   *request*
 For Merci evere clepeth° to the°   *calls / thee*
 Til that the prison dilyvered be;
 And Ichul fleon and nevere come
520 Bote my sustren ben saught° and some.°" *at peace / in agreement*
  The kynges Sone al this con heren,
 Hou his sustren hem tobeeren,°   *quarreled*
 And seigh this strif so strong awaken
 And Pees and Merci al forsaken,
525 That withouten help of His wisdome
 Ne mihten heo nevere togedere come:
 "Leove° fader," quath he, "Ich am thi sone, *Dear*
 Of thi wit and of thi wone,°   *country*
 And thi wisdam [me]° clepeth° me;° *people / call / me*
530 And so muche thou lovedest me
 That al the world for me thou wroughtest
 And so thou me in° werke [broughtest];   *to*
 For we beoth on° in one fulnesse,   *united*
 In miht, in strengthe, and in heighnesse;° *exalted position*
535 Ichulle al don that thi wille is,
 For thou art Kyng rihtwis.
 So muche, fader, Ich nyme° yeme°   *take / heed*
 Of this strif that is so breme,°   *severe*
 That for the tale that Merci tolde the
540 Ful sore the prisun° reweth me;°   *prisoner / I pity*

Forthi he reweth me wel the more
For Merci evere clepeth thin ore.°   *forgiveness*
Thou art, Fader, so milsful° kyng: *merciful*
Hire° we schul heren of ° alle thing.   *Her / i.e., above*
545 Al Ichul hire wille° don   *will I*
And sauhten° Soth and hire ful sone.°   *conciliate / soon*
Nimen Ichulle the thralles weden°   *clothes*
As Soth and Riht hit wolden and beoden,°   *bid*
And alone Ichul holde the doom,
550 As Justice ouhte to don.
And maken Ichule Pees to londe come
And Pees and Riht cussen° and be saught and some,°   *kiss / be in agreement*
And dryven out werre, nuy,° and onde,°   *trouble / malice*
And saven al the folk in londe."

*   *   *

LEGENDS OF THE VIRTUOUS HEATHEN

From John Trevisa's Translation of Higden's Polychronicon†

[*Aigolandus Rejects Christendom*]

*   *   *

De libro Turpini.[1] In a day whan trewes° was   *truce*
i-graunted [in]° either side, Aigolandus, a strong prince   *i.e., on*
of Spayne, come to Charles to be cristned, and sigh°   *saw*
al that were at the bord° realliche° i-clothed and likyn-   *table / royally*

---

† Reprinted, with new punctuation, glosses, and notes, from *Polychronicon Ranulphi Higden Monachi Cestrensis*, ed. C. Babington and R. Lumby, 9 vols, Rolls Series 41 (London 1865–1886), VI, pp. 251–53. Ranulph Higden, a monk of the Benedictine Abbey of St. Werburgh Chester, composed the *Polychronicon* in Latin in successive versions before his death in 1364. It is an attempt to provide a universal history from Creation up to Higden's own time. John Trevisa's English translation of this work was commissioned by Thomas IV, Lord Berkeley, and completed in 1387. Higden compiled his work from many sources, including the very popular *Pseudo-Turpin Chronicle*, a history of Charlemagne's wars in Spain against the Saracens (Muslims) purported (falsely) to have been written by the Emperor's chief ecclesiastic, Archbishop Turpin.
    The excerpt printed here comes from a chapter in the *Pseudo-Turpin* where the Saracen king Aigolandus, having been defeated in battle by Charlemagne, agrees to be baptized. Langland may well have had the episode in mind when writing the analogy between the degree of salvation experienced by the repentant thief at the Crucifixion and the "beggar, not at the board but . . . on the ground" (Passus XII, 198–205; and cf. Passus XIII, 21ff.). The episode was abstracted into several other didactic works to which Langland could have had access, such as John Bromyard's manual of preaching, the *Summa Praedicantium*, and Thomas Brinton's sermons (about Brinton, see the selection, p. 488.) The episode is used in those texts, as it is in the *Pseudo-Turpin*, to reinforce the lesson that faith without good works is like a body without a soul (James 2:26), but Langland's treatment is ultimately used in aid of a remarkably generous argument justifying the salvation (however low ranking) of virtuous non-Christians such as Trajan. As if he is angry at an argument such as that made by Langland, Trevisa in his own comment at the end of the episode rejects—as he does in a sarcastic addendum to Higden's favorable account of Trajan (Rolls Series 41, V, p. 7)—the possibility of a non-Christian's salvation. Cf. the mixed verdict on Trajan in the selection from *The Golden Legend*, below, p. 416.
1. From the book of Turpin (i.e., the *Pseudo-Turpin Chronicle*).

gliche° i-fedde, and sigh afer° thrittene pore men sitte   *pleasingly / afar*
on the grounde and have foule mete° and symple   *food*
withoute eny bord, and he axede° what they were. Me°   *asked / Men*
answerde hym and seide, "These thrittene beeth°   *are*
Goddes° messangers, and prayeth for us, and bringeth   *God's*
to us mynde of the nombre of Cristes disciples." "As I
see," quod Aigolandus, "youre lawe is nought° right-   *not*
ful that suffreth° Goddes messangers be° thus evel°   *allows / to be / badly*
bylad;° he serveth evel his lord that so fongeth° his   *treated / receives*
servauntes." And so he was lewedliche° offended, and   *ignorantly*
despised cristenynge, and wente hoom agen; but
Charles worschipped° afterward pore men the more.   *honored*
Trevisa: Aigolandus was a lewed goost, and lewedliche
i-meved as the devel hym taughte,[2] and blende° hym   *blinded*
that he kouthe° nought i-knowe that men schulde be   *could*
i-served as here astaat axeth.[3]

From The Golden Legend
translated by William Caxton†

[*The Story of Trajan from the Life of St. Gregory.*]

* * *

In the tyme that Trajan th'emperour regned, and on a
tyme as he wente toward a batayll out of Rome, it
happed that in his way as he shold ryde, a woman, a
wydowe, cam to hym wepyng, and sayd, "I pray the,
sire, that thou avenge the deth of one, my sone,
whiche innocently and wythout cause hath be slayn."
Th'emperour answerd, "Yf I come agayn fro the
bataylle hool° and sounde, then I shal doo justyce for   *safe*
the deth of thy sone." Thenne said the wydowe, "Syre,
and yf thou deye° in the bataylle, who shal thenne   *die*
avenge his deth?" And th'emperour sayde, "He that
shal com after me." And the wydowe sayd, "Is it not
better that thou do to me justyce and have the meryte
therof of God than another have it for the?" Thanne
had Trajan pyté, and descended fro hys hors and dyde
justice in avengyng the deth of her sone.

On a tyme, Saynt Gregory wente by the market of
Rome whyche is called the Market of Trajan, and
thenne he remembered of the justice and the other

---

2. An ill-conditioned spirit, and ignorantly disposed as the the devil induced him.
3. Provided for according to their rank.
† Text of the Cambridge University Library copy. Reprinted by permission of Cambridge University
Library (Short Title Catalogue [2nd ed.]/24873), fols. 143ᵛ–144ʳ. The original *Golden Legend* or
Lives of the Saints was compiled by Jacobus de Voragine in 1275 and became the best-known compendium of saints' lives in the later Middle Ages; William Caxton, the first printer in England, published this, his own translation, in 1483. Cf. Langland's account of Trajan, *Passus* XI and XII. Cf.
also the titular footnote to *Polychronicon*, p. 415.

good dedes of Trajan, and how he had been pyteous
and debonayr,° and was moche sorowful that he had   *gracious*
ben a paynem;° and he torned to the Chyrche of   *pagan*
Saynt Peter, wayllyng° for th'orrour° of the mes-   *wailing / the horror*
creaunce° of Trajan.   *paganism*

Thenne answerd a voys fro God, seyeng, "I have
now herd thy prayer and have spared Trajan fro the
payne perpetuell." By thys, thus as somme saye, the
payne perpetuel due to Trajan as a mescreaunt was
somdele° take away, but for al that was not he quyte°   *somewhat / redeemed*
fro the pryson of helle, for the sowle may wel be in
helle and fele ther no payne by the mercy of God. And
after it is sayd that the angele in hys answere sayd
more to thus: "By cause thou hast prayd for a
payneme, God graunteth the to chese° of two thynges   *choose*
that one which thou wylt: or thou shalt be two dayes
in Purgatorye in payne, or ellis all the dayes of thy lyf
thou shalt languysshe in seknesse."° Thenne answerd   *illness*
Saynte Gregory that he had lever° to have seknesse all   *rather*
his lyf in this world, than to fele by two dayes the
paynes of Purgatorye. And ever after he had con-
tynuelly the fevres or axces,° or the gout in hys feet.   *seizures*

* * *

From The Examination of William Thorpe†

* * *

And I [Thorpe] seide thanne thus to [Archbishop
Arundel]: "Ser,° my fadir and my modir, whoos soulis   *Sir*
God asoile° if it be his wille, spendiden moche moneye   *redeem*
in dyverse placis aboute my lore,° in entent to have me   *for my education*
a preest° of God. But whanne I cam into yeeris° of dis-   *priest / years*
cressioun I hadde no wille to be preest—and herfore°   *for this*
my freendis° weren ofte right hevy° towardis me.   *relatives / displeased*
And thanne me thoughte her° grucchynge° ayens° me   *their / criticism / of*
was so disesi° to me that I purposide herfore to have   *harmful*
laft° her companye. And whanne thei perseyveden this   *abandoned*
in me, thei spaken sumtyme ful fair and plesyng
wordis to me; but forthi° that thei myghten not make   *because*
me to consente of good herte for to be preest, thei

† Text of Oxford, Bodleian Library, MS Rawlinson c. 208, fols. 19ʳ–26ᵛ, printed by permission of the Bodleian Library. Paragraphing follows the standard edition by Anne Hudson in *Two Wycliffite Texts*, EETS 301 (Oxford, 1993). The text purports to record the examination for heresy, held on 7 August 1407, of William Thorpe, who had been arrested for Lollardy (preaching the outlawed proto-Protestant doctrines of John Wycliffe). Thomas Arundel, Archbishop of Canterbury, a fierce opponent of Lollardy, is here cast as the principal examiner, whose primary objective will have been to compel Thorpe to recant. Although it is very unlikely that Langland would have been a Lollard, or even lived to see the outlawing of the movement, his reformist yearning and defiance in the face of the authoritative claims of churchmen is not dissimilar from that of Thorpe.

spaken to me fele° tymes ful rowgh° wordis and gre- *many / abrasive*
vous, thretynge° and manassynge° me in dyverse *threatening / menacing*
maners, schewynge to me ofte ful hevy cheere.° And *mood*
thus bothe in faire maner and in greete,° thei weren *haughty*
longe tyme as me thoughte ful bisie° aboute me or° *busy / before*
that I consentid to hem to be preest. But at the laste,
whanne in this mater thei wolden no longer suffre
myn excusaciouns, but eithir I schulde consente to
hem eithir I schulde bere evere her indignacioun—
yhe,° ser, her curse, as thei leten°—I thanne, seynge° *yea / said / seeing*
this, praiede hem that thei wolden fouchesaaf ° for to *promise*
yeve° me lycence for to gon to hem that weren named° *give / renowned*
wyse preestis and of vertues° conversacioun to have *virtuous*
her counseile, and to knowe of hem the office and the
charge° of preesthode. And herto my fadir and my *duty*
modir consentiden ful gladli and thei yaven to me her
blessyng and good leve to go, and thei token° me *granted*
money to spende in this jornay.° *undertaking*

"And so thanne I wente to tho preestis whom I herde
to ben losid° or named of moost holi lyvynge, and best *famed*
taught and moost wyse of hevenly wysdom. And, ser, I
comowned° with hem to° the tyme that I persayved, *communed / i.e., until*
bi her vertues and contynuel occupatioun, that her
honest werkis° and charitable passid° her fame which *works / surpassed*
I hadde herd biforehonde° of hem. Wherefore, ser, bi *formerly*
ensaumple° of the doctryne of these men, and speciali *example*
for the goodlich° and innocent werkis whiche I per- *benevolent*
seyvede thanne of hem and in hem, after° my kun- *according to*
nynge° and my power I have bisied me than,° and *ability / then*
tanne° into this tyme to knowe in partie Goddis lawe, *undertaken*
havynge a wille and a desyre to lyve theraftir, will-
nynge° that alle men and wymmen bisieden° hem *wishing / busied*
feithfulli heraboute. If thanne, ser, either for plesynge
or displesynge of hem that ben° neither so wise ne of *are*
so greet vertuous conversacioun in my knowynge (neither bi comoun fame in ony° othir mennes knowynge *any*
of this londe as these men weren, of which I tooke my
counseile and myn enformacioun)°, I schulde now for- *instruction*
sake, thus sodeynli, schortli, and unwarned, al the
lore° that I have bisied me for this thritti° yeer and *knowledge / thirty*
more, my conscience schulde ever be herwith over-
mesure unquyetid.° And also, ser, I knowe wel that *excessively disturbed*
manye men and wymmen schulden ben herthorugh° *by this act*
greetli troublid and sclaundrid,° and, as I seide, ser, to *scandalized*
you bifore, for myn untruthe and fals cowardise many
oon schulde be putt into ful greet repreef. * * * And
thanne I were moost wrecchidli overcomen and
undon° bothe bifor God and man. *destroyed*

"But, ser, bi ensaumple cheefli of Nycol Herforde,
of Joon Purveye, of Robert Bowland—and also bi the
present doynge of Filip Repingtoun, that is now

bicome bischop of Lyncolne[1]—I am now lerned,° *instructed* as
many other ben and many mo° *more* heraftir thorugh Goddis grace schulen° *shall* be lerned, to hate and to fleen al
sich sclaundre that these forseid men cheefli have
defouliden with principali hemsilf.[2] And in that that
in hem is, thei have envenymed° *poisoned* al the chirche of
God: for the sclaundres° *scandalous* revokinge, at the Cros of
Poulis,[3] of Herforde, Purveye, and of Bowland—and
how Filip of Repintoun pursueth now Cristen peple—
and the feynynge that these dissimylen now thorugh
worldli prudence * * * wolen not ben unponyschid of
God, for to the poynt of truthe that these men
schewiden out sumtyme,[4] these wolden not now strecche forth her lyves, but, bi ensaumple eche of hem of
other,[5] as her wordis and her werkis schewen,° *show* thei
bisien hem thorugh her feynyng for to sclaundre and
to pursue Crist in his membris[6] rather than thei wolde
be pursued."

And the Archebiscop seide to me, " * * * thei ben
wise men, though thou and sich other demen° *judge* hem
unwise. Natheles,° *Nevertheless* I wiste never noon right sad man
that was ony while[7] envenymed with youre contagious
doctrine."

And I seide to the Archebischop, "Ser, I gesse wel
that these men and such othere ben now wise men as
to this world, but as her wordis sowneden° *implied* sumtyme,
and her werkis shewiden° *showed / probable* outward, it was licly° to
many men that thei hadden eernis° *foretaste* of the wisdam of
God, and thei schulden have deserved myche grace
of ° *from* God to have saved her owne soulis and manye
other mennes if thei hadden perseyvered feithfulli in
wilful povert° *poverty* and in othir symple and vertues lyvyng,
and speciali if with these forseid vertues thei hadden
contynewid° *continued / fruitful* in her bisie and frutuous° sowinge of
Goddis word * * *—but wo worth° *evil befall / greediness* fals coveitise° and
yvel counseile and tirauntrie° *tyranny* bi whiche thei and many
other men and wymmen ben lad° *led / as dupes* blynelyngis° into an
yvel eende!"

* * *

1. The identity of Robert Bowland is uncertain, but Nicholas Hereford, John Purvey, and Philip Repingdon were all Oxford associates and outspoken followers of John Wycliffe. All, however, were eventually compelled to recant, Repingdon in 1382, Hereford in 1392, and Purvey in 1401. Repington was made bishop of Lincoln in 1404, thus officially becoming an important agent in the suppression of Lollardy.
2. *fleen al sich sclaundre . . . principali hemsilf*: flee all such harmful untruth with which these above-mentioned men have defiled principally themselves.
3. St. Paul's Preaching Cross, in the churchyard of St. Paul's Cathedral, London, was a traditional site for important religious proclamations.
4. *The feynynge . . . sumtyme*: their allegedly prudent regard for this world . . . will not go unpunished by God, for as far as the extreme of integrity these men once proclaimed. . . .
5. *bi ensaumple eche of hem of other*: each following the other's example.
6. *Crist in his membris*: those with true faith in Christ.
7. *I wiste never . . . ony while*: I never knew any truly serious man that was for a moment.

Guild Ordinances of St. Peter's Church, Cornhill†

Fyrst ordeyned it is that by the same fraternité shalle be maytened° and sustened on° honest and able Preeste devoutely syngyng° in the same chirche of Seint Petre for the bretherne and the susterne of the same fraternité quyke° and deed,° and for alle Christen.

maintained / one
singing Mass

alive / dead

* * *

* * * And every Monday; Wodenesday, and Fryday vij. psalmes penitencialle, and xv°.; and letanie° withe prayers and orysouns° that longen° thereto for the lyves and the soules aforseyde, save only whenne thes psalmes and latenie been sayde in other divine service of the day; and that the same preeste be able of cunning,° that is to say, of redyng and syngyng, and of covenable° understondyng and honest of conversacioun. And that he be present and helpyng at all divine service° done withe note in the forseyde chirche for his tyme, but if° grete and resonable cause it lette,° and that yit° with leve° of the parson of the same chirche for the tyme beyng.

Gradual Psalms / litany
prayers / belong

learning, knowledge
appropriate

i.e., worship
i.e., unless / hinder
yet / permission

ij. Also it is ordeyned that this same preest shalle reherce° every brethers and Sistres soule from the tyme of his deyng° unto the yeres ende next suyng,° or do be reherced every Sonday openly atte bedes° in the forsayde chirche of Seint Petre, and specially to pray ther or do to pray for it by name, and aftir that yeres ende alwey in generalle.

commemorate
dying / following
prayers

iij. Also it is ordeyned that this same preest shalle reherce by name eche brother and sister of this fraternité quyke and dede in the pulpit aftir the offertorie eche yere atte the masse of Requiem that shalle be do in that forsaide chirche solemnly for the deede of this fraternité, withe this salme for the qwyke *Deus misereatur nostri,*[1] as the custume is in Sondays in paroche° chirches, and withe the psalme for the deede *De profundis*[2] also as custume is in paroche chirches the Sondays: And that the preest abovesaide be dwellyng in the same paroche of Seint Petre aforsaide, or

parish

† Reprinted, with new glosses and punctuation, from the *Sixth Report of the Royal Commission on Historical Manuscripts* (London, 1877), pp. 407–14. Cornhill is the area of London in which the speaker of the "autobiographical" passage of the C-text of *Piers Plowman* claims to live (see p. 364, l. 1, n.). The guild ordinances here printed were written in the fourth year of the reign of Henry IV (September 1402–September 1403), a time potentially within living memory of the period when the C-text was produced, and sufficient to suggest that the concerns articulated in both texts represent a substantial contextual intersection. A substantial ideological agreement, however, seems less secure, the source of the difference emerging largely from an agenda of corporate self-interest and comfort characteristic of medieval guilds.
1. "God be merciful unto us," Psalm 67.
2. "Out of the depths," Psalm 129.

nyghe therto: And that he take every yere for his sell-
arie° x. marcz° and clothyng ones in the yere yif it be   *salary / marks (£⅔)*
hoole clothyng or hodyng°, savyng° the state° of the   *hood/notwithstanding/*
same fraternité.   *finances*

iiij. Also it is ordeyned that thoughe this preest falle
in age or febillnisse of body or any other secknesse,
and noughte thurghe his owen mysreule qwerfore he
may noughte fulfille the charges and th'ordinances
aboveseyed, he shalle nevertheles have his salarie
alhole° als longe as he levythe. But if he be ony time,   *fully*
that god forbeyd, on notorie° lechour, or an nyghte   *a notorious*
wandrer, or oute of mesure;° or taverne or alhous°   *intemperate / alehouse*
haunter or otherwyse criminous or mysproude° or   *arrogant*
debate-maker in chirche or elleswhere, and he amend
noght his vices withinne the warnynges that the parsone or wardeyns that shall be for that time yeve° hym   *give*
therof warnyng, but he is fondyne° aftirwarde defauty   *found to be*
therinne, and therof convict, by honeste and trewe
wittenesse byfore the forsayde parsone and wardeyns
excuse hym, than shalle the parsone in presence of
these wardeyns and parisshens° of Seint Petres chir-   *parishoners*
che aforseide denunce hym privyde° of alle manere   *deprived*
righte to this aforeseide chaunterie³ and of alle thynges that longethe therto, and, withowte ony othir processe of lawe, chese° and sette inne onothir honest   *select*
and able priest in his stede: And if this preest take
upone hym ony othir office, chaunterie, or benefice,
than anon° aftir that, withe-outene ony more processe,   *immediately*
shall the parsone and wardeyns aforseide cheese and
sette in his steede an other honest and able preest.

v. Also it is ordeyned that this preest no tymes at
ones ne at diverse tymes absente hym out of Seint
Petres Cirche aboveseide overe xl. dayes in a yere, and
yit nevere withe-out leve of the parsone aboveseide
and for resonable cause, and in honeste companie
and place wele knowene, and, er° than he go out,   *before*
especified to the parson aforsaide:

* * *

* * * Also it is ordeyned that every man or woman
that be resceyved into the forseid fraternité hereaftir
shalle paie to the wardeyns of the same fraternité at
his first entré as they accordene withe the same
wardeyns, and every quarter aftir that yere iijd.° And   *three pence*
also that no manne ne womanne be resceyved into
that fraternité but that he or she be knowen of good
loose,° fame, and condicioun.   *reputation*

---

3. An endowment for the maintenance of a priest or priests to sing daily Mass for the souls of the guild.

* * *

ix. Also it is ordeyned and accorded that every brother and sister of the same fraternité byquethe in his testament summe almes as he goodly may and wille of his devocioun to the same fraternité, unto tyme that [a] Chaunterie of ij. preestes be sufficyently endowed.

* * *

xj. Also it is ordeynad that the Saterday next suyng° aftir the fest of Seint Petir and Poule, all the bretherne and sisterne of the same fraternité shulle come and assemble togedir at the forseid chirche of Seint Petir in Cornhille, in the lyveré of the same fraternité, and ther have and here *placebo et dirige*[4] solempnly saide be note, for alle the soules of the same fraternité and for alle Christen soules: And the Sonday next aftir, afore mete° tyme, they shulle been alle present in the same chirche in the lyveré aforseide, ther to here a solempne masse of Requiem for the same soules, atte wiche masse all the forseid bretherne and sisterne shulle offre for the same soules, and atte wiche masse the preest of the same fraternité openly in the pulpit shall reherce and recomende to alle good prayers by name all bretherne and sisterne quyke and deed of the forseid fraternité, and all Cristene; and in this same Sonday shall alle this fraternité have and hold a fest or a semblé° as the Wardeyns for the tyme beyng willene ordeyne; And that every persone atte that same tyme shulle paie for her lyveré als it commythe to, and here quarterage° also, if he owe any atte that tyme, and for the fest also, that is to seye, every man xij*d*. and for his wyfe viij*d*.; and everybody for his gest in the same manere, and for the assemblé as the Wardeyns resonabilly ordeyne;

following

meal

assembly

quarterly dues

* * *

xiiij. Also it is ordeyned that if ther be ony° brother or sistir of the same fraternité deed, that alle this same fraternité shulle come and assemble hem togedir in her liveré of the same fraternité atte forsaid chirche of Seint Peter, to go togedir to the chirche theras they ben warned by the wardeyns or by the bedelle° of the same fraternité, and on the morowe to come ayen° togedir on that same maner, and ther to offre° for the soule and alle cristene soules. * * *

any

constable
again
make offerings

* * *

4. See the "autobiographical" passage from the C-text, p. 365, line 45 and n.

xv. Also it is ordeyned if ther be ony brother or sister deed, and what brothir of the same fraternité wille have the compaynie of the same fraternité togethir to come to the *dirige* and to offre atte masses of the deed, the executors and frendes of the deed shall warne therof the bedelle° of the forsaide fraternité, and he shalle warne and doo° come togedir the fraternité at suche tyme in maner aforesaide; for the wiche travaille the forsaide bedelle shalle have of the frendys of the deed xij*d*. or elles as they mewe° accorde.

bailiff
cause to

may

*   *   *

xvj. Also it is ordeyned the box° and the tresour° of the same fraternité shall abyde alwey in holde° withinne the forsaide chirche of Seint Petir, and the keyes thereof shulle abide on° in the kepyng of the wardeyns of the same fraternité the wiche wardeyns be also parochenis° of Seint Petir chirche aforsaide, and other in the kepyng of the parsone of Seint Petris cherche aforsaide; and alle other keyes of the same tresour shulle abyde in the kepyng of two or iij more discrette and sadde° menne bretherne of the same fraternité duellyng in the parisshe aforseid.

lockbox / treasury
a locked place

one

parishioners

dutiful

*   *   *

xviij. Also it is ordeyned that if ther be ony persone of the same fraternité y-falle° in myschief and povereté by Godys sonde,° and nought thurghe his owene° evelle° governaunce, and may noght susteyn hymself by his labour and connynge,° nether by his aver° and frenshippe, thanne hym shalle be rewarded of the same fraternité viij*d*. to his sustenaunce, if the box may suffice therto and to the remenant° of the charges of the same fraternité; It is ordeyned netherteles that no persone shall have the almose° aforsaid, but if he have stonde° atte leste vij yere in the same fraternité and atte all tymes trewli payde his quarterages to the mayntenaunce and sustenaunce of the prestes and almose of the same fraternité in manere aforsaid, and also have honestely and goodly obeyde atte alle tymes to the wardeyns of the same fraternité for the tyme of their wardeynshippe, commyng to here° their summaunce° to feste, to assemblé to *dirige*, to offeryng, in manere abovesaide, and fulfillyng alle ther ordenaunces that bene for the honesté° and encrece° of the same fraternité

fallen
ordinance / own
ill
ability / wealth

remainder

donation
stood

hear / call

wholesomeness / growth

*   *   *

xx. Also, it is ordeyned that if it may be founde prevyd° that ony of the same fraternité be ony comune° contectour, hasardour, lechour, chider, fals

proved
common

usurour, or usethe ony othir shrewed tacches,[5] and
thanne therof be resonabilly warned and repreved
onys° twyis,° thriys,° by the wardeyns of the same fra-   *once / twice / thrice*
ternité withe vij or viij the more discrete and wele-
consciencyd mene of the same fraternité, and he thus
warnyd and reprevyd wille noghte be correctyd,
thanne he that so is founde defectyf and wille noghte
be correcked, shalle be put out of the same fraternité
for evermore by the self autorité of the wardeyns and
of the bretherne next aforsayde.

Kepe well x, and flee fro vii†

Kepe well x,[1] and flee fro vii;[2]
Rule well v,[3] and come to heven.

Mesure††

In a semely° someres tyde°	*agreeable / time*
Als° I gan° walke in a wild woude°	*as / started to / wood*
Undre a bowe° I sawe abyde°	*bough / resting*
A company of clerkes gude°	*good*
In a stody° als thai stode.	*quandry*
Thus thai gan mene° in thaire spekyng:	*declare*
"In ilke° manere of mans mode°	*every / state of mind*
Mesure° is best of alle thyng;	*Moderation*
Crist that alle thynge has undre cure°—	*keeping*
Hevene and erthe and also helle—	
Alle He made undre mesure,	
As holy writte wytenes° welle."	*witnesses*
Thou spare° no poynt of thaire spelle°	*ignore / argument*

---

5. *contectour . . . shrewed tacches:* brawler, gambler, lecher, scold, deceitful money-lender, or one who
   engages in any other wicked practices.
† From Maxwell S. Luria and Richard L. Hoffman, eds. *Middle English Lyrics,* A Norton Critical Edition (New York: W. W. Norton & Company, 1974), p. 122. Reprinted by permission of W. W. Norton & Company. Mnemonic-catechistic texts like this—texts designed to assist the laity in
   remembering key elements of the Faith—are extremely common in manuscripts from Langland's
   time: other typical examples are *The Sixtene Condiciouns of Charité, XII Degrees of Humility, Foure
   Errours, Four Tokens of Salvation, The Five Wits, Nine Virtues,* and so on (few have been published
   in modern editions, but Volume 7 of *The Manual of the Writings in Middle English* [New Haven:
   Yale UP, 1986] provides a useful guide to the variety and content of such works—see pp.
   2255–2378 and 2467–2582). So popular was such material that Langland probably saw in it a
   challenge to personal responsibility for salvation; in his personification of the Seven Deadly Sins
   in Passus V, for instance, one can detect a kind of counter-mnemonic procedure which rejects the
   notion that each sin can be understood through systematic ritual.
1. The Ten Commandments (cf. p. 369).
2. The Seven Deadly Sins.
3. The Five Wits (Senses).
†† Reprinted, with new glosses and punctuation, from *The Middle English "Harrowing of Hell" and
   "Gospel of Nicodemus,"* ed. William Henry Hulme, EETS, ES 100 (London, 1907), pp. xxx–xxxi.
   The poem was probably composed in the fourteenth century, and demonstrates a traditional opening and theme. Cf. the opening lines of *Piers Plowman,* and Passus I, lines 12–42.

Bot leve° wele in this lernynge;°   *believe / teaching*
And take this tale as I the° telle,   *thee*
That mesure is best of alle thyng.

To° litille or to gret excesse   *Too*
Bothe arne° wike and vicyous   *are*
And greve° God bothe, as I gesse,   *grieve*
For bothe the partise° arne° perillouse.   *extremes / are*
Then were a mene° fulle vertuouse   *midpoint*
And proved prisse° in prechynge;   *excellent*
And therefore bothe in hille and house,
Mesure is best of alle thynge.

God graunt that His grace so grete°   *great*
Be wele mesured tille° ilka° man,   *unto / every*
And to His grace He take hym mote°   *may*
With crafte° to kepe° hym as he kan!   *skill / watch over*

Political and Historical

THE PLAGUE, 1348–1349

THOMAS OF WALSINGHAM

On the Great Mortality in England, Now Called the "First Pestilence"†

In the year of grace 1349, which was the twenty-third year of King Edward III . . . a great mortality of humankind ran riot throughout the world, beginning in the tracts of the East and North, and concluding in such a great disaster that barely half of the people remained. Then the towns, formerly filled with people, became destitute of their inhabitants, and at such a rate did the pestilence increase in power that the living were barely able to bury the dead—truly, in certain houses of men of religion, barely two out of twenty men remained alive. It was estimated by many that barely a tenth part of humankind might have been left alive. After this pestilence a pestilence among animals followed immediately; then revenues ceased; then the land, on account of the failure of tenants, who were nowhere to be found, remained uncultivated. And such great misery followed out of these evils, that afterwards the world at no time had the ability to return to its former condition.

ROBERT OF AVESBURY

On the General Pestilence in England††

The pestilence, which first began in the land occupied by the Saracens, increased so much in power that, in the sparing of no dominion, it stretched out from that land with the scourge of sudden death to the different parts of all the kingdoms, extending northward, including as far as Scotland, destroying the major part of the people. It began in England in Dorsetshire, around the feast of St. Peter, which is called Ad Vincula, in

---

† Translated by Stephen H. A. Shepherd, from *Gesta Abbatum Monasterii S. Albani, a Thomas Walsingham, regnate Ricardo Secundo, ejusdem ecclesiae Prae centore, compilata*. Ed. H. T. Riley. 3 vols. London, 1867–1869. (Rolls Series no. 28, part IV). For documents reflecting the social, political, and economic eventualities of the Plague, 1348–1349—the cataclysmic event that is estimated to have killed off as much as half of the population—see the selections on pp. 428–30. Cf. *Piers Plowman*, Prologue, lines 83ff.

†† Translated by Stephen H. A. Shepherd from *Adae Murimuth Continuatio Chronicarum. Robertus de Avesbury De gestis mirabilibus regis Edwardi Tertii*. Ed. E. M. Thompson. London, 1889. (Rolls Series 93).

the year of the Lord 1348, and at once advancing from place to place without warning it cut down for the most part those who were healthy—of those striken in the morning it despatched many from human affairs before noon; it permitted no one whom it willed to die to live longer than three or four days. Further, there was no choice of persons (with the exception, at any rate, of a small number of rich people). In the same day twenty, forty, sixty of the dead, and indeed many times more corpses of those who had died, were brought to church burial together in the same pit at the same time. About the feast of All Saints, reaching London, daily it deprived many of their life, and increased so greatly that, from the feast of the Purification until after Easter, in the cemetery which had been then newly made near Smithfield, more than two hundred bodies of those who had died, besides the bodies which were in other cemeteries of the city, were buried daily. The grace of the Holy Spirit finally intervening, that is to say about the feast of Pentecost, it ceased in London, toward the north continuously proceeding, in which parts also it ceased, about the feast of St. Michael, in the year of the Lord 1349.

STATUTES OF THE REALM

The Statute of Labourers, 1351†

EDWARD by the Grace of God, etc. to the Reverend Father in Christ, William, by the same grace Archbishop of Canterbury, Primate of all England, Greeting. Because a great Part of the People, and especially of Workmen and Servants, late died of the Pestilence, many seeing the Necessity of Masters, and great Scarcity of Servants, will not serve unless they may receive excessive Wages, and some rather willing to beg in Idleness, than by Labour to get their Living; We, considering the grievous Incommodities, which of the lack especially of Ploughmen and such Labourers may hereafter come, have upon deliberation and treaty with the Prelates and the Nobles, and Learned Men assisting Us, of their mutual counsel Ordained:

THAT every Man and Woman of our Realm of England, of what condition he be, free or bond, able in body, and within the age of threescore years, not living in Merchandize, nor exercising any Craft, nor having of his own whereof he may live, nor proper Land, about whose Tillage he may himself occupy, and not serving any other, if he in convenient Service, his estate considered, be required to serve, he shall be bounden to serve him which so shall him require; and take only the Wages, Livery, Meed, or Salary, which were accustomed to be given in the places where he oweth to serve, the xx. year of our Reign of England, or five or six other common years next before. Provided always, that the Lords be preferred before other in their Bondmen or their Land Tenants, so in their Service to be retained:

---

† Reprinted from *Statutes of the Realm* (London, 1810–1828), 23 Edw. III, c. 5–7 (1349), vol. 1., pp. 307–309. The statute was issued by Edward III as a severe (and ultimately ineffective) response to the economic and social chaos which ensued after the excessive depopulation brought about by the Black Death of 1347–1349 (for medieval accounts of what is also known as the Plague, see pp. 427–28). The statute was originally issued in Latin.

so that nevertheless the said Lords shall retain no more than be necessary for them; and if any such Man or Woman, being so required to serve, will not the same do, that proved by two true Men before the Sheriff, or the Bailiffs of our Sovereign Lord the King, or the Constables of the Town where the same shall happen to be done, he shall anon be taken by them or any of them, and committed to the next Gaol, there to remain under strait keeping, till he find surety to serve in the form aforesaid.

ITEM, If any Reaper, Mower, or other Workman or Servant, of what estate or condition that he be, retained in any Man's Service, do depart from the said Service without reasonable Cause or Licence, before the Term agreed, he shall have Pain of Imprisonment. And that none under the same Pain presume to receive or to retain any such in his Service.

ITEM, That no Man pay, or promise to pay, any Servant any more Wages, Liveries, Meed, or Salary than was wont, as afore is said; nor that any in other manner shall demand or receive the same, upon Pain of doubling of that, that so shall be paid, promised, required, or received, to him which thereof shall feel himself grieved, pursuing for the same; and if none such will pursue, then the same to be applied to any of the People that will pursue; and such Pursuit shall be in the Court of the Lord of the Place where such Case shall happen.

ITEM, If the Lords of the Towns or Manors presume in any Point to come against this present Ordinance either by them, or by their Servants, then Pursuit shall be made against them in the Counties, Wapentakes, Tithings, or such other Courts, for the Treble Pain paid or promised by them or their Servants in the form aforesaid; and if any before this present Ordinance hath covenanted with any so to serve for more Wages, he shall not be bound by reason of the same Covenant, to pay more than at another time was wont to be paid to such Person; nor upon the said Pain shall presume any more to pay.

ITEM, That Sadlers, Skinners, White-tawers, Cord-wainers, Taylors, Smiths, Carpenters, Masons, Tilers, Shipwrights, Carters, and all other Artificers and Workmen, shall not take for their Labour and Workmanship above the same that was wont to be paid to such Persons the said twentieth year, and other common years next before, as afore is said, in the Place where they shall happen to work; and if any Man take more, he shall be committed to the next Gaol, in manner as afore is said.

ITEM, That Butchers, Fishmongers, Regrators, Hostelers, Brewers, Bakers, Pulters, and all other Sellers of all manner of Victual, shall be bound to sell the same Victual for a reasonable Price, having respect to the Price that such Victual be sold at in the Places adjoining, so that the same Sellers have moderate Gains, and not excessive, reasonably to be required according to the distance of the Place from whence the said Victuals be carried; and if any sell such Victuals in any other manner, and thereof be convict in the manner and form aforesaid, he shall pay the Double of the same that he so received, to the Party damnified, or, in Default of him, to any other that will pursue in this behalf: And the Mayors and Bailiffs of Cities, Boroughs, Merchant-Towns, and others, and of the Ports of the Sea, and other Places, shall have Power to inquire of all and singular which shall in any thing offend the same, and to levy the said Pain to the Use of them at whose Suit such Offenders shall be convict; and in case that the same Mayors and Bailiffs be negligent in doing Execution of the Premises, and thereof be convict before our Justices, by Us to be assigned, then the same Mayors and Bailiffs shall be compelled by the same Justices to pay the Treble of the Thing so sold to the Party damnified, or to any other in Default of him that will pursue; and nevertheless towards Us they shall be grievously punished.

ITEM, Because that many valiant Beggars, as long as they may live of begging, do refuse to labour, giving themselves to Idleness and Vice, and sometime to Theft and other Abominations; none upon the said Pain of Imprisonment shall, under the colour of Pity or Alms, give any thing to such, which may labour, or presume to favour them towards their Desires, so that thereby they may be compelled to labour for their necessary Living.

The Statute of Pleading, 1362†

ITEM, Because it is often shewed to the King by the Prelates, Dukes, Earls, Barons, and all the Commonalty, of the great Mischiefs which have happened to divers of the Realm, because the Laws, Customs, and Statutes of this Realm be not commonly holden and kept in the same Realm, for that they be pleaded, shewed, and judged in the French Tongue, which is much unknown in the said Realm; so that the People which do implead, or be impleaded, in the King's Court, and in the Courts of other, have no Knowledge nor Understanding of that which is said for them or against them by their Serjeants and other Pleaders; and that reasonably the said Laws and Customs the rather shall be perceived and known, and better understood in the Tongue used in the said Realm, and by so much every Man of the said Realm may the better govern himself without offending of the Law, and the better keep, save, and defend his Heritage and Possessions; and in divers Regions and Countries, where the King, the Nobles, and other of the said Realm have been, good Governance and full Right is done to every Person, because that their Laws and Customs be learned and used in the Tongue of the Country: The King, desiring the good Governance and Tranquillity of his People, and to put out and eschew the Harms and Mischiefs which do or may happen in this Behalf by the Occasions aforesaid, hath ordained and stablished by the Assent aforesaid, that all Pleas which shall be pleaded in any Courts whatsoever, before any of his Justices whatsoever, or in his other Places, or before any of His other Ministers whatsoever, or in the Courts and Places of any other Lords whatsoever within the Realm, shall be pleaded, shewed, defended, answered, debated, and judged in the English Tongue, and that they be entered and inrolled in Latin; and that the Laws and Customs of the same Realm, Terms, and Processes, be holden and kept as they be and have been before this Time; and that by the ancient Terms and Forms of the Declarations no Man be prejudiced, so that the Matter of the Action be fully shewed in the Declaration and in the Writ. * * *

---

† Reprinted from *Statutes of the Realm* (London, 1810–1828), 36 Edw. III. *Stat.* 1. c. 15, vol. 1., pp. 375–76. The statute was issued by Edward III as a response to a growing demand for the use of English, rather than the official French, in courts of law. That the document was originally written in French suggests something of the resistance to change which the statute would encounter; but the existence of the statute at all also suggests something of the power of public outcry in the period following the Black Death.

SHORTER POEMS

Pees maketh plenté†

Pees° maketh plenté;°   *peace / plenty*
Plenté maketh pride;
Pride maketh plee;°   *plea (law suit)*
Plee maketh povert;°   *poverty*
Povert maketh pees.

Bissop lorles††

Bissop° lorles°   *bishop / without learning*
Kyng redeles,°   *ill-advised*
Yung man rechles,°   *reckless, thoughtless*
Old man witles,°   *witless*
Womman ssamles:°   *shameless*
5   I swer° bi Heven Kyng,   *swear*
    Thos beth° five lither° thing.   *are / evil*

Vertues and good lyvinge is cleped ypocrisie†††

Vertues° and good lyvinge is cleped° ypocrisie;   *Virtuous / called*
Trowthe and Godis lawe is clepud heresie;
Povert and lownes° is clepud loselrie;°   *humility / wretchedness*
Trewe prechinge and penaunce is clepud folie;
Pride is clepud honesté,
5   And coveityse° wisdom;   *covetousness*
    Richesse° is clepud worthynes,   *Wealth*
    And lecherie kyndely° thing,   *a natural*
    Robberie good wynnynge,°   *success, profit*
    And glotenye but murthe;°   *mirth*
10 Envye and wraththe men clepen° rightfulnes;   *call, name*
    Slouthe men clepen nedfulnes°   *necessity*
    To norshe° mennes kynde.°   *nourish / natural strength*

---

† Reprinted, with new punctuation, from Maxwell S. Luria and Richard L. Hoffman, eds., *Middle English Lyrics,* A Norton Critical Edition (New York: W. W. Norton & Company, 1974), p. 119. Reprinted by permission of W. W. Norton & Company. This fatalistically encircling lyric is found in more than a dozen Middle English manuscripts, and in French and Latin versions dating from the late twelfth century. Note the use of alliteration and a single verb to emphasize, in a way reminiscent of Langland, the association of conditions which one might normally tend to see as dissociated. Cf. Passus XIV, lines 71ff.

†† Text of London, British Library MS Harley 913, fol. 6ᵛ, printed by permission of the British Library. The text, with slight variations, appears to have been quite popular, having been preserved in at least nine MSS dating from the thirteenth to fifteenth centuries.

††† Text of Oxford, Bodleian Library MS Bodley 416, fols. 108ᵛ–109ʳ, printed by permission of the Bodleian Library. The MS, which preserves the poem uniquely, dates from the second half of the fourteenth century. Cf. Avarice's misappropriation of language, Passus V, lines 230ff.

And thus mannes lif that shulde be holi
Is turned into cursednes.°   *i.e., wickedness*
15 Rithtwis° dom° is not dred,°   *righteous / judgment / feared*
And mercy is but scorned;
Lesinges° and fables ben clepude good lore,°   *lies / teaching*
And Cristes gospel but a chape.°   *jest*
20 And thus for defaute° of trewe techinge,   *default, lack*
Men wenden° to helle by many weies.°   *go / ways*
 The joye of hevene men setten not bi,
But al bi wordli likinge.[1]
And herefore° venjaunce God wol take   *for this*
25 On us, but yif ° we amende,°   *if / make amends*
And with sorwe° oure synne forsake   *sorrow*
Or° we hame° wende—   *before / home (i.e., to heaven)*
Whanne hit° shal be, we knowen not.   *it*

God Kepe the Kyng, and Save the Croune†

Glade° in God, call hom° youre herte,   *glad / home*
In joye and blisse youre merthe° encres,° *happiness / increase*
And kepe Goddis lawe in querte;°   *wholly*
Thes° holy tyme, lete sorwe ases;°   *this / cease*
Among oureself, God sende us pes!°   *peace*
5 Therto eche man be boun:°   *committed*
To letten° fooles of here° res,°   *hinder / their / actions*
Stonde with the kyng, mayntene the croun!

What doth a kynges crowne signyfye,
Whan stones and floures on sercle° is bent? *circlet of the crown*
10 Lordis, comouns,° and clergye   *commons*
To ben° all at on° assent—   *be / one*
To kepe that crowne—take good tent.°   *notice*
In wode, in feld, in dale, and downe,
The leste° lyge-man,° with body and rent,° *lowest / liege-man / income*
15 He is a parcel of the crowne.

What signyfyeth the stones aboute?
Richesse, strengthe, and gret bounté;
Oure townes and castels, the reme° withoute,   *realm*
They are oure stones of gret pousté.°   *power*
20 In pes° they kepe all this contré,   *peace*
Holynes, contemplacioun.
God, let hem never skaterid be,
And save the kyng, and kepe the crowne!

1. Men set the value of the joy of heaven at nothing, but set all their value on worldly pleasure.
† Text (and title) from Oxford, Bodleian Library, MS Digby 102, fols 110ᵛ–111ᵛ. Reprinted by permission of the Bodleian Library. For an edition of this and related poems from the same MS, see J. Kail, ed., *Twenty-Six Political and other Poems*, EETS 124 (London, 1904). Sometimes the poem is known by the title "God Save the King and Keep the Crown." The poem was written in 1413 after a failed conspiracy to usurp Henry V. Like Langland's work, it contemplates a traditional view of an ideal relationship among Crown, Church, and commons.

25 By-yonde the see, and° we had nought,°   *i.e., if / nothing*
    But all oure enemys so neyghe° us were,[1]   *near enough*
    Though all here gold were hider° brought,   *to here*
    I wolde set hit° at lytel store.°   *it / value*
    Oure enemys wolde coke° therfore   *do battle*
30 With ordynaunce and habergeoun,°   *armor*
    Wynne that, and wel more:
    Oure landes, oure lyves, the reme,° the crowne.   *realm*

    Yif° we among oure self debate,   *if*
    Than endeth floure° of chyvalrie;   *i.e., the best*
35 Alle othere londis that doth us hate,
    Oure feblenes wole aspye;
    On every syde they wole in hye.°   *hasten*
    The stalworthe° cast the feble a-doun;   *bold*
    Yif they with myght have maystrye,°   *victory*
40 Fro the right heire° wolde take the crowne.   *heir*

    Yif sercle and floures and riche stones
    Were eche a pece fro° other flet;°   *from / separated*
    Were the crowne broken ones,
    Hit were ful hard ayen° to knet.°   *again / knit together*
45 Avyse yow° er° ye suffre that fit;   *take heed / before*
    Amende ye, that mende mown!°   *can*
    Ye that ben wysest, cast youre wyt;
    Stonde with the kyng to kepe the crowne.

    To kepe the crowne, God graunte yow grace,
50 And let it nevere be to-broken;
    For word of wynd° lityl trespase;   *air*
    Non harm nys° don, though word be spoken.   *is not*
    Let wysdom be unloken,°   *released*
    Apert° and prevyly° to rowne.°   *openly / privately / speak*
55 For non evyll wille no man be wroken,°   *driven out*
    But stonde with right, mayntene the crowne.

    A man myghte be forborn°   *restrained*
    Fer° fro° a kynges place,   *far / from*
    Wolde make a kyng to be forsworn°   *treacherous*
60 To lette° the lawe—it most not passe!—   *hinder*
    And make hym wene° that he hath grace,   *believe*
    And holy in condicioun,
    And mayntene hym in his trespace,
    While he pyketh the stones out of the crowne.

65 A kyndom must be governed by right,
    To chastyse false° that ar aspyed.   *deceivers*
    Falsed° and Trouthe togydre wole fight,   *Falsehood*
    Til oon that other hath distroyd;
    Til Trouthe be fro treson tryed,°   *separated*

1. The principal enemies of England at this time were Scotland and, especially, France, where England claimed, and in some cases held, possession of extensive territories.

70 Shal nevere be pes in regyoun.
   In all kyngdomes that man hath gyed,°   *ruled*
   To the place of vertues, God geveth the crowne.

   Though Falsed trouthe defame,
   Trouthe secheth non hernes° to shewe his speche;   *hiding places*
75 Trouthe, of his craft thenketh° no shame;   *intends*
   He is bold alle folk his craft to teche;
   And evere by Trouthe stondes Wreche,°   *Retribution*
   For Wreche is Goddis champioun.
   Or° Wreche smyte, God be leche,°   *before / healer*
80 And save the kyng, and kepe the crowne.

   Loke° of thyng that ye bygynne;   *beware*
   Caste before how it wole ende,
   Gostly,° bodyly, what mowe° ye wynne.°   *spiritually / may / gain*
   Eche man destroyghe his best frend:
85 So dede Flaundres²—how dede it wende?°   *death / turn out*
   Of noblay° they han° lore° the sown;°   *nobleness / have / lost / renown*
   Pray we God His bowe of wraththe unbende,°   *to unbend (i.e., unload)*
   And save the kyng, and kepe the crowne.

   God yeveth° his doom° to alle kynges that be;   *gives / power of judgment*
90 As a god, in erthe a kyng hath myght.
   Holy writ byd, blissed be he
   In alle tymes that demeth ryght.
   Men do in derk, God seeth in lyght;
   Synne, morthere,° derne° tresoun,   *murder / secret*
95 Not may be hyd fro° Goddis syght.   *from*
   To ryghtwys° juge,° God yeveth the crowne.   *righteous / judge*

   That lord loveth lityl hymselve,
   That yeveth° his blisse for sorwe and woo,   *gives up*
   For the love of ten° or twelve,   *ten (people)*
100 Make alle folk his foo,
   And lese the love of God also,
   For fawte° of perfeccyone.   *lack*
   Though he had no vauntage° but of tho,°   *gain / those*
   He myghte were° a symple crowne.   *wear*

105 Eche a kyng hath Goddis power,
   Of lyf and leme° to save and spille.°   *limb / kill*
   He muste make God his partener,
   And do not his owen wille.
   For God resceyveth eche pore mannys bille,°   *petition*
110 And of here playnt,° God hereth the sowne.°   *complaint / sound*

---

2. In 1407 John, Duke of Burgundy and Flanders, arranged the murder of his rival, Louis, duke of
   Orleans, after both had sworn an oath of friendship.

Sette youre in evene skille;[3]
Counseile the kyng, to kepe the crowne.

The fadir the wanton child wole kenne,°   *instruct*
Chastyse with yerde,° and bete hit sore.   *yardstick, rod*
115 So after, the fadyr the yerde wole brenne,°   *burn*
When child is wys, and taketh to lore,°   *learning*
We han ben Goddis yerde yore,°   *in the past*
Chastysed kyngdom, castell, and towne;
Twyggis of oure yerde we have forlore.
120 God save the kyng, and kepe the crowne!

Englischemen dede maystryghes° make;   *victories*
Thurgh all the world, here word it sprong.
Cristen and hethen they mad° to quake,   *made*
Tok° and slowen° kynges strong.   *Captured / slew*
125 God let nevere werre be us among,
To lese that blo° of gret renowne,   *fame*
Ne nevere oure right be turned to wrong.
God save the kyng, and kepe the crowne!

Among oureself, yif fight be raysed,
130 Than stroye° we oure awen° nest.   *destroy / own*
That° hath victor,° wole be evel payed,   *(He) that / victory*
So many good men ben lest;°   *lost*
Yit is beter bowe° than brest.°   *bend / burst*
Eche man is bounden to resoun;
135 Ye that ben wysest, take the best—
Conseile the kyng, mayntene the crowne!

A comons myght sone be shent°   *destroyed*
Withouten kyng or governour;
And a kyng withoute rent°   *revenue*
140 Myght lightly trussen° his tresour,   *pack up*
For comons mayntene lordis honour,
Holy chirche, and religyoun—
For comouns is the fayrest flour
That evere God sette on erthely crown.

145 God, lete this kyngdom nevere be lorn°   *lost*
Among oureself, in no distance!
Other kyngdomes laughe us not to skorn,
And sey, for synne God send vengeance.
God, yeve° us space of repentance,   *give*
150 Good lyf, and devocioun;
And God, kepe in they° governance   *thy*
Oure comely kyng, and save the crowne!

3. Formulate your petition properly.

Plowman Poems

I-blessyd be Cristes sonde†

The merthe of alle this londe
Maketh the gode husbonde,°   farmer
With erynge° of his plowe.   plowing

I-blessyd be Cristes sonde,°   dispensation
5   That hath us sent in honde
Merthe and joye y-nowe.°   (more than) enough

The plowe gothe° mony a gate,°   goes down / course
Bothe erly and eke° late,   also
In wynter in the clay.

10 Aboute barly and whete,
That makethe men to swete,°   sweat
God spede the plowe al day!

Browne Morel and Gore[1]
Drawen the plowe ful sore,°   sorely, earnestly
15 Al in the morwenynge.°   morning

Rewarde hem° therfore   them
With a shefe° or more,   sheaf
All in the evenynge.

Whan men bygynne to sowe,
20 Ful wel here° corne° they knowe   their / i.e., wheat
In the mounthe of May.

Howe-ever Janyuer° blowe,   January
Whether hye or lowe,
God spede the plowe allway!°   always

25 Whan men bygynneth to wede°   weed out
The thystle fro the sede,
In somer° whan they may,   summer

---

† Text of Oxford, Bodleian Library, MS Arch. Selden B. 26, fol. 19ʳ. Printed by permission of the Bodleian Library. The poem's date of composition is held to be c.1450. The first three lines, printed in italics, constitute a refrain, and the whole was intended to be sung. About the poem's performative elements, see Rossell Hope Robbins, *Historical Poems of the 14th and 15th Centuries* (New York, Columbia UP 1959), pp. 97–98. Unlike the next selection ("God Spede the Plough," p. 437), this "plowman poem" is not satirical. Like the next selection, it belongs to a group of post-Langlandian works which have been called "plowman writings," about which see James M. Dean, ed., *Medieval English Political Writings* (Kalamazoo, Michigan: U of Western Michigan P, 1996). In some editions this poem is confusingly entitled "God Spede the Plowe."
1. I.e., the (generic) names of the two oxen pulling the plow.

God lete hem wel to spede°—   *prosper*
And longe gode° lyfe to lede,   *good*
30 All that for plowemen pray.

God Spede the Plough†

*A processe or an exortation to tendre the chargis
of the true husbondys[1]*

As I me walked over feldis° wide,[2]   *fields*
When men began to ere° and to sowe,   *plough*
I behelde husbondys,° howe faste they hide°   *farmers / hastened*
With their bestis and plowes all on a rowe.
5 I stode and behelde the bestis well drawe
To ere the londe that was so tough;
Than to an husbond I sed° this sawe,°   *said / saying*
"I pray to God, spede° wele the plough."   *prosper*

The husbondys helde up harte and hande,
10 And said, "That is nedefull for to praye!
For all the yere we labour with [the lande,]
With many a comberous° clot [of claye,]   *heavy*
To mayntayn this worlde yf that we maye,
By downe and by dale and many a slough.°   *swamp*
15 Therefore it is nedefull for to saye,
'I praye to God, spede wele the plough.'

"And so shulde of right the parson praye,
That hath the tithe shefe[3] of the londe;
For our sarvauntys we moste nedis° paye,   *necessarily*
20 Or ellys ful still the plough may stonde.
Than cometh the clerk anon at hande,
To have a shef of corne there° it growe,   *where*
And the sexten° somwhate° in his hande— *sexton / something of it*
'I praye to God, spede wele the plough.'

25 "The kyngis purviours° also they come,   *purveyors*
To have whete and otys° at the kyngis nede;   *oats*
And over that, befe and mutton,
And butter and pulleyn,° so God me spede!   *poultry*
And to the kyngis courte we moste it lede,

† Text of London, British Library, MS Lansdowne 762, fols. 5ʳ–6ᵛ. Printed by permission of the British Library. Several words that are torn away in the manuscript, indicated here in brackets, have been reconstructed following the edition of W. W. Skeat (in *Pierce the Ploughmans Crede*, EETS OS 30 [London, 1867]). The poem was composed c.1500, its use of alliteration and its use of ploughing as a focal point for social satire suggesting the influence of Langland's poem. For a useful introduction to the heritage of *Piers Plowman* in later poetry, see Anne Hudson, "Epilogue: The Legacy of *Piers Plowman*," in *A Companion to Piers Plowman*, ed. John A. Alford (Berkeley: The U of California P, 1988), pp. 251–266.
1. To show consideration to the duties of the true farmers.
2. This line appears on the side of the manuscript.
3. Who is entitled to receive a tenth part of the produce.

30 And our payment shal be a styk a bough;[4]
    And yet we moste speke faire for drede°—   *fear*
    'I praye to God, spede wele the plough.'

    "To paye the fiftene[5] ayenst our ease—
    Beside the lordys rente of our londe—
35 Thus be we shepe shorne, we may not chese,
    And yet it is full lytell understonde.
    Than bayllys° and bedellis° woll put to their hande   *bailiffs / beadles*
    In enquestis° to doo us sorwe inough,°   *inquests / more than enough*
    But yf we quite° right wele the londe—   *repay the use of*
40 'I praye to God, spede wele the plough.'

    ["Than cometh] prisoners and sheweth their nede,
    [What gret] sorowe in prison theye drye:°   *endure*
    ['To buye the kyngis] pardon we most take hede;'
    For man and beste° they woll take money;   *beast*
45 Than cometh the clerks of Saint John Frary,°   *Friary*
    And rede in their bokis mennyis namyis inough;
    And all they live by husbondrye—
    'I praye to God, spede wele the plough.'

    "Then comme the Graye Freres[6] and make their mone,°   *complaint*
50 And call for money our soulis to save;
    Then comme the White Freres and begyn to grone,
    Whete or barley they woll fayne have;
    Then commeth the Freres Augustynes and begynneth to crave
    Corne or chese, for they have not inough;
55 Then commeth the Blak Freres which wolde fayne have—
    'I praye to God, spede wele the plough.'

    "And yet, amongest other, we may not forgete
    The poore Observauntes that been so holy;[7]
    They muste amongis us have corne or mete;
60 They teche us alway to fle° from foly,   *flee*
    And live in vertue full devowtely,
    Preching dayly sermondys° inough   *sermons*
    With good examples full graciously—
    'I praye to God, spede wele the plough.'

65 "Than cometh the sompner° to have som rente,   *summoner*
    And ellis he woll teche us a newe lore,°   *knowledge*
    Saying we have lefte behynde unproved som testament,

---

4. And our payment shall be beating from a stick.
5. A tax amounting to a fifteenth of one's property.
6. The Franciscans were known as Grey Friars, the Carmelites as White Frairs, The Augustinians as
   the Austin Frairs, and the Dominicans as the Black Friars.
7. The Observants were members of a reformed branch of the Franciscan order.

And so he woll make us lese° moche more;   *lose*
Then commeth the grenewex[8] which greveth us sore,
70 With ronnyng in reragis° it doth us sorowe inough,   *arrears*
And after, we knowe nother why ne wherefore°—   *why*
'I praye to God, spede wele the plough.'

"Then commeth prestis° that goth to Rome   *priests*
For to have silver to singe at *Scala celi*;° *Ladder of heaven (a chapel in Rome)*
Than commeth clerkys of Oxford and make their
75   mone,
To her° scole hire° they most° have money;   *their / fees / must*
Then commeth the tipped-staves° for the Marshalse,[9] *constables*
And saye they have prisoners mo than inough;
Then commeth the mynstrellis° to make us gle°— *minstrels / entertainment*
80 'I praye to God, spede wele the plough.'

"At London also yf we woll plete,°   *plead*
We shal not be spared, good chepe nor dere.°   *expensive*
Our man of lawe° may not be forgete,°   *lawyer / forgotten*
But he moste have money every quartere;
85 And somme comme begging with the kyngis charter,
And saye, 'bisshoppis have graunted ther-to pardon
     inough'—
And wymen° commeth weping on the same maner—   *women*
'I praye to God, spede wele the plough.'"

And than I thanked this good husbond,
90 And prayed God the plough to spede,
And all tho that laboreth with the londe,
And them that helpeth them with worde or dede.
God give them grace such life to lede,
That in their concience maye be mery inough,
95 And heven blisse to be their mede°—   *reward*
And ever I praye, "God spede the plough."

London Lyckpeny†

To London once my stepps I bent,°   *directed*
Where trouth in no wyse° should be faynt;°   *way / feigned*
To Westmynster-ward° I forthwith went, *i.e., toward Westminster*

8. A notice of a fine, sealed with the green wax seal of the Exchequer.
9. The Marshalsea was a combined court and prison in London.
† Text of London, British Library, MS Harley 367, fols. 126ʳ–127ʳ. Printed by permission of the British Library. This poem, composed in the first half of the fifteenth century, resonates well with the often pejorative accounts of law and metropolitan life found in *Piers Plowman* (beginning with the Prologue, lines 211–216). The standard edition of this version of the poem is by Eleanor Hammond, in *English Verse between Chaucer and Surrey* (Durham: Duke UP, 1927), pp. 238–239 and 476–478. A "lyckpeny" is that which "licks up" the pennies.

To a man of law to make complaynt.
5 I sayd, "For Marys love, that holy saynt,
Pyty the poore that wold proceede"°—   *litigate*
But for lack of mony I cold not spede.°   *succeed*

And as I thrust the prese° amonge   *crowd*
By froward° chaunce° my hood was gone!   *unlucky / accident*
10 Yet, for all that, I stayd not longe,
Tyll at the Kynges Bench[1] I was come.
Before the judge I kneled anon,
And prayd hym for Gods sake to take heede—
But for lack of mony I myght not speede.

15 Beneth them sat clarkes° a gret rout,°   *clerks / company*
Which fast dyd wryte by one assent;
There stood up one and cryed about
"Richard, Robert, and John of Kent!"
I wyst° not well what this man ment;   *knew*
20 He cryed so thycke there in dede—
But he that lackt mony myght not spede.

Unto the Common Place I yode thoo,[2]
Where sat one with a sylken hoode.[3]
I dyd hym reverence for I ought to do so,
25 And told my case as well as I coolde,
How my goode were defrauded me by falshood.
I gat not a "mum"°of his mouth for my meed°—   *i.e., word / reward*
And for lack of mony I myght not spede.

Unto the Rolls[4] I gat° me from thence   *got*
30 Before the clarkes of the Chauncerye,[5]
Where many I found earnyng of pence;
But none at all once regarded mee.
I gave them my playnt° uppon my knee;   *complaint*
They lyked it well, when they had it reade—
35 But lackyng mony I could not be sped.°   *i.e., assisted*

In Westmynster Hall I found out one
Which went in a long gown of raye.[6]
I crowched and kneled before hym anon—
For Maryes love, of help I hym praye.
40 "I wot not what thou meanest," gan° he say;   *did*
To get me thence he dyd me bede°—   *command*
For lack of mony I cold not speede.

---

1. The King's Bench was one of the three courts of common law in London; the King's Bench normally heard criminal cases; the Court of Common Pleas normally heard civil actions; the Exchequer normally handled the financial concerns of the court.
2. Unto the Court of Common Pleas I then went.
3. Silk hoods were worn by sargeants at law; that is, by lawyers.
4. The office of Chancery records.
5. The Chancery acted as a court of appeals.
6. According to Hammond, "Ray, a striped cloth, was much worn by lawyers."

Within this hall, nether rych nor yett poor
Wold do for me ought,° although I shold dye;   *anything*
45 Which seing, I gat me out of the doore,
Where Flemynges[7] began on me for to cry,
"Master, what will you copen° or by?°   *purchase / buy*
Fyne felt hattes, or spectacles to reede?
Lay down your sylver, and here you may speede!"

50 Then to Westmynster Gate I presently went,
When the sonn was at hyghe pryme.°   *i.e., noon*
Cookes to me they tooke good entent,
And profered me bread with ale and wyne,
Rybbs of befe,° both fat and ful fyne—   *beef*
55 A fayre cloth they gan forto sprede—
But wantyng mony I myght not speede.

Then unto° London[8] I dyd me hye,°   *i.e., into / hasten*
Of all the land it beareth the pryse;°   *carries the prize (as the best)*
"Hot pescodes!"° one began to crye,   *peapods*
60 "Strabery rype!" and "Cherryes in the ryse!"°   *branch*
One bad me come nere and by some spyce;
Peper and safforne° they gan me bede°—   *saffron / offer*
But for lack of mony I myght not spede.

Then to the Chepe[9] I gan me drawne,°   *go*
65 Where mutch° people I saw forto stand;   *many*
One ofred me velvet, sylke, and lawne;°   *linen*
Another he taketh me by the hande:
"Here is Parys thred, the fynest in the land!"
I never was used to such thynges in dede—
70 And wantyng mony I myght not spede.

Then went I forth by London stone,
Throughout all Canwyke[1] streete;
Drapers mutch° cloth me offred anone.   *much*
Then comes me one, cryed, "Hot shepes feete!"
One cryde, "Makerell!"—"Ryshes° grene!" another gan   *rushes*
75   greete;°   *cry*
On bad° me by° a hood to cover my head—   *bade / buy*
But for want of mony I myght not be sped.

Then I hyed° me into Estchepe:[2]   *hastened*
One cryes, "Rybbs of befe, and many a pye!"

7. Inhabitants of Flanders, the Flemings came to England to further the wool trade, eventually creating resentment in England for their skill in cloth-making.
8. According to Hammond, "Our countryman crossed LongDitch after leaving Westminster Hall by
the gate, walked by the White Hall along the Strand, entered the City through Ludgate, and passed
along Fleet Street to St. Paul's and the west end of Cheapside."
9. Cheapside was one of the largest market areas of London.
1. Candlewick Street, one of the wards of the city.
2. Eastcheap contained a number of market stalls.

80 Pewter pottes they clattered on a heape;
    There was harpe, pype, and mynstralsye.
    "Yea, by cock!—Nay, by cock!"³ some began crye;
    Some songe of Jenken and Julyan for there mede°—   reward
    But for lack of mony I myght not spede.

85 Then into Cornhyll⁴ anon I yode°   went
    Where was mutch stolen gere° amonge;   goods
    I saw where honge myne owne hoode
    That I had lost amonge the thronge.
    To by° my own hood I thought it wronge—   buy
90 I knew it well as I dyd my Crede°—   Creed
    But for lack of mony I coulde not spede.

    The taverner tooke mee by the sleve:
    "Sir," sayth he, "wyll you our wyne° assay?"°   wine / try
    I answerd, "that can not mutch me greve;
95 A peny can do no more then it may."
    I drank a pynt, and for it dyd paye;
    Yet sore a-hungerd from thence I yede°—   went
    And wantyng mony I colde not spede.

    Then hyed I me to Belyngsgate,⁵
100 And one cryed, "Hoo! go we hence!"
    I prayd° a bargeman, for Gods sake,   begged
    That he wold spare me my expence.
    "Thou scapst° not here," quod he, "under .ii. pence; escape
    I lyst° not yet bestow my almesdede!"°   wish to / gift of alms
105 Thus lacking mony I could not speede.

    Then I convayd me° into Kent,   betook myself
    For of the law wold I meddle no more,
    Because no man to me tooke entent;
    I dyght° me to do as I dyd before.⁶   set myself
110 Now Jesus that in Bethlem was bore,
    Save London, and send trew lawyers there mede°—   reward
    For whoso wantes mony, with them shall not spede.

3. *Cock*: a euphemism for God.
4. Cornhill was another large market area of London; for more on this area, see n. 1, p. 364.
5. One of the city's gates.
6. Another version of this poem appears in MS Harley 542, where the narrator returns to his accustomed work of plowing.

From Symonye and Covetise†

* * *

Trewthe was somtyme redy fore pouer° men to speke,	*poor*
And now the pouer goun aldoun—God almyghti hem wreke![1]	
For Pride and Covetise gyvet° overal jugement	*render*
And tornethe the lawe op-so-down,° so the pouer is	*upside-down*
schent°	*ruined*
95 [Al clene].°	*utterly*
Noman tellet be° Trewthe more than of a bene.°	*values / bean*

For tho that han al the wel in fright and in [feld,][2]	
Bothe erl and baroun and a knyght of o cheld,°	*with a coat of arms*
Al they beth swore Holy Chirche holde to righte;	
Therfore was ordre of knyt math° for Holy Chirche to	*instituted*
100 fighte,	
Sans faile°—	*Without doubt*
And now they [beth] the ferste men that wil hit° assaile.°	*it / attack*

They make strout° and strountnesse° that scholde be	*strife / foolishness*
pes.°	*peace*
They scholde go to the Holy Lond and mak ther here	
res,°	*assault*
And fighte for the Holy Cross and schew° ordre° of	*display / proper role*
105 knyght,	
And wreke° Jhesu Crist, with suerd and launce to fight—	*avenge*
And scheld.	
Ac now they beth leouns in halle and haris° in the	*hares (i.e., cowards)*
feld.°	*battlefield*

Knyghtes aghte for to were wedes in here manere,	
110 After that here ordre wolde, as wel as a frere.[3]	
Now they beth disgiseth and grislich° y-dight,°	*grotesquely / dressed*
And unethe° schal me knowe now a gleman° fro a	*with difficulty / minstrel*
knyght,	
Wel nye.°	*very nearly*
So his dever dryve a-doun, and Pride risith an hye.[4]	

† Text of Oxford, Bodleian Library, MS Bodley 48, fols. 325ᵛ–328ᵛ, printed by permission of the Bodleian Library. Emendation and line numbering are modeled on the edition by Thomas W. Ross, "On the Evil Times of Edward II," *Anglia* 75 (1957) 173–93; damaged or illegible text is supplied from versions of the poem found in Edinburgh, National Library of Scotland, MS Advocates 19.2.1 and Cambridge, Peterhouse, MS 104. The poem predates *Piers Plowman* by as much as fifty years. Sometimes it is also entitled "The Simonie" or "A Satire of Edward II's England." *Symonye*: simony, the sin of buying and selling ecclesiastical pardons, offices, or rewards (cf. Acts 8:18–19, though not a theme of the present selection). *Covetise*: covetousness.
1. And now the poor are being oppressed—God almighty avenge them!
2. For those who hold all the wealth in forest and country (i.e., landowners).
3. Knights ought to wear clothing (i.e., armor) for its proper purpose, according to the proper role of their order—just as friars do.
4. So is proper duty suppressed, and Pride takes over.

115 Thus is the ordre of knyghtes y-torneth op-so-doun.
Also wel can a knyght chide as a scolde° in a toun;   *abusive woman*
They scholde be as hende° as lady of londe.°   *noble / landed status*
To speke al maner of rybawdrie° now wil no knyght   *obscenity*
    wonde°   *cease*
        For schame,
And thus is knyghtschip a-cloyd° and almest°   *encumbered / almost*
    fot-lame.°   *crippled*

                        *   *   *

And thes atornés° in contré, they gete silver fore noght;°   *attorneys / nothing*
200 They make men begynne ple° that never had it thoght,°   *a lawsuit / intended*
But whanne they come to the ryng, hoppe yif they
    conne.[5]
Al that ever they mow° gete, they thenke hem y-wonne°   *may / earned*
    [With skyle],
Ne trust no man to men; they beth fals in gyle.

                        *   *   *

Than began beggeris to bolde° that erst° bigan to   *be emboldened / formerly*
    schrynke,
And° al that ever they myghte gete fore to frete° and   *i.e., and get / devour*
260   drynke;
So fore no schepe° that falleth° whiles enyman may lyve,   *wages / avail*
Som ther beth° that no thrifte wil opon hem clyve°   *are / cling*
    Olyve.°   *while alive*
While eny goth° ale is in londe, wil they never tryve.°   *good / thrive*

And thow men threte hem to the derthe that hath
265   slawe so fele
And bidde hem thenke ther-opon, hit nys bot duele,[6]
Fore right also as hit is gete, hit schal ford° als yerne°   *go forth / quickly*
At cheker° and at peny-prikke-thrie;° they fynde   *checkers / a penny game*
    taverne
    [Ful son].°   *soon*
Of here wombe° thei make here° God, fore other have   *belly / their*
270   they [non].

But thus Pride ros° ageyn° Hordon° and Glotonye   *eft / beside / Whoredom*
And han° geten° other to to° hem, Falsnesse and   *had / gotten / two more with*
    Trecherye;
The sone wile begile the father, and the doghter the
    mother,
So ther is no trewthe, ne no man loveth other
275   A fyn—°   *in the end*
And in this we beth worse than Jwe or Sarsyn.

_____

5. They will make them join the dance (i.e., come to trial) without counsel.
6. Even though men warn them about the famine that has slain so many and bid them think about
    it, nothing but grief comes of it.

* * *

Al wite° we wel hit is our gilt, the wo that we beth   *know*
355   inne,
But no man knowet that hit is fore his owe° synne;   *own*
Everich witeth other the wrecche and the wow,[7]
But wolde ech man knowe himself, al were goth ynow
       Y-wroght.[8]
But now can ech man deme° other, and hymself right   *judge*
       noght.

* * *

Hit is rewthe° to speke therof-ho-so° right durst [deme]—   *pity / whosoever*
Of bedeles° and of bayleffes° that hath the townes to   *beadles / bailiffs*
       [yeme],°   *care for*
375 That suffer such falsnesse reyne in breth and ale,[9]
And thow the pouer° hem pleyne,° ne mow they get no   *poor / cry to them*
       bale,°   *release*
[I wen]°—   *believe*
And haulf is stole that they take of wretchethe° pouer   *wretched*
       men.

A sely° workman in a toun that lyve in [trewthe fre]   *innocent*
380 And hath a wif or children, peraunter° to° or thre,   *two / possibly*
He sueteth° many a suetes drope and swynk° he never   *sweats / labors*
       so sore
Al day fore a peny, or fore a peny more
       Be cas,°   *perhaps*
At eve whan he setteth° hit, half is stole, alas.   *i.e., counts*

385 Thes bakers and this brewers beth so bold in here yifte°   *bribes*
That fore a litel mercyment° or fore a symple gifte,   *fine*
On may fore xii d. at a court do xl[ti] schilli[n]gwerd
       [schame];[1]
But howsoever hit falle, the pouer han al the grame°   *harm*
       At [mele].°   *meal*
Now God amende pouer men that can wel dight° and   *dig*
390   dele.°   *delve*

That riot reyneth now in londe everiday more and
       [more],
The lordis beth wel apaith° therwith and listneth to   *satisfied*
       here° [lore];°   *i.e., the beadles' / account*
But of the pouer mannes harm, therof is now no
       speche.

---

7. Each person ascribes to the other the wretchedness and the woe.
8. Everything would be made well enough.
9. Who allow such deceit to reign in the selling of bread and ale (cf. Passus V.218; XIII. 358).
1. One may for twelve pence at court do forty shillings' worth of injury.

This bondes warien[2] and widous wepen and crie to
    God for [wreche]°   *vengeance*
395 So fast—
How myghte hit be but such men mystymeth° ate last?   *suffer misfortune*

Fore al is long on lordis that suffre thus hit go;[3]
They scholde mayntene the porayle,° and they do noght   *poor*
    therto,
But take methe° and sle° the folc inasmoche as they [may].   *bribes / slay*
400 The pore han here her° purgatorie; the riche kepe her day   *their*
    [In helle],
That so scorneth God and hise,° can I non other telle.   *his (poor)*

*   *   *

But Lord, fore that blisseth bloth° that ran out of thi   *blood*
    side,
410 Graunt us rightfol lif to lede wile we here abide,
So that we mow oure giltis knowe° with sorwe and   *acknowledge*
    schrifte° of mouthe.   *confession*
And ever to serve God the bet,° for that I haf yow seith,°   *better / said*
    nowthe°   *now*
    Y-told,°   *finished*
And come to Hym that fore us was to the Jwes sold.

Explicit° *Symonie and Covetise*   *(Here) ends*

Longer Poems

From Wynnere and Wastoure†

Here begynnes a tretys and god schorte refreyte bytwixe Wynnere and Wastoure[1]

Sythen° that Bretayne was biggede° and Bruyttus it   *since / built /*
    aughte,°[2]   *conquered*
Thurgh the takynge of Troye with tresone withinn,[3]
There hathe selcouthes° bene sene in seere° kynges   *wonders / various*
    tymes,

---

2. These husbandmen curse.
3. All is due to lords who allow it to happen this way.
† Text of London, British Library, MS Additional 31,042, fols. 176ᵛ–183ᵛ. Printed by permission of the British Library. The poem was composed in the third quarter of the fourteenth century, possibly as early as 1353, and is likely to predate *Piers Plowman*. The poem's allegorical satire of contemporary social conditions—especially the economic turmoil that ensued under the reign of Edward III, in part due to the Hundred Years' War, in part due to the Black Death—is often compared to *Piers Plowman*. The standard edition of *Wynnere and Wastoure* is by Stephanie Trigg, EETS 297 (Oxford, 1990).
1. Here begins a treatise and a good short debate between Winner and Waster.
2. A number of alliterative poems open with reference to Brutus (the legendary great grandson of Aeneas) as the founder of Britain. The legend has its orgins in Geoffrey of Monmouth's *Historia Regum Britanniae* ("History of the Kings of Britain," written c. 1137).
3. Through the taking of Troy because of treason within.

Bot never so many as nowe by the nyne dele.°   *ninth part*

5 For nowe alle es° witt and wyles° that we with delyn,°   *is / wiles / deal with*
Wyse wordes and slee,° and icheon° wryeth° othere.   *sly / each / obscures*
Dare never no westren wy° while this werlde lasteth   *person*
Send his sone southewarde to see ne° to here,°   *nor / hear*
That he ne schall holden byhynde when he hore eldes.[4]

10 Forthi° sayde was a sawe° of Salomon the wyse—   *thus / proverb*
It hyeghte° harde appone° honde, hope I no nother°—   *hastens / upon / other*
When wawes° waxen schall wilde and walles bene doun,   *waves*
And hares appon herthe-stones schall hurcle° in hire   *crouch*
   fourme,°   *lairs*
And eke° boyes of blode° with boste and with pryde, *also / churls of low rank*
15 Schall wedde° ladyes in londe° and lede hem at will, *marry / of landed status*
Thene dredfull Domesdaye it draweth neghe° aftir.   *near*
Bot whoso sadly° will see and the sothe° telle,   *soberly / truth*
Say it newely° will neghe° or es neghe here.   *soon / come near*
Whylome° were lordes in londe that loved in thaire°   *once / their*
   hertis°   *hearts*
20 To here° makers of myrthes that matirs° couthe° fynde, *hear / subjects / could*
And now es no frenchipe° in fere° bot fayntnesse of hert, *friendship / company*
Wyse wordes withinn that wroghte° were never,   *made*
Ne redde° in no romance that ever renke° herde.   *read / man*
Bot now a childe appon chere,° withowtten chyn-   *in appearance*
   wedys,°   *beard*
That never wroghte° thurgh witt thries° wordes   *composed / three*
   togedire,
25 Fro he can jangle als° a jaye° and japes° telle,   *as / bluejay / jokes*
He schall be levede° and lovede and lett of° a while *believed / esteemed for*
Wele more than the man that made it hymselven.
Bot, never-the-lattere,° at the laste when ledys° bene *nevertheless / men*
   knawen,
Werke° wittnesse will bere who wirche kane beste.   *poetic work*

30 Bot I schall tell yow a tale that me° bytyde° ones *to me / happened*
Als I went in the weste, wandrynge myn one,°   *on my own*
Bi a bonke° of a bourne;° bryghte was the sone   *bank / stream*
Undir a worthiliche° wodde° by a wale° medewe: *attractive / wood / pleasant*
Fele° floures gan folde° ther° my fote steppede.   *many / unfold / where*
35 I layde myn hede one ane hill ane hawthorne besyde;
The throstills° full throly° they threpen° togedire, *thrushes / boldly / competed*
Hipped° up heghwalles° fro heselis° tyll othire, *hopped / woodpeckers / hazels*
Bernacles with thayre billes one barkes thay roungen,[5]
The jay janglede one heghe,° jarmede° the foles.° *high / chirped / birds*
40 The bourne full bremly° rane the bankes bytwene;   *swiftly*
So ruyde° were the roughe stremys and raughten° so *rough / reached*
   heghe
That it was neghande° nyghte or° I nappe myghte, *approaching / before*
For dyn of the depe watir and dadillyng° of fewllys.° *chattering / birds*

4. That he (the son) will not hold himself back (i.e., at home) when he (the father) grows old and gray.
5. Barnacle geese peck with their beaks on the bark of trees.

45 Bot as I laye at the laste than lowked° myn eghne,°   *closed / eyes*
 And I was swythe° in a sweven° sweped belyve.°   *at once / dream / quickly*
 Me thoghte I was in the werlde, I ne wiste° in whate   *know*
  ende,
 One a loveliche lande° that was ylike° grene,   *clearing / all over*
 That laye loken° by a lawe° the lengthe of a myle.   *surrounded / hill*
 In aythere holte° was ane here° in hawberkes° full   *wood / army / armour*
50 brighte,
 Harde hattes appon hedes and helmys° with crestys;   *helmets*
 Brayden° owte thaire baners, bown° for to mete,   *unfurled / prepared*
 Schowen° owte of the schawes,° in schiltrons° thay   *rushed / woods / phalanxes*
  felle,
 And bot the lengthe of a launde° thies lordes bytwene.   *field*
55 And alle prayed for the pese till the prynce come,
 For he was worthiere in witt than any wy° ells   *person*
 For to ridde and to rede° and to rewlyn° the wrothe° *counsel / control / angry*
 That aythere here appon hate had untill othere.[6]
 At the creste of a clyffe a caban was rerede,
60 Alle raylede° with rede° the rofe° and the sydes,   *decorated / red / roof*
 With Ynglysse besantes° full brighte, betyn of golde,   *coins*
 And ichone gayly umbygone with garters of inde,[7]
 And iche a gartare of golde gerede° full riche.   *decorated*
 Then were ther wordes in the webbe werped° of he,°   *woven / high*
65 Payntted of plunket,° and poyntes° bytwene,   *light blue / points*
 That were fourmed full fayre appon fresche lettres,
 And alle was it one sawe appon Ynglysse tonge,
 "Hethyng° have the hathell° that any harme thynkes."[8]   *shame / knight*
 Now the kyng of this kythe° kepe hym Oure Lorde!   *nation*

                    * * *

85 And als I waytted withinn I was warre° sone   *aware*
 Of a comliche° kynge crowned with golde.   *attractive*

                    * * *

 Bot than kerpede° the kynge, sayd, "Kythe° what ye   *spoke / make known /*
  hatten°   *are called*
 And whi the hates° aren so hote youre hertis bytwene.   *hatreds*
220 If I schall deme° yow this day, dothe° me to here."   *judge / allow*
 "Now certys, lorde," sayde that one, "the sothe for to
  telle,
 I hatt Wynnere, a wy that alle this werlde helpis,
 For I lordes cane lere° thurgh ledyng of witt.   *teach*
 Thoo that spedfully° will spare° and spende not to   *profitably / save*
  grete°   *too much*
225 Lyve appon littill-whattes,° I lufe hym the bettir.   *small amounts*
 Witt wiendes° me with, and wysses° me faire;   *goes / guides*

---

6. That either army in hatred had for the other.
7. And each one gaily surrounded with fastenings of blue.
8. This line is a translation of the French motto of the Order of the Garter, *Honi soit qui mal y pense*.
 Founded circa 1348 by Edward III, this chivalric order consisted of the king and twenty-six knights,
 each of whom wore a blue and gold garter symbolizing their loyalty to one another.

Aye, when gadir° my gudes° than glades myn hert. *increase / goods*
Bot this felle° false thefe that byfore yowe standes *wicked*
Thynkes to strike or° he styntt° and stroye° me for *before / stops / destroy*
    ever.
230 Alle that I wynn thurgh witt he wastes thurgh pryde;
I gedir, I glene, and he lattys goo sone;
I pryke° and I pryne,° and he the purse opynes. *sew / stitch*
Why hase this cayteffe° no care how men corne sellen? *wretch*
His londes liggen° alle ley,° his lomes° aren solde, *lie / untilled / tools*
235 Downn bene his dowfehowses,° drye bene his poles;° *dovecots / pools*
The devyll wounder one the wele he weldys at home,[9]
Bot° hungere and heghe° howses and howndes full *nothing but / high*
    kene.
Safe a sparthe° and a spere sparrede° in ane hyrne,° *ax / shut up / corner*
A bronde° at his bede-hede, biddes he no nother *sword*
240 Bot a cuttede capill° to cayre° with to his frendes. *gelding / ride*
Then will he boste with his brande and braundesche
    hym ofte,
This wikkede weryed° thefe that Wastoure men calles, *accursed*
That if he life may longe this lande will he stroye.° *destroy*
Forthi deme us this daye for Drightyns° love in heven *the Lord's*
To fighte furthe with oure folke to° owthire° fey° *until / both of us / dead /*
245   worthe."° *comes to be*
"Yee, Wynnere," quod Wastoure, "thi wordes are hye.° *arrogant*
Bot I schall tell the° a tale that tene° schall the better. *you / vex*
When thou haste waltered° and went° and wakede alle *tossed / turned*
    the nyghte,
And iche a wy in this werlde that wonnes° the° abowte, *dwells / thee*
And hase werpede° thy wyde howses full of wolle
250   sakkes— *filled*
The bemys benden at the rofe, siche bakone° there
    hynges,° *bacon / hangs*
Stuffed are sterlynges° undere stelen bowndes°— *silver coins / bonds*
What scholde worthe° of that wele° if no waste come? *become / wealth*
Some rote, some ruste, some ratons° fede.[1] *rats*
Let be thy cramynge of thi kystes° for Cristis lufe of *chests*
255   heven!
Late the peple and the pore hafe parte of thi silvere;
For if thou wydwhare° scholde walke and waytten° the *far and wide / seek*
    sothe,
Thou scholdeste reme° for rewthe,° in siche ryfe° bene *weep / pity / plenty*
    the pore.
For and° thou lengare° thus lyfe, leve° thou no nother, *if / longer / believe*
Thou schall be hanged in helle for that thou here
260   spareste;° *hoard*
For siche a synn haste thou solde thi soule into helle,
And there es ever wellande° woo,° worlde withowtten *boiling / woe*
    ende."
"Late be thi worde, Wastoure," quod Wynnere the riche;

9. The devil may wonder at the wealth that he wields at home.
1. For this line and following see Matthew 6:19–21 and Matthew 25:31–46.

"Thou melleste° of a mater, thou madiste it thiselven.   *speak*
With thi sturte and thi stryffe thou stroyeste up my
265   gudes²
In playinge and in wakynge in wynttres nyghttis,
In owttrage,° in unthrifte,° in angarte° pryde.   *outrage / extravagance / arrogant*
There es no wele° in this werlde to wasschen thyn   *wealth*
          handes
That ne es gyffen° and grounden° are° thou it   *bestowed / established / before*
          getyn have.
270   Thou ledis° renkes° in thy rowte wele rychely attyrede;   *lead / men*
Some hafe girdills° of golde that more gude coste   *waistbands*
Than alle the faire fre londe that ye byfore haden.
Ye folowe noghte youre fadirs that fosterde yow alle,
A kynde herveste to cache and cornes to wynn
For the colde wyntter and the kene with gleterand
275   frostes,
Sythen° dropeles drye° in the dede monethe.°   *then / drought / i.e., March*
And thou wolle to the taverne, byfore the tonne-hede,°   *spigot*
Iche beryne° redy with a bolle° to blerren° thyn eghne,   *man / bowl / blear*
Hete° the° whatte thou have schalte and whatt thyn   *order / thee*
          hert lykes,
280   Wyfe, wedowe, or wenche that wonnes° there aboute.   *dwells*
Then es there bott "fille in" and "feche forthe,"
          florence to schewe,³
"Wee hee," and "worthe up," wordes ynewe.°   *enough*

                    *   *   *

"Yee, Wynnere," quod Wastoure, "thi wordes are vayne.
295   With oure festes° and oure fare we feden the pore;   *feasts*
It es plesynge to the Prynce that paradyse wroghte.
When Cristes peple hath parte, Hym payes° alle the   *it pleases*
          better
Then here ben hodirde and hidde and happede in
          cofers,⁴
That it no sonn may see thurgh seven wyntter ones,
300   Owthir freres it feche when thou fey worthes,⁵
To payntten with thaire pelers° or pergett° with thaire   *pillars / plaster*
          walles.

                    *   *   *

Bot than this wrechede Wynnere full wrothely° he lukes,°   *angrily/looks*
325   Sayse, "This es spedles° speche to speken thies wordes.   *unprofitable*
Loo! this wrechide Wastoure, that wydewhare° es   *far and wide*
          knawenn,°   *known*
Ne es nothir kaysser,° ne kynge, ne knyghte that the°   *caesar / thee*
          folowes,

---

2. With your quarreling and strife you destroy my goods.
3. Then is there but "fill up" and "fetch it forth," to make you show your money.
4. Than if goods be covered up, hidden, or hoarded in chests here.
5. Or friars receive it when you die (Friars were often left goods in wills).

Barone, ne bachelere, ne beryn° that thou loveste,   *man*
Bot foure felawes or fyve, that the° fayth° owthe,°   *thee / allegiance / owe*
And he schall dighte° thaym to dyne with dayntethes°   *summon / delicacies*
330   so many
That iche a wy° in this werlde may wepyn° for sorowe."   *man / weep*

*   *   *

"If fewlis° flye schold forthe and fongen° be never,[6]   *fowls / caught*
385 And wild bestis in the wodde wone al thaire lyve,
And fisches flete° in the flode, and ichone ete other,   *swim*
Ane henne at ane halpeny by halfe yeris ende,[7]
Schold not a ladde be in londe a lorde for to serve.[8]
This wate° thou full wele witterly° thiselven,   *know / certainly*
390 Whoso wele schal wyn, a wastour moste he fynde,
For if it greves one gome,° it gladdes another."   *man*
"Now," quod Wynner to Wastour, "me wondirs in hert
Of thies poure penyles° men that peloure° will by,   *penniless / fur*
Sadills of sendale,° with sercles° full riche.   *fine cloth / rings*
395 Lesse and ye wrethe ° your wifes, thaire willes to folowe,   *Lest you anger*
Ye sellyn wodd° aftir wodde in a wale tyme,°   *wood / quickly*
Bothe the oke and the assche, and all that ther growes;
The spyres° and the yonge sprynge° ye spare to your   *shoots / sapling*
    children,
And sayne God wil graunt it His grace to grow at the last,
400 For to save to your sones: bot the schame es your ownn.
Nedeles save ye the soyle, for sell it ye thynken.°   *intend*
Your forfadirs were fayne,° when any frende come,   *glad*
For to schake to the schawe and schewe hym the estres,[9]
In iche holt° that thay had ane hare for to fynde,   *woods*
405 Bryng to the brod lande bukkes ynewe°   *enough*
To lache° and to late goo, to lightten thaire hertis.   *catch*
Now es it sett and solde, my sorowe es the more,
Wastes alle wilfully, your wyfes to paye.°   *please*
That are° had lordes in londe and ladyes riche,   *formerly*
Now are thay nysottes° of the new gett,° so nysely° *new fools / fashion / foolishly*
410   attyred,
With side slabbande° sleves, sleght° to the grounde,   *sloping / let down*
Ourlede° all umbtourne° with ermyn[1] aboute,   *trimmed / around*
That es as harde, as I hope, to handil in the derne,°   *dark*
Als a cely° symple wenche that never silke wroghte.   *innocent*

---

6. (Waster is speaking here.)
7. A hen would cost a halfpenny by the end of half a year.
8. *And wild bestis . . . for to serve*: These lines suggest that without consumption, food would become so plentiful that the poor would lose their motivation to work. For an analogous point, see the plowing of the half acre in Passus VI of *Piers Plowman*.
9. To go into the woods and show him the recesses of the estate.
1. The white fur of the ermine (a kind of weasel), evenly punctuated by the black tip of the creature's tail, is a distinctive feature ideally reserved for royal robes.

415 Bot whoso lukes on hir lyre,° Oure Lady of Heven,   *misfortune*
How scho fled for ferd° ferre° out of hir kythe,°   *fear / far / known home*
Appon ane amblande° asse, withowtten more pride,   *ambling*
Safe a barne° in hir barme,° and a broken heltre°   *baby / lap / halter*
That Joseph held in hys hande, that hend° for to   *noble (child)*
   yeme,°   *guard*
420 Allthofe scho walt° al this werlde, hir wedes° wer pore   *ruled / clothes*
For to gyf ensample of siche,° for to schewe° other   *such / show*
For to leve° pompe and pride, that poverté ofte   *leave*
   schewes."°   *teaches*
Than the Wastour wrothly castes up his eghne,
And said, "Thou Wynnere, thou wriche!° Me wondirs   *wretch*
   in hert
425 What hafe oure clothes coste the, caytef, to by,°   *buy*
That thou schal birdes° upbrayd of thair bright wedis,   *ladies*
Sythen that we vouchesafe that the silver payen?"

* * *

The kynge lovely lokes on the ledis° twayne,   *men*
Says, "Blynnes,° beryns, of youre brethe and of youre   *Stop*
   brode worde,
And I schal deme yow this day where ye duelle schall,
Aythere° lede° in a lond ther he es loved moste.   *either / person*
460 Wende, Wynnere, thi waye over the wale° stremys,°   *swift / streams*
Passe forthe by Paris to the Pope of Rome;
The cardynalls ken° the° wele, will kepe the ful faire,   *know / thee*
And make thi sydes in silken schetys to lygge,°   *lie*
And fede the° and foster the and forthir thyn hert,   *thee*
465 As leefe to worthen wode as the to wrethe ones.²
Bot loke, lede, be thi lyfe,° when I lettres sende,   *on your life*
That thou hy° the to me home on horse or one fote;   *hasten*
And when I knowe thou will co[me],³ he schall cayre°   *go*
   uttire,°   *further away*
And lenge° with another lede, til thou thi lefe° [take];   *stay / leave*
For thofe° thou bide in this burgh to thi be[ryinge-   *although*
470   daye],°   *death*
With hym happyns the never a fote for [to holde].
And thou, Wastoure, I will that thou wonn[e° scholde]   *dwell*
Ther° moste waste es of wele, and wyng° [ther until].   *where / hasten*
Chese the forthe into the Chepe, a chambre thou rere,⁴
475 Loke thi wyndowe be wyde, and wayte the aboute,
Where any potet° beryn thurgh the burgh passe;   *drunk*
Teche hym to the taverne till he tayte° worthe,°   *merry / becomes*
Doo° hym drynk al nyghte that he dry be at morow,   *Make*
Sythen ken° hym to the crete° to comforth his vaynes,   *direct / Cretan wine*
480 Brynge hym to Bred Strete—bikken° thi fynger—   *beckon*
Schew hym of fatt chepe° scholdirs ynewe,   *sheep*

2. As willing to go mad as to anger you once.
3. 468–73: The emendations here reconstruct a missing part of the text according to Stephanie Trigg's suggestions.
4. Go forth into Cheapside and set up a chamber there.

"Hotte for the hungry!" a hen other twayne,[5]
Sett hym softe one a sege,° and sythen send after,   seat
Bryng out of the burgh the best thou may fynde,
And luke thi knave° hafe a knoke° bot° he the clothe   servant / beating / unless
485   sprede.
Bot late hym paye or° he passe, and pik° hym so clene   before / pick, i.e., rob
That fynd a peny in his purse and put owte his eghe.[6]
When that es dronken and don, duell ther no lenger,
Bot teche hym owt of the townn to trotte aftir more.
490 Then passe to the Pultrie,° the peple the° knowes,   Poultry / thee
And ken° wele thi katour° to knawen thi fode,   instruct / buyer
The herons, the hasteletez, the henne wele serve,
The pertrikes,° the plovers, the other pulled° byrddes,   partridges / plucked
The albus, this other foules, the egretes dere;
The more thou wastis° thi wele,° the better the Wynner   waste / wealth
495   lykes.
And wayte to me, thou Wynnere, if thou wilt wele   prosper
        chefe,°
When I wende appon werre° my wyes to lede;   war
For at the proude pales° of Parys the riche[7]   place
I thynk to do it in ded, and dub the to knyghte,
500 And giff giftes full grete of golde and of silver,
To ledis of my legyance that lufen me in hert.
And sythen kayre as I come, with knyghtes that me
        foloen,
To the kirk° of Colayne[8] ther the kynges ligges . . . [9]   cathedral

GEOFFREY CHAUCER

From The General Prologue *to* The Canterbury Tales†

Whan that April with his shoures sote°   sweet showers
The droghte° of Marche hath perced to the rote,°   dryness / root
And bathed every veyne° in swich licour,°   vein / such moisture
Of which vertu° engendred is the flour;   By power of which
5 Whan Zephirus° eek with his swete breeth   the west wind
Inspired° hath in every holt° and heeth°   Breathed into / wood / heath

---

5. These calls describing food for sale echo the prologue of *Piers Plowman*.
6. That if anyone find a penny in his purse, let him have his eyes put out.
7. Possibly the Palais de la Cité.
8. A reference to the shrine of the Three Magi in Cologne cathedral.
9. The poem breaks off at this point.
† From V. A Kolve and Glending Olson, eds. *The Canterbury Tales: Nine Tales and the General Prologue*, A Norton Critical Edition (New York: W. W. Norton & Company, 1989). Reprinted by permission of W. W. Norton & Company. To place Chaucer's great work merely under the heading of
"Political and Historical" background is, of course, highly misrepresentative; but the placement is
intended to draw attention to a common interest between Chaucer and Langland in inviting critical thought about the spiritual and institutional conditions of their society. Common also to both
is a dedication to satire as a principal means of exploring those conditions, though Chaucer's satire
is perhaps less direct, and neither poet can be said to be working satirically at all times. Indeed, it is
difficult not to read Chaucer's unequivocal representation of the Plowman (p. 460) as an approv-
ing acknowledgment of Langland's poem. Chaucer died in 1400, leaving his compendium of tales
incomplete.

The tendre croppes,° and the yonge sonne   *sprouts*
Hath in the Ram his halfe cours y-ronne;[1]
And smale fowles° maken melodye,   *birds*
10   That slepen al the night with open yë°—   *eye(s)*
So priketh hem Nature in hir corages[2]—
Than longen° folk to goon° on pilgrimages,   *Then long / go*
And palmeres for to seken straunge strondes,[3]
To feme halwes,° couthe° in sondry londes,   *far-off shires / known*
15   And specially, from every shires ende
Of Engelond to Caunterbury they wende,
The holy blisful martir[4] for to seke,°   *seek*
That hem hath holpen,° whan that they were seke.°   *helped / sick*
Bifel° that, in that seson on a day,   *It befell*
20   In Southwerk at the Tabard° as I lay°   *(an inn) / lodged*
Redy to wenden° on my pilgrimage   *depart*
To Caunterbury with ful devout corage,°   *heart*
At night was come into that hostelrye°   *inn*
Wel nyne and twenty in a companye
25   Of sondry folk, by aventure° y-falle°   *chance / fallen*
In felawshipe, and pilgrims were they alle,
That toward Caunterbury wolden° ryde.   *wished to*
The chambres° and the stables weren wyde,°   *bedrooms / spacious*
And wel we weren esed° atte beste.°   *made comfortable / in the best (ways)*
30   And shortly, whan the sonne was to° reste,   *at*
So hadde I spoken with hem everichon°   *each and every one*
That I was of hir felawshipe anon,
And made forward° erly for to ryse,   *agreement*
To take oure wey, ther as I yow devyse.°   *(will) tell*
35   But natheles,° whyl I have tyme and space,   *nevertheless*
Er that I ferther in this tale pace,°   *pass on*
Me thinketh it acordaunt to resoun[5]
To telle yow al the condicioun[6]
Of ech of hem, so as it semed me,°   *seemed to me*
40   And whiche° they weren, and of what degree,°   *what / status*
And eek in what array° that they were inne;   *clothing*
And at a knight than wol° I first biginne.   *will*

*   *   *

The Prioress

Ther was also a Nonne, a PRIORESSE,
That of hir smyling was ful simple and coy°—   *modest*
120   Hir gretteste ooth was but by Seynte Loy°—   *Eligius (Fr. Eloi)*

---

1. Has run his half-course in the Ram; i.e. has passed through half the zodiacal sign of Aries (the Ram), a course completed on April 11. A rhetorically decorative way of indicating the time of year.
2. Nature so spurs them in their hearts.
3. And pilgrims to seek foreign shores.
4. Thomas Becket, archbishop of Canterbury, murdered in 1170 and canonized shortly thereafter. The place of his martyrdom was the greatest shrine in England and much visited by pilgrims.
5. It seems to me reasonable (proper).
6. Character, estate, condition.

And she was cleped° madame Eglentyne.   *called*
Ful wel she song° the service divyne,   *sang*
Entuned° in hir nose ful semely;°   *Intoned / becomingly*
And Frensh she spak ful faire and fetisly,°   *elegantly*
125 After the scole of Stratford atte Bowe,[7]
For Frensh of Paris was to hire unknowe.
At mete[8] wel y-taught was she with alle:
She leet° no morsel from hir lippes falle,   *let*
Ne wette hir fingres in hir sauce depe.°   *(too) deeply*
130 Wel coude she carie a morsel, and wel kepe[9]
That no drope ne fille° upon hire brest.   *fell*
In curteisye° was set ful muchel° hir lest.°   *etiquette / much / delight*
Hir over°-lippe wyped she so clene,   *upper*
That in hir coppe was no ferthing° sene°   *small drop / seen*
135 Of grece,° whan she dronken hadde hir draughte.   *grease*
Ful semely after hir mete she raughte,°   *reached*
And sikerly° she was of greet disport,°   *certainly / cheerfulness*
And ful plesaunt, and amiable of port,°   *deportment*
And peyned hire° to countrefete chere°   *took pains / imitate behavior*
140 Of court, and to been estatlich° of manere,   *stately*
And to ben holden digne° of reverence.   *considered worthy*
But, for to speken of hire conscience,°   *sensibility*
She was so charitable and so pitous,°   *compassionate*
She wolde wepe, if that she sawe a mous°   *mouse*
145 Caught in a trappe, if it were deed or bledde.
Of[1] smale houndes hadde she, that she fedde
With rosted flesh, or milk and wastel-breed.°   *fine white bread*
But sore° wepte she if oon of hem were deed,   *sorely*
Or if men° smoot it with a yerde° smerte;°   *(some)one / stick / sharply*
150 And al was conscience and tendre herte.
Ful semely hir wimpel° pinched° was,   *headdress / pleated*
Hir nose tretys,° hir eyen° greye as glas,   *graceful / eyes*
Hir mouth ful smal, and therto softe and reed.
But sikerly° she hadde a fair forheed—   *certainly*
155 It was almost a spanne° brood, I trowe°—   *span / believe*
For hardily° she was nat undergrowe.°   *certainly / undersized*
Ful fetis° was hir cloke, as I was war.°   *elegant / aware*
Of smal coral[2] aboute hire arm she bar
A peire of bedes, gauded al with grene;[3]
160 And theron heng a broche° of gold ful shene,°   *ornament / bright*
On which ther was first write° a crowned A,[4]   *written*
And after, *Amor vincit ominia*.°   *Love conquers all*

*   *   *

7. I.e., in the English fashion, as it was spoken at Stratford at the Bow—a suburb some two miles east of London and home of the Benedictine nunnery of St. Leonard's.
8. I.e., at table.
9. She knew well how to raise a portion (to her lips) and take care.
1. I.e., some.
2. I.e., small coral beads.
3. A string of beads (a rosary,) its groups marked off by special stones, called "gauds," of green.
4. The letter A with a symbolic crown fashioned.

The Monk

A MONK ther was, a fair for the maistrye,°	*a very fine one*
An outrydere° that lovede venerye.°	*estate supervisor / hunting*
165	A manly man, to been an abbot able.	
Ful many a deyntee° hors hadde he in stable,	*valuable*
And whan he rood, men mighte his brydel here°	*hear*
Ginglen° in a whistling wind als° clere	*Jingling / as*
And eek° as loude as dooth the chapel belle,	*also*
170	Ther as° this lord was kepere of the celle.⁵	*Where*
The reule of Seint Maure° or of Seint Beneit,°	*Maurus / Benedict*
By cause that it was old and somdel streit,°	*somewhat strict*
This ilke° monk leet olde thinges pace,°	*same / pass away*
And held after the newe world the space.°	*meanwhile*
175	He yaf° nat of° that text a pulled° hen,	*gave / for / plucked*
That seith that hunters ben° nat holy men,	*are*
Ne that a monk, whan he is reccheless,°	*negligent of his vows*
Is lykned til° a fish that is waterlees°	*likened to / out of water*
(This is to seyn,° a monk out of his cloistre);	*say*
180	But thilke° text held he nat worth an oistre.°	*that same / oyster*
And I seyde his opinioun was good:	
What° sholde he studie, and make himselven wood,°	*Why / mad*
Upon a book in cloistre alwey to poure,°	*pore over*
Or swinken° with his handes, and laboure,	*work*
185	As Austin° bit?° How shal the world be served?	*Augustine / bids*
Lat Austin have his swink° to him reserved!	*work*
Therefore he was a pricasour° aright,°	*hard rider / truly*
Grehoundes he hadde, as swifte as fowel° in flight;	*bird*
Of priking° and of hunting for the hare	*riding*
190	Was al his lust,° for no cost wolde he spare.	*pleasure*
I seigh° his sleves purfiled° at the hond	*saw / trimmed*
With grys,° and that the fyneste of a lond,°	*gray fur / land*
And, for to festne° his hood under his chin,	*fasten*
He hadde of gold y-wroght° a ful curious pin:	*made*
195 | A love-knotte⁶ in the gretter° ende ther was. | *larger* |

* * *

The Friar

A FRERE° ther was, a wantowne° and a merye,	*Friar / gay (one)*
A limitour,⁷ a ful solempne° man.	*distinguished*
In alle the ordres foure⁸ is noon that can°	*knows*
So muchel of daliaunce and fair langage.	
He hadde maad° ful many a mariage	*arranged*
210	Of yonge wommen, at his owne cost.⁹	
Unto his ordre he was a noble post.°	*pillar*

5. A priory or dependent house.
6. An elaborate knot symbolizing true love.
7. One licensed to beg within a certain region or limit.
8. The four orders of friars (Franciscan, Dominican, Carmelite, and Augustinian).
9. I.e., he gave them dowries out of his own funds, perhaps after having first seduced them himself.

215 Ful wel biloved and famulier was he
     With frankeleyns over al in his contree,[1]
     And eek with worthy wommen of the toun;
     For he hadde power of confessioun,
     As seyde himself, more than a curat,°   *parish priest*
220 For of his ordre he was licentiat.°   *licensed to hear confessions*
     Ful swetely herde he confessioun,
     And plesaunt was his absolucioun;
     He was an esy man to yeve° penaunce   *give*
     Ther as he wiste to have a good pitaunce.[2]
225 For unto a povre° ordre for to yive°   *poor / give*
     Is signe that a man is wel y-shrive°—   *shriven*
     For if he yaf,° he dorste make avaunt,°   *gave / (the Friar) dared assert*
     He wiste° that a man was repentaunt.   *knew*
     For many a man so hard is of his herte,
230 He may nat wepe al-thogh hym sore smerte.°   *it sorely pain him*
     Therfore, in stede of wepinge and preyeres,
     Men moot° yeve silver to the povre° freres.   *may / poor*
     His tipet° was ay farsed° ful of knyves   *scarf / always stuffed*
     And pinnes, for to yeven° faire wyves.   *give to*
235 And certeinly he hadde a murye note,°   *pleasant voice*
     Wel coude he singe and pleyen on a rote,°   *stringed instrument*
     Of yeddinges he bar outrely the prys.[3]
     His nekke whyt was as the flour-de-lys;°   *lily*
     Therto° he strong was as a champioun.   *Moreover*
240 He knew the tavernes wel in every toun,
     And everich hostiler° and tappestere°   *innkeeper / barmaid*
     Bet than a lazar or a beggestere,[4]
     For unto swich° a worthy man as he   *such*
     Acorded nat, as by his facultee,[5]
245 To have with seke lazars° aqueyntaunce: *sick lepers*
     It is nat honest,° it may nat avaunce°   *respectable / be profitable*
     For to delen with no swich poraille,°   *such poor people*
     But al with riche and selleres of vitaille.°   *victuals*
     And over al,° ther as° profit sholde aryse,   *everywhere / wherever*
250 Curteys he was, and lowely of ° servyse.   *humble in*
     Ther nas° no man nowher so vertuous.°   *was not / capable*
     He was the beste beggere in his hous,
252a [And yaf ° a certeyn ferme° for the graunt: *gave / payment*
252b Noon of his bretheren cam ther in his haunt.]°   *area of begging*
     For thogh a widwe° hadde noght a sho,°   *widow / shoe*
     So plesaunt was his *In principio*,°   *"In the beginning"*
255 Yet wolde he have a ferthing,° er he wente.   *farthing*
     His purchas was wel bettre than his rente.[6]

---

1. With rich landholders everywhere in his region.
2. Wherever he knew (that he could expect) to have a good gift in return.
3. At narrative songs, he absolutely took the prize.
4. Better than a leper or beggar woman.
5. It was not fitting, considering his position.
6. His profit from begging was much greater than "his regular income," or "the fee he paid for his exclusive begging rights." (Meaning uncertain.)

And rage he coude, as it were right a whelpe;[7]
In love-dayes° ther coude he muchel° helpe,   *legal arbitrations / much*
For there he was nat lyk a cloisterer,[8]
260 With a thredbare cope,° as is a povre scoler.   *cape*
But he was lyk a maister° or a pope: *Master of Arts*
Of double worsted was his semi-cope,°   *half-cape*
That rounded as a belle out of the presse.°   *mould*
Somwhat he lipsed, for his wantownesse,[9]
265 To make his English swete upon his tonge;
And in his harping, whan that he hadde songe,
His eyen° twinkled in his heed aright   *eyes*
As doon° the sterres° in the frosty night.   *do / stars*
This worthy limitour was cleped° Huberd.   *called*

* * *

The Wife of Bath

A good WYF was ther of bisyde BATHE,°   *from near Bath*
445 But she was somdel° deef, and that was scathe.°   *somewhat / a pity*
Of clooth-making she hadde swiche an haunt,°   *such practiced skill*
She passed° hem of Ypres and of Gaunt.[1]   *surpassed*
In al the parisshe wyf ne was ther noon
450 That to the offringe° bifore hir sholde goon;°   *offering in church / go*
And if ther dide, certeyn so wrooth° was she,   *angry*
That she was out of alle charitee.
Hir coverchiefs° ful fyne were of ground;°   *kerchiefs / texture*
I dorste° swere they weyeden° ten pound   *would dare / weighed*
455 That on a Sonday weren upon hir heed.
Hir hosen° weren of fyn scarlet reed,   *hose*
Ful streite y-teyd,° and shoos ful moiste° and newe.   *tightly tied / soft*
Bold was hir face, and fair, and reed of hewe.°   *hue*
She was a worthy womman al hir lyve:
460 Housbondes at chirche dore[2] she hadde fyve,
Withouten,° other companye in youthe—   *Not to mention*
But therof nedeth nat to speke as nouthe°—   *at present*
And thryes° hadde she been at Jerusalem.   *thrice*
She hadde passed many a straunge streem:[3]
465 At Rome she hadde been, and at Boloigne,°   *Boulogne (France)*
In Galice at Seint Jame, and at Coloigne;[4]
She coude° muchel of wandringe by the weye.°   *knew / along the road(s)*
Gat-tothed° was she, soothly for to seye.   *Gap-toothed*
Upon an amblere° esily° she sat,   *saddle-horse / comfortably*
470 Y-wimpled° wel, and on hir heed an hat   *Covered with a wimple*

7. And he knew how to play and flirt, as if he were a puppy.
8. A religious who knows only the enclosed life of the cloister.
9. He lisped a little, out of affectation.
1. Cloth-making in the Low Countries (here represented by Ypres and Ghent) was of high repute.
2. The medieval marriage ceremony was customarily performed by the priest on the church porch. Afterward the company entered the church to hear the nuptial mass.
3. She had crossed many a foreign river.
4. In Galicia (in Spain) at (the shrine of) St. James of Compostella, and at Cologne.

As brood as is a bokeler or a targe;[5]
A foot-mantel° aboute hir hipes large,   *outer skirt*
And on hir feet a paire of spores° sharpe.   *spurs*
In felawschipe wel coude she laughe and carpe.°   *talk*
475 Of remedyes of love she knew per chaunce,°   *as it happened*
For she coude° of that art the olde daunce.°   *knew / (steps of the) dance*

The Parson and the Plowman

A good man was ther of religioun,
And was a povre PERSOUN° of a toun,   *poor parson*
But riche he was of holy thoght and werk.
480 He was also a lerned man, a clerk,°   *scholar*
That Cristes gospel trewely wolde preche;
His parisshens° devoutly wolde he teche.   *parishioners*
Benigne° he was, and wonder° diligent,   *Kindly / very*
485 And in adversitee ful pacient,
And swich he was y-preved ofte sythes.[6]
Ful looth° were him to cursen° for his tithes,   *loath / excommunicate*
But rather wolde he yeven,° out of doute,°   *give / there is no doubt*
Unto his povre parisshens aboute
Of° his offring, and eek of his substaunce.°   *From / income*
490 He coude in litel thing han suffisaunce.[7]
Wyd was his parisshe, and houses fer asonder,
But he ne lafte° nat, for reyn ne° thonder,   *ceased / nor*
In siknes nor in meschief,° to visyte   *misfortune*
The ferreste in his parisshe, muche and lyte,[8]
495 Upon his feet, and in his hand a staf.
This noble ensample° to his sheep he yaf,°   *example / gave*
That first he wroghte,° and afterward he taughte.   *did (what was right)*
Out of the gospel he tho° wordes caughte,°   *those / took*
And this figure° he added eek therto,   *metaphor, image*
500 That if gold ruste, what shal iren° do?   *iron*
For if a preest be foul,° on whom we truste,   *corrupted*
No wonder is a lewed man to ruste;[9]
And shame it is, if a preest take keep,°   *head (it)*
A shiten[1] shepherde and a clene sheep.
505 Wel oghte a preest ensample for to yive,°   *give*
By his clennesse, how that his sheep sholde live.
He sette nat his benefice to hyre,[2]
And lee° his sheep encombred in the myre,   *left*
And ran to London unto Seynte Poules°   *St. Paul's cathedral*
510 To seken him a chaunterie for soules,
Or with a bretherhed to been withholde,[3]

---

5. Both buckler and targe are shields.
6. And he was proved (to be) such many times.
7. He knew how to have enough in very little.
8. The furthest (members) of his parish, great and humble.
9. It is no wonder that an unlearned man (should go) to rust.
1. I.e., covered with excrement.
2. He did not hire out (i.e., engage a substitute for) his benefice (church appointment).
3. To seek for himself an appointment as a chantry-priest singing masses for the souls of the dead, or to be retained (as a chaplain) by a guild. (Both sorts of position were relatively undemanding, and paid enough for such a priest to retain a curate at home and have money to spare.)

But dwelte at hoom, and kepte° wel his folde,   *took care of*
So that the wolf ne made it nat miscarie,°   *come to harm*
He was a shepherde and noght a mercenarie.
515 And though he holy were, and vertuous,
He was to sinful men nat despitous,°   *scornful*
Ne of his speche daungerous ne digne,°   *haughty nor disdainful*
But in his teching discreet and benigne.
To drawen folk to heven by fairnesse,
520 By good ensample, this was his bisinesse;°   *endeavor*
But it were° any persone obstinat,   *were there*
What so° he were, of heigh or lough estat,°   *Whatever / condition, class*
Him wolde he snibben° sharply for the nones.°   *rebuke / on such an occasion*
A better preest I trowe° that nowher noon is.   *believe*
525 He wayted after° no pompe and reverence,   *looked for*
Ne maked him a spyced conscience,[4]
But Cristes lore,° and his apostles twelve,   *teaching*
He taughte, and first he folwed it himselve.
    With him ther was a PLOWMAN, was his brother,
530 That hadde y-lad° of dong° ful many a fother.°   *hauled / dung / cartload*
A trewe swinkere° and a good was he,   *worker*
Livinge in pees° and parfit charitee.   *peace*
God loved he best with al his hole° herte   *whole*
At alle tymes, thogh him gamed or smerte,[5]
535 And thanne his neighebour right as himselve.
He wolde thresshe, and therto dyke° and delve,°   *make ditches / dig*
For Cristes sake, for every povre wight,°   *poor man*
Withouten hyre,° if it lay in his might.°   *wages / power*
His tythes° payed he ful faire and wel,   *tithes*
540 Bothe of his propre swink° and his catel.°   *own work / possessions*
In a tabard° he rood upon a mere.°   *smock / mare*

                              *   *   *

The Summoner and the Pardoner

    A SOMONOUR[6] was ther with us in that place,
That hadde a fyr-reed cherubinnes face,[7]
625 For sawcefleem° he was, with eyen° narwe.   *pimpled / eyes*
As hoot° he was and lecherous as a sparwe.°   *passionate / sparrow*
With scalled° browes blake, and piled berd;°   *scabby / scraggy beard*
Of his visage° children were aferd.°   *face / afraid*
Ther nas quik-silver, litarge,° ne brimstoon,   *lead oxide*
630 Boras,° ceruce,° ne oille° of tartre noon,   *Borax / white lead / cream*
Ne oynement that wolde clense and byte,°   *sting*
That him mighte helpen of ° his whelkes° whyte,   *cure / pimples*
Nor of the knobbes° sittinge on his chekes.   *lumps*

---

4. Nor affected an overly scrupulous nature.
5. At all times, whether he was glad or in distress.
6. A summoner was an officer who cited ("summoned") malefactors to appear before an ecclesiastical court: in this case, an archdeacon's, having jurisdiction over matrimonial cases, adultery, and
   fornication.
7. Cherubim, the second order of angels, were sometimes painted brilliant red ("fire-red") in medieval
   art. The summoner resembles them, not through beatitude, but through a skin disease.

Wel loved he garleek, oynons, and eek lekes,°   *leeks*
635 And for to drinken strong wyn, reed as blood.
Thanne wolde he speke, and crye° as° he were wood;°   *shout / as if / mad*
And whan that he wel dronken hadde the wyn,
Thanne wolde he speke no word but Latyn.°   *(in) Latin*
A fewe termes° hadde he, two or three,   *technical phrases*
640 That he had lerned out of som decree—
No wonder is,° he herde it al the day;   *it is*
And eek ye knowen wel, how that a jay°   *a chattering bird*
Can clepen "Watte" as well as can the Pope.[8]
But whoso coude in other thing him grope,°   *question*
645 Thanne hadde he spent° al his philosophye;   *exhausted*
Ay "*Questio quid iuris*" wolde he crye.[9]
He was a gentil° harlot° and a kinde,°   *worthy / rascal / natural one*
A bettre felawe° sholde men noght finde: *companion*
He wolde suffre,° for a quart of wyn,   *allow*
650 A good felawe to have his concubyn
A° twelf-month, and excuse him atte fulle;°   *(For) a / fully*
Ful prively a finch eek coude he pulle.[1]
And if he fond° owher° a good felawe,   *found / anywhere*
He wolde techen him to have non awe°   *fear*
655 In swich cas of the erchedeknes curs,[2]
But—if° a mannes soule were in his purs,   *Unless*
For in his purs he sholde y-punisshed be.
"Purs is the erchedeknes helle," seyde he.
But wel I woot° he lyed right in dede: *know*
660 Of cursing oghte ech gilty man him drede—
For curs wol slee, right as assoilling saveth—
And also war him of a *significavit*.[3]
In daunger° hadde he at° his owene gyse°   *his power / in / way*
The yonge girles° of the diocyse,   *wenches*
665 And knew hir counseil,° and was al hir reed.°   *their secrets / adviser to them all*
A gerland° hadde he set upon his heed,   *garland*
As greet as it were for an ale-stake,°   *tavern sign*
A bokeler° hadde he maad him of a cake.°   *shield / round bread*
With him ther rood a gentil PARDONER[4]
670 Of Rouncival,[5] his freend and his compeer,°   *companion*
That streight was comen fro the court of Rome.
Ful loude he song,° "Com hider,° love, to me."   *sang / hither*
This sommour bar to° him a stif burdoun,°   *accompanied / sturdy bass*
Was nevere trompe° of half so greet a soun.°   *trumpet / sound*
675 This pardoner hadde heer° as yelow as wex,°   *hair / wax*

8. Knows how to say "Walter" as well as does the Pope.
9. He would always cry. "The question is what point of law applies?"
1. He was skilled in secretly seducing girls. ("To pull a finch," i.e., to pluck a bird, was an obscene expression.)
2. Curse, the power of excommunication.
3. Every guilty man ought to be fearful of excommunication, for it will slay (the soul eternally), just as absolution (the forgiveness granted through the sacrament of penance) saves—and (he ought) also beware a *significavit* (a writ of arrest).
4. A pardoner was a seller of papal indulgences (remissions of punishment for sin), whose proceeds were often intended to build or support a religious house. Many pardoners were fraudulent, and their abuses were much criticized.
5. Near Charing Cross in London.

But smothe it heng,° as dooth a strike of flex;°   *hung / bunch of flax*
By ounces° henge his lokkes that he hadde,   *In thin strands*
And therwith° he his shuldres overspradde;°   *with it / covered*
But thinne it lay, by colpons° oon and oon;   *in small bunches*
680 But hood, for jolitee,° wered he° noon,   *sportiveness / wore*
For it was trussed° up in his walet.°   *packed / pouch*
Him thoughte he rood al of the newe jet;
Dischevele, save his cappe, he rood al bare.[6]
Swiche glaringe eyen° hadde he as an hare.   *staring eyes*
685 A vernicle[7] hadde he sowed on his cappe.
His walet lay biforn° him in his lappe,   *in front of*
Bretful of pardoun comen from Rome al hoot.[8]
A voys he hadde as smal as hath a goot.°   *goat*
No berd hadde he, ne nevere sholde have,
690 As smothe it was as it were late shave:°   *recently shaved*
I trowe° he were a gelding or a mare.   *believe*
But of his craft, fro Berwik into Ware,[9]
Ne was ther swich another pardoner.
For in his male° he hadde a pilwe-beer,°   *bag / pillowcase*
695 Which that he seyde was Oure Lady veyl.°   *Our Lady's veil*
He seyde he hadde a gobet° of the seyl°   *piece / sail*
That seynt Peter hadde, whan that he wente°   *walked*
Upon the see, til Jesu Crist him hente.°   *took hold of*
He hadde a croys° of latoun,° ful of stones,°   *cross / metal / gems*
700 And in a glas° he hadde pigges bones.   *glass container*
But with thise relikes,° whan that he fond   *relics*
A povre person dwellinge upon lond,[1]
Upon a° day he gat him more moneye   *In one*
Than that the person gat in monthes tweye.°   *two*
705 And thus, with feyned flaterye and japes,°   *tricks*
He made the person and the peple his apes.°   *fools*
But trewely to tellen, atte laste,°   *after all*
He was in chirche a noble ecclesiaste.°   *preacher*
Wel coude he rede a lessoun or a storie,°   *religious tale*
710 But alderbest° he song° an offertorie;   *best of all / sang*
For wel he wiste,° whan that song was songe,   *knew*
He moste preche, and wel affyle° his tonge   *make smooth*
To winne silver, as he ful wel coude—
Therefore he song the murierly° and loude.   *more merrily*

*   *   *

6. It seemed to him he rode in the very latest fashion; (his hair) loose, he rode bareheaded except for his cap.
7. A copy of the veil St. Veronica gave to Christ when He was carrying the cross, that He might wipe His brow; it received the imprint of Christ's face.
8. Brimful of pardons, come all hot (fresh) from Rome.
9. I.e., from north to south.
1. A poor parson living in the country.

From Richard the Redeless†

[*Prologue*]

And as I passid in my preiere° ther° prestis° were at   *prayer / where / priests /*
  messe,°   *mass*
In a blessid borugh that Bristow° is named,   *Bristol*
In a temple of the Trinité the toune even amyddis,°   *in the middle*
That Cristis chirche is cleped° amonge the comune°   *called / common*
  peple.
5 Sodeynly° ther sourdid° selcouthe° thingis—   *suddenly / arose / wondrous*
A grett wondir° to wyse men, as it well mygth—°   *wonder / might seem*
And dowtes for to deme for drede° comynge after.   *to assess for fearful things*
So sore° were the sawis° of bothe two sidis,°   *bitter / words / sides*
Of Richard that° regned° so riche and so noble,   *who / regined*
10 That whyle° he werrid° be° west on the wilde Yrisshe,   *while / waged war / in*
Henrri was entrid° on the est° half,[1]   *advanced / east*
Whom all the londe° loved, in lengthe and in brede,°   *land / breadth*
And ros° with him rapely° to rightyn his wronge,   *rose up / quickly*
For he shullde hem serve of the same after.
15 Thus tales me troblid,° for they trewe where,°   *troubled / were*
And amarride° my mynde rith° moche and my wittis   *troubled / right*
  eke:°   *also*
For it passid° my parceit° and my preifis° also   *surpassed / perception / proofs*
How so wondirffull werkis° wolde have an ende.   *deeds*
But in sothe whan they sembled° some dede repente,   *assembled*
20 As knowyn is in cumpas° of Cristen londis,   *throughout*
That rewthe° was, if reson ne had reffourmed°   *pity / reformed*
The mysscheff° and the mysserule that men tho° in   *misfortune / then*
  endurid.
I had peté° of his passion,° that prince was of Walis,°   *pity / suffering / Wales*
And eke° our crouned kynge, till Crist woll no lenger.°   *also / longer*
25 And as a lord to his liage,° though I lite° hade,   *liege / little*
All myn hoole° herte° was his while he in helthe   *whole / heart*
  regnid.
And for I wuste° not witterly° what shulde fall,°   *know / fully / happen*
Whedir° God wolde geve° him grace sone to amende,   *whether / give*
To be oure gioure° ageyn or graunte it another,   *leader*
30 This made me to muse many tyme and ofte,
For to written him a writte,° to wissen° him better,   *writing / to educate*
And to meuve° him of mysserewle, his mynde to   *make aware*
  reffresshe
For to preise° the prynce that paradise made   *pray to*
To fullfill him with feith and fortune above,

---

† Text reprinted with new punctuation, glosses, and notes from *The Vision of William concerning Piers the Plowman . . . together with Richard the Redeless*, ed. W. W. Skeat (Oxford, 1886). The poem is concerned with the causes of the removal of Richard II from the throne in 1399, whereupon his usurper, Henry of Lancaster, was crowned Henry IV. A number of verbal and thematic echoes of *Piers Plowman* are found throughout the poem. The most recent full edition is in *Richard the Redeless and Mum and the Sothsegger*, James Dean, ed. (Kalamazoo, Michigan: U of Western Michigan P, 2000.) *Redeless*: heedless, without judgment.
1. Henry of Lancaster landed at Ravenspur on the lower Humber on July 4, 1399, while Richard II was waging war against the Irish (see l. 10).

35 And not to grucchen° a grott° ageine Godis sonde,°   *grudge / bit / order*
     But mekely to suffre what-so° him sente were.   *whatsoever*
     And yif him list° to loke a leef° other° tweyne,   *is desirable / page / or*
     That made is to mende° him of his myssededis,   *amend*
     And to kepe him in confforte° in Crist and nought°   *comfort / nothing*
        ellis,°   *else*
     I wolde be gladde that his gost° myghte glade° be° my   *spirit / be glad / by*
40   wordis,
     And grame° if it greved him, be God that me boughte.°   *distressed / redeemed*
     Ther nys no governour on the grounde ne sholde gye°   *guide*
        him the better;
     And every Cristen kyng that ony° croune bereth,°   *any / bears*
     So° he were lerned on the language, my lyff durst I   *as long as*
        wedde,°
45 Yif ° he waite° well the wordis and so werche° therafter,   *if / study / act*
     For all is tresour of the Trinité that turneth men to
        gode.
     And as my body and my beste° oughte° to be my liegis,   *beast / ought*
     So rithffully° be reson° my rede° shulde also,   *rightfully / reason / advice*
     For to conceill,° and° I couthe,° my kyng and the   *counsel / if / I could*
        lordis;
50 And therfor I fondyd° with all my fyve wyttis   *attempted*
     To traveile° on this tretis, to teche° men therafter   *work / teach*
     To be war° of wylffulnesse, lest wondris arise.   *wary*
     And if it happe° to youre honde, beholde the book   *happens to come*
        onys,°   *once*
     And redeth on him redely° rewis° an hundrid,   *readily / rows, i.e., lines*
55 And if ye savere° sum dell,° se° it forth overe,   *savor / part / look*
     For reson is no repreff,° be° the rode° of Chester.   *reproof / (I swear) by / cross*
     And if ye fynde fables or foly ther amonge,
     Or ony fantasie y-ffeyned,° that no frute° is in,   *feigned / fruit*
     Lete youre conceill° corette° it, and clerkis togedyr,   *wisdom / correct*
60 And amende that ys amysse,° and make it more better.   *which is / amiss*

✻   ✻   ✻

[Third Passus]

✻   ✻   ✻

     But now to the mater that I before meved,°   *mentioned*
     Of the gomes° so gay that grace hadde affendid°   *men / offended*
     And how stille that steddeffaste° stode amonge this   *i.e., Wisdom*
        reccheles° peple,   *careless*
210 That had awilled° his wyll as wisdom him taughte: *determined*
     For he drough° him to an herne° at the halle ende,   *drew / corner*
     Well homelich° y-helid° in an holsume gyse,°   *modestly / covered / outfit*
     Not overelonge, but ordeyned° in the olde schappe,°   *conceived / style*
     With grette browis° ybente and a berde° eke,   *eyebrows / beard*
215 And y-wounde in his wedis,° as the wedir° axith.°   *clothes / weather / required*
     He wondrid° in his wittis, as he well myghthe,   *wandered*
     That the hie housinge° herborowe° ne myghte   *building / lodge*

Halfdell° the houshould but° hales° hem helped;   *Half / unless / halls*

But for craft that he coude caste thenne, or bethenke,

He myghte not wonne° in the wones,° for witt that he   *dwell / place*

220   usid,

But, aroutyd° for his ray° and rebuked ofte,   *routed / array*

He had leve° of the lord and of ladies alle   *leave*

For his good governaunce to go or° he drank.   *before*

Ther was non of the mené° that they ne merveilid°   *company / marveled*

    moche

225   How he cam to the courte and was not y-knowe.

But als° sone as they wiste° that Witt° was his name,   *as / knew / Wisdom*

And that the kyng knewe him not, ne non of his

    knyghtis,

He was halowid° and y-huntid and yhote trusse,°   *heckled / sent away*

And his dwellinge y-demed a bowe-drawte° from hem,   *bow-shot*

230   And ich man y-charchid° to schoppe° at his croune,°   *charged / chop / head*

Yif he nyhed° hem ony° nere,° than they had him   *approached / any / nearer*

    nempned.°   *named*

The portir with his pikis° tho° put him uttere,°   *pikes / then / outside*

And warned° him the wickett° while the wacche durid;°   *denied / gate / endured*

"Lete sle° him!" quod the sleves° that   *kill / long-sleeved ones*

    slode° uppon the erthe,   *slid (with their sleeves)*

235   And alle the berdles° burnes° bayed on him evere,   *beardless / young men*

And schorned° him, for his slaveyn° was of the olde   *scorned / hood*

    schappe.

Thus Malaperte° was myghtffull° and maister of hous,   *Impudence / powerful*

And evere wandrid Wisdom without° the gatis.   *outside*

"By Him that wroughte this world!" quod Wisdom in

    wrath,

240   "But yif° ye woll° sumtyme I walke in amonge you,   *if / allow*

I shall forbede you burnes° the best° on this erthe,   *men / i.e., best thing*

That is, governance of gettinge° and grace that him   *avarice*

    follwith:

For these two trewly twynned° yet nevere."   *separated*

And so it fell on hem,° in feith, for fautis° that they   *befell them / faults*

    usid,

245   That her grace was agoo° for grucchinge° chere,°   *gone / grudging / conduct*

For the wrong that they wroughte° to Wisdom affore°   *did / before*

For tristith,° als trewly as tyllinge° us helpeth,   *trust / plowing*

That iche° rewme° under roff° of the reynebowe°   *each / realm / roof / rainbow*

Sholde stable and stonde be these thre degrés:

250   By governaunce of grete and of good age;

By styffnesse and strengthe of steeris° well y-yokyd,°   *oxen / well yoked*

That beth myghthffull° men, of the mydill age;   *powerful*

And be° laboreris of lond that lyfflode° ne fayle.   *by / livelihood*

Thanne wolde right dome reule, if reson were amongis°   *among*

    us,

255   That ich leode° lokide° what longid° to his age,   *person / attended to / belongs*

And nevere for to passe more oo° poynt forther   *one*

To usurpe the service that to sages bilongith,

To become conselleris er° they kunne° rede,°   *before / know how / to read*

In schenshepe° of sovereynes, and shame at the last.   *destruction*

260 For it fallith° as well to fodis° of four and twenty yeris,   *pertains / men*

Or yonge men of yistirday to geve good redis,°   *advice*

As becometh a kow° to hoppe in a cage!²   *cow*

It is not unknowen to kunnynge° leodis°   *perceptive / people*

That rewlers of rewmes° around all the erthe   *realms*

265 Were not y-ffoundid° at the frist tyme   *established*

To leve° al at likynge and lust of the world,   *live*

But to laboure on the lawe, as lewde° men on plowes,   *unlearned*

And to merke° meyntenourz³ with maces ichonne,   *hit*

And to strie strouters that sterede ageine rithis,⁴

270 And alle the myssedoers that they myghte fynde,

To put hem in preson,° a peere° though he were;   *prison / peer of the realm*

And not to rewle as reremys° and rest on the daies,°   *bats / all day*

And spende of the spicerie° more than it neded,   *spices*

Bothe wexe° and wyn,° in wast° all aboute,   *wax / wine / waste*

275 With deyntés y-doublid° and daunsinge to pipis,   *doubled*

In myrthe with moppis,° myrrours of synne.   *fools*

Yit forbede I no burne° to be blithe° sum while;   *person / happy*

But all thinge hath tyme, for to tempre glees:°   *enjoyment*

For caste° all the countis° that the kyng holdith,   *reckon / accounts*

280 And loke how these lordis loggen° hemself,°   *lodge / themselves*

And evere shall thou fynde, as fer as thou walkiste,

That wisdom and overewacche° wonneth° fer asundre.   *late nights / dwell*

But whanne the governaunce goth thus with tho° the   *those*

    hous gie° shulde,   *guide*

And letith° lyghte° of the lawe and lesse of the peple,   *thinks / lightly*

285 And herkeneth° all to honour and to ese° eke,   *hearkens / those at ease*

And that ich wyght with his witt waite on him evere,

To do hem reverence aright, though the rigge° brest,°   *back / break*

This warmnesse in welth° with wy° uppon erthe   *wealth / person*

Myghte not longe dure,° as doctourz° us tellith.   *endure / learned men*

290 For ho-so° thus leved° his lyff to the ende,   *whoever / lived*

Evere wrappid in welle, and with no wo mette,

Myghte seie that he sawe that seie° was nevere: *seen*

That hevene were unhonge° out of the hookis,   *unhinged*

And were boun° at his bidding yif it be myghte.   *ready*

295 But clerkis knew I non yete that so coude rede

In bokis y-bounde, though ye broughte alle

That ony° wy° welldith° wonnynge° uppon erthe;   *any / man / owns / living*

For in well° and in woo° the werld evere turneth.   *prosperity / woe*

Yit ther is kew-kaw,° though he come late,   *reversal*

300 A new thing that noyeth° nedy men and other,   *annoys*

Whanne realles° remeveth° and ridith thoru° tounes,   *royals / move / through*

And carieth° overe contré ther° comunes dwelleth,   *wander / where*

---

2. The line comprises a proverbial figure for ungainliness.

3. Maintainers were men or warriors "maintained" by a lord. They often wore distinctive clothes and badges.

4. And to destroy proud men who acted against right.

To preson° the pillourz° that overe the pore renneth;   *imprison / pilferers*
For that were evene° in her weye if they well ride.   *exactly*
305 But yit ther is a foule faute° that I fynde ofte: *flaw*
They prien° affter presentis or pleyntis° ben y-clepid,°   *beg / pleadings / called*
And abateth° all the billis° of tho° that noughth°   *void / legal actions / those /*
     bringith;   *nothing*
And ho-so grucche or grone ageins her° grette° willes   *their / great*
May lese her lyff lyghtly and no lesse weddis.°   *legal pledges*
310 Thus is the lawe louyd° thoru myghty lordis willys,   *brought low*
That meyneteyne myssdoers more than other peple.
For mayntenaunce many day—well more is the   *pity*
     reuthe!°
Hath y-had mo° men, at mete and at melis,°   *undone more / meals*
Than ony Cristen kynge that ye knewe evere:
315 For, as reson and rith° rehersid to me ones,   *right*
Tho ben men of this molde° that most harme worchen.   *earth*
For chyders° of Chester where° chose many daies°5   *troublemakers / were*
To ben of conceill for causis that in the court hangid,°   *were pending*
And pledid pipoudris⁶ alle manere pleyntis.
320 They cared for no coyffes° that men of court usyn,°   *wigs / wear*
But meved° many maters that man never thoughte,   *raised*
And feyned° falshed,° till they a fyne° had,   *contrived / falsehoods / settlement*
And knewe° no manere cause,° as comunes   *understood / legal proceeding*
     tolde.
Thei had non other signe to schewe the lawe
325 But a prevy° pallette° her pannes° to kepe,°   *trusty / head-piece / heads / protect*
To hille° here lewde heed in stede of an hove.°   *cover / lawyer's wig*
They constrewed° quarellis to quenche the peple,   *settled*
And pletid° with pollaxis and poyntis of swerdis,   *pleaded*
And at the dome-gevynge° drowe out the bladis,   *judgment*
330 And lente° men lyverey° of her longe battis.°   *gave / delivery / clubs*
They lacked alle vertues that a juge shulde have:
For, er a tale were y-tolde, they wolde trie the harmes,°   *assess the damages*
Withoute ony° answere but ho° his lyf hatid.   *any / except for him who*
And ho-so pleyned to the prince that pees shulde kepe,
335 Of these mystirmen,° medlers° of wrongis,   *officials / provokers*
He was lyghtliche° y-laughte° and y-luggyd° of many,   *quickly / seized / goaded*
And y-mummyd° on the mouthe and manaced° to the   *silenced / menaced*
     deth.
They leid° on thi leigis,° Richard, lasshis° ynow,   *laid / lieges / lashes*
And drede nevere a dele° the dome of the lawe.   *bit*
340 Ther nas° rial° of the rewme that hem durste rebuke,   *was not / nobleman*
Ne juge° ne justice that Jewis° durste hem deme   *judge / i.e., outlaws*
For oute° that thei toke or trespassid to the peple.   *anything*
This was a wondir world, hoso° well lokyd,   *whosoever*
That gromes° overegrewe so many grette maistris;   *serving-men*
For this was the rewle in this rewme while they here
345   regnyd.

---

5. Richard II kept a private army of archers known as the Chester guard, who were known for their
     brutality.
6. And pleaded as if at summary courts held for itinerants at markets and fairs.

Though I satte° sevenenyght° and slepte full selde,   *sat up / a week*
I myghte not reche° redili° to rekene the nombre,   *succeed / readily*
Of many mo wrongis than I write couude;
For selde were the sergiauntis° soughte for to plete,°   *sergeants-at-law / plead*
350 Or ony prentise° of courte preied° of his wittis,   *apprentice / asked*
The while the degonys° domes weren so endauntid,°   *churls' / esteemed*
Tille Oure Sire in His see° above the seven sterris,°   *throne / i.e., planets*
Sawe the many mysschevys that these men dede,
And no mendis° y-made, but menteyned evere   *amends*
355 Of° him that was hiest, y-holde° for to kepe   *by / required*
His liegis° in lawe, and so her love gette.   *subjects*
He sente for his servauntis that sembled° many,   *assembled*
Of baronys° and baccheleris,° with many brighth   *barons / young knights /*
     helmes,°   *helmets*
With the comunes of the contres° they cam all at ones;   *districts*
360 And as a duke doughty° in dedis of armes,   *strong*
In full reall° aray he rood uppon° hem evere,   *royal / against*
Tyll Degon and Dobyn,[7] that mennys doris° brastyn,°   *doors / broke down*
And were y-dubbid of a duke for her while° domes,   *former*
Awakyd for wecchis° and wast that they usid,   *night revels*
365 And for her breme° blastis buffettis henten.°   *bitter / received*
Than gan it to calme and clere all aboute,
That iche man myghte, hoso° mynde hadde,°   *whosoever / had a mind to*
Se,° be the sonne° that so brighte schewed,   *see / i.e., King Richard*
The mone° at the mydday meve,° and the   *i.e., lords / move*
     sterris,°   *i.e., officers*
370 Folwinge felouns for her false dedis,
Devourours of vetaile° that foughten er thei paide.   *provisions*

*   *   *

From Pierce the Ploughman's Crede[†]

Cros, and curteis Crist, this begynnynge spede,°   *help*
For the Faderes frendchipe, that fourmede hevene,
And thorugh the speciall Spirit that sprong of hem°   *them*
     tweyne,°   *two*
And alle in on godhed endles dwelleth.
5 A and all myn *A-B-C* after have I lerned,[1]
And patred° in my *Pater Noster* iche° poynt after other,   *repeated / each*
And after all myn *Ave Marie* almost to the ende.

---

7. Degon and Dobyn are evidently generic names for churls.
† Reprinted with new punctuation, glosses, and notes from *Pierce the Ploughman's Crede*, ed. W. W. Skeat, EETS 30 (London, 1867). This late fourteenth-century poem is thought to have been influenced by Lollard thinking; that is, by the critics of the established Church who followed the teachings of John Wycliffe. The poem imitates Will's search for the truth, although in this poem the focus is almost entirely on antifraternal satire (that is, criticism of the friars), cf. *Piers Plowman, Passus* VIII. The most recent full edition with extensive notes is that of James Dean, *Piers the Plowman's Crede* in *Six Ecclesiastical Satires* (Kalamazoo, MI: U of Western Michigan P, 1991).
1. The narrator knows his alphabet, which suggests he can read; later in lines 6–7, we learn he also knows his *Pater Noster* (Our Father). He now wishes to learn the creed (cf. the Athanasian Creed, printed herein, p. 373).

But al my kare is to comen, for I can° nohght my   *know*
   Crede.
Whan I schal schewen myn schrift, schent mote I
   worthen.[2]
10 The prest wil me punyche,° and penaunce enjoyne.   *punish*
The lengthe of a Lenten,° flech° moot I leve°[3]   *lent / meat / abstain from*
After that Estur ys y-comen, and that is hard fare;
And Wednesday iche wyke° withouten flech-mete.   *week*
And also Jesu hymself to the Jewes he seyde:
15 "He that leeveth nought on me, he leseth° the blisse."[4]   *believes / loses*
Therfor lerne the byleve levest me were[5]
And if any werldly wight° wille me couthe,°   *person / teach*
Other° lewed° or lered,° that lyveth therafter,   *either / unlearned / learned*
And fulliche° folweth the feyth, and feyneth° non   *completely / feigns*
   other,
20 That no worldliche wele° wilneth no tyme,   *material goods*
But lyveth in lovynge of God, and his lawe holdeth,
And for no getynge of good never his God greveth,°   *grieves*
But followeth him the full wey, as he the folke taughte.
But to many maner° of men this matter is asked,   *kinds*
Bothe to lered and to lewed, that seyn that they
25   leveden°   *believed*
Hollich° on the grete God, and holden alle his hestes.°   *wholly / commands*
But by a fraynyng° forthan° faileth ther manye.   *asking / about it*
For first I fraynede the freres, and they me fulle tolden,
That alle the frute of the fayth was in here foure
   ordres,[6]
30 And the cofres of Cristendam, and the keye bothen,
And the lok° of beleve lyeth loken in her hondes.   *lock*
Thenne wende I to wyten,° and with a whight° I mette,   *know / man*
A Menoure[7] in a morow-tide, and to this man I saide:
"Sire, for grete Godes love, the graith° thou me telle.[8]   *plain truth*
35 Of ° what myddelerde° man myghte I best lerne   *from / earthly*
My Crede? For I can° it nought, my kare° is the more;   *know / care*
And therfore, for Cristes love, thi councell I praie.
A Carm° me hath y-covenaunt° the Crede me to teche[9]   *Carmelite / agreed*
But for thou knowest Carmes well, thi counsaile I
   aske."
40 This Menour loked on me, and lawghyng he seyde,
"Leve° Cristen man, I leve° that thou madde!°   *dear / believe / are mad*
Whough° schulde thei techen the° God, that con° not   *why / thee / know*
   hemselve?°   *themselves*

2. When I shall reveal my confession, I must be ruined.
3. Lent in the Christian Church is a period from Ash Wednesday to Easter Eve for fasting and penitence. The forty weekdays are in memory of the forty days Christ spent in the wilderness fighting
the devil's temptations (See Matthew 4:1–11).
4. See John 3:15, 18.
5. Therefore, I had best learn the belief (i.e., the creed).
6. The four orders of friars were the Franciscans (the "Menoures"), the Dominicans (the "Preachers"
or "the Prechours"), the Augustinians (the "Austens"), and the Carmelites (the "Carmes").
7. A Minorite; that is, a friar minor or a Franciscan. St. Francis founded the Franciscans in 1209.
8. Wycliffites often claimed that the truth was plain and simple.
9. The narrator claims a Carmelite friar has promised to teach him the Creed, which inspires the
Minorite to criticize the Carmelites.

Thei ben but jugulers° and japers,° of kynde,°   *tricksters / jokesters / by nature*
Lorels° and lechures, and lemmans° holden.°   *villains / lovers / keep*
45 Neyther in order ne out, but unnethe° lybbeth,°   *hardly / live (by rule)*
And byjapeth° the folke with gestes° of Rome.   *dupe / stories*
It is but a faynt° folk, ifounded upon japes,   *weak*
Thei maken hem° Maries men—so thei men tellen—   *themselves*
And lieth on Our Ladie many a longe tale.
50 And that wicked folke wymmen bitraieth,
And bigileth hem of her good° with glaverynge° wordes, *possessions / flattering*
And therwith holden her° hous in harlotes werkes.   *their*
And, so save me God, I hold it gret synne
To gyven hem any good, swiche glotones to fynde,°   *support*
To maynteyne swiche° maner men that mychel° good   *such / much*
55   destruyeth.
Yet seyn they in here° sutilte° to sottes° in townes,   *their / subtlety / fools*
They comen out of Carmeli Crist for to followen,[1]
And feyneth hem with holynes, that yvele hem
    bisemeth.°   *ill suits them*
Thei lyven more in lecherie and lieth in her tales
60 Than suen any god liife—but lurken in her selles,[2]
And wynnen werldliche° god,° and wasten it in synne.   *worldly / goods*
And yif thei couthen° her Crede other° on Crist   *knew / or*
    leveden,°   *believed*
Thei weren nought so hardie° swich harlotri usen.°   *bold / practice*
Sikerli° I can nought fynden who hem first founded,   *certainly*
65 But the foles° foundeden hemself, freres of the Pye,[3]   *fools*
And maken hem mendynauns,° and marre° the puple.   *mendicants / harm*
But what glut of tho gomes may any good kachen,[4]
He will kepen it hymself, and cofren° it faste,°   *put it in a coffer / securely*
And theigh his felawes fayle good, for him he may
    sterven.[5]
70 Her money may biquest and testament maken,
And no obedience bere, but don as hym luste,°   *act as they wish*
And ryght as Robertes men° raken° aboute   *robbers / roam*
At feires and at ful° ales,° and fyllen the cuppe,   *full / ale-fests*
And precheth all of pardon to plesen the puple°—   *people*
75 Her° pacience is all pased° and put out to ferme,°   *their / gone / pasture*
And pride is in her poverté, that litell is to preisen—
And at the lulling of Oure Ladye, the wymmen to
    lyken,[6]
And miracles of mydwyves, and maken wymmen to
    wenen°   *think*
That the lace of oure Ladie smok lighteth° hem of   *i.e., gives birth for*
    children.

---

1. The Carmelites, or White Friars, were originally established at Mt. Carmel; they came to England in 1244.
2. Than follow any good life, but lurk in their cells.
3. Pied Friars or Fratres de Pica, friars with habits of black and white like a magpie.
4. But whatever glutton of those men may catch any goods.
5. And although his fellows may lack goods, as far as he is concerned they all can die.
6. And at the time when the lullabies of the Virgin (are sung), to please the women.

Thei ne prechen nought of Powel,° ne penaunce for   *St. Paul's doctrine*
80   synne,
But all of mercy and mensk° that Marie may helpen.°   *grace / provide*
With sterne° staves and stronge they over lond   *fierce*
     straketh°   *wander*
Thider as° her° lemmans liggeth,° and lurketh in   *There where / their / lie*
     townes,
Grey grete-hedede° quenes° with gold by the eighen,°   *head-geared / crones / eyes*
And seyn that her sustren thei ben that sojourneth
85   aboute;
And thus about they gon and Godes folke bytraieth.
It is the puple° that Powell preched of in his tyme.   *people*
He seyde of swich° folk that so aboute wente,   *such*
Wepyng, I warne yow of walkers aboute.[7]
90 It beth enemyes of the cros, that Crist upon tholede.°   *suffered*
Swich slomerers° in slepe slauthe° is her ende,[8]   *slumberers / sloth*
And glotony is her god, with gloppyng° of drynk,   *gulping*
And gladnes in glees,° and gret joye y-maked;   *songs*
In the schendyng° of swiche schall mychel° folk   *downfall / many*
     lawghe.°   *laugh*
95 Therfore, frend, for thi feyth, fond° to don betere,   *try*
Leve nought on tho losels,° but let hem forth pasen,   *louts*
For thei ben fals in her° feith, and fele° mo° othere."   *their / many / more*
"Alas! frere," quath° I tho, "my purpos is i-failed,°   *said / lost*
Now is my counfort a-cast; canstou no bote,[9]
Where I myghte meten with a man that myghte me
100   wissen°   *teach*
For to conne° my Crede, Crist for to folwen?"   *know*
"Certeyne, felawe," quath° the frere, "withouten any   *said*
     faile.
Of all men opon mold° we Menures° most scheweth   *earth / Minorite Friars*
The pure Apostell[e]s life, with penance on erthe.[1]

*   *   *

[*The narrator is dissatisfied with the Minorites, who attack the Carmelites,
and moves on to test the Dominicans, who criticize the Augustinians; he goes
on to the Augustinians, who criticize the Minorites; then on to the Carmelites,
who criticize the Dominicans. All four orders refuse to help the narrator
unless he gives them money.*]

*   *   *

Thanne turned I me forthe and talked to myselve
Of the falshede of this folk, whou feithles they werne.
420 And as I wente be the waie, wepynge for sorowe,
I seigh a sely° man me by, opon the plow hongen.   *poor, innocent*

7. Lines 89–93: cf. Phillipians 3:18–19.
8. See Ephesians 5:14.
9. Now my comfort is cast away; do you know no remedy?
1. The friars based their order on the imitation of the apostolic life.

His cote was of a cloute° that cary² was y-called,   *cloth*
His hod° was full of holes, and his heer oute,°   *hood / sticking out*
With his knopped schon clouted full thykke.³
425 His ton° toteden° out as he the londe treddede,   *toes / poked*
His hosen overhongen his hokschynes° on everiche a   *ankles*
    side,
Al beslombred° in fen° as he the plow folwede.   *slathered / mud*
Twey myteynes, as mete, maad all of cloutes⁴
The fyngers weren forwerd° and ful of fen° honged.   *were worn out / muck*
430 This whit° waselede° in the fen almost to the ancle,   *man / wallowed*
Foure rotheren° hym byforn that feble were worthen.°   *heifers / become*
Men myghte reken° ich° a ryb, so reufull° they weren.   *count / each / pitiful*
His wiif walked him with, with a longe gode,°   *goad (whip)*
In a cutted° cote,° cutted full heyghe,   *short / coat*
435 Wrapped in a wynwe schete to weren hire fro weders,⁵
Barfote on the bare iis,° that the blode folwede.   *ice*
And at the londes° ende° laye a litell crom-bolle,°   *field's / edge / scrap-bowl*
And theron lay a litell childe lapped° in cloutes,   *wrapped / rags*
And tweyne° of tweie° yeres olde opon another syde,   *two / two*
440 And alle they songen o° songe, that sorwe was to heren;   *one, a single*
They crieden alle o cry, a careful° note.   *sorrowful*
The sely° man sighede sore and seide, "Children, beth   *simple*
    stille!"
This man loked opon me, and leet the plow stonden,
And seyde, "Sely° man, why syghest thou so harde?   *Poor*
445 Yif the lakke liflode,° lene° the ich will   *sustenance / lend*
Swich good as God hath sent. Go we, leve° brother."   *dear*
I saide thanne, "Naye, sire, my sorwe is wel more,
For I can° nought my Crede, I kare well harde.   *know*
For I can fynden no man that fully byleveth
450 To techen me the heyghe° weie, and therfore I wepe.   *high*
For I have fonded° the freres of the foure orders,   *tried*
For there I wende have wist, but now my wit lakketh;⁶
And all my hope was on hem, and myn herte also.
But thei ben fully feithles, and the fend° sueth."°   *the fiend / follow*
455 "A, brother," quath he tho, "beware of tho foles!°   *fools*
For Crist seyde himselfe 'of swich I you warne,'⁷
And false profetes in the feith he fulliche° hem calde,°   *utterly / called*
'In vestimentis ovium, but onlie° withinne⁸   *except*
Thei ben wilde wer-wolves° that wiln° the folk robben.'   *man-wolves / wish*
460 The fend° founded hem first the feith to destroie,   *devil*
And by his craft thei comen in to combren° the   *burden*
    Chirche,

2. A kind of coarse material.
3. With his lumpy shoes bound with rags.
4. Two mittens, matching (the shoes) made all of rags.
5. Wrapped in a winnowing sheet to protect her from bad weather.
6. For there I thought I would have learned, but now my wits lack (i.e., I am at my wit's end).
7. Christ warns often of false prophets. See, for example, Matthew 24:11, 23–5 and the next n.
8. *In vestimentis ovium*: in the clothing of sheep. Matthew 7:15: "Beware of false prophets who come to you in the clothing of sheep but inwardly they are ravening wolves."

By the coveitise of his craft the curates to helpen.
But now they haven an hold, they harmen full many.
Thei don nought after Domynick, but dreccheth° the   *oppress*
     puple,
465 Ne folwen nought Fraunces, but falslyche lybben,°   *live*
And Austynes rewle thei rekneth but a fable,
But purchaseth hem pryvylege of popes at Rome.
Thei coveten confessions to kachen some hire,[9]
And sepultures° also some wayten to cacchen.   *administering burials*
470 But other cures° of Cristen thei coveten nought to have,   *spiritual duties*
But there as wynnynge liith—he loketh none other."[1]
"Whough schal I nemne thy name that neighboures
     the kalleth?"[2]
"Peres," quath he, "the pore man, the plowe-man I
     hatte."°   *am called*
"A, Peres," quath I tho, "I pray the, thou me telle
475 More of thise tryflers, hou trechurly° thei libbeth?°   *treacherously / live*
For ichon° of hem hath told me a tale of that other,   *each one*
Of her° wicked liif, in werlde that° hy lybbeth.   *their / where*
I trowe that some wikked wyght wroughte this orders
Thorughe that gleym of that gest that *Golias* is y-calde,[3]
480 Other° ells° Satan himself sente hem fro° hell   *or / else / from*
To cumbren° men with her craft, Cristendome to   *burden*
     schenden?"°   *destroy*
"Dere brother," quath Peres, "the devell is ful queynte.°   *sly*
To encombren° Holy Churche he casteth ful harde,   *oppress*
And fluricheth° his falsnes opon° fele° wise,°   *flaunts / in / many / ways*
485 And fer he casteth to-forn, the folke to destroye.[4]
Of the kynrede° of Caym° he caste° the freres,[5]   *kindred / Cain / fashioned*
And founded hem on Farysens,° feyned for gode.[6]   *Pharisees (hypocrites)*
But thei with her fals faith michel° folk schendeth;°   *many / destroy*
Crist calde hem° himself 'kynde ypocrites.'°[7]   *them / 'hypocrites by nature'*
490 How often he cursed heme, well can I tellen.
He seide ones himself to that sory puple:°   *people*
'Wo worthe° you, wyghtes, wel lerned of the lawe!'[8]   *come unto*
Eft° he seyde to hemselfe,° 'Wo mote you worthen,   *Again / them*
That the toumbes of profetes tildeth° up heighe!   *raise*
Youre faderes fordeden° hem and to the deth hem   *killed*
495   broughte.'°   *(Matt. 23:29–31)*
Here I touche this two,° twynnen° hem I thenke,   *(see ll. 486–7) / to compare*
Who wilneth° ben wisere of lawe than lewde° freres,   *wishes / unlearned*

---

9. They covet hearing confessions to make some money.
1. But where profit lies—they look to nothing else.
2. How shall I name you by the name that your neighbors call you?
3. Through that trick of that story that is called The Apocalypse of Bishop Golias. This remark refers
     to a twelfth-century satire on the monastic orders.
4. And thoroughly he contrives beforehand to destroy people.
5. The friars were believed to have descended from Cain.
6. The friars were often compared to the Pharisees whom Christ condemned as hypocrites. See
     Matthew 15 and 23.
7. See Matthew 23:28.
8. See Matthew 23:23: "Woe to you scribes and Pharisees, hypocrites; because you tithe mint, and
     anise, and cummin, and have left the weightier things of the law; judgment and mercy and faith."

And in multitude of men ben 'Maysters' y-called,°   (*cf. Matt.*23:7)
And wilneth worchips of the werlde, and sitten with
    heye,°   *the nobility*
500 And leveth lovynge of God and lowness° behinde.   *humility*
And in beldinge° of tombes thei travaileth grete   *building*
To chargen° her chirche-flore, and chaungen it ofte.   *overload*
And the fader of the freers defouled hir soules—
That was the dygginge° devel that dreccheth° men ofte.*undermining / troubles*
505 The divill° by his dotage° dissaveth° the Chirche,   *devil / derangement*
And put in the Prechours, y-paynted withouten.   */ deceives*
And by his queyntise° they comen in, the curates to   *deceitfulness*
    helpen,
But that harmede hem harde, and halp° hem full litell!   *helped*
But Austines° ordynaunce was on a good trewthe,   *Augustine's*
510 And also Domynikes dedes weren dervelich° y-used,   *diligently*
And Frauncis founded his folke fulliche on trewthe,
Pure parfit prestes, in penaunce to lybben,
In love and in lownesse, and lettinge° of pride,   *hindering*
Grounded on the godspell,° as God bad himselve.   *Gospel*
515 But now the glose° is so greit° in gladding° tales   *gloss / got-up / cheerful*
That turneth up two-folde, unteyned° opon trewthe,   *unfastened*
That thei bene cursed of Crist, I can hem well prove;

✳   ✳   ✳

"Sur," I seide myself, "thou semest to blamen.
Why dispisest thou thus thise sely° pore° freres,   *poor / poor in spirit*
None° other men so mychel,° monkes ne preistes,   *no / much*
Chanons° ne Charthous,° that in Chirche serveth? *Canons / Carthusian Monks*
It semeth that thise sely men han somwhat the°   *thee*
675   greved°   *grieved*
Other° with word or with werke, and therfore thou   *either*
    wilnest
To schenden° other° schamen hem with thi sharpe   *destroy / or*
    speche,
And harmen holliche,° and her hous greven."°   *wholly / persecute*
"I praie the," quath Peres, "put that out of thy mynde.
680 Certen for sowle hele° I saie the° this wordes.   *health / to you*
I preise nought possessioners but pur° lytel;[9]   *very*
For falshed of freres hath fulliche encombred
Many of this maner men, and maid° hem to leven°   *made / abandon*
Here° charité and chasteté, and schosen° hem to   *their / devote themselves*
    lustes,
685 And waxen to° werldly, and wayven° the trewthe,   *too / abandon*
And leven the love of her God, and the werlde serven.
But for falshed of freres I fele in my soule
(Seynge° the synfull liif) that sorweth myn herte   *seeing*
How thei ben clothed in cloth that clennest scheweth;°   *appears*
690 For aungells and arcangells all thei whiit° useth,   *white*

---

9. Friars were not allowed to own property. *Possessioners*: clergy who were allowed to have possessions.

And alle aldermen° that bene *ante tronum*.°¹   *elders / before the throne*
Thise tokens° haven freres taken; but I trowe that a   *outward signs*
    fewe
Folwen fully that cloth, but falsliche that useth.
For whiit in trowthe bytokneth clennes° in soule;   *purity*
695 Yif he have undernethen whiit, thanne he above wereth
Blak, that bytokneth bale° for oure synne,²   *sorrow*
And mournynge for misdede of hem that this useth,
And serwe for synfull liif—so that cloth asketh.
I trowe ther ben nought ten freres that for synne
    wepen,
700 For that liif is here° lust,° and theryn thei libben.°   *their / object of desire / live*

                    ✢   ✢   ✢

"Leve° Peres," quath I tho, "I praie that thou me tell   *dear*
Whou I maie conne my Crede in Cristen beleve."
"Leve brother," quath he, "hold° that I segge,°   *remember / say*
795 I will techen the° the trewthe, and tellen the the sothe."   *thee*

                    ✢   ✢   ✢

                Credo°   *The Creed (lit. "I believe")*

Leve thou on oure Louerd° God, that all the werlde   *Lord /*
    wroughte,°   *created*
Holy heven opon hey° hollyche° He fourmede,   *high / wholly*
And is almighti Himself over all His werkes,
And wrought, as His will was, the werlde and the
800   heven;
And on gentyl Jesu Crist, engendred of Himselven,
His own onlyche° Sonne, Lord over all y-knowen,   *only*
That was clenly° conseved° clerly, in trewthe,   *purely / conceived*
Of the hey° Holy Gost; this is the holy beleve;°   *high / belief*
805 And of the mayden Marye man was he born,
Withouten synnfull sede°—this is fully the beleve;   *seed*
With thorn y-crouned, crucified, and on the Crois
    dyede,
And sythen his blessed body was in a ston byried,°   *buried*
And descended adoune to the derk helle,
810 And fet oute our formfaderes, and hy full feyn weren;³
The thridde daye rediliche° himself ros° fram deeth,   *quickly / arose*
And on a ston there° he stod he steigh° up to hevene,   *where / ascended*
And on his Fader° right hand redeliche he sitteth,   *Father's*
That almighti God over all other whyghtes;°   *creatures*
815 And is hereafter to komen Crist, all Himselven,
To demen° the quyke° and the dede withouten any   *judge / living*
    doute;
And in the heighe Holly° Gost holly° I beleve,   *Holy / wholly*

1. An apparent assemblage of details from Rev. 4:4 (the 24 elders dressed in white); 4:9 (the elders before the throne); and 7:9 (the multitude in white robes before the throne).
2. The habit of the Dominicans is black over white.
3. And fetched out our forefathers, and they were very glad.

And generall Holy Chirche also, hold this in thy minde;
The communion of sayntes, for soth I to the° sayn;°   *thee / say*
820 And for our great sinnes forgivenes for to getten,
And only by Christ clenlich to be clensed;
Our bodies again to risen, right as we been here,
And the liif everlasting leve ich to habben. Amen.
And in the sacrement also that sothfast God on° is—   *in*
Fulliche His fleche and His blod—that for us dethe
825   tholede.°   *suffered*
And though this flaterynge freres wyln,° for her° pride,   *will / their*
Disputen of this Deyté,° as dotardes° schulden,   *Deity / fools*
The more the matere is moved, the masedere hy
worthen.[4]
Lat the losels° alone, and leve° thou the trewthe,   *fools / believe*
830 For Crist seyde it is so, so mot it nede worthe;°   *it needs must be*
Therfore studye thou nought theron, ne stere° thi   *stir*
wittes:
It is his blissed body, so bad° he us beleven.   *bade*
Thise maystres of dyvinitie many, als I trowe,
Folwen nought fully the feith, as fele° of the lewede.   *much*
Whough° may mannes wiit,° thorugh werk of   *how / wits*
835   himselve,
Knowen Cristes pryvitie, that all kynde passeth?[5]
It mot ben a man of also° mek° an herte   *so / meek*
That myghte with his good liif that Holly Gost fongen;°   *receive*
And thanne nedeth him nought never for to studyen.
He mighte no Maistre ben kald—for Crist that
840   defended°—   *forbade*
Ne puten no pylion° on his pild° pate;   *priest's cap / bald (i.e., tonsured)*
But prechen in parfite liif, and no pride usen.
But all that ever I have seyd, so it me semeth,
And all that ever I have writen is soth, as I trowe,
845 And for amending° of thise men is most that I write;   *reforming*
God wold hy° wolden ben war and werchen the better!   *they*
But, for° I am a lewed man, paraunter° I mighte   *since / perhaps*
Passen par aventure, and in som poynt erren;[6]
I will nought this matere maistrely° avowen.°   *like a master / insist on*
850 But yif ich have myssaid,° mercy ich° aske,   *misspoken / I*
And praie all maner men this matere amende,
Iche° a word by himself,° and all, yif it nedeth.   *each / itself*
God of his grete myghte and his good grace
Save all freres that faithfully lybben,
855 And alle tho that ben fals, fayre hem amende,
And gyve hem wiit and good will swiche dedes to
werche
That thei maie wynnen the lif that ever schal lesten.

Amen.

4. The more the matter is broached, the more confused they become.
5. Know Christ's hidden wisdom that surpasses all the natural world.
6. Go too far by chance and in some point make a mistake.

From Mankind†

* * *

MANKYNDE   Of the erth and of the cley we have our
    propagacyon;°   *origin*
By the provydens of Gode thus be we derivatt,°   *derived*
To whos mercy I recomende this holl° congrygacyon.   *whole*
I hope onto° hys blysse ye be all predestynatt—°   *unto / predestined*
190   Every man for hys degre° I trust xall° be partycypatt°—*rank / shall / included*
Yf we will mortyfye our carnall condycyon
Ande our voluntarye dysyres,° that ever be   *desires /*
    pervercionatt,°   *perverse*
To renunce them and yelde us under Godys
    provycyon.
My name ys Mankynde. I have my composycyon
195   Of a body and of a soull, of condycyon contrarye;
Betwyx them tweyn ys a grett dyvisyon:
He that xulde° be subjecte, now he hath the victory.   *should*
Thys ys to me a lamentable story,
To se my flesch of ° my soull to have gouernance.   *i.e., over*
200   Wher the goodewyff ° ys master, the goodeman° may   *wife / husband*
    be sory.
I may both syth° and sobbe, this ys a pytouse°   *sigh / pitiable*
    remembrance.
O thou my souell,° so sotyll° in thy substance!   *soul / subtle*
Alasse, what was thi fortune and thi chaunce
To be assocyat with my flesch, that stynking
    dungehill?
205   Lady, helpe. Souerens, yt doth my soull myche yll[1]
To se the flesch prosperouse and the soull trodyn°   *trampled*
    under fote.
I xall go to yondyr man and asay° hym Y wyll.   *test*
I trust of gostly° solace he wyll be my bote.°   *spiritual / help*
All heyll,° semely father! ye be welcom to this house.   *hail*
210   Of the very° wysdam ye have partycypacyon.   *true*
My body wyth my soule ys ever querulose.°   *quarrelsome*
I prey, for sent° charité, of your supportacyon.°   *holy / support*
I beseche you hertyly of your gostly° comforte.   *spiritual*
I am onstedfast° in lyvynge. My name ys Mankynde.   *unsteady*
215   My gostly enmy the Devill° wyll have a grett dysporte°   *Devil / sport*
In synfull° gydynge° yf he may se me ende.   *sinful / behavior*

MERCY   Crist sende you goode comforte. Ye be
    welcum, my frende.

---

† Selections transcribed from the facsimile of *The Macro Plays*, ed. David Bevington (Washington,
D.C., 1972), Folger Shakespeare Library, MS v.a. 534, fols. 124ʳ–134ʳ. Printed by permission of
the Folger Shakespeare library. This "morality play"—a form of allegorical drama produced by tour-
ing troupes for mixed audiences and typically depicting personifications of virtues and vices competing for a human soul—was composed c. 1465–1470. It nevertheless presents a form which had
begun to develop in Langland's day. Bevington provides a full edition with comprehensive glosses
in his anthology, *Medieval Drama* (Boston, 1975), pp. 901–938.
1. Our Sovereign Lady [Mary], help. It does my soul much ill.

Stonde uppe on your fete, I prey you aryse.
My name ys Mercy. Ye be to me full hende;°   *gracious*
220 To eschew vyce I wyll you avyse.

MANKYNDE   O Mercy, of all grace and vertu ye are the
    well°—   *i.e., source*
I have herde tell of ° ryght worschyppfull clerkys°   *from / scholars*
Ye be approxymatt to Gode and nere of hys consell.
He hat° instytut° you above all hys werkys.   *has / instituted*
225 O, your lovely wordys to my soull are swetere then
    hony.

MERCY   The temptacyon of the flesch ye must resyst
    lyke a man,
For ther is ever a batell betwix the soull and the
    body:
Vita hominis est militia super terram[2]
Oppresse your gostly enmy and be Crystys own
    knyghte;
230 Be never a cowarde ageyn° your adversary.   *against*
Yf ye wyll be crownyde, ye must nedys° fyghte.   *necessarily*
Intende well and Gode wyll be you° adjutory°   *to you / helpful*
Remember, my frende, the tyme of contynuance°—   *i.e., duration of life*
So helpe me Gode, yt ys but a chery tyme.°—   *cherry season (i.e., short)*
235 Spende yt well. Serve Gode wyth hertys° affyance.°   *heart's / loyalty*
Dystempure° not your brayn wyth goode ale nor wyth   *cloud /*
    wyn.°   *wine*
Mesure° ys tresure—Y forbyde you not the use—   *moderation (cf. p. 424)*
Mesure yourself ever; beware of excesse.
The superfluouse gyse° I will that ye refuse;   *manner*
240 When nature ys suffysdye,° anon that ye sese.°   *satisfied / cease*
Yf a man have an hors and kepe hym not to hye,°   *i.e., too well fed*
He may then reull° hym at hys own dysyere;°   *rule / desire*
Yf he be fede overwell he wyll dysobey
Ande in happe° cast hys master in the myre.   *by chance*

245 NEW GYSE°   Ye sey trew, ser, ye are no faytour.°   *Fashion / liar*
I have fede my wyff so well tyll sche ys my master;
I have a grett wonde on my hede—lo! and theron
    leyth° a playster°—   *lies / bandage*
Ande another ther° I pysse my peson.°   *where / pea soup*
Ande° my wyf were your hors, sche wold you all to-   *if*
    bann.°   *curse*
250 Ye fede your hors in mesure, ye are a wyse man.
I trow,° and° ye were the kyngys palfreyman,°   *trust / if / horseman*
A goode horse xulde° be gesumme.°   *should / a rarity*

MANKYNDE   Wher spekys this felow? Wyll he not com nere?

---

2. "The life of man on earth is a battle, a struggle," Job 7:1.

MERCY   All to° son,° my brother, I fere me, for you.°   *too / soon / your sake*
255   He was here ryght now, by hym that bowte° me   *ransomed*
        dere,°   *dearly*
        With other of hys feloyse;° they kan° moche sorow.   *fellows / know*
        They wyll be here ryght son, yf I owt° departe.   *at all*
        Thynke on my doctryne; yt xall° be your defence.   *shall*
        Lerne wyll° I am here—sett my wordys in herte—   *while*
260   Wythin a schorte space° I must nedys hens.°   *i.e., time / hence*

NOWADAYS   The sonner the lever,° and yt be evyn   *better*
        anon!°   *if it be right away*
        I trow° your name ys Do Lytyll, ye be so long fro°   *believe / away from*
        hom.
        If ye wolde go hens, we xall cum everychon,°   *everyone*
        Mo° then a goode sorte.°   *more / many*
265   Ye have leve,° I dare well say,   *permission to leave*
        When ye wyll go forth your wey.
        Men have lytyll deynté° of your pley   *delight*
        Because ye make no sporte.

NOUGHT   Your potage xall be forcolde, ser; when wyll
        ye go din?³
270   I have sen a man lost twenty noblys° in as lytyll tyme;   *gold coins*
        Yet yt was not I, be Sent Qwintyn,°   *Quentin*
        For I was never worth a pottfull a° wortys° sithyn° I   *of / vegetables / since*
        was born.
        My name ys Nought. I love well to make mery.
        I have be sethen° with the comyn°   *before now / common*
        tapster° of Bury   *bartender*
275   And pleyde so longe the foll° that I am evyn° very —   *fool / even*
        wery°   *weary*
        Yit xall I be ther ageyn to-morn.°   *tomorrow*

MERCY   I have moche care for you, my own frende;
        Your enmys wyll be here anon, thei make ther
        avaunte.°   *boast*

                        *   *   *

344   NEW GYSE   Ey, Mankynde, Gode spede you with your
        spade!°   *(i.e., emblem of hard work)*
        I xall tell you of a maryage:
        I wolde your mowth and hys ars that thys° made   *(i.e., the spade)*
        Wer maryede° junctly° together.   *married / jointly*

MANKYNDE   Hey° you hens, felouse,° wyth   *hasten / fellows /*
        bredynge.°   *reproach*
        Leve your derysyon and your japying.°   *joking*
350   I must nedys labure; yt ys my lyvynge.

---

3. Your soup will be completely cold, sir. When will you go dine?

NOWADAYS   What, ser, we cam but lat° hethyr.°   *just lately / hither*
Xall all this corn grow here
That ye xall have the nexte yer?
Yf yt be so, corne hade nede° be dere,°   *necessarily / costly*
355   Ellys ye xall have a pore lyffe.

NOUGHT   Alasse, goode fadere, this labor fretyth° you   *devours*
    to the bon.
But for your croppe I take grett mone;°   *sorrow*
Ye xall never spende° yt aloune.   *finish*
I xall assay to geett° you a wyffe—   *get*
360   How many acres suppose ye here by estymacyon?

NEW GYSE   Ey, how ye turne the erth uppe and down!
I have be° in my days in many goode town   *been*
Yett saw I never such another tyllynge.

MANKYNDE   Why stonde ye ydyll? Yt ys pety° that   *pity*
ye were born!

365   NOWADAYS   We xall bargen with you and nother°   *neither*
    moke° nor scorne.   *mock*
Take a goode carte in hervest° and lode yt wyth your   *harvest*
    corne,
And what xall we gyf ° you for the levynge?°   *pay / crop-yield*

NOUGHT   He ys a goode starke° laburrer, he wolde   *strong*
    fayn° do well;   *gladly*
He hath mett wyth the goode man Mercy in a
    schroude° sell.°   *hard / season*
370   For all this he may have many a hungry mele°—   *meal*
Yyt° woll ye se he ys polytyke.   *yet*
Here xall be goode corn, he may not mysse° yt;   *fail of*
Yf he wyll have reyn° he may overpysse° yt;   *rain / piss on*
Ande yf he wyll have compasse° he may overblysse°   *compost / bless*
    yt
375   A lytyll wyth hys ars lyke.°   *in the same way*

MANKYNDE   Go and do your labur! Gode lett° you   *prevent /*
    never the°   *prosper*
Or with my spade I xall you dynge,° by the Holy   *bash*
    Trinyté.
Have ye non other man to moke°, but ever me?   *mock*
Ye wolde have me of your sett?°   *group*
380   Hye° you forth lyvely, for hens I wyll you dryffe.°   *hasten / drive*

NEW GYSE   Alas, my jewellys°—I xall be schent° of my   *testicles / deprived*
wyff!

* * *

525 TITIVILLUS[4]   * * * To speke wyth Mankynde I wyll tary
      here this tyde,°   *time*
      Ande assay hys goode purpose for° to sett° asyde.   *i.e., so as / i.e., set it*

* * *

541 MANKYNDE   Now Gode of hys mercy sende us of° hys   *a portion of*
      sonde.°   *grace*
      I have brought sede here to sow wyth my londe;
      Qwyll° I overdylve yt,° here yt xall stonde.   *while / dig up its ground*
      In nomine Patris et Filii et Spiritus Sancti now I wyll
      begyn.[5]
545 Thys londe ys so harde yt makyth wn° unlusty° and   *one / lacking in desire*
      yrke;°   *irked*
      I xall° sow my corn at wynter and lett Gode werke.   *shall*
      Alasse, my corn ys lost! here ys a foull werke;
      I se well by tyllynge lytyll xall I wyn.
      Here I gyff uppe my spade for now and for ever;
550 To occupye my body I wyll not put me in dever.°   *endeavor*
      (Here Titivillus goth out wyth the spade)°   *(a stage direction)*
      I wyll here° my envynsonge here or° I dyssever.°   *hear / before / leave*
      Thys place I assyng° as for my kyrke.°   *assign / church*
      Here in my kerke I knell on my kneys.
      Pater noster qui es in celis.[6]

555 TITIVILLUS   I promes you I have no lede° on my helys;°   *lead / heels*
      I am here ageyn to make this felow yrke.

* * *

609 MANKYNDE   Adew, fayer masters! I wyll hast me to the
      ale-hous
      Ande speke with New Gyse, Nowadays, and Nought
      And geett me a lemman with a smattrynge° face.   *attractive*

NEW GYSE   Make space, for cokkys° body sakyrde,°   *God's (see n. 3 p.442) /*
      make space!   *sacred*
      A ha! well overron!° Gode gyff hym° evyll grace! *escaped / i.e., my hangman*

* * *

MERCY   What how, Mankynde! Fle that felyschyppe, I
      you prey!
726 MANKYNDE   I xall speke wyth the° another tym, to-   *thee*
      morn, or the next day.
      We xall goo forth together to kepe my faders yer-day.° *death anniversary*
      A tapster, a tapster! Stow,° statt,° stow!   *i.e., come on, let's go / slut*

---

4. A devil often associated with the sin of sloth and errors of inattentiveness.
5. In the Name of the Father, the Son, and the Holy Ghost. (A conventional beginning or ending to
   a spiritual oration.)
6. Our Father who art in heaven. (The first line of the Lord's Prayer.)

* * *

734 MERCY   My mynde ys dyspersyde, my body trymmelyth
          as the aspen leffe.[7]
     The terys xuld trekyll down by my chekys, were not
          your reverrence.[8]
     Yt were to me solace, the cruell vysytacyon of deth.
     Wythout rude behaver I kan° expresse this   *can hardly*
          inconvenyens;
     Wepynge, sythynge,° and sobbynge were my   *sighing*
          suffycyens°   *sustenance*
     All naturall nutriment to me as caren° ys odybull.°   *carrion / odious*
740 My inwarde afflixcyon yeldyth° me tedyouse unto   *makes*
          your presens.
     I kan not bere yt evynly° that Mankynde ys so   *serenely*
          flexybull.°   *fickle*

* * *

756 O goode Lady and Mother of mercy, have pety° and   *pity*
          compassyon
     Of the wrechydnes of Mankynde, that ys so wanton
          and so frayll!
     Lett mercy excede justyce, dere Mother, amytt° this   *grant*
          supplycacyon,
     Equyté° to be leyde° in party,° and Mercy to prevayl;   *justice / set aside / part*
760 To sensuall lyvynge ys reprovable that ys nowadays,[9]
     As be° the comprehence° of this mater yt may be   *by / contents*
          specyfyde.
     New Gyse, Nowadays, Nought, wyth ther allectuouse°   *enticing*
          ways
     They have pervertyde Mankynde, my swet sun,° I have   *son*
          well espyede.°   *found out*

* * *

799 MYSCHEFF   How, Mankynde! Cumm and speke wyth
          Mercy, he is here fast by.
     MANKYNDE   A roppe,° a rope, a rope! I am not worthy.   *(hangman's) rope*

* * *

811 MERCY   Aryse, my precyose redempt son! ye be to me
          full dere.
     He ys so tymerouse, me semyth hys vytall spryt doth
          exspyre.
     MANKYNDE   Alasse, I have be so bestyally dysposyde,° I   *inclined*
          dare not apere;°   *appear*

7. My mind is distracted, my body trembles like an aspen leaf.
8. The tears should trickle down my cheeks, were it not for your (the audience's) reverence.
9. What happens nowadays is blamable on sensual living.

To se your solaycyose° face I am not worthy to   *solac-giving*
   dysyere.°   *desire*

*   *   *

835 MANKYNDE Than mercy, good Mercy! What ys a man
      wythowte mercy?

*   *   *

879 MERCY Mankynde, ye were oblivyous of my doctrine
      manyterye°   *admonitory*
    I seyd before, Titivillus wold asay° you° a bronte;°   *try / on you / assault*
    Beware fro° hensforth of hys fablys° delusory.   *from / fables*
    The proverbe seyth, *Jacula prestita minus ledunt*.[1]
    Ye have iii aduersaryis and he ys mayster of hem all:
    That ys to sey, the Devell, the World, the Flesch and
      the Fell°—   *Skin*
885 The New Gyse, Nowadayis, Nought, the World we
    may hem° call—   *them*
    And propylly° Titivillus syngnyfyth the Fend of helle; *properly*
    The Flesch, that ys the unclene concupissens of your
      body.
    These be your iii gostly enmyis, in whom ye have put
      your confidens.
    Thei browt you to Myscheffe to conclude your
      temporall glory
890 As yt hath be schewyd° before this worscheppyll° *shown / worshipful*
    audiens.
    Remembyr how redy I was to help you—fro swheche
      I was not dangerus[2]—
    Wherfore, goode sunne, absteyne fro syn evermore
      after this.
    Ye may both save and spyll° your soule that ys so   *kill*
      precyus.
    Libere welle, libere nolle, God may not deny, iwys.[3]
895 Be ware of Titivillus wyth his net and of all enmys°   *inimical*
    will,
    Of your synfull delectacion that grevyth your gostly
      substans.
    Your body ys your enmy; let hym not have hys wyll.
    Take your leve whan ye wyll. God send you good
      persverans!°   *perseverance*

    MANKYNDE Syth I schall departe, blyse° me, fader, her   *bless*
    then I go.
900 God send us all plenté of hys gret mercy!

---

1. Darts anticipated wound less.
2. Remember how eager I was to help you; from such I was not hesitant.
3. Freely to choose or freely not to choose, God may not deny you truly.

MERCY   *Dominus custodit te ab omni malo*⁴
*In nomine Patris et Filii et Spiritus Sancti. Amen!*⁵
*Hic exit Mankynde*⁶

*   *   *

The Letter of John Ball,
Sent to the Commons of Essex†

Johan Schep,¹ somtyme Seynte Marie prest of York,	
and now of Colchestre, greteth wel Johan Nameles,	
and Johan the Mullere, and Johon Cartere, and bid-	
deth hem° that thei bee war° of gyle in borugh,° and	*them / cautious / town*
stondeth togidere° in Godes name, and biddeth Peres	*together*
Ploughman go to his werk, and chastise wel Hobbe	
the Robbere,² and taketh with yow Johan Trewman	
and alle hiis felawes, and no mo,° and loke schappe	*more*
you to on heved,³ and no mo.	

Johan the Mullere hath y-grounde smal, smal, smal;⁴	
The Kynges Sone of hevene schal paye for al.	
Be war or the be wo;⁵	
Knoweth your freend fro your foo.	
Haveth ynow, and seith "Hoo!"⁶	
And do wel and bettre,⁷ and fleth° synne,	*flee*
And seketh° pees,° and hold you therinne.	*seek / peace*

And so biddeth Johan Trewman and alle his felawes.

---

4. God protects you from all evil.
5. Cf. line 544.
6. Here exits Mankind.
† Text of London, British Library, Royal MS 13. E.ix., fol 287ʳ. Printed by permission of the British Library. Edited also by James M. Dean in his anthology, *Medieval English Political Writings* (see above, p.436, n.†). The text—a prose letter, followed by a poem—is one of several ascribed to various leaders of the so-called Peasants' Revolt of 1381, a series of uprisings among the artisan classes against, among other things, what they claimed to be excessive and corrupt taxation. The manuscript includes this note (originally in Latin): "John Ball confessed that he wrote this letter and sent it to the commons and that he made many others. For which reason . . . he was drawn, hanged, and beheaded before the king at St. Albans, the ides of July; and his body was quartered and sent to four cities of the kingdom."
1. John Shepherd: no doubt an allegorical alias for Ball himself, who was reputed to be a former priest (evidently of St. Mary's church in York, according to this letter). The other allegorical names may have been intended to serve similarly as aliases for specific rebels, but unequivocal identifications have not proved possible. For further commentary, see the essay by Anne Middleton, printed herein, p. 572 (and esp. pp. 582–83).
2. Cf. *Piers Plowman*, Passus V, line 463.
3. And see that you follow but one leader.
4. A proverbial reference to hard times, when grain is ground finer to make it go further.
5. Be wary before woe befall thee.
6. Have what you need, and say "Stop!" (I.e., show restraint in your actions.)
7. An evident allusion to Do-wel and Do-bet in *Piers Plowman*.

From the Chronicon Angliae†

[Alice Perrers and Edward III]¹

* * *

There was at this time in England a tempest brought about by an unchaste woman, a manipulative harlot, named Alice, surname Perrers, of low birth, originally the daughter of some tiler of the village of Henney, but who obtained great fortune, being neither beautiful nor noble, but who knew how to make up for these defects through flattering speech.

Blind Fortune elevated her to such heights that she who was necessarily accustomed to go about a handmaid and an unclean housemistress, to carry water with her own arms, was advanced much more than was appropriate into a close intimacy with the king—and with the queen still living, the king would prefer her in love. After this insurgence into intimacy with the king, she made such a fool of him that he permitted the high and great business of the kingdom to be determined by her counsel.

Thereafter she alone began to seduce the king, and knew she had also captivated his mind, and she began to administer all matters without justice, to support false suits, everywhere to acquire unauthorized possessions for her own use; and if on occasion she herself encountered legal resistance, she approached the king, who soon either legally or illegally helped with her defense, and brought about a decision in her favor. Englishmen tolerated this for many years, because they loved the king sincerely and guarded against offending him.

* * *

[Eventually, the lords and magnates, their patience worn out by the persistent outrages of Alice and her favorites—including Sir William Latimer and her husband William Windsor—are moved in the "Good Parliament" of 1376 to have her banished from the presence of the king. She agrees to this, but later that year she is permitted to return, as Edward weakens and draws near to death.]

* * *

As soon as [Alice] realized that the king was at death's door, she planned her escape; but before her flight * * * she stole the rings of state from the royal hands—such that no one might doubt the truth of the old proverb: no courtesan can abstain from petty theft. * * * Nothing indeed besides nature was at work, because her female condition was fulfilled.

* * *

---

† "Chronicle of the English," selection translated by Stephen H. A. Shepherd from Chronicon Angliæ 1328–88, ed. E. M. Thompson, Rolls Series 64 (London, 1874), pp. 95–100, 142–143.
1. Cf. Langland's account of Lady Meed, Passus II–IV, who, it is conventionally argued, is modeled in part on Alice Perrers. An excellent point of departure for further study of the relationship between Langland's work and accounts of Alice Perrers is Stephanie Trigg, "The Traffic in Medieval Women: Alice Perrers, Feminist Criticism and Piers Plowman," The Yearbook of Langland Studies 12 (1998): 5–29.

THE CROWNING OF A KING

THOMAS OF WALSINGHAM

From the Historia Anglicana†

[*The Coronation of Richard II, July 16, 1377*][1]

* * *

Thus came to pass the charmed and joyous day * * * the day a long time awaited, of the restoration of the peace and the law of the land that for a long time had been banished by the indolence of the old king and the greed of his fawning followers.

In honor of the king, the people had arranged for fountains to flow continually—for the three or more hours of the procession's duration— with an abundance of wine. Above the market named "Chepe" they also made a mock fortification having four towers, through which from two sides the wine also flowed out abundantly. Four of the most beautiful maidens had been placed in the towers, one in each of the towers, dressed in white, with a regal bearing and stature; at a distance from the approaching king they blew out golden leaves in his direction, and as he drew closer, skilfully they threw out gold coins over him and to his right. When he came in front of the fortification, they took golden bowls and filled them with wine from the founts of the said fortification and offered them to the king and the lords. At a part of the fortification raised between the four towers a golden angel was placed, holding a golden crown in its hands, which angel had been constructed in such a manner that, bending, it might stretch out the crown to the king.

Many other tributes to the king were devised throughout the community, each of which would take a long time to enumerate. * * * Thus with so many of the people and so many of the lords and magnates joyfully he is led to the Palace of Westminster, where he rested that night.

On [Thursday], the sixteenth day of July * * * in the late morning the congregation of the Archbishop and the bishops and the nobility made way to Westminster in a procession with caped monks; and the Bishops with monks reached the entrance to the royal chamber, finding the king prepared in that place by attendants who assisted him at his side. They led him to the church of St. Peter, singing antiphons in honor of the Apostle, with corresponding prayers—and with this prayer:

> Truly the king, in order to come soon to the altar, has prostrated himself alone before the altar.[2]

---

† "History of the English," translated by Stephen H. A. Shepherd from *Thomas Walsingham . . . Historia Anglicana*, ed. H. T. Riley, 2 vols, Rolls Series 28 (London, 1863), II (A.D. 1272–1381), pp. 331–332.

1. Richard II came to the throne at the age of ten, and so the unprecedented exuberance of his coronation reflected more a hope for the reform of a state damaged by the corruption of Edward III's later years than certainty over the new administration's abilities. Partly through this hope, the coronation procession and ceremony was the longest ever, replete with the symbolism of an idealized kingship. On Edward III's decline, see p. 485 above.

2. I.e., before the coronation, which takes place in front of the high altar, the king must engage in a gesture of submission to the power of the King of Kings.

Meanwhile, the floor had been spread with cloths and tapestries. Following the said prayer, the archbishop, when assisted by the bishops, prostrated himself upon the floor near the king. At the same time, two bishops devoutly sang the liturgy, after which the risen king was conducted to his seat, with the chorus chanting this antiphon:

Strong is thy hand.[3]

Then the bishop gave a sermon on the subject of kings and royal power in relation to the people, how the king had it from the people, and which the people themselves must obey.[4]

* * *

From The Maner and the Forme of the Coronacioun of Kyngis and Quenes of Engelonde†

[*The King's Coronation Oaths*]

* * *

The kyngis othe the day of his coronacioun: The Archebishop of Cauntirbery schall oppose° and aske the kynge the same day if he will holde, graunte, and kepe the lawes and the customes grauntid to his pepill of° olde, devoute, and rightwise kyngis aforehande,° and yf he will swere it—and namely the lawes and the customes and the libertees of the gloriouse kynge Edwarde°—to the pepill and to the clergie. And the kynge schall behote° that he will kepe all these forseyde thingis. Than schall the Archebishop schewe and declare certeyne articles, to the which the kynge shall swere.

question

i.e., by previously

Edward I (d. 1307)
promise

The first poynt of the othe: "Thou schalt kepe full pese° and acorde in God to the chirche, to the pepill, and to the clergie." And the kynge schall answere, "I schall doo."

peace

The secunde poynte: "Thou schalt doo kepe in all this domys° rightfull, and every rightwiseness° and discrecioun with mercy and trouthe." And the kynge shall swere, "I schall do."

judgments / act of justice

The thirdde poynte: "Grauntest thou all rightfull lawes and customes to beholde, and wilt thou behote° that thou will defende and strengthe° them to the wor-

promise
support

---

3. Psalm 89:13.
4. For an account of the coronation oaths sworn by the king and bishops, see the next selection.
† Reprinted, with new glosses and explanatory notes, from Harold Arthur, Viscount Dillon, "On a MS. Collection of Ordinances of Chivalry of the fifteenth century, belonging to Lord Hastings," *Archaeologia* 57.i (1900):29–70 (51–52). Dillon's transcription is from a MS produced c. 1461, but which records details of the ceremony that could date back as far as 1385.

shipe of God to thi myght and powere, the which the
comoun° schall chese?" And the kynge shall answere,   *people*
"I graunt and behote it."

* * *

*The amonicioun of bishopis to the kynge that schall be
radde of oon.*[1] "Sir kynge, we aske that it be grauntid
and pardonid to us and to eche of us and all oure
clergies that is yevyn°and takyn to us, ye will kepe and   *given*
gaunte the privilege of holy chirche and dewe° lawe   *due*
and rightwisnesse, and them defende, as a kynge
owith° and schulde in his reme,° to every bisshop and   *ought / realm*
abbot and to ther clergies." And the kynge schall
answere in this wise: "With glad wille and devoute
sould I yeve and behote to yow and to eche of yow
and to yowre clergies the priviligis of lawe canoun°   *canon law*
and of holy chirche, and I shall kepe and doo dewe
lawe and rightwisness and defende it in as moche as
I may, with Goddis helpe, as a kynge owith to doo in
his rewme to every bisshop and abbot and to ther clergies, bi resoun and right."

* * *

THOMAS BRINTON, BISHOP OF ROCHESTER

Sermon 69

[*The Parliament of the Mice and Rats*]†

* * *

But now it is known and almost everywhere proclaimed how, not the virtuous people, but those who live viciously and scandalously have for many a
season had the principal government of this kingdom. Although we uni-
versally murmur and protest about the government of such people, yet we
dare not speak the unmitigated truth about the appropriate remedy. * * *
Yet in this behaviour [the bishops] all make clear they are mercenaries, not
shepherds. * * *

---

1. The counsel of the bishops to the king, to be read by one (of the bishops).
† Translated by Stephen H. A. Shepherd from *The Sermons of Thomas Brinton, Bishop of Rochester*
   (*1373–1389*), ed. Sister Mary Aquinas Devlin, 2 vols, Camden Series 75–76 (London, 1954), II,
   pp. 316–317. Like Brinton, Langland employs the fable in an allegory of ineffective government
   (Prologue, 146ff.), although his account of the motivations of the rodents differs. Brinton preached
   this sermon probably on May 18, 1376, at a clerical convocation held during the so-called Good
   Parliament, where Brinton and other bishops would have served in the House of Lords. It is possible that Brinton is Langland's source, and suggests one of the later dates at which Langland could
   have completed the B-version. For further discussion, see G. R. Owst, "The 'Angel' and the
   'Goliardeys' of Langland's *Prologue*," *Modern Language Review* 20 (1925):270–279 and *Literature
   and Pulpit in Medieval England* (Cambridge: Cambridge UP, 1933), pp. 579–586; Eleanor Kellogg,
   "Bishop Brinton and the Rat Parliament," *PMLA* 1 (1935): 57–68; and see the selections from
   Ralph Hanna III, *William Langland*, reprinted in this Norton Critical Edition, p. 591.

Some would verify the psalm, "Have the workers of iniquity no knowledge? who eat up my people as they eat bread" [Psalm 53:4], saying, that
is, "let the Commons, who effectualy support the king and parliament like
the foundations of the state, deal with the problem." Not so, however, reverend fathers! lest our parliament be compared to the fabled parliament of
the mice and rats; of which it is told how, in their parliament, when they
proposed arranging for someone to set a bell around the neck of the cat—
so that the mice, safeguarded by the sounding of the bell, would without
peril be able to retreat to the refuge of their holes in the walls of the
building—an old rat stood in opposition. Of which innovation this rat
inquires if a mouse could tell the truth about the difficulty it would involve.
[A mouse answered,] "This arrangement is good if there is someone in parliament who has the disposition to perform such difficult work." And the
former did respond, "This cannot be determined in parliament and as a
consequence is unfounded and vain."

For the love of Christ and for the defense of the kingdom brought to so
great a crisis, we should not be such great talkers but doers—and so "Let
us, therefore, cast off the works of darkness, and let us put on the armor of
light" (Romans 13[:12]); in order that our life be emended and the kingdom be governed in accordance with justice, recall afresh also of the
Psalms, "Blessed are they that observe justice" [Psalm 106:3]; and so just
as the words of [my] theme, "the doer of the work, this man shall be
blessed" [James 1:25].

✳   ✳   ✳

The Case of the Earl of Devonshire†

Esturmy versus *Courtenay, 1392*

The records and process touching the earl of Devonshire.

Be it remembered that upon a complaint made to the king by William
Esturmy knight against Edward Courtenay earl of Devonshire, our lord the
king sent his writ to the said earl that he should be before the king and
his council on Thursday following the feast of Candlemas, the fifteenth
year of the said king, bringing with him one Robert Yeo his retainer.
On this day the said William declared, before the said council that whereas
one William Wyke of the county of Devonshire, tenant of the lord of
Huntington and of himself, recently pursued divers writs of our lord the

---

† Reprinted from I. S. Leadman and J. F. Baldwin, eds., *Select Cases Before the King's Council
1243–1482* (Cambridge, MA, 1918), pp. 77–81. Notes have been deleted. The Case of the Earl of
Devonshire sheds light on the verisimilitude of the Trial of Wrong in Passus IV. In 1391, Edward
Courtenay the Earl of Devonshire was charged with protecting his retainer Robert Yeo, whose servant at his instigation murdered William Wyke, a man who tried to sue Yeo. The Earl encouraged
Yeo to ignore any legal proceedings against him, and threatened the local justices of the peace. The
quarrel grew to involve many of the gentry of Devonshire and a civil war threatened to erupt. The
Earl was implicated then in what is known as "maintenance"; that is, "an attempt on the part of the
earl to sustain the quarrel of another." Finally, the King's Council called the Earl himself to appear
with Yeo away from the corruptible or intimidated local officials. The charges that had been made
by William Esturmy on behalf of the justices of the peace were there investigated. The Earl could
not refuse this call nor could he fail to admit his and his retainer's wrongs. He then appealed to the
king's mercy, whereupon, because of his high social status, both the Earl and Yeo were pardoned.
The Trial of Wrong follows many of the twists and turns of such a case, although in the poem the
King ultimately refuses to grant mercy to Wrong (Passus IV, lines 98–109).

king against the said Robert Yeo, and one of the said writs was taken by force from the hands of the said William Wyke by the said Robert Yeo and John Langford his servant and thrown into a well, and then other writs were directed to the sheriff of Devonshire and delivered to him at the suit of the said William Wyke to seize the bodies of the said Robert and John. Whereupon on Lady Day last passed the said John lying concealed in a ditch attacked the said William Wyke as he was coming to the church bare-foot on a pilgrimage, and horribly murdered him by command and at the instigation of the said Robert Yeo. And afterwards the said William Esturmy sat with John Wadham justice of the peace in this county, when the said Robert and John Langford were indicted of the aforesaid murder by the most worthy knights and esquires of this county, and then the said William Esturmy went to the house of the said earl expecting to find good favour, and the said earl said to him in the presence of John Grenville knight that he and his ally the false justice and others had indicted his servant the said Robert Yeo falsely, whereof he swore on the cross of his chapel that the said William Esturmy should answer with his body, calling him repeatedly false traitor, and said that he should have respite no longer than this day of his aforesaid promise, and moreover the earl sent (word) to him the same day by the said John Grenville that he should keep faith of what he had promised and then he said the same words to Walter Cornu, and at last he sent to the said William Esturmy William Gouys as messenger, who told him in the presence of Sir James Chudlegh, the said John Grenville and William Hankford on behalf of the said earl that he was false and that he should answer with his body, that he knew all the roads by which he must come and go, and that he should not escape the hands of the earl who was sure of him. And also the said William Esturmy says that the said earl had threatened and reproached William Beaumont, John Coppleston, William Burleston, Thomas Credy, and John Wotton because they had taken part in the inquest indicting the said felons. Wherefore these men as well as the said James, John Grenville, and Walter Cornu were required to come on the said Thursday before the said council to be examined upon the matters aforesaid. Whereupon the said John Grenville, having been sworn and examined before the said council said that he heard the very words that the earl spoke to the said William Esturmy, and that he took the message of the said earl just as the said William Esturmy had declared. And Walter Cornu having been sworn and examined before the said council said that the said earl spoke to him the same words as the said William Esturmy had said, but the earl discharged him of taking such a message; and the said James, John Grenville, and William Hankford, having been sworn and examined before the said council, said that they heard the message given to the said William Esturmy by the said William Gouys on behalf of the said earl just as the said William Esturmy had alleged. And the said John Wadham, having been examined before the said council, says that while he was sitting in a session of the peace at Exeter on Tuesday following the last feast of St. Hilary, holding process upon the said felons, the said John Grenville told him in the presence of the said William Esturmy and William Hankford that the said earl sent word to him that he should sit more uprightly without partiality in this session than he had at the last session. And the said William Esturmy said that the said John Grenville did not give his message fully, for he said that he had been

charged to say that the said John Wadham was a false justice; and as to this
the said John Grenville, having been sworn and examined before the said
council, says that his message was the same as the said John Wadham and
William Esturmy had declared; and also the said William Beaumont, having been sworn and examined before the said council, says that he was
vilely reproached by one John Folk, esquire of the said earl, and afterwards
by the earl himself, that he was perjured in the aforesaid indictment, but
this would be true of others more than of himself whom it behooved to
kneel and cry "mercy." And also the said John Folk said to the said William
Beaumont that the said James Chudlegh was false. And also the said earl
said to the said William Beaumont that the said Robert Yeo would be delivered in spite of the teeth of the said John Wadham and William Esturmy.
And John Coppleston, having been sworn and examined before the said
council, says that the said earl reproached him, saying he had perjured
himself for the aforesaid cause. And the said William Burleston, having
been sworn and examined before the said council, says that the said earl
reproached him saying he had falsely perjured. And John Wotton, having
been sworn and examined before the said council, says that the said earl
reproached him saying he had perjured, etc. And inasmuch as the said earl
had been commanded by writ to be before the king and his council at
Westminster on the aforesaid Thursday to answer to the things that
should be laid against him on behalf of the king, on this day the said earl
came before the said council and was given one day after another until the
king should be pleased to attend to this business. Whereupon after the following Thursday in the presence of our lord the king and of the lords spiritual and temporal remaining with him, namely the duke of Guienne and
Lancaster, the archbishop of Canterbury and the archbishop of York,
chancellor, the bishops of London, Winchester, Durham, St. David's,
Chester, the bishop of Salisbury, treasurer, the bishops of Hereford and
Chichester, the dukes of York and Gloucester, the earls of Derby, Rutland,
Arundel, Huntington and the earl marshal, Lord Roos, and many others,
wherein was propounded the entire matter aforesaid touching the said earl
of Devonshire, as well as the fact that the said Robert Yeo was indicted of
felony before the justices of the peace from whom the said earl of Devonshire had knowledge of the same indictment, but he did not put the said
Robert under arrest, rather the earl harboured him. To this the said earl
of Devonshire answered as regards the message that he sent to the said
John Wadham justice that this was true, and for this he threw himself on
the grace of our lord the king, and as to his having reproached the men
who had sworn in the said inquest, suggesting that they had perjured, he
acknowledged that he spoke to some of them declaring that it weighed
heavily upon him that they had perjured, not with the intent of reproach-
ing them, and for this also he placed himself in the king's grace; and as to
his having threatened the said William Esturmy who had the king's commission to take the said Robert Yeo as had been alleged against the said
earl of Devonshire, he answered saying that he had no knowledge of the
said William having such a commission, but he did say that he would like
to break his head, and for this also he placed himself in the king's grace.
Whereupon it was adjudged by our lord the king and his said council that
the said earl of Devonshire should be committed to prison, there to remain
until he paid to our lord the king fine and ransom at the pleasure of our

said lord the king. Immediately thereafter all the aforesaid lords, spiritual
as well as temporal, prayed our lord the king to do grace to the said earl of
Devonshire, having regard for the fact that he was of royal blood and one
of his uncles, and that it was the first time any such complaint had been
made to our lord the king against the said earl of Devonshire. Our lord the
king at the aforesaid request extended to the earl grace and pardon in his
behalf on condition that he should aid and sustain according to his power
the laws of our said lord the king and the execution thereof as well as his
ministers in guarding the laws and making execution thereof, so that if any
default on his part should be found in time to come contrary to this
(understanding), our said lord the king would take cognisance of the trespasses and the execution aforesaid, as (though they were) trespasses and
malfeasances committed and perpetuated by him anew.

CRITICISM

E. TALBOT DONALDSON

[Summary of the Poem]†

The Poem

The headings in the manuscripts of all three versions distinguish between
two major sections, the first of which (the *Visio*) is called by the same name
some of the explicits use for the whole poem, "The Vision of William Concerning Piers the Plowman": this consists of two dreams, after each of
which the narrator wakes. The second section (the *Vita*) is called "The Life
of Do-Well, Do-Better, and Do-Best According to Wit and Reason": this
consists of a single dream in *A*, but of seven in *B* and six in *C*. The concept
of Do-Well is one that comes to Will suddenly at the very end of the *Visio*
and becomes the object of his search for much of the rest of the poem. In
the *Visio* the narrator's dreams come to him while he is merely wandering
about the country in search of "wonders." As a result, Will is a more passive observer than he is when he is engaged actively in a search and par-
ticipating more directly in the action. In his dreams in the *Visio*, he is
granted only one interview with an allegorical figure, Lady Holy Church,
while in the *Vita* he meets and questions a host of allegorical figures and
sometimes takes strong exception to their replies, though their loquacity is
often such that he has a hard time getting a word in edgewise.

The *A*-text breaks off with Will's eloquent denial of the usefulness of
learning in obtaining salvation, but in *B* and *C* he continues his often
obstreperous search through dream and dream-within-dream until, as the
poem nears its end, he gradually withdraws from his active role and
becomes once more the passive observer he had been in the *Visio*. *Visio* and
Vita are alike in their sharp satire, especially of friars and corrupt clergy-
men, in their mingling of digressive homily with poetry of great intensity,
and in their constant discussion of the most basic tenets of Christianity.
Will's questions imply that the poet believed that the answer to the question of why the well-taught Christian society of late fourteenth-century
England was so badly behaved lay in a general failure to apprehend first
principles.

Society and its behavior are the subject of Will's first dream, which
comes to him while he is lying by a brook in the Malvern Hills. He sees in
a dream a fair field full of folk, situated between a lovely tower on a hill
and a dreadful donjon in a dale. The folk are of all sorts, from the top to
the bottom of society, behaving as people of the world do in all sorts of
occupations. Langland's penchant for satire ensures that most seem to be
doing their work badly or dishonestly. The dream of the fair field is
expanded in the *B*-text to include a rather cryptic glimpse of the political
situation in England under the young King Richard. While Will is still
surveying the field, Lady Holy Church appears to him and speaks of the
behavior of the folk and of the significance of the two towers. The fair one
is occupied by Truth or God, the other by Wrong or the Devil. It is characteristic of the poem that while Truth's abode is visible from the field at

† From *Dictionary of the Middle Ages* (New York: Charles Scribner's Sons, 1986), ed. Joseph R. Strayer,
vol. 7, pp. 331–337. Reprinted by permission of Charles Scribner's Sons.

the very beginning, the search for Truth is a constantly recurring theme throughout, as if what seems present and immediate is actually remote and elusive.

Will, who often shows the slow-wittedness shared by many medieval first-person narrators, does not recognize Lady Holy Church when she appears despite the fact that she speaks in terms of basic Christian doctrine. When he learns who she is, he at once asks her how he might save his soul. How one may attain salvation is a question often asked, and often answered, in the poem, so often that the search for salvation is sometimes said to be the chief theme. But as is customary with Langland, the very obviousness of the question conceals the extreme difficulty implicit in the seemingly simple answer it is apt to evoke. Thus when Holy Church explains that Will must practice charity, which she identifies with Truth, he objects that her answer is unsatisfactory for he has no "natural knowledge" of Truth; she must teach him better "by what power it originates in my body and where." Holy Church is angered by Will's obtuseness, but her reply, that knowledge of Truth is "a natural knowledge that teaches one in one's heart to love God," simply imputes to him the very thing he claims he lacks. Like other of Langland's seemingly august allegorical personifications such as Conscience and Reason, Holy Church is both human and fallible: she is like a Sunday school teacher impatient of her pupils' failure to grasp what seems to her self-evident.

The exchange between Will and Holy Church is paradigmatic of much that occurs in the poem. The questions he asks his interlocutors are usually simple, and the answers are generally (though not always) right, but the suggestions, like those offered by Lady Holy Church, are easier stated than acted upon. If things were as simple as she suggests, there would be no need for a poem based on the premise that Christianity has little reality except within the human heart, where it is to be apprehended not merely by the intellect but by the entire spirit. To gain such an apprehension, Will (and the human will) must live long, travel far, and dream much. The poem is a dramatization of an individual's attempt to learn the Truth in his heart.

Having been told, if unsatisfactorily, how to know the Truth, Will asks Holy Church to teach him how to know the False. Her answer is a protracted illustration of falseness: she points to a beautiful woman clad in rich scarlet (characters come and go in Will's dreams with truly dreamlike abruptness) who is her greatest enemy, Lady Meed. The following incident is Langland's most sustained piece of narrative and affords him a fine opportunity to exercise his powers as a satirist. It also affords him another opportunity to illustrate the complexity of the seemingly simple. Lady Meed (Reward) is about to be wedded to False with the assistance of unsavory allegorical figures such as Favel (Flattery), Liar, and Fickle-Tongue, as well as a number of officials of the church and of the civil service. But Theology, hearing of the wedding, objects that Meed must not be wedded to False since God has granted that Meed be given to Truth, despite Holy Church's contempt for her. To determine the true nature of Meed—to straighten out her ambiguity—is the object of much of the subsequent action. Theology recommends that Meed and her fiancé False go to London to find out in the law courts whether their marriage would be valid. The whole wedding party takes off in a marvelously grotesque procession: Meed rides on a sheriff "shod all new," Simony and Civil Law ride on summoners, and Liar becomes a "long cart" to carry some of the rabble. But when the King hears of what is going on and orders that False and his fellows be arrested, all run away, leaving Lady Meed alone to be taken into custody.

Treated as a privileged prisoner, Lady Meed at once begins to corrupt the secular and ecclesiastical authorities with bribes and promises of bribes. The King, who, like Theology, thinks she is of some potential benefit to society, offers her as wife to one of his knights, Conscience. But Conscience indignantly refuses her, and in a long speech he condemns her as a whore who gives illicit rewards to all comers, perverting justice with her largesse. Meed replies to these charges by arguing that meed in the sense "reward" is an absolutely necessary principle in society, which, since all work or serve for pay, could not function without it. She argues that even Conscience makes use of reward. In an extended topical reference, she accuses Conscience of causing the King (here Edward III) to settle the French wars by accepting only a "little silver"—a reference to the Treaty of Bretigny of 1360, by which Edward gave up his claim to the French throne in return for a huge sum. If Meed had been in charge, she says, the King would have defeated the French and rewarded his followers with parcels of the captured country.

The King is greatly impressed by Meed's defense, and Conscience is forced to offer a rebuttal. He tries to refute her claim that she represents payment for services rendered by making distinction between true meed, which is what God awards the just in the afterlife, and "meed measureless," which seems to denote any reward given on earth: Lady Meed is the latter. But so ideal a definition is too simplistic, leaving society with no word for legitimate compensation. The point bothered Langland, who in the C-text adds a passage in which Conscience, using an ingenious analogy from grammar, argues that the system of rewards by which society seems to function does not properly depend on the desire for gain but rather on the love and loyalty which exist between the servant and the served, of which reward is merely the tangible token. The idealism of B's definition remains; but another aspect of Langland's idealism is seen in C's determination not to let B's oversimplification remain unmodified.

In her final appearance, Meed resolves any lingering doubts by her own bad behavior. She appears in the judgment hall and interferes with the King's justice by offering to settle criminal cases with cash payments to the victims. The King, influenced by Reason, now realizes that Meed is a perverter of justice. He vows to rule his realm henceforth with the aid of Conscience and Reason—a moment of the triumph of virtue which, like other such moments in the poem, seems short-lived.

In all three texts Will wakes after Meed's condemnation, but in A and B he goes to sleep almost immediately to continue his dreaming. He hears a sermon, preached by Conscience in A and by Reason in B, to all the folk on the field, exhorting them to live better. As a result they go to confess their sins to Repentance, confessions that Will hears as emanating from personified deadly sins. These confessions, six in A and all seven in B, are probably the best-known part of the poem. Though Pride and Lechery receive only a few lines, Envy, Avarice, Gluttony, Sloth, and Wrath (omitted in A) are developed with great art, as allegorical figures, to be sure, but speaking as people in conditions appropriate to the sins they represent.

This extraordinary mingling of allegory and realism generates a vitality that rivals that of the pilgrims in Chaucer's General Prologue to the *Canterbury Tales*. Here follows, in the C-text, the quasi-autobiographical episode (described above) relating to Langland's clerical status.

After Will falls asleep following this incident, the C-text proceeds as had A and B (though C amplifies the confessions with material transferred from a later part of B). When the confessions are completed, in all three texts "a thousand of men" set off penitently in search of St. Truth. But no one knows where to find him—a palmer they meet has never heard of him—until a plowman suddenly "puts forth his head": this is the first appearance of Piers, the simple farmer whose name became the poem's. Piers knows the elusive Truth well, having served him, he says, for many years, and he instructs the pilgrims how to reach him. But the folk say they need a guide, since they find confusing Piers's directions, which lead the traveler through the Ten Commandments and other basic Christian precepts. Piers offers to lead them himself if they will first help him plow his half acre.

All agree to this proposal and they work hard for a time; but then their enthusiasm wanes, and many sit about idly. Piers, whose natural leadership is made stronger by a good measure of righteous wrath, calls upon Hunger to get the idlers back to work, and Hunger's arrival makes everyone work strenuously. Piers, highly conscious of his obligation to feed society, asks Hunger how he should treat people who refuse to work, and receives good moral advice. But having proved to be a helpful moralist, Hunger, like other of Langland's allegorical personifications, then shows an unexpected though not unnatural aspect of himself—he refuses to depart until he has been well fed. Piers and the people have to labor frantically to satisfy him, whereupon he goes to sleep like an overfed glutton, and everyone stops work. Langland knew that hunger made men both overwork and, when they could, overeat—hunger's effect is not simple, but cyclical.

At the beginning of the final section of the *Visio*, Truth sends Piers a message telling him to stay home and plow his field, and sends a pardon for him and those who help him plow. Truth's message to stay at work confirms Piers's function as the economic basis of society, while his being the principal recipient of the pardon tends to make him the spiritual basis as well. Langland discusses the pardon at some length and the matter of who will or will not qualify for it: in general it will apply to all those who behave as they should. At the end of this discussion, a priest approaches Piers and asks to see his pardon so that he may interpret it for him. Will himself sees that the pardon consists of only two lines: "They that have done good shall go into life everlasting; and they that have done evil into everlasting fire." In these lines, actually from the Athanasian Creed, the priest says he can find no pardon, presumably because the reward of good and the punishment of evil do not involve pardon, which applies only to sin. Of course, the very fact that a virtuous man can achieve everlasting life is itself a pardon, effected by Christ's sacrifice, but the priest is technically correct within the limited context of his thought.

In the A- and B-texts, Piers reacts surprisingly by tearing the pardon apart "in pure anger," after which he vows to cease from manual labor and to devote himself henceforth to prayers and to penance. The poet gives us no hint for the motive of his anger, which is exacerbated when the priest scornfully asks him where he got the learning he shows when he quotes Scripture as a reason for his sudden vow. No wholly satisfactory explanation for the tearing of the pardon has been advanced, but the analogy with Moses' destruction of the tablets of the law after his descent from Sinai, while far from exact, is suggestive. Moses was also angered at the behavior of a priest, Aaron, who led the people to worship the golden calf. Furthermore, in the patristic tradition, Moses' angry action was considered a type of the replacement of the Old Law by the New, an action signifying a movement from something supremely good to something better. Piers himself is clearly moving from his position as simple farmer to that of a dedicated and authoritative exponent and teacher of Christian doctrine, which is what he is when we next meet or hear of him in the B- and C-texts (he does not reappear in A).

In Piers's imitation of Moses we get an illustration of the poet's belief that the individual Christian must relive Scripture historically as well as spiritually. But the C-poet, perhaps yielding to complaints that the scene made Piers seem impious by destroying a pardon sent from Truth, breaks off with the priest's announcement that he can find no pardon, omitting the tearing of the pardon and Piers's quarrel with the priest. Thereafter in all three texts Will awakens and broods upon the meaning of his dream. He comes to the conclusion (as so often, one a little aside from the point) that, while papal pardons are efficacious, at Judgment Day the surest pardon is Do-Well. It is here that Do-Well first appears, soon to be joined by his grammatical kinsmen Do-Better and Do-Best.

Here the *Visio* ends; and with the *Vita* begins Will's search for Do-Well. While still awake, he questions two Franciscan friars, who tell him Do-Well dwells with them. Will denies this stridently, sharing his author's scorn for the friars' self-satisfaction. Once more asleep, Will encounters "a much man, like to myself," who turns out to be Thought. Like many of the allegorical personifications Will meets, Thought is an aspect of his own psyche. In answer to Will's question, Thought gives a definition of the three Do's that fails to satisfy him. Wit (Intelligence) suddenly appears and gives other definitions, which still do not satisfy Will. Wit's wife, Dame Study, rebukes Wit for wasting advice on one whose motives she suspects. She excoriates Will for wanting knowledge that she assumes he will misuse. Will's courtesy pacifies her, and she sends him on to Clergy (Learning). Will is warmly welcomed by Clergy and his wife, Dame Scripture, and Clergy again defines the Do's.

All these definitions Will receives vary, but in general Do-Well appears to be a person in active, secular life who lives and makes a living in accord with Christian teaching; Do-Better seems more contemplative, withdrawn from secular activity, living in patience and charity, and helping and teaching others; Do-Best seems to be an ecclesiastical executive, one who punishes the wicked and cares for the good, a bishop or a pope. These definitions accord roughly with the several manifestations of Piers Plowman. We have already seen him making a transition from Do-Well to Do-Better in the Pardon scene, and his handling of the people who helped him plow his field foreshadows his final appearance as executive.

A misconstruction of some of Clergy's remarks starts Will thinking of predestination, fear of which brings him to the not entirely logical conclusion that learning is of little help in attaining salvation, and the A-text

breaks off with Will's eloquent condemnation of learning: apparently Langland had introduced into his poem issues he was unable to solve in poetry.
In B and C the action is resumed with a kind of allegory of the poet's abandonment of his quest in favor of more worldly though unspecified activity,
which he pursued for a number of years. When Fortune, to whom he had
submitted himself in this period, abandons him he returns to the quest.
After a series of dialogues with Scripture, with Lewte (Justice), and, in B,
with an unnamed interlocutor who becomes in C Recklessness, an aspect
of Will, he has a marvelous inner dream in which Kind (Nature) takes him
up on a mountain and shows him a vision of the natural world without
humanity. But Will has reached his lowest point in understanding, and the
reverence he feels for God's ways as they appear in the natural world is dis-
pelled when he takes his vision to prove that all the animals save man are
guided by reason: therefore he rebukes Reason for not guiding men. Reason tells him to mind his own business, and Will awakes back into the outer
dream, ruefully aware that he has spoiled an opportunity to make progress
in his search.

   This conclusion is confirmed by a figure who appears to him and tells
him that he should not have rebuked Reason. Will follows the newcomer,
who introduces himself as Imaginative, actually Will's own constructive
memory, the faculty that enables human beings to make proper sense of
their experience. Imaginative answers a number of questions that have
puzzled Will, and most especially explains to him the importance of clergy,
learning, in the Christian scheme. With characteristic Langlandian irony,
Imaginative chides Will for writing when there are already enough books
to teach what Do-Well is—and enough pairs of friars.

   But Imaginative suddenly vanishes, and Will awakes. When he sleeps
again, it is Conscience who comes to comfort him. He is invited to take
dinner with Clergy, and finds himself at a side table with Patience, eating
sour food of penance while a fat doctor of divinity sits at the head table
munching victuals of the best. The doctor is thought to be modeled on a
contemporary Dominican, and Will's outrage at his smugness provides a
fine bit of double-edged satire. Will asks his usual question about the Do's,
and after the doctor gives his definition, Conscience calls upon Clergy for
his. Clergy refuses to answer on the grounds that Piers Plowman has
denied learning any value except for love, that is, except insofar as it
teaches love. In B, Patience then defines the Do's as to learn, to teach, and
to love God and one's enemies, placing stress on the last. In C, Piers suddenly appears and speaks the definition given to Patience in B, after which
he disappears.

   The treatment of Piers in this scene helps explain how he eventually
took on a life almost independent of his creator. Will, the poet's surrogate,
has just treated the guest of honor with ill-tempered satirical wit that we
have come to associate with the poet himself, and has had to be hushed
by Conscience and Patience. These same august allegorical figures recognize Piers as a superior authority. Thus at the same time that we are
encouraged to identify the poet with the badly behaved Will, we see the
poet's other creation, Piers, at his most exalted, and the difference in the
moral order of the two makes it seem impossible that the person Will
resembles could possibly have created Piers. It is hardly surprising that
some critics have supposed that Piers Plowman must have had mythic

existence before Langland wrote his poem. And at the end of the scene Conscience takes on his own independent life when he suddenly vows to leave Clergy and to become a pilgrim with Patience, despite Clergy's claim that he can teach him more than Patience can.

Will follows the pilgrims, who soon come upon a person identified as both a minstrel and a wafer-seller, the busiest of men, Hawkin the Active Man, whose coat is stained with many spots of dirt. These are his sins, which he confesses to Patience at length, a kind of repetition of the earlier confessions of sin that C avoids by transferring much of the confession to them. Patience preaches Hawkin a sermon on the life of patient poverty, through which one may avoid the deadly sins. Patience seems to suggest that Do-Well cannot be made actual in an active life. Paradoxically, in order to do well, one must really move toward Do-Better by living the life of patient poverty. After Patience's sermon Hawkin is left wailing for his sins. In *B*, Will wakes to wander the country like a lunatic, still in search of Do-Well, despite the discouraging example of Hawkin. Reason finally takes pity on Will and rocks him to sleep. There appears to him an extraordinary creature with many names, the chief of which is Anima (Soul or, in the theological sense, Life). In *C*, Will does not wake, and the creature, renamed Liberum Arbitrium (Free Will), appears to him in a continuation of his previous dream.

Anima–Liberum Arbitrium, a kind of model of the human psyche with all its functions such as thought, reason, and memory, takes Will a step further along the path Piers has already trod, from the active outer world into his own soul, where, conditioned by patient poverty, one learns to practice love. Anima–Liberum Arbitrium speaks most eloquently of Charity, whom Will says he has never known. In *B*, Anima tells Will that without Piers Plowman's help one will never know Charity, for Piers alone can look into men's wills. Anima then conflates two biblical texts (1 Cor. 10:4; Matt. 16:18) into a kind of identification of Piers with Christ: *Petrus id est Christus*. Apparently Piers is seen as an aspect of Christ, human nature at its best, historically that human nature which craved redemption and which Christ took upon himself when he became man. Piers the simple virtuous farmer has left his half acre to become the Christlike exponent of Christian charity, has gone all the way from Do-Well to Do-Better.

In *C*, Anima's association of Piers with Christ is weakened, and in the following scene, where in *B* Piers plays a major role, he is replaced in *C* by Liberum Arbitrium. In *B*, Anima, responding to Will's inevitable objection that despite Anima's discussion he still does not know what charity means, describes it as the fruit of a tree named Patience which grows in an orchard called man's heart. This tree is in the care of Piers Plowman and his associate Liberum Arbitrium. At the mention of Piers's name, Will faints, and in a dream-within-a-dream Piers shows him the tree. In *C*, Liberum Arbitrium takes Will directly to the tree, and there is no secondary dream.

The Tree is the most complex of all Langland's images. It symbolizes both Patience and Charity, and since it is propped by the three piles of the Trinity, it symbolizes also the Trinity, the interaction of whose three parts is the cause of charity. Since man is made in the image of God, the Tree grows within man's heart. Its fruits are marriage, widowhood, and virginity—analogues of the three parts of the Trinity. Piers (Liberum Arbitrium in C) describes how he defends the tree with the three piles, and Will asks if he might taste an apple; when the tree is shaken, the fruit that falls from it turns out to be the prophets and patriarchs. This fruit the Devil seizes as it falls and bears off to limbo. It appears that the tree has become also an image of that Tree of the Garden of Eden whose fruit tempted Eve to original sin. In B, Piers angrily seizes the second pile of the Trinity, the Son, and hits out after the Devil. This action is at once followed by—seemingly causes—Christ's Incarnation. Gabriel visits the Virgin and Christ is conceived. The poet then gives a summary narrative of Christ's life and death. In C, the final violent section is taken by Libera Voluntas Dei, the free will of God, into whom Liberum Arbitrium has suddenly metamorphosed.

The summary of Christ's life and death is a kind of reading of Scripture, but as always Will must not only read it but live it, and he now begins a journey that will take him to Jerusalem on the first Good Friday. On a mid-Lenten Sunday he meets successively with Abraham (Faith) and Moses (Hope), each of whom is seeking a knight named Christ, who alone can release the souls lying in Abraham's bosom and seal the commandment Moses received on Mt. Sinai. Will and his companions are overtaken by a Samaritan riding on a mule who is hastening to a joust in Jerusalem. He is not specifically identified as Charity or as Piers or as Christ, but his succor of a man who falls among thieves (whom neither Faith nor Hope could help) shows him to be in some sense all three. He explains the doctrine of the Trinity to Will at great length and with considerable ingenuity, though the relevance of the doctrine to Christ's sacrifice, which we are about to witness, is hard for the modern reader to understand.

When the Samaritan hurries away to Jerusalem, Will wakes and wanders wildly until he once more sleeps. He dreams he is in Jerusalem on Palm Sunday, where he sees one who is "like the Samaritan and somewhat like Piers Plowman" riding barefoot on an ass's back, like a knight who comes to be dubbed. Will witnesses the Crucifixion, which he describes simultaneously as a tournament in which the Christ-knight jousts with Death and as a literal crucifixion. When Christ dies, Will follows him to hell. Here he hears the Four Daughters of God disputing about the great light before hell's gates, with Mercy and Peace arguing that Mary's son has come to release the souls of the patriarchs and prophets, while Truth and Righteousness indignantly deny that those in hell can ever be let out. As Christ appears at hell's gates the devils argue with one another about whether he can despoil hell of their prey. In a marvelous passage, Christ explains that he has come to claim what was stolen from him in the Garden of Eden, and that he has become man in order to redeem man—a trick to cheat a trickster. Hell's gates break open, Christ frees those souls he wishes, the Daughters of God kiss one another, and Will wakes to summon his wife and daughter to Easter Mass.

With this triumphant scene a poet more sanguine might well have closed his poem. But, surprisingly, Christ's triumph is not man's Do-Best, nor does the universal hope it brings long survive. In the last two passus of the poem (unrevised in the C-text), Will witnesses the founding of the church and its ultimate subversion by the friars, and the poem ends like a true apocalypse. In Piers Plowman's final appearance, he has become St. Peter and the type of the good pope, and as such he is also Do-Best. Conscience

tells Will that before ascending to heaven Christ gave Piers power to forgive all men their sins who pay what they owe to Piers's pardon. Will himself watches the descent of the Holy Spirit on the Apostles at Pentecost,
and sees the Spirit in the form of Grace join with Piers. In a reversion to
the agricultural imagery of Piers's first appearance, Grace distributes
seeds—skills by which men may earn honest livings and the four cardinal
virtues by which they may govern themselves. The half acre becomes the
whole earth on which Piers and Grace cultivate Christianity, and a barn
called Unity or Holy Church is erected wherein Christians may store their
grain and take refuge against the attacks of Antichrist.

The latter begins his attacks as soon as Grace and Piers go off to cultivate the earth. Conscience has the common people fortify Unity and withdraw into it for safety. But the cardinal virtues are perverted into tools of
self-gratification, and Antichrist's attack on Unity becomes fiercer. Will
awakes from his sleep not knowing where to find food to support himself.
While still awake, he meets Need, who advises him to pervert the cardinal
virtue of temperance by making a virtue of necessity, that is, to be needy,
as Christ was, but to make of neediness an excuse for begging his livelihood. Will goes to sleep and dreams how Antichrist ultimately overcomes
Unity when, at Clergy's request, Conscience allows the begging friars to
enter: their easy confessions poison Contrition, and Unity is wholly corrupted. The narrator, now an old man ready for death, hears Conscience in
despair vow to become a pilgrim and go to find Piers Plowman, who alone
may remedy what has happened. Conscience cries after Grace until Will
awakes for the last time. Like Truth so many times in the poem, Do-Best
has been found and lost. Piers has become the elusive symbol of the leader
of the true church whom many in the Reformation were to adopt as their
own.

ROBERT CROWLEY

[A Renaissance Reader's Response]†

The Printer to the Reader.

Beynge desyerous to knowe the name of the Autoure of this most worthy
worke (gentle reader) and the tyme of the writynge of the same: I did not
onely gather togyther suche aunciente copies as I could come by, but also
consult such men as I knew to be more exercised in the studie of antiqui-
ties, then I my selfe have ben. And by some of them I have learned that the
Autour was named Roberte langelande, a Shropshere man borne in Cley-
birie, aboute viii myles from Maluerne hilles.'

For the time when it was written: * * * We that may justly conject therfore
that it was firste written about two hundred yeres paste, in the tyme of Kynge
Edwarde the thyrde. In whose tyme it pleased God to open the eyes of many
to se hys truth, geving them boldenes of herte, to open their mouthes and
crye oute agaynste the worckes of darckenes, as did John wicklefe, who also
in those dayes translated the holye Bible into the Englishe tonge, and this

---

† From *The Vision of Pierce Plowman* (London, 1550), pp. lxxiii–lxxiv.

writer who in reportynge certaine visions and dreames, that he fayned him selfe to have dreamed: doeth moste christianlye enstruct the weake, and sharply rebuke the obstinate blynde. There is no maner of vice, that reigneth in anye estate of men, whiche this wryter hath not godly, learnedlye, and wittilye, rebuked.

* * *

C. S. LEWIS
[On Langland's "Intellectual Imagination"]†

* * *

* * * Scholars more interested in social history than in poetry have sometimes made this poem appear much less ordinary than it really is as regards its kind, and much less extraordinary as regards the genius of the poet. In fact, its only oddity is its excellence; in *Piers Plowman* we see an exceptional poet adorning a species of poetry which is hardly exceptional at all. He is writing a moral poem, such as Gower's *Miroir de l'homme* or Gower's Prologue to the *Confessio Amantis*, and throwing in, as any other medieval poet might have done, a good deal of satire on various 'estates'. His satire falls heaviest where we should expect it to fall—on idle beggars, hypocritical churchmen, and oppressors. Like Chaucer he reverences knighthood. Even as a moralist he has no unique or novel 'message' to deliver. As a cure for all our ills he can offer us only the old story—do-wel, do-bet, and do-best. His advice is as ancient, as 'conventional', if you will, as that of Socrates; not to mention names more august. It is doubtful whether any moralist of unquestioned greatness has ever attempted more (or less). * * * Langland is a learned poet. He writes for clerks and for clerkly minded gentlemen. * * * He offered to his educated contemporaries fare of a kind which they well understood. His excellent satiric comedy, as displayed in the behaviour of the seven Deadly Sins belongs to a tradition as old as the *Ancren Riwle*; and his allegorical form and pious content were equally familiar.

What is truly exceptional about Langland is the kind, and the degree, of his poetic imagination. His comedy, however good, is not what is most characteristic about him. Sublimity—so rare in Gower, and rarer still in Chaucer—is frequent in *Piers Plowman*. The Harrowing of Hell, so often and so justly praised, is but one instance. There is not much medieval poetry that does not look pale if we set it beside such lines as these:

> Kinde huyrde tho Conscience, and cam out of the planetes
> And sente forth his foreyours, fevers and fluxes—
> Ther was 'Harow!' and 'Help! Here cometh kynde,
> With Deth that is dredful to undo us alle!'
> The Lord that lyuede after lust, tho aloude criede

† From *The Allegory of Love* (Oxford: Oxford UP, 1936), pp. 159–61.

After Comfort, a knyght, to come and bere hus baner.
'Alarme, alarme!' quath that Lord, 'eche lyf kepe hus owene![1]

In a quieter mood, the great vision wherein the poet beholds 'the sea, and the sun, and the sand after' and sees 'man and his make' among the other creatures, is equally distinctive.[2] There is in it a Lucretian largeness which, in that age, no one but Langland attempts. It is far removed from the common, and beautiful descriptions of nature which we find in medieval poetry—the merry morning and the singing birds; it is almost equally far from the sterner landscapes of *Gawain and the Greene Knight*. It belongs rather to what has been called the 'intellectual imagination'; the unity and vastness were attained by thought, rather than by sense, but they end by being a true image and no mere conception. This power of rendering imaginable what before was only intelligible is nowhere, I think, not even in Dante, better exemplified than in Langland's lines on the Incarnation. They are, so far as I know, perfectly accurate and clear in doctrine; and the result is as concrete, as fully incarnate, as if the poet were writing about apples or butter:

> Love is the plonte of pees and most preciouse of vertues;
> For hevene holde hit ne my3te so hevy hit semede,
> Til hit hadde on erthe 3oten hym-selue.
> Was never lef upon lynde lyghter ther-after,
> As whanne hit hadde of the folde flesch and blode ytake.
> Tho was it portatyf and pershaunt as the poynt of a nelde.[3]

Doubtless such heights are rare in Langland, as they are rare in poetry at all; but the man who attains them is a very great poet. He is not, indeed, the greatest poet of his century. He lacks the variety of Chaucer, and Chaucer's fine sense of language: he is confused and monotonous, and hardly makes his poetry into a poem. But he can do some things which Chaucer cannot, and he can rival Chaucer in Chaucer's special excellence of pathos.

ROBERT WORTH FRANK

From *Piers Plowman* and the Scheme of Salvation†

* * *

The poet, I believe, used the triad Dowel, Dobet, and Dobest, not as a set of terms, but as a literary device to elaborate his meaning. He used the triad to express the divisions of the idea contained in the generic term Dowel as he first used it in the poem: Dowel is the good life that leads to salvation. Because the personifications vary in their capacity to inform the Dreamer, and because various activities considered good fall into two or three parts, statements about Dowel are sometimes broken into two parts

---

1. *P. Plowman*, C, xxiii, 80 et seq.
2. Ibid. C, xiv. 135 et seq.
3. Ibid. C, ii. 149 et seq.
† From *Piers Plowman and the Scheme of Salvation: An Interpretation of Dowel, Dobet, and Dobet* (New Haven: Yale UP, 1957), pp. 37–39, 118. Reprinted by permission of the publisher. Notes have been renumbered.

(Dowel and Dobet) or into three (Dowel, Dobet, and Dobest). If Conscience tells the Dreamer about penance as a necessary part of the good life, he must observe the threefold division of penance and tell him about contrition, confession, and satisfaction. The threefold division of ideas in medieval thought is, of course, a commonplace. Moreover, there are degrees of effort in the struggle to lead the good life. And the triad Dowel, Dobet, and Dobest is, after all, a comparison of the adverb "wel" and therefore represents degrees of effectiveness in the effort to "do well."

As evidence that the triad is an elaboration of what is contained in the generic term Dowel, consider first the contrast between the first mention of Dowel and the first mention of the triad. Dowel's introduction is dramatic. It comes in the Pardon Scene after considerable suspense has been created about the pardon; the term carries the important message that good deeds rather than indulgences will lead to salvation; and it leads to an explosive argument between Piers and the priest. The triad, on the contrary, is introduced quite casually. The character Thought, asked about Dowel, replies that Dowel, Dobet, and Dobest the third are three fair virtues and not far to find.[1] The triad is mentioned without any preparation and is pointed up by no comment from the Dreamer. The manner of introduction suggests that Dobet and Dobest have no meaning apart from the meaning of the generic term Dowel.

There is the same contrast between Dowel alone and the triad in their final appearances. Except for an isolated passage where it is applied to Christ's life, the triad is last used when Conscience tells Haukyn that Dowel is contrition, Dobet is confession, and Dobest is satisfaction.[2] There is a reference to Dowel a few lines later, and perhaps an implied reference to the other terms, though they are not used.[3] And in this casual fashion the triad disappears from the poem. There are, however, two more references to Dowel, and both reveal its importance. The first occurs at the conclusion of *Dowel*. Haukyn, moved by Patience's speech on poverty, bewails the fact that after his christening he had not died and been buried "for doweles sake."[4] A few lines later the Dreamer, awakening, says it was a wondrous long time before he could "kyndely knowe what was Dowel."[5] At length, Soul gives him his answer.[6] Significantly, it is of Dowel alone that we hear at the last, not the triad. The triad is abandoned casually, and the poem discusses what it has been discussing all along, Dowel, the good life. Dowel, it should be noticed, begins and ends the inquiry. The triad appears in the midst of the discussion of Dowel and is dropped shortly before it ends. This is difficult to explain if Dobet and Dobest have some significance apart from Dowel.[7]

1. viii. 78 ff.
2. xiv.18–23.
3. xiv.87, 89–94.
4. xiv.320–1.
5. xv.1–2.
6. xv.23 ff., esp. 145 ff., the passage on charity.
7. Both B. xiv.320–1 and B. xv.1–2 are omitted in C. But in C, as in B, Dowel takes his final bow alone. The last reference to the triad is at C. xvii.25–36. But at C. xvii.177 the phrase "do wel" is used. Likewise, when the A-text is brought to what is apparently a premature conclusion, Dowel alone is referred to: A. xii.2, 32, 36–37, 54. And cf. the final reference, A. xii.94–95: " 'And therfore do after Do-wel · whil thi dayes duren, That thi play be plentevous · in paradys with aungelys!' " Part of A. xii is the work of one John But (cf. A. xii.106); how much, is a matter of wide disagreement. See the note on A. xii.117 in *Piers the Plowman: A Critical Edition of the A-Version*, ed. Thomas A. Knott and David C. Fowler (Baltimore, 1952), p. 170.

A study of the manner in which the poet uses the triad also suggests that it is a device for elaborating on the meaning of Dowel. There are several peculiarities to be observed. First, the relationship between the terms and their specifically assigned meanings is very unstable. Second, Dobet or Dobest is sometimes omitted from the triad without any apparent significance attaching to the omission. Third, Dowel is frequently used as a synonym for all three terms.

If the poet had in mind some concept, such as the Active Life, for which Dowel was his term, another concept for Dobet, and another for Dobest, he would be using the terms with the general meaning of each already clearly established. But the relationship between the terms and their meanings is very unstable. The poet has difficulty in assigning meanings to a term in specific situations. Again, he feels free to use the terms at times without any intention to communicate meaning (except their literal meaning). And he will give a meaning to one term and then later assign it to another. Yet if he has in mind a specific, over-all meaning for each term and expects the reader to perceive it, such treatment of the terms is puzzling.

✳   ✳   ✳

The poet's artistic vision is moralistic rather than raptly prophetic, realistic rather than mystical. The poem closes with both a warning and a note of hope.[8] There is neither universal darkness nor the supernal vision. The climactic battle with the sins and Antichrist has produced splendid Beethovian thunder, but the final chords are muted and unresolved. This is neither a tragedy nor a comedy, for the drama of salvation continues as long as mankind exists and as long as there is a Piers Plowman, a goodness and a divinity in man. There is nothing trivial, however, in this conclusion in which nothing is concluded. Conscience's cry for grace which closes the poem is nothing less than a cry for and a faith in the salvation of man. And the salvation of man is the great theme of the whole poem. It is the poem's reason for being.

MORTON BLOOMFIELD

From *Piers Plowman* as a Fourteenth-Century Apocalypse[†]

✳   ✳   ✳

In what formal tradition of genre was *Piers Plowman* conceived? What kind of work was it, and in what form did the author choose to express himself? Actually, it seems that Langland never could decide what form he

---

8. Burdach comments that the final vision "trembles in fear and hope for the future of mankind" (Konrad Burdach, *Der Dichter des Ackermann aus Böhmen und seine Zeit* [Berlin: Weidmann, 1926–32], p. 314). I have reviewed some of the varying comments on the mood of the poem at its close in "The Conclusion of *Piers Plowman*," *JEGP*, 49 (1950), 309. The discussion of Sister Rosa Bernard Donna, *Despair and Hope, A Study in Langland and Augustine* (Washington, D.C., 1948), pp. 65–73, 176–82, pertains to theological hope and despair, not the poet's mood. See E. Talbot Donaldson's review in *MLN*, 68 (1953), 141–42.

† From *Piers Plowman* as a Fourteenth-Century Apocalypse (New Brunswick, New Jersey: Rutgers University Press, 1961), pp. 8–10. Reprinted by permission of the publisher. Notes have been deleted.

was using, and from beginning to end, part of the difficulty of *Piers* to its readers is its confusion and even clash of genres. Just as Langland could never come to rest in his search for perfection, so he could never find the one genre in which to express himself. In other literary works there is a mixing of genre—indeed it is a characteristic of much medieval literature, but a deliberate one—but in *Piers* it seems that the mingling is more extensive than in most and is intimately related to the quest for perfection that is the basic subject of the poem. And it is not entirely deliberate on the poet's part.

This is not the place to enter into a discussion of the importance of genre as one of the literary boundaries for the artist. Some have denied the validity of considering genre in assessing art; but without any reference to other periods, it is obvious that the medieval writer was very conscious of the kind of form in which he chose to present his artistic vision and that it is against the customary lines of this form that an author's innovations and uniqueness can best be understood. With a certain form went certain expectations which the writer felt he must at least satisfy.

Genre analysis is not a scientific subject. What is one man's genre may be another man's theme or motif. Some genres are artificially created by modern critics even when they have gone beyond the romantic notion that rhetoric implies insincerity. One must, however, accept as genres only literary forms defined as such before the time of the composition of the work being considered; for some forms are esoteric and others are so broad that they lose the distinguishing marks of a genre—a literary type that has a certain general organization and arouses certain definite expectations in its readers and listeners.

This problem of definition comes to the fore in connection with the quest around which *Piers Plowman* is mainly organized. The quest has been a most popular unifying principle in literature in all ages, but in the later Middle Ages it reached its apogee. "Then indeed," says R. W. Southern, "it meets us on all sides—in the Arthurian Romances, in allegories of love, in descriptions of the ascent of the soul towards God. The imagery of movement seemed at this time to lay hold on the imagination, and it invaded secular as well as religious literature." The quest is the literary counterpart of the new or revived twelfth-century conative attitude towards life, of the general Christian image of life as a pilgrimage, of actual travel, which increased as a result of the Crusades and greater wealth, and of what may be termed the idea of the Crusade itself, which seized all Europe. But Mr. Southern's opinion, that it is a theme or dominant image rather than a genre, is probably correct. It is certainly the commanding image of *Piers*.

A simple answer to the question of the genre of *Piers Plowman* would be to say that it is an apocalypse. The classic Judeo-Christian apocalypse is cast in dream form, or consists of several dreams, is a revelation from some superior authority, is eschatologically oriented, and constitutes a criticism of, and warning for, contemporary society. In the Old Testament and Apocrypha, we may see such literary forms in Daniel and Second Esdras and in early Christian literature in Revelation, the *Shepherd of Hermas*, and in the *Visio sancti Pauli*, to take only a few examples. The form of the apocalypse owes something to the late classical aretalogy, a narration of the theophany of a god among men with emphasis on his miracles for the furtherance of his cult. But its actual origins are obscure, and the matter need not be pursued further.

These apocalypses and others were known to the Middle Ages, and there is even a parody of one, in the *Apocalypsis Goliae* of the twelfth century, possibly by Walter Map but certainly connected with the British Isles. It is fundamentally a satire on the Church, and the superior guide is Pythagoras. It is closely modeled on the Revelation of St. John.

In many ways *Piers Plowman* seems to fit the category of apocalypse, yet there are certain fundamental differences. The emphasis on the quest is foreign to the apocalypse as we know it. There is no single guide in *Piers*, but rather a search for guides, although Holy Church and Conscience have a certain authority. The use of personifications is not a characteristic of the apocalypse, and there is a strong vein of irony in the figure of Will that is not consonant with the apocalypse. Although *Piers* does criticize contemporary society, is in dream form, and is eschatologically oriented, these characteristics of the apocalypse can be accounted for otherwise.

The chief objection to taking the form of *Piers* to be an apocalypse is that it is doubtful whether such a literary form existed. I agree with Father H. Musurillo when he writes, "The form known as 'apocalypse' creates a problem, and perhaps no useful purpose is served in making the term a technical one applicable both to the Revelation of St. John and the so-called Shepherd of Hermas." He says that the *Shepherd* is rather "allegorical fiction disguised as a primitive Christian prophecy."

The problem of the genre of *Piers Plowman* is thus complex, but in some sense it can be said to be formally an apocalypse. The apocalypse as it appeared in the Bible and early Christian literature and in the occasional late parody of it may have prepared the way for *Piers* and made it possible in a very fundamental sense. However, the particular shifting organization of *Piers* can be understood only in terms of other and more common high medieval literary forms. In a basic sense, it is an apocalypse, but because we cannot clearly accept this form of literature as an established genre, we had better see it in another light.

It appears that *Piers Plowman* is based on three literary genres: the allegorical dream narrative; the dialogue, *consolatio*, or debate; and the encyclopedic (or Menippean) satire. And it is influenced by three religious genres (or forms): the complaint, the commentary, and the sermon. These genres are not mutually exclusive, and some are related. The *consolatio* in its classic medieval form is also a dream vision; the religious complaint owes something to classical satire and to the diatribe; and no doubt the sermon and complaint are difficult at times to keep apart. It is still true that in the Middle Ages these six forms were distinct in tradition, had a definite organization, and were designed to satisfy certain expectations in an audience.

※   ※   ※

CHARLES MUSCATINE

From The Locus of Action in Medieval Narrative†

* * *

By the time of Langland's *Piers Plowman* (late fourteenth century), then, medieval narrative shows a strong geometry (or geography) of locus of action that is used structurally. I mention *Piers Plowman* because I should like to conclude my remarks by examining the locus of action in that poem. Though I shall confine my attention to the A-text (to avoid the authorship problem), my remarks will in fact apply equally well to Text B.

Langland's space seems surrealistic, unlike the space of any predecessor. For while he knows and in part uses flat, geometric, schematic, Romanesque space; knows and uses in particular scenes naturalistic space; knows and intermittently uses the linear, pilgrimage form, none of these becomes a controlling locus of his narrative. The locus of the characters and actions and their spatial environments are continually shifting. This has a profound relevance to the peculiar character of the poem, and I am tempted to see in it a symptom, too, of Langland's period.

His opening suggests a single schematic locus, like that of Prudentius: a fair field full of folk, with a tower on a hill above and a dungeon in a dale below. In the description of the activity in the field we notice at once Langland's Gothic doubleness, his capacity to inject into his schematic plan figures, scenes, and tiny settings of realistic depth and vigor. The technique here is even swifter and more suggestive than Dante's. In the Prologue of the A-text no single scene is allowed extensive development; each gives way to the next with a curious inconsequence of spatial relations. There is a kind of artistic logic here in that no coherence but only a heaping and piling of tiny scenes is used to picture man's activities in this wilderness earth. But as this scheme dissolves, as one setting reels and melts into the next, as characters (sometimes whole troops of them) appear and disappear without notice and without trace, we become aware that something more than literary tactics is involved. Dante, at any turn of the road, can suddenly expose us to a shift of perspective, a change of scale, without this surrealistic feeling. In Canto IV of the Inferno, in the midst of darkness, we reach all of a sudden a seven-walled castle, and within it a green field in a place "open, luminous, and high," where the heroes of antiquity are visible. But then we turn back with the narrator and guide to "the part where there is nothing that shines"—that is, back to the spatial and locational frame that organizes the whole. In *Piers Plowman* there is no going back. The fair field, the vale, and the mountain are transformed without notice into a great encampment—with ten thousand tents for all the onlookers at the marriage of Meed. We suddenly witness the dickering over the marriage articles. Thence we go—by what road I know not—to Westminster, before the King.

In the next vision, the extraordinary shift of locus brought by the realistic tavern scene is righted by the continuity of the confessions of the deadly sins. But then in a completely unspecified locus, "a thousand men

† From *Romance Philology* 17.1 (1963): 115–22 [120–22]. Reprinted by permission.

thronged together and prayed for grace to seek truth." They wander aim-
lessly as beasts over valleys and hills. After a long journey they meet a pilgrim who says he has never heard of St. Truth. At that instant: "Peter!" says
a plowman. "I know him"—and from nowhere Piers Plowman materializes
into the poem. He describes to them the road, by way of meekness and conscience and the ten commandments, to where truth resides in the human
heart. The next spatial reference finds them all on a rather different pilgrimage: helping Piers plow his half-acre. . . . And so the poem goes, existing in no one system of space and locations, invoking successive spatial
concepts for limited and temporary effects, without tending to the relations
between them. The peculiarity of space in *Piers Plowman* cannot alone
account for the poem's character. But it works powerfully in concert with
such other traits as the periodic establishment and collapse of the dream
frame, the alternation of allegory and liberalism, the violent changes of
tone and temper, the peculiar equivalence of concrete and abstract terms,
and the indistinctness of the genre. Along with these, the shifting locus of
action produces an effect that, for lack of a better term, I have called "surrealistic."

Such a formal trait in poetry must have a profound consequence for
meaning. It almost explains why this, among medieval English poems, is
the greatest paradox. His sense of space almost betrays the poet. For while
at every turn the discrete, isolable episodes—the overt statements—
proclaim conservative Christian doctrine, the surrealistic spatial context
creates a sense of instability. Thus it is, perhaps, that the preachers of 1386
could so easily use Langland's social orthodoxy as food for revolt, and later
reformers make of him a violent Protestant. The poem's spatially isolated
scenes invite being wrenched from so shifty a context. That sense of
earnestness, of extraordinary urgency in the poem derives partly from the
insecurity of its structure. Unlike Dante's, Langland's fulminations seem
not to be issued from under the arching security of a stable, permanent
structure. The episodes, fragmentary in relation to one another, suggest
shorings, passionately and hastily assembled—from heaven or earth—
against some impending ruin.

In this, perhaps, the poem also reflects its time. Langland's knowledge of
the great medieval formal schemes and his comparative failure with them—
his failure to organize and to "see" by means of them—argues, in the context
of his other traits, more than a lack of narrative skill. It means perhaps that
for a man of his extreme sensitivity those schemes had begun to lose their
clarity, hence their meaning and efficacy. The levels of goodness, "Do-Well,
Do-Bet, and Do-Best the third," mentioned in the A-text as if they were
clearly defined levels, might have been used to impose on the poem a
Romanesque or Dantean clarity; but they were not. And the same is true of
the consecutive, linear processional form. For Langland, the pilgrimage road
to the New Jerusalem has too many detours to be called a road at all. His use
of place and location—along with the other traits I have mentioned—
suggests that for him, despite his doctrinal orthodoxy, the structure of the
moral world—to which most of his predecessors could give coherent spatial
expression—had become a thing newly problematic.

※   ※   ※

GEORGE KANE

[Who Is William Langland?]†

There is some great poetry which conveys to its readers the liveliest impression of a personality in and behind it. * * * But when biographical documentation is lacking, and when at the same time the poetry creates in its reader a strong sense of a distinctive, individual authorial presence, that poetry can take on the aspect of a source of information about the poet. This has been the case with Chaucer and Langland. Out of their poetry these two men have emerged as legendary national figures: the one, roly-poly, whimsical, but also a shrewd observer, hiding his perceptivity behind a pretence of genial condonation; the other a lanky, embittered malcontent in a rusty cassock, striding arrogantly about the Malvern Hills, or, variously, the City of London.

* * *

The life-records of Chaucer relate mainly to his career as a royal servant; the various facts of office and employment tell us relatively little about the man as a private individual; and of Langland we actually have no information beyond his paternity and possibly, his birthplace. Yet it seems to us that we know them both. There are not many studies of Chaucer where discussion is not rounded out by the author's impression of a Chaucerian personality, inferred from his poetry; and all the 'biographies' of Langland have been constructed.

* * *

My argument will be that our notions of the personalities of these two poets, and our sense that we 'know' them as men, are attained by inferences both logically dubious in themselves, and unauthorized by the literary history of the fourteenth century.

* * *

I have spoken so far about Chaucer; but *Piers Plowman* studies afford instances of even wilder aberrations of biographical inference. I must in charity no more than mention the worst offender; he did not have a scholar's training and his enthusiasm for Langland exceeded his capabilities. I will say only that *New Light on Piers Plowman* is the ultimate demonstration of the fallacy, with respect both to farfetched identification of the autobiographical in the poem, and to absurdly subjective criteria of behaviour appropriate to the poet.[1] But many *Piers Plowman* scholars (I shamefacedly include myself) have at some time and in some way thought or argued in terms of the fallacy; to find one secure against it, and also believing in single authorship, is the exception.[2] The situation is not with-

---

† From "The Autobiographical Fallacy in Chaucer and Langland Studies," in *Chaucer and Langland* (Berkeley and London: University of California Press, 1965), pp. 1–4. Reprinted by permission of the publisher. Notes have been renumbered.
1. A. H. Bright, *New Light on 'Piers Plowman'* (Oxford, 1928); and see also his 'Langland and the Seven Deadly Sins', *MLR*, xxv (1930), 133–39.
2. Lawlor's care in this respect deserves to be noticed. See, e.g., J. Lawlor, *Piers Plowman: An Essay in Criticism* (London, 1962), pp. 281, 285, 313, 319.

out its comedy. An article surveying, with great parade of judiciousness, forty years of *Piers Plowman* scholarship, argues that when the dreamer in the B version recounts a youthful lapse into unregeneracy this cannot be autobiographical because 'it is not credible that the conscientious author of A fell victim to the sins of the flesh after writing A'.[3] Arming us against one element in the fallacy, the author of this article demonstrates the other in his appeal to a manifestly questionable subjective notion of appropriate behaviour. Sitting in judgement he too registers, however absurdly, the powerful impact of what has been aptly called 'the imagination inhabiting *Piers Plowman*'.[4] The brutal fact is that all 'biographies' of Langland are constructed on the basis of the fallacy. Some of them seem wise, perceptive, full of insight; they may be full of truth; but all are purely speculative; all are, in the present state of knowledge, unverifiable.

* * *

* * * For all their confidential asides to the audience, their apologies for digression, the dreamers and narrators of Chaucer and Langland are, if I may use jargon, constructs. They bear the poets' names, and speak of writing down their dreams. But things happen to them which could not, except in imagination, have happened to the poets; thus their ultimate reality is imaginative only. They are manipulated by the poet. When it suits his purpose they surrender the speaking voice to him without signal, just as readily as on other occasions they licence him to report for truth the most extravagant incidents, to adopt as his own the most preposterous attitudes. Their nature is enigmatic.

The poets invite us to identify the narrators with themselves, and then, by the character of what is narrated, caution us not to carry out the identification. This they do consciously, creating an ambiguity which they then variously exploit: the enigma is deliberate.

* * *

* * * Whatever sense of reality a dreamer or narrator awakens in us, we have no historical authorization, just as we have no good logic, for imputing that dreamer's particular attributes and circumstances and attitudes to the actual poet. Meanwhile, by reference to the convention, it is almost certainly the case that the dreamers and narrators of Chaucer and Langland are not fictions in any total sense; that they do mirror to some extent the actual men who created them. The question is to what extent and in what respects they are fictions, and that question, having been made designedly difficult for contemporaries in the first instance, has as far as we are concerned become unanswerable.

We can then, as things are, have no biography of Langland, only speculative 'lives', without historical necessity. The general probability that there is autobiography in his poems becomes, in respect of any particular detail, only a possibility, for the establishment of which there is neither logic nor support from literary history.

---

3. J. R. Hulbert, '*Piers the Plowman* after Forty Years', *MP*, xlv (1947–48), 221.
4. Lawlor, *op. cit.*, p. 315.

* * *

* * * As far as the lives of these poets go we are in the hardest position of scholarship: obliged, in the face of tantalizing biographical possibilities, to acknowledge that we cannot, and strictly speaking should not try to, establish these.

* * *

ELIZABETH SALTER AND DEREK PEARSALL

Allegory *and* Realism and the Figural Approach to Reality†

Allegory

* * *

It would be a pity, when describing the richness of Langland's allegorical invention, to lose sight of this 'openness' of aim and technique, and to risk creating false barriers between the poem and present-day readers. *Piers Plowman* has sometimes been recommended as a work susceptible of many-levelled interpretation,[1] as if it could command the same kind of attention from us as the text of the Bible from the medieval scholar—

> Blessed are the eyes which see divine spirit through the letter's veil . . .[2]

But its wealth of significance cannot be charted in any very precise and rigorous way. No one would deny that from the moment when the dreamer looks out over his dream province, and recognizes not only the familiar, turbulent scenes of his own day—'al the welthe of the world and the wo bothe'—but also the symbolic tower of Truth and the deep dale of Death (Prologue 10ff.), *Piers Plowman* engages with some kind of allegorical mode. * * *

* * *

But if, by the mingling of 'real' and 'allegorical' characters, and by frequent references to the 'meaning' of phenomena, Langland very early on in his poem makes us conscious of appearance and its further significance, he is certainly not laying down or taking for granted specific rules for the realization of that significance. * * *

* * *

The real test is not so much the historical probability of 'multiple meaning' in *Piers Plowman*, but our own experience of the work. If Langland

† From Elizabeth Salter and Derek Pearsall, eds., *Piers Plowman* (Evanston, Illinois: Northwestern U. Press, 1969), Introduction, pp. 3–27. Reprinted by permission of the publisher. Notes have been renumbered.
1. In particular, by D. W. Robertson and Bernard F. Huppé, in *Piers Plowman and Scriptural Tradition* (Princeton, 1951).
2. Quoted from Claudius of Turin by B. Smalley, *The Study of the Bible in the Middle Ages* (Oxford, 1952), p. 1.

did not see the dreamer's quest as an investigation on four separable planes of significance, he did see it as a search for a Truth which was complex, often contradictory, and cumulative.

It need not then surprise us that his methods of charting that search are most various. We should be sceptical of critics who recommend to us one kind of allegorical writing as 'characteristic' of *Piers Plowman*, or who try to convince us that we have a straight choice between 'allegorical' and 'literal' methods of reading it. In fact, a whole spectrum of allegorical modes is characteristic of the poem: it displays almost every type of allegory known to the medieval period. To give a comprehensive account of the sources of Langland's allegory, we should have to range over popular sermon literature, courtly poems in French and English, moral treatises, and, in all probability, illustrations to tracts. Not only can we observe diversity of forms, but also widely differing stages of growth. Moreover, even when Langland appears to dispense, temporarily, with allegory, his 'realism' is by no means as simple to define as our first contact with it might suggest.

Allegorical Categories and Modes

Personification Allegory. * * * Various attempts have been made to sort and regroup allegorical writings. For instance, one of the major methods of procedure in allegory is that of personification, and Langland's poem has been called, in company with other English and French poems, 'personification allegory'.[3] In this, abstract qualities or faculties are given human form, and display their natures or re-enact some experience by means of a typical human activity—a debate, a fight, a feast, a trial, a journey.

          *   *   *

The point to make is that the category 'personification allegory' is only of limited help in placing *Piers Plowman*, as, indeed, it may be in placing other medieval works. Personification is a weapon for many allegorists, but they can only be properly distinguished by their ability and inclination to handle it. And, as we shall see, personification is not the whole story: allegory has many faces.

The same difficulty arises when we try to assign *Piers Plowman* to any particular allegorical class or category, and it seems more useful to begin by recognizing its comprehensive allegorical span. This involves not only recognition of the variety of traditional methods Langland draws upon, but also his unique use and combination of those methods.

Dramatic Allegory. Usually—and rightly—singled out for attention is the kind of allegory we find in the Lady Meed episodes of *Piers Plowman* (C. III-V) or in the Feast of Patience (C. XVI). Here a central subject is investigated by means of an actively developing allegorical narrative, with conceptional and fictional elements in perfect, continuous adjustment. The whole sequence of events involving Lady Meed—the arranging of the marriage, the journey to Westminster, the arraignment at the king's court—is dramatically convincing, as well as deeply meaningful. No detail is imprecise in significance, or flat in design.

3. R. W. Frank, "The Art of Reading Medieval Personification Allegory," ELH 20 (1953): 237–250.

*   *   *

It is a master stroke of dramatic writing, but it is also a highly appropriate witness to the dreamer's unreformed, and therefore rebellious, state of mind.

In both of these sequences—and in others like them—Langland mingles personifications with 'real' figures: Meed, Falsehood, Liar, Conscience, Peace, and Wrong thread their way through undefined crowds of the medieval world—pardoners, lawyers, soldiers.

*   *   *

* * * But there are growing-points for such writing all the way through the poem—embryonic allegory. Langland frequently rests on the very brink of 'realizing' an allegorical sequence. A quotation may suggest to him a theme for development, and he makes a brief, telling sketch for a larger design. The words 'Multi enim sunt vocati, pauci vero electi' (*Matthew* 22:14) are rapidly set as an allegorical feast-scene:

> *Multi* to a mangerie and to the mete were sompned,
> And whan the peuple was plener come, the porter unpynnede the gate,
> And plyghte in *pauci* pryueliche and leet the remenant go rome.
> (B.XI.112–114)

*   *   *

These little episodes, arrested between concept and allegorical action, and rich in potential, show how Langland was constantly drawn to allegory (cf. 16.84–5). But the fact that they remain undeveloped is interesting too: if Langland's movement towards allegory was instinctive, it was also controlled. For him, allegory vivified and clarified doctrine; its form and scope depended intimately upon the needs of the sense at any given moment. We can compare his compact treatment of these quotations with his elaborate drawing-out of a Biblical quotation in the 'Four Daughters of God' debate which prefaces the Harrowing of Hell (B.XVIII. 121ff.) Here *Psalm* 85, verse 10, 'Misericordia et veritas obviaverunt sibi: iusticia et pax osculate sunt', is expanded into a full-scale encounter and debate on the reasons for man's salvation.[4] The positioning of this debate is all-important: the length and detail of the allegory are closely related to Langland's concern for absolute clarity on the subject of atonement and salvation. Differences between such passages are those of extent rather than of nature; the minuscule sketches are capable of expansion into robust allegorical scenes—they cry out for lively development.

Diagrammatic Allegory. But there are forms of allegory in *Piers Plowman* which make no such claims upon us. By comparison, they are flat and unspectacular, and it is all the more important for us to understand their nature and function. Very frequently Langland uses an allegorical mode which is closely connected with a particular kind of medieval art: in fact, 'diagrammatic' is the best descriptive term to use of it. Although no exact sources have been identified, it seems possible that Langland was influenced by schematized drawings when he devised his allegory of the Tree

---

4. He had many precedents for this in art and literature: the verse had been dramatized and illustrated from the 9th century onwards. See A. Katzenellenbogen, *Allegories of the Vices and Virtues in Medi-aeval Art* (New York, 1964), pp. 40–41 and plate xxv, fig. 44: see also 15.117n.

of True-Love, growing in man's heart (C. XIX. 6 foll.). Medieval moral treatises constantly used the image of the tree, formally divided into branches,
leaves and fruit, as a way of expressing man's life, and his relationships to
God. * * *

* * *

But if our knowledge of particular sources must remain incomplete, we
can still use art to help us define the character of Langland's diagrammatic
allegory. For like the didactic illustrations of the period, it is static, precise,
and formalized: what it lacks in evocative power it makes up in faithful
accuracy of communication. The description of the way to St. Truth,
offered by Piers Plowman (C. VIII. 157 foll.), illustrates this well. It is a
route plan, laid before the 'thousand of men' who have been stirred by
Repentance to 'go to Treuthe'. The passage has often been dismissed as dull
and wooden. But like the maps and diagrams of medieval religious art, it is
not meant to be visualized *in depth*. It is a blue-print for action, not a picture or a full description of the action itself. * * *

* * *

Non-visual Allegory. But Langland can, on occasion, deal even more
severely with our visual expectations. The way to Truth may have to be 'realized' as a map, and not as a picture, but there are times when his allegorical writing is clearly not meant to be visualized in any form whatsoever. We
should be mistaken in trying to make ordinary visual sense out of the
descriptions of Book, Wit and Anima:

> Thenne was ther a wihte with two brode yes,
> Boke hihte that beau-pere, a bolde man of speche.
> (C. XXI. 240–1)

> He was long and lene, ylyk to noon other.
> (C. XI. 114)

> Tyl I seigh, as it sorcerye were, a sotyl thinge withal,
> One withouten tonge and teeth . . .
> (B. XV. 12–13)

In these, the eye is refused any help: the details do not build up into a
logically and visually acceptable whole, but are isolated symbolic features.
Thus the protean shape of Anima—by turns Love, Conscience, Memory,
Spirit, Reason—is properly denied a physical identity because this would
limit and confine it: it is 'spirit specheles' (B. XV. 36) and only assumes bodily form to operate God's will in man. The staring eyes of Book refer us
directly to the double authority of the opened Gospel pages—an immediate confrontation with the revealed word of authority, rather than with 'a
bold man' *representing authority.*

* * *

If, to us, this seems a somewhat cold and intellectualized allegorical
mode,[5] we may be taking for granted that visual clarity and forcefulness

5. Such non-visual allegorical 'picturing' is to be found in some of the Latin literature of the earlier
   fourteenth century; see B. Smalley, commenting upon the work of the Franciscan John Ridevall:
   '. . . all this fancy is verbal. not visual; the "pictures" will serve as aural aids to preaching' (*English
   Friars and Antiquity*, Oxford, 1960), p. 118.

are always the most effective means of communication for poet or artist. Langland's readers—many of whom were by no means unsophisticated— may have found the very impossibility of visualizing Book a short-cut to grasping its full significance. Clearly Langland could count upon a sensitive response to widely differing allegorical methods, and it is not surprising if, with his comprehensive and complex subject matter, he availed himself of all known devices to capture the understanding.

Allegory through Exempla. Somewhere between the full-scale allegorical sequence and the formal allegorical design lie numerous passages of illustrative material, presented very much like parables or 'exempla' in the sermon literature of Langland's time. They do not make use of personification, and they are not diagrammatic: occurring mostly within the speeches of allegorical characters, they are short narratives within narratives. Their function is essentially allegorical; the events they describe are meant to be translated into more significant conceptual terms—and, in fact, are often translated on the spot. But their most distinctive feature is their positioning, for they are experienced by the dreamer at one remove. They are reported allegory. And, like their counterparts in the sermon literature of the Middle Ages, they are vivid and authoritative. Their message is trenchant, but it is also limited: because of their special, circumscribed position in the poem, they can only be developed to a certain extent. Sometimes Langland uses them to make a moral point more tellingly than subtly: the rough effectiveness of the friar's 'forbisene' (in 7.32: C. XI. 32 foll.) is deliberate. Here sinful man is likened to a man in a boat in peril of the waves and the wind, and 'waggynge of the bote', but saved by the very condition of his humanity, which is set in faith and love. Man falls, but not into the sea; he only stumbles within the boat, and is saved: he sins, but only within the body, which, in its frailty, draws God's compassion to it:

> 'So hit fareth', quod the frere, 'by the ryhtful mannes fallynge;
> Thogh he thorw fondynges falle, he falleth nat out of charite . . .'
> (C. XI. 41–42)

It is immediately obvious that the 'equivalences' will not stand up to rigorous analysis—the boat as the body is a tricky concept and, indeed, Langland's purpose in the whole episode is to show us a spiritual teacher who is only superficially clever. The friars are a constant butt of his irony and anger for their glib, popular methods and their presumption. But Langland will also use the 'forbisene' in a favourable context, as a swift means of clinching a protracted argument, or as a sudden—but not necessarily final—simplification of a complex debate. So Ymaginatif (in C. XV. 103 foll.) offers the puzzled dreamer a chance to resolve, temporarily, some of the long-worked-over problems of the debate on salvation by faith, good works, or learning. The man with learning, he says, can be compared to a man in the water who knows how to swim—he is more likely to be able to save himself from sinking, because of his knowledge:

> 'Ryght so,' quath that renke, 'reson hit sheweth,
> That he that knoweth cleregic can sonnere aryse
> Out of synne, and be saf, thow he synegy ofte.'
> (C. XV. 110–12)

The sense of relief, shared by dreamer and reader, when they come upon what seems to be a neat and apt analogy, is short-lived. It soon becomes clear that there is much more to say about 'cleregie', and that Ymaginatif is certainly not envisaging it simply as a useful sort of expertise. Neither is he convinced that it is always as efficacious as his parable would have; his last words dwell upon truth, hope, and love, not upon learning:

'And where hit worth other nat worth, the byleyve is gret of treuthe,
'And hope hongeth ay theron to have that treuthe deserueth;
Quia super pauca fidelis fuisti, supra multa te constituam:
And that is love and large huyre yf the lord be trewe,
And cortesie more than covenant was, what so clerkes carpen.'
(C. XV. 213–16)

But as an interim comment, the parable had value: it helped to concentrate the dreamer's diffuse thoughts, and it encouraged him to use his reason as well as his feelings when tackling the thorny problem of salvation for the simple and the learned.

But if we can distinguish four or five allegorical methods at Langland's easy command, we should not think of them as operating independently of each other. Whatever approach is made—diagrammatic, exemplary, active—it is chosen to display or to investigate subject matter most effectively at that particular point, and may be preceded or superseded by an entirely different kind of approach. The merging of one type of allegory into another is a characteristic of *Piers Plowman*, not shared by many other poems of its time, though frequent enough in some types of devotional prose writing.[6] The most striking example of this comes in C. XIX. 106 foll. when the static allegory of the Tree of Trewe-love quickens, and in the presence of the dreamer becomes an active allegorical drama of man's subjection to the devil—

* * *

Nor should we think that all in *Piers Plowman* which cannot be categorized as one or other type of allegory is therefore the very reverse of allegory, with only literal or realistic force. In the passages discussed so far, realism has been either subtly adjusted or subordinated to conceptual truth: no problem has arisen. But there are many parts of *Piers Plowman* in which Langland does not appear to be working in any allegorical mode at all. Moreover, it will be obvious that some very important characters in *Piers Plowman*—Piers himself, Abraham, Trajan, the Good Samaritan—are not easily accounted for 'allegorically'. And yet they are hardly to be described as 'real', or 'historical': Trajan is accepted by the poet as 'real', but also as 'symbolic' of salvation by works (C. XIII, 74 foll.): Abraham, is double-named "Faith" (C. XIX, 186, 200, 275, etc.).

* * *

The Figural Approach

This easy commerce between a vivid sense of the real, the actual, and an equally vivid sense of spiritual implication is as characteristic of *Piers Plow-*

---

6. See, for instance, the section on Love in the 13th-century spiritual guide, the *Ancrene Wisse*, ed. G. Shepherd (Nelson's Medieval and Renaissance Library, 1959), pp. 21–3. This work was highly influential in the 14th and 15th centuries.

man as it is of the whole outlook of the Middle Ages. And when we have finally distinguished and categorized all types of allegory in the poem, we are left with many vigorous creations which, without any loss of their 'reality', may still be intended as 'figures and foreshadowings of great things'.[7] For an understanding of these, we must look not to allegorical processes of thought and composition, but no *figural*.[8] The difference is important: in terms of biblical study, for instance, the allegorical method uses the literal, historical narrative merely as point of departure for various kinds of spiritual interpretation—the figural method maintains the historical truth of Biblical events, while seeing in them, simultaneously, a 'foreshadowing of greater things'. So the Old Testament is 'real', but is also a 'figure' of the New Testament: in its turn, the New Testament, fulfilling the Old, is an incarnation not quite complete. It is itself a promise or augury of the ultimate truth which will be revealed after the Last Judgment. It was an attitude which had far-reaching consequences, in art and literature: 'No student of the Middle Ages can fail to see how it provides the medieval interpretation of history with its general foundation and often enters into the medieval view of everyday reality' (Auerbach, p. 61). It is this which underwrites not only Langland's acceptance of the concrete, historical actuality of the life of Christ ('Jesus Christ on a Jews douhter alight'), of Abraham, or of the life of the patient poor in the 14th century, but also his ability to place them in a 'perspective of eternity' (ibid., p. 42). *Piers Plowman* bases itself firmly on a figural interpretation of reality,[9] upon 'the idea that earthly life is thoroughly real, with the reality of the flesh into which the Logos entered, but that with all its reality it is only *umbra* and *figura* of the authentic, future, ultimate truth, the real reality that will unveil and preserve the *figura*'.[1]

Such a statement makes it easier to understand the whole complex relationship between the real, the literal, the dramatic and the spiritual in *Piers Plowman*. It is easier, in particular, to understand 'characters' such as Abraham, the Good Samaritan, and Piers Plowman himself. For they are not presented as 'allegorical' in the same way as the personified abstractions Clergy, Study, Reason, are presented. On the other hand, they are not dealt with in terms of unequivocal realism. They shift easily between literal and symbolic modes.

*   *   *

Similarly, Langland presents his Good Samaritan in a manner not totally realistic, but certainly not allegorical. Accepting Christ's parable as virtual sacred history, he develops the man warmly and vividly—but we are not

---

7. Quoted and translated from Lactantius, *Divinae Institutiones*, by E. Auerbach, in his essay 'Figura', *Scenes from the Drama of European Literature* (New York, 1959), p. 35.
8. The best short exposition of the figural outlook is by Auerbach, in the essay noted above. But see also C. Donahue, 'Patristic Exegesis: Summation', in *Critical Approaches to Medieval Literature*, ed. D. Bethurum (Columbia UP, 1960), p. 81, who comments perceptively that the figural or typological approach 'might turn imaginative writers towards realism rather than towards allegory'.
9. See the clear 'figural' statement about Christ at C.XV.3–9:

> Lawe of louue oure lord wrot, longe er Crist were.
> And Crist cam *and confermede*, and holy kirke made . . .

1. Auerbach, p. 72. The figural or typological view of history is especially clear in the double row of personages and events from the Old and the New Testaments in medieval choir stall carvings, for instance, and in the series of Old Testament episodes chosen for the Miracle Play Cycles.

allowed to forget that the action of the Good Samaritan is a 'figure' of Christ's rescue of wounded mankind.

*   *   *

The 'character' of Piers Plowman might also be regarded as a natural product of figurative thinking. This highly complex creation of Langland's cannot be dealt with in terms of allegory or social realism. Piers comes before us with particular historical and dramatic force: he is rooted in the life of the 14th-century peasant—

> 'Bothe to sowe and to sette, the while I swynke myhte'
> (C. VIII. 186)

He provides all classes of men with the very stuff of their earthly lives— grain *is* life. But from the beginning, we are made conscious that he 'figures' much more than this; he is in touch with mysteries, and it is instantly clear that he has it in his power to provide spiritual sustenance, as well as material. He expounds, to the crowd of waiting pilgrims, not only the Ten Commandments of the Way to God, but also the miraculous heart of the matter—the ultimate recognition of God, dwelling in man:

> 'And yf Grace graunte the to go in in this wyse,
> Thow shalt se Treuthe sitte in thy sulve herte,
> And solace thy soule, and save the fram payne. . . .'
> (C. VIII. 254–56)

Here he hints at his own 'fulfilment', as incarnate spiritual wisdom and love: at the height of the poem, he comes before the dreamer's astounded gaze as the human 'form' of Christ (C. XXI. 8, and C. XXII. 6 foll.). His constant function—for dreamer and mankind—is that of guide to salvation and to the knowledge of God. In fact, when Christ says (in C. XXII. 260–61)

> 'My prower and my plouhman Peers shall beo on erthe;
> And for to tulye treuthe, a teome shall he have.'

we accept his words as a confirmation of what has already been understood: Piers is 'incarnate revelation, that part of the divine plan of salvation which . . . is the miracle whereby men are raised above other earthly creatures . . .'[2] But, as is proper and natural to the figurative view, the 'man Piers' is never lost to our sight: indeed, for his complete spiritual fulfilment to take place, he must remain recognizable. What Langland shows us in Piers the Plowman is the operation of God through a man in a state of grace; he is not propounding, by personification, a theological concept of grace in humanity. Consequently, Piers is always familiar, always sought for, acclaimed by the dreamer and other characters—'the historical reality is not annulled, but confirmed and fulfilled by the deeper meaning' (Auerbach, p. 73).

*   *   *

What then seems to be true is that some of the most significant parts of *Piers Plowman* cannot be dealt with in terms of allegory: neither can they be satisfactorily dealt with as areas of dramatic or social realism. Allegory

---

2. Auerbach, op. cit., p. 75, writing of Beatrice, in the *Divine Comedy*.

provides Langland with a wide variety of literary methods for examining and
displaying his wealth of material: it allows him freedom of play in many
poetic styles and genres, ranging from fictions of strong visual content to
designs of flat diagrammatic clarity. But allegory is no help to us when we
come to consider how Langland 'built' his central character, Piers, nor is it
helpful to our understanding of Langland's basic attitude to historical and
spiritual truth—to his concept of 'reality'.

   The essential structure of his thought is figural, with all that this implies
about the co-ordination of the real and the spiritual. No-one could have
felt more intensely and described more vividly the often claustrophobic
'reality' of later 14th-century England: this did not prevent Langland from
'interpreting' it in a perspective of eternity, both in the first disturbing long
shots, and in the last terrifying close-ups of the poem.* * *

MARY C. SCHROEDER (CARRUTHERS)

The Character of Conscience in *Piers Plowman*†

It has long been recognized by students of *Piers Plowman* that the personifications in the poem embody particular and definable theological concepts.[1] The tendency of some commentators has been, however, to regard
personifications as wholly static figures, mere sign-posts pointing to the
dictionary, instead of moving, acting characters in a long poem. This I think
is a mistake, for it is apt to limit the meaning of a personification to what
the figure may denote at a single point in the poem rather than taking into
account what is the fact—namely, that the personifications act, interact
with each other, and reappear in different contexts in the poem, all of
which can significantly affect the meaning they carry.

                              *   *   *

   * * * Of all the personifications in *Piers Plowman* Conscience is the
most complex, with regard not only to the concept he embodies but also
to the way in which his character is constructed. Conscience has not
received the careful critical attention he deserves.[2] He is, along with Will
and Piers, one of the major figures in the poem, but while great amounts
of energy and acumen have gone in pursuit of Piers, and only slightly less
after Will, Conscience has most often been either ignored or relegated to
a few pages in an appendix. This I suppose is because of his name, which
is apt to seem entirely self-explanatory at least until one looks in the
dictionary and sees how many widely different meanings the word could

† From *Studies in Philology* 67.1 (1970): 13–30. Reprinted by permission of the publisher.
  1. To take a few examples, see Morton W. Bloomfield, *Piers Plowman as a Fourteenth-Century Apoc-
     alypse* (New Brunswick, 1961), pp. 170–74 (on Ymaginatif) and pp. 167–69 (on Conscience); E.
     Talbot Donaldson, *Piers Plowman, the C-Text and Its Poet* (New Haven, 1949), pp. 170–74 (on
     Recklessness); and D. W. Robertson, Jr. and Bernard F. Huppé, *Piers Plowman and Scriptural Tra-
     dition* (Princeton, 1951), esp. pp. 33–34, 240–42 (on Will).
  2. A recent and thorough study of the concept in Middle English, with special reference to *Piers Plow-
     man*, is that of Günter Spitzbart, *Das Gewissen in der mittelenglischen Literatur* (Inaugural-
     Dissertation, Köln; Köln, 1962). Spitzbart mentions most of the meanings of the word I have
     developed here, but does not analyse them systematically in terms of the action of Langland's per-
     sonification.

have in the fourteenth century, and considers how various Conscience's role is in *Piers Plowman*.

The concept which Conscience embodies is a large one. He is especially in Passus III–IV, basically a blend of the scholastic terms synderesis and conscience.[3] However, as Bloomfield notes, Conscience's function in the later parts of *Piers Plowman* "has been considerably widened";[4] he is not just "the scholastic quality of the natural, reasonable soul, but much more,"[5] having a quasi-mystical function which seems to reflect an older conception of the role of conscience. Then too, there is the fact that he is a knight.[6] This gives him a social role which both corresponds to and complicates, sometimes in limiting ways, his psychological and spiritual roles.

The most familiar of Conscience's roles is that assigned to the concept in scholastic psychology. This is the function defined by the *OED* as "moral sense."[7] Unlike Langland, who includes aspects of both in his conception,[8] St. Thomas distinguishes between synderesis and conscience. Synderesis is a habit, a natural disposition of the practical intellect, "the first practical principles bestowed on us by nature,"[9] by means of which the practical intellect is inclined to the good and is able "to discover, and to judge of what [it has] discovered."[1] Conscience is formed by a number of secondary habits, all derived from and based upon the primary habit of synderesis,[2] and is defined by St. Thomas as the act by which these intellectual habits are applied to something:

> Conscience, according to the very nature of the word, implies the relation of knowledge to something. . . . But the application of knowledge to something is done by some act. Wherefore . . . it is clear that conscience is an act.[3]

Thus Conscience, in the scholastic conception of it, becomes the judge of right and wrong:

> For conscience is said to witness, to bind, or incite, and also to accuse, torment, or rebuke. And all these follow the application of knowledge or science to what we do.[4]

The perfection of conscience-synderesis depends upon the perfection and accuracy of one's knowledge. Conscience thus is closely connected

---

3. See Randolph Quirk, "Langland's Use of *Kynde Wit* and *Inwit*," *JEGP, LTT* (1953), 188, and Morton Bloomfield, *Piers*, pp. 167–69.

4. Bloomfield, *Piers*, p. 168.

5. *Idem.*

6. The king tells Lady Meed, "I haue a knyghte, Conscience, cam late fro biyunde" (III. 109). Textual references, unless otherwise noted, are to the B-Text, upon which this discussion of Conscience is chiefly based.

7. *OED, s.v. Conscience*, II: "Consciousness of right and wrong; moral sense." The *MED*'s definitions of the term accord in the main with those of *OED*, and I refer the reader to the many examples of its use given there to supplement the ones I have mentioned.

8. Bloomfield, *Piers*, p. III. Cf. Quirk, "*Kynde Wit*," 186–88, who says that for Langland conscience is "inwit in action," *inwit* being defined as "human . . . comprehension," not only of the intellect but also of feeling or the heart.

9. "Principia operabilium nobis natura indita"; *ST* I^a, Q. LXXIX, a. 12. I have used the complete edition of St. Thomas Aquinas's works edited by Vernon J. Bourke (New York, 1948–50).

1. "Ad inveniendum, et judicamus inventa"; *ST* I^a, Q. LXXIX, a. 12.

2. St. Thomas implies that many habits form conscience: "Habitus autem ex quibus conscientia informatur, esti multi sunt, omnes tamen efficaciam habent ab uno primo principio, scilicet ab habitu primorum principiorum, qui dicitur syndereis." *ST* I^a, Q. LXXIX, a. 13.

3. *ST* I^a, Q. LXXIX, a. 13. Translation by the Fathers of the English Dominican Province.

4. *ST* I^a, Q. LXXIX, a. 13. Translation by the Fathers of the English Dominican Province.

with knowledge. Randolph Quirk notes that *inwit* (which he defines as synonymous with *intellectus agens*, the practical intellect)[5] is frequently confused with conscience, as in Michael of Northgate's famous treatise, for *inwit* is "concerned with the apprehension of truth, [and] it is therefore concerned with the distinction between true and false, good and evil; hence its functions can come near to, and be confused with, those of conscience."[6] But if *inwit* could be confused with conscience, conscience could also be confused with *inwit* and mean "consciousness," "inward knowledge," or "mind."[7] The role of conscience was able to include not only the function of moral judge but also that of intellectual judge distinguishing between truth and falsehood. Indeed, such an extension of meaning is almost implicit in the scholastic definition of the term, since the action of conscience implements the knowledge of the *intellectus agens*, or *inwit*.

* * *

Conscience also plays an important social role, particularly in the two final passus of the poem, which is dependent upon and emphasized by the fact that he is a knight. As Bloomfield believes,[8] this role may indeed reflect an aspect of the monastic conception of conscience—not only as the guide and protector of the individual soul but as a collective conscience defending the collective soul of the Church. Langland need not have gotten the idea from the monastic theologians, however, for in *Piers Plowman* the social and individual realms tend to be held in a parallel, metaphoric relationship to each other. Langland frequently gives his personifications social roles which are analogous to their psychological or moral ones—Reason is the king's chief advisor, for example.[9] Similarly, Conscience's role as a knight is analogous to his psychological one. Just as the function of conscience is to protect the soul and guide it to truth, so the function of a knight is to protect the kingdom. As Piers tells the knight who offers to help him plow his half-acre:

> I shal swynke and swete and sowe for us bothe,
> And other laboures do for thi love al my lyf-tyme,
> In covenaunt that thow kepe holikirke and my-selve
> Fro wastoures and fro wykked men that this worlde struyeth.
>   (VI. 26–29)[1]

Knights are also, in a more spiritual role, to protect Truth itself; as Lady Holy Church teaches Will, they are to "holden with him and with hir that [asken the] treuthe" (I. 100).

Conscience's knightly role is also linked with one final and less exalted meaning of the word, "conscientious observance or practise" or "tender-

5. Quirk, "*Kynde Wit*," 187.
6. *Idem*.
7. *OED, s.v. Conscience*, I: "Inward knowledge, consciousness; inmost thought, mind." The etymological note states that "in ME. *conscience* took the place of the earlier term INWIT in all its senses." See also Spitzbart, *Das Gewissen*, pp. 9–40.
8. Bloomfield, *Piers*, pp. 168–69.
9. IV. 177–91.
1. All references are to W. W. Skeat's Oxford text of *Piers Plowman* (Oxford, 1886). Though the text is basically Skeat's, I have adopted certain emendations kindly suggested to me by Prof. E. T. Donaldson, which are indicated by square brackets. I have omitted the medial point in Skeat's text and have instead substituted when necessary, such punctuation as seemed reasonable.

ness of conscience."[2] This is the meaning of conscience which is especially applicable to knights of courtly romance, models of courtesy and gentle practise. But in *Piers Plowman*, purely aristocratic or courtly motifs are used almost always for ironic purposes. Langland never demonstrates any real trust in courtesy, and the good manners and tenderheartedness which Conscience shows on many occasions serve only to get him into trouble. Thus two types of knighthood are utilized in the poem, one the high ideal of Christian chivalry culminating in the image of the Christ-knight jousting with death at Jerusalem,[3] and the other the aristocratic knight of the courtly tradition, a figure whom Langland distrusts mightily.

But it is not enough simply to enumerate the different meanings which Conscience can have at certain points in the poem. For these meanings are not discrete—they are all attached to the same figure who appears in each scene, and thus while his character may be deepened and informed as Conscience progresses through the poem, his other aspects are still a part of him. The meaning of any personification in *Piers Plowman* results from an accretive process; it depends not only on how the figure looks and moves and speaks in a particular situation, but more importantly on how he responds to other figures embodying different concepts both at a given point in the poem and in his previous appearances. This is particularly and richly true of Conscience, for Conscience is actually educated during the course of the poem. This fact itself is a dramatization of one of his meanings, for according to St. Thomas, conscience is educable, and develops as knowledge increases.[4] The process for Conscience in *Piers Plowman* is entirely like that of human education, as older psychologies conceived of it. Conscience has, as his limit, the nature defined by the four different meanings discussed above. But these meanings are not all in evidence at the same time, though they are all present possibilities in his nature. The problem for Conscience, like that for Christian men, is to grow and inform his nature, to evolve from being simply a human, fallible faculty to a faculty purified by grace, to acquire that mystical function which Bloomfield so well defines. Conscience's meaning is clarified, deepened, and refined by the various contexts in which he appears, but the process is not one of simply imposing different meanings on him; it is one of education wrought by his encounters with the other figures in the poem.

Conscience has three major scenes: the debate with Lady Meed in Passus III–IV, the dinner with Clergy and the drunken friar in Passus XIII, and the defense of Unity in Passus XIX–XX. His role as judge of truth and falsehood is evident in his debate with Meed. Conscience is associated with truth from the start. Theology warns Civil to beware of trying to wed Meed to False because "witty is Truthe, / And Conscience is of his conseille and knoweth yow uchone" (II. 137–38). Conscience does indeed know

2. *OED*, s.v. *Conscience*, III: "Conscientious observance or practise; tenderness of conscience." *Cf.* *MED*, s.v. *conscience*, 3(a): "scrupulousness, conscientiousness," and 4: "tenderness of conscience, solicitude." Noteworthy examples of these meanings (often overlapping) occur in *The Canterbury Tales*: "Stomak ne conscience ne knowe I noon" (D. 1441), and "And al was conscience and tendre herte" (A. 150).
3. For a detailed discussion of this motif, with special reference to its sources and development, see Wilbur Gaffney, "The Allegory of the Christ-Knight in *Piers Plowman*," PMLA, XLVI (1931), 155–68.
4. This is implied not only in *ST* I[a], Q. LXXIX, a. 13 quoted above (n. 2, p. x), but also in St. Thomas's discussion of the nature of habits, *ST* I[a], QQ. LII and LIII.

them all for what they are, including Lady Meed, and paints a graphic picture of how she corrupts society:

> 'She leteth passe prisoneres and payeth for hem ofte,
> And gyveth the gailers golde and grotes togideres,
> To unfettre the fals, fle where hym lyketh;
> And taketh the trewe bi the toppe and tieth hym faste,
> And hangeth hym for hatred that harme dede nevre.'
>
> (III. 136–40)

Conscience's choice of words here is significant, for he expresses the confusion of guilt and innocence, the corruption of Law, in terms of the confusion of true and false, the corruption of Knowledge. In other words,
moral decay is an aspect of falsehood and is due to a lack of knowledge. A
few lines later Conscience warns the king that Meed "is favorable to the
fals and fouleth trewthe ofte" (III. 153). Conscience, being of Truth's
counsel, knows the false when he sees it and, unlike the king, is not confused by it. His victory over Meed begins when he is able to distinguish her
two opposite meanings, meed as rightful reward, and meed as bribery.
Clearly then, Conscience's role involves more than a simple blend of
the scholastic synderesis and conscience. He is a fully conscious figure,
his effectiveness being directly dependent upon the refinement of his
comprehension.

But the kind of comprehension and knowledge that Conscience must
possess in order to be pure involves far more than mere intellectual acumen. This becomes evident during the course of his debate when, in trying
to explain to the king what Meed is, he gives as an example Saul's ill-fated
expedition against the Amalekites:

> 'Such a myschief mede made Saul the kynge to have
> That god hated hym for evere and alle his eyres after.'
>
> (III. 276–77)

The issues shift from the comparatively limited ones of the court at Westminster to the ultimate battle itself, in which the enemy is still Meed, but
a Meed so powerful that she can be routed only by "love and lowenesse
and lewte togederes" (III. 289). Conscience's role in this apocalyptic
description is central. He is the companion of "kynde love" (III. 297).
Together they will set up a millennial society of peace and perfect truth.
This role seems to reflect the monastic conception of conscience as the
dwelling-place of God in the soul. But the difference between Conscience's
conception of what his perfection entails and that of the monastic theologians should be noted. Langland's Conscience foresees here a social har-
mony and order based solely upon law, the reign of reason, as he calls it in
III. 283, and though he says that the world will be ruled by one Christian
king (III. 287) and that priests will be made to behave themselves (III.
309–12), the element of *grace*, necessary for any genuinely Christian society, is entirely lacking. What Conscience envisions is no reign of the saints
on earth, but a society of enlightened, reasonable men. The love which sus-
tains it is not Christian grace but "kynde love," natural love, and Conscience's
acknowledged instructor is Kind Wit (III. 282). Kind Wit, according to Quirk, is the scholastic *vis cognitiva*, a natural faculty which man
shares with animals, and distinct from *ratio particularis*, which man alone

possesses.[5] Langland regards Kind Wit rather more highly than some critics would have us believe,[6] but it is never more to him than a purely natural mental power.

After listening to Conscience's arguments, his emphatic and entirely reasonable rejection of Meed, the king still does not perceive the danger. He interrupts at the beginning of Passus IV, tired of the argument, and commands Conscience to shut up and kiss Meed, for they shall both serve him. Conscience responds rudely to this silly request and decides to call in Reason as his ally. In doing so he is not so much appealing to a higher authority as simply getting a second voice to support him. The king has not been convinced—perhaps if he hears it from somebody else he will be. After having been instructed by Conscience concerning the situation at court (IV. 33–41), Reason's argument, to which the king favorably responds, turns out to be no more than a summary of what Conscience has already said, even to an echo of his own words.[7] Thus the relationship of Conscience and Reason seems to be one of equals rather than of servant and master. This emphasizes not only Conscience's importance but, by what it leaves out, his limitations. His guides are only Reason and Kind Wit. His is a wholly natural consciousness, human comprehension in an eminently rational form, but not yet a Christian conscience illumined by grace. For all his intellectual keenness he still has a great deal to learn.

His education begins in Passus XIII, during the dinner he gives for Clergy, Will, Patience, and the drunken doctor. It is in this passus also that Conscience's knightly qualities become particularly evident, but they are important in Passus III–IV as well. Conscience is very concerned to preserve the truth and expose falsehood. This role is identical with the one Langland assigns to knights—to hold with those "that [asken the] treuthe" (I. 100). He is also keeping the kingdom against the wicked men "that this worlde struyeth" (VI. 29). These knightly duties entirely accord with and support Conscience's moral ones. But to be a knight can mean simply to be a polite aristocrat and, as I suggested earlier, this kind of knighthood reflects another meaning of conscience, correct behavior or conscientiousness.

This aspect of knights and of Conscience is a distinct liability as far as Langland is concerned. The only time he even approaches the style of the courtly romances is in the Lady Meed episodes. The *descriptio* of her in Passus II—the only example of that form in the poem—is sheer romantic convention with its emphasis upon the brilliant color and richness of her jewelry and costume:

> Fetislich hir fyngres were fretted with golde wyre,
> And there-on red rubyes as red as any glede,

---

5. Quirk, "*Kynde Wit*," 184–85.
6. Huppé and Robertson, *Piers*, pp. 27–29. For a criticism of their understanding of the term, see a review of their book by M. W. Bloomfield, *Speculum*, XXVII (1952), 245–26.
7. Compare Conscience's words in describing the millennial society:

> 'And make of lawe a laborere suche a love shal arise,
> And such a pees amonge the peple and a perfit trewthe.'
>   (III. 298–29)

Reason's words are a direct echo of this:

> 'Lawe shal ben a laborere and lede a-felde donge,
> And Love shal lede the londe as the lief lyketh!'
>   (IV. 147–48)

And diamantz of derrest pris and double manere safferes,
Orientales and ewages envenymes to destroye.
Hire robe was ful riche of red scarlet engreyned,
With ribanes of red golde and of riche stones;
Hire arraye me ravysshed suche ricchesse saw I nevere.

(II. 11–17)

When she arrives at Westminster she is treated as befits a courtly heroine:[8]

Curteysliche the clerke thanne as the kyng hight,
Take Mede bi the middel and broughte hir in-to chaumbre,
And there was myrthe and mynstralcye Mede to plese.
They that wonyeth in Westmynstre worschiped hir alle;
Gentelliche with joye the justices somme
Busked hem to the boure there the b[u]rde dwelled.

(III. 9–14)

Everyone including the king bends over backwards to be nice to her. Adverbs like "curteysliche" and "gentelliche" in the above passage are paralled by Meed's responses, "mildeliche" (III. 20) and "hendeliche" (III. 29). When Meed comes before the king he speaks to her "curteisliche" (III. 103), and his whole treatment of her is velvet gloved—"The kynge graunted hir grace with a gode wille" (III. 171). That is much too nice a way to handle someone like Lady Meed. The king's anxiety to avoid a quarrel and effect a reconciliation makes it extremely difficult for Conscience to win his argument; as we have seen, he has to bring in Reason to repeat what he has already said before the king will believe it. The court, in fact, is so courtly that its concern for the outward forms of polite, conscientious behavior has blinded it entirely to the truth about the woman standing before it. Meed may be introduced in the most elegant terms but the fact is that she is clothed in scarlet and closely allied to False. Meed is not only the dangerous pun which Conscience is at pains to define, but a rhetorical flourish as well. The ambiguous nature of the word "quen" (*queen-quean*)[9] which ends the A-Text's version of her *descriptio* puts the situation most succinctly: "*there* nis no quen queyntere that quyk is o lyve" (A-Text, II.

---

8. J. A. Burrow has noted the high percentage of courtly vocabulary found in this passage, "The Audience of *Piers Plowman*," *Anglia*, LXXV (1957), 81.
9. I have used George Kane's edition of the A-Text (London, 1960). There is perhaps no actual, phonological pun here, although there is some evidence to indicate that in certain dialects of the West Midlands which derive from West-Saxon and Mercian such a pun might have been possible. ME *quen* ("quean"), from OE *cwene*, had $\bar{e}$, due to the lengthening of the vowel in open syllables. The regular form of ME *quen* ("queen"), from OE *cwēn*, had $\bar{e}$. The vowel of OE *cwēn* developed by i-mutation from Prim. OE $\bar{o}$, the normal development of Prim. OE nasalized $\bar{a}$. There are, however, a number of spellings in WS and Mercian texts for *cwēn* and words of similar derivation with $æ$ instead of $\bar{e}$ (see Alastair Campbell, *Old English Grammar* [Oxford, 1957], paragraph 198, and note 4). Indeed, Bosworth-Toller lists *cwǣn* as an alternate spelling for *cwēn*. If these graphs are phonologically significant, and their status is somewhat dubious (see Campbell, *loc. cit.*), WS and Mercian *cwǣn* would give West Midlands *quen* with $\bar{e}$, the same sound as ME *quen* from OE *cwene*. Until the evidence is more complete, however, the possibility of a true pun on linguistic grounds must remain doubtful. Yet there can be no doubt that Langland had noted the similarity of the two words and used them in a punning fashion. An example occurs in the C-Text:

> At church in the charnel cheorles aren vuel to knowe,
> Other a knyght fro a knave, other a queyne fro a queene.
> (C, IX. 45–46)

This would seem to suggest that in the line from the A-Text, where it is impossible to tell by the spelling which word is intended, the ambiguity is probably deliberate (the scribes seem to have split on what was intended—see Kane's textual notes on this line).

14). The king and his court see only the gorgeous romance queen before them and not the quean beneath all the layers of rhetorical ornament.

Conscience sees much more clearly than the court in Passus III, but he does not lack courtesy towards Meed. He speaks harshly to her in his argument, not mincing terms and consistently addressing her in the familiar form, "thow." But when he has won the victory (or so he thinks) he switches to the polite form of address, "ye," and calls her "lady" and "madame" (III. 333–49). One critic interprets this as "exaggerated deference" which "parodies the respect paid her at . . . first."[1] But this is surely not parody. Conscience's deference is not particularly exaggerated; it is the kind of address which a courteous knight would use to a lady. The trait is, however, a liability. Even genuine courtesy is demonstrated by polite forms of speech and behavior and is in turn apt to be blinded by outwardly polite forms of speech and behavior. The king, though not himself a corrupt man, is fooled by Meed's rhetorical shimmer, both of speech and dress, and her courteous behavior.

Thus Conscience is by no means an infallible figure. As he is presented in Passus III–IV, he possesses two major weaknesses. He has no divine guide but only his natural comprehension and knowledge, and he is inclined to be too polite and tenderhearted. He takes both liabilities with him to his dinner in Passus XIII. Conscience's courtesy is immediately apparent, and it extends equally to all his guests. To Patience he speaks "curteisliche" (XIII. 31); to Scripture he is "ful curteis" (XIII. 46); the loud-mouthed doctor he knows well and "welcomed hym faire" (XIII. 27), a fact which seems surprising since even Will can see that that friar is something of a fraud. Will tries to start a quarrel with the learned man, who has been dining sumptuously while he and Patience have had to settle for sour leaves and draughts of *diu-perseverans*. As Will rudely points out, the doctor has not been doing well, since he has eaten all the pudding at dinner and left none for anyone else. Will is entirely right in his denunciation of the friar, but Conscience steps in at once and tries to smooth things over:

> Thanne Conscience curteisliche a contenaunce he made,
> And preynte upon Pacience to preie me to be stille,
> And seyde hym-self, 'sire doctour and it be yowre wille,
> What is Dowel and Dobet? ye devynours knoweth.'
> (XIII. 111–14)

His treatment of the doctor is reminiscent of the king's treatment of Lady Meed and just as misplaced.

But the main issue for Conscience here is not his courtesy so much as his knowledge. He has confidently subscribed to rational knowledge heretofore; in Passus XIII he becomes troubled by its limitations. The doctor and Clergy (learning) answer Conscience's questions about Dowel in terms of intellectual knowledge as opposed to practice and knowledge of the heart. Clergy says he will not say what Dowel is until he has consulted his seven sons, the seven liberal arts (XIII. 121–22). Furthermore he complains that "one Pieres the Ploughman hath inpugned us alle, / And sette alle sciences at a soppe save love one" (XIII. 123–24). Piers, he says, refuses to define Dowel at all in intellectual terms, thus undermining

---

1. John Lawlor, *Piers Plowman: An Essay in Criticism* (London, 1962), p. 34.

Clergy's authority. Conscience is dubious of Clergy's charge—"I can nought here-on" (XIII. 130)—for he knows Piers and cannot believe that he would say anything against Holy Writ. It is important to note Conscience's honesty in this debate. He is a fair judge and his decision is made with scrupulous logic. In this spirit he turns to Patience, who "perauntre croweth / That no clerke ne can" (XIII. 133–134). Patience replies that love is the only true teacher of Dowel, Dobet, and Dobest. The love Patience describes is human love proceeding outward from the self to others and thence to the divine:[2]

> "Thow love lelly thi soule al thi lyf-tyme;
> And so thow lere the to love for the lordes love of hevene,
> Thine enemye in al wyse evene-forth with thi-selve."
>   (XIII. 141–43)

This love is still only "kynde love" as Patience says (XIII. 150), but it sets man on the path of doing well.

Conscience finds this argument more satisfactory than Clergy's. He has spoken before in Passus III of the "kynde love" which with law and lewte must be the basis for a just society, and this same attitude informs his reply to Patience. Charity fears nothing, as the Bible says, and so it is the most reasonable basis for action (XIII. 158–63). Every ruler must rule through this doctrine, for this is evident to "puyre reson" (XIII. 166). Once any king hears Patience's teaching he will "thorugh wit" (XIII. 168) make his judgments in accordance with it. There are two important things to notice here: first, that Patience has now replaced Reason as the king's best counsellor in Conscience's estimation, and secondly, that Conscience arrives at this decision because of its eminent reasonableness. Thus, although he has gone a step further than he had in Passus III, his intellectual equipment is the same. He is not inspired by grace but convinced by reason. And the love of which Patience speaks is, as Conscience interprets it, only natural love—the love of self turned outward to one's fellow creatures in "kynde love." Patience refers to "the lordes love of hevene" but Conscience does not respond to this. Instead, he is convinced by its *self-evident* truth, apprehensible by pure reason and wit, and not dependent upon supernatural revelaton to be understood—as he says, he knows it "Nought thorugh wicche-craft but thorugh wit" (XIII. 168). Unlike Patience (who is after all a Christian virtue and not a rational faculty), Conscience is still firmly bound by the limits of unaided human comprehension, but he has at least learned that love is a better teacher than simple learning. He is no longer satisfied with mere intellectual keenness of the sort that enabled him to see through the verbal intricacies of Lady Meed.

Conscience and Patience then set out on a pilgrimage together, leaving Clergy behind. It is at this point that one begins to see a real change in Conscience. He becomes a student, wishing to learn what Patience has to teach him:

---

2. The process of perfection which Patience describes here is very like that of St. Bernard of Clairvaux's way of charity. Several commentators have seen a Bernardine influence in the poem. It was first noted, to my knowledge, by Donaldson, *Piers*, pp. 188–93. It has been developed most elaborately by Helmus Maisack, *William Langlands Verhältnis zum zisterziensischen Mönchtum* (Inaugural-Dissertation, Tübingen; Balingen, 1953). The problem is discussed with some caution by Bloomfield, *Piers*, pp. 63–66.

'For I wil go with this gome, if god wil give me grace,
And be pilgryme with Pacience til I have preved more.'
(XIII. 181–82)

He has not lost his respect for Clergy, but he has come to realize that he must "prove more" with Patience's help. He has learned all that the intellect, unaided, can teach him—now he must learn the knowledge that comes only through love. It is significant that he asks for God's grace before undertaking the pilgrimage, for he has never before acknowledged a need of it. Conscience's education toward perfection has begun. At the end of Passus IV his companion is Reason; at the end of XIII it is Patience, the Christ-like virtue of patient poverty,[3] whose *lemman* is Love.

Conscience disappears from the poem after the instruction of Hawkyn in Passus XIV, during which he defers to Patience (rather as though both he and Hawkyn were learning about patient poverty). He comes back in Passus XIX, having learned the lessons of patience and love well enough to be entrusted by Grace with the defense of Unity-Holychurch. Grace tells the folk of the field, "crouneth Conscience kynge" (XIX. 251). He has now attained through grace that primary purity which conscience has in the monastic writings. When Grace appears in the form of a dove, Conscience is the first to recognize him, kneeling and singing "*veni, creator spiritus*" (XIX. 205). It is the Holy Spirit who is descending, and the fact that Conscience knows him and leads the people in welcoming him is a clear expression of the role which conscience plays in such mystical writings as *The Abbey of the Holy Ghost*. Here Conscience does indeed lead God into men's souls. He has been purified enough for the dwelling of the Spirit to be built "in a place that es called 'conscyence.'"

To say this, however, is not to say that Conscience's basic nature has been wholly transformed. He is still only human comprehension, and though Grace has illumined and strengthened him, in himself he has no inherently divine understanding. Without grace, he is still liable to error and to being deceived. He knows perfectly well, as he tells the folk, "we beth noughte of strengthe/To gone agayne Pryde but Grace were with us" (XIX. 355–56). Unfortunately neither Grace nor Piers is with them, and so Conscience is left again to his own woefully limited resources. His helpers are all purely natural: Kind Wit instructs him in preparing the defence of Unity, and in Passus XX his supporters are Kind, Death, Elde, and Need. It is all too obvious that this is a world without grace of any sort. At this point, without divine guidance and with only the treacherous natural world to fight for him, Conscience's peculiar limitation betrays him. He is taken in by his conscientiousness, his courtesy and tenderheartedness. As in Passus XIII, he makes the mistake of being too gentle with a friar. This time the result is disastrous.

Conscience's courtesy is suspiciously evident even as he leaves on his pilgrimage with Patience. Far from denouncing the fraudulent, sophistical doctor, he "curteislich . . . congeye fyrst the frere" (XIII. 198). Now there is nothing inherently wrong with being polite even to rascals, except when politeness blinds judgment and becomes the unwitting aid of treachery. It

---

3. For the identification of Patience with patient poverty, see Donaldson, *Piers*, pp. 170, 175–78, and R. W. Frank, Jr., *Piers Plowman and the Scheme of Salvation* (New Haven, 1957), pp. 70–75.

is no accident that the figure who admits Friar Flattery to Unity, over the vigorous protests of Peace, is called Hende-speech (gracious words). Hende-speech has very idealistic reasons for doing as he does—he wishes to bring about an accord between Conscience and the (now thoroughly corrupt) figure of Life, so that they may "kisse her either other" (XX. 351). Naked idealism, however, is inadequate to deal with the subtle and evil enemies of Unity. And Conscience continues what Hende-speech has begun. Several parallels exist between the confrontation of Conscience and Friar Flattery and the debate of Conscience and Lady Meed in Passus III. Hende-speech's desire for a kiss of peace to terminate the battle (as if *that* were a solution to Armageddon) is reminiscent of the king's similar desire at Westminster. It is a measure of the darkness of Passus XX that this time Conscience is unable to see through the courtesy and flattery of his enemy, even though he knows much more than he did in Passus III. The friar greets Conscience "curteisly" (XX. 352), much as Lady Meed greeted the court. Conscience responds politely out of solicitous concern for Contrition's pain:

> 'Thow art welcome,' quod Conscience, 'canstow hele the syke?
> Here is Contricioun,' quod Conscience, 'my cosyn, ywounded;
> Conforte hym,' quod Conscience, 'and take kepe to his sores.
> The plastres of the persoun and poudres biten to sore.'
> (XX. 354–57)

The repetition of the phrase "quod Conscience" sounds the warning. Conscience is indeed speaking, but it is the wrong kind of conscience. The gentleman-knight and tenderhearted companion has betrayed what he himself as heralder of the Holy Spirit had tried so valiantly to defend. What makes this moment so believable and so moving is that his liability has been in evidence from Conscience's first appearance in the poem.

Conscience has come to mean something very complex during the course of *Piers Plowman*, and the way in which Langland makes his various meanings interact and illuminate each other is masterly. Though all these meanings have been implicit since his earliest appearances, each of his major scenes emphasizes a different aspect of his nature. Against Lady Meed, we see Conscience primarily in the role of judge, a just arbitrator of right and wrong. Then, in the scene at dinner, Conscience becomes aware of the necessity for charity and begins to assume a more mystical role. This aspect of his nature is most apparent at the beginning of Passus XIX, when he kneels in welcome to Grace and is made the defender of Unity. After Grace departs, we see Conscience hard pressed by foes too powerful for him to face alone, and he is finally betrayed not by the Friar so much as by his own weakest aspect, his conscientiousness. At the very end, having learned the bitter lessons of Passus XX, we see him starting out in search of the one figure that can save him, Piers the Plowman.

At no point does Conscience overstep the limitations of his nature. What he is and does is determined, as in the case of all the other personifications in the poem, by the nature of the concept. Yet he often seems to us to be more of a character, in the sense of having a distinct consciousness and awareness, than many of Langland's other personifications. This is due partly, I think, to the sheer complexity of the concept and the depth to which it is explored. We see Conscience more often and more variously than practically any other figure. But I think the chief reason for our sense of his consciousness is that we see him being educated during the course of the poem. He gains a sense of the needs and potentials of his character—in short, he develops. As I have shown, this is in itself an aspect of his nature, but what Langland achieves in exploring the concept of conscience through the device of personification is to give us a vivid sense of the inter-relatedness of all the various meanings the word can have. What is involved is much more than simply applying separate meanings out of the diction-ary at given points in the poem; all the meanings together step out of the dictionary in the person of a single figure acting within a narrative, and so become potentialities, assets, and liabilities of the character rather than separable definitions imposed from without. Because of this the word itself, through the figure embodying it, takes on a richness, vitality, and vivid com-plexity that can be given to it only in poetry and only at the hands of a mas-terful allegorist like Langland.

JILL MANN

Eating and Drinking in *Piers Plowman*†

> Grex fidelis triplici cibo sustentetur,
> corpore Dominico, quo fides augetur,
> sermonis compendio, quod discrete detur,
> mundano cibario, ne periclitetur.[1]

[The company of the faithful may be sustained by threefold food, by the body of the Lord, by which faith is increased, by the distillation of the ser-mon, which may be given separately, by daily food, lest it be in danger.]

When we think of metaphor or of allegory (which can defensibly be glossed as narrative metaphor),[2] we tend to assume that it illuminates the complex by means of the simple—that it seeks to express the elusive mysteries of the emotions and the spirit by using the familiar features of the concrete physical world we know and understand. It is the purpose of this essay to explore one particular aspect of Langland's use of metaphor and allegory,

---

† From *Essays and Studies* 32 (1979):26–42. Reprinted by permission of the publisher. All the Latin quotations in this essay are translated by Elizabeth Robertson.

1. These lines occur in the (12th–13th c.) poem 'Viri venerabiles, sacerdotes Dei', printed by B. Hau-réau, *Notices et Extraits de Quelques Manuscrits Latins de la Bibliothèque Nationale* vol. 6 (Paris, 1893), p. 14. They may serve as a small indication of the extensive use of the images of eating and drinking in medieval Latin poetry. This essay is a preliminary version of part of a book on some aspects of allegory, language, metaphor and concept in *Piers Plowman* on which I am at present working, and in which I hope to be able to include fuller consideration of the rich background for these metaphors in medieval Latin and vernacular literature. Some general studies which may use-fully be cited here are Klaus Lange, 'Geistliche Speise', *Zeitschrift für Deutsches Altertum*, 95 (1966), 81–122, and the chapter on 'Banquet Imagery' in Mikhail Bakhtin, *Rabelais and his World*, trans. H. Iswolsky (Cambridge, Mass., 1968), pp. 278–302. A. C. Spearing has discussed the development of the theme of hunger in the C-text from the episode of Hunger in Passus IX, with its emphasis on physical food, to the speech of Activa-vita and Patience's reply to it in Passus XVI, which shifts the emphasis on to the spiritual aspect of the problem of food ('The Development of a Theme in *Piers Plowman'*, *Review of English Studies*, n.s. 11, 1960, 241–53). Elizabeth Kirk has also pointed to the importance of the images of food and drink, both physical and spiritual, in the poem (*The Dream Thought of Piers Plowman*, New Haven and London, 1972, pp. 132–33, 153 and 197).

2. See the beginning of the stimulating chapter on allegory in Pamela Gradon, *Form and Style in Early English Literature* (London, 1971), pp. 32–92.

the images of eating and drinking in *Piers Plowman*, in order to show that in his poetry the material world is not merely a vehicle for expressing the immaterial, but on the contrary contains the heart of its meaning and its mystery. If on the one hand the material world is interpenetrated by a spiritual reality which transcends material laws, on the other hand the laws of the material world interpenetrate spiritual reality and resolve some of its most fundamental problems.

As a consequence, this discussion must include Langland's representation of actual hunger and thirst, and actual eating and drinking, as well as their more obviously metaphorical applications, and I use the term 'image' as one which will cover both metaphorical and concrete uses. It is, of course, largely due to the general structure of the allegory that we can see even the most apparently concrete activities as metaphorical, and vice versa. In the lengthy account of the ploughing of Piers' half-acre in Passus VI, it might seem that Langland is primarily concerned with the concrete rôles of the real members of fourteenth-century society in the production and consumption of food—but because the ploughing which was meant to be a prelude to the pilgrimage to Treuthe eventually comes to be seen as an allegorical replacement for it, it acts as nourishment for the spirit as well as the body. Conversely, when in Passus XIX (260 ff.) we hear of Piers 'ploughing' with the four evangelists as his oxen, and sowing in man's heart the seeds of the four cardinal virtues, it might seem that only spiritual food is in question; but the harvest of this sowing is celebrated in the Eucharist, which offers bodily as well as spiritual refreshment:

> 'Cometh', quod Conscience   ·   Cristene, and dyneth,
> That han laboured lelly   ·   al this lente-tyme.
> Here is bred yblessed   ·   and goddes body ther-under.'[3]
> (381–83)

Often, however, Langland is not content to rely on the structure of the allegory, and adopts special means to make us simultaneously conscious of both real and metaphorical dimensions for the image, as in his complaint of the avarice of 'chapeleynes':

> Unkynde to her kyn   ·   and to alle cristene,
> Chewen here charite   ·   and chiden after more.
> (I. 190–91)

Metaphorically, the chaplains are greedy of their charity—wish, 'cormorant-like', to swallow it up for themselves—but the image also suggests that they do so by actually eating food which they could give to others. It is easy to see from these instances the difficulties in dividing Langland's food and drink images into concrete *or* metaphorical, bodily *or* spiritual. But for the sake of convenience in discussion, I shall start with those images which seem to have most emphasis on the concrete; secondly, move on to more metaphorical usages; and finally, show how even the most apparently metaphorical examples ultimately resolve themselves into concretions.

* * * So we may begin discussion of the importance of concrete food

---

3. All quotations are from the B-text unless it is otherwise stated. I cite from W. W. Skeat's two-volume edition (Oxford, 1886), with occasional corrections from the edition of the B-text by G. Kane and E. T. Donaldson (London, 1975).

in *Piers Plowman* by looking at its rôle in the formation and regulation of social relationships in the ploughing of Piers' half-acre in Passus VI. In the course of the ploughing, the various social groups define themselves and their relationships to each other (see especially ll. 7–97). Moreover, although in providing food for those 'that feithfulliche libbeth' (71), Piers and his fellows serve Treuthe, it is not only obedience to Treuthe which acts as stimulus to their labour; it is the simple driving force of natural needs. We see this clearly when some of the lazier workers refuse to continue, and the knight's attempts to coerce them prove fruitless; only Piers' summons of Hunger is effective.

> Hunger in haste tho   ·   hent Wastour bi the mawe,
> And wronge hym so bi the wombe   ·   that bothe his eyen wattered;
> He buffeted the Britoner   ·   aboute the chekes,
> That he loked like a lanterne   ·   al his lyf after.
>
>   (176–79)

The control of this society is not solely in the hands of its human members. They depend on the power of Hunger to drive them to work—and in that sense Hunger plays a beneficial rôle in society. But Hunger is not always so conveniently subservient to human interests; once installed in society he refuses to depart, and eventually has to be put to sleep with a whole banquet of homely fare, which Langland clearly enjoys enumerating with concrete specificity: 'two grene cheses', 'A fewe cruddes and creem · and an haver cake', 'percil and porettes · and many kole-plantes', 'Benes and baken apples', 'Chibolles and chervelles · and ripe chiries manye' (283–97). The society envisaged in this Passus is thus not ruled solely by moral laws—nor even by the physical coercion exerted by one social group on another. It is ruled, ultimately, by the laws of physical nature. Natural laws may embrace moral laws, but they cannot be confined to them; Hunger cannot be summoned and dismissed as morally appropriate even though his rôle may have a morally appropriate effect (the punishment of wasters).

One conclusion that can be drawn from this episode is that Langland sees justice as naturally 'built in to' the world. He does not quote the biblical text 'If any would not work, neither should he eat' (2 Thess. 3:10), but it is clearly fundamental to his thought. But if justice is thus an inherent part of the nature of things, rather than humanly or divinely imposed, how can it ever fall into abeyance?—as it clearly does when Hunger is finally put to sleep and the wasters take over. Partly, this state of affairs is due to the fact that individual human beings can pervert nature by the sin of gluttony, which overrides the moderation that nature would dictate. (The cloak of Hawkin the Active Man is soiled with Gluttony because he has eaten and drunk more 'then kende might defie'.[4]) But partly it is due to the possibility for wasters to live off the labour of others, to win food by begging. So Langland introduces a long discussion between Hunger and Piers on the question of whether Piers is perverting justice and nature if he gives food to those who do not work. The problem is of more than local interest, since it forms part of the larger problem of how mercy can be exercised without undermining justice, which occupies Langland through-

---

4. XIII. 404. In the C-text, this line forms part of Gluttony's confession (VII. 430).

out the poem. Hunger's answer to Piers on this question is that beggars *should* be given food (albeit only coarse food), if they are needy.

'And alle maner of men   ·   that thow myght asspye,
That nedy ben, and naughty   ·   helpe hem with thi godis,
Love hem and lakke hem noughte   ·   late god take the venjaunce.'[5]
(225–27)

It is need which thus creates the suspension of vengeance. Need overrides the dispensation of reward and punishment according to moral deserts; physical need takes precedence over moral laws. And it is hunger that teaches us this.

The lines quoted above, however, are hardly sufficient by themselves to indicate the importance of need, and Langland gives it independent treatment in a very curious and isolated incident at the beginning of Passus xx. The dreamer is looking for somewhere to eat, and being unable to find anywhere, around midday he appropriately meets Need. Need berates him for failing to provide for his physical requirements by any means available, as would be legitimate if he took no more than Need taught him, for

. . . . Nede ne hath no lawe   ·   ne nevre shal falle in dette
For thre thynges he taketh   ·   his lyf forto save,
That is, mete, whan men hym werneth   ·   and he no money weldeth,
Ne wyght none wil ben his borwe   ·   ne wedde hath none to legge.
And he caughte in that cas   ·   and come ther-to by sleighte,
He synneth noughte sothelich   ·   that so wynneth his fode.
And though he come so to a clothe   ·   and can no better chevysaunce,
Nede anon righte   ·   nymeth hym under meynpryse.
And if hym lyst for to lape   ·   the lawe of kynde wolde
That he dronke at eche diche   ·   ar he for thurste deyde.
So Nede at grete nede   ·   may nymen as for his owne,
Wyth-oute conseille of Conscience   ·   or cardynale vertues,
So that he suwe and save   ·   *spiritus temperancie*.'[6]
(10–22)

Need continues to define himself for another twenty-five lines, and the dreamer then falls asleep—leaving this little episode without an obvious sequel, as it is without an obvious introduction. Its full significance will only become clear later; for the moment it may stand as demonstration that Langland's reference to need in Passus IV is not a casual one, but part of a clearly thought out conception of the relationship between physical and moral laws.

In the C-text, Langland's insistence that no one should beg 'bote yf he haue nede' leads to a description of the life of the needy which is an excellent example of his fully concrete realization of hunger and thirst (Cx. 71–97). Langland does not try to win our sympathy for the poor by directly describing them and their pitiful appearance (as does, for example, his less

5. Kane and Donaldson's text differs considerably at this point, but the references to need and vengeance are unaffected.
6. The punctuation of line 10 follows Kane and Donaldson's edition; Skeat's punctuation is clearly wrong. The images of debt, pledge and bail ('meynpryse') strengthen the link (which I shall be suggesting later) between this passage and the account of the Harrowing of Hell in Passus xviii (see esp. ll. 182–85). An excellent and illuminating study of the legal imagery in *Piers Plowman* is to be found in Dr. Anna Baldwin's unpublished Ph.D. dissertation (Cambridge 1975), 'The Law of the King in the C-text of Piers Plowman', to which I am much indebted; on debt, surety and 'mainprise', see esp. pp. 118–42.

sensitive follower, the author of *Pierce the Ploughmans Crede*, in his picture of the poor ploughman);[7] instead, he makes poetry out of the things
that make up the lives of the poor, and thus re-creates the texture of those
lives around us as we read. Their barrenness, their pinched quality can be
felt especially in the concrete details of food and drink: 'papelotes' made of
'mylk' and 'mele', 'To a-glotye with here gurles   ·   that greden after fode',
'payn and peny-ale', 'Colde flessh and colde fyssh', 'a ferthyng-worth of
muscles . . . other so fele cockes' (Cx. 75–6, 92–5). The poverty of the poor
is most clearly shown in the simple fact that they are *not there* in the lines
describing their lives; they are, as it were, only the emptiness which is filled
up with the daily round of wearing tasks and pitiful items of food and drink.
The spare, matter-of-fact tone registers the fact that even emotion is a luxury which the poor cannot afford, so that we are left to confront hunger in
its most concrete and simple reality:

> Al-so-hem selve   ·   suffren muche hunger . . .
> Both a-fyngrede and a-furst   ·   to turne the fayre outwarde,
> And beth abasshed for to begge   ·   and wolle nat be aknowe
> What hem needeth at here neihebores   ·   at non and at even.
>   (Cx. 77, 85–87)

Such passages work cumulatively to establish hunger and thirst, food
and drink as subjects of major importance in the poem. It is only when we
see them as subjects in their own right that we can properly understand,
for example, Langland's frequent outbursts against those social classes that
are guilty of corrupting food—'Brewesteres and bakesteres   ·   bocheres
and cokes' who

> . . . rychen thorw regraterye   ·   and rentes hem buggen
> With that the pore people   ·   shulde put in here wombe.
>   (III. 78, 83–84)

—and who would otherwise seem rather minor villains to be singled out for
attack. We also might interpret as merely 'conventional' the recurrent
denunciations of gluttony, such as the following one which emerges, to our
surprise, in the middle of an elaborate explanation of Inwitte:

> Moche wo worth that man   ·   that mys-reuleth his Inwitte,
> And that be glotouns globbares   ·   her god is her wombe;
>   *Quorum deus venter est.*
> For thei serven Sathan   ·   her soule shal he have;
> That liveth synful lyf here   ·   her soule is liche the devel.
> And alle that lyven good lyf   ·   aren like god almighti;
>   *Qui manet in caritate, in deo manet, &c.*
>   (IX. 59–63)

The importance of food in this passage becomes even clearer if we take into
account Skeat's comment (vol. 2, p. 141) that the text 'Qui manet in caritate . . .' (1 John 4:16) 'was commonly repeated in the Graces before and
after meat'.[8] The importance of food and drink in the poem similarly
explains why Gluttony is given the most vivid and elaborate of the confessions of the Seven Deadly Sins; Langland wishes to develop an image of

---

7. Ed. W. W. Skeat, EETS, o.s. 30 (London, 1867), ll. 422–27.
8. Skeat also notes (vol. 2, p. 207) several other Latin texts used as graces which are quoted by
Langland.

the dissipating and futile nature of gluttony which will serve as a powerful contrast to the rôle of hunger in regulating productive work and social interchange.[9] Further, food and drink enter into the portraits of all the other sins except the half-dozen lines devoted to Pride. Lecher's short confession includes a vow of fasting. Envy suffers from indigestion—

> I myghte noughte eet many yeres · as a man oughte,
> For envye and yvel wille · is yvel to defye.
>
> (v. 120–21)

Wrath works in a convent kitchen as 'potagere' and 'cooks up' quarrels out of gossip and slander: 'Of wikked wordes I, Wrath · here wortes i-made' (v. 157–64); conversely, he is 'starved out' of monasteries by 'unthende fisshe · and fieble ale drynke' (177). Avarice and his wife are corrupters of ale (v. 219–25), and Sloth concludes his confession by acknowledging that he has let food go to waste through his laziness (v. 442–45).

Wrath's rôle as cook, making 'wortes' out of 'wordes', serves to introduce us to a major metaphorical use of the image of eating and drinking— the idea of eating words. The associative connection between food and speech is something almost entirely lost to us, except in such unthinkingly used phrases as 'I'll make him eat his words' or 'he swallowed the story whole'. But in the Middle Ages the two functions of the mouth were much more commonly related to each other, and a traditional cluster of ideas and imagery expressed this connection.[1] In medieval English literature, we have only to think of Chaucer's *Pardoner's Tale* (which the Pardoner cannot tell until he has had a drink), and its use of the mouth (the Pardoner's flow of rhetoric) to castigate the sins of the mouth (gluttony and oaths) to see the strength and integration of the tradition.[2] The connection does not just reside in the notion that the mouth takes in food and 'spews up' words; it has, for example, a simple experiential foundation in the fact that the table is a place for talk, and drink loosens a man's tongue. Speech accompanies eating and drinking and is influenced by them. The consequence of this is that a perversion in eating and drinking leads to a perversion in words, and vice versa. In a long passage at the beginning of Passus X we can see many aspects of this idea. Dame Study attacks contemporary lords for preferring to be entertained at dinner by the base kind of minstrels that

> Spitten and spewen · and speke foule wordes,
> Drynken and dryvelen · and do men for to gape.
>
> (40–41)

—instead of one that 'hath holy writte · ay in his mouth' (32). In addition, the clerks who share in these feasts practise a kind of verbal *gourmandise*:

> Thanne telleth thei of the trinite · a tale other tweyne,
> And bringen forth a balled resoun · and taken Bernard to witnesse,
> And putten forth a presumpsioun · to preve the sothe.

---

9. Cf. the picture of gluttony frustrating social order and productivity at Prol. 22.
1. See Bakhtin, *Rabelais and his World*, pp. 283–86.
2. See John Leyerle, 'Thematic Interlace in "The Canterbury Tales"', *Essays and Studies*, 29 (1976): 113–14, on the importance of food and drink in the *Pardoner's Tale*, and cf. F. Tupper, 'Chaucer's Sinners and Sins', *Journal of English and Germanic Philology*, 15 (1916): 67–71, on the tale's use of the traditional medieval links between gluttony, swearing and blasphemy.

Thus thei dryvele at her deyse · the deite to knowe,
And gnawen god with the gorge · whan her gutte is fulle.

(x. 53–57)

And the new and perverted habit of eating meals in private rooms (and thus denying the social importance of food, the benefit to the community from meals in hall which can be shared by travellers or beggars) leads lords themselves, 'etyng atte table', to 'Carpen as thei clerkes were · of Cryste and of his mightes', and to quibble over theological doctrines in 'crabbed wordes' (x. 96 ff.).

There is however yet another connection—and a more purely metaphorical one—which is described in Jean Leclercq's book on the culture of medieval monasticism, *The Love of Learning and the Desire for God*.[3] He is commenting on the significance of the medieval habit of reading texts aloud, rather than silently to oneself:

> This repeated mastication of the divine words is sometimes described by use of the theme of spiritual nutrition. In this case the vocabulary is borrowed from eating, from digestion, and from the particular form of digestion belonging to the ruminants. For this reason, reading and meditation are sometimes described by the very expressive word *ruminatio* . . . To meditate is to attach oneself closely to the sentence being recited and weigh all its words in order to sound the depths of their full meaning. It means assimilating the content of a text by means of a kind of mastication which releases its full flavour. It means, as St Augustine, St Gregory, John of Fécamp and others say in an untranslatable expression, to taste it with the *palatum cordis* or *in ore cordis*. (pp. 89–90)

It is not necessary to assume that Langland was or had ever been a monk (although aspects of his work which suggest monastic connections have been commented on in the past)[4] to envisage his being familiar with the notion thus described, and his having memorized and contemplated many passages of scripture in this way. His poem itself makes clear that Langland had meditated on a large number of biblical texts—and also on their relationship to each other, so that one text called another to mind in a manner that habitual contemplation and study of the Bible made natural.[5] Leclercq claims that the monks were so deeply imbued with the text of scripture that they had no need of artificial aids to underpin the development of their associative stream of thought. But such aids did, nevertheless, exist, in the form of the so-called *distinctiones*. These aids to biblical study 'amount to alphabetical concordances of key words from Scripture . . . accompanied by citations or quotations from the Biblical text', which 'served as a guide to the Biblical *sentence* of important objects or concep-

3. Translated by C. Misrahi (New York, 1974), originally printed as *L'Amour des Lettres et le Désir de Dieu* (Paris, 1957).
4. See Morton W. Bloomfield's article 'Was William Langland a Benedictine Monk?', *Modern Language Quarterly*, 4 (1943): 57–61. Bloomfield's book, *Piers Plowman as a Fourteenth-Century Apocalypse* (New Brunswick, New Jersey, 1961), is a more general discussion of the influence of monastic ways of thinking (*Denkform*) on Langland's poem. (This book is hereafter cited as *Apocalypse*.)
5. Cf. John A. Alford's article on the influence of such meditation on Richard Rolle's prose style: 'Biblical *Imitatio* in the Writings of Richard Rolle', *ELH*, 40 (1973): 1–23. Alford's unpublished dissertation, '*Piers Plowman* and the Tradition of biblical *Imitatio*' (U of North Carolina, 1969) was unfortunately not available to me.

tions'.⁶ Headings such as 'Fames' [Hunger], 'Sits' [Thirst], 'Cibus' [Food], 'Esca' [Victuals], 'Vinum' [Wine], 'Vinea' [a Vineyard], etc., appear regularly in collections of *distinctiones*. The entry under 'Cibus' in the twelfth-century *distinctiones* of Peter the Chanter will give an idea of their method:

> The food, that is sustenance, is of the will, about which Christ says, 'My etc.' Of the soul, in Christ, that is contemplation of the divinity, from which Christ has never abstained; thus: 'I have set the Lord in my sight always'—Of the Scripture; thus: 'Man shall not live by bread alone.'—Of human intercourse, from which he abstained in the passion, because he did not join anyone to himself but the thief, about which it is said: 'And I have subdued my soul by fasting'—Of the body, by which Christ fasted, thus: 'When he had fasted for 40 days, etc.'— Of beginners, in penance, thus; 'Tears have been my bread day and night?'—Of those making progress, in holy Scripture; thus: 'do you sit at the feast? Consider carefully what is put before you and know that it is fitting for you to prepare such things.'—And in the Eucharist; thus: 'Let a man prove himself, etc.'—For those reaching the end, at the eternal feast; thus, 'so that you may eat and drink at my table.'⁷

Whichever collection of *distinctiones* Langland knew—Peter's, or that of his contemporary Alan of Lille, or the thirteenth-century *Distinctiones monasticae*, or yet another—the influence of their structure is fundamental to his meditation on the many biblical texts which involve the ideas of eating and drinking, hunger and thirst. The importance of eating is therefore twofold: firstly it is metaphorically applied to the texts in the practice of *ruminatio*, and secondly, the texts which are thus 'digested' are themselves passages which use the images of eating and drinking.

We can see a vivid animation of the concept of *ruminatio* in the description of the dinner-party at Conscience's house in Passus XIII. The 'doctoure on the heigh dese' eats real food, 'mortrewes and puddynges, / Wombecloutes and wylde braune · & egges yfryed with grece' (62–63). But Patience and the dreamer are nourished by the text of scripture; they eat words.

> And than he brought us forth a mees of other mete · of *Miserere-mei-deus*;
> And he broughte us of *Beati-quorum* · of *Beatus-virres* makynge,
> *Et-quorum-tecta-sunt-* · *peccata* in a disshe
> Of derne shrifte, *Dixi* · and *confitebor tibi!*
> (52–55)

6. D. W. Robertson Jr and Bernard F. Huppé, *Piers Plowman and Scriptural Tradition* (Princeton, New Jersey, 1951), p. 5. Robertson and Huppé have related the content of the *distinctiones* (and to some extent their method) to *Piers Plowman*. See also A. C. Spearing's comment that those familiar with the *distinctiones* 'would surely have seen many common Scriptural images as exemplifying themes, and hence as pregnant with potential meanings' (*art. cit., Review of English Studies* n.s. 11, 1960, p. 252).
   For printed texts of *distinctiones*-collections, see: *Spicilegium Solesmense*, ed. J. B. Pitra, vols. 2–3 (Paris, 1855), in which extracts from Peter the Chanter and the *Distinctiones monasticae* are printed in conjunction with the so-called *Clavis S. Melitonis*; *Allegoriae in Universam Sacram Scripturam* (Ps.-Rabanus; see A. Wilmart, *Revue Bénédictine*, 32 (1920), 47–56, *PL*, 112. 849–1088; Alan of Lille, *Distinctiones Dictionum Theologicalium, PL*, 210. 685–1012. See also C. Spicq, *Esquisse d'une Histoire de l'Eexégèse Latine au Moyen Age* (Paris, 1944), pp. 175–77, and Beryl Smalley, *The Study of the Bible in the Middle Ages* (2nd edn., Oxford, 1952), pp. 247–48.
7. The biblical texts cited are the following: John 4:34 (cf. *PPl*, xiv. 48 and xv. 174): Matt. 4:41; Luke 4:4 (quoted at *PPl*, xiv 46); Ps. 68: 11; Matt. 4:2; Ps. 41:4 (quoted at *PPl*, vii. 123); cf. Prov. 23:1; 1 Cor. 11:28; Luke 22:30.

This whole scene could itself be seen as the result of Langland's meditation on the text: 'Man shall not live by bread alone, but by every word that proceedeth out of the mouth of God' (Matt. 4:4; Luke 4:4). Such texts often provide a sort of 'hidden structure' in the poem, organizing and articulating its development—or at the very least, they are nodal points which serve both to generate and concentrate its ideas.[8] Thus, behind the description of Charity's livelihood—

> *Fiat-voluntas-tua*   ·   fynt hym ever-more
> And if he soupeth, eet but a soppe   ·   of *spera-in-deo*.
>   (xv. 174–75)

—is the scriptural text: 'Jesus saith unto them, "My meat is to do the will of him that sent me"' (John 4:34). And in the famous scene where Piers tears the pardon and renounces his concern for his 'bely-joye', he quotes from the Psalms (Vulgate 41:4) to mark the transition to a new kind of food:

> *Fuerunt michi lacrime mee panes die ac nocte.*
> ["My tears have been my bread day and night."]
>   (vii. 117–23)

Yet spiritual food never supersedes real food in importance, as we see, for example, in Langland's formulation of the duties of bishops:

> . . . Ysaie of yow speketh   ·   and Osyas bothe,
> That no man schuld be bischope   ·   but if he hadde bothe,
> Bodily fode and gostly fode   ·   and gyve ther it nedeth;
>   *In domo mea non est panis neque vestimentum, et ideo nolite*
> *constituere me regem.*
> Ozias seith for such   ·   that syke ben and fieble,
>   *Inferte omnes decimas in oreum meum, vt sit cibus in domo mea.*
>   (xv. 565–68)

All these aspects of the images of eating and drinking find their richest concentration and expression in Langland's meditation on the central mysteries of Christianity—the sin of Adam and Eve, its redemption by the crucifixion of Christ, and the participation of Christians in that redemption through the Eucharist. And here we shall see how the concrete aspect of the images of eating and drinking asserts itself again. We may begin with the image of Christ's redemption as satisfying the thirst of the sinful:

> For Cryste cleped us alle   ·   come if we wolde,
> Sarasenes and scismatikes   ·   and so he dyd the Jewes,
>   *O vos omnes scicientes, venite, &c.;*
> And badde hem souke for synne   ·   saufly at his breste,
> And drynke bote for bale   ·   brouke it who so myghte.
>   (xi. 114–17)

Christ is here presented as ministering to our spiritual thirst. And in Passus v (in a passage which anticipates in miniature compass the themes, images and action of the Harrowing of Hell in Passus xviii), he is presented as ministering to our spiritual hunger.

---

8. Cf. Alford, *art. cit.*, 12, and Bloomfield, *Apocalypse*, pp. 30–32.

The sonne for sorwe ther-of   ·   les syghte for a tyme
Aboute mydday whan most lighte is   ·   and mele tyme of seintes;
Feddest with thi fresche blode   ·   owre forfadres in derknesse.
                                                              (499–501)

(The passage is prefaced by the text 'Qui manet in caritate', which acts as
a kind of grace before this 'meal', and it is followed by the text 'Verbum caro
factum est'—the Word becomes flesh, and thus people can eat it.) The
power of the lines I have quoted arises not only from the matter-of-factness
which aligns this with everyday (and therefore real) meal-times, but also
from the double reference in the word 'fresche'; fresh in the sense of
'recently poured forth', and fresh in the sense of 'not stale'. In the painful
fusion of our responses to fresh food and our responses to fresh blood, we
can feel both the relief offered and the pain of its cost; but the sharpness
of the sensation arises from the way the image causes us to apprehend this
food as a concrete experience.

And the drinking of Christ's blood, the eating of his body, is not a metaphorical notion only; in the service of the Mass, it is actually performed.
God's grace enters the body through the physical act of eating and drinking.[9] The sin of Adam and Eve was also a physical action: 'Adam and Eve
·   eten apples unrosted' (v. 612)—the homely addition of 'unrosted' makes
these *real* apples to us.[1] It may be objected that this is to concentrate merely
on the outward performance of their sin, which was really constituted by
the desire to 'be as gods, knowing good and evil' (Gen. 2:5). It is certainly
true that Langland attributes their action to this desire:

Coveytise to kunne   ·   and to knowe science
Pulte out of paradys   ·   Adam and Eve;
    Science appetitus hominem inmortalitatis gloria spoliauit.
And righte as hony is yvele to defye   ·   and engleymeth the mawe,
Right so that thorw resoun   ·   wolde the rote knowe
Of god and of his grete myghtes   ·   his graces it letteth.
For in the lykyng lith a pryde   ·   and a lycames coveitise,
Ayein Crystes conseille   ·   and alle clerkes techyng,
    That is, *non plus sapere quam oportet sapere.*
                                                              (XV. 61–67)

But it is not just that Langland uses a metaphor of eating (from Prov.
25:27)—the indigestibility of honey—to describe the consequences of an
excessive desire for knowledge; it is that the image of eating is actually *contained in* the desire to know, since it is an *appetite* ('*appetitus sciencie*') and
since the Latin verb *sapere* means first 'to taste' and only secondly 'to know'.
The desire to know is thus a 'lycames coueitise'—a bodily desire. Thus
when the dreamer expresses a desire to eat an apple from the Tree of Charity to see 'what sauoure it hadde'—to 'know' it in the Latin sense (XVI. 74)—
there is, I think, nothing in his desire which is sinful or absurd. The only
way you can know apples, for Langland, is to eat them.

If the desire to know is an appetite, in order to understand it we must
go back to everything we have learned from the poem about concrete
appetites (real hunger, real thirst). One thing we learned was that they were

---

9. Notice also that the Eucharist is, like other food, to be taken at need (XIX. 387).
1. Cf. the description of their sin as a sin of eating at XVIII. 189 ff.

natural forces—driving needs which can legitimate otherwise illicit actions in finding their fulfilment. This is of crucial importance in understanding the Harrowing of Hell Passus and its justification of salvation. Righteousness insists that the sin of Adam and Eve carries eternal punishment as a natural consequence of eating the apple:

'. . . late hem chewe as thei chose   ·   and chyde we nought, sustres,
For it is botelees bale   ·   the bite that thei eten.'
(XVIII. 199–200)

But Peace argues against this. Firstly, she says that Adam had to learn to know 'wel' by learning 'wo', just as the knowledge of hunger gives us the capacity to recognize its satisfaction (XVIII. 203–205). But secondly, and surprisingly, we find that God too had to go through this process of learning, 'to see the sorwe of deyinge':

'And after god auntred hym-self   ·   and toke Adames kynde,
To wyte what he hath suffred   ·   in thre sondri places,
Both in hevene, and in erthe   ·   and now til helle he thynketh,
To wite what al wo is   ·   that wote of al Joye.'
(220–23)

The union of God and man in 'kynde' means that they are united in their thirst for knowledge. The appetite for knowledge which drove man to sin drives God to redeem him, since it sends him down to earth to become flesh and die.[2]

The rôle of appetite is merely implicit in these references to the desire for knowledge. But it is made explicit when Christ himself proclaims to Lucifer the redemption of souls.

For I, that am lorde of lyf   ·   love is my drynke,
And for that drynke to-day   ·   I deyde upon erthe.
I faughte so, me threstes yet   ·   for mannes soules sake;
May no drynke me moiste   ·   ne my thruste slake,
Tyl the vendage falle   ·   in the vale of Josepath,
That I drynke righte ripe must   ·   *resurreccio mortuorum*,
And thanne shal I come as a kynge   ·   crouned with angeles,
And han out of helle   ·   alle mennes soules.
(363–70)

Behind the image of the champion of the vintage lies the beginning of Isa. 63:

1 Who is this that cometh from Edom, with dyed garments from Bozrah? this that is glorious in his apparel, travelling in the greatness of his strength: I that speak in righteousness, mighty to save.
2 Wherefore art thou red in thine apparel, and thy garments like him that treadeth in the winefat?
3 I have trodden the winepress alone; and of the people there was none with me: for I will tread them in mine anger, and trample them in my fury; and their blood shall be sprinkled upon my garments, and I will stain all my raiment.

2. See the important article of Sister Mary Clemente Davlin, '*Kynde Knowyng* as a Major Theme in *Piers Plowman* B', *Review of English Studies*, n.s. 22 (1971): 1–19, in which she argues that '*Kynde knowyng* is not only man's goal; it is God's as well' (p. 13), but does not bring out the strange similarity thus created between God's 'curiosity' and that of Adam and Eve.

4 For the day of vengeance is in mine heart, and the year of my
redeemed is come.[3]

I think that the reason that Langland incorporates this passage into the
Harrowing of Hell Passus, where justice and mercy are to be reconciled, is
his 'rumination' on the hidden connection between its picture of God treading the 'grapes of wrath' in fury and in vengeance, and the lyrical gentleness of the immediately following passage in Isaiah: 'I will mention the
lovingkindnesses of the Lord. . . .' But in Isaiah there is no mention of thirst,
or of drink. Yet once this text has been 'digested', it becomes clear that it is
possible to see as mysteriously present in it the simple fact that if one treads
the vintage, it is because one wants drink. From the grapes of wrath flows
the wine of lovingkindness. Langland discovers this as the deep and hidden
impulse behind Isaiah's words, not by reflecting on them alone, but by jux-
taposing them with another scriptural text, which is quoted at this point in
the C-text: the gospel account of Christ's words from the cross—'Sicio', 'I
thirst'. The God whom we have previously seen as offering drink to the
thirsty is now himself one of the thirsting—and not metaphorically, but in
the most cruel reality. And Langland suggests, I think, that the reasons for
the crucifixion and redemption can only be understood as thirst. He does not
offer us an abstract explanation made vivid by a concrete image; the con-
cretion is the heart of his conception of the redemption. For if the desire to
know is an appetite, so is love, as the very first Passus of the poem had made
clear to us; it is an appetite which cannot be resisted until it has 'of the erthe
yeten his fylle' (I. 152) and magically transformed earth into itself. God is
driven by a need which is as concrete, as impossible to paraphrase, as the
need of hunger or thirst. And it is, finally, this need which legitimates the
suspension of the letter of the law that would leave mankind in damnation,
because, as we have seen, 'need ne hath no lawe'. The daring of Langland's
imagination is nowhere more clearly seen than in the way he legitimates the
redemption not by man's need, but by God's.

ANNA BALDWIN

From The Theme of Government of Piers Plowman†

Langland's political ideals are not inconsistent. They seem to change,
depending on whether he is addressing the present king of England, or the
subjects and Christians who are reading the poem. It is only parts of the
Prologue and Passus II–IV which appear as a kind of 'Fürstenspiegel', a Mirror for Princes, in which England's governors are blamed for their weak tolerance of the over-powerful subject epitomized by Lady Meed or Wrong.
But when similar problems are raised in the last two Passus, it is the individual Christians who are blamed for their own tolerance of Pride and
Antichrist, their own treason to the Conscience who should rule all their
actions. Then again, in the great allegories of the Atonement in Passus

---

3. Langland probably also had in mind the apocalyptic vintage of Apoc. 14:15, but there too the pre-
   dominant idea is of the wrath of God.
† From Piers Plowman Studies 1 (1981): 81–107. Reprinted by permission of the publisher.

XVIII–XX, it is not Christ the King who is addressed, but the Christian reader. He can only wonder at Christ's obedience to the Old Law, epitomised by the laws of mainprise, charter, duel and pardon, and strive to obey Christ's New Law in return. Piers the Ploughman himself, whether tilling his half-acre or the whole of Christendom, is an ideal to be embraced not by kings and popes, but by fellow-ploughmen and subjects. If the king will not put England to rights, then it is the individual subject who must set about it, particularly as no king, not even Christ Himself, will take the responsibility for reforming man's free soul.

It would seem then that, like most 'political' poets of the time, Langland does not separate the political from the moral. When addressing the 'commune', this tends to make him a political conservative, teaching men to obey their own Consciences by keeping the laws, rather than (as the B-text Prologue implied) by helping the king to shape the laws. When addressing the king, Langland's reliance on the individual Conscience makes him hope for an absolute royal authority over both the subjects and the law, of a kind one would associate more with Edward I than with Edward III or the younger Richard II. In fact Langland's political ideals, both for the community and for the king, go counter to his own experience of law and government.

It seems to me that this is not because Langland was unaware of contemporary political developments, but because he did not mean the *Visio* kingdom to be read simply as an analogy for English society. It is also an analogy for the society of the Church, in which the king is contrasted with Christ, and the labouring subjects are contrasted with Christians. The *Visio* king's successful assertion of justice over Meed and Wrong may in one sense be a model for Richard II. It is also a foil for Christ, who chooses not to judge Adam or his sinful descendants with the same severity, but instead to obey the conditions of the law on their behalf. Similarly, Piers' unwillingness to punish his own recalcitrant but free employees reflects Christ's refusal to force men to obey their Consciences. Viewed in this light it does not really matter that Lady Meed remained at large in Langland's own kingdom, or that labourers generally preferred to abuse their new-found freedoms. A poem is not a political programme, however firmly it is rooted in contemporary life. Only Christ can truly combine in His double nature the ideal subject who obeys the law, and the ideal king who overturns it in favour of a new kind of justice and mercy.

JOHN BURROW
The Action of Langland's Second Vision†

I

The second of the ten visions in the B version of *Piers Plowman* contains some of the poem's most famous episodes. It has the confession of the Seven Deadly Sins in Passus V, the ploughing of the half-acre is Passus

† From *Essays on Medieval Literature* (Oxford: Oxford UP, 1984), pp. 79–101. Reprinted by permission of the publisher.

VI, and the tearing of the pardon in Passus VII. Critics have devoted a good deal of attention to these episodes; but they have generally failed to see them as parts of that whole to which they most immediately belong—the action, that is, of the second vision. I hope to show that, so far as its action is concerned, this vision *is* a whole, and that its more difficult episodes make better sense if we see them as parts of it. This is in the general belief that readers and critics of Langland have made too little of his vision-structure. I suppose that many people do not even know that the B version has ten visions.

*   *   *

*   *   * In the second vision at least there is a well-constructed plot, however incoherent our usual memories of it may be. The parts of this plot are not confession, ploughing, and pardon, but sermon, confession, pilgrimage, and pardon.

This series may itself seem somewhat arbitrary; but Langland wrote for readers who would appreciate its coherence. A sinful man hears a SERMON. This is the beginning of the action: it is 'not itself necessarily after anything else'; but it 'has naturally something else after it' in so far as it moves its hearer to contrition, and so sends him on to CONFESSION. This is a middle, not an end, because the priest's absolution, though it wipes away the guilt ('culpa') and the eternal punishment, leaves a debt of temporal punishment to be paid. Hence penance necessarily follows confession; and a usual form of penance, in hard cases, is PILGRIMAGE. But a pilgrimage is not an end either, for it is not normally thought sufficient in itself to pay off the whole debt of temporal punishment. This is done by the plenary PARDON (or indulgence), the usual object of major fourteenth-century pilgrimages. The pardon is a true end, both because it follows the pilgrimages as its 'usual consequent', and because it requires nothing else after it. By its power the penitent is freed from the last consequences of his sin; and the arc of penitential action is therefore complete.

*   *   *

One should realize that it was quite common in the Middle Ages for great public sermons to be followed by mass confession and a mass pilgrimage in search of pardon. An early example is the First Crusade (1095). After the Pope's sermon at Clermont, the audience knelt, recited the Confiteor, and undertook an armed pilgrimage to Jerusalem, the Pope promising plenary pardon to all who took part. Norman Cohn, in his book *The Pursuit of the Millennium*, discusses this and many other examples of what he calls the 'collective quest for salvation'. The quest was often associated, as in the case of the First Crusade, with a period of natural calamity. People were specially ready at such times to 'cluster in devotional and penitential groups'—just like Langland's thousand men—and set out on crusades, or on other more pacific kinds of pilgrimage. It is perhaps worth noticing here that the very calamities referred to by Langland's Reason in his sermon—the winds and pestilences of 1361–2—provoked just such a reaction. John of Bridlington, a contemporary of Langland's, reports that on account of the pestilence certain English lords received the sign of the Cross to go to the Holy Land.[1] Such movements were less frequent in

1. See *Political Poems and Songs*, ed. Thomas Wright, Rolls Series (London, 1859–61), vol. i, p. 183.

England than on the Continent, where 'hordes' of penitential pilgrims seem to have been almost commonplace; but Langland must have known about them. For his presentation of the conversion of the 'commune' as a collective or horde response to natural calamity implies knowledge, if not approval.

II

The plot described in the last section provides the essential ground-plan of the second vision.

* * *

The vision begins with Reason's sermon to the 'commune' (identified with the 'feeld ful of folk' of the Prologue). Reason preaches to 'al the reaume', with a cross, and in the King's presence. These details suggest a great episcopal occasion, rather than an ordinary parochial one; and the character of the sermon itself rather supports this impression. It is a 'sermo ad diversos status hominum', such as fourteenth-century bishops are known to have preached on special occasions—an address to the various 'states' of men, calling upon husbands, fathers, priests, etc. to amend their ways. Yet the preacher is Reason, not a fourteenth-century bishop; and his homely tone suggests the personification rather than the parson:

> 'My sire seide so to me, and so dide my dame,
> That the levere child the moore loore bihoveth;
> And Salomon seide the same, that Sapience made—
> "*Qui parcit virge odit filium*:
> Whoso spareth the spryng spilleth hise children." '
> (V. 37–40)

This represents what any man's reason will tell him about his duties; and it is this reasoning with oneself, rather than any grand public preaching, which Langland sees as the beginning of the conversion of the folk of the field. People have only to take thought to see that all is not as it should be. Yet we should note, in view of developments later in the vision, that the substitution of Reason for the usual priest or bishop is not polemical. Langland, that is, does not seem concerned to score points off the priests and bishops by suggesting that self-examination is *better* than sermon-going.

There is a like absence of polemic in the second stage of the action—the confession. Here Langland substitutes the personifications of the Seven Deadly Sins (representing the sins of the folk) for the penitents, and the personification of Repentance for the confessor. The latter substitution is not an altogether happy one: 'confessing to Repentance', unlike 'listening to Reason', makes little sense when one tries to convert it into literal terms. But the general point of the episode is quite clear. Once a man has taken thought and recognized his imperfections, he must then repent and confess. It must be admitted that Langland is vague about the externals of the confession. For example, Repentance speaks, in the manner of a confessor, of absolving the Sins individually (V. 184 and 272); but his actual absolution, which must be looked for in V. 479–506, is of a purely general and supplicatory character. He simply prays that God may have mercy on them all. The fact that this prayer ends with Hope blowing his horn of '*Deus tu conversus vivificabis nos*' (507) suggests that Langland is here thinking of public liturgical, rather than private sacramental, penance; for this verse from the Psalms occurs after the Confiteor and the absolution-prayer Misereatur in the Mass.[2] But such inconsistencies are typically Langlandian. We do not conclude that he thought sacramental absolution unnecessary or *merely* external.

It is, I want now to argue, exactly because he did think this way about pilgrimages that the third stage of his action presented him with a special challenge. The fact is beyond dispute. Langland, to put it bluntly, though he believed in sermons and confessions, did not believe in pilgrimages. His opinion of pilgrims is clearly stated in the Prologue:

> Pilgrymes and palmeres plighten hem togidere
> For to seken Seint Jame and seintes at Rome;
> Wenten forth in hire wey with many wise tales,
> And hadden leve to lyen al hire lif after.
> (Prol. 46–49)

Later in the first vision Reason says that, in his ideal society, St. James would be sought 'there I shal assigne' (IV. 126). The point of this enigmatic remark is made clear in the C text, where Reason requires that

> 'Seynt Iame be souht ther poure syke lyggen,
> In prisons and in poore cotes for pilgrymages to Rome'.
> (C V. 122–23)

Reason, in other words, tells us that it is better to do good works at home than to travel abroad on pilgrimages. The B text has a very similar passage later on, when Anima, speaking of Charity, says that it is his custom

> 'to wenden on pilgrymages
> Ther poore men and prisons liggeth, hir pardon to have'.
> (XV. 182–83)

Good works *instead* of pilgrimage: this is surely also the point of the pilgrimage to Truth proclaimed by Reason at the end of his sermon in the second vision:

> 'And ye that seke Seynt James and seyntes of Rome,
> Seketh Seynt Truthe, for he may save yow alle'.
> (V. 56–57)

Seeking St. James and the saints of Rome is not an acceptable form of penance—the echo of the Prologue is sufficient proof of that. So the substitution of St. Truth (i.e., God) for these saints, unlike the substitutions of Reason and Repentance for preacher and confessor, *is* polemical. There is a new tension here between the allegorical action and that which it signifies. The pilgrimage proposed by Reason signifies, one might almost say, *anything but* actual pilgrimage.

Langland makes this point dramatically in the last part of his long fifth passus. After the confession of the Sins and Repentance's great prayer, a

---

2. I owe this information to Fr. S. Tugwell, who also points out that the source of the verse (wrongly given by Skeat) is Psalm 84:7 (Vulgate).

thousand men from the field full of folk cluster (Langland uses the word 'thrungen') into a devotional and penitential group, and set out on the expiatory pilgrimage proclaimed by Reason. But they are not yet real pilgrims by any standards—Langland's or the world's—for they have no sense of where they are going. So they just roam about like a herd of animals, until they meet the Palmer:

> blustreden forth as beestes over baches and hilles,
> Til late was and longe, that thei a leode mette
> Apparailled as a paynym in pilgrymes wyse.
>
> (V. 514–16)

The Palmer is a pure grotesque, embodying everything Langland most hated in the pilgrims of his day—the worldliness, the meaningless rigmarole of place-names and keepsakes, and above all the bland complacency:

> 'Ye may se by my signes that sitten on myn hatte
> That I have walked ful wide in weet and in drye
> And sought goode Seintes for my soule helthe'.
>
> (V. 529–31)

The Palmer knows all the 'good saints', it appears, except Truth. He represents the business of worldly pilgrimage, and so stands to be contrasted with Piers, the representative of the true or spiritual pilgrimage, who 'puts forth his head' for the first time at this point in the poem. The contrast is boldly stated, and there is no need to enlarge upon it. Piers knows Truth well, and he knows the way to his place. It leads through Meekness, Conscience, Love of God, Love of Neighbour, and the Ten Commandments.

By the end of the fifth passus, then, Langland has established his third substitution—that of St. Truth for St. James and the saints of Rome—and has made sure, one would have thought, that the reader sees its polemical point. So we have every reason to expect, as we begin the sixth passus, that he will proceed with the account of the conversion of the commune by showing them following the road described by Piers, reaching Truth's shrine, and receiving his pardon. The actual course of events in the sixth passus is therefore disturbing—and, I think, deliberately so.

The opening of the passus gives no particular cause for alarm. Piers offers to guide the people on the way to Truth; but first he has a 'half acre . . . by the heighe weye' to plough and sow. One may not quite see the point of this interruption; but it does not seem to matter very much. Ploughing and sowing a single half-acre cannot take very long—it seems in fact to have been no more than a customary 'long morning's work'[3]—and the land is right 'by the heighe weye', the road which the pilgrims are to travel (described in the C text as the 'alta via ad fidelitatem'). So one expects the company to resume its journey very shortly. True, when Piers enlists the help of the pilgrims and instructs them in their various duties—the ladies to sew church vestments, the common women to spin and weave, the knight to hunt and fight, etc.—he seems to be treating the long morning's interruption in the half-acre as if it were a lifetime in the world; but we are comforted by his repeated assurances that he will lead the pilgrims on shortly, as soon as he is ready:

---

3. See G. C. Homans, *English Villagers of the Thirteenth Century* (Cambridge, Mass., 1941), p. 49.

'Hadde I eryed this half acre and sowen it after.
I wolde wende with yow and the wey teche'

(VI. 5–6)

'And I shal apparaille me,' quod Perkyn, 'in pilgrymes wise
And wende with yow I wile til we fynde Truthe'

(57–58)

'For I wol sowe it myself, and sithenes wol I wende
To pilgrymage as palmeres doon, pardon for to have'

(63–64)

'To penaunce and to pilgrimage I wol passe with thise othere;
Forthi I wole er I wende do write my bequeste'.

(84–85)

The 'bequest', or will, which these last lines introduce seems at first to
provide further reassurance; for the making of a will was a customary part
of the preparations for a pilgrimage, it being necessary to set one's house
in order in case one did not get back safely. Surely, we feel, Piers *is* going
to set out on the journey. Yet it is the will which, in its closing passage, first
positively suggests that this is not so. After bequeathing his soul to God, his
body to the Church, and his lawful winnings to his wife and children, Piers
speaks of what is left:

'And with the residue and the remenaunt, by the Rode of Lukes!
I wol worshipe therwith Truthe by my lyve,
And ben His pilgrym atte plow for povere mennes sake.
My plowpote shal be my pikstaf, and picche atwo the rotes,
And helpe my cultour to kerve and clense the furwes'.

(VI. 100–104)

This noble passage strongly suggests that Langland has in mind, however
bewilderingly, a second polemical substitution. The opening lines recall a
bit of anti-pilgrimage polemic in the confession of Sloth in the previous
passus (a parallel which is even closer in the A text where Piers refers, like
Sloth, to the rood of Chester):

'And with the residue and the remenaunt, bi the
Rode of Chestre,
I shal seken truthe erst er I se Rome!'

(V. 460–61)

But the present passage goes further than that. Having substituted the pilgrimage to Truth, proclaimed by Reason and described by Piers, for the
false and meaningless Rome-running represented by the Palmer, Langland
now has Piers talk of a 'pilgrimage at the plough', as if the ploughing of the
half-acre was to be substituted for the pilgrimage to Truth.

The rest of the sixth passus, together with the beginning of the seventh,
seems to me to provide decisive evidence that this was indeed Langland's
intention, despite the opinion of several good critics (T. P. Dunning and R.
W. Frank among them) to the contrary. The main point to note in Passus
Six is the disintegration of the time-scheme proposed in its opening passage. The long morning's work stretches out to a whole year. The action

of the passus begins round about Michaelmas, at the beginning of the husbandman's year, with the ploughing and sowing of the winter corn field—Piers's half-acre. Then, after the intervention of Hunger, there follows a threshing:

> Faitours for fere herof flowen into bernes,
> And flapten on with flailes fro morwe til even.
> (VI. 183–84)

This comes in its right place, for, as Homans observes in his excellent account of the medieval farming year, 'after the sowing of the winter corn field, the husbandman would be likely to turn from the land to the barn, where he would busy himself with the sheaves of the last harvest' (op. cit., p. 356). There follows the discussion between Piers and Hunger about poor-relief, after which we learn from Piers that the people are to live sparsely until Lammas (1st August).

> 'And by that I hope to have hervest in my croft'.
> (290)

Then, with dream-like suddenness, 'hervest' or autumn (the period between Lammas and Michaelmas) approaches once more, bringing the wheel round in a full circle:

> By that it neghed neer hervest and newe corn cam to chepyng;
> Thanne was folk fayn, and fedde Hunger with the beste.
> (299–300)

So the people, it would seem, are no longer merely pausing by the highway on their pilgrimage to Truth. They are living, under Pier's guidance, through the whole yearly cycle of dearth and abundance which determined the everyday life of the medieval 'commune'.

But the decisive indication that the pilgrimage is not to be resumed comes at the beginning of the following passus:

> Treuthe herde telle herof, and to Piers sente
> To taken his teme and tilien the erthe,
> And purchased hym a pardoun *a pena et a culpa*
> For hym and for hise heires for everemoore after;
> And bad hym holde hym at home and erien hise leyes,
> And alle that holpen hym to erye, to sette or to sowe,
> Or any maner mestier that myghte Piers availe—
> Pardon with Piers Plowman Truthe hath ygraunted.
> (VII. 1–8)

Two things, for the moment, are particularly to be noticed in this passage. First, Truth sends a message to Piers telling him to 'holde hym at home' and plough his lands once more—in preparation for another year of sowing and reaping. This surely means that on one level—the literal level—the pilgrimage is abandoned. For St. Truth himself, the very object of the proposed pilgrimage, commands his servant to stay at home. At the same time, the fact that Truth obtains a plenary pardon for Piers, his heirs, and his helpers, suggests equally clearly that the pilgrimage is, in another sense, completed. Critics have not generally drawn this inference; but it seems quite unavoidable. Piers himself said, towards the beginning of the sixth passus, that he would go

> 'To pilgrymage as palmeres doon, *pardon for to have*'.
> (VI. 64)

Truth's pardon is the object of the pilgrimage to Truth; so the granting of it can only mean that the object of the pilgrimage has been attained. There seems no alternative to this simple explanation of why the pardon comes at this point in the action. We are forced to recognize a second substitution. Piers will not lead the folk on a pilgrimage 'as palmeres doon'. *His* pike-staff is a 'plowpote', *his* scrip a seed-hopper, and *his* pilgrimage a pilgrimage at the plough.

In the third stage of his action, then, Langland first substitutes an allegorical pilgrimage for a real one, and then substitutes for that allegorical pilgrimage something which is not a pilgrimage at all, even in the allegorical action. Pilgrimage first becomes an allegorical form or 'vehicle', then dwindles into a mere metaphor. The point of both transformations is essentially the same; but the second involves a more explicit emphasis on the idea of 'holding oneself at home'.

* * *

I hold, then, that Piers and his faithful followers—'alle kynne crafty men that konne lyven in truthe'—are on the highway to Truth, 'non pedibus, sed moribus' [not by foot, but by death], when they stay at home labouring in their vocations and helping their neighbours, since this is the way of truth which Truth himself taught. They are worshipping him not in Jerusalem but in spirit—'by their lives' as Piers says (VI. 101). It is therefore not surprising that they win his pardon. Holy Church promised that they would:

> Ac tho that werche wel as Holy Writ telleth,
> And enden as I er seide in truthe, that is the beste,
> Mowe be siker that hire soules shul wende to hevene,
> Ther Treuthe is in Trinitee and troneth hem alle'.
> (I. 130–33)

III

I believe that many of the difficulties in the controversial fourth stage of the vision, to which I now turn, will disappear once we realize that Langland handles the pardon in very much the same ways as he handled the pilgrimage. In each case there is a tension between the literal action and that which it signifies; and in each case Langland eases this tension by a twice-repeated gesture of substitution.

It cannot be said of pardons, as of pilgrimages, that Langland simply did not believe in them. In the epilogue to the second vision he goes out of his way to assert that the Pope *has* power to grant pardon:

> And so I leve leelly (Lord forbede ellis!)
> That pardon and penaunce and preieres doon save
> Soules that have synned seven sithes dedly.
> (VII. 177–79)

The protestation is doubtless sincere; yet it seems clear that Langland's deepest feelings on the matter are represented in the following lines (where 'triennals' * * * probably refers to pardons):

> Ac to trust on thise triennals—trewly, me thynketh,
> It is noght so siker for the soule, certes, as is Dowel.
>
> (180–81)

Langland's fear, as so often, is that the external form or institution—even though it is acceptable in itself—may come to usurp the place of the inner spiritual reality. It is this fear which determines his treatment of the pardon in Passus VII. His chosen action required that the final reward for the converted members of the commune should take the form of a pardon. But this was no more than a 'form', embodying the spiritual truth, stated by Holy Church in the first vision and spelt out in the epilogue to the second, that those who turn from their wickedness and do well will receive their reward in heaven. And Langland explicitly says that this Dowel—represented, again, in the life of the half-acre[4]—is more 'siker for the soule' than any pardon. So Truth's pardon, like his pilgrimage, is not—emphatically not—to be taken literally. It is in his anxiety to make this point that Langland resorts once more to a somewhat bewildering double transformation of his primary action.

The first of these transformations is basically quite straightforward, in that it follows directly from the substitution of St. Truth for St. James and the saints of Rome as the object of the pilgrimage. But it led Langland into certain complications, to understand which the reader must know that a pardon involves three parties—a producer, a distributor, and a consumer. The producers are Christ and the saints, who by their lives and deaths have accumulated a 'treasury of merit' which is available to the faithful. The distributor is the Pope.

* * *

* * * The main points are the same in all three versions: that the pardon is purchased by St. Truth, and that it is available (whoever actually 'grants' it) to all who help Piers:

> Alle that holpen hym to erye, to sette or to sowe,
> Or any maner mestier that myghte Piers availe—
> Pardon with Piers Plowman Truthe hath ygraunted.
>
> (B VII 6–8)

The essence of the first substitution is here. This is not an ordinary saint's pardon, such as could be obtained at any registered shrine; it is *Truth's* pardon.

After a longish passage (VII. 9–104) specifying the various benefits the pardon brings for various classes of men—kings, knights, bishops, merchants, etc.—Langland proceeds to dramatize his point by confronting Piers with a representative of ordinary pardons: the Priest. There have been considerable differences of opinion about this character, whom Langland seems rather to have taken for granted; but I would agree with Nevill Coghill that he is 'a sophist who understands the letter but not the spirit'.[5]

4. See Nevill Coghill, "The Character of Piers Plowman," *Medium Aevum* II (1933), pp. 108–35 passim.
5. See 'The Pardon of Piers Plowman', *Proceedings of the British Academy* 30 (1944): 319.

Those who share this view will see here a notable parallel between the third
and fourth stages of the action. The Priest stands to Piers with respect to
the pardon exactly as the Palmer stands to Piers with respect to the pilgrimage. In each case a representative of the unsubstituted, literal institution challenges the spiritual version for which Piers stands. The Palmer
does not recognize the pilgrimage to Truth:

> 'I seigh nevere palmere with pyk ne with scrippe
> Asken after hym er now in this place';
> (V. 535–36)

and the Priest does not recognize Truth's pardon:

> 'Peter!' quod the priest tho, 'I kan no pardon fynde
> But "Do wel and have wel, and God shal have thi soule,"
> And "Do yvel and have yvel, and hope thow noon oother
> That after thi deeth day the devel shal have thi soule!"'
> (VII. 111–14)

It is natural that a priest should want to see the pardon, since priests were
responsible for seeing that false pardons were not distributed in their
parishes. But this priest, it would seem, is so much concerned with proper
drafting and proper sealing that he does not recognize the word of God.

Some critics have held that the Priest's attack on the pardon is supported
by the author; but I cannot believe that this is right. The pardon is 'purchased' by Truth / God, and, in the B and C texts, 'granted' by him too; and
it carries a message from the Athanasian Creed:

> 'Et qui bona egerunt ibunt in vitam eternam;
> Qui vero mala, in ignem eternum.'[6]

This recalls the words of Holy Church in Passus I (128–33, quoted in part
above), and harmonizes with the whole argument of the second vision,
especially Passus VI. Those who 'werche wel' (live the life of truth, do well,
'bona egerunt') will, by the grace of God, be saved; those who don't, won't.
It is true that the message is very simple, and can be reduced, as the Priest
reduces it, to a common proverb: 'Do well and have well . . .' ('est notan-
dum quod proverbialiter solet dici, "bene fac et bene habe"', Brunton,
1376). But Langland respected proverbs and admired simplicity.

*   *   *

First, Piers responds to the Priest's attack on the pardon by tearing it up:

> And Piers for pure tene pulled it atweyne.
> (B 116)

This is, of course, the most notorious crux in the whole vision. * * * R. W.
Frank believes, as I do, that the pardon is valid and that Piers does not
reject it. He explains the tearing in terms of a 'clash between form and content' [*Speculum* xxvi (1951), 322–23]. The pardon, he argues, 'contains a
message which is by implication an attack on pardons and which does
in fact lead to such an attack by the Dreamer' (in the epilogue). It is definitely not an ordinary pardon. Indeed, 'in trusting its message, Piers is
rejecting bulls with seals. In tearing the parchment, Piers is symbolically

6. For a full translation of the Creed, see p. 373.

tearing paper pardons from Rome.' So the tearing, 'because of the special character of the pardon, was intended by Langland as a sign that Piers had rejected indulgences and accepted the command to do well. Unfortunately, it was a very confusing sign'.

This reading enables us to see a clear parallel between the tearing of the pardon and the shelving of the pilgrimage. The 'clash between form and content' is the same in each case; for the pilgrimage, like the pardon, contains a message which is by implication an attack on itself. And in each case Langland responds in the same fashion. First he allegorizes the 'form' polemically (pilgrimage to *Truth*, *Truth's* pardon); then, as if not content with this, he has Piers turn against even the allegorized version. And the significance of this 'second substitution' is the same in each case. Piers does not reject the 'content' of Truth's pardon (Dowel etc.) when he tears it up, any more than he rejects the content of Truth's pilgrimage (Meekness, Conscience, etc.) when he distracts the folk from that. He is demonstrating angrily ('for pure tene'), and on Langland's behalf, against the 'form'.

What makes the pardon-tearing a somewhat obscure demonstration, however, is that in this case Langland could find nothing concrete or dramatic—no vehicle, form, objective correlative, or what you will—to convey positively what was to be substituted *for* pardon-mongering, as the ploughing of the half-acre conveys what is to be substituted for pilgrimage. It is one thing to show Piers living 'truly' at home, quite another to show— really *show*—him trusting in Dowel. Trust in Dowel is an idea not easy to present dramatically. In the event, Langland was content to follow the tearing with a single quotation from the Psalms:

> And Piers for pure tene pulled it atweyne,
> And seide, 'Si *ambulavero in medio umbre mortis*
> Non time bo mala, quoniam tu mecum es'.
> (VII. 115–17)

Langland, I think, cuts a corner here. I would suggest that he is trying to convey in a single verse Piers's trust in the saving power of Dowel or Truth. The evidence for this is that Imaginative expresses the same trust with the very same verse at the end of Passus XII:

> 'Ne wolde nevere trewe God but trewe truthe were allowed.
> And wheither it worth or noght worth, the bileve is gret of truthe,
> And an hope hangynge therinne to have a mede for his truthe;
> For *Deus dicitur quasi dans vitam eternam suis, hoc est fidelibus*.
> Et alibi, Si *ambulavero in medio umbre mortis etc*.
> The glose graunteth upon that vers a gret mede to truthe.'
> (XII. 288–92)

The relevant passage from Psalm 23 runs as follows: 'He leadeth me in the paths of righteousness for his name's sake. Yea, though I walk through the valley of the shadow of death, I will fear no evil: for thou art with me'. Peter Lombard, author of the most widely used commentary ('glose') on the Psalms, takes 'thou art with me', following Augustine, to refer to the reward enjoyed after death by the man who walks 'in the paths of righteousness'.[7] The 'gret mede to truthe' is God's company in heaven. This,

7. See Frank's article cited in the text, p. 323, for quotations and references.

surely, is the point of Piers's enigmatic quotation: that righteousness ('truth') can be trusted, as pardons cannot, to win the reward of
eternal life.

*   *   *

IV

Perhaps the most peculiar and perplexing feature of the second vision, as
I have described it, is the degree of interference on the literal level of the
allegory. This is sufficiently common in Langland's work to be considered
characteristic. It contributes to the general 'lack of a sustained literal level'
noted by Miss Woolf among the chief 'non-medieval qualities' of *Piers Plowman.*[8] A good example, to add to the shelving of the pilgrimage and the tearing of the pardon, is provided by Passus XVIII. By the beginning of this
passus Langland has already made quite elaborate preparations for presenting the passion as a joust between Jesus and the powers of evil. Jesus
is a young knight, instructed by Piers and wearing his mentor's armour, who
rides into Jerusalem, announced by the herald Faith, to do battle with his
enemies in a joust presided over by Pilate.

*   *   *

* * * This mode of movement, as the case of the second vision shows,
runs counter to the demands of the 'sustained literal level'; but it seems
essential to the progress of Langland's poem. Without the tearing of the
pardon, the second vision would in itself be a more perfect whole; but it
would, after all, stop the poem dead.

DAVID AERS

From Community, Gender, and Individual Identity†

Passus VI begins by reaffirming the traditional social model in the face of
the challenges it has had to sustain, in the poem and in the poet's society.
Here the knight so loves the peasant that he offers to share his manual
labour and the peasant so loves maintaining the knightly class in its power
and privilege that he quickly rejects the offer in favour of the status quo (VI
21–26). With a few strokes of the pen all contemporary struggles over
villeinage, rents, fines, and rights of hunting are dissolved (VI 27–56). A
miracle has transformed peasant consciousness while leaving the systems
of exploitation, power, and privilege untouched, safe in the hands of benevolent gentlemen in the current demographic collapse. The poet, however,
was fortunately well aware of the crazy abstractionism this involved and
once more submits his cherished social model to the unpalatable conflicts
of his historical moment. The result is the breakdown of the good ploughman's enterprise and the collusion with the knight to which he had sought

8. 'Some Non-Medieval Qualities of *Piers Plowman*', *Essays in Criticism* 12 (1962): 112.
† From *Community, Gender, and Individual Identity: English Writing 1360–1430* (London and New
    York: Routledge, 1988), pp. 41–48. Reprinted by permission of the publisher. Notes have been
    edited.

to commit his community.[1] Here I will focus on one aspect of this complex breakdown, the problems of the 'wastours' the knight was meant to repress (VI 28) together with those posed, to use Langland's terms, by bold big beggars and the unfortunate needy.

Before the breakdown the working people do just what the employers and their Statute demanded. They work hard and unquestioningly. The ploughman's task includes overseeing their work, fulfilling the role of the good reeves and bailiffs so essential to the gentry in its extractions from peasant communities. (Zvi Razi recalls how one year 'all men on the manor of Hales' were amerced ten pounds for refusing to elect a reeve for the Abbot's use [*ad opus abbatis*], an episode which symbolizes the place of such overseers).[2] Piers, the ploughman, insists that only those who work best will be hired at harvest time. The specific direction of this threat is interesting. Middling and wealthy peasants, those with holdings of more than about thirty acres would not usually need to hire themselves out as wage-labourers—on the contrary, they would need some help from hired labour. It was the large group holding less than twelve acres who would certainly need supplementary or even the bulk of their income from wage-labour, and in most late medieval communities this seems to comprise at least 40 per cent of the population.[3] Piers's stick-and-carrot approach is thus plainly addressed to poorer peasant families and the many landless labourers who were totally dependent on wage-labour for their very survival. This distinction is important in grasping the real orientations of Passus VI. The point is that however resistant peasant families were to the extractions of gentry and state, they never needed urging to work their own holdings—their survival, let alone self-respect, self-identity, and relative comfort demanded it. The situation of those dependent on wage-labour was different, and this is what Langland addresses.

Contrary to their overseer's exhortations the 'werkmen' who have 'wroghten ful faste' (VI 109) decide that they have done and got enough for their present wishes: 'Thanne seten somme and songen atte Nale / And holpen ere the half acre with "how trolly lolly"' (VI 115–16). In thus withdrawing to the pub, the 'werkmen' actually reject the tempo and labour discipline imposed on them; imposed on them by employers, not by nature—a different psychological and economic position to that of middling and substantial peasants. Already Langland has represented the village ale house as a demonic anti-Church, the location of 'wastours', and the present scene recapitulates the earlier one. In doing so it confirms the analysis offered above of the ideological nature of the term 'wastours' in quite particular social conflicts, sharpening our understanding of those who are repeatedly called wasters in the Passus (VI 25–26, 130, 133, 152, 161, 162, 173, 174, 201, 302, 323). As soon as 'werkmen' reject the employer's work ethic they are classified as 'wastours'. For these people, responding perfectly

---

1. On this breakdown, see Aers, *Chaucer, Langland*, chapter 1.
2. Z. Razi (1981), 'Family, land and village community', *Past and Present* 93: 15.
3. On peasants both as wage-labourers and employers of labour see, for example: Edward Miller and John Hatcher, *Medieval England* (London, New York: Longman, 1978), pp. 49–53, 219–24; M. Postan, The Medieval Economy and Society; an Economic History of Britain, 1100–1500 (Berkeley Univ. of California Press, 1972), pp. 147–50, 257–8; R. Hilton (1973), *Bond Men Made Free*, pp. 154–6, 171–5, 235: McIntosh, *Autonomy and Community: The Royal Manor of Havering 1200–1500* (Cambridge: Cambridge UP, 1986), pp. 149–50, 157, 160–6; L. R. Poos (1983), "The Social Context of Statute of Labourers Enforcement," *Law and History* Review 1:27–52.

rationally to their place in the existing division of labour, land, and resources, work is no more than a means to acquire wages for immediate enjoyment of material comforts and the convivial pleasures found in the pub. Their work is in itself of no special concern, hardly the case for those working holdings which could be made to yield their families' subsistence and cultural needs. Nor will those who have to sell their labour-power at whatever rates current market conditions dictate have quite the same attitudes to work, time, and the future as those who do not.

Langland does not accept this fact and his response to the 'werkmen' become 'wastours' is to have Piers angrily warn them that unless they hurry 'to werche' now they will be starved out, to death if necessary (VI 117–20). At this moment the poet makes a move which was to have a long future before it. He turns the independent 'werkmen' / 'wastours', those who have been seen both working and singing in the ale house, into able-bodied beggars, pseudo-cripples, and vagrants (VI 121–28). The shift inevitably involves a further implication: those who may *look* poor are likely in reality to be 'wastours', work-shy scroungers, to use the characteristic term from the fully fledged ethos we now know so well. Piers responds by asserting a simple classification: either such people are physically disabled, in which case they are the deserving poor, or they are able-bodied vagrants who should be selling their labour-power 'as truth wolde', not jugging it up 'in lecherie and in losengerie'. To the former alms are due, to the latter punishment (VI 129–51). The poem is plainly addressing the contexts and conflicts outlined in section I of this essay. We quoted from the 1376 petition against 'wandering labourers' and have observed how useful it was for employers to classify migrant workers in search of the best wages on the current market as 'mendicant beggars' pursuing 'an idle life'. In this struggle against workers' mobility they demanded a law forbidding 'any sustenance and alms to be given to such false mendicants and beggars': 'let it be established by statute that all such false beggars as well as the said "staff strikers" shall be . . . placed in stocks or led to the nearest gaol, until they show themselves willing to submit and return to their own areas', thus accepting the wage-freeze imposed by employers at pre-plague levels.[4] The allegiances of the poem to the employers' work ethos and ideological imagery seem rather unequivocal, at this stage.

As it elaborates the scene in which Piers assures the 'werkmen' / 'wastours' / mendicants that the employers' views represent 'truth', the poem displays a prominent feature of those classified as 'undeserving' poor:their individual and collective self-agency, the very opposite quality to the passivized and deferential poor so pleasing to the pious:

> Thanne gan wastour to wrathen hym and wold have yfoughte;
> To Piers the Plowman he profrede his glove.
> A Bretoner, a braggere, he bosted Piers als
> And bad hym go pissen with his plowgh: pyvysshe sherewe!
> Wiltow, neltow, we wol have oure wille
> Of thi flour and thi flessh, fecche whanne us liketh,
> And maken us murye therwith maugree thi chekes
>   (VI 152–58)

---

4. Dobson, *The Peasants' Revolt*, p. 74.

Not surprisingly the poet has the secular élite summoned by the overseer to impose labour discipline, that is, the gentry's current labour legislation, 'the statut' (VI 318, 320, 150–70). The knight, acting as a justice of labour or the peace, warns 'wastour' to do better, 'Or thow shalt abigge by the lawe, by the ordre that I bere' (VI 166). His threat is made yet more explicit in the later C version of the poem: 'Or Y shal bete the by the lawe and brynge the in stokkes' (VIII 163). One recalls the new law: those who refuse to work at the wages fixed by the employing gentry 'shall be put in the stocks for three days or more by the said lords, stewards, bailiffs and constables of the vills or sent to the nearest gaol, there to remain until they are willing to submit to justice.'[5] The poem resolves this encounter not with the harmonious melodies heard by some nostalgic critics but in terms of the gentry's anxious perception of the current balance of forces illustrated in the parliamentary petitions of 1376 and 1377 against vagrants, malicious labourers, and bondsmen. So the worker-wasters reject the gentry's rhetoric and their law, as so many were to do in 1381—and on many, many other occasions through the later Middle Ages. They 'leet light of the lawe and lasse of the knyghte' (VI 168).

At this point the poet hopes for a subsistence crisis. This would force working people into the kind of disciplined and docile labour force required by Piers and the gentry (VI 171–78). It does just this, and Langland allows himself the pleasure of imagining hungry wasters and able-bodied beggars turning into fanatically dedicated labourers, all content to work for minimal subsistence wages and ready to receive any bonuses with unquestioning gratitude (VI 183–201). We glimpse a vision of the new work ethos triumphant over rebellious labourers, an employer's utopia. In these circumstances the disciplinary dimension of 'charity' emerges as we watch its transformation into a discriminatory instrument of poor relief under lay control, itself an important part of the new ethos and its gradual institutionalization.[6] 'Of beggeris and bidderis what best to be doone' (VI 203)? Alms must be just enough to keep able-bodied labourers alive—'lat hem ete with hogges' (VI 181)—but certainly not enough to allow them any independence from the demands of the employers.

But Langland was deeply committed to traditional moral theory and could not remain happy with a solution in terms of the newer ethos. He now has Piers note that the reformed 'wasters' actually work so obediently and hard 'for defaute of foode': remove famine conditions and 'thei wol werche ille' (IV 204–206). That is, the production relations remain impersonal and fundamentally antagonistic, hardly a state of affairs congenial to Langland's traditional social model or equally traditional moral theology. As Piers points out, the labourers

> are my blody bretheren for God boughte us alle;
> Truthe taughte me ones to loven hem ech one
> (VI 207–208)

The recognition of the Gospel's demands for Christian fraternalism will become increasingly prominent in the poem, and it had been foreshadowed

---

5. Dobson, *The Peasants' Revolt*, p. 65.
6. Piers is unequivocally a layman—see, for example, V 17–32, 91–3, 546–8.

in Repentance's moving oration.[7] Its social meaning and current potential, however, was far from simple, although John Ball had some challenging views on this. Whatever the difficulties here, Piers has lost confidence in the moral justification of solutions centred on hunger and forced labour. Hunger assures him that justification is available in the distinction between 'Bolde beggeris and bigge' and the impotent, deserving poor (VI 212–28). Yet in mid-stream Hunger seems to shift away from the emphasis on discriminatory and disciplinary charity. He tells Piers to feed and give money to the poor:

> Love hem and lakke hem noght; lat God take the vengeaunce;
> Theigh thei doon yvele lat thow God yworthe.
>
> (VI 225–26)

This could certainly be read as an abandonment of the punitive surveillance involved in the discriminatory relief from which he had begun, for now even *blame* of the 'undeserving' poor is to be left to God[8] This wobble makes Piers's reaction open to more than one interpretation as he asks, 'Mighte I synnelees do as thow seist?' (VI 230). Is he asking whether the solution centred on hunger, forced labour, and discriminatory charity is compatible with Christ's teaching in the Gospels? Or is he questioning the possible shift Hunger has made from the newer ethos backed by gentry, clerics, parliament, law, and courts? It could well be that Langland himself was uncertain at this stage, an uncertainty he later resolved in the C version by eliminating Hunger's 'wobble'. That revision makes Piers's question unambiguously one about the evangelical authority of Hunger's defence of discriminatory charity and all that goes with that mentality.[9]

Hunger's reply to Piers is, however, clear, and it anticipates the C revisions of his speech. First he invokes God's curse on humanity in the third chapter of Genesis, adding to it. Where the Bible has 'In the sweat of thy face shalt thou eat bread' (3.19), the poem adds 'and swynk . . . And laboure'.[1] Next he uses another part of the Old Testament which contained some useful texts for those seeking Biblical underpinnings to the newer ethos, the 'wisdom' literature we saw FitzRalph using: the idle beggar shall not be relieved (VI 235–37; c.f. Proverbs 20:4). Then, seeking New Testament support he turns the parable of the talents, one that exhorts Chris-

---

7. See V 483–505.
8. See Kane and Donaldson, *Piers Plowman*, p. 361, critical apparatus to VI 223: the manuscripts they have chosen to alter here make the shift very explicit by advising Piers to help out not only the needy but the 'noughty' with his 'goodes'. It is unjustifiable to use the C-version to tell us what the poet's earlier version or versions must have been, since this only short-circuits the processes of the poet's struggles to find his way through complex moral and social issues. For a different view of work and wasters (in A-version, VIII) see Guy Bourquin (1978) *Piers Plowman* 2 vols, Lille: University of Lille, p. 714.
9. C VIII 232ff. and see Pearsall's commentary pp. 154–5 on C VIII 210, useful despite its stance being uncritically a gentry/clerical one which blurs the cultural shifts and conflicts. This last comment applies with far greater force to some recent books on *Piers Plowman*: J. M. Bowers (1986) *The Crisis of Will in Piers Plowman*, Washington, DC: Catholic University of America Press, pp. 105–6 (including an unwary but typical enough homogenization of 'the nation' under the interests of gentry); A. Baldwin, with her unquestioning assumption of gentry interests in her version of 'fair' and 'honest', in (1981) *The Theme of Government in Piers Plowman*, Cambridge: Boydell & Brewer Press; M. Stokes with her ranting about 'the Marxist rhetoric of the down-trodden proletariat' and 'the authentic note of self-righteous whining against the "bosses"' in Passus VI, is perhaps the most striking case (1984) *Justice and Mercy in Piers Plowman*, London: Croom Helm, pp. 210–12.
1. C VIII 242 even *latinizes* the addition, giving it 'real' authority.

tians to make full use of *spiritual* gifts, into a lesson on the divine punishment awaiting those who will not work (VI 238–46).[2] Pursuing his increasingly confident elaboration of the work ethos, Hunger wisely leaves the New Testament and makes the startling claim that,

> The freke that fedeth hymself with his feithful labour
> He is blessed by the book in body and in soule
> (VI 25–52)

Theologically this seems very crudely Pelagian, but what interests me in the present discussion is the unqualified claim it makes for religious salvation as the reward of productive labour. As striking is the exegesis of 'the book'. The passage quoted in the next line is Psalm 127:2, 'thou shalt eat the labours of thy hands'; yet it would hardly be more forced to read the Psalm as a verse promising devout Christian peasants that God will deliver them from the class that coercively extracts their labour and produce, thus at last enabling them to 'eat the labours of their hands'—a reading that would be congenial enough to radical Christian preachers like John Ball and to the communities which rose up in 1381 and formulated their demands at Mile End and Smithfield in June 1381. But as Hunger anticipates, *orthodox* Christianity was to continue adapting to the employers' changing needs and ethos, in its moral teaching as in its exegesis.[3]

Langland, however, was sure that whatever texts could be mustered in support of Hunger's doctrine, labourers would continue to resist, rejecting the work ethos propagated by justices of the peace, employers, and orthodox clerics. So he again presents their outlook as one in which work is solely a means to immediate enjoyments. As soon as their arduous labour completes the agricultural year and 'newe corn cam to chepyng' (VI 299), the labourers responses are unreformed and memorably imagined:

> And tho nolde Wastour noght werche, but wandred aboute,
> Ne no beggere ete breed that benes inne come,
> But Coket or clermatyn or of clene whete,
> Ne noon halfpenny ale in none wise drynke,
> But of the beste and the brunneste that brewsteres selle.
> Laborers that have no land to lyve on but hire handes
> Deyneth noght to dyne a day nygh olde wortes.
> May no peny ale hem paie, ne no pece of bacoun,
> But if be fressh flessh outher fissh yfryed,
> And that *chaud* and *plus chaud* for chillynge of hir mawe.
> (VI 302–11)

Once more, people who have been represented as the hardworking essential producers, the 'winners' of society, are reclassified as 'wastours', vagrants, and greedy labourers guilty of demanding 'excessive' wages to support living conditions better than those endured by preceding genera-

---

2. Matthew 25.14–30: see Pearsall's astute comments on C VIII 247, p. 157.
3. See the examples of FitzRalph's exegesis in section one of this chapter, and the story told in L. K. Little (1978), *Religious Poverty and the Profit Economy*, St Albans: Elek, as well as in Mollat, *Poor*, J. C. Schmitt (1978), *Mort d'une hérésie*, Paris: Mouton, and, for a later period, R. H. Tawney (1926), *Religion and the Rise of Capitalism*, Harmondsworth: Penguin.

tions on the margins of survival.[4] The passage deploys the terms in which
horrified gentry and clerics perceived working people's increased expectations and assertiveness. * * * The poet locates the problems in the contemporary struggles over the price and terms of labour-power. He attributes
the source of rebellion to *landless* labourers, that is to the workers most
directly dependent on market fluctuations and incentives for their survival,
as well as for relatively improved possibilities in the present. These opportunities could only be grasped if working women and men opposed the
classes who sought to ensure that their own material privileges and power
were not in any way eroded. Oppose them they did, and one should not forget that the poet writes this in the period immediately preceding the rising which involved representatives from 'the whole people below the
ranks of those who exercised lordship in the countryside and established
authority in the towns':[5]

> But he be heighliche hyred ellis wole he chide;
> That he was werkman wroght warie the tyme.
> Ayeins Catons counseil comseth he to jangle:
> *Pauperlatis onus pacienter ferre memento;*
> He greveth hym ageyn God and gruccheth ageyn Reson,
> And thanne corseth the kyng and al the counseil after
> Swiche lawes to loke laborers to chaste.
>   (VI 312–18)

These 'werkmen' see that what counts as practical 'Reason', labour 'lawes',
and social virtue tends to be shaped by the current interests of the ruling
classes, a tiny but immensely powerful fraction of the population. To the
gentry (lay or ecclesiastic), views such as those expressed by Langland's
labourers are not only rank sedition but blasphemous—the powerful have
habitually found it difficult to distinguish a threat to their own privileges
from a threat to God and all religion.[6] Langland concludes the Passus
bemoaning how labourers strive 'ayeins the statut' and threatening 'yow
werkmen' with hunger and apocalyptic vengeance (VI 319–31). Perhaps not
surprisingly, neither he nor the gentry see a benevolent divine hand shifting
forces in favour of 'Laborers that have no land to lyve on but *hire* handes'!

                              *   *   *

4. The precarious existence on the very margins of survival led by so many European people in the
long thirteenth century (amply documented in Miller and Hatcher, *Medieval England*, Postan,
Economy and Society, Mollat, *Poor*, and others) makes the approach of literary scholars such as
Stokes rather foolish in its equation of justice and fairness with the employers' efforts to force working people to remain in that miserable state under changed circumstances, to make the poorer
people of the community pay for the (relative) economic problems of the more affluent.
5. Hilton, *Bond Men Made Free*, p. 184.
6. A commonplace, illustrated plainly in Gower's *Vox Clamantis*, trans. Stockton, e.g., pp. 58, 70, 72,
75, 80, 90, 94–5, or Walsingham's celebration of the suppression of the 1381 rising, Dobson, *The
Peasants' Revolt*, pp. 310–13.

DEREK PEARSALL

Poverty and Poor People in *Piers Plowman*†

'On exorcise la misère par son image idéale, la pauvreté'[1]

The persistence of Langland's concern for the sufferings of poor people is remarkable, as many of his readers have recognised,[2] and seems unusual for a medieval writer. It is a concern that is announced in the A version of *Piers Plowman*, developed extensively, and towards some sort of resolution, in the B version, and then returned to, with renewed intensity and at some length, in the C version. An exceptionally large proportion of the new material in C has to do with questions of poverty, and it is clear that to the end of his life Langland was still painfully conscious of the actual sufferings of poor people, and of the rebuke that they constituted to himself, to his fellow human beings, and to the notion of good government. The revisiting in C of problems apparently resolved in B is characteristic of Langland, and of the anxious movement of his social conscience.

* * *

The extensive medieval literature of poverty * * * is marked by its pursuit of philosophical and ideological issues: it rarely touches on the lives of poor people, except in a conventional way for purposes of demonstration. When poor people, or issues of poverty, are present in other kinds of writing there is usually some similar purpose that they are brought in to serve: as a means to attack the ostentation of wealth, for instance, in the Judgement Day sermons cited by Owst, or to criticise certain kinds of economic measure (*The Song of the Husbandman*), or to reveal the hypocrisy of the so-called poor friars (*Pierce the Ploughman's Crede*).[3] When the chronicler Henry Knighton describes children crying from hunger on the streets of Leicester in 1390, it is not because he has had a sudden rush of compassion but because he wants to demonstrate the consequences of a policy which prohibits the export of wool.[4] It might seem that the literature of poverty represents it as a theme for argumentation, as well as a very relative matter of perception, and certainly medieval historians find themselves somewhat nonplussed when they come to look for the documents that will tell them about the realities of poverty. 'Most obscure of all', says

† From *Medieval English Studies Presented to George Kane*, ed. Edward Donald Kennedy, Ronald Waldron, and Joseph S. Wittig (Cambridge: Cambridge UP, 1988), pp. 167–85. Reprinted by permission of the publisher.

1. Roland Barthes, *Mythologies* (Paris, 1957), p. 51. Quoted in Claus Uhlig, *Chaucer und die Armut: Zum Prinzip der kontextuellen Wahrheit in den Canterbury Tales*, Akademie der Wissenschaften und der Literatur (Mainz), Abhandlungen der Geistes- und Sozial-wissenschaftlichen Klasse, no. 14 (Wiesbaden, 1973), p. 46. ["One exorcizes misery with its ideal representation, poverty." *Editors*.]

2. Two recent essays worthy of particular remark are those of David Aers, 'Piers Plowman and Problems in the Perception of Poverty: A Culture in Transition', in *LeedsSE*, new series 14: Essays in Memory of Elizabeth Salter (1983), 5–25, and Geoffrey Shepherd, 'Poverty in *Piers Plowman*', in *Social Relations and Ideas: Essays in Honour of R. H. Hilton*, ed. T. H. Aston, P. R. Coss, Christopher Dyer, Joan Thirsk (Cambridge, 1983), pp. 169–89.

3. See G. R. Owst, *Literature and Pulpit in Medieval England* (Cambridge, 1933), pp. 290–307. *The song of the Husbandman is edited in Historical Poems of the XIVth and XVth Centuries*, ed. R. H. Robbins (London, 1959), pp.7–9 [and for *Pierce the Ploughman's Crede*, see p. 468. *Editors*].

4. Henry Knighton, *Chronicon*, ed. J. R. Lumby, Rolls series (London, 1895), II. 314–15, quoted in F. R. H. du Boulay, *An Age of Ambition: English Society in the Later Middle Ages* (London, 1970), p. 37.

one historian, 'in late medieval England were the really poor and those, relatively few, who remained tied with the yoke of legal bondage'. He goes on: 'To find out how the poor themselves felt we have to search many kinds of literature'.[5] But the search, except in rare instances (of which Langland himself is the most notable),[6] will be likely to turn up not the feelings of the poor but the views and opinions of their various spokesmen. Other historians hardly mention the poor. Economic historians, perhaps understandably, have tended not to be interested in the non-productive poor: an economic history of indigence might seem to them something of a contradiction in terms. The most authoritative general historian of late fourteenth-century England speculates on whether there was much poverty in the countryside, quotes Chaucer and Langland, and concludes reassuringly that 'unrelieved misery can hardly have been general'.[7] And then again, she says, there were the consolations of religion; landlords could be quite kind; and there were lots of opportunities. 'Society as a whole was mobile, active, and fundamentally healthy. No power known to medieval man could have prevented the able and enterprising peasant from going up, the slack, the feeble, and the unlucky from going down' (p. 346).

* * *

The first half of the fourteenth century was * * * a time of economic depression, especially after the fierce winters and bad harvests of 1314–17. The existence of the poorest classes of society had been a precarious subsistence at best: a large proportion, perhaps as much as half, of the rural population had always lived 'at or even under subsistence minima', and had always had to eke out a living by supplementing the produce of their tiny plots with the most menial wage-labour.[8] Now those who had been living on the starvation line fell below it, and comparatively minor accidents of fire, flood, theft, or injury could undo many lives.[9] As always, pauperism had its roots in the rural economy, but its most devastating effects are now seen in the towns, especially after the Black Death of 1347–49 created a tide of immigration from the country into the towns.[1] Urban poverty is not like traditional poverty: it is not spread through a community which is economically able and socially prepared to sustain and relieve the poor. There is now, in the towns, a depressed class of part-time, casual and unemployed workers, many of them unqualified, many recently immigrated. In Lille, it is a steady, grinding, unspectacular, mostly secret, chronic poverty, a life of those who are poorly fed, poorly clothed, poorly housed, and without access to the aid traditionally given to the 'marginaux'.[2] Many turn to begging (sometimes simulating disablement to

5. Du Boulay, An Age of Ambition, pp. 59, 77.
6. So G. G. Coulton, Chaucer and his England (1908; 3rd edn. London, 1921), p. 268, commenting on Chaucer's Nun's Priest's Tale: 'For glimpses of the real poor, the poor poor, we must go to "Piers Plowman."'.
7. May McKisack, The Fourteenth Century 1307–1399 (Oxford, 1959), p. 343. Cf. J. E. Thorold Rogers, Six Centuries of Work and Wages (1884), p. 415: 'The grinding, hopeless poverty under which existence may be just continued, but when nothing is won beyond bare existence, did not, I am convinced, characterise or even belong to mediaeval life'.
8. Lis and Soly, Poverty and Capitalism, p. 11.
9. Mollat, Les Pauvres, p. 198; Goglin, Les Misérables, p. 54.
1. Mollat, Les Pauvres, p. 242; Little, Religious Poverty, p. 28. McKisack (The Fourteenth Century, p. 337) comments that 'there was a steady drain of villeins to London' from Barnet in the aftermath of the Black Death.
2. Mollat, Les Pauvres, p. 296.

improve their prospects), or to vagabondage, or prostitution, or crime. The passage from poverty to criminality is an easy one, and the records frequently attribute the cause of crime to poverty, and specially to being 'chargé de femme et de petitz enfantz'.[3] Examples from Florence in the same period from 1340 onwards show small artisans and textile workers falling below the poverty line. In the past there had usually been some special cause for poverty—age, infirmity, accident—but now a low-paid worker can be one of 'the poor', and earn insufficient to maintain a proper diet. The poor begin to settle in segregated areas, in ghettoes, or in the new 'suburbs'.

※ ※ ※

※ ※ ※ The increase in the number of the poor is only one factor in the new situation: more and more people are now chronically poor and concentrated in urban centres, where they constitute an anonymous and rootless class, more and more perceived as a threat to the social order. Poor people had once had the advantage of being a small and uncomplaining group, manageable, even desirable, as the recipients of private and organised charity. Now, by their numbers, and above all by their conspicuousness, they have become a source of disquiet and irritation.[4] Where Dante spoke of poverty as a value which it is necessary to affirm and defend against worldliness, and of the poor as the possessors of a spiritual riches which makes them specially pleasing to God, his near-contemporary, Francesco de Barberino, speaks of poverty as a social evil which should be eradicated or at least opposed, and of the poor as a scourge and a menace.[5]

※ ※ ※

The denial of the Franciscan principle of the absolute poverty of Christ, in the papal bull *Cum inter nonnullos* of 1323,[6] was in part the product of an anti-mendicant move within the Church, but it was a sign of the times. The great debate about Franciscan poverty had acted in a way to obscure the social realities of poverty and to divert attention to more intellectually manageable issues. Instead of adding an edge to concern about poverty, it actually deflected it,[7] and one of the effects of the bull *Cum inter nonnullos* was to make it easier for an anti-mendicant writer like Richard FitzRalph to downgrade poverty as an absolute value, to advocate discrimination in charity, even to argue that Christ's invitation to the poor (Luke 14:12–14) excludes the 'stalworthe and stronge' poor who might work.[8] Meanwhile the friars, the representatives of the traditional ethos of poverty, found themselves justifying the financial activities of the urban rich, from whom they obtained most of their endowments and support, on the grounds that profit was the necessary prerequisite of philanthropy.[9] The friars' further

---

3. Mollat, *Les Pauvres*, p. 298.
4. Jean Batany, 'Les pauvres et la pauvreté dans les revues des "estats du monde"', in *Etudes sur l'Histoire de la Pauvreté*, ed. Mollat, pp. 469–86 (p. 484); Mollat, *Les Pauvres*, p. 304.
5. Raoul Manselli, 'De Dante à Coluccio Salutati: Discussions sur la pauvreté à Florence au XIVe siècle', in *Etudes*, ed. Mollat, pp. 637–59 (p. 645).
6. Lambert, *Franciscan Poverty*, p. 234.
7. Mollat, *Les Pauvres*, p. 222.
8. Cited by Aers, 'Piers Plowman and Problems in the Perception of Poverty' (n. 2, above), p. 9. Aers places much emphasis on the 'materialism' of the new ethic of discrimination.
9. Little, *Religious Poverty*, pp. 203, 213.

recommendation to discrimination in charity was more precise and
pointed: it should go to them.[1]

*　*　*

*　*　* Langland's response to the social realities he perceives is as always
that of a devout Christian, who sees all change and transformation as a
form of decay, and who struggles to comprehend the nature of change
within the structures of a traditional mode of thought. But it is also the
response of an individual and a poet, whose power of imagination, allied to
an implacable honesty and urgent personal sense of impending disaster,
enables him to see more penetratingly than other men. He shows himself,
in the particular context of the present discussion of poverty, keenly aware
of and deeply engaged with the problems of traditional rural society in
the aftermath of agricultural depression and the Black Death, and with
the threat posed to its stability by the landless and workless labourers who
have left their villages in search of better-paid wage-labour and now drift
the country as vagrants and beggars.

*　*　*

*　*　* In his vision of the Ploughing of the Half-Acre, the allegory of the
setting up of the ideal social and economic order, he sees the class of unemployed labourers, whom he personifies in *Wastour*, as the threat to the new
order. Their idleness and insolence drive even Piers Plowman to anger and
violence: his response to their refusal to work is to call in Hunger (as we
might say, to administer a sharp dose of deflation to the economy) so as to
coerce them into submission.

*　*　*

At the same time, Langland faces squarely the problem of the chronic poor,
not only those who are poor through misfortune (the 'safe' traditional poor)
but also the able-bodied unemployed, or 'sturdy beggars', as they came later
to be called. The question is not, and never is in the Middle Ages, how to
eliminate poverty, but how to discriminate between the deserving and the
undeserving poor, and then what to do with the latter. The difference here,
between Langland's view of the matter and the contemporary move towards
discrimination in charity, is the continued scrupulous concern that Langland has for the 'undeserving' poor, and the debate that he enters concerning their entitlement to personal or organised charity. The government, by
contrast, had no interest in any such debate.

*　*　*

*　*　* The government's answer was imprisonment, though this was an
empty threat and not a practical solution, and clearly the bureaucracy of
the day was incapable of distinguishing between the relief of poverty and
the suppression of vagrancy.

Nor could the Church do any better. The problem for a Christian community was in the conflict between economic realism, to which were allied
the Biblical texts recommending discrimination in charity ('If any would
not work, neither should he eat', 2 Thess. 3:10, cf. Gen. 3:19) and the

1. Chaucer, Summoner's Tale, *Canterbury Tales*, III, 1954–73.

clear exhortation of the gospels ('Give to every man that asketh of thee', Luke 6:30, cf. 2 Cor. 9:7, 1 John 3:17). This conflict was not reconciled in the debates on the subject in canon law. What was needed, says Tierney, was 'a kind of scholastic critique of employability in able-bodied vagrants', but it was not forthcoming from a canon law which was by now hardened into rigidity and incapable of adaptation to change.[2]

It was to these problems that Langland addressed himself. At one point Piers had suggested in a fit of exasperation, 'in puyre tene', that idlers should be left to starve:

> 'But ye aryse the rather and rape yow to worche
> Shal no grayn that here groweth gladyen yow at nede,
> And thow ye deye for deul, the devel have that reche!'
> (VIII. 125–27)

A more characteristic compassion makes him ask later, of Hunger:

> 'Of beggares and biddares what beste be to done? . . .
> . . . hit are my blody bretherne, for god bouhte us alle.
> Treuthe tauhte me ones to lovye hem uchone
> And to helpe hem of alle thynges ay as hem nedeth.'
> (VIII. 210, 217–19)

Hunger argues that Piers, as manager of the economy, has a responsibility to ensure that no one should starve, though no responsibility to maintain life beyond the meanest level (VIII. 223–35). Similar thinking concerning the 'dole', of course, produced the Elizabethan poor law and the workhouse, and Piers evidently has his reservations:

> 'Y wolde nat greve god', quod Peres, 'for al the good on erthe!
> Myhte Y synneles do as thow sayst?' sayde Peres the plouhman;
> (VIII. 236–37)

Yet the many reservations one might have about such a system of administering poor relief should not encourage a belief that Hunger's solution is implicitly rejected by Langland.

*   *   *

There is no sentimentalisation of the poor in Langland's analysis of the problem of poverty in the Ploughing of the Half-Acre. He is rigorous as well as compassionate, conscious both of the reality of need and of the need for realism, as well as for justice and charity. As he returns to the question in the next passus, describing those who are to receive Truth's pardon, his first reaction, in offering a spiritual analysis of the social and economic order, is to affirm the orthodoxy of his day: mercantile profit is legitimate so long as the surplus (beyond what is 'needed') is dedicated to almsgiving and charitable works (C. IX. 22–42),[3] and beggary is condemned:

> Beggares and biddares beth nat in that bulle
> Bote the sugestioun be soth that shapeth hym to begge.
> (IX. 61–62)

2. Brian Tierney, *Medieval Poor Law: A sketch of canonical theory and its application in England* (Berkeley, 1959), p. 119.
3. See Little, *Religious Poverty*, pp. 178–9.

The account of professional beggary (IX. 153–74), of those who make a
trade out of poverty, is, as Geoffrey Shepherd says, 'as hateful a passage as
any in the poem'.[4] It is notable, too, how insistent Langland is on the distinction between those beggars who go forth, like the apostles, 'withoute
bagge and bred' (IX. 120), who 'bereth none bagges ne boteles under clokes'
(IX. 139), and the 'beggares with bagges' (IX. 98), the professional beggar
who goes about

> With a bagge at his bak in begyneld wyse.
> (IX. 154)

Langland is referring here to a dominant theme in the Franciscan ideali-
sation of poverty: to have a bag is to betray Christ (Judas 'was a thief, and
had a bag', John 12:6); to renounce it is to join him. Judas's bag is an image
of all care for the world: ["so much more does he endanger the soul with
his money-bag"].[5]

But the power of Langland's imaginative vision and loving compassion
does not permit him to rest content with these assertions of the offensive-
ness of beggary. He adds in the C-text a prolonged meditation upon the
opposed injunctions of Cato, *Cui des videto*, and of the gospels in relation
to alms-giving. The meditation is pursued with characteristic tenacity,
probing, questioning, objecting, qualifying, so that one has the liveliest
sense that Langland is working at the problem, 'ruminating' upon it, as
Coghill puts it, rather than presenting in a rhetorically persuasive manner
a conclusion he has already arrived at.[6] In one particularly moving passage,
he turns aside from the condemnation of beggary and the question 'Who is
worthy to have?' to a contemplation of needs of the real poor, those who
never ask, who are ashamed to beg, who try to make ends meet by taking
on all the most menial jobs that society allows them—washing and patch-
ing clothes, scraping flax, winding yarn, peeling rushes to make tapers:

> Woet no man as Y wene, who is worthy to have;
> Ac that most neden aren oure neyhebores, and we nyme gode hede,
> As prisones in puttes and pore folk in cotes,
> Charged with childrene and chief lordes rente;
> That they with spynnyng may spare, spenen hit on hous-hyre,
> Bothe in mylke and in mele, to make with papelotes
> To aglotye with here gurles that greden aftur fode.
> And hemsulve also soffre muche hunger,
> And wo in wynter-tymes, and wakynge on nythes
> To rise to the reule to rokke the cradel,
> Bothe to carde and to kembe, to cloute and to wasche,
> And to rybbe and to rele, rusches to pylie,
> That reuthe is to rede or in ryme shewe
> The wo of this wommen that wonyeth in cotes;
> And of monye other men that moche wo soffren,
> Bothe afyngred and afurste, to turne the fayre outward,
> And ben abasched for to begge and wolle nat be aknowe
> What hem nedeth at here neyhebores at noon and at eve.
> (IX. 70–87)

4. Shepherd, 'Poverty in *Piers Plowman*', p. 171.
5. Lambert, *Franciscan Poverty*, p. 63. Cf. also C. V. 52.
6. N. K. Coghill, 'The Character of Piers Plowman considered from the B text', *MÆ*, 2 (1933): 108–35 (p. 128).

The revelation that Langland is writing about women, 'this wommen that wonyeth in cotes', is a gradual one, and it might seem that women (presumably widowed), being members of the 'safe' traditional poor, are an easy choice for the exercise of social compassion. Yet the focus is not exclusively on women; and furthermore the specificity of detail is such as to identify the reality of this class of women in relation to the European context we sketched in earlier. These are women in part-time or casual employment, often in the most poorly paid jobs in the textile trade, widowed or otherwise responsible for their familes ('charged with childrene' poignantly recalls the phrase in the Lille records). It is, I would have thought, specifically an urban class that Langland is describing, and the reality and extent of this class is indicated by Gwyn Williams, who, though he deals only with the period of London history up to 1337, speaks of 'the submerged population of non-citizens and paupers', working in shops that 'measured as little as five or six feet by ten, with a living-room above; thousands lived, worked, ate and slept in an airless solar in some alley tenement'.[7] It is a class for which Langland has on many previous occasions shown concern. An example is his attack on those traders who exploit the economic weakness of the poor people who must buy in small quantities, 'parselmele' (C. III. 86), and who are specially vulnerable to even small price-rises.

The passage stands out from its surroundings in Langland's poem, and stands out too in the history of the representation of poor people, remarkable both for its unsentimental loving compassion and for its raw truth. Geoffrey Shepherd has said that it is 'probably the earliest passage in English which conveys the felt and inner bitterness of poverty', and adds: '[Langland] is precocious in that he often presents the inner life of the unvocal unassertive people who live in powerlessness and poverty and he draws them into the cultural reality of his time'.[8]

*   *   *

The rawness of Langland's honesty stands in sharp contrast. What he records with such unwavering accuracy, furthermore, is what he would not wish to see, something that constitutes itself an objection to his own passionate orthodoxy. There is no sense that the contemplation of the miseries and indignities suffered by poor people provides the fuel for indignation at economic oppression and for programmes for reform (the 'chief lordes' are a cipher in this account). It is not at all like *The Road to Wigan Pier*, nor indeed, in the end, like Blake, for Langland has no proposals to make, no plans for reform which will remove the problem. The question remains, 'Who is worthy to have?', and, having spoken earlier of a discriminating charity, Langland now insists that charity must actively seek out the needy in order to fulfil the promise that God will provide whilst accepting the ban on beggary. Those who have must give so that those who have not need not ask.

*   *   *

Langland returns on a number of occasions in the *Vita* to the theme of poverty, but it is now always patient poverty that he writes about—not

7. Gwyn A. Williams, *Medieval London: From Commune to Capital* (London, 1963), p. 24.
8. Shepherd, 'Poverty in *Piers Plowman*', pp. 172, 175.

poverty as a social evil and human indignity, but poverty as a means to the strengthening and purifying of the moral and spiritual life. Poor people slip out of focus and grow blurred in the imaginative vision, as they are subsumed among the *pauperes Christi* and into the rich imagery of voluntary poverty. The image of Christ as a poor man has all its traditional resonance:

> [For] oure Joye and oure [Ivel], Iesu Crist of hevene,
> In a pouere mannes apparaille pursue[th] us evere,
> And loketh on us in hir liknesse and that with lovely chere . . .
> (B. XI. 185–87)

Langland may be affected by certain considerations not present in the *Visio*, such as the complications that have entered into any simple eulogy of poverty as a result of the Franciscan debate about the absolute poverty of Christ and the Wycliffite insistence on the poverty of the priesthood, but the pattern of spiritualised interpretation is now set, and it is recurrently exemplified.

*   *   *

If we look elsewhere, we shall find that the discourse of Patience has lost none of that earlier vivid realisation of the sufferings of poor people, even though the mitigation may be offered exclusively in terms of the hereafter:

> Ac poore peple, thi prisoners, lord, in the put of meschief,
> Conforte tho creatures that muche care suffren
> Thorugh derthe, through droghte, alle hir dayes here,
> Wo in wynter tymes for wantynge of clothes,
> And in somer tyme selde soupen to be fulle.
> Conforte thi carefulle, Crist, in thi rich[e],
> For how thow confortest alle creatures clerkes bere witnesse.
> (B. XIV. 174–80)

The physical reality in this passage of 'summer' and 'winter' is now, however, more usually commuted into figurative language: the winter of purgatorial suffering here which is to be endured in the hope of the summer of heavenly joy hereafter:[9]

> Muche murthe is in May amonge wilde bestes
> And so forth whiles somur laste here solace duyreth,
> And moche murthe among ryche men is that han meble ynow and hele.
> Ac beggares aboute myssomur bredles they soupe,
> And yut is wynter for hem worse, for weet-shoed they gone,
> Afurste and afyngered and foule rebuked
> Of this world-ryche men, that reuthe is to here.
> Now lord, sende hem somur somtyme to solace and to joye
> That al here lyf leden in lownesse and in poverte!
> (XVI. 10–18)

9. So Gautier de Coincy, in his sermon *De la misere d'omme et de fame*, speaks of the rich having their summer here, their winter in hell, while 'Li boen povre qui en povrece, / En maladie et en tristrece / En ceste vie aront esté, / Aprés yver aront esté' (lines 487–90), in *Miracles de Gautier de Coincy*, ed. A. Langfors, Annales Academiae Scientiarium Fennicae, B, 34 (Helsinki, 1937), pp. 207–92 (cited in *Etudes*, ed. Mollat, pp. 479–80).

Humble acceptance of poverty as a manifestation of divine will—

> For al myhtest thou haue ymad men of grete welthe
> And yliche witty and wys and lyve withoute nede—
> Ac for the beste, as Y hope, aren som pore and ryche.
>
> (XVI. 19–21)

makes of it a spiritual benefit. The rich lack the opportunity for this exercise, and the assertion of the poem's now firmly established priorities is made clearest in the sorrowing over their deprivation:

> Allas! that rychesse shal reve and robbe mannes soule
> Fro the love of oure lord at his laste ende.
>
> (XVI. 1–2)

'Rychesse', like 'poverte', has been totally abstracted from the economic context in which it exists, in which rich people are visible, and in which they are the cause that there are poor people.

This, then, finally, is the way in which Langland, conscious as he is of every suffering and every harrowing indignity to which poor people are subject, springs open the trap of economic circumstance. It is a traditional enough solution, but Langland has arrived at it, as is his custom, by his own personal and painfully honest route. There is nothing of which he forces himself to become oblivious, no wilful obscuring of uncomfortable realities, and the frankly outspoken personification Need appears at the beginning of the very last passus to reassert the primacy of the claim of the indigent upon society:

> So nede at greet nede may nyme as for his owne
> Withouten consail of Consience or cardinale vertues,
> So that he sewe and save *Spiritus Temperancie*.
>
> (XXII. 20–22)[1]

But the scrupulousness of Langland's record of reality can end only, for him, in the necessity of raising the eyes to a higher reality.

---

1. On the right of the poor, in extreme need, to seize what is needed to maintain life, see the note in Pearsall (ed.) to C. XXII. 15; Mollat, *Les Pauvres*, p. 139; Little, *Religious Poverty*, pp. 178–79. For an important discussion of the Need passage, putting forward views very different from those advanced in this paper, see Robert Adams, 'The Nature of Need in "Piers Plowman" XX', *Traditio*, 34 (1978): 273–301. Adams does not believe that Langland endorses the views of Need at this point (p. 288), and, more generally, argues that 'Langland never shifts his basic principles on the issues associated with poverty' (p. 289). The appearance of self-contradiction is not due to any ruminative process of lived experience, such as I have argued for, but to the extraordinary effort Langland makes to give fair representation to a great wealth and complexity of 'legitimately canonical views' (p. 290).

ANNE MIDDLETON

[Kynde Name]†

A Poet Nearly Anonymous

Why is the author of *Piers Plowman* a poet nearly anonymous? William Langland, an older contemporary of Chaucer, spent at least two decades making and revising the first English poem to attain a national readership and influence while its author lived. Its survival to the present century in over fifty manuscripts, none clearly a direct copy of any of the others, implies that copies of the poem must have numbered in the hundreds by 1400.[1] The poem was immediately and widely imitated, but those who adopted its distinctive idiom did not credit Langland with its invention. Rather, the poem's fictive hero Piers Plowman, who is rarely present in the narrative and seldom speaks, was widely taken to be the center and source of authority for the poet's powerful innovation. * * *

* * *

For twentieth-century interpreters of Langland's poem, the apparently idiosyncratic qualities of the text as a literary production—its heterogeneous literary form, the affinities of its style—have with remarkable consistency seemed explicable only by reference to the identity of the author: the course of inquiry has repeatedly enacted a kind of scholarly ascesis, an ascent from the unknown to the unknown. Indeed, to the early twentieth-century scholars who first posed and debated the "authorship question," the very boundaries of the literary text were (as for different reasons they still are) at issue: in its initial version, the questions under most intense dispute were whether the same writer composed all three surviving versions of the poem, and what circumstances conditioned the course of its production as a sequence of revisions. Since these indeterminacies arose from ambiguous "internal evidence," they seemed capable of resolution only by appeal to information that lay outside the text. Scholars sought decisive "external" documentation, either in the form of extraliterary biographical records that might corroborate or supply a name for this elusive writer, or through comparative investigation of analogous examples of authorial self-presentation in other medieval poems that might establish the norms within which Langland's authorial self-disclosures within the poem might be understood. Both kinds of "external" inquiry were conceived as factual constraints upon interpretation, "historically" grounded controls of the almost limitless interpretive inferences that are everywhere tantalizingly invited by the poem itself concerning the actual social identity and life-circumstances of the author. Biography—a text or tissue of data woven by inference into knowledge but conceived as distinct in character and truth-value from a literary record—would in this view

† From "William Langland's 'Kynde Name': Authorial Signature and Social Identity in Late Fourteenth-Century England" in *Literary Practice and Social Change in Britain, 1380–1530*, ed. Lee Patterson (Berkeley: U of California P, 1989), pp. 15–82. Reprinted by permission of the publisher. Notes have been renumbered.
1. A. I. Doyle, "Remarks on Surviving Manuscripts of *Piers Plowman*," in *Medieval English Religious and Ethical Literature: Essays in Honour of G. H. Russell*, (Cambridge, 1986).

stabilize the range of legitimate inferences that the poetic text can not in itself contain or disclose.

The chief "external" record of authorship cited in these debates seems to offer all the documentary solidity that turn-of-the-century scholars sought. It is a Latin note written about 1400 in the Trinity College Dublin manuscript of the C version of the poem. The earliest surviving manuscript of any version of the poem, it originated and for some time remained (as did most of the surviving C texts) in the southwest Midland region of the poet's own origin, as determined by dialect evidence. The memoranda among which this Latin note appears show considerable local knowledge of South Wales border events and families: there is, in other words, good reason to trust its report as informed about the matters it records.[2] It declares "willielmus . . . de Langlond" to be the maker of the poem, names Langland's father as a member of the gentry who held land of the Despensers in Oxfordshire, and reveals that Langland, at least as a writer, did not use his father's surname.[3] One early inference from this note—that William was illegitimate—is certainly itself illegitimate: individuals in the fourteenth century might be known by more than one surname. * * *

* * *

Forms and Methods of Literary Signature

Langland's internal self-naming takes two main forms, both widely used in contemporary French and English writings. The first, the "open" or referential method, requires little discussion—and causes little interpretive controversy; it is familiar in the writings of Chaucer and Gower as well as Langland. By this device, especially frequent in dream-visions, persons in the fiction simply address or refer to the first-person narrator or dreamer by name, or the subject introduces himself (examples from the poem are A-3, C-1, and C-3 * * *). Generally this open referential form is used by Langland to display the baptismal name of Will alone, but it also aids in the recognition of more indirect forms of signature, such as the famous anagram of the surname in Will's speech to Anima, the creature of many names, retrospectively summarizing his quest thus far: "I have lyved in londe . . . my name is longe wille" (B.15.152, B-3 * * *).

2. On this and other external attributions of authorship, see Kane, *Evidence for Authorship*, 26–51. For the most recent argument about the dialect evidence on the poet's native place, see M. R. Samuels, "Langland's Dialect," *Medium Aevum* 54 (1985): 232–47. Malcolm Parkes has recently determined that the Trinity College Dublin manuscript "must have been made in the first half of the 1380s" and is thus the earliest surviving manuscript of any version of the poem (cited in George Kane, "The 'Z Version' of *Piers Plowman*," *Speculum* 60 [1985]: 912).

3. The fortunes of the Despenser family—their spectacular rise and as spectacular fall in royal favor and power—roughly brackets the poet's lifetime. The chief magnate adherents of Edward II in the 1320s, they had consolidated their standing during the Welsh border wars and continued to prosper under the reign of Edward III. The family's already declining political fortunes went into ultimate eclipse with the accession of their long-standing opponents, the house of Lancaster, in 1399, and with the lack of male heirs after that date; see *Dictionary of National Biography* (Oxford: Oxford University Press, 1917–) 5:860–67, s.v. Henry le Despenser (d. 1406), Hugh le Despenser (d. 1265), Hugh le Despenser the elder, Earl of Winchester (1262–1326), Hugh le Despenser the younger (d. 1326), and Thomas le Despenser, Earl of Gloucester (1373–1400). As Paul Strohm has argued for the post-1400 alteration of the "Chaucer tradition," it may be that the death or decline from social power of Langland's immediate circle of readers and kindred intellects—and possibly patrons—by the mid-1380s has as much to do with the pattern of transmission and reception of the poem as changing literary fashions per se ("Chaucer's Fifteenth-Century Audience and the Narrowing of the 'Chaucer Tradition,'" *Studies in the Age of Chaucer* 4 [1982]: 3–32).

While open referential self-naming may be accompanied by further deictic marking, more indirect forms virtually require it, and for this purpose there are several kinds of local signals that an authorial name is to be read in the discourse. Among the more patent devices, illustrated in the example cited, are the depiction in the narrated events of social or ceremonial occasions (the formal introduction of a new character on the scene to other persons present, formal confession, or juridical testimony) or textual forms (such as the last will and testament) that require explicit self-naming for their execution as gestures. In these performative moments the subject's intent is rendered "for the record," and the representation of these acts in narrative thus calls attention to the constitutive and stabilizing power socially attributed to written documents as such. A more subtle and mobile device, exploited by Chaucer as well as more exhaustively by Langland, is locally intensified allusion to the first-person's physical characteristics or social circumstances. Jokes about bodily stature and habit (Chaucer's doll-like "shap" or "noyous" weight, Langland's tall leanness and "long clothes") are not simply descriptive specifications, for verisimilitude or "authentication," but invariably in both poets' work coincide with—and, in effect, announce—complex and very often "signed" accounts of the poetics of the work. The presence of self-references to physical characteristics, like that of the signatures to which they usually point, calls redoubled attention to the author's modal contract with the user of the text, and evokes as part of that contract both reader's and writer's embodiment in a specific sociohistorical situation. We shall find Langland using such moments of bodily self-awareness and occulted signature to translate writerly into readerly self-consciousness.

At the opposite end of the spectrum from these explicit, and explicitly pointed, open forms of signature are the wittier and more occulted devices based on anagrammatic methods, in which wordplay upon the name is made by an anatomy of its parts.[4] It is the "occulted" technique of anagram, Langland's second main signature method and the basis for his system of cross-referencing signature mnemonics in the B and C versions of the

---

4. I borrow the term "occultation" from a highly self-conscious and mannered textual interpreter, almost an exact contemporary of Langland, John Ergome or Erghome, who wrote, some time between 1364 and 1373, an extensive Latin commentary on the so-called Bridlington Prophecies—and may have written the prophecies themselves as well; see Michael J. Curley, "The Cloak of Anonymity and the *Prophecy of John of Bridlington*," *Modern Philology* 77 (1980): 361–69, who presents the arguments for and against Ergome's authorship of the prophecies; and Rigg, "John of Bridlington's *Prophecy*," 596–613, who argues against the attribution. Ergome introduces his work with a commendation of his endeavors to Duke Humphrey de Bohun, in which he encodes "against envious detraction" his own name in an elaborate riddle, one of the most complicated signatures I have found in this period: "si super consequentiae notam caput miserationis vellitis adjungere, nomen obscurum et obsequium salutare"; it was M. R. James who unlocked the syllables of Frgome's name in it: "The Catalogue of the Library of the Augustinian Friars at York, now first edited . . . ," in *Fasciculus J. W. Clark dicatus* (Cambridge, Eng.: Cambridge UP, 1909), 11.

Following this introduction, Ergome provides three prologues to the commentary, each in a different mode. The first is a highly ramified example of the "four-cause" scholastic prologue, the third a summary of its *forma tractatus*; see A. J. Minnis, *Medieval Theory of Authorship* (London: Scholar Press, 1984), 161, 168. The second, however, expounds, with examples from the text, the ten "methods of occultation" used in the prophecies to represent names, dates, and historical events. Among these are the representation of noble persons by their cognomens or heraldic badges, bilingual anagrams of the syllables of names, and the representation of numbers in the letters of Latin words used as common nouns (e.g., cuculi=ccli, 251). It therefore seems appropriate to collect under the term "occulted" all those signature methods that involve some rearrangement or reconstruction of the discourse in order to yield a name. It is also worth noting that for Ergome, anagrams, number codes and heraldic cognomens were classified together as forms of secret or initiate's language.

poem, that will require our closer attention—as indeed the device itself demands a peculiar kind of self-conscious attention to be legible, as well as a sustaining repertory of accompanying conventions, some of them requiring social as well as textual skills for recognition.

*   *   *

Unlike open referential signatures, those made by occultation require the reader to reassemble the proper name dispersed among the common terms of the poem ("I have lyved in londe . . . my name is longe wille" [B.15.152]). Their power to disclose a name not only resides in but calls attention to the beholder's share, as they displace his attention momentarily from the referential to the formal aspect of words. Occulted signatures induce in the reader a momentary high awareness of his operative arts of reading, a perception that is the counterpart of the bodily self-consciousness that both heralds authorial self-reference and supports its use in indicating an operative poetics. By foregrounding for an instant the textual medium itself, forcing one to notice not only the arts of making and reading such disclosures but also the shared social space and physical circumstances within which that art is exercised, they insist on the embodied social dimension of literary processes.

Syllabic anagram, Langland's second main signature device, shares with his first, simple vocative naming, the property of audibility: we can hear as well as see on the page the name, distributed into separate monosyllabic words rather than as a whole.

*   *   *

The acrostic signature, depending for its legibility largely on the physical layout of the page and book, rules the order of the parts in which it appears, and it can only be seen, not heard.

*   *   *

The wit of the anagrammatic signature thus derives from the perpetual double life of tshe text, its claim to represent the spoken and audible voice of someone's "menyng" as well as visible signs representing the meaning of things.

*   *   *

There could be no more decisive mark of this absorption than a signature that transforms the author's name into the place-name of his own *selva oscura*, the Lond of Longyng.

*   *   *

* * * It is only with the B version that the surname is introduced into the signature system, and only at this stage, therefore, that Langland begins to exploit anagrammatic methods: a syllabic anagram requires more than the monosyllable Will to exist. An extreme skeptic might even wish to argue that only here do signatures as such first appear at all: that all occurrences of the baptismal name Will alone denote only the common noun, the faculty, personified in the dreamer, and not a proper name, and hence need not be regarded as references to the author.

* * *

In B, as in A, three signatures have been identified, two of them survivals
from A: the first and last of A's three are retained, while A's second, in which
Will as a copyist is rewarded by the merchants, is rewritten so that the merchants' gratitude is now directed to Piers, "that purchased this bulle." The
keystone for all demonstration that the poem contains an authorial signature in any form is therefore the third instance in B, the anagram of Will
Langland in "'I have lyved in londe,' quod I, 'my name is longe wille.'"
Despite Manly's dissent, and what appears to be skepticism in John Norton-
Smith's recent observation that the line "hints at an English equivalent for
the Latin noun *longanimitas, longanima*, 'long-sufferance'", there has been
no convincing account of this line that succeeds in explaining away its sig-
natory function—although as we have already seen, that function need not
exclude (and in this poem often conspicuously and efficiently includes)
other figurative significances.[5] Like the third signature of A (now the second
in B), this one collects and secures those that precede it: Will's long leanness, twice evoked in the A passage we have examined, is now elevated from
a visible to a verbal distinction, no longer a bodily trait but a cognomen.

* * *

The texts of St. Bernard that Anima adduces to support his rebuke designate the thematic terms and the kind of narrative incident within which
Will's identity is disclosed to himself as well as the reader repeatedly
throughout the poem. *Beatus est qui scripturas legit et verba vertit in opera*
(blessed is he who reads the scriptures and turns their words to works) and
Sciencie appetitus hominem inmortalitatis gloriam spoliavit (the appetite for
knowledge has robbed man of the glory of immortality) recall the contraposition of words and works that anchor Will's pivotal formal function in
the narrative and embed them in its verse language.[6] They also call up in
the reader's memory several earlier occasions of reversal, framed in like
terms: Will's ambitious ransacking of the world for intricate answers to
increasingly subdivided questions is repeatedly disrupted and transformed
by encounters that humiliate this ambition. On such occasions, Will's illu-
sory progress through the world of knowledge is deflected inward, toward
a strenuous confrontation of the self and its motives. By this point in the
poem this recurrent oscillation between ambition and shame has become
the governing pattern of narrative development: each humiliation of Will's
striving shatters the preceding line of narrative figuration and in turn
becomes the site of a new one.[7] It is these restorative ruptures that are the
locus of authorial signatures. We have examined one such moment of self-

5. John Norton-Smith, *William Langland* (Leiden: E. J. Brill, 1983), 89.
6. The sources of these two texts are, respectively, Bernard's *Tractatus de Ordine Vitae* (*Patrologia Latina* 184:566), based on Matt. 7:24, and *Sermo IV in Ascensione Domini* (*Patrologia Latina* 183.311); the latter is incorporated by Hugh of St. Cher in his commentary on Ephesians 4:9–10 (*Post. in Univ. Bbl.* vol. 7, fol. 174ᵛ): see John Alford, "Some Unidentified Quotations in *Piers Plowman*," *Modern Philology* 72 (1975): 396, 397. On the importance of this alliterating triad of terms in linking thematic and self-referential authorial disclosures, see John A. Burrow, "Words, Works, and Will: Theme and Structure in *Piers Plowman*," in *Piers Plowman: Critical Approaches*, ed. S. S. Hussey (London: Methuen, 1969), 111–24.
7. See my essay, "Narration and the Invention of Experience: Episodic Form in *Piers Plowman*," in *The Wisdom of Poetry: Essays in Early English Literature in Honor of Morton W. Bloomfield*, ed. Larry D. Benson and Siegfried Wenzel (Kalamazoo, Mich.: Medieval Institute Publications, 1982), 91–122.

reflexivity in Will's A encounter with Thought and Wit. Anima's rebuke in B—the one that evokes Will's anagram of his name—most vividly recalls, however, an earlier one by Dame Scripture, *multi multa sciunt et seipsos nesciunt* (many know many things, but know not themselves, B.11.3), the humiliation that had sent him in despair into the Lond of Longyng. By looking forward in the poem from this moment, we also begin to apprehend what is at stake in looking backward, and to grasp the terms of their equivalence.

Conceding to Anima that what he really seeks is not many things (the nice distinctions of the soul's many names) but only one, charity, Will's contrite return to a project of self-understanding marks the penultimate turning point in the poem. It initiates the long and sublime narrative sequence, the most sustained of the entire poem, that culminates in the narrator's vision of Christ's victory at the Crucifixion. With a fine and characteristic irony, that scene of redemption is realized in precisely the two dramatized forms that Will here indicates to Anima that he least expects: as both "champions fight" and "chaffare" (exchange, B.15.164). That one whom he looks forward to knowing "soothly," he concedes, is neither knight nor merchant and embodies the antithesis of that pride of which Will himself has just been accused—*non inflatur, non est ambiciosa, non querit que sua sunt* (he is not boastful, nor overweening; he asks not after his own goods, 1 Cor. 13:4–5). Though he has been told that this Christ, the goal of all his longing, "is in all places," Will admits that thus far he has not found him "bifore ne bihynde," having glimpsed him only "figuratyfly" (C.16.294), "as myself in a mirour" (B.15.162); *hic in aenigmate, tunc facie ad faciem*, 1 Cor. 13:12).

Emphasizing, like A's major signature, the subject's insufficiencies and his renewed commitment to his project, Will's anagrammatic introduction of himself in B likewise becomes a moment of long perspectives for the reader. From here forward to Will's Good Friday sleep lies an unbroken thematic path toward his one "face to face" vision of charity, the thing itself, acting in human form "in Piers armes." And just as it is a brief reflection on Will's name and on the proprieties of naming in general that begins this long motion, it is the true identity and proper name of the champion himself, not at first fully blazoned as he approaches the ground of trial, that as in chivalric romance becomes a focus of interest at the end of this long arc of development, both before and after the redeemer's battle (B.18.10–25; 19.10–29). Christ's blazoned name is thus made to designate the central, unique, unrepeatable event in history that measures and renders intelligible what goes before and after, while Will's reiterated signature becomes the sign of historical recursiveness and narrative repetition as the condition of the subject in temporal life.[8] Yet while Will's anagrammatic signature-speech to Anima offers a conspectus of what lies "bifore" Will, it also makes present to memory as "in a mirour" what lies "bihynde" him: an earlier signed moment of humiliation and self-confrontation in the Lond of Longyng, an event that in turn recalls and reframes the starting point of his quest.

On that antecedent occasion, in the opening lines of the B continuation,

---

8. See my essay, "Making a Good End: John But as a Reader of *Piers Plowman*," in *Medieval Studies Presented to George Kane*, ed. Edward Donald Kennedy, Ronald Waldron, and Joseph S. Wittig (Cambridge, Eng.: D. S. Brewer, 1988), 243–66; esp. 248–50.

when Will looked at "myself in a mirour," his gaze met only mortality as far as the eye could see. "Scorned" by Scripture for his inability to find himself and his place amid the speculative intricacies that are all he sees when he gazes at the sacred page—*multi multa sciunt et seipsos nesciunt*—he falls into Fortune's tutelage and finds his place in the world. In "a Mirour that highte middelerthe" she shows Will his land of heart's desire, promising all the "wonders" he has sought since the opening lines of the poem. The place where Fortune rules is called by his "kynde" name: the Lond of Longyng. This "avanture" into Fortune's realm, occurring at about the midpoint of the poem in its two long versions, proclaims a new beginning, a re-vision of the nature of his project, enabled by yet another act of retrospection. Will's fall into the Lond of Longyng restages the first adventure of the poem, his first inquiry into the ownership and end of all worldly provisions, paradoxically instigated by the tutelage of Holichurche.

From the moment in the first dream when Will asks Holichurche about the disposition of the "money of this molde" as if the fate of the world's treasure were inextricably parallel to that of his soul, the mixed motives of the subject's inquiry and interests are thrown into high relief, and they set the terms for the oscillating order of narrative development. For the duration of his life—made coextensive with that of the poem—he seems determined to approach truth by a kind of peripheral vision, along a circuitous route lying always "on thi left half," through the perpetually "ravishing" distractions of the false. In such terrain, significance can reveal itself only in opposition, in a series of unrelenting exposures of Will's apparent progress as merely thriftless repetition. Will's fall into the Lond of Longyng, a few lines into the B continuation, underscores this pattern of narrative reversal with a chilling economy, for it repeats, motif for motif, his first exploratory "avanture" out into the visionary terrain called up by his first dream of the poem. Just as in his first dream he had looked on his "left half" to be "ravysshed" at the sight of Lady Meed, Will is again "ravished" by the "wondres" Lady Fortune presents, and the similarity of their blandishments suggests that they are sisters under the skin: riches, array, carnal favors, a retinue compliant to her followers' pleasures, and the highly visible aura of public respectability that attends lofty kinship.

*   *   *

The Lond of Longyng is thus patently and schematically a place of temptation for Will-as-common-noun, as the power of ethical volition: Fortune's two "damsels" are *concupiscencia carnis* and "Coveitise of eighes," and "Pride of parfit lyvynge pursued hem bothe" (B.11.13–15).[9] But it is also a place for Will as author to disclose the massively revised terms of his art in the long versions. It is "Elde" who offers, in contraposition to Fortune's, a version of Will's life-history that throws narrative emphasis on making a good end rather than on the mediate enchantments and negotiations of the prime of life. With the approach of old age Will comes to regret the "forward" (agreement or contract) he made with the friars, while Fortune was his friend, to be buried by them instead of in his parish churchyard. Under Elde's tutelage he now desires to dispose his life within

---

9. See Donald Howard, *The Three Temptations: Medieval Man in Search of the World* (Princeton: Princeton UP, 1966), 161–214.

the integrity of a biographical circle rather than the open and episodic form of adventure-tale: "At kirke there a man were cristned by kynde he sholde be buryed" (B.11.67). But it is within the terms of his revised desire to represent himself "kyndely" that Langland inscribes his name in the scene.

As Will vehemently castigates the friars' mercenary trade in such spiritual "forwards" as the one he had made at Fortune's behest and now wishes to rewrite, Lewte intervenes to ask Will to explain and justify his anger (B.11.84–85); from this point the scene begins explicitly to bring the terms of its own literary "forward" into the foreground of attention. Lewte's challenge, Priscilla Martin has suggested, raises the question of the morality and limits of satire, particularly the danger to the subject in taking immoderate pleasure in exposing the faults in others while, as a condition of its rhetorical posture, it appears to allow the criticizing subject to remove his own condition, and the limits of his ethical charter, from the field of scrutiny. "It is only on the question of satire," she argues, "that Langland can formulate the problem latent in the entire poem: . . . that the 'personality' of a literary work may color its 'doctrine.' "[1] This formulation is, however, not an incidental effect in this scene, but defines the terms of its structural centrality and the memorial role of the signature in the poem.

In the Lond of Longyng, as in the later anagrammatic signature that points backward to it, the author's name accompanies a disclosure and renegotiation of the literary terms of the work. Will, who was in the early visions situated at the periphery of the community of the folk as it turns toward its collective penitential enterprise, an engaged observer who forecasts and mimes in his own weeping and seeking the canonical motions by which journeying becomes a penitential labor, here fully introjects this massive social project as his own—indeed, as *himself*: he does not so much abandon the field full of folk as *become* it, his wanderings now a prophetically significant mimesis of the story of his people. He marks this development, which enables the B–C continuation, by making his name signify not only the person but the place in which this labor is undertaken: a *longe launde* is, among other things, the strip of land a plowman plows.[2] As a place-name, his authorial surname has the surface form of many that were to become fixed and heritable in this century: it seems to specify the landholding, dwelling, or birthplace that could serve to distinguish him in written record from a neighbor or relative with the same baptismal name. Yet the addition that in contemporary usage serves to mark a socially significant difference here serves to redouble the force of the given name alone, underscoring its generic power: though formally a proper name or surname, the "long land" designates what he possesses in common with all mortals, his unsatisfied desire or will. At once disclosing and occulting his identity, Will's enigmatic authorial name is paradoxically both proper and common, a condensed confession and a device that enables him to go on "writing and hiding himself." As inhabitant and heir of the Lond of Longyng that has so far defined the space of his life, he has, in Augustine's words, "become a problem to himself"—a project of social reclamation and cultivation in the first person—and his literary signature, with its accom-

1. Priscilla Martin, *Piers Plowman: The Field and the Tower* (London: Macmillan; New York: Harper and Row, 1979), 70.
2. *OED*, s.v. "land," sb., I.7.

panying moments of intensive self-reference, has become a narrative and
critical, not an attributive, mnemonic.

* * *

   This "heighe wey" to Scripture traverses a figurative landscape much like
the one Piers had delineated for the folk who asked his guidance to truth,
but where Piers's way led through the social discipline of the commandments and sacraments, Study's lies through the marked and unmarked hazards of individual temptations:

> And rid forth bi ricchesse, ac reste thou not therinne,
> For yif thou couple the with hym to clergie comist thou nevere;
> And ek the longe launde that leccherie hatte,
> Leve hym on thi left half a large myle or more,
> Til thou come to a court, kepe wel thi tunge
> Fro lesinges and lither speche and likerous drinkes.
> Thanne shalt thou se sobirte, and simplite of speche,
> That iche wight be in wille his wyt the to shewen.
>   (A.11.116–23)

It is this "longe launde that leccherie hatte"—lying, like the domain of
Lady Meed, "on thi left half"—that is developed and populated in the
opening moments of the B–C continuation to produce a more extended
trial of Will's motives, not only as pilgrim but as maker. The Lond of Longyng, built up on a slender strip of terrain merely glimpsed by the way in
the first version, is in the long versions resituated *in medias res*, in several
senses: Fortune addresses her gratifications to the desires and powers
characteristic of the middle of life, and her appeal presents itself both
about midway in the poem and midway in Will's life's journey. As the name
of the place, and the surname of the person, from which the long versions
begin, it reframes the fundamental narrative premise of the poem by an act
of superimposition: Will's satiric critique of his world is now subsumed in
a massive historical reclamation of the subject's life in the light of salvation history. It is by proclaiming at this point his full name that the poetic
subject assumes the prophet's mantle, and his representative status. He
becomes, to adopt a phrase whose contemporary legal usage will prove res-
onant in understanding the social significance of this move, a "son of the
people."

LANGLAND'S "KYNDE NAME" AND NARRATIVE "KYNDE"

If the anagram of Will's name in his meeting with Anima initiates the final
progression of the poem—a penultimate turning point much like that experienced by Dante when for the first time in the poem the poet hears his own
name in the first syllables Beatrice addresses to him—then the Lond of
Longyng, to which that later signature alludes narratively, may be understood as Will's *selva oscura*, encountered, like Dante's, *nel mezzo del cam-
min de nostra vita* (midway in our life's journey).

* * *

Names Proper and Improper: Identities for the Record

It is hardly incidental to our story that it is in precisely this period that most historians of personal names place the final general stabilization of the English surname in its modern form: that is to say as the heritable and conventional paternal addition.

* * *

This comparison succinctly declares the chief function of the surname in common law, and explains why in England by the fourteenth century, well before this occurred anywhere else in Europe, anybody who had occasion to appear in or make a written record of any kind—and by this time that included peasants, many of whom possessed their own personal seals for the purpose—already had a name that followed the common modern form: a given or baptismal name plus a heritable surname that matched that of the father, whether or not it any longer actually declared either the father's own given name (as, say, the name Robertson does) or his occupation (consider, for example, Chaucer, whose father was not a shoemaker but a winemerchant).[3] It was by this sustained continuity of heritable surname across generations as a regulatory convention, rather than by its real reference to paternal given name or occupation, that rights, tenant as well as free, were claimed and maintained through time: to be a copyholder was to hold one's rights by "copy of the court roll" in the manorial court, and it was in this practical sense that the functional name of the father, as the name of one's paternal ancestors, was powerful.

The two names, first and last, virtually divide between them one's spiritual and civil identity.[4] For virtually all matters before God's tribunal one acted under the given or baptismal name, the name that proclaimed the individual's beginning in this world as a moral agent and marked all his new beginnings of spiritually significant relations. Examples include the custom of the confession and the practice that still survives in the marriage service: both are sacramental performative occasions in which the parties avow their intentions and constitute their own spiritual "estate" by given name only ("I William take thee Catherine . . ."). This notion of the individual as capable of making provision for the benefit of his soul extended to the making of wills for the disposition of personal property, even by peasants holding in villein tenure, a practice no longer unusual by the latter fourteenth century.

* * * A family in which the same two or three male given names recur

---

3. See C. M. Matthews, *English Surnames* (London: Weidenfeld and Nicolson, 1966), 43–44; P. H. Reaney, *The Origin of English Surnames* (London: Routledge and Kegan Paul, 1967), 300–316.
4. Here and throughout this exposition, I use the term "civil" for those temporal and publicly accountable activities that fall outside the specific concern of spiritual authority and ecclesiastical jurisdiction and are governed by common and statutory law—in other words, those that in a later age might be said to occupy "public" space and identity and come to be the concern of the "state." The term should not be understood to imply the jurisdiction of the civil, as against common, law.

    Like "public," "civil" is a term that must be applied with caution, and with alertness to its specific local utility in marking distinctions of heuristic and expository use in interpretation. I do not contend that these were the terms in which medieval writers and thinkers conceived the terms of their worldly relations. The special and limited senses in which a nascent "public" sphere was available as an imaginative ground for distinctive forms of late medieval thought and action is a topic beyond the scope of this essay. I would contend, however, that such a space—in Habermas's sense of an arena in which participants tacitly agree to relinquish for purposes of discursive exchange their class status and identifications—exists as at least a literary idea, or ideal, in this period, and that it is a distinctive notion of this cultural moment. * * *

in two or more adjacent generations may distinguish the holdings of a son
from those of a nephew of about the same age by referring to one by the
name of the holding that was or would be his, rather than by the sire's surname: William Langlond, for example, rather than William de Rokayle.[5]
Which surname William used, and under what circumstances, would
depend on the claims and distinctions he and his family wished it to make
for him, and therefore to some degree on where he lived and worked in relation to this proprietary identity—just as a boy tends to lose the appellation
Junior to the extent that he moves as an adult outside the territorial and
social range of its utility in marking a difference. Whatever we may infer
about Langland's practice in this regard, then, we are not entitled to
assume that the difference of his sire's surname from his own meant that
he was a bastard, as a few early critics argued.

                                    *   *   *

A second way in which it might be perceived as disadvantageous to have
one's traceable and stable familial or household name a matter of record
became immediately apparent with the first Poll Tax, and dramatically more
so with its second and third collections not long afterward, when a nation-
wide investigation into massive tax evasion was met with what quickly
became the Peasants' Revolt of 1381. The Poll Tax was the first tax to be
levied by the "head" (poll), or individual person, instead of, for example, by
the household or the village, the units of taxation drawn upon by the Lay
Subsidies, that fiscal innovation which had immediately preceded the
invention of the Poll Tax and remained in place after the disastrous civil
consequences of the latter measure had become all too obvious.[6] The Poll
Tax was imposed at the rate of 4d. per person on all lay men and women
over fourteen years of age; only those who regularly begged for a living were
exempt.

                                    *   *   *

Such fears, and a variety of civil fictions to articulate them, are abun-
dant in the literature of the 1381 Revolt. The representative status of the
named actors in these events has proved to be very hard to interpret.
Actual persons, craft typenames, nonce names, sectarian code names,
obvious pseudonyms, and patent evasions mingle in the chronicles under
the same naming conventions as purported actors in a newly defined arena
of civil events. Persons of indeterminate status between the fictive and the
actual become the "one head" under which the rebels, those previously
unnamed in chronicles of significant public actions, enter the records and
are comprehended by the chroniclers as an improvised, indeterminate,
unnameable, and therefore threatening new social body; a "great society"
made by common volition and bound together by oath—made, that is to say,
chiefly of words and deeds, confected names and improvised identities. A
rich collection of such indeterminate beings, suspended between the hypo-
thetical and the actual, populate the so-called Letter of John Ball, recorded

---

5. Oscar Cargill, in "The Langland Myth," *PMLA* 50 (1935): 36–56—a largely tendentious argument
   against the evidential solidity of opposition to Manly's view of the authorship of the poem—
   nevertheless contains some valuable if incomplete information from various fourteenth-century
   records of the Rokayle and But family names, including just the circumstance we have described
   occurring within three adjacent generations of the Rokayle family (48).
6. M. W. Beresford, *Lay Subsidies and Poll Taxes* (Canterbury: Phillimore, 1963).

by Walsingham as having been addressed to the men of Essex.[7] * * * The mix of kinds of signification in these names is dizzying. While a William Trueman is named in King's Bench records as having berated Nicholas Brembre for injuries suffered during his mayoralty as the latter rode with the king to meet the rebels at Mile End, John Treweman "and alle his felawes" looks to be a coinage allied to the generic typename Lollards gave themselves, distinguishing the correct beliefs of "trewe men" from the false opinions of all outside their sect. Hobbe the Robbere may or may not be Langland's coinage, though Piers certainly is, and Ball's exhortation later in the letter to "do wel and bettre and fleth synne" seems to close the case for some knowledge on the part of the speaker or writer of these key terms of Langland's text. John Carter and John the Miller may be meant as typenames of the skilled rural and town craftsmen groups among which the revolt spread most deeply and quickly—though other chroniclers, such as Knighton, soberly list them along with Jack Straw (to whom he attributes the actions assigned by other chroniclers to Wat Tyler) as actual persons in the crowd that descended on London. (Knighton's version of this report makes Ball's letter several messages, spoken by Jakke Mylner, Jakke Carter, and Jakke Trewman). The Dieulacres Chronicler also attributes Wat Tyler's deeds to Jack Straw—and goes on to name Piers Plowman as one of his confederates. And what are we to understand of John Nameless? Possibly that the surname Nameless in this context itself counts as an act of defiance and solidarity—that a parody of the common name-form calls into question the social function to which it is perceived to be attached, landed proprietorship.

* * *

Authorship, Improvisation, and the Rhetoric of Presence

The violence, perceived as well as actual, of 1381, together with considerable interpretive depth in representing a phenomenon that in their explicit moral pronouncements upon it both Commons and chroniclers profess to find an inexplicable and sinister breach in nature, testifies to a "crisis of the proper" in the latter decades of the fourteenth century. Proper names, like the proprietary rights they represented and regulated, go into a kind of liquefication in these documents:

* * *

What Langland's self-reference seems rather to have in common with these late medieval discourses, both orthodox and dissenting, is a paradoxical skepticism and anxiety about the established agencies for textual distribution of authority. It is important to avoid attributing a necessarily "progressive" or revolutionary character to these phenomena: indeed, those who enacted them saw them rather as restorative of some simpler and more directly mediated form of exemplification and authority.

Orthodox or dissenting, the contemporary discourses to which Langland's practice of self-representation has its closest affinities are based on a rhetoric of presence, on resistance to the independent intelligibility of texts without reference to their authorship as actions. These late medieval

7. See p. 484 herein for the text [Editors].

forms of social and spiritual piety enact a powerfully nostalgic rearguard action on behalf of ideas of communal and personal integrity disposed locally and face-to-face rather than from above or outside. They envision individual and communal life as so permeated by lived scripture that its integrity is wholly transparent, as St. Francis had insisted, "without a gloss." Like Langland they speak on behalf of an ethic based on the lived rather than formalized deployment of authorizing texts, and propose a renegotiation of traditional relations between textual fixity and human action. If graven images were profoundly suspect, those that formed spontaneously in the individual memory and imagination steeped in direct assimilation of canonical texts of scripture and the lives of the saints—metonymies or images of equivalence that suggested themselves to Margery Kempe in daily domestic life—were fundamentally trustworthy, because their syntax of relation was implicit in a customary grammar of living. Inscribing in his poem a name and equivocal occupation that loosely allied his improvisatory activities with these, Langland claims for himself and those who undertake to define their own actions within this terrain an extremely risky social authority. That such a move was fully self-conscious I do not doubt. That it assured that he would *as author* join the John Namelesses of his age to the memory of posterity is one of the profound witticisms of historical process he shows every sign of having accepted with equanimity.

* * *

JAMES SIMPSON

From *Piers Plowman*: An Introduction to the B-Text†

Preface

The main aim of this book is to convince undergraduate readers of *Piers Plowman*'s centrality in any account of the literary and cultural history of the later English Middle Ages. I seek to do this by trying to demonstrate how the poem, despite being deeply anchored in a conservative literary, ecclesiastical and social culture, in fact questions that culture in moving towards positions of doubt and dissent, and in reimagining social and religious institutions.

I argue that Langland consistently develops one theme throughout the poem, that of the relations between justice and mercy. In following this theme, certain psychological, institutional, and literary changes become necessary: broadly speaking, the poem moves away from a rational to an affective approach to problems; from a hierarchical to a more horizontal sense of ecclesiastical and social institutions; and from authoritarian, 'closed' literary forms to more exploratory and open-ended procedures.

I seek meaning in the poem less out of the development of 'character', than out of the relationship of different genres of writing which constitute

---

† From *Piers Plowman: An Introduction to the B-Text* (London: Longman Group UK Limited, 1990), pp. viii–ix, 14–16, 78–80, 248–51. Reprinted by permission of the publisher.

the poem. I do this not because the notions of 'character' and personhood are irrelevant in this work; on the contrary, I will argue that the narrative structure of the poem is shaped out of Langland's conception of what it is to be a person. But exclusive focus on the personal development of Will seems to me to eclipse Langland's interest in corporate institutions, and in the ways in which individuals and institutions intersect. In trying to encompass both Langland's sense of the self, and his sense of institutions, my approach has been to begin with the formal, textual choices Langland has made, and to work out from there to his sense both of institutions and the self.

The argument will take into serious account Langland's theology, his idea of the Church as an institution, and, in a broad sense, his politics. But I will also try to make sense of the formal qualities of the work, by showing how ecclesiastical and political attachments are written into the formal choices Langland makes—how, that is, the formal characteristics of the poem have historical significance. The questions I will consistently ask of the poem (though in no consistent order) are these: What genre is being practised here? What claims to authority does such a genre make? What aspect of the self does it appeal to? What social or ecclesiastical institution is it produced by and does it support? And, finally, in what ways are authoritative genres (what I call 'discourses') found by Langland to be inadequate?

*   *   *

Introduction

'DISCOURSE'

* * * Langland's poetry might be projected from the margins of literary discourses, but it is projected from the theoretical centre of different institutional discourses. * * * Langland brings ideological, institutional attachments to the surface of his narrative, and explores the theoretical bases of those institutions: thus the main actants in the first vision, for example, are Holy Church and the King, representing the two fundamental institutions of Langland's age.[1] This is not to say that Langland is unconcerned either with poetry as a craft, or with the status of specifically poetic modes of apprehension; in fact he is deeply concerned both with the craft and with the status of poetry.[2] But this commitment to specifically poetic modes of apprehension is not a given in the poem; instead it becomes part of the poem's own subject, as other, institutional ways of saying things fail. For Langland's initial commitment in the poem is not to poetry as a self-justifying art; on the contrary, his commitment is rather to the reformation of both social and ecclesiastical institutions, and his initial reliance is on genres of writing and speaking which ideally sustain these institutions.

A working assumption of this book, then, will be that Langland's poem cannot be understood within standard literary categories;[3] Langland is essentially concerned to transform institutions, and as such he often

---

1. I use the word 'actant' in this book simply to designate the generators of action in any given narrative; I use this neutral word to avoid the complications of personhood involved with words like 'actor', 'character', which may not be relevant to personification allegory.
2. A. V. C. Schmidt, *The Clerkly Maker: Langland's Poetic Art* (Cambridge: Cambridge UP, 1987).
3. For the problems of reading much medieval writing 'as literature', see J. A. Burrow (1982, 12–23).

adopts the textual (or oral) forms of those institutions. These forms cannot readily be called 'literary' forms, since their presuppositions are distinct from those of a body of writing which may be described as 'literary' in Langland's England. The word 'genre' will serve to designate the formal characteristics of these textual forms, and I will continue to use it throughout this book. But in adopting such genres, Langland is exploiting or questioning the authority of those genres, and, thereby, exploiting or questioning the authority of the institution from which the genre derives. It is for this reason that I use the word 'discourse', since while denoting the formal characteristics of a way of writing or speaking in the way 'genre' does, the word 'discourse' also denotes (in a branch of contemporary theory, at least) the claims to power made by a given genre.[4] So the word 'discourse', as used in this book, will never denote anything less than the word 'genre' (i.e., the stylistic and structural characteristics of a given way of writing), but it will denote something more—the authoritative claims made by a given way of writing or speaking.

A word of caution should be added about the terms 'genre' and 'discourse' as applied to Langland's poem: Langland often merges recognisable genres in the one sequence of his poem (e.g., dream-vision and sermon in Passus I), often with the effect of creating poetry which is distinctively Langlandian, and beyond the reach of traditional generic categories. It remains true that the poem is constituted by distinct blocks of kinds of writing, discussion of which requires formal analysis.

*   *   *

Chapter Three

*   *   *

When Langland discusses rewards from God, he does so in economic terms, of both wages and gifts: payments fully deserved, that is, and payments given out of the giver's generosity.[5] In Passus II Theology had defined reward from God as 'mede', which, as we know from Conscience's definitions in Passus III, indicates a reward beyond desert, a gift.

> For Mede is muliere of Amendes engendred;
> And God graunted to gyve Mede to truthe,
> And thow hast gyven hire to a gilour—now God gyve thee sorwe!
> The text telleth thee noght so. Truthe woot the sothe.
> For *Dignus est operarius* his hire to have.

(II. 119–23)

Theology indicates that God's reward is for honestly performed works, with his image of the *operarius*, or workman. But the reward given is not a wage strictly deserved; it is a 'mede' rather than a 'mercede', to use the term

4. The branch of 'contemporary' theory which defines the notion of 'discourse' and points to the claims to power made by different discourses, is that derived from the writing of Michel Foucault. Foucault's notion of discourse is more far reaching than the one I propose here, since he is concerned to define the underlying conceptual rules which govern 'forms of co-existence between statements' (Foucault 1972 [*Archaeology of Knowledge*], 73). But this does involve questions of style (Foucault 1972, 33–34), and it certainly involves questions of power (particularly institutional power) which the use of a particular way of speaking raises (Foucault 1972, 50–52). See Lawton (1987) for a discussion of how the notion of discourse affects subjectivity in *Piers Plowman*.
5. James Simpson, "Spirituality and Economics in Passus 1–7 of the B-Text." *Yearbook of Langland Studies* 1 (1987): 83–103.

used in the C-Text to denote strictly deserved payment, which is given in exact proportion to works performed. It may be helpful to cite that passage to recall the exact distinctions Conscience makes. Having defined 'mede' as the undeserved reward paid before payment is merited, Conscience goes on to define 'mercede' as a payment paid

> When the dede is ydo and the day endit;
> And that is no mede but a mercede, a manere dewe dette,
> And but hit prestly be ypayed the payere is to blame . . .
> And ther is resoun as a reve rewardynge treuthe
> That bothe the lord and the laborer be leely yserved.
>
> (C. III. 303–309)

endit; ended; *prestly*: readily, *reue*: reeve; *leely*: justly.

If Theology uses the word 'mede' to denote reward from God, this necessarily implies that reward from God to man is undeserved by man; and in the definition of 'mede' given by Theology, we can see that such a reward from God does imply that man has failed to deserve reward fully, as a 'mercede', or 'maner dewe dette for the doynge', since Theology's Mede is 'of amendes engendred'. Theology's reward from God, that is, implies a failure on man's behalf to merit full reward, which is compensated for by the making of amends, or penitence for sins committed.

If Theology defines 'mede' as the model of man's reward from God, Piers, on the other hand, merits a 'mercede', or wage. When Piers first introduces himself he describes the payment he receives from Truthe:

> I have ben his folwere al this fourty wynter—
> Bothe ysowen his seed and suwed hise beestes . . .
> For though I seye it myself, I serve hym to paye:
> I have myn hire of hym wel and outherwhiles moore.
> He is the prestete paiere that povere men knoweth:
> He withhalt noon hewe his hire that he ne hath it at even.
>
> (V. 542–52)

The terms of Piers's reward from God here evoke the definition Conscience had given of a just reward, which is no 'mede'—what 'laborers and lewede [leodes] taken of hire maistres, / It is no manere mede but a mesurable hire' (III. 255–56). Piers, as the apparently perfect Christian, does not require a gift from God (even if God, out of his generosity, might give 'outherwhiles moore'), but is able to meet the requirements of God's justice, and to merit the 'mesurable hire', or 'mercede' proportionate to his labour.

These two categories of reward, the wage and the gift, derive from one of the most controversial doctrinal issues of the Christian tradition: how does man receive the reward of salvation, by works or by grace? On the one hand, the Christian tradition as it developed placed great emphasis on the existence of free will, by which humans are responsible for their actions, and by which they deserve or fail to deserve salvation by the worth of their works. On the other hand, the Judeo-Christian tradition conceives of man as radically debilitated by the wound of original sin, so that it is only through the free gift (or grace, from Latin *gratia*) of redemption that God has rendered humanity capable of good deeds and salvation.[6]

---

6. Robert Adams, "Piers's Pardon and Langland's Semi-Pelagianism." *Traditio* 39 (1983): 369–70.

To stress the importance of works and independent human virtue in achieving salvation is to undermine the omnipotence of God, since it renders God *obliged* to reward virtue; it also undermines the omniscience of God in making His knowledge dependent on the decisions of humans. The doctrine which stressed the independent possibility and worth of human works was labelled as Pelagianism, after the late fourth-century British monk Pelagius, who was considered to maintain this position. On the other hand, to stress the omnipotence and omniscience of God in awarding salvation through His grace as a gift, is radically to diminish the worth of human action, and can lead to a position which attributed salvation only to God's predestination of souls. This was the position of St Augustine's (AD 354–430) later writings.

The images of 'gift' and 'wage', then, arise out of this larger doctrinal debate concerning the nature of reward from God: if the reward God gives is a wage, then man deserves it and God is obliged to give it (the potentially 'Pelagian' position); if the reward God gives is a gift, then man has not deserved it, and God is not obliged to give it (the more Augustinian position). Langland's use of these images is not original, and he is indebted to central currents of fourteenth-century theology in his use of them. For fourteenth-century theologians the questions of how man could be said to merit from God was of central importance. Theologians drew on a thirteenth-century distinction between two kinds of merit, *condign* merit and *congruent* merit. Condign merit is an absolute, strict merit, whereby man can be said to merit the reward of salvation absolutely and justly. Congruent merit, on the other hand, is relative and conditional, whereby man receives reward from God out of God's generosity.[7] When we look to the image used by theologians to describe these two kinds of reward, we see that they described condign reward as wages, and congruent reward as a gift.[8] The early fourteenth-century theologian Durandus of St Pourçain, for example, defines two kinds of merit, correlating them with two kinds of debt:

> Just as there are two kinds of debt, so too are there two kinds of merit. One is condign debt, which is debt in a simple sense. [This debt pertains] when, for example, it is just that a labourer, through the nature of his work, be given a reward on account of the equality between the work and the payment. The other kind of debt is congruent debt, where such a reward is not deserved through the nature of the work, but rather through the generosity of the giver. For it is allowed to offer some generous gift which someone did not merit condignly. Condign merit pertains to the first kind of debt, while congruent merit pertains to the second kind.[9]

The categories of reward offered by this passage correspond exactly to the categories of reward from God defined in *Piers Plowman*: 'mercede', or 'mesurable hire' (a wage) corresponds with condign reward, and 'mede' (a gift) with congruent reward. Besides being indebted to this theological

---

7. Heiko A. Oberman, *Archbishop Bradwardine: A Fourteenth-Century Augustinian* (Utrecht: Kemink and Zoon, 1957), pp. 149–51; 155–59, and *The Harvest of Medieval Theology: Gabriel Biel and Late Medieval Nominalism* (Cambridge: Harvard UP, 1963), pp. 169–74.
8. Samuel Overstreet, "'Grammaticus Ludens': Theological Aspects of Langland's Grammatical Vocabulary." *Traditio* 40 (1984): 281–87.
9. Durandus of St Pourçain (1556). I cite the Latin text (Simpson 1987, 94) with slight emendation of the edition.

tradition for his categories of rewards, it should not be forgotten that Langland is also indebted to the Bible for images of salvation as a wage for works performed, found in the Parable of the Vineyard, for example (Matthew 20.1–16), and at John 4.36: 'And he that reapeth receiveth wages, and gathereth fruit unto life eternal'.

❊ ❊ ❊

Conclusion

❊ ❊ ❊

In my consideration of corporate institutions, and especially of the Church, I have tried to show that Langland's position with regard to the Church is not a static one, but one which can only be defined by tracing the process of the poem, whereby institutional attachments come under strain, and give way to others. Theological 'truthe' seems to be a unitary principle in Passus I, automatically implying ecclesiastical and political allegiances of a conservative kind; but as Langland follows through the logic of his central question (concerning the relations of justice and love), the reader discovers competing voices *within* the institution of Holy Church. In its broadest terms, my arguments has been that the movement of the poem is from allegiance to feudal, authoritarian, vertically organised institutions (where the dominant quality is 'truthe') to fundamentally non-hierarchical, brotherly, horizontally organised institutions (where the dominant quality is charity). The meaning of the poem lies less in the conservative or the more dissenting positions (despite their interest and importance), than in the movement between them.

So in tracing the development of the poem's central concern with the relations of justice and love, I have tried to give an account not only of selfhood in *Piers Plowman*, but also of the corporate institutions by which the self is shaped. The areas so far considered in this conclusion require students of literature to take quite serious account of theology, psychology, and institutional history. But for students of literature, perhaps the biggest challenge offered by the poem is its poetic form. My own students (and, no doubt, many other readers of the poem) have often complained that the work is 'dogmatic'. My argument in response to this complaint has been that the poetic form of the work is correlative with its theological, psychological and institutional attachments. As Langland moves theologically from consideration of God as Truthe to consideration of God as Kynde, so too do the poetic forms of the poem change from being authoritarian to being more personal. As the poem moves psychologically from the reason to the will, so too do the poetic forms of the poem change from rational and analytical to being affective and synthetic. The poem's form is determined by the soul's form. And as Langland moves institutionally from a hierarchical to a 'brotherly' sense of institutions, so too do the discourses of the poem change from being those whose authority is centred outside the self, to those whose authority is centred in the self. Holy Church's commitment to 'truthe' in Passus I seemed to imply not only conservative institutional allegiances, but also, concomitantly, authoritarian discourses. As the poem proceeds, I have argued that Langland explores the premises of such authoritarian discourses, and as those premises are found to be inadequate, the poem adopts a range of discourses which, while never outside the institution 'Holy Church', are not authoritarian and closed.

Another way of putting the point about the formal changes in the poem is to say that the structure of the poem is unstable and self-consuming, undercutting itself as the inadequacy of its means of progressing is recognised. In fact the poem is full of tiny models of verbal subversion. Holy Church recommends that 'mesure is medicine' (I. 35), neatly using the model of 'medicine' to undercut it: if one is temperate, medicine will be unnecessary. This strategy, of which there are many examples, also characterises larger narrative units in the poem, such as that of using pilgrimage as a narrative model to subvert the normal practice of pilgrimage, in the second vision. And if we were looking to the poem to provide us with textual models of this procedure, we might go to the treatment of documents in the poem. Langland often uses documents as the model for his poetry: take, for example, the marriage charter of Mede and False in Passus II; the pardon Piers receives in Passus VII; the 'patente' of Patience in Passus XIV, and the writ carried by Moses in Passus XVII. I have treated each of these individually in the body of this book, but by putting them together, it is possible to see a common strategy applied to each: they are proposed as documents in order to undercut the premises of the document. Mede's marriage charter uses legal forms to subvert law; Piers's 'pardon' undermines the premises of a normal pardon; the 'patente' of Patience must be written on the parchment of 'pure pacience', which undercuts the purely legal, documentary status of the patent; and the writ of Moses will be sealed by Christ 'hanging' from the cross, which evokes, but overbears the idea of a seal hanging from a legal document. In their strategy, at least, these 'texts' are more like *Piers Plowman* than the texts which are promoted as models from within the poem—the pious stories of 'Tobye and of the twelve Apostles', for example, that Study recommends (X. 33).

If formal change is in part explicable in terms of changes in institutional attachment represented in the poem, this has implications for cultural history more generally: we can see the way in which the literary category of form bears historical significance within it. But formal change in the poem also has implications for literary history, and for the history of reading. A sub-theme of this book has been that biblical texts are used in different ways as the poem proceeds;[1] without specifying each kind of use, we might notice that Will changes in the poem from being a passive receiver of biblical texts designed for moral instruction at the beginning of the poem, to being an active 'reader', especially from Passus VIII forwards. Holy Church uses scriptural texts in an authoritarian and dogmatic way in Passus I, but when in Passus XI Will comes face to face with the ultimate text of the tradition to which Langland is committed, Scripture, the event is not one of passive reading, submissively accepting a 'closed' text; instead, Will responds to the text of Scripture in a personal and liberating way. From this vision on in the poem, Will's 'reading' of scriptural texts is more inward and poetic, and designed to appeal to the deeper reaches of the self. So despite the initial commitment to habits of reading which are purely subservient, Langland represents a movement towards a more intu-

---

1. Helen Barr, "The Use of Latin Quotations in *Piers Plowman* with Special Reference to Passus XVIII of the 'B' Text," *Notes and Queries*, n.s. 33, pp. 440–48.

itive, personal reading. In its testing and revaluation of textual authority, it could be said that *Piers Plowman* is much more like Chaucer's *House of Fame* than it is like, for example, Chaucer's *Parson's Tale* (setting aside the very different institutional and textual traditions within which *Piers Plowman* and *The House of Fame* are working). Again, the meaning of the poem lies not so much in one kind of reading or another, but in the movement between them.

Langland's culture might be foreign, or at best ancestral, to our own; readers in a secular, liberal culture might find much in *Piers Plowman* that they want to resist. But for anyone who agrees that we know ourselves through cultural history (and not just the cultural history of our own, immediate tradition), Langland's poem affords an extraordinary occasion for self-knowledge.

RALPH HANNA III

[Dating the A, B, and C Versions][†]

*   *   *

Dating the A Version

The A Version is the earliest and most eccentric form of Langland's poem. Just over 2500 lines long, it comprises but three visions. The first two of these, the *Visio*, social and satirical in emphasis, survey 'contemporary conditions'; this version, more emphatically than either subsequent revision, thus may fruitfully be considered within pre-existent traditions of alliterative social satire, e.g. *Winner and Waster* (contentiously dated 1352) or 'The Song of the Husbandman' and other lyrics in BL MS. Harley 2253 (before 1340). In the third, fragmentary vision, the *Vita*, the dreamer Will initiates a different mode, an inner spiritual search for 'dowel'. But this narrative breaks off, with the dreamer in despair, probably early in the twelfth passus of the poem.[1]

Skeat lays out the broad outlines for dating the three versions.[2] He places the A Version in 1362 on the basis of two references: Meed's and Conscience's protracted debate before the king about the Brétigny campaign of 1359–60 (A Version III. 176–95) and the allusion to the great storm of Saturday, 15 January 1362 (A Version V. 13–14). To this placement, one should object that the two events provide only a *terminus a quo* and that Skeat too readily sees the states of the poem as something like 'spontaneous effusions', completed within short order.[3]

Later scholars have adduced evidence suggesting a slightly later begin-

---

† From *William Langland* (Aldershot, UK: Ashgate, 1993), pp. 11–17. Reprinted by permission of the publisher.
1. On the authenticity of A Version XII, see, most recently, Middleton 1988 [in *MESPGK*].
2. See Skeat 1886, 2, ix–x (the A Version) and xi–xiv (the B Version).
3. For the Brétigny campaign, see Bennett [*PMLA* 58], 568–70 and [his edition,] 1972, 139–40 nn. 188ff. and 206; for the 1362 storm, [*PMLA* 58] 571 and n. 14; 1972, 152 n. 14. For the 'dym cloude' (III. 80), see also the English prose *Brut*, EETS o.s. 136 (1908), 310/34–311/9; and for the 1362 storm, 315/1–8. With regard to Skeat's early dating, note Kane's caveats [in Alford] 1988, 185–86.

ning, that Langland worked on this version c. 1365–70.[4] Since the first Victorian investigations of the poem, scholars have insisted that the character Meed involves some satire of Edward III's mistress, Alice Perrers; the earliest record taken to testify to such a liaison is dated 9 December 1364.[5] The reference to 'rome-renneris' (A Version IV. 111) appears the latest datable allusion in this version, which is sensible only in the context of Urban V's removal of the papacy to Rome (October 1367–September 1370).[6]

The circulation of the A Version, so far as it is recoverable, is extremely peculiar. The manuscripts capable of dialectical placement survive from peripheral areas; large numbers cluster in East Anglia (below, MSS. 6, 8, 9, 10, 16, 19, and by provenance 11), second in the West Midlands (MSS. 12, 13, 17).[7] Moreover, few of the copies are as old as many B and C Version copies; the only certainly fourteenth-century A Version manuscripts are the copies MSS. 1, the archetype available to John But behind 5 + 6, 11, and 12. Peculiarly, several scholars claim that such apparently limited circulation provides the best argument for the extensive general circulation of this version. But it is more probable that the A Version was a text which never achieved independent general circulation: the success of the later versions, which is attested by larger numbers of pre- or *circa* 1400 copies (as well as by John Ball's appropriation of the B Version in 1381), may have drawn the A Version into a wider public view. Yet even then, this version occurs primarily as a *faute de mieux* substitute in regions where these later versions had limited circulation. Moreover, the A Version was widely perceived as incomplete or superseded; seven of the eighteen full copies, generally codices which cannot be mapped dialectically, fill out this 'fragment' with a C Version 'conclusion'.[8]

Dating the B Version

The process by which Langland converted the A Version into the B Version had two stages. First, Langland took up the A Version where he had left it and extended the poem for an additional eight dreams (two within dreams) and ten passus (B XI–XX). Secondly, he went through the A Version with great care, most usually expanding it, e.g. adding a confession by Wrath and substantially extending that of Sloth (B Version V. 135–87, 385–440a), inserting the account of the foundation of the Commonwealth and associated Rat Parliament (B Prologue 112–210, the former surely inspired by A Version VII. 3–53). The resulting text (some 7700 lines) roughly tripled the previous version in length. The distribution of historical

4. Bennett [*PMLA* 58] effectively destroys such earlier views as Cargill [*PMLA* 47] and Huppé [*PMLA* 54], which would place composition during the first half of the seventies. Recently, Selzer [*PQ* 59] returns to this older view, but not to my mind convincingly.
5. See Bennett [*PMLA* 58], 566 and n. 1.
6. So Bennett [*PMLA* 58], 568 (cf. A. Gwynn, "The Date of the B Text of *Piers Plowman*," *Review of English Studies* 19 (1943): 1–24, p. 4), followed by Kane 1988, 184; cf. the *Brut* 323/15–21. The term *rome-renner* (the activity implied by *ren* presumably indicates that physical, rather than intellectual, pursuits are at issue) here is certainly a neologism, but given its recurrence in two Lollard tracts from later in the century, probably not Langland's own invention, rather his appropriation of contemptuous slang; see further MED Rome n., sense 2(b). Bennett's effort ([*PMLA* 58] 566; 1972, 139 n. 288ff.) to connect A Version III. 185 'And made [my lord] merthe mournyng to leue' with the death of queen Philippa (1369) and Alice Perrers' 'comfort' seems to me forced.
7. For manuscript placements and general comments on their distribution, see Samuels [*ES* 44], 94; [*Medium Ævum* 55].
8. Cf. such claims for extensive hidden circulation of A as Samuels [*Medium Ævum* 55], Kane [in Alford] 1988, 184 and 186, and Doyle's more moderate statement, 36–37. On the belated circulation of this version, see further Adams [*SB* 45], 60–63; Hanna [*YLS* 7].

allusions in the B Version implies that Langland first extended the poem and only later rewrote the existing A Version portions, presumably to accord with his new and fuller perceptions of the work.[9]

Skeat dates the B Version 1377, largely on the basis of Prologue 193–96. These lines imply that Richard II was a minor heir or king, and thus must postdate the death of his father Edward the Black Prince on 8 June 1376; Richard's formal recognition as heir, his elevation as prince of Wales, occurred on 20 November. But the earliest new allusion, as Skeat sees, appears at XIII. 268–70 where Langland exactly dates John Chichester's service as mayor of London (1369–70). And the likely identification of the fatuous doctor of divinity with William Jordan O.P. (cf. B Version XIII. 84) also speaks for a date in the early 1370s. Jordan drops out of the historical record after 1368, and the joke would lose its force through time. Such allusions to events of c. 1366–70 early in the B *Vita* imply that the extension of the A Version into the B Version followed on the preparation of what would become the archetype behind all A Version copies without appreciable delay. The only historical reference in this portion of the poem which contradicts such a view occurs at XIII. 243–49a, where Hawkin alludes to a papal indulgence against the plague, granted in 1375 or 1376.[1]

In contrast, the latest allusions in the B Version occur in the Prologue. The fable of the Rat Parliament (Prologue 146–210) retells an anecdote associated with Bishop Brinton of Rochester's sermon on the occasion of The Good Parliament in 1376, albeit to an effect contrary to that urged by the bishop.[2] Similarly, Langland's foundation of the Commonwealth at Prologue 112–45 draws on the ceremony of the coronation of Richard II in July 1377.[3]

Efforts to link the poem with later events are considerably more tenuous. Perhaps the most persuasive potential allusion adduced occurs at Prologue 107–08:

> Ac of the cardinals at court that kaughte of that name
> And power presumed in hem a pope to make

The precision of 'at court' may specifically imply Avignon (rather than the Curia more generally), and the 'power presumed' may claim that the cardinals acted presumptuously, on their own initiative and not as a result of canon law or some special grace. If so, the lines may refer to the rump of French cardinals who elected the anti-pope Clement VII in September 1378 and thus precipitated the Great Schism (only resolved with the election of Martin V in 1417). But other possible allusions to events early in the Schism (e.g., B Version XIII. 173–76, XIX. 417–23, 428–29, 442–46a) prove less compelling; they may either represent abstract moral exhortations, unattached to any specific occasion, or, in a century during which

9. See Gwynn [*RES* 19], 16, 18–19, preferable to Bennett [*Medium Ævum* 12]:59.
1. On Jordan, see Gwynn [*RES* 19], 2–4, 23–24; and BRUO 2, 1022. For the papal indulgence, see Skeat, *loc. cit.*, followed by Bennett [*Medium Ævum* 12], 61–62; cf. the *Brut* 328 / 24–34.
2. For the sermon, see Devlin 1954, sermon 69, 2, 315–21. [For a translation of the anecdote, see p. 488 herein–*Editors.*] Delvin dates the sermon 18 May 1376, delivered to the convocation of clergy during the Good Parliament (see further 1, xxv–vi); for this parliament, cf. the *Brut* 329/25–330/26. The bishop urges his audience not to be rats because the rodents do not carry through their plan, not because, as Langland argues, their effort represents misbegotten self-interest. For further discussion, see Owst [*MLR* 20]; Kellogg [*PMLA* 50]; Orsten [*MS* 23]. For Brinton, see BRUO 1, 268–69.
3. See Bennett [*Medium Ævum* 12], 57; Donaldson 1949, 116–18.

both nations and popes waged war frequently, general references to repeated actions, not specific events of 1379.[4]

B Version manuscripts survive from an early date—at least five are probably of the 1390s—and they cluster in two areas.[5] Many show mixtures of linguistic forms which render exact placement of their scribes' origins impossible, but a substantial number of these include dialectical layers indicative of some stage of London copying. Nearly half of the sixteen full copies provide evidence of production in the metropolis (nos. 20, 24, 35; one underlay of 33) or adjacent areas (nos. 25, 34), and a trio (nos. 28–30) closely related in their physical similarities imply an ongoing formalized system of production which may be metropolitan. But equally prominently, other forms indicate some earlier West Midland transmission, especially in Worcestershire or adjacent counties; such western forms appear sporadically even in metropolitan copies. Manuscripts displaying evidence of such antecedents include nos. 21, 24 (Oxford), 28–30, 31, 32, and 33.

Dating the C Version

Informed discussion of the revision which produced the C Version must await the appearance of the Athlone edition. However, one can see that certain features of this activity are distinctly puzzling; the C manuscripts routinely blend many readings inherited from errors in the lost common ancestor behind the surviving B MSS. (i.e., many of the most plausible emendations which Kane and Donaldson adopt in their edited text do not appear here) with authorial revisions foreign to B. At the same time, many passages arguably show Langland in his revision wrestling with B Version scribal readings which he knew could not be what he had previously written but equally could not see how to restore.[6] It remains unclear how to account for this state of affairs, especially since the revision is of a piece with Langland's earlier expansion of the A Version. Given the evidence provided by manuscript provenance, the poet may have been physically separated from his B holograph (and thus forced to revise from scribal copy) in Worcestershire, not London, where he may even have given up his original to facilitate the production of copies of the B Version.

Discussion of this version has been handicapped by the assumptions that C is both an 'incomplete revision' and one reflecting a substantial diminution of poetic powers. But such views presume that Langland's response to his text should always have resembled the earlier, and necessarily extensive, activity by which he carefully converted the A Version into the B. And C can scarcely be faulted as poetry; although Langland may often remove verbal brilliances from B (B Version V. 495/C Version VII. 136 has often provided critics with a *locus classicus*), an addition like IX. 70–158 has struck many readers as more powerful than, yet perfectly harmonious with, the poetry of the earlier versions.

---

4. See, for Prologue 107–08, Bennett [*Medium Ævum* 12], 56; and for other such allusions, 62–63; Huppé 1941 (and cf. [Huppé, *SP* 46]). But Gwynn [*RES* 19], 4, 13–14 seems equally plausible in identifying such allusions with events of 1369–70 (cf. Kane's approval [in Alford] 1988, 184). * * *

5. For the information in this paragraph, see Samuels [*Medium Ævum* 55]. Although individual scribal profiles only identify that locale in which the scribe received his training, persistent repetition of forms associated with a single geographical area within a single textual tradition can be taken as testimony to repeated copying in that area.

6. See Kane-Donaldson 1975, 98–127 (123–27 especially address the nature of the C revision).

Perhaps the most distinctive feature of the C revision is the advancement of certain topics Langland had introduced in his B continuation so that they now occur within the C *Visio*. Examples include the consolidation of the two extensive passages on the Seven Deadly Sins (portions of B V and XIII are fused as C VI.1–VII.119), the advancement of many materials associated with minstrelsy, and the replacement of several late passages, excised in C, by more extended analogues (e.g. B Version XII. 1–27 now appears transformed as C V. 1–104, XIII. 150–57 as III. 332–405a). In addition, Langland added a small number of long passages, such as those on the poor, beggars, and lunatic lollares in C IX (which may compensate for the most remarkable C Version excision, Piers's tearing of the pardon) and extensively reworked a substantial, but still limited, number of others. This revision typically proceeds through large structural changes, not the persistent detailed work of the B revision; Langland did not worry over every line, as he did previously; hence he tacitly accepts many scribal alterations of his B Version holograph.

Moreover, as suggested above, this revision does not appear to have been completed; the final passus, C XXI and XXII, are unchanged from the B Version. Yet to take this as a sign of incompleteness assumes that Langland in revising the B Version proceeded sequentially though his poem and that he had not, at the end of the B composition, been satisfied with what he had done and then turned to revise the remainder of his poem into a commensurate form.[7] But Russell alleges that there remain signs that dissemination of the C Version was supervised by an editor, rather than the poet himself.

Establishing a *terminus a quo* for the C Version has proved as contentious as establishing the date of the poet's death. Kane suggests that C Version Prologue 135 indicates that Wycliffe's work *De potestate pape* was already in circulation, probably in 1379–80.[8] But *De potestate* deals with issues of ecclesiology a good deal more inflammatory than simply that of disputing papal elections, and Langland's position in the B version of these lines is probably just as orthodox as that in the C Version, if less directly stated.

Since Langland's C revision is usually thematic, rather than topical, inference has often been invoked in dating the C Version. Most commonly, scholars have tried to find revisions stimulated by the appropriation of Langland's work in June 1381 by John Ball, both in the sermon which, according to Thomas Walsingham, he delivered at Blackheath on 12 June and in the letter he addressed to the commons of Essex. Here argument has usually centered upon Langland's attitude toward the 'commune' and its political role; scholars have found evidence of antipathy toward the 'commune's' participation in government in the revision of C Version Prologue 140 (either alone or in conjunction with the excision of B Version Prologue 143–45 from the C Version).[9]

A similar example has perhaps better textual support. Langland also excised the 'trewe wedded libbing folk' of B Version IX. 110 and extensively revised Wit's disquisition on spiritual genetics. This decision may represent a direct response to John Ball's association of salvation with marriage and

7. Cf. Donaldson 1949, 32.
8. See Kane [in Alford] 1988, 185; and for Wycliffe, BRUO 3, 2103–06.
9. See Kane [in Alford] 1988, 185; Baldwin 1981, 15–18, but contrast Donaldson 1949, 108.

of virtuous marriage with Adam and Eve (an opinion which is certainly not Lollard, as other views which chroniclers attribute to Ball are) and which he might well have derived from the B Version, which his letter shows he knew. Not only would such a revision provide a direct sign of Langland's seeking to distance himself from revolutionary appropriation in 1381, but it would indicate a *terminus a quo* for at least part of his work.[1] Given the evidence for the poet's reliance on the 1388 promulgation of the Statute of Labourers, Langland may have worked on the C Version throughout the 1380s.

The dialectically localizable C manuscripts cluster geographically to a degree unparalleled by the manuscripts of the other versions, and some of them—at least eleven may be of the fourteenth century—are among the oldest copies of the poem. On this evidence the C Version appears to have been disseminated from south-western Worcestershire, perhaps specifically the Malvern area. Of the twenty unconflated C copies, six (nos. 39, 40, 41, 42, 44, 49), show Worcestershire forms, although four (39, 41, 42, and 49) certainly, or likely, were copied in London, as were the C portions of the conflated no. 35 and the fragment no. 58). In addition, nine other copies (nos. 43, 46, 48, 51, 52, 53, 55, 56, 57) may be placed in counties adjacent to Worcestershire, and two other copies come from Oxfordshire (nos. 47, 54). Such localizations of the scribes' origins support the theory that Langland returned late in life to Malvern, and that the C Version was distributed at an early date from that provincial centre, perhaps by another individual who took over the poet's papers.

*   *   *

C. DAVID BENSON

Piers Plowman and Parish Wall Paintings†1

More than fifty years ago, at the conclusion of his article "The Present State of *Piers Plowman* Studies," Morton Bloomfield called for "a general study of the backgrounds" of Langland's poem in such areas as folklore, art, theology, and homilies: "The basic purpose is not to find sources, necessarily, but to make possible a new understanding of the intellectual and social atmosphere of fourteenth-century England" (25).[2] Many scholars have responded to Bloomfield's call, and we now have detailed discussions of *Piers* in relation to such things as the liturgy, biblical exegesis, sermons, and the academic *moderni*. Studies of the second item on Bloomfield's list—art—have been relatively infrequent, however, perhaps because

1. See Justice * * * 1994—*Writing and Rebellion: England in 1381* (Berkeley: U of California P).
† From *The Yearbook of Langland Studies* 11 (1997): 1–38. Reprinted by permission of the publisher.
1. I want especially to thank David Park for his interest and help throughout this project and James Simpson for his stimulating analysis and suggestions for improving an early version of this paper. I am also grateful to Thorlac Turville-Petre, Douglas Gray, Derek Pearsall, Vincent DiMarco, Eamon Duffy, and Kathleen Scott for reading and commenting on various drafts of the essay. Finally, I want to thank a number of audiences in England and the United States (especially the Southeastern Medieval Association), who challenged and encouraged my attempts to explore the visual in *Piers Plowman*.
2. See "Works Cited" at the end of this essay for full citations [*Editors*].

scholars have been uneasy about exactly what form of art can properly be compared with *Piers Plowman*.[3] Illuminations in expensive manuscripts (the images most frequently used by scholars when discussing medieval literature) seem inappropriate to such a popular work, though a lone *Piers* manuscript (Douce 104) has an extensive series of lively colored drawings. But there is one kind of visual art that would have been known to everyone in medieval England: the wall paintings in local parish churches. Although murals, like sermons and plays, are a significant contemporary religious discourse, they have been largely ignored in studies of *Piers Plowman*.[4]

* * *

The great age of English wall painting was between the twelfth and sixteenth centuries—roughly from the Norman Invasion to the Reformation. We know that there were Anglo-Saxon wall paintings, but few are extant.[5] The most ambitious medieval mural schemes in England, those in royal palaces and cathedrals, are largely gone, though a few fragments remain to suggest something of what we have lost. Two superb examples are a tender thirteenth-century Madonna and Child from the bishop's private chapel in Chichester, and the late fourteenth-century paintings of the Virgin and other saints from the Byward Tower in the Tower of London.[6] Most English wall paintings that survive today are found in rural parishes, which were less likely to have been remodeled than cathedrals or city churches. Once such works were everywhere. * * * In what follows, I shall discuss only parish murals (ignoring those few that survive in cathedrals and private buildings) because these are the works that would have been most available (and available most constantly) to the author and, of even more importance for this study, to the lay and clerical audience of *Piers Plowman*.

3. Derek Pearsall's recent *An Annotated Critical Bibliography of Langland*, which is not exhaustive, lists only five articles in his section on *"Piers Plowman* and the Visual Arts." By far the most influential of these is by Elizabeth Salter, which will be discussed below.
4. Only three articles known to me discuss *Piers Plowman* in relationship to English wall paintings. All are brief treatments that attempt to identify the source or influence of specific passages with results that are either wrong or unconvincing. Early in the century E. W. Tristram claimed that the fairly common late-medieval subject of Christ surrounded by tools and other daily objects, such as that at Hesset, Suffolk, or Breage, Cornwall, was directly inspired by our poem and showed Piers the laborer as Christ ("Piers Plowman in English Wall-Painting"; see also Tristram, *14th*, 121–25). For the Breage painting, see Rouse, *Medieval Wall Paintings*, illus. 72, and Caiger-Smith, pl. 20).
   Charlotte D'Evelyn quickly disputed Tristram's explanation of this image and instead identified the tools as the instruments of the Passion. Subsequent research, however, suggests that the image is actually a warning to those who work or play on the Sabbath, like the merchants in passus 7 of *Piers Plowman* who "holde noght hir haliday as Holy Chirche techeth" (B.7.20). Rouse describes a similar image in San Miniato, Florence, with an accompanying inscription that identifies it as a warning against Sabbath breaking (*Medieval Wall Paintings* 68; see also Binski 15).
   A section of a third article by Robert Kaske proposed that the mirror of Middle Earth in *Piers* (B.11.9) may have been suggested to Langland by wall paintings of the Wheel of Life near his Malvern home, such as the one still extant (but very obscure) at Kempley, Gloucestershire, though even Kaske admits that the evidence is not completely convincing. The loss of so many medieval murals and our almost complete ignorance of the life of the poet of *Piers Plowman* make any attempt to identify the precise source of particular images in the work difficult if not impossible.
5. Perhaps the best surviving example is the angels at Nether Wallop, Hampshire; for this and other early paintings, see the introduction and essays in the collection edited by Cather, Park, and Williamson.
6. For the paintings in the Byward Tower, see Tristram, *14th*, plates 8b, 9a–b, 10; Alexander and Binski, catalogue 696. Other examples of wall paintings in cathedrals or royal buildings include the twelfth-century St. Paul from St. Anselm's Chapel in Canterbury Cathedral (Rouse, *Medieval Wall Paintings*, illus. 19), the paintings at Winchester discussed by David Park in "The Wall Paintings of the Holy Sepulchre Chapel," and the fourteenth-century biblical episodes formerly in St. Stephen's Chapel, Westminster, and now in the British Museum (Alexander and Binski, catalogue 680).

*   *   *

I make four assumptions about wall paintings for the purposes of this study. First, such painting was highly conventional in order to communicate to a wide audience: although no two churches would have had identical mural schemes (and their quality varied greatly), a relatively limited number of recognizable subjects are used.[7] Second, every image now extant represents many that were present in the Middle Ages. If several images survive today, we can be reasonably confident that many more existed in the Middle Ages. Third, there seems to have been no great difference in the subjects of wall paintings from one part of England to another (with the exception of local saints), and therefore murals that now survive largely in the east and south can represent the entire country. Fourth, we need not restrict ourselves to paintings from Langland's lifetime because many earlier schemes survived unchanged into the fourteenth century, and later works are often repaintings of earlier work.[8]

My study might seem doomed from the start by the famous condemnation of stained glass and wall painting in *Piers Plowman* itself. After she arrives in Westminster, Meed corruptly promises the friars that if they will go easy on lecherous lords in confession, she will decorate their church: "Wowes do whiten and wyndowes glazen, / Do peynten and portraye who paied for the makynge" (B.3.61–62).[9] Although the narrator goes on to condemn all such prideful displays, the criticism of religious art may be less severe than it first appears. Primarily concerned with the making of windows (though painting is mentioned), the lines are specifically aimed at those who use art to boast publicly about good deeds that should be known only to God: "To writen in wyndowes of youre wel dedes" (3.70). Image making for the right reasons is not necessarily forbidden, any more than the biblical citation that immediately follows, which criticizes ostentatious alms giving, is a prohibition against genuine charity (3.71–75). By restating Christian doctrine and stories, wall paintings are doing in images what *Piers Plowman* does in poetry—not that Langland finds his own artistic practice unproblematic.

The connections I want to suggest between *Piers Plowman* and contemporary paintings are not direct or clear-cut. As Bloomfield's words quoted at the beginning of this essay had urged, I am not looking for sources (or influences), but instead I hope "to make possible a new understanding of the intellectual and social atmosphere of fourteenth-century England."[1]

7. Murals can be roughly divided into five categories: (1) decorative schemes; (2) the Last Judgment or Doom; (3) narratives of the life of Christ, especially the Nativity and Passion; (4) lives or single figures of saints, apostles, and the Virgin, including the single most frequent image in parish churches, St. Christopher carrying the Christ child; and (5) moralities, especially the Seven Deadly Sins and the Seven Works of Mercy. Rouse gives a slightly different list of categories, *Medieval Wall Paintings* 35.

8. Many twelfth-century mural schemes must have been visible in Langland's time, like the Apocalypse scene in the chancel at Kempley near Malvern (the same church mentioned by Kaske, though he discussed a different and later image). Such older paintings might possibly have had some influence on what some have seen as the occasionally old-fashioned spirituality of *Piers*. The images I shall directly compare with *Piers* were extant before the third quarter of the fourteenth century, unless otherwise indicated, though precise dating of parish painting, in the almost total absence of surviving records, is extremely difficult.

9. Caiger-Smith quotes the citation of St. Bernard in *Jacob's Well* on the vanity of wall paintings while the poor are naked and needy (90). I use the B text of *Piers Plowman* throughout, unless otherwise noted. Quotations are from the 1995 Everyman edition by A. V. C. Schmidt. References to the C text are to Pearsall's edition.

1. Unlike Kaske, my interest is not in the author's particular sources or in the author alone. Neither, unlike V.A. Kolve in his study of imagery and Chaucer, am I attempting to find images in the

* * *

Let me give a brief example of what an awareness of wall painting may contribute. By far the most stimulating discussion of *Piers Plowman* and the
visual arts is by Elizabeth Salter, though the only murals she mentions are Ital-
ian. In one section of her essay, Salter argues that the exemplar for Langland's
Tree of Charity might have been illustrations of allegorical trees in religious
treatises such as British Library Additional 37049, though she also notes the
difference between these simple drawings and the complexities that Langland
creates. I agree that the poet's actual inspiration might have been one of these
manuscripts, but allegorical trees would also have been widely known to him
and to his audience from their frequent appearance on church walls. * * *
Common mural examples from the second half of the fourteenth century are
trees of the Seven Deadly Sins, as at Hesset (fig. 1), which has branches ending in dragon heads supporting the individual sins, or at Hoxne, Suffolk, and
corresponding trees of the Seven Works of Mercy at Hoxne and Barnby, Suffolk.[2] A different but common kind of tree on parish walls is the genealogical
Tree of Jesse, as at Black Bourton, Oxfordshire, or Weston Longville, Norfolk.[3]

Such paintings thus provide a historical context for the Tree of Charity
that has not previously been noted. At the same time, on the formal level,
they remind us just how fundamentally schematic *Piers Plowman* is. For all
its intellectual sophistication, the poem keeps returning to diagrammatic
allegories, such as Piers's account of the route to Truth (5.560–629) or the
description of the castle made by Kind at the beginning of passus 9. Yet, as
Salter cautioned, such visual images, whether from manuscripts or church
walls, do not begin to equal the dynamism of Langland's poetic practice. For
example, Anima's initial description of the Tree of Charity (16.4–9) associates each part with a virtue (e.g., the root is mercy and the leaves faithful
words); similar to the simple didactic meanings that can be read out from
one of the mural trees of the sins or virtues. When Piers the Plowman is
mentioned, however, the narrator suddenly falls into an inner dream, and
the tree, now actually present before him, changes into what David Aers has
called a disclosure rather than picture model (79–107), a complex and shifting allegory: now the Trinity, now the three states of chastity, now those who
lived before the birth of Christ (16.60–85). The genealogical and moral
trees, which remain separate in wall paintings, are fused in the poem, so that
the static diagram becomes something like a motion picture. * * *
In contrast to manuscript illuminations, murals are especially appropriate for *Piers* because they are not elite art designed for the privileged few,

---

narrative that an audience might hold in its mind as it reads and thinks about the poem. Indeed, I
do not have space in this essay to deal with all the aspects of Langland's special kind of visual imagination. I am, however, encouraged by Kolve's call for new kinds of interdisciplinary scholarship:
"We are only beginning to understand the issues involved in using pictures as a means of recovering the meaning of literary texts, only beginning the hard tasks of historical scholarship, method-
ological refinement, and sympathetic imagination necessary if we would restore what was once a
vital and viable relation between the two" (3).
2. The Hesset tree seems to be from c. 1400 (Caiger-Smith 173). Tristram, *14th*, notes that the
Deadly Sins and Works of Mercy, along with the Doom, are the subjects "more often found after
c. 1350 than any others" (20), and he discusses the frequency of trees of the Sins and Works in
the fourteenth century (102).
3. For the thirteenth-century Jesse tree at Black Bourton, see Tristram, *13th*, pl. 108b; for the later
one at Weston Longville, see Tristram, *14th*, plates 22–24.

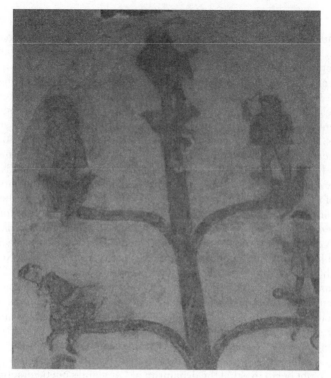

Figure 1. The Seven Deadly Sins (Hesset)

but rather the most prominent religious art in everyday life.[4] The subjects and style of wall paintings would have been known from childhood to the poet and his entire audience, whatever their social status. Although the poet assumes literacy in his readers, he must never have been confident about what the national audience he sought to reach had actually read. But everyone had always seen wall paintings. They were one of the most widely shared cultural experiences of both author and audience. They provided a common grammar, a ubiquitous repertoire of images, and an aesthetic, which the poet draws on (whether consciously or not) for his own more challenging religious discourse.[5]

※   ※   ※

4. The difference between elite and popular art is dramatically shown at Thornham Parva in Suffolk. Today this little country church displays on its altar the Thornham Parva Retable, one of the great achievements of East Anglian medieval painting. In the Middle Ages, the retable was not to be found in the parish church but probably on the high altar of the Dominican priory at Thetford. The non-cloistered clergy and laymen of Thornham had to make do with the wall paintings in the church (of the Nativity and the Life of St. Edmund), whose vigorous narrative style is in many ways more like Piers Plowman than the courtly, iconic retable.
5. Wall paintings may have also helped readers of Piers understand its irony. For example, at the end of passus 10 the Dreamer argues against the need for works and learning because some, such as Mary Magdalene and the Apostle Paul, who acted wickedly during their lives, are now saved (10.421–24). The clerically trained reader might well perceive the dubiousness of the Dreamer's reasoning here even before Imaginatif's correction in passus 12, but so would less educated contemporaries (unlike some modern critics) who had seen the Magdalene and Paul portrayed so often and so positively on their church walls.

II

Medieval churches of all sizes and importance often made a clear distinction between the chancel, the domain of the clergy, and the nave, the place of the people, frequently separating the two by a rood screen. Often, though certainly not always, there was a difference of mural subjects in the two spaces. As Tristram has written about twelfth-century painting, "The nave, devoted to the laity, represented the world, and its walls were therefore reserved for the delineation of events more closely associated with ordinary human existence, including the earthly life of Christ, the Virgin, and the Saints. . . . The chancel was conceived as Heaven, as Heaven would be after the Last Day."[6] This distinction can clearly be seen at Kempley, Gloucestershire, only a few miles from the Malvern Hills, where the nave contains a variety of earthly subjects painted in the fourteenth century (one of which, an apparent Wheel of Life, is discussed by Kaske), whereas the chancel has a remarkably well-preserved twelfth-century vision of the New Jerusalem based on John's *Apocalypse*, with Christ in heavenly majesty adored by angels and apostles (Caiger-Smith, plates 1 and 2). From roughly the same period is a narrative sequence of the Passion of Christ on the north wall of the nave at Ickleton, Cambridgeshire, with the painful martyrdoms of apostles depicted below. Subjects that are even more of this world are the practical moralities found in many naves, such as warnings against Sabbath breaking (see note 4 above) or against idle chatter and dispute, as in a vivid fourteenth-century image at Melbourne, Derbyshire, of devils urging on two women.[7]

The common if not inevitable distinction between a Christianity of this world in the nave and a Christianity of the hereafter in the chancel can help us to see a crucial way in which *Piers Plowman* differs from other contemporary religious writing. Despite the intensity of its spirituality, *Piers* remains with the earthly subjects of the nave. It contains none of the mystical flights of such works as the *Cloud of Unknowing* nor any attempt to describe the divine realms as is done with such virtuosity in *Pearl*. From the plowing of the half-acre through the jousting of Christ at Jerusalem to the assault on the barn of Unity (for all its apocalyptic coloring), *Piers Plowman* is about achieving the Christian life in this world. Three of the most popular mural schemes of the nave illuminate aspects of *Piers Plowman*: the first is a spectacle, the Doom or Last Judgment; the second is a narrative, the life of Christ; and the third is a morality, the Seven Deadly Sins, often paired with the Seven Works of Mercy.

The Doom or Last Judgment was the most prominent and dramatic scene in English wall painting.[8] A powerful fifteenth-century example is found in the parish church of St. Thomas, Salisbury, which because it is

---

6. Tristram, *12th* 9; see also Caiger-Smith 1–2. In general, parishioners seem to have been responsible for the upkeep and decoration of the nave, and rectors for the upkeep and decoration of the chancel; see Cook 23, Platt 37, and Binski 40.

7. On warnings against idle gossip, see Rouse, *Medieval Wall Paintings* 68 (and illus. 78), and Alexander and Binski, catalogue 557, which records nine examples of the subject in the thirteenth and fourteenth centuries and notes that the Melbourne image "may also contain a witchcraft element, with the object the women are exchanging possibly to be identified as the Host" (444).

8. The elements of the Doom are based on Matt. 24:30–31; 25:31–34, 41, 46. See Caiger-Smith 31–43. For a full discussion and catalogue of English Dooms, see the admirable study by Ashby. In his *Testament*, Villon has his mother say that she is a poor old woman who cannot read but that on the walls of her parish church she can see painted paradise and hell. She prays to the Virgin that she might go to the good place (lines 893–902).

repainted gives a sense of the visual impact of the Doom when new (fig. 2). As at Salisbury, the Doom was usually, though certainly not always, placed over the chancel arch directly facing the congregation (Tristram, *14th* 19). As this location suggests, the Doom is a transitional subject between the chancel and the nave, picturing both the last day of earth and the eternal destinations—heaven and hell. Many surviving Dooms are from the fifteenth century, but most of its elements are found as early as the late eleventh or early twelfth century at Clayton, Sussex (Tristram, *12th*, plates 36–43; Baker; and Park, "Lewes Group"). At the center of the chancel arch is Christ in a mandorla displaying his wounds flanked by the apostles (fig. 3). At Clayton the scheme fills the entire nave: on the north wall, the dead rise from graves to be weighed for salvation or damnation by the Archangel Michael and Peter welcomes the saved into the New Jerusalem; on the south wall the damned are driven into hell by a devil on a horse.

Three centuries later, in the crude, fragmentary remains from a fourteenth-century Doom at Ickleton, the central image is still recognizably similar, though Christ now sits on a rainbow, and the apostles have been replaced by two beseeching figures, John the Baptist on his left (often this is John the Apostle, as in images of the Crucifixion) and the Virgin on his right (in this case baring her breasts in supplication).[9] The Salisbury Doom includes the two beseeching figures as well as the apostles. In another late Doom from Wenhaston, Suffolk, painted on wood but originally placed over the chancel arch, we find Christ with Mary and John (though unusually on the same side), whereas below, as on the walls of Clayton, are the dead rising from their graves and Michael weighing their souls, who are then either welcomed by Peter to the New Jerusalem on Christ's right or herded into hell on his left (fig. 4).

The Doom is a neglected contemporary context for *Piers Plowman*. Critics have long recognized the Dreamer's powerful desire to save his soul, but it has perhaps not been sufficiently appreciated that salvation and damnation were not just orthodox doctrine known intellectually by the poet and his audience, but the most vivid and complex image in their churches. The Day of Doom is repeatedly referred to in *Piers*, as at the anguished conclusion of Robert the Robber's plea: "Dampne me noght at Domesday for that I dide so ille!" (5.471). Truth's pardon, which is given such attention at the end of the Visio, is all about the Last Judgment: "*Et qui bona egerunt ibunt in vitam eternam; / Qui vero mala, in ignem eternum*" (7.110a–b). The starkly opposed destinations of the pardon echo those of the Doom. Near the end of the poem, in the important *redde quod debes* section, we hear of Christ's second coming, when he will judge humans "at domesday, bothe quyke and dede— / The goode to the Godhede and to greet joye, / And wikkede to wonye in wo withouten ende" (19.197–99).[1]

Although *Piers Plowman* never describes the complete visual scheme of the Doom, the poet could rely on his audience's familiarity with specific

9. Park, "Ickleton," pl. 14. For another example of Mary baring her breast (in a Doom on the side wall of what seems to have then been a one-cell church at North Cove, Suffolk), see Rouse, *Medieval Wall Paintings*, illus. 69.
1. Other references, direct or implicit, to the Day of Judgment include 1.128–32 (an early version of Truth's pardon); 2.103–07; 5.20, 274, 293; 7.172, 188, 201; 10.358, 410; 11.134; 12.91; 18.386; 20.294.

Figures 2 and 3. The Last Judgment (St. Thomas, Salisbury, and Clayton, Sussex)

elements. The "tour" and "dongeon" at the very beginning of the poem may owe something to the staging of contemporary drama, as has been suggested (Carruthers 28), but readers are just as likely to have associated this awesome duality of good and evil places with the New Jerusalem and hell of the more frequently seen Doom. Here also appears the only example in the wall paintings of the social criticism of Church and State in *Piers Plowman*. Kings, queens, clergy, and bishops (whose otherwise naked figures reveal their offices by their somewhat incongruous headgear) are often welcomed into heaven in Dooms such as that at Wenhaston (fig. 4); but in others, such as the magnificent if restored Doom at South Leigh, those who hold these powerful positions in church and state are sent chained to hell.[2]

---

2. Avarice, which John Yunck has identified as the "great, tawdry sin" of Langland's world (145), is prominently punished in many Dooms, as in the damned soul with money bags from the fifteenth-

Figure 4. The Last Judgment (Wenhaston, Suffolk)

For all its potential terror (perhaps overemphasized by modern commentators), the Doom tempers justice with mercy, especially in the figures of Mary and John who were introduced to the scheme as intercessors. Over time the weighing of souls by the archangel Michael, which was part of the early Last Judgment at Clayton, also became less severe through the addition of the Virgin, who often tips the balance in favor of the sinner. Wenhaston has a late weighing without the Virgin but with the Devil holding a scroll of indictment, whereas Slapton, Northhamptonshire, has a weighing separated from the Doom (as often in the later period) in which the Virgin intercedes for the soul by placing her prayer beads on the scale in its favor (fig. 5).

The popular wall painting of the weighing of a soul at death by Michael seems to be evoked when Truth promises merchants their own pardon if they use their profits for good causes:

> "And I shal sende yow myselve Seynt Michel myn angel,
> That no devel shal yow dere ne drede in your deying,
> And witen yow fro wanhope, if ye wol thus werche,
> And sende youre soules in saufte to my Seintes in joye."
> (7.33–36)[3]

The common mural image possibly evoked by these lines has not been recognized, and the relationship between painting and poetry may be even more complex. Truth's Michael is as strict as Truth's pardon; he will shield only those merchants who have used their winnings profitably. There is no

---

century mural at Chesterton, Cambridgeshire. Perhaps the most dramatic example of social criticism is the thirteenth-century Ladder of Salvation scheme, a variation of the standard Doom, at Chaldon, Surrey (fig. 6; Caiger-Smith, pl. 12), in which devils punish a variety of trades for their commercial sins. A central figure subject to special punishment is a man with money bags around his waist from whose mouth burning coins fall.

3. The weighing is not explicitly mentioned in these lines, and the reference might be generally to the traditional Christian belief that the saved were escorted to heaven by angels, especially archangels, as suggested to me by Kathleen Scott: see Sheingorn. Nevertheless, given the popularity of the weighing in parish murals, the specific naming of St. Michael would probably have evoked this image to contemporaries. For the weighing, see Caiger-Smith 58–63. His plate 21 has a weighing with Virgin from Swalcliffe, Oxfordshire.

Figure 5. Intercession of the Virigin at a Weighing of a Soul (Slapton, Northamptonshire)

grace for evildoers, perhaps because there is no Virgin. Or is she only deferred? In fact, Mary does appear at the very end of the passus, offering a more merciful (though still demanding) hope for humans at Domesday:

> Forthi I counseille alle Cristene to crie God mercy,
> And Marie his moder be oure meene bitwene,
> That God gyve us grace here, er we go hennes,
> Swiche werkes to werche, while we ben here,
> That after oure deth day, Dowel reherce
> At the day of dome, we dide as he highte.
> (7.196–201)[4]

These lines are a powerful expression, repeated often in the poem, of the human need for both works and mercy: Mary's grace saves the sinner not absolutely but by permitting him to do well. In contrast to the promiscuous mercy to all who call on her when in trouble that is found in contemporary Miracles of the Virgin and implied in the murals of the weighing, Mary's help in *Piers Plowman* demands an active response during one's lifetime.

In keeping with its theology of the nave, *Piers Plowman* does not directly portray either of the eternal destinations of the Last Judgment. Perhaps more surprising than the absence of the New Jerusalem in *Piers* is the poet's refusal to describe the terrors of hell, which are so prominent in Dooms. The demonic torments of damned sinners, found as early as the Clayton Doom and portrayed dramatically in a thirteenth-century variation of the Last Judgment at Chaldon (fig. 6), would seem well suited to the

4. Nigel Morgan argues that although Mary interceding with her beads at the weighing of souls is found in the thirteenth-century *Golden Legend*, it does not appear in English art until the third quarter of the fourteenth century (50–51). Even if this late dating is correct, Mary as a more general intercessor is a prominent theme in thirteenth- and fourteenth-century Dooms.

Figure 6. Ladder of Salvation or Last Judgement (Chaldon)

poet's deep interest in social abuses and his thirst for justice against the wicked.[5]

Yet the lively devils of the Doom are not wholly absent from *Piers Plowman*. They are found during an optimistic event, the Harrowing of Hell. When fiends and fiendkins appear, it is not triumphantly to drag men and women into eternal damnation; instead the devils are themselves conquered by Christ during the Harrowing, which occupies so much of passus 18. The repetition of an identical image in two different mural schemes may help us understand what the poet has done. In English wall paintings the whale-like hellmouth of the Doom, as in the Wenhaston Doom (fig. 4), is also found in depictions of the Harrowing of Hell, as in an early fourteenth-century example from North Cove, Suffolk (fig. 7).[6] *Piers* contains the Harrowing, whose special prominence in the poem has long been recognized, but not the damnation. Hellmouth with its many active devils is present in the poem only in a context of hope and mercy. We are shown not the terrible execution of the law on the sinful but their rescue. Because of the moral intensity of *Piers Plowman*, its emphasis on Christ's redemption and grace is sometimes downplayed. The positive and negative contexts of the hellmouth in wall paintings can help us redress the balance and remind us of how often the poem portrays mercy.[7] * * *

---

5. The Chaldon scheme, a ladder of salvation, shows some human beings led to salvation; others, especially those guilty of commercial sins, tortured by devils (Caiger-Smith, pl. 12). This social criticism, prominent in *Piers*, anticipates the increased number of professional abusers (from lawyers to alewives) among the damned in fifteenth- and sixteenth-century Dooms (Ashby 175–81).

6. Other examples of the Harrowing include a huge (though now obscure) thirteenth-century Harrowing at Brent Eleigh, Suffolk (which may not have had a hellmouth), and a fourteenth-century image at Chalgrove, Oxfordshire (Tristram, *14th*, pl. 32). A later, though clearer (because repainted) example is at Pickering, Yorkshire.

7. Knowledge of wall paintings may thus contribute further answers to Morton Bloomfield's question, "Why did Langland concentrate on the Harrowing of Hell rather than, say, the Incarnation or Passion in [passus 18]?" (*Apocalypse* 123).

Figure 7. The Harrowing of Hell (North Cove, Suffolk)

The focus of the Crucifixion in *Piers* is less on divine suffering than on human benefit because of the prominence given to the figure of the blind knight Longinus, who is made to spear Jesus's dead body on the cross. As he does so, the blood from the Savior's body restores his sight, prompting the knight to fall to his knees and beg for mercy [B.18.78–87]. This powerful scene is frequently marked by the scribes and early readers of B-text manuscripts of *Piers Plowman*. The emphasis on Longinus, which surprises some modern readers, would not have surprised the original audience of *Piers*. Although the poet himself may be depending on a written source as he claims, even the least learned among his readers would have known the story from wall paintings, for it was one of the most popular images in English parish churches, as it was in expensive Books of Hours.[8]

Like the Harrowing of Hell, Longinus is an answer to the Doom. He is an example of God's mercy and redemption: his evil act brings salvation, a reversal best summed up in one single, punning line: "The blood sprong doun by the spere and unspered the knyghtes eighen." The poet seems here to be building on a paradoxical treatment of the knight that would already have been familiar to his audience. The murals frequently show Longinus still with the spear in his hand as he points to his now opened or unspeared eye. At Peakirk, Cambridgeshire, an image from about 1360 is particularly compressed and thus close to the passage in *Piers* (fig. 8). As Clive Rouse has demonstrated, four separate incidents (two bad and two good) are merged into this single scene: Longinus is shown both attacking and kneeling in homage; he points to his healed left eye while his right eye remains closed and blind ("St. Pega"; see also Rouse, *Medieval Wall Paintings* 18 and illus. 5). The image is crudely painted, but it has the fused layers of meanings, which must be unpacked by the audience, so often found in the concentrated poetry of *Piers Plowman*.

---

8. Longinus is pictured in thirteenth- and fourteenth-century wall paintings at Croughton; North Cove; Duxford, Cambridgeshire; Great Tew, Oxfordshire; Barnby (perhaps later) and Wissington, Suffolk; and Wisborough, Sussex.

Figure 8. Longinus (Peakirk, Cambridge)

I shall conclude by suggesting that wall painting can help us appreciate both the complex structure of *Piers Plowman* and the way it was meant to be read. What most bothers modern critics about *Piers* is its sometimes bewildering mixture of allegory, description, and narrative, which seems to lack any principle of organization or coherence. Thus C. S. Lewis asserts that Langland "hardly makes his poetry into a poem" (161), and Salter and Pearsall counsel us to accept that "Langland is not committed to a narrative structure in any continuous way" (32). Those more used to Chaucer's storytelling, which never loses its coherence even in the digressions of the Wife of Bath's Prologue, are continually frustrated by the narrative discontinuities of *Piers Plowman*.

An audience brought up on parish wall paintings, rather than novels and films, would have been much more comfortable than we are with the poem's disharmonies, as we can see in the crowded and eclectic interior of the little church at Slapton. In addition to various decorative motifs and a large St. Christopher mural, which contains a delightful mermaid looking at herself in a mirror, the images at Slapton include St. Michael weighing a soul at death with the Virgin intervening, which I have already noted (fig. 5); St. Francis receiving the stigmata; a resurrection scene with donor; St. Anne teaching the Virgin; the devil urging on two gossiping women; a mysterious man with a tree, who may be Judas; an annunciation scene; a scene from the life of St. Eligius; and the remains of a "three living and three dead" motif (in which three rich kings confront the three skeletons they shall become). There are fragments of other paintings and evidence that there were once many more.[9]

---

9. See Tristram, *14th* 247, who dates the paintings at Slapton "c. 1350 or just after the early part of the following century," without explaining whether he means that some are earlier and some later or that the dating of all is uncertain.

Two other examples of churches that still preserve a wide variety of fourteenth-century imagery include Barton, Cambridgeshire, and Belchamp Walter, Essex. At Belchamp Walter, the east end

Long familiarity with the art in such churches must have prepared contemporary readers of *Piers Plowman* in ways that are denied to us. Murals such as those at Slapton would have provided the poet's audience not only with a range of specific religious images, but also with the experience of stylistic and narrative variety within a single structure. Like *Piers* but unlike some other forms of medieval art, murals contain a variety of genres: narrative sequences as well as icons and didactic moralities. The violent transitions and juxtapositions of material in the poem, which appear so difficult and even perverse to modern readers, would have seemed more natural to contemporary readers—as it will to us once we are aware of this neglected form.

Murals may also help us understand something that I can only hint at here: the way that *Piers Plowman* was meant to be read (see also Benson, "The Frustration of Narrative"). Wall paintings, unlike modern art in a museum, were not seen on only a few special occasions; instead they would have been gradually absorbed over many years. In a similar way, *Piers Plowman* was not designed to be read straight through like a novel (which is why those who do so are disappointed or confused), but rather, like other religious treatises, read piecemeal, not necessarily always in the same order, and repeatedly. * * *

Indeed, the audience of both the poem and the painting might have received a range of different messages. Although parish murals are orthodox and may have been used by homilists for direct instruction, sometimes the images on the walls must have been more attractive than the words from the pulpit. The very variety of the murals would have made them susceptible to individual interpretation. Observers could choose to look at some rather than others, and understand them idiosyncratically. What lessons did women parishioners draw from images of the Virgin, for example, or from the frequent stories of heroic female saints? As modern criticism has shown us, *Piers Plowman*, despite its apparent didacticism, is also open to multiple interpretation, which is perhaps only truly possible in the comfort of a widely shared system of belief like that of late-medieval Catholic England.

✳   ✳   ✳

Works Cited

Adams, Robert. "Langland's Theology." *A Companion to Piers Plowman.* Ed. John A. Alford. Berkeley: University of California Press, 1988. 87–114.

---

of the north wall of the nave has a compressed Passion sequence (from the entrance into Jerusalem to Christ before Pilate) and below that a martyrdom of St. Edmund, a pelican feeding her children with the blood from her own breast, and a "three living and three dead" motif. Further west on the north wall are a charming icon of the Virgin and Child and the remains of a rebirth of the phoenix. On the south wall are fragments of a Resurrection scene, and further east the remains of a Seven Deadly Sins, with a central Pride being attacked by Death with a lance.

Although twelfth-century parish schemes are often very coherent (such as the Last Judgment that fills three walls at Clayton), murals in the next two centuries may be a jumble of diverse subjects. Some scholars find this change a decline, though my argument makes no such value judgment. For example, Park, "Wall Painting," argues that in the thirteenth century the "coherence of organization and subject-matter of all but the most major schemes begins to break down," which results in an "odd diversity of subjects" (126; cf. 129).

Aers, David. *Piers Plowman and Christian Allegory*. London, 1975.

Alexander, Jonathan, and Paul Binski, eds. *Age of Chivalry: Art in Plantagenet England 1200–1400*. London, 1987.

Ashby, Jane E. *English Medieval Murals of the Doom: A Descriptive Catalogue and Introduction*. M. A. Thesis. York University, 1980.

Aston, Margaret. "Lollards and Images." *Lollards and Reformers: Images and Literacy in Late Medieval Religion*. London, 1984. 135–92.

———. *England's Iconoclasts*. 2 vols. Oxford, 1988.

Baker, A. M. "The Wall Paintings in the Church of St. John the Baptist, Clayton." *Sussex Archaeological Collections* 108 (1970): 58–81.

Benson, C. David. "The Frustration of Narrative and the Reader in *Piers Plowman*." *Art and Context in Late Medieval English Narrative: Essays in Honor of Robert Worth Frank, Jr.* Ed. Robert R. Edwards. Cambridge, 1994. 1–15.

Binski, Paul. *Medieval Craftsmen: Painters*. Toronto, 1991.

Bloomfield, Morton. *Piers Plowman as a Fourteenth-century Apocalypse*. New Brunswick, nd (1961).

———. "The Present State of *Piers Plowman* Studies," *Speculum* 14 (1939): 215–32. Rpt. in Blanch 3–25.

Bowers, John. *The Crisis of Will in Piers Plowman*. Washington, 1986.

Burrow, John. "The Audience of *Piers Plowman*." *Anglia* 75 (1957): 373–84.

Caiger-Smith, A. *English Medieval Mural Paintings*. Oxford, 1963.

Camille, Michael. "Seeing and Reading: Some Visual Implications of Medieval Literary and Illiteracy." *Art History* 8 (1985): 26–49.

Carruthers, Mary. *The Search for St. Truth*. Evanston, Ill., 1973.

Cather, Sharon, David Park, and Paul Williamson, eds. *Early Medieval Wall Paintings and Painted Sculpture in England*. Oxford, 1990.

Cook, C. H. *The English Medieval Parish Church*. London, 1954.

D'Evelyn, Charlotte. "*Piers Plowman* in Art." *MLN* 34 (1919): 247–49.

Dives and Pauper. Ed. Priscilla Heath Barnum. EETS 275 and 280. London, 1976 and 1980.

Duffy, Eamon. *The Stripping of the Altars*. New Haven, 1992.

Kane, George. *Middle English Literature*. London, 1951.

Kaske, Robert. "*Piers Plowman* and Local Iconography." *JWCI* 31 (1968): 159–69.

Keyser, C. E. *A List of Buildings in Great Britain and Ireland Having Mural and Other Painted Decorations*. Rev. ed. London, 1883.

Kolve, V. A. *Chaucer and the Imagery of Narrative*. Stanford, 1984.

Lawlor, John. *Piers Plowman: An Essay in Criticism*. London, 1962.

Lewis, C. S. *Allegory of Love*. 1936; London, 1948.

Middleton, Anne. "The Audience and Public of 'Piers Plowman.'" *Middle English Alliterative Poetry and Its Literary Background: Seven Essays*. Ed. David Lawton. Cambridge, 1982. 101–23, 147–54.

Morgan, Nigel. "Texts and Images of Marian Devotion in Fourteenth-Century England." *England in the Fourteenth Century: Proceedings of the 1991 Harlaxton Symposium*. Ed. Nicholas Watson. Harlaxton Medieval Studies 3. Stamford, 1993. 34–57.

Owst, G. R. *Literature and Pulpit in Medieval England*. Oxford, 1966.

Park, David. "The 'Lewes Group' of Wall Paintings in Sussex." *Anglo-Norman Studies* 6 (1983): 201–37.

————. "The Wall Paintings of the Holy Sepulchre Chapel." *British Archaeological Conference* 6 (1983): 38–62.

————. "Romanesque Wall Paintings at Ickleton." *Romanesque and Gothic: Essays for George Zarzecki.* Bury St. Edmunds, 1987. 1: 159–69.

————. "Wall Painting." *Age of Chivalry: Art in Plantagenet England 1200–1400.* Ed. Jonathan Alexander and Paul Binski. London, 1987. 125–30.

Pearsall, Derek. *An Annotated Critical Bibliography of Langland.* Ann Arbor, 1990.

————. "Manuscript Illustration of Late Middle English Literary Texts, with Special Reference to the Illustration of *Piers Plowman* in Bodleian Library MS Douce 104." *Suche Werkis to Werche: Essays on Piers Plowman.* Ed. Míceál F. Vaughan. East Lansing, Mich., 1993. 191–210.

Pecock, Reginald. *The Repressor of Over Much Blaming of the Clergy.* Ed. Churchill Babington. Rolls Series. London, 1860.

Piers Plowman: A Facsimile of Bodleian Library, Oxford, MS Douce 104. Introduction by Derek Pearsall, catalogue by Kathleen Scott. Cambridge, 1992.

Platt, Colin. *The Parish Churches of Medieval England.* London, 1981.

Rouse, E. Clive. "Wall Paintings in the Church of St. Pega, Peakirk, Northants." *Archaeological Journal* 110 (1953): 135–49.

————. *Medieval Wall Paintings.* 4th ed. Princes Risborough, Buckinghamshire, 1991.

Salter, Elizabeth, and Derek Pearsall, eds. *Piers Plowman.* York Medieval Texts. Evanston, Ill., 1969.

Salter, Elizabeth. "*Piers Plowman* and the Visual Arts." *Encounters: Essays on Literature and the Visual Arts.* Ed. John Dixon Hunt. London, 1971. 11–27; rpt. *English and International: Studies in the Literature, Art and Patronage of Medieval England.* Ed. Derek Pearsall and Nicolette Zeeman. Cambridge, 1988. 256–66.

Scott, Kathleen. "The Illustrations of *Piers Plowman* in Bodleian Library MS. Douce 104." *YLS* 4 (1990): 1–86.

Sheingorn, Pamela. "'And flights of angels sing thee to they rest': The Soul's Conveyance to the Afterlife in the Middle Ages." *Art into Life.* Ed. Kathleen Scott and Carol Fisher. East Lansing, Mich., 1995.

Shepherd, Geoffrey. "The Nature of Alliterative Poetry in Late Medieval England." Gollancz Memorial Lecture. *PBA* 56 (1970): 57–76.

Tristram, E. W. "Piers Plowman in English Wall-Painting." *Burlington Magazine* 31:175 (October 1917): 135–40.

————. *English Medieval Wall Painting: The Twelfth Century.* Oxford, 1944.

————. *English Wall Painting: The Thirteenth Century.* 2 vols. Oxford, 1950.

————. *English Wall Painting of the Fourteenth Century.* London, 1955.

Tristram, E. W. and M. R. James. "Wall-Paintings in Croughton Church, Northamptonshire," *Archaeologia* 76 (1927): 179–204.

Villon, François. *The Poems of François Villon: A Dual Language Edition.* Trans. Galway Kinnell. Boston, 1977.

Woolf, Rosemary. "Some Non-Medieval Qualities of *Piers Plowman.*" *Essays in Criticism* 12 (1962): 111–25.

————. *The English Mystery Plays.* London, 1972.

Yunck, John. "Satire." *A Companion to Piers Plowman.* Alford. 135–54.

612

MARY CLEMENTE DAVLIN, O.P.

[The Place of God in *Piers Plowman*]†

What follows is a study of 'the place of God' in this poem, because the view of God in *Piers Plowman* is peculiarly expressed in terms of locus or place. Although 'his was not a pictorial poetry' (Schmidt, ed. xxvii) and his space was 'unlike the space of any predecessor' (Muscatine, 'Locus' 120/61), Langland[1] had a markedly spatial imagination.[2]

I do not mean that in *Piers Plowman* God is imagined in particular geographical localities,[3] that plot is organized by means of place, or that the poem describes many places (although it is admired for a few 'realistic' descriptions).[4] I mean rather that the question 'where?' is a driving force in the whole narrative, that the poet seems to think of God as of other realities in directional or locational terms, and that characters who are forever moving about are identified by their places of origin or destination. There are comparatively few specific physical places described in *Piers Plowman*. The 'locus of action' is often a symbolic place like the heart of a generalized or abstract place like nature or the church, for it is usually 'moral space' rather than 'physical space' which, as Charles Muscatine has shown, is characteristic of allegory and which interests Langland ('Locus' 117/57). God is vividly 'placed' in moral and physical space. Where God is, is always important in the poem.

* * *

Outside the Corpus Christi plays, *Piers Plowman* is the only English poem before *Paradise Lost* in which God is an actor: talked about and sought at the beginning, active though unseen in the middle, and present and speaking at length near the end. In the poem, God is three Persons and has

---

† From *The Place of God in "Piers Plowman" and Medieval Art* (Aldershot, U.K.: Ashgate, 2001), pp. 2–12. Reprinted by permission of the publisher.

1. There is still some dispute about whether *Piers Plowman* was written by a single author. The debate is extraneous to my interests here, but I use 'Langland' as a convenient name for the author(s) of the *Piers Plowman* texts.

2. By 'spatial,' here and throughout, I mean 'apprehending or perceiving . . . extension' (*OED* 4); denoting movement, relation, or position in space. On place and space, see Muscatine, 'Locus' ° ° °. *Piers Plowman* is certainly influenced in its use of spatial language by the gospel and first letter of John (see Davlin, 'John' 111–16) and probably by Augustine's *Confessions*, which were known and copied in the Middle Ages. Medieval manuscripts of the *Confessions* are still extant; for example, a twelfth-century copy exists in the Hereford Cathedral Library (MS O.4.8). Langland quotes the *Confessions* once in A, B, and C (Alford, *Piers* 70). See C. D. Benson, 'Augustinian' 51–54. For spatial language about God and self in *Confessions*, see, for example, Book 1, Chs 2–6, 18; 2:10; 3:6; 4:7, 11–12; 5:2; 6:3; 7:1, 7, 10–11, 15–16; 8:3, 7–8; 9:4; 10:3, 8–9, 16–17, 24–27, 39–40. Aquinas uses spatial language in questions like, 'Whether God is in all things' (ST Ia.8:1) and 'Whether God is everywhere' (Ia.8:2), as Peter Lombard does in the Sentences, for example, 'In what ways it may be said that God is in things' (Bk. 1, Dist. 37). See Georgianna on the sense of self in *Ancrene Wisse*, and Harwood, 'Dame' 3–4 on orality and self.

3. Unlike *Piers Plowman*, the Prologue to Chaucer's 'Clerk's Tale,' for example, insists on geographical detail as meticulous as that of a map drawing, although the Clerk attributes it to Petrarch and judges it 'a thyng impertinent' (54):

> . . . descryveth he
> Pemond and of Saluces the contree,
> And speketh of Apennyn, the hilles hye,
> That been the boundes of West Lumbardye,
> And of Mount Vesulus in special,
> Where as the Poo out of a welle smal
> Taketh his firste spryngyng and his sours (IV 43–49).

4. See, for example, Salter, *English* 125–27.

many names. When Truth is reported to be present in the tower (Passus 1)[5] and sought by pilgrims (Passus 5); when he sends a pardon (7.1–4); when Kynde[6] (as nature but probably also as God) takes Will into nature (11.324–25); when Christ comes as the Samaritan (17) and as a knight, harrowing hell (18), then walking among worshipers at Mass (19); when the Holy Spirit as Grace comes on Pentecost (19.201–202) and founds the church (19.214–337); and when Kynde talks with Will in his extremity (20.201–11), God is acting in the poem as what narratologists call a 'character . . . foregrounded . . . in the narrative' (Prince 71). Such divine action seems ordinary and probable in the narrative; it is treated with understatement and analogy rather than overstatement. Although Will sets out 'wondres to here' (Pro. 4), there is little emphasis in the poem on 'merveilles.'

* * *

* * * In this study, I am primarily concerned, not with space, but with place, that is, with where God is believed or imagined to be in the poem and in art. Aristotle says that 'the parts and kinds of place' include 'the six dimensions . . . right and left . . . above and below, and ahead and behind' (*Physics* 208b, 12–22, qtd. in Casey [1997,] 53). Although Casey sees an important 'issue . . . [as] place versus space' (104), this seems to be the case principally when 'space' means 'something undelimited and open-ended' (77). I shall use the word 'space' not to mean 'Continuous, unbounded, or unlimited extension in every direction, regarded as void of matter' (*OED* 7), but as 'area or extension' (*OED* II); '2a. a limited extension in one, two, or three dimensions' or '2d.(2) The representation or effect of three-dimensional forms and volumes in paintings' (Webster's *Third*). Thus, with Muscatine, I use 'spatial relations' to mean 'being above or below, to the right or to the left,' ahead or behind, whether in 'a single continuous space' or in a discontinuous 'flat—planimetric . . . schematic' 'spatial environment' ('Locus' 116/56).

The frequent reference to place in language about God in *Piers Plowman* derives from the importance of place and spatial relations in the poem as a whole.[7] A sense of place in literature can express itself in realistic concrete description of physical environment or simply in a reliance upon the directional language of prepositions: 'up' and 'down,' 'in' and 'out,' 'through,' 'under,' 'between,' and the like, or upon nouns like 'somewhere' and verbs like 'come' and 'go,' without any concrete physical description at all. One of the peculiarities of *Piers Plowman* is that its narrative relies upon such directional or locational language without much physical description or even identification of setting and without reliance on a con-

5. I am using Schmidt's 2nd edition of the B-Text with attention to his parallel text edition, to the Kane-Donaldson B-Text ["K.-D."], and to parallel passages in Pearsall's C-Text. Line numbering follows Schmidt's 2nd ed. When I refer to 'Schmidt, ed.' I mean that edition. Where variations in text affect my argument, I quote K.-D. or Pearsall. When a passage I am referring to does not appear in C, I use an asterisk (*) next to the B-citation to note this. In general, I am concerned here only with the longer versions (B and C), not A or Z. Translations are mine.

6. Hugh White notes the 'virtual replacement of Truth by Kynde as the poem's designation of God the Father' in and after Passus 9 (61).

7. Webster defines 'place' as a 'physical environment . . . physical surroundings' (1), 'a particular region' (3a) or 'specific locality' (4a), but also as 'an indefinite region or expanse' (2a). The word 'place' always has, as E. S. Casey says, 'holding-locating properties' (20). He notes, too, that Heidegger viewed 'place as dwelling, nearness' (335). For Muscatine, place, or locus, is setting, and 'the sense of place [is a sense of] the here, the elsewhere, the there' ('Locus' 116 / 57).

sistent allegorical spatial scheme. As Muscatine makes very clear, although Langland 'knows and in part uses flat, geometric, schematic, Romanesque space; knows and uses in particular scenes naturalistic space; knows and intermittently uses the linear, pilgrimage form, none of these becomes a controlling locus of his narrative. The locus of the characters and actions and their spatial environment are continually shifting' ('Locus' 120/62).

The major metaphor throughout the poem, both in the waking narrative (the story at the beginning and end of the poem, and between dreams) and within dreams, is of walking: 'And thus I wente widerwher [all over], walkyng myn one' [by myself] (8.62). The poem begins with images of the people of the world 'wandrynge' (Pro. 19) and ends with Conscience setting out on foot through the world to find Piers Plowman who, somewhere, is planting Truth's crop. In between, Will is almost always walking in his dreams, meeting most of his interlocutors along the way. For example:

> Thus yrobed in russet I romed aboute
> Al a somer seson for to seke Dowel (8.1–2).[8]

> [Thus, robed in russet, I roamed around
> Throughout the summer season to seek Do Well.]

The spatial flow of the poem includes three major pilgrimages: the people's pilgrimage to Truth,[9] which begins with their question to the palmer, 'Koudestow wissen us the wey wher that wye dwelleth?' [Could you teach us the road to where that person lives?] (5.533),[1] the pilgrimage of Conscience with Patience to mourn for his sins (13.192, 216–17), and the pilgrimage of Conscience at the end:

> . . . I wole bicome a pilgrym,
> And walken as wide as the world lasteth,
> To seken Piers the Plowman (20.381–3).[2]

> [I will become a pilgrim
> And walk to the world's end
> To seek Piers the Plowman.]

The importance of walking in *Piers Plowman* may be related to its paucity of specific places, for, as DeCerteau points out, 'To walk is to lack a place' ([1984,] 103).[3]

Where Will is, is most often defined not by a named place but by the

---

8. K.-D.: [Th]us I wente widewher [dowel to seke,
9. Pamela Raabe calls this a 'non-spatial pilgrimage' because it 'ends where it starts, with the sinners' discovery and willing acceptance of faith and love within. The journey is accomplished the moment it begins' (41). Yet even though the tenor or meaning of the metaphor is non-spatial, its vehicle or imagery remains spatial.
1. K.-D.: '[Kanstow] wissen . . .' (5.532). C: 'Kouthest wissen vs the way whoder out Treuth woneth?' (7.178).
2. K.-D.: 'And [wenden] as wide as the world [renneth]' (20.381). C: 'And wenden as wyde as the would regneth' (22.381).
3. 'The ordinary practitioners of the city . . . walk . . . [and] the paths that correspond in this intertwining . . . elude legibility. It is as though the practices organizing a bustling city were characterized by their blindness. The networks of these moving, intersecting writings [what Holy Church calls a 'maze'] compose a manifold story. . . . Pedestrian movements . . . are not localized; it is rather they that spatialize' (DeCerteau 93, 97). On walking in Husserl, see Casey 224–28. For Merleau-Ponty, bodily movement is 'productive of space' (*Phenomenology of Perception* 387, qtd. in Casey 229).

interlocutor(s) he is with in a world almost empty of objects and landscape. Movement in medieval allegories is ordinarily 'inward and heavenward' (Nolan 216), and thus in *Piers Plowman*, the sinner is described as one who may 'rome fro home' (11.129).⁴ But although some of the most important movement in the poem is 'inward' or 'heavenward,' much of the movement in *Piers Plowman* seems to be horizontal, and we have no idea of its direction: 'I have sued [followed] thee this seven yeer' (8.75); 'Thoght and I thus thre daies we yeden [went] / Disputyng upon Dowel day after oother' (8.114–15). Dowel, Dobet, and Dobest 'ben noght fer to fynde' [are not far to find] (8.79); the good person finds that 'Dowel hym folweth' [follows him or her] (8.83). A person may 'ronne [run] into religion' (8.90). Will is brought 'into the lond of longynge and love' (11.8). Christ calls us all to 'come if we wolde [want to] . . . *venite*' [come] (11.119, 120a). Horizontal motion becomes almost frenzied in Passus 16 when Piers, in pursuit of the devil, 'hitte [hit out] after hym' (87), and when Jesus 'soughte out the sike' (16.108),⁵ 'Justed in Jerusalem' (16.163*), and 'On cros upon Calvarie . . . took the bataille' (16.164*). Will pursues the Samaritan (17.85), descends into hell (18.111), and finally, after Antichrist comes, desires to 'ben hennes' [get away] (20.203) and journeys 'into Unitee' [unity] (20.204).⁶

The frame story of *Piers Plowman*, often called the waking narrative, in which the dreamer introduces his dreams, is always a journey narrative, and therefore implicitly at least it has to do with moving from place to place, but description of place is almost non-existent. The poem opens in the outer world, with a locational vagueness like that of Dante's opening '*per una selva oscura*' [in a dark wood] (*Inf.* 1:2): 'I . . . / Wente wide⁷ in this world wondres to here' [to hear wonders] (Pro. 2, 4). The only place name used anywhere in the waking narrative is the Malvern Hills (Pro. 5; 7.142). In the rather long waking narrative that leads into the third dream, Will hints at a large world in general terms: the friars he meets 'moost wide walken, / And knowen contrees and courtes and many kynnes places— / Bothe princes paleises and povere mennes cotes' [walk far / And know countries and courts and many sorts of places—/ Both princes' palaces and poor men's houses] (8.14–16). When Will leaves the friars, he gives a brief, rather general physical description of a landscape which could be the Malvern Hills:

> And thus I wente widewher, walkyng myn one,
> By a wilde wildernesse, and by a wode side;

---

4. K.-D.: 'recchelesly rennen aboute' (11.130).
5. C: 'a lechede hem' (18.120).
6. Jill Mann states that 'in *Piers Plowman* movement is morally suspect' ('Allegorical' 200), and Anne Middleton documents 'the control, enforcement, and punishment of mobility as such, in the social as well as spatial sense' in the Statute of 1388. 'Will's reply [in C 5] thus appears to be an effort to defeat the statute's most fundamental premise: that everyone ultimately belongs to a single local habitation, presumptively identified with a native place, which serves both as a fixed workplace with a primary claim upon his or her labors, and as the venue charged with the support of its disabled indigents. . . . By claiming that his regular "place" is not single but multiple, Will in the first instance attempts to defeat the determination of a proper "place" to which he can be committed if found indigent. Yet with the same gesture—"*and so*"—he also claims the deeper legitimacy of his apparently irregular and vagrant existence' ('Acts' 218, 253–54). See * * * Aers, 'Justice' 182.
7. C: 'wente forth . . . in the world' (Pro. 4). Papka notes the similarity in the openings of the two poems (237).

Blisse of the briddes abide me made,
And under lynde upon a launde lened I a stounde
To lythe the layes that the lovely foweles made (8.62–66).

[And thus I went all over, walking alone
By a wild wilderness, and by the side of a forest;
The birds' joy made me stop,
And under a linden on a plain I rested a while
To hear the songs the lovely birds sang.]

The spatial[8] character of the lines derives from verbs of motion and rest, 'wente,' 'walkyng,' and 'abide'; and of posture, 'lened'; the adverb 'wide-wher,' and the prepositions 'by' and 'under.' Every noun is general. At the end of the Paschal dream, Will and his family go to church (18.429, 19.2).[9] There is no further reference to physical places anywhere in the waking narrative, and Will's psychological state therein is indicated, if at all, not by locational language but by clothing (Pro. 2–3; 8.1; 18.1; 19.2)[1] and by explicit statements (5.3–4,* 7.143–46).

Within the eight dreams and two inner dreams framed by this waking narrative, Will, as he walks and pauses, is sometimes observer, sometimes participant, and occasionally the center of action or passion. Where is he?[2]

* * *

ELIZABETH D. KIRK

"What is this womman?"
Langland on Women and Gender†

Some of the most valuable work on Chaucer in recent years has focused on gender. Langland's treatment of this subject, in contrast, presents problems so awkward that such analysis is barely beginning. Chaucer has a unique array of women characters who invite examination in their own right, not only as characters but even (occasionally) as narrators. In a larger sense, Chaucer's whole oeuvre conducts a kind of inquest on four hundred years of texts that reflect seminal developments in western culture's attitudes to desire. Though Chaucer has been called the friend of women at least since Gavin Douglas in the early sixteenth century, traditional scholarship has often overtly endorsed medieval misogyny in the name of his-

---

8. See note 2 above.
9. Economou discusses the significance of the second and seventh dreams being set in church.
1. In C, 5.2 also mentions Will's clothing.
2. Although it is perhaps true that in *Piers Plowman* 'there are two geographical landscapes: the waking one is England's and of the fourteenth century; the visionary one is Biblical and of all time' (Bolton Holloway 91), the Biblical landscape is such not in a consistent or developed geographical sense but in the sense that Will meets (mentally, through the liturgy) Biblical characters.
† This essay is derived from a long paper on Langland and Chaucer presented to the National Endowment for the Humanities Langland and Chaucer Institute in Boulder, Colorado, in the summer of 1995 and is reprinted by permission of the author. The author is grateful to all the participants and to the co-directors, David Benson, James Simpson, and Elizabeth Robertson for invaluable discussion. Special thanks are given to Elizabeth Robertson and Stephen Shepherd for numerous suggestions, and for the opportunity to revisit the subject here. All references are to the works cited in the bibliography.

torical professionalism. More often critics respond to Chaucer's women naively, as if they provide transparent and agenda-less windows on medieval reality, raw data for the historian. John Gardner's and Donald Howard's biographies of Chaucer want to say simply that Chaucer liked, enjoyed, appreciated women, in passages that smack, to the female reader at least, of patronizing jocularity or condescension by one narrator or another if not by the author. More recently debate has raged over whether Chaucer is to be regarded as proto-feminist, or whether he is to be attacked for perpetuating patriarchal notions of gender, since his superficially realistic and sympathetic portrayals seduce readers into responding as if these figures offered direct access to the realities of female experience. Some respond to the very subtlety of these portrayals with an outrage that might be paraphrased as "I actually believed he was playing straight with me as a female reader, when all the time he had his hand up my skirt." "Geoffrey Chaucer, friend of women" has acquired an opposite number, "Geoffrey Chaucer, purveyor of poisoned candy," whose texts purport to provide a crack in the wall of patriarchal textuality, but which prove on inspection to be right at home there, wolves in sheep's clothing. Note that this is not a strictly modern problem; the question of whether Chaucer is anti-feminist was clearly a subject of debate in his own time, to judge by the Prologue to the *Legend of Good Women*, if not by the defensiveness of the *Troilus* narrator.

In contrast, there seems at first sight practically nothing about women and gender in *Piers Plowman*. Of course that is not literally true. Terence Dolan's "Langland's Women"[2] notes a number of passages, mostly offering women what he calls "walk-on parts" (127), some favorable to women, some stereotypically pejorative; he concludes that on balance Langland's references to women are more "consistently" favorable than Chaucer's. It is certainly true, however, that women are relatively inconspicuous in the poem's foreground, a phenomenon of interest in itself in considering that the poem is attempting an overview, microcosm, or icon of society as a whole. The poem's "discourses of authority" and its interwoven Latin citations are drawn, as David Lawton argues (6), from the "non-fictional discourses of social and intellectual power" as opposed to the "nonliterary discourses" on which Chaucer plays ("Subject," 6).[3] *Piers Plowman* does not appear, on the face of it, to draw upon the mainstream of medieval literary discourse about love, gender roles, or the erotic as Chaucer does.

The most exciting material on gender in Langland is to be found in the last place we might expect, his least psychologized, least realistic, least representational material, his personification allegory. His epistemology especially examines systemic patterns of thought and social construction by transposing marriage and the feminine into metaphors that explore not actual women, but rather the social and intellectual structures behind gendered experience. David Aers, following Charles Taylor, has called these structures the "webs of interlocution" about class and gender within which texts and people exist, the "networks of power in medieval culture, their sources and effects," which offer "heuristic guides in our inquiries" into

---

2. One of the few attempts at an overview, its title plays on Arlyn Diamond's essay of more than twenty years earlier, "Chaucer's Women, Women's Chaucer," noting that it attempts only an equivalent to the first of the issues her title suggests.
3. See also Martin, "Indirect Relations," 185–86.

particular texts and communities ("Class" 59, 73). His personifications are tools in an attempt to extrapolate what he observes into an analytical dramatization of his world's intellectual, religious, and economic dynamics. Langland seems to erase gender as part of the literal level while, in the very act of so doing, he raises that very issue in other ways. The classic embodiment of this strategy is his portrait of Lady Meed's wedding party setting off for London with Reward / Profit-Motive coalesced into the image of a gorgeous lady perched on "a Sherreve shoed al newe" (B II, 164–65). The (female) personification is superimposed on a supposedly "real life" (male) functionary, who has just had horseshoes applied to his feet, thus yoking discordant levels of representation and thought together as drastically as Samuel Johnson accused the metaphysical poets of doing.

Before pursuing this train of thought, however, the question remains whether "real" women are actually as invisible as all that in *Piers Plowman*. The poem includes set-piece overviews of society: the Visio Prologue's opening Fair Field full of Folk or the *Vita de DoBest's* closing enumeration of those who make their last stand in Piers's barn Unity. Here economic and political work is generally pictured as male. Conceptual schemes like the king's procession in the Prologue, which structures society in terms of the Three Estates, offers no category for women's production, biological or economic. The tripartite model of mankind divided into *laboratores, bellatores*, and *oratores* had long ceased to be an adequate diagram of contemporary economic and political reality, and Langland plays boldly with this model in a number of respects. But not with its elision of gender. Women are not even among the "lewed men" whose "rynges and broches" the Pardoner is snatching with his "brevet" in the Prologue. Women (and children) are often equally inaccurately excluded from the enumeration of citizens, pilgrims or crowds except as unruly hangers-on that men are exhorted to beat for their ill behavior. They appear prominently as prostitutes or as the mistresses of land-leaping hermits who refuse to marry them; according to Cooper, at least half of the total references to women in the B-text are to whores and concubines.[4] Only occasionally do women and children appear as model subordinates in a patriarchal family such as Piers's.

This invisibility disappears, however, when Langland gets to more specific portrayals of social process. The economic role of women of different classes is explicitly addressed, for example, when a division of labor is set up on Piers's half-acre. Lower-class women are responsible for making cloth, sewing harvest sacks, and clothing the needy (while Piers and the men produce food). Upper-class "lovely ladies with youre longe fyngres" (B VI, 10) are to embroider vestments for the Church. Other well-established roles of aristocratic women, such as patronizing the arts, literature, and religion; setting the religious and social tone of great houses; and modeling courtesy and decorum are only indirectly referred to here if at all. The aristocratic woman (though not her middle- and lower-class sister) is seen largely in terms of household management and charity, like a proto-Victorian relegation of women to the domestic sphere—kinder, kirche, kuche.

In the Confession of the Seven Deadly Sins, however, Langland offers a different take. He acknowledges the pervasiveness of women's economic

4. Note that *harlot* and *harloterie* at this date mean "dirty *talk*," and appear in *Piers Plowman* about male behavior.

role, foregrounding their cloth-making, brewing, and tavern-keeping, reflecting accurately the function of women in the early stage of commodity production studied by Martha Howell and others. The elaborately detailed stratagems of "Rosie the Retailer" ("Rose the Regrator," Avarice's wife) define sharp practice by the publican and by the cloth-making entrepreneur who, like the Wife of Bath, mediates between the cottage industry spinners and weavers and the larger market. Betty the Brewer's tavern, into which she sweet-talks Glutton, has many women customers as well as men, and though they include prostitutes, there are women in other trades, apparently present on their own. This offers a striking contrast to Chaucer, where women as businessmen, as opposed to heiresses, customers, or objects of sexual exchange, are limited almost exclusively to the Wife of Bath (and the shopkeeper/prostitute in the fragmentary Cook's Tale). This is what leads Lee Patterson to assume that Chaucer relegated women to a realm of proto-bourgeois subjectivity existing exclusively in the private, not the political domain.

Langland, though offering nothing like the "Marriage Group" and its related tales, devotes much explicit attention to the institution of marriage and to the ethics that ought to govern it. Wit (Intelligence) opens his discussion of human nature with a gendered, (in this case romance) image of the relationship between soul and body. A human being is comprised of a courtly lady (*Anima*, the soul) who has been installed in a castle (*Caro*, the flesh—note that the flesh is *not* gendered female) by her absent lover. The lover has delegated the defense of the castle against "a proud prikere of fraunce, Princeps huius mundi" (B IX, 8) to its Warden, DoWell, and his sons, the five senses, until the day when the lover can send to fetch her, or come to care for her, himself. The lover is Kynde: in the poem's terminology, kynde—nature—can mean the natural order, or natural phenomena, but as a personification Kynde is one of the two principle names of God (the other being Truth).

Wit then shifts from a romance model of the individual to a marriage model of society. The Prologue had pointed to the labor of the commune, epitomized in plowmen, as the undergirding support of civilized society. Wit assigns that role to marriage: "Dowel in this world is trewe wedded libbynge folk. / For thei mote werche and wynne and the world sustene" (B IX, 110–11). The married couple is the economic and productive as well as the psychological and legal base of society. The woman is subordinated but not elided. Wit's remarks are clearly addressed to men about women, rather than to women; he cautions the randy male, "Whiles thow art yong [and yeep] and thi wepene [yet] kene / Wreke the with wyuyng if thou wolt ben excused" (185–86). No comparable advice is given to women (a proto-Victorian idea that decent women don't desire? an assumption that women who do are beyond the reach of advice?). Yet he does not entirely elide female desire. He condemns choosing ill-matched spouses for their money or forcing young women into marriages with old men: "It is an uncomly couple, by Crist! As me thynketh / To yeven a yong wenche to [a yolde] feble" (165–66); women as well as men are entitled to some sexual satisfaction (compare the Dreamer's wife's response to his impotence in old age in Passus XX). Wit emphasizes (correctly in canon law but radically to the modern ear) that what makes a marriage is the assent of the two people to each other, not the priest's acknowledgment and proclamation, though couples are exhorted to follow in an orderly way the go-between's negotiations, the father's (not mother's) advice, and the counsel of friends. The wife is assenting to a subordinate position: "The wif was maad the wye for to helpe werche" (115). Work is again the defining sphere of the male, but the wife is helpmate to her husband not just domestically, psychologically, and sexually, but in his capacity as worker; women do not occupy a domestic sphere separate from work and production, as tends to be assumed in industrial and post-industrial economies. Marriage is an economic and political building block, not a romantic one; Wit confines his romantic metaphor to the relationship of body and soul.

Langland is equally firm that in the economic sphere, no less than in any other, a stable social order requires treating people in such a way as to allow them reasonable subsistence, decency, and such autonomy as their status permits. Wit asserts that the Church is the institution of last resort to care for those who lack the inwit, or practical intelligence—the common sense, to take care of themselves in society. This group includes the insane and the feeble-minded (but not drunks whose incapacity is self-inflicted). But this category does *not* include women as such—their gender does not in itself constitute lack of inwit—but only certain categories of women: "maydenes," marriageable girls, and unsupported widows with no marketable skills. Young girls (as opposed to children) are by definition vulnerable to economic exploitation, but widows, even if left unprovided for, are expected to constitute a self-supporting unit of some sort and not to be wards of society under normal circumstances. As we know from contemporary documentation, widows regularly assumed the responsibility of their husband's businesses and became guild members in their own right. Similarly, the letter to merchants appended to the Pardon lists providing dowries for otherwise impoverished girls as a charitable duty along with building hospitals and repairing roads and bridges as ways of atoning for receiving unearned increment. There are two crucial points here: Langland sees a direct connection between minimal psychological and cognitive empowerment (inwit) and minimal economic impowerment; and gender as such does not disqualify a person from economic autonomy, though during a marriage the woman's civil existence is erased. Langland takes the position, then, that such personal autonomy and accountability an individual has is a social and economic artifact, an aspect of the nature of things which the situation of women throws into relief. (Compare Chaucer's giving the Wife of Bath not just a room of her own but an income of her own as well as residence in an area where she can continue to possess and manage her own property as a *femme sole* even if she remarries.)

Langland is keenly aware of how impoverished or exploited women suffer not just under exceptional circumstances but as part of the constraints of normal life. One of the C-poet's most striking additions (to the letter to the merchants) is in answer to the question of who the truly needy are, for whom we should provide. It offers a poignant and realistic picture of women's experience not in disaster or abandonment, but in ordinary poverty, recognizing their painful efforts to care for and feed children in the cold, going hungry themselves, and their efforts to help pay the rent by their spinning, cloth-making, dairy production, and other earnings, however limited, while trying to maintain appearances by "turning the fair side outward" (86).[5]

> Ac that most neden aren oure neyhebores, and we nyme gode hede,
> As prisones in pittes and pore folk in cotes,
> Charged with childrene and chief lordes rente;
> That they with spynnyng may spare, spenen hit on hous-huyre.
> Bothe in mylke and in mele, to make with papelots
> To aglotye with here gurles that greden after fode.
> And hemselves also suffre muche hunger,
> And wo in wynter-tymes, and wakynge on nyghtes
> To rise to the reule to rokke the cradel,
> Bothe to carde and to kembe, to cloute and to wasche,
> And to rybbe and to rele, rusches to pylie,
> That reuthe is to rede or in ryme schewe
> The wo of this wommen that wony in cotes;
> And of monye other men that moche wo suffren,
> Both afyngered and afurste, to turne the fayre outward,
> And ben abasched for to begge and wollen nat be aknowe
> What hem nedeth at here neyhebores at noon and at eve.
>   (C, IX. 71–87)

> But those that are most needy are our neighbors, if we were to pay real attention, like prisoners in dungeons, and poor folk in hovels who are burdened with children and especially with the rent due the lord of the manor; what they can eke out by [?extra] spinning they spend on the rent, and on milk and flour, to make porridge to fill the stomachs of their children [of both sexes] who cry for food. And they themselves suffer much hunger, and woe in winter time, and waking at night to get up into the space between the bed and the wall to rock the cradle, to card and comb [wool], to patch clothes and wash [them], and to scrape flax and wind yarn, to peel rushes [to make rush lights], so that it is painful to explain or to show in rhyme the woe of these women who live in hovels; and of many other men that suffer much woe, both of hunger and thirst, in order to keep up a respectable appearance [turn the fair side of the situation to face outward], and are ashamed to beg, and don't want it to be apparent what they need from their neighbors at noon and at night.

Note that being in prison and living in a "cote" are comparably desperate situations. Note how much work women have to be do at night, presumably because the family's few garments are needed (or have to look respectable) in the daytime, and because the day is full of its own labors. The spinning and other craft work that goes toward rent, milk, and having grain ground is extra ("with spynnyng may spare"—74), either above quota, or on top of ordinary labor, and may be where the family gets cash from, as distinct from what they produce. The C-Dreamer tells us (at the beginning of his confession to Reason and Conscience) that he and his wife and daughter live in a "cote" clothed like down-and-outs ("lolleres"). Whether or not that is sufficiently based on biographical truth to account for the poet's remark-

---

5. Note that the passage begins and ends as if it were non-gender-specific, but actually deals explicitly with women—the generic "pore folk in cotes" of line 72 become "this wommen that wonyth in cotes" by line 83, before reverting to "men" in line 84.

able empathy with women who live in cotes, the passage is marked by its complete lack of the condescension that would be expected of an outsider who can shrug his shoulders and utter the old bromide that "the poor ye have always with you."

Piers Plowman in general is marked by its comparative—only comparative, of course—lack of religious misogyny (like its comparative lack of anti-Semitism and comparatively respectful view of Muslims). Langland almost never uses formulas that attribute the Fall entirely to Eve (Piers's early reference to opening the wicket-gate that the woman shut [B V, 601] is an exception that may reflect alliteration). Hawkyn attributes his filthy coat in part to having a wife, servants, and children, but the overall thrust of the passage is to suggest that the fault is not theirs, though they may be the occasion. Among the Seven Deadly Sins, Lecher is, astonishingly, male, and Langland does not seem to associate lechery with the female body which precipitates it in others and is consequently blamed for it. Rather, lechery appears primarily in association with male desire for, aggression toward, and violence against women. Helen Cooper observes, moreover, that Langland offers "more . . . in praise of marriage than of virginity" ("Gender," 44). Indeed, Langland's ethics in general are remarkable (though, canonically correct) in placing sexual sins a distant third behind gluttony and sloth, which are not particularly associated with the feminine, and all of them a long way behind self-aggrandizement or the exploitation of others, especially economically. Too Much Sex may be the staple of pulpit rhetoric and confessor's manuals.[6] But *Piers Plowman* has more to say about merchants who have figured out that the big money is made from the poor who buy in small quantities, or parents who cripple their children to make them more effective beggars.

Langland's Meed is a useful crux to examine in this respect. At first sight she seems a standard Whore of Babylon figure in which luxury and sexual greed are combined in a female figure onto which responsibility for sin is displaced. The responsibility for sin is deflected from the desirer to the desired. Several recent commentators, however, especially Helen Cooper, Elizabeth Fowler, Claire Lees, Colette Murphy and Elizabeth Robertson have called attention to how Langland's portrayal of Meed is actually the reverse of the stereotypical female whose desire has run amok. Fowler argues that Langland plays on the civil death of the woman who passes into male possession on marriage (*femme couvert*) in order to portray Meed as "'pure' agency, agency without intentionality . . . dangerously operating out of coverture" (6) even though the forces she embodies are very active indeed and produce activity in others.

Conscience, of course, is convinced that Meed is intrinsically vicious, promiscuous, and predatory; Conscience would, by definition, reject anything like an extraneous incentive. It is important to note, however, that only this specific character considers Meed's function intrinsically and monolithically evil, just as misogyny does women. The larger drama attributes the economic adventurism she represents not to her but to the men who use her; she acquiesces to, and colludes in, everything she is asked for, but desire is precisely what she does *not* embody. The Peace episode, with its emphasis on rape, is instructive. Here Meed seems to play an active

---

6. See Tentler, *Sin and Confession on the Eve of the Reformation* (Princeton: Princeton UP, 1977).

role and take initiative, and her money can temporarily convince Peace himself (if not the various raped and molested women) that his grievance has been addressed. But the thrust of the story turns out to be that Meed's ability to allay Peace's feelings by economic satisfactions is quite beside the point. Her "solution" is not a solution, and the king properly ignores it. Langland's choice of rape here plays on the fact that medieval law regarded rape as an offense not against the woman but against the man deprived of her, just as he would be by kidnapping or seduction. But he then goes on to show that appeasing the man does not begin to address the real problem of sexual violence. Chaucer's Wife of Bath's Tale too focuses on rape, but takes the story a step further: He shows women as unsatisfied when the rape is dealt with man on man. This is not because the sentence is a light one—the rapist knight has been condemned to death—but because they feel he should be accountable to *them*. When he is handed over to them, they prove to be less interested in making him suffer than in forcing him to recognize women's autonomy (their right to reject unwelcome desire).

Langland's metaphor of economic incentive is that of a woman with money to bestow. He is addressing, as the fourteenth century was having to begin to do, the difference between two concepts of money. In the older view money is a neutral "short-hand" for just equivalence between the values of different contributions to society (so much food-raising is equivalent to so much shoe-making), so that money is a superficial tool to facilitate exchange in what can be still thought of as a barter system. In the newly emerging one, money is a social force in and of itself, which can make things happen and create more wealth than there was before: money is capital. Claire Lees comments that the image "displace[s] the newly pressing issue of the circulation of money onto the issue of the more traditional institutions of patriarchal marriage. The narrative . . . enacts the process of men's desire for her: . . . Meed is therefore rightly the object—not the subject—of the narrative, even when she is presented as the giver, not the receiver, of gifts" (117). Murphy sees here "The operations of the traffic in women. . . . If men are shown to be the natural power brokers in a feudal model of society, so are they too in a market-economy model" (152). Reward-incentive turns out to be a far more complicated issue than Conscience as such is qualified to pronounce on. He does, however, persuade the king to split the concept of Meed in two, differentiating the notion of incentive above and beyond the facts of the situation (reward) from "measurable hire" (equivalence, that is, justice). As a result, the king decides to rule without "profit motive" or extrinsic inducement. He turns back to the older values of Reason, Conscience, and Obedience as the basis for a just order. This sounds like a good plan. But it turns out, as the story continues, that he has elided a factor that goes right on functioning anyway. It may now be out of sight, out of mind, but it is still there, because nobody "married" Meed. In spite of a promising start, doing without her simply leads to even more social disorder which, this time, can not be displaced onto a feminine figure. The appeal to higher intention, and then to the disincentive of compulsion (or the law of cause and effect) ought to work better, but ends in a disaster that even Pardon cannot avert, because Reason and Conscience can't affect human motivation on the large scale social order requires.

The complexities Langland can address by placing a female personification in the midst of male characters opens a larger question of female personifications in Langland's epistemology. Whether personification allegory
is really allegory at all is a problem; it is not a way of saying one thing and
meaning another. Personification can be considered, as it was by many
medieval exegetes, a rhetorical device that remains part of the literal level,
as is metonymy where a part of something is shorthand for the whole. Mary
Carruthers argues in *The Search for St. Truth* that the status of verbal signs
is central to Langland's epistemology as well as to his narrative strategy.
Langland's personifications don't do what the factor of the same name does
in the real world; they do what the *word* for that thing does in that culture's
language system. A word represents not a thing but a hypothesis about that
thing, a model of how it works, because we feel the need to differentiate it
from other comparable things in order to refer to it. The analysis of the reality a given language's vocabulary embodies could be, and often is, different
from that of other languages.[7] The word for a thing is the end product of a
cultural process of thinking about that thing, about what a given culture
perceives and also what it evades about reality. Evelyn Fox Keller puts this
very well with respect to the analogous role of gender in the development
of western science, which was underway in Langland's time:

> A feminist perspective on science confronts us with the task of exam-
> ining the roots, dynamics, and consequences of this interacting net-
> work of associations and disjunctions—together constituting what
> might be called the "science-gender system." It leads us to ask how ide-
> ologies of gender and science inform each other in their mutual con-
> struction, how that construction functions in our social arrangements,
> and how it affects men and women, science and nature.[8]

In Langland's English, the abstract words he wants to explore were no
longer gender-marked as they had been in the ancient and continental languages in which these personifications developed.[9] Therefore concepts
that were once grammatically feminine need no longer necessarily become
feminine characters, so that the femaleness or maleness of such characters is optional and can mean more. Many characters that were traditionally female—Nature, Reason, the Vices and Virtues—become masculine
in Langland. His Lecher is male. His Kynde is a masculine figure who is
master of all natural phenomena (except unruly man), as well as the lover
and protector of Lady Anima in her castle of the flesh. Feminist re-
examination of the development of the western scientific world view has
stressed the importance of the shift from Nature as a figure exercising
authority over the male scientist/philosopher to a newly feminized Nature
who, so far from being authoritative, becomes the passive object, even the

7. The debate on this matter (whether words stand for real things or only for concepts in the human
mind) was, of course, central to medieval philosophic debate. By Langland's time the Nominalists,
rather than the Realists, held the field.
8. See Evelyn Fox Keller, *Reflections on Gender and Science* (New Haven: Yale UP, 1985), 8.
9. English pronouns, on the other hand, are still inescapably gender-marked—English has no human
pronoun that is singular yet does not specify male or female, causing us to tie ourselves up in knots
trying to prevent unintentional sexism without using an ungrammatical "they." Consider the problems about pronouns encountered by Ursula LeGuin (in *The Left Hand of Darkness*) and other science fiction writers when they seek to problematize gender by hypothesizing a genderless, or a
plurigendered society. The equally difficult problem of a narrator who is desiring but not specified
as to gender, on the other hand, is elegantly handled in Melissa Scot's *The Kindly Ones.*

raped or enslaved victim of the scientist who tortures her secrets out of her. Particularly telling is Francis Bacon's often quoted portrayal of the scientist saying to his son, "I am come in very truth leading to you Nature with all her children to bind her to your service and make her your slave."[1] Langland's masculinizing of nature while retaining its authoritative status may mark a key stage in this historical process.

Thus Langland can manipulate allegorical figures and the reader's response to them by setting up "marriages" between concepts. He can create characters who are nontraditionally gendered, display gender slippage, or a multigendered, like Anima who is female in Wit's castle image but becomes both male and female in Passus XV. Because Langland can personify as female some but not all characters who represent authority, he can problematize authority by doing so. Lady Holy Church is a case in point. Those who administer the Church as a temporal institution are strictly male and at least ostensibly celibate, whereas *Lady* Holy Church can shift from a nurturing if irascible mother, responsible for her children's early religious and intellectual education, to a shrewish lover who is jealous of Meed, thus demystifying an institution which, at least in its temporal form, was becoming the object of increasing criticism. She is then revised retroactively by the accretion of other characters representing the Church, especially Clergy, Scripture, and Piers himself as St. Peter. The problem is not as simple as "Holy Church all good, Meed all bad." Culture did not create sex, but it did create gender, and because gender does not offer a stable and unambiguous iconographic system, introducing gender into ostensibly ungendered problems provides destabilizing effects where Langland's epistemological strategy requires them.

Langland's use of the marriage metaphor develops further in his most consistently epistemological section, the *Life of DoWell*. The figure of Thought is followed by a progressive series of intellectually and religiously authoritative figures, Intelligence (Wit), Study, Clergy (Learning and Clerics), and Scripture (the Bible and other authoritative writings). Two of them are female; furthermore they form two married couples. But the wives are anything but meek subordinates or *femmes couvertes*—quite the reverse. Study is the classic shrewish wife who reduces Intellect to groveling subservience as if he had been a bad little boy. Scripture takes the discussion away from Clergy when he gets bogged down on the fuzzy border between the political and the religious and precipitates the decisive turning point in the Dreamer's experience. It accords with common sense that Scripture should be the authority to which Clergy answers, as well as the raw material he interprets; one cannot help thinking ahead to the *sola scriptura* of the Reformation. Equally obviously Study is the necessary condition using intellect responsibly, without which it becomes frivolous, self-indulgent, and misguided, as is the case with musical or athletic talent, or in the crafts for which Study takes credit.[2] But in that

1. See Evelyn Fox Keller and Carolyn Merchant, *The Death of Nature: Women, Ecology, and the Scientific Revolution* (1980; San Francisco: Harper and Rowe, 1983). Compare Chaucer's take on this transition to science in his treatment of alchemy, where the Canon and his Yeoman are anything but triumphant masters in their laboratory.
2. One might also instance the fact that in the complex theology of Langland's Crucifixion and Harrowing of Hell in Passus XVIII, "Book," who guarantees Christ's Resurrection, is male, but the Four Daughters of God, one of whom, Peace, presents some of Langland's most original theological work on the Incarnation, are female. See Elizabeth D. Kirk, "Langland's Narrative Christology." In *Art and Context in Late Medieval Narrative* (Cambridge: D. S. Brewer, 1944), 17–35.

case why make them the wives instead of the husbands, and why present their authority as if it represented the normal order being turned topsy-turvy? Why not make Scripture and Study the husbands, unless to problematize and examine that authority, or show the incongruity between social reality and a trans-social order? Or to attempt to say something which neither term of an accepted either-or polarity can express? An analogy might be the way Chaucer presents the Wife of Bath (and her Hag as well) as insisting that what she wants is "sovereignty," when what she really wants is clearly something else, since once she has obtained sovereignty (and, as a student of mine once observed, if someone "gives" it to you, do you have it?) she uses it to obey her husband in everything that might please him. What does she really want— self-determination? The right not so much to choose different things, as to choose them for different reasons? Such paradox is intrinsic to any attempt by a writer to force the social and intellectual categories which are all that's available in order to talk about something which these categories are incapable of expressing, something that is problematic precisely because the culture's assumptions make it hard either to understand, or even to perceive.

Answers to such questions are a long way off. But this preliminary conclusion is evident: Langland, like Chaucer, doesn't seem to be able to think about teaching and learning, religious institutions and religious authority, greed and justice, truth or falsehood, without thinking about gender. He problematizes any idea he is laboring with through the use of gender. Langland studies are only beginning to address this dimension of *Piers Plowman*. This means that extraordinarily rewarding work is waiting to be done, and that Langland's text can be mesmerizing to students in ways our curriculum has not allowed it to be. This in turn will open the poem to its scholars in ways that studying the poem without teaching it cannot do. For both Langland and Chaucer, gender is not just part of our bodies and our social behavior. It is part of our minds, and will be working in everything we do whether or not we can catch a glimpse of it out of the corner of our eyes.

Gloss

(The function of the Gloss is explained in the Introduction, under "Using This Edition.")

Ambrose, St. (340?–397) one of the four great Fathers of the Western Church, Bishop of Milan, a teacher of St. Augustine, and author of major commentaries and hymns.

anchorites like hermits, they were vowed to a life of solitude and meditation, but they chose to live in a populous area walled into a small dwelling, usually attached to a church. They often taught and counseled through a window to the outside world and participated in the life of the church through a second window, opening into it.

Anima the soul. Medieval thought attributed many more functions to the soul than are generally associated with the modern word. These functions are discussed in detail in IX.5–59 and XV.22–39.

Aristotle (384–322 B.C.) the Greek philosopher who had the greatest influence on the development of medieval scholastic philosophy and theology.

assizers members of the assize or inquest, which was the ancestor of the modern jury. Serving on the assize was considered a great hardship, not simply because this function, like jury duty today, was time consuming; instead of assessing evidence, medieval "jurors" took oaths vouching for the credibility of one of the parties to the lawsuit. This would be a demanding responsibility in the best of times, but under the problematic conditions of medieval "justice" (of which Langland is so critical) jurors were often subjected to great pressures in the form of bribes, threats, or even blackmail. It is understandable that as late as the fifteenth century it was not uncommon for an individual to have more faith in trial by ordeal or combat than in a jury.

Augustine, St. (354–430) one of the four major Fathers of the Western Church, Bishop of Hippo, most often cited by Langland in connection with his autobiography, the *Confessions*, and his treatise on the Trinity, *De Trinitate*, and often referred to in the poem as Austin or Austin the Old. He was later claimed by the Austin Friars as their founder.

Austin, Austin Friars see **Augustine**.

bachelor Bachelor of Divinity, but also, occasionally, novice knight, as in the case of Longeus in **Passus** XVIII.

Benedict, St. (480?–543?) the founder of the Benedictine Order, whose Rule became the central influence on Western monasticism. In addition to binding the monk to poverty, chastity, and obedience, the Rule divided his day into thirds: one for liturgical prayer, one for study, and one for manual labor. Unlike the later orders of friars, monks were committed to living their lives in a single, enclosed community. See **friars**.

Bernard, St. (1091–1153) Abbot of Clairvaux and one of the founders of the Cistercian Order, which attempted a return to strict observance of the original Benedictine Rule. A mystic, preacher, and religious writer, Bernard was also a major political leader, who played a central role in mobilizing the Second Crusade (1146).

bought   often means "redeemed," in the sense that Christ's sacrifice on the Cross "purchased" salvation for the human race.

bull   an official document issued by the pope and sealed with his *bulla*, or seal. **Pardoners** (see below) had, at least in theory, to have such a papal permit, which had also to be endorsed by the local bishop.

burgess   a town-dweller, not necessarily of great wealth, who had full rights as the citizen of a municipality. Towns, which had a status outside the feudal system of land tenure, operated under governmental and legal systems quite distinct from those of rural areas.

Cato   Dionysius Cato, supposed author of the *Distichs of Cato*, an early fourth-century collection of Latin maxims, one of the first books studied in medieval grammar schools.

civil   civil as opposed to criminal law, especially noted for its bribery and corruption in the later Middle Ages. This corruption resulted at least partly from the fact that law, particularly as it affected ownership of property, was changing drastically; people were devising ways to own land and possessions outright, rather than simply as part of a feudal contract by which land was held in return for service.

clergy, clerks   the Middle English word *clergie* has two meanings that Langland sometimes connects and sometimes differentiates: (1) intellectual learning or book learning; (2) clerics, those who traditionally were the only ones to have such learning (though this situation was beginning to change in the later Middle Ages). Hence the character Clergy is married to Scripture, but in some contexts the term means intellectual learning pure and simple. Theology was the culminating science in medieval university training and was based on the interpretation of Scripture. Knowledge of Scripture, in turn, as Study explains in Passus X, presupposed the "seven arts," which formed the basic curriculum in medieval education and which are, therefore, allegorically Scripture's "siblings." They consist of the trivium, comprising grammar, rhetoric, and logic, which teach language and rational discourse, and the quadrivium, comprising arithmetic, geometry, astronomy, and music. Clerics were under canon rather than secular law, so that proving one's power to read (usually by translating a verse from the Psalms) could remove a person from the jurisdiction of the secular law even in the case of a crime as serious as murder.

common (adjective)   in common, not peculiar to particular individuals or groups. See also **common** (noun).

common, commons (noun)   the Middle English word *commune, communes* has several distinct meanings on which Langland plays: (1) the community taken as a whole; (2) the common people or working classes as opposed to the aristocracy and clergy; (3) the food that supports the whole community. A fourth meaning, the members of the lower house of Parliament, was just coming into use but does not appear to be one that Langland uses (though the possibility has sometimes been suggested).

Compostela   see **James**.

conscience   the Middle English word, like the modern one, includes as its dominant meaning "ethical integrity"; but, like its other descendant, the modern word "consciousness," it also includes a wider range of awareness. Langland's major character who bears this name develops in importance and complexity as the poem progresses, so that both aspects of the word's meaning must be borne in mind in following his role. See also the discussion of mental faculties under **wit** below.

consistory   literally, a bishop's court or the "senate" of cardinals convened by the pope to deliberate on church affairs. Langland often uses the term metaphorically, especially as a term for the Day of Doom (see **doom**).

contra "on the contrary!" or "I object!"—the technical term used to introduce a rebuttal in scholastic philosophical argument.

Distichs see **Cato**.

doctor normally, Doctor of Divinity, though Langland does occasionally mean a medical doctor by the term.

Dominic, St. (1170–1221) contemporary of St. Francis, founder of the Dominican Order of Friars, who were primarily intellectuals and preachers (see **friars**).

doom, Doomsday the word "doom" means "judgment" or "verdict," not necessarily in a negative sense; "Doomsday" is the Last Judgment, when Christ at his Second Coming will separate humanity into the good and the evil.

ergo "therefore"—like *contra*, a central term in scholastic argument. Ergo introduces the logical conclusion of the propositions, or arguments, advanced.

evensong vespers, the evening prayer service said just before sunset. On the seven canonical "hours" of the liturgical day, see **hours**.

farthing a coin worth a quarter of a penny.

florin a gold coin, so called by analogy with the gold coins of Florence, whose coinage was viewed as an international standard. It was worth about two shillings or twenty-four silver pennies.

Francis, St. (1182–1226) founder of the Franciscan Order of Friars, originally dedicated to a life of complete poverty, not only personal but also institutional. That is, as Francis envisaged his order, a brother was not to possess a house, a horse, or money himself; more radically still, he was not to have use of such things, on the grounds that they belonged to his order, rather than to himself. Franciscans were at first dedicated to preaching to and caring for the poorest and most outcast, those least served by the regular church parish system. By the fourteenth century, however, many were major university intellectuals ("masters," that is, masters of divinity), and only a few extremists held to the ideal of institutional poverty.

friar members of a new kind of religious order that developed in the early thirteenth century. Unlike monks, they were not committed to an enclosed life in one place (cf. **Francis** and **Dominic**). They lived, in principle, entirely on donations and were therefore called mendicant or begging orders. Friars generally traveled in pairs and had license to beg in a limited geographical area and, hence, were also known as *limiters*. The four orders of friars in Langland's England were the Franciscans, Dominicans, Austin (Augustinian) Friars, and Carmelites.

gentle, gentleness the Middle English word combined the class meaning "aristocratic, chivalric, or genteel" with the moral and social meaning preserved in the modern word "gentle," a quality originally thought of as class-based. Some of Langland's uses of the term reflect contemporary discussion by the emerging middle class about what meaning the term could have for them other than mere social upward mobility.

Gregory the Great, St. (Pope 590–604) one of the four major Fathers of the Western Church, a great organizational as well as intellectual leader and author of religious works; he is most often mentioned by Langland as the author of the *Moralia*, a moral and allegorical commentary on the Book of Job.

groat a silver coin worth four pennies.

hermits vowed to a life of solitude, austerity, and meditation in the wilderness (in contrast to **anchorites**, see above).

Holy Kirk Holy Church. The term "kirk," particularly in Scotland, has acquired a Protestant aura, which the Middle English word did not, of course, have. The translation, like Langland's text, uses the terms "kirk" and "church" interchangeably for alliterative purposes.

hours   clerics and monastic orders organized their day around seven canonical "hours," or periods of liturgical prayer: matins (with lands), prime, terre, sext, none, vespers, and complin.

Imaginative   not "imagination" in the modern, especially Romantic and post-Romantic sense, but the faculty of forming mental images of things in the exterior world or in the past. Imaginative thus makes it possible for the mind to work since it cannot act on the data given by experience and the senses directly but must interiorize them before it can do so. Medieval psychology did not generally associate this faculty with the creation of art, but rather with memory and with the power of the mind to make analogies and abstractions for use in reasoning. Langland's association of the figure of Imaginative in Passus XII with poetic composition, which seems quite normal to the modern reader, was a highly unusual, if not unique, defense of the writing of poetry in his time. See also the "autobiographical" passage from the C-text printed in the Appendix.

inwit   see the discussion of various related intellectual faculties under **wit**.

James, St.   one of the original twelve Apostles, whose name is especially associated with the New Testament Epistle of St. James and with his great shrine at Compostela, in Galicia, in Spain, the goal of one of the most important medieval pilgrimage routes.

Jerome, St. (340?–420)   one of the four major Fathers of the Western Church, whose translation of the Bible into Latin is termed the "Vulgate" text.

kaisers   emperors, from the Latin Caesar.

kind   nature or the nature of things in general. A crucial term in *Piers Plowman*, kind has three main meanings: (1) God conceived of primarily in his creative aspect (as distinguished from his other major aspect in the poem, as Truth—see **truth**); (2) the nature of something, as in the modern expression "this kind of thing rather than that kind" (Langland uses the expression "the law of kynde" to cover what we would call the law of nature as well as the instinctual morality of decent human beings, insofar as the latter seems to be cross-cultural; (3) kindness in the modern sense, i.e., benevolence, but conceived of as the norm of human behavior rather than as some special sort of altruism: to be "unkind" is to be distorted and unnatural as well as cruel. *Kind love*, "natural love": a love that is an instinctive and a natural expression of a benevolent will and cannot be taught, just as "natural [*kind*] faith" is. Langland's most crucial (and perhaps most controversial) use of the word is in the term *kind knowing*, "natural knowledge": experiential knowledge—whether interiorly or exteriorly derived—as opposed to reasoning and to book learning. The Dreamer uses the term when he responds to a character's intellectual explanation of something with the comment that he has no "natural knowledge" of it and must find another way to learn it. He is not rejecting the explanation or even finding it unintelligible; rather, he is saying he has not interiorized it in such a way that it can become a part of his life. Contrast *kind knowing* with the other intellectual faculties discussed under **wit**, particularly *kind wit* and *inwit*.

kind love   see **kind**.

kind wit   see **kind** and **wit**.

kirk   see **Holy Kirk**.

know naturally   see **kind**.

law-sergeants   important lawyers whose badge of office was a silk coif or scarf.

lewté   the primary meaning is "justice," as distinct from "law" as such. The medieval conception of justice, however (as the fact that the modern descendant of this word is "loyalty" illustrates), is more oriented toward relationships than ours, and so the translation has opted to maintain the Middle English word.

limiter see **friar.**

lovedays manor courts set aside certain days to try to reconcile adversaries in a negotiated settlement; this laudable aim was too often achieved by bribery rather than by genuine resolution of the problem. Friars were also associated with the holding of such sessions of reconciliation, which, while in the spirit of the order's original function, were widely perceived as motivated by a desire for additional income, with little concern for either justice or repentance.

low, lowly, lowliness humble, humility, without the negative connotation ("coarse or vulgar") that has become attached to the modern word.

mark equivalent to 160 pennies, several weeks' wages.

master Master of Divinity.

matins the first of the seven canonical "hours," or periods of liturgical prayer into which the day was divided—"morning prayer," as distinct from Mass.

meat food, nourishment (not just flesh).

Meed reward, recompense, the profit motive. A major concept that develops throughout the poem, Meed is defined by various characters in terms ranging as widely as "bribery," "heavenly reward," and "wages." It is a crucial term in the poem's analysis of the relationship between ethics and economic structure. Because of the wider range of meanings carried by Meed than by any single modern equivalent, the translation has kept the Middle English word.

might, mighty the Middle English term "might" simply means the strength necessary to do a particular thing, not necessarily the overwhelming force implied by the modern word.

Moralia see **Gregory the Great.**

natural knowledge see **kind.**

noble a gold coin worth eighty pennies.

palmer a virtually professional pilgrim who took advantage of the hospitality offered pilgrims everywhere to go on traveling year after year. As transients dependent on charity, palmers earned a somewhat unsavory reputation for tall tales and more general dishonesty. Strictly speaking, palmers were pilgrims who had been to Jerusalem, or who had made a lifelong commitment to pilgrimage.

pardoner an official empowered to transmit temporal indulgence (i.e., remission of some part of the punishment due in purgatory for one's sins on earth) from the pope in return for contributions to charitable enterprises. These contributions were not considered purchases of forgiveness but gifts freely given in return for God's free gift of mercy, which the Church administered through its agents; they were part of the "satisfaction," in the sequence "contrition, confession, satisfaction," required for the forgiveness of sins. But in practice the gifts were widely perceived as financial transactions, and their receipt came to be regarded as a fundamental abuse of the power entrusted by Christ to the Church. In theory, a pardoner had to have a papal authorization (see **bull**), which had also to be endorsed by the local bishop, and, since he was not a cleric, he was not allowed to preach as one. In practice, most of these safeguards were routinely evaded and many pardoners were con men, pure and simple. As a group they were as sharply criticized by thoughtful medieval Catholics as they were later by Protestant critics. Cf. p. 460.

Paternoster "The Lord's Prayer" ("Our Father, who art in heaven . . .").

penny a silver coin, quite valuable in medieval England. This Gloss defines other coins in relation to it. The term was also used as shorthand for money *per se.*

provisors clerics who, instead of being appointed to their offices by the local or national hierarchy, had obtained them by petitioning the pope directly, going over the heads of the intervening officials. Such "petitions" were routinely accompanied by bribes.

Psalter the Book of Psalms, or a separate volume containing it, sometimes in conjunction with other prayers for private use. The Psalms were collectively attributed to King David and regularly interpreted, like the rest of the Hebrew Scriptures, as foreshadowing the events recorded in the New Testament.

reason the process considered by medieval thinkers to be the unique and distinctive capacity of human beings, as opposed to animals, of reaching truth by discursive logic or rational argument. See **wit**.

reeve the superintendent of a large manor or farming estate. The reeve was a member of the manor community; that is, a peasant or even a serf, and elected by them, though paid by the lord of the manor, to organize and account for the work. As a result, he generally understood his social superiors' finances better than they did, and frequently profited at their expense.

religion, religious the translation almost never uses this word in the usual modern sense, but in a now less common one—the members of religious orders or their way of life, as opposed to other kinds of clerics, such as parish priests. E.g., "you religious" means "you monks and nuns"; "run into religion" means "join a religious order."

Rood a crucifix, i.e., a cross with a figure of the crucified Christ on it, though the term is sometimes applied to a large cross without a figure.

St. James see **James**.

Sapience four "Wisdom Books" are attributed to King Solomon; two, The Book of Wisdom and Ecclesiasticus, are considered part of the Bible by Catholics but not by Protestants, while the other two, Proverbs and Ecclesiastes, are accepted by both groups.

Scripture the term often means the canonical Bible strictly defined, but can also include sacred writings more generally.

sergeants see **law-sergeants**.

simony buying and selling the functions, spiritual powers, or offices of the Church for money. The word derives from the name of Simon Magus, a magician who tried to persuade the early Apostles to sell him their power to perform miracles through the Holy Spirit (Acts 8).

sloth not merely, as in modern English, laziness, but a more fundamental irresponsibility or parasitic way of living (defined by Dante as "love deficient"). *Wanhope*, "despair," was considered its ultimate form.

soothness, sooth; soothfast truth or reality; truthful or honest. Middle English had two words for "truth": see **truth**.

summoner an official who served summonses to the ecclesiastical courts, which dealt with many issues we now regard as part of private morality rather than the concern of judicial action, whether clerical or secular. Summoners, who were not clerics themselves, were among the most feared and hated of church officials because of their power to blackmail and to demand bribes. Cf. p. 460.

truth the Middle English term *trouthe* has three meanings on which Langland plays: (1) fidelity, integrity (as in modern "troth"); (2) reality, actuality, or a statement in conformity with what is; (3) the ultimate reality, God, who appears directly in the poem under the figure of two allegorical characters, of which Truth is one (**Kind**—see above—is the other).

unkindness see **kind**.

Walsingham an English town, site of a famous shrine to the Virgin Mary and often referred to by Langland as the destination of pilgrimages of dubious motivation.

wanhope   see **sloth**.

Westminster   area (now part of London) famous for its courts of justice.

wit   mental capacity, intellectual ability. Wit is the dimension of the mind that permits human beings to perform their distinctive function, reasoning (see **reason**). The translation never uses the term in its later meaning of "witticism, humor." Wit is a quality that, like learning itself, can be put to bad use as well as to good. The allegorical character Wit is scolded by his wife Study for trying to explain intellectual matters to a morally unqualified person, and Warren Witty and his fellow Wisdom are among the hangers-on who stand ready to profit from the trial of Lady Meed. Langland differentiates wit from **conscience**, a more intuitive faculty (see above), and from two others: one is *inwit*, which seems to mean consciousness of the kind that permits a person to use mental faculties and which was believed to be absent in drunks, the insane, the immature, and those especially vulnerable to exploitation. The other is kind wit, which sometimes clearly means "common sense" or "practical thought," as opposed to formal or abstract reasoning or book learning, but is also related to the term "natural knowledge," *kind knowing* (see **kind**).

wits, the five   the five senses—sight, hearing, touch, taste, and smell. Langland sometimes speaks as if they can have normative or moral value as well, as when he makes them the five sons of "Sir Inwit" (see **wit**), whose function is to guard Lady Anima, the soul, in the "castle" of the body in which Kind—God—has placed her.

Selected Bibliography

• indicates items included or excerpted in this Norton Critical Edition.

Editions of Piers Plowman

Complete Texts

THE A-TEXT

Kane, George, ed. *The A-Version. Will's Visions of Piers Plowman and Do-Well.* London: Athlone Press, 1960. Reprint. London and Berkeley: Athlone Press and U of California P, 1988.
Knott, Thomas A., and David C. Fowler. *Piers the Plowman: A Critical Edition of the A Version.* Baltimore: Johns Hopkins UP, 1952.

THE B-TEXT

• Kane, George, and E. Talbot Donaldson, eds. *Piers Plowman: The B-Version. Will's Vision of Piers Plowman, Do-Well, Do-Better and Do-Best.* London: Athlone Press, 1975.
Schmidt, A. V. C. *William Langland: The Vision of Piers Plowman: A Critical Edition of the B-Text Based on Trinity College Cambridge MS B. 15. 17.* London: J. M. Dent, 1995.

THE C-TEXT

Pearsall, Derek, ed. *Piers Plowman by William Langland, An Edition of the C-Text.* York Medieval Texts, second series. London: Edward Arnold, 1978. Reprint. Berkeley and Los Angeles: U of California P, 1979.
Russell, George, and George Kane, eds. *Piers Plowman: The C Version, Will's Visions of Piers Plowman, Do-Better and Do-Best.* London and Berkeley: The Athlone Press and the U of California P, 1997.

the z-text

Rigg, A. C., and Charlotte Brewer, eds. *Piers Plowman, the Z-Version.* Studies and Texts, 59. Toronto: Pontifical Institute of Mediaeval Studies, 1983.

Abridged Texts

Bennett, J. A. W. *Langland: Piers Plowman: The Prologue and Passus I–VII of the B-Text as found in Bodleian MS. Laud 581.* Oxford: At the Clarendon Press, 1972.

A, B, and C Texts

Schmidt, A. V. C. *William Langland: Piers Plowman: A Parallel-Text Edition of the A, B, C and Z Versions, Volume I. Text.* London and New York: Longman, 1995.
• Skeat, W. W. *The Vision of William Concerning Piers the Plowman in Three Parallel Texts together with Richard the Redeless by William Langland, Volumes I and II.* Oxford: Oxford UP, 1886. Reprint. 1954, 1961, 1965, 1968, 1969.

Facsimiles

Pearsall, Derek, and Kathleen Scott. *Piers Plowman: a facsimile of Bodleian Library Oxford, MS Douce 104.* Woodbridge, Suffolk, UK, and Rochester, N.Y.: D. S. Brewer, 1992.

Rigg, A. C., and Charlotte Brewer. *Piers Plowman: A Facsimile of the Z-Text in Bodleian Library, Oxford, MS. Bodley 851.* Cambridge: D. S. Brewer, 1994.

Electronic Edition

Hoyt N. Duggan and Ralph Hanna. *The Piers Plowman Electronic Archive. Vol. 4, Oxford, Bodleian Library MS Laud misc. 581* (CD-ROM). Rochester, NY, and Woodbridge, Suffolk: Boydell & Brewer, 2005.

Selected Translations

Attwater, Donald, and Rachel Attwater. *The Book of Piers the Plowman.* London and New York: Dent and Dutton, 1953.
Coghill, Neville. *Visions from Piers Plowman.* London: Phoenix Hill, 1964.
• Donaldson, E. Talbot, trans. *Piers Plowman: An Alliterative Verse Translation.* Ed. Elizabeth D. Kirk and Judith H. Anderson. New York: Norton, 1990.
Goodridge, J. F. *Piers the Plowman.* Hammondsworth, Middlesex: Penguin, 1959.
Schmidt, A. V. C. *Piers Plowman: A New Translation of the Three Texts.* Oxford and New York: Oxford UP, 1992.

Glossary

Kane, George, *Piers Plowman Glossary: Will's Visions of Piers Plowman, Do-Well Do-Better and Do-Best.* London and New York: Continuum Publishing Group International, 2005.

Concordance

Wittig, Joseph S. *Piers Plowman: Concordance. A Lemmatized Analysis of the English Vocabulary of the A, B, and C Versions as Presented in the Athlone Editions, with Supplementary Concordance of the Latin and French Macaronics.* London and New York: Athlone Press, 2001.

Bibliographies and Other Useful Resources

Annual Bibliographies appear in *The Yearbook of Langland Studies.*
Baldwin, Anna. *Piers Plowman: A Reader's Guide.* Forthcoming.
Pearsall, Derek. *An Annotated Critical Bibliography of Langland.* Ann Arbor: U of Michigan P, 1990.
• Simpson, James. *Piers Plowman: An Introduction to the B-Text.* London and New York: Longman, 1990.

Related Primary Sources

Andrew, Malcolm, and Ronald Waldron, eds. *The Poems of the 'Pearl' Manuscript: 'Pearl,' 'Cleanness,' 'Patience,' 'Sir Gawain and the Green Knight.'* York Medieval Texts, 2d ser. London: Edward Arnold: 1978.
Aquinas, Thomas. *Summa Theologiae. Vol. 1, Christian Theology.* Ed. Thomas Gilby. London: Blackfriars, 1964.
Augustine. *De Doctrina Christiana.* Ed. K. D. Daur. Corpus christianorum. Series latina. Vol. 32. Turnholt: Brepols, 1962.
• Babington, Churchill, and R. Lumby, eds. *Polychronicon Ranulphi Higden, with the English Translations of John Trevisa.* London: Longman, Green, Longman, Roberts and Green, 1865.
Benson, Larry, et al., eds. *The Riverside Chaucer.* 3d ed. Boston: Houghton Mifflin, 1988.
• Brinton, Thomas. *The Sermons of Thomas Brinton, Bishop of Rochester (1373–1389).* Ed. Sister Mary Aquinas Devlin, O. P. Camden Society, 3d ser., nos. 85–86. London: Royal Historical Society, 1954.
Brown, Carleton, ed. *English Lyrics of the Thirteenth-Century.* Oxford: At the Clarendon Press, 1932.
Colledge, Edmund, and James Walsh. *Julian of Norwich: Showings.* New York: Paulist Press, 1978.
Davis, Norman, J. R. R. Tolkien, and E. V. Gordon, eds. *Sir Gawain and the Green Knight.* Oxford: At the Clarendon Press, 1967.
Gordon, E. V., ed. *Pearl.* Oxford: At the Clarendon Press, 1953.
Hector, L. C., and Barbara F. Harvey. *The Westminster Chronicle, 1381–94.* Oxford: At the Clarendon Press, 1982.
Hodgson, Phyllis, ed. *The Cloud of Unknowing and the Book of Privy Counselling.* EETS OS 218. London: Oxford UP, 1944.
Hudson, Anne. *English Wycliffite Sermons.* Vol I. Oxford: At the Clarendon Press, 1983.
Knighton, Henry. *Chronicon.* 2 vols. Ed. J. R. Lumby. London: Rolls Series, 1889–95.
Macaulay, G. C., ed. *The English Works of John Gower.* Vol. I. EETS ES 81. London: Oxford UP, 1900.

Skeat, W. W. *The Testament of Love in Chaucerian and Other Pieces.* Oxford: At the Clarendon Press, 1897.
Stahl, William H., trans. *Commentary on the Dream of Scipio.* New York: Columbia UP, 1952.
• *The Statutes of the Realm.* Vols. I and II. London, 1810 and 1816.
• Trigg, Stephanie, ed. *Winner and Waster. EETS OS* 297. London: Oxford UP, 1990.

General Historical, Theological, and Cultural Studies

Church and Theology

Bloomfield, Morton. *The Seven Deadly Sins: An Introduction to the History of a Religious Concept, With Special Reference to Medieval English Literature.* East Lansing, Michigan: Michigan UP, 1952.
Bolton, Brenda. *The Medieval Reformation.* London: Edward Arnold, 1983.
Chenu, M. D. *Nature, Man and Society in the Twelfth Century.* Ed. and trans. Jerome Taylor and Lester Little. Chicago: U of Chicago P, 1957.
Fleming, John V. *An Introduction to the Franciscan Literature of the Middle Ages.* Chicago: Franciscan Herald Press, 1977.
Gilson, Etienne. *A History of Christian Philosophy in the Middle Ages.* London: Sheed and Ward, 1955.
Harvey, E. Ruth. *The Inward Wits, Psychological Theory in the Middle Ages and the Renaissance.* Warburg Institute Surveys. Vol. 6. London: The Warburg Institute, 1975.
Hudson, Anne. *Lollards and their Books.* London: Hambledon Press, 1985.
———. *The Premature Reformation: Wycliffite Texts and Lollard History.* Oxford: Clarendon Press, 1988.
Leclercq, Jean. *The Love of Learning and the Desire for God.* Trans. Catherine Mishrahi. London: SPCK, 1974.
Leff, Gordon. *Bradwardine and the Pelagians, a Study of his 'De Causa Dei' and its Opponents.* Cambridge Studies in Medieval Life and Thought n.s. Vol. 5. Cambridge: Cambridge UP, 1957.
———. *Heresy in the Later Middle Ages.* 2 vols. Manchester: Manchester UP, 1967.
Little, Lester K. *Religious Poverty and the Profit Economy in Medieval Europe.* London: Paul Elek, 1978.
Oberman, Heiko A. *Archbishop Bradwardine: a Fourteenth Century Augustinian.* Utrecht: Drukkerijen Uitgevers-Maatschappij, 1957.
———. *The Harvest of Medieval Theology: Gabriel Biel and Late Medieval Nominalism.* Cambridge, Mass.: Harvard UP, 1963.
Owst, G. R. *Literature and Pulpit in Medieval England.* Cambridge: Cambridge UP, 1963.
———. *Preaching in Medieval England: An Introduction to Sermon Manuscripts of the Period c. 1350–1450.* Cambridge: Cambridge UP, 1926.
Smalley, Beryl. *English Friars and Antiquity in the Early Fourteenth Century.* Oxford: Blackwell, 1960.
———. *The Study of the Bible in the Middle Ages.* Notre Dame, Ind.: U of Notre Dame P, 1964.
Southern, Richard. *St. Anselm and his Biographer: A Study of Monastic Life and Thought 1059–c. 1130.* Cambridge: Cambridge UP, 1963.
Wenzel, Siegfried. *The Sin of Sloth: Acedia in Medieval Thought and Literature.* Chapel Hill: U of North Carolina P, 1960.

Literacy and Education

Clanchy, M. T. *From Memory to Written Record: 1066–1307.* 1979. Oxford: Blackwell, 1993.
Courtenay, William J. *Schools and Scholars in Fourteenth-Century England.* Princeton: Princeton UP, 1987.
Orme, Nicholas. *English Schools in the Middle Ages.* London: Methuen, 1973.
Thompson, James Westfall. *The Literacy of the Laity in the Middle Ages.* Publications in Education 9. Berkeley, California, 1939.

Pilgrimage

Dyas, Dee. *Pilgrimage in Medieval English Literature, 700–1500.* Cambridge: D.S. Brewer, 2001.
Sumption, Jonathan. *Pilgrimage: An Image of Medieval Religion.* London: Faber and Faber, 1975.

Art

Emmerson, Richard K. *Antichrist in the Middle Ages: A Study of Medieval Apocalypticism, Art and Literature.* Seattle: U of Washington P, 1981.
Mâle, Emile. *The Gothic Image.* Trans. from the 3d edition by D. Nussey. London: Collins, 1961.

History and Economics

Bennett, Judith. *Ale, Beer, and Brewsters in England: Women's Work in a Changing World, 1300–1600.* New York and Oxford: Oxford UP, 1996.

Bolton, Brenda. "*Paupertas Christi*: Old Wealth and New Poverty in the Twelfth Century." *Renaissance and Renewal in Christian History, Studies in Church History.* 14 (1977): 95–103.

Bolton, J. L. *The Medieval English Economy.* Everyman's University Library, Vol. 1274. London: J. M. Dent, 1980.

Dobson, R. B. *The Peasants' Revolt of 1381.* London: Macmillan, 1970.

Gervase, Matthew. *The Court of Richard II.* London: John Murray, 1968.

Hilton, Rodney H. *Bond Men Made Free: Medieval Peasant Movements and the English Rising of 1381.* London: Temple Smith, 1973.

———. *The Decline of Serfdom in Medieval London.* London: Macmillan, 1969.

———. *The English Peasantry in the Later Middle Ages.* Oxford: Clarendon Press, 1975.

Justice, Steven. *Writing and Rebellion: England in 1381.* Berkeley: U of California P, 1994.

Keen, M. H. *England in the Middle Ages: A Political History.* London: Methuen, 1973.

Lewis, N. B. "The Organization of Indentured Retinues in Fourteenth Century England." *Transactions of the Royal Historical Society,* 4th ser. 27 (1945): 2–39.

McFarlane, K. B. "Bastard Feudalism." *Bulletin of the Institute of Historical Research,* 20 (1944): 161–80. Rpt. in K. B. McFarlane, *England in the Fifteenth Century: Collected Essays.* London: Hambledon, 1981, pp. 23–43.

———. *The Nobility of Later Medieval England. The Ford Lectures for 1853 and Related Studies.* Oxford: Clarendon Press, 1973.

Mollat, Michel. *The Poor in the Middle Ages.* Trans. Arthur Goldhammer. New Haven and London: Yale UP, 1986.

Morris, W. A. and J. R. Strayer, eds. *The English Government at Work, 1327–1336.* Cambridge, Mass.: Medieval Academy of America, 1947.

Platt, Colin. *The English Medieval Town.* London: Granada, 1979.

Postan, M. M. "Some Social Consequences of the Hundred Years' War." *Economic History Review* 12 (1942): 1–12.

———. "England." *The Agrarian Life of the Middle Ages. The Cambridge Economic History of Europe.* Vol. I. 2d ed. Ed. M. M. Postan. Cambridge, Cambridge UP, 1971, pp. 549–632.

Roth, C. *A History of the Jews in England.* Oxford: Clarendon Press, 1941.

Saul, Nigel. *Richard II.* New Haven and London: Yale UP, 1997.

Thrupp, Sylvia L. *The Merchant Class of Medieval London 1300–1500.* Chicago: U of Chicago P, 1948.

Ziegler, Philip. *The Black Death.* New York: Harper and Row, 1969.

Literary Sources

Burrow, J. A. *Ricardian Poetry: Chaucer, Gower, Langland and the Gawain-Poet.* London: Routledge & Kegan Paul, 1971.

———. *Medieval Writers and their Work: Middle English Literature and its Background 1100–1500.* Oxford: Oxford UP, 1982.

Carruthers, Mary J., and Elizabeth D. Kirk, eds. *Acts of Interpretation: Essays on Medieval and Renaissance Literature in Honor of E. Talbot Donaldson.* Norman, Oklahoma: Pilgrim Books, 1982.

Coleman, Janet. *English Literature in History 1350–1400: Medieval Readers and Writers.* London: Hutchinson, 1981.

Gradon, Pamela. *Form and Style in Early English Literature.* London: Methuen, 1971.

Lohr, C. H. "The Medieval Interpretation of Aristotle." *CHLMP* (1982): pp. 80–98.

Mann, Jill. *Chaucer and Medieval Estates Satire.* Cambridge: Cambridge UP, 1979.

Minnis, A. J. *Medieval Theory of Authorship: Scholastic Literary Attitudes in the Later Middle Ages.* London: Scholar Press, 1984.

———. *Middle English Poetry: Texts and Traditions: Essays in Honour of Derek Pearsall.* York Manuscripts Conferences 5. Woodbridge, Suffolk; Rochester, NY: York Medieval Press in association with Boydell Press, 2001.

Nolan, Barbara. *The Gothic Visionary Perspective.* Princeton: Princeton UP, 1977.

Peebles, R. J. *The Legend of Longinus in Ecclesiastical Art and in English Literature.* Bryn Mawr Monographs. Vol. 9. Bryn Mawr, 1911.

Peter, John. *Complaint and Satire in Early English Literature.* Oxford: Clarendon Press, 1956.

Simpson, James. *The Oxford History of Medieval Literature.* Volume 2. 1350–1547. *Reform and Cultural Revolution.* Oxford: Oxford UP, 2002.

Smith, D. Vance. *The Book of the Incipit: Beginnings in the Fourteenth Century.* Minneapolis: U of Minnesota P, 2001.

Spearing, A. C. *Medieval Dream Poetry.* Cambridge: Cambridge UP, 1976.

Szittya, Penn. "The Anti-Fraternal Tradition in Middle English Literature." *Speculum* 52 (1977): 287–313.

Travers, Hope. *The Four Daughters of God.* Bryn Mawr Monographs. Vol. 4. Bryn Mawr, 1907.

Turville-Petre, Thorlac. *The Alliterative Revival.* Cambridge: D. S. Brewer, 1977.

Wallace, David, ed. *The Cambridge History of Medieval English Literature.* Cambridge: Cambridge UP, 1999.

Gender and Sexuality

Bennett, Judith. *Ale, Beer, and Brewsters in England: Women's Work in a Changing World, 1300–1600.* New York and Oxford: Oxford UP, 1996.

Brundage, James A. *Law, Sex, and Christian Society in Medieval Europe.* Chicago: U of Chicago P, 1987.

Bynum, Caroline. *Holy Feast and Holy Fast: The Religious Significance of Food to Medieval Women.* Berkeley: U of California P, 1987.

Goldberg, P. J. P. *Women, Work, and Life Cycle in a Medieval Economy: Women in York and Yorkshire c. 1300–1520.* Oxford: At the Clarendon Press, 1992.

Meale, Carol. *Women and Literature in Britain: 1150–1500.* Cambridge: Cambridge UP, 1993.

Sheehan, Michael M. *Marriage, Family, and Law in Medieval Europe: Collected Studies.* Ed. James J. Farge. Toronto: U of Toronto P, 1996.

Secondary Sources on the Poem

Book-Length Studies

Aers, David. *Chaucer, Langland and the Creative Imagination.* London: Routledge and Kegan Paul, 1980.

———. *Piers Plowman and Christian Allegory.* London: Edward Arnold, 1975.

Alford, John A. *A Companion to Piers Plowman.* Berkeley and Los Angeles: U of California P, 1988.

———. *Piers Plowman: A Glossary of Legal Diction.* Piers Plowman Studies, no. 5. Cambridge: D.S. Brewer, 1988.

Anderson, Judith. *The Growth of a Personal Voice: Piers Plowman and the Faerie Queene.* New Haven and London: Yale UP, 1976.

• Baldwin, Anna. "The Theme of Government in *Piers Plowman*." Piers Plowman Studies, vol. I. Cambridge: D. S. Brewer, 1981.

Barney, Stephen A. *Allegories of History: Allegories of Love.* Hamden, Conn: Archon Books, 1979.

Benson, C. David. *Public Piers Plowman.* University Park, PA: Pennsylvania State UP, 2003.

• Bloomfield, Morton W. *Piers Plowman as a Fourteenth-Century Apocalypse.* New Brunswick: Rutgers UP, 1961.

Bowers, John M. *The Crisis of Will in Piers Plowman.* Washington, D.C.: The Catholic U of America P, 1986.

Carruthers, Mary Jean. *The Search for St. Truth: A Study of Meaning in Piers Plowman.* Evanston, Illinois: Northwestern UP, 1973.

Clopper, Lawrence M. *"Songes of Rechlesnesse": Langland and the Franciscans.* Ann Arbor: The U of Michigan P, 1997.

Coleman, Janet. *Piers Plowman and the "Moderni."* Rome: Letture di Pensiero e d'Arte, 1981.

Davlin, Sister Mary Clemente. *A Game of Hevene: Word Play and the Meaning of Piers Plowman B.* Piers Plowman Studies, 7 Cambridge: D.S. Brewer, 1989.

• ———. *The Place of God in "Piers Plowman" and Medieval Art.* Aldershot, Eng.; Burlington, Vt: Ashgate, 2001.

Donaldson, E. Talbot. Piers Plowman: *The C-Text and its Poet.* Yale Studies in English. Vol. 113. New Haven: Yale UP, 1949.

• Frank, Robert W. *Piers Plowman and the Scheme of Salvation: An Interpretation of Dowel, Dobet, and Dobest.* New Haven: Yale UP, 1957.

Goldsmith, Margaret E. *"The Figure of PP: The Image on the Coin."* Piers Plowman Studies, vol. II. Cambridge: D. S. Brewer, 1981.

Griffiths, Lavinia. *Personification in Piers Plowman.* Piers Plowman Studies, vol. III. Cambridge: D. S. Brewer, 1985.

• Hanna, Ralph. *William Langland: English Writers of the Late Middle Ages.* Authors of the Middle Ages, 3. Aldershot, Eng. and Burlington, Vt: Ashgate, 1993.

Hewett-Smith, Kathleen M., ed. *William Langland's Piers Plowman: A Book of Essays.* New York: Routledge, 2001.

Howard, Donald R. *The Three Temptations: Medieval Man in Search of the World.* Princeton: Princeton UP, 1966.

Hussey, S. S., ed. *Piers Plowman: Critical Approaches.* London: Methuen, 1969.

Justice, Steven, and Kathryn Kerby-Fulton. *Written Work: Langland, Labor and Authorship.* Philadelphia: U of Pennsylvania P, 1997.

• Kane, George. *Chaucer and Langland: Historical and Textual Approaches.* Berkeley and Los Angeles: U of California P, 1989.

———. *Middle English Literature: A Critical Study of the Romances, the Religious Lyrics, Piers Plowman.* London: Methuen, 1951.

———. Piers Plowman: *The Evidence for Authorship.* London: Athlone Press, 1965.

Kerby-Fulton, Kathryn, and Denise Despres. *Iconography and the Professional Reader: The Politics of Book Production in the ('MS. Douce 104') "Piers Plowman."* Minneapolis: U of Minneapolis P, 1999.

Kirk, Elizabeth. *The Dream Thought of Piers Plowman.* New Haven and London: Yale UP, 1972.

Krochalis, Jeanne, and Edward Peters, eds. and trans. *The World of Piers Plowman.* Philadelphia: U of Pennsylvania P, 1975.
Lawlor, John. *Piers Plowman: An Essay in Criticism.* London: Edward Arnold, 1962.
Martin, Priscilla. *Piers Plowman: the Field and the Tower.* London: Macmillan; New York: Harper and Row, Barnes and Noble, 1979.
Murtaugh, Daniel M. *Piers Plowman and the Image of God.* Gainesville: UP of Florida, 1978.
Quilligan, Maureen. *The Language of Allegory: Defining the Genre.* Ithaca: Cornell UP, 1979.
Salter, Elizabeth. *Piers Plowman: An Introduction.* Oxford: Blackwell, 1963.
Schmidt, A. V. C. *The Clerkly Maker: Langland's Poetic Art.* Piers Plowman Studies, vol. IV. Cambridge: D. S. Brewer, 1987.
Simpson, James. *Piers Plowman: An Introduction to the B-Text.* London and New York: Longman, 1990.
Stokes, Myra. *Justice and Mercy in Piers Plowman.* London and Canberra: Croom Helm, 1984.
Tavormina, Teresa M. *Kindly Similitude: Marriage and Family in Piers Plowman.* Cambridge: D. S. Brewer, 1995.
Vasta, Edward, ed. *Interpretations of Piers Plowman.* Notre Dame, Ind.: U of Notre Dame P, 1968.
Yunck, John A. *The Lineage of Lady Meed: The Development of Medieval Veniality Satire.* Notre Dame, Ind.: U of Notre Dame P, 1963.

Essays and Chapters

Adams, Robert. "Langland's *Ordinatio*: The *Vision* and the *Vita* Once More." *YLS* 8 (1994): 51–84.
———. "Langland and the Liturgy Revisited." *Studies in Philology* 73 (1976): 266–84.
———. "Langland's Theology." In Alford, pp. 87–114.
———. "Mede and Mercede: the Evolution of the Economics of Grace in the *Piers Plowman* A, B and C Versions." In *Medieval English Studies Presented to George Kane.* Ed. Edward D. Kennedy, Ronald Waldron, and Joseph S. Wittig. Woodbridge, Suffolk: D. S. Brewer, 1988. 217–32.
———. "The Nature of Need in *Piers Plowman* XX." *Traditio* 34 (1978): 273–302.
———. "Piers's Pardon and Langland's Semi-Pelagianism." *Traditio* 39 (1983): 367–418.
———. "The Reliability of the Rubrics in the B-Text of *Piers Plowman.*" *Medium Ævum* 54 (1985): 208–31.
• Aers, David. *Community, Gender and Individual Identity: English Writing 1360–1430.* London and New York: Routledge, 1988, pp. 20–72.
———. "Class, Gender, Medieval Criticism and *Piers Plowman.*" In *Class and Gender in Early English Literature: Intersections.* Ed. Britton J. Harwood and Gillian R. Overing. Bloomington: Indiana UP, 1994, pp. 59–75.
———. "Justice and Wage-Labour after the Black Death: Some Perplexities for William Langland." In Aers, *Faith, Ethics, and Church: Writing in England, 1360–1409.* Cambridge: D. S. Brewer, 2000, pp. 56–75.
———. "Imagination and Ideology in *Piers Plowman.*" *Literature and History* 7 (1978): 2–19.
———. "*Piers Plowman* and Problems in the Perception of Poverty: A Culture in Transition." *Leeds Studies in English* (1983): n.s., 14: 5–25.
Aers, David, and Lynn Staley. *The Powers of the Holy: Religion, Politics, and Gender in Late Medieval English Culture.* University Park, PA: Pennsylvania State UP, 1996, pp. 1–76.
Alford, John A. "The Gramatical Metaphor: A Survey of its Use in the Middle Ages." *Speculum* 57.4 (October 1982): 728–60.
———. "The Idea of Reason in *Piers Plowman.*" *Medieval English Studies Presented to George Kane.* Ed. Edward D. Kennedy, Ronald Waldron, and Joseph S. Wittig. Woodbridge, Suffolk: D. S. Brewer, 1988. 199–215.
———. "Haukyn's Coat: Some Observations on *Piers Plowman* B. XIV. 22–7." *Medium Ævum* 43 (1974): 133–38.
———. "The Role of Quotations in *Piers Plowman.*" *Speculum* 52 (1977): 80–99.
———. "The Idea of Reason in *Piers Plowman.*" In *MESGK*, pp. 199–215.
Allen, Judson. "Langland's Reading and Writing: Detractor and the Pardon Passus." *Speculum* 59 (1984): 342–62.
Baker, Denise. "From Plowing to Penitence: *Piers Plowman* and Fourteenth Century Theology." *Speculum* 55 (1980): 715–25.
———. "The Pardons of *Piers Plowman.*" *NM* 85 (1984): 462–72.
Baker, Joan, and Susan Signe Morrison. "The Luxury of Gender: *Piers Plowman* B.9 and *The Merchant's Tale.*" In Hewett-Smith, *Book of Essays*, pp. 41–67.
Baldwin, Anna. "The Double Duel in *Piers Plowman* B XVIII and C XXI." *Medium Ævum* 50 (1981): 64–78.
———. "Patient Politics in *Piers Plowman.*" *YLS* 15 (2001): 99–108.
Barney, Stephen A. "Langland's Mighty Line." In Hewett-Smith, *Book of Essays*, pp. 103–17.
———. "The Plowshare of the Tongue: The Progress of a Symbol from the Bible to *Piers Plowman.*" *MS* 35 (1973): 261–93.
Barr, Helen. "The Use of Latin Quotations in *Piers Plowman* with Special Reference to Passus XVIII of the 'B' Text." *N & Q* n.s., 33 (1986): 440–8.
Barratt, Alexandra, "The Characters 'Civil' and 'Theology' in *Piers Plowman.*" *Traditio* 38 (1982): 352–64.
Benson, C. David. "The Langland Myth." In Hewett-Smith, *Book of Essays*, pp. 83–99.

———. "The Function of Lady Meed in *Piers Plowman*." *English Studies* 61, no. 3 (June 1980): 193–205.

• ———. "Piers Plowman and Parish Wall Paintings." *YLS* 11 (1997): 1–38.

———. "What Then Does Langland Mean? Authorial and Textual Voices in *Piers Plowman*." *YLS* 15 (2001): 3–13.

Bishop, Louise. "Dame Study and Women's Literacy." *YLS* 12 (1998): 97–116.

———. "Will and the Law of Property." *YLS* 10 (1996): 23–42.

Bloomfield, Morton W. "*Piers Plowman* and the Three Grades of Chastity." *Anglia* 76 (1982): 227–53.

Burrow, J. A. "The Audience of *Piers Plowman*." *Anglia* 75 (1957): 373–84.

———. "The Action of Langland's Second Vision." *EC* 15 (1965): 247–68.

———. "Words, Works and Will: Theme and Structure in *Piers Plowman*." In Hussey, ed., 11–24.

Clopper, Lawrence M. "Langland's Persona: An Anatomy of the Mendicant Orders." In Justice and Kerby-Fulton, *Written Work*, 144–184.

———. "Langland and Allegory: A Proposition." *YLS* 15 (2001): 35–42.

Coghill, Nevill. "God's Wenches and the Light that Spoke: Some Notes on Langland's Kind of Poetry." In *English Studies Presented to J. R. R. Tolkien on the Occasion of his Seventieth Birthday*. Ed. Norman Davis and C. L. Wrenn. London: George Allen and Unwin, 1962.

Collins, Marie. "Will and the Penitents: *Piers Plowman* B X. 420–35." *LSE* n.s., 16 (1985): 290–308.

Cooper, Helen. "Langland's and Chaucer's Prologues." *YLS* I (1987): 71–81.

———. "Gender and Personification in *Piers Plowman*." *YLS* 5 (1991): 31–48.

Craun, Edwin D. "'Ye, by Peter and by Poul!': Lewte and the Practice of Fraternal Correction." *YLS* 15 (2001): 15–25.

Davenport, W. A. "Patterns in Middle English Dialogues." In *MESGK*, 127–45.

Davlin, Sister Mary Clemente. "Chaucer and Langland as Religious Writers." In Hewett-Smith, *Book of Essays*, 119–41.

———. "'Kynde Knowynge' as a Major Theme in *Piers Plowman* B." *RES* n.s., 22 (1971): 1–19.

———. "'Kynde Knowynge' as a Middle English Equivalent for 'Wisdom' in *Piers Plowman* B." *Medium Ævum* 50 (1981): 5–17.

———. "The Spirituality of *Piers Plowman*." In *The Mystical Gesture: Essays on Medieval and Early Modern Spiritual Culture in Honor of Mary E. Giles*. Ed. Robert Boenig. Aldershot, Eng., and Burlington, Vt.: Ashgate, 2000, 23–40.

———. "The Spirituality of *Piers Plowman*: a New Look in Memory of Conrad Pepler, O. P. (1908–1993)." *New Blackfriars* 81 (March 2000): 124–28.

Dillon, Janette. "*Piers Plowman*: A Particular Example of Wordplay and its Structural Significance." *Medium Ævum* 50 (1981): 40–48.

Dod, Bernard G. "Aristoteles Latinus." In *CHLMP*, 1982, pp. 45–79.

Dolan, Terence. "Langland's Women." In *A Wyf ther Was*. Ed. Juliette Dor. Liège: Liège Language and Literature, 1992, 123–28.

Donaldson, E. Talbot. "Apocalyptic Style in Piers Plowman B: XIX–XX." In *Essays in Memory of Elizabeth Salter*. Ed. Derek Pearsall, *Leeds Studies in English* NS 14 (1983): 74–81.

Dronke, Peter. "Arbor Caritatis." In *Medieval Studies for J. A. W. Bennett*. Ed. P. L. Heyworth. Oxford: Clarendon Press, 1981, pp. 207–53.

Duggan, Hoyt N. "Extended A-Verses in Middle English Alliterative Poetry." *Medieval English Measures: Studies in Metre and Versification*. Ed. Ruth Kennedy. *Paragon* 18.1 (2000): 53–76.

———. "Notes Towards a Theory of Langland's Meter." *YLS* I (1987): 41–70.

———. "Some Aspects of A-Verse Rhythms in Middle English Alliterative Poetry." In *Speaking Images: Essays in Honor of V. A. Kolve*. Ed. R. F. Yeager and Charlotte Morse. Asheville, NC: Pegasus Press, 2000, pp. 479–503.

Fichte, Joerg O. "'For coueitise after cros; the croune stant in golde': Money as Matter and Metaphor in *Piers Plowman*." In *Material Culture and Cultural Materialisms: In the Middle Ages and Renaissance*. Ed. Curtis Perry. Arizona Studies in the Middle Ages and Renaissance 5. Brepols: Turhout, 2001, pp. 59–74.

Fisher, John H. "*Piers Plowman* and the Chancery Tradition." In *MESGK*, pp. 267–78.

Fletcher, Alan J. "The Essential (Ephemeral) William Langland: Textual Revision as Ethical Process in *Piers Plowman*." *YLS* 15 (2001): 61–84.

Fowler, Elizabeth. "Civil Death and the Maiden: Agency and the Conditions of Contract in *Piers Plowman*." *Speculum* 70 (1995): 760–92.

Frank, Robert Worth Jr., "The Pardon Scene in *Piers Plowman*." *Speculum* 26 (1951): 317–31.

———. "The Art of Reading Medieval Personification Allegory." *ELH* 20 (1953): 237–50. Rpt. in Vasta, *Interpretations*, pp. 217–31.

Galloway, Andrew. "Intellectual Pregnancy, Metaphysical Femininity, and the Social Doctrine of the Trinity in *Piers Plowman*." *YLS* 12 (1998): 117–152.

———. "Making History Legal: *Piers Plowman* and the Rebels of Fourteenth-Century England." In Hewett-Smith, *Book of Essays*, pp. 7–39.

———. "*Piers Plowman* and the Schools." *YLS* 6 (1992): 89–108.

———. "*Piers Plowman* and the Subject of the Law." *YLS* 15 (2001): 117–28.

Gilbert, Beverly Brian. "'Civil' and the Notaries in *Piers Plowman*." *Medium Ævum* 50 (1980): 49–63.

Godden, Malcolm. "Plowmen and Hermits in Langland's *Piers Plowman*." *RES* n.s., 35 (1984): 129–63.

Goldstein, R. James. "'Why calle ye hym crist, sien Iewes called hym Iesus?': The Disavowal of Jewish Identification in *Piers Plowman* B Text." *Exemplaria* 13 (2001): 215–51.

Gradon, Pamela. "Langland and the Ideology of Dissent." *PBA* 66 (1980): 179–205.
———. "*Trajanus Redivus:* Another Look at Trajan in *Piers Plowman.*" In *Middle English Studies Presented to Norman Davis in Honour of His Seventieth Birthday.* Ed. Douglas Gray and E. G. Stanley. Oxford: Clarendon Press, 1983, pp. 93–114.
Gray, Nick. "The Clemency of Cobblers: A Reading of 'Glutton's Confession' in *Piers Plowman.*" *LSE* n.s., 17 (1986): 61–75.
Hailey, R. Carter. "'Geuyng Light to the Reader': Robert Crowley's Editions of *Piers Plowman* (1550)." *PBSA* 95.4 (2001): 483–502.
Hanna, Ralph, III. "School and Scorn: Gender in *Piers Plowman.*" *New Medieval Literatures* 3 (2000): 213–27.
———. "Brewing Trouble: On Literature and History—And Alewives." In *Bodies and Disciplines: Intersections of Literature and History in Fifteenth-Century England.* Ed. Barbara A. Hanawalt and David Wallace. Medieval Cultures 9. Minneapolis and London: U of Minnesota P, 1996, pp. 1–18.
———. "Reading Prophecy/Reading Piers." *YLS* 12 (1998): 153–58.
———. "Will's Work." In Justice and Kerby-Fulton, *Written Work,* pp. 23–66.
Harwood, Britton. "'Clergye' and the Action of the Third Vision in *Piers Plowman.*" *MP* 70: 4 (1973): 279–90.
———. "Langland's *Knde Knowyng* and the Quest for Christ." *MP* 80.3 (February 1983): 242–55.
———. "*Piers Plowman:* Fourteenth-Century Skepticism and the Theology of Suffering." *Bucknell Review* 19.3 (Winter 1971): 119–36.
Hewett-Smith, Kathleen M. "Allegory on the Half-Acre: The Demands of History." *YLS* 10 (1996): 1–23.
———. "'Nede ne hath no lawe': Poverty and the De-stabilization of Allegory in the Final Visions of *Piers Plowman.*" In Hewett-Smith, *Book of Essays,* pp. 233–53.
Hill, Thomas D. "'Dumb David': Silence and Zeal in Lady Church's Speech, *Piers Plowman* C.2.30–40." *YLS* 15 (2001): 203–11.
———. "The Problem of Synecdochic Flesh: *Piers Plowman* B.9.49–50." *YLS* 15 (2001): 213–18.
Huppé, Bernard F. "*Petrus id est Christus:* Word Play in Piers Plowman, the B-Text," *English Literary History* 17.3 (1950): 163–90.
Hussey, S. S. "Langland's Reading of Alliterative Poetry." *MLR* 60.2 (April 1965): 163–70.
———. "Langland the Outsider." In Minnis 2001, pp. 129–37.
Justice, Steven. "The Genres of *Piers Plowman.*" *Viator* 19 (1988): 291–306.
———. "Music 'Neither Unpleasant nor Monotonous.'" In *Medieval Studies for J. W. Bennett.* Ed. P. L. Heyworth. Oxford: Clarendon Press, 1981, pp. 43–63.
———. "The Text." In Alford *Companion,* pp. 175–200.
Kaske, Robert E. "'Ex vi transicionis' and its Passage in *Piers Plowman.*" *JEGP* 62 (1963): 32–60.
———. "The Character Hunger in *Piers Plowman.*" In Kennedy, Waldron, and Wittig, eds. (1988); pp. 187–97.
Kaulbach, Ernest N. "The 'Vis Imaginativa' and the Reasoning Powers of Ymaginatif in the B-Text of *Piers Plowman.*" *JEGP* 84 (1985): 16–29.
Kean, P. M. "Love, law and *Lewté* in *Piers Plowman.*" *RES* n.s., 15 (1964): 241–61.
Kellog, Alfred L. and Louis A. Haselmayer. "Chaucer's Satire of the Pardoner." In *Chaucer, Langland, Arthur: Essays in Middle English Literature.* Ed. Alfred L. Kellog. New Brunswick: Rutgers UP, pp. 212–44.
Kerby-Fulton, Kathryn. "Langland 'in his Working Clothes'?: Scribe D, Authorial Loose Revision Material, and the Nature of Scribal Intervention." In Minnis 2001, pp. 139–68.
———. "Langland and the Bibliographic Ego." In Justice and Kerby-Fulton, pp. 67–143.
Kerby-Fulton, Kathryn and Maidie Hilmo, eds. *The Medieval Professional Reader at Work: Evidence from Manuscripts of Chaucer, Langland, Kempe, and Gower. English Literary Studies* 85. Victoria, B.C.: U of Victoria, 2001.
Kirk, Elizabeth D. "Langland's Plowman and the Recreation of Fourteenth Century Religious Metaphor." *YLS* 2 (1988): 1–21.
Korolec, J. B. "Free Will and Free Choice." In *CHLMP,* 1982, pp. 629–41.
Lassahn, Nicole. "Literary Representations of History in Fourteenth-Century England: Shared Technique and Divergent Practice in Chaucer and Langland." *Essays in Medieval Studies* 17 (2000): 49–64.
Lawlor, John J. "The Imaginative Unity of *Piers Plowman,*" RES, n.s., 8.30 (April 1957): 113–26.
Lawton, David. "Lollardy and the 'Piers Plowman' Tradition." *MLR* 76.4 (October 1981): 780–93.
———. "Middle English Alliterative Poetry: An Introduction." In *Middle English Alliterative Poetry and its Literary Background.* Ed. D. A. Lawton. Cambridge: D. S. Brewer, 1982, pp. 1–19.
———. "The Subject of *Piers Plowman.*" *YLS* 1 (1987): 1–30.
———. "Alliterative Style." In Alford, *Companion,* pp. 223–249.
Lees, Claire. "Gender and Exchange in *Piers Plowman.*" In Harwood, *Class & Gender,* pp. 112–130.
• Mann, Jill. "Eating and Drinking in *Piers Plowman.*" *Essays and Studies* 32 (1979): 26–42.
Middleton, Anne. "Acts of Vagrancy: The C-Version 'Autobiography' and the Statute of 1388." In Justice and Kerby-Fulton, *Written Work,* pp. 208–319.
———. "The Idea of Public Poetry in the Reign of Richard II." *Speculum* (January 1978): 94–114.
———. "Two Infinities: Grammatical Metaphor in *Piers Plowman.*" *ELH* 39 (1972): 169–88.
———. "Narration and the Invention of Experience: Episodic Form in *Piers Plowman.*" In Benson and Wenzel, eds. *The Wisdom of Poetry* (1982): 91–122.
• ———. "William Langland's 'Kynde Name': Authorial Signature and Social Identity in Late Four-

teenth-Century England." In *Literary Practice and Social Change in Britain, 1380–1530*, ed. Lee Patterson. Berkeley: U of California P, 1989.

———. "Acks of Vagrancy: The C Version 'Autobiography' and the Statute of 1388." Justice and Kerby-Fulton, *Written Work*, 208–318.

Minnis, A. J. "Literary Theory in Discussions of *Forma Tractandi* by Medieval Theologians." *New Literary History*, II 133–45.

———. "Langland's Imaginatif and Late-Medieval Theories of Imagination." *Comparative Criticism* 3 (1981): 71–103.

Murphy, Colette. "Lady Holy Church and Meed the Maid." In *Feminist Readings in Middle English Literature: The Wife of Bath and All Her Sect*. Ed. Ruth Evans and Lesley Johnson. London and New York: Routledge, 1994, pp. 140–64.

• Muscatine, Charles. "The Locus of Action in Medieval Narrative." *Romance Philology* 17.1 (1963): 115–22.

Overstreet, Samuel. " 'Grammaticus Ludens': Theological Aspects of Langland's Grammatical Allegory." *Traditio* 40 (1984): 251–96.

Pates, Stella. *The Rock and the Plough: John Grandisson, William Langland and 'Piers Plowman': A Theory of Authorship*. Cirencester, Gloucs., and Eliot, ME: Fairford Press, 2000.

Paxson, James J. "Gender Personified, Personification Gendered, and the Body Figuralized in *Piers Plowman*." *YLS* 12 (1998): 65–96.

———. "Inventing the Subject and the Personification of Will in *Piers Plowman*: Rhetorical, Erotic, and Ideological Origins and Limits in Langland's Allegorical Poetics." In Hewett-Smith, *Book of Essays*, pp. 195–231.

Pearsall, Derek. "Langland's London." In Justice and Kerby-Fulton, *Written Work*, pp. 185–207.

• ———. "Poverty and Poor People in *Piers Plowman*." In *MESGK*, pp. 167–85.

Potts, Timothy. "Conscience." In *CHLMP*, pp. 687–704.

Quilligan, Maureen. "Langland's Literal Allegory." *EC* 28 (1978): 95–111.

Robertson, Elizabeth. "Measurement and the 'Feminine' in *Piers Plowman*: A Response to Recent Studies of Langland and Gender." In Hewett-Smith, *Book of Essays*, 167–92.

Russell, George. "The Imperative of Revision in the C Version of *Piers Plowman*." In *MESGK*, pp. 233–42.

St. Jacques, Raymond C. "The Liturgical Associations of Langland's Samaritan." *Traditio* 25 (1969): 217–30.

Salter, Elizabeth. "Langland and the Contexts of *Piers Plowman*." *E & S* n.s., 32 (1979): 19–25.

———. "*Piers Plowman* and *The Simonie*." *Archiv* 203.4 (January 1967): 241–54.

Samuels, M. L. "Langland's Dialect." *Medium Ævum* 54 (1985): 232–47.

Schmidt, A. V. C. "The Inner Dreams in Piers Plowman." *Medium Ævum* 55 (1986): 24–40.

———. "A Note on Langland's Conception of 'Anima' and 'Inwit.' " *N & Q* n.s., 15 (1968): 363–64.

———. "Langland and Scholastic Philosophy." *Medium Ævum* 38 (1969): 134–56.

———. "Langland's Structural Imagery." *EC* 30.4 (1980): 311–25.

———. "Langland and the Mystical Tradition." In Glasscoe, *Medieval Mystical Tradition* (1980): 17–38.

———. "The Inner Dreams in *Piers Plowman*." *Medium Ævum* 55 (1986): 24–40.

• Schroeder, Mary (Carruthers). "Conscience in *Piers Plowman*." *Studies in Philology* 67 (1970): 13–30.

Schweitzer, Edward C. " 'Half a Laumpe Lyne in Latyne' and Patience's Riddle in *Piers Plowman*." *JEGP* 73 (1974): 313–27.

Scott, Anne M. " 'Nevere noon so nedy ne poverer deide': *Piers Plowman* and the Value of Poverty." *YLS* (2001): 141–53.

Shepherd, Geoffrey. "The Nature of Alliterative Poetry in Late Medieval England." *Proceedings of the British Academy*, 1970, pp. 57–76.

Shepherd, Stephen H. A. "Langland's Romances." In Hewett-Smith, *Book of Essays*, pp. 69–81.

Simpson, James. " 'Et Vidit Deus Cogitationes Eorum': A Parallel Instance and Possible Source for Langland's Use of a Biblical Formula at *Piers Plowman* B. XV. 202a." *N & Q* n.s., 33 (1986): 9–13.

———. "From Reason to Affective Knowledge: Modes of Thought and Poetic Form in *Piers Plowman*." *Medium Ævum* 55 (1986): 1–23.

———. "The Power of Impropriety: Authorial Naming in *Piers Plowman*." In Hewett-Smith, pp. 145–65.

———. "The Role of *Scientia* in *Piers Plowman*." In *MERELGR*, pp. 49–65.

———. "Spiritual and Earthly Nobility in *Piers Plowman*." *NM* 83 (1985): 467–81.

———. "Spirituality and Economics in Passus 1–7 of the B-Text." *YLS* I (1987): 83–103.

———. "The Transformation of Meaning: A Figure of Thought in *Piers Plowman*." *RES* n.s., 37 (1986): 161–83.

Spearing, A. C. "The Art of Preaching and *Piers Plowman*." In *Criticism and Medieval Poetry*. 2d ed. New York: Edward Arnold, 1972, pp. 107–34.

———. "The Development of a Theme in *Piers Plowman*." *RES* n.s., 11.43 (1960): 241–53.

———. "Verbal Repetition in *Piers Plowman* B and C." *JEGP* 62.4 (1963): 722–37.

Trigg, Stephanie. "The Traffic in Medieval Woman: Alice Perrers, Feminist Criticism and *Piers Plowman*." *YLS* 12 (1998): 5–30.

Waldron, R. A. "Landland's Originality: The Christ-Knight and the Harrowing of Hell." In *MERELGR*, pp. 66–81.

Wenzel, Siegfried. "Medieval Sermons." In Alford, *Companion*, pp. 15–72.

White, Hugh. "Landland's Ymaginatif, Kynde and the Benjamin Minor." *Medium Ævum* 55 (1986): 241–8.

Wittig, Joseph. "*Piers Plowman* B, Passus IX–XII: Elements in the Design of the Inward Journey." *Traditio* 28 (1972): 211–80.
———. "'Culture Wars' and the Persona in *Piers Plowman.*" *YLS* 15 (2001): 167–95.
Yunck, John A. *The Lineage of Lady Meed: The Development of Mediaeval Venality Satire.* Notre Dame: U of Notre Dame P, 1963.
———. "Satire." In Alford, *Companion,* pp. 135–54.
Zeeman, Nicolette. "'Studying' in the Middle Ages and in *Piers Plowman.*" *New Medieval Literatures* 3 (2000): 185–212.
———. *Piers Plowman and the Medieval Discourse of Desire.* Cambridge: Cambridge University Press, 2006.